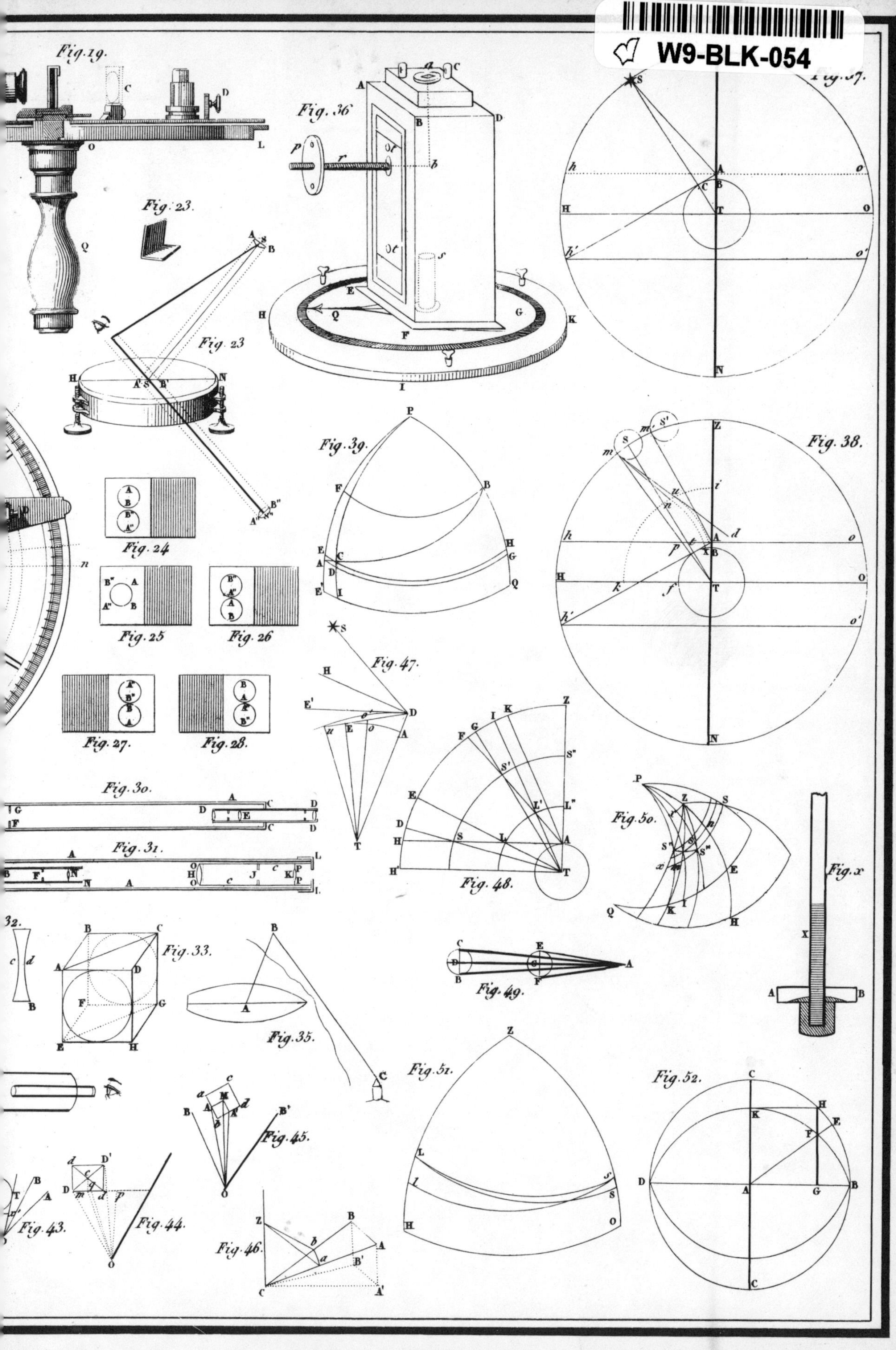
Fig. 19.
Fig. 23.
Fig. 23
Fig. 24
Fig. 25
Fig. 26
Fig. 27.
Fig. 28.
Fig. 30.
Fig. 31.
Fig. 33.
Fig. 35.
Fig. 36
Fig. 37.
Fig. 38.
Fig. 39.
Fig. 43.
Fig. 44.
Fig. 45.
Fig. 46.
Fig. 47.
Fig. 48.
Fig. 49.
Fig. 50.
Fig. 51.
Fig. 52.
Fig. x

DUTTON'S
Navigation & Piloting

Merry Christmas, Dad

love,

Judy

THIRTEENTH EDITION

DUTTON'S
Navigation & Piloting

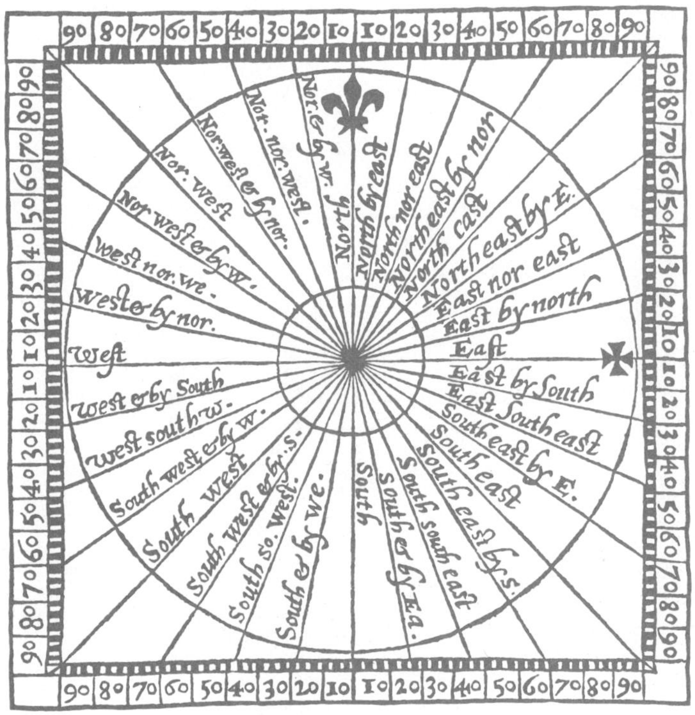

BY ELBERT S. MALONEY

NAVAL INSTITUTE PRESS
Annapolis, Maryland

Library of Congress Catalog Card Number: 77-87943
ISBN: 0-87021-164-1

Printed in the United States of America

End paper illustrations from *D'Astronomie Nautique* by Gueprate, 1839.

Cover and frontispiece illustrations reproduced by permission of Ministry of Defense, London.

Credit by figure number is acknowledged to the following individuals and organizations:

Alden Electronic & Impulse Recording Equipment Co., Inc.: 4108; Applied Physics Laboratory, The Johns Hopkins University: 3403a, 3403c, 3404, 3407a, 3407b; Autonetics Division of North American Aviation: 3505b, 3507a, 3507b, 4005c; Chesapeake Instrument Corporation: 710a, 710b, 1714; Convair Division, General Dynamics: 203a, 203b, 205a, 205b, 205c, 207a, 207b, 302, 310, 312a, 2122, 2203, 2204, 2303, 2902; C. Plath: 2108d; Danforth/White: 409d; Decca Navigation Systems, Inc.: 3225a, 3225b, 3225c; Edo Canada: 715a, 3602a; F. W. Keator: 3005b; Hamilton Watch Company: 2221; Hartman-Huyck Systems Company, Inc.: 723a, 723b; The Institute of Navigation, London: 4104a, 4104b, 4106a, 4106b; Kenyon Marine: 712; Kollmorgan Corporation: 3805, 3807; Kollsman Instrument Corporation: 3802a, 3802b; Northrop Nortronics: 3303a, 3308a, 3309; NOS: 304b, 314b, 315, 316; Peabody Museum: 2101; Rand McNally & Company: 4002, 4003; Raytheon: 1702a, 1702b, 3704b, 3704c; Robert A. Raguso: 4107a, 4107b; SI-TEX/KODEN: 1716; Sperry Rand Corporation: 430a, 430b, 438, 439a, 439b, 440, 3506a, 3506b, 3506c, 3507c, 3512a, 3512b, 4005a, 4005b, 4007; U.S. Coast Guard: 502, 513, 515, 516, 523; U.S. Naval Oceanographic Office: 312b, 904a, 904b, 904c, 1008, 1009, 1805b, 3105, 3108b, 3110, 4009; U.S. Navy: 436, 713, 715b, 1812c, 3602b, 3602c.

Contents

Preface

This book, under its original title of *Navigation and Nautical Astronomy,* was first written in 1926 by Commander Benjamin Dutton, U.S. Navy, for the instruction of midshipmen at the U.S. Naval Academy. Commander Dutton himself prepared five editions under that title before his death in 1937. The title was changed with the 11th Edition both to perpetuate the name of the original author and to describe the contents more accurately. Widely recognized as a standard authority in its field, *Dutton's Navigation & Piloting* is familiar to hundreds of thousands of students of the art and science of navigation.

This 13th Edition has been extensively revised and updated. It covers the latest changes in navigation practice, including the many advances in radionavigation systems. It also discusses the new chart numbering system and the recent changes in navigational publications, and reflects the standardized labeling and plotting procedures adopted by the Navigation Symposium. There is a new appendix which describes the use of hand-held electronic calculators in solving navigational problems. As well, numerous applications of electronic calculators are shown throughout the text. Celestial navigation has not been slighted: there are thirteen chapters devoted to the subject.

Many new illustrations and more comprehensive sample navigational problems have been added to aid the reader. Because of the importance of the effects of tides and currents, these subjects are now treated in separate chapters. To make space for this and other new material, several chapters of marginal value to students and most practicing navigators have been deleted, as were the extracts from sight reduction tables. The navigator should refer to DMAHC Publications No. 229 and 249, and to Table 35 in Pub. No. 9, Volume II, as required.

As was the case with its predecessors, this edition is intended for use by students of navigation, either enrolled in a class or studying on their own. It is equally suitable as a reference for practicing navigators at sea. While not intended to be encyclopedic in coverage, it should well meet the needs of students and navigators.

The "article" format of text organization has been retained from previous editions, along with the numbering of illustrations to correspond with the applicable article of text; but, by "popular demand," the index now refers to pages rather than article numbers.

This edition has been prepared by the undersigned, who accepts the responsibility for any errors. This task would not have been possible, of course, without the suggestions and assistance of many other persons. I approach the task of extending acknowledgments with much trepidation, as the list is long and I fear that someone will be inadvertently overlooked.

Comments and suggestions were made by many professors and instructors in the field as well as by those putting their knowledge to work on the high seas. Much appreciated and valued were the comments of Ernest B. Brown, Elbert S. Maloney, Jr., Alton B. Moody, and William T. McMullen. (Throughout these acknowledgments, names are listed alphabetically since any attempt to evaluate each contribution in order of importance would be hopeless.) From the Educational Department of the United States Power Squadrons, helpful comments and advice were received from Allan E. Bayless, Charles H. Bowles, Charles W. Brannen, O. B. Ellis, Charles B. Minnich, Louis Spector, and others. Technical information and suggestions were received from many offices of the Navy, Coast Guard, Defense Mapping Agency Hydrographic Center, and National Ocean Survey. Individuals whose assistance is gratefully acknowledged include: Anthony S. Basile, Raynard Cardascia, Barry Chapman, LeRoy E. Doggett, James E. Gearhart, R. G. Hall, G. W. Hockins, Donald R. Lesnick, Frank C. Leyden, Cornell H. Mayer, Harold M. Nordenberg, David C. Scull, P. K. Seidelmann, and W. G. Walker.

From nongovernmental activities, assistance was received from, and thanks are extended to, the following individuals and their organizations: Carl Andren (Decca Navigation); A. L. Comstock (Teledyne Hastings-Raydist); Jerry Fisher (Hewlett-Packard); Captains Richard James and John Underwood (Maritime Institute of Technology and Graduate Studies); R. A. Sleiretin (Raytheon); T. A. Stansell, Jr. (Magnavox); and Reed Trask (Texas Instruments).

A general acknowledgment is made to the many individuals and activities who contributed to the 12th and earlier editions, and whose efforts have been carried over into this edition wholly or in part.

Special thanks for a critical review of the manuscript go to Richard A. Hobbs and the officers of the Navigation Department of the Naval Academy under Commanders William M. Ross, Jr., and John F. Hopper, U.S. Navy. Many navigational problems in the text were checked by Charles B. Minnich.

The manuscript was typed (and retyped and retyped . . .) by Sharon L. Lannon, whose continued cheerful attitude in the face of demanding schedules was a great help. To Sharon, my most grateful appreciation.

And finally, my thanks to my wife, Mary, for her forbearance and understanding during the many long months of the preparation of this edition when I was too often unavailable for family activities.

Annapolis, Maryland
January 1978

Elbert S. Maloney

DUTTON'S
Navigation & Piloting

1 Introduction to Navigation

Derivation and definition

101 *Navigation* (from the Latin *navis,* a ship, plus *agere,* to direct) is the process of directing the movement of a vehicle from one point to another—the "vehicle" can be a surface craft or ship, a submarine, an aircraft, or a space craft. To make the definition complete, the qualification of "safely" or "successfully" should be added.

Navigation can properly be described as both an art and a science. It is a science in that it involves the development and use of instruments, methods, tables, and almanacs; an art in that it involves the proficient use of these tools and in the application and interpretation of information gained from such use. Much work must be done with precise instruments and exact mathematical tables—yet when the observations have been taken, and the calculations made, the seasoned navigator applies a measure of judgment when he says "We are here on the chart."

Primary categories of navigation

102 Navigation can be divided into four primary classifications: piloting, dead reckoning, celestial navigation, and radionavigation. These are convenient and logical categories; this is also the sequence in which they probably developed as man's knowledge and abilities grew over the centuries.

Piloting

Piloting may be defined as the determination of the position and the direction of the movements of a vessel, involving frequent or continuous reference to landmarks, aids to navigation, and depth soundings. Man first directed his movements on land by referring to familiar objects and views. When he took to the water to transport himself and his goods, he carried over the same techniques. Later, when water travel became more widely practiced, man-made aids to navigation, at first quite primitive but soon more advanced, were needed and were developed. Piloting is now done by referring to natural land features and structures and other objects ashore which, although not constructed for that purpose, can guide the mariner; by making use of specific aids to navigation such as lights, buoys, daybeacons, and fog signals; and by measuring the depth of the water. Man once depended entirely on his senses of sight and sound for piloting. Now he is aided by modern developments such as radio, radar, and electronic depth sounders which vastly expand the navigator's range of perception.

Because these devices are electronic extensions of the senses of sight and sound, and are frequently used in modern-day piloting, they are treated in the section on piloting rather than in the section on complex radionavigation systems. Piloting normally will provide a vessel's position with precision and accuracy.

Dead reckoning

Dead Reckoning (DR) is the projection of a present position, or anticipated future position, from a previous position using known directions and distances. As man became bolder in his ventures on the seas, he traveled beyond the range of visual reference to natural or man-made landmarks and into waters too deep to measure. He then developed procedures to help him estimate his position. The term is derived from the "deduced reckoning" of sailing ships, which was abbreviated "ded. reckoning." In dead reckoning, projections are made from planned courses and speeds without allowance for wind or current. Courses are determined from the compass, magnetic or gyro, and speed is taken from a log or count of engine revolutions. The plot of DR positions can be done either manually or by a dead-reckoning tracer which automatically analyzes directions and distances and plots a continuous track. The very modern systems of inertial and Doppler navigation are, in reality, extensions of dead reckoning using the capabilities of present-day technology.

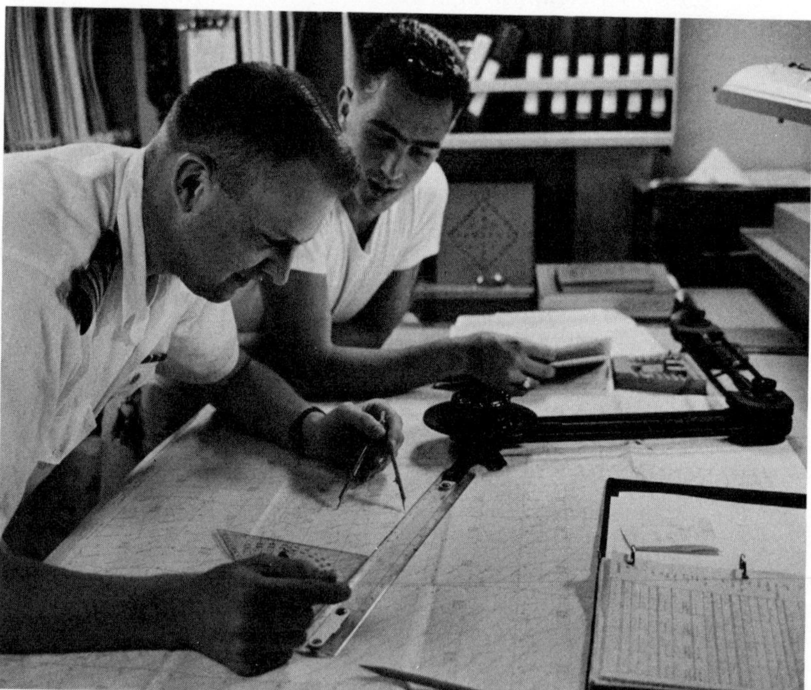

Figure 102. All phases of navigation involve some form of plotting.

Celestial navigation

Celestial navigation is the determination of position by observing the celestial bodies—the sun, moon, planets, and stars. Navigators, recognizing the deficiencies of dead reckoning when carried on for days without knowing the effects of wind and current, soon developed techniques for observing heavenly bodies. Instruments were crude at first but soon became more precise; even today, improvements are still being made in observational instruments and the techniques for using them. Although presently somewhat overshadowed by electronic systems, celestial navigation remains a basic and widely used procedure for determining positions at sea. Positions plotted by celestial navigation are much less precise than those derived from piloting, but as the plotting is done on the high seas, the accuracy is quite sufficient for the vessel's safety.

Radionavigation

Radionavigation is the determination of position—and to a lesser extent, course direction—using information gained from radio waves received and processed on board a vessel or aircraft. Radar navigation and satellite navigation are a part of this primary classification, but will be considered separately from radionavigation systems. Radar is essentially "electronic piloting," and the use of satellites is a unique application of radio waves. The term "electronic navigation," sometimes used, more properly includes *all* electronic devices from depth sounders and gyrocompasses to inertial systems and Doppler equipment.

Radionavigation systems in general provide coverage of a few hundred to many thousands of miles with accuracies from ±5 miles or so down to several hundred yards or less. Radionavigation systems and celestial techniques complement each other well at sea—celestial navigation is simple and self-contained, but requires fair weather in order to observe the heavens and horizon; radio systems are generally usable regardless of the weather, but are subject to power and equipment failures. Radionavigation systems are continually being improved by research and development; already the earlier systems are being phased out and replaced with improved versions or entirely new systems.

The problems of navigation

103 Regardless of the specific method of navigation, or combination of methods, used by a navigator, the procedures he applies must furnish him with a solution to the three basic problems of navigation. These problems are:

1. How to determine his *position;*
2. How to determine the *direction* in which to proceed to get from one position to another; and
3. How to determine *distance* and the related factors of *time* and *speed* as he proceeds.

Position Of these three problems facing every navigator, the most basic is that of locating his position. Unless he knows where he is, he cannot direct the movements of his vessel with accuracy, safety, and efficiency. The term *position* refers to an identifiable location on the earth or a point within a man-made system of artificial coordinates. The word *position* is frequently qualified by such adjectives as "fixed," "estimated," or "dead reckoning"; these will be further discussed in later chapters.

Direction *Direction* is the orientation of an imaginary line joining one point to another without regard to the distance between them. Direction is measured in angular units—*degrees* of arc from a reference—using a polar coordinate system. The usual reference is *true north,* although others will be defined and used later in this book. The subdivision of a degree may be either *minutes* and *seconds* ($1° = 60'$; $1' = 60''$), or *decimal fractions.*

It is the knowledge of the spatial relationship between two positions—the direction from one to another—that makes it possible for a navigator to lay a course from where he is to where he wants to go, and then proceed to that destination.

Distance *Distance* is the spatial separation between two points without regard to direction. In navigation, it is measured by the length of a line on the surface of the earth from one point to the other; customary units are yards, miles, or kilometers. The "mile" commonly used by navigators

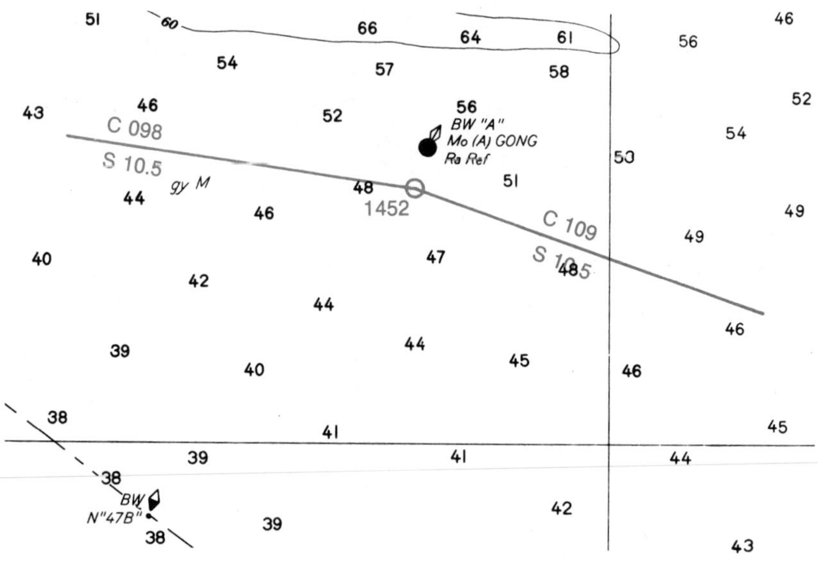

Figure 103a. Plots show a vessel's position, course, speed, and other essential data.

Figure 103b. Time is an essential element in all types of navigation.

is the *international nautical mile* of 6076.1 feet (approximately). This is longer than the *statute mile* used on land, 5280 feet; a close approximation of the ratio is 38/33, but 8/7 is often used because of its simplicity. *Time* may be either the time of day of an event as indicated by a watch or clock, or it may be the interval between two successive events. Units used are hours, minutes, and seconds; decimal fractions of a second are rarely needed. Time is written as four digits in a 24-hour system. Four minutes after midnight is 0004; 9:32 A.M. would be written as 0932; and 8:15 P.M. would appear as 2015. (The word "hours" is *not* written or spoken after the four digits.) *Speed* is defined as the time rate of movement and in navigation is usually measured in nautical miles per hour, or *knots*. Note that the time element is included in the definition of "knot"; the use of "knots per hour" is incorrect.

Metric system of measurement

104 The United States is moving increasingly toward the use of the *metric* system of measurement. The Metric Conversion Act of 1975 declared that the policy of this country was to increase the use of metric units on a voluntary basis with the goal of "a nation predominantly, although not exclusively, metric." Accordingly, this edition will introduce metric units where appropriate as approximate equivalents to the customary (English) units.

The nautical mile is expected to remain the basic unit of distance at sea. Depths and heights, however, are increasingly being shown in meters and decimeters (tenths of meters). (1 nautical mile = 1.852 km; 1 fathom = 1.829 m; 1 foot = 0.3048 m.)

Additional information on the metric system of measurement is given in Appendix D.

Navigational mathematics

105 A navigator will constantly be working with mathematics regardless of the type of navigation being practiced or the particular problem being solved. Standards of accuracy and precision, and general mathematical rules, are given in Appendix C.

Summary

106 The study of navigation is learning how to measure and use position, direction, distance, time, and speed. The practice of navigation, in any of its forms, is the application of this knowledge to ensure the safe and expeditious passage of a vessel.

2 The Earth and its Coordinates

Size and shape of the earth

201 That the earth is round—but not perfectly so—is well known. The earth can be described more exactly as a "spheroid," which simply means a less-than-perfect sphere. The equatorial diameter of the earth is not quite 6,888 nautical miles (12,757 km); the polar diameter is nearly 6,865 nautical miles (12,714 km), or about 23 miles (43 km) less.

If the earth is represented by a globe with an equatorial diameter of 12 inches (30.48 cm), the polar diameter, to be exact, should be 11.96 inches (30.38 cm), or 0.04 inches (0.10 cm) less.

The earth has a much smoother surface than might be imagined. Mt. Everest reaches a little less than 30,000 feet (9,144 m) above mean sea level; the greatest ocean depths yet known extend a little more than 35,000 feet (10,668 m) below the water's surface. On the same globe as above, these heights and depths would only be about 0.01 inch (0.025 cm) above or below the mean surface unless the vertical scale was deliberately much exaggerated for emphasis and clarity.

Since these variations from a truly spherical shape are so slight, for most navigational purposes the earth can be considered a sphere, and solutions of navigational problems based on this assumption are of practical accuracy. In the making of charts, however, consideration is given to the *oblateness* of the earth.

Reference lines on the earth

202 Points on the surface of a sphere at rest are similar because they are equidistant from its center. Lines passing through the center of the sphere, between two points on its surface, are also similar. None of the lines has distinguishing characteristics which render it suitable as a reference for navigational measurements.

But if the sphere is rotated, one line becomes distinguishable from all others; this line is the *axis* on which the sphere rotates. The earth's axis meets its surface at the *north pole* and *south pole*.

Halfway between the two poles, a plane perpendicular to the axis intersects the surface of the earth in a line known as the *equator*. All points on the equator are equidistant between the two poles, and the plane of the equator divides the earth in half, into the *northern* and *southern* hemispheres.

Great circles **203** A *great circle* is a circle formed on the surface of the earth by the intersection of a plane passing through the center of the earth, thereby dividing the earth into two equal parts. Great circles are illustrated in Figure 203a.

A *small circle* is a circle formed on the surface of the earth by the intersection of a plane which does *not* pass through the center of the earth and does not divide the earth into two equal parts. Although "small circles" may actually be quite large, they are always smaller than any great circle of the earth. Figure 203b illustrates several examples of small circles.

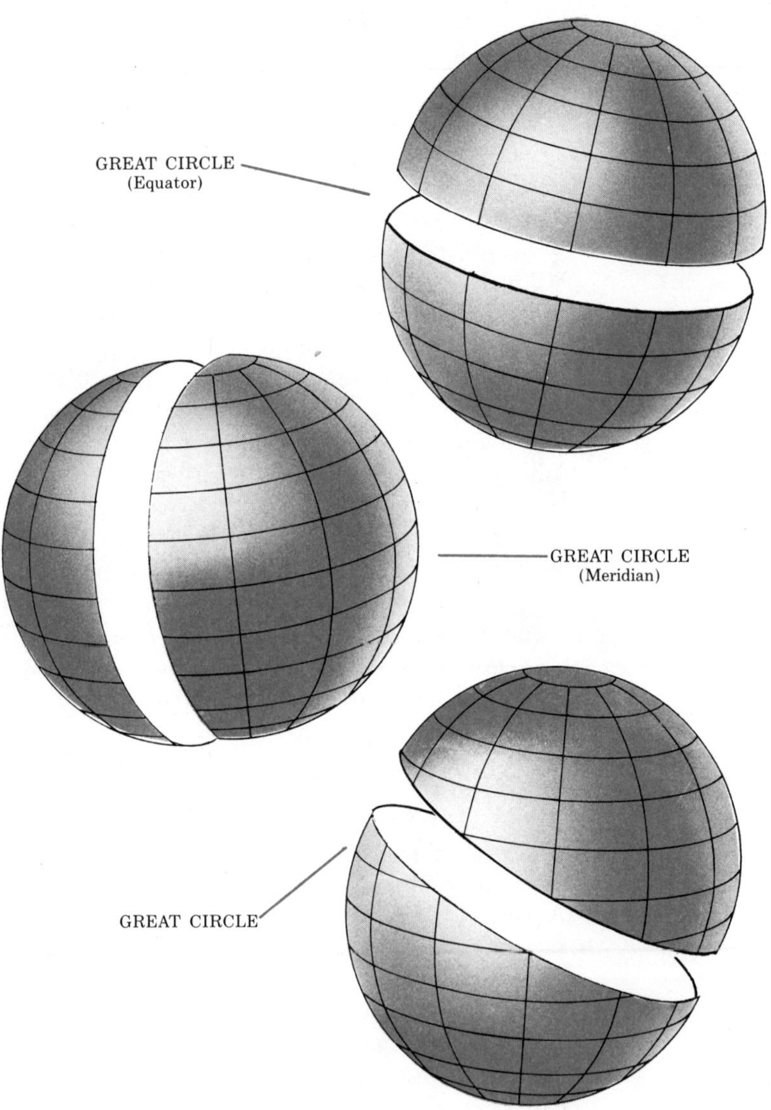

Figure 203a. Great circles.

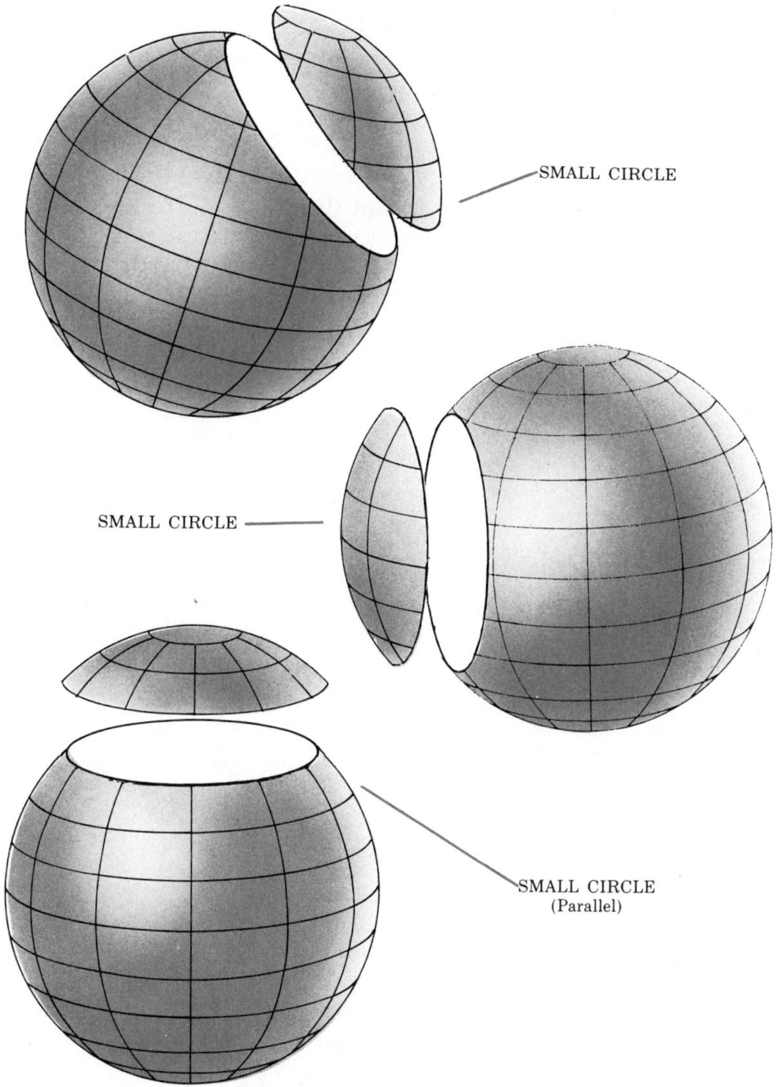

Figure 203b. Small circles.

Parallels and meridians

204 Certain great and small circles have applications in navigation. A *parallel* is a small circle on the earth's surface whose plane of intersection is parallel to the plane of the equator. The equator itself is a special parallel in that it is a great circle. See Figure 204a and b.

A *meridian* is a great circle formed by a plane which contains the earth's axis and its poles; see Figure 204c. That half of a meridian extending from the north to the south pole on the *same* side of the earth as an observer is considered by him as the *upper branch* of the meridian. The other half of the meridian, which is on the *other* side of

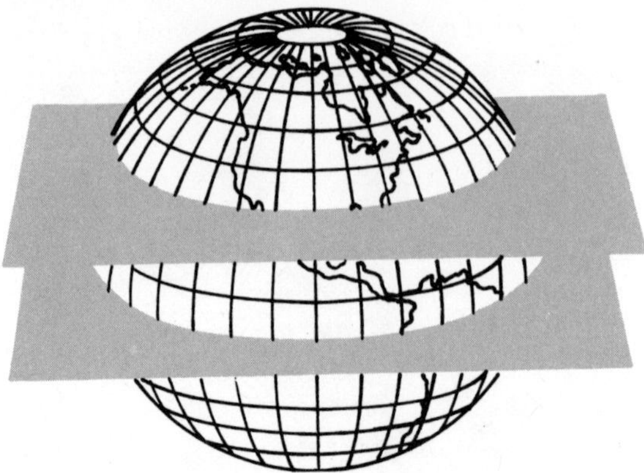

Figure 204a. Parallels of latitude are formed by planes perpendicular to the axis of the earth.

Figure 204b. The equator is formed by a plane perpendicular to the earth's axis and equidistant from the poles.

Figure 204c. Meridians of longitude are formed by planes that contain the earth's axis.

the earth and seems to the observer to be beneath him, is referred to as the *lower branch.* (The term "meridian" is often applied to the upper branch only.)

Terrestrial coordinates **205** The location of any point on the earth may be defined in a system of *terrestrial coordinates.* The earth's surface is laid out in a grid of *parallels* of latitude (usually called merely "parallels") and *meridians* of longitude.

Latitude *Latitude* (abbreviated as Lat.; symbol L) is measured north or south from the equator, where it is 0°, to the poles, where it is 90°. The latitude of a point may be considered either as the angular distance measured from the center of the earth or as an arc on the surface. Latitude is normally measured in degrees, minutes, and seconds, or in degrees, minutes, and decimal fractions of a minute; the suffix "north" or "south" is an essential part of the description and must always be included. Figure 205a shows measurements of the angles for 15° and 45° *north* latitude and for 30° *south* latitude.

Longitude *Longitude* (abbreviated as Long.; symbol Lo or λ) is measured using meridians, but a particular meridian must be selected as the starting point. In the early days of map making, a number of meridians were used for starting points. Each map maker or seafaring nation used its own reference meridian, and charts often had four or more longitude scales. Now, however, the *prime meridian,* longitude 0°, is universally taken as the upper branch of the meridian which passes through the original site of the Royal Observatory, Greenwich, England. All modern

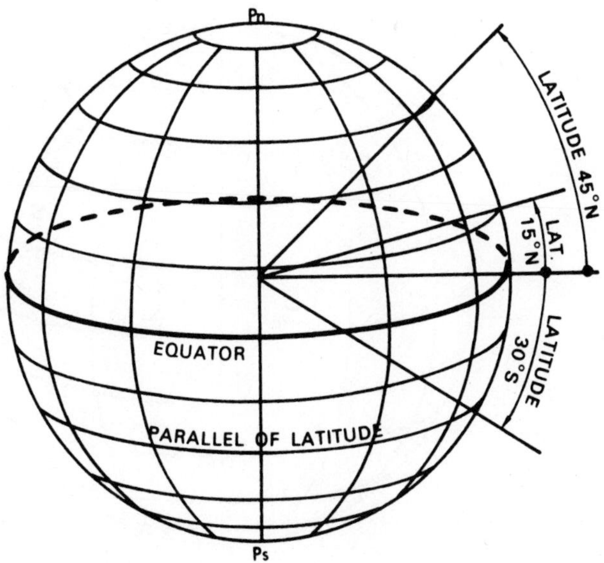

Figure 205a. Latitude; parallels of latitude; the equator.

charts use the prime meridian as the starting point for the measurement of longitude.

Figure 205b illustrates the measurement of longitude. The longitude of any point on earth may be defined as the angular distance between the meridian of Greenwich and the meridian passing through the point. It is measured in degrees of arc, from 0° to 180° east (*east longitude*) or west (*west longitude*) from the prime meridian (Greenwich). It may be thought of:

1. as measured along a parallel of latitude, as in the figure;
2. as measured along the equator; or
3. as the angle between the two meridians as they converge and meet at the pole.

Having established a set of reference lines for the sphere (meridians and parallels), any position on earth may be precisely pin-pointed as "so many degrees north (or south) latitude, and so many degrees east (or west) longitude." (Latitude is always stated first.)

Degree length

The length of a degree of latitude (measured *along* a meridian) is everywhere the same on a sphere, from the equator to the poles. On the earth, for practical navigational purposes, it is equal to 60 nautical miles (111.12 km), and 1 minute of latitude is equal to 1 nautical mile (1.852 km).

The length of a degree of longitude (measured along a parallel) decreases from 60 nautical miles (111.12 km) at the equator to 52.10 nautical miles (96.48 km) at latitude 30° north or south, and to 30.13 nautical miles (55.80 km) at latitude 60°; it is zero at latitude 90°, the north and south poles. See Figure 205c.

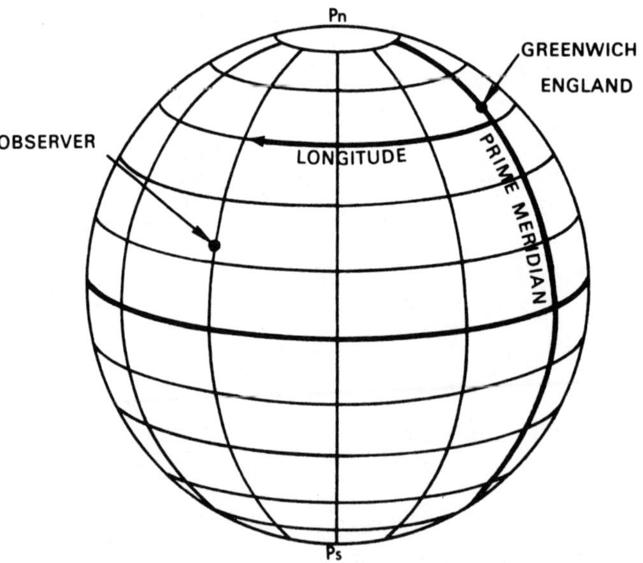

Figure 205b. Longitude, meridians; prime meridian.

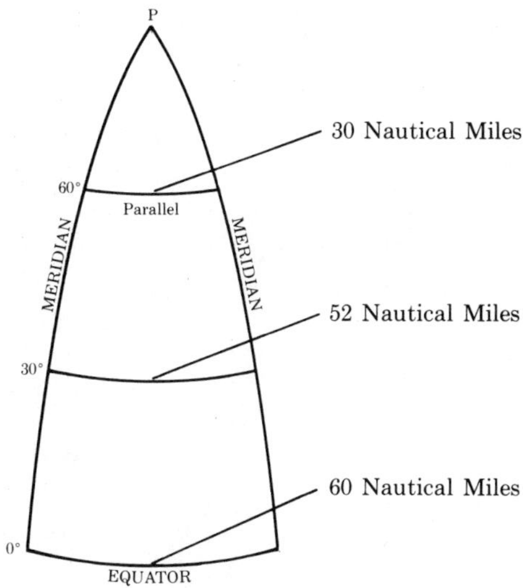

Figure 205c. Length of a degree of longitude at various latitudes.

Departure The linear distance between two meridians at any given parallel of latitude is termed *departure* (abbreviated Dep.; symbol p); it is normally expressed in nautical miles.

Difference of latitude and longitude **206** In some problems of navigation it is necessary to know the *difference of latitude* (*l*), or the *difference of longitude* (DLo) between two points.

In determining the difference of latitude, the two points may both be on the same side of the equator, in which case they are said to be of the "same name" (that is, both are *north* latitude, or both are *south* latitude); or they may be on opposite sides of the equator, and of "contrary name" (one *north* latitude, one *south*). The difference of latitude (*l*) is always measured as though the two points were both on the same meridian, with one point due north or south of the other, regardless of the direction between them. Thus, in Figure 206a, *A* is 45° north, *B* is 30° south (*contrary name*); obviously, the total difference of latitude between them is obtained by *adding* the two distances from the equator: $45° + 30° = 75° = l$. This gives rise to the formal rule:

for latitudes of contrary name, add.

Again, in Figure 206a, *A* is 45° north, *C* at 15° north (*same name*) and the difference of latitude, 30°, is obtained by subtracting the smaller from the larger. The rule in this case becomes:

for latitudes of same name, subtract.

In the same way, the *difference of longitude* (DLo) is always measured as though both points were on the same parallel, or on the equator.

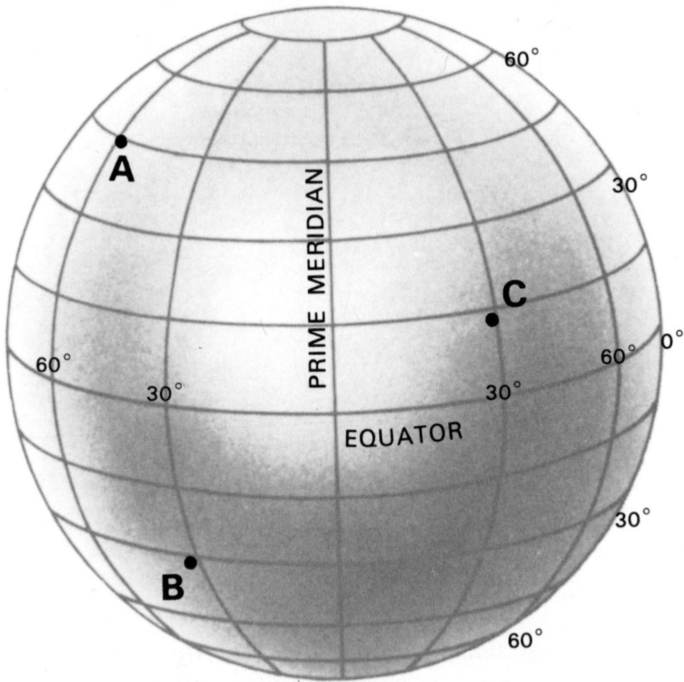

Figure 206a. Difference of latitude (*l*) and difference of longitude (DLo).

Both points may be on the same side of the prime meridian (Greenwich), and therefore of the "same name"—both *east* longitude, or both *west* longitude. They may also be on opposite sides of the prime meridian, and therefore of "contrary name"—one in *east* longitude, the other in *west* longitude.

In Figure 206a, *B* is at longitude 30° west, *C* at 30° east (*contrary name*); the total DLo is obtained by adding the two distances from the prime meridian: 30° + 30° = 60° = DLo, and the rule is still:

for contrary name, add.

A slight complication may appear if the sum of the two longitudes is greater than 180°, but in this case the DLo is *360° minus the sum.* This may be seen from Figure 206b, in which the circumference *GWE* is the equator, and *P* is the north pole. *PG* is the meridian of Greenwich. *PW* is the meridian through the point *W,* at 120° west longitude, *PE* the meridian through *E,* at 90° east longitude (*contrary name*): sum, 120° + 90° = 210°. Obviously, the DLo sought is the *shorter* arc between them (*WXE*), or 360° − 210° = 150°, not the longer arc of 210°.

Again, in Figure 206a, *A* is at 60° west longitude, *B* at 30° west longitude (*same name*). The DLo of 30° is obtained by subtracting the smaller from the larger, and the rule again is:

for same name, subtract.

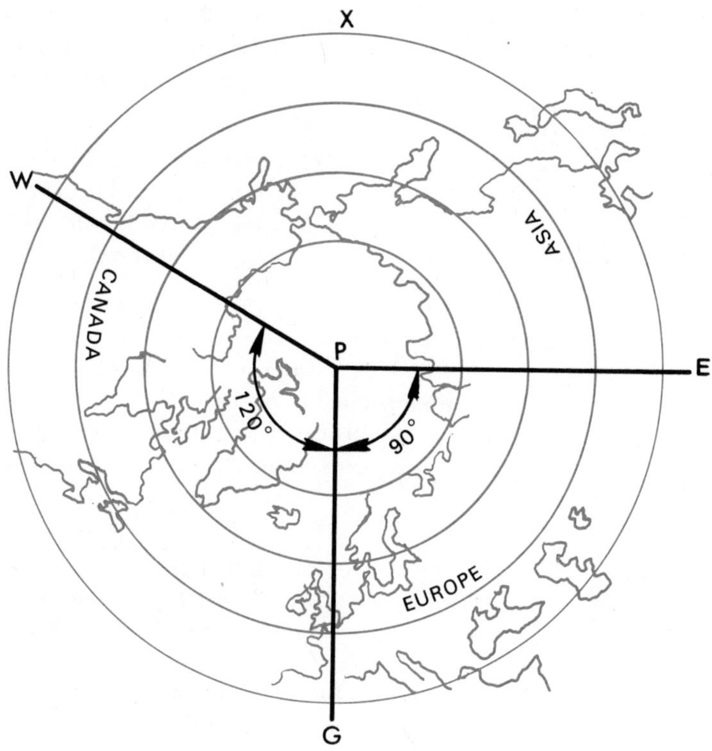

Figure 206b. Difference of longitude (DLo) for "contrary names," and when greater than 180°.

Some navigation problems are solved by means of *latitude and departure* (*latitude,* here, is the difference of latitude already discussed). *Departure* is the difference in longitude, but here expressed in nautical miles rather than degrees and minutes of arc; mathematically, it is DLo multiplied by the cosine of the latitude. As described in Chapter 29, DLo or departure can be found graphically; it can be computed; or it can be found using Table 3 of Volume II, Publication No. 9, *American Practical Navigator* (generally referred to as *Bowditch*).

Mid-latitudes For some navigational calculations, the *mid-latitude* (Lm) is needed. To be quite precise, this is the latitude at which the arc length of the parallel between the meridians of the two points concerned is exactly equal to the departure when proceeding from one point to the other. As this is difficult to calculate, the *mean* latitude is normally used; this gives fully satisfactory results for practical navigational purposes. When both points are on the same side of the equator, this is the arithmetical mean of the two latitudes. For example, in Figure 206a, Lm for points *A* and *C* is (45° + 15°) ÷ 2 = 60° ÷ 2 = 30°.

If Lm is ever required for points on opposite sides of the equator, the procedure is readily apparent in Figure 206a. Thus, Lm for *A* and

B (contrary names) is: (45° + 30°) ÷ 2 = 75° ÷ 2 = 37°30′. In this case, however, 37°30′ is not the Lm sought. It is the difference of latitude between *either* of the two points and the desired Lm; that is, it is either

45° − 37°30′ = 7°30′ north latitude; or
30° − 37°30′ = −7°30′ (that is, 7°30′ on the other side of the equator from *B*, which is, as before, at 7°30′ north latitude).

Although charts and globes are printed with meridians and parallels at regular intervals of 1, 2, 5, or more degrees, a navigator must remember that *any* point on earth lies on a meridian and on a parallel; and that the absence of a printed line does not alter the fact that the longitude and latitude of a point is the measurement of the meridian and parallel passing through that point, described earlier.

Distance in navigation

207 On a *plane* surface, a straight line is defined as "the shortest distance between two points." With the help of a straightedge, such a line may be drawn on an engineering plan and the *distance* measured at the scale of the drawing. Similarly, the *direction* from one point to another may be measured by using an ordinary protractor to determine the angle which the line makes with the rectangular reference lines of the drawing.

Great circles

The shortest *distance* (abbreviated as Dist., symbol D) between any two points on the surface of the earth is always along the great circle between them. The more closely the plane of a small circle approaches the center of the earth, the more closely will distance measured along it approach the shortest distance. The converse is also true, of course.

Since a great circle is the shortest distance between two points on the surface of a sphere, it might be supposed that it would always be the route selected unless there were intervening dangers, such as reefs or shoals. The practical objection to following a great-circle route is that the direction of a great circle is constantly changing; it makes a different angle with each meridian it crosses from starting point to destination. This means that the ship's heading on a great-circle route would be subject to continuous alterations.

Since constant heading changes are scarcely practical, it is customary to follow a *rhumb line,* or a series of rhumb lines, rather than to follow a great circle.

Rhumb lines

For practical purposes, a *rhumb line* (also known as loxodromes or loxodromic spirals) can be defined as a line which crosses every meridian of the sphere at the same angle. In other words, a ship may maintain a true heading without change from starting point to destination (if, for the moment, one disregards factors such as currents, wind, and changing magnetic variation). Figure 207a shows a rhumb line ex-

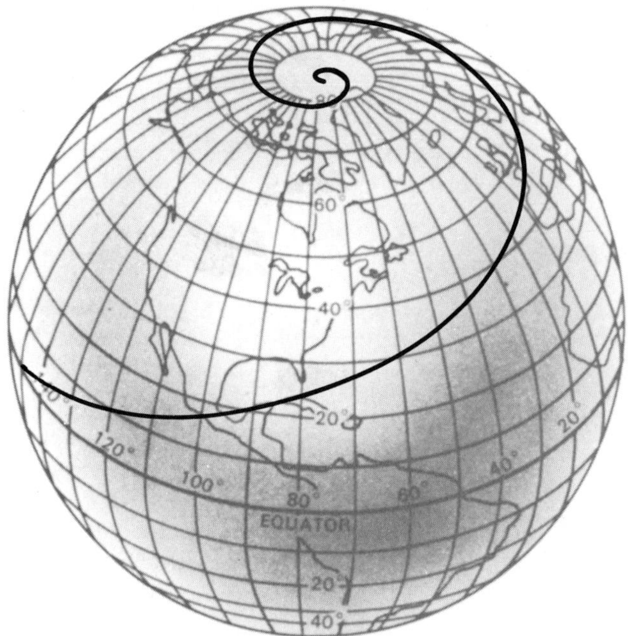

Figure 207a. A rhumb line or loxodrome.

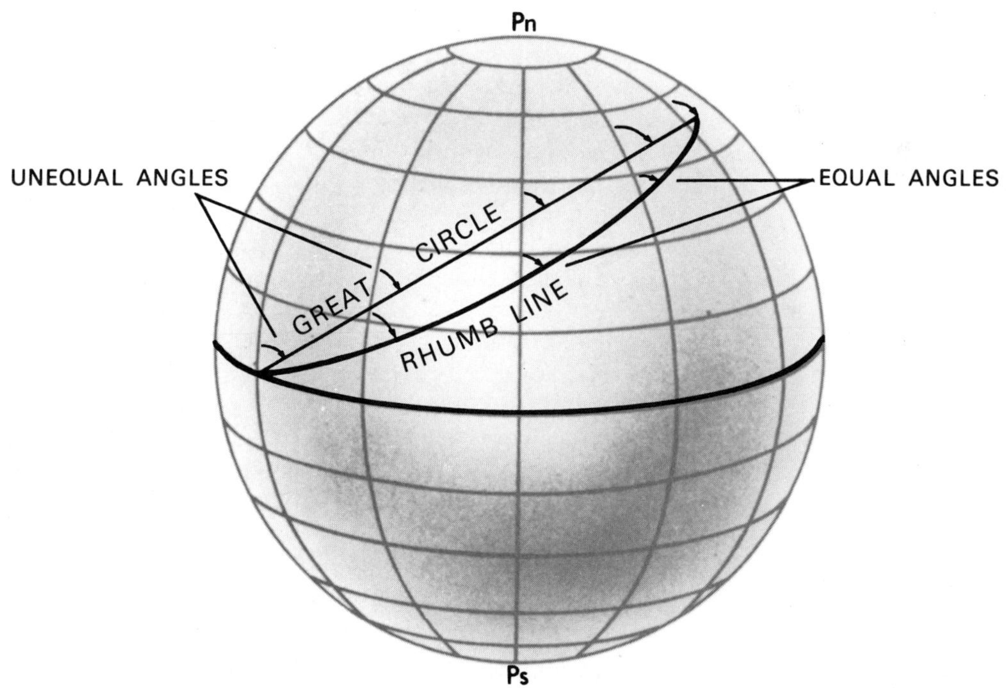

Figure 207b. Great circle and rhumb line on surface of the earth.

tending in a continuous spiral from the equator to the north pole, crossing each meridian at a constant angle of about 70°.

Figure 207b shows the sphere with its meridians and parallels. A great circle and the corresponding rhumb line are also shown, both lines from a point on the equator to a point about 135° of longitude toward the east and at a latitude near 52° north. In this rendition of the sphere it is not possible to show angular relationships correctly, but reference to a globe will show that the great circle leaves the equator at an angle of a little less than 30° with the meridian there; near the middle of the route, the angle with the meridian has increased to about 50° and, near the end of the route, to more than 100°. The rhumb line crosses each successive meridian at a constant angle of about 65°.

Comparative distances

208 A navigator is concerned with both great-circle distances and rhumb-line distances. Except for a few special cases where they are the same, great-circle distances are shorter than rhumb-line distances, the difference depending upon various combinations of latitude and longitude.

In Article 204 it was seen that the equator is a great circle. But the equator is also a rhumb line, with a constant direction of 090° or 270°. Along the equator, then, great-circle distance and rhumb-line distance are identical; there is no difference at all.

As a ship moves farther from the equator toward either pole, the saving in distance by way of the great circle becomes greater, and is always greatest for east-west courses (090° or 270°).

All meridians, too, are great circles by definition; they are also rhumb lines of constant direction, 000° or 180°. It should be obvious that along a meridian (as along the equator) great-circle distance and rhumb-line distance are identical, and there is no difference. The difference begins to increase as the great-circle direction moves away from the north-south direction, reaching a maximum in an east-west direction.

Near the equator, then, the saving in distance by way of a great circle is negligible. For an east-west distance of 1,000 nautical miles, the saving is only about 1.5 miles at latitude 40°, and 10.5 miles at latitude 60°. For the route from New York City to London (mid-latitude about 46°), the great-circle distance is 3,016 nautical miles and the rhumb-line distance is 3,139 nautical miles—a difference of 123 nautical miles.

Great-circle distances are sometimes computed, rather than measured on the chart. In this case, they are obtained in degrees and minutes of arc. As is true of any great circle (such as a meridian), one degree of arc is equal, for practical navigational purposes, to 60 nautical miles, and 1 minute essentially equals 1 nautical mile. The total number of minutes, then, can also be taken as the distance in nautical miles.

Directions in navigation

209 From the preceding it is apparent that there are two kinds of direction, both of which are of interest to the navigator:

Rhumb-line directions are most commonly used in determining the course to be followed, or the track made good.

Great-circle directions are used chiefly in connection with radio direction finding or star sights, and are generally referred to as *bearings* or *azimuths.*

In navigation, *true direction* is the direction from one point on the earth's surface to another, without regard for the distance between them; it is expressed as an angle in degrees from 000° to 360°, referenced to true north. Direction is always expressed in three digits; for example, a direction 8° east of north is expressed as 008°, and one 34° east of north as 034°. True north may be considered as either 000° or 360°, according to the problem at hand.

In Figure 209, the true direction from *A* to *B* is 060°. The true direction from *B* to *A* is 240°; this is called the *reciprocal* direction and is 180° greater, or less, than the other direction. It is axiomatic that every line has two directions, hence the direction intended should be

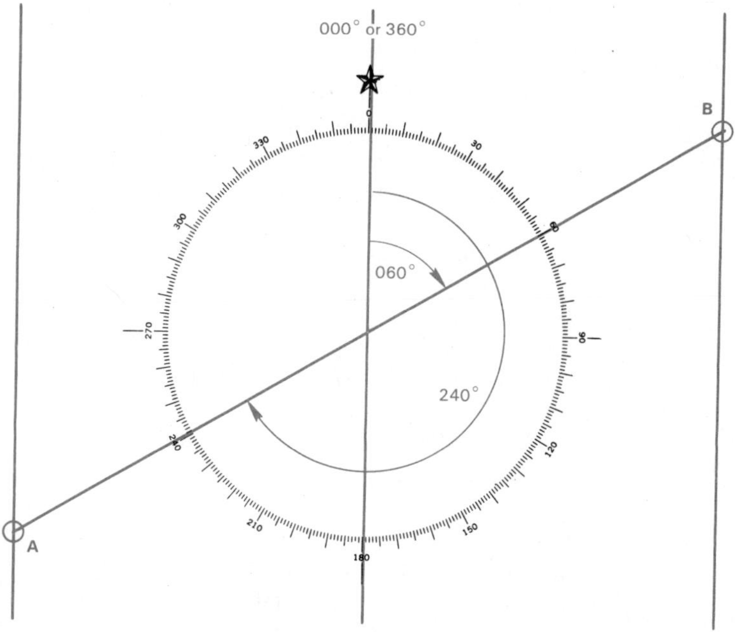

Figure 209. Measurement of direction (course or track) in navigation.

clearly indicated by arrow heads or some system of labeling. Direction can be shown as clearly by the *order of letters* used: thus *AB* is the direction from *A* to *B*; the reciprocal direction from *B* to *A* is *BA*.

All directions, whether great circle, rhumb line, or other, are *true* directions when measured from the true geographic meridian printed on the chart; *magnetic* directions when measured from magnetic north; and *compass* directions when measured with respect to compass north as indicated by the vessel's compass. *Relative* directions are those measured from the ship's head (the direction in which the ship is pointed).

Definitions, abbreviations, and symbols

210 Certain terms are widely used in navigation. A few that have already been touched upon, together with several related ones, will be defined here, together with their commonly used abbreviations and symbols.

Azimuth (Zn). The great-circle direction of any place or object from a given point; chiefly used to designate the direction of a heavenly body in celestial navigation. When referred to true north, azimuth is written as Zn. Aximuth angle (Az or Z) is measured either east or west to 90° using either north or south as the reference direction.

Bearing (B). Same as azimuth, but commonly used in radio direction finding, or in visual sights. As mentioned in Article 208, azimuths and bearings (or any other directional term) may be true, magnetic, compass, or relative, according to the reference line or point used.

Course (C). As applied to marine navigation, the direction in which a vessel is to be steered, or is being steered; the direction of travel through the water. Course may be designated as *true, magnetic, compass,* or *grid* as determined by the reference direction. The course is measured from 000° clockwise from the reference direction to 360°.

Heading (Hdg. or SH). The direction in which a ship points or heads at any instant, expressed in angular units, 000° clockwise through 360°, from a reference direction. The heading of a ship is also called ship's head. Heading is a constantly changing value as a ship oscillates or yaws across the course due to effects of the sea and of steering error.

Track (TR). The intended (anticipated, desired) direction of movement with respect to the earth.

Course Over Ground (COG). The actual path of a vessel with respect to the earth; this will not be a straight line if the vessel's heading varies as she yaws back and forth across the course.

Course Made Good (CMG). The single resultant direction from a given point of departure to a subsequent position; the direction of the net movement from one point to the other. This may differ from the track by inaccuracies in steering, varying current effects, etc.; see Figure 210.

Mile. The unit of distance used in navigation at sea is the *international nautical mile* (n.mi.) of 6076.1 feet (1.852 km). In practical terms, it is equivalent to one minute of latitude, or one minute of arc of any great circle. The *statute mile* (st. mi.) of 5280 feet (1.609 km) is used on land and some inland U.S. waters such as the Great Lakes and the Intracoastal Waterways. One nautical mile equals approximately 1.15 statute miles. Unless otherwise qualified, the term "mile (mi.)" in this book will mean the international nautical mile. (For short distances, a nautical mile and 2,000 yards are often used interchangeably; the error is only 1¼ percent.)

Knot (kn, or occasionally kt). The unit of speed; one knot equals one nautical mile per hour. It is redundant and incorrect to refer to speeds in "knots *per hour.*"

Latitude (Lat.; L or occasionally ϕ, the greek letter phi). The arc distance of a point measured from the equator toward either pole. In problems involving latitude at two or more points, latitude of the first point is usually written as L_1; second point L_2, etc. *Difference* of latitude between two places is indicated by *l*; *mid-latitude* (the mean latitude) is indicated by Lm.

Longitude (Long.; Lo or λ, the Greek letter lambda). The angular distance along the equator or a parallel between the prime meridian at Greenwich and the meridian of a particular point. In problems involving the longitude of two or more points, the longitude of the first point is written as Lo_1 (or λ_1), the second point as Lo_2 (or λ_2), etc. The

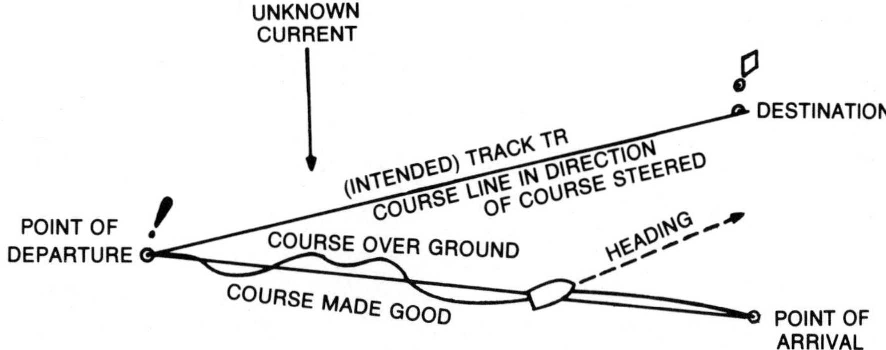

Figure 210. Course, track, course over ground (exaggerated), and course made good.

east-west separation of two points is termed *difference of longitude* (DLo) when expressed in angular units, or as *departure* (p) when expressed in nautical miles.

Summary

211 This chapter has described the earth and the basic reference lines which are essential in determining geographical position in terms of latitude and longitude. It has also outlined the general problems of distance and direction and their solutions by way of great circles, small circles, and rhumb lines. This information is basic and fundamental. Without it, solution of the problems of navigation is impossible.

3 Chart Projections and Chart Interpretation

Introduction **301** The nautical chart is one of the mariner's oldest and most widely used navigational aids; the term is derived from the Greek *chartēs,* a leaf of papyrus. The Greeks used sailing directions several hundred years before the birth of Christ. They may also have had charts, as it is easier to draw a diagram to show how to get to a place than it is to explain the process in writing; however, there is no proof that such charts actually existed.

In the third century B.C, the Greek scientific writer, Eratosthenes of Alexandria, reasoned that the earth must be a sphere, as at high noon on the day of the summer solstice objects of the same height at two locations on the same meridian did not cause shadows of the same length. He proceeded to determine the zenith distances at Alexandria and Syene (now Aswan), which he estimated to be the equivalent of 500 statute miles to the south, and found them to differ by about 7.5°. Since 7.5° is 1/48 of the circumference of a circle, he calculated that the earth's circumference must be 48 × 500 or 24,000 statute miles. This was a surprisingly accurate determination as the actual length of a meridian is 24,820 statute miles. This seems to be the first measurement of latitude using the degree as a standard of measurement.

In the second century A.D., the great astronomer and mathematician, Ptolemy, constructed many maps, among them a famous world map which listed several thousand places by latitude and longitude. Unfortunately, he did not use Eratosthenes' calculations but those of a Greek philosopher, who had estimated the earth's circumference to be the equivalent of 18,000 statute miles. Ptolemy's work remained a standard through the middle ages, and led Columbus to believe that he had reached the East Indies in 1492.

The earliest charts of the middle ages still in existence are the Portolan charts prepared in Spain in the fourteenth century. They are remarkably accurate in their portrayal of the Mediterranean. In 1515, Leonardo da Vinci drew his famous map of the world, which shows America extending farther east and west than north and south.

Gerardus Mercator, the Flemish cartographer who produced a world chart constructed on the basis of the projection which bears his name, is the father of modern cartography. The accuracy of charts continued to improve, but as they had to be printed by hand, they were extremely expensive. The mariner considered them much too valuable to be used for plotting; this led to wide use of the *sailings* (various forms of calculated dead reckoning). These mathematical methods of determining DR position remained in wide use aboard ship through much of the nineteenth century. (See chapter 29.)

U.S. chart agencies

The *U.S. Coast and Geodetic Survey* was established by Congress in 1807 and charged with making a survey of the coasts, harbors, and off-lying islands of the United States. The Navy, in 1830, established the *Depot of Charts and Instruments* which later became the *Hydrographic Office* and then the *Naval Oceanographic Office.*

As a result of several governmental reorganizations, the present agency for charting U.S. coastal waters and those of U.S. possessions is the *National Ocean Survey* (NOS), an element of the National Oceanic and Atmospheric Administration (NOAA) in the Department of Commerce. NOS publishes charts for coastal rivers and the Great Lakes; the Army Corps of Engineers prepares "navigational maps" for the Mississippi River and its tributaries.

The charting (and navigational publications) functions of the U.S. Navy were consolidated with roughly similar activities of certain other government offices into the *Defense Mapping Agency.* Of primary interest to navigators is that agency's *Hydrographic Center* (DMAHC). This activity is charged with the production of charts of the rest of the world, either from its own field work or by reproduction of the charts of other nations. Both NOS and DMAHC conduct continuing surveys, and their highly accurate charts are generally available to the mariners of all nations. (A few DMAHC charts are restricted to official use only.) Specialized charts for aviation interests and for other purposes are published by various other government agencies.

Maps and charts

A *map* is a representation, in miniature, on a flat surface, of a portion of the earth's surface. It shows physical features; cities, towns, and roads; political boundaries; and other geographic information.

A *chart* is also a representation of a portion of the earth's surface, but has been specially designed for convenient use in navigation. It is intended to be worked upon, not merely to be looked at, and should readily permit the graphic solution of navigational problems, such as distance and direction or determination of position, in terms of latitude and longitude.

A *nautical chart* has to do primarily with areas of navigable water. It features such information as coastlines and harbors, depths of water, channels and obstructions, and landmarks and aids to navigation. Charts provide a means of describing a position in terms of latitude and longitude.

Aeronautical charts show elevations, obstructions, prominent landmarks, airports, and aids to navigation. Although frequently depicting only land areas, they may differ from ordinary maps of the same areas by emphasizing or exaggerating landmarks or other features of special importance to air navigators.

For use at sea there are also a number of "special purpose" charts, such as pilot charts to provide weather and other information, tidal current charts, star charts, etc. In the remainder of this chapter, primary consideration will be given to nautical charts, to the projections upon which they are constructed, and to the navigator's use of them.

The round earth on flat paper

302 A simple experiment will prove that no considerable portion of a hollow rubber ball can be spread out flat without some stretching or tearing. Conversely, a sheet of tissue paper cannot be wrapped smoothly around a sphere; there will be numerous wrinkles and overlaps.

The earth also being round (a "spheroid"), it cannot be represented on a flat piece of paper without some distortion. The smaller the portion of the globe to be mapped, the less the distortion that will

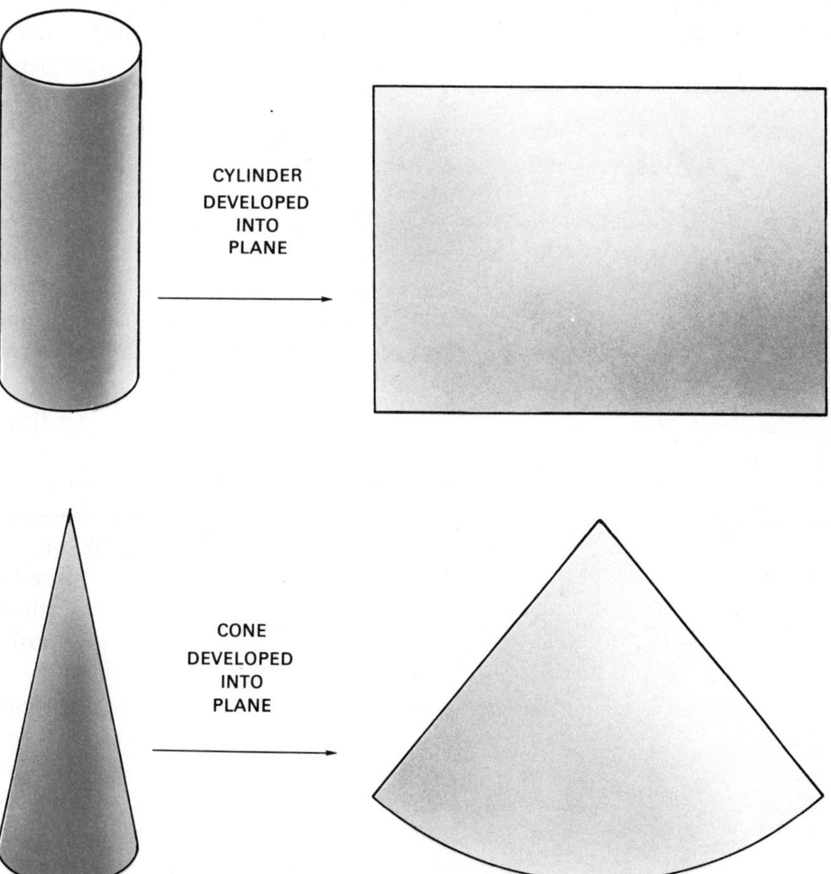

Figure 302. Development of a cylinder and a cone.

be present—conversely, the greater the area, the greater the distortion.

Because the surface of a sphere cannot be represented accurately upon a plane surface, it is called "undevelopable." There are other surfaces, however, which *are* developable, and can be spread out flat without change in any design or pattern drawn upon them. Two such surfaces are those of a cone and a cylinder. A paper cone or cylinder can be cut from top to bottom and rolled out flat without distortion of any kind, as indicated in Figure 302. It is also true that a *limited portion* of the earth's surface can be shown ("projected") directly upon a plane surface while keeping distortion within acceptable limits.

Reference lines

It is customary, therefore, to think of the reference lines of the non-developable sphere as first projected upon some developable surface (a plane, cone, or cylinder) and then developed or spread out flat. A chart projection may be loosely defined as any orderly arrangement of the meridians and parallels of the sphere. There are several hundred projections, each with some particular property that may make it desirable for some specific purpose. Of these, not more than about half a dozen have ever been of much use for navigation.

Properties and projections

303 For navigation, certain properties are desirable in a projection. Among them are:

1. *True shape* of physical features such as bodies of land or water;
2. *True scale and size* of various areas of land or water;
3. *Correct angular relationships;*
4. *Great circles as straight lines;*
5. *Rhumb lines as straight lines.*

A chart of a very small area may closely achieve most or all of these characteristics with any method of projection. As the area grows larger, however, only one or two of the characteristics can be achieved; for example, in a large area chart either great circles or rhumb lines can be straight lines, but not both. The projection method used for any particular application must weigh and balance the various characteristics against each other. *All* of them can be obtained *only* on a *spherical* surface.

Conformal charts

All of the projections commonly used for navigational charts (with one exception) are *conformal.* This is generally interpreted to mean depiction of both *true shape* and *correct angular* relationships, but this is true only in a quite limited sense.

Conformality does provide true shape for small areas. For example, the Mercator projection is conformal. Along the rugged coast of Alaska it preserves the shape of a single inlet accurately enough, but for Alaska as a whole this projection stretches out the northerly portion much more than the southerly portion, and the overall shape is not true at all.

Conformality is also said to yield correct angular relationships. It might therefore be expected that on a Lambert conformal map of the United States, one might draw a straight line from Miami to Seattle, and that the line so drawn would make the correct angle with each of the meridians between, but this is not the case (see Article 312). With only minor exceptions, no straight line "from *A* to *B*" can be said to represent *exactly* correct angular relationships, even on a conformal map or chart.

Classification of projections

304 Perhaps it is most practical to classify projections in accordance with the developable surface from which they are considered to be derived; that is, as plane, conical, or cylindrical projections.

The *plane* projections best known by navigators are the *gnomonic* and the *stereographic.*

Conic projections include those with a tangent cone, those with a cone cutting the earth's surface at two parallels of latitude, and those with multiple cones tangent at several parallels. The best known is the *Lambert conformal* projection.

The most-used cylindrical projection is the *Mercator;* it has several variations.

Classification by reference point

This classification by developable surfaces can be further broken down according to the point from which the reference lines (meridians and parallels) are projected upon the developable surface. Figure 304a shows the method of projection for the *gnomonic, stereographic,* and *orthographic* projections.

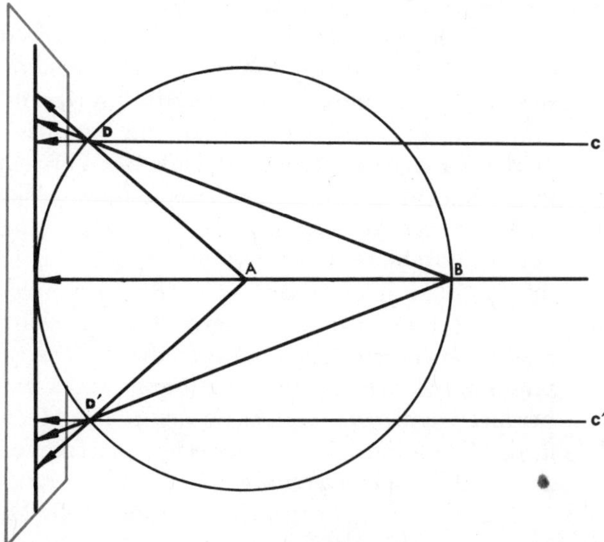

Figure 304a. Gnomonic projection from center of sphere A; stereographic projection from B; orthographic projection from C and C′ (parallel rays).

For the *gnomonic* projection the points *D, D'* on the sphere in Figure 304a are projected from *A,* the center of the sphere, upon a plane tangent at the equator. Because of the point of projection this is classed as a *central perspective* (or geometrical) projection. Since the plane is tangent at the equator, it is also known as the *equatorial* gnomonic. For a chart of the north polar regions the plane could have been made tangent at the pole, and the resulting projection from *A* would have been a *polar* gnomonic. The plane could also have been made tangent at any point between the equator and either pole, in which case the projection obtained from the same central point *A* would have been an *oblique* gnomonic.

Figure 304a also shows the method of projection for the *stereographic.* Instead of being projected from the center of the sphere, points are projected upon the tangent plane from the opposite end of the diameter from the point of tangency (from *B* in the figure). As described in the preceding paragraph, the case shown in the figure yields an equatorial stereographic. A *polar* stereographic or an *oblique* stereographic is as readily obtained. In each case, the point of projection is always the opposite end of the diameter from the point of tangency.

The third type of projection onto a tangent plane illustrated by Figure 304a is the *orthographic.* Here the projection "rays" are from infinity, shown as C and C', and thus are all parallel. The plane of the projection is usually tangent at the equator to depict half of the earth, such as the western hemisphere, although without conformality or equal area representation.

Cylindrical projections

A central perspective projection can readily be obtained by projecting the reference lines of the sphere upon a cylinder tangent to the sphere along the equator. The resulting projection is shown in Figure 304b (at left), with the meridians represented by a series of equally spaced vertical lines, the parallels by a series of lines at right angles to the meridians; spacing between the parallels expands rapidly with increasing distance from the equator. This expansion is, in fact, so great that the *central perspective cylindrical* projection is never used.

A *Mercator projection* is often visualized as the placement of a cylinder around the earth touching it at a great circle; see Figure 304b. For this reason, it is generally classified as a cylindrical projection. Strictly speaking, however, the modern Mercator chart is derived from rigid mathematical equations in order that a straight line between any two points will represent a rhumb line; this is a property that the central perspective projection does not have. The Mercator is conformal, and its distortion in high latitudes is less than that which would occur with a central perspective chart.

Accepting the general classification of the Mercator as a cylindrical projection, the "cylinder" may be thought of as tangent along the equator (its most common form), and become the *equatorial* case. The cylinder may also be turned through 90° and become tangent along

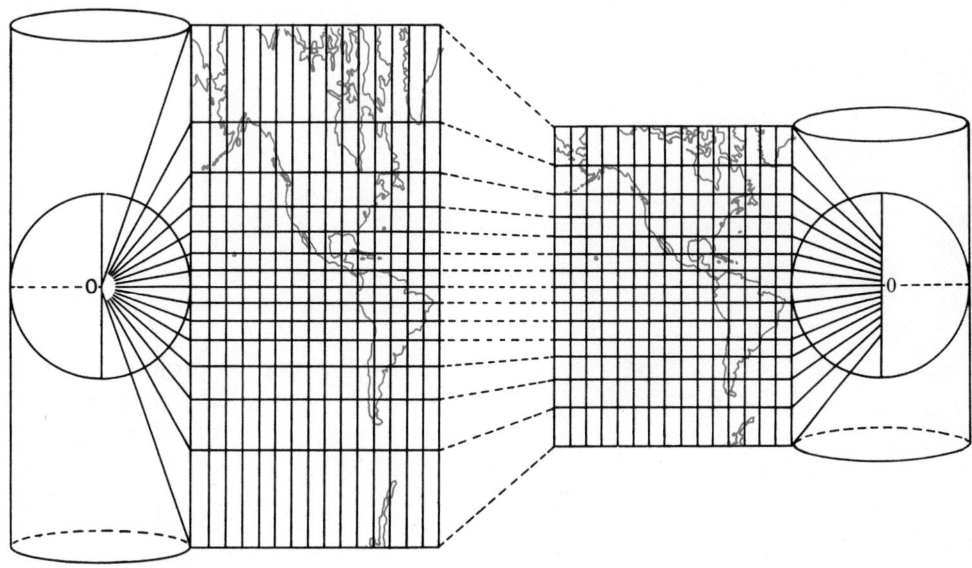

Figure 304b. Central projection upon a cylinder (left) compared with Mercator conformal projection (right).

a selected meridian, and thus tangent also at both poles. According to previous terminology, this should be known as the polar case, but is actually called the *transverse Mercator*—and, sometimes, the *inverse Mercator.*

The cylinder may also be made tangent to some selected great circle, in any direction, anywhere on the surface of the sphere, as along a great-circle route between Miami and Lisbon; see Figure 304c. This is generally known as the *oblique Mercator,* since the cylinder in this case is neither vertical nor horizontal with reference to the earth's axis; only a small area on either side of the line of tangency is used.

For conic projections, the axis of the cone usually coincides with the axis of the sphere, but it also may be turned to any other position, resulting in a transverse or oblique conic.

Azimuthal projections

Other classifications are common. For example, most polar projections are *azimuthal* (or zenithal). By this it is meant that all directions (azimuths) from the center of the projection are true. The polar stereographic projection is azimuthal as well as conformal. All gnomonic projections are azimuthal, affording true directions from the point of tangency, regardless of the position of the point on the sphere.

In any family of projections it is possible to obtain different properties simply by varying the spacing of the parallels. The *polar stereographic* projection is conformal, and scale along the meridians varies. The *polar equidistant* yields true scale along each meridian. A *polar equal area* projection is also obtainable by another variation in the spacing of the parallels. All three are azimuthal.

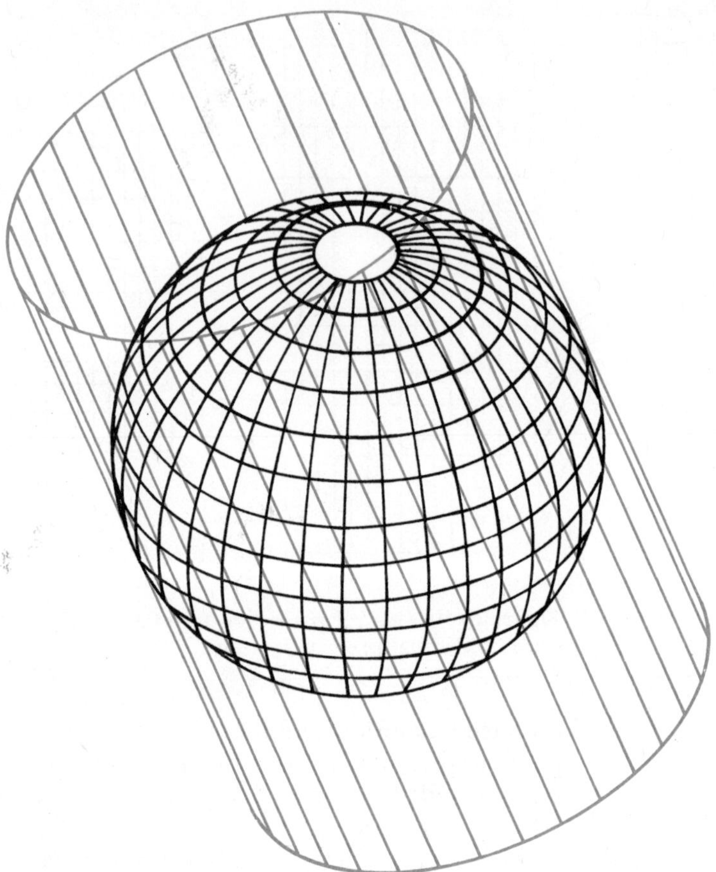

Figure 304c. An oblique Mercator projection.

In the same way, a cylindrical projection may be conformal (the ordinary Mercator) or equal area, by varying the spacing of the parallels. Conic projections, too, may be either conformal (as the Lambert conformal) or equal area (as the Albers).

Mercator projection

305 Most of the charts used for marine navigation, and a good many of those used for air navigation, are based on the Mercator projection. In many cases this is completely justifiable; in others, its use appears to be based in part on its past success, and on a reluctance to adopt more suitable projections because of slightly different procedures from those which have become customary. It is thought by some that modern methods of radionavigation might be better adapted to a projection on which a straight line represents a great circle rather than a rhumb line. It has also been pointed out that, even for ordinary nautical charts, other projections could replace the Mercator with appreciable advantage, especially in higher latitudes.

Rhumb lines For conventional methods of navigation—largely based on dead reckoning, or the determination of position by course and distance from some charted point—the Mercator projection has its advantages. On its rectangular graticule, latitude and longitude are conveniently plotted; the *rhumb line* (see Article 207) between any two points is the straight line between them; and the direction of a rhumb line may be measured at any convenient meridian.

Distances along a course line can be determined without great difficulty although not with the same ease of measurement as on a Lambert. Great-circle distances and directions are not readily determinable without first plotting the great circle on a gnomonic chart (Article 309) and transferring points along the line to the Mercator.

When compared with a globe, a Mercator projection shows great exaggeration of shape and area in high latitudes. The example most often cited is that Greenland, when shown complete on the Mercator, appears to be larger than South America, although it actually is only one-ninth as large as that continent.

Figure 305 may help in understanding this weakness of the projection. In the figure, at *A,* one gore or section of an ordinary school room globe has been peeled off and stands vertically. Two true circles of the same size have been drawn on the gore, to serve as "test patterns."

At *B* the sides of the gore have been stretched horizontally so that the two outer meridians are parallel to the central meridian of the gore. In the stretching the two circles have become ellipses (repre-

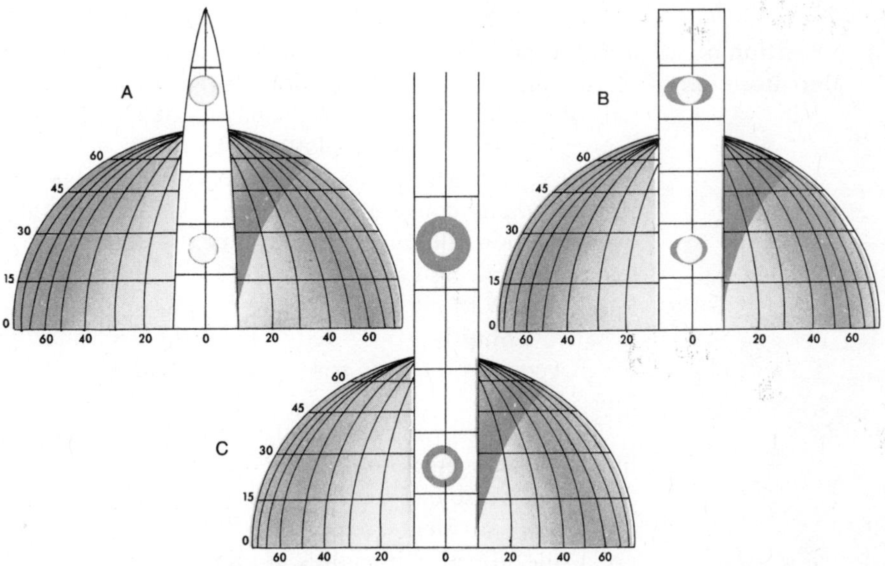

Figure 305. Relationship between areas on a globe and their representations on a Mercator projection.

sented by the shaded areas), the northerly one having been stretched much more than the southern one.

Since the Mercator projection is to be conformal, true shapes of small areas must be preserved, so the horizontally stretched gore must now be stretched vertically until the ellipses again become (approximately) circles, the diameter in each case approximating the major axis of the ellipse. The result is shown at *C* in Figure 305.

Distortion Note that, since the upper part of the gore has been stretched more than the lower part, the upper circle has become appreciably greater in diameter than the lower one. Also, the upper edge of the gore at *C* is shown ragged and broken. It can no longer be extended all the way to the pole, for the pole has been stretched northward all the way to infinity. Consequently, most Mercator projections extend no farther from the equator than about 70°; rarely beyond 80°.

Part of the definition of *conformality* is that the scale at any point must be the same in all directions. This means that when a given parallel of latitude has been expanded from its length as shown at *A* to the length indicated in *B*, the scale of the meridian at that latitude must be expanded proportionately. It can be shown mathematically that the expansion at any place on the Mercator approximates the secant of the latitude of the place. Figure 304b (right) shows the graticule of a Mercator projection for the western hemisphere.

Many navigation charts cover a much smaller area, on which the distance scale is almost constant and there is little variation between the rhumb line and great circle. It is on the small-scale charts of large areas (see Article 322) that distinctive features become evident.

Position on a Mercator chart **306** A position of known latitude and longitude can be quickly plotted on a Mercator projection, using a plotter or straightedge and a pair of dividers. For example, a navigator's fix at 1635 (Lat. 41°09′ N, Long. 70°44′W) may be plotted as follows: note the given latitude, 41°09′ N, on the latitude scale. Place a straightedge through this point parallel to any convenient parallel of latitude, aligning it in an east-west direction. Then set one point of the dividers at 71°00′ W on the longitude scale and the other at 70°44′ W, a spread of 16.0 minutes of longitude. Without changing the setting of the dividers, lay off this distance along the straightedge from the 71st meridian eastward, in the direction of the fix. Circle this point and label with the appropriate time (1635).

The reverse problem—determining the latitude and longitude of a fix that has been plotted at the intersection of two or more lines of position—is also easily accomplished; see Figure 306. Place one point of a pair of dividers on the 1635 fix and swing the other point in an arc, while adjusting its radius, until it becomes tangent to a parallel of latitude. The spread of the dividers then equals the difference of latitude from this reference parallel. Transfer the dividers to the latitude

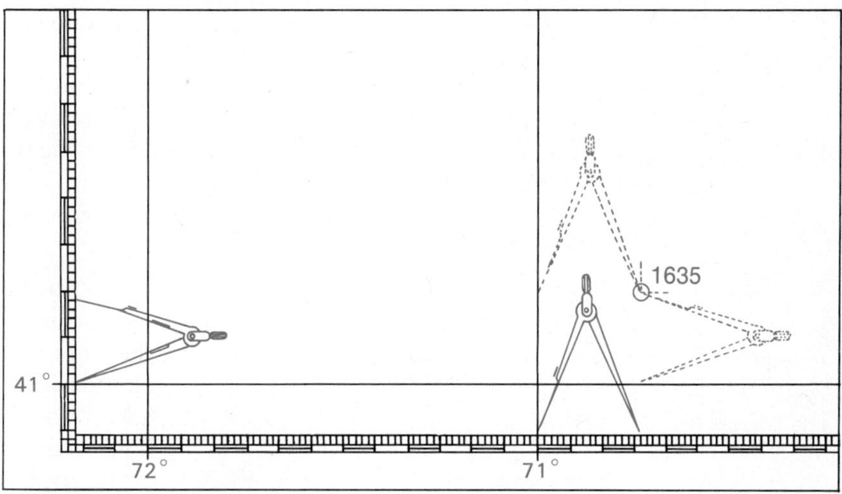

Figure 306. Locating a position on a Mercator chart.

scale and, placing one point at the reference parallel, read the latitude of the fix at the other point. A similar procedure, measuring from the fix to a meridian of longitude, will provide the longitude of the point. Be careful in each case to lay off the difference of latitude and longitude in the proper direction from the reference parallel or meridian. With practice, this can easily be done with one hand while aligning the straightedge or recording with the other.

Direction on a Mercator chart

307 As pointed out in Article 209, two kinds of direction are important to a navigator: *great-circle* directions and *rhumb-line* directions.

On a sphere, the great circle is the direct (shortest) route, and may be thought of as a straight line, while the rhumb line is a longer curved line, always between the great circle and the equator; see Figure 207b. The purpose of the Mercator projection is to introduce exactly the right amount of distortion to show every rhumb line as a straight line; see Figure 307a. When this has been done, in order to keep all parts of the chart in their correct *relative* positions, the great circle has been distorted into a curved line, always farther from the equator than the rhumb line, and always concave toward the equator; see Figure 307b. If a mental picture of this relationship is kept in mind, it will help in the solution of navigational problems.

Measurement of the rhumb-line direction (Figure 307a) can be made at any convenient meridian, with any available protractor; or the direction of the rhumb line can be transferred to a nearby compass rose by means of parallel rulers or a drafting machine, and read from the compass rose. In any case, care must be taken to read the direction at the circumference of the compass rose *toward* the destination, not in the opposite direction, a difference of 180°.

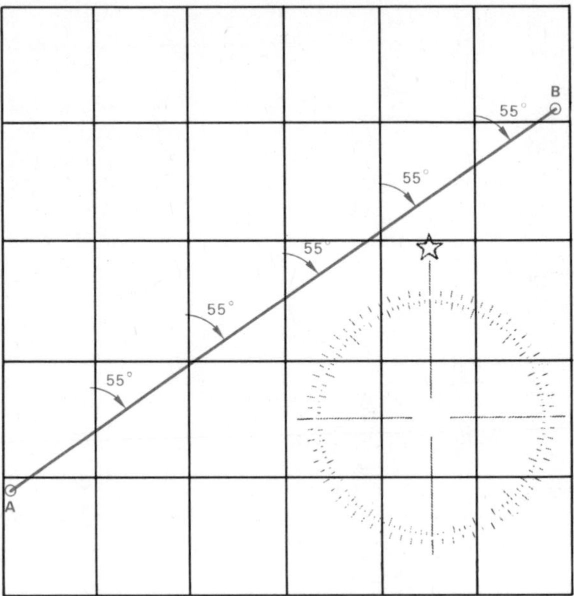

Figure 307a. Measuring direction on a Mercator chart.

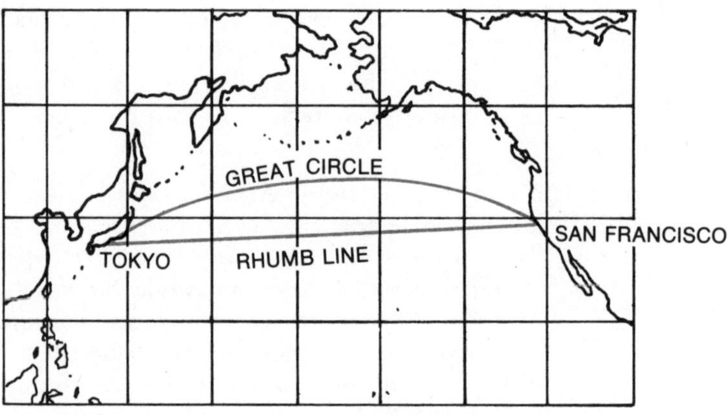

Figure 307b. On a Mercator chart, a great-circle course plots as a curved line with its vertex on the side of the equivalent rhumb line away from the equator.

Distance on a Mercator chart

308 For practical purposes, 1° of latitude everywhere on the earth's surface may be considered to be 60 nautical miles in length; the length of 1° of longitude varies with the latitude, from 60 miles at the equator to zero at the poles (Figure 205c). Since 1 *minute* of latitude, then, is everywhere equal to 1 *mile,* it is the *latitude scale* that must be used for measuring distance—*never the longitude scale.*

Because the latitude scale of a Mercator chart expands increasingly with distance from the equator, the scale of miles is increasing accordingly. That is, in the northerly part of a Mercator chart in the northern hemisphere the length of each mile on the chart has been stretched and there are fewer miles in an inch than in the southerly part. That part of the latitude scale should be used which is at the mean latitude of the distance to be measured (Figure 308a). Except for small-scale charts, this may usually be done with sufficient accuracy by placing one point of a pair of dividers at *A*, the other point at *B*, then placing the dividers on the latitude scale with the middle of the dividers at about the mid-latitude. The difference of latitude in minutes on the latitude scale, is the distance in nautical miles.

When the distance is great enough that the dividers cannot reach all the way from *A* to *B* in one step, one point of the dividers might be placed at *A*, the other point at a position about halfway between *A* and *B*. The length of this portion of the route could then be measured from the latitude scale with the dividers centered at about the mid-latitude of that part. Similarly, the length of the remainder could be read with the dividers centered at about the mid-latitude of the other part. The two distances then would be added to obtain the total distance.

Distance measured at mid-latitude of route

When the distance is too great for one or two settings of the dividers, some convenient unit (10 miles, in Figure 308a) can be taken from the latitude scale at the mid-latitude and stepped off along the route, as shown. In the figure it was stepped off five times: 5 × 10 = 50 miles, with a little left over. The small amount left over is then set on the dividers and laid off along the latitude scale, where it is found to measure 2 miles: 50 + 2 = 52 miles, the total distance from *A* to *B*.

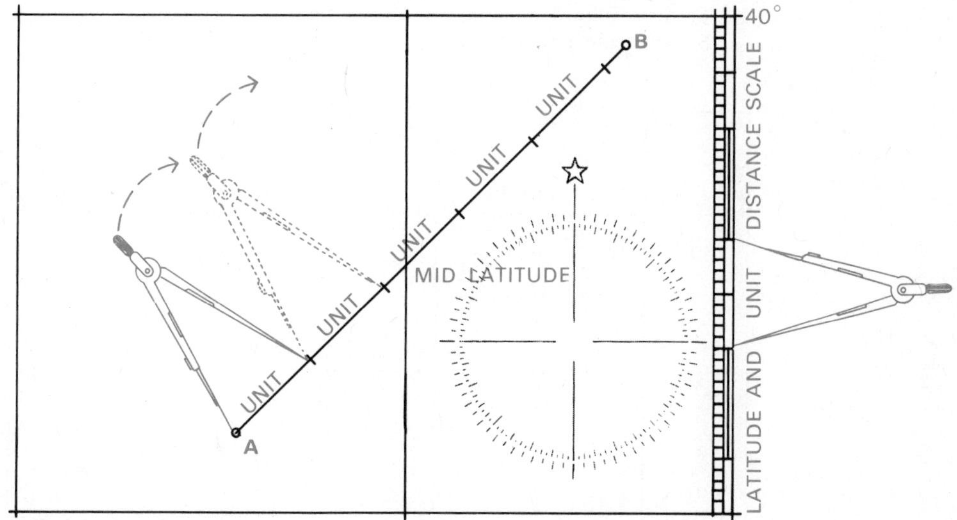

Figure 308a. Measuring distance on a Mercator chart.

Large-scale charts, which cover a limited area, with little change of scale, often carry a simple graphic "bar scale" for measuring distance. This may be simply a line, or a double line, divided into miles, or some other appropriate unit such as yards or kilometers; fractions of one major unit are marked to the *left* of the zero point. Frequently, such a chart will carry two or three such graphic scales, each with different units; see Figure 322.

When using the bar scale, a distance to be measured between two points on the chart is set on the dividers and referred to the bar scale. Assume that the distance is between 2 and 3 miles; one point of the dividers is set on the graduation for 2 miles, and the other point falls at 0.5 miles to the left of zero. The total distance is determined as 2.5 miles.

For smaller scale charts covering a wide band of latitude a "scale diagram" (Figure 308b) is sometimes used. This is, in effect, simply a series of bar scales, in parallel lines, with zero of each scale in the same vertical line. Smooth curves are then drawn through the corresponding graduations of each scale.

Each scale in the diagram is correct for the latitude indicated, and distances should be measured with the scale for the average latitude of the distance required. Obviously, the correct scale for any latitude intermediate between two adjacent lines is also available. For example,

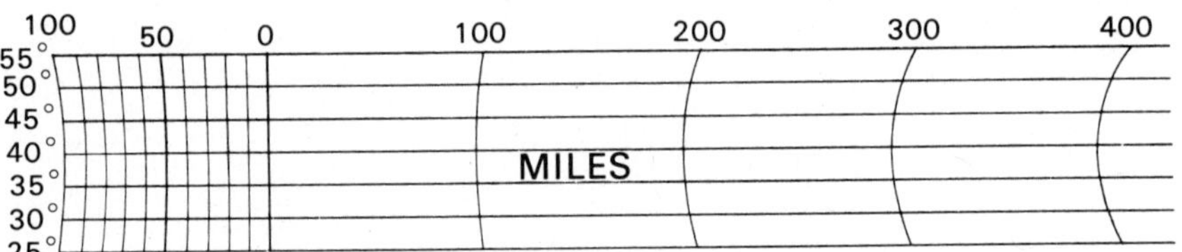

Figure 308b. Scale diagram for a Lambert conformal chart of the United States; scale 1:5,000,000.

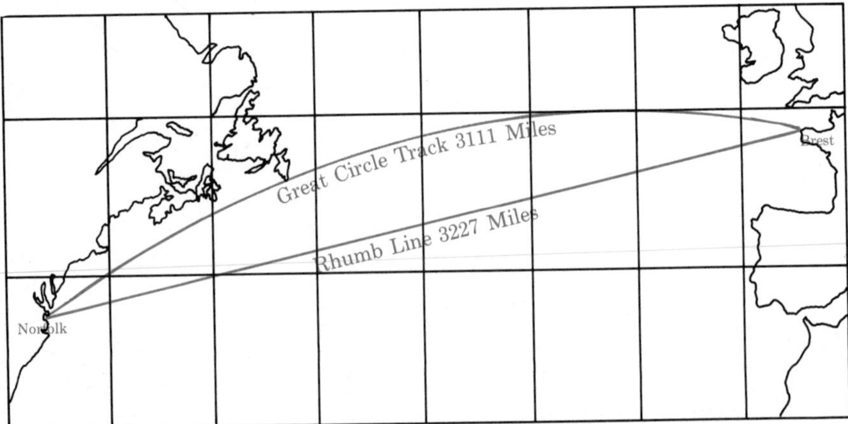

Figure 308c. Great circle and rhumb line on a Mercator chart.

if the average latitude between *A* and *B* is determined as about 27°30′ the dividers can be set on the diagram about halfway between the scales for 25° and 30°.

Figure 308c is a portion of a Mercator chart showing both the great-circle route and the rhumb line between Norfolk, Virginia (Chesapeake Bay Entrance), and Brest, France. As always on a Mercator chart, the great-circle route *appears* to be appreciably longer but, when measured as shown in Figure 308a, the longer line is found to cover fewer miles.

Transverse and *oblique* Mercator projections are described in Article 314 on pages 44–47.

Gnomonic projection

309 The gnomonic projection (Figure 304a) is a perspective (geometrical) projection in which the reference lines of the sphere are projected from the center of the earth upon a tangent plane. The point of tangency may be on the equator (*equatorial*); at either pole (*polar*); or at any other latitude (*oblique* gnomonic). For the oblique gnomonic, shown in Figure 309a, convergency of the meridians increases with the latitude of the point of tangency, from 0° in the equatorial case to 1° for each degree of longitude in the polar case.

Great circle as a straight line

The Mercator projection was developed for the purpose of showing every rhumb line as a straight line. The gnomonic projection has been adapted to a number of special uses, but in navigation it is chiefly used because it shows every *great circle* as a straight line. Figure 309b shows the great circle and rhumb line of Figure 308c. For the latter figure, the great circle was first drawn as a straight line on the gnomonic, then transferred to the Mercator by plotting a number of geographic positions along it. For the navigator, this is the principal use of the gnomonic or great-circle charts. If a rhumb line is desired on the gno-

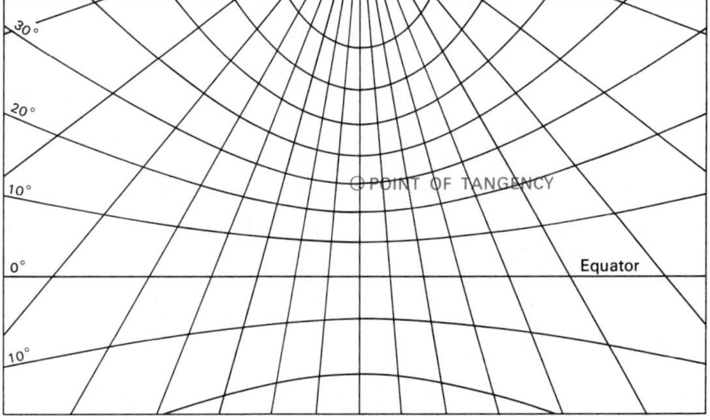

Figure 309a. Gnomonic great-circle chart.

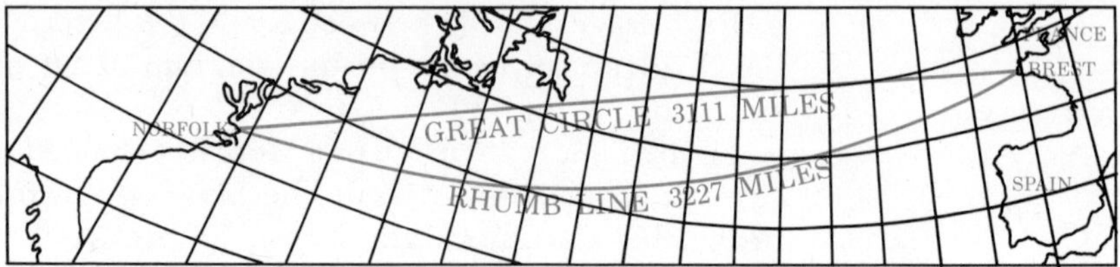

Figure 309b. Rhumb line and great circle on a gnomonic chart.

monic, this process must be reversed: a straight line is first drawn on the Mercator, then transferred to its geographic position on the gnomonic.

Combining great-circle and rhumb-line courses

Great-circle courses yield the shortest distances; rhumb-line courses are easier to sail because of the unvarying heading. For routes where the saving in distance is sufficient to justify it, the advantages of great-circle *and* rhumb-line navigation can be combined. As it is obviously impractical to follow a path of constantly changing direction (great circle), the course is changed in steps at convenient intervals; the result is a series of rhumb lines closely approximating the great-circle course. This is done by first plotting the great-circle route on a *gnomonic* chart, on which every straight line is a great circle (Figure 309a). The great-circle route is then transferred to the Mercator chart by plotting the latitude and longitude of a number of points lying on the great circle. Finally, the great circle as plotted on the Mercator is divided into sections of convenient length; and the rhumb-line direction of each section is measured, and *followed* in turn. In this way the great-circle route is approximated by a number of rhumb-line "chords."

(Great-circle courses and intermediate points can also be calculated mathematically; see Chapter 29.)

Gnomonic distortion

In all three cases of the gnomonic, distortion of shape and scale increases as distance from the center of the projection (the point of tangency) increases. Within about 1,000 miles of the point of tangency, this distortion is not objectionable; beyond that, it increases rapidly. Distance and direction cannot be measured directly, but instructions are usually printed on the chart for determining great-circle distances and the initial direction of a great circle. It is useless as a working chart for normal plotting of navigational data.

It is impossible to include as much as a hemisphere in a single gnomonic chart. At 90 degrees from the center of the projection (the point of tangency) the projecting line is parallel to the plane of the projection, and would meet it only at infinity.

Lambert conformal projection

310 Like the Mercator, the Lambert is derived from rigid mathematical equations. To aid in visualizing the general form of the projection, it is convenient to think of it as in Figure 310, which illustrates a Lambert chart of the United States.

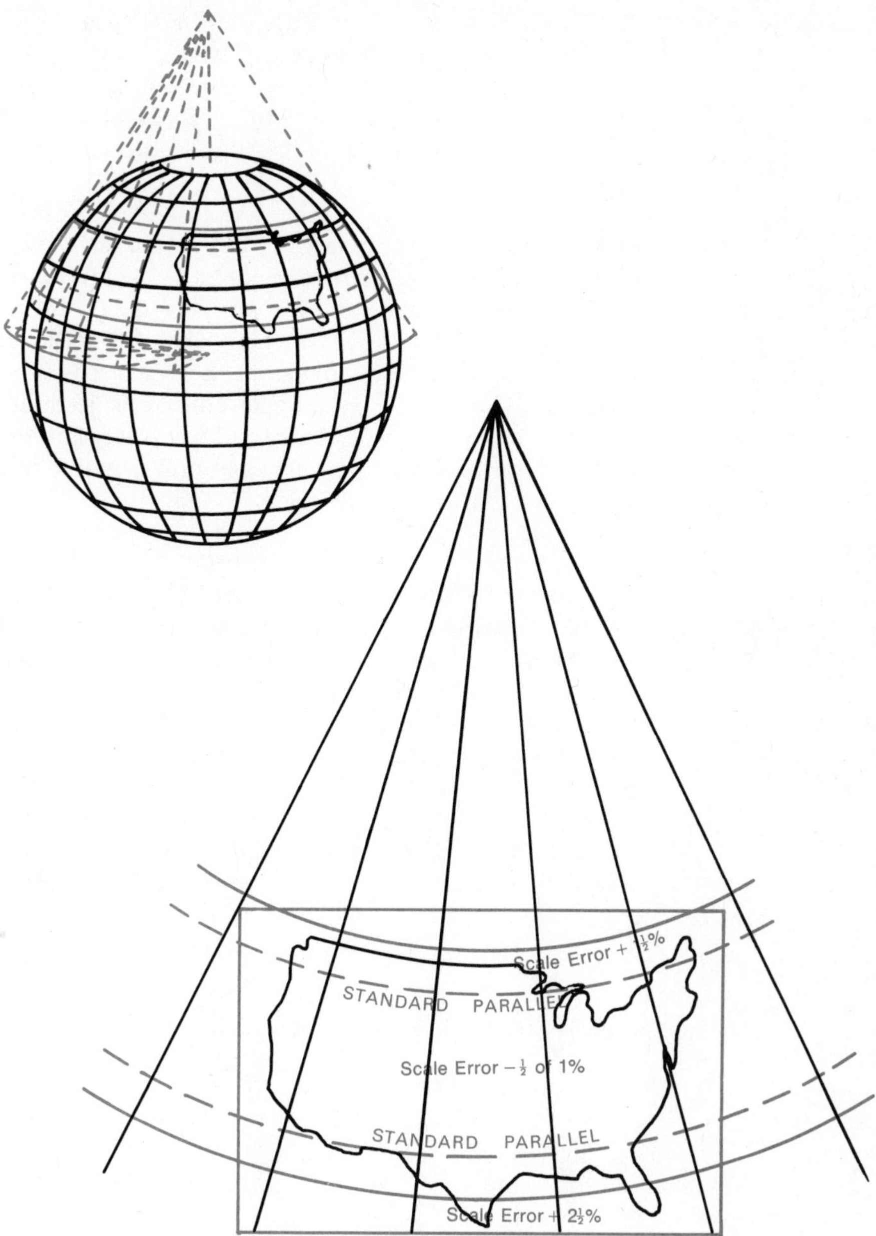

Figure 310. Development and scale properties of Lambert conformal projection.

The cone is represented, not as tangent to the earth, but as *intersecting* the earth along two *standard parallels* of true scale. Between the standard parallels the scale is somewhat compressed, the maximum error being about 1/2 of 1 percent (minus); outside them, the scale is slightly expanded, reaching a maximum of nearly 2½ percent at the tip of Florida. Stated another way, the *total* change in scale within the United States is about 3 percent. That is, from a point in the central United States to the tip of Florida, each 100-mile section would measure about 103 miles (Figure 310). By way of comparison, the total change of scale for a Mercator chart of the United States would be approximately 40 percent.

As illustrated in Figure 310, all parallels are concentric circles, all meridians are straight-line radii of the parallels, meeting when extended at a common point, the apex of the developed cone.

This projection first came into use during World War I, for military maps. Since then it has been widely used for aeronautical charts; its use for marine navigation has been largely confined to the Great Lakes. In Article 305 it was suggested that projections other than the Mercator might well be considered for modern radionavigation. The Lambert conformal projection has several desirable properties for this application.

Position on a Lambert chart

311 Many meridians and parallels of a Lambert chart are subdivided for easy plotting of latitude and longitude. The subdivision interval varies with the scale of the particular chart, or chart series. Figure 311 represents a portion of the Aircraft Position Chart No. 3071 published by the National Ocean Survey at a scale of 1:6,250,000 (85.72 n.mi. to 1 inch); meridians and parallels are both clearly subdivided into 10′ intervals.

Assume that a fix has been obtained at 0932, at Lat. 36°40′ N, Long. 13°20′ W, and is to be plotted on the chart. First, the longitude is plotted by laying a straightedge through the appropriate subdivi-

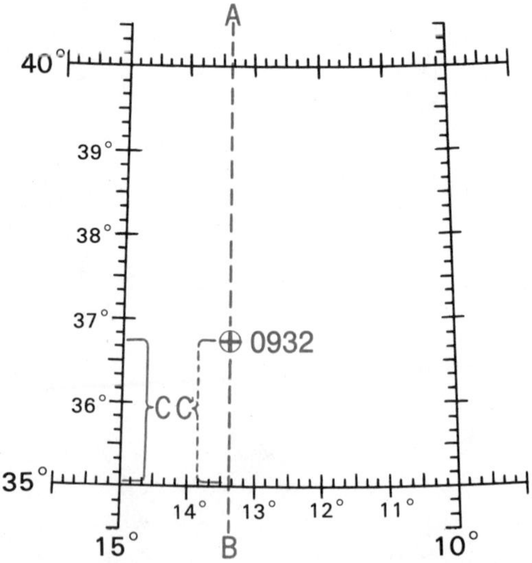

Figure 311. Position on a Lambert chart.

sions for 13°20′ W, on the parallel for 35° N and on the parallel for 40° N, and drawing at least a part of the line *AB* (Figure 311). Plot the latitude by setting the dividers for the distance from the 35th parallel up to the subdivision for 36°40′, along any meridian, as at *C*; then lay off the same distance from the 35th parallel along the line *AB* (as at *C′*) to obtain the position of the fix. Note that the latitude cannot be plotted by use of a straightedge, as all parallels are curved lines.

The problem of determining the geographic position of a fix obtained on the chart by graphic methods is solved quite easily by reversing the procedure just outlined.

Direction on a Lambert chart

312 On a Lambert chart, for most practical purposes, a straight line may be considered a great circle; a rhumb line is a curved line, as on the sphere itself. In Figure 312a the straight lines *AB* and *CD* are approximate great circles; the line *EF,* which coincides with a meridian, *is* a great circle, and also a rhumb line. As with great circles on the sphere, straight lines such as *AB* intersect each successive meridian at a different angle, but the direction of the rhumb-line course may be measured at the intersection of the straight line with the meridian nearest halfway between *A* and *B,* as in Figure 312a.

Radio signals travel great-circle (shortest distance) routes. In Figure 312b, assume *G* is a radio station and *H* is a ship. The angle with the meridian nearest *H* is the direction of the station as measured by a radio direction finder aboard the ship. The protractor scale of a standard plotter has been used to measure the bearing. (Conversely, the direction of the ship from the radio station, if this were of any interest, would be measured by the same technique with respect to the meridian nearest *G*.)

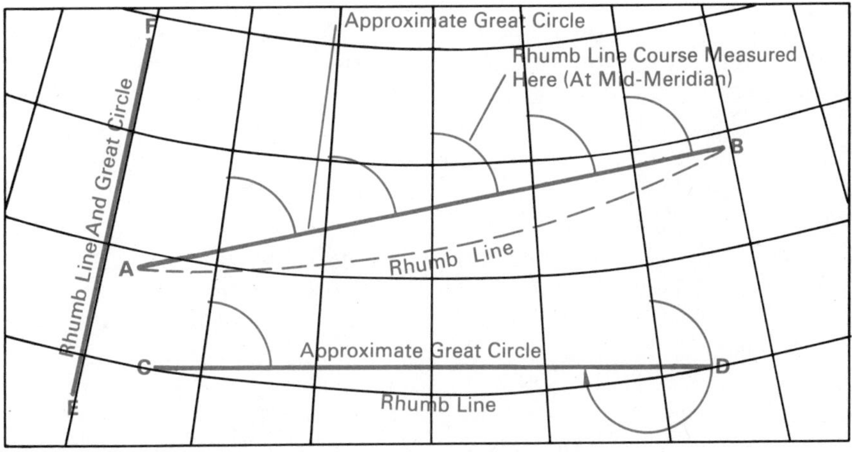

Figure 312a. Directions on a Lambert chart.

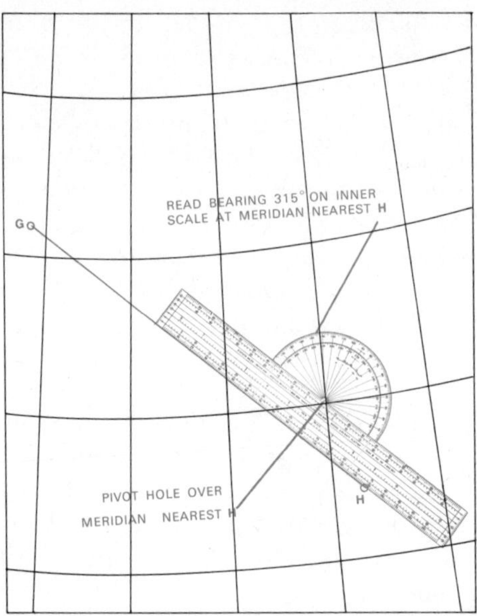

Figure 312b. Measuring a bearing on a Lambert chart using an AN plotter. Note that measurement is made at the meridian nearest the vessel.

Series of rhumb lines For long voyages, a ship is normally sailed along a series of rhumb lines approximating a great-circle track; the course is changed every few degrees of longitude. Using a Lambert chart, the track is laid down by drawing a single line on the chart representing the great circle and measuring the rhumb-line courses at various meridians. This is a far simpler process than using a great-circle gnomonic chart to determine the great circle, then determining the latitude and longitude of a number of points and transferring these to a Mercator where they are replotted and the rhumb-line courses measured. On long routes, the advantages of using a Lambert projection for the chart work become apparent. When the course is plotted as illustrated, a ship sailing that course does not exactly track the straight line, but follows a curved rhumb line, which is always between the straight line and the equator.

The higher the latitude the greater is the departure of the rhumb line from a great circle. This is due to the increasing curvature of the parallels with increasing distance from the equator. As the equator is approached, the curvature of the parallels becomes less; the distance between great circle and rhumb lines also decreases until, at the equator, as along the meridians, the great circle and rhumb lines coincide.

In the central part of the projection, about halfway between the standard parallels, there is less distortion than in any other area. There is less difference here, too, between a *true* great circle and a straight line on a Lambert chart, which *approximates* a great circle.

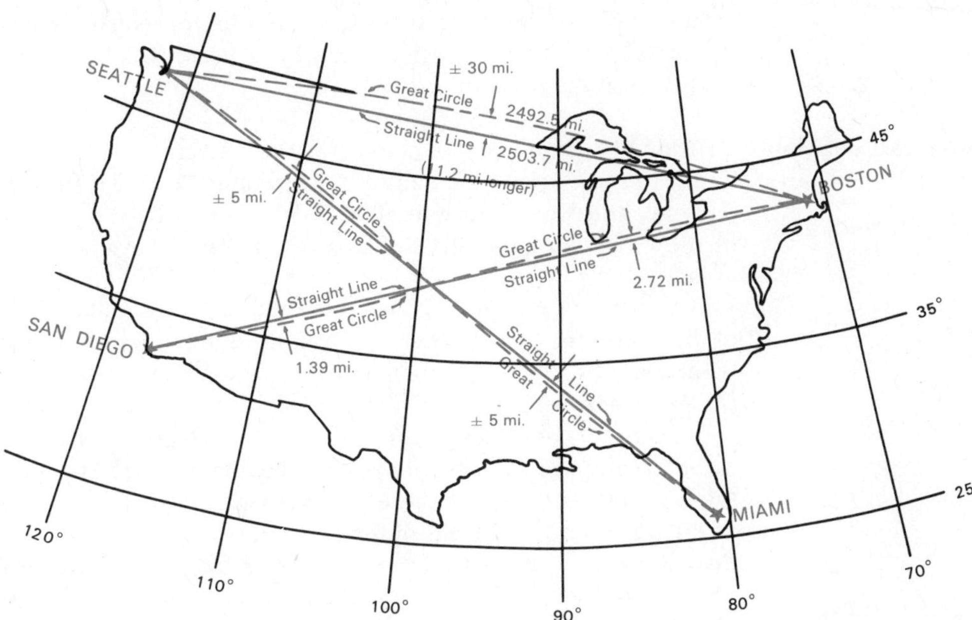

Figure 312c. Straight lines on a Lambert chart are close approximations of great circles.

Figure 312c shows the results of careful measurements on a Lambert chart of the United States with standard parallels at latitudes 33° and 45°, the center of the projection being about latitude 39°. It illustrates maximum error of a great circle on a Lambert chart. Most navigational charts will cover a smaller area and have even less distortion.

Distance on a Lambert chart

313 On a Lambert chart selected meridians are subdivided into degrees and minutes of latitude (Figure 311), the subdivision interval varying according to the scale of the particular chart. As with the Mercator projection, the subdivided meridians provide convenient scales of nautical miles. In general, distances are measured as though the chart had a constant scale. As shown in Figure 310, however, there *is* some variation in scale. If a distance to be measured is long and is appreciably far from the center of the projection, more accurate results may be obtained by using that part of the meridional scale at about the same latitude as the line between the two points in question, although this is by no means as necessary as in the case of the Mercator (Article 308).

Bar scales and scale diagrams similar to Figure 308b are printed on many Lambert charts. Special plotters are available which combine the functions of protractor, parallel rule, and a straightedge graduated to show mileage scales for some of the most commonly used charts. In aircraft navigation, dividers and parallel rules have been almost completely replaced by these special plotters for measuring course and distance. Even on a small-scale chart of the entire North Atlantic, practical accuracy can be attained.

Aircraft position charts

Article 311 referred to the series of Aircraft Position Charts. Three of these are on the Lambert projection: No. 3071, for the North Atlantic, and Nos. 3087 and 3094 for the North Pacific. Other charts of the series, on generally similar projections, are available for other areas.

The Aircraft Position Charts show, among other data, Loran lines of position and other radio aids. While designed primarily for air navigation, they are also suitable for surface navigation in long-range planning and cruising.

Because of the smaller scale and consequent greater extent of latitude, as compared with the chart of the United States, the total variation of scale in any one of these charts is slightly greater than that indicated in Figure 310. By any of the procedures just described, however, distances may be measured directly from the chart with practical accuracy. Even the slightly greater distance by way of the Lambert straight line, as compared with the true great-circle distance, is seldom great enough to be important. Figure 312c shows that for a route completely across the northern United States, in the poorest area of the projection, the straight-line distance is only about 11 miles greater than the great-circle distance.

Aeronautical charts on the Lambert projection are available for almost the entire earth, in a number of series and in several projection bands. In all cases, the standard parallels of the band of which the chart is a part are noted in the margin. For most of the smaller scale charts of the band, the standard parallels actually appear on the chart. Larger scale charts of the same area are constructed as though they were pieces cut out of the small-scale charts. In this case, the marginal notes indicate the standard parallels of the projection band, but the graphic scales printed on the chart are based on the true scale for the mid-latitude of the chart on which they appear. Consequently, they may generally be used anywhere on the chart with negligible error.

Transverse and oblique Mercator projections

314 Mercator also devised projections other than the Mercator conformal described in Articles 305–308. In speaking or writing of some other projection bearing his name, one must take care to give the complete designation, such as *Mercator equal area.* Whenever reference is made to "the Mercator projection" or to "a Mercator chart," it is always understood as meaning the Mercator *conformal,* his best-known projection and the one most commonly used in navigation.

It might seem that the transverse or oblique forms of the Mercator should have directly followed the description of the latter. While they are derived from the Mercator, they are actually more similar to the Lambert (Articles 310 to 313) in appearance and use, and are therefore considered at this point.

The Mercator is commonly pictured as being developed from a cylinder tangent to the earth's equator. For the transverse Mercator, the cylinder has been turned through 90° and is tangent along a selected meridian; see Figure 314a.

Figure 314b shows a transverse Mercator chart. For the polar regions it has the same desirable properties that the original Mercator possesses near the equator. As with the original Mercator projection, there has to be expansion of the parallels as one moves away from the line of tangency in order to maintain the relative shapes of areas. Now, however, the areas of size distortion are those *distant from the pole.*

The transverse Mercator has been used for some charts of the polar regions, where its properties and methods of use are practically identical with those of the Lambert. Its chief disadvantage is the curvature of the meridians, making them less suitable for measurements with a protractor. Within the limits of a single chart, however, this is usually negligible. The transverse Mercator is also known, confusingly enough, as the *inverse* Mercator. If its use is confined to regions not too far removed from the central (vertical) meridian—the shaded area of Figure 314b—it represents meridians and parallels with little distortion, and it is sometimes used by cartographers for polar maps.

The cylinder of the Mercator *could* have been turned through some angle other than 90°—any angle, and at any latitude between the equator and either pole. In this case it is often known as the *oblique Mercator,* though it is also referred to—and probably just as often—as the transverse Mercator.

Figure 314c shows a portion of a cylinder tangent to the great circle joining Miami and Lisbon. On the resulting *oblique Mercator* projection, whether it is visible or not, this great circle becomes, in effect, the "equator" of the projection. Meridians will be *S* curves, the direction

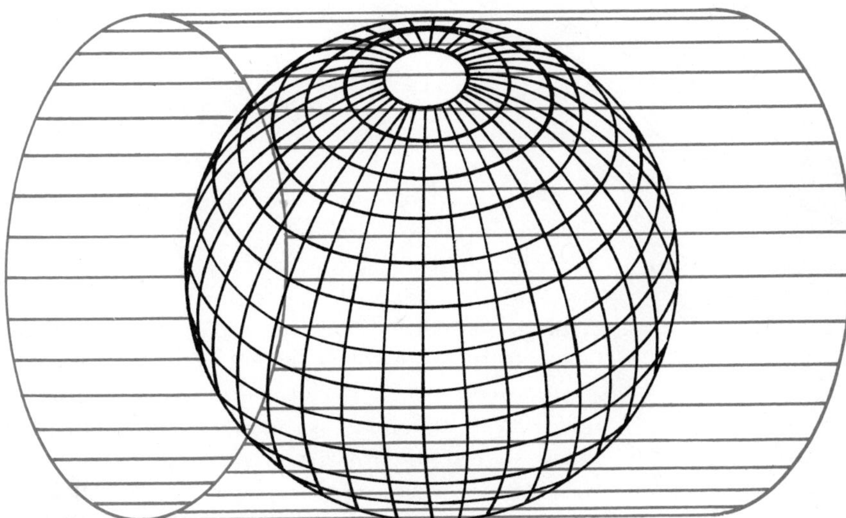

Figure 314a. Transverse Mercator projection.

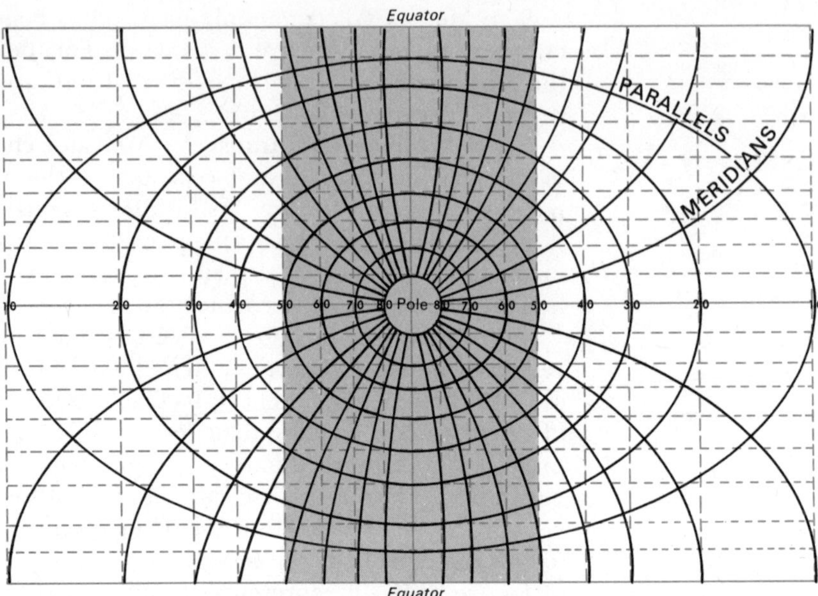

Figure 314b. Transverse Mercator projection as derived from a Mercator conformal projection.

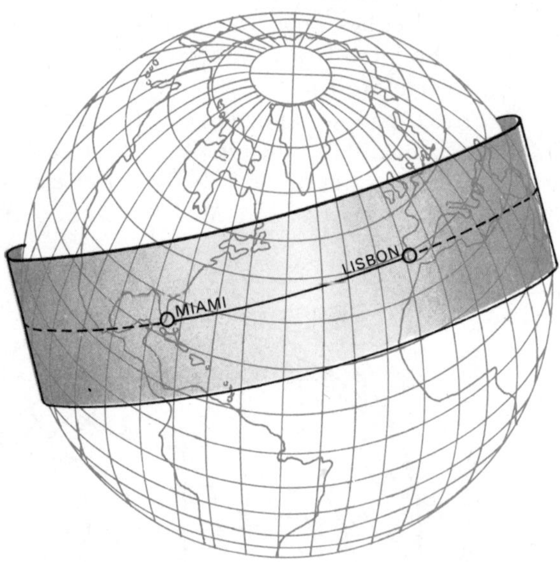

Figure 314c. Oblique Mercator projection in which a selected great circle (Miami to Lisbon) serves as the "equator" of the projection.

of curvature reversing as the meridian crosses the fictitious "equator" but the curvature is scarcely noticeable for areas within 700 to 800 miles on either side of this central line. Parallels are also curved lines.

In appearance, in its advantages and disadvantages, and in its methods of use, the oblique Mercator is generally similar to the Lambert conformal projection. It has been used for several of the Aircraft Position Charts: No. 3097, for great-circle routes between the west coast of the United States and the west coast of Europe; and No. 3096 for great-circle routes between the west coast of the United States and Tahiti and the nearby South Pacific. For each chart, when within 15 degrees (900 nautical miles) of the new equator (or selected great circle), the new projection possesses all the desirable properties afforded by the Mercator conformal when within 15 degrees of the earth's equator, *except* for straight-line meridians.

Stereographic projection

315 The polar stereographic is used for aeronautical charts of the polar regions, from about latitude 75° to the pole. It is also used for a few charts of interest in marine navigation. Figure 315 shows a polar stereographic map of the northern hemisphere. Note that in this case the parallels are concentric circles, and all meridians are straight-line radii. The polar form of the projection is, in fact, a special case of the Lambert projection. It possesses all the properties of the latter and is used in the same way.

A modified Lambert conformal projection is also used for some charts of polar areas. For such charts, the upper parallel of intersection, "standard parallel," is one very near to the pole. It is essentially conformal and has little distortion down to latitudes of 60° to 65°. It is easily used by navigators familiar with more conventional Lambert charts.

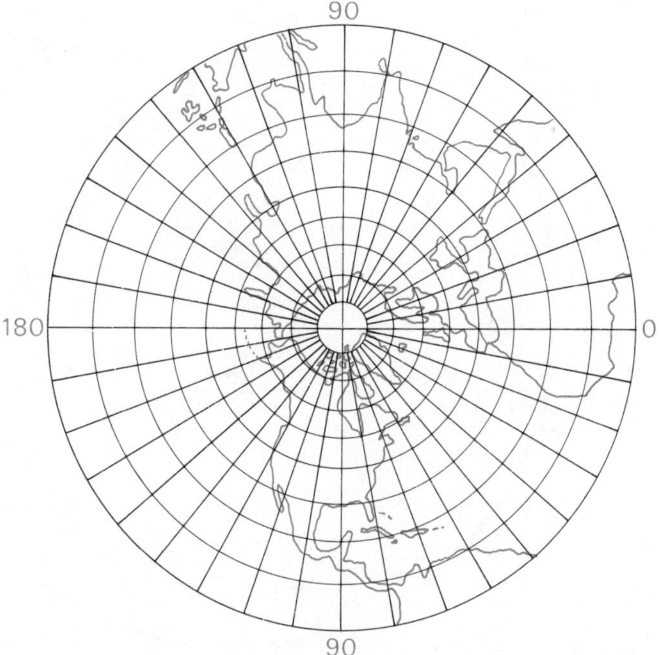

Figure 315. Polar stereographic projection.

Azimuthal equidistant projection

316 A specialized type of chart is the *azimuthal equidistant,* which is actually mathematically derived rather than being "projected." It is always centered on some place of particular significance, such as a nation's capital city or a major communications center. On this "projection," it is possible to show the *entire* surface of the earth in one flat chart, though with *great* distortion. For example, the *point* at the opposite end of the earth's diameter from the central point of the projection is stretched into a *line* throughout the entire 360° of the limiting circle, as in Figure 316.

From the chosen central point of the projection all distances are true (equidistant), and the distance to any place on earth may be measured as accurately as the scale of the chart permits.

From the same central point all directions are true, and the direction (azimuth) of any place on earth may also be measured directly. A 360° scale is usually printed around the edge of the chart for this purpose.

Charts using the azimuthal equidistant projection are particularly useful in communications as the great-circle paths followed by radio waves appear as radial lines and the proper orientation for a directional antenna is easily obtained. For aviation interests, direct great-circle routes are easily plotted and the various areas to be overflown are readily apparent. A number of these charts, centered on points of typical interest, are published by the Defense Mapping Agency Hydrographic Center.

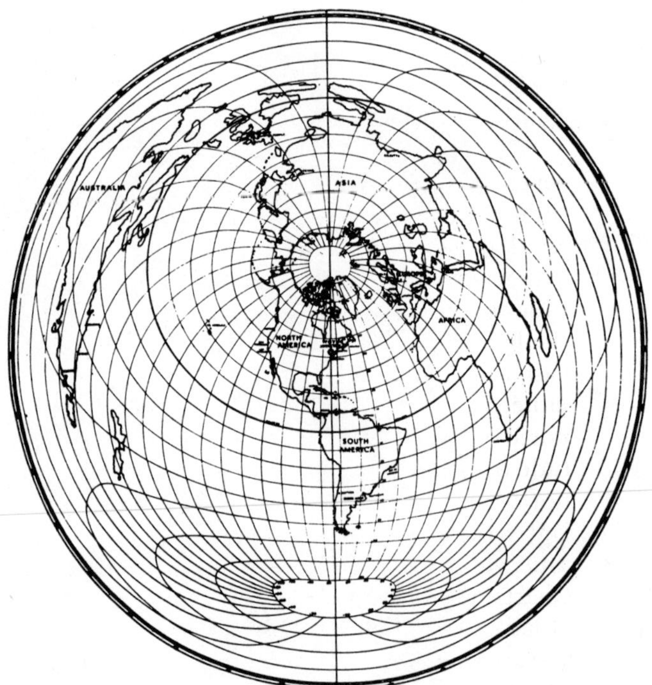

Figure 316. An azimuthal equidistant chart centered on Washington, D.C.

Other projections **317** There are a considerable number of other types of projections that can be used for making charts. Most, but not all, of these are variations of the types just discussed. They will not, however, be of general interest to the marine or air navigator.

Extensive information on many other forms of chart projections can be found in Volume I of DMAHC Publication No. 9, *American Practical Navigator* (*Bowditch*).

Orthophoto charts **318** The National Ocean Survey publishes some charts using a combination of aerial photographs and conventional chart symbology—these are called *orthophoto charts.* Usually of harbor areas, such charts assist a navigator by providing greater land details for use in fixing his position on the water. The orthophoto format also aids in the production of charts by eliminating the laborious hand drafting and scribing of intricate land details such as roads, buildings, and other man-made objects. Photographs of these features and the natural vegetation surrounding them are combined with the conventional nautical charting of water and marginal areas.

Plotting sheets **319** Plotting sheets are designed for use by the navigator at sea when no large-scale charts are available. They are basically Mercator charts showing only the graticule of meridians and parallels with a compass rose, without any other chart data. Plotting sheets are particularly useful in plotting celestial fixes on a large scale. The position of the fix is then transferred to the working chart. There are two types available; those printed for a given band of latitude, and Universal Plotting Sheets (UPS) which can be used at any latitude.

The Defense Mapping Agency Hydrographic Center publishes several series of plotting sheets at different scales; the value of the latitude is printed on the parallels of latitude. The meridians are left blank and the navigator inserts the longitude of his area of operations. When labeling the meridian it must be remembered that in west longitude the longitude becomes numerically greater towards the west, to the left on the sheet. In east longitude it increases numerically to the east, to the right on the sheet. The same plotting sheets can be used for either north or south latitudes by inverting the sheet. As on any chart, north is always at the top. When plotting sheets are used in north latitude the value of the latitude becomes numerically larger towards the north or top of the sheet. In south latitude the reverse is true. DMAHC charts No. 900–910 are plotting sheets covering 8° of latitude with a longitude scale of 1° = 4 inches. At the same latitude scale, Charts 920–933 are smaller in overall size and cover varying amounts of latitude from 8° near the equator to 3° at 65° latitude. Charts 934–936 are the same size but at higher latitudes and 1° latitude = 2 inches. Charts 960–975 cover 4° of latitude and 1° of longitude = 4 inches, but the series only extends to 49° north or south latitude. Charts 940–953 are the smallest in overall size, intended for use in lifeboat navigation, and the latitude coverage varies from 7° to 5° with a latitude scale of 1° = 2 inches (except that plotting sheets for the two highest latitudes, 952 and 953, are at a scale of 1° = 1 inch).

Universal plotting sheets (*UPS*) have a compass rose, unnumbered parallels of latitude, and a single meridian in the center of the sheet. They are unusual in that they can be used for any latitude and longitude, exclusive of the polar areas where a Mercator chart is not practical. On the UPS the navigator draws in meridians properly spaced for the mid-latitude of the area to be covered. To draw meridians on the UPS the mid-latitude of the area desired is determined and the parallels labeled accordingly. Points on the compass rose, representing angles from the horizontal numerically equal to the mid-latitude, are determined and a meridian drawn through these points, as in Figure 319. The Universal Plotting Sheets are published by DMA Aerospace Center with the designation of VP-OS. They are 13″ by 14″ and have a scale of 20 miles per inch. The AN plotter shown in Figure 312b has distance scales to fit the UPS; this greatly facilitates plotting distance and direction.

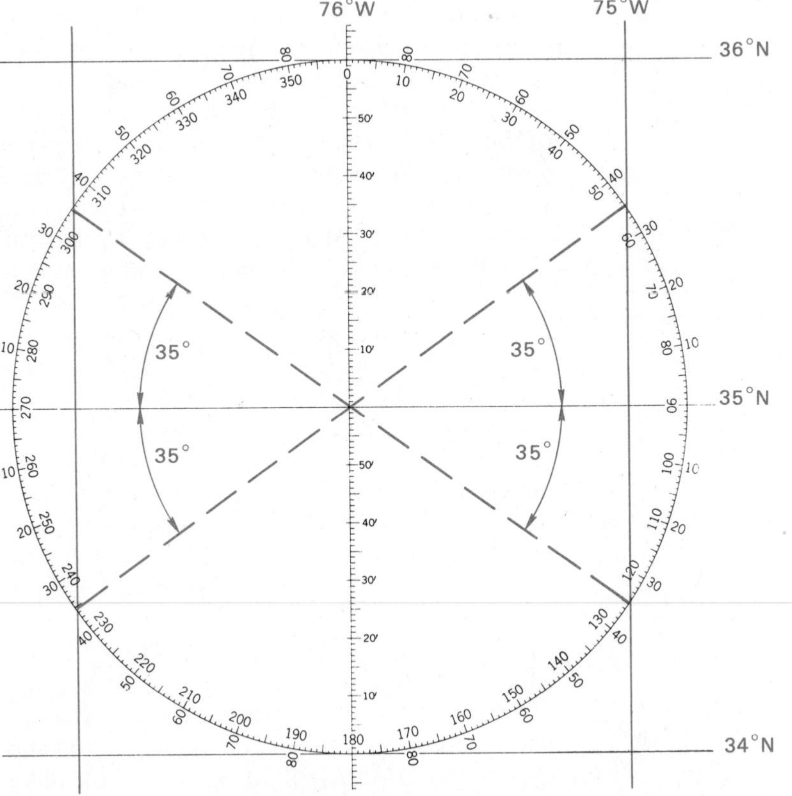

Figure 319. Universal plotting sheet.

If a small-area plotting sheet is needed, and no printed forms are available, a navigator can construct his own by drawing a circle of convenient size and marking it as a compass rose for the latitudes with which he is concerned. Lines are then drawn for parallels and meridians in the same manner as for a universal plotting sheet.

Comparison of chart projections

320 In the preceding articles of this chapter, the basic principles of chart projection have been presented, with comments on the selection of the different projections and how to use them.

By way of summary, the items of practical importance for selected projections have been combined into the following table, for further study and convenient reference.

	Mercator	Lambert*	Oblique gnomonic
Parallels	Horizontal straight lines	Arcs of concentric circles	Curved (conic sections), except equator
Meridians	Vertical straight lines perpendicular to parallels	Straight-line radii of parallels, converging at the pole	Straight lines
Appearance	See Figure 304b	See Figure 310	See Figure 309a
Conformal	Yes	Yes	No
Great circle	Curved lines (except meridians and equator)	Approximates straight line	Straight line
Rhumb line	Straight line; course angle measured with *any* meridian	Curved line; course angle measured at intersection of straight line and mid-meridian	Curved line
Distance scale	Varies; scale at mid-latitude of a particular course to be used	Nearly constant	No constant scale; can be measured by rules printed on most charts
Increase of scale	Increases with distance from equator	Increases with distance from central parallel of projection	Increases with distance from center of projection (point of tangency)
Derivation	Mathematical; tables available (only one table required)	Mathematical; tables available for various standard parallels	Graphic or mathematical
Navigational uses	Dead reckoning; may be adapted to almost any type	Dead reckoning and electronic; may be used for almost any type	Great-circle route determination

* Includes Lambert conformal, transverse and oblique Mercator, and polar stereographic. Statements in this column are true for the Lambert conformal; approximately correct for others.

CHART INTERPRETATION

Accuracy of charts **321** A chart is no more accurate than the survey on which it is based. In order to judge the accuracy and completeness of a survey, note its source and date, which are generally given in the title. Besides the changes that may have taken place since the date of the survey, the earlier surveys often were made under circumstances that precluded great accuracy of detail. Until a chart based on such a survey is tested, it should be regarded with caution. Except in well-frequented waters, few surveys have been so thorough as to make certain that *all* dangers have been found. Noting the fullness or scantiness of the soundings is another method of estimating the completeness of the survey, but it must be remembered that the chart seldom shows all soundings that were obtained. If the soundings are sparse or unevenly distributed, it should be taken for granted, as a precautionary measure, that the survey was not in great detail.

Large or irregular blank spaces among soundings mean that no soundings were obtained in those areas. Where the nearby soundings are deep, it may logically be assumed that in the blanks the water is also deep, but when the surrounding water is shallow, or if it can be seen from the rest of the chart that reefs or banks are present in the vicinity, such blanks should be regarded with suspicion. This is particularly true in coral regions and off rocky coasts. These areas should be given a wide berth.

Compromise is sometimes necessary in chart production as various factors may preclude the presentation of all data that has been collected for a given area. The information shown must be presented so that it can be understood with ease and certainty. Putting more information on a chart than is really necessary might increase "accuracy" at the expense of utility.

Chart scales **322** The *scale* of a chart is the ratio of a distance unit on the chart to the actual distance on the surface of the earth; as this is a ratio, it does not matter what size the unit is, or in what system it is measured. For example, a scale of 1:80,000 means that one unit (inch, foot, meter, etc.) on the chart represents 80,000 such units on the earth. Such a ratio is commonly called the *natural* or *fractional scale.*

At times, the scale will be stated in descriptive terms, such as "4 miles to the inch" or "2 inches to a mile"; these are called *numerical* or *equivalent scales,* and are often used as a generalization rather than an exact statement of scale. On a Mercator chart it may be stated that "1° of longitude equals 1.25 inches." Scale is stated in this form because the spacing between meridians is the one constant on a Mercator projection.

All charts have their scale shown in fractional form; charts on a scale of 1:80,000 or larger will generally also carry *graphic* (bar) *scales* of distance, usually in more than one set of units; see Figure 322.

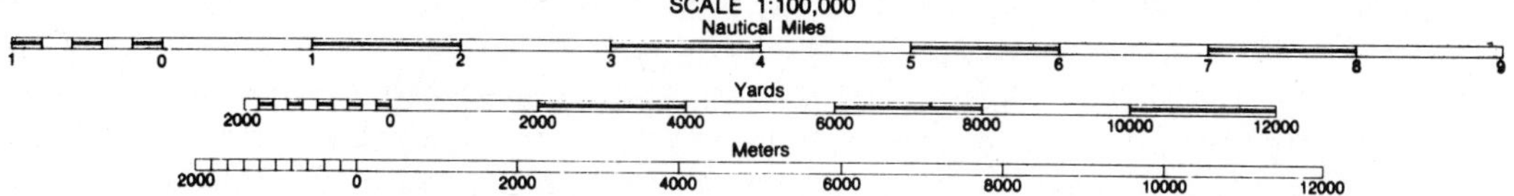

Figure 322. Various chart graphic (bar) scales.

Large and small scale charts

The terms "large scale" and "small scale" are often confusing to people who are not accustomed to using charts.

For example, if a chart is printed at scale 1: 5,000,000, the very bigness of the second number makes it seem of larger scale than one at 1:150,000. Remember that these scales can also be written as fractions —1/5,000,000 or 1/150,000—and the larger the denominator of a fraction, the smaller is the quantity.

At a scale of 1:5,000,000, one mile is only 0.015 inch in length; at 1:150,000, it is 0.486 inch—roughly 33 times as long.

The 1:5,000,000 means that 1 inch on the chart represents 5,000,000 inches on the earth's surface; or 1 centimeter represents 5,000,000 cm.; or 1 of any other unit represents 5,000,000 of the same units.

There is no firm definition for the terms large-scale charts and small-scale charts; the two terms are only relative. Thus, as compared with a chart at 1:150,000, the chart at 1:5,000,000 is a *small-scale* chart; it becomes a *large-scale* chart when it is compared with one at 1:10,000,000. The chart that shows any particular feature, such as an island or bay, at a larger size and in more detail is considered—comparatively, at least—as a *large-scale* chart.

In summary, remember that opposites go together, "Small scale, large area; large scale, small area."

Scales of principal chart series

323 The scales of nautical charts range from about 1:2,500 to about 1:5,000,000. Charts published by the National Ocean Survey are classified into "series" according to their scale.

Sailing charts. Scales 1:600,000 and smaller. These are used in fixing the mariner's position as he approaches the coast from the open ocean, or for sailing between distant coastwise ports. On such charts, the shoreline and topography are generalized and only offshore soundings, the principal lights, outer buoys, and landmarks visible at considerable distances are shown. Charts of this series are also useful for plotting the track of major tropical storms.

General charts. Scale 1:150,000 to 1:600,000. These are used for coastwise navigation outside of outlying reefs and shoals when the vessel is generally within sight of land or aids to navigation and her course can be directed by piloting techniques.

Coast charts. Scale 1:50,000 to 1:150,000. These are used for inshore navigation, for entering bays and harbors of considerable width, and for navigating large inland waterways.

Harbor charts. Scales larger than 1:50,000. These are used in harbors, anchorage areas, and the smaller waterways.

Small-craft charts. Scale 1:40,000 and larger. These are special charts of inland waters, including the Intracoastal Waterways, or special editions of conventional charts. They are printed on lighter weight paper and folded. These "SC" charts contain additional information of interest to small-craft operators, such as data on facilities, tide predictions, weather broadcast information, and so forth.

Charts published by the Defense Mapping Agency Hydrographic Center are classed as *general* or *approach* charts, with the latter category being used for those with scales of roughly 1:150,000 or larger.

Mariners are urged to obtain and study thoroughly the largest scale charts available for a particular route, even if a smaller scale is used for keeping track of position in passage.

Planes of reference

324 Each chart will carry information on the *planes of reference* used for the measurement of depths and heights. The *datum* for soundings is generally some form of average low water so that at most stages of tide the mariner has at least the charted depths. Among the various levels used are *mean low water, mean lower low water,* and *mean low water*

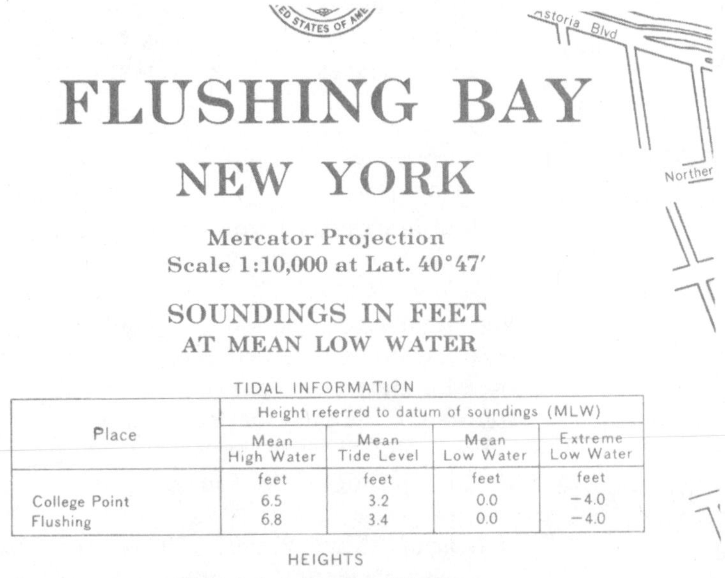

Place	Height referred to datum of soundings (MLW)			
	Mean High Water	Mean Tide Level	Mean Low Water	Extreme Low Water
	feet	feet	feet	feet
College Point	6.5	3.2	0.0	−4.0
Flushing	6.8	3.4	0.0	−4.0

Figure 324. Chart legend showing datum used for depth and for heights.

springs; for more details, see Article 905. It must always be remembered that tidal stages *below* a mean level will occur at times, and depths will then be *less than charted.* On bodies of water not significantly affected by tidal action, such as the Great Lakes and the Baltic Sea, an arbitrary reference plane is designated.

The plane of reference for the measurement of heights is usually chosen so that the mariner will have, at most times at least, the charted vertical clearance under bridges and other overhead obstructions such as power transmission lines. Mean high water is commonly used and is assumed to be the reference plane on U.S. charts unless information to the contrary is shown. As with mean lows, some tide levels will be *above* mean high water and caution must be exercised if vertical clearances are critical.

Chart symbols and abbreviations

325 Many symbols and abbreviations are used on charts. These constitute a kind of shorthand which tells the navigator the physical characteristics of the charted area, and details of the available aids to navigation. The symbols used are quite standardized, but are subject to some variation, depending on the scale of the particular chart or chart series. It simply is not possible on a small-scale chart to show all the details that can be shown on a large-scale chart.

Many pages of text would be needed to describe all the symbols and abbreviations employed to present the detailed information available on a modern chart. Instead of a written description, these symbols and abbreviations are shown in Chart No. 1 issued jointly by the Defense Mapping Agency Hydrographic Center and the National Ocean Survey; see Appendix G. New editions of this list of symbols and abbreviations are issued at intervals of about five years.

Nearly all charts employ color to distinguish various categories of information such as shoal water, deep water, and land areas. Color is also used with aids to navigation to make them easier to locate and interpret. "Nautical purple" ink is used for much information as it is more easily read under the red night-time illumination normally used on the bridge of a ship to avoid interference with the watchstander's night vision.

Even the style of lettering on a chart provides information. For example, features that are dry at high water are identified in roman lettering such as this; submerged and floating hydrographic features (except the sounding figures, showing depths) are identified in *italic* lettering. Often, on small-scale charts, it may be difficult to distinguish a small reef from a small islet, but the style of lettering will indicate the difference.

Chart notes

Much valuable information is printed on charts in the form of *notes* and as *boxes* of data. Notes will relate to such topics as regulatory restrictions, cautions and warnings, unusual magnetic conditions, etc. Boxes of data may show depths in major dredged channels, mean and

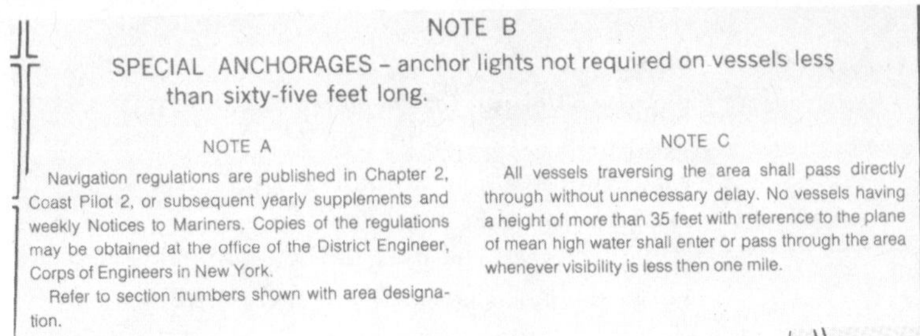

NOTE B
SPECIAL ANCHORAGES - anchor lights not required on vessels less than sixty-five feet long.
NOTE A
Navigation regulations are published in Chapter 2, Coast Pilot 2, or subsequent yearly supplements and weekly Notices to Mariners. Copies of the regulations may be obtained at the office of the District Engineer, Corps of Engineers in New York.
Refer to section numbers shown with area designation.
NOTE C
All vessels traversing the area shall pass directly through without unnecessary delay. No vessels having a height of more than 35 feet with reference to the plane of mean high water shall enter or pass through the area whenever visibility is less then one mile.

Figure 325. Chart "notes" are used to provide information that cannot be shown by symbols or abbreviations.

extremes of tidal stages at selected points on the chart (charts with scales of 1:75,000 and larger), etc. Notes and boxes may be printed in the margins or on the face of the chart at locations where they will not obscure navigational information.

Editions and revisions

326 A chart is issued with a date and edition number. When many changes have been made to the information on a chart, a new edition is published; the interval between editions can vary from a year or less to more than 50 years. A chart is sometimes issued with a "Revised" date when the stock level requires another printing and only a few changes have been incorporated; in this case a new edition number is not warranted.

CHART/PUB. CORRECTION RECORD DMAHC-8660/9 (11-74)

CHART/PUB. NO.	PORTFOLIO NO.	EDITION NO./DATE	CLASS	PRICE	CORRECTED THRU N. TO M., NO./YR. OR PUB. CHANGES

TITLE

APPLICABLE NOTICE TO MARINERS

N/M YR	PUB. PAGE NO.	CORRECTION MADE DATE	CORRECTION MADE INITIAL	N/M YR.	PUB. PAGE NO.	CORRECTION MADE DATE	CORRECTION MADE INITIAL	N/M YR.	PUB. PAGE NO.	CORRECTION MADE DATE	CORRECTION MADE INITIAL	N/M YR.	PUB. PAGE NO.	CORRECTION MADE DATE	CORRECTION MADE INITIAL

CHART/PUB. NO.

Figure 326. File card for recording chart and publication corrections.

All charts in regular use on board ships and boats should be kept corrected according to the latest information from all official sources such as *Notice to Mariners* (see Article 610). Also, procedures should be established whereby charts that are not used regularly can be quickly brought up to date when needed; the use of a file of *Chart/Publication Record* cards (DMAHC No. 8860/9) will help to organize and expedite this task.

A navigator should use only the latest edition of any chart, and this chart should be corrected as fully as possible. An old edition of a chart is not safe to use.

Metric system **327** A program is underway in the United States to make use of the metric system of measurement on nautical charts issued by DMAHC, and, to a lesser degree, on those published by NOS. The object of this program is to conform to bilateral chart-reproduction agreements with other nations. Heights and water depths will be shown in meters. Land contours will be shown in meters if the source information is in meters; when source information is in feet this measurement will be retained. As the program progresses, the change to the metric system will have widespread effects and will, for example, necessitate changes in echo-sounder equipment to provide dual scales for use with either the customary (English) or the metric system.

Nautical charts which use the metric system will carry in *bold purple* type the legend "Soundings in Meters" on the upper and lower margins and the word "Meters" superimposed over the metric depths on the face of the chart when space allows. A few charts were produced with the land areas in green to alert the navigator to the fact that depths were in meters, but the basic color for land on DMAHC charts is gray (NOS charts have used a solid yellow tint for land areas, but are now being changed to a screened gold color that is more suitable when viewed with the red illumination often used on the bridge of a ship or boat at night).

Appendix E provides a table for the easy and accurate conversion of measurements in feet, fathoms, or meters to both of the other two units.

Using a chart **328** Charts must be used intelligently, not blindly. The degree of reliance to be placed on a given chart or portion of a chart is no less of an art than is navigation itself. With experience, however, comes the skill that makes the chart a much more useful and dependable aid.

Read carefully all notes appearing on the chart. Do not merely look at it as though it were a picture. Check the scale, determine the date of the survey on which it is based, and see whether or not it is corrected and up to date. Check whether soundings are in feet, fathoms, or meters. Check that the sounding coverage is complete and, if not, note the areas where lack of information may indicate danger. Note the system of projection used, so that you can be sure of how to measure direction and distance when using it. Check the tidal reference plane. Remember that a chart is a basic tool in the art of navigation. Learn to use it skillfully.

Summary

329 This chapter has described the basic chart projections on which almost all the nautical charts of the world are, or are likely to be, constructed. Only by becoming familiar with the way in which one type of chart may be used to complement another, and by learning the weaknesses, advantages, and methods of using the different projections, may the various available charts be used to the best advantage.

Chart symbols have been referred to as a kind of shorthand. Until the mariner can read this shorthand and can relate the appearance of objects he observes around him to their corresponding symbols on the chart, the chart will remain merely a piece of paper.

No tool is more important to the art of navigation than the mariner's chart. This tool requires intelligent and practiced use in order that the most efficient service may be gained from it.

4 Compasses

THE MAGNETIC COMPASS

Introduction

401 The magnetic compass is one of the oldest of the navigator's instruments. Its origin is unknown, but apparently the Vikings were familiar with it in the eleventh century. Although records are scanty and inexact, it is probable that the magnetic compass was independently developed by the Chinese at about the same time. The earliest compasses probably consisted of an elongated piece of lodestone, iron ore having magnetic properties, placed on a wood chip and floated in a bowl of water. Rather quickly, this developed into an iron needle thrust through a straw and floated on the surface of a container of water; the lodestone had to be applied to the needle each time the "compass" was to be used.

Initially, a compass was used only to indicate north, but soon the concept of marking other directions around the rim of the bowl was introduced. The directions were given the names of the various winds, now known as North, East, South, and West; these are the *cardinal* directions. Next are the *intercardinal* directions: NE, SE, SW, and NW. Still finer subdivisions are the *combination* directions: NNE, ENE, ESE, etc.; and the *by-points*: N×E, NNE×N, NNE×E, etc. This system results in a complete circle divided into 32 points (1 point = $11\frac{1}{4}°$) and there are half-points and quarter points. The point system was widely used until relatively modern times, but is now obsolete except for some minor use on sailing craft.

Because of the difficulty at sea in using a needle floating freely in an open bowl of water, the next development was that of using a pivot at the center of a dry bowl. Not for some centuries was the liquid put back in, this time in an enclosed chamber, as now is the case in modern magnetic compasses.

The magnetic compass still retains its importance, despite the invention of the gyrocompass. While the latter is an extremely accurate instrument, it is highly complex, dependent on an electrical power supply, and subject to mechanical damage. The magnetic compass, on the other hand, is entirely self-contained, simple, comparatively rugged, and not easily damaged.

Standard and steering compasses

Most vessels of any size carry at least two magnetic compasses; these are the *standard compass* and the *steering compass.* The standard compass, whenever possible, is located on the ship's centerline, and on a

	Points	Angular measure		Points	Angular measure
NORTH TO EAST		° ′ ″	SOUTH TO WEST		° ′ ″
North	0	0 00 00	South	16	180 00 00
N¼E	¼	2 48 45	S¼W	16¼	182 48 45
N½E	½	5 37 30	S½W	16½	185 37 30
N¾E	¾	8 26 15	S¾W	16¾	188 26 15
N by E	1	11 15 00	S by W	17	191 15 00
N by E¼E	1¼	14 03 45	S by W¼W	17¼	194 03 45
N by E½E	1½	16 52 30	S by W½W	17½	196 52 30
N by E¾E	1¾	19 41 15	S by W¾W	17¾	199 41 15
NNE	2	22 30 00	SSW	18	202 30 00
NNE¼E	2¼	25 18 45	SSW¼W	18¼	205 18 45
NNE½E	2½	28 07 30	SSW½W	18½	208 07 30
NNE¾E	2¾	30 56 15	SSW¾W	18¾	210 56 15
NE by N	3	33 45 00	SW by S	19	213 45 00
NE¾N	3¼	36 33 45	SW¾S	19¼	216 33 45
NE½N	3½	39 22 30	SW½S	19½	219 22 30
NE¼N	3¾	42 11 15	SW¼S	19¾	222 11 15
NE	4	45 00 00	SW	20	225 00 00
NE¼E	4¼	47 48 45	SW¼W	20¼	227 48 45
NE½E	4½	50 37 30	SW½W	20½	230 37 30
NE¾E	4¾	53 26 15	SW¾W	20¾	233 26 15
NE by E	5	56 15 00	SW by W	21	236 15 00
NE by E¼E	5¼	59 03 45	SW by W¼W	21¼	239 03 45
NE by E½E	5½	61 52 30	SW by W½W	21½	241 52 30
NE by E¾E	5¾	64 41 15	SW by W¾W	21¾	244 41 15
ENE	6	67 30 00	WSW	22	247 30 00
ENE¼E	6¼	70 18 45	WSW¼W	22¼	250 18 45
ENE½E	6½	73 07 30	WSW½W	22½	253 07 30
ENE¾E	6¾	75 56 15	WSW¾W	22¾	255 56 15
E by N	7	78 45 00	W by S	23	258 45 00
E¾N	7¼	81 33 45	W¾S	23¼	261 33 45
E½N	7½	84 22 30	W½S	23½	264 22 30
E¼N	7¾	87 11 15	W¼S	23¾	267 11 15
EAST TO SOUTH			WEST TO NORTH		
East	8	90 00 00	West	24	270 00 00
E¼S	8¼	92 48 45	W¼N	24¼	272 48 45
E½S	8½	95 37 30	W½N	24½	275 37 30
E¾S	8¾	98 26 15	W¾N	24¾	278 26 15
E by S	9	101 15 00	W by N	25	281 15 00
ESE¾E	9¼	104 03 45	WNW¾W	25¼	284 03 45
ESE½E	9½	106 52 30	WNW½W	25½	286 52 30
ESE¼E	9¾	109 41 15	WNW¼W	25¾	289 41 15
ESE	10	112 30 00	WNW	26	292 30 00
SE by E¾E	10¼	115 18 45	NW by W¾W	26¼	295 18 45
SE by E½E	10½	118 07 30	NW by W½W	26½	298 07 30
SE by E¼E	10¾	120 56 15	NW by W¼W	26¾	300 56 15
SE by E	11	123 45 00	NW by W	27	303 45 00
SE¾E	11¼	126 33 45	NW¾W	27¼	306 33 45
SE½E	11½	129 22 30	NW½W	27½	309 22 30
SE¼E	11¾	132 11 15	NW¼W	27¾	312 11 15
SE	12	135 00 00	NW	28	315 00 00
SE¼S	12¼	137 48 45	NW¼N	28¼	317 48 45
SE½S	12½	140 37 30	NW½N	28½	320 37 30
SE¾S	12¾	143 26 15	NW¾N	28¾	323 26 15
SE by S	13	146 15 00	NW by N	29	326 15 00
SSE¾E	13¼	149 03 45	NNW¾W	29¼	329 03 45
SSE½E	13½	151 52 30	NNW½W	29½	331 52 30
SSE¼E	13¾	154 41 15	NNW¼W	29¾	334 41 15
SSE	14	157 30 00	NNW	30	337 30 00
S by E¾E	14¼	160 18 45	N by W¾W	30¼	340 18 45
S by E½E	14½	163 07 30	N by W½W	30½	343 07 30
S by E¼E	14¾	165 56 15	N by W¼W	30¾	345 56 15
S by E	15	168 45 00	N by W	31	348 45 00
S¾E	15¼	171 33 45	N¾W	31¼	351 33 45
S½E	15½	174 22 30	N½W	31½	354 22 30
S¼E	15¾	177 11 15	N¼W	31¾	357 11 15
South	16	180 00 00	North	32	360 00 00

Figure 401. Conversion table, points to degrees from Pub. No. 9.

weather deck near the bridge, at a point where it will be least affected by unfavorable magnetic influences. Headings read from this compass are termed *per standard compass* (*psc*). The steering compass in most ships is also located on the centerline, just forward of the steering wheel, where it can be seen easily by the helmsman. Its headings are termed *per steering compass* (*p stg c*).

This section is intended primarily to stress the continuing importance of the magnetic compass, despite the great advances made in the field of the gyrocompass. It will deal only briefly with the theory of magnetism, and is not intended as a treatise for the professional compass adjustor. The theory of compass adjustment is covered in detail in the *Handbook of Magnetic Compass Adjustment and Compensation,* DMAHC Pub. No. 226.

Magnetic principles

402 *Magnetism* is a fundamental physical phenomenon which occurs both naturally, as in a lodestone mentioned above, and artificially by induction. It is the property of certain metals to attract or repel items of like material or certain other metals; it is also an effect of electrical currents. An object which exhibits the property of magnetism is called a *magnet.* It can be elongated, as in a *bar* magnet, shaped like a horseshoe, or take other forms. The space around each magnet in which its influence can be detected is called its *field;* this can be pictured as being composed of many *lines of force.* Figure 402 illustrates a typical bar magnet and the lines of force which represent its field. The lines concentrate at both ends, or *poles,* of a magnet. Each magnet always has two—no more, no less—areas of opposite polarity; one is termed *north* and the other *south.*

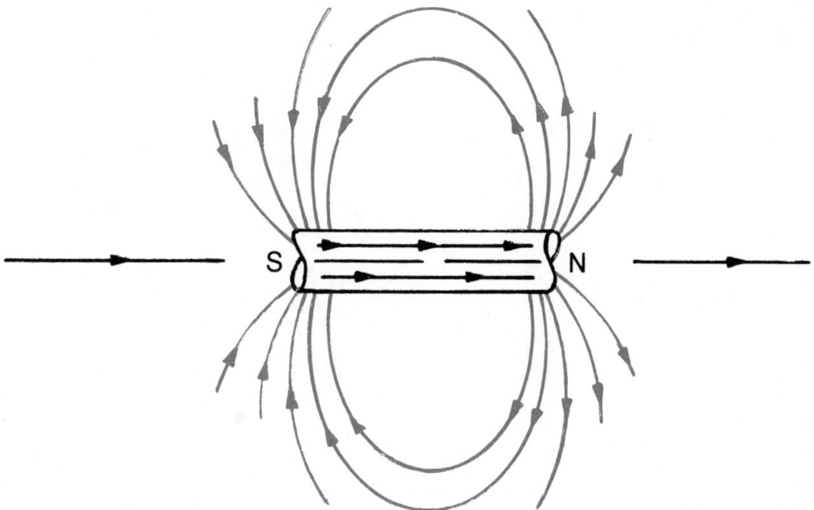

Figure 402. Lines of force representing field around a bar magnet.

The basic law of magnetism

The *basic law of magnetism* is that poles of the *same polarity repel* each other and those of *opposite polarity attract.* Thus an N pole (sometimes colored red in illustrations) attracts an S (blue) pole, but repels another N pole.

The earth as a magnet

403 The earth may be visualized as having a bar magnet within it radiating lines of force that may be detected on the surface. Figure 403 illustrates this concept of the earth as a magnet. The "internal magnet" is not exactly aligned with the earth's axis. The consequence of this divergence is that the magnetic poles are *not* at the location of the geographic poles; furthermore, the location of the magnetic poles varies with time. These two facts complicate the use of a magnetic compass. The north magnetic pole is currently in the vicinity of latitude

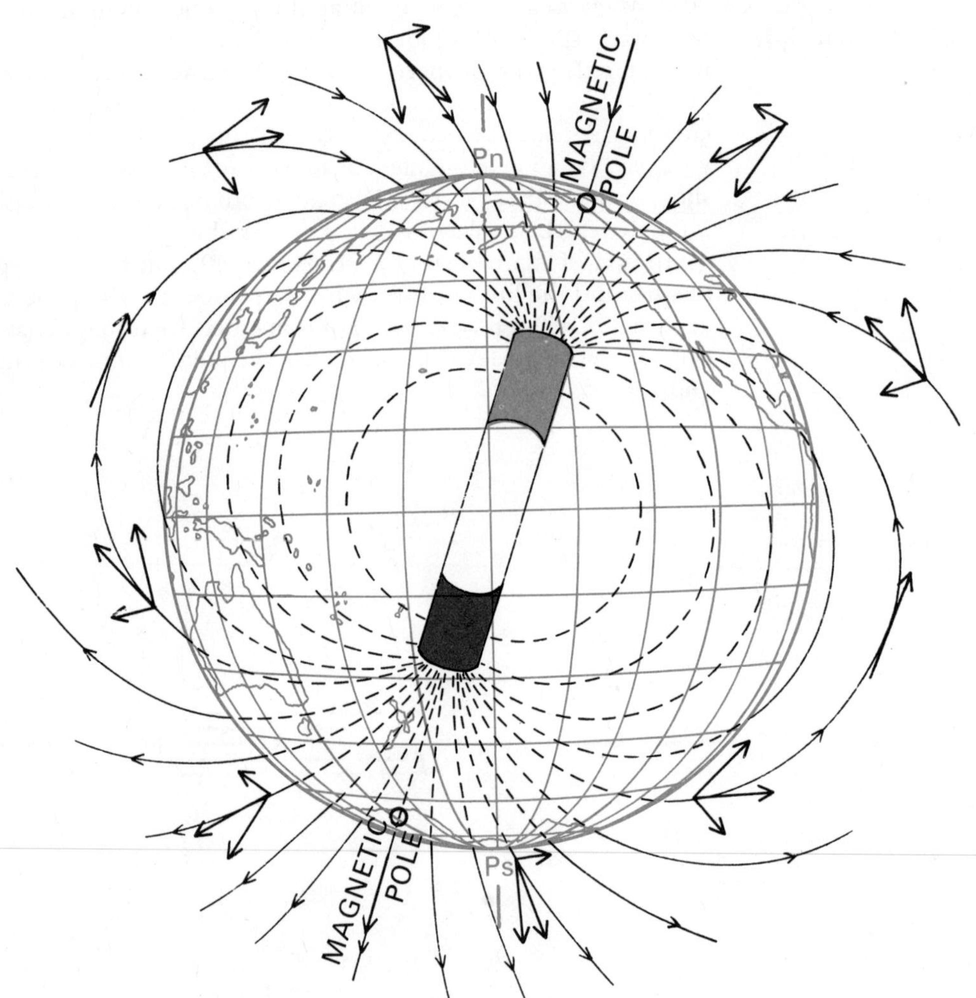

Figure 403. The earth's magnetic field.

76.1° N, longitude 100.0° W and the south magnetic pole is near 65.8° S, 139.4° E; these locations are somewhat indefinite and change irregularly over a period of years. Some studies have shown that the poles appear to move in daily cycles over an elliptical path having a major axis of about 50 miles; such movement is, of course, too slight to affect practical navigation in nonpolar latitudes.

Magnetic meridian At the surface of the earth, the lines of force become magnetic *meridians.* These are irregular lines which cannot be printed on charts covering large areas; their irregularity is primarily caused by the nonuniform distribution of magnetic material in the earth.

The magnetic lines of force can be divided into components. For the navigator, the horizontal and vertical components are important, and are discussed as *variation* and *dip* in subsequent articles.

Variation **404** Magnetic meridians indicate the direction of the earth's magnetic field; but only in a very few places do the magnetic and true meridians coincide. The difference at any location between the directions of the magnetic and true meridians is the *variation,* sometimes called *magnetic declination.* It is called easterly (E) if the compass needle, aligned with the magnetic meridian, points eastward or to the right of true north, and westerly (W), if it points to the left. Variation results from the horizontal component of the earth's magnetic field.

Variation is important to the navigator because the magnetic compass, responding to the earth's magnetic field, is in error in measuring true geographic direction by the amount of the variation (*Var.* or *V*). The magnetic variation and its annual change are shown on charts, so that directions indicated by the magnetic compass can be corrected to true directions. Since variation is caused by the earth's magnetic field, its value changes with the geographic location of the ship, but is the same for all headings of the ship.

Secular change The earth's magnetic field is not constant in either intensity or direction. The changes are *diurnal* (daily), *yearly,* and *secular* (occurring over a longer period of time). The changes in intensity are too small to have any effect in navigation. The same is true of diurnal changes in direction, except in polar regions, where diurnal changes of 7° have been observed.

The secular change in direction, however, is a real factor in navigation. Although it has been under observation for more than 300 years, the length of its period has not been fully established. The change generally consists of a reasonably steady increase or decrease in the *variation,* which is the inclination of the magnetic meridian to the true meridian at a given place. This change may continue for many years, sometimes reaching large values, remain nearly stationary for a few years, and then reverse its trend.

Change in variation The secular change is extremely complex. However, if the change of inclination of the magnetic meridian to the true meridian is measured over a period of several years at a given location, its future values for the next few years can be predicted with considerable accuracy. Charts generally indicate the values of the variation for a stated year, and note the annual amount and direction of the secular change, so that the value for any subsequent year, within a reasonable period, may be calculated. This annual change is printed within the compass rose on the chart as shown in Figure 404. Predictions of the change of variation are intended for short term use—a period of a few years. Values derived from the predictions on an old chart may be considerably in error; the latest charts available should always be used.

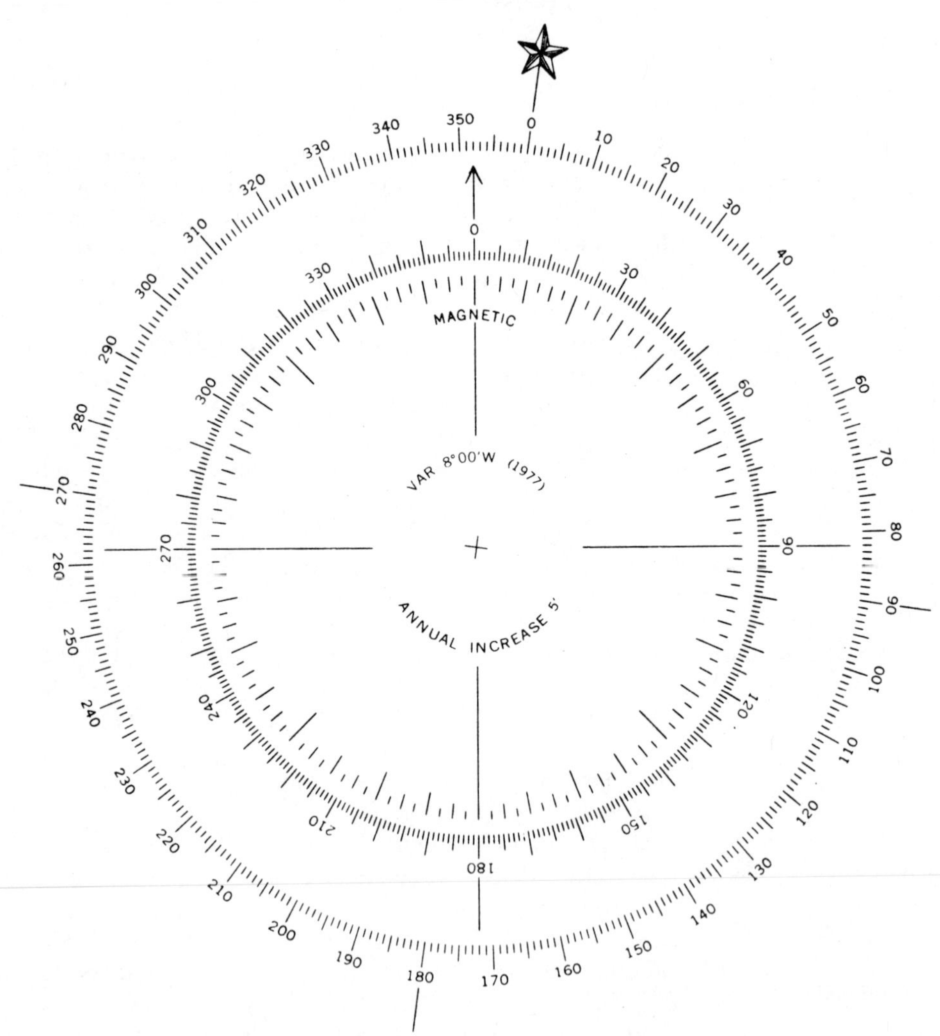

Figure 404. Compass rose, showing variation and annual rate of change.

Dip **405** The earth and its surrounding magnetic field are illustrated in Figure 403. Note that the lines of force are horizontal, or parallel to the earth's surface only at the *magnetic equator,* which is defined as the line connecting points of zero dip. At all other points they are inclined to the horizontal, the degree of inclination increasing as the magnetic poles are approached, where the inclination reaches 90°. The amount of this inclination is called the *dip, magnetic inclination,* or *magnetic latitude,* and the instrument which measures it is called a *dip circle.*

As the compass magnets are constrained to remain essentially horizontal, they are acted on only by the horizontal component of the earth's total magnetic force. This is greatest at the magnetic equator, where the dip is 0°, and disappears altogether at the magnetic poles, where the dip is 90°. Thus it can be seen that the aligning force on a magnetic compass will be considerably diminished at the higher magnetic latitudes.

Magnetic charts **406** Lines on a chart which connect points of equal magnetic variation are called *isogonic lines;* the line of zero variation is the *agonic line.* The Defense Mapping Agency Hydrographic Center publishes a series of magnetic charts of the earth as a whole (Mercator projection) and for the North and South polar areas (azimuthal equidistant projection). Separate charts are prepared for variation and vertical in-

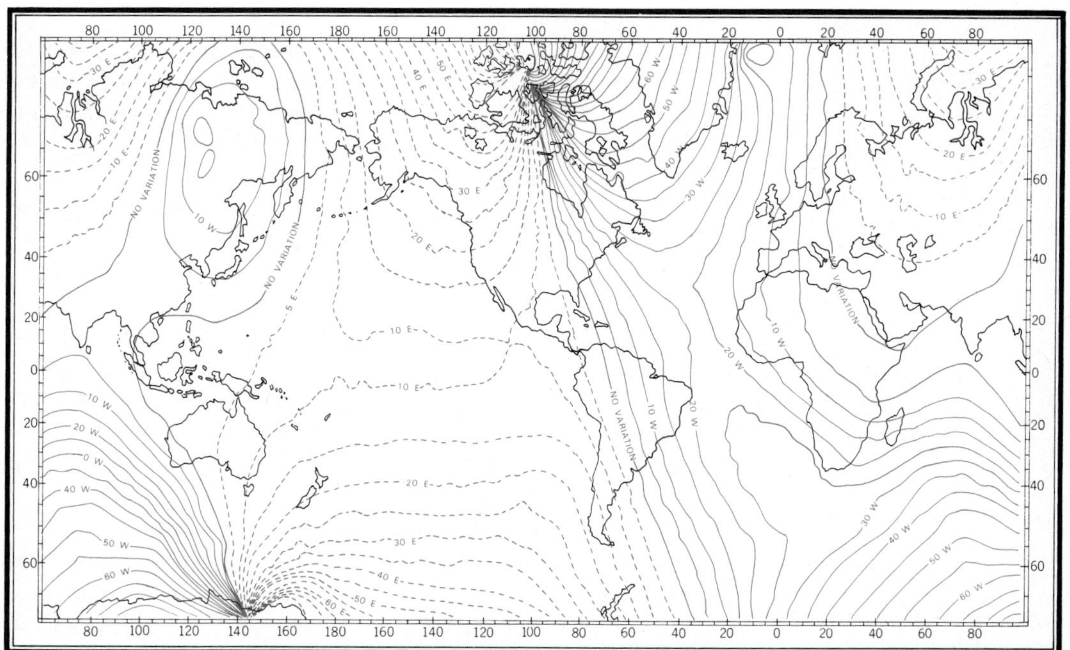

Figure 406. Simplified chart of magnetic variation of the world, from Chart 42. Shown are isogonic and agonic lines.

clination (dip) and for intensity of field, horizontal, vertical, and total; they are revised when required by changes in the earth's magnetic field. Of greatest interest to a navigator is DMAHC Chart 42, Magnetic Variation Chart of the World for the Year 1975, a simplified adaptation of which is shown in Figure 406.

While these charts are useful for planning purposes, the large-scale chart of the area involved should always be consulted in setting a course by magnetic compass or converting a magnetic compass bearing to a true bearing for plotting, since there are many small irregularities in variation that cannot be shown on the small-scale world charts. In addition, there are very small areas of local magnetic disturbance that may or may not be indicated on the chart. At one place off the coast of Australia, near Cossack, the variation changes from 56° E to 26° W in a distance of about 180 yards, less than the length of a ship; areas of local disturbance of lesser magnitude extend over nearly three miles of navigable water. There are many others of less extreme nature, but still of a magnitude and extent that must be taken into account by a navigator.

Modern compass construction

407 The basic mechanism of modern magnetic compasses is exactly the same as that of the very earliest ones used—a small bar magnet freely suspended in the magnetic field of the earth. Refinements have been added for greater accuracy, steadiness of indication, and ease of reading, but the basic mechanism remains unchanged.

Compass components

The modern marine magnetic compass is contained in a glass-topped bowl made of nonmagnetic material. Figure 407a presents a sectional view, and Figure 407b a photograph, of a Navy standard No. 1 seven and one-half inch compass. The letter *C* indicates the bowl with its cover secured by the bezel ring, *G*. The letters in the following description refer to the corresponding components in this illustration. At the forward side of the bowl is the *lubber's line,* which indicates the direction of the ship's head (355° in the photograph). At the center of the bottom of the bowl is a vertical pin, the pivot, upon which the compass card (*B*) rests. To the bottom of this card are attached two or more magnets (*A*) aligned with the north-south axis of the compass card. The card is marked around its outer edge with graduations at suitable intervals, 1°, 2°, or 5°, from 000° at the point where the card indicates compass north clockwise through 360°; cardinal and intercardinal directions may also be shown on the card in some designs.

In order to reduce friction on the pivot and to dampen vibration, the compass bowl is filled with a clear fluid (*D*) which is not subject to freezing at normal temperatures. The card has a *float* or air chamber (*E*), designed so that it will support all but a minute percentage of the weight of the card with the attached magnets. Lastly, the bowl is fitted with an *expansion bellows* (*F*) which permits the bowl to remain filled as the liquid expands and contracts with temperature changes.

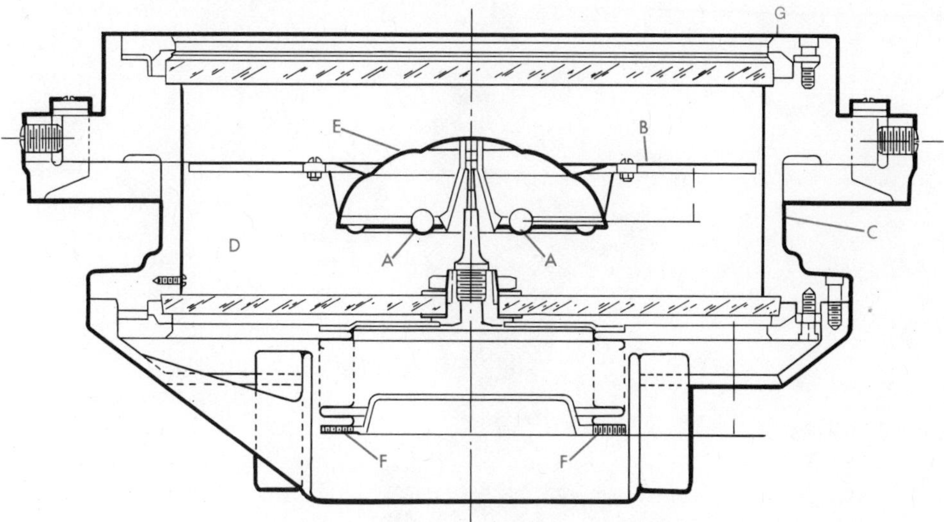

Figure 407a. Cutaway view of a magnetic compass.

Figure 407b. U.S. Navy standard No. 1 7½-inch varsol-filled compass.

The bowl is supported in *gimbals*, or double rings, hinged on both the fore and aft and athwartships axes. These gimbals permit the compass bowl to remain horizontal, or nearly so, regardless of the ship's rolling or pitching. A gimbal is illustrated in Figure 407b.

The gimbaled compass is mounted in a *binnacle,* or stand, made of nonmagnetic material. A typical binnacle is shown in Figure 407c. (The balls on either side are called "quadrantal spheres"; their function is explained in Article 415.)

Figure 407c. Binnacle for standard U.S. Navy compass.

Requirements for a marine compass

408 Much research has gone into the development of the magnetic compass to bring it to its present high state of accuracy and reliability. Metallic alloys have been intensively studied in order that magnets of increased strength and retentivity might be produced. Alloys of nickel, cobalt, and other metals have proven far superior to the iron formerly used in both these respects. In addition, great advances have been made in protecting the needle from mechanical disturbances, in reducing its oscillations, or *hunting*, and in the presentation of the directional readout.

On some modern compasses a circular or ring magnet is used, replacing the bar magnets attached to the compass card. The ring magnet, due to its circular shape, causes less friction with the fluid in the compass bowl as the ship turns; this produces an exceptionally steady card.

Typical marine compasses

409 The *No. 1 seven and one-half inch compass* described in Article 407 is the magnetic compass used most widely in the U.S. Navy. It has proven itself to be an excellent instrument. Two other typical compasses are the five-inch model shown in Figure 409a and the three-inch model illustrated in Figure 409b. Merchant ships use compasses of generally similar design.

Figure 409a. U.S. Navy standard No. 3 5-inch alcohol-filled compass in binnacle.

Figure 409b. U.S. Navy standard No. 5 3-inch varsol-filled top-reading compass.

Periscopic compass

The periscopic reflection compass and binnacle is coming into increasing use as a combined steering and bearing compass on most maritime vessels. It permits installing the compass on the level above the wheelhouse; the image of the compass card is reflected down periscopically and presented in the field of view of the helmsman. This type of installation has several advantages. The compass itself is removed from the enclosed wheelhouse, where it would be surrounded by metal and much electrical and electronic equipment. Also, on the open deck above, bearings and azimuths may be obtained directly on the compass itself, either for navigation or for checking the compass. A schematic representation of a typical periscopic reflection compass is shown in Figure 409c.

A *spherical compass* is illustrated in Figure 409d. This type of compass is becoming increasingly popular among yachtsmen, as well as with commercial operators, as it offers several advantages compared to the conventional flat-topped compass. These compasses are internally gimbaled, and the compass card is pivoted at the center of the sphere, assuring maximum stability of the card in all conditions of pitch, roll, and heave. In addition, the transparent spherical dome of the compass acts as a powerful magnifying glass, and greatly increases the apparent size of the compass card in the area of the lubber's line. A recent development, a "dished" card, slightly concave upward, together with spherical dome, permits such a compass to be read accurately from a distance of 10 feet (3 m) or more. When fitted with shock-absorbing mounts, a spherical compass gives excellent results in high-speed boats, despite continuous vibration and shock in heavy seas.

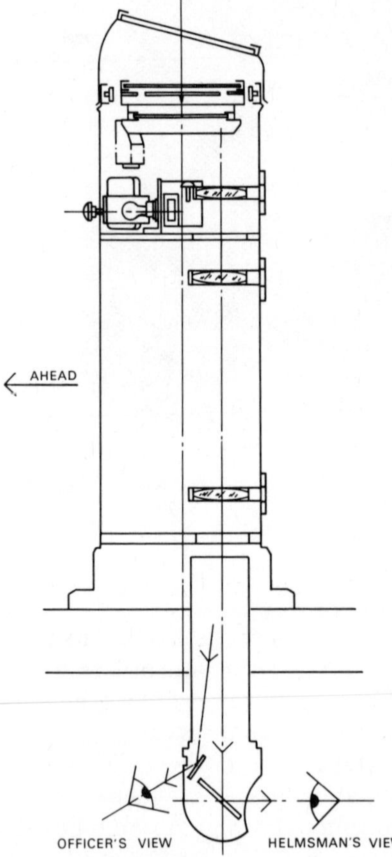

Figure 409c. Cutaway view of a reflection binnacle.

Figure 409d. A spherical compass.

Operation of the magnetic compass

410 When a compass is mounted on a vessel, its magnets align themselves with the magnetic field in which they exist. Assuming for the moment that there are no local influences (objects of magnetic material or electrical currents), this alignment will be parallel to the horizontal component of the earth's magnetic field. *The compass card will maintain this alignment regardless of the vessel's heading.*

As the compass card is attached to the magnets, the 000° mark on the card always points in the direction of *compass north,* and the ship's *compass heading* is indicated by the lubber's line. If there are no local disturbing influences, no *deviation* (see Article 411 below), then this is also the *magnetic heading.* When a compass is installed, great care must be taken to align the lubber's line exactly parallel to the center line of the ship. The compass bowl and lubber's line are constrained to turn with the ship, thus the direction of the lubber's line from the center of the compass always represents the direction of the ship's head. Since the 000° mark on the card is always toward the magnetic north, the direction indicated on the compass card opposite the lubber's line is the ship's heading. As the ship turns, the lubber's line turns with it, while the compass card remains aligned with compass north, so that the heading at any moment is indicated at the lubber's line. *Remember that it is the lubber's line, and not the compass card, that turns.*

Deviation

411 As stated above, a compass needle free to turn horizontally tends to align itself with the earth's magnetic lines of force. Unfortunately, it is not free to do so in a steel ship; such ships have marked magnetic properties of their own, and these tend to deflect the compass from the magnetic meridian. The divergence thus caused between the north-south axis of the compass card and the magnetic meridian is called *deviation* (Dev. or D). Even in a vessel made of wood or fiberglass there is enough magnetic material on board—engines, fuel and water tanks, rigging, etc.—to cause deviation.

The possibility of deviation from electrical circuits must not be overlooked. Direct currents flowing in straight wires establish magnetic fields. Care must be taken that all wiring in the vicinity of a compass is properly installed to eliminate or reduce any effect on the compass; checks must be made for deviation with the circuits turned on and off.

Although deviation differs from variation in that the latter is caused by the *earth's* magnetism, the two are designated in the same manner. Thus, if no deviation is present, the compass card lies with its axis in the magnetic meridian and its north point indicates the direction of *magnetic* north. If deviation is present and the north point of the compass points eastward of magnetic north, the deviation is named *easterly* and marked E. If it points westward of magnetic north, the deviation is named *westerly* and marked W.

The navigator can easily find the correct variation by referring to the chart of his locality. Deviation, however, is not so simple to ascertain. It varies not only on different ships, but on any particular ship it varies with changes in the ship's heading. Also, it often changes with large changes in the ship's latitude.

Compass error

412 The algebraic sum of variation (Article 404) and deviation (Article 411) is *compass error.* The navigator must understand thoroughly how to apply variation, deviation, and compass error, as he is frequently required to use them in converting one kind of direction to another.

From the foregoing it should be apparent that there are three ways in which a direction can be expressed:

As *true*, when referred to the *true* (geographic) meridian as the reference of measurement.

As *magnetic*, when referred to the *magnetic* meridian as the reference of measurement.

As *compass*, when referred to the axis of the *compass* card as the reference of measurement.

Any given direction may be expressed in all three of these ways, if it is understood that:

True differs from *magnetic* by *variation.*
Magnetic differs from *compass* by *deviation.*
Compass differs from *true* by *compass error.*

Figure 412a outlines a ship in which is shown the card of the standard compass. *OC* is the direction of the compass needle. *OM* is the magnetic meridian, and *OT* the true meridian. The two outer circles, concentric with the standard compass card, represent magnetic and true compass roses, thus indicating magnetic and true directions. The observer is at *O*. The magnetic meridian is 12° eastward (right) of the true meridian; therefore, the variation of the locality is 12° E. It is added to the magnetic direction of *M* (0° on magnetic rose) to obtain the true direction of *M* (12° on true rose). The compass needle is 8°

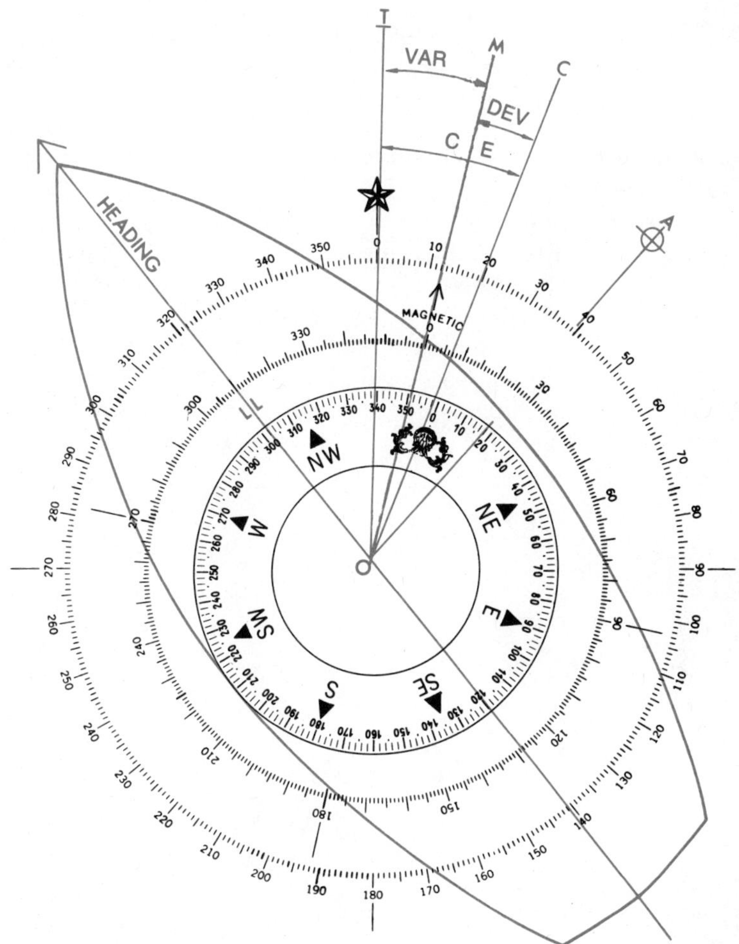

Figure 412a. Compass error.

eastward (right) of the magnetic meridian; therefore, the deviation is 8° E on the ship's heading shown. It is added to the compass direction of *C* (0° on compass card) to obtain the magnetic direction of *C* (8° on magnetic rose). The compass error is the algebraic sum of the variation and deviation or CE = 20° E. It is added to the compass direction of *C* (0° on compass card) to obtain the true direction of *C* (20° on true rose). The bearing of object *A* from the ship is shown as 20° psc, 30° magnetic, and 40° true. In practice, bearings are expressed in three-numeral groups—e.g., 020°, 030° and 040°. The ship's heading is 300° psc (note lubber's line *LL*), 308° magnetic, and 320° true.

As already noted, easterly deviation is added (+) to compass in converting to magnetic, easterly variation is added (+) to magnetic in converting to true, and easterly compass error is added (+) to compass in converting to true. Conversely, they are subtracted (−) when converting in the reverse order.

Figures 412b and c show westerly variation and deviation and demonstrate that the above rules of application should be reversed for westerly errors.

Rules for applying compass errors

It is convenient to have a thumb rule to serve as an aid to the memory in applying the above principles. The following will serve: *When correcting, easterly errors are added,* or simply, *correcting add east.* When applying this rule, it is necessary to consider a *compass* direction as the "least correct" expression of direction as it contains *two errors,* variation and deviation. *Magnetic* direction is thus "more correct" than compass as it contains only *one error,* variation. This is so even when the axis of the compass card is closer to the true meridian than is the magnetic meridian. Magnetic direction is, however, "less correct" than *true* direction, which contains *no errors.* Hence the process of converting a

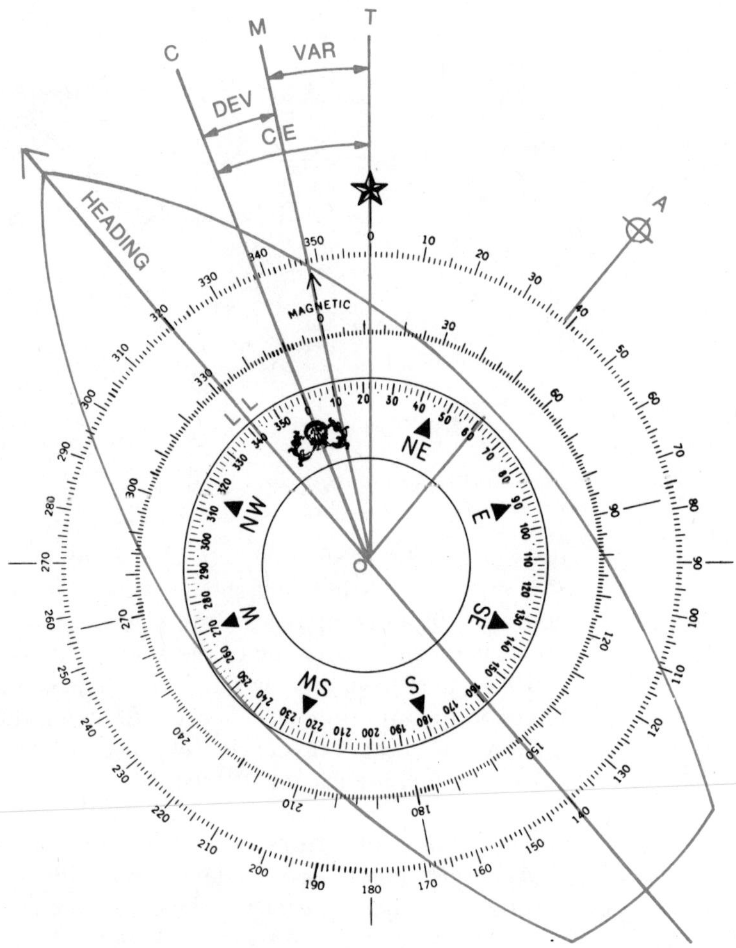

Figure 412b. Westerly variation and deviation.

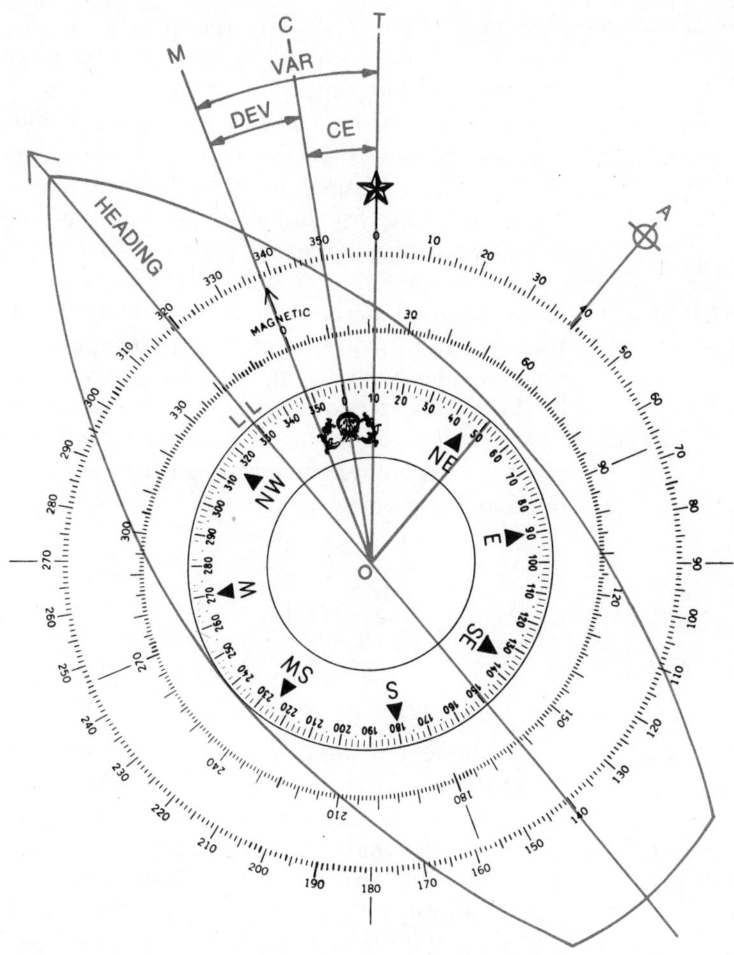

Figure 412c. Westerly variation, but easterly deviation.

Correcting and uncorrecting

compass direction to a magnetic or true direction or of converting a magnetic direction to a true direction is one of "correcting," or removing errors. If easterly errors are added, it is obvious that westerly errors are subtracted, and no separate rule is needed.

The opposite of *correcting* is called *uncorrecting.* The process of uncorrecting is one of converting a true direction to a magnetic or compass direction or a magnetic direction to a compass direction by applying errors. If easterly errors are added and westerly errors subtracted when correcting, then the reverse is true when uncorrecting. Hence, the one rule, *correcting add east*, is sufficient to cover all four possible situations:

Correcting, add east, subtract west.
Uncorrecting, add west, subtract east.

C-A-E

Note that to get the other three forms from the basic statement "correcting add east (which can be memorized as "C-A-E"), you must change two, but only two, of the three words. If "correcting" is changed to "uncorrecting," then *either add* must be changed to *subtract,* or *east* to *west.* If "correcting" is not changed to "uncorrecting," but "east" is changed to "west," then "add" must be changed to "subtract." The basic phrase, C-A-E, and the rules to change only two words will suffice to meet all problems of correcting and uncorrecting.

C-D-M-V-T

An alternative method for remembering the rules of correcting and uncorrecting involves using the first letters of the following words: Compass, Deviation, Magnetic, Variation, and True and letting these be the initial letters of words that form an easy-to-remember sentence. A convenient one to use is *Can Dead Men Vote Twice?* Using this sentence to remember the order, write down just the initial letters and arrange them vertically:

W	C	______
↑	D	______
+	M	______
↓	V	______
E	T	______

To the left of the column, draw a double-ended arrow, placing a *W* at the top, and *E* at the bottom and a *plus* sign in the center as illustrated. The addition of "At Elections" to the sentence above will assist in remembering that in the direction C-D-M-V-T the procedure is to *A*dd *E*ast. The arrow heads have nothing to do with actual direction but apply only to the direction of proceeding through the initial letters of the memory phrase, whether correcting from compass to true or uncorrecting from true to compass.

Now, by placing the given information in the corresponding blanks, the unknown values can easily be computed following the rule of the form.

Examples of correcting and uncorrecting

Example 1: A ship is heading 127° per standard compass. For this heading the deviation is 16° E and the variation is 4° W in the area.

Required: (1) The magnetic heading. (2) The true heading.

Solution: The problem is one of correcting. Since the deviation is easterly, it must be added. Hence, the magnetic heading is 127° + 16° = 143°. To find the true direction we are again correcting, and since the variation is westerly, it is subtracted. Hence, the true heading is 143° – 4° = 139°. In this case the compass error is 16° E – 4° W = 12° E. Applying this directly to the compass heading, we find the true heading is 127° + 12° = 139°, as previously determined.

Answers: (1) MH 143°, (2) TH 139°.

Example 2: A ship's course is 347° psc. The deviation is 4° W and the variation is 12° E.

Required: (1) The magnetic course. (2) The true course.

Solution: Again the problem is one of correcting. The deviation is subtracted and the magnetic course is 347° − 4° = 343°. The variation is added and the true course is 343° + 12° = 355°.

Answers: (1) MC 343°, (2) TC 355°.

Example 3: A ship's course is 009° psc. The deviation is 2° W and the variation is 19° W.

Required: (1) The magnetic course. (2) The true course.

Solution: The problem is one of correcting and since both errors are westerly, they are subtracted. The magnetic course is 009° − 2° = 007°. The true course is 007° − 19° = 348°. Since 000° is also 360°, this is the same as 367° − 19° = 348°.

Answers: (1) MC 007°, (2) TC 348°.

Example 4: From a chart the true course between two places is found to be 221°. The variation is 9° E and the deviation is 2° W.

Required: (1) The magnetic course. (2) The compass course.

Solution: It is necessary to uncorrect; the easterly variation is subtracted and the westerly deviation is added. The magnetic course is 221° − 9° = 212°. The compass course is 212° + 2° = 214°.

Answers: (1) MC 212°, (2) CC 214°.

Naming variation, deviation, or compass error

Another problem that can arise is that of assigning a "name"—east or west—to variation, deviation, or compass error when the numerical value has been found by subtraction between two directions. Here, the simple phrase rhymes as follows:

Compass least, error east.
Compass best, error west.

"Least" means lesser numerically, and "best" means greater numerically. For variation from true directions, "magnetic" can be substituted for "compass" in the rhyme.

Example 5: A navigator sets up a compass at a spot on shore near the ship's anchorage. This compass, not being affected by the iron and steel of the ship, is free from deviation and indicates magnetic direction. From the chart the navigator determines the true bearing of a distant mountain peak to be 320°. By compass it bears 337°. The ship bears 076° by compass from the observation spot ashore.

Required: (1) The variation. (2) The true bearing of the ship.

Solution: The numerical difference between the true and magnetic bearings is 17°; since the magnetic bearing is greater—"best" by the rhyme—the variation is westerly, 17° W. To find the true bearing of the ship is "correcting," and we use the previous rule—correcting, subtract west; thus, the true bearing of the ship is 076° − 17° = 059°.

Answers: (1) V 17° W, (2) TB 059°.

Example 6: Two beacons are so placed ashore that when seen in line from seaward they mark the direction of a channel, 161° T. Seen in line from a ship heading up the channel, they bear 157.5° by compass. The chart shows the variation for the locality to be 2.5° E.

Required: (1) The compass error. (2) The deviation.

Solution: The numerical difference is 161° – 157.5° = 3.5°. Since "compass is least" the "error is east." The compass error is the algebraic sum of the variation and deviation. Hence, the deviation is the algebraic *difference* or 3.5° – 2.5° = 1.0° E.

Answers: (1) CE 3.5° E, (2) D 1.0° E.

The table below summarizes the six examples; answers that were determined in each problem are underscored. A line for compass error (CE) has been added.

		1	2	3	4	5	6
W	C	127°	347°	009°	214°	337°	157°.5
↑	D	16° E	4° W	2° W	2° W	0°	1° E
+	M	143°	343°	007°	212°	337°	158°.5
↓	V	4° W	12° E	19° W	9° E	17° W	2°.5 E
E	T	139°	355°	348°	221°	320°	161°
	CE	12° E	8° E	21° W	7° E	17° W	3°.5 E

Deviation table **413** As stated in Article 411, the deviation changes with a change in the ship's heading. The deviation is determined by comparing a direction shown on the compass with the known magnetic direction. Several methods of accomplishing this will be explained later. The deviation on various headings is tabulated on a form called a *deviation table,* or *magnetic compass table,* and posted near the compass. A copy of the table should also be kept posted in the chart house.

Figures 413a and 413b illustrate the standard U.S. Navy form, used for tabulating deviation, compass history, and performance data.

It provides blanks for filling in certain information regarding the compass and the correctors used to reduce the deviation. Two different columns of deviation are shown, one marked "DG OFF" and the other "DG ON." "DG" refers to the ship's degaussing coils. Since the deviation may be somewhat different when the degaussing coils are energized, it is necessary to determine the deviation under both conditions. A deviation table for a vessel without degaussing coils would be simpler by half.

The deviations shown in this illustration are somewhat larger than would be acceptable under normal conditions of a properly adjusted compass. Such larger values are given here to provide practice in calculation and interpolation, the procedure for determining an intermediate value between two tabular listings.

A deviation table can be made for ship's heading by compass as in Figure 413c or, more commonly, by ship's heading magnetic as shown in Figure 413a. *When the deviations are small* (5° or less), *compass and magnetic courses being close together, little significant error is introduced in entering the deviation table with either compass or magnetic heading.* When the deviations are large and change rapidly, great care must be exer-

MAGNETIC COMPASS TABLE NAVSHIPS RPT. 3530-2
NAVSHIPS 3120/4 (REV. 6-72) (FRONT) *(Formerly NAVSHIPS 1104)*
S/N 0105-601-9521

U.S.S. S. P. Lee NO. AG 192 *(BB, CL, DD, etc.)*

[X] PILOT HOUSE [ ] SECONDARY CONNING STATION [ ] OTHER

BINNACLE TYPE: [ ] NAVY ST'D [ ] OTHER

COMPASS 7½" MAKE Lionel SERIAL NO. 12792

TYPE CC COILS K DATE 15 Sept 1977

READ INSTRUCTIONS ON BACK BEFORE STARTING ADJUSTMENT

SHIPS HEAD MAGNETIC	DEVIATIONS		SHIPS HEAD MAGNETIC	DEVIATIONS	
	DG OFF	DG ON		DG OFF	DG ON
0	4.0 W	4.5 W	180	4.0 E	3.5 E
15	4.0 W	4.0 W	195	5.5 E	5.0 E
30	3.5 W	4.0 W	210	6.5 E	6.0 E
45	3.0 W	3.5 W	225	6.5 E	6.0 E
60	2.5 W	3.0 W	240	6.0 E	5.5 E
75	2.5 W	2.5 W	255	4.5 E	4.0 E
90	2.0 W	2.5 W	270	3.0 E	2.5 E
105	2.0 W	2.0 W	285	0.5 E	0.5 E
120	2.0 W	2.0 W	300	1.0 W	1.0 W
135	1.5 W	1.5 W	315	2.5 W	3.0 W
150	0.5 W	0.5 W	330	3.5 W	3.5 W
165	1.5 E	1.5 E	345	4.0 W	4.0 W

DEVIATIONS DETERMINED BY: [ ] SUN'S AZIMUTH [X] GYRO [ ] SHORE BEARINGS

B 4 MAGNETS RED [ ] FORE [ ] AFT AT 13" FROM COMPASS CARD

C 6 MAGNETS RED [ ] PORT [ ] STBD AT 15" FROM COMPASS CARD

D 2-7" [X] SPHERES [ ] CYLS AT 12" [X] ATHWARTSHIP [ ] SLEWED ____° [ ] CLOCKWISE [ ] CTR. CLOCKWISE

HEELING MAGNET: [X] RED UP [ ] BLUE UP 18" FROM COMPASS CARD FLINDERS BAR: [X] FORE [ ] AFT 15"

[ ] LAT [X] H 0.190 [ ] LONG [ ] Z +0.530

SIGNED (Adjuster or Navigator) APPROVED (Commanding)

VERTICAL INDUCTION DATA
(Fill out completely before adjusting)

RECORD DEVIATION ON AT LEAST TWO ADJACENT CARDINAL HEADINGS

BEFORE STATING ADJUSTMENT: N 5.5W; E 4.0W; S 5.5E; W 6.0E.

RECORD BELOW INFORMATION FROM LAST NAVSHIPS 3120/4 DEVIATION TABLE:

DATE 1 Mar 1977 [X] LAT [ ] H 41° 22' N [X] LONG [ ] Z 71° 18'W

15" FLINDERS BAR [X] FORWARD [ ] AFT DEVIATIONS N 4.5W; E 2.0W; S 4.5E; W 3.0E.

RECORD HERE DATA ON RECENT OVERHAULS, GUNFIRE, STRUCTURAL CHANGES, FLASHING, DEPERMING, WITH DATES AND EFFECT ON MAGNETIC COMPASSES:

Annual shipyard overhaul:
3 June - 7 Sept 1977
Depermed Boston NSY: 12 Sept 1977

Abnormal deviation observed

PERFORMANCE DATA

COMPASS AT SEA: [ ] UNSTEADY [ ] STEADY

COMPASS ACTION: [ ] SLOW [X] SATISFACTORY

NORMAL DEVIATIONS: [X] CHANGE [ ] REMAIN RELIABLE

DEGAUSSED DEVIATIONS: [X] VARY [ ] DO NOT VARY

REMARKS

None

INSTRUCTIONS

1. This form shall be filled out by the Navigator for each magnetic compass as set forth in Chapter 9240 of NAVAL SHIPS TECHNICAL MANUAL.
2. When a swing for deviations is made, the deviations should be recorded both with degaussing coils off and with degaussing coils energized at the proper currents for heading and magnetic zone.
3. Each time this form is filled out after a swing for deviations, a copy shall be submitted to: Naval Ship Engineering Center Hyattsville, Maryland 20782. A letter of transmittal is not required.
4. When choice of box is given, check applicable box.
5. Before adjusting, fill in section on "Vertical Induction Data" above.

NAVSHIPS 3120/4 (REV. 6-72) (REVERSE) C-24855

Figure 413a. Left, deviation table (front), NAVSHIPS 3120/4; 413b., right, deviation table (reverse), NAVSHIPS 3120/4.

cised in using the table of deviation to ensure that the proper deviation is obtained for the heading desired.

If it is desired to find the compass course when a magnetic heading deviation table is available, proceed in the manner discussed in the following examples.

Example 1: A ship is to steer course 201° true. The variation is 10.5° W. DG is off.

Required: The compass course using deviation table of Figure 413a.

Solution: Applying the variation, the magnetic course is 201° + 10.5° = 211.5°.

Enter the table with 211.5°. The deviation is 6.5° E. The compass course is 211.5° − 6.5° = 205.0°.

Answer: CC 205.0°.

SHIPS HEAD MAGNETIC	DEVIATIONS		SHIPS HEAD MAGNETIC	DEVIATIONS	
	DG OFF	DG ON		DG OFF	DG ON
0	4.0 W	4.5 W	180	4.5 E	4.0 E
15	4.0 W	4.0 W	195	6.0 E	5.5 E
30	3.5 W	4.0 W	210	7.0 E	6.0 E
45	3.0 W	3.5 W	225	6.5 E	6.0 E
60	2.5 W	3.0 W	240	5.5 E	5.5 E
75	2.5 W	2.5 W	255	4.0 E	3.5 E
90	2.0 W	2.5 W	270	2.5 E	2.5 E
105	2.0 W	2.0 W	285	0.5 E	0.5 E
120	2.0 W	2.0 W	300	1.0 W	1.0 W
135	1.5 W	1.5 W	315	2.5 W	3.0 W
150	0.5 W	0.5 W	330	3.5 W	3.5 W
165	2.0 E	1.5 E	345	4.0 W	4.0 W

Figure 413c. Deviations tabulated by compass headings.

Example 2: The ship's head is 210° magnetic. A lighthouse bears 136° by compass. The variation is 3° E. DG is off.

Required: The true bearing using deviation table of Figure 413a.

Solution: The deviation depends on the ship's head, *not* the bearing. Hence, we enter the table with 210°. The deviation is 6.5° E + 3.0° E = 9.5° E. The true bearing is then 136° + 9.5° = 145.5°.

Answer: TB 145.5°.

Example 3: Using the deviation table of Figure 413a, determine the compass courses corresponding to the following true courses in an area where the variation is 12° W and with DG off: 093°, 168°, 238°.

Answers: CC 107°, CC 176°, CC 245°.

When it is desired to find a compass course if deviations for compass headings only (Figure 413c) are available, proceed as shown in Example 4.

Example 4: A ship is to steer course 187° true. The variation is 6° E. DG off.

Required: The compass course (CC) using the deviation table of Figure 413c.

Solution: Find the magnetic course first: 187° – 6° = 181°. Enter the deviation table with the compass courses, which when converted to magnetic courses, will bracket the desired magnetic course of 181° as follows:

Ships Hd. Compass	Deviation	Ships Hd. Magnetic
165°	2.0° E	167.0°
		181.0°
180°	4.5° E	184.5°

Interpolate between 167.0° and 184.5° to find the deviation corresponding to MH 181° as follows: for a change in magnetic heading of 17.5° (184.5° – 167.0°), the corresponding change of deviation is +2.5 E. For a change of magnetic heading of 14° (181.0° – 167.0°), the change of deviation is found by the ratio 2.5/17.5 = Δd/14, and Δd = 2.0° E. The deviation for MH 181° is then the deviation for MH 167° plus Δd determined above, or 2.0° E + (+2.0° E) = 4.0° E. Combining this deviation with the magnetic course of 181° corresponding to the true course given of 187°, the compass course is found to be 177°.

Answer: CC 177°.

The degree of precision to which calculations are carried will be determined by the application of the final figures. In this book, interpolation and other calculations of direction will be carried to the nearest half-degree. In the practice of navigation at sea, it is not likely that any greater degree of precision in the steering of a vessel could be obtained, and in smaller craft even this would be most improbable.

It should be noted that the deviation tables illustrated tabulate deviations for either compass or magnetic headings. Usually only one or the other of these deviations is prepared by the navigator and is available.

If the deviations are large, interpolating for headings between those tabulated can be difficult. A convenient way of interpolating for large deviations is to use a *Napier diagram,* as discussed in the following article.

Napier diagram or Curve of Deviations

414 When the maximum deviation is considerable, roughly 10° or more, a *Napier Diagram* or *Curve of Deviations* is a convenience to the navigator as it permits quick, easy, and accurate interpolation between recorded values of deviation. The user can find the deviation for any heading, compass or magnetic, and obtain the magnetic course corresponding to a compass course, or vice versa, simply by drawing two short lines.

Figure 414 shows a Napier diagram. The solid blue curves are drawn through the points established by plotting the deviations given in the following table:

Compass	Magnetic	Deviation
N 000°	012°	12° E
NE 045°	049°	4° E
E 090°	087°	3° W
SE 135°	128°	7° W
S 180°	174°	6° W
SW 225°	224°	1° W
W 270°	278°	8° E
NW 315°	238°	13° E

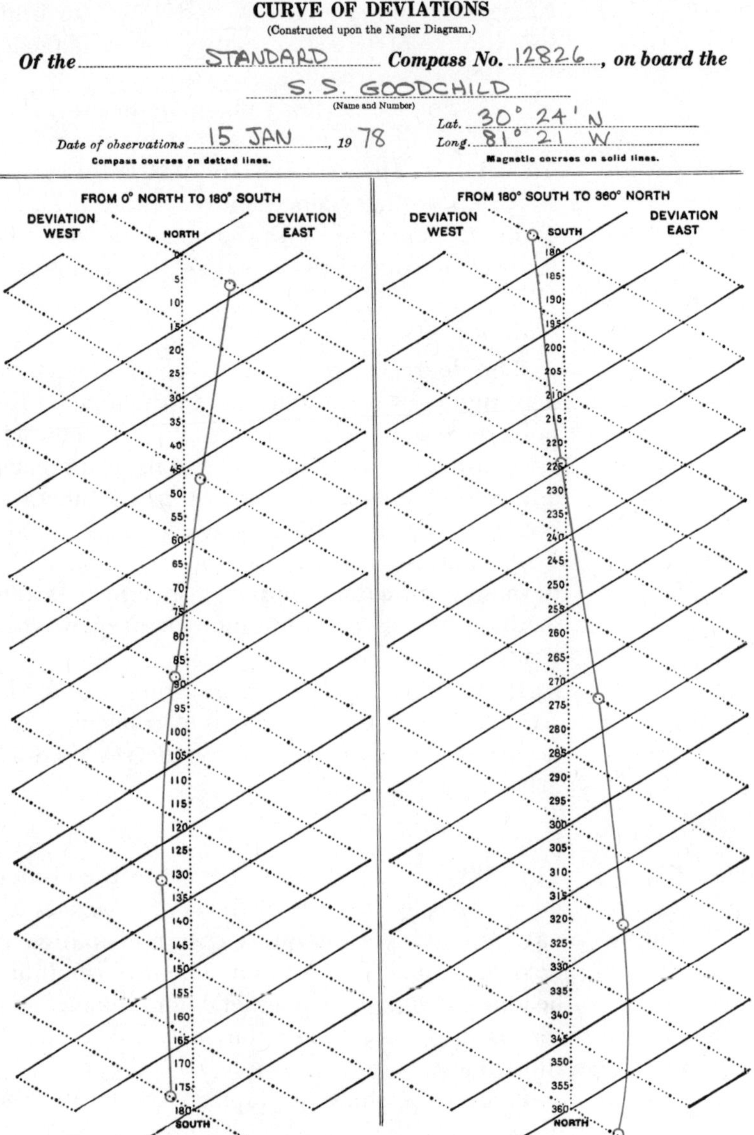

Figure 414. Napier diagram with curves drawn.

For simplicity, only whole degrees have been used in this table and there are fewer data points than would be normal. The values here are excessive; they indicate that the compass is in need of adjustment (see Article 415), but they serve to illustrate the construction and use of a Napier diagram.

The central dotted line of the diagram with the numerals of every fifth degree represents the rim of a compass card cut at the north point and straightened into a vertical column. For convenience, it is usually arranged in two columns, as shown in the illustration. The method of constructing and using the curve can best be explained by describing the preparation of the *curve of deviations* shown in the figure, and by examples.

Just above the left half of the curve is the precept, "compass courses on dotted lines." This means that to plot the deviation of 12° E on north (000°) by compass, the dotted line is followed toward "deviation east" from the "0" to the twelfth dot. This dot is enclosed in a small circle. Because the table is in two halves, the full circle back to zero ends with the "360" at bottom of the right half of the diagram; here again the twelfth dot toward "deviation east" is circled for the deviation of 12° E. In similar fashion the deviation of 4° E on compass heading of 045 is represented by a circle around the fourth dot from the "45" toward "deviation east," and the 3° W on 090 by compass is shown by the circle around the third dot from the "90" toward "deviation west," etc. A faired curve is drawn through all the circled points. When a deviation to a fraction of a degree is to be plotted, the correct position between the dots for the whole degrees on each side is estimated by eye and marked by a circled dot.

Wherever the curve crosses a diagonal dotted line, the deviation for that 15° rhumb of the compass headings may be read directly, as 15° E for 330° and 345° and 5° W for 105°. For a compass heading which does not have a diagonal dotted line through it, a broken line drawn parallel to those dotted lines, from the dot of the desired heading to the curve, will give the deviation. For example, for compass heading 009° the broken line, from the ninth dot on the central line to the curve, will be found to be about 11 dots long toward "deviation east," showing the deviation to be 11° E.

The second precept, "magnetic courses on solid lines," is applied this way: A *solid* line drawn parallel to the *solid* lines, say, from the 323d dot to the curve will be found to be 13 dots long toward "deviation east." This shows that the deviation for 323° *magnetic* is 13° E.

When using the "curve of deviations" to determine directly the magnetic courses corresponding to compass courses, or vice versa, the following old jingle may help in applying the two precepts:

From compass course, magnetic course to gain,
Depart by dotted and return by plain.
From magnetic course to steer the course allotted,
Depart by plain and then return by dotted.

The first half of this jingle is applied as follows: From the point on the central dotted line, draw a light penciled line from the known compass heading, parallel to the *dotted* diagonal lines, out until it intersects the curve. From this point draw a light line, parallel to the *solid* diagonal lines back until it intersects the central dotted line. At this point, read a value for the desired magnetic heading.

Example 1: The compass heading is 310°. What is the correct magnetic heading? *Answer:* 323°.

The second half of the jingle is applied in a similar fashion. Draw a light construction line from the known magnetic course, parallel to the solid diagonal lines, out to its intersection and then parallel to the dotted diagonal lines, back to the central vertical line where the intersection is the value of the desired compass course.

Example 2: A magnetic course of 020° is desired. What is the compass course to be steered? *Answer:* 009°.

PRACTICAL COMPASS ADJUSTMENT

Introduction

415 Article 411 stated that the deviation of the magnetic compass is caused by the magnetic properties of a steel ship. A complete analysis of the many separate magnetic components which combine to cause deviation is beyond the scope of this book; however, an understanding of the basic concepts and terminology is desirable. The various magnetic components or parameters of the total magnetic field of a vessel are referred to as coefficients, and different correcting magnets are used to compensate for their effects on the compass. Figure 403 illustrates the concept of the earth as a magnet, with the north magnetic pole colored blue, in accordance with the usual practice. Article 402 states that materials of opposite polarity attract each other; the polarity of the magnetic hemisphere and the north-seeking end of a compass magnet are therefore opposite. To identify their polarity, the ends of compensating bar magnets used in binnacles are color-coded, the *north* end being painted *red,* and the *south, blue.*

Coefficients of deviation

The total local magnetic effects which cause deviation of a vessel's compass can be broken down into a series of components termed *coefficients;* these are arbitrarily defined and designated by letters. As used below, "soft iron" is material in which magnetism is induced by the earth's magnetic field. This magnetism changes as its orientation with respect to the earth's magnetic field changes. In contrast, the ship's "hard iron" has the relatively permanent magnetism acquired during construction and fitting-out. Soft and hard iron are also classified as "horizontal" or "vertical" as determined by the orientation of their magnetic axes when induced by components of the earth's field.

Coefficient A is constant on all headings and may be a combination of other parameters or may be mechanical, as from an incorrectly placed lubber's line.

Coefficient B is maximum on compass headings east or west and zero on compass headings north or south.

Coefficient C is maximum on compass headings north or south and zero on east or west. *Coefficients B and C* are caused by permanent magnetism and to some extent by induced magnetism in vertical soft iron. On small craft constructed mainly of wood and/or fiberglass, adjustment is normally made only for these coefficients. Most boat compass mountings will have built-in small correcting magnets for this purpose.

Coefficient D is quadrantal deviation. It is maximum on intercardinal headings: 045°—135°—225°—315°, and zero on cardinal compass headings: north—south—east—west.

Coefficient E is quadrantal deviation which is maximum on the cardinal compass headings and zero on the intercardinal headings.

Coefficients D and E are caused by induced magnetism in horizontal soft iron and are compensated for by the use of the soft iron *quadrantal spheres* normally mounted on brackets athwartship on the binacle. These spheres should be used on all vessels constructed of steel.

Heeling error *Coefficient J* is defined as the change of deviation for a heel of 1° while the vessel is on compass heading 000°. It is, in effect, the error caused because the compass, with its gimballing arrangement, remains in a horizontal plane while the ship, with its magnetic field, rolls and pitches. A slight change in the relative positions of the compass and ship is therefore introduced. This change in deviation caused by the motion of the ship can cause the compass card to oscillate. Coefficient *J* is compensated for by a heeling magnet placed in a vertical tube directly below the center of the compass.

Flinders bar On the magnetic equator (Article 405) there is no vertical component of the earth's magnetic field and consequently no induced magnetism in vertical soft iron. At other locations, notably in higher latitudes, the vertical component can cause the compass to become unreliable in a much larger area than if the force is neutralized. This statement represents an oversimplification of the problem as the various coefficients are of course interrelated. To compensate for or neutralize any induced magnetism in vertical soft iron, a *Flinders bar* is used. This consists of sections of soft iron having no permanent magnetism; as many sections as required are installed vertically in a tube on the side of the compass opposite to the effective pole of the ship's field.

The theory of compass adjustment hinges on a more complete analysis. The following articles will dispense with theory, and follow empirically the procedure which experience indicates is satisfactory for adjusting the great majority of compasses. It is assumed that the compass is in correct alignment with the ship's centerline, has no internal malfunctions, and that only comparatively minor adjustment is required.

If the procedure outlined hereafter does not give acceptable results, the services of a professional compass adjustor should be sought. For a detailed discussion of compass adjustment, see *Handbook of Magnetic Compass Adjustment and Compensation,* DMAHC Pub. No. 226.

Compass binnacle and correctors

416 The *compass binnacle* is the case and stand in which a magnetic compass is mounted. The type used by the Navy for mounting its standard 7½-inch compass is illustrated in Figure 407c. It consists of a casting of nonmagnetic material about 3½ feet (1.07 m) high with an opening in the top to receive the compass, and provision for holding the correctors used for adjusting the compass. Inside the binnacle, which has access doors, are trays or holders for fore-and-aft magnets and for athwartship magnets. The trays are supported on screws so they can be raised or lowered, with about 12 inches (30 cm) of travel available, and provision is made for as many as eight 4-inch (10-cm) magnets in each set of trays. These are the *B* and *C* correcting magnets. Most modern binnacles now have provision for under-lighting the compass. In the center of the interior of the binnacle a tube is located to hold the heeling magnets, which can be moved up and down in the tube and secured as desired. The soft-iron spheres are mounted on either side of the binnacle in grooved brackets which permit the spheres to be moved in a horizontal plane, toward or away from the binnacle. The binnacle in Figure 407c is also equipped with degaussing compensating coils mounted around the binnacle at the level of the compass, with the junction boxes for the coils shown near the base of the stand. Binnacles for non-naval vessels are generally of similar design but without degaussing coils.

Preparations for adjustment

417 The preparatory steps for adjusting the compass can be made before getting underway. The vessel should be on an even keel. All movable magnetic gear in the vicinity of the compass should be secured in the position it will occupy at sea. Several types of personal articles occasionally taken onto the bridge of a vessel—small transistor radios, photoelectric light meters, and hand calculators—are highly magnetic and should never be permitted in the vicinity of the compass.

Degaussing coils should be secured and compass coils given a "dockside" compensation.

The binnacle should be exactly on the midship line and should be so solidly secured as to avoid any chance of movement.

The compass bowl should be in the center of the binnacle. To center a compass bowl in its binnacle, with the ship heading north or south or nearly so, and on an even keel, put the compass bowl in place and adjust its position by the screws at the ends of the outer gimbal ring knife-edges, until no change of heading by compass is observed as the heeling magnet is raised and lowered. Secure the compass bowl in this position by tightening the screws to prevent any sliding back and forth athwartships. In case there is excessive looseness from wear in the gimbal rings, they should be repaired or new ones obtained. The compass bowl should not move either fore-and-aft or athwartships in the gimbal rings.

The lubber's line of the compass should be exactly in the fore-and-aft plane of the ship. This should be carefully verified. It is best done by sighting with the azimuth circle on straightedges erected on the midship line at some distance forward and abaft the compass; this may be done very accurately when in drydock.

The lubber's line of each pelorus should also be checked. This can be done by taking simultaneous bearings of a distant object from the magnetic compass and the pelorus.

Preparations should be made to record details of the adjustment.

Flinders bar

418 If the *Flinders bar* is in place, it should be left there. If not, do not use it until expert advice has been obtained.

Quadrantal spheres

The *quadrantal spheres* should be left in the same position in which they were placed when the compass was last adjusted. If there is uncertainty as to where they should be located, place them in the middle of each athwartships arm.

Heeling magnet

If the *heeling magnet* is in place, with the correct end up—*red* end *up, north* of the magnetic equator, and *blue* end *up, south* of the magnetic equator—leave it in place. If not, place it in the bottom of the tube with the appropriate end up. The proper height for the heeling magnet can be determined after the other steps of the adjustment are completed, by heading north or south when the ship has a steady roll. Observe the oscillations of the compass, and raise the magnet until the compass steadies. This can readily be accomplished on smaller vessels;

Figure 418. Compasses on bridge of a ship.

it is more difficult on larger ones. The position of the heeling magnet may have to be readjusted to keep the compass steady if the ship moves to a substantially different magnetic latitude.

Remove all other correctors, except the degaussing coils.

Underway procedure

419 Having arrived in a clear area, with plenty of room to maneuver, the ship must be steadied *accurately* on selected *magnetic* headings in a definite sequence. Then when the proper corrector described below is so placed as to cause the compass to read the known *magnetic* heading, the deviation becomes zero. For example, if the ship is on magnetic north but the compass shows the heading as 358°, when it should read 000°, the deviation is 2° E, and the corrector should be so placed as to cause the compass to read 000°. Various methods of putting the ship on the desired magnetic headings are given later in this chapter.

The sequence of magnetic headings is as follows:

1. A cardinal point—N, S, E, or W.
2. The cardinal point 180° from the first point.
3. A cardinal point 90° from the first.
4. The cardinal point 180° from the third.
5. An intercardinal point—NE, SE, SW, or NW.
6. An intercardinal point 90° from the point used in step 5.
7. Separate runs, steadying for at least one minute on headings 15° apart—000°, 015°, 030°, etc., through 360°—to find the residual deviations.

Assume that the first heading is north. After the ship has been steadied on 000° *magnetic,* the compass is read and the deviation noted. The required correcting magnets will go in the *athwartship* holders below the compass, which should be cranked down to near, but not quite at, the bottom of their travel. The correct direction in which to place the red ends of the magnets may be determined by holding one magnet above the compass parallel to the position it will have in the holder. If the card swings in the proper direction, magnets should be inserted in the holders with that orientation; if the swing is in the wrong direction, the magnet should be turned end for end before it is inserted. The number of magnets to be used is determined by trial and error. *Several magnets near the bottom of travel are preferable to one or two close to the compass;* if more than one magnet is used, all red ends must point in the same direction. When enough magnets have been put in the holder to remove approximately all the deviation on that heading, a fine adjustment is made by cranking the holders up or down until the compass indicates the correct magnetic heading, zero deviation.

The ship is now brought to the second heading, 180° from the first —in this case, south. After she steadies down, the deviation, which should be small, is again noted. *Half* of the deviation is removed, by cranking the holders containing the athwartship magnets up or down, as necessary.

Proceed next to the third heading, which in this case will be east or west. All deviation on this heading is removed, using magnets in the fore-and-aft holders. The correct direction of the red ends is determined as on the first heading. The holders should again be cranked down near the lower end of their travel; magnets will be inserted as required. The holders are cranked up or down to remove all deviation.

The ship now comes to the fourth heading, 180° from that of the third. *Half* the deviation is removed, by cranking the fore-and-aft magnets up or down as required.

She is next brought to the fifth heading, an intercardinal point, and all deviation found on this heading is removed by moving the two iron spheres. *Both the spheres are moved in or both out,* as required, until the magnetic heading and heading by compass are identical. If the inboard limit of travel is reached without fully removing the deviation, larger spheres are needed; if overcorrection exists at the outward limit of movement of the spheres, smaller ones must be used. It is preferable to use large spheres farther away from the compass rather than smaller ones nearer the compass.

Come next to the sixth heading, an intercardinal point 90° from the one used for the fifth heading, and remove *half* the deviation found by moving the iron spheres. Both spheres must be moved in, or out, and by the same amount.

At this point the number and positions of all correctors should be carefully logged.

Finally, the ship is swung through 360°, steadying on each 15° heading *for not less than a minute;* if the compass appears sluggish, steady up for at least two minutes on each heading. The *residual deviation,* the deviation remaining after adjustment, is recorded for each 15° change of heading. If time is very short, or the residuals only 2° or less, deviations may be taken on only eight headings, or every 45°.

If the ship is fitted with degaussing gear, all circuits for normal operation are now energized, the ship is swung again and the residuals for degaussing on (DG ON) are noted on each 15° heading.

The degaussing equipment is intended to give the ship some measure of protection against magnetic mines and torpedoes, by reducing the ship's magnetic field. Degaussing is normally accomplished by permanently installed cables in the form of coils through which an electric current is passed, thus setting up a magnetic field which tends to neutralize the ship's field. The degaussing currents do, however, have a strong effect on the magnetic compass, and the deviation caused by these currents is usually larger than that caused by the ship's magnetism. Some of the deviation caused by the degaussing circuits is offset by degaussing compensating coils mounted on the binnacle as described in Article 416. They are not completely efficient, hence the deviation must also be determined with the degaussing gear activated.

A deviation table, as described in Article 413, and if desired, a Napier diagram, are now completed. Copies of the deviation table should be posted at the compass, in the compass record book, and in the ship's log.

Coming to a magnetic heading and finding deviation

420 There are five methods for coming to a magnetic heading and finding the deviation, but the first method listed below is probably the most accurate, as well as the one most commonly used:

By taking azimuths of a celestial body.
By comparison with a gyrocompass.
By comparison with a magnetic compass having known deviations.
By taking bearings of a distant object.
By using ranges.

Azimuths of a celestial body

421 The body most frequently used for this purpose is the sun. A time of day should be selected when the sun's altitude is below about 30°, because it is quite difficult to measure its azimuth, or direction, accurately at high altitudes. The azimuths must be computed in advance, usually for every eight minutes of the period that it is anticipated will be required for the adjustment. Azimuths can be computed from DMAHC Publication No. 229 or special tables of Azimuths of the Sun, such as Publication No. 260. Having determined the azimuth at eight-minute intervals, the variation for the locality is applied to obtain magnetic azimuths. These are plotted on graph paper, and a smooth curve is drawn through the various points; the coordinates are time and magnetic azimuths. The method of computing the azimuths and plotting the curve is discussed in Chapter 28.

To put the ship on a desired magnetic heading, pick the magnetic azimuth off the curve for the appropriate time, then find the angle between the desired magnetic heading and the magnetic azimuth. Rotate the azimuth circle on the compass so that the line of sight through the vanes forms this same angle with the lubber's line. Adjust course right or left until the sun appears in the vanes. Recheck the time and the corresponding magnetic azimuth, and adjust the setting of the azimuth circle, if necessary.

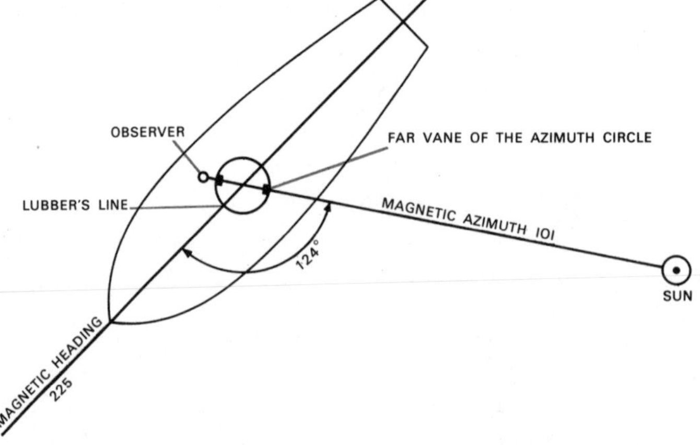

Figure 421. Placing a vessel on a magnetic heading of 225° by azimuth of the sun.

Example: How would you place a ship on magnetic heading 225° when the magnetic azimuth of the sun is 101°?

Solution: When the ship is on the required heading, the sun will be 225° – 101° = 124° to the *left* of the ship's head. See Figure 421.

Answer: Place the far vane 124° to the left of the ship's head and maneuver the ship until the sun is in line with the vanes.

If a pelorus is used, it can be set with the required magnetic heading, 225°, at the lubber's line and the far vane at the magnetic azimuth, 101°.

The deviation is determined by comparing the observed azimuth with its computed value at that moment. The difference is the deviation, which is easterly if the computed azimuth is the greater, and westerly if the observed azimuth is the greater. Again the jingle "Compass least, error east; compass best, error west" can serve as a memory aid.

Example: At a given time the azimuth of the sun is observed by the standard compass, and is found to be 105.5°. The magnetic azimuth taken from the curve for the same moment is 103.5°.

Required: The deviation of the standard compass on the present heading.

Answer: Dev. 2.0° W.

By comparison with a gyrocompass

422 When a gyrocompass is available, the comparison of the course as shown by gyro and the course as shown by magnetic compass will give the compass error, provided the gyro is running true. If the gyro has an error it must be allowed for. The deviation can then be found by combining the compass error thus determined and the charted variation. This is the method most frequently used by ships with a reliable gyrocompass.

To bring the ship to a desired magnetic heading, apply the variation to the desired magnetic heading to obtain the corresponding true heading, and bring the ship to this heading by gyro.

Example 1: A ship is heading 214° by gyrocompass and 201° by magnetic compass. The gyro error is 1° W and the variation is 5° E.

Required: The deviation of the standard compass on the present heading.

Solution: If the ship is heading 214° by gyrocompass and the gyro error is 1° W, the heading is 213° true. Applying the variation, the magnetic heading is found to be 213° – 5° = 208°. The deviation is 208° – 201° = 7° E.

Answer: Dev. 7° E.

Example 2: Find the gyro heading to place a ship on magnetic heading 000°, if the variation is 23° E and the gyro error is 1° W.

Solution: The true heading is 000° + 23° = 023°. The gyro heading is 023° + 1° = 024°.

Answer: GH 024°.

By comparison with a magnetic compass of known deviation

423 This method is similar to that of comparison with a gyrocompass, except that it is not necessary to know the variation. The method is often used when two or more magnetic compasses are adjusted at the same time. For example, the deviation of the standard compass may be found by a curve of magnetic azimuths or some other method and the steering compass then compared with it. This is a method frequently used when there is no gyrocompass installed in the ship.

To bring the ship to a desired magnetic heading apply the deviation to the desired magnetic heading to obtain the compass heading.

Example 1: A ship is heading 173° by standard compass and 175° by steering compass. The deviation of the standard compass on this heading is 4° E.

Required: The deviation of the steering compass.

Solution: The magnetic heading is 173° + 4° = 177°. The deviation of the steering compass is 177° – 175° = 2° E.

Answer: Dev. 2° E.

Example 2: Find the compass heading to place a ship on magnetic heading 180°, using the deviation table of Figure 423 (DG OFF).

Solution: The deviation table is made out for compass headings. Entries of compass heading 165° and 180° are converted to magnetic headings of 167° (Dev. 2.0° E) and 184.5° (Dev. 4.5° E). Interpolation is done for magnetic heading of 180° (rounded to the nearest half degree), and deviation is found to be 4° E. Applying this to the magnetic heading, the required compass heading is 180° – 4° = 176°.

Answer: CH 176°.

SHIPS HEAD MAGNETIC	DEVIATIONS		SHIPS HEAD MAGNETIC	DEVIATIONS	
	DG OFF	DG ON		DG OFF	DG ON
0	4.0 W	4.5 W	180	4.5 E	4.0 E
15	4.0 W	4.0 W	195	6.0 E	5.5 E
30	3.5 W	4.0 W	210	7.0 E	6.0 E
45	3.0 W	3.5 W	225	6.5 E	6.0 E
60	2.5 W	3.0 W	240	5.5 E	5.5 E
75	2.5 W	2.5 W	255	4.0 E	3.5 E
90	2.0 W	2.5 W	270	2.5 E	2.5 E
105	2.0 W	2.0 W	285	0.5 E	0.5 E
120	2.0 W	2.0 W	300	1.0 W	1.0 W
135	1.5 W	1.5 W	315	2.5 W	3.0 W
150	0.5 W	0.5 W	330	3.5 W	3.5 W
165	2.0 E	1.5 E	345	4.0 W	4.0 W

Figure 423. Deviation table.

By bearings of a distant object

424 If a ship swings about an anchor, the bearings of a fixed object at least six miles distant will not change materially during the swing. By observing the bearing of the object by a magnetic compass as the ship heads in various directions, the deviation can be obtained for each heading for which an observation is taken, by comparison with the magnetic bearing.

If the distant object is shown on the chart, its magnetic bearing is obtained simply by applying the charted variation to the true bearing by compass rose. If not charted, its magnetic bearing may be taken as the average of a round of compass bearings of the object, observed on equidistant headings of the ship. The explanation of the last statement is that, theoretically, if a ship is swung through a circle and deviations are determined on equidistant compass headings, the sum of the easterly deviations found will equal numerically the sum of the westerly deviations, the resulting net deviation for all headings being zero. The error introduced by this assumption is generally very small unless there is a constant error, such as a misaligned lubber's line.

A ship may be underway when obtaining a table of deviations by this method. In this case an object at a great distance must be chosen, and the ship should remain in as small an area as possible while making the observations. A buoy may be anchored and the ship maneuvered to keep as close as possible to this buoy while taking the observations.

Example 1: A ship plants a buoy, and, remaining close to this buoy, takes bearings of an unidentified prominent peak on a distant mountain.

Required: The deviations of the standard and steering compasses, the observations being as shown in the columns below.

Solution:

A	B	C	D	E	F	G
Ship's head psc	Bearing of peak psc	Magnetic bearing of peak	Deviation standard compass	Ship's head magnetic	Ship's head per steering compass	Deviation of steering compass
°	°	°	°	°	°	°
000	340.7	330.5	10.2 W	349.8	342.4	7.4 E
045	338.0	330.5	7.5 W	037.5	038.0	0.5 W
090	332.5	330.5	2.0 W	088.0	097.0	9.0 W
135	328.0	330.5	2.5 E	137.5	154.0	16.5 W
180	325.0	330.5	5.5 E	185.5	193.7	8.2 W
225	321.5	330.5	9.0 E	234.0	232.6	1.4 E
270	326.0	330.5	4.5 E	274.5	263.5	11.0 E
315	332.3	330.5	1.8 W	313.2	294.0	19.2 E
Sum	2644.0					
Mean	330.5					

Columns *A*, *B*, and *F* are observed during the swing. Column *C* is the average of column *B*. Column *D* is the difference between columns *B* and *C*. Column *E* is found by applying column *D* to column *A*. Column *G* is the difference between columns *E* and *F*.

If bearings can be read to a tenth of a degree, it is good practice to so measure, but then to round off to the nearest half-degree when preparing the deviation table. When deviation values have been determined for headings at irregular intervals, as the steering compass in the above example, it is desirable to calculate values for the more normal intervals of the table. Plot the deviations on cross-section paper and fair a curve through the points. The deviation at regular intervals such as 000°, 045°, 090°, etc., can then be read from the curve to the nearest half-degree.

With deviations as large as those shown, the ship should be swung on headings differing by 15°, rather than 45° as shown, if it is not possible to adjust the compasses and reduce the deviations. The example uses headings differing by 45° for brevity.

Note that this example includes the method of comparing a compass with one of known deviation.

To bring the ship to a desired magnetic heading, determine the magnetic bearing of the object, and find the difference between this and the desired magnetic heading. Set the far vane of the bearing circle to the right or to the left as with an azimuth of a celestial body, and maneuver the ship until the distant object is in line with the vanes.

Example 2: How would you place a ship on magnetic heading 180° if the true bearing of a distant mountain peak is 227° and the variation is 12° W?

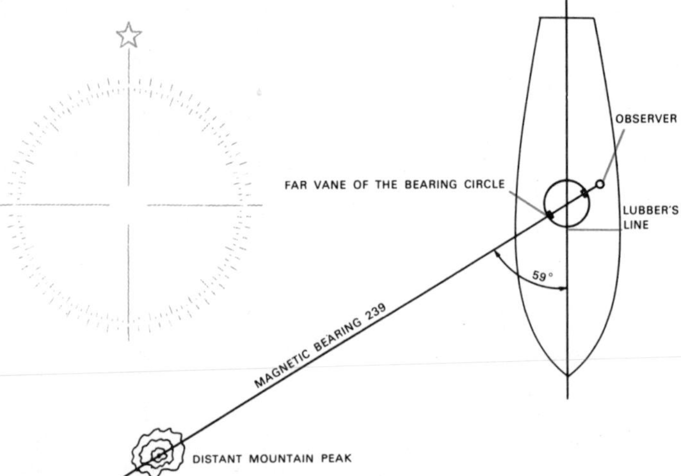

Figure 424. Placing a ship on a magnetic heading of 180° by bearings on a distant object.

Solution: The magnetic bearing is 227° + 12° = 239°. Set the far vane 239° − 180° = 59° to the *right* of the ship's head. See Figure 424.

Answer: Set the far vane 59° to the right of the ship's head and maneuver until the mountain is in line with the vanes.

By ranges **425** Two fixed, identifiable objects appearing in line constitute a *range.* Aids to navigation consisting of two range marks are often used to mark midchannels, turning points, measured mile courses, etc. Ranges of natural or man-made objects can often be found. If it is necessary to *swing ship*—take multiple bearings for compass compensation—it should be done where it will not interfere with normal ship traffic. The true direction of the range is determined by measurement on the chart. (The direction of ranges that are aids to navigation can be found in the *Light List.*) The magnetic direction is then determined by applying the variation of the locality. The deviation is found by crossing the range on the desired heading and observing the compass bearing at the instant the objects are in line.

To bring the ship to a desired magnetic heading, proceed as outlined in Article 424.

Refer to Figure 425. Beacons *A* and *B* form a range, the direction of which is 030.5° true. The local variation is 20° W. Hence, the magnetic direction of the range is 050.5°. If the observed bearing of the range is 045°, the deviation is 050.5° − 045.0° = 5.5° E.

Example: For determining the deviations of the standard compass, a ship uses the two ranges marking the measured mile off Kent Island, Chesapeake Bay. The true direction of the ranges is 091.5° and the variation for the locality is 7.8° W. As the ship crosses a range on the

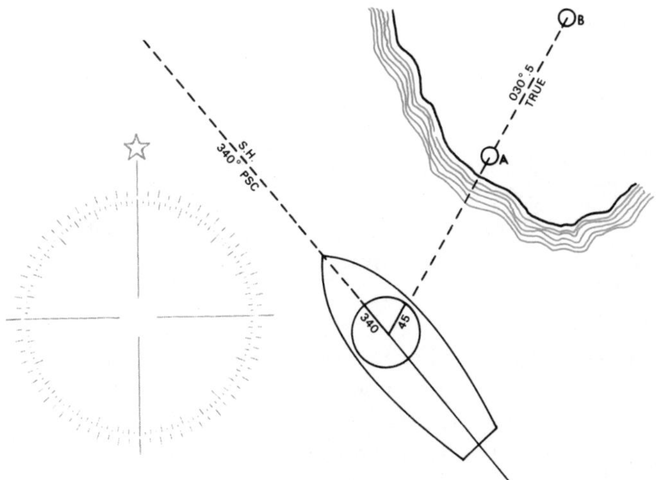

Figure 425. Finding compass deviation by a range.

headings shown in the first column of the following table, the navigator observes the corresponding directions of the range as noted in the third column.

Required: The deviations of the standard compass.

Ship's head psc	Magnetic direction of range	Direction of range psc	Deviation
°	°	°	°
000	099.3	103.2	3.9 W
015		103.1	3.8 W
030		102.6	3.3 W
045		102.1	2.8 W
060		101.8	2.5 W
075		101.7	2.4 W
090		101.5	2.2 W
105		101.4	2.1 W
120		101.3	2.0 W
135		100.8	1.5 W
150		099.9	0.6 W
165		097.2	2.1 E
180		094.8	4.5 E
195		093.3	6.0 E
210		092.5	6.8 E
225		092.9	6.4 E
240		093.8	5.5 E
255		095.3	4.0 E
270		096.8	2.5 E
285		098.8	0.5 E
330		100.3	1.0 W
315		101.8	2.5 W
330		102.7	3.4 W
345		103.3	4.0 W

Solution: The magnetic direction of the range is 091.5° – 7.8° = 099.3°.

The deviation table (Figure 413c—DG OFF) is made up from this solution, by rounding off the deviations to the nearest half degree.

Critical values tables

426 A different style of deviation table is often used on smaller vessels where deviation and headings are only used in whole degrees. It is quicker and easier to use, requiring no interpolation for any heading. This is a *critical values* table. The spread of headings is shown for each one degree increment of deviation. For example, the DG-OFF portion of Figure 423, disregarding fractions of a degree, might appear as seen in Figure 426.

Ship's Heading Compass	Deviation DG Off
000–034	4W
035–077	3W
078–133	2 W
134–150	1 W
151–159	0 W
286–293	0 W
294–303	1 W
304–314	2 W
315–330	3 W
331–360	4 W

Figure 426. Deviation shown by a table of critical values (extract).

THE GYROCOMPASS

Introduction to the gyrocompass

427 The first section of this chapter was devoted to the magnetic compass which was for many centuries the only instrument available at sea for the determination of direction. In the search for an instrument which would indicate true north rather than magnetic north, the gyrocompass was developed early in this century. Parallel advances have been made in America and Europe; the American Sperry Gyrocompass was developed on the basis of the use of a single rotor or spinning wheel as compared with the multiple rotors of the early Anschutz compasses built in Germany.

Schuler pendulum

As will be explained in Article 433, the gyrocompass inherently is capable of oscillating about its vertical, or azimuth-indicating axis. Damping is employed to suppress this tendency. Professor Max Schuler showed that the effects of accelerations, due to speed and course changes, are minimized when the period of this oscillation is made equal to approximately 84 minutes. This is the period a simple pendulum would have if its length were equal to the radius of the earth. This has come to be known as the Schuler pendulum, and the principle has basic application in all inertial navigation systems.

The gyro is used increasingly in navigation aboard ships today, not only as a steering or heading reference, but also to indicate the ship's roll and pitch data needed for instruments used for celestial navigation (Chapter 38). The gyro is also a basic component of inertial navigation systems (Chapter 35).

Gyroscopic laws Of the four natural laws or facts upon which gyrocompass operation depends, the first two are inherent properties of the gyroscope, namely, *gyroscopic inertia* (rigidity in space) and *precession*. The third and fourth relate to the earth and are the earth's rotation and gravitation. The interrelationship of these natural phenomena is explained briefly in this chapter to enable the navigator to understand the basic concept of a gyrocompass and, more importantly, to enable him to realize the limits of its accuracy, and to know the sources of inherent error of the gyroscope when used as a compass in the shipboard environment.

Basic gyroscope **428** A rapidly spinning body having three axes of angular freedom constitutes a gyroscope (from the Greek *gyro,* meaning turn or revolution, and *skopein,* meaning to view). This is illustrated by a heavy wheel rotating at high speed in supporting rings or gimbals, as shown in Figure 428. One degree of freedom for the mass of the wheel or rotor is provided by the spin axis (1) itself. The remaining two degrees of freedom, which allow the spin axis to be pointed in any direction, are provided by the axes of the supporting gimbals. Corresponding to the arrangement used in the simple gyrocompass, these are designated in Figure 428 as the horizontal axis (2) and the vertical axis (3).

Gyroscopic inertia **429** Newton's first law of motion states that a body in motion will continue to move at constant speed in the same direction unless it is acted upon by an outside force. If the gyroscope could be constructed entirely free of mechanical error, with no bearing friction on the axis of the rotating wheel or its gimbals, and operated in a vacuum with no air friction on the rotating wheel, the result would be a perpetual motion machine. The direction of the spin axis would be fixed in inertial space parallel to its original position when placed in motion, and

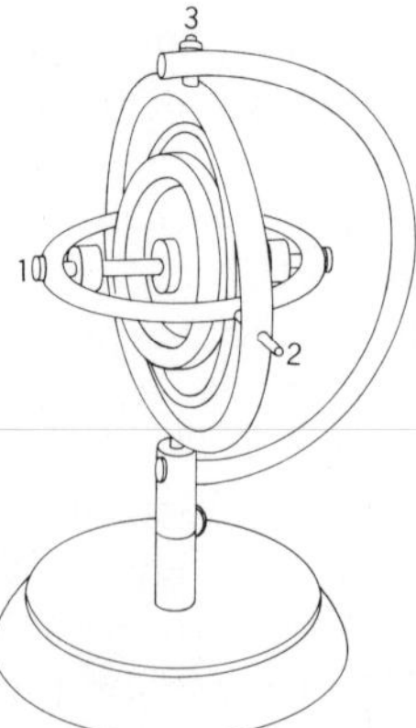

Figure 428. A gyroscope has three axes of freedom.

the gyroscope would rotate forever. Obviously this perfection has not been accomplished, although electrostatically supported gyros have been constructed which will spin, or coast, for many months. Gyroscopic inertia thus tends to keep the rotating wheel in the same plane and resists any force which tries to change its plane of rotation. The strength of this force depends on the moment of inertia and velocity of the spinning rotor.

A basic model of the gyroscope as shown in Figure 428 can be used to illustrate the principle if the rotor is kept spinning with sufficient velocity. If the base of the gyroscope is slowly tipped, the rotor or wheel will maintain its original plane of rotation as the base is moved about in any direction and the relative position of the gimbals is changed. A simple model of this type is useful in demonstrating gyroscopic inertia and precession.

Precession **430** If force is applied to the axis of the spinning gyroscope, the axis rotates not in the direction in which the force is applied, but 90° from this. This reaction is known as *precession,* which is defined as that property of a gyroscope which causes the spin axis to change direction when a torque or force is applied to the gyro. The phenomenon was observed by Foucault, the French physicist who first observed the laws of the gyroscope and gave the device its present name. Figure 430a illustrates precession when a force is applied to the horizontal axis. (Note that here the horizontal axis is the outer axis, rather than inner axis of Figure 428; this does not affect the gyroscope.) The applied

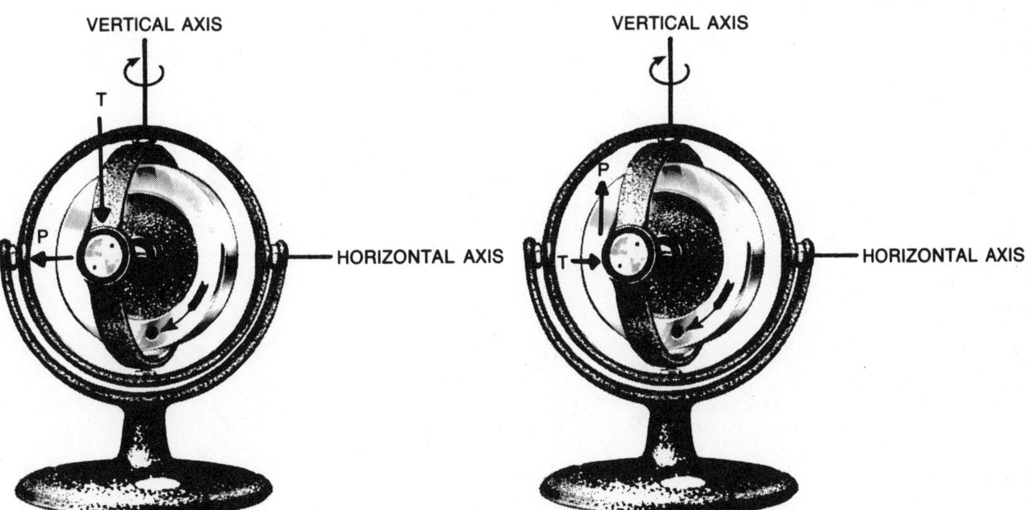

Figure 430a. Left, precession about the vertical axis; 430b., right, precession about the horizontal axis.

force or torque, T, meets with resistance and the reaction of the gyro, rather than turning about its horizontal axis as it would do if the rotor were stationary, is to rotate about the other, vertical, axis in the direction indicated by the arrow P in the figure. Similarly, in Figure 430b, if the force (torque), T, is applied around the vertical axis, the gyro turns (precesses) about its horizontal axis in the direction shown by the arrow P. A convenient way to remember the direction in which precession takes place is to regard the pressure or torque as though it acted at a single point on the rim of the wheel, as indicated by the black dot in Figure 430a and 430b. This point will not move in response to the pressure, but a point 90° beyond (in the direction of the wheel's rotation) will move away instead. The speed of precession is directly proportional to the force applied and to the speed of rotation of the wheel.

Effect of earth's rotation

431 As stated in Article 429 the direction of the spin axis tends to be fixed in inertial space due to gyroscopic inertia. Inertial space may be conceived as a region in which the sum of all acceleration and gravity forces is zero. For purposes of illustration, if the spin axis were directed toward a star, the axis would continue to point toward the star during its apparent motion across the sky.

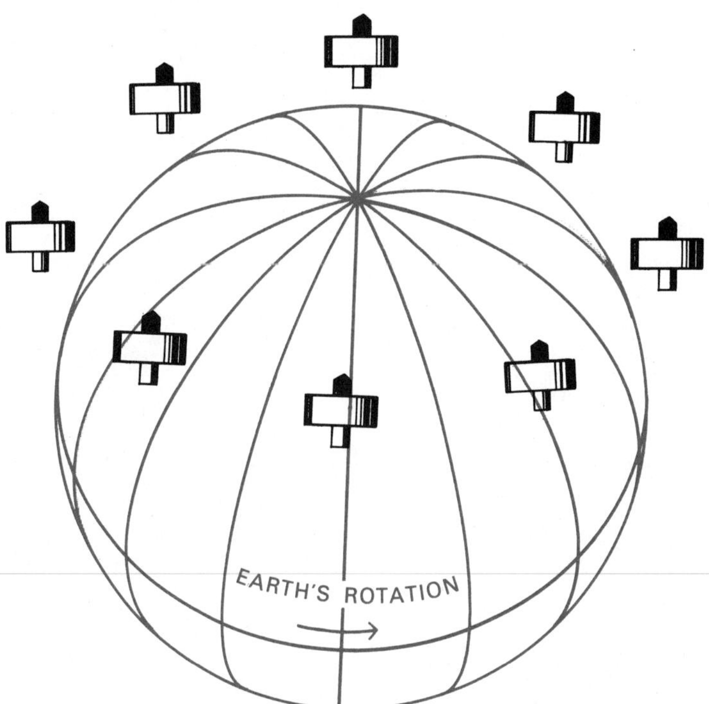

Figure 431a. A gyroscope set with its spin axis horizontal at any point away from the equator; observed from a point in space above the gyroscope.

To an observer on earth the spin axis would appear to change direction as the earth rotated eastward. This is illustrated in Figure 431a, in which it can be seen that with one rotation of the earth the direction of the spin axis relative to the earth would have moved through a complete 360°; it therefore becomes apparent that the gyroscope in this form is not suitable as a compass as it is not *north-seeking.* To make the gyroscope useful as a direction-indicating instrument with respect to the earth rather than space, a torque must be applied which causes it to precess an amount exactly opposite to the apparent movement caused by the rotation of the earth. In Figure 431b, the gyroscope is considered to be mounted at the equator with its spin axis pointing east and west. From a point in space beyond the south pole the relative position of the gyro and of the earth is illustrated for a 24-hour period. If observed while standing on the earth the gyro appears to rotate about its horizontal axis with a velocity equal to but in the opposite direction of the rotation of the earth. This effect is commonly referred to as *horizontal earth rate.* Similarly, if the gyro is assumed to be mounted at the north or south pole with its axis horizontal as shown in Figure 431c, the gyro will appear to rotate about its vertical axis. This effect is commonly referred to as *vertical earth rate.* At points between the poles and the equator the gyro appears to turn partly about the horizontal axis and partly about the vertical axis. This can be visualized in Figure 431a. The relative magnitudes of the vertical and horizontal rates are a function of latitude. The effect of horizontal earth rate is maximum at the equator and zero at the poles, and varies as the cosine of the latitude. The effect of the vertical earth rate will

Earth rate

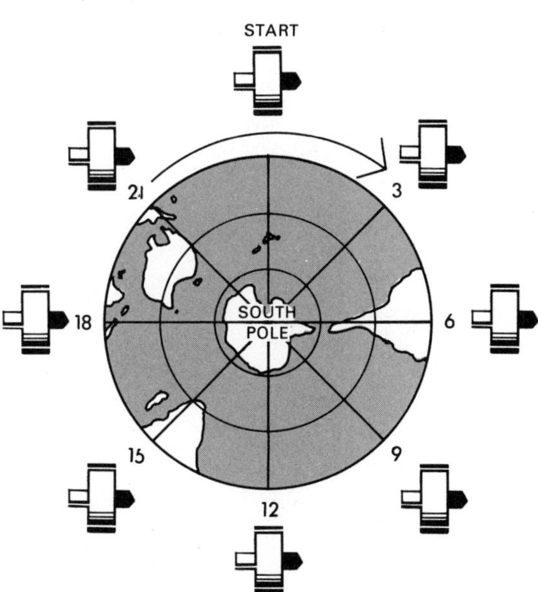

Figure 431b. A gyroscope with its spin axis set in an east-west position at the equator; observed from a point in space beyond the earth's south pole.

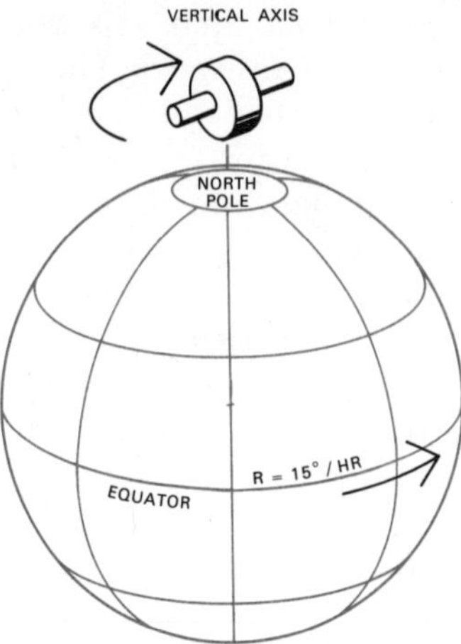

Figure 431c. A gyroscope set with its spin axis horizontal at the north pole; observed from a point in space beyond the equator.

vary as the sine of the latitude being maximum at the poles and zero at the equator.

In general the horizontal earth rate causes the gyro to tilt and the vertical earth rate causes it to move in azimuth with respect to the earth.

Gravity effect **432** As previously stated, the horizontal earth rate causes the gyro spin axis to tilt in relation to the surface of the earth. The precession effect on a gyroscope when a force or torque is applied has been discussed briefly. The effect of this application of force is precisely the same whether it be a force applied mechanically or whether it be the force of gravity, or of acceleration. The use of gravity to cause the spin axis to precess into a north-south plane, in a pendulous type gyro, can be visualized in an overly simplified manner as follows: picture the spinning gyroscope mounted in a hollow sphere with the spin axis horizontal and aligned in an east-west direction and with a weight mounted in the bottom of the sphere. The unit is located on the equator (Figure 432 at A). As the earth rotates, the spin axis, which is fixed in space, tends to become inclined to the horizontal, with the east end rising. The weight applied to the bottom of the sphere is therefore raised against the pull of gravity and consequently causes a torque about the horizontal axis of the gyro, as at position B.

This torque causes a precession about the vertical axis causing the spin axis of the gyroscope to align itself with the axis of rotation of the earth, the north-south direction, position C. When this alignment has taken place there will no longer be a tendency for the heavy bottom of the sphere to rise and produce further precession. The gyroscope now performs as a crude north-seeking instrument or gyrocompass. Gravity reference systems vary with different compass designs and will be

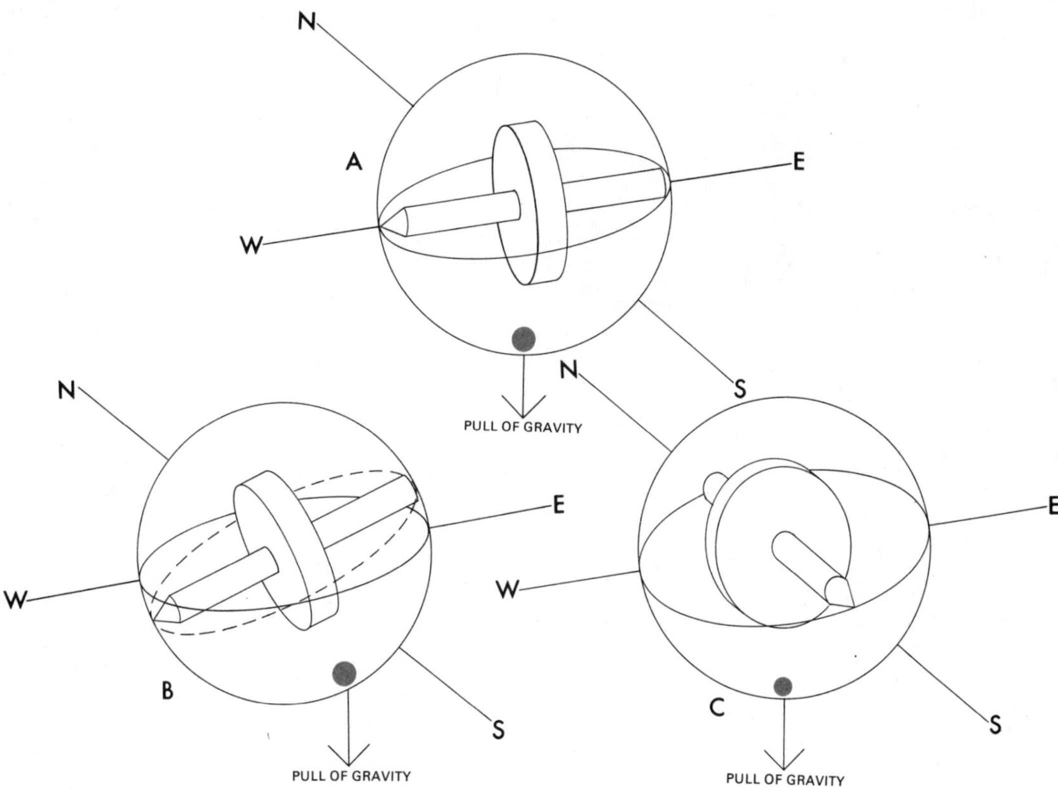

Figure 432. Gravity effect on a gyroscope.

discussed in the following articles. Older designs of gyrocompass were described as *pendulous* or *nonpendulous* according to the type of mechanical device used. Newer models use an electrical gravity reference system. There are, however, other essentials of a practical gyrocompass, such as damping and latitude and speed compensation.

Basic gyrocompasses

433 A gyrocompass basically consists of one or more north-seeking gyroscopes with suitable housing, power supply, etc. It must have a scale for reading direction and usually has some method for electrically detecting direction and transmitting this information as signals to other equipment.

Various mechanical and electrical arrangements have been devised to take advantage of the natural laws described in the four previous articles. The mercury ballistic described below constitutes a basic method which produces the nonpendulous system used in older Sperry compasses. A pendulous system is used in Arma compasses and by some European manufacturers to achieve the same results.

One method of utilizing precession to cause a gyroscope to seek north is illustrated in Figure 433a. Two reservoirs connected by a tube are attached to the bottom of the case enclosing the gyro rotor, with one reservoir north of the rotor and the other south of it. The reser-

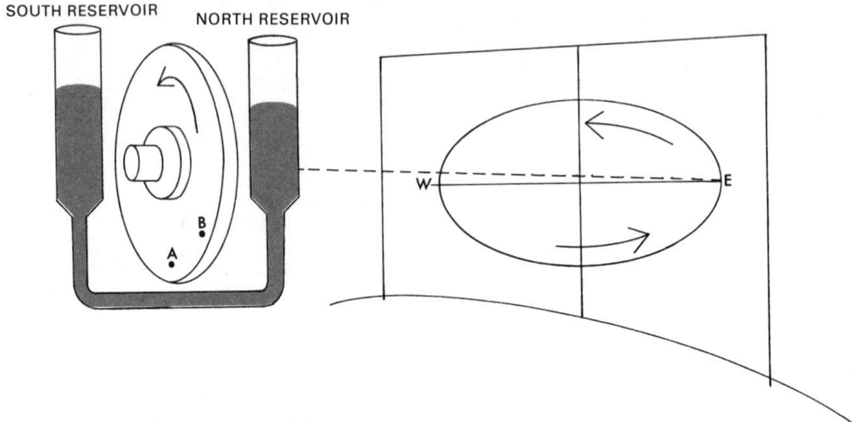

Figure 433a. A mercury ballistic (left) and the elliptical path (right) of the axis of spin without damping.

voirs are filled with mercury to such a level that the weight below the spin axis is equal to the weight above it, so that the gyroscope is non-pendulus. The system of reservoirs and connecting tubes is called a *mercury ballistic.* In practice, there are usually four symmetrically placed reservoirs.

Suppose that the spin axis is horizontal but is directed to the eastward of north. As the earth rotates eastward on its axis, the spin axis tends to maintain its direction in space; that is, it appears to follow a point, such as a star rising in the northeastern sky. With respect to the earth, the north reservoir rises and some of the mercury flows under the force of gravity into the south reservoir. The south side becomes heavier than the north side and a torque is thus applied to the rotor case; this is equivalent to a force being applied to the rotor at point A. If the rotor is spinning in the direction shown, the north end of the spin axis precesses slowly to the westward, following an elliptical path. When it reaches the meridian, upward tilt reaches a maximum. Precession continues, so that the axis is carried past the meridian and commences to sink as the earth continues to rotate. When the sinking has continued to the point where the axis is horizontal again, the excess mercury has returned to the north reservoir and precession stops. As sinking continues, due to continued rotation of the earth, an excess of mercury accumulates in the north reservoir, thus reversing the direction of precession and causing the spin axis to return slowly to its original position with respect to the earth, following the path shown at the right of the illustration. One circuit of the ellipse requires about 84 minutes. This is the Schuler period mentioned previously.

The elliptical path is symmetrical with respect to the meridian, and, neglecting friction, would be retraced indefinitely, unless some method of damping the oscillation were found. One method is by offsetting the point of application of the force from the mercury ballistic. Thus, if the force is applied not in the vertical plane, but at a point to the eastward of it, as at *B* in Figure 433a, the resulting precession causes the spin axis to trace a spiral path as shown in Figure 433b and eventually to settle near the meridian. The gyroscope is now north-seeking and can be used as a compass. Some compasses are provided with automatic means for moving the point of application to the center line during a large change of course or speed, to avoid introduction of a temporary error.

Another method of damping the oscillations caused by the rotation of the earth is to reduce the precessing force of a pendulous gyro as the spin axis approaches the meridian. One way of accomplishing this is to cause oil to flow from one damping tank to another in such a manner as to counteract some of the tendency of an offset pendulous weight to cause precession. Oscillations are completely damped out in approximately one and one-half swings.

Details of construction differ considerably in the various models. Each instrument is provided with a manual giving such information and operating instructions. A navigator should read carefully the instruction manual accompanying the specific gyrocompass installed in his vessel. In the latest designs, methods have been developed to measure the tilt of the gyro axle, due to earth rate, and to use control devices about the vertical and horizontal axes to produce torques proportional to the tilt. This eliminates the necessity for using weights or a mercury ballistic to produce torques and damping.

On the Mark 19 gyrocompass, now in wide use in U.S. naval vessels, this is accomplished by the use of a special electrolytic level which transmits an electrical signal with magnitude and phase according to tilt. The gravity reference and the gyro axle are parallel and rigidly fixed with respect to one another. The signal emitted by the gravity reference is amplified and applied to the control fields of electrical torquers which are used to precess the gyro.

Detailed descriptions of various systems using sensing devices in the form of electrolytic levels, special pendulums, and electromagnetic pick-off units for sensing orientation are included in the operating

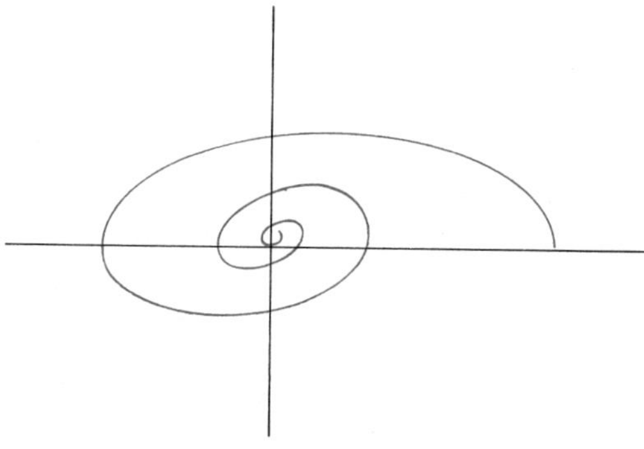

Figure 433b. Spiral path of axis of spin with damping.

manual provided with the compass. A comparative analysis of mechanical and electrical features of different compass designs is beyond the scope of this text.

Fundamentally, a gyrocompass is a gyroscope to which has been added control elements to apply *torques* of the correct magnitude and phase to the gyroscope in order that: the gyroscope will precess in such a manner that the spinning axis is brought parallel to the meridian within a reasonable time after the wheel is set spinning, and quickly returned to the meridian if it becomes displaced. The gyroscope will precess about the vertical axis at the proper rate and direction so as to cancel the effect of the earth's rotation; the *spinning axis* will remain nearly level when parallel to the meridian and prevent the instrument from oscillating across the meridian.

Gyrocompass components

434 A modern gyrocompass system consists of a *master unit,* a *control cabinet,* a *power supply unit,* a *speed unit,* and *auxiliary electrical transmission* and *alarm units.*

The master unit is the heart of the compass system and contains the gyroscopic north-seeking, and in the more complex newer compasses, the vertical-seeking sensitive elements, necessary gimballing, and related electrical components and wiring.

The control cabinet is the "nerve center" of the system. It contains all the computing and amplifying circuitry and components, and in addition provides on its front panel all the controls, meters, and dials necessary for proper control of the operation of the compass.

On major U.S. naval ships, present standards provide for two master compasses with the necessary control units and auxiliary apparatus. At steering stations two repeaters are provided in order that indications of both master compasses may be constantly available at those stations for purposes of comparison and checking. On smaller naval vessels, and on most merchant ships, only one gyrocompass is installed; repeater compasses are provided as necessary for navigation and fire control.

Most naval ships are also supplied with dead-reckoning equipment to plot automatically, to the scale of various charts, the track of the vessel during action or maneuvers. Latitude and longitude indicators and course recorders are also included in the tracer equipment.

By being employed to actuate a contact maker, which causes the rudder to respond instantly to slight variations of the vessel's head from the prescribed course, the gyrocompass has become the control element of the gyro pilot for mechanical steering, and for the mechanical recording of the courses pursued.

Gyro repeater compasses mounted as peloruses on the wings of the bridge give true bearings. Self-synchronous alidades also include gyro repeaters. In the event of gyrocompass failure, gyro or self-synchronous alidade repeaters, set to the true course, may be used as ordinary peloruses.

Gyrocompass transmission system

435 One of the features of the gyrocompass system is the ability of the master compass to transmit to remotely located indicators electrical data representing the ship's heading, and on the more complex newer compasses, electrical data representing ship's roll and pitch. These data are used in navigating the ship and on warships provide a necessary input to radar, sonar, fire-control, and other ship's systems.

Gyrocompass repeaters (ship's course indicators)

436 Gyrocompass repeaters are accurate electronic servomechanisms which reproduce the indications of the master gyrocompass at remote locations anywhere on the ship.

Older types of repeater compasses consist essentially of a compass card fixed to the end of the shaft of a step or synchromotor, the rotor of which turns in synchronism with the transmitter indications of the master gyrocompass. In appearance it looks much the same as any compass, but it may be mounted rigidly in any position; it may be attached to a bulkhead as well as placed horizontally in a pelorus stand or binnacle. There are several models, each best adapted to the use intended.

Most repeaters are entirely self-synchronous, so that if they become out of step with the master gyro, as through temporary power failure, they will automatically line up with the transmitter when power is restored. Repeaters are generally provided with a damping device to prevent undesirable oscillation when the heading is changed rapidly.

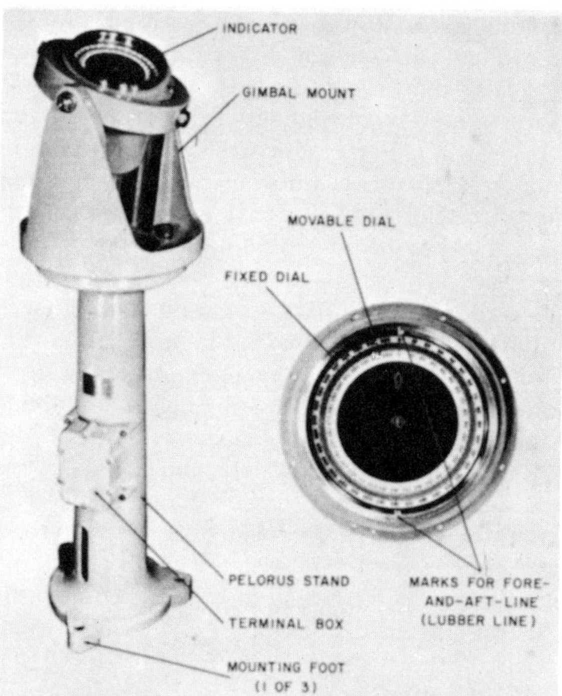

Figure 436. Gyro repeater.

A gyro repeater is used as a compass. As far as the user is concerned, the repeater *is* a compass. Lighting is provided by making the dial of translucent material with dark or colored markings or of opaque material with translucent markings, and placing a light behind the dial.

There is no practical limit to the number of repeaters that can operate from a single master gyrocompass.

Preparation for use

437 The gyrocompass is normally kept in continuous operation at sea. Most compasses are equipped with a stand-by power supply and a compass failure annunciator to indicate any malfunction of the compass or failure of the ship's electrical power supply. The stand-by power supply will automatically operate the compass for a short period of time until ship's power can be restored. When in port for a considerable period of time the gyro can be switched off. The navigator must be aware of the fact that when the gyro is restarted, several hours may be required for the rotor to attain operating speed and for the compass to settle on the meridian. The instruction manual contains methods to precess the compass to speed up this settling period. If the ship is apt to be ordered to get underway on short notice, the gyrocompass should be kept running.

Latitude, speed, and course correction

438 When a vessel is underway, the movement over the earth resulting from course and speed, as well as the latitude in which the vessel is operating, is detected by the gyroscope as a change in horizontal and vertical earth rate (Article 431). The gyro cannot distinguish between a force caused by movement of the vessel and that caused by rotation of the earth. On an east or west course there is no effect on the gyrocompass, as the vessel's movement merely adds to or subtracts from the rate of rotation of the earth. This motion is in the plane of the rotor when the spin axis is settled on a meridian and therefore causes no precession. A vessel steaming north or south produces a maximum effect upon the compass indication. On older compasses speed and latitude were compensated for by applying a torque which could be set by hand, generally by moving pointers along speed and latitude scales.

Applying corrections

Course was compensated for by the use of a built-in cosine cam automatically driven by the compass itself. On the Mark 19 and other new models, no insertion of latitude and speed correction by the navigator is necessary. The control cabinet contains an electronic computer which generates an electrical signal to torque the gyro. The computer has an input for speed directly from the vessel's speed-measuring instrument and an input for heading generated from within the compass itself. The computer is set for latitude when started and thereafter produces both a constant display of latitude and an electrical compensating signal to the gyrocompass.

U.S. Navy Mark 19, Mod 3 gyrocompass

439 The Mark 19, Mod 3 gyrocompass, manufactured by Sperry, is in general use on larger vessels of the U.S. Navy. It constitutes a system which includes two gyroscopes, the meridian and slave gyros, to which certain control devices have been added. The system consists of four principal components: these are the master compass, the control cabinet, the compass failure annunciator, and the standby power supply.

The Mark 19 has two gyroscopes within a sensitive element. The spin axis of the meridian gyro is aligned with the earth meridian as in any gyro compass. The slave gyro mounted on the same phantom or support has its spin axis oriented in an east-west direction. In addition to indicating the meridian, this arrangement defines the true vertical, useful for fire control and other purposes. This two-gyro arrangement should not be confused with the multiple gyro arrangement originated by Anschutz in Germany, wherein a two- or three-gyro configuration is used to produce heading information.

The force of gravity, instead of acting directly to control the compass, merely acts on a special type of electrolytic bubble level, called the gravity reference, which generates a signal proportional to the tilt of the gyro axle. This signal is used to apply torque electromagnetically about the vertical or horizontal axes to give the compass the desired period and damping. The gyro unit is enclosed in a gyrosphere.

The gyrosphere is the heart of the meridian gyro assembly, as it is the north-seeking component of the compass. It derives its name from the fact that the gyro wheel is mounted within a spherical enclosure.

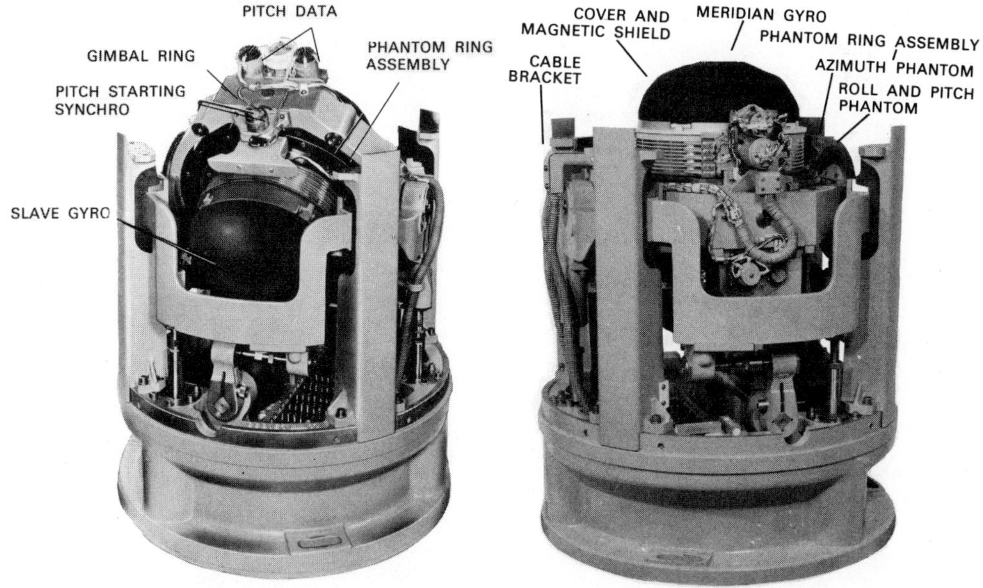

Figure 439. Master gyrocompass with sensitive element components labeled.

The gyrosphere is immersed in oil, and is of the same specific gravity as the oil. It is therefore in neutral bouyancy, and exerts no load on the vertical bearings, which serve only as guides. This flotation not only reduces pivot friction, but also serves to protect the gyrosphere from destructive shock.

Figure 439 shows the sensitive element in the master compass—the gyrosphere for the meridian gyro in the upper part of the sensitive element, and that for the slave gyro in the lower portion.

Mark 23, Mod 4 gyrocompass

440 The Sperry Mark 23, Mod 4 gyrocompass was designed as a small compass capable of withstanding the severe operating conditions encountered by amphibious vessels, such as LSTs, without sacrificing the primary function of furnishing accurate heading data. It is also used as an auxiliary compass aboard larger ships. It combines electronic compass control and oil flotation, and uses an electronic control to make it north-seeking.

The electrolytic bubble level is used to sense the force of gravity in the same manner as on the Mark 19 compass.

AN/WSN-2 gyrocompass

441 The latest gyrocompass design for the U.S. Navy is the AN/WSN-2, manufactured by the Guidance & Control Systems division of Litton Industries; it will be used aboard vessels from patrol boats to cruisers. Its components, within a single console, can provide for full

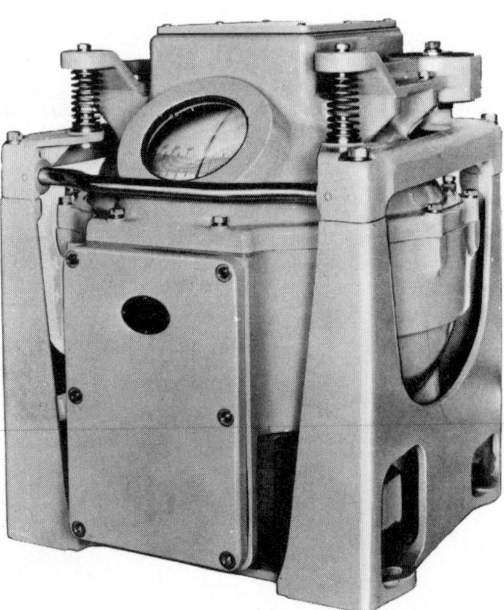

Figure 440. Mark 23 Mod 4 (Sperry) gyrocompass.

inertial navigation: weapons system, radar, and ship's stabilization; automatic piloting; and collision avoidance. The AN/WSN-2 will combine improved performance with significantly reduced weight and volume.

Advantages **442** The gyrocompass has the following advantages over the magnetic compass:

It seeks the true meridian instead of the magnetic meridian.

It can be used near the earth's magnetic poles, where the magnetic compass is useless.

It is not affected by surrounding magnetic material which might seriously reduce the directive force of the magnetic compass.

If an error exists, it is the same on all headings, and correction is a simple process.

Its information can be fed electronically into automatic steering equipment, course (DR) recorders, and inertial navigation systems. On warships, data can be injected into weapons control systems.

Limitations **443** In spite of the many advantages and undoubted capabilities of a modern gyrocompass, there are certain disadvantages inherent in its design:

It requires a constant source of electrical power.

It requires intelligent care and attention if it is to give the kind of service of which it is inherently capable.

The accuracy decreases when latitudes above 75 degrees are reached.

If operation is interrupted for any length of time long enough for it to become disoriented, a considerable period of time, as much as four hours, may be required for it to settle back into reliable operation.

Despite these limitations, the modern gyrocompass, if given proper attention, will render reliable and satisfactory service. This should not cause the navigating officer to neglect his magnetic compass. When the gyrocompass does fail, as any intricate instrument may, the prudent navigator who has a properly adjusted magnetic compass, with an accurate deviation table, will be well repaid for his efforts.

Errors **444** When a gyrocompass is mounted on land, it is affected only by gravity and the earth's motion. When it is mounted in a ship at sea, consideration must be given to additional factors due to motions of the ship, such as roll, pitch, turning, speed over the ground, course being steered, and the latitude. The effect of these factors differs in compasses of different basic design. Reference should be made to the appropriate instruction books for a detailed exposition of the theory of a particular compass design, including a description of the automatic and manual corrective features incorporated in the design.

Accuracy

445 Even after all the corrections have been made, a gyrocompass is not perfect. However, the error of a modern, properly adjusted gyrocompass seldom exceeds 1°, and is usually such a small fraction of this that for practical purposes it can be considered zero. This does not mean that it must not be checked frequently. A small error carried for a long time will take a ship far to one side of the desired objective. Large errors introduced by temporary mechanical failure, when undetected, have meant disaster.

Comparing gyro and magnetic compasses

446 Whenever a new course is set, and at regular intervals thereafter, the magnetic compass, master gyrocompass, and gyro repeaters should be compared. A record of these comparisons should be kept in a compass comparison book. Any erratic operation of either gyrocompass, or of either steering repeater, will be apparent at once by such comparisons.

Determining gyro error

447 At both the gyrocompass itself and its repeaters a compass card is attached to or activated by the sensitive element and is graduated in degrees from 0° to 360°. Just as with a magnetic compass, the direction of the ship's head is indicated by the *lubber's line,* a vertical line on the compass housing exactly aligned in the fore and aft axis of the ship. As the ship turns, the lubber's line turns with it so that the changing heading is properly indicated on the card. *It is the lubber's line and not the compass card* which actually turns. The 0° point on the card always points toward true north if there is no compass error. If there is compass error, the 0° point on the compass will not indicate true north but a direction either to the left or to the right of the meridian. If the 0° point is to the left or west of the meridian, gyro error (GE) is the numerical difference between the two directions and is labeled west (W). If the 0° point is to the right or east of the meridian, gyro error is again the numerical difference between the two directions and is labeled east (E).

When a ship is at sea, the navigator should determine the gyrocompass error at least once each day; this is required for naval vessels and is desirable on any ship. Over and above this bare minimum, the prudent navigator will take advantage of every opportunity to check the accuracy of his gyro. The importance of so doing is emphasized by a grounding case on record where the failure of a ship's gyro went undetected for a period of over twelve hours, with the result that, at the time of grounding, the vessel was more than 110° off course and more than 200 miles from the DR position.

There are several methods of checking the accuracy of a gyrocompass, the most important of which are summarized and briefly discussed as follows:

By comparing the observed gyro bearing of an artificial or natural range with the charted true bearing of the range. When entering or leaving a port, the method of checking the gyrocompass by ranges should be used regularly, as the varying speed of the ship, even though compensated for by the proper setting of the speed corrector, causes the compass to oscillate to a certain extent across the meridian. This makes it necessary for the navigator to be constantly on the alert to note in which direction and by what amount his compass is swinging off, and to correct his bearings accordingly.

By comparing the gyro bearing of an object ashore with the charted true bearing of the same object from a fixed position. The fixed position is obtained by means of the three-point problem using a sextant and a three-arm protractor. (See Article 1110.) The right and left angles for any three well-defined objects are taken with the sextant at the gyro repeater which is to be used in the checking. At the same time, the bearings of the three objects are taken with the repeater. By means of the sextant angles set on the three-arm protractor, the position of the ship at the time of observation can be accurately plotted on the chart. From this position, the bearings of the three objects can be found by plotting. A comparison of the bearings so found, with the bearing taken by the repeater, shows the error of the gyrocompass. The repeater should be checked against the master gyro each time a set of these observations is made.

By comparing the gyro bearing of a celestial body, usually the sun, with the computed true bearing (azimuth) of the same body. At sea, the azimuth method is the only one available and any time a sight of a celestial body is taken for a line of position, the bearing of the body observed may be taken at the same instant (see Chapter 28). Azimuths of the sun at sunrise and sunset, and when its altitude is low in the early morning and late afternoon, are particularly useful for this purpose. The azimuth obtained by computation, when compared with the gyro azimuth, gives a check on the accuracy of the compass. Polaris is very useful for checking the azimuth at night in low northern latitudes.

By "trial and error" adjustment of the observed bearings of three or more lines of position obtained on charted objects equally spaced around the ship until a point fix is obtained. A set of bearings are taken with the repeater on three objects that will yield suitable angles of intersection; these are plotted on the chart. If they meet in a point, the repeater is "on" and there is no gyro error. If the three lines form a triangle, the lines can be adjusted to meet in a point by trial and error; that is, 1° is added to or subtracted from each bearing, and they are again plotted. If the size of the triangle is reduced, the proper estimate of the direction of the error has been made, and after a sufficient correction is applied, the lines should meet in a point. When they do meet, the total amount of correction applied to any one bearing is the error of the compass.

By comparison with a compass of known error, as for example, a standby gyro compared with a master gyro. If a compass of unknown error is compared with one whose errors are known, the difference in their readings on various headings will provide information from which the errors of the former can be determined. This comparison is generally only possible in ships having two gyrocompasses installed aboard.

As previously mentioned, error as determined by using one of these methods is known as *westerly* or *easterly* gyro error, depending upon its direction. If the 0° point on the compass card is to the *west* of true north, the card has been rotated counter-clockwise and all readings of course and bearing made with this error will be too high. If the 0° point on the compass card is to the *east* of true north, the card has been rotated clockwise and all readings will be too low. The principles of applying compass error to obtain true course and bearing hold true both for the application of magnetic compass error discussed in Article 423 and for the application of gyro error discussed in the next article.

Gyro error calculations

448 By any one of several methods it is a relatively easy process for a navigator to determine the numerical value of the gyro error using simple arithmetic. The difficulty arises in determining the *label,* east or west, of the error. A simple memory-aid phrase can be used as before.

Compass least, error east;
Compass best, error west.

As with magnetic compasses, "compass best" means that the compass reading is numerically greater than the true value.

Example 1: Two beacons in line are sighted with a gyrocompass repeater, and found to be bearing 136.5° per gyrocompass. According to the chart, the bearing of these beacons when in line is 138° true.

Required: The gyro error (GE).

Solution: Numerically, the gyro error is the difference between gyro and true bearings of the objects in range, or 138° – 136.5° = 1.5°. Since this 1.5° would have to be added to the gyro bearing to obtain true bearing, the direction of the error is easterly.

Answer: GE 1.5° E.

Example 2: A light ashore is sighted, and by gyrocompass repeater is observed to bear 310.0° per gyrocompass. From the ship's fixed position, the charted true bearing of the light is measured as 308.5° true.

Required: The gyro error (GE).

Solution: As before, the gyro error is the difference between the gyro and the true bearing, or 310° – 308.5° = 1.5°. Since this 1.5° would have to be subtracted from the gyro bearing to obtain true bearing, and since westerly errors are subtracted, the direction of the error is westerly.

Answer: GE 1.5° W.

Example 3: A round of gyro bearings was taken on three terrestrial objects with results as follows:

Tower: 058.0°
Light: 183.0°
Beacon: 310.0°

The three lines of position, when plotted, formed a small triangle. By trial and error, it was found that when 2.0° was *added* to each bearing, a point fix resulted.

Required: The gyro error (GE).

Solution: Since 2.0° had to be added to each bearing to obtain a perfect fix, and since easterly errors are added, the gyro error is 2.0° E.

Answer: GE 2.0° E.

Gyro error must be added to or subtracted from true or gyro headings and bearings to go from one form of direction to the other. The two basic rules to be applied in such calculations can be stated as follows:

When converting from gyro to true, add easterly error and subtract westerly error.

When converting from true to gyro, add westerly error and subtract easterly error. Here, too, the memory aid for magnetic compasses, Correcting Add East, or C-A-E, is applicable.

Example 4: A ship is heading 130° per gyrocompass (GH). The gyro error (GE) is 1° E.

Required: The true heading (TH).

Solution: Since error is easterly, it must be added. Hence the true heading is 130° + 1° = 131°.

Answer: TH 131°.

Example 5: A ship is heading 020° per gyrocompass. The gyro error is 1° W.

Required: The true heading.

Solution: Since the error is west it must be subtracted. Hence, the true heading is 020° – 1° = 019°.

Answer: TH 019°.

Example 6: From a chart the true course between two places is found to be 151°; the GE is 1° E.

Required: The heading per gyrocompass to steer 151° true.

Solution: Since easterly errors are added to gyro to obtain true, they must be subtracted when converting from true to gyro, or 151° – 1° = 150°.

Answer: GH 150°.

Another simple, easily remembered expression combines the first letters of the words Gyro, Error, and True to form the short word GET. This is then written as G + E + T indicating that from Gyro to True it is Plus (add) East. The westerly error procedure and the reverse direction, True to Gyro, can be worked out from the basic equation.

Summary **449** Primary emphasis in this section has been placed on the basic concept of the gyro and the determination of errors affecting the accuracy of the gyrocompass, and their application once the errors are known. When properly operated, serviced, and maintained, the gyrocompass is an extremely accurate instrument, but as is the case with all such instruments it is subject to failure and error. Total failure of the gyrocompass is immediately evident and corrective measures can be taken quickly to eliminate the trouble, or to shift to the stand-by compass. Even with known error, the gyrocompass is eminently serviceable, since account can be taken of this error, and correction to course and bearing can be applied accordingly. It is the unknown error that contributes to marine disasters, particularly so in those instances in which the dead reckoning plot was laid in navigable water whereas the actual track finally terminated at the point of grounding. For example, if a ship had an undetected error in its gyrocompass of 2° during a 24-hour run at 18 knots, the 24-hour DR position would be in error by more than 15 miles, a margin which, if the course were planned to clear a certain hazard, probably would not be sufficient.

The gyrocompass is a tool of the navigator and, as with any other tool, it demands intelligent operation to obtain the accurate directional reference which it is designed to supply.

5 Aids to Navigation

Introduction **501** The term "aid to navigation" means any object or device, external to a vessel, that is intended to assist a navigator in fixing his position or determining a safe course past hazards to navigation. In this chapter, it includes both fixed and floating objects such as lights, lightships, buoys, daybeacons, and fog signals, plus electronic aids to navigation such as radiobeacons, Loran, Omega, and others discussed in later chapters. Prominent features ashore, both natural—such as mountain peaks—and man-made—such as water tanks and radio towers, may often assist the navigator in fixing his position or directing his course; these, however, are excluded from the definition of an "aid to navigation," which is considered to be an object established for that primary or sole purpose.

The *U.S. Coast Guard,* which absorbed the functions of the Lighthouse Service in 1939, has responsibility for the operation and maintenance of all lights and other aids to navigation along 40,000 miles of coastline in the United States and its possessions, plus additional thousands of miles along the shores of the Great Lakes and on most inland rivers. This includes more than 12,000 primary, secondary, and minor lights, over 26,000 lighted and unlighted buoys, and additional thousands of daybeacons. There are some "private aids," those maintained by individuals, local governments, or federal agencies other than the Coast Guard, but these are relatively few in number.

Importance These aids are of tremendous assistance to the navigator in making a landfall when approaching from seaward, and in all coastal navigation. Their importance was first recognized by the ancient Mediterranean mariners; a lighthouse was built at Sigeum, near Troy, before 600 B.C., and the famous Pharos of Alexandria was built in the third century B.C. Wood fires furnished their illumination, and wood and sometimes coal remained in general use for this purpose until the eighteenth century. The first lighthouse in the United States was built at Boston in 1716, and logs and kegs were used as buoys in the Delaware River in 1767.

Major categories **502** Aids to navigation take a wide variety of forms; some are very simple unmanned objects, others are complex and costly devices, sometimes with operating crews in attendance. All serve the same goal

—the safety of vessels and those on board; differences in type, size, etc., are determined by the circumstances of location and use.

Buoys *Buoys* are perhaps the largest category of aids to navigation and come in many shapes and sizes. These are floating objects, heavily anchored to the bottom, that are intended to convey information to a navigator by their shape or color, by the characteristics of a visible or audible signal, or a combination of two or more such features. (Lightships fit such a definition but form a separate category by themselves.) Buoys often have bands or patches of reflective material to enhance their detection at night; these reflect brightly in the beam of a vessel's searchlight. Many buoys have *radar reflecters.*

Daybeacons In shallower inland waters, *daybeacons* are often used instead of buoys, because they are less expensive to maintain. These are single piles or multiple-pile structures (dolphins) driven into the bottom, on which are placed one or more signboards called "*daymarks*" which convey information through their color, shape, and lettering or numbers. Daymarks normally have reflective material as part of their design.

Lights and lightships The term "light" covers a wide variety of aids to navigation—from the simple short-range *minor light* on a single pile in inland waters to the multi-million-candlepower *primary seacoast light* on a structure a hundred feet or more tall established to aid ships in making a safe landfall. These lights, and the *secondary lights* between these extremes, are assigned characteristics of color and off-on periods for ease of identi-

Figure 502. Buoys are found in almost all waters.

fication. In some instances, the shape and color of the supporting structure will be of assistance in identification. (The classification of "major light" includes both primary seacoast and secondary lights.)

When a light is required offshore, a *lightship* may be established. This is a specially designed vessel, anchored in a precisely determined position, equipped with a high intensity light of specified characteristics and usually with other types of aids to navigation as well. The current trend is to replace lightships either with lights on fixed structures (sometimes called "Texas Towers") or with large navigational buoys, both of which are much more economical to operate and maintain.

Ranges *Ranges* are pairs of aids to navigation, lighted or unlighted, so positioned with respect to each other that a line between them extended over water marks a preferred channel. When the *front* and *rear* marks or lights are aligned, a navigator is guided safely past shoals or obstructions. Ranges can also be used to mark turning points on channels or to establish specific directions for compass adjustment.

Fog signals *Fog signals* are audible signals used to indicate the location of an aid to navigation when it cannot be seen due to conditions of reduced visibility. They are usually, but not always, co-located with another form of aid such as a light; they may be on shore, on a fixed structure in the water, or on a buoy. (See, also, Article 523.)

Radio and radar beacons *Radiobeacons* supplement visual aids to navigation and permit bearings to be obtained at greater distances, at night and under conditions of reduced visibility; they are often co-located with primary or secondary lights. See Articles 3203–3208.

Radar beacons, known as *racons* and *ramarks,* are used to give a stronger radar return from specific locations; they are often co-located with other aids to navigation. See Article 1718.

Light Lists **503** *Light Lists* for the United States and its possessions, including the Intracoastal Waterway, the Mississippi and its navigable tributaries, and the Great Lakes including both the U. S. and Canadian shores, are published annually by the U.S. Coast Guard. A portion of a typical page is reproduced in Figure 503.

Similar publications, called *Lists of Lights,* covering foreign coasts, are published by the Defense Mapping Agency Hydrographic Center as Publications No. 111A, 111B, and 112 through 116.

These *Light Lists* give detailed information regarding navigational lights, light structures, radiobeacons, and fog signals. In addition, the *Light Lists* for the United States, published by the Coast Guard, give data on lighted and unlighted buoys and daybeacons.

Corrections to both sets of light lists are published weekly in *Notices to Mariners* (and *Local Notices to Mariners* for USCG *Light Lists* only); see

SEACOAST		MAINE				FIRST DISTRICT
(1)	(2)	(3)	(4)	(5)	(6)	(7)
No.	Name Characteristic	Location Lat. N. Long. W.	Nominal Range	Ht. above water	Structure Ht. above ground Daymark	Remarks Year
	(Chart 13260)					
	(For Gulf of Maine, see No. 199)					
1 227 *J48*	**MOUNT DESERT LIGHT** .... **Fl. W.**, 15^s	On Mount Desert Rock, 20 miles south of Mount Desert Island. 43 58.1 68 07.7	24	75	Conical gray granite tower 58	RBN: 314 kHz (▬ • • •)I. Antenna at light tower. HORN: 2 blasts ev 30^s (2^{s}bl-2^{s}si-2^{s}bl-24^{s}si). 1830
2 239 *J116*	**MATINICUS ROCK LIGHT** .... **Gp. Fl. W.** (1 + 2), 15^s 0.2^{s}fl., 5.8^{s}ec. 0.2^{s}fl., 2.8^{s}ec. 0.2^{s}fl., 5.8^{s}ec. 3 flashes.	On south part of rock. 43 47.0 68 51.3	23	90	Cylindrical gray granite tower and dwelling. 48	RBN: 314 kHz (• ▬ ▬ •)II. Antenna 105 feet 053° from light tower. HORN: 1 blast ev 15^s (2^{s}bl). 1827–1857
3 282 *J128*	**MONHEGAN ISLAND LIGHT** ..... **Fl. W.**, 30^s (2.8^{s}fl)	Near center of island. 43 45.9 69 19.0	21	178	Gray conical tower covered way to dwelling. 47	Within 3 miles of island the light is obscured between west and southwest. 1824–1850
4 283 *J130*	Manana Island Fog Signal Station.	On west side of island, close to Monhegan Island. 43 45.8 69 19.7	....	....	Brown brick house	RBN: 314 kHz (▬ ▬ ▬ •)III. Antenna 2,880 feet 259° from Monhegan Island light tower. HORN: 2 blasts ev 60^s (3^{s}bl-3^{s}si-3^{s}bl-51^{s}si). 1855–1870
5 297 *J146*	**SEGUIN LIGHT** .... **F. W.**	On island, 2 miles south of mouth of Kennebec River. 43 42.5 69 45.5	19	180	White cylindrical granite tower connected to dwelling. 53	HORN: 2 blasts ev 20^s (2^{s}bl-2^{s}si-2^{s}bl-14^{s}si). 1795–1857
6 320 *J176*	**HALFWAY ROCK LIGHT** .... **Fl. R.**, 5^s	On rock, midway between Cape Small Point and Cape Elizabeth. 43 39.4 70 02.2	19	76	White granite tower attached to dwelling. 77	RBN: 314 kHz (• • • • • ▬ •)IV. Antenna on light tower. HORN: 2 blasts ev 30^s (2^{s}bl-2^{s}si-2^{s}bl-24^{s}si). 1871
	(Chart 13286)					
7.10 334.10	**Portland Lighted Horn Buoy P** .... **Fl. W.**, 2^s	In 150 feet 43 31.6 70 05.5	14	....	Red	RBN: 314 kHz (• ▬ ▬ • • • • •)VI. HORN: 1 blast ev 30^s (3^{s}bl). RACON: M (▬ ▬).

Figure 503. *Light List* (extract).

Article 610. It is of the utmost importance that all corrections be entered in the appropriate *Light List,* as well as on any applicable chart, before either of these is used for navigation.

Types of buoys **504** A complete system of buoyage includes several different types of buoys, each type designed to meet the requirements of certain specific conditions. All buoys serve as guides during daylight; those having lights are also available for navigation at night; those having sound signals are more readily located in times of fog or other conditions of reduced visibility.

Can buoy. A buoy built of steel plates with the portion above water having the shape of a tin can, flat on top when seen from a distance.

Nun buoy. A buoy built of steel plates with the portion above water terminating in a cone with a rounded tip.

Lighted buoy. A steel float on which is mounted a short skeleton tower at the top of which a light is placed. A set of electric batteries (or other sources of power) which operate the light, is placed in the body of the buoy.

Bell buoy. A steel float topped with a short skeleton tower in which there is a bell fixed with several clappers—usually four—hung externally so that they will strike the bell as it rocks with the motion of the sea. A few of these bell buoys have clappers activated mechanically by electricity or compressed gas; these are placed where sea motion may not always be enough to operate them reliably.

Gong buoy. Generally similar in construction to a bell buoy except that rather than a bell it has several, usually four, gongs mounted in a vertical stack, each of which sounds a different note; each gong has its own clapper of a length so as to strike only that gong.

Whistle buoy. A buoy generally similar in construction to a bell or gong buoy but which has a low-pitched whistle signal that is activated by the rise and fall of the buoy in a seaway. A *horn buoy* is much the same except that its sound signal is electrically powered by batteries within the lower part of the buoy.

Combination buoy. A buoy having a light signal and a sound signal, such as a lighted bell buoy, a lighted gong buoy, etc.

The overall shape and general physical characteristics of these buoys may be seen in Figure 507.

Significance of buoys

505 The primary function of buoys is to warn the mariner of some danger, some obstruction, or change in the contours of the sea bottom, and to delineate the channels leading to various points; occasionally, a buoy may be placed offshore merely to assist a navigator in establishing his position before approaching a harbor (a "sea buoy"). Valuable information is obtained from buoys when they are considered as marking definitely identified spots, for if a mariner knows his location at the moment and is properly equipped with charts, he can plot a safe course on which to proceed. Such features as size, shape, coloring, numbering, and signaling equipment of buoys are but means to warn, orient, and guide the navigator.

Station buoys

Buoys do not always maintain exact positions; therefore, they should always be regarded as warnings and not as fixed navigational marks, especially during the winter months or when moored in exposed waters. A smaller nun or can buoy called a *station buoy,* is sometimes placed in close proximity to a major aid, such as a sea buoy, to mark the station in case the regular aid is accidentally shifted from station. Station buoys are colored and numbered the same as the major aid to navigation. Lightship station buoys bear the letters "*LS*" above the initials of the station.

Reflectors Unlighted buoys and daybeacons are marked with reflective tape. This greatly facilitates locating the buoys at night with a searchlight. Reflective areas may be red, green, white, or yellow, and have the same significance as lights of these colors.

Caution Despite their usefulness, buoys must be used with caution. The buoy symbol on a chart is used to indicate the *approximate* position of the buoy and the anchor which secures it to the seabed. This position is termed "approximate" because of the practical limitations in positioning and maintaining buoys in precise geographic locations. These limitations include, but are not limited to, inherent imprecisions in position-fixing methods, prevailing wind and sea conditions, the slope and the make-up of the seabed, and the fact that buoy positions are not under continuous surveillance but are normally checked only during periodic maintenance visits which may occur a year or more apart. It must also be remembered that buoys are moored to an anchor with varying lengths of chain (a scope of three times the depth of the water is typical, but it may be more) and a buoy can be expected to swing in a circle under the varying influences of current, wind, and waves. Buoys are subject to being carried away, shifted, capsized, or sunk; lighted buoys may become extinguished and sound signals may malfunction.

Buoys marking wrecks will normally *not* be directly over the hazard due to possible danger to the vessel placing the buoy in position. Such buoys are usually put on the seaward or channelward side of the wreck; if two buoys are used, the wreck may lie between them. Wrecks may shift position due either to normal currents or storm conditions; care must always be exercised in the vicinity of wreck buoys.

As useful as buoys are, a prudent navigator will not completely rely on the position or operation of floating aids to navigation, especially those in exposed waters; he will, whenever possible, give preference to bearings on fixed aids to navigation or natural landmarks.

U.S. buoyage system **506** The waters of the United States are marked for safe navigation by the *lateral system* of buoyage. This system employs a simple arrangement of colors, shapes, numbers, and light characteristics to indicate the side of the vessel on which a buoy should be passed when proceeding in a given direction. The characteristics are determined by the position of the buoy with respect to the navigable channels as the channels are entered *from seaward.* As all channels do not lead from seaward, arbitrary assumptions must at times be made in order that the system may be consistently applied.

The characteristics of buoys and other aids to navigation along the coasts, in the Intracoastal Waterways, and on the Great Lakes are as if a vessel were "returning from seaward" when she is proceeding in a westerly and southerly direction along the Maine coast, and in a southerly direction along the remainder of the Atlantic coast, in a northerly and westerly direction along the Gulf coast, in a northerly direction on the Pacific coast, and in a northerly and westerly direction on the Great Lakes (except southerly in Lake Michigan). Canada maintains a buoyage system which is in general accord with that of the United States lateral system.

Identification of buoys

507 In the U.S. lateral system, the following rules for daytime buoy identification are applied.

All buoys in the lateral system are painted distinctive colors to indicate their purpose or the side on which they should be passed. The meaning of these buoys, *when returning from seaward,* is indicated by their colors as follows:

Buoy colors

Black buoys mark the port (left) side of channels, or the location of wrecks or obstructions which must be passed by keeping the buoy on the port (left) hand.

Red buoys mark the starboard (right) sides of channels, or the location of wrecks or obstructions which must be passed by keeping the buoy on the starboard (right) hand.

Red and black horizontally banded buoys mark junctions in the channel, or wrecks or obstructions which may be passed on either side. If the topmost band is black, the preferred channel will be followed by keeping the buoy on the port (left) hand, as if the whole buoy were black. If the topmost band is red, the preferred channel will be followed by keeping the buoy to starboard.

However, in some instances it may not be feasible for larger vessels to pass on either side of such a buoy, and the chart should always be consulted.

Black and white vertically striped buoys mark the fairway or midchannel. Such buoys are also used in Vessel Traffic Separation Schemes at the entrances to busy ports or in narrow passages congested with heavy traffic.

Special-purpose buoys

These buoys are not part of the lateral system. Their meaning is indicated by their colors as follows:

White buoys mark anchorage areas.

Yellow buoys mark quarantine anchorage areas.

White buoys with green tops are used in connection with dredging and survey operations.

White and black horizontally banded buoys mark fishnet areas.

White and international orange buoys alternately banded, either horizontally or vertically, are for special purposes to which neither

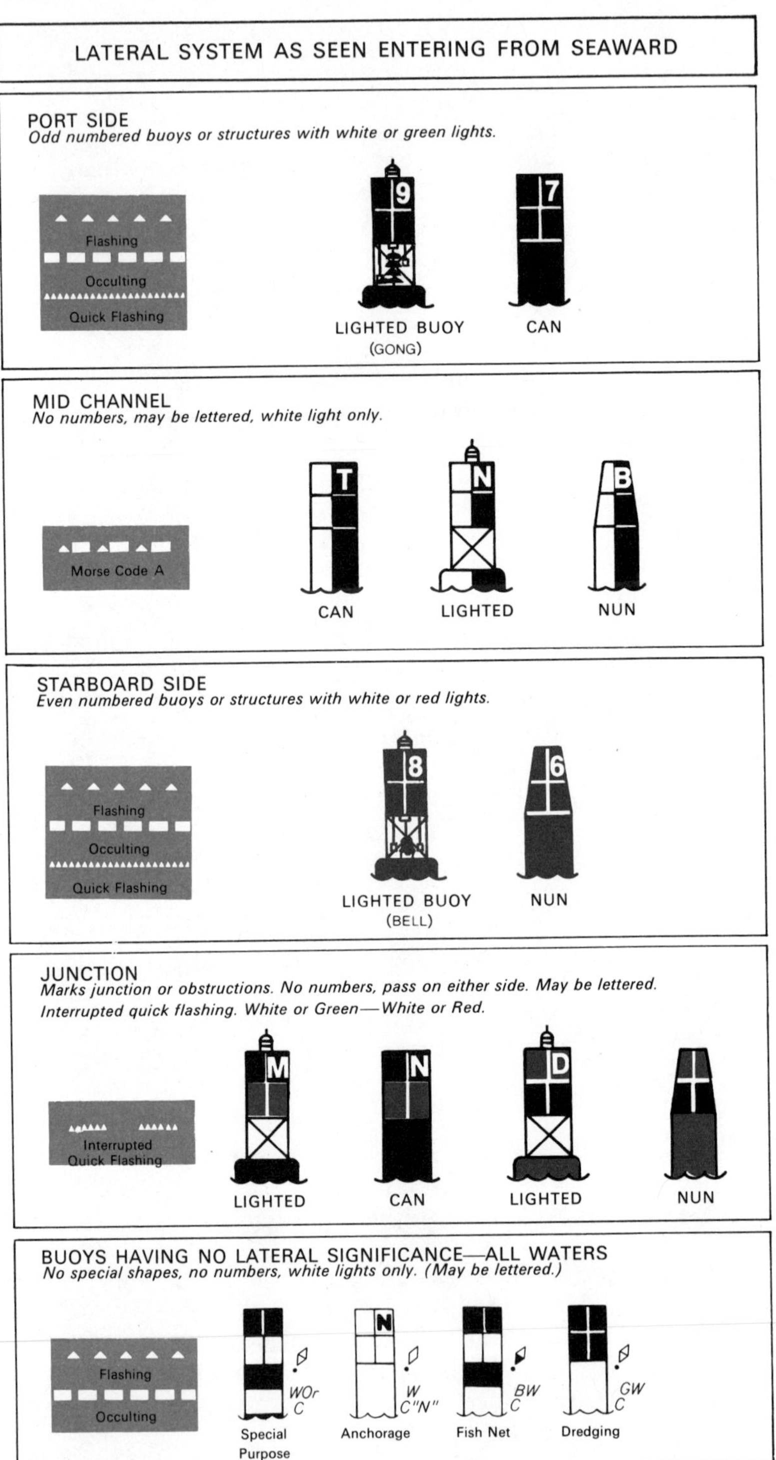

Figure 507. Buoy identification. More complete illustrations are provided in Appendix H.

the lateral-system colors nor the other special-purpose colors apply.

Yellow and black vertically striped buoys are used for seadrome markings and have no marine significance.

Buoy numbers Most buoys are given numbers, letters, or combinations of numbers and letters which are painted conspicuously upon them. These markings facilitate identification and location of the buoys on the charts.

All solid-colored red or black buoys are given numbers, or combinations of numbers and letters. Other colored buoys may be given letters. Numbers increase sequentially from seaward; numbers are sometimes omitted when there are more buoys of one type than another. Odd numbers are used *only* on solid black buoys. Even numbers are used *only* on solid red buoys. Numbers followed by letters are used on solid-colored red or black buoys when a letter is required so as not to disturb the sequence of numbers, such as when an additional buoy is placed after the numbering system has been established. Letters may also be used on certain important buoys, particularly those marking isolated offshore dangers. An example of the latter case would be a buoy marked "6 WQS." In this instance the number has the usual significance, while the letters "WQS" indicate the place as Winter Quarter Shoal. Letters without numbers are applied in some cases to black and white vertically striped buoys, red and black horizontally banded buoys, solid yellow or white buoys, and other buoys not solid-colored red or black.

The numbers and letters (as well as portions of the buoy) are of reflective material for better visibility at night.

Buoy shapes In order to provide easier identification under certain light conditions where the color may not be readily discerned, certain unlighted buoys are differentiated by their shape.

Nun buoys are used for red buoys or for red and black horizontally banded buoys where the topmost band is red.

Can buoys are used for black buoys or red and black horizontally banded buoys where the topmost band is black.

In the case of other unlighted buoys and nonlateral system special-purpose buoys, shape has no significance; for example, an unlighted black and white vertically striped buoy may be either a can or nun buoy.

Full reliance should not be placed on the shape of an unlighted buoy alone. Charts and light lists should be consulted to ascertain the significance of unlighted buoys as determined by their colors.

Lighted buoys and sound buoys are not differentiated by shape to indicate the side on which they should be passed. Since no special significance is attached to the shapes of these buoys, *their purpose is indicated by the coloring, numbering,* or *light characteristics.*

Buoy sound signals If both bell and gong buoys are used to mark a channel, the gongs are usually to port and the bells to starboard.

Daybeacons Where daybeacons are substituted for buoys in the U.S. lateral system, the color of the daymark will be the same and the shape will be roughly similar—red daymarks will be triangular, approximating the shape of the top of a nun buoy; square daymarks, corresponding to can buoys, will be green (preferred), or black, or white. They will be numbered (and/or lettered) with retro-reflective material in the same manner as a buoy and have a border of that material. (See Appendix H.) Some channels may be marked with a combination of buoys and daybeacons.

Buoy lights **508** Buoys of the U.S. lateral system may be lighted as well as unlighted; the colors used and the light-phase characteristics aid in their proper identification at night.

Color of lights. The three standard light colors used for lighted aids to navigation are white, red, and green. *Red lights* on buoys are used only on red buoys, or red and black horizontally banded buoys with the topmost band red. *Green lights* on buoys are used only on black buoys, or red and black horizontally banded buoys with the topmost band black. *White lights* are used on any color buoy when required to distinguish it from other buoys in the vicinity or because of the greater intensity of a white light. Since white lights may be shown on buoys of any color, the color of the light has no lateral significance; and the purpose of the buoy must be found in its body color, number, or light-phase characteristic.

Light-phase characteristics Lights shown from buoys and other aids to navigation have distinct characteristics to assist in their identification. These are illustrated, and their abbreviations are given, in Figure 508. Lights are described as *flashing* when the time on is less than the time off. Lights are termed *occulting* when they are on more than they are off ("eclipsed"). If the times on and off are equal, the light is designated as *equal interval* or *isophase*. The *period* of a light is the time for it to complete one full cycle of on-and-off changes. By varying the lengths of the periods and the elements of a cycle, a considerable variety of light-phase characteristics can be obtained. Advantage is taken of this to provide the necessary distinction between aids in the same area or to aid in the recognition of a primary seacoast light by the navigator of a vessel making her landfall.

Light characteristics in the lateral system **509** Lighted buoys and minor lights in the lateral system are assigned phase characteristics as follows:

Flashing Lights (flashing at regular intervals and at a rate of not more than 30 flashes per minute) are placed only on black buoys, red buoys, or special purpose buoys, and on minor lights equivalent to black and red buoys.

Quick Flashing Lights (not less than 60 flashes per minute) are placed only on black buoys and red buoys, and on equivalent minor lights, at

Illustration and phase description	Symbols and meaning	
	Lights which do not change color	Lights which show color variations
A continuous steady light.	F. = Fixed . . .	Alt. = Alternating.
A fixed light varied at regular intervals by a flash of greater brilliance.	F.Fl. = Fixed and flashing.	Alt.F.Fl. = Alternating fixed and flashing.
A fixed light varied at regular intervals by groups of 2 or more flashes of greater brilliance.	F.Gp.Fl. = Fixed and group flashing.	Alt.F.Gp.Fl. = Alternating fixed and group flashing.
Showing a single flash at regular intervals, the duration of light always being less than the duration of darkness; not more than 30 flashes per minute.	Fl. = Flashing	Alt.Fl. = Alternating flashing.
Showing at regular intervals groups of 2 or more flashes.	Gp.Fl. = Group flashing.	Alt.Gp.Fl. = Alternating group flashing.
Light flashes are combined in alternate groups of different numbers.	Gp.Fl. (1+2) = Composite group flashing.	. . . .
Light in which flashes of different duration are grouped in such a manner as to produce a Morse character or characters every 8 seconds.	Mo.(A) = Morse Code.	. . . .
Shows not less than 60 flashes per minute.	Qk.Fl. = Quick flashing.	. . . .
Shows a series of 6 quick flashes repeated at intervals of 10 seconds.	I.Qk.Fl. = Interrupted quick flashing.	. . . .
Light with all durations of light and darkness equal.	E.Int. = Equal interval. *(Isophase)*	. . . .
A light totally eclipsed at regular intervals, the duration of light always greater than the duration of darkness.	Occ. = Occulting.	Alt.Occ. = Alternating occulting.
A light with a group of 2 or more eclipses at regular intervals.	Gp.Occ. = Group occulting.	. . . .
A light in which the occultations are combined in alternate groups of different numbers.	Gp.Occ. (2+3) = Composite group occulting.	. . . .
Light colors used and abbreviations: W = white, R = red, G = green.		

Figure 508. Light phase characteristics.

points where it is desired to indicate that special caution is necessary; for example, at sharp turns, where a channel narrows, or to mark wrecks or other obstructions which must be passed *on one side only.*

Interrupted Quick-Flashing Lights (groups of six quick flashes repeated at intervals of ten seconds) are placed only on buoys painted with red and black horizontal bands, or on a minor light whose square or triangular daymark is colored red and black divided horizontally, at points where it is desired to indicate junctions in channels, or to mark wrecks or other hazards that may be passed *on either side.*

Morse (A) Lights (groups consisting of a short flash and a long flash repeated at intervals of eight seconds) are placed on buoys with black and white vertical stripes, and on minor lights whose daymarks are octagonal, colored black and white vertically, placed at points where it is desired to indicate fairways or midchannels, and they should be passed close to on either side. These lights are always white.

Miscellaneous light information

The lights on U.S. buoys are operated by means of electricity supplied from batteries stored in the body of and wired to a flashing mechanism in the base of the lantern. At minor lights, the batteries are in a weatherproof box on a platform near the top of the structure.

In order that lighted buoys and minor lights may function for a reasonably long period of time without requiring a replacement of the batteries, the length of the light flashes is quite short in comparison with the intervening periods of darkness. To further conserve electricity, lights are now equipped with a "daylight control" (photoelectric cell) to turn the light off during the day. Battery power supplies at isolated locations are frequently good for a year or more of operation. An automatic bulb-changing mechanism is included to increase the dependability of the light; if a bulb burns out, an internal device operates to put into use one of several spare bulbs.

Navigation lights on bridges

In U.S. waters, the Coast Guard prescribes certain combinations of lights for bridges and other fixed structures across waterways. In general, red lights are used to mark piers and supports, and green lights mark the centerline of the navigable channel through a fixed bridge; if there is more than one channel through the bridge, the preferred route is marked by three white lights placed vertically. Green lights are also used on some drawbridges to indicate that the draw is open and the vessel may proceed.

Full details on the lighting of bridges will be found in the introductory pages of each volume of the *Light List.* Some bridges may also be equipped with sound signals (see Article 523).

Cardinal system of buoyage

510 In some waters, particularly those of foreign nations, the *cardinal* system of buoyage is used. The location of each mark indicates its direction from the danger that is is marking. There are four quadrants (North, East, South, and West), bounded by the true bearings

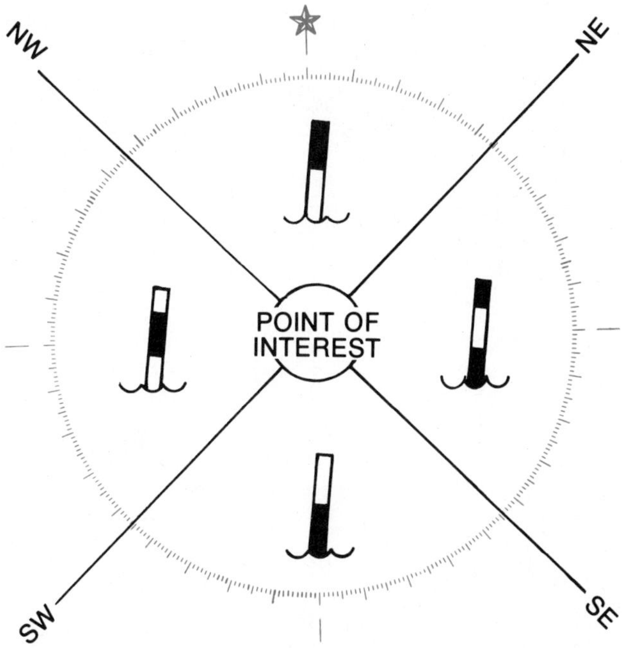

Figure 510. The cardinal system of buoyage.

NW-NE, NE-SE, SE-SW, and SW-NW, respectively, *from* the point of interest. A distinctive shape, color, and light characteristic (and "topmark" if one is used) is assigned to each quadrant.

A cardinal mark is named after the quadrant in which it is placed, and it should be passed on the named side of the mark. A cardinal mark may be used to indicate that the deepest water is on the named side of the mark, or it may be used to indicate the safe side on which to pass a danger. Such a mark may also be used to draw attention to a feature in a channel such as a bend, a junction, or the end of a shoal.

Closely related to the cardinal system are two other types of aids to navigation. An *isolated danger mark* is one erected on or moored over an isolated hazard that has navigable water all around it and thus may be passed on any side. Somewhat similarly, a *safe-water mark* also has navigable water all around it, but it does *not* mark a danger at or beneath it; these include buoys marking midchannel or the centerline of a fairway. A safe-water mark may also be used as an alternative to a cardinal or lateral mark to indicate a landfall.

Buoys on the chart

511 Harbor buoys are normally shown only on harbor charts. An approach chart displays sea buoys, approach buoys, and the beginning of channel buoys or lights. Smaller scale charts show sea buoys only. The position of a buoy is indicated on the chart by a diamond symbol with a dot or small circle marking the approximate position of the anchor. The diamond may be black or nautical purple (magenta)

Figure 511. Symbols from charts.

for black and red buoys respectively, or half of each color for horizontally banded buoys; it may be an "open" diamond with appropriate abbreviations for other colors or combinations of colors. A larger overprinted disc in nautical purple indicates a lighted buoy and the accompanying legend notes the color (if other than white) and its characteristics. Additional printed information shows the sound signal (BELL, GONG, etc.), if any; the presence of a radar reflector is sometimes indicated by an addition to the symbol or the lettering "Ra Ref." The number or letter designation is shown adjacent to the symbol in quotation marks (to differentiate it from figures for water depths). For unlighted buoys, the letter C or N indicates a can or nun buoy respectively. The information given for any buoy is limited by the available space on the chart.

Daybeacons in the U.S. lateral system of buoyage are charted in the same general manner. A triangular symbol is used for all daybeacons regardless of the shape of the daymark. This is colored black, nautical purple, or a combination, or is left "open" in the same fashion as for buoys.

Minor lights may be used in lieu of lighted buoys where water depths permit. The symbol is a dot with a nautical purple "flare" making the symbol as a whole appear much like a large exclamation mark. The light color (if other than white) and characteristic will be shown by abbreviations near the symbol.

Lighthouses **512** Lighthouses called "lights" in the *Light Lists* are found along most of the world's navigable coastlines and many of the interior waterways of the various countries. Such structures are so well known as to require little description. Lighthouses are placed where they will be of most use, on prominent headlands, at entrances, on isolated dangers, or at other points where it is necessary that mariners be warned or guided. Their principal purpose is to support a light at a considerable height above the water. The same structure may also house a fog signal and radiobeacon equipment, and contain quarters for the keepers. However, in the majority of instances, the fog signal, the radiobeacon equipment, and the operating personnel are housed in separate buildings grouped around the tower. Such a group of buildings constitutes a *light station.*

The location of a lighthouse, whether in the water or on shore, the importance of the light, the kind of soil upon which it is to be built, and the prevalence of violent storms, have a direct bearing upon the type of structure erected and on the materials with which it will be built. Engineering problems will not be entered into here, but it is important to note that the materials used and types of construction differentiate one lighthouse from another and hence aid in identification.

Lighthouses vary markedly in their outward appearance because of the points already mentioned and also because of the great difference in the distances from which their lights should be seen. Where the need for a powerful light is great and the importance and density of traffic warrant, a tall tower with a light of great candlepower is erected. Conversely, at points intermediate to the major lights, where the traffic is light, and where long range is not so necessary, a less expensive structure of more modest dimensions suffices.

Classes of lights **513** The terms *primary seacoast light, secondary light,* and *river* or *harbor lights* (also called *minor* lights) indicate in a general way the wide variety of lighted aids to navigation that are "fixed" as distinguished from "floating" as a buoy. The specific definition of each class is not of

Figure 513. A primary seacoast light (Cape Hatteras Light).

importance to a navigator. Such lights may be displayed from massive towers, or may be shown from almost any type of inexpensive structure. The essentials of a light structure are: best possible location dependent on physical conditions of the site, sufficient height for the location, a rugged support for the lantern, and a housing for the tanks of compressed gas or electric batteries by which the light is operated. There are many types of structures meeting these essentials—small tank houses surmounted by a short skeleton tower, a cluster of piles, or even a single pile supporting a battery box and the light, and countless other forms.

Lighthouses and major light structures are painted to make them readily distinguishable from the background against which they are seen, to distinguish one structure from others in the same vicinity, and for positive identification by a navigator making an uncertain landfall. Solid colors, bands of colors, and various patterns are used for these purposes. Minor lights, such as river or harbor lights that are part of a lateral system, will normally have a numbered daymark of the appropriate shape and color.

Many primary and secondary lights that formerly were manned by resident keepers are now *automated;* often the proper operation of such lights is remotely monitored so that any failure is immediately known at a central control point.

Lightships **514** Lightships serve the same purpose as lighthouses, being equipped with lights, fog signals, and radiobeacons. Ships are used only when it is impracticable or impossible to construct a lighthouse at the desired location. Lightships mark the entrances to important harbors or estuaries, dangerous shoals lying in much-frequented waters, and also serve as leading marks for both transoceanic and coastwise traffic.

Lightships in United States waters are painted red with the name of the station in white on both sides. Superstructures are white; masts, lantern galleries, ventilators, and stacks are painted buff. Relief lightships are painted the same color as the regular station ships, with the word "RELIEF" in white letters on the sides.

Relief vessels may be placed at any lightship station, and when practicable, will exhibit lights and sound signals having the characteristics of the station. Relief ships may differ in outward appearance from the regular station ship in certain minor details.

The masthead lights, fog signals, and radiobeacon signals of lightships all have distinguishing characteristics, so that each lightship may be differentiated from others and also from nearby lighthouses. As with lighthouses, details regarding these signals are shown briefly on charts and more completely in the *Light Lists* and *Lists of Lights.*

A lightship underway or off station will fly the International Code signal flags "*LO,*" signifying that the light ship is not at anchor on her station. It will not show or sound any of the signals of a lightship, but will display the lights prescribed by the International or Inland Rules for a vessel of her class. While on station a lightship shows only the masthead light and a less brilliant light on the forestay. As lightships ride to a single anchor, the light on the forestay indicates the direction from which the combined wind and current effect is coming and the direction in which the ship is heading. By day, whenever it appears that an approaching vessel does not recognize the lightship or requests identification, the lightship will display the call letters of the station in flags of the International Code.

Lightships are anchored to a very long scope of chain, and thus the radius of the swing circle is considerable. The charted position is the approximate location of the anchor. A navigator must set his course to pass lightships with sufficient clearance to avoid any possibility of collision. Experience has shown that lightships cannot be safely used as "leading marks" to be passed close aboard; they must always be left broad off the course whenever sea room permits. Most lightships will have a station buoy which also must be avoided.

Light towers **515** A number of lightships have been replaced by *offshore light towers.* One of the first of these was the Ambrose Offshore Light Tower, shown in Figure 515; it is painted red with the exception of the radiobeacon antenna, which is painted in accordance with the Federal

Figure 515. An offshore primary light tower (Ambrose Light).

Aviation Administration requirements. The quarters in the upper deck, just below the helicopter platform, are painted white. The Ambrose Tower is located at the entrance to New York Harbor approximately seven miles east of Sandy Hook, New Jersey, in 75 feet of water. The main light beacon operates at a high intensity of six million candlepower and at a low intensity of 600,000 candlepower, with a nominal range of 24 miles. A horn fog signal with an audible range of 4 miles and a radiobeacon with a range of 100 miles are mounted on the tower. An oceanographic laboratory is also located on the tower.

Some offshore light stations have resident crews; others are automated and unmanned.

Large navigational buoys

516 The light towers were developed as a more economical means than a lightship for maintaining a light in an offshore location. Now, however, the trend is toward the use of *large navigational buoys,* Figure 516. These provide a platform for a light, a fog signal, and a radiobeacon, plus sensors for sea and weather conditions which can be telemetered ashore over a radio link. Such buoys can be put on station at only a small fraction of the cost of a light tower and require no onboard operating crews.

Figure 516. A large navigation buoy (Delaware Lighted Horn Buoy "D").

Identification of lights **517** In order to obtain full benefit from lights, the navigator must not only understand their use and be able to interpret all data concerning them given in the *Lights Lists* and on charts, but he must also be able to identify each light correctly.

One of the most frequent causes of groundings is the failure to identify lights correctly. When making a landfall, the navigator should consult the charts and the *Light Lists* to learn the exact characteristics of the light or lights that he expects to see first. When a light is observed, its color is noted and, by means of a watch or clock with a second hand, a note is made of the time required for the light to perform its full cycle of changes. If color, cycle, and number of flashes per cycle agree with the information in the *Light List,* correct identification has been made. The *Light List* should be examined to ascertain if any other light in the general locality might be seen and mistaken for the desired light. If there is doubt, a careful timing of the length of all flashes and dark intervals, and comparison with the *Light List,* is usually conclusive.

In approaching a light with a complex characteristic of different intensities, due allowance must be made for the lesser range of the portion with inferior brightness. For example, a *fixed* and *flashing* light will have flashes brighter than the fixed light. When observed initially from a distance, it is likely that only the flashes will be seen and the full characteristic will not develop until the observer has come within the range of the fixed light. Another example might be a light with a characteristic of alternating flashing, white and red. The red flashes will be less bright and such a light, when first seen from a distance, will most likely be seen as a simple flashing white characteristic; the intervening red flashes will be seen only after the observer comes closer. At short distances and in clear weather, some flashing lights may show a continuous faint light; this results from the fact that the light does indeed burn continuously with the "flashes" being created by a revolving lens.

It is important to note that in *Light Lists* all bearings are stated in degrees true, reading clockwise from 000° at north; bearings relating to visibility of lights are given as observed *from a vessel;* distances are in nautical miles unless otherwise stated; heights are referred to mean high water; depths are referred to the plane of reference on charts. The great majority of lights have no resident crew tending them; such lights are called "unwatched." Unwatched lights have a high degree of reliability; however, they may become irregular or extinguished. Latitudes and longitudes in the *Light Lists* are approximate, and are intended only to facilitate reference to a chart.

Light sectors **518** Sectors of colored glass are placed in the lanterns of certain lighted aids to navigation to mark shoals or to warn mariners off the nearby land. Lights so equipped show one color from most directions and a different color or colors over definite arcs of the horizon indicated in the *Light Lists* and upon the charts. A sector changes the color of a light, when viewed from certain directions, but *not* the characteristic. For example, a flashing white light having a red sector, when viewed from within the sector, will appear flashing red. (But remember, the red may not be visible at all distances from which the white flashes can be seen.)

Sectors may be but a few degrees in width, marking an isolated rock or shoal, or of such width as to extend from the direction of the deep water toward shore. Bearings referring to sectors are expressed in degrees as observed from a vessel *toward* the light.

For example, the *List of Lights* describes a certain light as displaying a red sector from 045° clockwise to 120°. Both are true bearings as observed from seaward. Figure 518 is a sketch of this light indicating the limits through which the light would appear red as observed from aboard ship.

In the majority of cases, water areas covered by red sectors should be avoided, the exact extent of the danger being determined from an examination of the charts. In some cases, instead of indicating danger a narrow sector may mark the best water across a shoal.

In some atmospheric conditions white lights may have a reddish hue; the mariner therefore should not trust solely to color where there are sectors, but should verify the position by taking a bearing of the light. On either side of the line of demarcation between white and a colored sector there is always a small sector (about 2°) of uncertain color as the edges of a sector cannot be cut off sharply. Note here also that the bearings given on the lines of demarcation on the chart are true bearings of the light as seen *from the ship*.

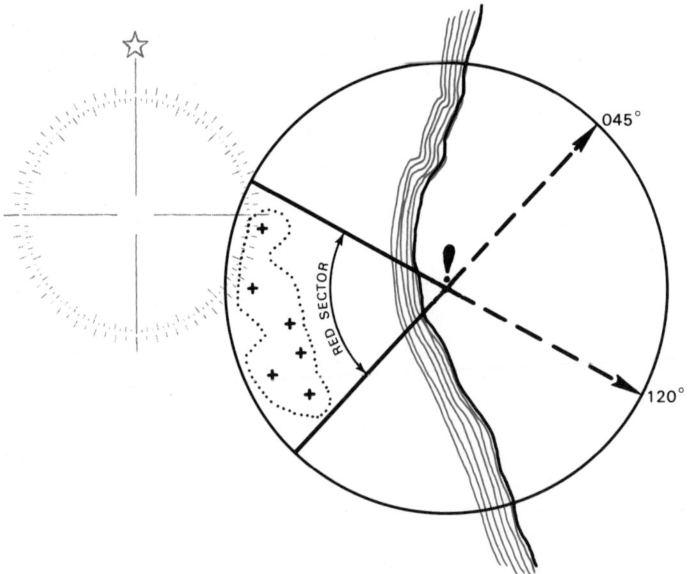

Figure 518. Red sector of a light marking a hazardous area (reef).

When a light is cut off by adjoining land or structures, the obscured sector is shown on the chart and described in the *Light List.* The bearings on which the light is cut off are stated as for colored sectors, from ship toward the light. The exact bearings of cut-off may vary with the distance of the observer and his height of eye.

Visibility of lights

519 In order for a lighted navigational aid such as a lighthouse to be seen at a distance, it must have sufficient elevation above sea level, and sufficient intensity or power. The navigator frequently desires to know at what specific distance he can expect to sight a given light. The first step is always to refer to the appropriate *Light List* or *List of Lights* for the necessary data.

The following terms and their definitions as used in current editions of the *Light List* are employed in connection with the range of visibility of a light.

Horizon distance (or distance of visibility) is the distance, expressed in nautical miles, from a position above the surface of the earth along the line of sight to the horizon. It is the approximate range of visibility of an object of known height to an observer whose eye is at sea level. Horizon distances for various heights are given in Table 8 of *Bowditch,* an extract from which appears as Figure 519. A similar table can be found in the introductory pages of each volume of the *Light Lists.* These tables are calculated for standard conditions of weather and refraction.

The distance to the horizon, D, in nautical miles, may be calculated by the formula $D = 1.144\sqrt{h}$, where h is the height of eye in feet. For height of eye in meters, the constant is 2.072, and D is still in nautical miles.

Nominal range is the maximum distance at which a light may be seen in clear weather (meteorological visibility of 10 nautical miles—see International Visibility Code, Figure 520a) expressed in nautical miles. Nominal range is listed for all Coast Guard lighted aids except range and directional lights.

Luminous range is the maximum distance at which a light may be seen under the existing visibility conditions. By use of the diagram in Figure 520b, luminous range may be determined from the known nominal range and the existing visibility conditions. Nominal and luminous ranges take no account of elevation, observer's height of eye, or the curvature of the earth.

Geographic range is the maximum distance at which a light may be seen under conditions of perfect visibility, limited only by the curvature of the earth. It is expressed in nautical miles for a height of observer's eye at sea level.

Computed range is the geographic range plus the observer's distance to the horizon based on his height of eye.

Computed visibility is the visibility determined for a particular light, taking into consideration its height and nominal range, and the height

Height Feet	Nautical Miles	Height Feet	Nautical Miles	Height Feet	Nautical Miles
1	1.1	33	6.6	125	12.8
2	1.6	34	6.7	130	13.0
3	2.0	35	6.8	135	13.3
4	2.3	36	6.9	140	13.5
5	2.6	37	7.0	145	13.8
6	2.8	38	7.1	150	14.0
7	3.0	39	7.1	160	14.5
8	3.2	40	7.2	170	14.9
9	3.4	41	7.3	180	15.3
10	3.6	42	7.4	190	15.8
11	3.8	43	7.5	200	16.2
12	4.0	44	7.6	210	16.6
13	4.1	45	7.7	220	17.0
14	4.3	46	7.8	230	17.3
15	4.4	47	7.8	240	17.7
16	4.6	48	7.9	250	18.1
17	4.7	49	8.0	260	18.4
18	4.9	50	8.1	270	18.8
19	5.0	55	8.5	280	19.1
20	5.1	60	8.9	290	19.5
21	5.2	65	9.2	300	19.8
22	5.4	70	9.6	310	20.1
23	5.5	75	9.9	320	20.5
24	5.6	80	10.2	330	20.8
25	5.7	85	10.5	340	21.1
26	5.8	90	10.9	350	21.4
27	5.9	95	11.2	360	21.7
28	6.1	100	11.4	370	22.0
29	6.2	105	11.7	380	22.3
30	6.3	110	12.0	390	22.6
31	6.4	115	12.3	400	22.9
32	6.5	120	12.5	410	23.2

Figure 519. Table of distance to the horizon for various heights of eye.

of eye of the observer. In computing the visibility of a light, it is assumed that the computed visibility will never exceed the light's nominal range; however, under certain atmospheric conditions a light may occasionally be visible far beyond its nominal range.

Determining visibility

520 The following examples illustrate the recommended form for determining the visibility of a light. *The computed visibility is the lesser of the computed range or the luminous range.*

Example 1: Determine the visibility of Mount Desert Light (L. L. No. 1) for an observer with a height of eye of 70 feet.

Solution: From the *Light List* (Fig. 503) determine the nominal range (column 4), 24 miles, and the height above water (column 5), 75 feet, of the light. Determine horizon distance from Figure 519, and place in the form shown below.

Geographic Range for 75 feet	9.9 miles
Horizon Distance for 70 feet	9.6 miles
Computed range	19.5 miles
Nominal range	24 miles

Answer: 19.5 miles

Example 2: Determine the visibility of Seguin Light (L.L. No. 5) for an observer with a height of eye of 11 meters.

Solution: From the *Light List* determine the nominal range (column 4), 19 miles, and the height of the light above water, 180 feet. Determine geographic range for the light from Figure 519, 15.3 miles. Determine horizon distance for height of eye using formula, 6.9 miles.

Geographic range for 180 feet	15.3 miles
Horizon distance for 11 meters	6.9 miles
Computed visibility	22.2 miles
Nominal range	19 miles

Answer: 19 miles (assuming standard "clear visibility")

Variations due to refraction

As stated earlier, the distance at which a light may be sighted may, due to abnormal atmospheric refraction, be far greater than its nominal range. Conversely, the nominal range may be greatly lessened by fog, haze, rain, snow, or smoke. In clear weather, the loom of a powerful light may appear before the light itself comes into sight.

Variations due to weather conditions

The nominal ranges, tabulated in column 4 of the *Light Lists* for major lights, are predicted on the existence of "clear" weather, with a meteorological visibility of 10 nautical miles; this falls in code No. 7 of the International Visibility Code, reproduced in Figure 520a. It may

METEOROLOGICAL OPTICAL RANGE

Code	Weather	Yards	Code	Weather	Nautical Miles
0	Dense fog	Less than 50	4	Thin fog	½ to 1
1	Thick fog	50 to 200	5	Haze	1 to 2
2	Moderate fog	200 to 500	6	Light haze	2 to 5½
3	Light fog	500 to 1000	7	Clear	5½ to 11
			8	Very clear	11.0 to 27.0
			9	Exceptionally clear	Over 27.0

Figure 520a. International Visibility Code.

be noted that under "very clear" and "exceptionally clear" conditions, visibility is greatly increased, and the luminous range of a given light may be increased by several miles. Conversely, in the lower ranges, visibility tends to fall off very rapidly. By means of the diagram in each *Light List,* Figure 520b, the luminous range of a light may be approximated for existing conditions of visibility. The diagram is entered vertically from either top or bottom using the nominal range in column 4, Figure 503. The selected vertical line is followed until the appropriate curve for the existing visibility is reached (intermediate values are interpolated visually, the scale is logarithmic). Horizontally opposite this point on the scale at the left, the approximate luminous range for

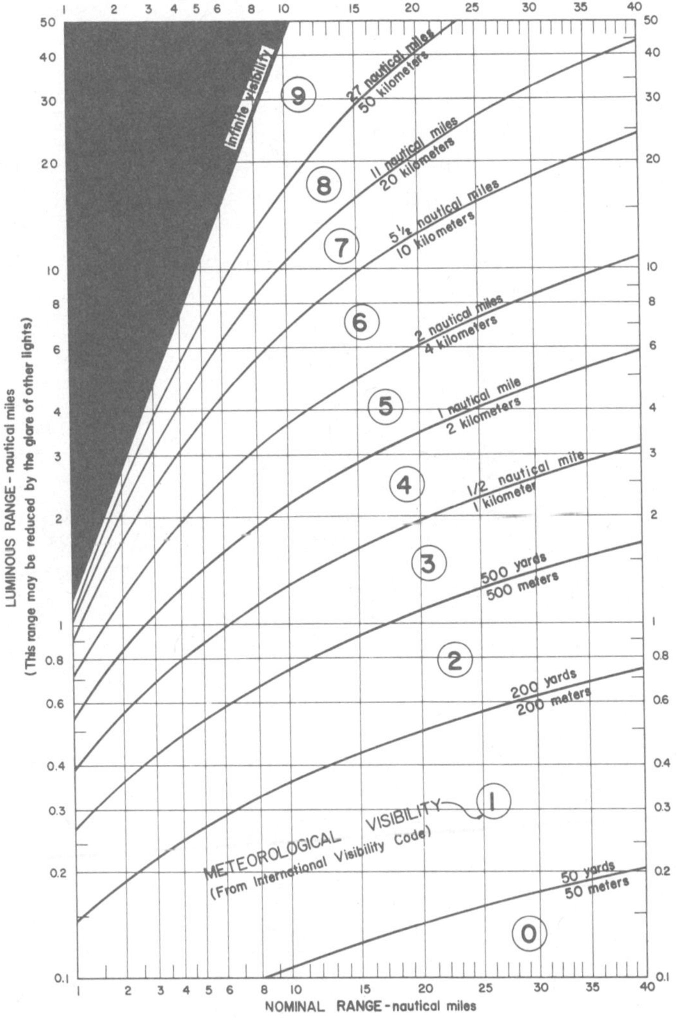

Figure 520b. Luminous range diagram; its method of use is explained in the text.

the existing meteorological conditions may be read off. For example, using the diagram, the luminous range of Monhegan Island Light (L.L. No. 3) may be determined for different conditions of visibility. The nominal range, from Figure 503, is 21 nautical miles. When the meteorological visibility is 20 miles, the light could be sighted at a distance of about 35 miles, but this would require a height of eye of roughly 300 feet. When the meteorological visibility is only 2 miles, it would be sighted at 6½ miles.

The diagram can also be used to obtain an approximate value for meteorological visibility. For example, Monhegan Island Light with a nominal range of 21 miles is sighted at 10 miles; the meteorological visibility is about 4 miles, International Code 6, light haze.

Predicting time and bearing for sighting a light

521 When the visibility of a light for the appropriate height of eye has been determined, an arc can be drawn on the chart; this arc is centered at the charted position of the light, and its radius is the computed visibility. It is labeled with the name of the light above the arc, and the visibility below it. The point at which this circle intersects the dead reckoning plot indicates the position at which the light should become visible. The time of arrival at this point is determined by dead reckoning; the bearing on which the light should be sighted is its direction from this point. Such a plot is illustrated in Figure 521. The true bearing obtained from the chart is frequently converted to a relative bearing to assist lookouts in locating the light. If the dead reckoning plot crosses the computed visibility arc at an acute angle, the pre-

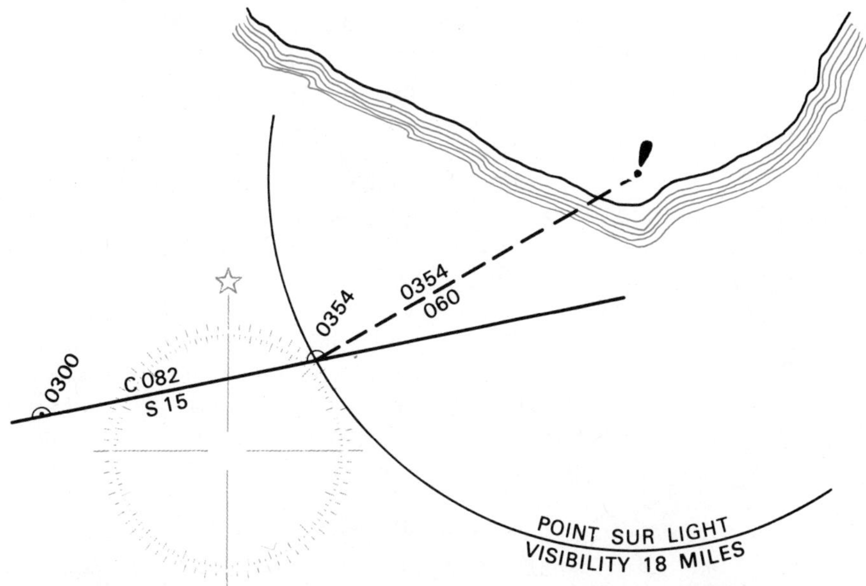

Figure 521. Predicting the time and bearing for sighting a light.

dicted time and bearing may be considerably in error, as a small set to the right or left will make a considerable difference in the location of the point of intersection.

Bobbing a light When a light is first seen on the horizon, it will disappear if the observer tries to sight it from a point several feet, or one deck, lower, and reappear when he returns to his original position. This is called *bobbing a light,* and can be helpful in estimating its distance. When a light can be bobbed, it is at the limit of its visibility for the observer's height of eye. By determining geographic range for the height of the light, and for the observer's height of eye, and combining these two values, an approximation of the distance may be obtained. This distance, combined with a bearing will give an *estimated position;* distances obtained in this way are not sufficiently accurate to yield a fix.

Range lights **522** Two lights, located some distance apart and one higher than the other, visible usually in one direction only, are known as *range lights.* They are so positioned that a mariner can place his ship on the axis of a channel by steering to make the lights appear one above the other (the farther away "rear" light above the nearer "front" light). If he continues to steer his vessel so that the lights stay aligned vertically, his vessel will remain within the limits of the channel.

Entrance channels are frequently marked by range lights. The Delaware River and the St. Johns River on the Atlantic coast, and the Columbia River on the Pacific coast are examples of successive straight reaches marked in this manner.

The lights of ranges may be any of the three standard colors, and may also be fixed, flashing, or occulting, the principal requirement being that they stand out distinctly from their surroundings. Recently, however, the U.S. Coast Guard has standardized on a quick-flashing characteristic for the range front light and an equal-interval, 6-second, characteristic for the rear light. Range light structures are usually fitted with conspicuously colored daymarks for daytime use. Most range lights lose brilliance rapidly as a ship diverges from the range line. On some ranges, the sector of visibility of the lights is very narrow; for example, the Cape May Harbor range lights are described in the *Light List* as "visible on range line only"; other range lights are variously listed as "visible 2° (or 4°) each side of range line."

Ranges should be used only after a careful examination of the charts, and it is particularly important to determine how far the range line can be followed safely; this is not obtainable from the *Light Lists.*

The proper turning point for leaving, or joining, any range must be known and the turn itself anticipated.

Directional lights In a limited number of situations, it is not practicable for one reason or another to install a pair of range lights. A less effective, but generally acceptable, substitute is a *directional light.* This is a single light which projects a high-intensity beam of very narrow width; often three colors are used, with a sharp white beam flanked on one side by a broader, but still rather narrow, red sector and with a similar green sector on the other side.

The same cautions regarding use apply as were discussed above for range lights. The entry in the *Light List* must be consulted for information on the beamwidth(s) involved, as normally there is space on the chart for only the color(s) and characteristics.

Fog signals **523** Any sound-producing instrument operated in time of reduced visibility (caused by fog, snow, haze, smoke, etc.) from a definite point shown on the charts, such as a lighthouse, lightship, or buoy, serves as a useful fog signal. To be effective as an aid to navigation, a mariner must be able to identify it and to know from what location it originates. The simpler fog signals are bells, gongs, or whistles on buoys. As such signals on buoys are operated by the motion of the sea, they will not produce sounds in a calm sea without swells. The only buoy that will signal its location under such conditions is the horn buoy whose sounds are mechanically produced by electrical power from the buoy's batteries.

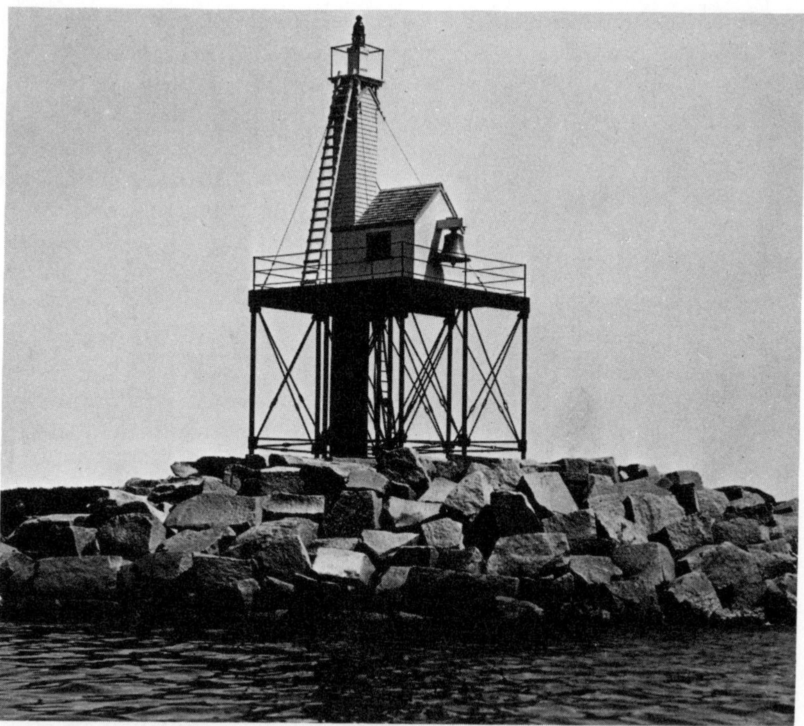

Figure 523. Fog signal at end of a jetty.

At primary and secondary lights, and on lightships, fog signals are operated mechanically. There are several types of such fog signals.

Diaphones produce sound by means of a slotted reciprocating piston actuated by compressed air. Blasts may consist of two tones of different pitch, in which case the first part of the blast is high and the last part is low. These alternate-pitch signals are called "two-tone."

Diaphragm horns produce sound by means of a disc diaphragm vibrated by compressed air, steam, or electricity. Duplex or triplex horn units of differing pitch produce a chime signal.

Reed horns produce sound by means of a steel reed vibrated by compressed air.

Sirens produce sound by means of either a disc or a cup-shaped rotor actuated by compressed air, steam, or electricity.

Whistles produce sound by compressed air or steam directed through a circumferential slot into a cylindrical bell chamber.

Bells are sounded by means of a hammer actuated by hand, by a descending weight, compressed gas, or electricity.

Identification As signals on buoys which are operated by the motion of the sea do not produce sounds on a regular time schedule, identification may be difficult or impossible. While it is easy to differentiate a bell buoy from a gong buoy or a whistle buoy, it is not possible to identify one specific buoy from another of the same type solely by the sound it makes.

Mechanically operated fog signals, however, are placed on a regular cycle of operation, and different types of signals and characteristics can be assigned various locations in the same general area for identification purposes. Fog signals at primary seacoast and secondary lights are usually *horns* with characteristics varying from one to three blasts in cycles of 10 to 60 seconds length; each blast is normally two or three seconds in duration with pauses of similar duration between blasts if there are more than one. Lightships are usually fitted with a *two-tone diaphone;* these, too, are assigned an identifying characteristic in terms of number of blasts and length of a cycle. Occasionally, a diaphone is installed on shore, or a siren or bell is used for some local purpose.

Operation Fog signals of the U.S. Coast Guard at locations where a continuous watch is maintained are placed in operation when the visibility decreases to 5 miles, or when the fog signal of a passing ship is heard. Fog signals at stations where no continuous watch is maintained may not always be sounded promptly when fog conditions develop or may operate erratically due to mechanical difficulties. At some stations, fog signals are operated continuously for a portion of each year; the operating period is stated in the *Light Lists.*

Caution The navigator must always bear in mind that sound signals in fog can be very deceptive. At times, they may be completely inaudible even when near at hand. Again, they may be somewhat refracted; that is, they may appear to be coming from a direction other than the actual bearing of the signal source. Constant soundings should be obtained when operating in fog in coastal areas.

Aids to navigation on ICW

524 The Intracoastal Waterway (ICW) is a largely sheltered waterway, suitable for year-round use, extending some 2,400 miles along the Atlantic and Gulf coasts of the United States. In general it follows natural waterways.

Aids to navigation along the ICW carry special identification marks. The usual daymark and buoy painting schemes are used, but an additional *yellow* stripe is added under the number. (The former distinctive marks of yellow borders on daymarks and yellow bands on buoys are being phased out.) The various types of aids are shown on page H-3 of Appendix H.

Colors

The colors used for ICW aids are governed by the following rules:

> The *left side* of the channel, entering from the north and east, and traversing towards the south and west, is marked with *black aids,* bearing *odd numbers.*
>
> The *right side* of the channel, entering from the north and east, is marked with *red aids,* bearing *even numbers.*
>
> All *green* or *black* daymarks on daybeacons are *square,* while the *red* markers are *triangular* in shape.

In certain areas, the ICW coincides with other waterways, which are buoyed in accordance with the standard practice; that is, black buoys on the left hand when proceeding from seaward, and red buoys on the right, as described in Article 507. In such joint waterways the standard system of coloring prevails for buoys, and the ICW numbers and yellow markings are omitted, but yellow triangles or squares are added on the regular aids to designate the ICW. The system of marking where the ICW and another waterway coincide is shown on page H-3 of Appendix H. An inspection of the sketch on that page shows that the color of aids may be reversed under such conditions. A vessel proceeding south down the ICW has red aids on her right hand until the nun "6" is reached where the channel becomes a joint waterway; at this point the red aids will be on her left hand. However, along this reach of the channel the yellow shapes painted on the buoys can be of assistance, as the squares will be on the red buoys as a reminder that in this joint waterway a red buoy may be on the left-hand for vessels proceeding south.

Western Rivers buoyage system

525 Aids to navigation on the "Western Rivers" of the U.S.—the Mississippi River and its tributaries—are generally similar to those on other U.S. waters, but there are a few differences that should be noted. Buoys are not numbered; their color system conforms to the U.S. lateral system or red-right-returning from sea, with white tops added for improved visibility. (The descriptions "right side" and "left side" are sometimes used but in terms of a person on a vessel proceeding downstream *toward* the sea.) Lights and daybeacons are numbered, but *not* in the even-odd style of the lateral system; numbers relate to the distance upstream in statute miles from some arbitrary point of origin. Lights and lighted buoys on the starboard side proceeding downriver show a single green or white flash; those on the port side show a *double* red or white flash. Special "crossing" daymarks are used at bends where the deeper water channel crosses from one side of the river to the other. See page H-4 of Appendix H.

Uniform State Waterway Marking System

526 To provide for consistent marking of U.S. internal waters not subject to federal jurisdiction, there has been established the Uniform State Waterway Marking System (USWMS). This consists of regulatory signs and buoys, plus buoys in either the lateral system or a "cardinal" system (see Article 510).

Information on the USWMS can be found on page H-5 of Appendix H of this book.

Systems of other nations

527 The buoyage system of other nations may or *may not* be similar to that of the United States. If a lateral system is used, the buoys to be left to starboard may be *black,* rather than red. In other cases, the color of the buoy may not be significant, information being conveyed only by the buoy's overall shape or its "topmark" (an added shape of one or two spheres, cones, etc., at the top of a buoy—not used on U.S. buoys). Some nations make regular use of buoys in a cardinal system (see Article 510).

Northwestern Europe buoyage system

The nations of Northwest Europe—England and France, north to Sweden and Norway, west to Ireland, and east to Poland—are establishing a uniform system of buoyage using both the lateral and cardinal systems, plus marks for isolated dangers, safe waters, and special indications. Not all types will be used in each area, but where used, the colors, shapes, topmarks, and light characteristics will be consistent with the established rules which are known as "System A—The Combined Cardinal and Lateral System (Red to Port)."

Navigator's responsibility

A navigator must be familiar with the system of buoyage that he will encounter before he enters the pilot waters of a foreign country. Advance study of the appropriate *List of Lights* or the appropriate volume of *Sailing Directions* is absolutely essential.

6 Navigational Publications

Introduction **601** In the United States Government there are several agencies that are responsible for the publication of various documents to aid in the greater safety of navigation at sea. The term "document" here is used in a broad sense to include charts, tables, books and pamphlets, and devices which relate to navigation. These agencies conduct field surveys and research studies of their own, and collaborate with each other and with similar activities in many foreign nations in order that their charts and other publications will contain the most recent and accurate information.

U.S. agencies The documents of the following agencies will be discussed in this chapter.

Defense Mapping Agency Hydrographic Center (DMAHC), Department of Defense.

National Ocean Survey (NOS), a part of National Oceanic and Atmospheric Administration (NOAA) in the Department of Commerce.

Naval Observatory, Department of the Navy.

U.S. Coast Guard (USCG), Department of Transportation.

Corps of Engineers, Department of the Army.

National Weather Service, NOAA, Department of Commerce.

Naval Oceanographic Office, Department of the Navy.

Hydrographic services of varying degrees of completeness are maintained by practically all maritime countries. The smaller countries restrict such service to their own coastal waters, but the larger countries, whose maritime interests embrace large parts of the globe, issue charts and other publications that cover the entire world. Most of these institutions are members of the International Hydrographic Organization, and hold periodic conferences to promote international uniformity in nautical publications and to collaborate in the collecting and disseminating of hydrographic information. As a result of this effort, there is a marked improvement in the quality and coverage of hydrographic surveys in many parts of the world and an increasing uniformity in charts and nautical books, both of which make navigating easier for mariners of all nations. There is a free exchange of hydrographic publications among the various maritime countries. As a result of this arrangement, the U.S. agencies, in preparing nautical documents for any particular area, make full use of the hydrographic and other marine information that has been compiled and published by the country having jurisdiction.

The various agencies responsible for navigational publications do not depend solely upon official sources of information. They serve as clearing houses for appropriate nautical data from any and all sources and in this way give navigators in general the benefit of observations noted by ships' officers in the routine performance of their duties. Many observers from time to time contribute valuable data concerning currents, aids and dangers to navigation, port facilities, and related subjects, which help materially in keeping the charts, *Sailing Directions, Coast Pilots,* and *Light Lists* in agreement with prevailing conditions. These publications solicit such cooperation and greatly appreciate the receipt of any data that may increase their accuracy and completeness. Direct contact with ships' officers is facilitated by branch offices (see Article 602) maintained at a number of ports in the United States and its possessions where the most recent marine information is made available to ships' masters and navigators.

Nautical charts

602 The principal U.S. agencies involved with nautical charts are the National Ocean Survey (NOS) and the Defense Mapping Agency Hydrographic Center (DMAHC). Both of these agencies have branch or regional offices, plus a network of local sales agents from whom charts and other publications can be obtained. Charts of some inland rivers, chiefly the Mississippi, Ohio, Tennessee, and their tributaries are prepared by the Army Corps of Engineers; these are sometimes called "navigational maps." Such charts or maps are normally purchased from District Engineer Offices.

Charts by geographic area

Charts of the coastal United States and its territories and possessions are published by the National Ocean Survey and distributed through its sales agents. These charts are listed in the NOS *Nautical Chart Catalog 1, the Atlantic and Gulf Coasts, including Puerto Rico and the Virgin Islands; Nautical Chart Catalog 2, the Pacific Coast, including Hawaii, Guam, and Samoa Islands; Nautical Chart Catalog 3, Alaska, including the Aleutian Islands;* and *Nautical Chart Catalog 4, the U.S. Great Lakes and Adjacent waterways,* which includes Lake Champlain, the New York state Barge Canal, and the St. Lawrence River above St. Regis and Cornwall, Canada.

Charts of foreign waters and coasts are published by the Defense Mapping Agency Hydrographic Center. These charts are listed in the Catalog of Nautical Charts, DMAHC Pub. No. 1-N (see Article 609).

Chart numbering system

To provide an orderly system for the numbering of U.S. charts, a world-wide scheme has been adopted which generally identifies a chart by means of a scale range and geographic location. U.S. charts have numbers consisting of one to five digits as follows:

One Digit	No scale involved
Two Digits	1:9,000,001 and smaller

Three Digits	1:2,000,001 to 1:9,000,000
Four Digits	Various non-navigational items
Five Digits	1:2,000,000 and larger

The one-digit category comprises the symbol and abbreviation sheets for the United States and some other nations. Also included is the chart of International Code Flags and Pennants published by DMAHC.

The two- and three-digit categories contain charts of very large areas such as entire oceans or major portions thereof. For these numbers, the world's waters have been divided into nine *ocean basins* numbered as shown in Figure 602a. The first digit of a two- or three-digit chart number (with limited exceptions) indicates the ocean basin concerned. (There are no two-digit chart numbers used for Ocean Basins 3 and 4 as the limited areas of the Mediterranean and Caribbean seas make such very small scale charts valueless; thus two-digit chart numbers beginning with 3 or 4 do not fit into the overall numbering scheme.)

The four-digit category consists of a series of *non-navigational,* special-purpose charts. These are numbered by arbitrarily assigning blocks of new numbers to existing series and to new series when originated.

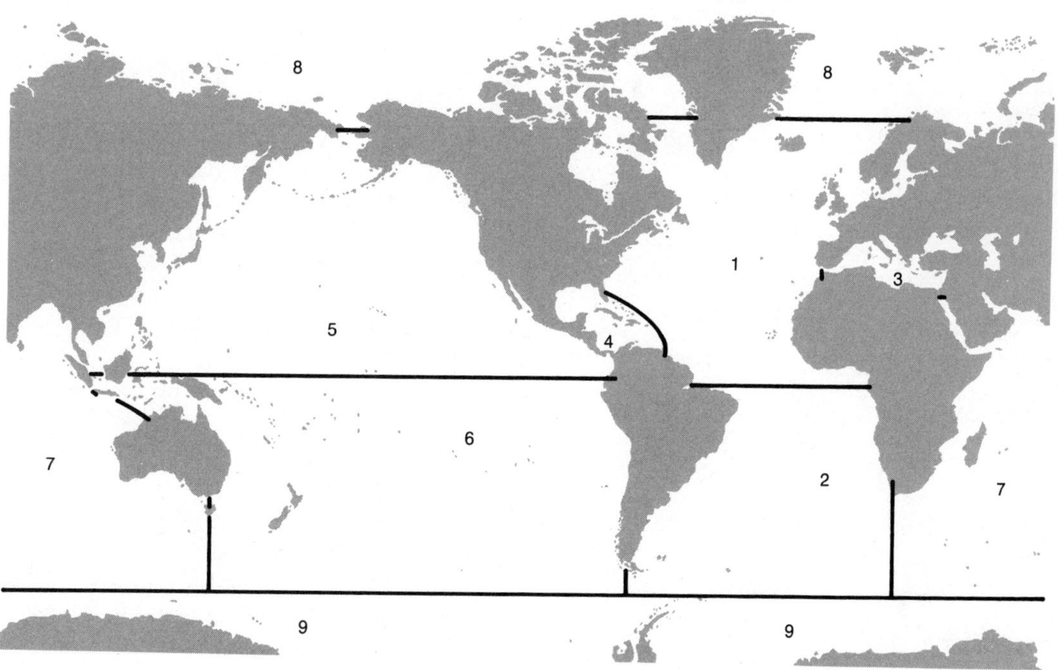

Figure 602a. The "ocean basins" of the DMA chart numbering system; first digit of a two- or three-digit chart number.

The five-digit category includes those charts most often used by navigators. Except for bathymetric charts, the first of the five digits indicates one of the nine *coastal regions* of the world in which the chart is located; see Figure 602b. (Note that this "coastal region" number is *not* the same as the "ocean basin" number used in the two- and three-digit number series.) The second of the five digits identifies a subregion; again see Figure 602b. The final three digits associate the chart with a specific location; they are assigned counterclockwise around the subregion.

Many gaps are left in the assignment of numbers so that any future charts may be smoothly fitted into the system. Although the numbering system covers the world, it has as yet been applied only to U.S.-produced charts and foreign charts reissued by DMAHC.

By virtue of their scale, bathymetric (bottom contour) charts would normally be assigned a five-digit number. These charts, however, are not of coastal areas as are the others in the five-digit series. To distinguish them, they are assigned a one-letter, four-digit number. The letter *C* indicates that they are overprinted with Loran-C lines of position; the letter B indicates Loran-A or no Loran information. The first

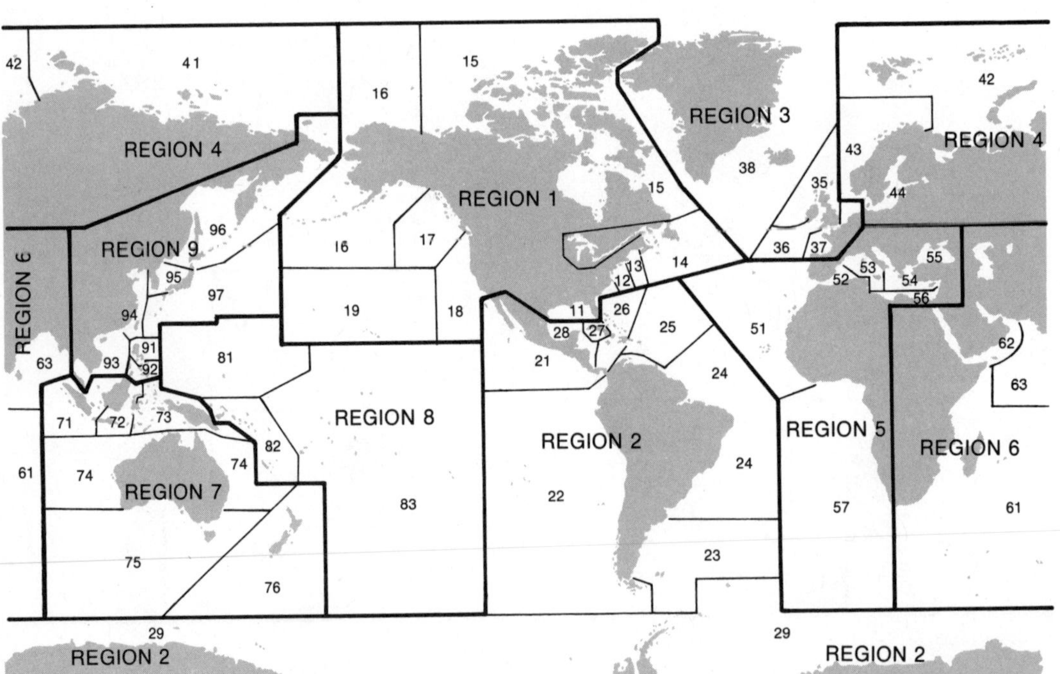

Figure 602b. The "coastal regions" of the DMA chart numbering system; first digit of a five-digit chart number.

two digits indicate a band of longitude, and the second two digits designate a latitude band; see Figure 602c. Ocean sounding selection sheets from the General Bathymetric Chart of the World (GEBCO), available to the public, will have the letter *G* preceding the numbers. Bottom contour charts, available only to the U.S. Navy, will have the letter *C* indicating that they are overprinted with Loran-C lines of position, or *B* indicating Loran-A lines or no Loran information.

Portfolios The chart numbering system based on regions and subregions provides an organized method of keeping track of charts issued by many various agencies, such as DMAHC, NOS, Canadian Hydrographic Service, British Admiralty, and others. All such charts are now referred to in U.S. usage by a five-digit number. In addition, each subregion is termed a *portfolio* and is subdivided into *A* and *B* sections; for example, charts of Subregion 26 are placed in Portfolios 26A and 26B (these include most, but not all, of the charts of the subregion).

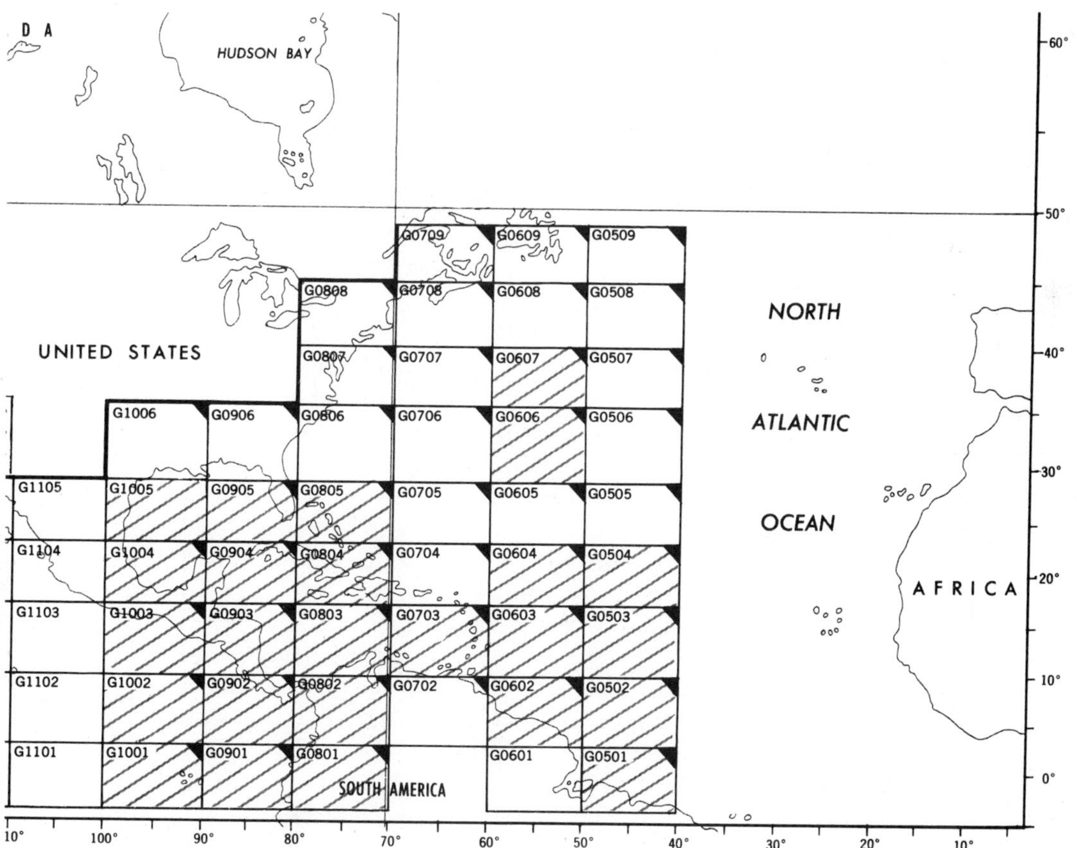

Figure 602c. Numbering system for bathymetric charts.

Portfolios are indicated in DMAHC Pub. No. 1-N-L; the first letter following the initial two digits of the stock number for each chart (the number of the subregion) will be an *A* or a *B* for the respective portfolio (or an *X* if the chart is one of those not a part of a portfolio). For each subregion, the *A* portfolio contains all the general charts and the principal harbor and approach charts; the *B* portfolio supplements the *A* coverage of nautical charts within the subregion.

There are also three portfolios of general charts: Atlantic, Pacific, and the World. Bottom contour charts have been grouped into two portfolios: Eastern Pacific and Western Pacific.

The chart portfolio system provides a simple method for ordering all the charts of a subregion, rather than ordering them individually. Although intended primarily for use by navigators of Navy, Coast Guard, and other federal vessels, it may also be used by nongovernmental individuals and activities. Some charts listed in the portfolios in Pub. No. 1-N-L are not available for purchase from DMAHC offices: these include NOS charts (obtainable from NOS offices and sales agents) and charts not available to civilians.

Chart editions, revisions, and changes

For safety in navigation, every chart when used, must be the latest edition (and revision, if applicable) and fully corrected for changes that have occurred since the edition date. Every chart shows an edition number and date; at times, charts are "revised" and printed with a revision date although retaining the same edition number. Between revisions and/or editions, changes are published in *Notices to Mariners* and *Local Notices to Mariners:* urgent information on chart discrepancies or changes is disseminated by radio in the appropriate series of warning notices (see Article 610).

Light Lists

603 Charts show as much information as possible regarding the many aids to navigation, but practical limitations of space necessitate a less-than-complete description. To supplement what is shown on the chart, and to provide the full amount of data to assist a navigator in locating, identifying, and using aids to navigation, there are two other series of publications; these are the *Light Lists* (see Figure 503) prepared by the U.S. Coast Guard (printed and sold by the Government Printing Office) and the *List of Lights* published by DMAHC.

The Coast Guard *Light Lists* are published in five volumes covering the U.S. coasts, including island possessions, the Great Lakes, and the Mississippi River system. These are complete listings of all lights, buoys, daybeacons, ranges, fog signals, and radiobeacons; detailed information is given on each aid including position (where necessary), shape, color, and characteristics. Typical of details *not* shown on a chart, but shown in a *Light List,* is information that the aids to navigation along a certain channel are 150 feet back from the channel limits rather than at the edge, or that certain lighted buoys are replaced during specified months because they may be endangered by ice.

H. O. 113

(1) No.	(2) Name and location	(3) Position lat. long.	(4) Characteristic and power	(5) Height	(6) Range (miles)	(7) Structure, height (feet)	(8) Sectors. Remarks. Fog signals
	FRANCE—WEST COAST						
		N. W.					
	GIRONDE ENTRANCE:						
	— Passe Sud:						
2390 *D 1310*	— — Entrance range, front, Saint Nicolas.	45 34 1 05	**F. G** .... Cp. 100,000	72 **22**	14	White quadrangular tower; 29.	Intensified 2° each side of axis.
2390. 1 *D 1310. 1*	— — — Rear, **Pointe de Grave,** 63° from front.	45 34 1 04	**Occ. W. R. G** .... period 4^{s} lt. 3^{s}, ec. 1^{s} Cp. W. 20,000 R. 4,000 G. 2,500	85 **26**	14	Square white tower, angles and top black; 82.	W. 330°–233°30′, R.–303°, W.–312°, G.–330°. **Radiobeacon.**
2395 *D 1312*	— — **Le Chay** Range, front.	45 37 1 03	**F. R** .... Cp. 20,000	105 **32**	16	White tower, red top; 44 ...	Intensified 1°30′ each side of axis.
2395. 1 *D 1312. 1*	— — — Rear, **Saint Pierre,** about 1,990 yards 41° from front.	....	**F. R** .... Cp. 10,000	197 **60**	14	Light gray water tower, red support; 128.	Intensified 2^{s} each side of axis.
	GIRONDE:						
2400 *D 1314*	— Port Bloc, head of N. mole.	45 34 1 04	**Fl. G** .... period 4^{s} fl. 1^{s}, ec. 3^{s} Cp. 60	18 **5**	7	Black pylon; 13	
2410 *D 1316*	— — Head of S. mole	....	**Iso. W** .... period 4^{s} Cp. 120	26 **8**	8	White tower, red top; 20 ...	
2420 *D 1328*	— Le Verdon sur Mer, head of pier.	45 33 1 02	**Gp. Fl. W. G. (3)** ..... period 12^{s} Cp. W. 500 G. 60	56 **17**	W. 12 G. 7	White pylon, green top; 42 .	G. 215°–172°, W.–215°.
2425	— — Range, front	45 32 1 02	**Qk. Fl. W**	16 **5**	9	White rectangular daymark with black stripe on dolphin.	
			Fl. G .... period 2^{s}	......	.....	On same dolphin	
2425. 1	— — — Rear, 435 yards 172° from front.	....	**Qk. Fl. W**	30 **9**	11	White rectangular daymark with black stripe on dolphin.	
			Fl. G .... period 2^{s}	......	.....	On same dolphin.	
2430 *D 1330*	— Pointe de la Chambrette .	45 33 1 03	**F. G**	25 **8**	3	Iron column	2 F. G. lights are shown 185 yards 73°, marking extremities of a jetty.
	— Royan:						
2460 *D 1304*	— — South Jetty	45 37 1 02	**Gp. Occ. W. R. (1+3)** . period 12^{s} lt. 1^{s}, ec. 1^{s} lt. 1^{s}, ec. 1^{s} lt. 3^{s}, ec. 1^{s} lt. 3^{s}, ec. 1^{s} Cp. W. 1,200 R. 240	36 **11**	10	White tower, red base; 30..	R. 199°–220°, W.–116°. **Horn:** 2 bl. ev. 30^{s}.
2470 *D 1306*	— — North Jetty	45 37 1 02	**Gp. Occ. W. R. (1+3)** . period 12^{s} lt. 3^{s}, ec. 1^{s} lt. 3^{s}, ec. 1^{s} lt. 1^{s}, ec. 1^{s} lt. 1^{s}, ec. 1^{s} Cp. W. 1,200 R. 240	52 **16**	W. 11 R. 10	White pylon, red base; 43..	W. 95°–285°, R.–35°. Synchronized with No. 2460.

Figure 603. *List of Lights* (extract).

In addition, each *Light List* volume contains introductory pages with general information on aids to navigation and their use, and the Loran radionavigation systems; color illustrations are included of various aids in the U.S. lateral system and the Uniform State Waterway Marking System. Aids are tabulated in the same sequence as lights are numbered—basically, clockwise around the U.S. coasts from Maine to Florida to Texas, California to Washington, east to west on the Great Lakes, upriver in the Mississippi River System; seacoast aids are listed first in the applicable volumes, followed by harbor and river aids, and then intracoastal waterways aids, if applicable. Each volume of the *Light List* is republished annually, but should be kept continuously corrected from *Notices to Mariners* and *Local Notices to Mariners* (see Article 610).

The DMAHC *Lists of Lights*, seven volumes, cover foreign coasts of the world (and limited portions of U.S. coasts); these are Pub. No. 111A, 111B, and 112 through 116. They include descriptive information similar to *Light Lists,* but, because of their greater coverage areas, they list only lighted aids to navigation and fog signals (lighted buoys within harbors are omitted). Each *List of Lights* is published in a new edition at intervals of approximately twelve months; changes and corrections are included frequently, as they are required, in *Notices to Mariners* (see Article 610).

Coast Pilots* and *Sailing Directions

604 Just as for aids to navigation, charts are limited in what can be shown by symbols and abbreviations regarding channels, hazards, winds and currents, restricted areas, port facilities, pilotage service, and many other types of information needed by a navigator for safe and efficient navigation. These deficiencies are remedied by the *Coast Pilots* published by NOS and the *Sailing Directions* published by DMAHC.

U.S. Coast Pilots are published in nine numbered editions to cover the waters of the United States and its possessions. (The former *Great Lakes Pilot* is now designated as *Coast Pilot 6.*) They are of great value to a navigator when used with charts of an area both during the planning stage of a voyage and in the actual transit of the area. *Coast Pilots* have been stored in a computerized data bank and are reprinted annually with all intervening changes included. Interim changes are published in *Notices to Mariners* and *Local Notices to Mariners* (see Article 610).

The DMAHC *Sailing Directions* provide information comparable to the *Coast Pilots* but for foreign coasts and coastal waters, and again contain much data that cannot conveniently be shown on charts. The appropriate volume of *Sailing Directions,* used with charts of the proper scale, should enable a navigator to approach strange waters with adequate information for his vessel's safety. They are being converted from a series of 70 looseleaf volumes to a new set of 43 publications;

Figure 604. Limits for *Enroute* volumes of *Sailing Directions,* North Atlantic Ocean.

8 *Planning Guides* for ocean basin transits and 35 *Enroute* directions for coastal waters and ports.

The new-style *Sailing Directions* are based on a division of the world's waters into eight "ocean basins" (but these are *not* the same as those used for two- and three-digit chart numbers). The revised *Sailing Directions* are given three-digit DMAHC Pub. Nos. starting with a "1"; the second digit is a number according to the ocean basin concerned; the third digit is "0" for the *Planning Guide,* and "1" through "9" for the various *Enroute* directions. (An exception is ocean basin 5, the North Pacific; here the Planning Guide is Pub. No. 152, as the number "150" was already assigned to the World Port Index and "151" to the table of Distances Between Ports.

The two components of the new *Sailing Directions* contain information as follows:

Planning Guide. Each covers an ocean basin (see Figure 604) containing chapters of useful information about countries adjacent to that particular ocean basin; information relative to the physical environment and local coastal phenomena; references to publications and periodicals listing danger areas; recommended ship routes; detailed electronic navigation systems and buoyage systems pertaining to that ocean basin.

Enroute. Each includes detailed coastal and port approach information, supplementing the largest-scale chart available from DMAHC. It is intended for use in conjunction with the Planning Guide for the ocean basin concerned. Each *Enroute* volume is divided into a number of *sectors,* and for each sector information is provided on available charts (with limits shown on an overall diagram in U.S. chart catalogs); winds, tides, and currents (shown on an outline chart); off-lying dangers; coastal features; anchorages; and major ports (an annotated chartlet with line drawings of aids to navigation and prominent landmarks).

The port facilities data, formerly scattered throughout the old *Sailing Directions,* has been computerized and tabulated in a new expanded edition of Pub. No. 150, *World Port Index,* designed as a companion volume to be used in conjunction with the new *Sailing Directions.*

Fleet Guides **605** The Defense Mapping Agency Hydrographic Center publishes, for U.S. Navy use only, *Fleet Guides.* These are Pub. No. 940, Atlantic Area, and Pub. No. 941, Pacific Area. These guides contain a number of chapters, each of which covers a port of major interest to naval vessels. They are prepared to provide important command, navigational, repair, and logistic information. This information is much like that contained in *Coast Pilots* and *Sailing Directions* but is oriented toward naval interests and requirements; they are not needed by, nor are they available to, non-naval vessels.

Data in *Fleet Guides* are corrected and updated through the publication of changes and/or new editions when required; interim corrections are published in *Notices to Mariners* if the urgency so warrants.

Navigational tables **606** Navigational tables are published to meet many different needs. Some of those most often used by navigators include:

Tide Tables: prediction tables published by National Ocean Survey, in four volumes—*East Coast of North and South America, including Greenland; West Coast of North and South America, including the Hawaiian Islands; Europe and the West Coast of Africa, including the Mediterranean Sea;* and *Central and Western Pacific Ocean and the Indian Ocean* (annual editions). Each volume includes data on the height and time of high and low water at thousands of locations; also included are data on times of sunrise and sunset, moonrise and moonset, and other astronomical phenomena (see Chapter 9).

Tidal Current Tables: prediction tables published by NOS, two volumes—*Atlantic Coast of North America,* and *Pacific Coast of North America and Asia* (annual editions); each volume includes data on the times and strengths of flood and ebb currents, and the time of slack water, for thousands of locations; also included are diagrams for certain heavily traveled bodies of water which facilitate determination of optimum transit times and speeds, and astronomical data similar to that in *Tide Tables* (see Chapter 10).

Tables of Distances Between United States Ports: published by NOS; tabulates approximately 10,000 distances along the shortest routes marked by aids to navigation.

Table of Distances Between Ports, Pub. No. 151; published by DMAHC; supplements the NOS publication with more than 40,000 distances between U.S. and foreign ports, and between foreign ports.

Sight Reduction Tables for Marine Navigation, Pub. No. 229; published by DMAHC, in six volumes, each volume covering 16° of latitude (1° overlap between volumes); see Chapter 24.

Sight Reduction Tables for Air Navigation, Pub. No. 249: published by DMAHC in three volumes; offers somewhat greater ease and speed in sight reduction, but has limited range of declination values and gives a lower order of precision as to position; see Chapter 24.

Azimuths of the Sun and Other Celestial Bodies of Declination 0° to 23°, Pub. No. 260: published by DMAHC; declination values 0° to 23°; see Chapter 28.

Azimuths of Celestial Bodies, Declination 24° to 70°, Pub. No. 261: published by DMAHC; declination 24° to 70°; see Chapter 28.

Metric Conversion Tables for Nautical Charting, Pub. No. 17503: published by DMAHC.

Almanacs **607** Volumes tabulating the positions of various celestial bodies used by navigators, and times of sunrise, sunset, moonrise, moonset, and other astronomical data of interest to navigators, are prepared jointly by the U.S. Naval Observatory and the Royal Greenwich Observatory in England. However, the almanacs are printed separately (in the United States by the Government Printing Office). The *Nautical Almanac,* published annually, and the *Air Almanac,* published three times each year, give ephemeristic data for marine and air navigation respectively. They are used in many other countries with minor modifications in language in the page headings and explanatory material. These almanacs are discussed in Chapter 23. The *American Ephemeris and Nautical Almanac,* published annually by the Naval Observatory, contains the information in the *Nautical Almanac* and a considerable amount of additional data of interest primarily to astronomers.

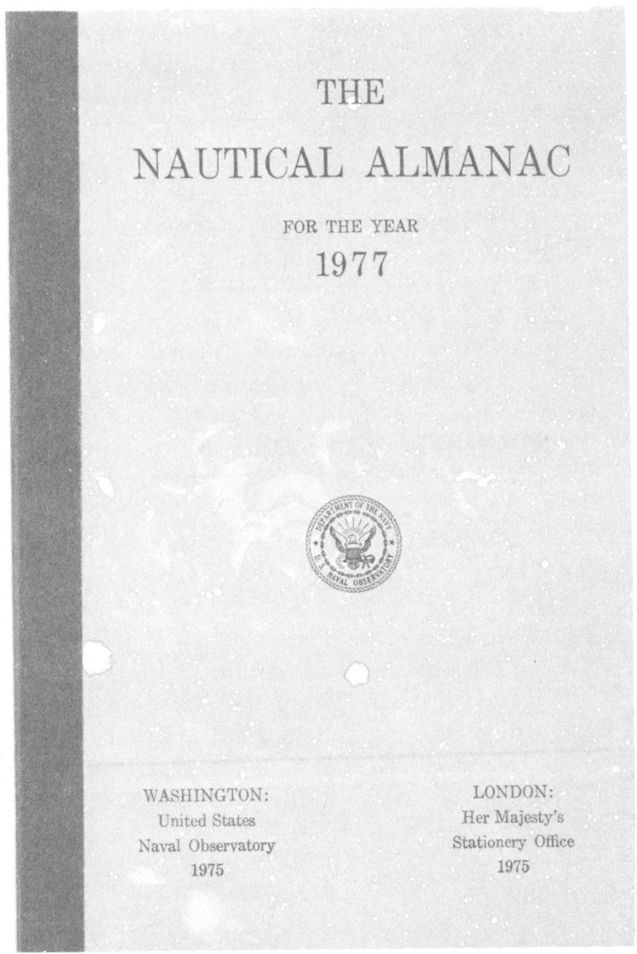

Figure 607. The *Nautical Almanac*, published in annual editions.

Books and manuals **608** Perhaps the best known and most encyclopedic of all navigation books is the *American Practical Navigator,* DMAHC Pub. No. 9, generally referred to simply as *Bowditch.* It first appeared in 1802 and has since been revised many times. The book was originally published because of the need for a simply written, complete text on navigation, with the necessary tables and explanations to permit the relatively uneducated mariner of a century and a half ago to navigate. The book immediately became popular because it was so much better and more reliable than any other book of its time. It has now become primarily a reference book, and will be found in any collection of books on navigation. The latest revision, 1975–1977, is completely updated and is published in two volumes.

Other useful and often used navigation books are:

Navigation Dictionary: DMAHC Pub. No. 220.

Handbook of Magnetic Compass Adjustment & Compensation: DMAHC Pub. No. 226.

Maneuvering Board Manual: DMAHC Pub. No. 217.

Radar Navigation Manual: DMAHC Pub. No. 1310.

609 There are other publications that are of interest to navigators but which do not fit easily into one of the above categories; among these are:

Pilot Charts: published by DMAHC for the North Atlantic Ocean, Chart No. 16, and for the North Pacific Ocean, Chart No. 55. These charts present available data in graphic form which will assist the mariner in selecting the safest and fastest routes. Besides timely information of a varied nature, Pilot Charts graphically depict magnetic variation, currents, prevailing winds and calms, percentage of gales, tracks of tropical and extratropical cyclones, wave heights, surface air and water temperatures, percentage of fog, surface barometric pressure, ice and iceberg limits, the location of ocean weather-station ships, and recommended routes for steam and sailing vessels. Additionally, such topics as winds (including gales and cyclones), pressures, temperatures, visibilities, and wave heights are discussed in brief paragraphs at the sides of each chart. Pilot Charts are now published quarterly with each sheet containing three monthly charts and an article of general information. They are furnished without charge to contributing observers, and automatically to naval vessels after an initial request; they may be purchased in the usual manner by others interested in their contents.

Pilot Charts are published in atlas form (for certain specific prior years) for Central American Waters and the South Atlantic, Pub. No. 106; for the South Pacific and Indian Oceans, Pub. No. 107; and for the Northern North Atlantic, Pub. No. 108.

Radio Navigational Aids: Pub. No. 117A for the Atlantic and Mediterranean Area, and Pub. No. 117B for the Pacific and Indian Ocean Area: published by DMAHC, they contain information on marine direction-finder stations, radiobeacons, Consol stations, Loran, Decca, Racon, Radar, time signals, times and transmission frequencies of navigational warnings, the delineation of *Hydrolant* and *Hydropac* areas, medical advice and quarantine stations, long-range navigational aids, and radio regulations for territorial waters.

Worldwide Marine Weather Broadcasts: published by the National Oceanic and Atmospheric Administration.

International Code of Signals: DMAHC Pub. No. 102: for visual, sound, and radio communications.

Catalog of Nautical Charts: published by DMAHC as Pub. No. 1-N-A, Miscellaneous and Special Purpose Navigational Charts, Sheets, and Publications; Pub. No. 1-N-L, Numerical Listing of Charts; and Pub. No. 1-N (Region No.), nine regional chart catalogs. There is also Pub. No. 1-N-S, Catalog of Classified Charts, for those carrying a security classification; and Pub. No. 1-N-P, Allowance Requirements for Nautical Charts and Publications, for U.S. Navy use only.

Guide to Marine Observing and Reporting: Pub. No. 606 is a collaborative effort of several U.S. governmental agencies to provide detailed guidance for submitting hydrographic and oceanographic reports. Check lists of key questions are included, where appropriate, as a means of ensuring that no essential facts will be inadvertently omitted from a report.

Mariners Weather Log: a pamphlet, and other publications of primary interest in weather observing, instruments, forecasting, cloud forms, etc., are issued by the Environmental Data Service, National Oceanic and Atmospheric Administration (NOAA), Department of Commerce.

Corrective information

610 As charts and other publications accumulate a sufficient number of changes and corrections, they are reprinted as a revision with the same edition number or as a new edition. Certain publications, such as *Light Lists* and *Coast Pilots,* are reprinted on an annual schedule. Other publications may have numbered "changes" issued, usually in the form of reprinted pages for direct insertion into the volume after the superseded pages are removed.

Notices to Mariners

In many instances the importance of the corrected or updated information is such that it cannot be delayed until the next scheduled transmittal of changes, or the revised or new edition. In such cases, the information is included in the weekly *Notice to Mariners* published by DMAHC with the cooperation of NOS and the Coast Guard. This printed pamphlet includes corrections for charts, listed in numerical order, with a separate entry for each chart affected; in order that corrections will not be overlooked, each entry also indicates the number of the *Notice* carrying the last previous correction. New charts and publications and new revised editions are announced in *Notice to Mariners.* This publication also carries corrections for other publications such as *Coast Pilots, Sailing Directions, Light Lists* and *Lists of Lights, Radio Navigational Aids,* and *Fleet Guides.* Small chartlets for pasting onto charts to correct limited areas are printed in the weekly *Notices,* as well as information of general interest to navigators. Broadcast NAVAREA WARNINGS for Areas IV and XII, and *Hydrolant* and *Hydropac* messages for the preceding week are printed in each *Notice.* Quarterly, an issue of *Notices to Mariners* will contain a summary, listing by number the charts affected by changes during that period, with the numbers of applicable *Notices.* Annually, *Notice to Mariners No. 1* includes additional information of continuing interest.

A separate edition of *Notice to Mariners* for the Great Lakes is published by the 9th Coast Guard District for those waters and tributaries east to Montreal, Canada.

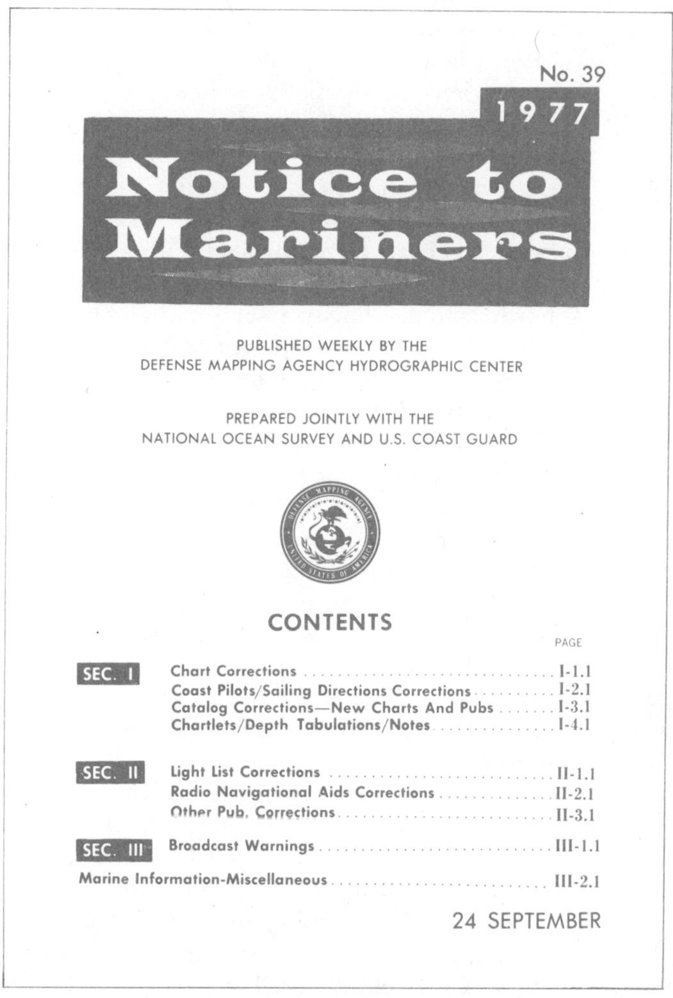

No. 39

1977

Notice to Mariners

PUBLISHED WEEKLY BY THE
DEFENSE MAPPING AGENCY HYDROGRAPHIC CENTER

PREPARED JOINTLY WITH THE
NATIONAL OCEAN SURVEY AND U.S. COAST GUARD

CONTENTS

		PAGE
SEC. I	Chart Corrections	I-1.1
	Coast Pilots/Sailing Directions Corrections	I-2.1
	Catalog Corrections—New Charts And Pubs	I-3.1
	Chartlets/Depth Tabulations/Notes	I-4.1
SEC. II	Light List Corrections	II-1.1
	Radio Navigational Aids Corrections	II-2.1
	Other Pub. Corrections	II-3.1
SEC. III	Broadcast Warnings	III-1.1
Marine Information-Miscellaneous		III-2.1

24 SEPTEMBER

Figure 610a. Information for the correction of charts and certain publications is published weekly in *Notices to Mariners.*

Summary of Corrections Semiannually, DMAHC publishes a *Summary of Corrections* in two volumes—Volume 1 covers the Atlantic, Arctic, and Mediterranean areas; Volume 2 covers the Pacific and Indian Oceans, and Antarctic. These volumes contain the full text of all changes to charts, *Coast Pilots*, and *Sailing Directions.* Each separate issue is cumulative, containing the corrections of previous issues as well as items from the *Notices* of the last six months; when the issues of the *Summary* get too voluminous for convenient use, the DMAHC begins a new series.

If a new edition of a chart is issued during the six-month period, corrections for the old edition are omitted. Charts listed as canceled in a previous *Summary* are not repeated.

Corrections are arranged into regions according to chart number and sequence of issue. The first region consists of World and Ocean Basin charts; this is followed by the geographic chart-numbering regions covered by that volume.

Paste-on corrections such as chartlets, depth tabulations, and chart notes are included in the back portion of the appropriate region. In cases where the paste-on corrections supersede previously issued similar items, only the latest item is included.

The *Summary of Corrections,* with the full text of all changes, is easier to use than the quarterly listings in *Notices to Mariners* which give only the numbers of the charts affected without providing the information necessary to make the change. The *Summary* is particularly valuable in bringing charts fully up to date when they have been obtained some time after their publication date, such as the initial set of charts for a newly commissioned vessel, or when charts have not been used and kept corrected for some time. The *Summary* is *not* a substitute for *Notices to Mariners;* these must still be used for changes affecting *Light Lists, Lists of Lights,* and other navigational publications.

Local Notices to Mariners Since the publications just described are worldwide in scope, changes that are of local interest only, of no concern to ocean-going ships, are omitted. Such information is published in *Local Notices to Mariners,* which are issued separately by each U.S. Coast Guard District at weekly intervals, or as required. The type of information is generally the same as for the worldwide *Notices.*

Radio broadcast warnings Often it is necessary for the safety of navigation to promulgate information without delay; radio broadcasts serve to accomplish this action. A worldwide navigational broadcast warning system having 16 long-range warning areas is operated by member nations of the International Hydrographic Organization; these NAVAREA are shown in Figure 610b. An Area Coordinator is designated for each and is responsible for assembling and evaluating information from various sources and then issuing an appropriate NAVAREA *Warnings* broadcast by a powerful radio station to cover the whole of that Area and parts of adjacent Areas. The various NAVAREAs are subdivided into *Subareas* (in which a number of countries have established a coordinated system for the transmission of coastal warnings) and *Regions* (portions of an Area or Sub-area in which one country has accepted responsibility for the transmission of coastal warnings). Radio broadcast details are contained in DMAHC Pubs. No. 117A and 117B, as kept current by changes published in *Notices to Mariners.*

The United States is Area Coordinator for Areas IV and XII, and is also providing worldwide coverage by continuing the *Hydrolant* and *Hydropac* Navigational Warning System outside Areas IV and XII. (*Hydrolants* cover the Atlantic Ocean, Gulf of Mexico, Caribbean Sea, and contiguous areas; *Hydropacs* cover the Pacific Ocean, Indian Ocean, and contiguous areas.) The location that is affected by information in these messages is indicated by the chart numbering system—region or subregion numerical designators are a part of the *Hydrolant/Hydropac* number.

For U.S. coastal and inland waters, Coast Guard radio stations transmit *Broadcast Notices to Mariners:* in some instances, these may also be transmitted by Navy and/or commercial (public correspondence) radio stations. Information remaining in effect is included in the next issue of *Local Notices to Mariners.* Other countries will generally have somewhat similar broadcasts of warnings relating to defective aids to navigation and other hazards; details on stations, frequencies, time, etc., will be found in *Radio Navigational Aids,* Pub. No. 117A and 117B.

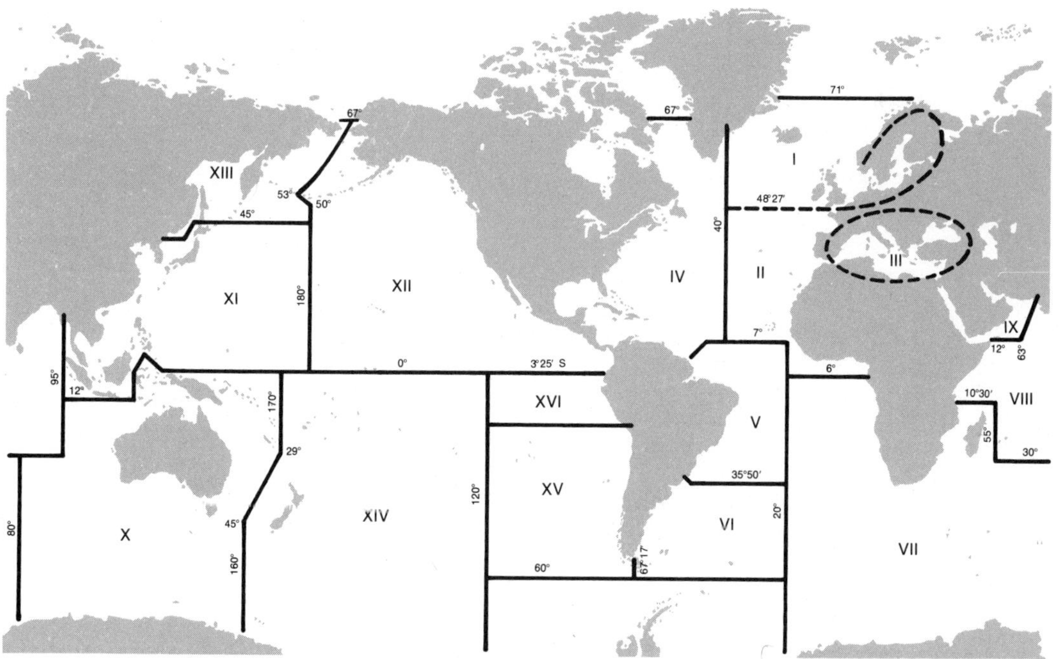

Figure 610b. A system of area responsibilities for radio broadcasts has been established to disseminate navigational safety information.

Other warnings The DMAHC *Daily Memorandum* is issued in two editions, Atlantic and Pacific; both are prepared at DMAHC Headquarters, Washington, D.C. This publication is of value to ships in port, both naval and merchant. Together with other items of navigational interest, each *Daily Memorandum* contains the text of applicable NAVAREA *WARNINGS* for Areas IV and XII and *Hydrolant* and *Hydropac* messages broadcast in the previous 24 hours, or since the last previous working day, with the exception of messages containing satellite ephemeral data.

Special Warnings supplement regular DMAHC messages such as *Hydrolants* and *Hydropacs*; they are used primarily for the dissemination of official governmental proclamations affecting commercial shipping restrictions. These warnings are consecutively numbered and are given further publicity in the *Daily Memorandum* and *Notices to Mariners.*

Summary **611** A navigator has many sources of information available to him to ensure the safe and efficient passage of his ship; a well-organized system exists to provide the latest data for keeping charts and other publications up to date. He should know what is available to him, and how to obtain it. The navigator of a vessel of any size should get and study the applicable publications and charts covering his operating areas; such studying should be done well in advance of the need for the knowledge—a time of danger or emergency is *not* the time to be hastily thumbing through an unfamiliar publication.

Failure to have on board and use the *latest* charts and other publications, *and to keep them corrected,* may adversely affect a mariner's legal position should he have a grounding, collision, or other mishap in which chart or publication information is involved.

7 Instruments for Piloting

Introduction **701** Navigation is both a science and an art, and the navigator must recognize this in the performance of his duties. This chapter will describe some of the instruments and devices available to the navigator in his practice of the science and art of navigation. These are the tools of his profession, which he uses in determining the position of his ship and in guiding it safely on its way.

Navigational instruments can be classified in various ways, any of which will result in some overlap. They will be considered here in groups according to their primary purpose—for measuring *direction, speed* and *distance, depth,* and *weather conditions;* for use in *plotting;* and for *miscellaneous* use. Earlier chapters have considered the compass, and other "instruments" such as charts and publications. Sextants and chronometers will be covered later in the chapters which describe celestial navigation.

DIRECTION

Compasses **702** The two general types of compasses are: *magnetic compass,* which depends on the earth's magnetic field for its directive force; and *gyrocompass,* which depends upon the inherent space stability of a rapidly spinning wheel plus mechanical or electrical torquing to keep its axis aligned with that of the earth. Marine compasses were discussed in Chapter 4.

Gyrocompass repeaters **703** A gyrocompass can transmit constant indications of true headings electrically to *gyrocompass repeaters* located at various positions throughout the ship. It resembles a magnetic compass in appearance, but unlike a magnetic compass it may be mounted in any position.

Azimuth circles **704** The term *azimuth,* as generally used, means the *bearing* of a celestial body. The terms *azimuth* and *bearing* are often used interchangeably to mean the *direction* of an object from the observer. Bearings and azimuths are expressed in degrees, using three digits, from 000° at north clockwise through 360°. True azimuth or bearing refers to the direction with respect to true north, magnetic azimuth with respect to magnetic north, and compass azimuth with respect to compass north. A *relative* bearing or azimuth is reckoned from the ship's head, measuring clockwise with 000° being dead ahead.

An *azimuth circle* is an instrument for determining both *bearings* of terrestrial objects and *azimuths* of celestial objects. It consists of a nonmagnetic ring formed to fit snugly over the top of a compass bowl (or onto the top of a gyrocompass repeater), about which it can be turned to any desired direction. Its inner lip is graduated from 0° to 360°, *counterclockwise,* for measuring relative bearings. An azimuth circle is shown in Figure 704. On one diameter of this ring is mounted a pair of sighting vanes, consisting of a peep vane (*A*) at one end of the diameter and a vertical wire mounted in a suitable frame at the other end (*B*). To observe the bearing of a terrestrial object the observer looks through the peep vane in the direction of the object and by means of the finger lugs (*C, C'*) provided on the circle, he turns the latter until the observed object appears on the vertical wire of the opposite vane. At the base of the opposite vane is a mirror (*D*) marked with a center line agreeing with the vertical wire of the vane. This mirror reflects the compass card into the field of view of the observer so that he can see the observed object and the compass card at the same time. The compass bearing of the observed object is then read by the position of the vertical wire on the compass card.

There is a reflector of dark glass (*E*) attached to the far vane (called *far* vane because it is *farther* from the eye, in observing, than the peep vane). The reflector is movable about a horizontal axis, enabling the observer to adjust it so that the reflected image of a celestial body can be brought to his eye, and a compass azimuth obtained as has been described for a terrestrial object.

At right angles to the line of sight of the pair of vanes just described, there is placed a second set of observing devices, designed

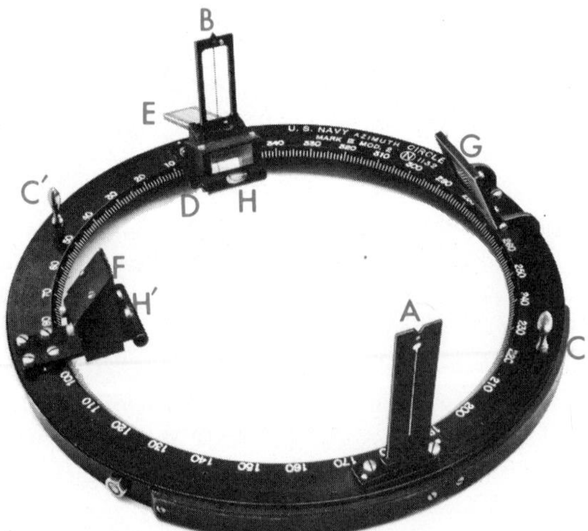

Figure 704. Azimuth circle to fit U.S. Navy standard 7½-inch compass.

especially for obtaining the compass azimuth of the sun. At one extremity of the diameter on which these appliances are mounted is a 45° reflecting prism encased in a metal housing (*F*). This housing is provided with a narrow slit in which light may be received from a concave mirror diametrically opposite (*G*), the slit being in the focus of the concave mirror. Light so received is reflected downward by the prism and appears on the graduations of the compass card as a bright narrow band. To observe the compass bearing of the sun with this arrangement, the observer turns the azimuth circle until the sun's rays are reflected by the mirror across the card to the prism, when the bearing can be read on the compass card by means of the narrow band of light.

Two leveling bubbles (*H, H'*) are provided, for the azimuth circle should be truly horizontal at the moment of observation if accurate azimuths or bearings are to be obtained.

Relative bearings or azimuths can be obtained by reading the graduations of the azimuth circle against a mark on the bezel ring, colinear with the lubber's line of the compass. (See Article 407.)

An azimuth circle without the prism-mirror appliance for sun observation is called a *bearing circle.* It serves the same purpose as an azimuth circle except that azimuths of the sun are not as conveniently measured.

Telescopic alidades

705 A *telescopic alidade* is similar to a bearing circle except that the azimuth circle mounts a telescope instead of the sighting vanes. The telescope contains a reticle for greater precision in taking bearings. The image is magnified, making distant objects appear larger to the observer. A prism arrangement which reflects the bearing of the object from the compass card enables the observer to sight the object and its bearing simultaneously.

Peloruses

706 Since a clear view in all directions may be unobtainable from the compass, *peloruses* (Figure 706) or dumb compasses may be mounted at convenient points, such as the wings of a bridge.

A pelorus consists essentially of a flat, nonmagnetic, metallic ring mounted in gimbals on a vertical stand. The inner edge of the ring is graduated in degrees from 0° at the ship's head clockwise through 360°. This ring snugly encloses a compass card called a *pelorus card.* The card, flush with the ring and the top of the bowl, is rotatable, so that any chosen degree of its graduation may be set to the lubber's line. A small set screw is provided for temporarily securing the card to the ring. Upon the card is mounted a pair of sighting vanes similar to those of a bearing circle. They may be revolved about the center of the card, *independently of the card itself,* and held in any desired position by a central clamp screw. On some models an electric light inside the stand illuminates the card from underneath for night work.

Figure 706. A pelorus.

Taking true bearings

True bearings are obtained as follows: set the pelorus to the ship's *true* course, by turning the card until its true-course graduation coincides with the lubber's line. Secure the card. Line up the sighting vanes approximately on the object to be observed. Direct the steersman to say "Mark! Mark! Mark!" when he is steady on his steering compass course, and when he does so, take the bearing exactly, and read the degree on the card as indicated by the sighting vanes.

As an alternative method of obtaining a true bearing, the navigator gives the steersman a warning "Stand by!" followed by a "Mark!" at the instant of the observation. If the steersman was on his course, the bearing was *true*. If not, it may be corrected by applying the number of degrees the steersman was off, being careful to apply the correction in the right direction.

Magnetic bearings

Magnetic or compass bearings are taken in exactly the same manner as true bearings, the pelorus card being set beforehand to the magnetic or compass course, respectively. By applying to such bearings the variation or the compass error, as appropriate, they can be converted to true bearings (Article 412) for plotting on a chart.

Relative bearings

The pelorus is used for taking relative bearings by setting the 0° graduation of the card to the lubber's line and observing the object. Relative bearings are converted to true bearings for plotting by adding to the bearings observed the true heading of the ship. In most modern installations, a gyro repeater is mounted in the pelorus stand in place of the pelorus card so that gyro bearings can be obtained directly.

SPEED AND DISTANCE

Types of logs **707** The *chip log,* or *ship log,* to determine a vessel's speed was invented in the sixteenth century; it consisted of a piece of wood in the shape of a quadrant, weighted with lead at the center of the circular side. This log chip, as it was called, was secured to a bridle at each corner; the bridle, in turn, was secured to the log line. At one corner of the log chip, the bridle was held by a wooden peg so arranged that a sharp tug on the log line would pull out the peg, allowing the chip to be hauled back on board readily.

The log line was wound on a free turning reel. To determine speed, the log chip was put overboard where it floated vertically due to its ballasting. A considerable length of log line was let out to get the log chip into undisturbed water astern where its resistance to forward motion kept it essentially stationary in the water; as the ship moved forward, the line was pulled off the reel. When the first knotted marker on the line passed off the reel, timing was started; at the end of a definite period, the line was seized and the number of knots in the line that had paid out were counted to determine the vessel's speed. From this arose the present use of the term *knot* to designate one nautical mile per hour.

The timing was originally done by reciting certain religious sentences, which, in theory, required an exact amount of time. Later, a sand glass was employed. This was usually a 30-second timer, and gave far more accurate results.

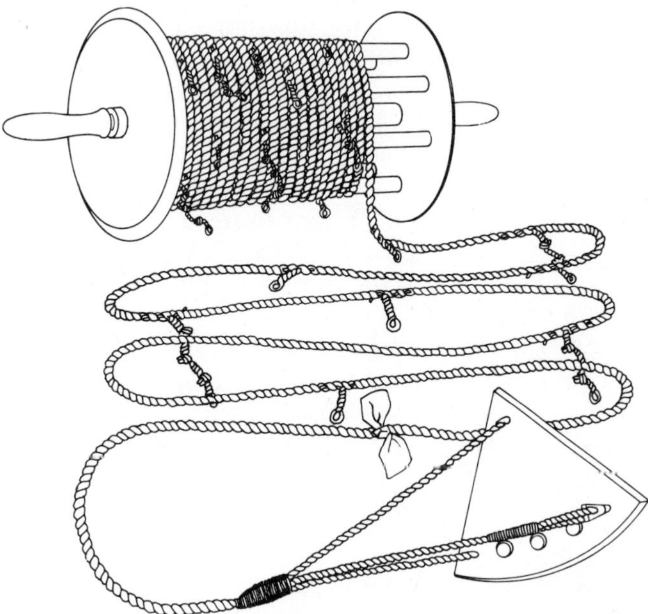

Figure 707. A chip log, or ship log formerly used to determine a vessel's speed.

Modern logs Three types of modern logs are in general use on ships, some of which determine distance traveled as well as speed. These are: the pitot-static log, the impeller type, and the electromagnetic (EM) log. These logs all require the use of a *rodmeter* projecting through the bottom of the ship into the water. The rodmeter contains the sensing device used to determine speed. As the rodmeter can be damaged by striking submerged objects, it may be necessary to retract the unit in shallow water. A sea valve forms a support for the rodmeter and provides a means for closing the hull opening when the rodmeter is withdrawn or housed. The various logs have a remotely located *indicator-transmitter* housing the electrical or electromechanical parts. The signal received from the sensing device is converted into a readout of speed and distance traveled which can be transmitted by synchronous motors or electronically to display units throughout the ship.

The dead-reckoning analyzer (Article 723), the modern gyrocompass, and various navigational computers require an automatic input of speed which is also transmitted from the indicator-transmitter unit of the log.

Pitot-static log **708** The rodmeter assembly of a pitot-static log detects both dynamic and static pressure. As a ship moves through the water, the forward side of the rodmeter is exposed to *dynamic* pressure which is proportional to the speed of the ship. Dynamic pressure is defined as the pressure on a surface resulting from a fluid in motion against that surface; it includes static pressure as well as that from the flow of the fluid. The pressure of still water is called *static* pressure. A *pitot tube* is a device by which the difference in dynamic and static pressures may be detected. Obviously, the difference of the two pressures will vary with the speed of the ship. The device consists of two tubes, one inside the other. One tube opens forward and is subjected to dynamic pressure when the ship is in motion; the other opens athwartship and is exposed only to static pressure.

The control unit for converting the pressure indications into speed units consists of a sensitive bellows arrangement connected to the dynamic and static orifices of the rodmeter. Suitable mechanical and electrical linkage converts the movement of the bellows into rotary motion for transmission to the speed and distance indicators by self-synchronous motors.

Two types differing slightly in construction but using the pitot-static principle are in general use. They are commonly known as the Pitometer Log and the Bendix Underwater Log.

Impeller-type logs **709** The *Impeller Type* Underwater Log System uses a propeller to produce an electrical impulse by which the speed and distance traveled are indicated. Typically, a rodmeter head is projected about 2 feet from the vessel through the sea valve. The head assembly contains an

8-pole, two-phase, propeller-driven frequency generator. The impeller is driven by the water as the impeller moves through it. The frequency generated is directly proportional to ship's speed.

The output of the generator is amplified and passed to a master transmitter indicator where the number of alternations, reduced by gears, shows the mileage on a dial. The frequency of the alternating current, being proportional to the speed of the ship, is transmitted to the tachometer mechanism which indicates the speed of the ship.

The speed and distance readings at the master transmitter indicator are repeated at remote indicators by means of electrical synchrotransmission.

Electromagnetic log

710 The *electromagnetic* (EM) log is generally calibrated for speeds from 0 to 40 knots. Components are shown in Figure 710a. The rodmeter (*A*), which can be fixed to the hull, is generally retractable through a sea valve (*B*), as described in Article 707. It is an induction device which produces a signal voltage that varies with the speed of the ship through the water. Any conductor will produce an electromagnetic field or voltage when it is moved across a magnetic field, or when a magnetic field is moved with respect to the conductor. It is this relative movement of the conductor and the magnetic field producing a measurable induced signal voltage which is used in the EM log.

Figure 710a. Underwater log equipment; electromagnetic type, 0–40 knots.

Figure 710b shows a cutaway view of the sensing unit in the rodmeter. The magnetic field, produced by a coil in the sensing unit, is set up in the water in which the ship is floating. Two Monel buttons, one on each side of the rodmeter, pick up the induced voltage as the ship moves through the water. A complete discussion of the principle involved and instructions for adjustment and repair is included in the manual supplied with each instrument.

The *indicator-transmitter*—labeled (*C*) in Figure 710a—contains all the electrical and electromechanical parts of the log except the components in the rodmeter and remote control unit. It indicates the ship's speed on a dial, and operates synchro-transmitters to generate corresponding synchro-signals for transmission to receivers located elsewhere in the ship. It also registers the number of miles the ship has steamed. Provision is made in the indicator-transmitter for calibrating the log.

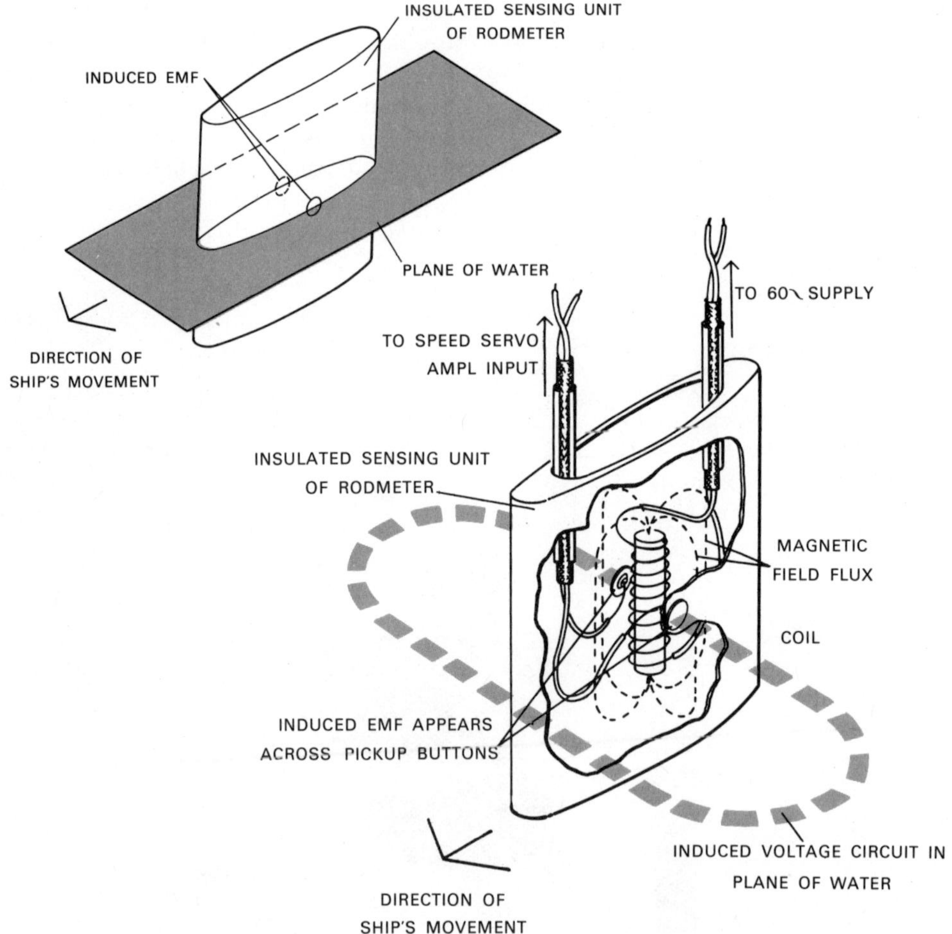

Figure 710b. Rodmeter sensing unit functional schematic.

The *remote control unit*—labeled (*D*) in Figure 710a—is used to set speed into the indicator-transmitter when the equipment is being operated as a dummy log. (See Article 711).

In addition to the ship's forward motion, pitching and rolling will produce output signals from the rodmeter, which could lead to an indicated speed that is too high. Provision is made in the indicator-transmitter so that these undesirable signals can be rejected.

RPM counters

711 The *engine revolution counters* provide a convenient means of determining speed and distance. One of these instruments is provided in the engine room for each shaft; repeating indicators may be installed on the bridge. They automatically count the revolutions of the propellers, and show the total count continuously on their dials. By means of a master counter, connected to the individual counters, the average revolutions made by all propellers can be obtained. The number of revolutions made during any interval of time can be determined by taking the difference in the readings at the beginning and the end of the interval, and if such difference is divided by the number of revolutions required to drive the ship one mile, then the distance traveled in miles is obtained. The records of the acceptance speed trials of a ship furnish data as to the revolutions required for a mile, as well as revolutions per minute (RPM) for various speeds. Such data can also be derived from trial runs made by the ship over a measured mile, a number of which are available for the purpose. This information is used to construct a curve with RPM as ordinates and corresponding speed in knots as abscissas. From the curve, a *revolution table* is made out for use on the bridge while underway. It gives the RPM required for each knot of speed. In making use of engine revolutions as speed indicators, the draft of the ship, the condition of its bottom as to cleanliness, and the state of the sea must be considered.

The *dummy log* is used underway when the ship's regular log is inoperative to supply speed information to the Dead Reckoning Tracer (DRT) (Article 723), the gyrocompass, and various computers throughout the ship. An estimate of the ship's speed, based on the propeller RPM, is set by hand on the dummy log.

Doppler

The use of highly complex *Doppler* equipment—see Chapter 37—gives speed *over the bottom* which can be integrated for distance made good; it does not yield speed through the water as do the devices previously described in this section.

Small-craft logs and speedometers

712 On small craft, the term *speedometer* is commonly used to designate devices which measure speed only. The term *log* is applied to instruments that measure speed or distance, or both. Simplified versions of all three types discussed for larger vessels are used on commercial and recreational boats.

On smaller, faster boats, the common type of speedometer is a simple form of pitot-static log with the indicating meter coupled directly to the sensing head by a length of tubing. The principal fault of this type is its lack of sensitivity at low speeds. On larger and slower boats, the impeller type is used in a rather "miniaturized" version. A small propeller-shaped or millwheel-design rotor projects from the hull a few inches; it may be fixed, or retractable for cleaning (problems of fouling with grass and weeds are not unknown). Indications of speed may be transmitted from the sensor to the indicator either mechanically or electrically. Many models include a means for determining and indicating distance as well as speed.

A design unique to boats is the *strut* type shown in Figure 712. The strut at the zero speed position is raked aft at an angle of about 45°, which helps to reduce fouling by weeds. As the boat moves forward, water pressure tends to deflect the strut; this deflection is sensed and converted to a speed reading. Electronic circuit design can yield very sensitive readings; some models can be switched into an ultrasensitive mode which, rather than indicating absolute speed, shows the slightest

Figure 712. Small-craft speedometer, strut type.

change in speed; this is valuable information for adjusting the trim of sails, especially in racing. Damping is also available electronically for a more steady reading in rough seas.

A few models of the electromagnetic type have appeared for boats. Although more expensive than the *impeller* type, this design avoids the problem of fouling with weeds or marine growth that will adversely affect an impeller which cannot be withdrawn into the hull when not in use.

The indicator-transmitter unit can also contain components, normally electronic, to *integrate* speed with respect to time in order to provide an output of distance.

Many boats depend upon a *tachometer* giving engine RPM for a determination of speed. An RPM vs. speed table is prepared on a measured mile or other course of known length, and a graph is plotted as described for ships in Article 711.

A few small craft, chiefly ocean-cruising sailboats, still use the traditional *taffrail log*. This consists of a rotor, streamed at the end of a braided log line sufficiently far astern to be clear of the wake effect. The log line is connected to an indicating device, usually reading nautical miles and tenths on two separate dials. In sailing ships, this indicator was frequently attached to the taffrail, the hand rail at the after end of the ship, hence the name.

Good taffrail logs are quite reliable, although all logs tend to over-read slightly when moving through a head sea, and to under-read with a following sea.

Stadimeters **713** The *stadimeter* is an instrument for measuring the distance of objects of known heights, between 50 and 200 feet, covering ranges from 200 to 10,000 yards. Other ranges can be measured by using a scale factor for the graduations. The two general types in use, the Fisk and the Brandon sextant type, are illustrated in Figure 713.

The Fisk type stadimeter consists of a rectangular metal frame upon which is pivoted an index arm graduated in feet. The arm bears an index mirror directly above the pivot. By moving the arm this mirror is rotated through a small arc, providing the necessary adjustment between the direct and reflected images as viewed through the sighting telescope. The stadimeter measures the angle subtended by the object of known height, and converts it into range, which is read directly from a micrometer drum attached to a pointer which moves the index arm. The instrument is initially set for the known height of the object by moving the carriage holding the drum and pointer along the index arm. The drum is then turned until the top of the reflected image is brought into coincidence with the bottom of the direct image, and the range read.

The Brandon sextant-type stadimeter uses the same principle as the Fisk type, but the construction is different. The frame, similar in appearance to a sextant frame, has mounted upon it two pivoted arms,

Figure 713. Stadimeter. Brandon sextant type (upper); Fisk type (lower).

the index arm and radius arm. The index arm bears the index mirror directly above the pivot. Rotation of the micrometer drum moves the index arm, accomplishing the rotation of the index mirror necessary for the desired coincidence of images.

The adjustment of the stadimeter is similar to that of a sextant as described in Chapter 21.

Distances of objects can also be ascertained by determining the angle subtended by an object of known height, as measured by a sextant. The angle so measured can be converted to distance by means of trigonometry or Table 9 in *Bowditch*.

DEPTH

Hand lead and deep sea lead

714 The *lead* (pronounced led), for determining the depth of water, consists essentially of a lead weight attached to one end of a suitably marked line. Developed from the *sounding pole,* it is undoubtedly the oldest of piloting instruments with an origin lost in antiquity. The practice of taking soundings probably began with man's earliest ventures onto the waters. The first man who ran his dugout onto a shoal soon learned that he needed some way to find the depth of the water, preferably as he was moving. Possibly he used a pole at first, but the sounding line soon followed. From the *Historia* of the Greek historian, Herodotus, one learns that it was in use in and about the mouth of the Nile in the fourth century B.C.: "When one gets 11 fathoms and ooze on the lead, he is one day's journey from Alexandria." Note that so long ago the term "fathom" was in use, and that the nature of the bottom was of navigational significance. Although rather completely replaced by electronic depth sounders, a lead can be a very valuable back-up "tool" for the navigator, particularly in "thick" (foggy) weather and shallow waters.

Two leads are used for soundings: the hand lead, weighing from 7 to 14 pounds, with a line marked to about 25 fathoms; and the deep-sea lead, weighing from 30 to 100 pounds, the line being 100 fathoms or more in length.

Lines are generally marked as follows:	*Metric Equivalent*
2 fathoms from the lead, with 2 strips of leather	3.66 meters
3 fathoms from the lead, with 3 strips of leather	5.49
5 fathoms from the lead, with a white rag	9.14
7 fathoms from the lead, with a reg rag	12.80
10 fathoms from the lead, with leather having a hole in it	18.29
13 fathoms from the lead, same as at 3 fathoms	23.77
15 fathoms from the lead, same as at 5 fathoms	27.43
17 fathoms from the lead, same as at 7 fathoms	31.09
20 fathoms from the lead, a line with 2 knots	36.58
25 fathoms from the lead, a line with 1 knot	45.72
30 fathoms from the lead, a line with 3 knots	54.86
35 fathoms from the lead, a line with 1 knot	64.01
40 fathoms from the lead, a line with 4 knots	73.15

Fathoms which correspond with the depths marked are called *marks* and intermediate fathoms are called *deeps.* The only fractions of a fathom used are a half and a quarter.

A practice sometimes followed is to mark the hand lead line in feet at the critical depths of the vessel using it.

Lead lines should be measured frequently while wet and the correctness of the marking verified. The distance from the leadsman's hand to the water's edge should be ascertained in order that proper allowance may be made in taking soundings at night.

A lead may be *armed* by filling its hollow lower end with tallow or salt water soap, by which means a sample of the bottom sediment is brought up.

Boatmen often use a lead with a weight of 2 to 5 pounds on a line of 20 to 30 feet. The line is normally marked with plastic tags giving the depth directly in feet or meters.

Echo sounder **715** A sound generated in the water will echo from the bottom and can be received by a microphone. Since the approximate speed of sound in water is known, the depth can be determined by measuring the time interval between the generation of the sound and the return of the echo, according to the formula, depth = speed $\times\frac{1}{2}$ time interval between sound and echo.

The speed of sound waves in water varies with temperature, salinity, and pressure; but an average value of 4,800 feet per second is sufficiently accurate for navigational depth finding (particularly if the same assumed speed was used for the surveys which produced the depth information on the charts used). This being equivalent to 800 fathoms per second, an elapsed time of one second would indicate a depth of 400 fathoms.

Devices for measuring depth in this manner are variously known as *echo sounders* or *electronic depth sounders.* (The term "fathometer" is sometimes used, but this is properly applied only to the equipment of one manufacturer whose trademark it is.)

The essential components of an echo sounder are a transmitter, a transducer, a receiver, and an indicator or recorder. Echo sounders are divided into two general classes: (1) sonic, those using sound waves

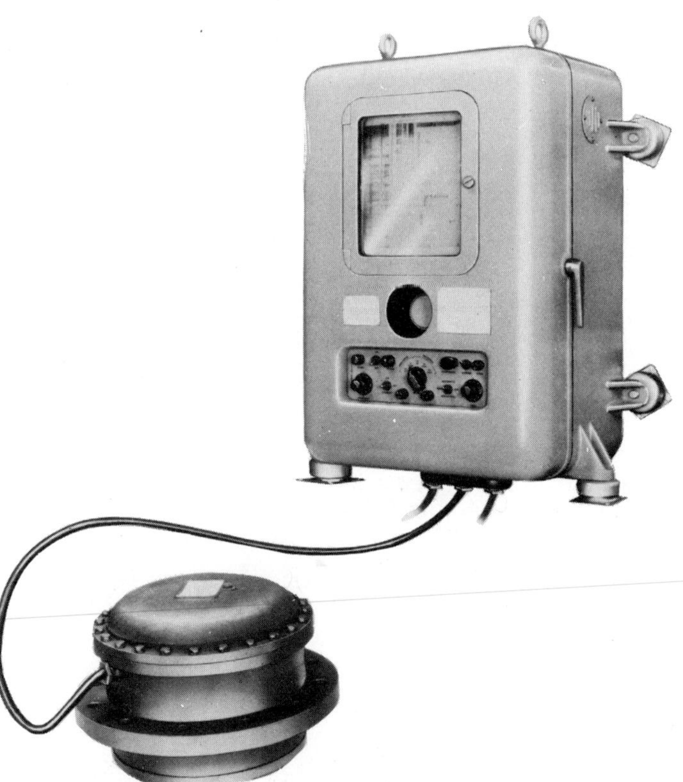

Figure 715a. Echo-sounding equipment, AN/UQN-1.

in the audible range and (2) ultrasonic, those using sound waves in the high-pitch range above audibility. In the first category, the sound is produced mechanically or by an oscillator, which is a diaphragm built into the ship's bottom. The echo is received by a microphone, amplified, and the energy thus obtained is used to flash a lamp in the depth indicator. In the second type, a diaphragm in contact with the water is vibrated by the contraction of quartz crystals in an electric circuit. The same diaphragm is used to receive the echo, which is amplified and fed into the depth indicator.

Echo sounders vary greatly in detail, but all operate on the same principle and measure the elapsed time for a signal to go to the bottom and echo back. A shaft driven by a constant-speed motor carries a contact maker and a device on an arm to illuminate the depth scale. The illuminating device, thus traveling in a circle, is just under a transparent scale graduated in fathoms or feet. When the arm passes under the zero of the scale, the contact maker closes and the signal is transmitted. When the echo is received, a flash of light is thrown on the scale, indicating the depth.

Many echo-sounding instruments are also equipped to record the depth graphically, usually by means of a hot stylus and sensitized paper. The AN/UQN-1 installed aboard many naval vessels is such an instrument. With this instrument, the operator has a choice of two indicators or direct depth readouts, one to a maximum depth of 100 feet, and the other to 100 fathoms. Alternatively, he has the choice of three graphic or recorder readouts, these depth ranges being to 600 feet, 600 fathoms, or 6,000 fathoms. Figure 715b illustrates depths recorded on these three scales; the trace on the left shows the depth

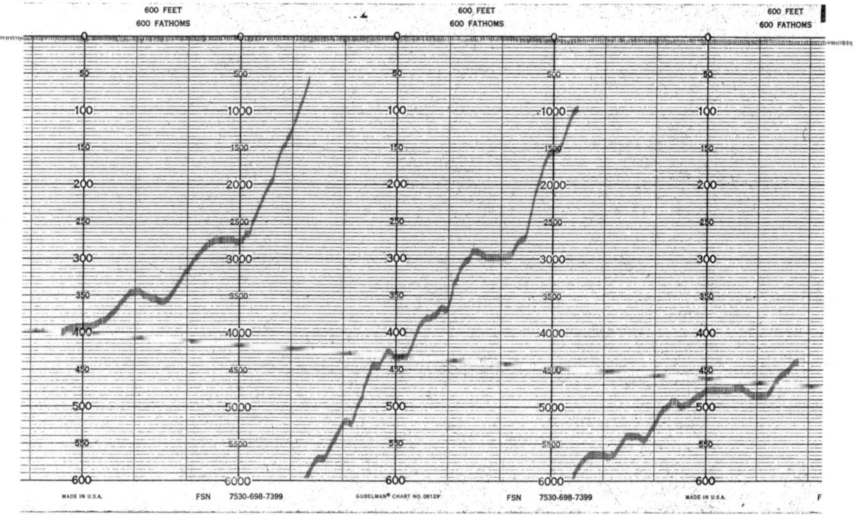

Figure 715b. Depth recording on three scales, showing a steady decrease in depth.

decreasing from 4,000 fathoms to roughly 600 fathoms, when the scale is shifted and the second trace starts; then at 100 fathoms, the scale is again shifted as the depths decrease from 600 feet to 450 feet. The horizontal trace at the top of the paper is the mark of the outgoing pulse. *It is essential that the navigator be certain which scale is being used at any time.*

Echo sounders of modern design used on small craft may indicate depths by a meter reading or direct digital readouts, in addition to the older flashing light and recording models. Scales emphasize the shallower depths of greater interest to boats, with readings in feet, fathoms, or meters.

A U.S. Navy precision echo sounder of more recent design, the AN/UQN-4, is described in Article 3603.

PLOTTING EQUIPMENT

Plotting tools **716** Most lines on a chart are ruled by means of a straightedge. Because of the width of the pencil lead and the conical shape of the sharpened end, the line ruled on the chart is a slight distance from the straightedge. Allowance for this distance must be made when placing the straightedge in position. The actual amount is easily determined by trial and error. The important point to remember is that the pencil must make the same angle with respect to the straightedge throughout the length of the line.

Use No. 2 pencils for plotting and keep a number of them handy and well sharpened. Hexagonal pencils are less likely to roll off a chart table than round pencils.

Draw only light lines on the chart, so that they can be easily erased. Avoid drawing lines longer than necessary and erase extra lengths. Label all lines and points as soon as drawn. An unlabeled line on a chart is a possible source of error. Avoid drawing lines through chart symbols for navigational aids, so that the symbols will not be indistinct when the line is later erased.

A soft eraser, such as the "Pink Pearl" type, should be used for making small erasures. An "art gum" eraser is best for the more general cleaning of a chart.

Dividers **717** Dividers are frequently used by the navigator. He keeps them handy for immediate use, primarily for measuring distance on the chart, but they have many other uses, also.

Learn to use the dividers with one hand, keeping the other hand free for other purposes. With a little practice this can be done easily and it will speed up plotting considerably. The dividers should be tight enough to remain as set, but not so tight that setting is difficult. If there is any choice, pick a pair of dividers with long legs, so that considerable distances can be measured with one setting; see Figure 717a.

It is frequently desirable to have a second pair of dividers of the "bow" style in which the distance between the points is set, and maintained, by a cross arm with a setting screw; see Figure 717b. These can be set to a specific distance and left with assurance that they will not be changed accidentally.

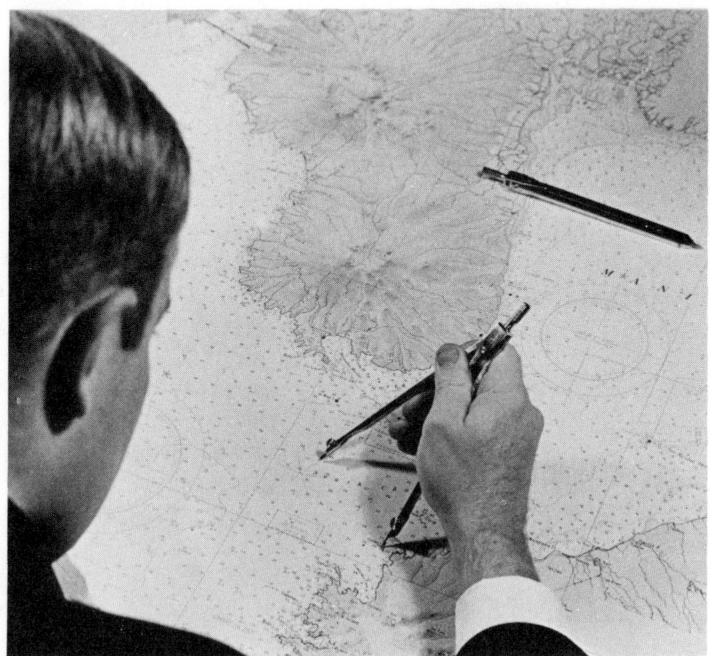

Figure 717a. Dividers are a basic plotting tool.

Figure 717b. "Bow" dividers are particularly useful as their setting cannot be accidentally changed.

Compasses **718** Compasses are convenient for drawing distance circles. They are used most frequently for drawing in computed visibility circles of lights, but they are also useful in drawing circles of position when the range of an object is known, for drawing circles of position for high altitude celestial observations, and other purposes.

The statement regarding the use, adjustment, and selection of dividers applies also to compasses. The pencil point must be kept well-sharpened for neat and accurate work.

Parallel rulers **719** Although various types of plotters have appeared, and some of these are widely used, parallel rulers are still used for measuring direction on a chart. Several types of parallel rulers are available. The best known consists of two bars of the same length connected in such a manner that when one is held in place on the chart and the other moved, it will move parallel to itself, or to its original direction.

Parallel rulers are used for drawing straight lines, moving lines parallel to themselves, as in advancing lines of position, and for measuring direction. When the direction of a line is to be measured, the line is moved parallel to itself to the center of a *compass rose* and its direction is read from the graduations of the compass rose. To plot a given direction from a point, the direction is transferred from the compass rose to the point.

Plotters **720** Parallel rulers are somewhat slow and it is sometimes difficult to keep them from slipping when a direction is to be moved a considerable distance across the chart. Moreover, they are of little value for measuring direction when no compass rose is shown on the chart, as on those of the Lambert conformal projection.

For these reasons and as a matter of personal preference, many navigators use one of the various plotters that are available. Most of these consist of some form of protractor and a straightedge.

A typical plotter is the *Weems Mark II;* it is a plotter-protractor of 180°, mounted on a scaled straightedge, intended primarily for measuring courses or bearings relative to a meridian. An auxiliary scale is included which permits measuring from a parallel. In Figure 720a this auxiliary scale is being used on a parallel of latitude to measure a true course from *A* to *B* of 186°. The Mark II Plotter was designed primarily for aircraft use, but it can be used on any chart which contains distance scales to match, or with plotting sheets. A similar plotter, the No. 641, contains distance scales at 20 miles to the inch matching the Universal Plotting Sheets.

The Paraline Plotter, Figure 720b, is a device that can be used as either a plotter or a roller-type parallel ruler. It is convenient for use on small craft and has been adopted by many ship navigators.

A pair of ordinary draftsman's triangles are also useful in plotting; they need not be of the same type or size. The two hypotenuse (long-

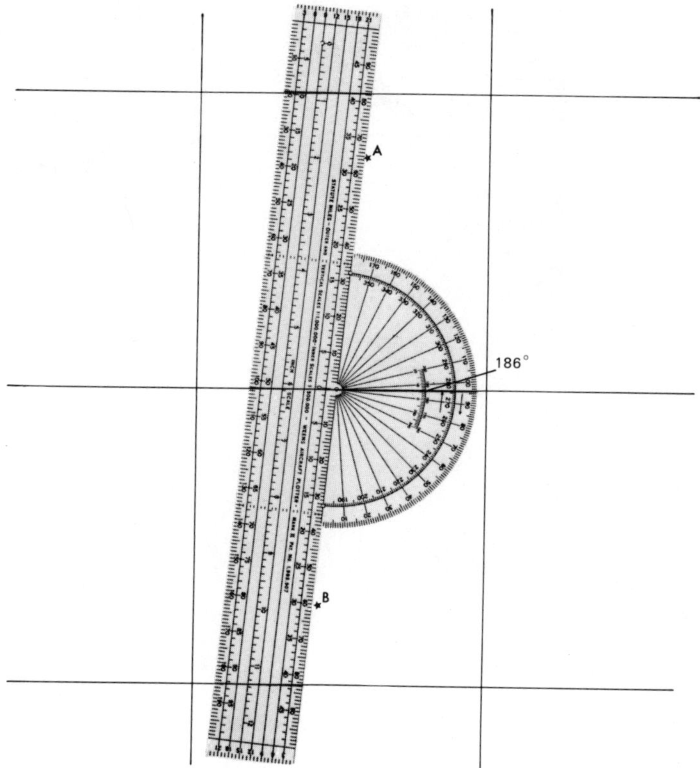

Figure 720a. Mark II Plotter.

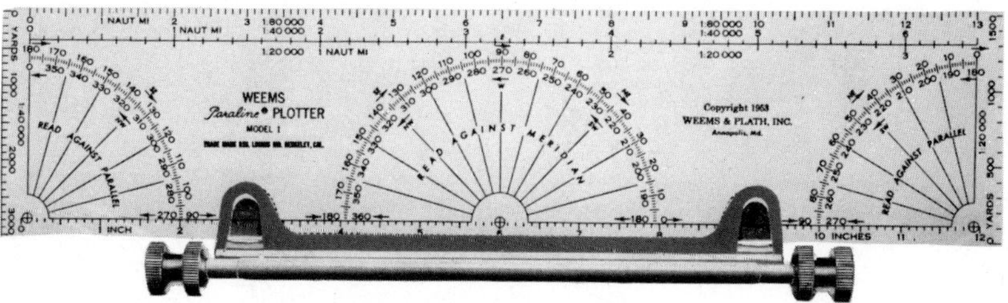

Figure 720b. Weems Paraline Plotter.

est) sides are placed together and the pair is aligned so that the chart line or desired direction is along one of the other four sides; see Figure 720c. By holding one triangle firmly in place and sliding the other with respect to it, alternating between them if the distance is great, the original direction, or one at right angles to it, can be transferred across the chart. The use of two triangles provides an easy and accurate means of drawing both a line and another line at right angles to the first one as is needed when plotting celestial sight reductions.

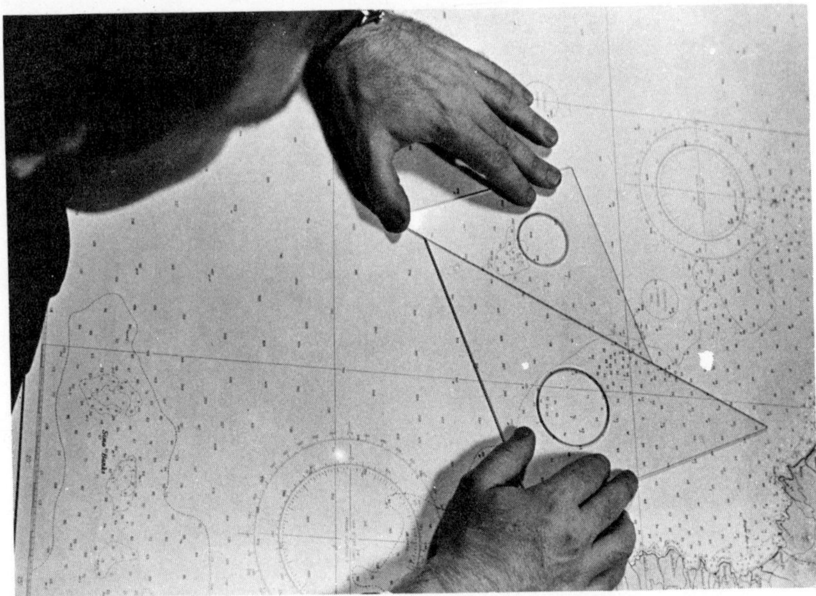

Figure 720c. Two drafting triangles can be used to transfer directions across a chart.

Universal drafting machine

721 Chart plotting on most large ships is done by means of a *drafting machine,* also called a *parallel motion protractor;* Figure 721 illustrates a typical model. The instrument consists of a protractor carried by a parallel-motion linkage system fastened to the upper left-hand corner of the chart table. The linkage permits the movement of the protractor to any part of the chart without change of orientation. Several graduated rulers of different length are provided. On some models any two of these can be mounted, one as shown and the other at right angles to the first, to facilitate plotting of lines of position from celestial observations. However, most navigators prefer to use a right triangle to obtain the perpendicular. The graduated protractor rim, or compass rose, can be rotated and clamped in any position desired. Hence, it can be oriented to directions on the chart.

Protractors

722 While not essential, a common protractor is sometimes useful for measuring angles. Any type will do, but a fairly large one made of transparent plastic is most desirable. One model has several small cutouts in its face so that it can be used for drawing standard plotting symbols. A special type of protractor with three arms is useful for plotting the position of a ship. The middle arm is fixed and the others movable so that they can be set at essentially any angle to the fixed arm. A complete description of this instrument and the method of using it is given in Article 1110; the instrument is illustrated in Figure 1110a.

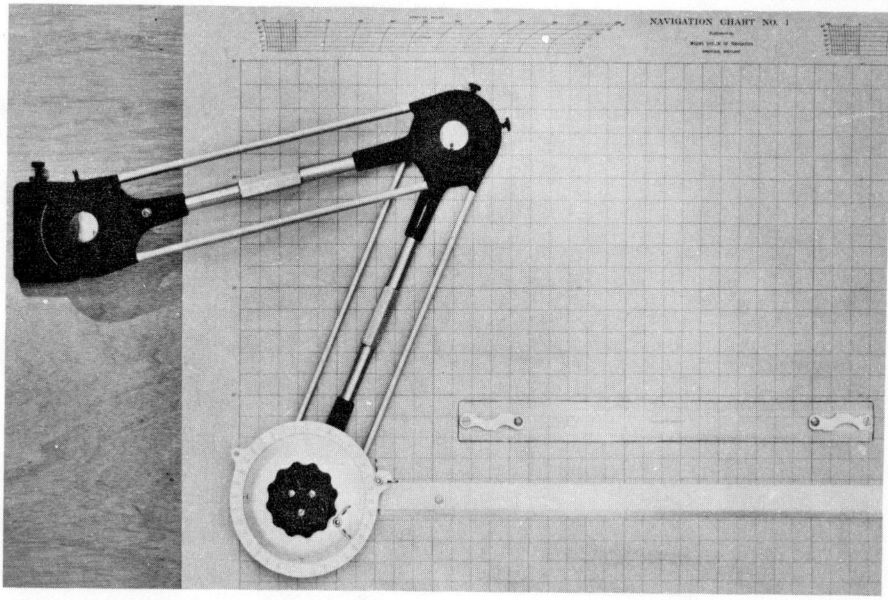

Figure 721. A universal drafting machine is excellent for plotting.

Dead reckoning equipment

723 Most naval vessels are supplied with a dead reckoning electromechanical computer. The basic part of this equipment is the *analyzer* (DRA); heading information is fed into the DRA from the ship's gyrocompass, and speed information is supplied by the log. The speed input is integrated with time to read distance. The DRA has three readouts: miles steamed north or south, miles steamed east or west, and total number of miles steamed.

Some DRAs also give latitude and longitude readouts, in which case they are usually called Dead Reckoning Analyzer-Indicator (DRAI). A Mark 9 Mod 4 DRAI is shown in Figure 723a.

The *Dead Reckoning Tracer* (DRT) receives its heading and speed inputs from the DRA, and provides a graphic trace of the ship's travel through the water. Some new models also trace the paths of two or more targets, permitting a constant readout of target range and bearing; target data are supplied from radar or sonar inputs. The DRT permits the choice of one of a number of scales, depending on the tactical situation, and the trace may be on a Mercator chart or a polar coordinate chart. The "own ship" trace may be made by a pencil moved across the chart; alternately the ship's position as well as that of the targets may be indicated by spots of light focused on the chart from underneath. Such a DRT is shown in Figure 723b; it is the PT-512 plotting table, designed primarily for use aboard ASW vessels. This plotting table permits a choice of eight scales, ranging from 200 yards per inch to 5 miles per inch, and gives a plotting area of 30 by 30 inches (76 by 76 cm).

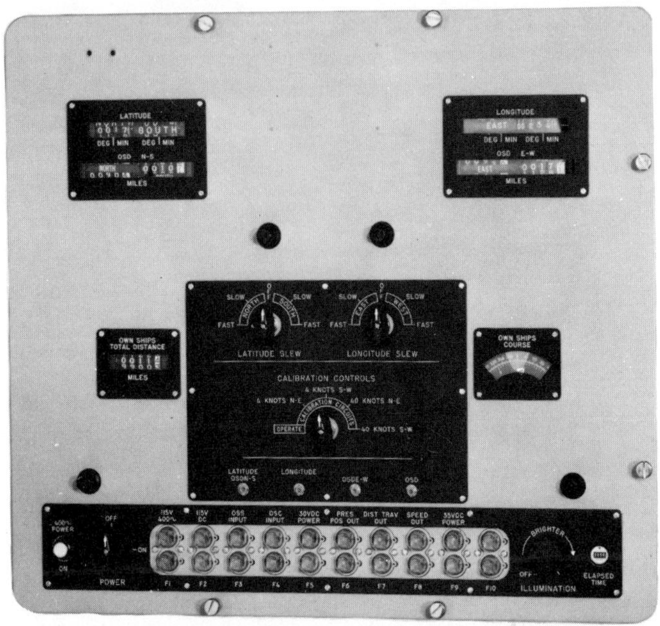

Figure 723a. Dead Reckoning Analyzer-Indicator, Mark 9 Mod 4.

Figure 723b. Plotting Table, PT-512.

Nautical slide rule

724 Circular plastic slide rules (Figure 724 is typical) are widely used for the rapid solution of problems involving time, distance, and speed. Given any two of these factors, the third may be obtained. The time scale gives hours in red figures, and minutes and seconds in black figures. Seconds are shown separately to 120; this scale must be used only for times of 120 seconds or less. Hours and minutes are both stated in units and decimals. If the hour scale is set to 2.5, the minute scale will read 150. Similarly, if the minute scale is set to 1.5, 90 seconds may also be read.

In the model shown, the distance scale is in miles in red figures and in yards in black figures. The yards scale is based on the assumption that 1 nautical mile equals 2000 yards; this is an assumption frequently used in marine surface navigation—the slight error, $1\frac{1}{4}$ percent, is ignored for the convenience gained. Therefore, if the distance scale is set at 3 miles, it will also read 6,000 yards. The figures on the distance scale may also be used in solving problems involving statute miles; however, in this case, the yard scale must *not* be used.

In using the slide rule, when the distance is one of the known factors, the distance setting should be made *first.* When speed is a known factor, it should always be set last, as the speed scale is read through both dials.

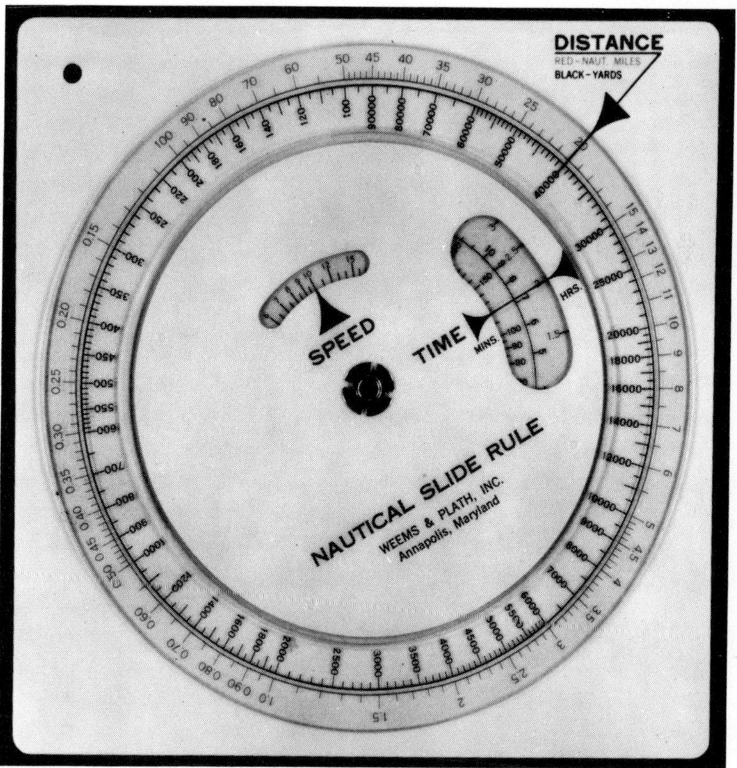

Figure 724. Nautical slide rule.

Figure 725. A personal electronic calculator.

Hand calculators

725 The rapid development of small hand-held electronic calculators has brought them onto the bridge of vessels, large and small, for the solution of many navigational problems. These have essentially replaced conventional slide rules; they permit quick, easy, and accurate solutions of problems of speed-time-distance, dead reckoning, current sailing, metric conversions, and many others related to navigation or general "ship's business." The more sophisticated personal calculators can be programmed and approach the capabilities of microcomputers. See Appendix F for more on these mathematical instruments.

WEATHER

Barometer

726 A *barometer* is an instrument for determining the atmospheric pressure, a meteorological element of considerable interest to a mariner, as its fluctuations provide an index useful in predicting weather, an important factor in navigation and ship handling. Because bad weather is usually associated with regions of low atmospheric pressure and good weather with areas of high pressure, a rapidly falling barometer usually indicates the approach of a storm.

Two general types of barometers are used. The *mercurial* barometer consists essentially of a column of mercury in a tube, the upper end of which is closed and the lower end open to the atmosphere. The height of the column of mercury supported by the atmosphere is read by a suitable scale. Readings are in inches of mercury. The *standard* atmospheric pressure is 29.92 inches.

The *aneroid* barometer consists essentially of a short metal cylinder from which the air has been partly exhausted. The ends of the cylinder, being of thin metal, expand or contract as the external pressure changes. This motion is transferred by a suitable linkage to a registering device which may be graduated in either inches of mercury or *millibars,* a metric unit of measurement. The reading of one scale can be converted to those of the other by table or arithmetically, since 29.92 inches of mercury is equivalent to 1013.2 millibars.

A *barograph* is a self-recording instrument that provides a permanent record of atmospheric pressure over a period of time.

Thermometer **727** Temperature is determined by means of a *thermometer.* Shipboard thermometers are generally graduated to the Fahrenheit scale (water freezes at 32° and boils at 212° at standard atmospheric pressure), but use of the metric scale of Celsius (formerly centigrade) degrees (0° is freezing, 100° is boiling) is increasing, particularly in international applications. The reading of one scale can be easily converted to that of the other by means of Table 15, *Bowditch*, or mathematically, since

$$°F = \tfrac{9}{5}C° + 32°$$

$$°C = \tfrac{5}{9}(F° - 32°)$$

in which °F = degrees Fahrenheit and °C = degrees Celsius.

Two thermometers are often mounted together in an *instrument shelter*, a wooden box with louvered sides to protect the instruments from direct rays of the sun and other conditions that would render their readings inaccurate. The instrument shelter is installed at some exposed position aboard ship. One of the thermometers has its bulb covered with a wet fabric and the other is exposed to the air. The rate of evaporation of the water is dependent on the *relative humidity* of the air, or the relative amount of water vapor in the air. The evaporating water cools the bulb of the thermometer, resulting in a lower temperature. Knowing the air temperature (reading of the *dry bulb thermometer*) and the difference between this and the reading of the *wet bulb thermometer,* the relative humidity and *dew point* (the temperature to which the air must be cooled for condensation to take place) can be easily determined; Tables 16 and 17 of *Bowditch* are applicable. Calculations of relative humidity and dew point are of interest to the mariner in connection with the formation of fog. A combination of wet and dry thermometers is known as a *psychrometer.*

Anemometer **728** An *anemometer* is an instrument for measuring wind force or speed, usually in knots. It must always be remembered that wind speed measured on a moving ship is *apparent* wind, or wind relative to the moving ship. Apparent wind can be converted to true wind, or vice versa, by means of a simple graphic solution (see Article 1417) or by the use of tables such as Table 10 in *Bowditch.*

MISCELLANEOUS EQUIPMENT

Binoculars **729** A pair of good binoculars is useful in visually detecting aids to navigation, especially small ones such as buoys, and in reading their identifying markings. The navigator should have a pair of binoculars for his own exclusive use, and they should be in a handy location, but sufficiently protected to prevent damage from dropping, being knocked off a table by the motion of the ship, or by weather. When they are being used, the strap should be placed around the user's neck. Like the other instruments used by the navigator, binoculars must receive proper care if they are to give reliable service.

The size of binoculars deemed most useful for marine work is 7 × 50; this describes glasses with a magnification of 7 powers and an objective lens 50 mm in diameter. This ratio of magnification is a satisfying compromise between need for magnification and the reduction of field of view that results as the magnification is increased. Objective lenses of 50-mm diameter have excellent light-gathering characteristics, making them particularly suitable for night use.

Other models, such as 6 × 30, may be used, but these are generally somewhat less satisfactory. The style in which each eye is *individually focused* has been adopted by the U.S. Navy, but many civilian mariners and boatmen use the *center focusing* style which focuses for both eyes simultaneously after an initial correction for any difference between the user's two eyes.

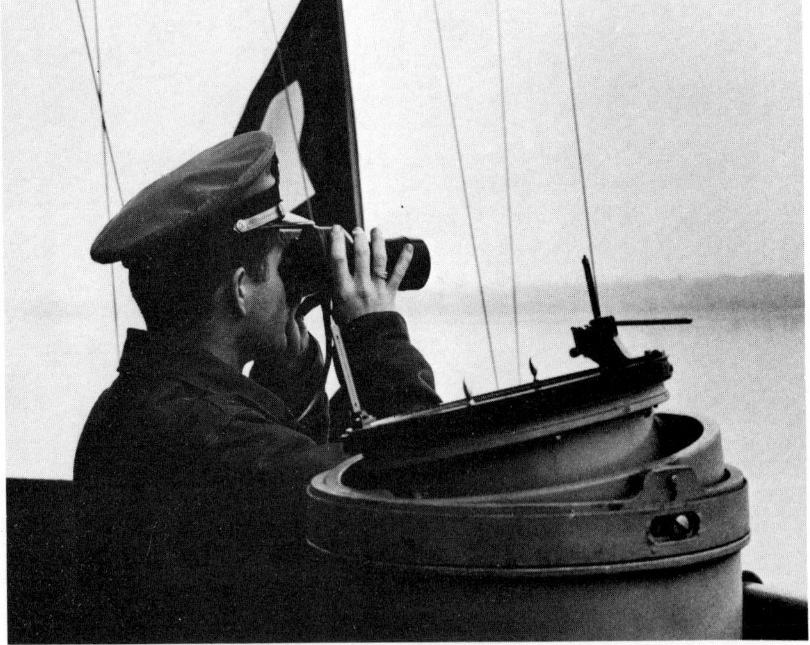

Figure 729. A pair of good binoculars is essential to the navigation of any vessel. Photo: Robert deGast

Flashlight

730 At least one good flashlight should be kept handy for accurate reading of the watch and sextant during twilight observations, if the latter is not equipped with its own light, and for timing light characteristics, etc., during the hours of darkness. To protect dark-adapted vision, this flashlight should be equipped with a red bulb, or a red lens. Lacking these, a red plastic or cellophane filter should be fitted.

If accurate twilight or night observations are to be made, the navigator must protect his eyes from any direct light. If no red flashlight is available, the quartermaster who is acting as recorder should stand with his back to the observer, with his light on the watch. After the altitude is obtained, if the sextant has no readout light it should be handed to the recorder for reading.

Timing devices

731 A stopwatch or a navigational timer, which can be started and stopped at will, is of particular value in timing the period of a navigational light to determine its characteristic for purposes of identification. When equipped with a luminous dial and sweep-second hand, the watch may be read without the use of artificial light, thereby maintaining night-adapted vision.

Split-second timers, sometimes referred to as split-action stopwatches, are now available. With this feature the watch continues to run and measure elapsed time; there are, in effect, two second hands that run together. When the side push button on the stopwatch is depressed, one of these second hands is stopped so that the exact interval can be read from the face of the watch. A second depression of the side push button causes the second hands to run together. This feature is also available on chronographs which can be kept running on GMT, with the split-second feature being used to determine the exact

Figure 731. A stopwatch (left) and a chronograph with a split-action capability.

time of an event, such as a celestial observation, without disturbing the time-keeping function of the watch.

Electronic stopwatches are now available with direct digital readouts. These generally have several modes of split-second operation suitable for the timing of different types of events.

Summary

732 This chapter has classified many of the usual navigation instruments used by the navigator in making his observations. No attempt has been made to describe all of the instruments and equipment with which the navigator must be familiar but only those which *are considered essential to basic navigation* and those not covered in detail elsewhere in the text. For this reason, instruments of direct concern to celestial navigation are discussed in the celestial navigation section, while various electronic instruments are described in separate chapters. The construction and operation of the gyro and magnetic compasses are described in Chapter 4.

8 Dead Reckoning

Introduction **801** *Dead Reckoning* (*DR*) is one of the four main divisions of navigation. When the earliest mariners became sufficiently daring and skilled to venture beyond their known waters in which they could *pilot* their vessel, they developed dead reckoning as a means of keeping track of their position. The term is derived from *deduced* or *ded.* reckoning, the process by which a ship's position was *deduced* or computed trigonometrically, in relation to a known point of departure. Although highly accurate modern charts permit solution by graphic methods, rather than by laborious mathematics, the term, in its present form, continues in use. While treated as a separate division of navigation in this text, dead reckoning is basic to all phases of navigation.

DR defined **802** Dead reckoning is the process of determining a ship's approximate position by applying to its last well-determined position a vector or a series of consecutive vectors representing the run that has since been made, using only the true courses steered, and the distance run as determined by log, engine revolutions, or calculations from speed measurements, *without considering current.* By projecting these course and speed vectors ahead of the present position, the ship's predicted DR position for any desired time can be determined.

Dead reckoning is normally a process carried out as a vessel advances along its passage. It can, however, be done in advance as the planned or projected plot of the movements of the vessel at a later time.

The key elements of dead reckoning may be summarized as follows:

Only the true courses steered are used to determine a DR position.

The distance used in determining a DR position is obtained by multiplying the ordered engine speed by the time involved in the run.

A DR plot is always started from an established position, that is, a fix or running fix. (See Article 804.)

The effects of current are *not* considered in determining a DR position.

The importance of DR

803 The importance of maintaining an accurate dead reckoning plot cannot be overemphasized. A means of fixing the ship's position is not always available, due to weather, equipment failure, etc. Under such conditions, a navigator must rely on his dead reckoning for an indication of his position. It is obvious that a DR position must be used with extreme caution in the vicinity of shoal water or other dangers to navigation.

If a ship made good the exact course and speed ordered, and there was no wind or current, dead reckoning would at all times provide an accurate indication of position. However, since such conditions rarely exist, a DR position is only an approximation of the true position, and the need for maintaining a constant and accurate dead reckoning plot should be obvious. A navigator must know his position, or approximate position, to determine when to make turns, to predict the time of sighting lights or other aids to navigation, and to identify landmarks.

Dead reckoning is customarily done graphically on a chart or plotting sheet appropriate to the area in which the ship is steaming. Graphic solutions enable the navigator to visualize his ship's position in relation to landmarks or to dangers to navigation.

DR terms defined

804 A number of terms used in dead reckoning must be defined. Unfortunately, not all books on navigation use exactly the same terms and definitions. The terms used in this book are defined below.

Heading (Hdg. or SH). The horizontal direction in which a ship points or heads at any instant, expressed in angular units, clockwise from 000° through 360°, from a reference direction (Figure 804). The heading of a ship is also called ship's head. Heading is a constantly

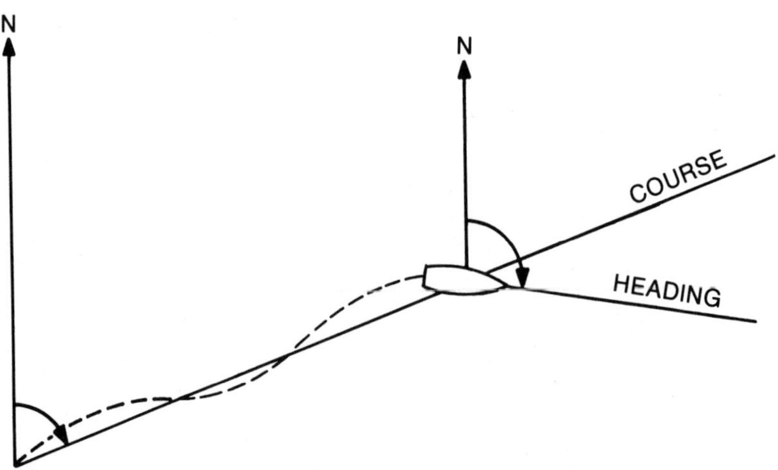

Figure 804. Heading and course.

changing value as a ship oscillates or yaws across the course due to the effects of the sea and of steering error.

Course (C). As applied to marine navigation, the direction in which a vessel is to be steered, or is being steered; the direction of travel through the water. The course is measured from 000° clockwise from the reference direction to 360°. Course may be designated as *true, magnetic, compass,* or *grid* as determined by the reference direction.

Course Line. In marine navigation, the graphic representation of a ship's course, normally used in the construction of a dead reckoning plot.

Speed (S). The ordered rate of travel of a ship through the water; normally expressed in knots. (In some areas, where distances are stated in statute miles, such as on the Great Lakes, speed units will be "miles per hour.") It is used in conjunction with time to establish a distance run on each of the consecutive segments of a DR plot.

Fix. A position established at a specific time to a high degree of accuracy may be determined by any of a number of methods discussed in Chapter 11. A *running fix* is a position of lesser accuracy based in part on present information and in part on information transferred from a prior time.

DR Position. A position determined by plotting a vector or series of consecutive vectors using only the true course, and distance determined by speed through the water, without considering current.

Estimated Position (EP). The more probable position of a ship, determined from incomplete data or data of questionable accuracy. In practical usage it is often the DR position modified by the best additional information available.

Dead Reckoning Plot. Commonly called DR plot. In marine navigation it is the graphical representation on the nautical chart of the line or series of lines which are the vectors of the ordered true courses, and distance run on these courses at the ordered speeds, while proceeding from a fixed point. The DR plot originates at a fix or running fix; it is suitably labeled as to courses, speeds, and times of various dead reckoning positions, usually at hourly intervals or at times of change of course or speed. A DR plot properly represents courses and speeds that have been used; a similar plot may be made in advance for courses and speeds that are expected to be used.

Estimated Time of Departure (ETD). The estimate of the time of departure from a specified location in accordance with a scheduled move to a new location.

Estimated Time of Arrival (ETA). The best estimate of the time of arrival at a specified location in accordance with a scheduled movement.

Course, speed, time, distance, and position will be stated to an order of precision suitable to the vessel concerned and prevailing conditions; see Appendix C.

A planned or intended path *with respect to the earth* rather than the water is labeled *Track* and *Speed of Advance;* see Chapter 12.

Labeling a DR plot

805 It is of the utmost importance that all points and lines plotted on a chart be properly labeled. The use of standardized methods will ensure that the plot will mean the same thing to others as it did to the navigator who made it; this is essential to the safety of the ship.

The principal rules for labeling DR plots are:

Immediately after drawing any line or plotting any point, it should be labeled.

The label for any point on a line should not be close alongside the line; labels for fixes and running fixes should be written horizontally, labels for DR positions at an angle to the horizontal.

The labels indicating direction and speed along a course line should be written along that line.

The label for direction should be the letter *C* followed by three digits indicating the true course in degrees; this is placed above the course line. (Should course be stated with reference to another base direction, an appropriate letter is added following the digits, such as *M* for magnetic.)

The label indicating the rate of movement along the course line is the letter *S* followed by digits indicating the speed, normally in knots. This is placed below the course line, usually directly underneath the direction label.

If a DR plot is drawn as a planning action in advance of actual vessel movement, distances are known; speeds may or may not be known prior to departure. If it is desired to label a DR plot with distance, this is done with the letter *D* followed by the distance in nautical miles (statute miles in some areas), usually to the nearest tenth of a mile; this is placed below the course line. (Some navigators will label a destination, usually in pilot waters, with its ETA and then intermediate points, marked by a heavy dot, with the ETA there plus the distance measured back from the final destination along the intended track.)

All labels should be printed clearly and neatly.

The symbol for a fix is a small circle surrounding a small dot; the time is written *horizontally* close nearby. (If the position is at the intersection of two lines, the dot may be omitted.) The symbol for a running fix is the same as for a fix but the letters "R FIX" are added following the time.

The symbol for a DR position is a small semicircle around a small dot; this will be a half-circle on a straight segment of a course line; it will be more or less than a half circle when plotted at a change in direction. The time is written nearby at *an angle to the horizontal.*

The dot in a fix, running fix, or DR position symbol is used to emphasize the point of the position; it should be small and neat. Course lines, properly labeled, are shown in Figure 805.

Times of DR position In addition to the rules for the symbols and labels, there are also six standard rules which will guide a navigator as to *when* DR positions and course lines are required to be plotted:

A DR position shall be plotted every hour on the hour.

A DR position shall be plotted at the time of every course change.

A DR position shall be plotted at the time of every speed change.

A DR position shall be plotted at the time of obtaining a fix or a running fix.

A DR position shall be plotted at the time of obtaining a single line of position.

A new course line shall be plotted from each fix or running fix as soon as the fix or running fix has been determined and plotted on the chart.

These rules of dead reckoning are considered adequate to meet the needs and requirements of navigation in the open waters of the sea. There are occasions, however, when a more frequent plot of the ship's dead reckoning position is essential to safe navigation, as when in the confined waters of channels, bays, straits and harbors. Knowledge of when to plot frequent fixes and even more frequent dead reckoning positions when in such waters will come with experience and judgment. This subject will be discussed more fully in Chapter 15.

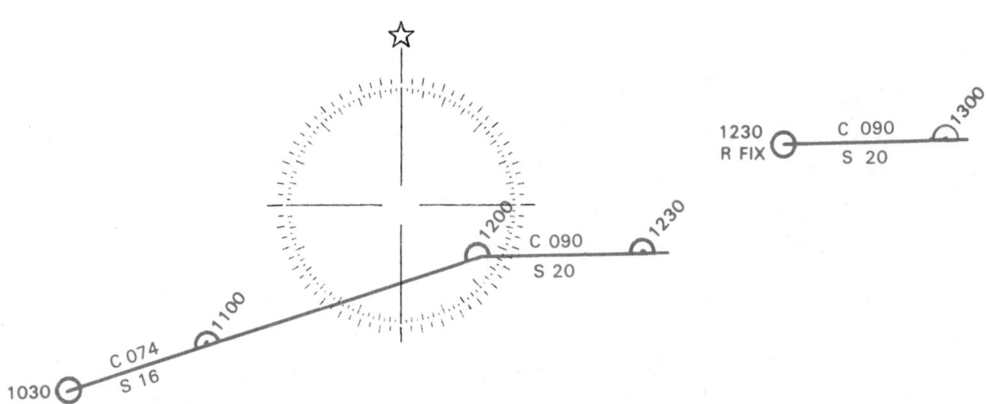

Figure 805. Labeling a DR plot.

Example of a DR plot

806 The following example outlines a typical dead reckoning problem: see Figure 806.

A partial extract from a ship's deck log reads as follows:

> 1045. With Tide Rip Light bearing 315°, distant 6 miles, took departure for operating area V-22 on course 090°, speed 15 knots. 1120-Changed speed to 10 knots to blow tubes. 1130-Changed course to 145° and increased speed to 20 knots. 1145-Changed course to 075°. 1210-Made radar contact on Buoy 1A bearing 010°, distant 8 miles, 1215-Changed course to 090° and changed speed to 18 knots to arrive at the rendezvous point at 1230 . . . .

It is well to review at this point the applicability of the rules for dead reckoning as they pertain to this example. Commencing at the initial known position, the 1045 fix, the navigator plotted the course line in a direction of 090° corresponding to the ordered course. The rate of travel, speed 15 knots, for an elasped time of 15 minutes and then 20 minutes enabled the navigator to make a scaled plot of the 1100 DR and 1120 DR positions respectively on his chart. Labeling the fix, the 1100 DR, the 1120 DR, and the course line itself completes the graphic description of the ship's travel to 1120. At 1120, only the speed was changed. At 1130, both the course and speed were changed, while at 1145, only the course was changed. Each of these occurrences requires a separate DR position on the plot, while segments of the course lines are labeled to indicate what specific change of the course and speed occurred at that time. The 1200 DR was plotted on the whole hour as prescribed. At 1210, since the navigator fixed his position by radar, he must then plot both the 1210 DR on the former course line and the 1210 radar fix from which he commences a new course line. The navigator plots the ship from the fix on a course of 075° at a speed of 20 knots to 1215, at which time the course is changed to 090° and the speed is reduced to 18 knots in order to arrive at the operating area at 1230 as scheduled. The DR plot reflects the course and speed change and includes the 1230 DR as shown.

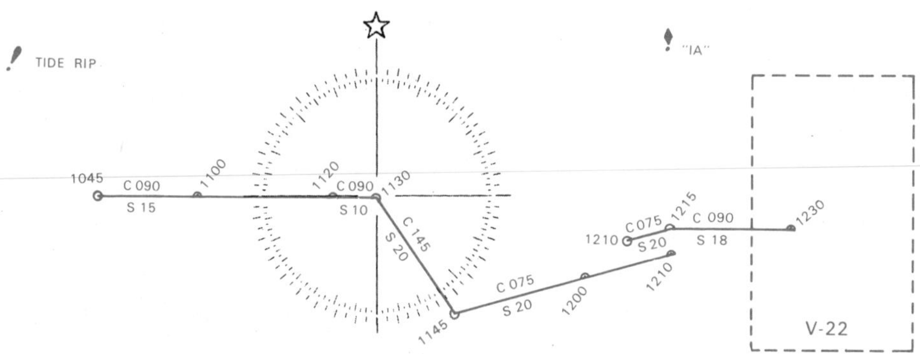

Figure 806. A typical navigator's DR plot.

Planned track **807** In actual practice, a preplanned track line is often plotted on a tentative basis before a ship ever gets underway. Called "navigational planning," it introduces a fundamental principle of safe navigation. Every passage, every departure from and entry into port must be planned in advance, based on all information available to the navigator. The material studied in the course of this planning includes the charts of the areas to be traversed, the navigational aids expected to be sighted, the availability of electronic coverage, estimates of currents and weather to be encountered, the contour of the bottom, and other factors that will be discussed later in this book. The preplanning phase also includes the construction of danger bearings, ranges, etc. The following description of a short voyage will serve to illustrate many of the principles and concepts enumerated so far in this chapter.

Referring to Figure 807a, assume that a ship is located at point *A*, and receives orders to depart at 0800 for point *B*, 90 miles distant, arriving at 1300. Immediately upon receipt of this information, the navigator located points *A* and *B* on the appropriate small-scale chart of the area. By measuring the direction of *B* from *A*, the course of 070° is determined and noted on the DR plot as "C 070." Dividing the rhumb-line distance between *A* and *B* by five hours, SOA is computed to be 18 knots and labeled accordingly. Next, starting at the known position, or fix, at 0800, the navigator stepped off and marked the successive hourly positions which the ship is expected to occupy. The plot is now a complete and graphic picture. The plan is complete and, barring any unforeseen circumstances, represents the track that the ship will follow from the point of departure to her destination. Note that in this case the vessel was able to order the planned course and speed and arrive at the destination as planned; this very seldom happens in actual practice. The technique of handling deviations from the plan is the subject of the next article.

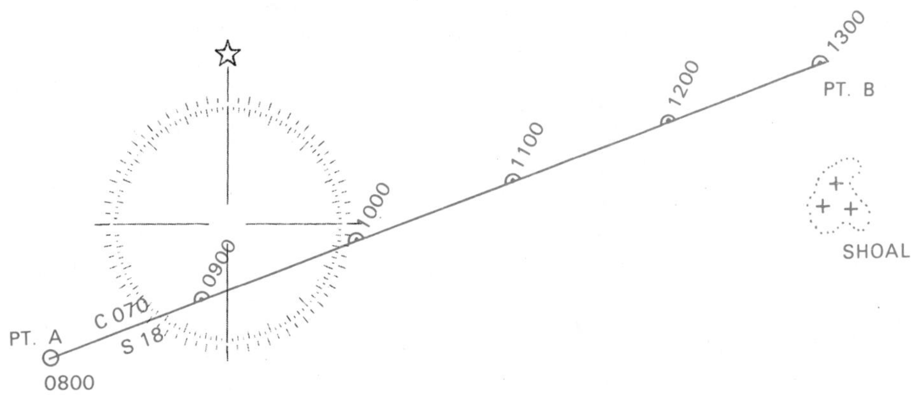

Figure 807a. Intended DR track, plotted and labeled in advance.

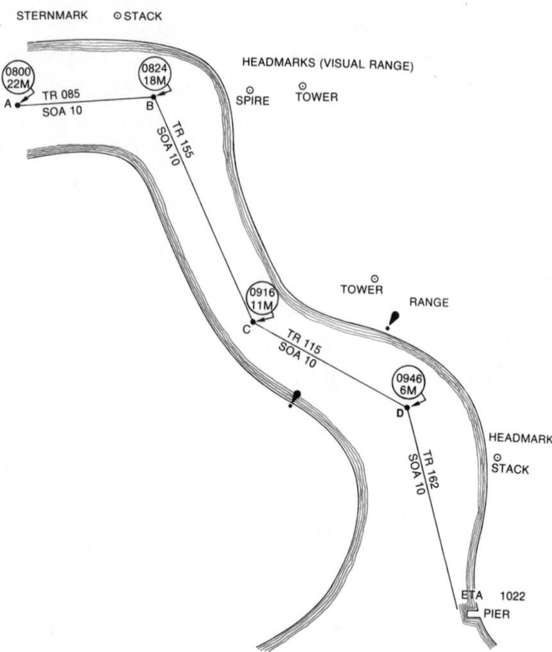

Figure 807b. Alternative labeling of a proposed track.

Departures from plan

808 The ship gets underway as scheduled and sets course 070° true and speed 18 knots to arrive at *B* at 1300. If the calculations are correct and there is no current or change of course to avoid shipping, the ship should arrive at *B* as planned. The navigator's work now consists of trying to establish his actual position from time to time, in order to be sure that the ship is following the intended track, or, if it is not following it, to recommend changes in course or speed, or both, which will bring the ship safely back to the intended track or to any selected point on it.

The navigator had poor weather and was unable to establish his position until about noon at which time he obtained a 1200 fix. When the fix was plotted, he found that the ship was actually about 10 miles south and a bit east of his 1200 DR position; see Figure 808. He further noted that if his ship maintained the same course on from the 1200 fix as it had from point *A*, she would be in danger of grounding on the indicated shoal.

Since the ship will not reach its destination on a course of 070° and a speed of 18 knots, the navigator must determine a new course and speed to arrive at point *B* by 1300, based upon the relationship between point *B* and the latest fix at 1200.

Since time was required to record the fix, evaluate it, and decide upon a new course and speed, this change cannot be effected from the 1200 fix but rather from a DR position some time later. Making a rough estimate of how long it will take him to determine a new course

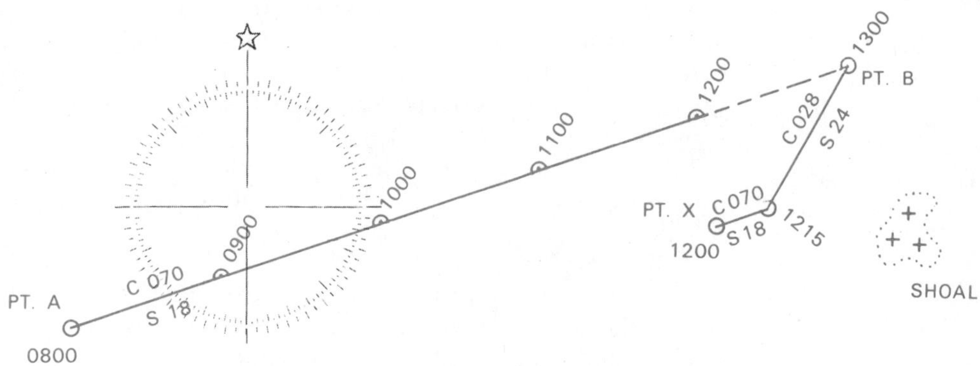

Figure 808. The practice of dead reckoning.

and speed, and get approval, the navigator plots a 1215 DR position based on the old, and still maintained, course and speed. From here he calculates a new course and a new speed (or new ETA if the ship is not capable of the greater speed needed to reach point *B* by 1300). It is very important to remember—*the course line will continue in the direction and at the speed originally ordered during the time required to obtain and plot the fix and decide upon a new course of action.* Upon the advice of the navigator in this instance, the captain ordered a course of 028° and a speed of 24 knots at 1215 to direct the ship to arrive at point *B* at 1300. Although it is apparent that a current existed, it is not considered in this example. The technique and procedures of computing and allowing for current are explained later in Chapter 12; they would have been used by the navigator in the computation of the new course and speed through the water.

The navigator believed that the ship was following the intended track until he obtained and plotted his 1200 fix. This illustrates the fundamental weakness of relying solely on dead reckoning, for dead reckoning is dependent on the assumption that the ship makes good over the ground the same direction that it is traveling through the water, and that the ship makes good over the ground the same speed that it is traveling through the water. Therefore, the dead reckoning position should not be relied upon if it is possible to obtain information to determine the position by other means. The many volumes of records on maritime disasters are filled with reports of instances of vessels having been put aground and lost because of a navigator's adherence to a course which was laid in safe waters, while the actual movement was an unknown path leading to danger.

Plotting techniques

809 As stated above, neatness and accuracy in plotting are essential for safe navigation. Skill will come with experience and practice, but a few hints and suggestions may be of assistance toward both accuracy and speed in plotting:

A drafting machine should be used whenever available to determine the direction of a line, as it is both more rapid and accurate than other methods. When a drafting machine is not available, a course plotter (or protractor or parallel rulers) is used. Various types are shown in Chapter 7.

Tape the chart to the table or desk used. This will maintain proper orientation of the chart. Tape is preferable to thumbtacks for this purpose.

If the chart is too large to fit on the desk used, determine the extent of the chart that must be used, then fold under the portions of the chart that will not be required to be exposed. Be sure to leave one latitude scale and one longitude scale available for measurement.

Use a *sharp* No. 2 pencil. A harder pencil will not erase well, and a softer pencil will smear.

Draw lines heavy enough to be seen readily, but light enough so that they do not indent the chart paper.

Avoid drawing unnecessary lines, and erase any lines used only for the purpose of measurement. Do not extend lines excessively beyond the point at which their direction is to be changed.

Hold the pencil against the straightedge in a vertical position throughout the entire length of a line when drawing it.

Measure all directions and distances carefully. Accuracy is the mark of good navigation. On Mercator charts, measure distance on the latitude scale using the portion of the scale which is opposite the line that is being measured. Be neat and exact in plotting work. Use standard symbols and labels and print neatly.

Learn to use dividers with one hand and with either hand if possible.

Lay down a new DR track from each new fix or running fix. Plot a DR position at every change of course, at every change of speed, at the time of obtaining a fix, a running fix, or a single line of position, and on the whole hour.

Time, speed, and distance calculations

810 The navigator may find it convenient to use a *nautical slide rule* (Figure 724) for the solution of time, speed, and distance problems. Small hand-held electronic calculators (Appendix F) are also useful for the easy, quick, and very accurate solution of these problems. Alternatively, he may use precomputed tables, such as those in *Bowditch,* for such solutions. He must, however, always be able to solve these problems quickly and accurately without the use of any equipment beyond pencil and paper.

Regardless of the tools used, however, it must *always be remembered in adding or subtracting values of time, there are 60 minutes in an hour, and 60 seconds in each minute;* don't forget and work in decimal terms of 100 units.

Time, distance, and speed calculations—finding the third quantity if the other two are known—can also be worked graphically using the logarithmic scale printed on larger-scale NOS and DMAHC charts, on some plotting sheets, and as the top line of the nomogram printed near the bottom of Maneuvering Board sheets, DMAHC Pub. No. 5090 and 5091; see Figure 810. The scale, together with a pair of dividers, is used as a slide rule. Let the right leg of a pair of dividers represent time in minutes and the left leg, distance. Consider speed as distance in 60 minutes.

The Maneuvering Board sheets also have a three-scale nomogram which can be used as described in Article 1404.

Thus, to obtain time, place the left leg of the dividers on the speed and the right leg on 60. Without changing the spread of the dividers, place the left leg on the required distance and read off the time at the right leg. If distance in a given time is desired, place the right leg on the given time and read off the distance at the left leg. If speed is required, set the left leg of the dividers at distance and the right leg at time and then, without changing the spread, place the right leg on 60 and read the speed at the left leg.

If the problem runs off the scale, solution can be made by using a fraction of the speed, or distance (only one), and multiplying the answer by the inverse of the same fraction.

If in doubt as to the accuracy of a solution, check it mentally or by simple arithmetic using the formula $D = S \times T$, where D is distance in miles, S is speed in knots, and T, is time in hours.

A useful rule to use in plotting in confined waters where frequent fixes and DR positions are required is the so-called *"three-minute rule,"* applied as follows: the travel of a ship *in yards* in three minutes is equal to the speed of the ship in knots multiplied by 100. (This uses the assumption that one nautical mile is equal to 2000 yards; not exact, but close enough for practical use.) Where a *six-minute* DR would be more appropriate than a three-minute plot, the travel of a ship *in miles* in six minutes is equal to the speed of the vessel divided by 10, a shift of the decimal point one place to the left.

Example 1: A navigator desires to plot a three-minute DR from his last fix in Brewerton Channel. The ship is making a speed of 12 knots. To compute the travel of the ship in yards in three minutes, he multiplies the speed in knots, 12, by the factor 100 and determines the DR advance to be 1200 yards.

Answer: Distance 1200 yards.

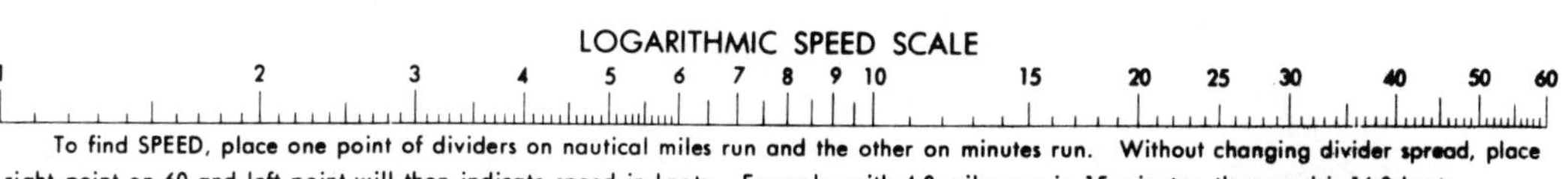

Figure 810. Logarithmic scales for determining speed or distance.

Example 2: A navigator desires to plot a six-minute DR from his last fix in Chesapeake Bay. The ship is making a speed of 15 knots. To compute the travel of the ship in miles, he divides the speed in knots, 15, by the factor 10 and determines the DR advance to be 1.5 miles.

Answer: Distance 1.5 miles.

Summary **811** This chapter has presented the basic information needed to understand the elements of the dead reckoning process. The mechanics of dead reckoning, the standard method of labeling, and when to plot DR positions have been discussed. Graphically portraying the travel of a vessel will come with practice.

The need for maintaining an accurate and readily understandable dead reckoning plot cannot be overemphasized. It is axiomatic that the navigator who demonstrates neatness and accuracy in plotting can be expected to demonstrate the same qualities in the other phases of navigation. It is the lack of these qualities which is frequently found to be a basic cause of groundings.

9 Tides and Tide Prediction

Introduction **901** When a navigator is preparing to take his vessel into port, one of his chief concerns is the available depth of the water at the time of arrival. In nearly every port, that depth will vary from time to time as a result of a natural phenomenon known as *tide.* A thorough knowledge of tidal action and how the height of tide—which in turn relates to depth of water—can be predicted and calculated is an essential part of the qualifications of anyone who would call himself "navigator."

In addition to concern over adequate depths of water in channels, across bars, alongside piers and wharves, etc., there may in some locations be concern as to sufficient vertical clearance beneath a fixed bridge. Here, too, tides play a major role, for as depths increase for safety, vertical clearances decrease by the same amount.

Definitions **902** The vertical rise and fall of the ocean level due to gravitational and centrifugal forces between the earth and the moon, and, to a lesser extent, the sun, is called *tide.* Local conditions cause considerable variations in tidal phenomena from place to place, but most places on the earth's oceans and connecting waters experience two high tides and two low tides each lunar day. *High tide* or *high water* is the highest level reached by an ascending tide. From high tide the level of the water decreases until it reaches a minimum level called *low tide* or *low water.* At high water and low water there is a brief period when no change in the water level can be detected. This period is called *stand.* The total rise or fall from low water to high water, or vice versa, is called the *range* of the tide. *Mean sea level* is the average height of the surface of the sea for all stages of tide, differing slightly from *half-tide level,* which is the plane midway between mean high water and mean low water.

Causes of tide **903** In any consideration of tidal theory, it is convenient to start with a spherical earth uniformly covered with water. It is also convenient to consider separately the effects of the moon and sun, following this with a consideration of the combined effects of both bodies; the effects of the moon will be studied first as it exerts the larger influence. Before 100 A.D. the Roman naturalist Pliny observed and wrote of the influence of the moon on tides, but full understanding had to wait for Newton's statement of the law of gravitation in 1687.

The effect of the moon The earth, and especially the oceans on it, are affected by the gravitational attraction between the earth and the moon, and by the centrifugal forces resulting from their revolution around a common center, a point located *within* the earth about 810 miles (1500 km) beneath the surface. The gravitational and centrifugal forces are in balance, and as a result, the earth and moon neither collide nor fly away from each other in space. Although the earth-moon system as a whole is in equilibrium, individual particles on the earth are not. The centrifugal force is the same everywhere, since all points on the earth's surface describe the same motion around the common center of mass; these forces are all parallel to each other and to a line joining the center of the earth and moon. On the other hand, the gravitational force is not everywhere the same; particles nearer the moon feel a greater attractional force than on those on the far side of the earth; these forces are not parallel, each being in the direction from that particle to the center of the moon. The combination of these forces, much exaggerated for emphasis, is shown in Figure 903a. Note that there are a series of resultant forces that will cause the surface water to flow toward the points on the earth's surface that are then nearest and farthest from the moon. This flow causes higher than normal levels of water at these points, and lower than normal levels at the areas from which the flow comes. Although at the nearest and farthest points there is an indicated outward force, this is very slight and not nearly enough to cause an appreciable tide; the true tide results from the near-horizontal forces causing the flow described above.

As the earth rotates each day on its axis, the line of direction toward the moon changes, and so each point has two highs and two lows. As a result of the tilt of the earth's axis, the highs and lows are not normally of equal levels.

The effect of the sun This overly simplified explanation must now be complicated by the presence of the sun, a body of immensely greater mass than the moon, but relatively so much more distant that its effect is less (about 46 per-

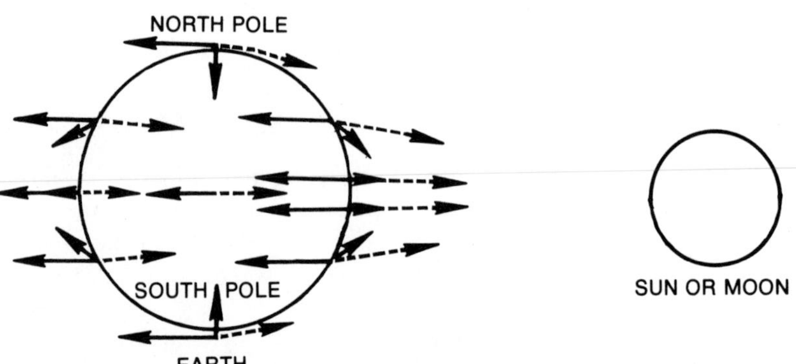

Figure 903a. Gravitational and centrifugal forces.

cent as great). The tides that occur on earth are the result of the lunar and solar influences. When these two bodies are in line with the earth—as at both new and full moon—the two influences act together and the result is higher than average high tides and lower than normal low tides; these are called *spring tides* (the word "spring" here has nothing to do with the season of the year of the same name). This is true regardless of whether the moon is between the earth and the sun or on the opposite side. Figure 903b illustrates these situations.

When the directions of the sun and moon are 90° apart—as at both first- and third-quarter moons—the effect of the sun is to partially counteract the moon's influence. At these times, the high tides and low tides are lower than normal; these are *neap* tides; Figure 903c shows this alignment of the moon and sun.

As the moon revolves about the earth once each lunar month of roughly 28 days, its transit of any meridian on earth occurs approximately every 24 hours and 50 minutes. This is the period for two high waters and two low waters and is called a *tidal day;* the period for one high and one low is sometimes referred to as a *tidal cycle.* In actuality, the daily rotation of the earth on its axis has a frictional effect on the tides so that high tides normally lag the time of the moon's transit across the meridian of any location.

The assumption of a spherical earth uniformly covered with water is, of course, solely hypothetical. Tides in the open oceans are only one to two feet high (with tides on the far side being about 5 percent less than those on the near side). Actual coastal tides are often much greater, in some places as much as 40 or 50 feet (12 to 15 m) or more. This is the result of large land masses restricting the flow of water, of

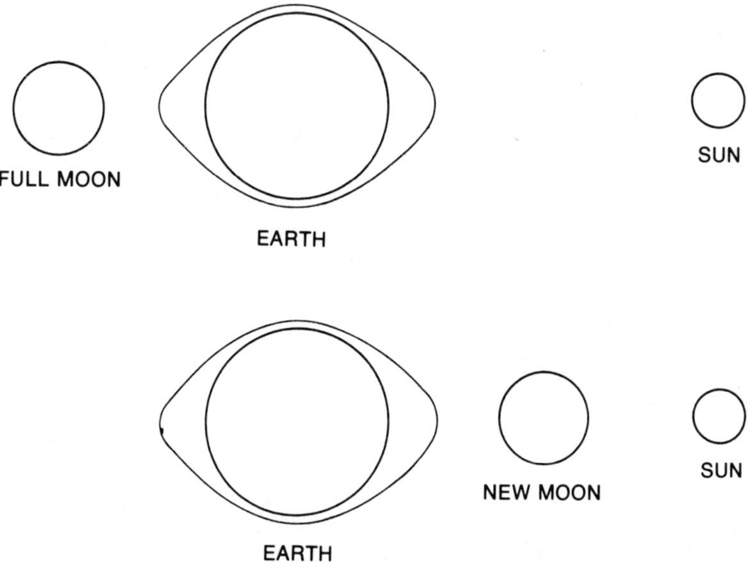

Figure 903b. Moon and sun acting together to produce spring tides.

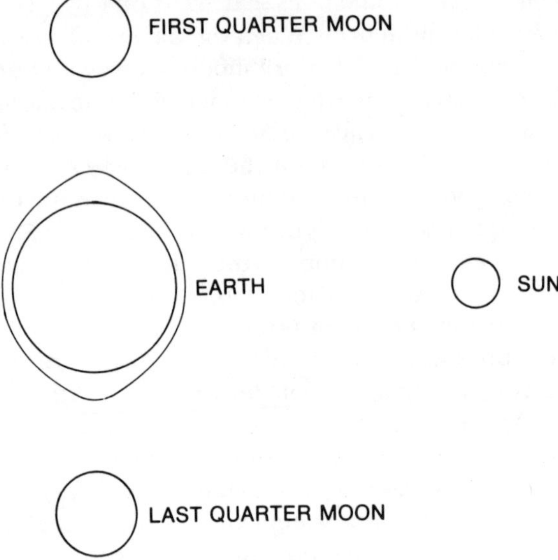

Figure 903c. Moon and sun acting in quadrature to produce neap tides.

ocean bottom and shoreline variations, the internal friction (viscosity) of the flowing water, and other factors. These interrelate to establish natural periods of oscillation for seas, gulfs, large bays, and estuaries, which combine with the basic tidal influences as described in the following article.

Types of tide

904 A body of water has a natural period of oscillation that is dependent upon its dimensions. No ocean appears to be a single oscillating body, but rather each one is made up of a number of oscillating basins. As such basins are acted upon by the tide-producing forces, some respond more readily to daily or diurnal forces, others to semidiurnal forces, and still others respond almost equally to both. Hence, tides at a given place are classified as *semidiurnal, diurnal,* or *mixed*—according to the characteristics of the tidal pattern occurring at that place.

Semidiurnal. In this type of tide, there are two high and two low waters each tidal day with relatively small inequality in the consecutive high and low water heights. Tides on the Atlantic coast of the United States are representative of the semidiurnal type, which is illustrated in Figure 904a.

Diurnal. In this type of tide, only a single high and a single low water occur each tidal day. Tides of the diurnal type occur along the northern shore of the Gulf of Mexico, in the Java Sea, in the Gulf of

Tonkin (off the North Vietnamese-Chinese coast), and in a few other localities. The tide curve for Pakhoi, China, illustrated in Figure 904b is an example of the diurnal type.

Mixed. In this type of tide the diurnal and semidiurnal oscillations are both important factors, and the tide is characterized by a large inequality in the high-water heights, low-water heights, or in both. There are usually two high and two low waters each day, but occasionally the tide may become diurnal. Such tides are prevalent along the Pacific Coast of the United States, and in many other parts of the world. Examples of mixed types of tides are shown in Figure 904c. At Los Angeles, it is typical that the inequalities in the high and low waters are about the same. At Seattle the greater inequalities are typically in the low waters, while at Honolulu the high waters have the greater inequalities.

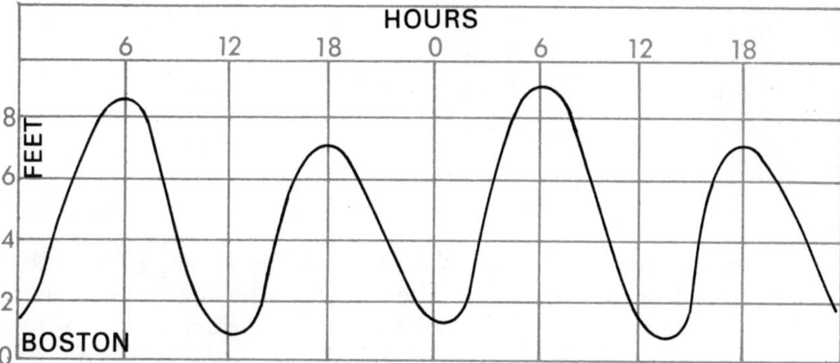

Figure 904a. Semidiurnal type of tides.

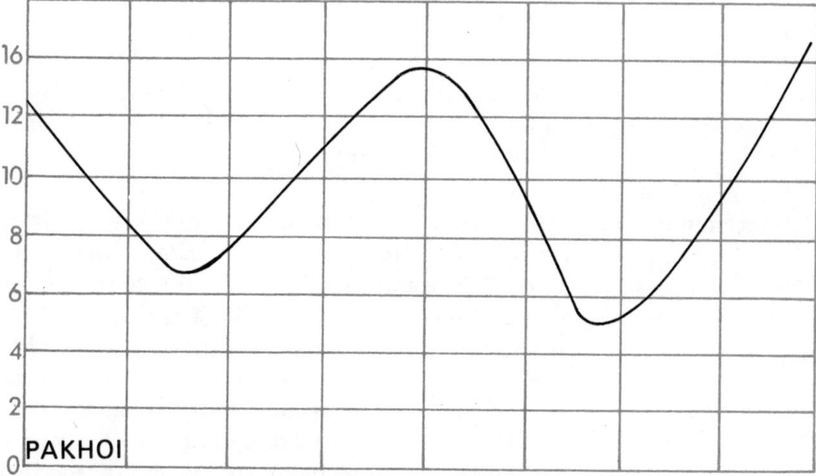

Figure 904b. Diurnal type of tides.

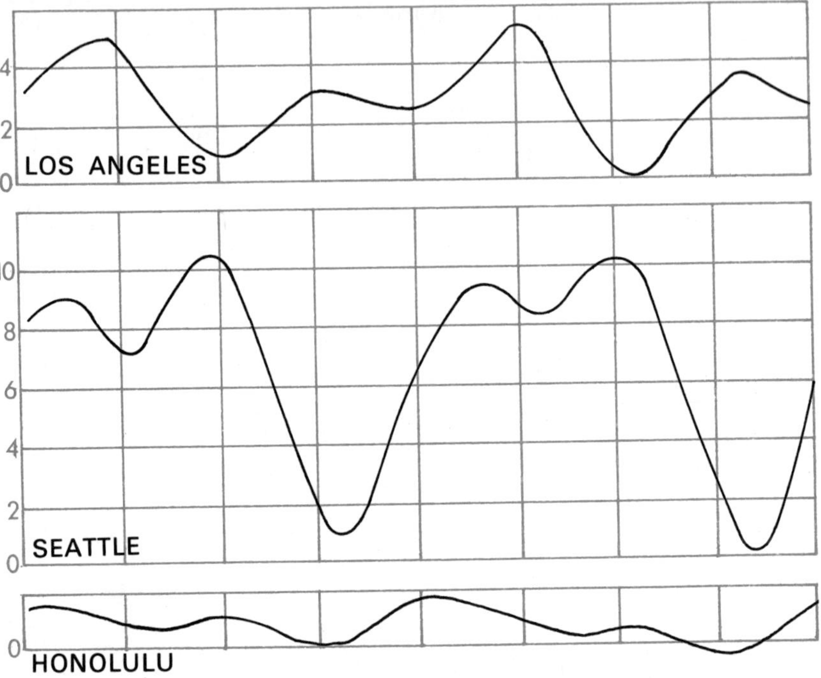

Figure 904c. Mixed type of tides.

Reference planes for tidal data

905 The expression *height of tide* is not to be confused with *depth of water.* The latter refers to the vertical distance from the surface of the water to the bottom; the former refers to the vertical distance from the surface of the water to an arbitrarily chosen *reference plane* or *datum*, such plane being based as a selected *low-water* average. The *charted depth* is the vertical distance from this reference plane to the ocean bottom. A second reference plane based on a selected *high water* average is used as a basis for the measurement of *charted heights* and *vertical clearances* of objects above the water. If the selected low-water average is mean low water, and the selected high-water average is mean high water, then the difference between these two planes is called the *mean range of the tide.* The relationship of these terms is shown in Figure 905.

Reference planes

It is important to remember that the water level is occasionally *below the reference plane.* That is, *the depth of water can be less than the charted depth.* This is indicated by a minus sign (−) placed before the height of tide as shown in the *Tide Tables*. The depth of water is equal to the algebraic sum of the charted depth and the height of tide, so that when there is a negative tide, the numerical value of the height of tide is subtracted from the charted depth to find the depth of water. In many coastal areas, the actual height of tide at any time may be considerably influenced by winds from a particular direction, especially if the winds are strong and persist for several days. At such times, the predicted

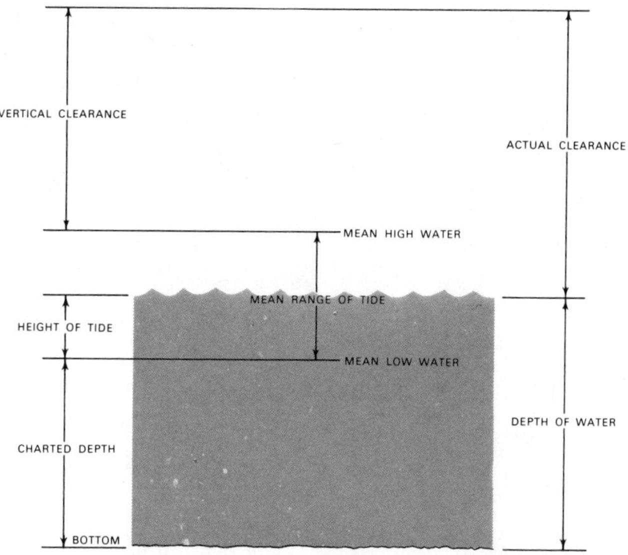

Figure 905. Relationship of terms measuring depths and heights.

tide variations may be completely masked by the temporary conditions. Periods of abnormally low barometric pressure may result in higher water levels for both high and low tides.

The arbitrarily chosen reference plane differs with the locality and the country making the survey on which the chart is based. The principal planes of reference used are derived from the approximation of:

Mean low water, the average of all low tides. This plane is used on NOS charts of the Atlantic coast, and on nearly all DMAHC charts. The *Gulf Coast Low Water Datum* is essentially the same plane.

Mean lower low water, the average of the lower of the two daily tides. This plane is used on charts of the Pacific coast of the United States, the Hawaiian Islands, the Philippines, and Alaska.

Mean low-water springs, the average of the low waters at spring tides, or *mean lower low-water springs,* the average of the lower of the two daily low tides at springs. Most British Admiralty charts are based on one of these two reference planes.

It is not necessary to know the reference planes of various localities, for the *Tide Tables* are always based on the same plane used for the largest scale charts of the locality. If the reference plane for a given locality differs from the three listed above, it is stated as being the same plane as that of another locality listed in the tables.

Each chart generally carries a statement of the reference plane used for soundings. However, the plane of reference may be in doubt on charts compiled from old or questionable data. If there is any doubt, assume that it is mean low water, for this assumption allows for the greatest margin of safety in that it is the *highest* of the low water datum planes in use on nautical charts. A cautious navigator knows that the depth of water at a given low tide (at a spring low water, for example) can often be less than the depth charted with reference to mean low water. (Note that for the month of June in Figure 906a, of the 58 low tides, 20 are minus heights.) He is also aware that the depth of the water will seldom be lower than the charted depth, *regardless of the state of the tide,* if mean lower low-water springs was used as a tidal reference plane. If he assumes the latter to be the plane used, his decision to take a ship drawing 24 feet over a shoal charted at a depth of 26 feet would prove disastrous if the height of the tide was (−) 3 feet from mean low water, the actual reference plane used, but not noted, on the chart.

Tide Tables **906** Predictions of tidal heights have been published annually by the National Ocean Survey (and its predecessor agency, the Coast & Geodetic Survey) since 1853. The *Tide Tables* now appear in four volumes as follows: *Europe and West Coast of Africa (including the Mediterranean Sea); East Coast, North and South America (including Greenland); West Coast, North and South America (including the Hawaiian Islands); Central and Western Pacific Ocean and Indian Ocean.* Together they contain daily predictions for 197 reference ports and difference data for about 6,000 stations.

Reference stations The format of the *Tide Tables* is shown in the following series of extracts. Table 1 lists the time and height of the tide at each high water and low water in chronological order for each day of the year at a number of places which are designated as *reference stations;* Figure 906a is an extract from Table 1 of the 1977 *Tide Tables for the West Coast of North and South America, including the Hawaiian Islands* for the months of April, May, and June at the reference station, Humboldt Bay, California. Depths are given in feet; these can be easily and quickly converted to meters by multiplying by 0.3.

All times stated in the *Tide Tables* are *standard times;* each page of Table 1 indicates the central meridian of the time zone used. Adjustment must be made for the use of daylight time or any other deviation from standard time at the locality concerned; see Article 2215.

Because the lunar or tidal day is a little more than 24 hours in length (an average of about 24^h50^m), the time between successive high or low tides is a little more than 12 hours. When a high (or low) tide occurs just before midnight, the next high (or low) tide occurs about noon of the following day, and the next one occurs just after midnight. Under these conditions, three consecutive high (or low) tides may occur on three different dates, although the total interval may be no more than the average period of a lunar day, 24^h50^m. This means that on the middle of the three days, there is but one high (or low) water. An example of this is seen in Figure 906a; only one high tide occurs at Humboldt Bay, California on 2 June.

HUMBOLDT BAY, CALIFORNIA, 1977

TIMES AND HEIGHTS OF HIGH AND LOW WATERS

APRIL

DAY	TIME h.m.	HT. ft.	DAY	TIME h.m.	HT. ft.
1	0348	1.6	16	0453	0.5
F	0945	5.8	SA	1102	5.3
	1612	0.5		1652	1.1
	2226	5.9		2302	6.1
2	0434	0.9	17	0531	0.2
SA	1036	6.0	SU	1148	5.2
	1651	0.5		1726	1.4
	2301	6.3		2331	6.2
3	0520	0.3	18	0607	0.0
SU	1126	6.0	M	1230	5.2
	1730	0.7		1800	1.7
	2334	6.6			
4	0606	-0.2	19	0000	6.2
M	1216	6.0	TU	0645	-0.1
	1810	1.0		1308	5.0
				1834	2.0
5	0012	6.9	20	0027	6.1
TU	0652	-0.6	W	0721	-0.2
	1308	5.8		1348	4.9
	1851	1.3		1905	2.2
6	0052	7.0	21	0057	6.1
W	0741	-0.8	TH	0759	-0.2
	1401	5.6		1428	4.7
	1936	1.6		1944	2.5
7	0134	7.0	22	0129	5.9
TH	0833	-0.9	F	0838	-0.1
	1459	5.3		1513	4.6
	2025	2.0		2021	2.7
8	0223	6.8	23	0205	5.7
F	0929	-0.7	SA	0921	0.1
	1603	5.1		1603	4.5
	2120	2.3		2110	2.9
9	0316	6.5	24	0248	5.5
SA	1031	-0.5	SU	1009	0.3
	1714	4.9		1658	4.4
	2229	2.6		2207	3.0
10	0418	6.1	25	0339	5.2
SU	1135	-0.2	M	1103	0.4
	1828	4.9		1757	4.5
	2346	2.6		2316	2.9
11	0533	5.7	26	0441	5.0
M	1240	0.1	TU	1159	0.6
	1935	5.1		1853	4.7
12	0104	2.4	27	0031	2.7
TU	0654	5.4	W	0554	4.8
	1343	0.3		1253	0.6
	2031	5.4		1941	5.0
13	0216	2.0	28	0137	2.2
W	0810	5.3	TH	0710	4.8
	1439	0.4		1346	0.7
	2116	5.7		2023	5.4
14	0317	1.4	29	0236	1.5
TH	0915	5.3	F	0823	4.9
	1527	0.6		1438	0.8
	2156	5.9		2100	5.8
15	0407	1.0	30	0327	0.8
F	1013	5.3	SA	0926	5.1
	1612	0.9		1523	0.9
	2230	6.0		2138	6.3

MAY

DAY	TIME h.m.	HT. ft.	DAY	TIME h.m.	HT. ft.
1	0417	0.0	16	0513	-0.3
SU	1023	5.3	M	1141	4.7
	1609	1.1		1651	2.0
	2217	6.7		2252	6.3
2	0502	-0.7	17	0551	-0.5
M	1120	5.4	TU	1223	4.7
	1654	1.3		1729	2.3
	2256	7.0		2322	6.3
3	0550	-1.3	18	0627	-0.6
TU	1213	5.5	W	1306	4.7
	1740	1.5		1805	2.4
	2338	7.2		2351	6.2
4	0637	-1.6	19	0702	-0.7
W	1306	5.5	TH	1343	4.7
	1828	1.8		1840	2.6
5	0021	7.3	20	0023	6.1
TH	0727	-1.7	F	0737	-0.6
	1401	5.4		1422	4.7
	1917	2.0		1915	2.7
6	0109	7.1	21	0057	6.0
F	0818	-1.6	SA	0814	-0.5
	1457	5.3		1502	4.7
	2009	2.2		2001	2.9
7	0201	6.7	22	0134	5.8
SA	0910	-1.3	SU	0853	-0.4
	1556	5.2		1544	4.7
	2112	2.4		2049	2.9
8	0257	6.2	23	0216	5.5
SU	1005	-0.9	M	0934	-0.2
	1658	5.2		1629	4.8
	2222	2.4		2144	2.9
9	0359	5.7	24	0304	5.2
M	1104	-0.4	TU	1019	0.1
	1801	5.3		1715	4.9
	2339	2.3		2253	2.7
10	0512	5.1	25	0405	4.8
TU	1202	0.1	W	1107	0.3
	1900	5.5		1757	5.2
11	0055	2.0	26	0004	2.4
W	0634	4.7	TH	0515	4.5
	1300	0.5		1157	0.6
	1950	5.7		1845	5.5
12	0204	1.5	27	0110	1.8
TH	0754	4.5	F	0638	4.3
	1356	0.9		1253	0.9
	2034	5.9		1928	5.9
13	0303	0.9	28	0210	1.0
F	0906	4.5	SA	0758	4.3
	1444	1.2		1348	1.2
	2114	6.1		2013	6.3
14	0352	0.4	29	0306	0.2
SA	1005	4.6	SU	0912	4.5
	1530	1.5		1439	1.5
	2148	6.2		2056	6.7
15	0436	0.0	30	0358	-0.6
SU	1058	4.6	M	1017	4.7
	1612	1.8		1533	1.7
	2221	6.2		2142	7.1
			31	0446	-1.3
			TU	1115	5.0
				1625	1.9
				2228	7.4

JUNE

DAY	TIME h.m.	HT. ft.	DAY	TIME h.m.	HT. ft.
1	0536	-1.8	16	0607	-0.8
W	1212	5.2	TH	1254	4.6
	1715	2.0		1739	2.7
	2314	7.5		2327	6.4
2	0625	-2.0	17	0642	-0.8
TH	1303	5.3	F	1329	4.7
	1806	2.1		1818	2.8
				2359	6.3
3	0002	7.4	18	0717	-0.8
F	0713	-2.0	SA	1401	4.8
	1353	5.4		1858	2.8
	1902	2.2			
4	0050	7.1	19	0035	6.2
SA	0801	-1.8	SU	0750	-0.7
	1445	5.4		1436	4.9
	1959	2.3		1940	2.8
5	0142	6.7	20	0113	5.9
SU	0849	-1.4	M	0826	-0.5
	1537	5.5		1512	5.0
	2102	2.3		2028	2.8
6	0238	6.1	21	0155	5.6
M	0938	-0.9	TU	0902	-0.3
	1629	5.6		1550	5.2
	2208	2.2		2122	2.6
7	0337	5.4	22	0244	5.3
TU	1029	-0.3	W	0940	0.0
	1722	5.7		1629	5.4
	2322	2.0		2226	2.4
8	0447	4.8	23	0340	4.8
W	1122	0.3	TH	1023	0.4
	1814	5.8		1711	5.7
				2333	2.0
9	0033	1.7	24	0453	4.4
TH	0605	4.3	F	1112	0.9
	1215	0.9		1756	6.0
	1903	5.9			
10	0142	1.3	25	0042	1.4
F	0731	4.0	SA	0615	4.1
	1306	1.4		1207	1.3
	1948	6.1		1845	6.3
11	0239	0.8	26	0145	0.6
SA	0848	4.0	SU	0741	4.1
	1357	1.8		1306	1.7
	2029	6.2		1934	6.7
12	0330	0.3	27	0247	-0.1
SU	0952	4.1	M	0903	4.2
	1447	2.1		1405	2.0
	2108	6.3		2025	7.1
13	0415	-0.1	28	0341	-0.8
M	1048	4.3	TU	1012	4.5
	1533	2.3		1504	2.2
	2143	6.4		2116	7.4
14	0454	-0.4	29	0432	-1.4
TU	1135	4.4	W	1107	4.8
	1618	2.5		1603	2.2
	2220	6.4		2207	7.5
15	0531	-0.6	30	0523	-1.8
W	1215	4.5	TH	1200	5.1
	1657	2.6		1658	2.2
	2252	6.4		2257	7.6

TIME MERIDIAN 120° W. 0000 IS MIDNIGHT. 1200 IS NOON.
HEIGHTS ARE RECKONED FROM THE DATUM OF SOUNDINGS ON CHARTS OF THE LOCALITY WHICH IS MEAN LOWER LOW WATER.

Figure 906a. *Tide Tables,* Table 1 (extract).

During portions of each month, the tide becomes diurnal at some stations; that is, there is only one high tide and one low tide each lunar or tidal day. This is indicated by blank entries in the tabulated data.

Subordinate stations Secondary or *subordinate stations* are listed in geographical order in Table 2; see Figure 906b. Each subordinate station is given a number, its location is described, and its position in latitude and longitude is given to the nearest minute. Data are then given which are to be applied to the predictions at a stated reference station (shown in bold type) to obtain the tidal information for the subordinate station; if there is more than one reference station on a page of Table 2, one must be sure to use the one printed *above* the subordinate station listing. For example, in Figure 906b, Nestucca Bay entrance in Oregon is subordinate station No. 763 at 45° 10′ N, 123° 58′ W; the time and height differences tabulated are to be applied to the daily predictions for the reference station of Humboldt Bay, California.

Determining time of high or low tide A separate time difference is tabulated for high and low water as shown in Figure 906b. Each time difference is added to or subtracted from the time of the respective high or low water at the reference station in accordance with its sign. A navigator must be alert to changes of date, either forward or backwards, when the time difference is applied. For example, if a high water occurs at a reference station at 2200 on 23 March and the tide at the subordinate station occurs 3 hours later, then high water will occur at 0100 on 24 March at the subordinate station. Conversely, if a high water at a reference station occurs at 0200 on 29 March, and the tide at the subordinate station occurs 5 hours earlier, the high water at the subordinate station will occur at 2100 on 28 March.

The height of the tide is found in several ways, depending on local conditions. If the difference for height of high water is given, with 0.0 feet tabulated as the low-water difference, apply the high-water difference in accordance with its sign to the height of high water at the reference station. The height of low water will be, of course, the same as that at the reference station. If a difference for height of low as well as high water is given, each must be applied in accordance with its sign to the height of the corresponding tide at the reference station, adding the difference if its sign is plus (+) and subtracting if its sign is minus (−). If a *ratio* of ranges is given, the heights of the tides at the subordinate station can be obtained by multiplying the heights of both high and low tides at the reference station by the respective ratios.

Any unusual conditions pertaining to a subordinate station, or any complex calculations required, are explained in keyed footnotes on the appropriate page of Table 2.

Tidal ranges The mean tide level and the ranges of tide (mean, plus spring, diurnal, or tropic) are listed in Table 2, but are seldom used by a navigator except as items of general interest. An explanation of them is given in the *Tide Tables.*

TABLE 2.—TIDAL DIFFERENCES AND OTHER CONSTANTS

No.	PLACE	POSITION		DIFFERENCES				RANGES		Mean Tide Level
		Lat.	Long.	Time		Height		Mean	Diurnal	
				High water	Low water	High water	Low water			
		° ′	° ′	h. m.	h. m.	feet	feet	feet	feet	feet
	CALIFORNIA, Outer Coast—Continued *Time meridian, 120°W.*	N.	W.	on HUMBOLDT BAY, p.76						
719	Trinidad Harbor	41 03	124 09	-0 37	-0 40	+0.1	0.0	4.6	6.4	3.5
721	Crescent City	41 45	124 12	-0 32	-0 29	+0.6	0.0	5.1	6.9	3.7
	OREGON									
723	Brookings, Chetco Cove	42 03	124 17	-0 30	-0 26	+0.6	0.0	5.1	6.9	3.7
725	Wedderburn, Rogue River	42 26	124 25	-0 22	-0 14	+0.3	-0.1	4.9	6.7	3.6
727	Port Orford	42 44	124 30	-0 24	-0 21	+0.9	+0.1	5.3	7.3	3.9
729	Bandon, Coquille River	43 07	124 25	-0 08	-0 02	+0.6	-0.1	5.2	7.0	3.7
	Coos Bay									
731	Entrance	43 21	124 19	+0 02	+0 07	+0.7	0.0	5.2	7.0	3.8
733	Empire	43 24	124 17	+0 41	+0 50	+0.3	-0.1	4.9	6.7	3.5
735	Coos Bay	43 23	124 13	+1 30	+1 28	+1.0	-0.1	5.6	7.3	3.9
	Umpqua River									
737	Entrance	43 41	124 12	+0 09	+0 03	+0.6	0.0	5.1	6.9	3.7
739	Gardiner	43 44	124 07	+1 00	+1 09	+0.4	-0.2	5.1	6.7	3.5
741	Reedsport	43 42	124 06	+1 15	+1 24	+0.4	-0.2	5.1	6.7	3.6
	Siuslaw River									
743	Entrance	44 01	124 08	+0 10	+0 15	+0.6	-0.1	5.2	6.9	3.7
745	Florence	43 58	124 06	+0 48	+0 58	+0.3	-0.2	5.0	6.6	3.5
747	Waldport, Alsea Bay	44 26	124 04	+0 25	+0 31	+1.3	0.0	5.8	7.7	4.1
	Yaquina Bay and River									
749	Bar at entrance	44 37	124 05	+0 03	+0 09	+1.5	+0.1	5.9	7.9	4.2
751	Newport	44 38	124 03	+0 13	+0 12	+1.6	+0.1	6.0	8.0	4.3
752	Southbeach	44 38	124 03	+0 02	+0 03	+1.8	+0.1	6.2	8.2	4.4
753	Yaquina	44 36	124 01	+0 24	+0 25	+1.8	+0.1	6.2	8.2	4.4
755	Winant	44 35	124 00	+0 32	+0 46	+1.8	0.0	6.3	8.2	4.3
757	Toledo	44 37	123 56	+0 58	+1 09	+1.7	-0.1	6.3	8.1	4.2
759	Taft, Siletz Bay	44 56	124 01	+0 17	+0 43	+0.2	-0.3	5.0	6.6	3.4
761	Kernville, Siletz River	44 54	124 00	+0 53	+1 23	*0.95	*0.67	4.6	6.1	3.1
763	Nestucca Bay entrance	45 10	123 58	+0 24	+0 42	+1.2	-0.1	5.8	7.6	4.0
	Tillamook Bay									
765	Barview	45 34	123 57	+0 11	+0 26	+1.1	-0.1	5.7	7.5	3.9
767	Miami Cove	45 33	123 54	+0 44	+0 56	+1.0	-0.1	5.6	7.4	3.9
769	Bay City	45 31	123 54	+1 02	+1 30	+0.7	+0.2	5.4	7.1	3.7
771	Tillamook, Hoquarten Slough	45 28	123 51	+1 21	+2 45	*1.03	*0.58	5.2	6.6	3.3
	Nehalem River									
773	Brighton	45 40	123 56	+0 20	+0 24	+1.4	0.0	5.9	7.8	4.1
775	Nehalem	45 43	123 53	+0 46	+1 26	+0.8	-0.3	5.6	7.2	3.7
	OREGON and WASHINGTON Columbia River†			on ASTORIA, p.80						
777	Columbia River entrance (N. Jetty)	46 16	124 04	-0 46	-1 10	-0.7	+0.1	5.6	7.5	4.0
779	Ilwaco, Baker Bay, Wash	46 18	124 02	-0 15	-0 09	-0.5	-0.1	6.0	7.6	4.0
781	Chinook, Baker Bay, Wash	46 16	123 57	-0 15	-0 44	-0.2	0.0	6.2	7.9	4.2
783	Hungry Harbor, Wash	46 16	123 51	+0 02	-0 19	+0.1	+0.1	6.4	8.2	4.4
785	Point Adams, Oreg	46 12	123 57	-0 27	-0 48	+0.1	+0.1	6.4	8.3	4.4
787	Warrenton, Skipanon River, Oreg	46 10	123 55	-0 15	-0 29	+0.2	+0.1	6.5	8.3	4.4
789	Astoria (Youngs Bay), Oreg	46 10	123 50	-0 15	-0 24	+0.4	+0.1	6.7	8.6	4.5
791	Astoria (Port Docks), Oreg	46 11	123 52	-0 10	-0 13	-0.2	0.0	6.2	8.0	4.2
793	ASTORIA (Tongue Point), Oreg	46 13	123 46	Daily predictions				6.5	8.2	4.3
795	Settlers Point, Oreg	46 10	123 41	+0 20	+0 43	-0.2	-0.1	6.3	8.0	4.1
797	Harrington Point, Wash	46 16	123 39	+0 19	+0 42	-0.5	-0.2	6.1	7.7	3.9
799	Skamokawa, Steamboat Slough, Wash	46 16	123 27	+0 54	+1 35	-----	-----	5.6	6.9	----
801	Cathlamet, Wash	46 12	123 23	+1 13	+2 05	-----	-----	5.2	6.4	----
803	Wauna, Oreg	46 10	123 24	+1 15	+2 09	-----	-----	5.2	6.3	----
805	Eagle Cliff, Wash	46 10	123 14	+1 41	+2 51	-----	-----	4.5	5.5	----

*Ratio.

†The Columbia River is subject to annual freshets. Short range predictions are available at local river forecast centers. The data for stations above Harrington Point apply only during low river stages.

Figure 906b. *Tide Tables,* Table 2 (extract).

TABLE 3.—HEIGHT OF TIDE AT ANY TIME

Duration of rise or fall, see footnote	Time from the nearest high water or low water														
h. m.	*h. m.*	*h. m.*	*h. m.*	*h. m.*	*h. m.*	*h. m.*	*h. m.*	*h. m.*	*h. m.*	*h. m.*	*h. m.*	*h. m.*	*h. m.*	*h. m.*	*h. m.*
4 00	0 08	0 16	0 24	0 32	0 40	0 48	0 56	1 04	1 12	1 20	1 28	1 36	1 44	1 52	2 00
4 20	0 09	0 17	0 26	0 35	0 43	0 52	1 01	1 09	1 18	1 27	1 35	1 44	1 53	2 01	2 10
4 40	0 09	0 19	0 28	0 37	0 47	0 56	1 05	1 15	1 24	1 33	1 43	1 52	2 01	2 11	2 20
5 00	0 10	0 20	0 30	0 40	0 50	1 00	1 10	1 20	1 30	1 40	1 50	2 00	2 10	2 20	2 30
5 20	0 11	0 21	0 32	0 43	0 53	1 04	1 15	1 25	1 36	1 47	1 57	2 08	2 19	2 29	2 40
5 40	0 11	0 23	0 34	0 45	0 57	1 08	1 19	1 31	1 42	1 53	2 05	2 16	2 27	2 39	2 50
6 00	0 12	0 24	0 36	0 48	1 00	1 12	1 24	1 36	1 48	2 00	2 12	2 24	2 36	2 48	3 00
6 20	0 13	0 25	0 38	0 51	1 03	1 16	1 29	1 41	1 54	2 07	2 19	2 32	2 45	2 57	3 10
6 40	0 13	0 27	0 40	0 53	1 07	1 20	1 33	1 47	2 00	2 13	2 27	2 40	2 53	3 07	3 20
7 00	0 14	0 28	0 42	0 56	1 10	1 24	1 38	1 52	2 06	2 20	2 34	2 48	3 02	3 16	3 30
7 20	0 15	0 29	0 44	0 59	1 13	1 28	1 43	1 57	2 12	2 27	2 41	2 56	3 11	3 25	3 40
7 40	0 15	0 31	0 46	1 01	1 17	1 32	1 47	2 03	2 18	2 33	2 49	3 04	3 19	3 35	3 50
8 00	0 16	0 32	0 48	1 04	1 20	1 36	1 52	2 08	2 24	2 40	2 56	3 12	3 28	3 44	4 00
8 20	0 17	0 33	0 50	1 07	1 23	1 40	1 57	2 13	2 30	2 47	3 03	3 20	3 37	3 53	4 10
8 40	0 17	0 35	0 52	1 09	1 27	1 44	2 01	2 19	2 36	2 53	3 11	3 28	3 45	4 03	4 20
9 00	0 18	0 36	0 54	1 12	1 30	1 48	2 06	2 24	2 42	3 00	3 18	3 36	3 54	4 12	4 30
9 20	0 19	0 37	0 56	1 15	1 33	1 52	2 11	2 29	2 48	3 07	3 25	3 44	4 03	4 21	4 40
9 40	0 19	0 39	0 58	1 17	1 37	1 56	2 15	2 35	2 54	3 13	3 33	3 52	4 11	4 31	4 50
10 00	0 20	0 40	1 00	1 20	1 40	2 00	2 20	2 40	3 00	3 20	3 40	4 00	4 20	4 40	5 00
10 20	0 21	0 41	1 02	1 23	1 43	2 04	2 25	2 45	3 06	3 27	3 47	4 08	4 29	4 49	5 10
10 40	0 21	0 43	1 04	1 25	1 47	2 08	2 29	2 51	3 12	3 33	3 55	4 16	4 37	4 59	5 20

Range of tide, see footnote	Correction to height														
Ft.	*Ft.*	*Ft.*	*Ft.*	*Ft.*	*Ft.*	*Ft.*	*Ft.*	*Ft.*	*Ft.*	*Ft.*	*Ft.*	*Ft.*	*Ft.*	*Ft.*	*Ft.*
0.5	0.0	0.0	0.0	0.0	0.0	0.0	0.1	0.1	0.1	0.1	0.1	0.2	0.2	0.2	0.2
1.0	0.0	0.0	0.0	0.0	0.1	0.1	0.1	0.2	0.2	0.2	0.3	0.3	0.4	0.4	0.5
1.5	0.0	0.0	0.0	0.1	0.1	0.1	0.2	0.2	0.3	0.4	0.4	0.5	0.6	0.7	0.8
2.0	0.0	0.0	0.0	0.1	0.1	0.2	0.3	0.3	0.4	0.5	0.6	0.7	0.8	0.9	1.0
2.5	0.0	0.0	0.1	0.1	0.2	0.2	0.3	0.4	0.5	0.6	0.7	0.9	1.0	1.1	1.2
3.0	0.0	0.0	0.1	0.1	0.2	0.3	0.4	0.5	0.6	0.8	0.9	1.0	1.2	1.3	1.5
3.5	0.0	0.0	0.1	0.2	0.2	0.3	0.4	0.6	0.7	0.9	1.0	1.2	1.4	1.6	1.8
4.0	0.0	0.0	0.1	0.2	0.3	0.4	0.5	0.7	0.8	1.0	1.2	1.4	1.6	1.8	2.0
4.5	0.0	0.0	0.1	0.2	0.3	0.4	0.6	0.7	0.9	1.1	1.3	1.6	1.8	2.0	2.2
5.0	0.0	0.1	0.1	0.2	0.3	0.5	0.6	0.8	1.0	1.2	1.5	1.7	2.0	2.2	2.5
5.5	0.0	0.1	0.1	0.2	0.4	0.5	0.7	0.9	1.1	1.4	1.6	1.9	2.2	2.5	2.8
6.0	0.0	0.1	0.1	0.3	0.4	0.6	0.8	1.0	1.2	1.5	1.8	2.1	2.4	2.7	3.0
6.5	0.0	0.1	0.2	0.3	0.4	0.6	0.8	1.1	1.3	1.6	1.9	2.2	2.6	2.9	3.2
7.0	0.0	0.1	0.2	0.3	0.5	0.7	0.9	1.2	1.4	1.8	2.1	2.4	2.8	3.1	3.5
7.5	0.0	0.1	0.2	0.3	0.5	0.7	1.0	1.2	1.5	1.9	2.2	2.6	3.0	3.4	3.8
8.0	0.0	0.1	0.2	0.3	0.5	0.8	1.0	1.3	1.6	2.0	2.4	2.8	3.2	3.6	4.0
8.5	0.0	0.1	0.2	0.4	0.6	0.8	1.1	1.4	1.8	2.1	2.5	2.9	3.4	3.8	4.2
9.0	0.0	0.1	0.2	0.4	0.6	0.9	1.2	1.5	1.9	2.2	2.7	3.1	3.6	4.0	4.5
9.5	0.0	0.1	0.2	0.4	0.6	0.9	1.2	1.6	2.0	2.4	2.8	3.3	3.8	4.3	4.8
10.0	0.0	0.1	0.2	0.4	0.7	1.0	1.3	1.7	2.1	2.5	3.0	3.5	4.0	4.5	5.0
10.5	0.0	0.1	0.3	0.5	0.7	1.0	1.3	1.7	2.2	2.6	3.1	3.6	4.2	4.7	5.2
11.0	0.0	0.1	0.3	0.5	0.7	1.1	1.4	1.8	2.3	2.8	3.3	3.8	4.4	4.9	5.5
11.5	0.0	0.1	0.3	0.5	0.8	1.1	1.5	1.9	2.4	2.9	3.4	4.0	4.6	5.1	5.8
12.0	0.0	0.1	0.3	0.5	0.8	1.1	1.5	2.0	2.5	3.0	3.6	4.1	4.8	5.4	6.0
12.5	0.0	0.1	0.3	0.5	0.8	1.2	1.6	2.1	2.6	3.1	3.7	4.3	5.0	5.6	6.2
13.0	0.0	0.1	0.3	0.6	0.9	1.2	1.7	2.2	2.7	3.2	3.9	4.5	5.1	5.8	6.5
13.5	0.0	0.1	0.3	0.6	0.9	1.3	1.7	2.2	2.8	3.4	4.0	4.7	5.3	6.0	6.8
14.0	0.0	0.2	0.3	0.6	0.9	1.3	1.8	2.3	2.9	3.5	4.2	4.8	5.5	6.3	7.0
14.5	0.0	0.2	0.4	0.6	1.0	1.4	1.9	2.4	3.0	3.6	4.3	5.0	5.7	6.5	7.2
15.0	0.0	0.2	0.4	0.6	1.0	1.4	1.9	2.5	3.1	3.8	4.4	5.2	5.9	6.7	7.5
15.5	0.0	0.2	0.4	0.7	1.0	1.5	2.0	2.6	3.2	3.9	4.6	5.4	6.1	6.9	7.8
16.0	0.0	0.2	0.4	0.7	1.1	1.5	2.1	2.6	3.3	4.0	4.7	5.5	6.3	7.2	8.0
16.5	0.0	0.2	0.4	0.7	1.1	1.6	2.1	2.7	3.4	4.1	4.9	5.7	6.5	7.4	8.2
17.0	0.0	0.2	0.4	0.7	1.1	1.6	2.2	2.8	3.5	4.2	5.0	5.9	6.7	7.6	8.5
17.5	0.0	0.2	0.4	0.8	1.2	1.7	2.2	2.9	3.6	4.4	5.2	6.0	6.9	7.8	8.8
18.0	0.0	0.2	0.4	0.8	1.2	1.7	2.3	3.0	3.7	4.5	5.3	6.2	7.1	8.1	9.0
18.5	0.1	0.2	0.5	0.8	1.2	1.8	2.4	3.1	3.8	4.6	5.5	6.4	7.3	8.3	9.2
19.0	0.1	0.2	0.5	0.8	1.3	1.8	2.4	3.1	3.9	4.8	5.6	6.6	7.5	8.5	9.5
19.5	0.1	0.2	0.5	0.8	1.3	1.9	2.5	3.2	4.0	4.9	5.8	6.7	7.7	8.7	9.8
20.0	0.1	0.2	0.5	0.9	1.3	1.9	2.6	3.3	4.1	5.0	5.9	6.9	7.9	9.0	10.0

Figure 906c. *Tide Tables,* Table 3.

Height of tide at intermediate time

The height of the tide at a specific time other than those tabulated in Table 1 or computed using Table 2 can be found by means of Table 3, illustrated in Figure 906c, which is normally used without interpolation. This table is easy to use and the instructions given below the table are explicit.

Note that interpolation is not done when using Table 3. The predictions of times and heights of tide are influenced by local conditions to the extent that they are not exact enough to make meaningful any interpolation for more precise values.

Other information in *Tide Tables*

The various volumes of the *Tide Tables* also contain other information which may be of interest to a navigator.

The local mean time of sunrise and sunset is given in Table 4 for each two degrees of latitude. While this information is usually ob-

TABLE 4.-SUNRISE AND SUNSET, 1977

Date		30° N.		32° N.		34° N.		36° N.		38° N.		40° N.	
		Rise	Set	Rise	Set	Rise	Set	Rise	Set	Rise	Set	Rise	Set
		h. m.	h. m.	h. m.	h. m.	h. m.	h. m.	h. m.	h. m.	h. m.	h. m.	h. m.	h. m.
Jan.	1	6 56	17 11	7 01	17 07	7 06	17 02	7 11	16 57	7 16	16 51	7 22	16 45
	6	6 57	17 15	7 02	17 11	7 06	17 06	7 11	17 01	7 17	16 56	7 22	16 50
	11	6 57	17 19	7 02	17 15	7 06	17 10	7 11	17 05	7 16	17 00	7 22	16 55
	16	6 57	17 23	7 01	17 19	7 05	17 15	7 10	17 10	7 15	17 05	7 20	17 00
	21	6 55	17 28	6 59	17 24	7 04	17 20	7 08	17 15	7 12	17 11	7 17	17 06
	26	6 54	17 32	6 57	17 28	7 01	17 25	7 05	17 21	7 09	17 16	7 14	17 12
	31	6 51	17 36	6 55	17 33	6 58	17 29	7 02	17 26	7 06	17 22	7 10	17 18
Feb.	5	6 48	17 41	6 51	17 37	6 54	17 34	6 58	17 31	7 01	17 27	7 05	17 24
	10	6 44	17 45	6 47	17 42	6 50	17 39	6 53	17 36	6 56	17 33	6 59	17 30
	15	6 40	17 49	6 43	17 46	6 45	17 44	6 48	17 41	6 50	17 39	6 53	17 36
	20	6 36	17 53	6 38	17 50	6 40	17 48	6 42	17 46	6 44	17 44	6 47	17 41
	25	6 31	17 56	6 32	17 55	6 34	17 53	6 36	17 51	6 38	17 49	6 40	17 47
Mar.	2	6 25	18 00	6 27	17 58	6 28	17 57	6 29	17 56	6 31	17 54	6 32	17 53
	7	6 20	18 03	6 21	18 02	6 22	18 01	6 23	18 00	6 24	17 59	6 25	17 58
	12	6 14	18 06	6 14	18 06	6 15	18 05	6 16	18 05	6 16	18 04	6 17	18 04
	17	6 08	18 10	6 08	18 09	6 08	18 09	6 09	18 09	6 09	18 09	6 09	18 09
	22	6 02	18 13	6 02	18 13	6 01	18 13	6 01	18 13	6 01	18 14	6 01	18 14
	27	5 56	18 16	5 55	18 16	5 55	18 17	5 54	18 18	5 53	18 18	5 53	18 19
Apr.	1	5 50	18 19	5 49	18 20	5 48	18 21	5 47	18 22	5 46	18 23	5 45	18 24
	6	5 44	18 22	5 43	18 23	5 41	18 24	5 40	18 26	5 38	18 27	5 37	18 29
	11	5 38	18 25	5 36	18 26	5 35	18 28	5 33	18 30	5 31	18 32	5 29	18 34
	16	5 33	18 28	5 30	18 30	5 28	18 32	5 26	18 34	5 24	18 37	5 21	18 39
	21	5 27	18 31	5 25	18 33	5 22	18 36	5 20	18 39	5 17	18 41	5 14	18 44
	26	5 22	18 34	5 19	18 37	5 17	18 40	5 13	18 43	5 10	18 46	5 07	18 49
May	1	5 17	18 37	5 14	18 40	5 11	18 43	5 08	18 47	5 04	18 51	5 00	18 54
	6	5 13	18 40	5 10	18 44	5 06	18 47	5 03	18 51	4 59	18 55	4 54	18 59
	11	5 09	18 44	5 06	18 47	5 02	18 51	4 58	18 55	4 54	19 00	4 49	19 04
	16	5 06	18 47	5 02	18 51	4 58	18 55	4 54	18 59	4 49	19 04	4 44	19 09
	21	5 03	18 50	4 59	18 54	4 55	18 59	4 50	19 03	4 45	19 08	4 40	19 14
	26	5 01	18 53	4 57	18 57	4 52	19 02	4 47	19 07	4 42	19 12	4 36	19 18
	31	5 00	18 56	4 55	19 00	4 50	19 05	4 45	19 11	4 40	19 16	4 34	19 22
June	5	4 59	18 58	4 54	19 03	4 49	19 08	4 43	19 14	4 38	19 19	4 32	19 25
	10	4 58	19 01	4 53	19 05	4 48	19 11	4 43	19 16	4 37	19 22	4 31	19 28
	15	4 58	19 02	4 53	19 07	4 48	19 13	4 43	19 18	4 37	19 24	4 30	19 30
	20	4 59	19 04	4 54	19 09	4 49	19 14	4 43	19 20	4 37	19 26	4 31	19 32
	25	5 00	19 05	4 55	19 10	4 50	19 15	4 44	19 21	4 38	19 26	4 32	19 33
	30	5 02	19 05	4 57	19 10	4 52	19 15	4 46	19 21	4 40	19 27	4 34	19 33

Figure 906d. *Tide Tables,* Table 4.

tained from an *almanac,* it should be noted that values in Table 4 extend to latitude 76° N; this is 4° beyond the latitude range of American almanacs.

Table 5 provides a quick and convenient method for converting local mean time to standard time when the difference in longitude is known.

Table 6 lists the time of moonrise and moonset for a few selected locations. The inside back cover of each volume gives data for the phases of moon, apogee, perigee, and greatest north and south declinations, and crossing of the equator; it also gives solar data on equinoxes and solstices.

Examples of tidal calculations

907 The following examples illustrate the use of *Tide Tables;* all calculations are taken from the extracts shown in Figures 906a, b, and c.

TABLE 5.—ROTARY TIDAL CURRENTS

Great Round Shoal Channel, 4 miles NE. of Great Pt., Nantucket Sound. Lat 41°26′ N., long. 69°59′ W.

Time (Hours after maximum flood at Pollock Rip Channel, see page 28)	Direction (true) *Degrees*	Velocity *Knots*
0	80	0.8
1	88	1.1
2	96	1.3
3	104	1.0
4	129	0.5
5	213	0.5
6	267	1.1
7	275	1.4
8	280	1.2
9	284	0.7
10	328	0.2
11	42	0.4

Cuttyhunk I., 3¼ miles SW. of Lat. 41°23′ N., long. 71°00′ W.

Time (Hours after maximum flood at Pollock Rip Channel, see page 28)	Direction (true) *Degrees*	Velocity *Knots*
0	356	0.4
1	15	0.3
2	80	0.2
3	123	0.3
4	146	0.5
5	158	0.5
6	173	0.4
7	208	0.3
8	267	0.2
9	306	0.3
10	322	0.3
11	335	0.4

Gooseberry Neck, 2 miles SSE. of Buzzards Bay entrance. Lat. 41°27′ N., long. 71°01′ W.

Time (Hours after maximum flood at Pollock Rip Channel, see page 28)	Direction (true) *Degrees*	Velocity *Knots*
0	52	0.6
1	65	0.4
2	108	0.2
3	168	0.3
4	210	0.4
5	223	0.5
6	232	0.5
7	249	0.3
8	274	0.2
9	321	0.2
10	16	0.3
11	38	0.5

Browns Ledge, Massachusetts. Lat. 41°20′ N., long. 71°06′ W.

Time (Hours after maximum flood at Pollock Rip Channel, see page 28)	Direction (true) *Degrees*	Velocity *Knots*
0	330	0.3
1	12	0.3
2	28	0.3
3	104	0.4
4	118	0.4
5	123	0.4
6	168	0.3
7	205	0.2
8	201	0.3
9	270	0.3
10	282	0.4
11	318	0.5

Point Judith, Harbor of Refuge, Block Island Sound (west entrance). Lat. 41°22′ N., long. 71°31′ W.

Time (Hours after maximum flood at The Race, see page 34)	Direction (true) *Degrees*	Velocity *Knots*
0	197	0.2
1	160	0.2
2	151	0.4
3	159	0.5
4	146	0.5
5	124	0.5
6	109	0.4
7	104	0.2
8	90	0.1
9	30	0.1
10	336	0.1
11	209	0.1

Point Judith, 4.5 miles SW. of, Block Island Sound. Lat. 41°18′N., long. 71°33′ W.

Time (Hours after maximum flood at The Race, see page 34)	Direction (true) *Degrees*	Velocity *Knots*
0	264	0.6
1	270	0.6
2	270	0.5
3	280	0.2
4	62	0.2
5	70	0.6
6	78	0.7
7	95	0.5
8	105	0.3
9	120	0.1
10	286	0.1
11	277	0.3

Figure 906e. *Tide Tables,* Table 5.

TABLE 6—MOONRISE AND MOONSET, 1977

SAN FRANCISCO, CALIF.

Day	January		February		March		April		May		June		Day
	Rise	Set	Rise	Set	Rise	Set	Rise	Set	Rise	Set	Rise	Set	
	h. m.	h. m.	h. m.	h. m.	h. m.	h. m.	h. m.	h. m.	h. m.	h. m.	h. m.	h. m.	
1	14 26	03 58	15 36	05 09	14 20	03 44	16 12	04 13	17 13	03 58	19 28	04 52	1
2	15 10	04 51	16 35	05 52	15 20	04 26	17 19	04 50	18 24	04 39	20 31	05 51	2
3	15 58	05 42	17 36	06 33	16 22	05 05	18 28	05 27	19 36	05 24	21 27	06 56	3
4	16 51	06 30	18 39	07 11	17 27	05 43	19 38	06 07	20 44	06 15	22 16	08 02	4
5	17 47	07 15	19 43	07 47	18 33	06 20	20 49	06 50	21 49	07 11	22 58	09 09	5
6	18 46	07 57	20 48	08 23	19 40	06 56	21 58	07 37	22 47	08 11	23 35	10 14	6
7	19 47	08 36	21 54	08 59	20 49	07 34	23 02	08 28	23 37	09 15	.. ..	11 16	7
8	20 49	09 12	23 01	09 35	21 57	08 14	.. ..	09 25	.. ..	10 20	00 10	12 17	8
9	21 52	09 47	.. ..	10 15	23 05	08 57	00 02	10 25	00 21	11 24	00 43	13 16	9
10	22 57	10 21	00 08	10 58	.. ..	09 44	00 54	11 27	01 00	12 26	01 14	14 13	10
11	.. ..	10 56	01 13	11 45	00 10	10 35	01 41	12 29	01 35	13 26	01 46	15 09	11
12	00 02	11 33	02 17	12 38	01 11	11 31	02 22	13 32	02 08	14 25	02 19	16 04	12
13	01 09	12 13	03 17	13 36	02 07	12 31	02 59	14 32	02 39	15 22	02 54	16 58	13
14	02 15	12 58	04 11	14 37	02 57	13 33	03 33	15 32	03 11	16 18	03 33	17 50	14
15	03 22	13 49	05 00	15 41	03 41	14 35	04 05	16 30	03 43	17 14	04 15	18 41	15
16	04 26	14 45	05 43	16 45	04 21	15 37	04 36	17 27	04 17	18 09	05 00	19 29	16
17	05 26	15 47	06 23	17 48	04 57	16 39	05 08	18 24	04 54	19 03	05 49	20 14	17
18	06 20	16 51	06 58	18 50	05 31	17 39	05 41	19 19	05 33	19 55	06 41	20 56	18
19	07 07	17 57	07 32	19 50	06 04	18 37	06 16	20 14	06 16	20 44	07 36	21 34	19
20	07 49	19 02	08 04	20 49	06 35	19 35	06 54	21 07	07 03	21 31	08 33	22 10	20
21	08 27	20 05	08 36	21 46	07 08	20 32	07 35	21 59	07 53	22 14	09 32	22 44	21
22	09 02	21 06	09 08	22 42	07 41	21 27	08 19	22 47	08 46	22 54	10 32	23 18	22
23	09 34	22 05	09 43	23 38	08 17	22 22	09 07	23 33	09 42	23 32	11 33	23 52	23
24	10 05	23 03	10 20	.. ..	08 56	23 14	09 59	.. ..	10 40	.. ..	12 37	.. ..	24
25	10 36	23 59	11 00	00 31	09 38	.. ..	10 53	00 15	11 39	00 08	13 42	00 28	25
26	11 09	.. ..	11 43	01 23	10 24	00 04	11 50	00 55	12 41	00 42	14 50	01 06	26
27	11 45	00 54	12 31	02 13	11 14	00 52	12 50	01 32	13 45	01 16	15 58	01 49	27
28	12 23	01 48	13 24	03 00	12 07	01 37	13 52	02 08	14 51	01 52	17 06	02 37	28
29	13 05	02 41	.. ..	.. ..	13 04	02 19	14 57	02 44	16 00	02 30	18 11	03 32	29
30	13 51	03 33	.. ..	.. ..	14 04	02 59	16 04	03 20	17 10	03 12	19 11	04 34	30
31	14 41	04 22	.. ..	.. ..	15 07	03 37	.. ..	.. ..	18 21	03 59	.. ..	.. ..	31

Figure 906f. *Tide Tables,* Table 6 (extract).

Example 1: Determination of time and height of a tide at a reference station.

Required: The time and height of afternoon high water at Humboldt Bay, California on 5 June 1977. (Local time is then Pacific Daylight Time, PDT.)

Solution: From Table 1, shown in Figure 906a, extract the desired information.

Answer: High water is at 1537 Pacific Standard Time (PST), which would be 1637 PDT; height of 5.5 feet (1.7 m) above mean lower low water.

Example 2: Determination of time and height of a tide at a subordinate station.

Required: The time and height of the morning low water at Crescent City, California, on 5 June 1977.

Solution: Determine the time and height differences for the location from Table 1; apply these to the appropriate tide at the reference station.

ASTRONOMICAL DATA, 1977

Greenwich mean time of the moon's phases, apogee, perigee, greatest north and south declination, moon on the Equator, and the solar equinoxes and solstices.

January

	d.	h.	m.
N	3	17	..
○	5	12	10
E	10	17	..
◑	12	19	55
P	16	10	..
S	17	01	..
●	19	14	11
E	23	15	..
◐	27	05	11
A	28	06	..
N	31	02	..

February

	d.	h.	m.
○	4	03	56
E	7	00	..
P	11	04	..
◑	11	04	07
S	13	09	..
●	18	03	37
E	20	01	..
A	25	03	..
◐	26	02	50
N	27	11	..

March

	d.	h.	m.
○	5	17	13
E	6	08	..
P	8	23	..
◑	12	11	35
S	12	15	..
E	19	09	..
●	19	18	33
$\odot_1$	20	17	43
A	24	22	..
N	26	19	..
◐	27	22	27

April

	d.	h.	m.
E	2	18	..
○	4	04	09
P	5	21	..
S	8	21	..
◑	10	19	15
E	15	15	..
●	18	10	35
A	21	12	..
N	23	02	..
◐	26	14	42
E	30	05	..

May

	d.	h.	m.
○	3	13	03
P	4	05	..
S	6	06	..
◑	10	04	08
E	12	21	..
●	18	02	51
A	18	18	..
N	20	09	..
◐	26	03	20
E	27	14	..

June

	d.	h.	m.
P	1	15	..
○	1	20	31
S	2	17	..
◑	8	15	07
E	9	04	..
A	14	21	..
N	16	16	..
●	16	18	23
$\odot_2$	21	12	14
E	23	22	..
◐	24	12	44
P	30	00	..
S	30	04	..

July

	d.	h.	m.
○	1	03	24
E	6	13	..
◑	8	04	39
A	12	08	..
N	14	00	..
●	16	08	37
E	21	05	..
◐	23	19	38
S	27	15	..
P	28	02	..
○	30	10	52

August

	d.	h.	m.
E	2	23	..
◑	6	20	40
A	9	00	..
N	10	08	..
●	14	21	31
E	17	11	..
◐	22	01	04
S	23	22	..
P	24	09	..
○	28	20	10
E	30	09	..

September

	d.	h.	m.
◑	5	14	33
A	5	18	..
N	6	17	..
●	13	09	23
E	13	19	..
P	18	09	..
S	20	04	..
◐	20	06	18
$\odot_3$	23	03	30
E	26	17	..
○	27	08	17

October

	d.	h.	m.
A	3	14	..
N	4	01	..
◑	5	09	21
E	11	04	..
●	12	20	31
P	15	09	..
S	17	10	..
◐	19	12	46
E	24	00	..
○	26	23	35
A	31	08	..
N	31	08	..

November

	d.	h.	m.
◑	4	03	58
E	7	15	..
●	11	07	09
P	12	12	..
S	13	19	..
◐	17	21	52
E	20	06	..
○	25	17	31
N	27	16	..
A	27	21	..

December

	d.	h.	m.
◑	3	21	16
E	5	01	..
●	10	17	33
P	10	23	..
S	11	06	..
◐	17	10	37
E	17	13	..
$\odot_4$	21	23	24
A	24	21	..
N	24	23	..
○	25	12	49

●, new moon; ◐, first quarter; ○, full moon; ◑, last quarter; E, moon on the Equator; N, S, moon farthest north or south of the Equator; A, P, moon in apogee or perigee; $\odot_1$, sun at vernal equinox; $\odot_2$, sun at summer solstice; $\odot_3$, sun at autumnal equinox; $\odot_4$, sun at winter solstice.

0^h is midnight. 12^h is noon. The times may be adapted to any other time meridian than Greenwich by adding the longitude in time when it is east and subtracting it when west. (15° of longitude equals 1 hour of time).

This table was compiled from the American Ephemeris and Nautical Almanac.

Figure 906g. *Tide Tables,* inside back cover.

Differences at subordinate station: low water time -0^h29^m; height 0.0 feet.

Reference station: Humboldt Bay; low water at 0849; height −1.4 feet.

08 49	− 1.4 feet
− 0 29	0.0
08 20	− 1.4 feet

Answer: The A.M. low water occurs at 0820 with a height of 1.4 feet (0.4 m) *below* the datum of mean lower low water.

Example 3: Determination of height of tide at a given time at a reference station.

Required: Height of tide at Humboldt Bay at 1400 PDT on 5 June 1977.

Solution: Correct daylight time to standard time. Use Table 1 to determine heights of high and low tide on either side of specified time. Use Table 3 to determine height at specified time.

1400 PDT is 1300 PST, which is the time zone of Table 1 for this area.

The applicable times and heights of tide from Table 1 are:

0849	−1.4
1537	5.5

To use Table 3, calculate range of tide: 5.5 − (−1.4) = 6.9 feet. Calculate duration of rise or fall: 1537 − 0849 = 6^h48^m, rising. Calculate time interval from the desired time to the nearest high water or low water: 1537 − 1300 = 2^h37^m (from high water).

Entering Table 3 on the line for the nearest tabulated duration, 6^h40^m, go across to nearest tabulated value for time interval, 2^h40^m. Go down this column to line for nearest value of range, 7.0 feet; here read correction to height, 2.4 feet.

Since the time interval used was from high water, subtract this correction from height at high water: 5.5 − 2.4 = 3.1 feet.

Answer: The height of tide at 1400 PDT is 3.1 feet (0.9 m) above datum.

Example 4: Determination of height of tide at a given time at a subordinate station.

Required: Height of tide at 1225 PDT at Kernville, Oregon, on Siletz River on 5 June 1977.

Solution: (See Figure 907.) Convert daylight time to standard time. Use Table 2, then Table 1, to determine time and height of high and low waters at subordinate station on either side of specified time. Use Table 3, to determine height at specified time.

1225 PDT is 1125 PST, which is the time zone of Table 1 for this area.

The applicable factors from Table 2 are: high water + 0^h53^m, 0.95 ratio; low water + 1^h23^m, 0.67 ratio.

HT OF TIDE	
Date	5 June 77
Location	Kernville, #761
Time	1225 PDT (1125 PST)
Ref Sta	Humboldt Bay
HW Time Diff	+0 53
LW Time Diff	+1 23
HW Ht Diff	0.95 ratio
LW Ht Diff	0.67 ratio
Ref Sta HW/LW Time	1537 / 0849
HW/LW Time Diff	+053 +123
Sub Sta HW/LW Time	1630 1012
Ref Sta HW/LW Ht	5.5 / -1.4
HW/LW Ht Diff	.95 .67
Sub Sta HW/LW Ht	5.2 -0.9
Duration Rise Fall	6:18 rising
Time Fm Near Tide	1:13 fm LW
Range of Tide	6.1
Ht of Near Tide	-0.9
Corr Table 3	0.6
Ht of Tide	-0.3
Charted Depth	
Depth of Water	
Draft	
Clearance	

Figure 907. Calculation of height of tide at a given time at a subordinate station.

Use these factors to determine applicable high and low waters at Kernville on either side of 1225 PDT (1125 PST).

Low water	08 49	− 1.4	(Reference Sta.)
	+ 1 23	× 0.67	
	10 12	− 0.938	
		− 0.9	(rounded)
High water	15 37	5.5	(Reference Sta.)
	+ 0 53	× 0.95	
	16 30	5.225	
		5.2	(rounded)

With these data, calculate range of tide: 5.2 − (−0.9) = 6.1 feet. Calculate duration of rise or fall: 1630 − 1012 = 6^h18^m (rising). Calculate time interval from the desired time to the time of the nearest high or low water: 1125 − 1012 = 1^h13^m (from low water).

Entering Table 3 on the line for the nearest value of duration, 6^h20^m, go across to nearest tabulated value for time interval, 1^h16^m. Go down this column to line for nearest value of range, 6.0 feet; here read correction to height, 0.6 feet.

Since the time interval was from low water, add this correction to the height at low water: −0.9 + 0.6 = −0.3 feet.

Answer: The height of the tide at 1225 PDT is −0.3 feet, or 0.3 (0.1 m) feet below datum.

Example 5: Determination of the time that a specific height of tide will be reached during a specified portion of a day at a reference station.

Required: How early in the morning of 5 June at Humboldt Bay will the rising tide height reach the datum plane, a tide of 0.0 feet?

Solution: Study Table 1 and note the trend of the tide: low water at 0849, −1.4 feet; high water at 1537, 5.5 feet.

Determine the time of rise: 1537 − 0849 = 6^h48^m. Determine the range: 5.5 − (−1.4) = 6.9 feet. Determine the correction of height needed 0.0 − (−1.4) = 1.4 feet.

Use the lower part of Table 3 with nearest tabulated value of range, 7.0, and correction to height 1.4, to determine the column to be used. Go up this column to the line for the nearest tabulated value of duration, 6^h40^m; here read the time interval, 2^h00^m.

Since the interval is that of rising from low water, add this to time of low water 0849 + 2:00 = 1049 PST or 1149 PDT.

Answer: By 1149 PDT, the tide will have risen to a level of 0.0 feet, the local datum for charted depths.

Example 6: Determination of the available clearance under a fixed bridge at a given time.

Required: The available clearance under a bridge charted with clearance of 55 feet, chart datum is mean high water for heights and mean low water for depths.

Solution: Determine the height of tide at the specified time in accordance with the prior examples; assume for this example it is 3.7 feet. Determine the mean tide range from Table 2; assume for this example it is 5.2 feet. Calculate the water level at specified time with respect to mean high water 3.7 − 5.2 = − 1.5 feet. The water level is 1.5 feet *below* the datum for *heights*; there is this much additional clearance, which then is 55 + 1.5 = 56.5 feet.

Answer: The available vertical clearance at the time specified is 56.5 feet (17.2 m). (Note that the height of tide can be *above* mean high water, at which times clearance will be *less* than the charted value.)

Tidal data by calculator

908 The NOS *Tide Tables* state that Table 3, Height of Tide At Any Time, is based on the assumption that the rise and fall conform to a simple cosine curve. (This is actually only an approximation, but it is sufficiently precise for practical purposes since the actual heights and times will vary somewhat from predicted values due to short-term local effects of winds and barometric pressure.) With this cosine relationship, a personal electronic calculator makes the determination of height of tide at any time an easy task (see Appendix F).

For this procedure, the correction is always calculated *up* from low water, rather than up or down from the nearest low or high water as when using Table 3. The predicted height of tide at any given time (Ht_D) is the low-water predicted height (Ht_{LW}) plus a correction (C).

$$Ht_D = Ht_{LW} + C$$

The correction is equal to the product of the range of tide and a factor (F) based on time.

$$C = F(Ht_{HW} - Ht_{LW})$$

The factor, F, is found using a haversine relationship.

$$F = \frac{1 - \text{Cos}\left(\dfrac{T_D \sim T_{LW}}{T_{HW} \sim T_{LW}} \times 180^\circ\right)}{2}$$

Where T_{HW} is the time of high water

T_{LW} is the time of low water

T_D is the desired time, and indicates absolute difference, the smaller quantity subtracted from the larger.

(Times may be subtracted in either the format of hours and minutes or hours and decimal fractions, but must be stated decimally for division.)

Combining the above equations, the height of tide at any given time may be found from the following expression:

$$Ht = Ht_{LW} + (Ht_{HW} - Ht_{LW}) \left[\frac{1 - \text{Cos}\left(\dfrac{T_D \sim T_{LW}}{T_{HW} \sim T_{LW}} \times 180^\circ\right)}{2}\right]$$

This equation may be used directly for predictions at reference stations, and for predictions at subordinate stations after applying time and height differences.

Example: Determination of the height of tide at any given station at a reference station by use of a calculator.

Required: Height of tide at Humboldt Bay at 1400 PDT on 5 June 1977.

Solution: Daylight time is corrected to standard time by subtracting one hour. Values of time and height on either side of the given time are taken from Table 1 and used in the equation just developed.

$T_D = 1300$ PST
LW $= -1.4$ feet at 0849
HW$=$ 5.5 feet at 1537

Therefore:

$$Ht_D = (-1.4) + [5.5 - (-1.4)]\left[\frac{1 - \text{Cos}\left(\dfrac{1300 - 0849}{1537 - 0849} \times 180^\circ\right)}{2}\right]$$
$$= 3.27 \text{ feet.}$$

Expressed to the nearest tenth of a foot, as specified for height of tide, this is 3.3 feet. In some instances, a difference of one or two tenths may exist between the results obtained by the two procedures as Table 3 is used to the nearest tabulated values without interpolation. The calculator solution might be said to be "more precise," but, as noted above, normal variations in local conditions will render the predictions less accurate in practice than the calculations would indicate.

Notes on tide problem solutions

909 The use of a standard printed form (such as Figure 907) will expedite calculations and help ensure accuracy. A qualified navigator, however, *must* be able to solve any tide problem *without* dependence on such forms since they may not always be available.

In cases of doubt, particularly in working with Table 3 in the Tide Tables, and Tables 3 and 4 in the Current Tables, reference to the explanatory notes accompanying the tables will clarify the method of solution.

The most common errors in the completion of a tide table for a subordinate station are: applying the high-water difference to the height of low water at the reference station as well as to the height of high water; not being alert to a change in date at the subordinate station after applying the high-water or low-water time difference to the reference station; and failure to apply the difference factor from Table 3 (with the proper sign) to a rising or a falling tide at the station in question. When the nearest tide is high water, subtract the correction factor of Table 3 from nearest high tide; when the nearest tide is low water, add the correction to nearest low tide.

Summary

910 Knowledge of the height of tide can be of critical importance to a navigator when traversing shoals, using a channel of barely enough depth, or having to pass under a bridge with close vertical clearance. Prediction tables are available for essentially all waters of interest, but in many instances predictions may be upset by persistent winds of moderate or greater strength. A navigator must be able to calculate quickly and accurately the heights of tide at a given time at either a reference station or subordinate station. He must be aware that often low-water depths may be less than charted depths (or vertical clearances less than charted values), and he should use all available methods of measuring depths to confirm actual depths and thus ensure the safety of his vessel.

10 Currents and Current Predictions

Introduction **1001** The preceding chapter discussed the *vertical* motion of water, or *tides.* This chapter deals with the *horizontal* movement of water which is called *current.* The effects of current on a vessel can set it off its course or change its rate of movement with respect to the earth, or, more likely, cause both of these. Currents have their origin in two separate phenomena: long-term climatic and weather conditions, and the daily rise and fall of the tides.

The first part of this chapter will deal with the known ocean current systems, their location, and where data concerning them may be found. In considering these current systems, it must be borne in mind that strong winds, blowing contrary to the prevailing wind pattern for prolonged periods, can have a marked effect on the drift (speed) of an ocean current, and, to a lesser degree, on its set (direction) in the affected area; drift is often described in terms of miles per day, rather than knots. When the weather returns to normal, the current system will also return to its normal flow, which often can be predicted with considerable accuracy.

Ocean current systems **1002** A number of well-defined, permanent, current systems exist in the open oceans, as charted in Figure 1002. The chief cause of these currents is wind. Winds, such as the various *trade winds,* blow almost continuously with considerable force, and in the same general direction, over large areas of the globe. The direction, steadiness, and force of a prevailing wind determine to a large extent the set, drift, depth, and permanence of the current it generates. However, currents with a generally northerly or southerly drift are considerably affected by the *Coriolis force.* This is an apparent force, acting on a body in motion, caused by the rotation of the earth. In the northern hemisphere deflection is to the right, in a clockwise direction; in the southern hemisphere the deflection is counterclockwise. The *Coriolis force* is largely responsible for the circular pattern of the slow flow of currents in the North and South Atlantic, the North and South Pacific, and in the Indian Ocean. Because of seasonal variations in the wind systems, and due to other seasonal changes, the characteristics of most ocean currents change considerably, but quite predictably, at certain times of the year.

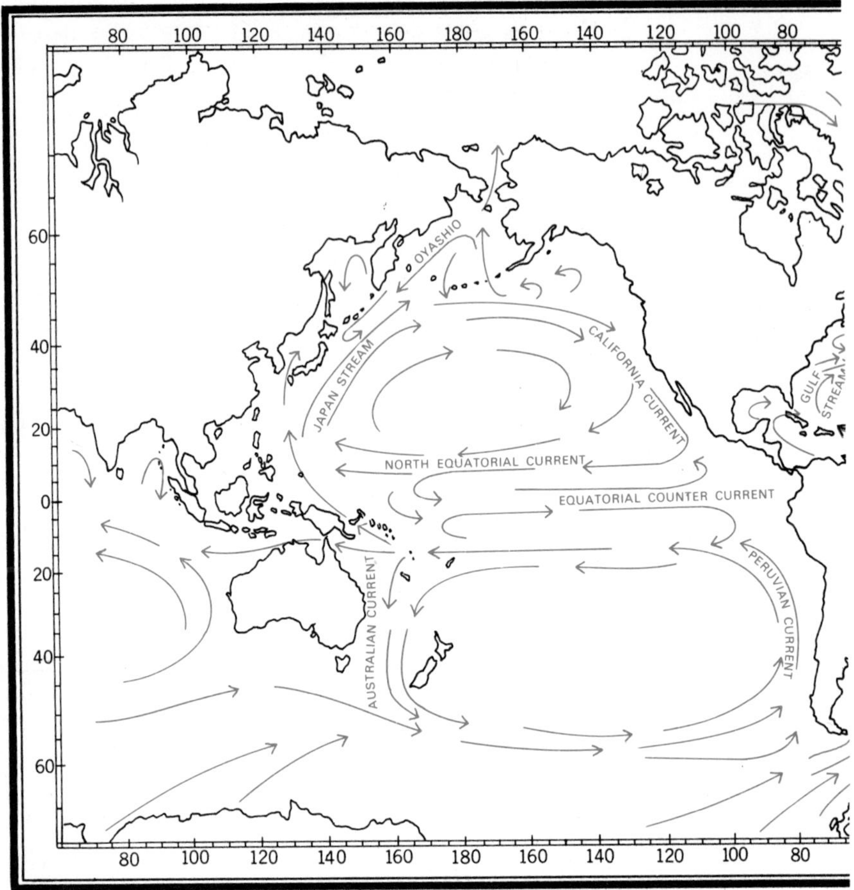

Figure 1002. The principal ocean currents.

Currents are often described as warm or cold. These terms are relative, and are based on the latitudes in which they originate, and on the effect they have on climate. For example, the northeast drift current off the northern coast of Norway is a "warm" current, although it may be lower in temperature than the southern extremity of the cold Labrador current off the New England coast.

Warm and cold currents

Currents as well as winds were of great importance in the days of sail. Clipper ships in the nineteenth century wool trade, bound from England for Australia, would go out via the Cape of Good Hope, but return via Cape Horn, thus taking advantage of both the strong prevailing westerlies in the "Roaring Forties" and the resultant westerly ocean currents; see Figure 1002. Similarly, the sixteenth century Spanish "treasure galleons" sailed from Acapulco, Mexico, for Manila, via the north equatorial current, but returned via the Japan Stream and the California current. Much useful information on these cur-

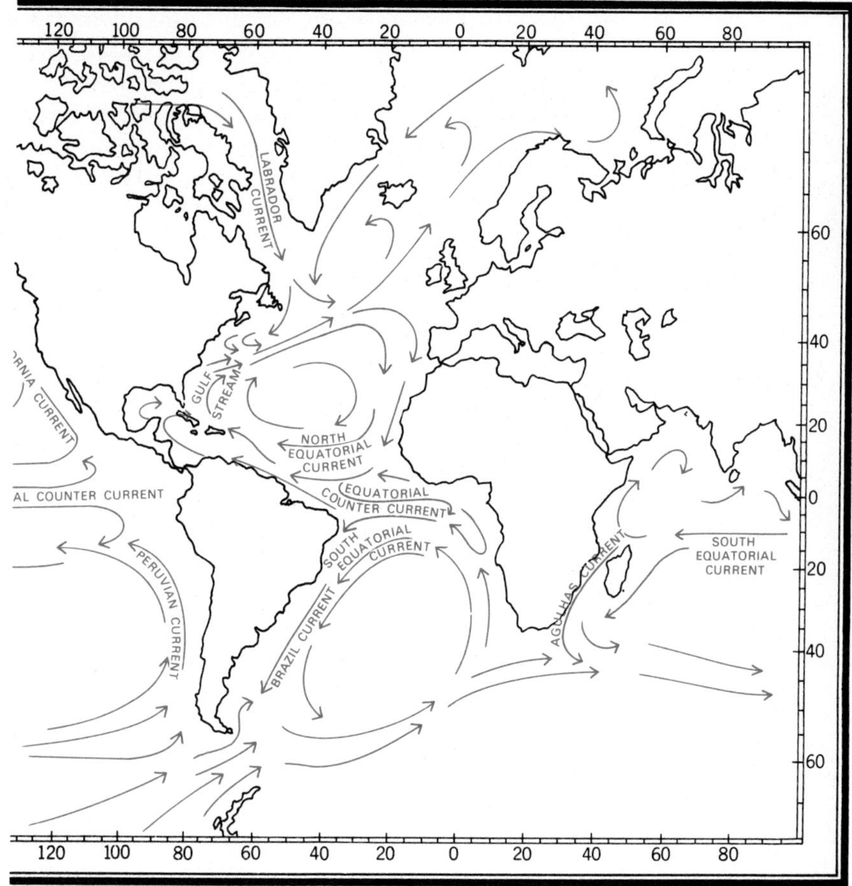

rents may be obtained from the *Pilot Charts* and *Pilot Chart Atlases* published by the Defense Mapping Agency Hydrographic Center. These publications, covering the principal ocean areas of the world, are, in most instances, designed to show for each month the mean direction and force of the surface currents in specific quadrangles of latitude and longitude, as well as the frequency of direction and average drifts. Brief summaries of the chief currents of the Atlantic, Pacific, and Indian Oceans follow.

Atlantic Ocean currents

1003 The effect of the trade winds is to form two *equatorial currents* flowing westward across the Atlantic at the rate of about two thirds of a knot. Between the *north* and *south* equatorial currents the somewhat weaker *equatorial counter current* flows to the eastward under the influence of the southwest monsoon.

At the western edge of the Atlantic, the south equatorial current divides at the eastern tip of South America, part of it flowing southward and part continuing on into the Caribbean or northwestward along the West Indies. This current is joined by the north equatorial current of the Atlantic which has flowed westward from an area to the north of the Cape Verde Islands. Water flows up the Caribbean, through the Yucatan Strait, across the Gulf of Mexico and back into the Atlantic through the Straits of Florida. Here it meets with the flow that came up to the eastward of the West Indies to form the famous Gulf Stream which flows northerly along the east coast of the United States, picking up even more flow from currents eastward of the Bahamas.

The indigo-blue water of this sharply defined current of warm water roughly follows the coast line as far as Cape Hatteras, where it curves eastward, widens, and gradually loses some of its velocity.

Off the Grand Banks the Gulf Stream loses its identity as such, but continues on eastward as a general circulatory flow or drift. It meets the cold water of the *Labrador current* in this area, part of which accompanies it towards the east. However, the water mass remains comparatively warm, and has a very marked effect on the climate of northwestern Europe. On the eastern side of the Atlantic it divides to form the *northeast, easterly,* and *southeast drift currents.*

The circulation of the South Atlantic is somewhat similar. That part of the south equatorial current curving southward forms the *Brazil current,* which roughly follows the coast of South America. Off the coast of Uruguay the current divides further, part of it continuing on to the south and part curving eastward across the south Atlantic. The part known as the *southern current* is joined in the eastern Atlantic by water flowing northward from the Antarctic and flows along the western coast of Africa to connect with the south equatorial current and complete the circulation, much as does the southeast drift current in the North Atlantic. The following are the principal Atlantic Ocean currents.

north equatorial (warm)	Gulf Stream (warm)
south equatorial (warm)	Labrador (cold)
equatorial counter (warm)	Brazil (warm)

Pacific Ocean currents

1004 The circulation in the Pacific is similar to that in the Atlantic. Here, as in the Atlantic, the *north* and *south equatorial currents* set westward, with the *equatorial counter current* between them setting to the east.

In the western Pacific the north equatorial current curves northward forming the *Japan Stream,* similar to the Gulf Stream, which roughly follows the coastline of the Japanese islands. The Japanese name for this current is *Kuroshio,* or "black stream," named for the dark color of the water. Part of this stream flows west of Japan into the Sea of Japan, but the main stream passes east of Japan and flows northward and eastward, widening as it does so, with a loss of velocity.

Part of the stream continues northerly as well as easterly to the region of the Aleutian Islands, and part continues on east where it joins the weak north and northeast drift currents in this area.

Similar to the Labrador current, the cold *Oyashio* flows out of the Bering Sea to the south and west close to the shores of the Kuril Islands and Japan. Like the Labrador current, the Oyashio often brings ice from the Arctic Ocean.

Along the Pacific coast of the United States the cold *California current* flows southward, generally following the coast line. This current, being 200 to 300 miles wide, is not as strong as narrower currents, but flows with an average velocity of about 0.8 knot.

In the western Pacific the south equatorial current divides, part of it continuing on to the west and part of it, the *Australia current,* curving southward past the east coast of Australia, where it bends toward the east and spreads out and is lost as a well-defined stream.

A current of cold water sets out of the Antarctic southwest of South America. The current divides at the southern tip of Patagonia, part of it, the *Cape Horn current,* crossing into the southern Atlantic and part of it continuing up the west coast of South America, as the *Peruvian current.* Near Cape Blanco the stream curves to the west past the Galapagos Islands and finally joins the south equatorial current. The following are the principal Pacific Ocean currents.

north equatorial (warm)	Oyashio (cold)
south equatorial (warm)	California (cold)
equatorial counter (warm)	Australia (warm)
Japan stream (warm)	Peruvian or Humboldt (cold)

Indian Ocean currents

1005 The circulation of the Indian Ocean bears a strong resemblance to the currents of the southern Atlantic and Pacific. North of the equator the currents are weak and variable with the seasons. South of the equator, the *south equatorial current* flows westward as in the other oceans.

Near the African coast this current divides, one part curving northward and eastward, but the main part curving to the south, dividing to flow down each side of Madagascar; at the southern end the two combine and narrow to form the warm *Agulhas* current, which bears a strong resemblance to the Gulf and Japan streams. Near the southern end of Africa this current curves more to the south and then eastward, where it widens and is generally lost as a well-defined stream.

Across the southern Indian Ocean the drift is generally eastward, the flow being fed by the Agulhas current and a weak flow from the Atlantic past the Cape of Good Hope. Near Australia this flow divides, part of it continuing on along the southern coast into the Pacific and part curving northward along the west coast.

As in the Atlantic and Pacific, there is a general weak flow from the Antarctic into the Indian Ocean. The Indian Ocean compares with the southern Atlantic or Pacific in size and general circulation, but lacks the cold currents of the others. The following are the principal currents of the Indian Ocean.

south equatorial (warm)	Agulhas (warm)

Temporary wind-driven currents

1006 Local and temporary wind-driven currents at times develop outside the well-defined ocean current systems. The drift of such a current depends largely on the force of the wind and its duration. However, if a wind has been blowing fairly steadily for some time at sea, a reasonable assumption would be that the drift of the current roughly equals 2 percent of the wind speed.

In the open ocean the set of a temporary wind current is not in the direction the wind is blowing. It is deflected by the *Coriolis force* (Article 1002); in the northern hemisphere, this deflection is to the right; in the southern hemisphere it is to the left. In the open sea, the deflection is about 40°; near a coast line it is considerably less, probably near 20°. Deflection of a wind-driven current is affected by the land structure and varies with depth, being more deflected at greater depths. The *Tidal Current Tables* (see Article 1011) give information on offshore conditions that may be expected in certain areas.

TIDAL CURRENTS

Basic causes

1007 Chapter 9 discussed briefly the causes of tides and noted that the waters in the oceans and connecting waterways rise and fall periodically. It follows that if the amount of water changes to vary its level, there must be a flow back and forth between different areas; these flows are *tidal currents.* Such water movements are little noticed on the high seas, but they become of significance, and sometimes of critical importance, along coasts and in bays, estuaries, and the lower reaches of rivers; this is particularly so in fog or thick weather. The horizontal movement of the water toward the land is called *flood current,* and the horizontal movement away from the land is called *ebb current.* Between these two, when the current changes direction, there is a brief period when no horizontal motion can be detected; this is *slack water*.

Rotary tidal currents

1008 Offshore, where the direction of flow under tidal influence is not restricted by any barriers, the tidal current is *rotary;* that is, it flows continuously, with the direction changing through all points of the compass during the tidal period. Due to the effect of the earth's rotation, the change is clockwise in the northern hemisphere, and counterclockwise in the southern hemisphere except where modified by local conditions. The speed usually varies throughout the tidal cycle, passing through two maximums in approximately opposite directions, and

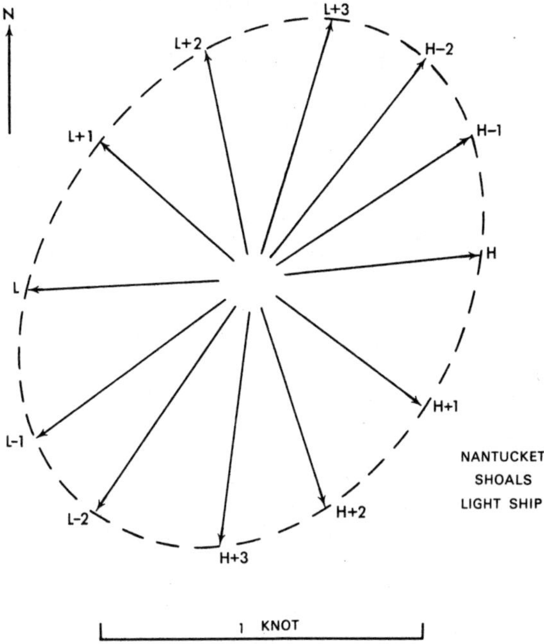

Figure 1008. Rotary tidal currents. Times are hours before and after high and low tides at a specified reference station (Nantucket Light Ship). The bearing and length of each arrow represents the direction and strength of the current at the labeled time.

two minimums about halfway between the maximums in time and direction. Rotary currents can be depicted as in Figure 1008 by a series of arrows representing the direction and speed of the current at each hour. This is sometimes called a *current rose.*

A distinguishing feature of a rotary current is that it has no time of slack water. Although the current varies in strength, the variation is from a maximum to a minimum and back to the next maximum without any occurrence of slack; see Figure 1011e.

Reversing tidal currents

1009 In rivers, bays, and straits, where the direction of flow is more or less restricted to certain channels, the tidal current is called a *reversing current;* that is, it flows alternately in approximately opposite directions, with a short period of little or no current, called *slack water*, at each reversal of the current. During the flow in each direction, the speed varies from zero at the time of slack water to the *maximum flood* or *ebb* about midway between the slacks. The symmetry of reversing currents is affected in certain areas by the configuration of the land and/or the presence of a natural flow of a river. Reversing currents can be represented graphically by arrows or curves that indicate the strength of the current at each hour, as in Figure 1009.

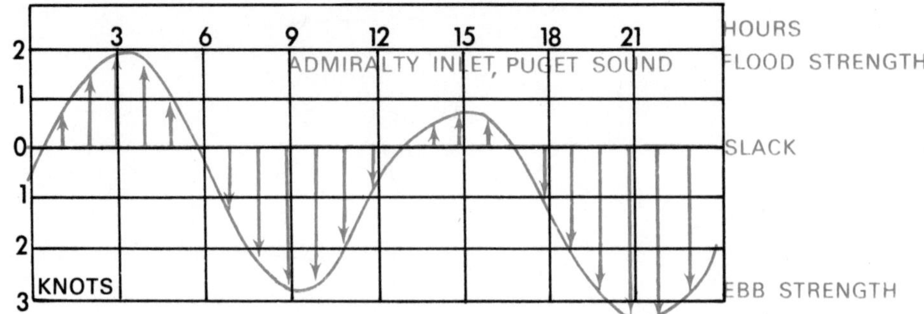

Figure 1009. Reversing tidal currents. (Such graphs may show only the curve without the arrows.)

In the navigation of vessels, it happens at times that the effect of tidal current is of more importance than the height of tide; in any body of water subject to tidal action, both must be considered. Mariners will sometimes speak of "the tide" as ebbing or flooding; this is incorrect terminology and should be avoided.

Along a relatively straight coast with shallow indentations there is usually little difference between the time of slack water and high or low tide, but where a large bay connects with the ocean through a narrow channel, the tide and current may be out of phase by as much as seven hours.

The effect of the tide in causing currents may be illustrated by two cases:

Where there is a small tidal basin connected with the sea by a large opening.

Where there is a large tidal basin connected with the sea by a small opening.

In the first case, the velocity of the current in the opening has its maximum value when the height of the tide within is changing most rapidly; i.e., at a time about midway between high and low water. The water in the basin keeps at approximately the same level as the water outside. The flood current corresponds with the rising of the tide and the ebb current with the falling of the tide.

In the second case, the velocity of the current in the opening has its maximum value when it is high water or low water outside the basin, for then there is the greatest difference in levels, and the maximum hydraulic pressure for producing motion. The flood current in such cases generally begins about three hours after low water and the ebb current about three hours after high water, slack water thus occurring about midway between the tides.

Along most shores not much affected by bays, tidal rivers, etc., the current usually turns soon after high water and low water.

The swiftest current in straight portions of tidal rivers is usually in the middle of the river, but in curved portions the most rapid current is toward the outer edge of the curve, and here the deepest water will generally be found.

Counter currents and eddies may occur near the shores of straits, especially in bights and near points. A knowledge of them is useful, that they may be used or avoided.

A swift current often occurs in a narrow passage connecting two large bodies of water, owing to their considerable difference of level at the same instant. The several passages between Vineyard Sound and Buzzards Bay are cases in point. A similar situation also occurs in connecting waterways such as the Cape Cod and Chesapeake & Delaware Canals, at Hell Gate on the East River in New York City, and on the Pacific Coast at such locations as Deception Pass and in Seymour and Sergius Narrows. With these *hydraulic currents,* strength is reached much more quickly after a very brief period of slack water, and the current remains strong for a greater part of the cycle than with normal reversing tidal currents.

Tide rips are generally made by a rapid current setting over an irregular bottom, as at the edges of banks where the change of depth is considerable, but they sometimes occur on the high seas.

Tidal current predictions

1010 Annual tables of predicted tidal currents have been published by the National Ocean Survey (and its predecessor agency, the Coast & Geodetic Survey) since 1890. Originally these also contained tide predictions but were made separate publications in 1923. There are now two volumes: *Tidal Current Tables for the Atlantic Coast of North America,* and *Tidal Current Tables for the Pacific Coast of North America and Asia.* Companion publications by NOS include *Tidal Current Charts* and *Tidal Current Diagrams.*

Description of *Tidal Current Tables*

1011 *Tidal Current Tables* have a format similar to the *Tide Tables* discussed in Chapter 9 and are used in much the same manner.

For a number of principal locations, called *reference stations*, Table 1 of these tables (Figure 1011a) lists the predicted times of slack water in chronological order in the left-hand column, and the predicted times and velocities of maximum flood (F) and ebb (E) currents, also in chronological order, in the center and right-hand columns respectively for each day of the year. Flood and ebb current directions appear at the top of each page.

All times in the *Tidal Current Tables* are *standard times;* each page of Table 1 indicates the central meridian of the time zone used. Adjustments must be made for the use of daylight time or any other deviation from standard time; see Article 2215.

Due to the length of the lunar day, approximately 24^h50^m, all days in Table 1 will not have a full set of four maximum currents and four slack waters.

Table 2 (Figure 1011b) contains a list of secondary or *subordinate stations,* arranged in geographic order. Given for each station is its position in terms of latitude and longitude to the nearest minute, its

ST. JOHNS RIVER ENTRANCE, FLA., 1977

F-FLOOD, DIR. 275° TRUE   E-EBB, DIR. 100° TRUE

MAY

DAY	SLACK WATER TIME H.M.	MAXIMUM CURRENT TIME H.M.	VEL. KNOTS
1	0327	0544	2.1F
SU	0824	1116	2.7E
	1528	1809	2.7F
	2105	2356	2.8E
2	0416	0634	2.2F
M	0914	1205	2.9E
	1613	1858	3.0F
	2156		
3		0049	3.0E
TU	0505	0723	2.3F
	1003	1256	3.0E
	1659	1948	3.1F
	2247		
4		0140	3.1E
W	0556	0813	2.4F
	1053	1347	3.1E
	1749	2037	3.1F
	2338		
5		0231	3.0E
TH	0648	0904	2.3F
	1144	1437	3.0E
	1842	2129	3.0F
6	0029	0322	2.9E
F	0742	0957	2.2F
	1238	1528	2.8E
	1939	2223	2.8F
7	0122	0414	2.8E
SA	0839	1052	2.1F
	1334	1623	2.6E
	2041	2316	2.6F
8	0216	0509	2.5E
SU	0938	1147	2.0F
	1432	1724	2.3E
	2147		
9		0013	2.3F
M	0311	0609	2.3E
	1037	1246	1.9F
	1534	1829	2.1E
	2254		
10		0111	2.0F
TU	0407	0715	2.2E
	1136	1347	1.8F
	1637	1946	1.9E
	2359		
11		0211	1.8F
W	0503	0824	2.0E
	1231	1446	1.8F
	1739	2107	1.9E
12	0100	0311	1.7F
TH	0558	0931	2.0E
	1324	1544	1.9F
	1837	2221	1.9E
13	0157	0405	1.6F
F	0650	1026	2.0E
	1413	1635	2.0F
	1930	2320	2.0E
14	0250	0457	1.6F
SA	0739	1107	2.0E
	1459	1722	2.1F
	2019	2359	2.0E
15	0338	0544	1.6F
SU	0824	1143	2.0E
	1542	1805	2.1F
	2104		

DAY	SLACK WATER TIME H.M.	MAXIMUM CURRENT TIME H.M.	VEL. KNOTS
16		0032	2.1E
M	0424	0625	1.6F
	0906	1211	2.1E
	1623	1846	2.2F
	2146		
17		0057	2.1E
TU	0508	0709	1.6F
	0947	1240	2.1E
	1702	1926	2.2F
	2226		
18		0125	2.2E
W	0551	0749	1.6F
	1026	1313	2.2E
	1740	2007	2.2F
	2306		
19		0154	2.2E
TH	0633	0831	1.6F
	1105	1350	2.2E
	1817	2051	2.2F
	2345		
20		0229	2.2E
F	0716	0914	1.5F
	1145	1431	2.2E
	1854	2134	2.1F
21	0025	0306	2.3E
SA	0758	1001	1.5F
	1226	1512	2.2E
	1932	2219	2.0F
22	0105	0346	2.3E
SU	0842	1047	1.4F
	1310	1555	2.2E
	2015	2308	1.9F
23	0148	0431	2.2E
M	0927	1136	1.4F
	1359	1646	2.1E
	2106	2355	1.8F
24	0233	0518	2.2E
TU	1013	1227	1.5F
	1452	1737	2.1E
	2207		
25		0047	1.7F
W	0322	0609	2.2E
	1059	1318	1.6F
	1551	1833	2.1E
	2312		
26		0141	1.7F
TH	0413	0702	2.3E
	1147	1411	1.0F
	1652	1932	2.1E
27	0015	0233	1.7F
F	0507	0758	2.4E
	1234	1505	2.0F
	1753	2033	2.2E
28	0115	0328	1.7F
SA	0602	0853	2.5E
	1322	1558	2.3F
	1852	2137	2.4E
29	0211	0424	1.9F
SU	0658	0950	2.6E
	1410	1651	2.6F
	1950	2238	2.6E
30	0305	0517	2.0F
M	0752	1045	2.8E
	1459	1743	2.9F
	2044	2335	2.7E
31	0357	0610	2.1F
TU	0846	1140	2.9E
	1549	1834	3.0F
	2138		

JUNE

DAY	SLACK WATER TIME H.M.	MAXIMUM CURRENT TIME H.M.	VEL. KNOTS
1		0032	2.9E
W	0448	0701	2.2F
	0940	1234	3.0E
	1640	1926	3.1F
	2229		
2		0125	3.0E
TH	0540	0753	2.3F
	1033	1329	3.0E
	1733	2018	3.1F
	2320		
3		0217	3.0E
F	0631	0845	2.3F
	1127	1422	2.9E
	1827	2109	3.0F
4	0011	0308	2.9E
SA	0724	0938	2.2F
	1222	1513	2.8E
	1925	2201	2.8F
5	0102	0401	2.8E
SU	0818	1030	2.2F
	1317	1609	2.5E
	2024	2255	2.5F
6	0152	0452	2.6E
M	0914	1124	2.1F
	1414	1708	2.3E
	2126	2350	2.2F
7	0244	0545	2.4E
TU	1009	1222	2.0F
	1513	1809	2.1E
	2230		
8		0045	1.9F
W	0335	0641	2.2E
	1105	1318	1.9F
	1612	1917	1.9E
	2332		
9		0141	1.7F
TH	0428	0740	2.0E
	1159	1414	1.9F
	1711	2029	1.8E
10	0033	0237	1.5F
F	0520	0836	1.9E
	1251	1511	1.9F
	1807	2140	1.8E
11	0130	0331	1.4F
SA	0611	0927	1.9E
	1341	1602	1.9F
	1901	2241	1.8E
12	0224	0422	1.4F
SU	0700	1016	1.9E
	1428	1650	2.0F
	1950	2329	1.8E
13	0314	0511	1.4F
M	0748	1056	1.9E
	1513	1733	2.1F
	2036	2358	1.9E
14	0401	0556	1.4F
TU	0833	1133	2.0E
	1555	1818	2.1F
	2120		
15		0033	2.0E
W	0445	0641	1.5F
	0916	1207	2.0E
	1636	1900	2.2F
	2201		

DAY	SLACK WATER TIME H.M.	MAXIMUM CURRENT TIME H.M.	VEL. KNOTS
16		0102	2.1E
TH	0528	0723	1.5F
	0958	1246	2.1E
	1714	1943	2.2F
	2242		
17		0132	2.2E
F	0610	0806	1.5F
	1040	1323	2.2E
	1752	2026	2.2F
	2321		
18		0207	2.2E
SA	0650	0850	1.5F
	1121	1406	2.2E
	1829	2109	2.2F
19	0000	0242	2.3E
SU	0730	0935	1.6F
	1203	1447	2.3E
	1907	2153	2.1F
20	0040	0323	2.4E
M	0809	1020	1.6F
	1248	1533	2.3E
	1948	2239	2.0F
21	0120	0404	2.4E
TU	0848	1107	1.6F
	1336	1622	2.3E
	2036	2327	1.9F
22	0202	0451	2.4E
W	0929	1157	1.7F
	1429	1713	2.2E
	2133		
23		0016	1.8F
TH	0248	0539	2.5E
	1013	1248	1.8F
	1526	1806	2.2E
	2238		
24		0111	1.7F
F	0338	0632	2.5E
	1102	1341	2.0F
	1626	1905	2.2E
	2345		
25		0205	1.7F
SA	0432	0725	2.5E
	1155	1436	2.2F
	1728	2007	2.2E
26	0049	0300	1.7F
SU	0529	0824	2.6E
	1249	1530	2.4F
	1829	2112	2.3E
27	0149	0357	1.7F
M	0628	0921	2.6E
	1344	1626	2.6F
	1928	2217	2.5E
28	0245	0451	1.9F
TU	0727	1023	2.7E
	1439	1722	2.8F
	2025	2320	2.6E
29	0339	0546	2.0F
W	0825	1122	2.8E
	1533	1815	3.0F
	2119		
30		0018	2.8E
TH	0431	0641	2.1F
	0921	1221	2.9E
	1627	1907	3.0F
	2211		

TIME MERIDIAN 75° W. 0000 IS MIDNIGHT. 1200 IS NOON.

Figure 1011a. *Tidal Current Tables,* Table 1 (extract).

TABLE 2.—CURRENT DIFFERENCES AND OTHER CONSTANTS

No.	PLACE	POSITION		TIME DIFFERENCES		VELOCITY RATIOS		MAXIMUM CURRENTS			
								Flood		Ebb	
		Lat.	Long.	Slack water	Maximum current	Maximum flood	Maximum ebb	Direction (true)	Average velocity	Direction (true)	Average velocity
		° ′	° ′	*h. m.*	*h. m.*			*deg.*	*knots*	*deg.*	*knots*
	ST. JOHNS RIVER—Continued	N.	W.	on ST. JOHNS RIVER ENTRANCE, p.88							
	Time meridian, 75°W.										
5380	St. Johns Bluff	30 23	81 30	+0 05	+0 50	0.8	1.0	245	1.6	060	2.2
5385	Drummond Point, channel south of	30 25	81 36	+2 00	+2 30	0.7	0.7	230	1.3	060	1.6
5390	Phoenix Park	30 23	81 38	+2 40	+3 10	0.6	0.4	190	1.1	350	1.0
5395	Chaseville, channel near	30 23	81 37	+2 35	+3 20	0.6	0.7	150	1.1	335	1.6
5400	Quarantine Station, Long Branch	30 21	81 37	+2 30	+3 05	0.6	0.5	185	1.1	000	1.2
5405	Commodore Point, terminal channel	30 19	81 38	+2 35	+3 10	0.5	0.4	210	1.0	060	1.0
5410	Jacksonville, off Washington St	30 19	81 39	+2 20	+2 50	0.9	0.8	280	1.8	120	1.9
5415	Jacksonville, F. E. C. RR. bridge	30 19	81 40	+2 20	+3 00	0.8	0.7	240	1.6	060	1.7
5420	Winter Point	30 18	81 40	+2 55	+3 10	0.6	0.5	200	1.1	015	1.1
5425	Mandarin Point	30 09	81 41	+3 00	+3 20	0.3	0.3	180	0.6	015	0.7
5430	Red Bay Point, bridge draw	29 59	81 38	(1)	(1)	0.5	0.3	115	0.9	300	0.6
5435	Tocoi to Lake George	-----	-----	*Current too weak and variable to be predicted.*							
	FLORIDA COAST			on MIAMI HARBOR ENTRANCE, p.94							
5440	Ft. Pierce Inlet	27 28	80 18	+0 50	+0 25	1.4	1.5	250	2.6	070	3.1
5445	Lake Worth Inlet (between jetties)	26 46	80 02	-0 10	-0 15	1.3	1.7	275	2.4	095	3.6
5450	Fort Lauderdale, New River	26 07	80 07	-0 40	-0 40	0.4	0.2	005	0.8	130	0.5
	PORT EVERGLADES										
5455	Pier 2, 1.3 miles east of	26 06	80 06	-----	-----	----	----	(2)	0.2	(2)	0.4
5460	Entrance (between jetties)	26 06	80 06	-0 40	-0 55	0.3	0.3	275	0.6	095	0.7
5465	Entrance from southward (canal)	26 05	80 07	+0 20	-0 15	0.7	0.8	165	1.3	000	1.7
5470	Turning Basin	26 06	80 07	-1 15	-1 20	0.1	0.2	320	0.2	155	0.5
5475	Turning Basin, 300 yards north of	26 06	80 07	-0 40	-0 55	0.5	0.9	350	0.9	160	1.8
5480	17th Street Bridge	26 06	80 07	-0 50	-1 05	1.0	0.9	350	1.9	170	1.9
	MIAMI HARBOR										
5485	Bakers Haulover Cut	25 54	80 07	-0 10	-0 15	1.5	1.2	270	2.9	090	2.5
5490	North Jetty (east end)	25 46	80 07	-0 40	-0 35	0.4	0.6	250	0.8	105	1.3
5495	Miami Outer Bay Cut entrance	25 46	80 06	See table 5.							
5500	MIAMI HARBOR ENT. (between jetties)	25 46	80 08	Daily predictions				290	1.9	125	2.1
5503	Fowey Rocks Light, 1.5 miles SW. of	25 35	80 07	*Current too weak and variable to be predicted.*							
	FLORIDA REEFS to MIDNIGHT PASS			on KEY WEST, p.100							
5505	Caesar Creek, Biscayne Bay	25 23	80 14	-0 05	-0 05	1.2	1.0	315	1.2	125	1.8
5510	Long Key, drawbridge east of	24 50	80 46	+1 40	+1 30	1.1	0.7	000	1.1	200	1.2
5515	Long Key Viaduct	24 48	80 52	+1 50	+1 40	0.9	0.7	350	0.9	170	1.2
5520	Moser Channel, drawbridge	24 42	81 10	+1 30	+1 40	1.4	1.0	340	1.4	165	1.8
5525	Bahia Honda Harbor, bridge	24 39	81 17	+1 25	+0 50	1.4	1.2	005	1.4	180	2.1
5530	No Name Key, NE. of	24 42	81 19	+1 10	+1 10	0.7	0.5	310	0.7	140	0.9
	Key West										
5535	Main Ship Channel entrance	24 28	81 48	-0 15	0 00	0.2	0.3	040	0.2	180	0.4
5540	Maine Ship Channel	24 30	81 48	(3)	3+0 30	(3)	0.2	065	(3)	135	0.4
5545	KEY WEST, 0.3 mi. W. of Ft. Taylor	24 33	81 49	Daily predictions				020	1.0	195	1.7
5550	0.6 mile N. of Ft. Taylor	24 34	81 49	+0 05	+0 15	0.6	0.7	040	0.6	200	1.2
5555	Turning Basin	24 34	81 48	+0 35	+0 55	0.8	0.6	050	0.8	215	1.1
5560	Northwest Channel	24 35	81 51	-0 10	-0 05	1.2	0.8	355	1.2	160	1.4
5565	Northwest Channel	24 37	81 53	-0 25	-0 20	0.6	0.4	345	0.6	170	0.6
5570	Boca Grande Channel	24 34	82 04	-0 20	-0 25	1.1	0.7	355	1.1	195	1.2
5575	New Ground†	24 39	82 25	+1 30	+1 35	0.7	0.4	070	0.7	245	0.7

[1] Flood begins, $+2^h\ 35^m$; maximum flood, $+3^h\ 25^m$; ebb begins, $+5^h\ 00^m$; maximum ebb, $+4^h\ 00^m$.
[2] Flood usually occurs in a southerly direction and the ebb in a northeastwardly direction.
[3] Times of slack are indefinite. Flood is weak and variable. Time difference is for maximum ebb.
† Current tends to rotate clockwise. At times for slack flood begins there may be a weak current flowing northward while at times for slack ebb begins there may be a weak current flowing southeastward.

Figure 1011b. *Tidal Current Tables,* Table 2 (extract).

reference station, the difference in time of slack water and time of maximum current in hours and minutes with respect to its reference station, the maximum flood and maximum ebb velocity ratios with respect to similar current at the reference station, and the direction and average velocities of the maximum flood and ebb currents.

The factors for any subordinate station are applied to the predictions of the reference station whose name is printed *next above* the subordinate station's listing in Table 2.

The respective time differences are added to or subtracted from, according to their signs, the time of slack water and strength of current (maximum flood or ebb) at the reference station to obtain the times of occurrence of the respective events in the current cycle at the subordinate station. The velocity of the maximum currents at the subordinate station is found by multiplying the velocity of either the flood or ebb current at the reference station by the respective velocity ratio listed for the subordinate station.

Note that the time differences for slack water and maximum current are usually *not* the same; however, only one time difference is given for maximum current and it is used for both flood and ebb. Where unusual conditions exist, keyed footnotes, applicable to specific subordinate stations, appear at the bottom of the page. The average flood velocity is the mean of all the maximum flood currents, and the average ebb velocity is the mean of all the maximum ebb currents.

Table 3, Figure 1011c, is used to determine the velocity of a current at any intermediate time between slack and maximum current. Instructions on its use appear beneath the tabulated factors. This table is in two parts, A and B. Table A is for use at nearly all locations. Table B is used for a limited number of places where there are "hydraulic" currents (see Article 1009); these locations for each volume of the *Tidal Current Tables* are listed beneath Table 3.

Table 4 (Figure 1011d) is used to find the duration of slack. Although slack water, or the time of zero velocity, lasts but an instant, there is a period each side of slack during which the current is so weak that for practical purposes it can be considered as being negligible. From Table 4, the period (half on each side of slack) during which the current does not exceed a given velocity (0.1 to 0.5 knot) is tabulated for various maximum currents. (This table also has a "Table B" whose use is similar but limited to a few specified locations.)

Table 5 (Atlantic tables only—Figure 1011e) gives information regarding *rotary tidal currents,* or currents which change their direction continually and never come to a slack, so that in a tidal cycle of about 12½ hours they set in all directions successively. Such currents occur offshore and in some wide indentations of the coast. The values given are average velocities due to tidal action only. When a steady wind is blowing, the effect of the current due to wind should be added vectorially to the current due to tidal action. This table is seldom used. Instructions for the use of this table as well as for Tables 1 through 4 are given in the publications themselves.

TABLE 3.—VELOCITY OF CURRENT AT ANY TIME

TABLE A

Interval between slack and desired time	Interval between slack and maximum current													
	h. m. 1 20	h. m. 1 40	h. m. 2 00	h. m. 2 20	h. m. 2 40	h. m. 3 00	h. m. 3 20	h. m. 3 40	h. m. 4 00	h. m. 4 20	h. m. 4 40	h. m. 5 00	h. m. 5 20	h. m. 5 40
h. m.	f.	f.	f.	f.	f.	f.	f.	f.	f.	f.	f.	f.	f.	f.
0 20	0.4	0.3	0.3	0.2	0.2	0.2	0.2	0.1	0.1	0.1	0.1	0.1	0.1	0.1
0 40	0.7	0.6	0.5	0.4	0.4	0.3	0.3	0.3	0.3	0.2	0.2	0.2	0.2	0.2
1 00	0.9	0.8	0.7	0.6	0.6	0.5	0.5	0.4	0.4	0.4	0.3	0.3	0.3	0.3
1 20	1.0	1.0	0.9	0.8	0.7	0.6	0.6	0.5	0.5	0.5	0.4	0.4	0.4	0.4
1 40	......	1.0	1.0	0.9	0.8	0.8	0.7	0.7	0.6	0.6	0.5	0.5	0.5	0.4
2 00	......	......	1.0	1.0	0.9	0.9	0.8	0.8	0.7	0.7	0.6	0.6	0.6	0.5
2 20	......	......	......	1.0	1.0	0.9	0.9	0.8	0.8	0.7	0.7	0.7	0.6	0.6
2 40	......	......	......	......	1.0	1.0	1.0	0.9	0.9	0.8	0.8	0.7	0.7	0.7
3 00	......	......	......	......	......	1.0	1.0	1.0	0.9	0.9	0.8	0.8	0.8	0.7
3 20	......	......	......	......	......	......	1.0	1.0	1.0	0.9	0.9	0.9	0.8	0.8
3 40	......	......	......	......	......	......	......	1.0	1.0	1.0	0.9	0.9	0.9	0.9
4 00	......	......	......	......	......	......	......	......	1.0	1.0	1.0	1.0	0.9	0.9
4 20	......	......	......	......	......	......	......	......	......	1.0	1.0	1.0	1.0	0.9
4 40	......	......	......	......	......	......	......	......	......	......	1.0	1.0	1.0	1.0
5 00	......	......	......	......	......	......	......	......	......	......	......	1.0	1.0	1.0
5 20	......	......	......	......	......	......	......	......	......	......	......	......	1.0	1.0
5 40	......	......	......	......	......	......	......	......	......	......	......	......	......	1.0

TABLE B

Interval between slack and desired time	Interval between slack and maximum current													
	h. m. 1 20	h. m. 1 40	h. m. 2 00	h. m. 2 20	h. m. 2 40	h. m. 3 00	h. m. 3 20	h. m. 3 40	h. m. 4 00	h. m. 4 20	h. m. 4 40	h. m. 5 00	h. m. 5 20	h. m. 5 40
h. m.	f.	f.	f.	f.	f.	f.	f.	f.	f.	f.	f.	f.	f.	f.
0 20	0.5	0.4	0.4	0.3	0.3	0.3	0.3	0.3	0.2	0.2	0.2	0.2	0.2	0.2
0 40	0.8	0.7	0.6	0.5	0.5	0.5	0.4	0.4	0.4	0.4	0.3	0.3	0.3	0.3
1 00	0.9	0.8	0.8	0.7	0.7	0.6	0.6	0.5	0.5	0.5	0.4	0.4	0.4	0.4
1 20	1.0	1.0	0.9	0.8	0.8	0.7	0.7	0.6	0.6	0.6	0.5	0.5	0.5	0.5
1 40	......	1.0	1.0	0.9	0.9	0.8	0.8	0.7	0.7	0.7	0.6	0.6	0.6	0.6
2 00	......	......	1.0	1.0	0.9	0.9	0.9	0.8	0.8	0.7	0.7	0.7	0.7	0.6
2 20	......	......	......	1.0	1.0	1.0	0.9	0.9	0.8	0.8	0.8	0.7	0.7	0.7
2 40	......	......	......	......	1.0	1.0	1.0	0.9	0.9	0.9	0.8	0.8	0.8	0.7
3 00	......	......	......	......	......	1.0	1.0	1.0	0.9	0.9	0.9	0.9	0.8	0.8
3 20	......	......	......	......	......	......	1.0	1.0	1.0	1.0	0.9	0.9	0.9	0.8
3 40	......	......	......	......	......	......	......	1.0	1.0	1.0	1.0	0.9	0.9	0.9
4 00	......	......	......	......	......	......	......	......	1.0	1.0	1.0	1.0	0.9	0.9
4 20	......	......	......	......	......	......	......	......	......	1.0	1.0	1.0	1.0	0.9
4 40	......	......	......	......	......	......	......	......	......	......	1.0	1.0	1.0	1.0
5 00	......	......	......	......	......	......	......	......	......	......	......	1.0	1.0	1.0
5 20	......	......	......	......	......	......	......	......	......	......	......	......	1.0	1.0
5 40	......	......	......	......	......	......	......	......	......	......	......	......	......	1.0

Use table A for all places except those listed below for table B.
Use table B for Cape Cod Canal, Hell Gate, Chesapeake and Delaware Canal and all stations in table 2 which are referred to them.

Figure 1011c. *Tidal Current Tables,* Table 3.

A limited amount of information is given on *wind-driven currents* and how such currents can be combined with predicted tidal currents to obtain a prediction of greater velocity. The astronomical data on the inside back cover is the same as that given in the *Tide Tables*—dates and times for the phases of the moon, apogee, perigee, and greatest north and south declinations, and crossing of the equator; also solar data on equinoxes and solstices.

TABLE A

Maximum current	Period with a velocity not more than—				
	0.1 knot	0.2 knot	0.3 knot	0.4 knot	0.5 knot
Knots	*Minutes*	*Minutes*	*Minutes*	*Minutes*	*Minutes*
1.0	23	46	70	94	120
1.5	15	31	46	62	78
2.0	11	23	35	46	58
3.0	8	15	23	31	38
4.0	6	11	17	23	29
5.0	5	9	14	18	23
6.0	4	8	11	15	19
7.0	3	7	10	13	16
8.0	3	6	9	11	14
9.0	3	5	8	10	13
10.0	2	5	7	9	11

Figure 1011d. *Tidal Current Tables,* Table 4A.

Difference of longitude between local and standard meridian	Correction to local mean time to obtain standard time	Difference of longitude between local and standard meridian	Correction to local mean time to obtain standard time	Difference of longitude between local and standard meridian	Correction to local mean time to obtain standard time
° ′ ° ′	*Minutes*	° ′ ° ′	*Minutes*	°	*Hours*
0 00 to 0 07	0	7 23 to 7 37	30	15	1
0 08 to 0 22	1	7 38 to 7 52	31	30	2
0 23 to 0 37	2	7 53 to 8 07	32	45	3
0 38 to 0 52	3	8 08 to 8 22	33	60	4
0 53 to 1 07	4	8 23 to 8 37	34	75	5
1 08 to 1 22	5	8 38 to 8 52	35	90	6
1 23 to 1 37	6	8 53 to 9 07	36	105	7
1 38 to 1 52	7	9 08 to 9 22	37	120	8
1 53 to 2 07	8	9 23 to 9 37	38	135	9
2 08 to 2 22	9	9 38 to 9 52	39	150	10
2 23 to 2 37	10	9 53 to 10 07	40	165	11
2 38 to 2 52	11	10 08 to 10 22	41	180	12
2 53 to 3 07	12	10 23 to 10 37	42		
3 08 to 3 22	13	10 38 to 10 52	43		
3 23 to 3 37	14	10 53 to 11 07	44		
3 38 to 3 52	15	11 08 to 11 22	45		
3 53 to 4 07	16	11 23 to 11 37	46		
4 08 to 4 22	17	11 38 to 11 52	47		
4 23 to 4 37	18	11 53 to 12 07	48		
4 38 to 4 52	19	12 08 to 12 22	49		
4 53 to 5 07	20	12 23 to 12 37	50		
5 08 to 5 22	21	12 38 to 12 52	51		
5 23 to 5 37	22	12 53 to 13 07	52		
5 38 to 5 52	23	13 08 to 13 22	53		
5 53 to 6 07	24	13 23 to 13 37	54		
6 08 to 6 22	25	13 38 to 13 52	55		
6 23 to 6 37	26	13 53 to 14 07	56		
6 38 to 6 52	27	14 08 to 14 22	57		
6 53 to 7 07	28	14 23 to 14 37	58		
7 08 to 7 22	29	14 38 to 14 52	59		

Figure 1011e. *Tidal Current Tables,* Table 5 (extract).

Use of *Tidal Current Tables*

1012 The use of the *Tidal Current Tables* will be illustrated by a series of examples. All problems will be worked from the tabular extracts of Figures 1011a, b, c, and d. These examples are sample calculations and do not cover all possible uses and computations.

Example 1: Determination of time of slack water, and time, strength, and direction of a maximum current at a reference station.

Required: The time of the mid-morning slack water at St. John's River Entrance, Florida, on 5 June 1977: and the time, strength, and direction of the next subsequent maximum current.

Solution: The desired information is obtained directly from Table 1 without calculation except to add one hour for Eastern Daylight Time (EDT).

Answer: The time of A.M. slack water is 0918 EDT; the next maximum current is at 1130, 2.2 knots, flooding. (These times are one hour later than the tabulated values to allow for daylight time (+4) that would be used locally at this time of the year.)

Example 2: Determination of the time of slack and following maximum current at subordinate station:

Required: The time of midafternoon slack water in the channel of the St. John's River just south of Drummond Point on 5 June 1977, and the time and strength of the next subsequent maximum current.

Solution: From Table 2, obtain the time difference and strength ratios as follows:

Time difference, slack water	h + 2^h00^m
Time difference, maximum water	+ 2^h30^m
Strength ratio, maximum flood	0.7
Strength ratio, maximum ebb	0.7

From Table 1 for the reference station, St. John's River Entrance, the following times are extracted:

Slack	1317
Maximum ebb	1609

The differences are applied as follows:

13 17	(slack at reference station)
+ 2 00	(Table 2 difference)
15 17	(+5)
+ 1 00	(for daylight time)
16 17	(+4) Slack, local time

16 09	(max. ebb at reference station)
+ 2 30	(Table 2 difference)
18 39	(+5)
+ 1 00	(for daylight time)
19 39	(+4) Maximum ebb, local time

The strength is calculated by multiplying the maximum current at the reference station by the Table 2 factor.

$2.5 \times 0.7 = 1.75$ kn.

Answer: The midafternoon slack is predicted to occur at 1617 EDT, with the next maximum current at 1939 which will be 1.8 knots, ebbing.

Example 3: Determination of current conditions at an intermediate time at a reference station.

Required: The strength and direction of the current at St. John's River Entrance at 1600 local time on 5 June 1977.

Solution: The applicable entries, those bracketing the desired time, in Table 1 are:

Slack	1317	
Maximum ebb	1609	2.5 kn

To use Table 3, the following calculations are made:

Interval between slack and maximum current:

```
  16 09
– 13 17
   2:52
```

Interval between slack and desired time after changing 1600 EDT to 1500 EST as used in the Tables:

```
  15 00
– 13 17
   1:43
```

Note: Caution must be used when subtracting times to remember that there are 60 minutes, and not 100, in an hour; this seemingly obvious fact is often overlooked, resulting in simple mathematical error. It is convenient when subtracting a larger number of minutes from a smaller number to restate the time as one hour less but 60 minutes more; for example,

```
1609 =    15 69        1500 =   14 60
        – 13 17                –13 17
           2:52                  1:43
```

Now applying these intervals to Table 3, we use the line for 1^h40^m and the column for 3^h00^m. The factor thus found is 0.8. (Note that the nearest values were used; predictions of current strength are not precise enough to justify the use of interpolation.) The factor from Table 3 is applied to the Table 1 value of maximum current.

$2.5 \times 0.8 = 2.0$ kn

Answer: The predicted current for 1600 EDT is 2.0 knots, ebbing.

Example 4: Determination of current conditions at an intermediate time at a subordinate station.

Required: The strength and direction of the current in the channel of the St. John's River at Jacksonville off of Washington Street at 1600 EDT on 5 June 1977.

Solution: (See Figure 1012.) The time differences of Table 2 are first applied to the predictions for the reference station (Table 1) to obtain the times at the subordinate station which bracket the desired time; the applicable velocity ratio is noted at the same time.

```
  10 30          2.2 kn, flooding            13 17
+  2:50            ratio 0.9               +  2:20
  12 80 = 1320                               15 37   slack
```

VEL OF CURRENT	
Date	5 June 77
Location	Jacksonville, Wash. St. #5410
Time	1600 EDT (1500 EST)
Ref Sta	St. Johns River Entrance
Time Diff Slack Water	+2 20
Time Diff Max Current	+2 50
Vel Ratio Max Flood	0.9
Vel Ratio Max Ebb	0.8
Flood Dir	280°
Ebb Dir	100°
Ref Sta Slack Water Time	1317
Time Diff	+220
Local Sta Slack Water Time	1537
Ref Sta Max Current Time	1030 flooding
Time Diff	+250
Local Sta Max Current Time	1320
Ref Sta Max Current Vel	2.5
Vel Ratio	0.9
Local Sta Max Current Vel	2.2
Int Between Slack and Desired Time	0:37
Int Between Slack and Max Current	2:17
Max Current	2.2
Factor Table 3	0.4
Velocity	0.9
Direction	Flooding, 280°

Figure 1012. Calculation of velocity of current at a given time at a subordinate station.

Note that the bracketing times are those at the subordinate station, which may be different from those of the reference station.

The maximum velocity at the subordinate station is obtained by applying the appropriate ratio.

$2.2 \times 0.9 = 1.98 = 2.0$ kn

Next, the desired time of 1600 EDT is converted to the standard time of the Tables, 1500, and the intervals are calculated as in the preceding example.

Interval between slack and maximum current:

15 37
− 13 20
2:17

Interval between slack and desired time:

15 37
− 15 00
0:37

Entering Table 3 on the line for 0^h40^m and the column for 2^h20^m, the factor of 0.4 is obtained; this is applied to the maximum current *at the subordinate station* as previously calculated.

$2.0 \times 0.4 = 0.8$ kn

Answer: The predicted current at 1600 EDT is 0.8 knots, flooding.

Example 5: Determination of the duration of a weak current (specified maximum strength) at a given point. (This information is frequently of considerable value when docking or undocking in a tidal current which has appreciable maximum velocities.)

Required: The times between which the current will be less than 0.3 knots in the terminal channel at Commodore Point on the St. John's River approximately midafternoon on 5 June 1977.

Solution: The time of applicable slack water is calculated from Table 1 and 2; the velocity of the maximum current on either side of this slack is also calculated.

13 17 Slack
+ 2:35 Table 2 difference
15 52

10 30   2.2 flooding
+ 3:10   × 0.5
13 40   1.1 maximum flooding

16 09   2.5 ebbing
+ 3:10   × 0.4
19 19   1.0 maximum ebbing

Table 4 is entered for a 1.0 maximum current as the difference between the two maximums is slight in this case. (If, however, the difference were great, separate periods on either side of slack water toward their respective maximums could be calculated.) One half of the duration of 70 minutes is taken on either side of the predicted time of slack water.

```
  15 52          15 52
–   :35        +   :35
  15 17          15 87 = 1627
```

These times are standard and must be converted to local daylight time by adding one hour.

Answer: It is predicted that the current will be less than 0.3 knots between 1617 and 1727 EDT.

Example 6: Determination of the time of a current of specified velocity.

Required: The time at which the velocity of the ebbing current at St. John's River Entrance will have decreased to 1.7 knots following its first maximum for 5 June 1977.

Solution: From Table 1,

0401	2.8 kn max. ebbing
0818	slack

Calculating the interval and factor to use in Table 3:

```
  08 18
– 04 01
   4:17 interval max-slack
```

$1.7 \div 2.8 = 0.607 = 0.6$

Table 3 is entered on the column for 4^h20^m; the line for a factor of 0.6 is located and identified as an interval between slack and desired time of 1^h00^m. This is applied to the time of slack water and the result is converted to local (daylight) time.

```
  08 18
–  1:40
  06 38 (EST)
+  1:00
  07 38 (EDT)
```

Answer: It is predicted that by approximately 0738 local time, the ebbing current will have decreased to 1.7 knots.

Current determination by calculator

1013 In a manner similar to that used for the determination of tidal heights in Article 908, predictions of current strength at any desired time can be made with a personal electronic calculator. The equation used is based on a cosine-curve variation in strength from one maximum to slack water.

$$S_D = S_M \times \text{Cos}\left[90° - \left(\frac{T_D \sim T_S}{T_M \sim T_S} \times 90°\right)\right]$$

Where S_D is strength at desired time
S_M is maximum current strength
T_D is desired time
T_S is time of slack water
T_M is time of maximum current

The direction of the current will be the same as that for the maximum current used in the equation; this should be the maximum current the time of which, with the time of slack water, brackets the desired time.

Example: Determination of the current strength and direction for a given time at a reference station using a calculator.

Required: The strength and direction of the current at St. Johns River Entrance at 1500 local time on 5 June 1977.

Solution: The desired time is converted to standard time by subtracting one hour to get 1500 EST. The slack water and maximum current that bracket the desired time are taken from Table 1:

Slack 1317

Maximum current 1609, 2.5 kn, ebbing

Therefore

$$S_D = 2.5 \times \text{Cos}\left[90° - \left(\frac{1500 - 1317}{1609 - 1317} \times 90°\right)\right]$$
$$= 2.02 \text{ knots}$$

Expressed to the nearest tenth of a knot, as specified for currents, this is 2.0 knots and the direction is ebbing. This is the same answer as was obtained in Example 3 of Article 1012 by use of Table 3. In some instances, the solution by calculator will yield an answer that is one or two tenths of a knot, or minutes of time, different from that obtained through use of Table 3. This results from the use of tabulated values in Table 3 without interpolation; the difference is of no practical significance.

Hydraulic currents

1014 At certain locations, where a narrow passage joins two bodies of water having very different times of high and low tides, the flow of water is termed a *hydraulic current.* Calculations for these areas are different and must be treated as special cases. These are the situations where "Table B" of Tables 3 and 4 must be used.

Diagrams in *Tidal Current Tables*

1015 The *Tidal Current Tables* for the Atlantic Coast contain diagrams of current direction and strength for certain bodies of water; this information is shown as a function of conditions at a specified reference station. These diagrams are very useful in determining a time of departure and speed so as to make maximum use of favorable ("fair") currents or minimize adverse ("foul") currents. Figure 1015 illustrates such a diagram for Chesapeake Bay. Note the "speed lines" for travel in each direction. A speed for a northbound ship can be selected which, with a properly selected starting time, will permit it to

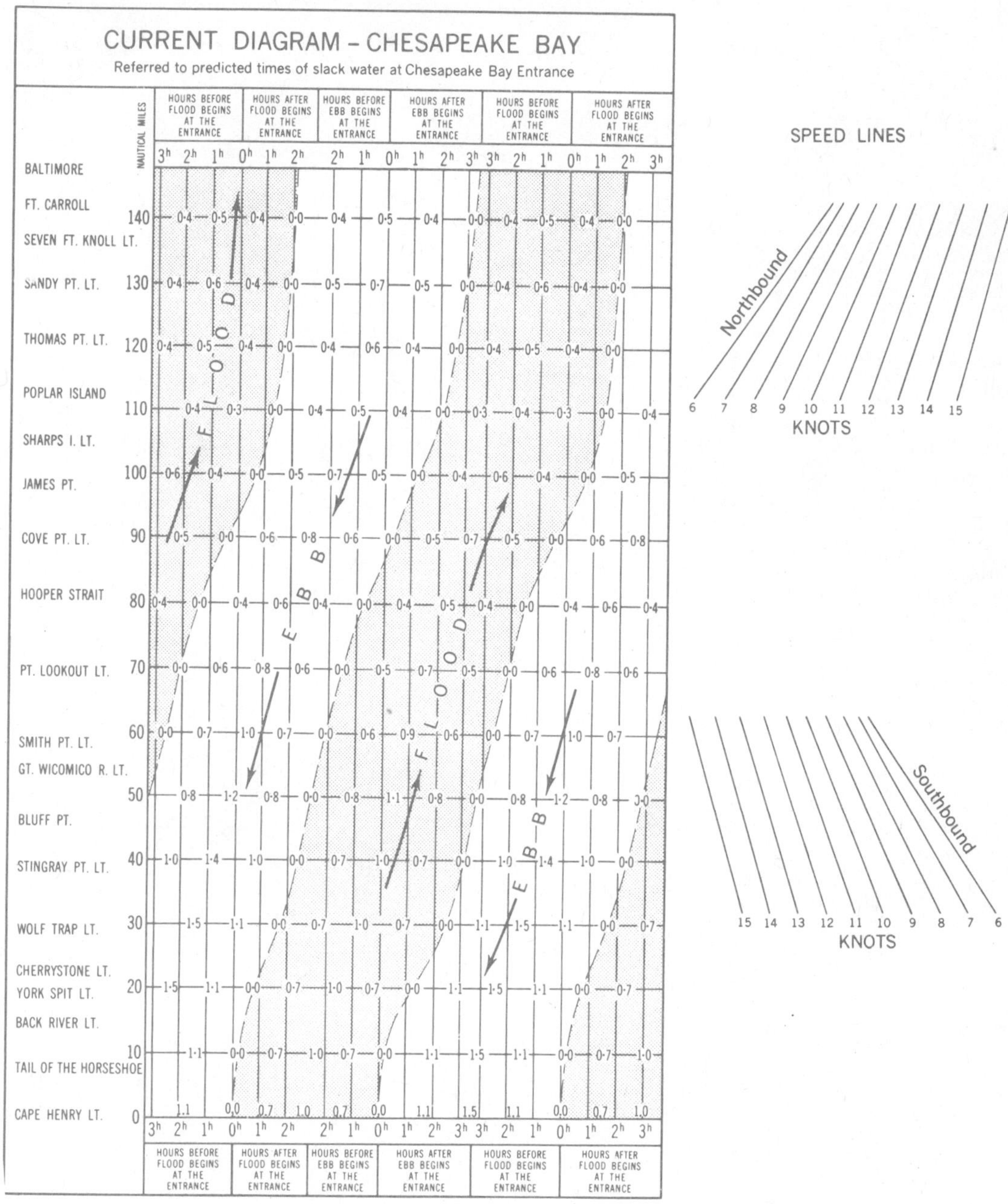

Figure 1014. Current Diagram from *Tidal Current Tables* (typical).

"ride the tide," have a favorable current, all the way from the Bay entrance to Baltimore near its northern end. Conversely, departure time and speed for a southbound passage can be selected to minimize the effects of unavoidable adverse flood currents up the Bay.

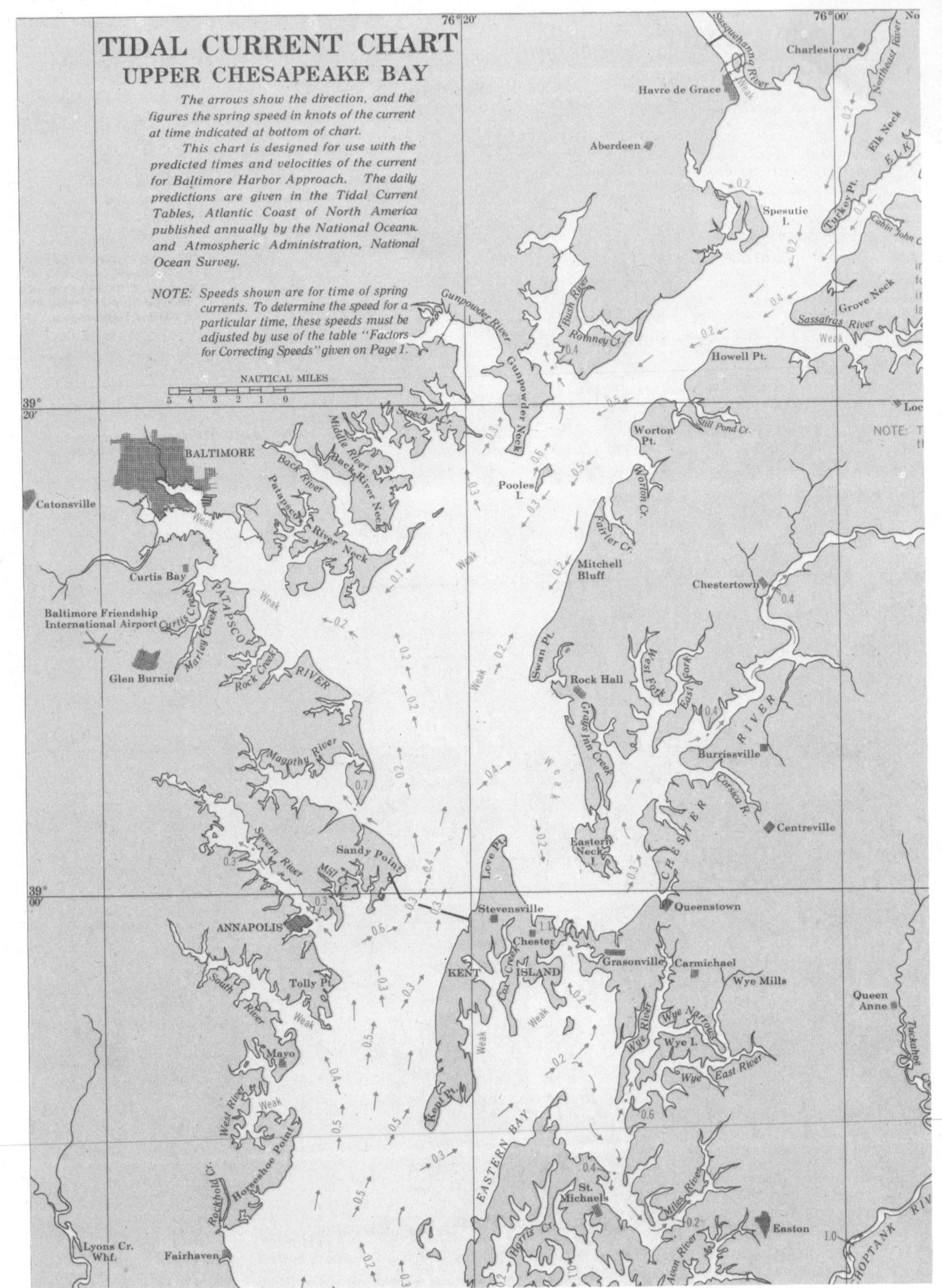

Figure 1015. *Tidal Current Chart* (extract).

In using these diagrams, as in using any of the predictions of the *Tidal Current Tables,* it must be remembered that they are for "normal" or "average" conditions. Periods of sustained winds of moderate or greater strength from certain directions will considerably alter both the times and strengths predicted.

Tidal Current Charts

1016 The National Ocean Survey also publishes a series of *Tidal Current Charts.* These cover eleven areas of heavy maritime activity.

Boston Harbor
Narragansett Bay to Nantucket Sound
Narragansett Bay
Long Island and Block Island Sounds
New York Harbor
Delaware Bay and River
Upper Chesapeake Bay
Charleston (S.C.) Harbor
San Francisco Bay
Puget Sound, Southern Part
Puget Sound, Northern Part

Tidal Current Charts each consist of a set of twelve reproductions of a small-scale chart of the area concerned. There is one chart for each hour of a tidal current cycle in terms of time before or after a stated event such as "slack, flood begins"; on each chart, there are numerous arrows and numbers which represent the current flow at that time; see Figure 1015.

The conditions for any hour of interest can be easily visualized. Some caution is necessary, however, as these are only for "normal" conditions, and currents can vary significantly under unusual circumstances; currents can also vary considerably over small distances and the *Tidal Current Charts* should be used as no more than a general guide. By following through a sequence of charts, the changes in currents at any point can be readily discerned.

Tidal Current Charts for Narragansett Bay and New York Harbor are used with the effective annual edition of *Tide Tables;* all others must be used with the effective edition of *Tidal Current Tables.* The former are prepared with respect to predicted tides, the latter with respect to predicted currents. New editions of *Tidal Current Charts* are published whenever conditions are found to be changed, or when additional information becomes available; only the latest edition should be used.

Tidal Current Diagrams

1017 For certain limited areas of water there are now available *Tidal Current Diagrams* which are published separately and should not be confused with the "current diagrams" contained in the East Coast volume of *Tidal Current Tables;* see Article 1015.

Tidal Current Diagrams are now available for Boston Harbor and for Block Island and Long Island Sounds. These are annual publications, sets of twelve monthly graphs to be used with the appropriate *Tidal Current Chart.* The *Diagrams* are more convenient than the *Tables* for determining conditions at any point, as the graphs indicate directly from the date and time which chart is to be used and what the strength correction factor is.

Summary **1018** Currents can help or hinder the passage of a vessel on the high seas or in pilot waters; her navigator must know where to get information on the various currents he may encounter and be able to make the necessary calculations.

Broad, general information on ocean currents can be found in books such as this or *Bowditch.* More specific information and predictions of ocean currents under *normal* conditions can be obtained from *Pilot Charts* and *Pilot Chart Atlases.* These can be used for planning purposes, but navigation should be based on the actual currents encountered as measured by the differences between DR positions and fixes.

Reversing tidal currents in bays, rivers, and harbors may affect the efficiency of a vessel's progress, or her safety in docking and undocking. Predictions of these are generally available in publications; they must, however, be used with a degree of caution as short-term, unusual local conditions may have made them inaccurate.

The solutions of problems relating to tidal current predictions may be expedited, and the possibility of error lessened, by the use of standard printed forms, but a navigator must *never* become dependent on the use of such forms since they are not always available.

11 Elements of Piloting

Piloting defined **1101** The direction of the movements of a vessel by reference to land and sea marks, by soundings, or by radar, is called *piloting*. All electronic methods of navigation are, in a broad sense, considered to be forms of piloting. The electronic methods, including radar, are discussed elsewhere in this text; this chapter deals with visual piloting, and, to a limited extent, with the use of depth information.

Piloting requires the greatest experience and nicest judgment of any form of navigation. Constant vigilance, unfailing mental alertness, and a thorough knowledge of the principles involved are essential. Mistakes in navigation on the open sea can generally be discovered and corrected before the next landfall. In piloting there is little or no opportunity to correct errors. Even a slight blunder may result in disaster involving, perhaps, the loss of life. The problems of piloting are fundamentally very simple, both in principle and in application. It is the proximity of danger which makes piloting so important. Avoiding a collision in the heavy traffic that exists in the harbors and along coast lines is essentially a problem of *seamanship*. The navigator is concerned with the problem of keeping his ship in navigable waters. Throughout this chapter a deep-draft vessel is hypothesized. The principles and procedures which will keep sufficient water under the keel of a large vessel will unquestionably bring safety to a smaller one.

In all phases of piloting, the navigator must constantly realize that he is dealing with the past, the present, and the future. He must continually analyze the situation that existed in the recent past and exists at present in order to plan for the future. He should constantly use every logical means at his disposal to:

obtain warnings of approaching danger;
fix the position of the ship accurately and frequently; and
determine the proper course of immediate action.

The keeping of a dead reckoning plot was described in Chapter 8. There it was noted that the plot was maintained without considering any offsetting effects of currents. Since it was seen in Chapter 10 that currents, both ocean and tidal, do exist, sometimes with considerable velocities, it becomes obvious that the ship may well *not* be where its DR plot indicates. Thus it is necessary to have techniques to determine not just where a vessel could be, but where she actually is; this is *positioning* and is the major topic of this chapter.

Lines of position (LOP)

1102 Probably the most important concept in piloting, as in almost all phases of navigation, is that of the *line of position* (LOP). A single observation does not establish a position; it does provide the observer with a line on some point of which he is located. This line is a segment of a great circle but in visual piloting the segment is so short that it may be plotted as a straight, or rhumb, line on a Mercator chart. In this chapter, only visual lines of position established by various methods will be discussed.

It should also be noted that a line of position can provide useful *negative* information. If the LOP is valid, then the observer, and his vessel, are *not* somewhere else, such as in shoal water. A single LOP of good quality, therefore, while not establishing a position, can at least rule out some worries if it crosses no hazards.

It must be borne in mind that there is no connection between the DR course line and lines of position. The DR course line and DR positions may be considered as statements of *intention,* or a graphic representation of ordered courses and speeds. The lines of position are statements of *fact,* as the ship is actually somewhere on the line of position, regardless of courses steered, and speeds used.

Labeling lines of position

1103 A single line of position, whether a bearing (Article 1105), a range (Article 1104), or a distance (Article 1106), is labeled on the upper side of the line with the time of observation expressed in four digits. A single line of position advanced to form a running fix (Article 1111) is labeled with the original time of observation and the time to which it has been advanced. (Direction is not normally labeled on an LOP, but, if desired, it can be added as a three-digit number directly

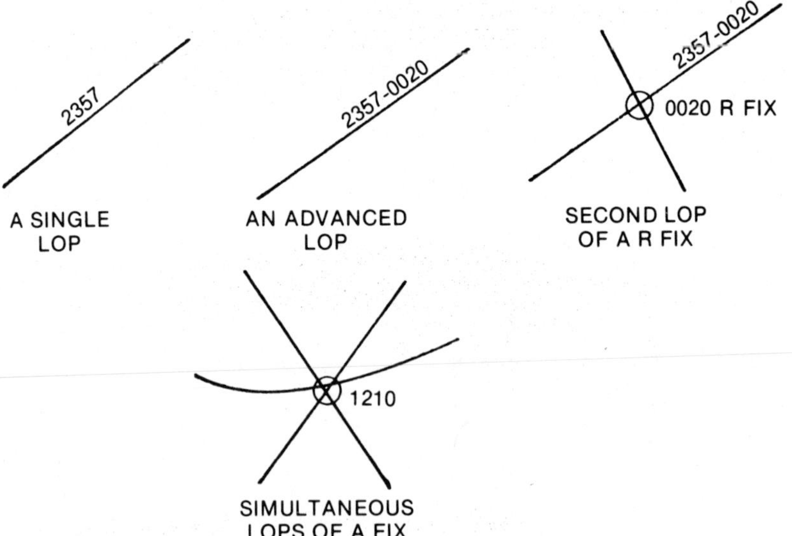

Figure 1103. Labels for lines of position and fixes.

beneath the time label; true direction is assumed unless "M" is suffixed indicating magnetic direction.) Simultaneous lines of position forming a fix need not be labeled, the time of the fix being sufficient. Similarly, the second line of position in a running fix is not labeled, taking its time as that of the running fix.

Every line must be labeled as soon as it is plotted; an unlabeled line can be a source of error, especially after a change of watch. There is enough uncertainty in piloting without adding to it by leaving doubt as to the meaning of a line. Care must be taken not to confuse a course line with a line of position (Article 1509).

Observing a range

1104 The simplest way to establish a line of position is to observe a range. If two fixed objects of known position appear to the observer to be in line, he must at that instant be somewhere on the line passing through the objects and extending beyond it. He can also take comfort from the negative aspects of his line of position; if he is on the range line, he is certainly *not* somewhere off of it such as in shoal water or headed into some other hazard.

Example: (Figure 1104). At 1205 a beacon and stack appear in line. The ship must then be somewhere along the straight line drawn through the symbols on the chart for these two objects.

Draw light lines on the chart and make them no longer than necessary. Particularly avoid drawing them through the chart symbols for

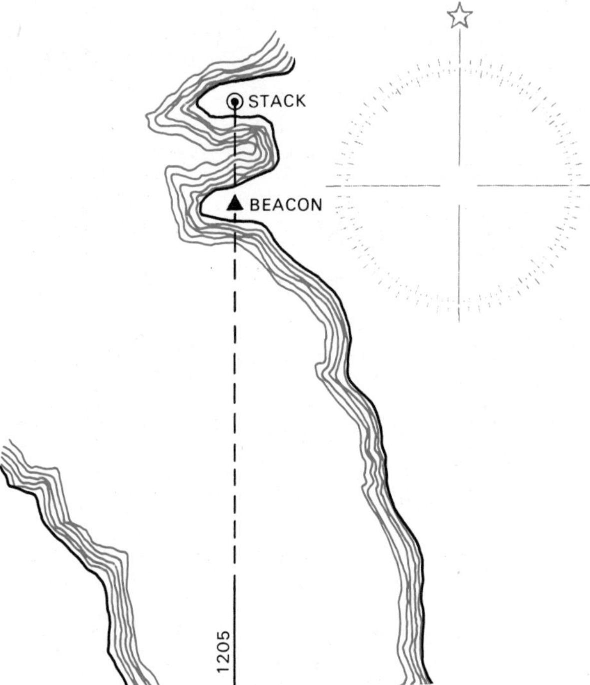

Figure 1104. Plotting a range.

aids to navigation, which may be rendered indistinct by erasures. In illustrations for this chapter, broken lines will be extended from the symbols on the chart to illustrate principles. *The solid segment of the line of position is all that is normally plotted on the chart.*

Most ranges used for navigation consist of two fixed aids to navigation, usually, but not always, lighted, and specifically established to constitute a range. A navigator, however, must not overlook the possibility of using natural or manmade objects fortuitously located to meet his needs, as in the example above.

In addition to using two objects in line to obtain a line of position, a *steering range* may often be used to direct the course of a vessel. Aids to navigation are located in pairs to assist a vessel in staying within a channel; see Articles 502 and 522. The danger in using any range, formal or informal, is that it can be used *beyond its safe limits.* A navigator must be careful to use any range over only that portion which is safe. He must especially be careful not to follow a range too far, either towards the front marker or away from it; he must be continually alert as to his position along the range line.

Plotting bearings

1105 It is not usually possible to find two fixed known objects in line at the time the navigator wishes to make an observation. Consequently, the line of position is normally obtained by plotting a *bearing* on the chart. The observer sights across his pelorus, hand-bearing compass, bearing circle, or gyro repeater toward a fixed, known object and thus determines the direction of the line of sight to that object; this is the *bearing* of the object. He then plots this bearing to the known object on his chart.

Example: (Figure 1105). At 1200 a spire bears 050°. The navigator plots this line as shown; at 1200 the ship must be somewhere on this

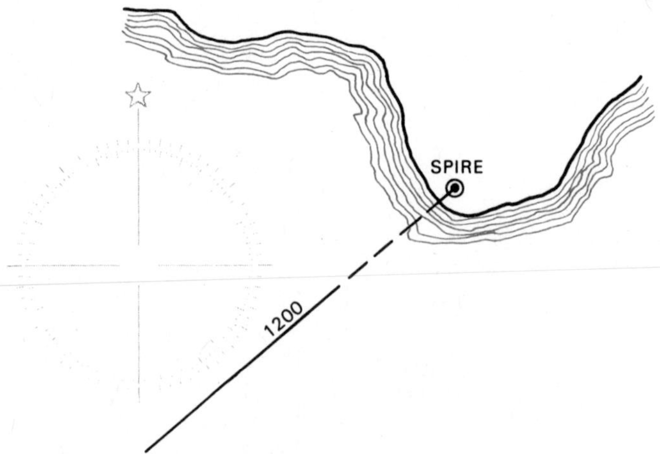

Figure 1105. A line of position from a bearing.

line. Direction is not labeled in Figure 1105; if it had been desirable to show it, the direction *toward the spire* would have been shown as a three-digit number beneath the time label.

Distance **1106** If the distance to an object is known, the ship must lie somewhere on a circle centered on the object, with the known distance as the radius. This circle is termed a *distance circle of position.* Figure 1106 illustrates a distance circle; at 1600, the navigator found the distance of the lighthouse, *D,* to be 6 miles. Obviously the ship must be somewhere on a circle of 6-mile radius, centered on the light. In most cases only a segment of the circle will be drawn on the chart. Distance may be obtained by radar, by range finder, or if the height of the object is known, by stadimeter or sextant; the latter two instruments are used for measuring angles by which distance may be determined. Table 9 in *Bowditch* permits a rapid solution for sextant angles. If the object observed is a lighthouse, the known height may be stated either as "height above water" or "height of structure"; the angle must be measured accordingly.

A distance circle is frequently combined with a bearing, as described in Article 1107 (example 6).

Getting a fix **1107** As noted in Article 1102, a single line of position does not give a navigator full and complete information as to his location—he is somewhere along that LOP, but just exactly where is undetermined.

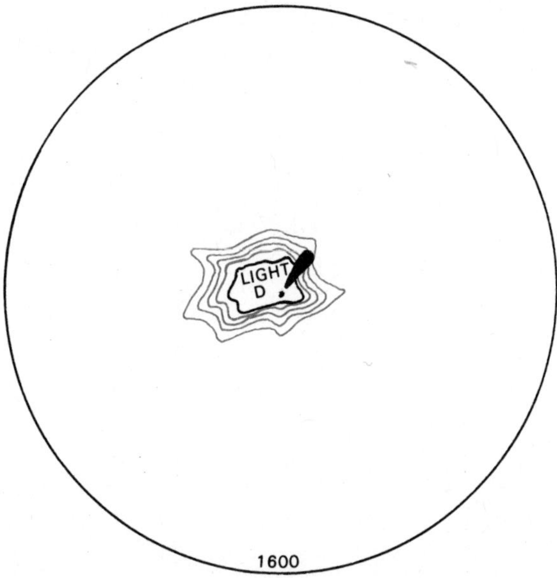

Figure 1106. A circular line of position from a distance measurement.

If, however, he has *two* simultaneous LOPs, he is on both of them and his only possible position (assuming the LOPs are accurate) is at their intersection—he has fixed his position; he has established a "fix." Obviously, if his vessel is moving, he is at his fix only at the time that the LOPs were obtained. Thus a time label must be added to the circle symbol of a fix. The two lines of position should cross at angles as near 90° as possible to define the position most precisely. Even more desirable would be three LOPs; in this case the bearings should differ by as close to 120° (or 60°) as possible. See Article 1109.

Lines of position can be combined to obtain fixes as follows:

Example 1: Two cross bearings (Figure 1107a). At 1545 a ship steaming on course 000°, speed 10 knots, observes a tower bearing 288°, and Danger Shoal Lightship bearing 194°.

The 1545 fix must lie at the intersection of the two lines of position; it is obtained by plotting the reciprocals of the observed bearings from the symbols of the tower and lightship on the chart of the area.

The intersection of the two lines of position at the 1545 fix is labeled as shown in Figure 1107a. A new DR course is then started from this position.

Example 2: Three cross bearings (Figure 1107b). At 1351, with the ship on course 285°, speed 15 knots, the navigator observes the following bearings by gyrocompass (gyro error is zero): left tangent of Smith Point, 005°; left tangent of Jones Bluff, 130°; Hall Reef Light, 265°.

Required: Plot and label the 1351 fix.

Solution: See Figure 1107b.

Note that in Examples (1) and (2) the bearings were taken simultaneously to obtain the fix, which is often the case in observing terrestrial objects. However, as will be explained more fully in Article 1111, if the bearings are taken at *different* times, they may be adjusted to a common time to determine what is known as a *running fix.*

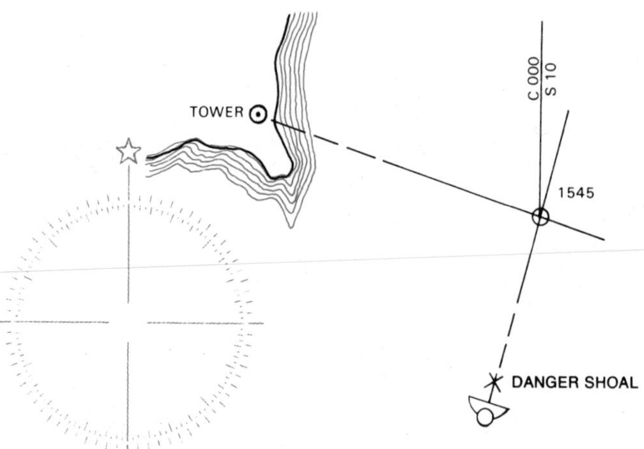

Figure 1107a. A fix from two crossed bearings.

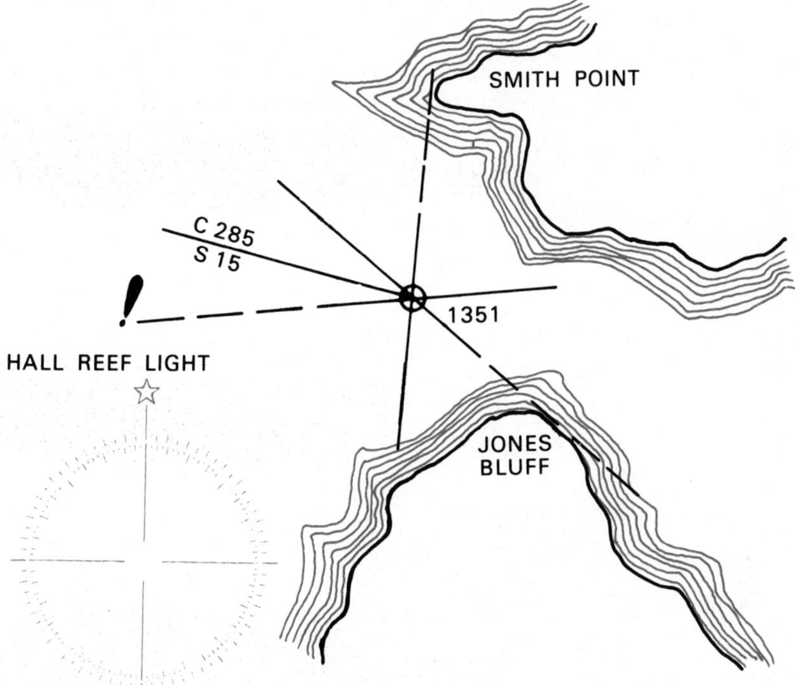

Figure 1107b. A fix from three intersecting bearings.

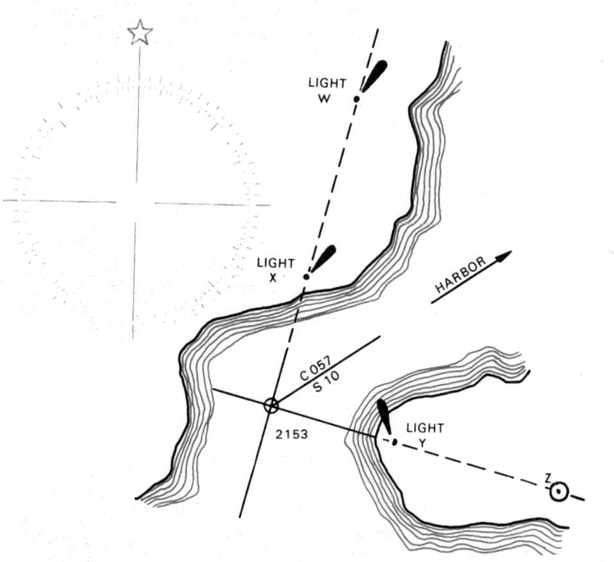

Figure 1107c. A fix from two ranges.

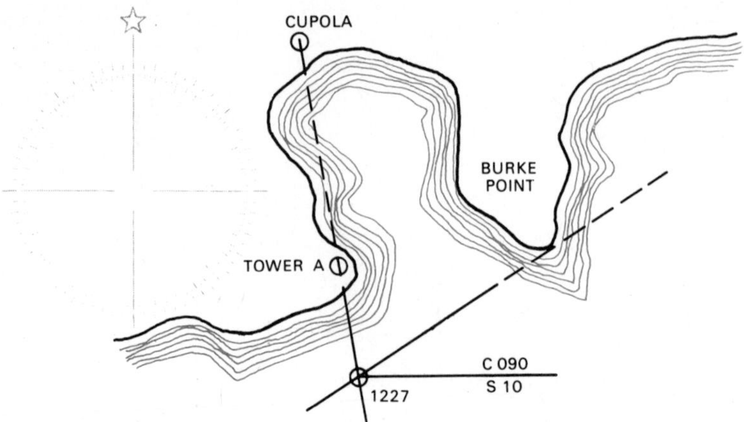

Figure 1107d. A fix from one range plus a bearing.

Example 3: Two ranges. A ship entering a harbor at 10 knots steams so as to keep range lights *W* and *X* (Figure 1107c) in line. At 2153, with *W* and *X* exactly in line, light *Y* and church spire *Z* are observed to be in line and the ship changes course to 057°.

Required: Plot and label the 2153 fix.

Solution: See Figure 1107c. The 2153 fix is at the intersection of the two range lines of position.

Example 4: One range and a bearing (Figure 1107d). A ship is on course 090°, speed 10 knots. At 1227 Radio Tower *A* and a cupola are in range. At the same time the right tangent of Burke Point bears 057°.

Required: Plot and label the 1227 fix.

Solution: The 1227 fix is at the intersection of the two lines of position.

Example 5: Bearing and distance on different objects (Figure 1107e). At 1425 radio tower *A* bears 350 degrees. At the same time, the radar range to Sandy Point Light is four miles. The ship is on course 050°, speed 18 knots.

Required: Plot and label the 1425 fix.

Solution: The 1425 fix is at the intersection of the line of position and the distance circle of position.

Example 6: Bearing and distance of the same object (Figure 1107f). At 1314, Double Point Light bears 347°. From a 1314 sextant observation its distance is computed to be 3 miles. Ship is on course 225°, speed 10 knots.

Required: Plot and label the 1314 fix.

Solution: Plot the observed bearing, 347°. With the lighthouse as the center, plot the distance circle of position. The point where the line of position is intersected by the circle of position is the 1314 fix.

Example 7: Passing close aboard an aid to navigation. The ship's position can also be determined approximately by passing close aboard a navigational aid, such as a buoy or offshore light tower, the position of

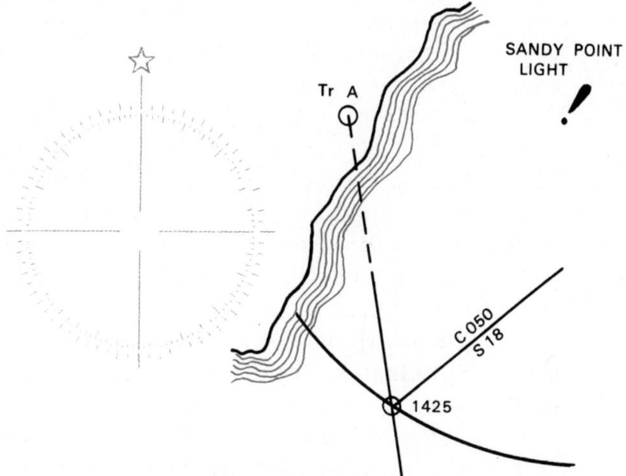

Figure 1107e. A fix by bearing on one object and distance from another.

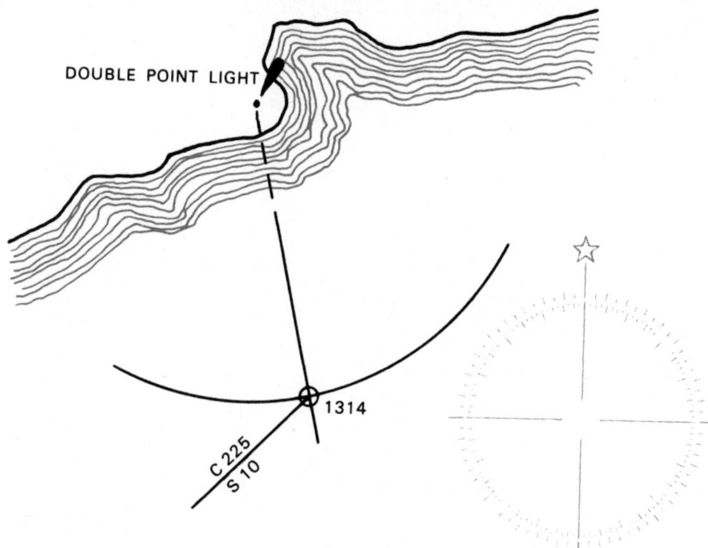

Figure 1107f. A fix by bearing and distance from same object.

which is indicated on the chart. This is a type of fix frequently employed by the navigator when plotting on a small-scale chart. The accuracy of a position obtained in this manner depends upon two factors: the accuracy of the measurement of the relationship between the ship and the observed aid, and the amount of displacement between the actual and plotted positions of the aid. If the aid is a fixed structure and the displacement can be accurately determined, this method gives an accurate and desirable fix. If a floating aid is involved, and there is any doubt as to its distance away from the ship, this procedure should be used only when other navigational aids are not available to establish a more accurate position.

Relative bearings **1108** The *relative bearing* of an object is its direction from the ship, relative to the ship's head. It is the angle between the fore-and-aft line of the ship and the bearing line of the object, measured clockwise from 000° at the ship's head through 360°. In Figure 1108 the relative bearings of objects *A, B, C,* and *D* are 135°, 180°, 270°, and 340°, respectively. The pelorus can be used for taking relative bearings by setting the 000° graduation of the pelorus card to the lubber's line, then observing the object and reading the card. The azimuth circle or the bearing circle are more frequently used, however.

Relative bearings are converted to true bearings before they are plotted. This is done simply by adding their value to the ship's true heading when the relative bearings were taken, subtracting 360° if the sum equals or exceeds that amount. Thus, assuming the ship is steady on 045° true during observations, the corresponding true bearings of *A, B, C,* and *D* are 180°, 225°, 315°, and 025°. Conversely, true bear-

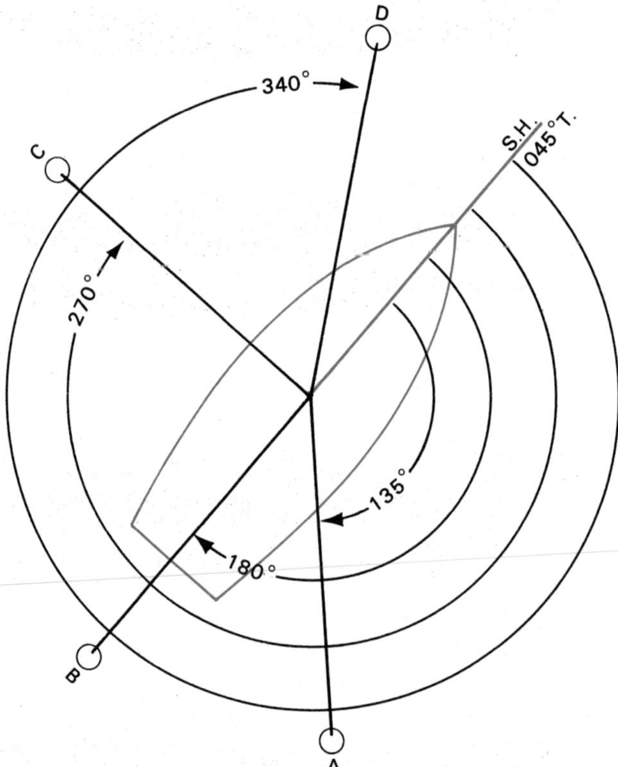

Figure 1108. Relative bearings.

ings can be converted to relative bearings by subtracting from them the ship's true heading, first adding 360° if necessary.

TB = RB + SH (−360°)
RB = TB (+ 360°) − SH

Selecting objects for obtaining a fix

1109 When selecting objects from which to obtain a fix, the primary consideration is the angle between the bearings. If only two visual bearings are available, the best fix results from two bearings crossing at 90°, in which case an error in either bearing results in minimal error in the plotted fix. As the angle between the objects decreases, a small error in either bearing throws the fix out by an increasing amount. Bearings of objects intersecting at less than 30° should be used only when no other objects are available, and the resulting fix should be regarded with caution. Figure 1109 illustrates the deterioration in accuracy of a fix caused by a given error in one bearing. (See also Article 3008.)

To check two bearings and to minimize fix error, three or more bearings should always be taken if possible. If three are taken, the optimum angle is 120° (or 60°) between bearings.

Figure 1109 compares the errors to a fix arising from a 5° error in one bearing, when the observed objects differ 90° in bearing and when they differ 20°. *A, B,* and *C* each represent known objects. *O* is the observer's true position. *AOC* = 20°, and *AOB* = 90°. If a 5° error is made in plotting the bearing of *B, OX* shows the resulting error; however, if a 5° error is made in plotting the bearing of *C, OY* is the error.

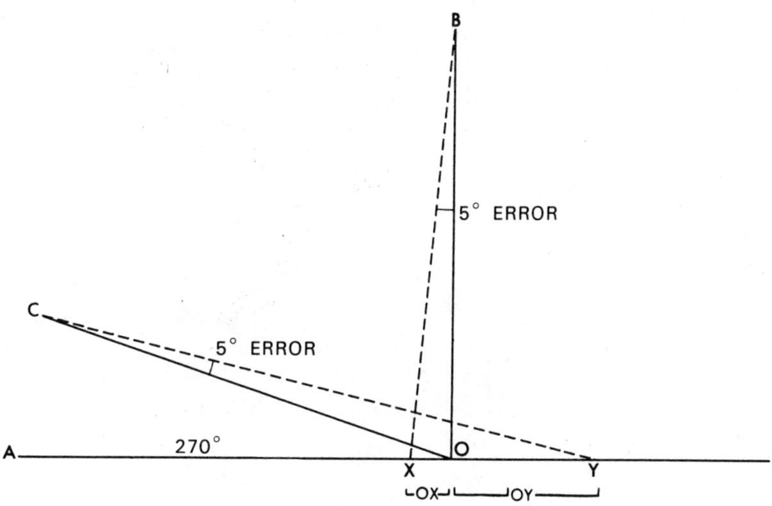

Figure 1109. The effect of errors in lines of position.

Fix by horizontal angles

1110 A fix can also be determined by the measurement of the two horizontal angles between three lines of sight to identifiable objects. The actual *directions* of these lines of sight are *not* measured; but the two angles must be measured simultaneously, usually when the ship has no way on. The angles are normally measured by a sextant held horizontally.

The three-arm protractor

The two angles so measured are usually plotted with a *three-arm protractor.* This instrument, made of brass or plastic, consists of a circular scale which can be read to minutes of arc, and to which the three arms are attached (Figure 1110a). The center or index arm is fixed, and the zero graduation of the protractor coincides with the straightedge of this arm. The other arms are rotatable, and can be set and locked at any angle relative to the fixed arm.

To obtain a fix, three fixed objects, which can be identified on the chart, must be visible. The angles between the right and central objects, and the left and central objects, are measured with the sextant. The two movable arms are set to these angles, and locked, and the protractor is placed on the chart, with the index arm passing through the center object. The instrument is now moved slowly across the chart until all three arms are aligned with the three objects. The ship's position may now be marked on the chart with the point of a pencil through the hole at the center of the protractor.

Care must be used in selecting the three objects to be observed; if they and the ship all lie on the circumference of a circle, no fix can be obtained. To avoid this possibility, the objects should be so selected, if a choice is available, that the center one is closer to the estimated position than the right and left objects.

The three-arm protractor gives chart positions of great accuracy; these positions are not affected by any error of the compass. If a three-arm protractor is not available, the method can be used by drawing a straight line on clear plastic or tracing paper, and laying off the two required angles from one end of this line; the piece of plastic or transparent paper is then placed on the chart and moved about until the

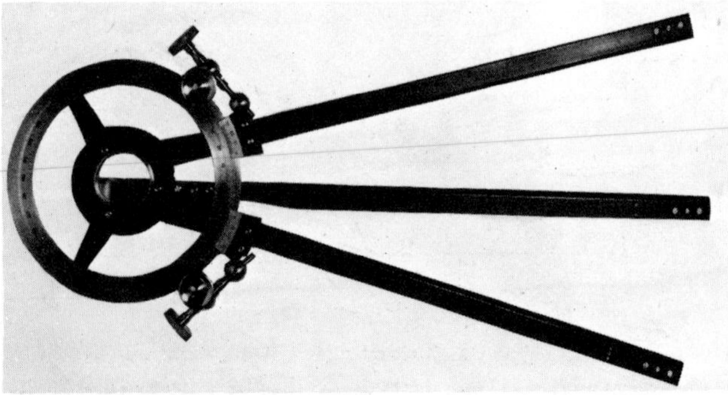

Figure 1110a. A three-arm protractor.

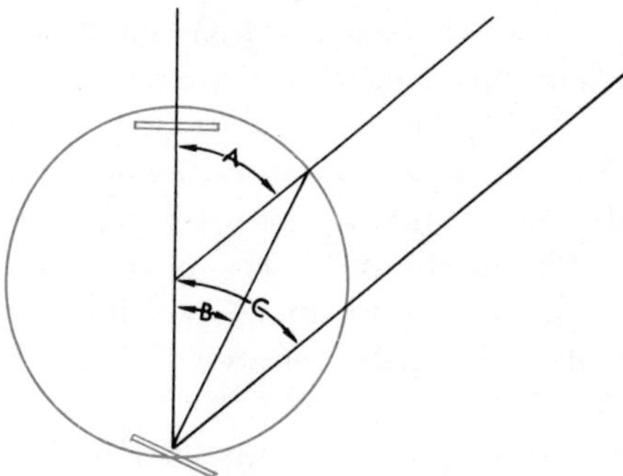

Figure 1110b. Optical principle of a position finder; B = ½A, C = A.

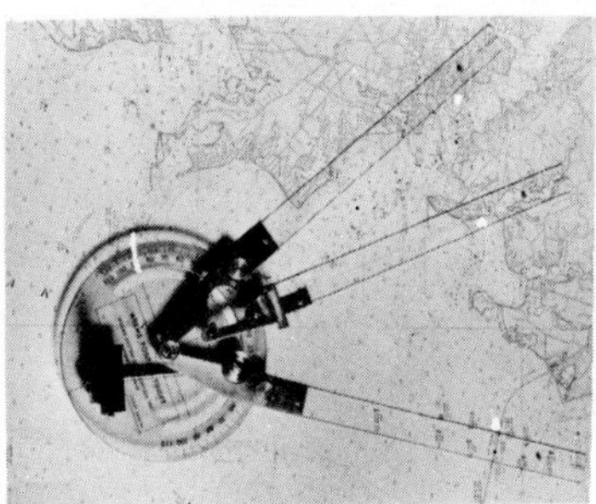

Figure 1110c. Using a position finder on a chart.

lines pass over all three objects; the position is beneath the intersection point of the lines.

On vessels not carrying a sextant a *position finder* can be substituted, because the accuracy required, for purposes other than surveying, is considerably less than the inherent accuracy of the sextant. The position finder is, in effect, a three-arm protractor with mirrors attached which permit using one instrument for observing and plotting. It is unnecessary to read the value of the angles measured as the plotting arms are properly positioned for plotting when making the observations. Figure 1110b illustrates the optics of the position finder and Figure 1110c shows it positioned on the chart for plotting.

The running fix

1111 It is not always possible to obtain two simultaneous observations. At such times the navigator must resort to a *running fix,* using two lines of position which are obtained by observations at *different times.* In order to plot a running fix, he must make allowance for the time elapsed between the first observation and the second. This is done by *advancing* the earlier line of position to the time of the second observation. (It is also possible to obtain a running fix by *retiring* the second LOP to the time of the first observation, but this is seldom desirable in actual navigation as the first method gives a more recent position.)

The navigator assumes that, for the limited period of time between the two observations, the ship makes good over the ground a definite distance in a definite direction. He moves the earlier line of position, parallel to itself, to this advanced position. The new advanced line now represents the possible positions of the ship at the time of the second observation.

When an accurate position has been determined by fix or good running fix, a new DR plot is started and the old one discontinued.

There is no rule as to how far a line of position can be advanced and still give a well-determined position. This is a matter of judgment and depends upon individual circumstances. But until judgment is developed, a good general rule is to avoid advancing a terrestrial line of position more than 30 minutes. The length of time should be kept as short as possible consistent with other considerations.

In the examples below, current effects are not considered.

Example 1: Advancing a line of position (Figure 1111a). A ship on course 012°, speed 12 knots, observes Light *E*, at 1500, bearing 245°. A subsequent observation on another object is made at 1520, at which time light *E* is no longer visible.

Required: Advance the 1500 line of position until it becomes a 1520 line of position.

Solution: In this case the navigator assumes that for the limited period of time (20 minutes) involved, the ship makes good both course 012° and speed 12 knots, or 4 miles in the direction of 012°. Plot and

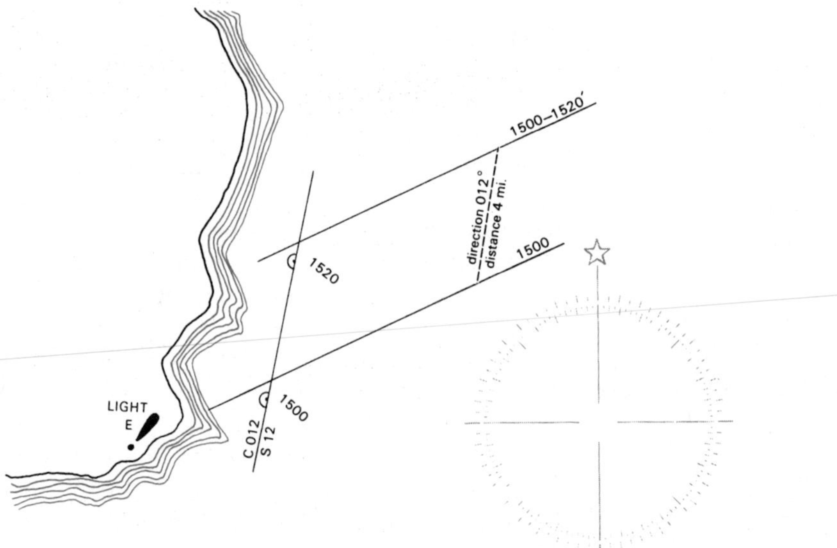

Figure 1111a. Advancing a line of position without consideration of current.

label the 1500 DR and the 1500 line of position. This line represents all possible positions of the ship at 1500. Note that the 1500 DR is not on the 1500 line of position, indicating that the DR position does not coincide with the true position of the ship, the location of which is not as yet known. From *any* point on the 1500 line of position (including but not limited to the point where the course line intersects this line of position), measure off 4 miles in the direction of 012° and draw a line through this point parallel to the original 1500 line. Label the new line with both the original time of observation, 1500, and the time to which the line has been advanced, 1520, as shown. Note that *any point* on the 1500 line advanced 4 miles in direction 012° arrives at the advanced line.

The label "1500–1520" really means "a 1500 line which has become a 1520 line by advancing all points of the 1500 line in a given direction at a given speed for the time interval indicated (1500–1520)." The given direction and given speed are the ordered course and the ordered speed, respectively.

Consider now the full problem of determining a ship's position by running fix.

Example 2: A running fix with bearings on different objects (Figure 1111b). The 1440 DR position of a ship is as shown. The ship is on course 012°, speed 12 knots. The weather is foggy. At 1500 light *T* is sighted through a rift in the fog bearing 245°. No other landmark is visible at this time. At 1520 stack *F* is sighted bearing 340°. Light *T* is no longer visible.

Required: Plot and label the running fix (1520 R Fix).

Solution: Plot and label both the 1500 and 1520 DR positions. (A DR position should be determined and plotted every time an LOP or fix is obtained.) Plot the bearing of Light *T* as a line of position and label with time. Advance this line parallel to itself in the direction (012°) of the ship's course being steered and a distance (4 miles) determined by the speed of the ship divided by elapsed time. (Depending upon the plotting technique used, it may be desirable to label the 1500 LOP with its direction, so that this direction can be used to draw an advanced line through an advanced point.) This distance will be the same as that between the 1500 and 1520 DR positions. Label this advanced line of position as shown in 1111b. Plot the second line of position through stack *F* bearing 340°. It is only necessary to draw a segment of this line, long enough to intersect the advanced LOP. The intersection of the two LOPs is the 1520 running fix; this is labeled with the time, and with the abbreviation "R FIX" so that the small circle symbol will not be thought of as a "fix," a position determined to a higher degree of accuracy. Since the position of the vessel has been relatively well established along an LOP to a better degree of accuracy than the simultaneous DR position, a new DR course and speed line is plotted from the running fix.

Care must always be exercised when plotting a running fix to ensure that the earlier line is advanced in the proper direction. This

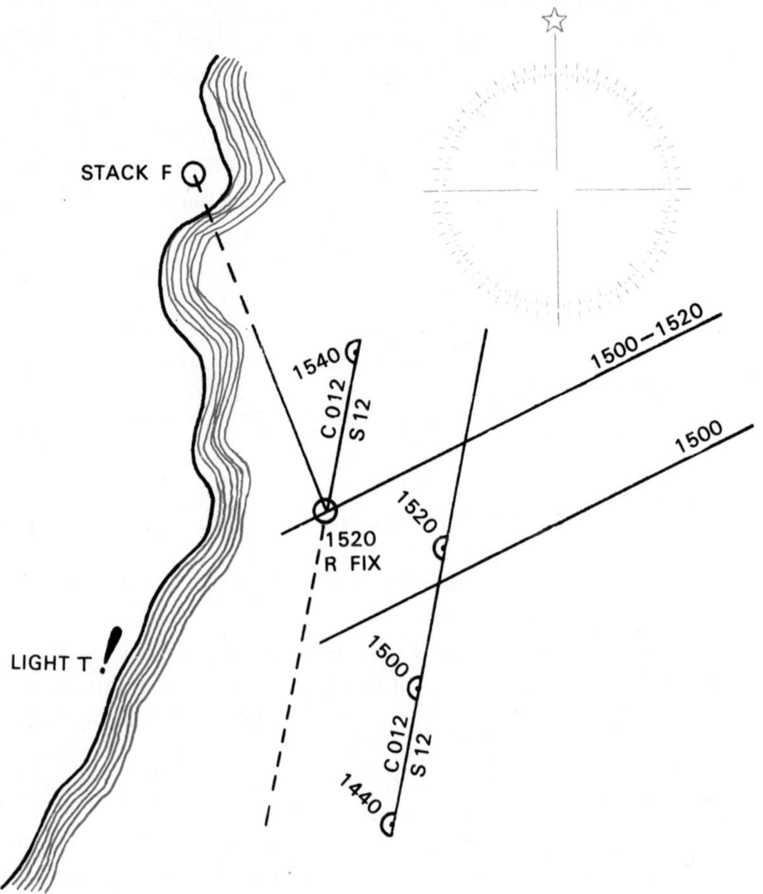

Figure 1111b. A running fix.

may be determined by close inspection of the labels on the DR course line and the lines of position.

Example 3: A running fix from successive bearings on the same object (Figure 1111c). A running fix can also be obtained by plotting two bearings on the same object as illustrated in this example.

A ship is on course 018°, speed 12 knots. At 1430, Light *G* bears 042° and at 1452, it is observed to bear 083°.

Required: Plot and label the 1452 running fix.

Solution: Plot the 1430 DR position on the course line which corresponds with the time of the first observation and plot the 1430 line of position on a bearing of 042° to the light, labeling the plot as indicated. In a like manner, plot the 1452 DR and its corresponding line of position on a bearing of 083°. Then advance any point on the earlier line of position in the direction of the course, 018°, for a distance of 4.4 miles ($\frac{22}{60} \times 12$ kts = 4.4 miles). Through this advanced point, construct a line parallel to the original 1430 line of position. (Again, it may be desirable to label direction on the initial LOP so that this informa-

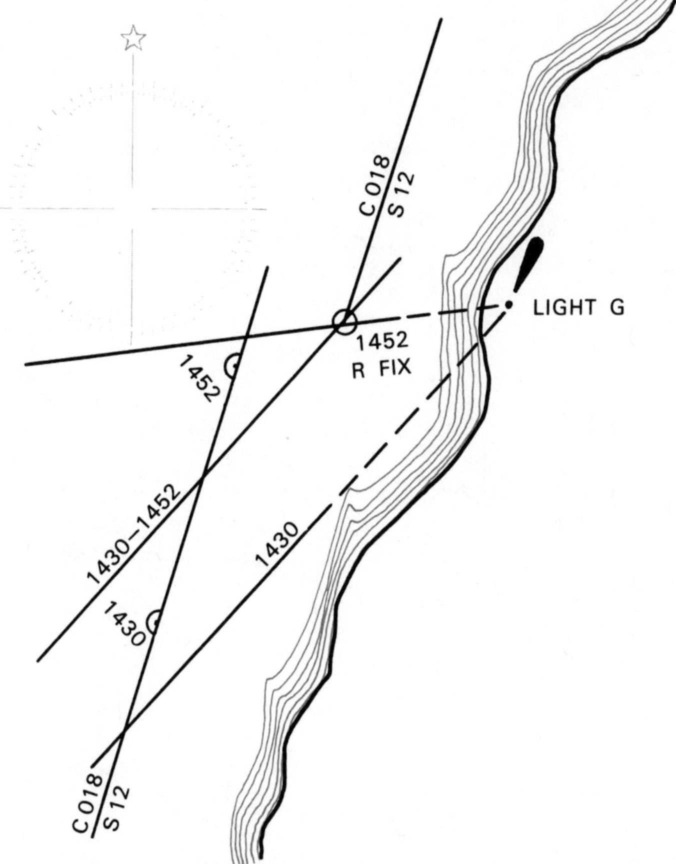

Figure 1111c. A running fix from two bearings on same object at different times.

tion can be used for drawing the advanced LOP.) The intersection of the 1430 LOP advanced to 1452 with the 1452 LOP determines the 1452 running fix. A new course line is started from the 1452 running fix as indicated.

Example 4: A running fix advancing a distance circle of position (Figure 1111d). A distance circle of position is advanced by moving the center of the circle as illustrated in this example.

A ship is on course 076°, speed 15 knots. The 1440 DR position has been plotted as shown. At 1440, the distance to Lightship *J,* obscured by fog, is found by radar to be 4.7 miles. At 1508, Light *H* is sighted bearing 040°, and the radar has become inoperable.

Required: Plot and label the 1508 running fix.

Solution: Note that the center of the circle (the lightship) is advanced in the direction 076° for a distance of seven miles ($\frac{28}{60} \times 15$ knots $= 7$ miles). From this point, the distance circle of position is constructed again with a radius of 4.7 miles and labeled as indicated. The 1508 line

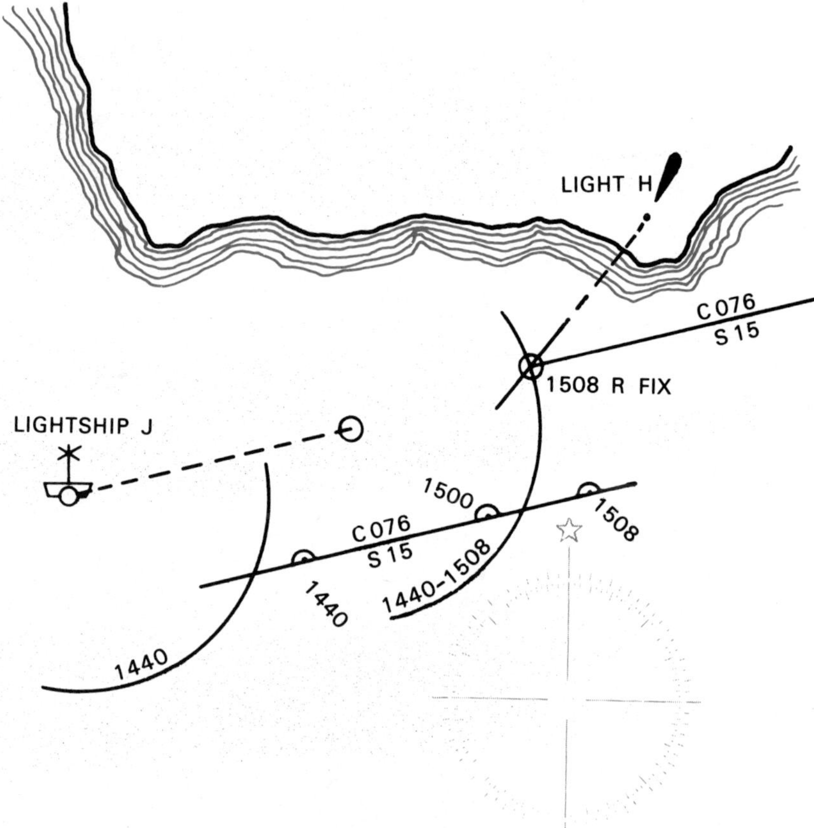

Figure 1111d. Advancing a circle of position.

of position to Light *H* is plotted on a bearing of 040°. The intersection of this line of position with the advanced distance circle of position determines the 1508 running fix, from which a new course line is started.

Note that there are two possible intersections of a bearing line of position with a distance circle of position, only one of which is shown. In ordinary circumstances, that intersection nearer the DR position is termed the running fix. In cases of doubt and in the absence of additional information which will confirm either one as the true running fix, commence a DR plot from both positions, assume the ship to be on the course that is potentially more dangerous, and govern future actions accordingly.

The running fix with changes of course and speed

1112 A line can be advanced to determine a running fix even though the ship's course or speed is changed in the period between the two observations, as illustrated in the following examples.

Example 1: A running fix with a single course change (Figure 1112a). A ship is on course 063°, speed 18 knots. The 2100 DR position is plotted

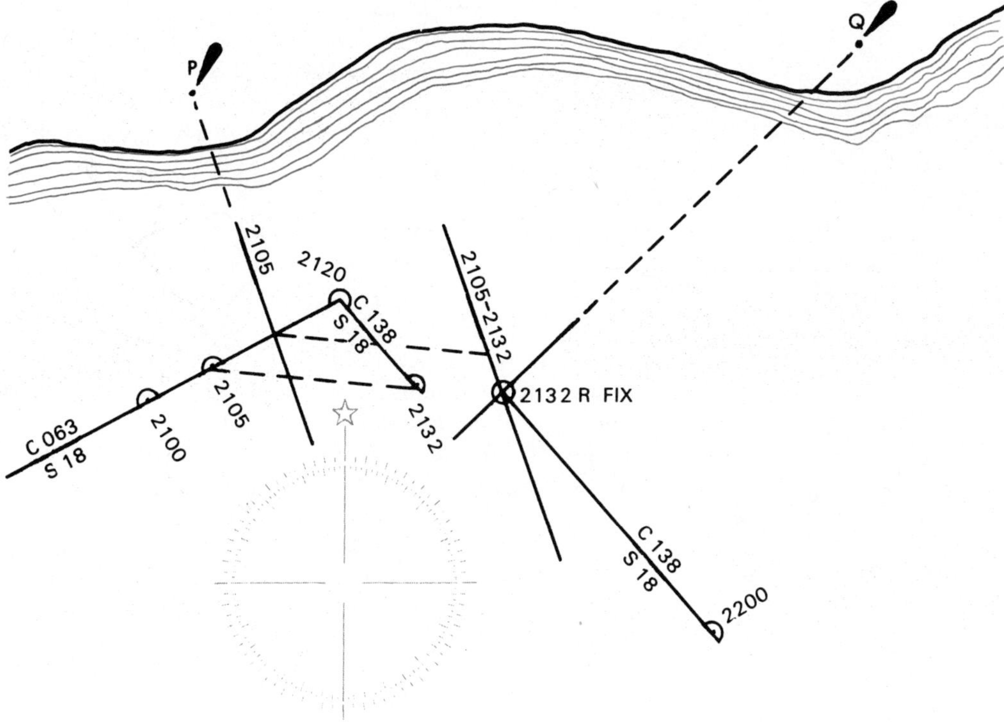

Figure 1112a. A running fix with a single course between times of bearings.

as shown. At 2105 Light *P* bears 340° and disappears shortly thereafter. The 2105 DR position is plotted. At 2120 the course is changed to 138° and the 2120 DR position plotted. At 2132 Light *Q* is sighted bearing 047°.

Required: Plot and label the 2132 running fix.

Solution: Plot the 2105 DR and 2132 DR positions. The 2105 line of position is advanced by using the course and distance made good through the water between the DR positions corresponding to the time of each visual observation. This is shown by a dashed line, usually not drawn in practice but used here for clarity, connecting the 2105 DR and the 2132 DR. By advancing the 2105 line of position parallel to itself in the direction of the *course made good* a distance equal to the *distance made good* between the 2105 and the 2132 DR, the 2105 line of position advanced becomes the 2105–2132 line of position. In this example, the point of origin for the measurement of this advance was at the intersection of the 2105 LOP with the DR course line as shown. Similar advance of any other point on the 2105 LOP would have produced the identical result.

Plot the 2132 line of position to Light *Q* on a bearing of 047°. The intersection of this line of position with the 2105–2132 LOP determines the 2132 running fix, from which a new DR is started. The plot is labeled as indicated.

Example 2: A running fix with multiple course and speed changes (Figure 1112b). At 0300, a ship is on course 125°, speed 20 knots. At 0302, Light *A* is observed on a bearing of 040° and is soon lost sight of in the haze. At 0310 course is changed to 195° and speed is reduced to 18 knots. At 0315, course is changed to 220°. At 0319, course is changed to 090° and speed is increased to 24 knots. At 0332, Light *B* is sighted on a bearing of 006°.

Required: Plot and label the 0332 running fix.

Solution: Use the "course and distance made good" technique described in the foregoing example to construct the 0332 running fix. The accuracy of measurement of "course made good—distance made good" displacement will depend, of course, upon the accuracy with which the DR plot was maintained between 0302 and 0332. *This principle is true for any running fix obtained by construction.*

The 0302 line of position is advanced parallel to itself in the direction of the course made good a distance equal to the distance made good between the 0302 and 0332 DR positions. This advanced line now defines the 0302–0332 LOP. The intersection of this line of position with the 0332 line of position on a bearing of 006° to Light *B* establishes the 0332 running fix, from which a new DR plot is started. The plot is labeled as indicated.

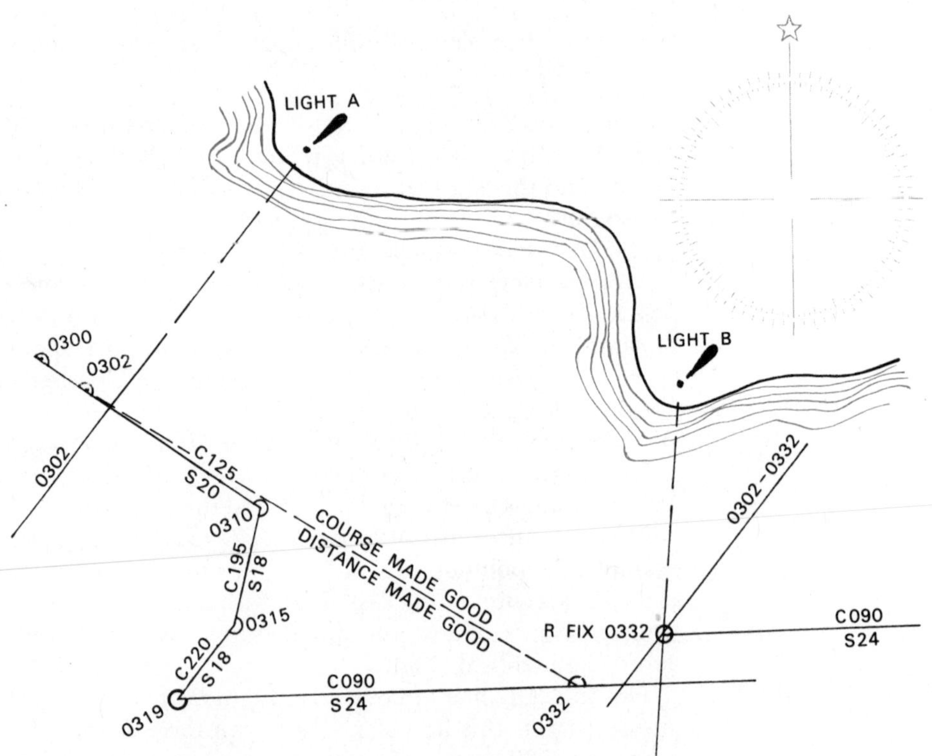

Figure 1112b. A running fix with multiple course and speed changes.

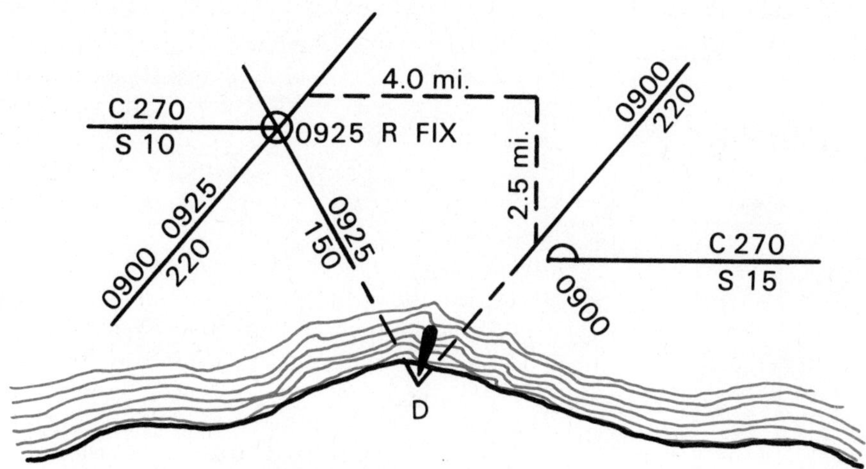

Figure 1112c. A running fix using a DRT.

Example 3: A running fix using the DRT (Figure 1112c). A ship is maneuvering with frequent changes of course and speed. The 0900 DR position is as shown. At 0900, Light *D* bears 220° by visual observation and at 0925 it bears 150°, at which time the ship is on course 270°, speed 10 knots. The DRT (Article 723) indicates that between 0900 and 0925 the ship makes good 2.5 miles north and 4.0 miles west.

Required: Plot and label the 0925 running fix.

Solution: Any point on the 0900 bearing line is advanced 2.5 miles north and 4.0 miles west, as indicated by the dashed line, and the advanced line of position is drawn through the point thus determined. A new DR track is started from the 0925 running fix.

Solution by trigonometry

1113 It is possible to solve the running fix by trigonometry; two angles are determined by measurement, and the length of the side between them is determined by the ship's run between the bearings. The distance off at the time of the second bearing can readily be found as can the predicted distance off when the object is abeam. These calculations can easily be done on any small hand calculator that has trigonometric functions; see Appendix F.

Solution by Table 7, *Bowditch*

It is not necessary to resort to trigonometry to obtain the solution. Table 7 of *Bowditch* (Figure 1113), tabulates both distance off at the second bearing and predicted distance off when abeam, for a run of one mile between relative bearings from 20° on the bow to 30° on the quarter. Since the distance rarely equals exactly one mile, the tabulations are in reality multipliers or factors, which, when multiplied by the actual run give the distance from the object at the time of the second bearing and the predicted distance at which the object should be passed abeam.

TABLE 7

Distance of an Object by Two Bearings.

Difference between the course and second bearing.	Difference between the course and first bearing.													
	20°		22°		24°		26°		28°		30°		32°	
30°	1.97	0.98												
32	1.64	0.87	2.16	1.14										
34	1.41	0.79	1.80	1.01	2.34	1.31								
36	1.24	0.73	1.55	0.91	1.96	1.15	2.52	1.48						
38	1.11	0.68	1.36	0.84	1.68	1.04	2.11	1.30	2.70	1.66				
40	1.00	0.64	1.21	0.78	1.48	0.95	1.81	1.16	2.26	1.45	2.88	1.85		
42	0.91	0.61	1.10	0.73	1.32	0.88	1.59	1.06	1.94	1.30	2.40	1.61	3.05	2.04
44	0.84	0.58	1.00	0.69	1.19	0.83	1.42	0.98	1.70	1.18	2.07	1.44	2.55	1.77
46	0.78	0.56	0.92	0.66	1.09	0.78	1.28	0.92	1.52	1.09	1.81	1.30	2.19	1.58
48	0.73	0.54	0.85	0.64	1.00	0.74	1.17	0.87	1.37	1.02	1.62	1.20	1.92	1.43
50	0.68	0.52	0.80	0.61	0.93	0.71	1.08	0.83	1.25	0.96	1.46	1.12	1.71	1.31
52	0.65	0.51	0.75	0.59	0.87	0.68	1.00	0.79	1.15	0.91	1.33	1.05	1.55	1.22
54	0.61	0.49	0.71	0.57	0.81	0.66	0.93	0.76	1.07	0.87	1.23	0.99	1.41	1.14
56	0.58	0.48	0.67	0.56	0.77	0.64	0.88	0.73	1.00	0.83	1.14	0.95	1.30	1.08
58	0.56	0.47	0.64	0.54	0.73	0.62	0.83	0.70	0.94	0.80	1.07	0.90	1.21	1.03
60	0.53	0.46	0.61	0.53	0.69	0.60	0.78	0.68	0.89	0.77	1.00	0.87	1.13	0.98
62	0.51	0.45	0.58	0.51	0.66	0.58	0.75	0.66	0.84	0.74	0.94	0.83	1.06	0.94

Figure 1113. Extract from Table 7 of *Bowditch*.

Arguments for entering Table 7 are arranged across the top and down the left side of each page. The multipliers or factors are arranged in *double columns.* The left-hand column lists the factors for finding the distance at the time of the second bearing. The right-hand column contains the factors for finding the predicted distance abeam.

Whenever the second bearing is 90° (relative), the two factors are the same. In this case the second bearing *is* the beam bearing and the element of *prediction* no longer exists.

In case the second bearing is greater than 90° (relative), the right-hand factor obviously no longer gives a *predicted* distance abeam, but the estimated distance at which the object *was* passed abeam.

Caution It must be remembered that the ship's heading (SH) may *not* be the same as the course being made good over the bottom (CMG); for example, the vessel may be "crabbing" slightly, heading a bit into a cross current in order to make good a desired track. In the general cases of this article, and in the more special cases of the following article, *the angles must be measured with respect to the course being made good over the bottom.* If there are any currents influencing the track of the ship with respect to the earth, appropriate corrections must be applied.

There is usually no need to interpolate when using Table 7, even though only the even-numbered relative bearings are given. As a rule it is easy to obtain even-numbered relative bearings if the bearing-taker or navigator exercises a little patience.

Example 1: A ship is on course 187°, speed 12 knots. At 1319 Light *A* bears 161° and at 1334 it bears 129° true.

Required: (1) Distance from Light *A* at 1334.

(2) Predicted distance at which Light *A* should be passed abeam.

Solution: (Figure 1113) Difference between course and *first* bearing (first relative bearing or first angle on the bow) = 26°. Difference between course and *second* bearing (second relative bearing or second angle on the bow) = 58°.

Factors (multipliers) = 0.83 and 0.70.

Run (1319 to 1334) = 15 minutes = 3 miles ($12 \times \frac{15}{60}$). (1) 3 × 0.83 = 2.49 = 2.5 miles (distance at 1334). (2) 3 × 0.70 = 2.10 = 2.1 miles (predicted distance abeam).

Example 2: A ship is on course 235° psc, speed 14 knots. At 2054 Light *X* bears 267° psc, at which time the patent log reads 26.7. At 2129 Light *X* bears 289° psc, at which time the patent log reads 34.9.

Required: (1) Distance from Light *X* at 2129.

(2) Predicted distance at which Light *X* should be passed abeam.

Solution: (Figure 1113) Difference between course and *first* bearing (first relative bearing or first angle on the bow) = 32°. Difference between course and *second* bearing (second relative bearing or second angle on the bow) = 54°.

Factors = 1.41 and 1.14.

Distance run = 8.2 miles. (1) Distance at 2129 (time of second bearing) = 11.6 miles. (2) Predicted distance abeam = 9.3 miles.

Special cases **1114** Certain cases of this problem (two bearings of an object and the intervening run) do not require the use of tables. Some of these *special cases* are as follows:

The *bow and beam* bearing (Figure 1114a and 1114b) in which the known run between the bow (45°) and beam (90°) bearings equals the object's distance abeam.

Doubling the angle on the bow (Figure 1114c). This is developed as follows:

$$b = 180° - 2a$$
$$a + b + c = 180°$$
$$a + 180° - 2a + c = 180°$$
$$a - 2a + c = 0°$$
$$\text{and } a = c$$
$$\therefore ABC \text{ is an isosceles triangle, and } AB = BC$$

Hence, when the angular distance of the object on the bow is doubled, the run between bearings equals the object's distance at the second bearing.

The *22½°–45° case*, or $\frac{7}{10}$ *rule.* This is a case of doubling the angle on the bow, explained in the preceding case, the distance run being equal

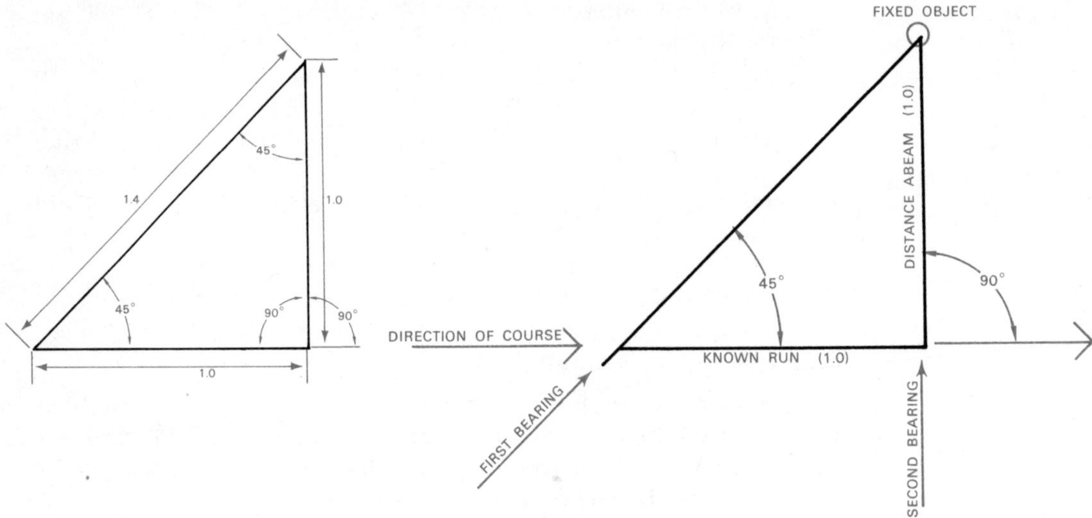

Figure 1114a, left. Proportions of a right isosceles triangle. Figure 1114b, right. Bow and beam bearings.

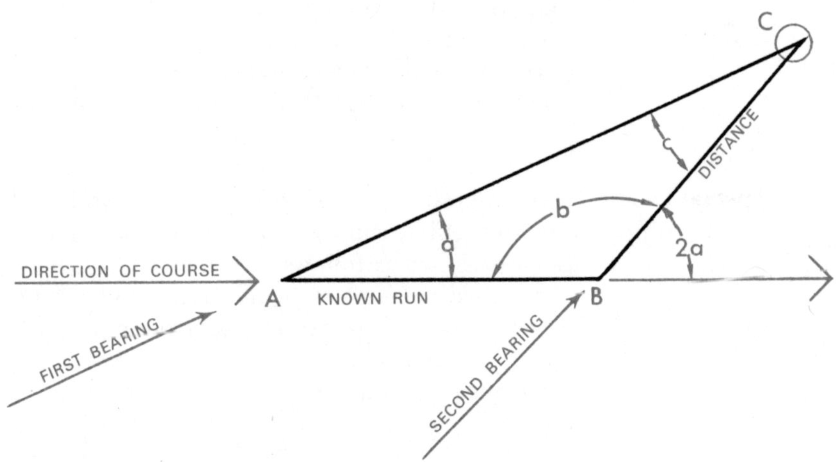

Figure 1114c. Doubling the angle on the bow.

to the object's distance at second bearing. Also, in this particular case, $\frac{7}{10}$ of the distance run equals the distance the object will be passed abeam.

The *30°–60° case,* or $\frac{7}{8}$ *rule,* in which the relative bearings are 30° and 60° on the bow. This being another case of doubling the angle on the bow, the distance run between bearings equals the object's distance at the second bearing. Also, $\frac{7}{8}$ of the distance run equals the distance the object will be passed abeam.

1st Bearing	2d Bearing	1st Bearing	2d Bearing	1st Bearing	2d Bearing
°	°	°	°	°	°
20	29¾	28	48½	37	71¼
21	31¾	*29	51	38	74¼
*22	34	30	53¾	39	76¾
23	36¼	31	56¼	*40	79
24	38¾	*32	59	41	81¼
*25	41	33	61½	42	83½
26	43½	34	64¼	43	85¾
26½	45	35	66¾	*44	88
*27	46	36	69¼	*45	90

Figure 1114d. Relative bearings.

The *26½°–45° case.* If the first bearing is 26½° on the bow and the second is 45°, the object's distance when abeam equals the run between bearings. This is true in other combinations of angles whose natural cotangents differ by unity. Some of these combinations are listed above in tabular form. The asterisked pairs are the most convenient to use, since they involve whole degrees only. In each case, the distance run between bearings equals the distance of passing the object abeam.

Keeping in safe water without a fix

1115 It is at times possible to ensure the safety of a vessel without obtaining a fix, even in the absence of a range. Under some conditions, such a method might be even more certain and even easier to use than those discussed previously.

Along a straight coast where the various depth curves roughly parallel the shore, the echo sounder or lead can be kept going and any tendency of the ship to be set in toward the beach will soon be apparent. Such a method, of course, must be used intelligently. If a given fathom curve is blindly followed, it may lead into trouble. It is necessary to look ahead and anticipate the results. If the given fathom curve makes a sharp turn, for instance, a ship following a steady course might find itself in rapidly shoaling water before it could make the turn. The given fathom line, while affording plenty of water under the keel, might pass close to isolated dangers, such as wrecks, shoals, or rocks.

In following a narrow channel, particularly one that is not well marked, a constant bearing on a distant object ahead or a range can be of inestimable value. A very slight deviation from the desired track is immediately apparent when piloting by means of a range dead ahead (or dead astern). Aids to navigation are often established in such a position as to form ranges to guide ships along channels, but when such an aid is not available, natural ranges can sometimes be found.

The navigator should be alert to recognize such a situation, for the value of ranges, either artificial or natural, as guides in navigation cannot be overemphasized. In using a range, it is important to know how far the range can be followed; that is, when to turn. Turns in a channel are usually marked by turn buoys. Excellent fixes to check the progress of a ship can be obtained by following a range and noting the instant other objects near the beam are in range. A study of the chart in advance will often reveal several good natural ranges to use as check points along a channel. One near a turn is especially valuable.

Danger bearings

1116 A *danger bearing* is used by the navigator to keep his ship clear of an outlying area of danger close to which the ship must pass. The area has been previously surveyed and is plotted on his chart but, in the vast majority of cases, it will give no warning of its presence to the eye. Examples of such dangers are submerged rocks, reefs, wrecks, and shoals. A danger bearing must be established between two fixed objects, one of which is the danger area. The other object must be selected to satisfy these conditions: visible to the eye; indicated on the chart; true bearing from the danger area should be in the same general direction as the course of the ship as it proceeds past the area.

As shown in Figure 1116, a ship is standing up a coast on course 000°, speed 15 knots. The 0430 DR is at Point *A*. A charted danger area of shoal water and sunken rocks off the coast must be avoided. On the chart draw line *GO* from Light *O* (the visible object), tangent to the danger area (the invisible object). The measured direction of this line from *G* to *O*, 015°, is the danger bearing. It is habitually drawn in red pencil, hachured on the dangerous side, and is labeled, also in red pencil, with "NLT 015" (meaning *Not Less Than* 015°) on the side

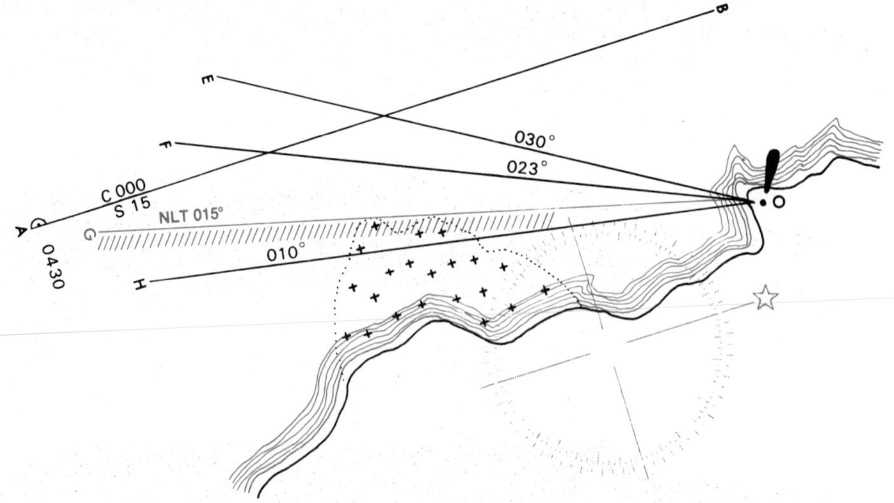

Figure 1116. A danger bearing.

opposite the hachures; any bearing less than 015° could indicate a hazardous situation. (If the chart is to be used under a red light at night, some other dark color may be desirable.)

As the ship proceeds up the coast, frequent visual bearings of Light *O* are taken. If each such bearing is numerically *greater* than the charted bearings *GO,* such as *EO* or *FO,* the ship must be in safe water. If, however, a bearing is observed to be *less* than *GO,* such as *HO,* the ship *may* be standing into danger as illustrated. In this case, if the position of the ship cannot be determined by a fix, the ship should change course radically to the left until the danger bearing is reached, after which it is safe to resume the original course.

Similarly, if the hazard were to the left of the course, a danger bearing could be plotted with hachures on the other side and a label reading "NMT" meaning *Not More Than.* In some waters, it is useful to use a pair of danger bearings, one NLT and one NMT, to keep the vessel on a safe course between hazards to either side.

The value of this method decreases as the angle between the course and the danger bearing increases. Unless the object is nearly *dead ahead,* the danger bearing is of little value in keeping the ship in safe water as the danger is approached. If there is a large angle between the course and the danger bearing, the object might better be used to obtain running fixes as the ship proceeds. However, if there is but one object in sight and that nearly ahead, it would be very difficult to get an exact position, but a danger bearing will show whether or not the ship is on a good course, and will, in consequence, be of the greatest value. Even if there were other objects visible by which to plot accurate fixes, it is a simple matter to note, by an occasional glance over the sight vane of the pelorus or compass, between fixes, that the ship is making good a safe course. It occasionally will occur that two natural objects will so lie that, when in range, they mark a danger bearing. Advantage should be taken of all such ranges.

When stated or recorded for use, a "danger bearing" should include not only the numerical value of the bearing, but also an amplifying statement of whether the bearing tendency should be greater or less for safety. In the previous example, the personnel concerned should be informed that *"bearings to Light O greater than 015° are safe"* or *"bearings to Light O less than 015° are dangerous,"* in order that the danger bearing be meaningful.

Danger angle **1117** To avoid sunken rocks or shoals, or other dangerous obstructions which are marked on the chart, the navigator may use what is known as a *danger angle.* There are two kinds, the horizontal and the vertical danger angle. The former requires two well-marked objects indicated on the chart, lying in the direction of the coast, and sufficiently distant from each other to give a fair-sized horizontal angle; the latter requires a well-charted object of known height. In Figure 1117a, let *AMB* be a portion of the coast along which a vessel is steam-

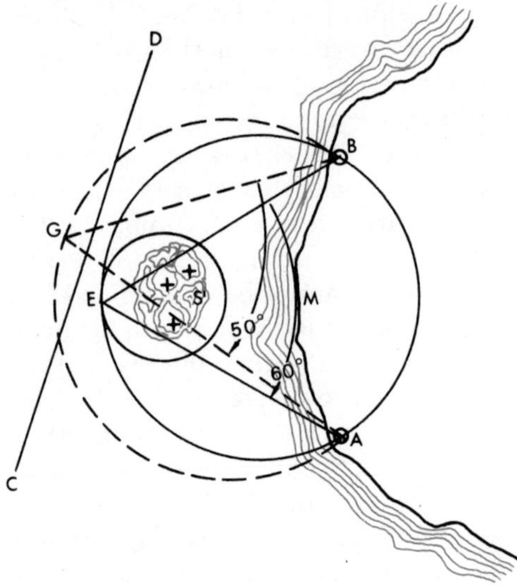

Figure 1117a. Horizontal danger angle, passing safely offshore of the hazard.

ing on the course *CD*. *A* and *B* are two prominent objects shown on the chart; *S'* is an outlying shoal or reef, or other danger. In order to pass offshore of the danger, *S'*, take the middle point of the danger as a center and the distance from that center at which it is desired to pass as a radius, and draw a circle. Pass a circle through points *A* and *B* tangent to the offshore side of the first circle (*E*). To do this, it is only necessary to draw a line joining *A* and *B* and draw a line perpendicular to the middle of *AB*, and then find by trial and error the location for the center of circle *AEB*. Measure the angle *AEB;* this is the *horizontal danger angle,* 60° in the example of Figure 1117a. (From any point on arc *AEB*, the same angle will be measured.) A sextant is set to the danger angle and frequent measurements are taken of the angle between *A* and *B*. In this situation, if the angle gets *less,* 50° in Figure 1117a, the trend is farther *away* from the danger, and the course is *safe.* If, on the other hand, the angle becomes greater, the vessel is closer in to the danger and the course is *hazardous.*

Horizontal danger angle

Alternatively, if the danger area is farther offshore, and it is desired to pass between it and the coastline, as at *S* in Figure 1117b, the danger angle is established by again drawing the smaller circle around the hazard and the larger circle tangent to it as before. Here any *decrease* in the observed horizontal angle between *A* and *B* would indicate that the vessel was getting farther out from the coastline and hence *closer to the danger area.* If the danger angle *increased,* it would indicate greater clearance from the danger area and greater safety, provided that the shore was not approached too closely.

The two situations described above can be combined into one if it is necessary to pass between two hazards, and suitable objects exist to serve as points A and B. In this case, the *safe* sextant angle will be between two limiting values with a decrease or increase beyond these limits being dangerous.

To simplify reference to the danger angle and to make the plot more meaningful, a notation can be made on the chart in red (or other color for night work) of the numerical value or values of the horizontal danger angles. In addition, trace over in red pencil the arc of the inscribed circle about shoal S and the arc of the circle AEB adjacent to which the ship will pass in the safe passage corridor between the danger areas. Unless the danger covers a large area, it is generally not necessary to draw the circles as described above. In many cases points E and G can be selected by eye at a safe distance from the dangers.

Vertical danger angle The *vertical danger angle* involves the same general principle, as can be seen by reference to Figure 1117c, in which AB represents a vertical object of known height. In this case the tangent circles are drawn with

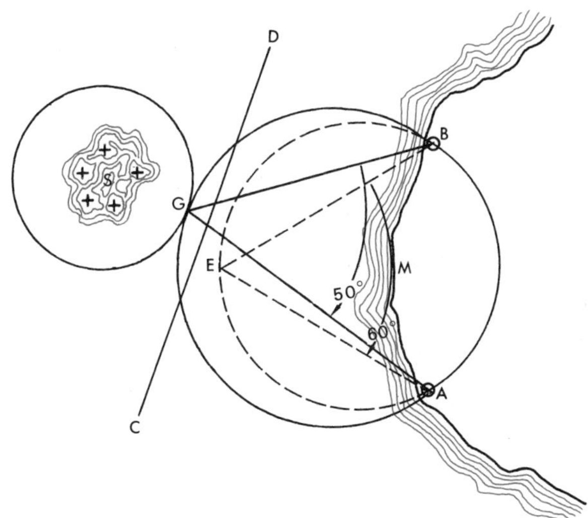

Figure 1117b. Horizontal danger angle, passing safely inshore of the hazard.

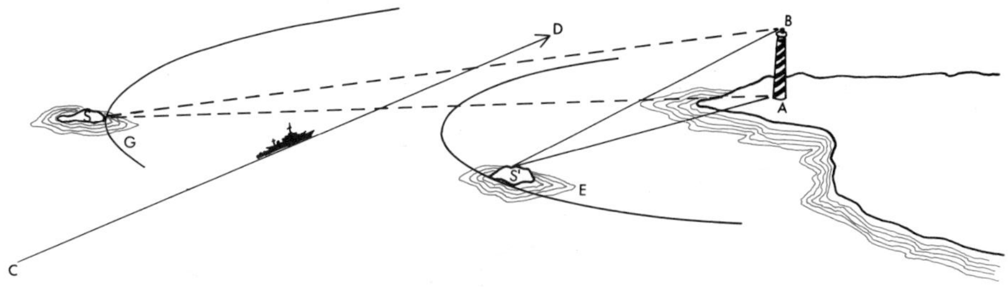

Figure 1117c. A vertical danger angle.

the charted position of the object as a center. The limiting angles are determined by computation or by means of Table 9, *Bowditch.* The addition of the measured values of the respective vertical danger angles and the marking of the limits of the safe passage corridor between the shoals in red pencil will measurably improve the graphic value of the plot.

The estimated position

1118 At times, the information available to the navigator is insufficient to fix the position of the ship accurately. However, under these conditions it is often possible to improve on the DR by using the data at hand. A position determined under these conditions is called an *estimated position* (EP). An EP is indicated on the chart by a small square and the corresponding time.

Estimated positions are determined in a variety of ways. In a heavy sea, it is sometimes impossible to obtain accurate bearings. Bearing lines determined electronically may vary considerably in accuracy; they are seldom as reliable as good visual bearings. Bearings obtained by magnetic compass are no more accurate than the deviation table. Estimates of current and leeway due to wind are rarely accurate enough to use in obtaining a fix. However, any of these factors may supply information, which, while not exactly correct, will tend to indicate the more probable position of the ship than that indicated by the DR.

An estimated position is the best position obtainable short of a fix or good running fix. A doubtful fix or running fix should appropriately be considered an EP. An estimated position is determined by considering all the data available, and giving due consideration to each factor. Each additional item of information results in a reconsideration of the estimated position, and the possible revision of the estimate.

One method of obtaining an estimated position from limited information involves ship's DR position. The DR position at the time of observation represents the best position available before a line of position is plotted. Once plotted, a line of position represents the locus of all the possible points the ship could have occupied at the time of the observation. The most probable position or estimated position (EP) of the ship is defined as that point on the line of position which is closest to the DR position.

Example 1: (Figure 1118) The 0600 DR of a ship is as indicated. Course is 025°, speed 10 knots. At 0627, Light *A* was observed through a rift in the fog, bearing 260°.

Required: Plot and label the 0627 EP.

Solution: Plot the 0627 LOP and the corresponding 0627 DR. From the 0627 DR, drop a perpendicular to the LOP. The intersection of the LOP and the perpendicular locates the 0627 EP, labeled as shown. This is the most probable position of the ship on the 0627 LOP, as it is not only on the observed line of position but it also represents the nearest point thereon to the 0627 DR.

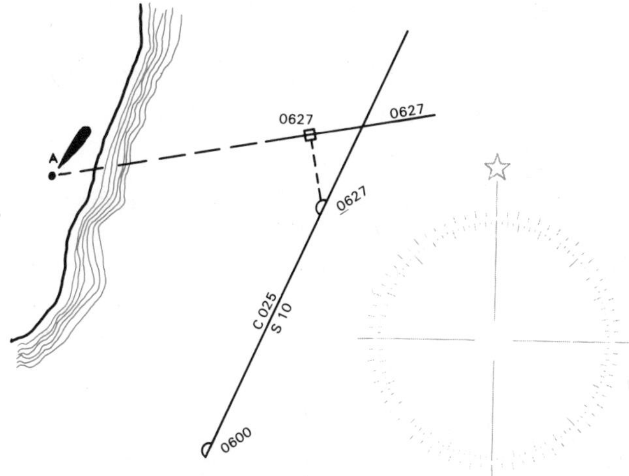

Figure 1118. Estimated position (EP).

EP from depth information **1119** The use of depth information to obtain an estimated position should not be overlooked. With modern electronic equipment, charts now show a number of precise depth soundings very accurately located; on many charts depth contours (lines of equal depths) are shown as light blue lines. If the bottom has a general slope, or there are areas of pronounced features, such as a sharp "valley" or ridge, a sounding can be combined with other positioning information to establish at least an estimated position. (This will not be possible on a flat, featureless bottom.)

One of the best ways to establish an estimated position by depth-curve navigation using soundings is as follows:

Draw a straight line on a piece of transparent paper or plastic. Along this line mark off distances between soundings according to the speed of the ship and the scale of the chart. For this purpose it is usually best to record soundings at regular intervals: every 6 to 10 minutes, or every mile, or oftener if desired. Record the times and corresponding soundings consecutively at the marks along the line. Then adjust the line of soundings on the paper to match the depth contours or individual soundings on the chart, using the DR plot and line of EP's, if there is one, as a guide and moving the paper so that it remains approximately parallel to the true course. Do not forget the possibility of a current setting the ship to one side of its course or affecting the speed made good. Soundings corresponding to depth curves shown on the chart are particularly valuable. These should be recorded even when they do not fall at the appointed time. Where tides are appreciable they must naturally be taken into account.

It is suggested that navigators use depth contours for position determination and for planning courses in advance, particularly where characteristic bottom features are available. They may be combined with other information such as radio bearings, visual bearings, or lines of position from celestial bodies.

In thick weather, or at times of poor radio reception, depth-sounding navigation can provide, where bottom characteristics permit, a highly practical means of obtaining an acceptable estimated position.

Using the EP **1120** Often the two methods just described in Articles 1118 and 1119 can be combined for a better EP than could be obtained from either alone. The negative value of depth information should never be overlooked—if the depths being measured at a location vary markedly from those shown on the chart, you are *not* at the position indicated by whatever other method is being used. Depth soundings may not be able to conclusively confirm an EP, but they can emphatically point to its inaccuracy.

Since an EP is not a well-determined position, it is not customary to run a new DR plot from such a position. However, a line representing the estimated course and speed being made good should be run from an EP to indicate the possibility of the ship standing into danger, allowing the navigator to take appropriate avoiding action before a dangerous situation develops.

Summary **1121** One of the most important responsibilities of a navigator is to often and accurately *fix* the position of his vessel. He can direct its further movement safely and efficiently *only* if he knows from where he is starting; he can be assured of his vessel's safety *only* if he knows where he is at a given time.

Lines of position are among the most valuable and useful "tools" of the navigator. An LOP of good quality tells a navigator that he is somewhere along that line, and *not* somewhere else. A single LOP provides useful information, but a second (and preferably more) are required to establish a *fix*. If he is on both lines, he can only be at their intersection. A *running fix* is a position obtained when two simultaneous observations cannot be made and one of the LOPs is advanced or retired in time to match the other; it is of lesser validity than a fix, but of sufficient value to be used as a starting point for a new DR track. An *estimated position* is of still lesser validity, but contains more input information than a *dead reckoning* position, which is the least likely to be the actual position of the vessel.

This chapter has described various methods of obtaining a fix, running fix, and estimated position. The use of danger bearings, and horizontal and vertical danger angles, has been considered, as well as the use of depth information. *At all times, a navigator must know to the best of his capabilities the position of his vessel and plan ahead for its safe future movement.*

12 Current Sailing

Introduction **1201** Several previous chapters have laid a foundation for the consideration here of *current sailing,* which is the determination of the effect of currents on the movement of a vessel with respect to the earth. In Chapter 8, it was seen that a dead reckoning plot ignored the effect of current and made use only of ordered courses and speeds. In Chapter 10, it was seen that in many areas there are horizontal flows of water of sufficient magnitude as to cause the path of a vessel with respect to the earth to differ significantly from its path through the water; often these *currents* can be predicted. Chapter 11 presented methods by which the ship's position could be fixed, and the DR plot verified or the need for correction seen. This chapter carries the process one step further showing how the net effect of current can be determined from the difference between DR positions and actual fixes, and how allowances can be made in advance for the anticipated effect of currents. This is *current sailing.*

In actuality, the term used in this chapter should be stated as "current"—in quotation marks—for more is to be considered than the horizontal movement of the waters. In navigation, especially in *current sailing,* the total of all the factors which may cause a ship to depart from its intended course and DR are termed *current.* Among the factors included in the term are:

- Ocean current
- Tidal current
- Wind current
- Windage on the ship
- Heavy seas
- Inaccurate steering
- Undetermined compass error
- Inaccurate determination of speed
  - Error in engine calibration
  - Error in log calibration
  - Excessively fouled bottom
  - Unusual conditions of trim

From the foregoing, it can be seen that *current,* unfortunately, has two meanings as commonly used in marine navigation. First, it refers to the horizontal movement of water due to ocean currents, tidal currents, or wind currents. Second, in common usage it refers to the combined effect of all the factors listed above. Thus the term current, as used in navigation, may or may not solely involve the motion of the water through which the ship is passing; in most cases, however, this factor, if it exists, will have the greatest effect on the ship's course.

Current sailing defined

1202 *Current sailing* is the art of determining course and speed through the water, making due allowance for the effect of a predicted or estimated current, so that upon completion of travel, the intended track and the actual track will coincide.

Current sailing may also be interpreted to include the determination of an existing current. Primarily, however, current sailing is the application of the best available current information to the intended track to determine what course and speed to order. Conversely, similar techniques are used to determine the actual current which has acted upon the ship.

Types of currents

1203 Three types of currents are of interest to the navigator:

Ocean current is a well-defined current, extending over a considerable oceanic area.

Tidal current is one resulting from tidal action. It will normally be of a *reversing* nature in harbors and estuaries, etc.; velocities are often enough to be significant in navigation. Along coasts, tidal currents are usually *rotary* in nature, with weak strengths, but these must still be taken into consideration in some navigational situations.

Wind current is one which affects a limited area and is created by the action of a strong wind blowing for twelve hours or more; it usually does not flow in the direction of the wind, as it tends to be deflected by Coriolis force. Details of this deflection were given in Chapter 10, which also covered tidal and ocean currents.

Current terms defined

Estimated current is determined by evaluating all the known forces which will contribute to make up the sum total of current effects in a given area.

Actual current is determined by the displacement of the ship from the DR position to a fix. It is determined only when an accurate fix can be obtained; the direction and distance between the actual fix and the DR position for the time of the fix establish the actual current.

Estimated position (EP) is the most probable position of a vessel, determined from all available data, when a fix or running fix is unobtainable; it includes the effect of the estimated current.

Current triangle is a graphic *vector diagram,* in which one side represents the set and drift of the current, one side represents the ship's course and speed, and the third side represents the actual track. If any two sides are known, the third can be determined by measurement or calculation.

The terms *heading, course,* and *speed* were employed in the discussion of dead reckoning in Chapter 8. Some additional terms to be introduced here include:

Track (TR): The intended (anticipated, desired) horizontal direction of travel with respect to the earth, taking into consideration known or predicted offsetting effects such as current, wind, and seas.

Speed of Advance (SOA): The intended (anticipated, desired) speed with respect to the earth, taking into consideration the effect of known or predicted current. SOA is also used to designate the average speed that must be made good to arrive at a destination at a specified time.

Set: The direction toward which the current is flowing; if the broader definition of "current" is used, the resultant direction of all offsetting influences. Note carefully that the description of the set of a current is directly opposite from the naming of a wind—a westerly *current* sets *toward* the west, a westerly *wind* blows *from* the west.

Drift: The speed of a current (or the speed of the resultant of all offsetting influences), usually stated in knots. Some publications, however, notably pilot charts and atlases, express drift in terms of nautical miles per day.

Course Made Good (CMG): The resultant direction from a given point of departure to a subsequent position; the direction of the net movement from one point to another, disregarding any intermediate course changes en route. This will differ from the Track if the correct allowance for current was not made.

Speed Made Good (SMG): The net speed based on distance and time of passage directly from one point to another, disregarding any intermediate speed change; speed along the Course Made Good.

Course Over the Ground (COG): The actual path of the vessel with respect to the earth; this may differ from CMG if there are intermediate course changes, steering inaccuracies, varying offsetting influences, etc. (Not used in current sailing triangles; CMG is used.)

Speed Over the Ground (SOG): The actual ship's speed with respect to the earth along the COG. (Not used in current sailing; SMG is used.)

The two current triangles

It should be carefully noted that there are *two* current triangles: before and after movement—anticipated and actual conditions. Track and Speed of Advance are used with the "before" triangle. Course Made Good and Speed Made Good are the corresponding components of the "after" triangle. Set and Drift are used with both triangles, although, of course, in one case it is estimated current and in the other, actual current. Course and Speed can be components of either the "anticipated" or the "actual" triangle.

Practical current sailing

1204 Point *D* (Figure 1204) bears 090° distant 20 miles from Point *A*. A current with an estimated set of 180°, and drift of 4 knots flows between the two points. If a ship were ordered to steam from *A* to *D* in a total elasped time of two hours, the navigator would be faced with a

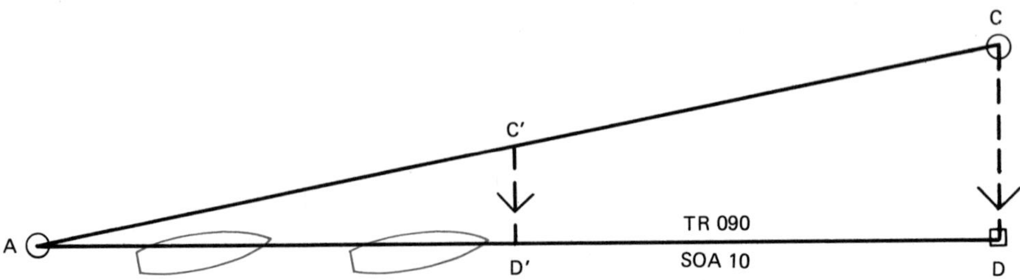

Figure 1204. Allowing for current.

typical problem in current sailing. It is obvious that the direction of the *TR* is 090°, and the *SOA* is 10.0 knots. It is equally obvious that if course 090°, and speed 10.0 knots were ordered, the ship two hours later would be some eight miles south of *D*. To allow for the estimated current on this two-hour trip, the ship should be steered on a course somewhat into the current in the direction of Point *C* some eight miles to the north of *D*, and at a speed slightly greater than 10 knots. *Provided the estimate of the current was correct,* the ship would arrive at *D* in two hours, the current effects having exactly countered the course and speed offset from the intended track.

Figure 1204 illustrates what has occurred. The ship headed for Point *C*, on course 070°, but actually made good 090°, constantly "crabbing" into the current, as shown. At the end of the first hour she reached *D′*, rather than *C′*, and at the end of the second hour she reached Point *D* rather than *C*. The track, *AD*, is the resultant of the vector sum of the velocity of the ship with respect to the water (*AC*) and the velocity of the current with respect to the earth, (*CD*), both of which were in action for the same length of time.

Point *C* represents the ship's DR position at the end of two hours, and Point *D* represents the *estimated position,* EP, which is the most probable position, short of a fix or running fix.

The EP plot

1205 It has been pointed out that in the absence of a fix or running fix, the navigator, on the basis of available information, may often estimate the ship's position to a greater accuracy than that indicated by the DR. For instance, if a navigator has good reason to believe that a current of well-determined set and drift exists, he can find the EP for a given time by plotting the predicted movement of the ship away from the DR position for a given time, due to the effect of the current. To do this, he plots the set and measures off along this line the *drift* multiplied by the number of hours it has been or will be acting. An alternate method, used chiefly when the ship steams on a single course at a constant speed, is to solve graphically a current triangle.

Example: (Figure 1205) The 0500 fix of a ship is as shown. The ship is on course 300°, speed 6 knots. A current has been estimated with a set of 250°, drift 1.0 knot.

Required: Plot and label the hourly DR positions and hourly EPs from 0500 to 0800.

Solution: Plot the course and the hourly DR positions up to 0800. From each DR position plot a line in the direction 250° and measure off 1 mile from the 0600 DR, 2 miles from the 0700 DR, and 3 miles from the 0800 DR. Enclose the points so obtained in small squares and label as shown in Figure 1205.

The accuracy of an estimated position depends on the accuracy with which the current is estimated. It is not safe to assume that a current determined by the last fix will continue, unless there is evidence to indicate that this is so. Unless there is information available to permit a reasonably accurate estimate of the current, it is best to assume zero current. It is especially unwise to expect a current to be regular and uniform near a coast, for local conditions are likely to cause irregularity, and tidal currents have greater effects here than on the open sea. When approaching pilot waters, it is often desirable to maintain two plots, allowing for anticipated current in one (the EP plot) and not in the other (the DR plot), and to consider both plots when laying a course to avoid danger.

Allowing for current

1206 Three problems frequently arise in connection with currents of estimated set and drift:

To find the anticipated track and speed of advance of a vessel steaming an ordered course at a specified speed through an estimated current.

To find what course a ship steaming at a given speed through an estimated current should take to make good an intended track.

To find what course and speed must be ordered to steam through an estimated current to arrive at the destination on time.

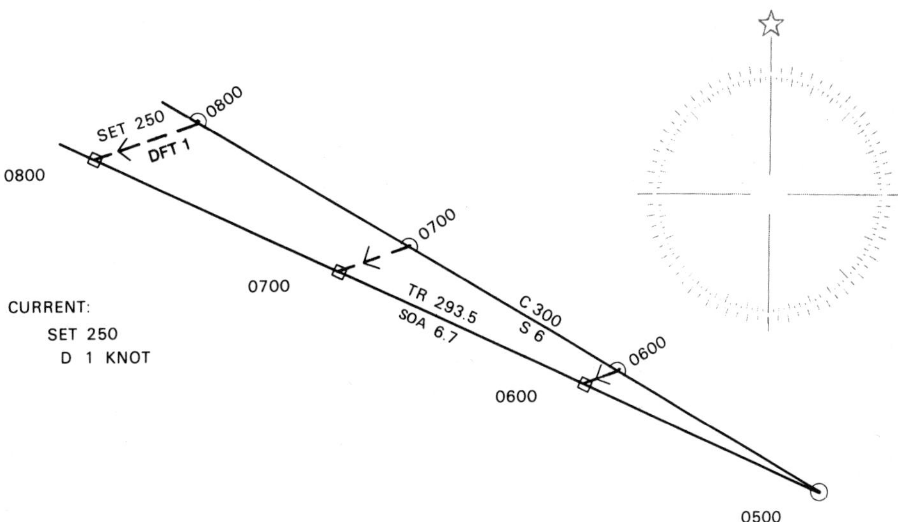

Figure 1205. An EP plot.

If a current is setting the same direction as the course, or its reciprocal, the track is the same as the course through the water. The effect on speed can be found by addition or subtraction; if in the same direction the speeds are added, and if in opposite directions, the smaller is subtracted from the larger. This situation happens frequently when a ship encounters tidal currents upon entering or leaving a port. If a ship is crossing a current, either at right angles or at a lesser or greater angle, the solution can be found graphically by a vector diagram since the velocity over the ground is the vector sum of the ship's velocity through the water and the current effects over the ground.

Such vector solution can be made to any convenient scale and at any convenient place, such as the center of a compass rose, on a separate sheet, or directly on the plot. The following examples will show the method of graphic solution:

Example 1: (Figure 1206a) Given the course and speed of the ship, and the estimated set and drift of the current, find the anticipated track (TR) and the anticipated speed (SOA) along this track. This example illustrates how the navigator not only finds the TR and SOA, but also, and perhaps more importantly, how he establishes an estimated position (*D*). It illustrates the first of the three cases of current sailing stated at the beginning of this article.

A ship will steam at 12 knots on a course of 211° true, through a current estimated to be setting 075° at drift of 3 knots. Find the anticipated track and speed of advance along that track.

Solution: In Figure 1206a, let point *A* be the location of the ship. From *A*, lay off the vector *AC* in the direction of the set of the current,

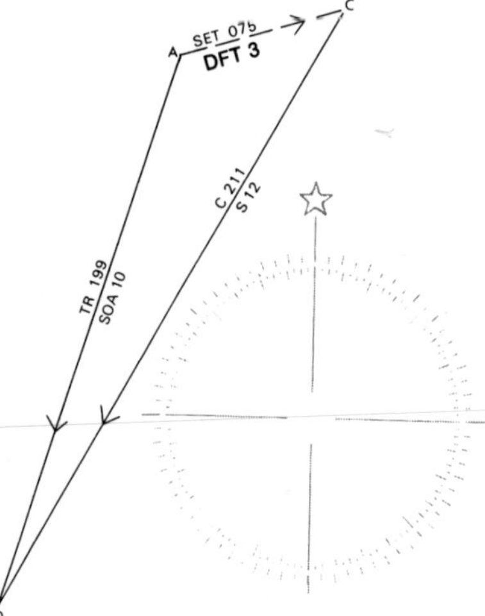

Figure 1206a. Determining track and speed of advance to determine an estimated position.

075°, for a length equal to the drift, 3 knots, at the scale selected (this represents motion of the ship due to current alone). From *C,* lay off a vector in the direction of the course, 211°, with length to scale of the speed, 12 knots, (this represents the travel of the vessel through the water with no consideration of current). Complete the current sailing vector diagram by drawing *AD*. The direction of *AD* is the direction of the anticipated track while its length represents, to the established scale, the speed that is anticipated along this track, if the current was predicted or estimated correctly. *D* is an *estimated* position only and must be used with caution until a fix can be obtained. The navigator is now able to apply this solution to the DR track from his last fix to obtain an estimated position.

Example 2: (Figure 1206b) Given the estimated set and drift of the current and the ordered speed of the ship, find what course must be steered to make good a given intended track (find also what the expected SOA will be along this TR).

Let the estimated set of the current be 075°, drift 3 knots. The ship will steam at 12 knots. The direction of the desired (intended) track is 195°, the speed of advance along that track is not specified and can be any value.

Solution: In Figure 1206b, from point *A*, the position of the ship, lay off the line *AD* of indefinite length in the direction 195°. Plot the current vector, *AC,* in the direction of the set, 075°, for a distance equal to the velocity of the drift, 3 knots. With *C* as a center, swing an arc of radius equal to the ship's speed through the water, 12 knots, intersecting *AD* at *D*. The direction, *CD,* 207.5°, is the course to order and the length *AD,* 10.2 knots, is the estimated SOA. Notice that vectors *AD* and *AC,* representing intended track and current respectively,

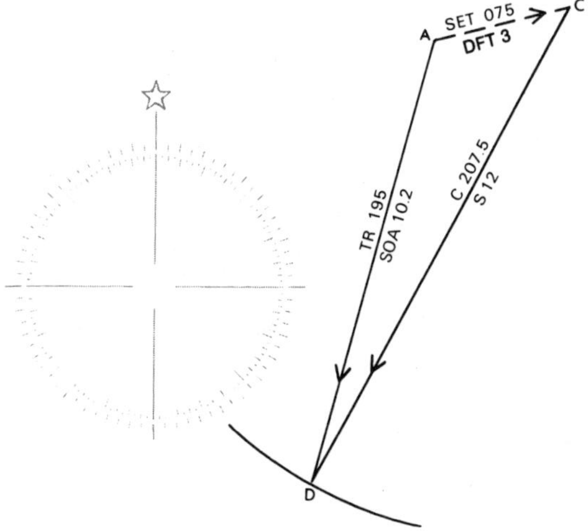

Figure 1206b. Determining course to steer to make good a desired track.

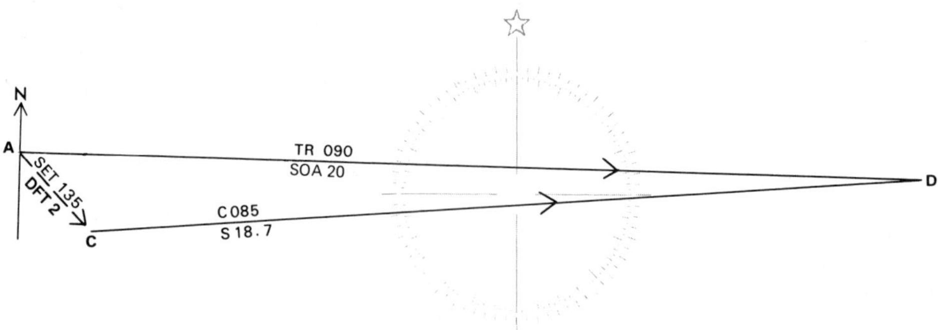

Figure 1206c. Determining course and speed to make good a desired track and speed of advance.

have been plotted with respect to the earth (point *A*), while vector *CD* has been plotted with respect to the water.

Example 3: (Figure 1206c) Given the set and drift of the estimated current, and the direction of the desired track and the required speed of advance, find the course and speed to be ordered.

A ship at 1300 is 100 miles due west of her desired destination. If the ship is to arrive at her destination at 1800, find the course and speed to order if a 2-knot current setting southeast (135°) is predicted.

Solution: In Figure 1206c, the ship is located at point *A* with point *D* as its destination, 100 miles due east. With five hours to reach this destination, the ship obviously must maintain a speed of advance of 20 knots. Lay off *AD* in the direction 090° to represent the intended track and of a length equal to the intended SOA, 20 knots. Lay off the current vector, *AC,* in the direction of its set, 135°, from Point *A* and of a length equal to the drift, 2 knots. Complete the current sailing vector diagram by drawing *CD.* The direction of *CD,* 085°, is the course to order while its length, 18.7 knots, is the speed to order to make the passage. Again notice that vectors *AD* and *AC,* representing *intended track* and current respectively, have been plotted with respect to the earth while vector *CD* has been plotted with respect to the water.

Determining actual current

1207 The preceding three examples have all included the use of "estimated currents." Another use of a current sailing triangle is the determination of "actual current" from a comparison of a DR position with a fix for the same time. If a course line is laid down from a fix (not a running fix) and at a later time a new fix is obtained which does not agree with the corresponding DR position, the difference between these two positions can be assumed to represent the actual "current" encountered during passage. It is immediately apparent that current so determined will include all of the factors mentioned in Article 1201 and, in addition, any errors in the fixes. (If the course line of the DR plot was last started from a *running* fix, actual current can still be determined but special procedures are needed; see Example 2 below.)

It should also be apparent that if the estimated position on the intended track coincides with the fix on the actual track, the estimated current computed prior to departure was exactly equal to the actual current encountered during passage. If the two positions are *not* identical, then the estimated current was in error by an amount directly proportional to the rate and direction of separation of the two positions.

Three problems most frequently arise in determining the set and drift of an actual current:

To find set and drift of an actual current, given the DR position based on a plot run from an earlier fix, and a new fix for the same time as the DR position.

To find set and drift of an actual current, given a DR position on a plot last started at a *running* fix, and a new fix at the same time as the DR position.

To find set and drift of an actual current, given a DR position and an estimated position, both based on an earlier fix, and a new fix for the same time as the DR position and EP.

Example 1: (Figure 1207a) Given the DR position based on an earlier fix and a fix for the same time, find the set and drift of the actual current.

The 1815 DR position has been run forward from a fix obtained at 0545 the same day. At 1815 a fix is obtained and when plotted, is located 7.5 miles from the 1815 DR.

Required: The set and drift of the actual current.

Solution: The set is the direction *from the DR position to the fix* for the same time. Drift is determined by measuring the distance between the DR position and the fix for the same time, and dividing it by the number of hours *since the last fix.* This is true regardless of the number of

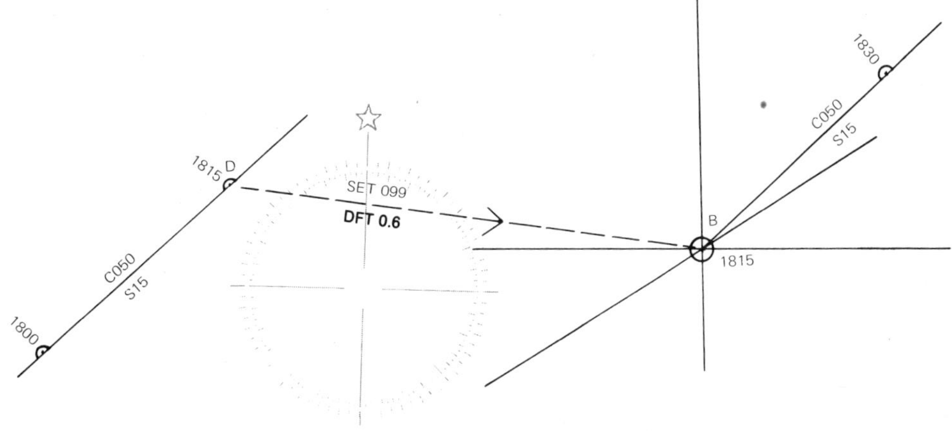

Figure 1207a. Determining the set and drift of the current.

changes of course and speed since the last fix. Since the 1815 DR position represents the position the ship would have occupied had there been no current, and the 1815 fix represents the actual position of the ship, the line *DB* joining them is the direction and distance the ship has been moved by current. The direction of this line from the DR to the fix, 099°, is the *set* of the current. The *drift* is its distance, 7.5 miles, divided by the time between the fixes, 12.5 hours, or 7.5/12.5 = 0.6 knots.

Answer: Set 099°, drift 0.6 knots.

Example 2: (Figure 1207b) Given the DR position based on an earlier running fix, and a fix for the same time, find the set and drift of the actual current.

Two methods may be used to determine the actual current when the DR position has been run forward from a running fix. Each method is explained below. At 0700 the navigator obtained a fix as shown. At 1152 a running fix is obtained from two LOP's, one at 0919, and the other at 1152, and a new DR plot is begun. At 1710 another fix is obtained as shown.

Required: The set and drift of the current.

Solution: (Method 1). The plotted DR position at 1710 (point *D'*) has been run forward from a running fix, and therefore cannot be used to obtain the set and drift of the current. Ignore the 1152 running fix, and continue the original DR course from point *C* until the DR position for time 1710 (point *D*) is determined. The set of the cur-

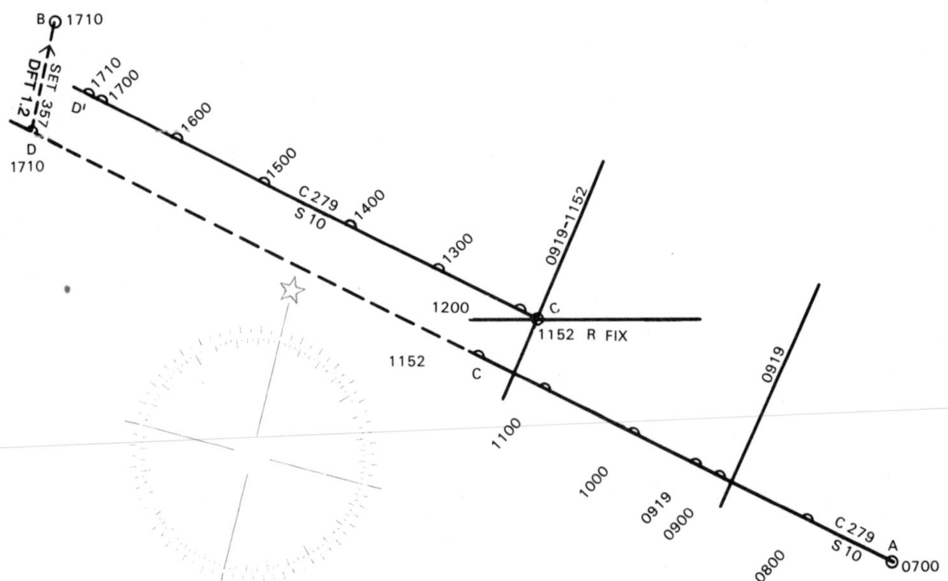

Figure 1207b. Determining the current when the DR plot has been carried forward from a running fix.

rent is the direction from point *D*, to the 1710 fix (point *B*), 357°, and the drift is this distance, 12.7 miles, divided by the time since the last fix, 10.2 hours, or 1.2 knots. (In this example the extension of the original course from *C* to *D* is shown as a broken line for clarity.)

Solution: (Method 2). Measure the direction and distance *CC′* from the original 1152 DR to the 1152 running fix. By applying the reciprocal of this direction and the same distance to the 1710 DR position, point *D* is established. It is noted that this is the same position as determined in method 1. The set of 357° and drift of 1.2 knots are obtained as before.

Answer: Set 357°, drift 1.2 knots.

Example 3: (Figure 1207c) Given a DR position and an estimated position based on an earlier fix, and a fix for the same time, find the set and drift of the actual current.

At 0900, a navigator fixed his position at *A* as shown. While proceeding to Point *D* bearing 090°, 20 miles from *A*, the navigator estimated that the current would be 135°, 6 knots, and therefore he set course 075° speed 16.3 knots to make good the intended track to Point *D*. At 1000, the navigator fixed his position at Point *B*.

Required: The set and drift of the actual current.

Solution: Since the 1000 DR represents the position the ship would have occupied had there been no current, and the 1000 Fix represents the actual position of the ship, the line *CB* joining them is the direction and distance the ship has been moved by the actual current. The direction of this line from the DR to the fix, 180°, is the set of the current. The drift is its distance, 8.0 miles, divided by the time between fixes, 1 hour, or drift = 8.0 knots.

As is evident from an inspection of the figure, the navigator's estimate of current was in error by the vector difference of *CD* and *CB*.

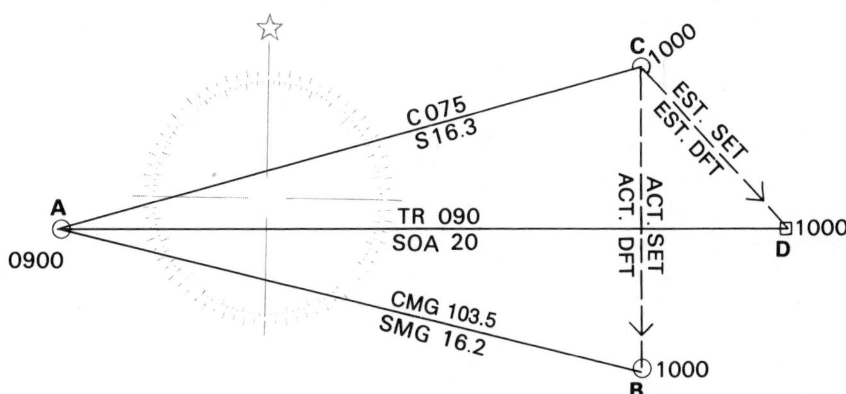

Figure 1207c. Determining actual current after having allowed for estimated current.

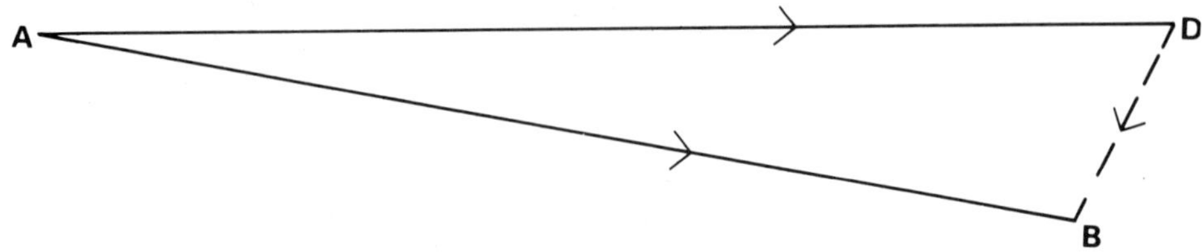

Part	Using Estimated Current	Using Actual Current
Point A	Present position (fix) of ship	Previous position (fix) of ship
Point D	DR position of ship at future time	DR position of ship at present time
Point B	Estimated position at future time	Present position (fix) at present time
Side AD	Course and speed vector	Course and speed vector
Side AB	Track and SOA	CMG and SMG
Side DB	Anticipated or expected current	Actual current encountered

Note: Points B and D are always for the *same* time.

Figure 1208. The current triangle and its parts.

Labeling the current triangle

1208 Many times it is desirable to construct a current sailing vector triangle to assist in the graphic solution of the problem. However, as has been demonstrated, the solution of the unknown parts of the triangle must be in terms of the given information of the known parts.

A complete current triangle equally applicable to the solutions of the current problem prior to departure, as well as to its solution after arrival, is illustrated in Figure 1208. A tabulation of the respective parts of each triangle is given in the accompanying table.

Other methods of solution

1209 Although the normal method of solving current sailing triangles is the graphic procedure described above, solutions are also possible by mathematics. In any of these triangles, there are six components, three sides and three angles (derived from the three directions): four of these factors will be known, two unknown. Solutions by plane trigonometry are unduly laborious if attempted by use of tables, but they can be quickly and easily found using a small electronic calculator, particularly a programmable model.

Advancing an LOP with current

1210 Article 1207 considered the fact that a running fix could not be used in the determination of current, as the earlier LOP used to obtain the running fix had in fact been acted upon by current during the time intervening between it and the second LOP. It follows, therefore, that if the navigator believes he knows the set and drift of the current within reasonable limits, he can increase the accuracy of the running fix by allowing for them when he advances the earlier LOP.

The following example illustrates the technique of plotting a running fix with a known current.

Example 1: (Figure 1210) The navigator of a ship on course 012°, speed 12 knots, observes Light *E* bearing 311° at 1500. He has reason to believe that a current exists with set 030°, drift 3.0 knots. Light *E* is subsequently observed bearing 245° at 1520.

Required: Plot the 1520 running fix, allowing for current.

Solution: In the twenty minutes between LOPs, the ship advanced 4.0 miles in the direction 012°, so the navigator advances the 1500 LOP as shown by line *AA'*. During this time the current has also moved the ship 1.0 mile in the direction 030°. The navigator must further advance the 1500 LOP to represent the additional travel of the ship caused by the current, or to the 1500–1520 LOP shown in the figure. The intersection of the 1500 LOP so advanced and the 1520 LOP marks the 1520 running fix. Had current not been taken into consideration, the running fix (see Article 1111) would have been located at the dotted circle, over one mile from the established running fix.

Errors inherent in running fixes

1211 In working with current, an inexperienced navigator may well make one of two errors, both about equally dangerous for his ship. He may either allow for too little or no current, or he may assume that a current is continuing without change when he is not justified in so doing. Judgment born of experience is the best guide. However, there are some considerations that even the beginner can learn to apply. The estimates of current given in current tables, pilot charts, etc., are usually quite accurate and should not be ignored. When there is a strong steady wind, its effect both in forming a temporary wind-driven current and in blowing the ship to leeward should be considered. The

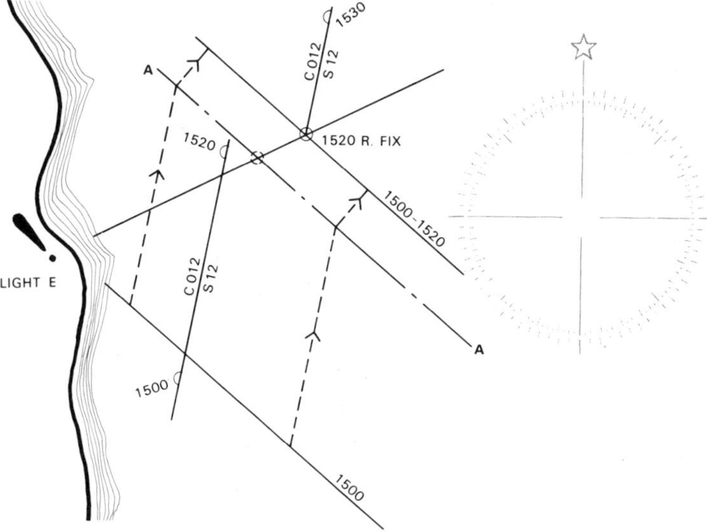

Figure 1210. Plotting a running fix with known current.

effect of wind on a ship differs with the type of ship, her draft, and the relative direction of the wind. The current acting on a ship is generally changing because of the tidal cycle, changes in wind, changes of geographical position, etc. The error in steering usually changes with a change of helmsman. Hence, it is generally unwise to assume that the current that has acted since the last fix will continue. All the factors mentioned above should go into the estimate of the current. In estimating current, the most unfavorable conditions possible should be assumed. It must be remembered that a running fix obtained by two bearings not taken simultaneously will be in error unless the course and distance are correctly estimated, the track and the distance over the ground being required. Difficulty will occur in estimating the exact course when there is bad steering, a cross current, or when the ship is making leeway; errors in the estimated run will arise when the vessel is being set ahead or back by a current or when the logging is inaccurate. Since the current is rarely known, the run between two bearings will often be in error, and therefore the running fix will give a false position, the amount and direction of the error depending upon the current that has *not* been taken into consideration during the run. Some indication of the current may be obtained by taking more than two successive bearings of the same object and plotting a series of running fixes, each using the three most recent lines of position. If the current actually is parallel to the course, its presence will not be revealed by this method since the fix will be a point either too far in to-

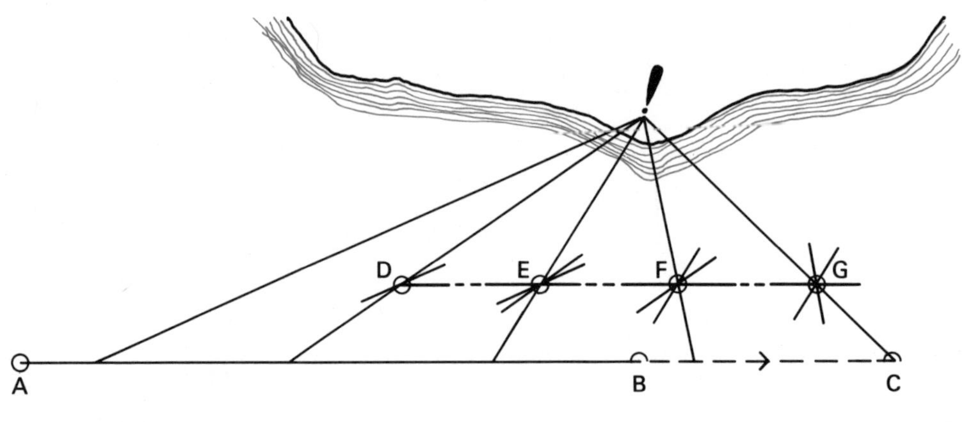

Figure 1211a. Error of a running fix with current parallel to course (following current).

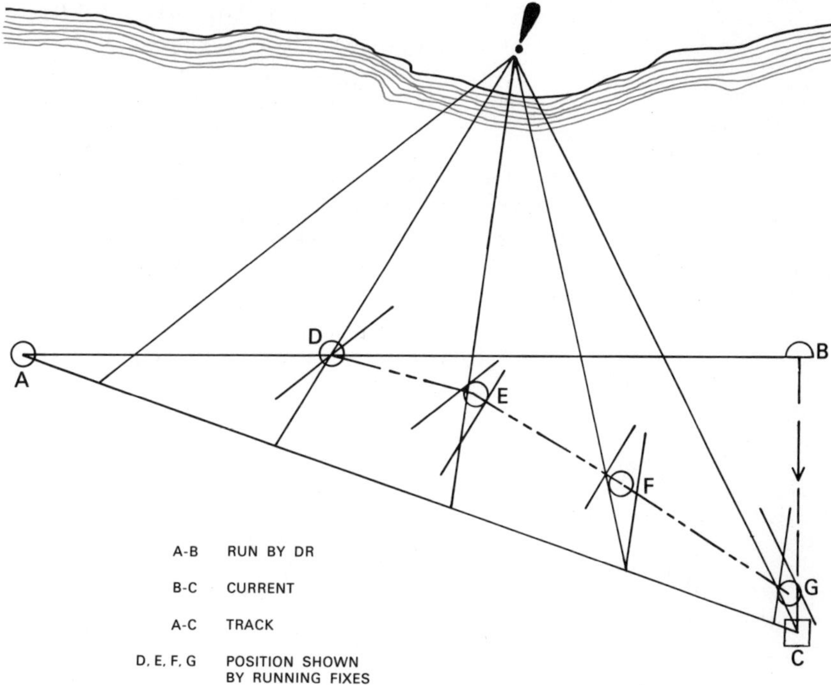

Figure 1211b. Error of a running fix with cross current.

ward the light or too far out, depending on whether the current is with or against the ship, respectively, and successive fixes will show a course parallel to that steered (Figure 1211a). If there is a cross current, however, the fix will result in a triangle, the size of which depends upon the cross component of the current; and the line through the mean points of the successive fixes will show a track oblique to the course steered, to the right or left depending upon whether the current is setting to the right or left, and it will plot between the course steered and the actual track (Figure 1211b).

Obviously, the presence of a current acting against the ship presents a hazard, since in this case the ship's positions as plotted by running fixes indicate a greater margin of safety to shoals, rocks, etc. extending out from the shore than actually exists. Hence, when there is a possibility that a head current exists, all dangers to navigation should be given a wider berth than indicated by running fixes. A better plan, when possible, is to obtain frequent fixes by simultaneous bearings of two or more fixed objects.

Summary **1212** This discussion on current sailing has involved aspects of DR and of piloting which are inseparable. Examples as "pure" or "simple" as those shown in this chapter are not normally encountered in actual navigation, but the ones shown serve to illustrate the vector analysis involved. Solutions are also possible using the considerable mathematical capabilities of small hand-held electronic calculators.

A DR plot must always be maintained. If data on current are not available, or cannot be trusted, the course and anticipated track are considered one and the same. If data of acceptable reliability are available, they should be used and an EP plot maintained. If in waters containing hazards, both plots should be maintained, at least to the extent of determining any possible danger to the ship. All possible data should be evaluated to give an estimated position, as it is a rare occasion when a fix is obtained that coincides precisely with the DR position, indicating no current effect whatsoever.

13 Ship Characteristics in Piloting

Introduction **1301** The phrase "tactical characteristics of a ship" refers to the manner in which a given naval vessel responds to engine and rudder orders; the more generalized term "handling characteristics" is used for merchant ships. So far in this book it has been assumed that at the instant of an ordered course change the vessel came immediately to the new course, and that when a new speed was ordered, the ship attained that speed instantly. Such, of course, is not the case. To increase or decrease speed by 10 knots may require from one to twenty minutes, or more, depending on the initial speed, the power available, and the flexibility of the engineering plant. A course change of 90° may require as much as a half mile, or more, of sea room to complete, depending on the type of ship, the rudder angle used, the wind and sea, and other factors. Each ship reacts in a different way to a given rudder or speed order, and reacts differently under different conditions of wind and sea.

When his ship is steaming singly at sea, the navigator may ignore the time and travel required to effect course and speed changes, for the scale of his plot is too small to be affected by the resulting errors.

Speed and course changes in restricted waters In restricted waters the situation is entirely different. Here, the navigator frequently needs to know his position within 10 yards, and the effect of the ship's travel in the time required to complete a change of course or speed is so comparatively large that it must be taken into account. The navigator must know his ship's handling characteristics; that is, how she will respond to a given order under existing conditions.

This chapter is concerned with the quantitive effects of course and speed changes on the travel of the ship, and the techniques and methods that a navigator uses to allow for these effects when piloting a ship in restricted waters. The term "precise piloting" is sometimes applied to the navigation of a vessel taking into consideration these small, but very important, factors. Bringing a ship to anchor in an assigned berth, which requires the use of these same techniques, will also be discussed in some detail.

Turning characteristics

1302 When approaching an anchorage, turning onto a range, piloting in a restricted channel, maintaining an intended track, or at any time when precise piloting is necessary, the navigator must allow for the *turning characteristics* of the ship. The standard method of finding a ship's turning characteristics is to turn her in a number of complete circles under varying conditions and to record the results for each. The variables used are: right and left rudder of specified angles, steady speeds of different value, and differences in draft and trim. When taking turning data, effects of wind and sea are allowed for. Most course changes are not as much as 360°, but by studying the complete turning circle, the ship's behavior for turns of any extent can be determined.

In considering the track actually followed by a ship during a turn, an understanding of the following definitions is essential. These terms may be understood more easily by reference to Figure 1302 in which a right turn is shown; a left turn would be generally similar, but actual distances might be slightly different in a single-screw vessel.

Definitions

1303 *Turning circle* is the path followed by the pivoting point of a ship in making a turn of 360° or more at a constant rudder angle and speed; the *pivoting point* is typically about one-third the way aft from the bow, but will vary from one vessel to another and may vary for a given vessel under different conditions of a longitudinal trim. The

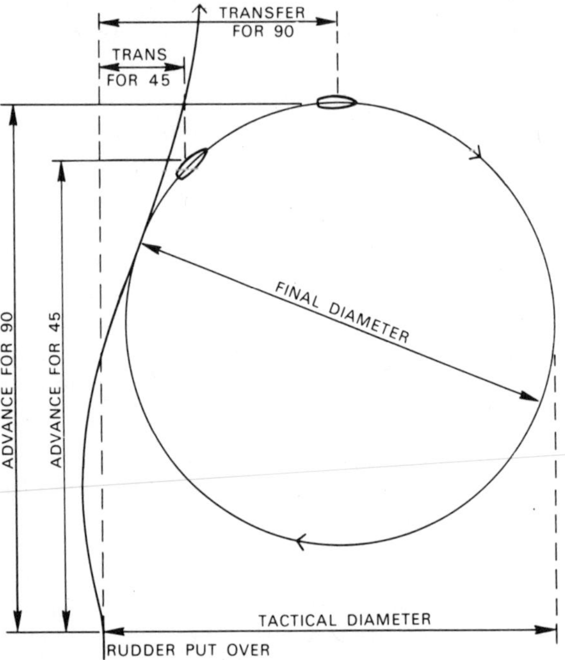

Figure 1302. Advance, transfer, and tactical diameter.

stem will turn on the inside of the turning circle and the stern outside this circle. The diameter of a turning circle for a given ship will vary with both rudder angle and speed through the water.

Advance is the distance gained in the original direction until the vessel steadies on her new course; it is measured from the point at which the rudder is put over. The advance will be a maximum when the ship has turned through 90°.

Transfer is the distance gained at right angles to the original course, measured from the line representing the original direction of travel to the point of completion of the turn.

Tactical diameter is the distance gained to the right or left of the original course when a turn of 180° has been completed.

Final diameter is the distance perpendicular to the original course between tangents drawn at the points where 180° and 360° of the turn have been completed. Should the ship continue turning indefinitely with the same speed and rudder angle, she will keep on turning in a circle of this diameter. It will nearly always be less than the tactical diameter.

Standard tactical diameter is a specific distance which varies according to naval ship type. It is laid down in tactical publications and is used when ships are maneuvering in company.

Standard rudder is the amount of rudder angle necessary to cause the ship to turn in the standard tactical diameter at standard speed.

Angle of turn (Figure 1304) is the arc, measured in degrees, through which the ship turns from the original course to the final course.

The speed at which a ship makes a turn may affect the turning diameter markedly if the "speed-length ratio" (ratio of speed to the square root of the length) is high enough. Thus a 300-foot ship at 30 knots has a considerably larger turning circle than at 15 knots. Tactical diameters are not inversely proportional to the rudder angle. While turning diameters decrease with increase in rudder angle (up to a certain point), the relationship is not an inverse proportion. Furthermore, the rudder angle for minimum turning diameter varies from one design to another. The rudder angle for minimum diameter depends upon many factors of ship and appendage form as well as speed. The majority of ships have a limiting rudder angle of 35°; some have larger ones. A short vessel will have a smaller turning circle than a longer one with the same general tonnage.

Sample tactical data for turning

Figure 1303 is a partial set of typical data on the turning characteristics of a naval ship; other values would be applicable for different speeds and rudder angles. These figures are representative of one particular ship and are for use *only* with problems in this book. It must be understood that the proper tactical data for the specific ship in which the navigator is embarked must be used when actually working under service conditions.

Handling characteristics are usually determined during the builder's trials of a new vessel (for the first of a class of naval ships).

Standard Tactical Diameter, 1500 Yards—Standard Rudder 15°					
Angle of Turn	Advance	Transfer	Angle of Turn	Advance	Transfer
15°	500	38	105°	993	853
30°	680	100	120°	933	1013°
45°	827	207	135°	827	1140
60°	940	347	150°	687	1247
75°	1007	513	165°	533	1413
90°	1020	687	180°	367	1500

Figure 1303. Typical amounts of advance and triangle for various angles of turn for a specific vessel.

Values of advance and transfer can vary slightly as a ship ages or is modified; they should be verified or updated when circumstances permit.

Tables of tactical characteristics are maintained on the bridge of all naval vessels. Coast Guard regulations require that U.S. merchant ships post data on handling characteristics where they can easily be seen by bridge watchstanders.

It will be noted that the table in Figure 1303 is prepared for every 15° of turn. Data required for increments between these 15-degree points may be obtained by interpolation. Instructions for obtaining tactical data for U.S. Navy ships are contained in NWP 50-A, *Shipboard Procedures,* and in the *Technical Manual,* NAVSEA 0901-LP-240-0003.

Computing the turning bearing

1304 From the preceding discussion it can be seen that during conditions when precise piloting is required the navigator must know at what point the rudder must be put over, so that when allowance has been made for the advance and transfer of the ship, she will steady on the desired heading at the time the desired track or point is reached. Having determined this point on his plot, his next task is to establish a means by which he will know when that point is reached.

Determining turning bearing

This is done by selecting a prominent mark, such as an aid to navigation or a landmark ashore, and predetermining its bearing. This is the *turning bearing* and the appropriate rudder angle is ordered when it is reached. Ideally, the object upon which the turning bearing is taken should be abeam at the time of starting the turn; this will give the greatest rate of change of bearing, and hence the most precisely determined point. In actual practice, relative bearings from roughly 30° to 150°, port or starboard, can be used if care is exercised at the extremes of this range; such bearings are usually used as true bearings. If practicable, preference is usually given to taking the turning bearing on the side toward which the turn is to be made, as the conning officer will be giving that side of the vessel the greater part of his attention.

In precise piloting, bearings will often be taken on objects that are at relatively close distances. Allowance must be made for the conditions of *parallax* that will then exist. Bearings on close objects will *not* be the same from peloruses on opposite wings of the bridge; directions, such as head bearings (Article 1306), will not be the same from bridge wings as those seen by the helmsman on the ship's centerline.

In allowing for the advance and transfer, the navigator should use standard tactical diameter and commence the turn using standard rudder. By so doing a margin for error remains and the rudder angle can be increased if the turn is commenced too late.

Example: (Figure 1304) A ship is standing up a channel on course 000° T and after rounding the point of land with Light *M*, must take up a new course of 075° T to continue up the river.

Required: The turning bearing on light *M* so as to be on course 075° upon completing the turn to proceed up the next reach of the river.

Solution: Draw the desired course line up the next reach of the river. Draw a line parallel to the vessel's present track at a distance out to the side equal to the transfer for a 75° turn (513 yards). The intersection of this line with the final course, 075° T, will be the point *B* at

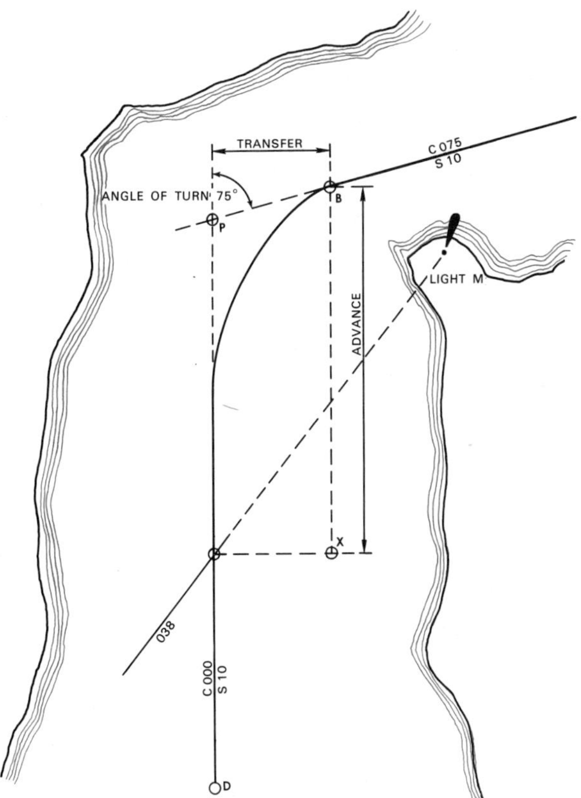

Figure 1304. A turning bearing.

which the turn must be completed. From this point, measure back along the line a distance equal to the advance, 1007 yards, locating point *X*. From point *X*, drop a perpendicular to the original course line. This will locate the point at which the rudder must be put over to complete the turn at the required point. The bearing, 038°, from that point to Light *M* is the *turning bearing.*

The problem is now complete and the data obtained are: The ship continuing on course 000° T arrives at a point *S*, from where Light *M* bears 038° T; here the order *"Right standard rudder"* is given. The turn is completed and the ship is heading on the final course at point *B*. The solid line *DB* represents the actual track of the ship.

Acceleration and deceleration

1305 Speed changes are usually of less concern to the navigator than are course changes. There are many times, however, when one may desire to allow for the acceleration or deceleration as in the cases described here.

Values for acceleration and deceleration rates vary widely for different ships. The values given in Figure 1305 are illustrative for one particular ship and are to be used *only* for examples in this book. A similar table must be prepared for or by a navigator on his own specific vessel.

The term "head reach" is used for the distance that a ship will travel from the point where action is taken to stop it to the point where it is dead in the water; this distance can be as much as several miles for large vessels of considerable tonnage but modest horsepower.

Determining time to change speed

Example 1: A ship is standing up a channel at speed 15 knots, and the captain desires to slow to 10 knots at the latest possible time so as to pass a construction barge at that speed.

Required: How far before reaching the barge should speed 10 knots be rung up so as to slow the ship to actual speed of 10 knots at the time the barge is abeam?

Solution: The table in Figure 1305 shows that to decelerate from 15 to 10 knots requires 1 minute. Since the rate of deceleration between these speeds is assumed to be constant, the average of the initial speed and the final speed will be the average speed for that minute, or 12½ knots. In a minute at 12½ knots a ship will travel 422 yards. Measure back 422 yards along the DR track from a point abeam of the construction barge to locate the point at which speed 10 knots should be rung up on the engines. (Note: A slightly different value, 417 yards, will be obtained if 2000 yards is used for a nautical mile rather than the more precise value of 2025.4 yards; the slight difference is of no practical significance.)

Example 2: A ship is standing down the channel at speed 10 knots. The captain has stated that he desired to order speed 24 knots as soon as the ship is clear of the channel, in order to make a rendezvous on time.

Knots		Minutes		Rate
Change of Speed From	To	Time Required for Change	Total Elapsed Time	Knots Change per Minute
		Acceleration		
0	10	3	3	$3\frac{1}{3}$
10	15	1	4	5
15	20	2	6	$2\frac{1}{2}$
20	24	4	10	1
24	28	6	16	$\frac{2}{3}$
28	31	9	25	$\frac{1}{3}$
		Deceleration		
31	28	3	3	1
28	24	4	7	1
24	20	2	9	2
20	15	1	10	5
15	10	1	11	5
10	0	2	13	5

Figure 1305. Acceleration and deceleration table.

Required: How far along the DR track line should the navigator consider the ship to have traveled between the time speed 24 is rung up on the engines, and the time the ship actually gets up to speed 24 knots through the water and how much time is required?

Solution: (Figure 1305) Note that three different rates of acceleration will be used for this speed change. For this reason it will be necessary to calculate the distance traveled during the period of acceleration in three separate parts, one part for each rate of acceleration. From speed 10 to speed 15 knots requires 1 minute, at an average speed of $12\frac{1}{2}$ knots. During this time the ship will travel 422 yards. From speed 15 to speed 20 requires 2 minutes at an average speed of $17\frac{1}{2}$ knots. During this time the ship will travel 1181 yards. From speed 20 to speed 24 requires 4 minutes at an average speed of 22 knots. During this time the ship will travel 2971 yards. Add the three distances computed to find the total distance traveled from the time the new speed is rung up until the ship is actually making it; the answer is 4574 yards, or about $2\frac{1}{4}$ miles. Elapsed time, the total of that noted in the table and used above, is 7 minutes.

As can be seen from these examples, the determination of distance traveled between the time a speed is ordered and the time a ship actually is making it good through the water is easily accomplished and can be quite accurate. The time involved can be determined by direct reading from the table. Many navigators use the average of the initial and final speeds as the effective average speed during the time of acceleration or deceleration. Although this is not as accurate as the method used in the examples above (it would yield 4017 yards, a difference of 557 yards, or 12 percent), it is usually sufficiently accurate for most navigational work.

Anchoring in an assigned berth

1306 Charts showing specific anchorage berths are published for many ports by either the National Ocean Survey, the Defense Mapping Agency Hydrographic Center, or the local maritime authorities for a foreign port. They are simply harbor charts with anchorage berths over-printed in colored circles of various diameters corresponding to the swinging area required by ships of various types and sizes. On these charts, series of berths of like size are laid out in straight lines, referred to as *lines of anchorages.* Usually, adjacent circles are tangent to each other. The center of the circle marks the center of the berth, and each berth is designated by a number or letter printed inside the circle.

This orderly arrangement greatly simplifies the assignment of anchorages, especially when a large group of ships is to occupy a harbor in company. In harbors for which no standard anchorage chart is available, berths are assigned by giving the bearing and distance from a known object to the center of the berth, together with the diameter of the berth. It is the duty of the navigator to cause the ship to be maneuvered in such a manner that the anchor may be let go in the center of the ship's assigned berth. This should be accomplished with a maximum permissible error of 10–50 yards (9–46 m), depending upon the type of ship.

Definitions of anchoring terms

For this discussion, the following terms are defined:

Approach track is the track that a ship must make good in order to arrive at the center of the berth.

Letting-go circle is a circle drawn around the center of the berth with a radius equal to the horizontal distance from the hawsepipe to the instrument used for taking bearings.

The *letting-go bearing* is the bearing from the point of intersection of the letting-go circle and the final approach track to any convenient landmark, generally selected near the beam.

Range circles are distance circles of varying radii from the center of the berth, with distance measured from the letting-go circle.

When the ship has been ordered to anchor in a specific berth (Figure 1306), the navigator consults the chart and prepares for the approach to the anchorage by laying off from the center of the berth the following:

The letting-go circle as described above.

The intended track, selecting appropriate approach courses and navigational aids for fixing the ship's position en route, and locating turning bearing marks at predetermined points where turns are necessary. The final approach should, if possible, be made with the ship heading

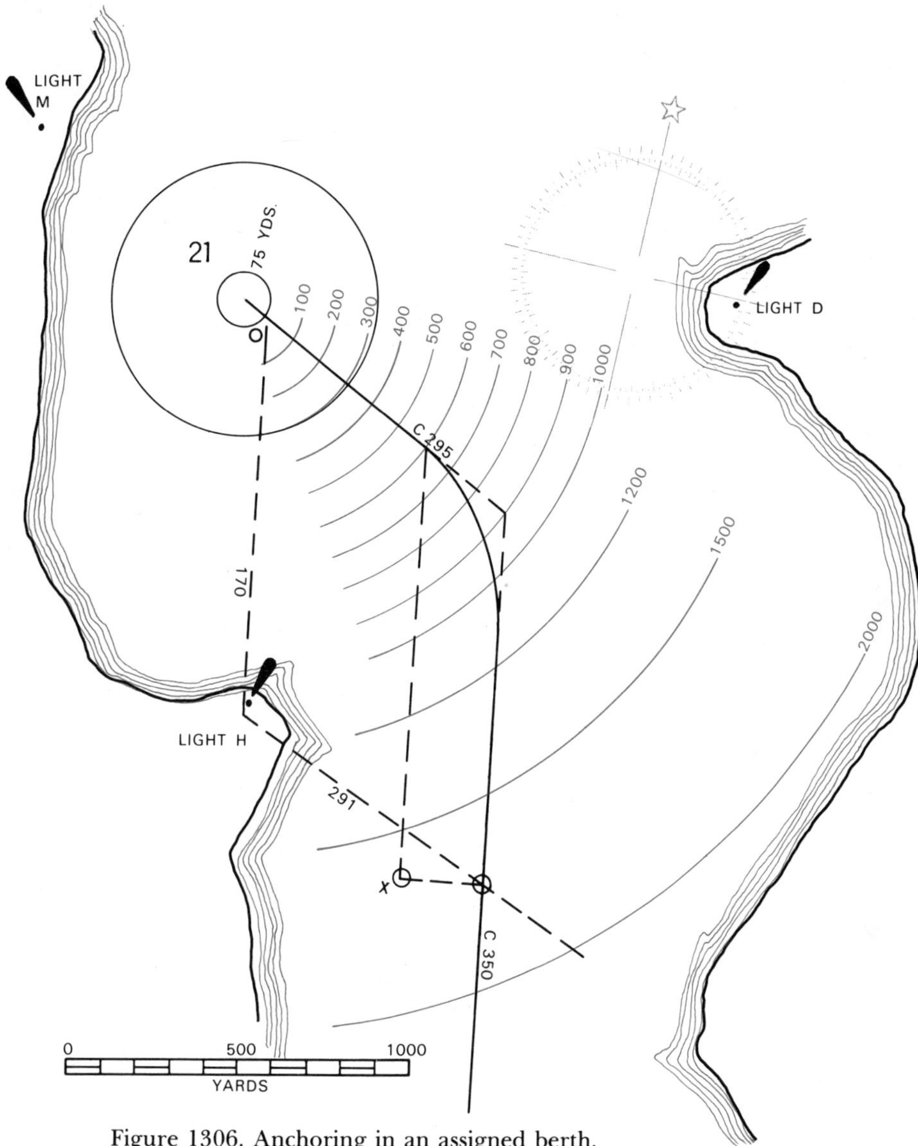

Figure 1306. Anchoring in an assigned berth.

into the current, or if the wind has the greater effect, then into the wind. The approach track must be long enough for the final turn to have been completed and any last-minute adjustments of track accomplished before reaching the center of the berth; this distance will vary with the ship concerned but should not be less than 500–1000 yards, increasing as the size of the vessel increases. It is also desirable that the approach track be directly toward an identifiable aid to navigation or landmark. As the approach is made, the constant bearing (termed a *head bearing*) of the aid or landmark can then be maintained. If no such aid is available, or if the aid previously selected becomes obscured, the positions of consecutive fixes with respect to the approach track (to the right of it or to the left of it) will permit the navigator to recommend a change of course to conn the ship back on the approach course.

Range circles of varying radii, including the radius of the letting-go circle. In most cases it is necessary to draw in only the arcs of the range circle adjacent to the approach track. In practice it is usual to draw arcs every 100 yards out to 1000 yards; then at 1200 yards, 1500 yards, and 2000 yards. The *letting-go circle* is labeled 0 yards; the other range circles are labeled with their distance from the *letting-go point* which is the intersection of the approach track and the letting-go circle.

When bringing a ship to anchor, the navigator should determine the depth of the water and the characteristics of the bottom as they may be shown on the chart, as well as the nature of and distance to any nearby areas of shoal water or other hazards. This information should then be passed to the captain and other officers directly concerned with the anchoring.

Example: A ship is assigned Berth 21 for anchoring, Figure 1306. The initial approach into the harbor is on a course of 350° T. An approach track directly toward Light *M* is possible and is selected. Distance from the hawsepipe to the gyro repeater used for taking bearings is 75 yards.

Required: 1. Approach track to the berth.
2. Letting-go bearing on Light *H*.
3. Turning point.
4. Turning bearing on Light *H*.

Solution: The selected approach track is plotted back from Light *M* through the center of the berth; its direction is measured (295°). The *letting-go circle* with a radius of 75 yards is plotted around the center of the berth. The intersection of this circle and the approach track is the *letting-go point* and is labeled 0 yards.

The initial approach track into the harbor is plotted. By use of the table of the ship's characteristics, the navigator can determine the advance and transfer of the final turn at the speed to be used. With this data, he determines the point at which the turn is to be completed and the point at which the rudder is to be put over. He plots this and determines the *turning bearing* on Light *H* (291°).

Range circles are plotted from the center of the berth, but ranges are measured from the *letting-go point.* Thus, the radius used to plot the "100-yard" range circle is actually 100 + 75 = 175 yards; similarly, all other range circles are plotted with a radius 75 yards greater than the labeled distance.

As the ship enters the harbor and proceeds along the track, frequent bearings are taken and fixes plotted to ensure that the desired track is maintained. As the range circles are crossed the navigator advises the captain of the distance to the letting-go point so that the speed may be adjusted to bring the ship nearly dead in the water when the letting-go point is reached.

When Light *H* bears 291° the rudder is put over and the turn commenced. The rate of turn is adjusted so that upon completion Light *M* bears 295°, dead ahead. The heading of the ship is adjusted so that a constant bearing of 295° is maintained on Light *M*. Bearings on Lights *H* and *M* are plotted continuously, and the captain advised of the distance to go. When Light *H* bears 170° and Light *M* 295°, the anchor is let go, and at that instant bearings are taken on all navigational aids visible, in order that the exact location of the anchor can be accurately determined. The ship's exact heading at the time of the final fix is also observed. A distance of 75 yards is then plotted from the fix, in the direction of the observed heading. The exact position of the anchor is then known. The anchor should be within 10 yards of the center of the berth.

Answers: (1) Approach track 295°
(2) Letting-go bearing 170°;
(3) See Figure 1306;
(4) Turning bearing 291°.

Port-anchoring procedures

1307 Immediately after the anchor is down and holding, and the intended length of chain has been let out, the navigator should plot the actual position of the anchor from the bearings taken at the moment it was dropped. Using this as a center, and a radius equal to the ship's length plus the horizontal component of the length of anchor chain in use, a *swing circle* is plotted and the chart is closely examined to be sure that no hazards exist within this circle, nor does it infringe on any other anchoring berth.

The navigator can also plot a *drag circle,* using the actual anchor position as a center and the horizontal component of the anchor chain length plus the hawsepipe to bearing instrument distance as the radius. Thereafter, any check bearing, taken to determine if the anchor is holding, must fall within this circle, which is of smaller diameter than the swing circle.

Effect of wind and current

1308 In discussing the computation of the turning bearing, the effects of acceleration and deceleration, and anchoring in an assigned berth, the assumption was made that these maneuvers were being carried out under conditions when there was no wind or current. In actual practice there almost always is some wind or current, and frequently both. Before entering or leaving harbor, and particularly if the channel is restricted in any way, the navigator must determine what currents may be encountered, and what effect they may have on the ship as she negotiates the channel. The effect of wind must also be taken into consideration; at times a strong wind may have a greater effect than the existing current. The navigator must always be prepared to modify his original plans to meet existing conditions.

When possible, constricted channels should be negotiated at slack water, or if this is impractical, when the ship can head into the current.

Summary

1309 This chapter has outlined the methods by which the navigator can use the known tactical data pertaining to his ship to keep it on the intended track in pilot waters and to bring it to anchor safely and accurately in its assigned berth. Every vessel has its own handling characteristics; the data for each will be slightly different. The tactical data for the ship must be available on the bridge at all times when underway, and in the most convenient form for use by the captain, the officer of the deck, and the navigator.

14 Relative Motion

Introduction **1401** Most of this book is concerned with the science and art of directing a vessel safely to her destination by avoiding fixed hazards such as shoals. These are stationary hazards; to avoid them, the navigator must know the actual or geographic movement of his ship. But moving hazards, such as other ships underway, are also encountered in the course of a voyage, and introduce a second kind of movement with which the navigator must become familiar. This is *relative movement* which deals with the apparent motion of moving objects. Sometimes, as when meeting another ship underway in constricted waters, both types of motion must be considered simultaneously.

The purpose of this chapter is to define the movement of a ship underway with respect to another moving vessel, and to the earth, and to show how the relationship between these two motions can be solved accurately and quickly, primarily to avoid the hazard of collision. For this purpose, it is assumed that all bearings and ranges on other vessels are obtained by radar. The technical and operational characteristics of radar equipment are covered in Chapter 17.

The Maneuvering Board here described can be used for many additional types of problems involving relative motion. In naval formations the conning officer is required to maintain a position relative to the guide, and to determine course and speed to move to a new station. These ship-handling problems and many other uses of this device are discussed in Pub. No. 217, *Maneuvering Board Manual,* published by the Defense Mapping Agency Hydrographic Center.

Motion **1402** Motion is the movement of an object from one point to another; it can be measured in terms of the direction and distance from the first point to the second. Alternatively, it can be measured in terms of the direction and speed of the object, as it moves from the first point to the second. All motion is relative to some reference, and it is necessary when discussing motion to define the reference. For purposes of this discussion, all fixed objects on the earth will be considered as being without motion.

To the navigator, the motion of his ship over the earth's surface is of primary importance. Assuming that there is no current, the course and speed of the ship through the water represents its movement *over the ground.* This is called *actual movement;* it is defined as *motion measured with respect to the earth*

Relative movement is motion measured *with respect to a specified object,* which may or may not have actual movement itself.

To illustrate the difference between relative and actual motion, suppose two ships are proceeding on the same course and at the same speed. Relative to each other, there is no motion, and the ships are at rest; however, both have the same actual movement relative to the earth.

Problems in relative movement are solved subconsciously in everyday life. A pedestrian wishing to cross the street sees a car coming. Without conscious thought he determines the car's approximate speed and converts it to speed relative to himself when walking; based on this determination he either crosses ahead of the car or waits for it to pass. The same type of reasoning, but at a conscious level, applies to the solution of problems of relative motion at sea.

In general, aboard ship, the problem is to determine the course and speed required to bring about the desired change in relative position. The navigator must learn to plot the position of any ship relative to any other ship. How this is done is discussed in the following articles.

General considerations regarding the use of radar and relative plotting in navigation

1403 The practical navigator may inquire as to what sort of accuracy can be achieved at sea, using radar bearings and ranges (distances), and relative plots similar to those to be described in this chapter. The answer depends on three factors—the characteristics of the radar set, the navigator's ability to read bearings and ranges accurately, and his care in plotting. Time, incidentally, should be stated to the nearest whole minute.

Assuming that the radar, when set on the 20-mile scale, gives bearings accurate to 0.5°, and ranges accurate to ±0.2 miles, and that the navigator uses reasonable care in plotting, he should be able to determine the closest point of approach (CPA) within 0.5 miles, the other vessel's course within 2°, and her speed within 0.2 knots.

It is most important that bearings and ranges be obtained on a continuing basis; the more there are, the more accurate and reliable the plot will be. Situations are known in which the other ship (in radar terms, the "target") has changed course or speed, or both, just after a navigator had decided that no more bearings were required as the separation at the closest point of approach (CPA) would be sufficient to be safe.

It is vital that the *Rules of the Road* be observed in making any decisions on course or speed changes based on radar or any other information. Article 1412 describes a situation in which two vessels are on a collision course, and one correctly changes course to the right, while the other changes to the left, contrary to the rules and common sense. But such things do happen. Some years ago the *Andrea Doria* and the *Stockholm,* both large passenger liners, and both equipped with radar, collided under rather similar conditions, resulting in the loss of the *Andrea Doria.* The admonition to motorists to "drive defensively" applies equally well on the high seas.

These suggestions are offered to simplify the task of relative plotting: A stopwatch is a great convenience in timing. It, as well as a pad

Figure 1403. Radar serves the dual functions of collision avoidance and navigation assistance. Photo: Raytheon Co.

of Maneuvering Board sheets or plastic Maneuvering Board, pencils, dividers, and plotting instruments should be ready to use at a moment's notice.

Tips on plotting

A series of readings should be made at convenient, but constant, time intervals. Readings should be made as long as there is any possibility that a change of course and speed on the part of the target ship might result in collision.

If the risk of collision exists, and action on your part is called for, make *big* changes in course and/or speed, rather than small ones, so that your actions will be readily apparent on the radar screen of the other vessel.

If the radar has concentric range rings, but no other range indicator, take bearings of the echo as it crosses these rings, and record the times.

Plot all bearings as true. If the radar does not have a gyro repeater, set the movable azimuth circle so that the bearings are true.

Plot all targets.

Aids for the graphic solution of relative movement problems

1404 The plotting necessary to obtain a solution to problems in relative motion can be done on plain paper. The solution is greatly facilitated, however, if the work is done on a polar coordinate form or "board."

Four such forms or boards designed especially for solving relative movement problems are available. They are the *Maneuvering Board,* the Navy *Mark I Mod 0 Plastic Maneuvering Board,* the *Radar Plotting Sheet,* and the *Radar Transfer Plotting Sheet.* The first two are intended to assist in the solution of all types of relative movement problems; the third and fourth are intended primarily for plotting radar contacts. Where a considerable amount of relative plotting is to be done, the Mark I Mod 0 Plastic Maneuvering Board is recommended as its design permits an extremely rapid solution; unfortunately, it is not available to non-naval navigators.

The Maneuvering Board comes in pads of 50 sheets; each sheet can be used on both sides. It is published by the Defense Mapping Agency Hydrographic Center (DMAHC) as Chart No. 5090 and 5091; the difference is in size—No. 5090 has a 10-inch diameter for the plot, while No. 5091 is larger with a 20-inch diameter. Sheets from the No. 5090, used to illustrate problems in this chapter, have ten concentric, equally spaced rings numbered 2 to 10 (the first ring is not numbered). All rings are dotted lines except the innermost and outermost; dotted arcs of rings beyond the tenth appear in each corner of the square working area. Dotted radial lines at 10° intervals extend out from the inner ring to the edge of the plotting area. These radials are labeled around the outer circle with 0° at the top of the sheet for larger figures around the outside of the outer ring and 0° at the bottom of the sheet for smaller figures around the inside of that ring. All dots indicate one-tenth subdivisions between the concentric circles and the radial lines; every fifth dot is replaced by a small + for more accurate plotting. Arranged vertically on either side of the paper are scales designed for rapid conversion for measuring distance or the length of vectors when a ratio of other than 1:1 in circle spacing is desired.

Aboard most ships moving targets are picked up at 20 miles or less and since most speeds at sea are less than 20 knots, a scale of 2:1 is generally convenient for plotting both ranges and speeds.

A nomogram is provided at the bottom of the Maneuvering Board, consisting of three logarithmic scales: one each for time, distance, and speed. If any two are known, the third may be determined by connecting the two known points with a straight line and extending it as necessary to intersect the third scale. The point so determined is the unknown quantity. If distance (D) is one of the known quantities, the nomogram can be used with a pair of dividers rather than drawing a line. Place one point of the dividers on the D value on the center scale; place the other point on the known value of S or T; swing the dividers, keeping the first point on the center scale; the second point will fall on the third scale at the unknown value of T or S. (The distance scale is marked off in both nautical miles and yards on the basis of one mile equalling 2000 yards.)

Time, speed, and distance problems may also be solved by using only the top logarithmic scale of the nomogram as a slide rule. This method is more accurate than using all three scales, and should be understood; see Article 810.

The *Mark I Mod 0 Plastic Maneuvering Board* illustrated in Figure 1414 offers the most rapid method of solving problems in relative motion. Solutions may be obtained without dividers or parallel rulers; only a pencil is required. This board consists of a transparent plastic plotting board upon which is engraved a compass rose. Beneath the board, and centered with the compass rose is a rotatable circular grid upon which are printed concentric circles, and a cross-section grid, as well as a compass rose. A transparent cursor, rotatable about the center, and mounted above the plotting board, is provided to facilitate the measurement of courses and bearings. A Speed-Time-Distance conversion computer is secured to the lower right-hand corner of the board. This computer or the nautical slide rule (Article 724) represents the most convenient method of solving the S-T-D problem. The navigator should not depend on mental conversion of the problem when a simple mechanical solution is readily at hand. A speed conversion scale from knots to yards per minute, appears at the upper right-hand corner. (Here again, for simplicity, a nautical mile is equated to 2000 yards; the slight error of this procedure, 1.27 percent, can be ignored in practical navigation and ship handling.) A detachable ruler clipped to the upper section carries a distance scale.

The *Radar Plotting Sheet* (Figure 1410) is generally similar to the Maneuvering Board. These are published by DMAHC as Chart No. 5092 and 5093 with 10-inch and 15-inch plotting areas respectively. There are four equally spaced concentric circles corresponding to the fixed range rings on the PPI scope of a radar set. Marks are shown for each degree around the outer circle, with labels every 10° and 0° at the top of the sheet (there are no radial lines). Distance and speed scales are printed in the side margins. A logarithmic time-speed-distance scale and nomogram are printed at the bottom of the sheet; brief instructions appear on the sheet.

The *Radar Transfer Plotting Sheet* (Figure 1413) is DMAHC Chart. No. 5089; it comes only in the 10-inch size. It is generally similar to the *Radar Plotting Sheet* described above, except that it has six concentric rings rather than four. Distance scales, of different values, appear in the left margin, and there is a single speed scale at the right. The logarithmic S-T-D scale is printed at the bottom, but the nomogram is omitted. Boxes are included in each corner of the sheet for recording data from each radar observation.

Either of the above sheets is extremely useful in the solution of radar plotting problems; solution is accomplished in the same manner as by the Maneuvering Board. (For relative movement problems other than those involving radar plots, the Maneuvering Board is generally more convenient.) The *Radar Navigation Manual,* DMAHC Pub. No. 1310 (formerly H.O. 257) covers the use of these sheets in detail; the latest revised printing is dated 1975.

The geographical plot

1405 A plot showing the successive positions of one or more ships, moving over the earth's surface, is called a geographic or navigational plot; this represents motion with reference to the earth. Such a plot is presented in Figure 1405; it can best be illustrated by an example. Your ship is on course 000°, speed 10.0 knots. At 2200, your ship is at point *A,* and a radar contact on another ship is obtained, bearing 067°, distance 10.8 miles.

Required: The other ship's course and speed, and the *closest point of approach* (CPA).

Solution: Draw your ship's course line from *A,* marking off the distance run for convenient periods of time; for this example, use 8 minutes. Then plot the target ship's 2200 position, bearing 067° distant 10.8 miles from *A.* Radar ranges and bearings on the target are obtained every 8 minutes, as shown in the table, and plotted from the position of your ship at that time.

Time	*Bearing*	*Range (Miles)*
2200	067°	10.8
2208	063°	9.4
2216	058°	8.2
2224	052°	7.2
2232	043°	6.2
2240	032°	5.4
2248	017°	4.9
2256	001°	4.8
2300	352°	4.9

Inspection will show that the bearing changed to the left, and that the range closed steadily until the target crossed ahead at about 2256, the CPA being about 4.8 miles (the actual CPA was about 4.75 miles, on bearing 004°). The plot will show that the target was on course 315°, speed 15.2 knots. Actually, all this information could have been predicted, after the first few points were plotted.

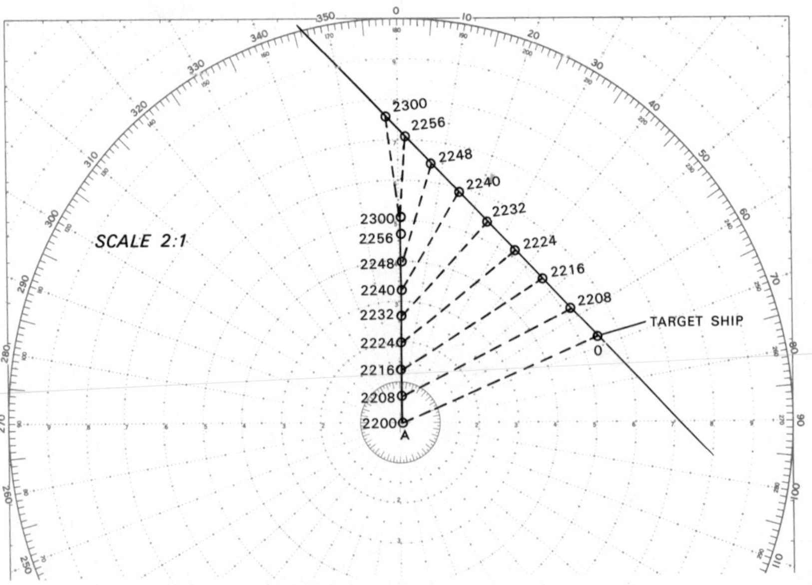

Figure 1405. Geographical plot shown on Maneuvering Board.

This geographical plot provides the required information; the difficulty is that its construction is extremely time consuming, some 30-odd steps being required. Fortunately, there is a simpler method of obtaining the desired information by means of the relative plot.

The relative plot

1406 In the geographical plot, the positions of both ships were plotted, using the earth as a reference; that is, course lines had to be drawn for both ships. But the requirement in that problem was the movement of the target ship, *relative* to your own. Now consider that your ship remains fixed at the center of the Maneuvering Board, which, of course, is the way it appears on most radar screens, and plot only the position of the target relative to your ship, using the bearings and ranges given in Article 1405.

Relative motion

This plot is shown in Figure 1406. The line joining M_1, M_2, M_3 through M_9 represents the movement of the target (other ships) in one hour, *relative to your vessel;* it is the *relative movement line,* and the direction of relative movement (DRM) is 274°. Measurement shows it is 10.6 miles long; as the target moved this distance in 60 minutes, target speed along this line must be 10.6 knots. This is the target speed with respect to your ship, or *speed of relative movement* (SRM).

This plot has provided data necessary to determine, by inspection, the CPA (about 4.8 miles on bearing 004° at 2256) and with a mini-

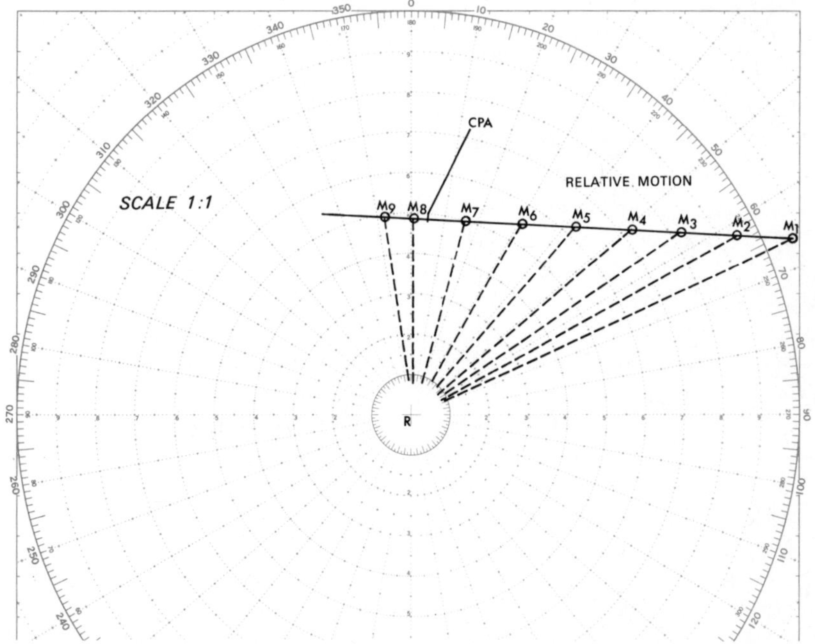

Figure 1406. Relative motion plot.

mum amount of work, as well as the SRM, and the DRM. It is frequently desirable to determine the distance at which another ship will pass ahead or astern of your ship. This is done by drawing a line from your ship's position (R, at center of the Maneuvering board) in the direction of the course; where this line crosses the direction of relative movement line locates the point where the other vessel will be directly ahead or astern.

Problems in relative motion require the use of two diagrams; the relative plot just discussed, and the speed triangle which will be discussed in the following article. These diagrams are entirely separate, although the solution of the problem consists of developing one diagram with the information gained from the other until the desired result is reached. Inasmuch as this development of the two diagrams consists largely in transferring similar directions from one to the other, it simplifies matters to use a common origin of direction (north) for the two so that these similar directions become parallel lines, readily transferred with parallel rules, protractors, or a drafting machine. It may also prove more convenient and will also save space if both diagrams are constructed from a common point of origin, but the diagrams as such remain separate and distinct nevertheless, and must not be confused. To help prevent confusion it is wise to use different types of lettering in the two diagrams. The common practice is to use small letters in the speed diagram and capital letters in the relative plot, but the same letter of the alphabet should be used to represent the same unit in both diagrams. In this text *e* is used for earth, *r* for own ship, and *m* for the target vessel.

The relative plot is a diagram comprising a fixed point of origin and one or more straight lines called relative movement lines. In the problems concerning collision avoidance, illustrated in this chapter, own ship is used as the point of origin as movement and position of other ships *relative to own ship* is the basis of the problem. In tactical naval maneuvers a guide ship is generally used as the origin, as the position and movement of your ship and others in the formation *relative to the guide* is the primary concern. The fixed point of origin is always plotted at the center of the Maneuvering Board.

The speed triangle

1407 So far, use of the relative plot has determined the relative speed and the direction of relative movement of the target, as well as the CPA. Still to be obtained are the target's course and actual speed; these may be determined by means of the *speed triangle,* sometimes called the vector triangle.

The speed triangle or vector diagram consists of a system of properly related straight lines called vectors. Each vector has a pointed end called the "head," and a plain end called the "foot," both appropriately lettered to indicate the units represented. These vectors indicate direction and rate of travel in accordance with the following vector definition applying to relative movement: "A vector is a straight line indicating by its orientation the direction, and by its length, the ratio of travel

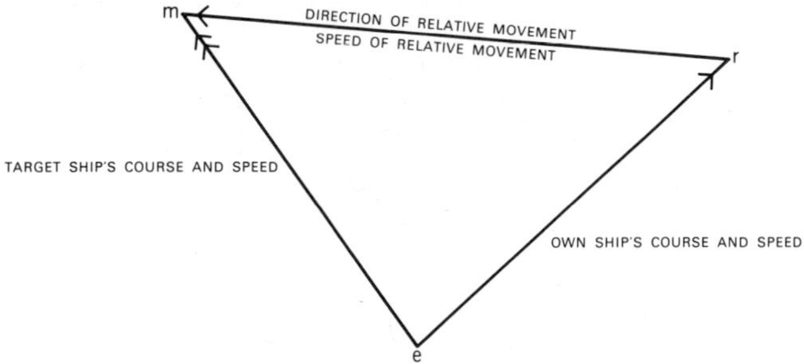

Figure 1407. The speed or vector triangle.

of a moving element, represented by the head of the vector, with respect to another element which is represented by the foot of the vector." It is essential that the distinction between the head and the foot of a vector be kept clearly in mind—the element or unit represented by the head moves relative to the element or unit represented by the foot of the vector. In order to form a vector diagram, the component vectors must represent movement taking place concurrently, they must be referred to a common origin of direction, and they must all be to the same scale. Since the vector diagram is composed entirely of vectors, and since vectors indicate only direction and speed, it follows that the diagram deals exclusively with direction and speed and will therefore yield only what is called course and speed.

The center of the plot is labeled with the small letter, *e,* for the "earth," since that is the reference for actual movement. The course and actual speed of own ship is represented by the vector *er,* while the course and actual speed of the target ship is represented by the vector *em.* The vector *rm* can be remembered as standing for relative movement; it represents both the direction of relative movement (DRM), and the speed of relative movement (SRM). *All actual course and speed vectors are drawn from e.* The directions of the vectors are also shown by arrows; the vector *rm* is always drawn in the direction from *r* towards *m.*

It is important not to confuse the speed triangle with the relative plot. The *relative plot* represents direction and *distance;* the *speed triangle* represents direction and *speed.*

Having plotted any two sides or vectors of the speed triangle, it is obvious that the third side can be determined, thus obtaining the direction and speed that is required.

The speed triangle and relative plot in use

1408 The procedure for obtaining the required data from the relative plot and speed triangle is illustrated in the following example.

Example: (Figure 1408) Own ship is on course 020°, speed 10.0 knots; at 2312, radar picks up a contact bearing 337°, distant 16.0 miles.

Required: The time and distance of the CPA, and course and speed of the target ship.

Solution: As the initial range to the target is 16.0 miles, 2:1 appears to be a convenient scale for distance. Accordingly, plot M_1 bearing 337° on the 8 circle; this is the first step in preparing the relative plot. As own ship speed is 10.0 knots, 2:1 also is a convenient scale for the speed triangle; draw *er,* course and speed vector.

Bearings and ranges are obtained on the target as tabulated below: the successive positions of the target are plotted as soon as noted.

Time	*Bearing*	*Range (Miles)*
2312	337°	16.0
2324	342°	15.0
2336	348°	14.0
2348	354°	13.3
0000	002.5°	12.6
0012	011°	12.3
0024	019°	12.2

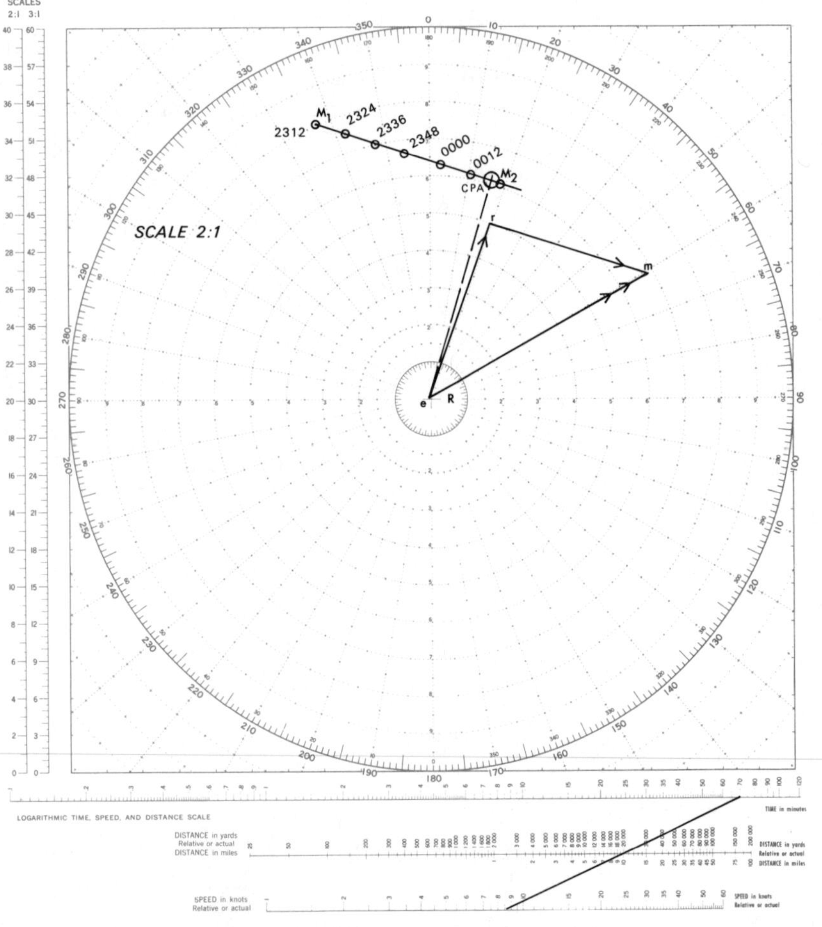

Figure 1408. Speed triangle and relative motion plot.

When the third bearing is obtained, it is evident that the bearing is changing quite rapidly, and that *no danger* of collision exists, *as long as both ships maintain their present course and speed.* When the 019° bearing and range are plotted at 0024, sufficient data are on hand to furnish answers of acceptable accuracy. A line is drawn in through all the bearings and range points that have been plotted and labeled M_1–M_2. Measure it, remembering to use a 2:1 scale to find the relative distance of 10.8 miles. The target ship, therefore, has traveled a *relative distance* of 10.8 miles in 72 minutes; by simple arithmetic, determine the *relative speed,* which is 9.0 knots ($\frac{10.8}{72} \times 60$), and check this answer by putting a straightedge across the nomogram, at the bottom of the board, as indicated.

Now draw the second vector or side in the speed triangle. From *r,* the head of own ship's course and speed vector, draw a line parallel to M_1–M_2, and to the *right,* as this is the direction of relative movement. This line is 4½ units in length, to correspond to the relative speed of 9.0 knots. The head of this line is labeled *m* and a line is drawn joining *em* to complete the triangle. This line, or vector, represents the target ship's course and speed; inspection shows target course 060.5°, speed 13.8 knots.

Data on the CPA is obtained by dropping a perpendicular from *e* to the line of relative movement, M_1–M_2. Measurement of this perpendicular shows that at the CPA, the target will be distant 12.2 miles, and the bearing will be 017.5°. To determine the time of the CPA, first determine its relative distance from M_1 which is 5.2 units or 10.4 miles. As the relative speed is 9.0 knots, it will take 68 minutes to move 10.4 miles. The time of CPA is 0020 (2312 + 68 min.). The nomograph or log scale may also be used to advantage in determining the time of CPA. Often the time of CPA can be estimated closely enough for practical purposes by judging its location with respect to time—labeled points on the relative motion line.

Relative movement problem involving a change of course

1409 The preceding article used an example in which the target was crossing the bow of your own ship, but the CPA was 12.2 miles. This is a comfortable distance at which to pass another ship and obviously no change of course or speed was indicated in the interests of safety.

Now consider the relative movement problem, when it appears that at the CPA, the target ship will be uncomfortably close to your ship, and you desire to take corrective action.

Example: (Figure 1409) Your ship is on course 200°, speed 14.0 knots. A pip appears on the radar screen, bearing 212°, range 20.0 miles. Plot the contact on the Maneuvering Board, using a scale of 2:1 and label it M_1, as shown. Observation of the pip shows that it is drawing left slowly, and that the range is closing. Ten minutes after the first contact, the bearing is 211.5°, range 18.2 miles. At time 20 minutes, the bearing is 211°, range 16.3 miles.

Enough data is now available to determine the CPA if both ships maintain present course and speed. Draw the relative movement line

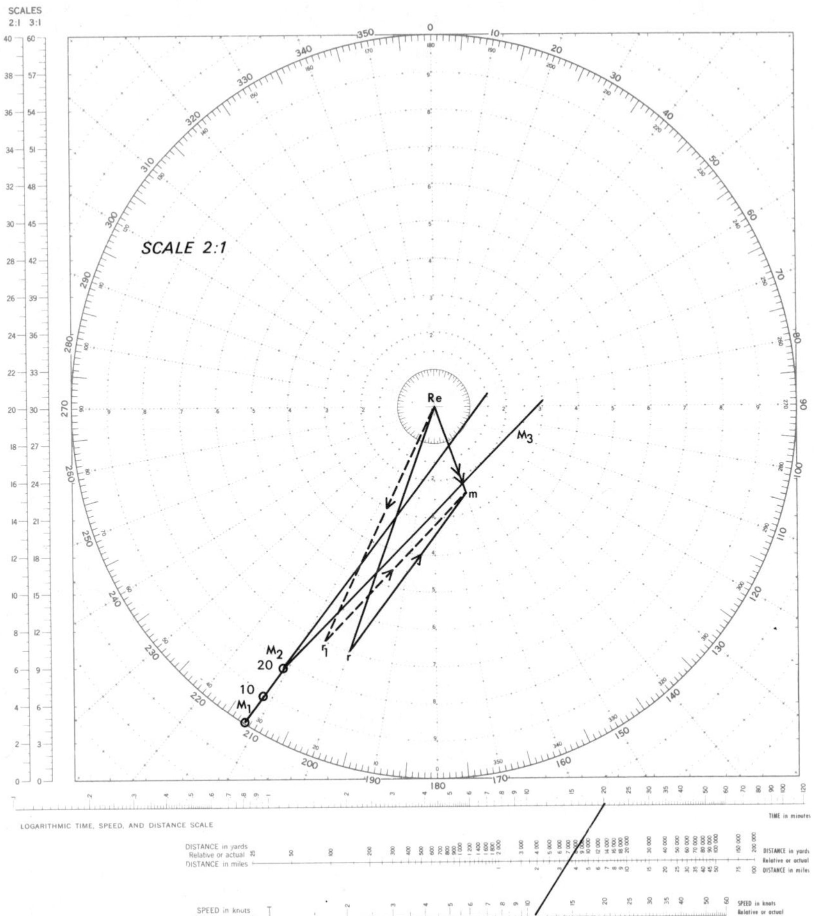

Figure 1409. Own ship changes course.

through the three points marking the target's bearings and ranges, and extend it past *e*, at the center of the Maneuvering Board. Note that this relative movement line shows that the range at the CPA will be slightly less than 2 miles.

The decision is made to pass the target at a range of 4.0 miles, by altering course immediately to starboard. To obtain the new course, first determine the target's course and speed. To do this, plot *er* own ship's present course and speed vector. Measure the relative distance traveled by the target between the first and third bearings (20 min); it is 3.6 miles. This gives a relative speed of 10.8 knots. Draw in the relative vector from *r* and parallel to the direction of relative movement (M_1–M_2). Now draw the target's course and speed vector from *e* to the end of the relative speed vector *m*. By inspection, the target is on course 160°, speed 5 knots.

To determine the new course, draw a line from M_2 tangent to the circle centered on *e*, and representing a distance of 4 miles. This line,

M_2–M_3, will be the new direction of relative movement. From *m* the end of the target's course and speed vector, draw the new relative speed vector parallel to the new line of relative movement, M_2–M_3. The point where this relative speed vector crosses the speed circle for 14.0 knots, r_1, defines the new course, 206°. Note that the target's range can be determined for the moment it crosses your ship's bow. The range is 12.3 miles.

Collision situation; own ship stops

1410 The following situation, shown using a *Radar Plotting Sheet,* is that of a burdened vessel which must first stop and then proceed at a reduced speed; it requires both a relative and a geographic plot. (In the International Rules of the Road, 1972, the burdened vessel is termed the "give-way" vessel, and the privileged vessel is referred to as the "stand-on" vessel.)

Example: (Figure 1410) Your ship is on course 145°, speed 10.0 knots. A radar contact is picked up, bearing 220°, range 18.0 miles and a relative plot of the target is commenced, with its present position

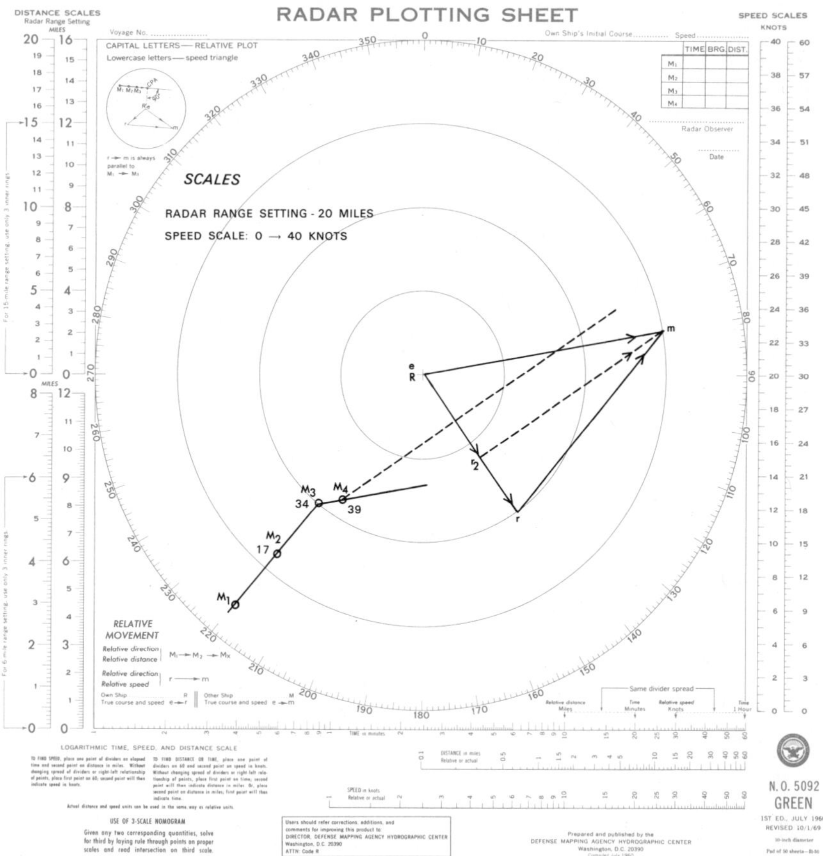

Figure 1410. Collision situation shown on radar plotting sheet.

labeled M_1. The range is closing, and there is no apparent change in the bearing. After 17 minutes, the range has closed to 14.0 miles but the bearing remains unchanged. At 34 minutes after the first contact the range is 10.0 miles; this position is M_3. Immediate corrective action is obviously required—it is not possible for your ship to change course to starboard as this would turn you into the other vessel's path—so stop engines, then back them until your ship has lost all way.

First, determine the target's course and speed. The direction of the relative movement is indicated by the successive plots of the target's position, along the line M_1–M_3, 040° as shown, and the relative distance traveled by the target is indicated by the length of the line M_1–M_2, which is 8.0 miles. The relative speed is 14.0 knots. With this data and own ship's course and speed vector, *er*, construct the speed triangle, *erm*. From the target's vector, *em*, determine the target to be on course 080°, speed 15.0 knots.

Next determine what the bearing and range of the target will be at 39 minutes, 5 minutes after your ship stopped. (For purposes of this problem, assume that your ship stopped short, with no advance while losing way.) Remember that your ship is now dead in the water and the situation has become a geographic plot rather than a relative movement plot. Draw a line in the direction 080°, the target's course, from M_3, its position at 34 minutes. Target speed is 15.0 knots, therefore in 5 minutes it will have moved 1.25 miles along this course line, and its position will be at M_4, bearing 215°, distant 9.2 miles.

At 39 minutes, you decide to go ahead on the original course, but at speed 6.0 knots. You wish to determine how far ahead of you the target will pass. You return to the speed triangle; the target's vector, *em*, remains the same, as it has not changed course or speed. Your own ship's vector, *er*, remains unchanged in direction, but is shortened to represent the new speed of 6.0 knots; call this vector er_2. By drawing in r_2m, obtain the new direction of relative motion, as well as the relative speed. Draw a line through M_4, the 39-minute position, parallel to r_2m; this crosses your own ship's course line at a distance of 3.2 miles, which will be the range when the target crosses ahead of you.

Collision situation; target alters course

1411 In the following situation, your vessel is the "stand-on" vessel, and the other, being the give-way vessel, is the one to alter course or speed. This problem, using a Maneuvering Board, requires only a relative plot. By now, the basic problems involved in solving relative movement problems should be coming clearer. A geographic plot is also shown in the lower left corner to assist in comprehension; it is not necessary to the solution of the problem at hand.

Example: (Figure 1411) Your ship is on course 350°, speed 12.0 knots. At 00 minutes a pip is seen on the radar screen, bearing 308°, range 20.0 miles. At 10 minutes, the range has closed to 16.5 miles; the bearing remains the same, and a plot is commenced. Subsequent plots show the bearing falling off to the left, and at 20 minutes, the

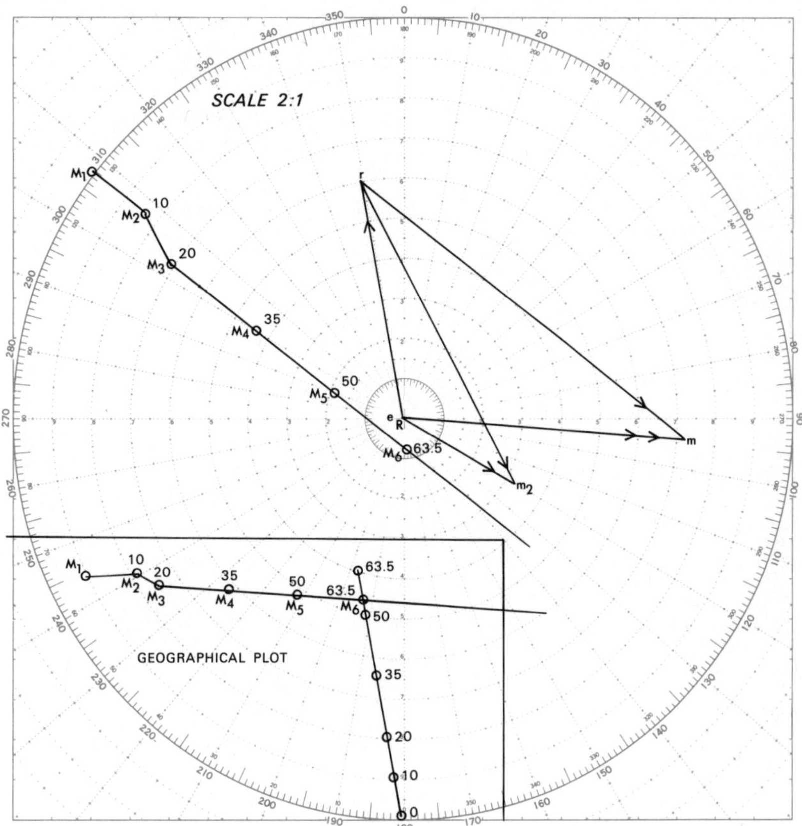

Figure 1411. Target ship changes course.

target bears 303°, range 14.0 miles, indicating a new relative movement line. A partial list of bearings and ranges appears below. (In actual practice, many additional bearings would have been obtained. Only the more important ones are included here.)

Time	*Bearing*	*Range (Miles)*
00 (M_1)	308°	20.0
10 (M_2)	308°	16.5
20 (M_3)	303°	14.0
35 (M_4)	300°	8.8
50 (M_5)	290°	3.7
63.5 (M_6)	170°	1.7

Required: 1. Target's course and speed from time 00 to 10.
2. What maneuver the target made at time 10.
3. What the target did at time 20.
4. The CPA.
5. The time of the CPA.

Solution: (Figure 1411) 1. Plot the ranges and bearings M_1 to M_6 establishing the relative motion line. Construct the speed triangle *erm*. From your ship's vector, *er*, lay off *rm* parallel to M_1–M_2, and for a relative speed of 21.0 knots (M_1–M_2 equals 3.5 miles; this distance was covered in 10 minutes). The vector *em* gives the target's course, 094°, and speed, 14.5 knots.

2. Draw a new relative speed vector from *r*. This vector, rm_2, is parallel to M_2–M_3, and for a relative speed of 16.8 knots. The vector em_2 shows that the target came right to course 120°, and slowed to 6.4 knots.

3. Use the relative movement line M_3–M_5, to obtain a new vector *rm.* This falls on the first vector *rm,* and is of the same length; the target therefore returned to her original course, 094°, and speed, 14.5 knots, at time 20 minutes.

4. Drop a perpendicular from *e* to the line M_3–M_5 extended, and find that the range at the CPA will be 1.2 miles, on bearing 217.5°.

5. Measure the relative distance from M_3 to the CPA. It is 14.0 miles; 14.0 miles at the relative speed of 21.0 knots will require 40 minutes, so the CPA will be reached at 60 minutes (40 + 20).

It should be pointed out again that considerably more bearings and ranges must be obtained than those tabulated in this example. There would have been considerable doubt as to the direction of the short leg, M_2–M_3, if only these two bearings had been obtained.

Relative movement problem, with both ships changing course

1412 A more complicated situation exists if *both* vessels change course, but it remains susceptible to a graphic solution using the *Maneuvering Board.* This example highlights the need to keep a *constant* check on a radar contact when danger of collision exists, and for plotting at frequent intervals.

Example: (Figure 1412) Your ship is steaming on course 000°, speed 10.0 knots. You obtain a radar contact bearing 029°, range 20.0 miles, start your stopwatch, and plot the target's relative position, M_1, as shown. At time 10 minutes the bearing has not changed, but the range has closed to 16.7 miles (M_2). You must obtain the target's course and speed. The relative speed is 19.8 knots (3.3 miles in 10 minutes) and the direction of relative movement is 209°. From the speed triangle, you determine that the target is on course 233°, speed 12.0 knots. The plot of the target's relative position is continued. At time 20 minutes, the bearing remains unchanged at 029°, but the range has closed at 13.4 miles (M_3). An immediate 20° course change to the right is ordered, and your ship steadies on course 020°.

This change of course should, of course, change the direction of the line of relative movement, as the latter is generated by the movement of one ship with relation to another, and any change in course or speed by either ship will change the relative movement line. You plot an er_1m vector.

Obviously, your ship's change of course to the right should cause the bearing to change to the left. This can be checked from the plot

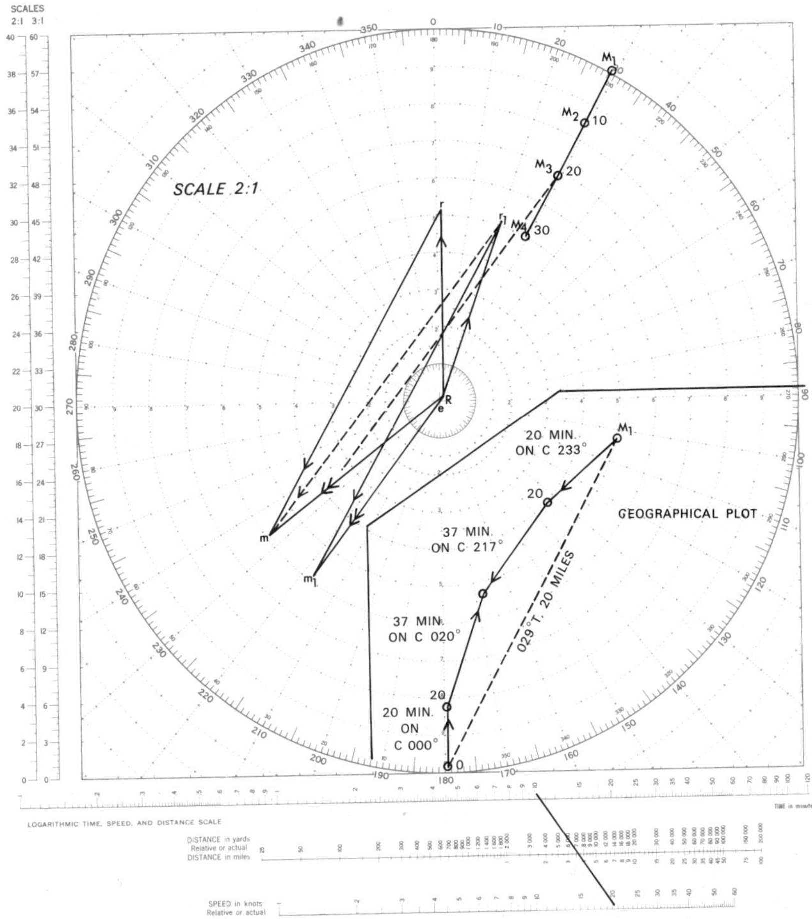

Figure 1412. Own ship and target ship both change course.

r_1m, which will now be the direction of relative movement; this direction, laid down from M_3, passes to the left of e. The CPA, incidentally, should be slightly more than 2 miles.

With your ship on her new course, 020°, you continue to watch the radar contact. Surprisingly, the range steadily decreases but the bearing remains unchanged. This can be due only to the fact that the target has also changed course or speed. You believe that it is probably maintaining speed of 12.0 knots, and that a course change is causing the bearing to remain constant. The target's new course must be determined.

Construct a new speed triangle, starting with the vector of your ship's new course, and speed of 10.0 knots; this is er_1. The relative speed line (r_1m_1) is then drawn in parallel to the direction of the relative movement, which has not changed. The terminus of the line, m_1, is determined by where the line cuts the 12-knot speed circle, at 217°. This shows the target's new course to be 217°, *and both ships are again on a collision course.*

The lower right corner of Figure 1412 shows a geographic plot for greater clarity of the situation as it is developing for both vessels.

At this time you must take drastic evasive action, as the range is closing at about 21.7 knots. At time 30 minutes, the bearing is still 029°, but the range has decreased to 9.8 miles. If your ship maintains speed of 10.0 knots, but comes right to 080°, can you determine the range and bearing at the CPA, assuming that the target makes no further changes in course or speed? The plotting necessary for this solution is not included in Figure 1412, which is already sufficiently complete. The answer is: Range 4.4 miles; bearing 327°.

Relative movement problem; own ship is being overtaken

1413 A quite different situation, but one which is frequently encountered at sea, is when your ship is being overtaken by another vessel.

Example: (Figure 1413) You are at sea, on course 320°, speed 10.0 knots. At 00 minutes a radar contact is made, bearing 201°, range 16.0

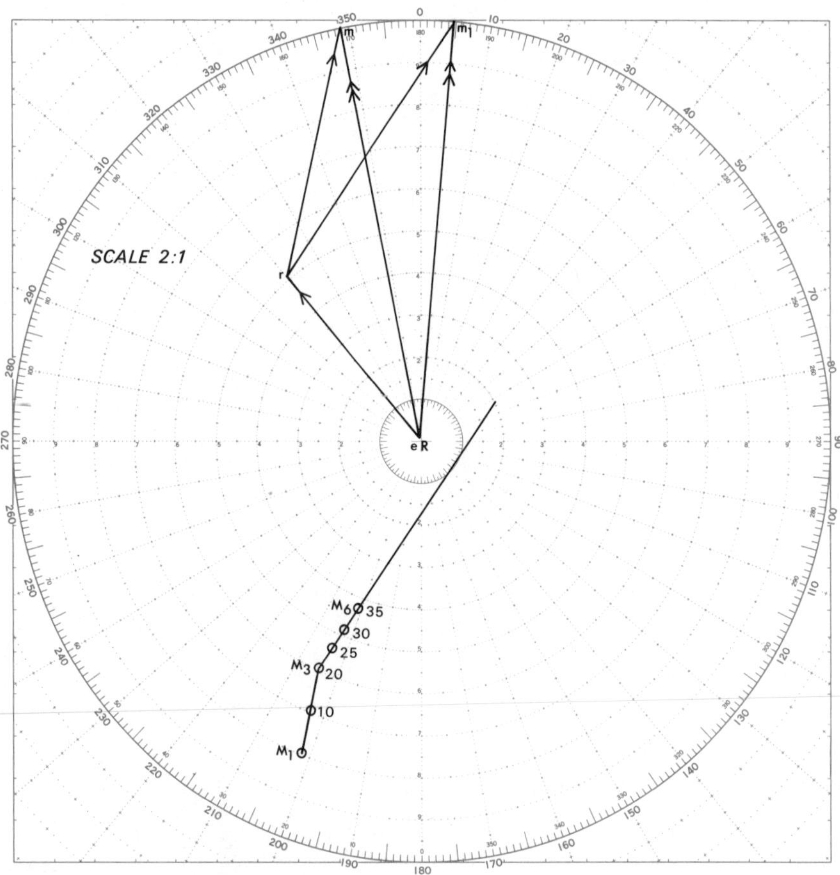

Figure 1413. Own ship is being overtaken.

miles. You continue to track and plot the target. A partial list of bearings and ranges is tabulated as follows:

Time (Min.)	*Bearing*	*Range (Miles)*
00	201°	16.0
10	202°	14.0
20 (M_3)	204°	12.0
25	203°	10.9
30	202°	9.7
35	200°	8.5

At time 20 minutes you decide to determine the target's course and speed based on the data so far obtained. The relative distance, M_1–M_3, is 4.1 miles, and this distance was traversed in 20 minutes: the relative speed is 12.3 knots, and the direction of relative movement is 012°. With these data draw the *rm* vector of the triangle: the target's vector, *em*, shows that it is on course 349°, speed 20.0 knots.

However, the bearings obtained after that are now changing in the opposite direction. As your ship has maintained course and speed, the target must have changed course and speed or both. With the data obtained after time 20 minutes, you must determine the target's new course and speed. The relative speed is 14.8 knots. By means of parallel rulers, the direction of relative movement is determined to be 033°. With these data, plot a new relative speed vector, rm_1 and determine that the target is now on course 005°, speed remaining at 20 knots. All that remains is to determine the range, the bearing, and the time of the CPA. Extend the M_3–M_6 line; it is tangent to the 2.0 mile circle, on bearing 123°. The target will reach the CPA at time 68 minutes (M_3–CPA = 11.8 miles). The relative speed is 14.6 knots; 11.8 miles at 14.6 knots requires 48 minutes; 48 + 20 minutes (M_3) = 68 minutes.

Plotting multiple targets

1414 Particularly in coastal waters, several targets may be on the radar screen at one time. The following example illustrates the plot for two targets which are on the screen at the same time; the plastic Maneuvering Board is well suited to the graphic solution of such a situation.

Example: (Figure 1414) Your ship is on course 000°, speed 8.0 knots. At time 00 there is a radar contact bearing 280.5°, range 10.0 miles. At time 43 there is another contact, bearing 070°, range 11 miles. Bearings and ranges are tabulated as follows:

TARGET *M*			TARGET *M′*		
Time (Min.)	*Brg.*	*Range (Miles)*	*Time (Min.)*	*Brg.*	*Range (Miles)*
00	280.5°	10.0	43	070°	11.0
30	286°	7.7	62	072°	8.1
45	291°	6.5	76	074°	6.3
61	300°	5.0	94	080°	3.8
87	313°	4.0	103	090°	2.5
105	336°	3.2			

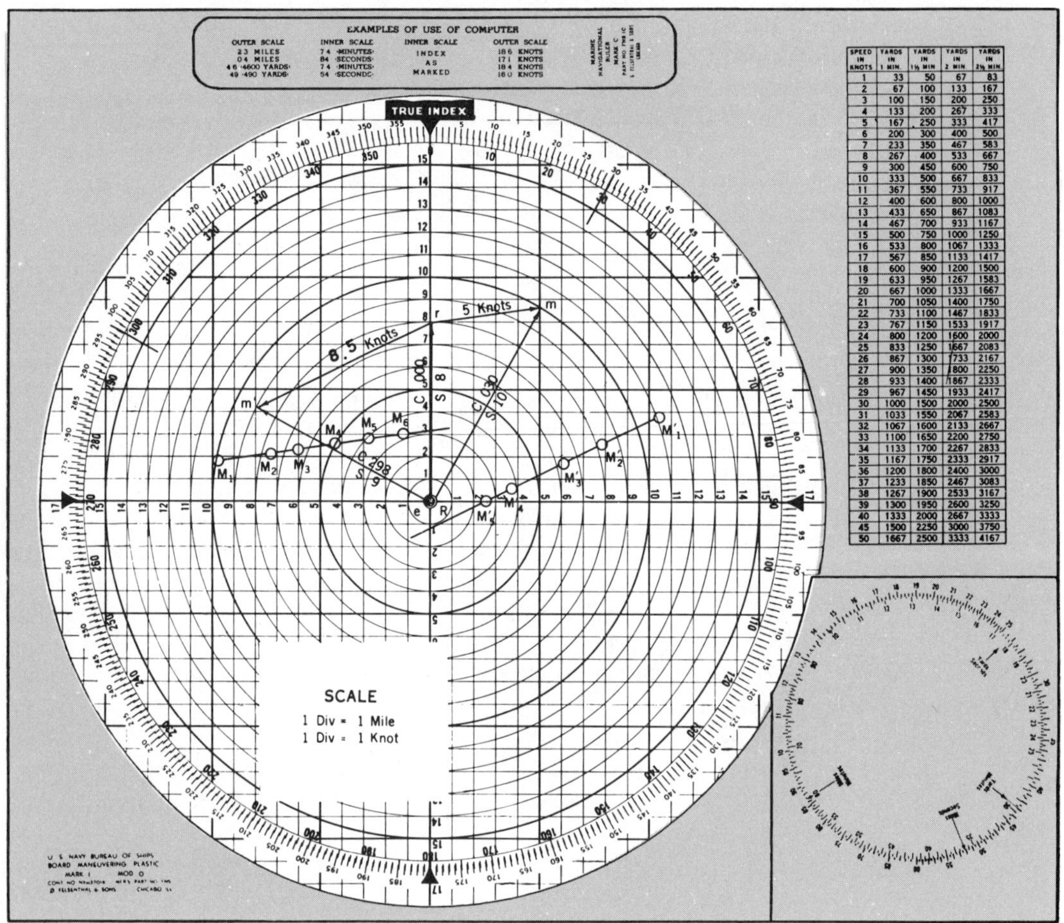

SPEED IN KNOTS	YARDS IN 1 MIN.	YARDS IN 1½ MIN	YARDS IN 2 MIN	YARDS IN 2½ MIN.
1	33	50	67	83
2	67	100	133	167
3	100	150	200	250
4	133	200	267	333
5	167	250	333	417
6	200	300	400	500
7	233	350	467	583
8	267	400	533	667
9	300	450	600	750
10	333	500	667	833
11	367	550	733	917
12	400	600	800	1000
13	433	650	867	1083
14	467	700	933	1167
15	500	750	1000	1250
16	533	800	1067	1333
17	567	850	1133	1417
18	600	900	1200	1500
19	633	950	1267	1583
20	667	1000	1333	1667
21	700	1050	1400	1750
22	733	1100	1467	1833
23	767	1150	1533	1917
24	800	1200	1600	2000
25	833	1250	1667	2083
26	867	1300	1733	2167
27	900	1350	1800	2250
28	933	1400	1867	2333
29	967	1450	1933	2417
30	1000	1500	2000	2500
31	1033	1550	2067	2583
32	1067	1600	2133	2667
33	1100	1650	2200	2750
34	1133	1700	2267	2833
35	1167	1750	2333	2917
36	1200	1800	2400	3000
37	1233	1850	2467	3083
38	1267	1900	2533	3167
39	1300	1950	2600	3250
40	1333	2000	2667	3333
45	1500	2250	3000	3750
50	1667	2500	3333	4167

Figure 1414. Multiple targets as shown on plastic Maneuvering Board.

As the plot develops, it becomes obvious from the two lines of relative movement M_1–M_6, M'_1–M'_5, that both ships are going to pass clear of you. The speed triangles are interesting, as they are both based on your ship's vector.

The course and speed of target *M*, from its triangle, are 030° and 10.0 knots. (The relative distance M_1–M_6 is 8.6 miles, the time is 105 minutes; the relative speed is 5 knots.)

Target *M′* is on course 298°, speed 9 knots. (The relative distance M'_1–M'_5 is 8.5 miles, the time is 60 minutes; the relative speed is 8.5 knots.)

You must determine the time each vessel will be at CPA, and the range at that time.

Relative movement problem; to intercept a moving ship on known course and speed

1415 The following example is that of a ship ordered to intercept another vessel whose course and speed are known, as well as her relative position at the start of the problem.

This is a common problem for Navy and Coast Guard vessels; it arises at times for other ships, as when called on to lend assistance. It is not based on radar data. The solution, on a Maneuvering Board, illustrates the use of different scales for speed and distance.

Example: Your ship at sea receives a message from ship *A* that she requires assistance. She gives her position, and states that she will remain on course 090°, speed 6.0 knots. The plot shows her to bear 030° from your position, distant 200 miles. Your ship can maintain 20 knots.

Required: (Figure 1415) (1) The course to reach *A* in minimum time, (2) How long will it take to rendezvous?

This is merely a new application of the other problems in this chapter. The relative plot differs in that ship *A* is at the center; your vessel

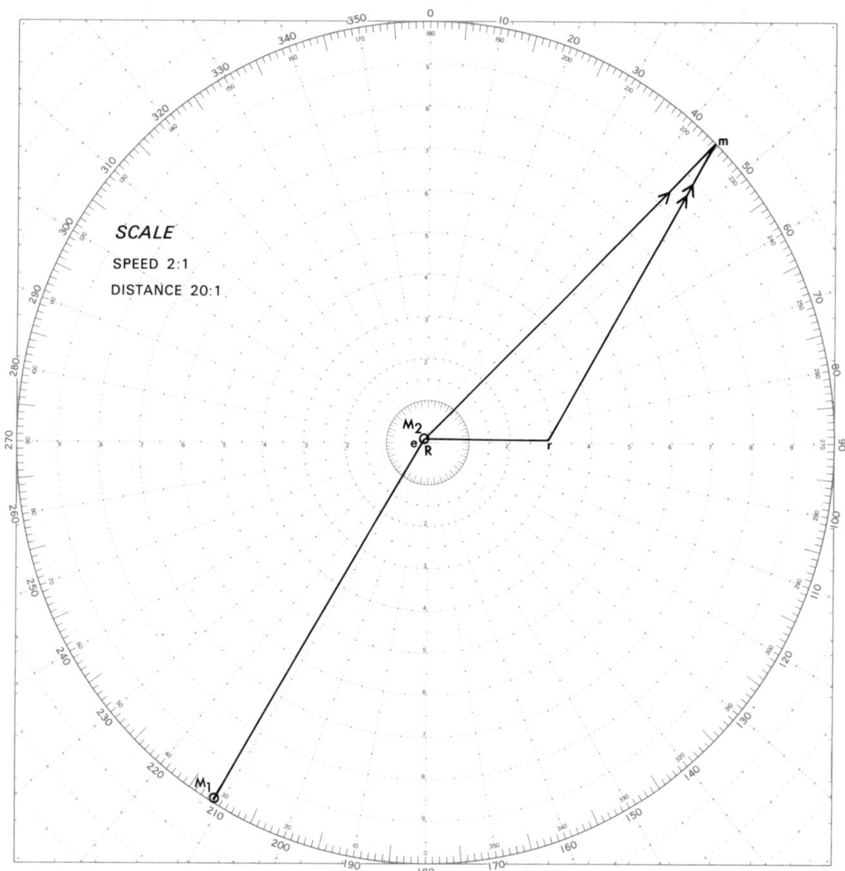

Figure 1415. Rendezvous problem.

will be at M_1 initially and your final position, M_2, is also at the center. In the speed triangle, *A*'s course and speed vector will establish the base with which to determine your ship's course, at 20.0 knots.

Solution: Plot initial position, M_1 bearing 210°, and distant 200 miles from *e* using a scale 20:1. Plot *A*'s course and speed vector, 090°, 6.0 knots, using a scale 2:1. The direction of relative motion is from M_1 towards $M_2(e)$, this is 030°. Plot the relative speed vector parallel to M_1–M_2 from *r* to where it intersects the relative speed circle at 20.0 knots; this intersection establishes the point *m*.

Answer: (1) The vector *em* establishes the course, 045°, to steer at 20.0 knots.

Your course is now established: all that remains is to determine how long it will take to come alongside *A*. The relative distance is 200 miles, the relative speed, *rm*, is found to be 16.3 knots.

(2) The time required will therefore be 12.3 hours, to the nearest tenth.

Other information can be obtained for this plot. For example, how many miles must your ship steam to reach *A*? The answer is 246—12.3 hours at 20.0 knots. Again, when should you pick up *A* on radar, at a range of 20.0 miles? *A*'s echo should appear in slightly over 11 hours (180 miles at 16.3 knots).

Changing station when in formation

1416 A common problem on board naval vessels is that of changing station within a formation.

Example: (Figure 1416) Your ship is in formation on course 020°, speed 12 knots, 9 miles ahead of the guide. The formation commander orders her to take station on the port beam of the guide, at a distance of 7 miles. The following information will be necessary before you can decide the most expedient way to make the maneuver:

1. Direction or relative movement of the guide with respect to your ship;
2. Own ship course at 18 knots;
3. Own ship course at 12 knots;
4. Own ship speed if you steer 295°;
5. Own ship speed if you steer 350°.

Solution: (a) Draw vector *em* to represent the true course, 020°, and speed, 12 knots, of the guide. Locate M_1 and M_2 as follows. Convert your relative bearing from the guide to true bearing as described above, which is 020°. Since own ship is the reference, M_1 bears the reciprocal of 020°, or 200° from the center. Hence, M_1 is located on the 9 circle in the direction 200° from the center. Similarly, M_2 is located on the 7 circle in the direction 110° from the center. The direction of relative movement (DRM) can now be determined.

(b) Draw vector r_1m parallel to M_1M_2. Since the direction of relative movement is from *r* to *m*, and *r* is to be found, the reciprocal of *rm* is drawn from *m* until it intersects the 18-knot circle. Thus, *rm* is in the required direction M_1M_2.

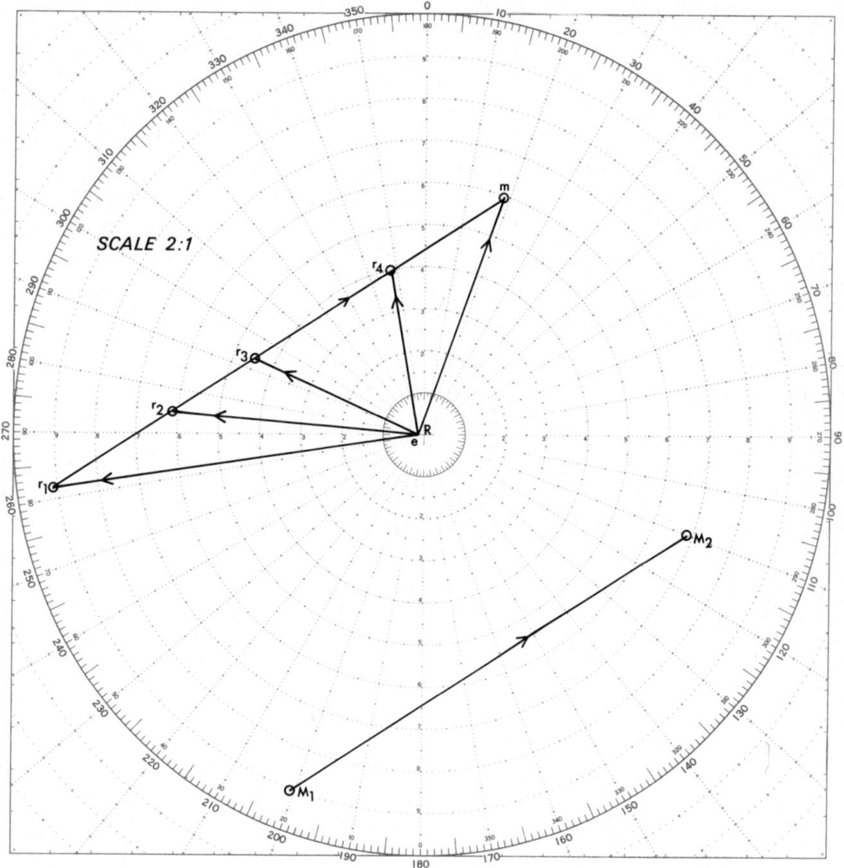

Figure 1416. Changing station maneuver.

(c) Complete the speed triangle by drawing vector er_1 from the center of the diagram to r_1.

(d) Draw vector er_2 from the center to the intersection of the r_1m vector with the 12-knot circle.

(e) Draw vector er_3 in the direction 295°.

(f) Draw vector er_4 in the direction 350°.

Answer: It can be seen that the DRM is 058°, the course at 18 knots is 262°, the course at 12 knots is 276°, the speed when steering 295° would be 8.8 knots and the speed for course 350° would be 7.9 knots. From this information you would be able to pick the course and speed to put your ship on the new station in the smartest manner.

Determining the true wind

1417 The Maneuvering Board lends itself well to determining both the speed (force) and the direction of the true wind by means of the speed triangle.

Apparent wind is the force and the relative direction from which the wind blows, as measured aboard a moving vessel. It can also be expressed as a true direction.

In this triangle, the vector *er* represents the course and speed of the ship, the vector *rw* the direction and speed of the relative or apparent wind, and the vector *ew* is the direction and speed of the true wind. The vector *er* is plotted first, the vector *rw* is then plotted from *r* in the direction the apparent wind is blowing, the length of *rw* representing the speed of the apparent wind. The third vector *ew* represents the direction and speed of the true wind. *True wind* is the force and the true direction from which the wind blows, as measured at a fixed point on the earth.

Example: (Figure 1417) Assume the ship is underway, on course 030°, speed 15 knots, and that true direction of the apparent wind is from 062° at 20 knots.

Required: Direction and speed of the true wind.

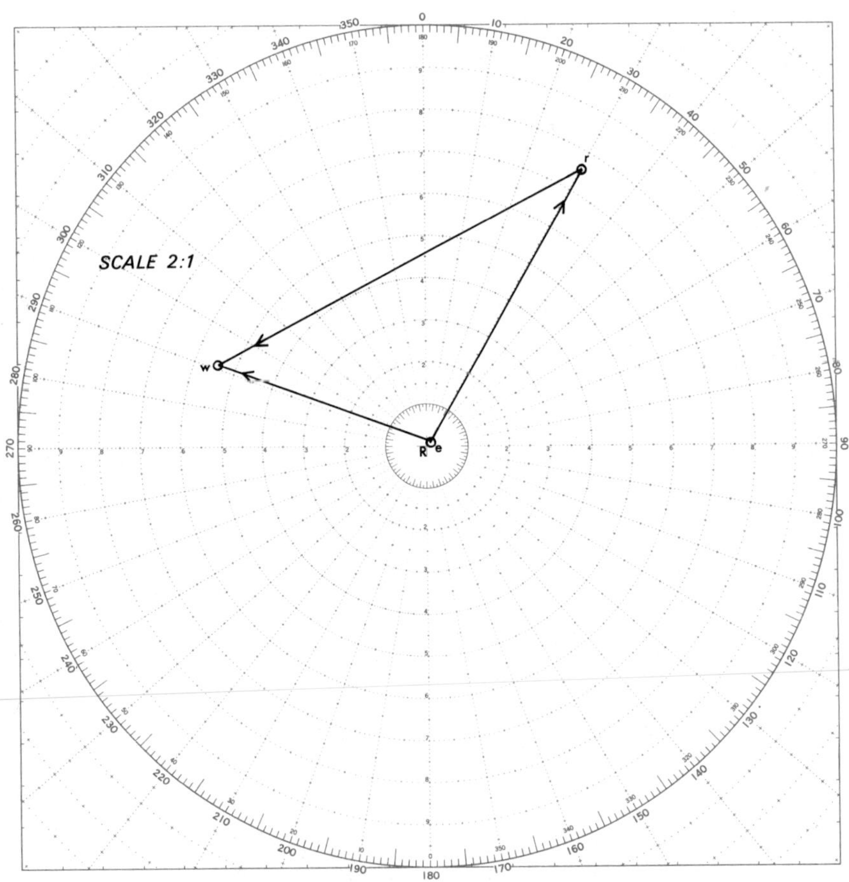

Figure 1417. Wind triangle.

Solution: Draw the speed triangle as shown, using a scale of 2:1. The vector *er* represents your course and speed. From *r,* plot the relative speed vector *rw* in the direction of 242° (the apparent wind direction, 062° plus 180°), and to a length representing 20 knots; the terminus of this vector is labeled *w;* join *e* and *w;* this vector, *ew,* represents the true wind direction, from 109.5°, and its speed, 10.8 knots.

Allowing for known current

1418 It is easy to determine the course to steer at a given speed, and the speed over the bottom, when the set and drift of a current are known. Solution is by the speed triangle method.

In this example, *er* is the vector representing the set and drift of the current; it is the vector on which the speed triangle is constructed. The vector *em* represents the intended track (TR) and speed of advance (SOA) to make good, and *rm* represents the course to steer and the speed through the water, to reach a given point at a desired time.

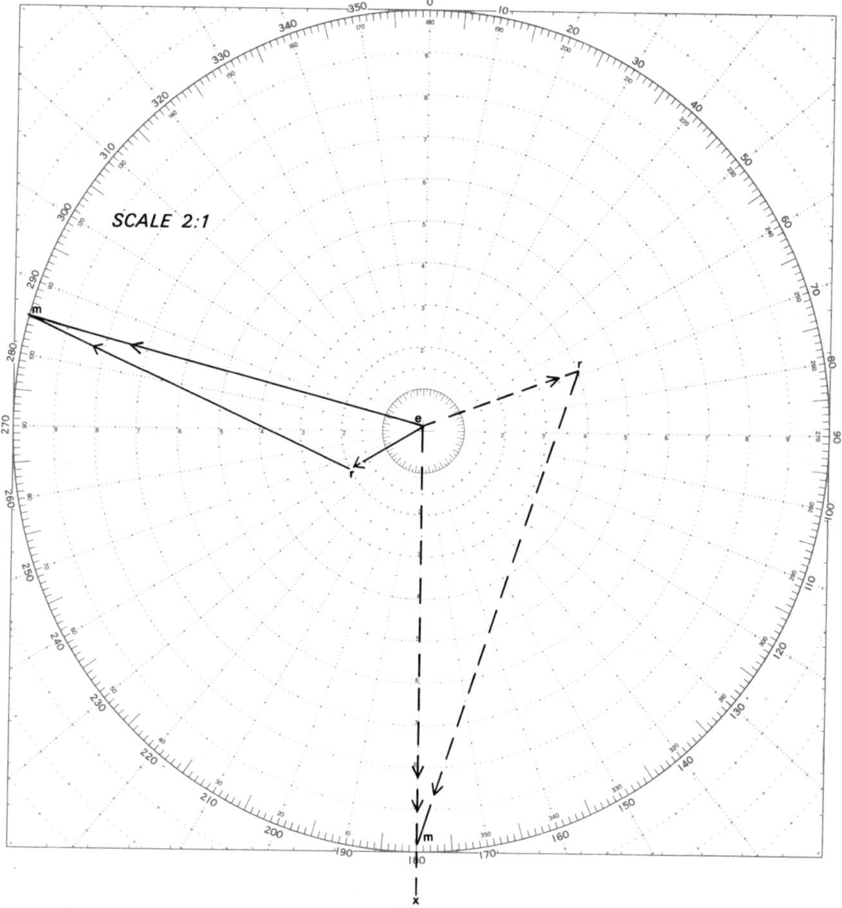

Figure 1418. Current vector problem.

Example 1: (Figure 1418) You have an intended track of 285° at a speed of 10.0 knots. The current is setting 240°, drift 2.0 knots.

Required: Course and speed to make to stay on the track line.

Solution: First draw the current vector *er* as shown in Figure 1418 (solid lines). Next, draw in the vector *em* for the intended track line in the direction 285°.

Answer: The vector *rm* represents the course to steer, 294.5°, and the speed to make, 8.6 knots, to travel along a track in the direction 285°, making 10.0 knots over the ground.

A similar problem arises when you want to travel along a given track line, and at a given speed, through a known current, and must determine the course to steer, and what will be the speed made good over the ground.

Example 2: (Figure 1418) A current sets 070°, drift 4.0 knots. You have an intended track of 180°, using a speed of 12.0 knots.

Required: Course to steer to stay on the track line, and speed made good over the ground.

Solution: (Figure 1418, broken lines) Plot the current vector, *er,* in the direction 070°, and for a speed of 4 knots. Next, from *e,* plot a vector *ex* in the direction 180°, but of indefinite length. Now from *r* swing an arc of a radius equal to 12.0 knots; the point at which this arc cuts *ex* is labeled *m,* and draw in *rm,* the vector representing the course you must steer. It is in the direction 198°; the length *em* indicates that you will need to make good 10.0 knots over the ground.

Summary

1419 Relative motion is of paramount importance to a navigator when his vessel is in the vicinity of others. A careful and continuous plot of bearings and distances, usually by radar, to the "target" ship is necessary to determine the closest point of approach, and hence any danger of collision. Four different plotting aids are available, but the Maneuvering Board and Radar Plotting Sheet are the most widely used.

Relative-motion solutions are also used for problems of movement within formations of ships, for determining true wind, and for applying current vectors.

Relative-motion problems require some reorientation of a navigator's normal perception of plots; sufficient practice with these problems and their solutions is mandatory so that he may work with them easily and accurately.

15 The Piloting Team

Introduction **1501** Thus far, this book has described most of the primary techniques and skills which enable a navigator to direct his ship safely in pilot waters. The techniques used in restricted waters were covered on the basis that the "input data," such as bearings, distances, and depths, were known. To obtain such data for use in piloting, in a systematic manner, requires several persons, each doing his or her small part of the overall job and organized as a group to provide the navigator with the proper information at the proper time. This group, known as the *piloting team,* is stationed whenever the ship gets underway in or enters into pilot waters.

Aboard most U.S. Navy vessels, the Combat Information Center (CIC) will also supply bearings and ranges, obtained by radar, to conn. The DRT in CIC will also be in operation, and will be updated frequently. However, the navigator must always bear in mind that he is charged with the safe navigation of the ship; and the information passed on from CIC is for "back-up" purposes.

This chapter is concerned with how the navigator obtains the necessary information in a timely and orderly manner from the various people on this team, how the team is organized to furnish this information, and some elements of doctrine and methods which have proven to be of assistance in the fleet in solving this problem. Not all of the combinations of information available to the navigator are used in the illustration herein; only a representative sampling of the everyday uses to show a typical method is given. It should be emphasized at the outset that the methods outlined here are only *one* way of accomplishing the result desired—namely, a smooth and timely flow of essential information to the navigator. Any method of organization will do, provided it achieves this desired result.

Although this chapter is written in terms of the activities aboard a U.S. naval vessel, the same broad principles will apply both to merchant ships and small craft. It is recognized that such vessels will be operating with fewer personnel and with less formalized procedures, but the same basic information is required for safe pilotage, even if it can only be obtained in lesser detail.

Sources of information **1502** The navigator is charged with using all available sources of information to fix the ship's position. The kinds of information needed, and the various places in a typical ship where it may be obtained, are listed in subsequent paragraphs.

Bearings of objects can be obtained by any of the following means in most ships of the Navy:

Visually, by means of a gyrocompass repeater, magnetic compass, pelorus, a self-synchronous alidade, or a gun director (5″ or larger).

By radar, using the surface-search radar equipment (either in CIC or the bridge PPI), or using a fire-control radar in a gun director.

By sonar, using the echo-ranging equipment.

Ranges (distances) of objects can be obtained in most ships of the Navy by the following means:

Optically, using an optical rangefinder in a gun director (5° battery or larger).

Visually, by use of the stadimeter.

By radar, using the surface-search radar equipment (either in CIC or the bridge PPI), or using fire-control radar in a gun director.

By sonar, using the echo-ranging equipment.

By sound, by computing ranges using the time difference of receipt at the ship between simultaneous audio and submarine sound signals, or simultaneous audio and radio signals transmitted from *a distance finding station.*

Depths of water can usually be obtained for most ships of the Navy, by the following methods:

Echo-sounder readings.

Lead-line soundings.

Required records

1503 Various U.S. Navy instructions require that a permanent record be maintained of all observations and computations made for the purpose of navigating the ship. This means that any organization established by the navigator to obtain navigational information must be so organized that the necessary information is recorded without hampering its flow to the navigator. Since in piloting the navigator normally relies on visual bearings of landmarks and other aids to navigation to fix the position of the ship, the primary record that must be maintained is of the bearings used to navigate the ship. To be complete, the time of the bearings and identification of the objects used must also be included. To accomplish this, a *Bearing Book* is maintained in each ship of the Navy; a standard form (OpNav Form 3530/2) is provided for this purpose. A sample page of a Bearing Book is shown in Figure 1503. Note that there is a place for the date, the port which the ship is entering or leaving and the gyro error. If distances are measured, they are recorded under the bearing (or in place of it) in the column for the object on which they were taken. An entry of this nature is seen for 0952 under Thimble Shoals.

Bearing Book

RECORD GYRO BEARINGS

PLACE: Entering Norfolk, Va. GYRO ERROR: 1°W

DATE TIME	Cape Henry Light	Cape Charles Light	Thimble Shoals Light	Lynn-Haven Bridge	Checkered Tank	Echo Sounder Reading
10 August 1977 0946	205.5	010.0	287.0			4
0949	201.0	012.5	287.0			
0952	197.0	016.0	287.0			3
			10870			
0955	192.5		287.0			3
0958	186.0		287.0			
1001	178.0		287.0	222.5		
1004	171.0		286.5	217.0		3
1007	164.0		287.0	211.0		
1010	155.0		287.0	206.5		3

Figure 1503. A U.S. Navy Bearing Book.

When bearings on one object are discontinued, the column previously used is relabeled when it is desired to use it for an object which is not already provided for, as was done in the *Cape Henry* column at 1016. Any bearing recorded in the Cape Henry column after the time when that column was relabeled *Stack* are bearings on the stack, and not on Cape Henry. Using this manner of relabeling, any number and sequence of landmarks employed for piloting can be recorded; for greater clarity a horizontal line can be drawn between the last of the bearings on the previous object and the name of the new object. The right-hand column should also be carefully noted; it provides a record of depth readings sent to the navigator at the times indicated.

Any book of convenient size may be used as a bearing book by simply ruling off the columns desired, and printing the appropriate information at the top of the page. There is the left-hand column for the *time* of each observation, normally at least four columns for *bearings* (and distances), and the right-hand column for *depth* readings. On most naval ships, it is required that the man keeping the Bearing Book sign his name when the piloting is completed, to indicate that the record made is a true one. In addition, most navigators have standing instructions posted in the front of the book prohibiting erasures, and directing the bearing recorder to draw a line through any mistake and to rewrite the correct bearing so that both are still legible. This is done to preserve the legality of the record, and to prevent any confusion as to the correct bearing.

Sounding Book All depth readings may not be sent to the navigator, for reasons which will be discussed later. However, all readings taken must be recorded, and a special *Sounding Book* is established for this purpose. Note that the right-hand column of the Bearing Book (Figure 1503) indicates the observed depth-sounding reading. This reading may or may not be the depth of water under the keel depending upon the location of the sounding head of the sonic depth finder. Since it is the comparison of the observed depth with the charted depth in which the navigator is primarily interested, a correction factor must be applied in any event to each reading to account for the distance from the sounding head to the water line. A record of this correction should be made on the inside front cover of the Sounding Book for ready reference. A recommended procedure that can be considered the least subject to error is to have the echo-sounder operator record and report depth measurements as read; the navigator and Bearing Book recorder will then apply the correction factor previously determined. The result will be the measured depth from the water line which can be compared directly with the charted depth corresponding to the estimate of the ship's position.

Selection of information **1504** Article 1502 lists the considerable number of sources of information available to the navigator in piloting. It is essential that he organize his piloting team so that the navigational aids are known in advance, and that he receives only the information which he requires at any particular time.

For normal piloting in good visibility, the navigator can accurately fix the position of the ship using two or three bearings or LOP's. As visual bearings are most accurate and normally the most easily obtained, they are the first choice. Should visibility become poor, the use of *radar ranges* (Article 1707) is the next most accurate method of positioning the ship.

When the ship is in pilot waters, continuous use of the echo sounder should be required. Depths obtained by the hand lead are useful in doubtful situations when the ship is proceeding slowly enough to permit accurate casts and readings. Both may then be used in comparison with charted depth data to ensure the greatest degree of safety. Merchant ships make little use of a hand lead line, except perhaps to take soundings around a vessel as she is loaded down to her safe loading lines.

From this brief summary of the effectiveness and accuracy of different types of fixes, it has been determined that provision should be made for obtaining the following sources of piloting information in the basic organization of a piloting team:

Visual bearings.

Radar information (ranges and bearings) from CIC and the bridge PPI.

Depth information from the echo sounder and by a hand lead line.

Stationing of personnel

1505 Since the chains (see Figure 1509) will be manned in pilot waters for the taking of soundings by means of a hand lead line (if the speed of the ship is slow enough), and the echo sounder will also be manned, two members of the team are thus stationed. As the typical ship has at least two peloruses or alidades, a man is assigned to each to obtain visual bearings. The careful navigator will request the operations officer to station his radar navigation team in CIC, which will include two additional surface plotters and an additional officer to supervise radar navigation, augmenting the normal watch personnel. Means must also be provided to transmit piloting information to the bridge on designated circuits. The echo-sounder operator can maintain the Sounding Book as well as operate the equipment, but an additional man is required to maintain the Bearing Book. Using these personnel, the basic team consists of the following:

The nagivator, plus possibly an assistant.
One leadsman in the chains, plus a talker to report his readings.
One echo-sounder operator.
Two or more bearing takers, each assigned to a pelorus.
One bearing recorder to maintain the bearing book.
One or more men to maintain communication with and receive radar information from CIC.

Should information be required from gun directors, special provision for this information must be made with the weapons officer. Sonar information is usually available through CIC, or by a direct telephone circuit to the bridge.

Communications

1506 Communications must be established between the various members of the team and the navigator. This is done in such a manner that the navigator has positive control of the communications used to reach any member of the team at any time. It is therefore customary for the piloting team to be connected by means of sound-powered telephones, with the bearing recorder acting as the navigator's talker on the circuit. In this way, the bearing recorder can obtain all information sent to the navigator and enter it in the bearing book as it is received. He can also act as a communication link with CIC, requesting and recording all radar data considered pertinent by the navigator. In practice, the talker for the leadsman is not normally on this telephone circuit with the other members of the team but sends his soundings over the anchoring and maneuvering circuit to the bridge. This information is usually desired by the captain and the officer of the deck as well as by the navigator. The lead-line soundings are repeated by the telephone talker on the bridge so that all can hear them, and the navigator notes the information as it is heard.

Thus a piloting telephone circuit has been established with the following stations:

The *bearing recorder* (who is the navigator's talker and controls the circuit).

A *bearing taker* at each pelorus.
The *echo-sounder operator.*
A *talker* in CIC.

The specific circuit used for this purpose will vary from ship to ship, but most ships have provision for such communications. In addition to sound-powered communications, many ships have and use voice tubes connecting these stations. Many navigators have found it helpful to use a call-bell system to indicate to the bearing takers the times to take a round of bearings. This system limits talking on the circuit, thereby reducing the noise level on the bridge, which is always desirable.

In addition, a separate circuit from CIC to bridge is usually established to provide a clear channel for the transmission of evaluated radar information during reduced visibility piloting.

Duties and doctrine

1507 For these stations it is desirable to establish specific reporting doctrine to assist the navigator in the advance selection of information that he will receive while piloting.

Bearing recorder

The *bearing recorder* is charged with four main duties:

Controlling the communication circuit and acting as the navigator's talker on that circuit.

Relaying all information received to the navigator.

Recording all bearings, ranges, and depths as he receives them.

At the direction of the navigator, giving *marks* to the bearing takers and CIC to indicate when to take bearings or ranges. In ships so equipped, the "*mark*" can be indicated by sounding a bell or buzzer installed on the bridge for that purpose. If this latter system is used, the officer doing the plotting frequently gives his own marks.

Bearing takers

The primary duty of each *bearing taker* is to take bearings on objects at times specified by the navigator, and to report them over the phone. In addition, a good bearing taker will be familiar with the landmarks and aids to navigation expected to be used, and will assist the navigator by reporting when they are in sight. He will also assist the navigator in identifying each landmark or aid as it is sighted. In addition, the bearing taker can assist the navigator by reporting other information, such as the set and estimated drift of current past buoys, other vessels which may lie along the intended track, when buoys and landmarks pass abeam, etc.

In most ships only two gyro repeaters are available, and since the navigator usually desires three LOP's to plot his fix, one bearing taker must take bearings on two objects. If it can be determined beforehand that a majority of the aids to navigation to be used will lie either to port or to starboard for the major part of the travel of the ship in pilot waters, the most experienced bearing taker should be assigned to the repeater on that side. In taking bearings of two objects from the same repeater, it is desirable that the two bearings be taken simultaneously insofar as possible. The bearing taker is trained to take the fastest moving bearing first. By this is meant taking the bearing of an object closest to the beam first, as it will be changing bearing most rapidly, and then taking the bearing of the object more nearly ahead or astern. In this manner the effects of the advance of the ship in the time between the two bearings will be minimized.

Echo-sounder operator The echo-sounding equipment is sometimes not on the bridge where the navigator can personally oversee the work of the operator. For this reason, the man assigned as *echo-sounder operator* should be thoroughly trained, and should realize the importance of his duties. As depths are normally used by the navigator only as a safety factor, readings are not actually required to be sent continuously to the bridge. Most ships establish a doctrine directing the operator to take soundings continuously, to record the soundings every minute, to send soundings to the bridge at regular specified intervals and whenever called for, or when a limiting depth is encountered. This depth is a safety factor determined by each navigator for his ship, and will depend upon the draft of the ship and the distance of the sonic transmitter below the water line. For instance, in a destroyer with a draft of 18 feet and with the sounding head located 12 feet below the water line, the navigator may direct the echo-sounder operator to report to the bridge immediately any reading less than 4 fathoms, while the doctrine on a carrier may prescribe a report at 8 fathoms. In addition, most navigators have a standing order to the operator to report immediately any rapid shoaling of the water. These limiting factors must occasionally be changed depending on the depth of water in which the ship expects to steam, for a minimum reading doctrine of 4 fathoms would have little practical significance if the destroyer were steaming inside the 5-fathom curve.

CIC talker The navigator does not provide the talker in CIC in most ships, as he is assigned from the CIC personnel. The talker usually sends up to the bridge only the information requested, in accordance with doctrine established by the navigator and approved by the commanding officer.

Frequency of fixes **1508** No fixed policy on the frequency of taking bearings and obtaining fixes by a navigator can be established. In practice, the frequency will vary with the situation, the navigator, and the wishes of the captain. If the ship is steaming comparatively slowly in coastal waters with no immediate dangers to navigation in the vicinity, a fix every 15 minutes could be sufficient; but if the ship is coming to anchor and exact accuracy is required, fixes should probably be taken every 30 seconds. However, a good rule for normal piloting in restricted waters, and at normal speeds, is to obtain a fix every three minutes. This will allow a navigator sufficient time to extend the DR track ahead for at least 6 minutes, to compute the current effects, and to keep the captain advised accordingly.

An international conference on this subject resulted in a consensus which is reproduced as the table below for general information and guidance.

Area	Distance From Nearest Danger	General Order of Depth of Water	Order of Accuracy	Fix Frequency
Pilot waters	Less than 3 miles	Up to 20 fathoms	±50 yds.	Every minute
Coastal waters	3–50 miles	20–100 fathoms	±$\frac{1}{4}$ mi.	Every 3–10 minutes
Ocean passage	Over 50 miles	Over 100 fathoms	±2–3 mi.	As conditions warrant, and at least 3 times daily

Assistant navigator Whenever possible, it is a practice in many ships to require the assistant navigator to assist in plotting under the supervision of the navigator. This procedure frees the navigator for overall piloting supervision, giving him the opportunity personally to check the identification of new landmarks and aids to navigation as they are sighted, and to instruct the team regarding which objects to plot, and when. The task of a navigator in pilot waters is an exacting one, and is a full-time duty, even with the assistance of a well-trained piloting team.

The team in operation **1509** A sketch of the bridge and related navigational positions on a typical destroyer-type ship is shown in Figure 1509. Personnel who wear sound-powered telephone headsets are shown, as are the telephone circuits. It should be noted in this diagram that the bearing recorder is located next to the navigator at the chart table. Frequently no provision has been made for the navigator to be on the open bridge, and consequently he must operate from inside the pilot house. This is acceptable if there is sufficient visibility, but it is preferable to have his chart desk on the open bridge. The chart table should have a clock mounted over it, or readily visible from it, as a record of time is important in piloting.

Charts In selecting the chart to be used, two conflicting factors must be considered and balanced against each other. It is desirable to use a large-scale chart for the greater degree of detail provided. However, the use of the largest scale chart available may often require one or more changes of charts during the run through restricted waters; this is time consuming and could lead to errors at the time of shifting from

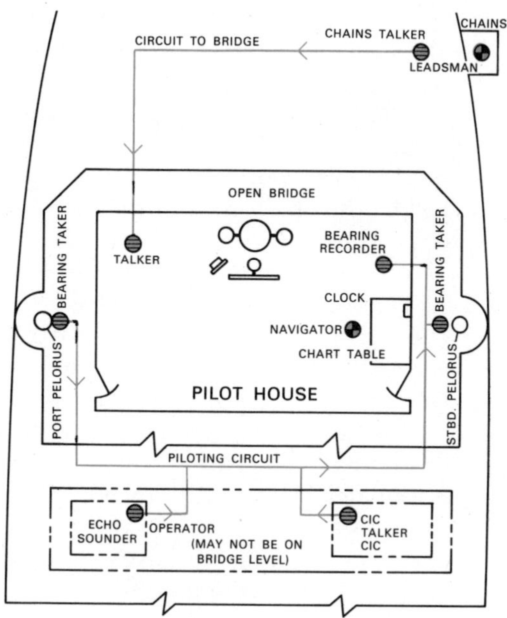

Figure 1509. Navigational stations on a destroyer-type ship.

one chart to the next. It is very helpful if the water area, which is too shallow to permit safe navigation, has been shaded on the chart in advance. This will permit the navigator to determine at a glance if the ship is standing into danger.

It is important that any and all charts used be fully corrected according to the most recently received *Notices to Mariners* and radio broadcast navigational warning messages.

Piloting team routine

Suppose that a destroyer is entering Chesapeake Bay en route Norfolk, and is about to pass into *Inland Waters.* The piloting team has been stationed. The navigator has a man stationed on both the port and the starboard gyro repeaters, the echo sounder is manned, a talker is in CIC, and the bearing recorder is at his station. Communications as shown in Figure 1509 have been established. It is a clear day, and Cape Charles, Cape Henry, and Thimble Shoals Lights are in sight. The bearing book has been set up as shown in Figure 1503 with columns headed by the names of the navigational aids expected to be used. The navigator directs the bearing recorder to sound the buzzer (or to give a "mark" over the circuit) every third minute, being careful to mark exactly when the second hand of the clock reaches the whole minute. The navigator also directs the bearing recorder to tell the port bearing taker to report Cape Henry and Thimble Shoals Lights, and the starboard bearing taker to report Cape Charles Light.

Plotting procedure When he is ready to plot, he directs the bearing recorder to obtain a round of bearings. At about 10 seconds before the minute, the bearing recorder informs the personnel on the circuit to "*standby.*" When the second hand reaches 60, he sounds the buzzer (or says "*mark*" over the circuit). The man on the port repeater who has two bearings to take, will report first. The first bearing, which he took on the *mark,* will be the object nearest the beam, Cape Henry Light. He reports, "Cape Henry bearing 205.5°." The starboard bearing taker has taken a bearing of Cape Charles Light when the *mark* was heard but does not report until the port bearing taker has reported his first reading. The quartermaster on the starboard side now reports "Cape Charles bearing 010.0°." While this report was being made, the port bearing taker has taken a bearing of Thimble Shoals Light, which he now reports: "Thimble Shoals bearing 287.0°." Since Thimble Shoals is nearly dead ahead, its bearing will not have changed appreciably during the time delay between the *mark* and the actual taking of the bearing.

When the bearing recorder gave the *mark,* the time was noted and recorded in the time column of the bearing book. As each of the bearings was reported by the bearing takers, the recorder wrote it down in the appropriate column of the bearing book, *and repeated it back over the circuit for confirmation.* This procedure enabled the navigator to hear it. The navigator commenced plotting as soon as the first bearing was reported, and should have all three bearings plotted in less than 30 seconds. As soon as the navigator has the fix plotted and labeled, he inspects it to see if it is on the intended track. If it is, he plots DR positions ahead from the fix for the next 6 minutes, which will enable him to be reasonably sure of his position should he be unable to obtain a fix for any reason at the next 3-minute mark. If the fix is not along the intended track, the navigator determines the course that should be steered, and recommends the new course to the captain. The navigator plots the DR, using the old course, up to the time of the course change, and then lays down the DR plot for the new course for the remainder of the 6 minutes from this position. In addition, an extended DR to compute the time of arrival at an expected turning point along the track, the identity of the turning point in terms of relative or true bearing, the range from an identifiable object, and the new course recommendation can be given to the captain. When the recorder, who has been watching the clock, sees that the next 3-minute mark is about due, he gives "standby" and "mark" at the proper time, and the procedure continues as before.

Plotting the LOP Previous chapters have covered the proper labeling of the DR plot, various lines of position, and fixes, including placing the time above an LOP and, in some instances, the direction below the line. The purpose of this was to ensure identification and provide a record of the data used to plot each LOP. On board ship, however, using a full piloting team, the time and true bearing of each LOP are recorded in the Bearing Book, as described above; and by using the information recorded therein, all plotting can be reconstructed should it become necessary. To facilitate plotting, labels may be left off LOPs in actual practice aboard naval ships and only the symbols, with times, used for fixes, EPs, and DR positions. If a series of fixes are being taken by two independent means, such as visually and by radar, a circle will be used for fixes from primary (visual) data and a triangle symbol may be used for fixes from secondary (radar) information.

Soundings Suppose that at about this time the echo-sounder operator reports "depth 4 fathoms." He has made this report in compliance with standard doctrine established in this particular ship for reporting a limiting reading of 4 fathoms, and a 6-fathom spot has just been crossed. Since 4 fathoms is the depth of water from the sounding head, the navigator must add to it the distance from the water line to the sounding head before he can compare it with the charted depth. If this distance is 12 feet, then the total depth of water according to the depth finder is 36 feet. The chart at the DR position for the time of the reading showed 34 feet; therefore, the two depths are basically in agreement, for the chart uses a mean low water datum and the height of the tide has been previously calculated to be approximately 2 feet. (For the approach to most harbors it is sufficient to calculate the height of the tide to the nearest foot for the mid-time of the entrance or departure. Where the range of the tide is considerable, and the entrance or departure will take several hours, the height of the tide should be calculated for several points of critical interest for the ETA at each such point.)

The navigator in piloting

1510 The foregoing example does not show all of the preparation which the navigator and his assistants made to achieve smooth results.

Prior to entering Chesapeake Bay, the navigator studied the charts of the area, studied the material in the *Coast Pilot, Fleet Guide, Light List, Tide and Tidal Current Tables,* and marked on the chart those landmarks and aids to navigation which he expected to use. He noted on the chart the physical appearance of each of these aids to navigation in order that he would have the information readily available and be able to use it in recognizing the landmarks as they were sighted. With this information firmly in mind, and with necessary notes on the charts, he assembled the bearing takers and the bearing recorder for a briefing. During this briefing he pointed out to each the location of every landmark expected to be used, its name, its appearance, and the order of expected sighting. In so doing he enabled each member of his team to become familiar, in some degree, with the objects which they would be using. The bearing takers knew in advance where to look and what to look for, and the bearing recorder knew the names of the landmarks he would have to record and transmit over the phones. In cases of entry into unfamiliar pilot waters, there is particular benefit to be gained from preparing and issuing a written brief to each man on the team in order that he can later refer to the printed information rather than trust it to memory. The brief should contain a written description of each expected navigational aid as recorded in the *Light List* and appropriate extracts from the *Coast Pilot* or *Sailing Directions.* Such a brief materially helps in the smooth operation of a piloting team, and is of particular importance when entering a strange port. If the port is a familiar one, such a written brief is usually not necessary.

When on the bridge, the navigator uses the knowledge he has gained in his preparation. As each landmark and aid to navigation is sighted, he personally checks its appearance to be sure it is correctly identified and compares it with the description in the *Light List,* not trusting to memory alone. The bearing takers, having been briefed in advance, can be of considerable help in preliminary identification, but the burden of final identification rests on the navigator. As the navigator plots his fixes, and as the ship proceeds up the channel, the prudent navigator visually checks all landmarks and aids to make sure that his ship is where it appears to be on the chart. The quick appraisal and good judgment of an experienced navigator have kept many ships out of danger, even though objects—particularly buoys—may previously have been incorrectly identified.

The navigator is responsible for the safe navigation of the ship, and if he is in doubt, *for any reason*, as to the ship's position, the only safe thing to do is so advise the captain and recommend slowing or stopping.

Summary **1511** This chapter has considered in detail the actions of each member of the *piloting team* in obtaining and recording the various bits of information that are used by a ship's navigator to direct his vessel through pilot waters safely. The responsibilities and actions of each member of a full team (such as is found on a major ship of the U.S. Navy) were analyzed. A useful guide was presented for the general frequency of taking fixes and their order of accuracy under offshore, coastal, and pilot waters situations. It was recognized that merchant ships and small craft have fewer persons to take bearings, soundings, etc., and to record and plot them. Nevertheless, essentially the same functions must be accomplished and specific duties will undoubtedly be doubled up. The prudent navigator of *any* vessel uses *all* available personnel and *every means* to obtain the information that he needs to direct his ship safely and efficiently.

16 The Practice of Piloting

Introduction **1601** The preceding chapters have discussed in detail the various charts, publications, instruments, procedures, and techniques customarily required for the safe piloting of a ship. The purpose of this chapter is to relate each of these individual treatments to the actual practice of piloting in order that the interrelationship of each may be understood, and the importance of each to intelligent voyage planning and execution may be appreciated. To accomplish this purpose, the initial articles discuss the steps which must be taken by a navigator in planning and executing any voyage in pilot waters, while the latter articles illustrate how these general requirements are applied to a specific piloting situation.

This chapter is written in terms of the plans and actions of a naval vessel. Many of these are applicable in general principles to merchant ships and yachts; others are of a purely naval nature. The non-naval navigator should carefully consider each step and adapt it to his needs if applicable.

Preliminary preparations **1602** As soon as it is known that the ship will get underway for a specified destination, the navigator assembles various data, charts, and publications for study so that he can *plan* the voyage in detail before submitting his plan to the captain for approval. Once underway, the navigator and his assistants will find that their time is well occupied with the routine mechanics and techniques of piloting, and that little or no time is available for completing the planning phase. For this reason, it is essential that all planning be done well in advance of the sailing date. In the following paragraphs, all essentials to the completion of adequate and safe planning are discussed. The order of accomplishing these steps is optional, although an attempt has been made to place the various items in the sequence most frequently encountered in practice.

Determining ETD and ETA **1603** Authority for a naval ship to get underway and proceed to a specified destination will usually be in the form of a message, fleet or type employment schedule, or operation order. This authority should be carefully studied, with dates and times of departure and arrival noted, as well as the route which may also be designated. It is customary for the authority directing the movement to specify only *dates* of departure and arrival, leaving the *times* of departure or arrival to the discretion of the commanding officer. This permits him to take advantage of the most favorable conditions of tide, current, and weather. Movement orders may specify other limiting factors such as time, date, and SOA; or perhaps only the time and date of arrival will be prescribed. Where exact ETA and ETD are not given, the navigator must complete his study of the various charts and publications as outlined below before these times may be accurately determined.

Determining chart requirements

Once the destination and other information prescribed in the movement order are known, the navigator must determine the charts available for use during the voyage. These are located by reference to the appropriate catalog of charts.

Most charts for United States waters are listed in the four catalogs of the National Ocean Survey. Charts of foreign waters, bottom contour charts, and charts restricted to naval usage are listed in the various sections of Defense Mapping Agency Hydrographic Center Publication 1-N. New editions of nautical chart catalogs are published when accumulated changes warrant such action; only the current edition of any catalog should be used. See also Article 602.

Using the appropriate catalogs, the navigator examines the *index diagrams* covering the area of interest. Each such diagram shows by colored outlines the area covered by each chart, with its corresponding number. With the chart numbers determined, he can consult a tabular listing for additional information such as chart name, scale, edition and date, and price.

From this information, the navigator compiles a list of the numbers of all available charts covering any part of the proposed route. These charts are then taken from the respective portfolios and are checked against Pub. No. 1-N-L to ensure that the latest edition is on board. (Pub. No. 1-N-L is periodically reprinted in new editions and is kept corrected between editions from information printed in *Notices to Mariners.*) Since most naval vessels are on the automatic distribution list maintained by DMAHC, it is usual for the charts on board to be the latest edition.

If the latest edition is not on board, immediate steps should be taken to obtain it before departure. Charts must be ordered by naval units using the quite complex procedures of the DMA Automated Distribution Management System (DADMS) as described in Pub. No. 1-N-L, which also lists the distribution points serving various geographical areas. Charts of the National Ocean Survey may be obtained through DADMS except for a few charts which must be obtained directly from NOS sources. Civilian users will normally obtain DMAHC charts from local sales agents, but can use the DADMS system with simplified procedures as set forth in Pub. No. 1-N-L; NOS charts should be purchased from local sales agents or directly from the NOS Distribution Division, Riverdale, MD 20840.

Publications required The navigator should have available all pertinent *Light Lists, Lists of Lights, Coast Pilots, Sailing Directions,* and other navigational publications for the area to be traversed. On board naval ships, the current allowances established for the type of ship and the fleet to which it is assigned will normally be adequate.

DMAHC Pub. No. 1-N-P sets forth these allowances. The various publications are described in detail in Chapter 6. After all necessary charts and publications have been assembled, they must be checked to ensure that each is the latest edition, and that the latest pertinent corrections have been entered.

Chart corrections. The Chart/Publication Correction Record card, DMAHC Pub. No. 8660/9, for each chart to be used is consulted to determine corrections which have been noted on the card, but which have not been entered on the chart. Each of these listed but unmade corrections must be completed before the chart can be used with safety. Charts may be corrected from either the on-board file of *Notices to Mariners* or a DMAHC publication, *Summary of Corrections,* a consolidated reprint of all still-valid changes published in *Notices to Mariners;* see Article 610. This quarterly *Summary* is more convenient to use for correcting charts, *Coast Pilots,* and *Sailing Directions,* but the file of *Notices* must still be used to update *Light Lists, Lists of Lights, Radio Aids to Navigation,* and other navigational publications. The *Summary* does not include chart corrections for the Great Lakes or inland bodies and routes that are not normally used by ocean-going vessels.

Corrections to publications. Each publication to be used must be checked to ensure that the latest corrections are available or have been entered. *Coast Pilots, Light Lists, Lists of Lights,* and some other publications are issued in annual editions (in a few cases, at somewhat longer intervals where the number of changes does not warrant annual editions). Between editions, changes are published in *Notices to Mariners.* In most instances, the change is published as an item that can be cut and pasted directly into the basic publication; few pen changes are required except for deletions. Each correction item published in *Notices to Mariners* carries information as to the last prior correction for that chart or publication published so that none will be inadvertently overlooked. Many publications contain a page where a record can be noted of the entry of each correction.

Tides and limiting conditions It is usually desirable to get underway or enter port at high water stand, and as near as possible to the time of slack water, although they seldom coincide. A large ship entering a harbor with comparatively shallow water will be primarily concerned with the time of high water, while a smaller ship entering a harbor with deep water but variable current, will be more interested in times when the current is slack.

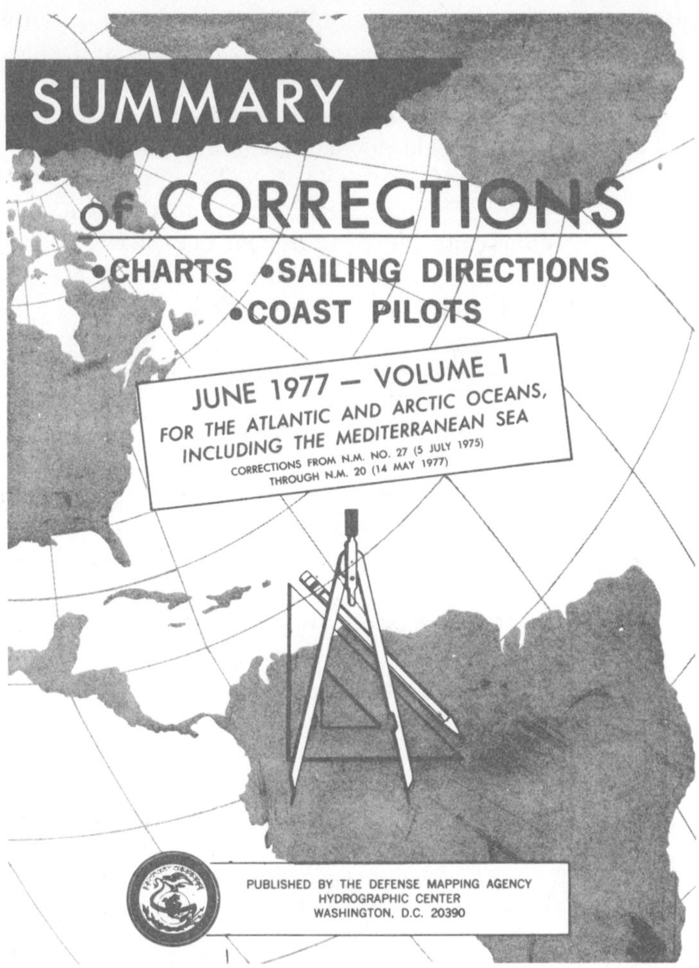

Figure 1603. *Summary of Corrections* (cover).

Draft Occasionally the draft of the ship will be greater than the charted depth (low water) of the harbor. This requires use of Table 3 in the *Tide Tables* to determine how long before and after high water the depth of the water will be sufficient to permit safe passage of the ship. Extreme care must be used in such cases, as the tide tables are only predictions, and there can be considerable difference between the predicted and the actual conditions.

Sortie plans Many ports with large naval concentrations place sortie plans in effect on certain days of the week, specifying times and order for ships to get underway. This plan is normally arranged so that ships nearer the harbor entrance get underway first. The SOPA (Senior Officer Present Afloat) instructions should be consulted for such standing procedures.

Determining distance and SOA Since the navigator normally recommends the times of departure and arrival and the SOA to the commanding officer, it is first essential that he determine the total distance to be steamed. This distance may be obtained by measurement from the charts to be used, or, in many cases, by reference to available publications. DMAHC Pub. No. 151, *Table of Distances Between Ports,* covering foreign ports throughout the world, or *Distance Between U. S. Ports,* published by the National Ocean Survey, should be consulted. Distances between many other combinations of ports will also be found in the pertinent *Coast Pilots* and *Sailing Directions.* If it is intended to travel the regular route between ports, the distance given in these publications should be used, as it is more accurate than can normally be determined by chart measurement.

Once favorable hours of departure and arrival have been decided upon, the required speed of advance (SOA) can be determined. Care must be taken not to exceed the maximum steaming speeds prescribed by fleet or type commanders in current directives. After the SOA has been computed, the speed to be ordered can be determined, taking into account the ship's displacement, condition of bottom, and trim; currents expected to be encountered; and other applicable factors.

Planning the passage **1604** After completing the preliminary preparations described above, the navigator is now ready to plan the voyage. Only by commencing the planning phase as far in advance as possible will the navigator have sufficient time to study the various publications, to give the proposed track careful consideration, and to obtain any needed charts and/or publications not presently on board.

Small-scale (large-area) charts Most captains and navigators prefer an overall plot of the entire voyage on one chart. This permits rapid determination of distance made good and distance to go at any desired time during the voyage, and presents clearly the relationship between the route selected and the coastline or adjacent land masses. Unless the voyage is very short, it is not possible to plot the entire track on one chart that is also suitable for piloting. For this reason, a small-scale (large-area) chart is initially used.

When the route has been established, the navigator must select those charts he will use for piloting. Many areas, such as the east coast of the United States, have charts available to four different scales. The overall plot referred to in the paragraph above will fit onto either one of the "sailing chart" series, such as Chart 13003, Cape Sable to Cape Hatteras at a scale of 1:1,200,000, or if not too great an area is required, one of the "general chart" series, such as Chart 12200, Cape May to Cape Hatteras at a scale of 1:416,944. Only occasionally will it be necessary to use a chart from both of these series.

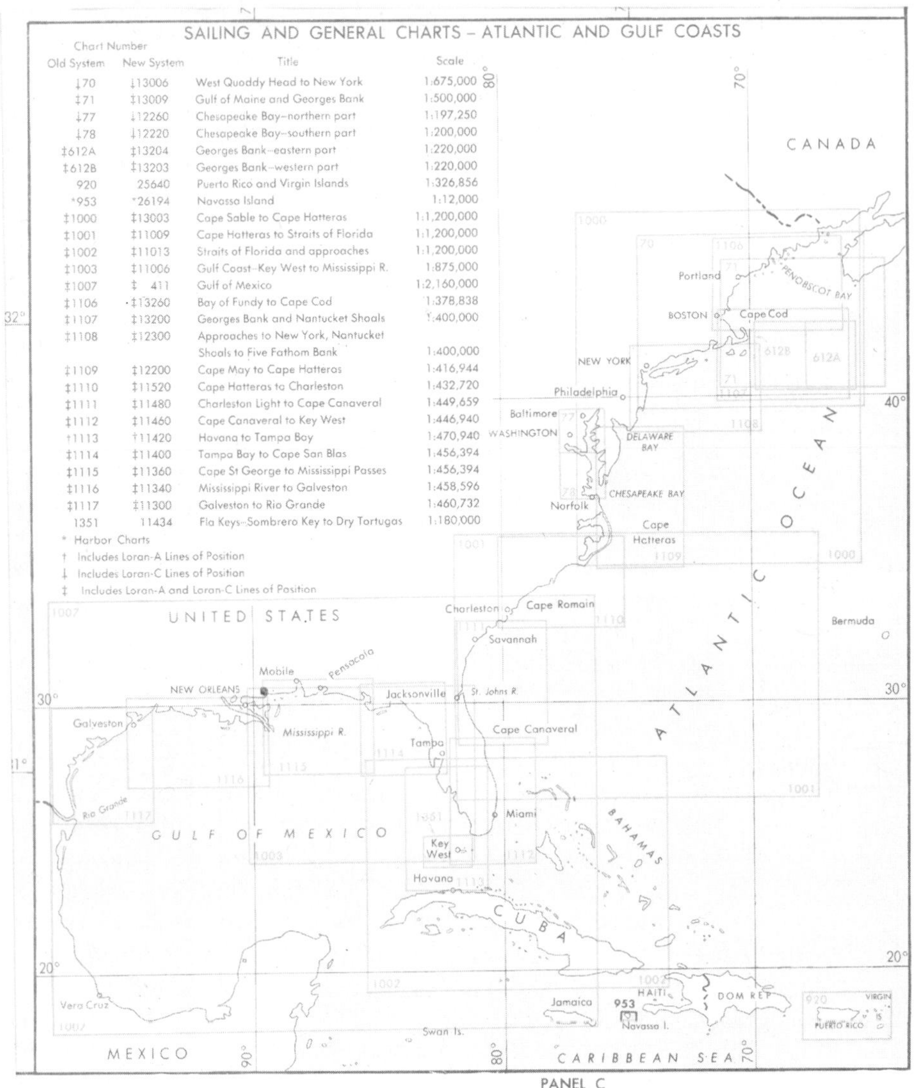

SAILING AND GENERAL CHARTS – ATLANTIC AND GULF COASTS

Chart Number Old System	New System	Title	Scale
↓70	↓13006	West Quoddy Head to New York	1:675,000
‡71	‡13009	Gulf of Maine and Georges Bank	1:500,000
↓77	↓12260	Chesapeake Bay–northern part	1:197,250
↓78	↓12220	Chesapeake Bay–southern part	1:200,000
‡612A	‡13204	Georges Bank–eastern part	1:220,000
‡612B	‡13203	Georges Bank–western part	1:220,000
920	25640	Puerto Rico and Virgin Islands	1:326,856
*953	*26194	Navassa Island	1:12,000
‡1000	‡13003	Cape Sable to Cape Hatteras	1:1,200,000
‡1001	‡11009	Cape Hatteras to Straits of Florida	1:1,200,000
‡1002	‡11013	Straits of Florida and approaches	1:1,200,000
‡1003	‡11006	Gulf Coast–Key West to Mississippi R.	1:875,000
‡1007	‡ 411	Gulf of Mexico	1:2,160,000
‡1106	·‡13260	Bay of Fundy to Cape Cod	1:378,838
‡1107	‡13200	Georges Bank and Nantucket Shoals	1:400,000
‡1108	‡12300	Approaches to New York, Nantucket Shoals to Five Fathom Bank	1:400,000
‡1109	‡12200	Cape May to Cape Hatteras	1:416,944
‡1110	‡11520	Cape Hatteras to Charleston	1:432,720
‡1111	‡11480	Charleston Light to Cape Canaveral	1:449,659
‡1112	‡11460	Cape Canaveral to Key West	1:446,940
†1113	†11420	Havana to Tampa Bay	1:470,940
‡1114	‡11400	Tampa Bay to Cape San Blas	1:456,394
‡1115	‡11360	Cape St George to Mississippi Passes	1:456,394
‡1116	‡11340	Mississippi River to Galveston	1:458,596
‡1117	‡11300	Galveston to Rio Grande	1:460,732
1351	11434	Fla Keys–Sombrero Key to Dry Tortugas	1:180,000

* Harbor Charts
† Includes Loran-A Lines of Position
↓ Includes Loran-C Lines of Position
‡ Includes Loran-A and Loran-C Lines of Position

Figure 1604. Extract from National Ocean Survey Chart Catalog No. 1.

Large-scale (small-area) charts

The most commonly used scale for coastal piloting is 1:80,000; such charts include those of the former "1200" series issued by NOS for the U.S. Atlantic and Gulf coasts. More detailed charts, at scales of 1:40,000 and larger, are desirable for harbor piloting, but are not suitable for offshore waters or approaches.

In selecting a chart to be used for a voyage in pilot waters, consideration should be given to the scale used, ascertaining that it includes all of the landmarks and aids to navigation desired or required in any one area. If the scale is too small, the chart coverage may exclude features best suited for visual observation and fixes.

Once the charts to be used are selected, the navigator should ensure that he is familiar with the details shown on each. The following should be particularly noted:

Whether depths are indicated in feet or fathoms.

Whether heights are indicated in feet or meters.

The distance indicated by the smallest division of the latitude scale.

The distance indicated by the alternately shaded divisions of the latitude scale.

The distance between adjacent printed meridians and parallels.

The significance of the length of the ship and its turning characteristics in relation to the scale of the chart.

The geographical limits covered by each chart.

Variation of the magnetic compass, correction to variation since printing of the chart due to annual change, and the differences in variation at different points along the track.

The patterns of shoal and deep water, and depths, as indicated by the fathom lines.

Abnormal patterns of bottom contour lines which may be useful for determining positions by echo sounder.

Land contours, marshes, bluffs, prominent mountain peaks, and landmarks which may be useful for radar piloting or identification, or which may affect radar PPI interpretation.

Intended track Having selected his charts, the navigator now plots the route to be followed on both the large- and the small-scale charts. The route is normally plotted first on the small-scale (large-area) chart or charts, and labeled as to track, speed, and distance between points. This permits the navigator to check visually the safety of the track initially laid down, and to make any adjustments apparent at this time.

DR positions for selected times are then plotted along the track, using the speed previously determined. The frequency with which these DR positions are plotted on the large-area chart will depend upon the judgment of the navigator, the proximity of land masses, and the course desired to be made good. When making an ocean passage, DR positions every twelve hours are normally sufficient; in coastal piloting, a DR position every hour is common practice.

At this time, any special information of interest in the broad planning of the voyage should be noted on the chart. These items may include limits of operational control areas, changes in communications responsibility, limits of special danger or restricted areas, etc. This information should be noted on the chart in the vicinity of the position at which the event is expected to occur.

The navigator should next translate the general voyage information portrayed on the small-scale chart into detailed graphic representations on the large-scale charts covering the same areas. At this time, careful reference should be made to the instructions and information given in the *Coast Pilots* and *Sailing Directions* for the areas of each chart. If specific routes are recommended or overprinted on the charts, these should be used to the greatest extent possible, for they represent known safe tracks which have been tested over many years. In deciding on details of the final track, the careful navigator will not only avoid all obvious dangers, but will also allow himself as much sea room as possible in the areas of these dangers.

Turning points, or points at which the course will be changed, are of particular interest to navigators and should always be marked on the chart. In operational movements of ships in company, it is frequently desirable to assign a name or number designation to these points for ease of reference. The ETA at each turning point should be plainly marked on the charts.

Danger areas, danger bearings, and limits of safe water

Frequently the intended track may of necessity place the ship in close proximity to dangers to navigation during the voyage. In addition to such natural dangers as rocks, shoals, and bars, various governmental agencies have reserved certain designated areas for hazardous operations. Gunnery practice and testing ranges, ammunition disposal areas, special anchorages, and spoil grounds are a few examples. Where particularly confined waters or heavy shipping concentrations prevail, special rules may be in effect to limit maximum speed and otherwise restrict vessel movement. At the entrance to many ports, there have been established Traffic Separation Schemes (TSS) consisting of inbound and outbound lines with a separation zone between them, special precautionary zones, and special communications arrangements. Each of these special areas, whether natural or man-made, constitutes an additional hazard for the mariner. Each chart should be carefully inspected to determine these dangers, with the *Coast Pilot, Sailing Directions,* and *Notices to Mariners* being consulted for detailed information concerning them, and appropriate annotations made on each chart in question. In addition, it is a good practice to outline all danger areas and the limits of water considered safe for the draft of the ship, using a colored pencil. Do not use a red pencil if the chart will be used under a red light on the bridge at night, as the red marking will not be visible. For this reason, "nautical purple" (magenta) is frequently used instead.

Where appropriate, danger bearings should be located, plotted, and the information noted on the chart.

Aids to navigation

Special attention should be given to the aids to navigation expected to be sighted during the voyage. A list in which has been recorded a complete description of the structures and their light characteristics, the expected times of sighting, and the approximate bearings at sighting is of particular use to the navigator.

Lights

Daytime identification. Under normal conditions of visibility, a primary seacoast light (a "lighthouse") can be seen in the daytime when within range and can be identified by its color and structural appearance. A complete description of the distinctive features of each is given in the appropriate *Light List,* and since this information seldom appears on the chart, notation should be made thereon. Photographs or drawings of many lights appear in the *Sailing Directions,* while many foreign charts include a sketch of the light near its symbol.

Nighttime identification. Harbor entrances, bays and rivers, coastal danger areas, and other hazards are normally well marked with lighted aids to navigation that the navigator should personally and positively identify on each initial sighting. Identification can be confirmed by using a stopwatch to time a light through a full cycle of its characteristics. Accurate identification of buoys is particularly important and should not be a matter of delegation, chance, or guesswork. The full characteristics of lighted buoys may not be printed on a chart, particularly small-scale charts and, even when using large-scale charts, information such as the length of each flash and eclipse of major aids does not normally appear. Only by use of the *Light List,* comparing the recorded information with those characteristics actually observed, can the navigator be absolutely certain of the identification of a lighted aid to navigation. Supplementary information appearing *only* in the *Light List* should be the subject of a special entry in a box adjacent to the charted symbol.

Visibility of lights. While preparing for the voyage, the computed visibility of all lights expected to be sighted en route is plotted and labeled on the charts. In United States waters, the *nominal range* is the extreme distance in nautical miles at which a light may be seen in clear weather (as defined in the International Visibility Code) without regard to the elevation of the light, observer's height of eye, or the curvature of the earth; see Article 518. In computing the geographic range at which the light might be sighted in clear weather, the navigator must allow for the elevation of the light and the height of his, and/or the lookout's eye; see Article 520.

Buoys While the color and shape of buoys that are a part of the lateral system used in United States waters are evident from the printed chart information, it is not always possible to predict the characteristics of a special purpose buoy by chart inspection alone. In like manner it is not possible to apply the rules pertaining to United States buoyage to the various buoyage systems in use in foreign countries, for each system is dissimilar except by coincidence. In such cases careful reference to the *Lists of Lights* and *Sailing Directions* is necessary to avoid misinterpretation.

Tide and current data Times and heights of the tides, and times and strengths of the currents, for the points of departure and arrival are computed for the respective dates. This information should be carefully studied before reaching a decision as to the time of departure and arrival. Some ports may have shoals or bars that can be crossed only near the time of high water, while others may have bridges of such vertical clearance that high-masted ships may be required to transit the channel at low water. Ships arriving at or leaving their berths will be assisted by a favorable current, while an unfavorable current may make the maneuver very difficult, especially for a single-screw ship.

When the decision as to the times of arrival and departure has been made, the navigator should consult the applicable National Ocean Survey tidal current chart, if available, for the ports or channels in question, and for the velocity and direction of the current at selected reference points along the track noted on the chart. Similarly, the current diagrams contained in the *Tidal Current Tables* should be consulted to determine the average current expected en route. This information, combined with the selected speed of advance, can be used to determine ordered speed at selected stages of the voyage. Occasionally these diagrams are used to plan the time of departure in order that advantage may be taken of a favorable channel current.

For ocean passages, the estimates of predicted currents contained in the monthly *Pilot Chart* and in the various current atlases should also be taken into consideration. These estimates have evolved after years of current observations, and warrant careful attention by the navigator.

Port information Information concerning the anchorage or berthing space assigned to the ship may not be received until the ship has reported its ETA to the port authority. If the destination is a port frequently used by naval vessels, an anchorage chart is usually available showing the exact location of all berths, the radius of each, and the range and bearing of its center from a prominent point or light. Additional information concerning the port such as pier space, tugs, pilots, communications, harbor facilities and other pertinent items of interest is contained in the appropriate *Coast Pilot* (U.S. waters), or *Sailing Directions* (foreign waters), and *Fleet Guide* (for U.S. Naval vessels only) which should be carefully read prior to arrival. In addition, the file of *NavArea Warnings, Hydrolant* or *Hydropac* messages, and *Local Notices to Mariners* (U.S. waters only) issued by the Coast Guard District concerned should be checked to ascertain if any recent changes in aids to navigation have been made, or if any special warnings concerning dangers to navigation have been issued for the area of interest.

Upon arrival, the latest copies of the *Daily Memorandum* and any other pertinent information available should be obtained from the DMAHC Branch Office if there is one at that port.

Every week, the office of the Port Director distributes a list of the exercises to be conducted in the designated operating and training area. This list should be carefully checked to make sure that the ship, upon departure, does not interfere with scheduled exercises in the area.

Berthing assistance The requirements for pilot and tug assistance vary from port to port, and the *Coast Pilot* (or *Sailing Directions*) and *Fleet Guide* must be consulted to determine the procedures in effect at each. Some ports with an elaborate pilot association require separate pilots for the approach to the harbor, the harbor itself, and the final berthing, whereas other ports may have no regular pilots engaged. In such cases, local fishermen, familiar with local conditions, can be of invaluable assistance to a ship making its first passage in strange waters.

Depending upon weather and other considerations, a large ship may require the assistance of two or more tugs, and smaller ships one, when berthing or undocking, and arrangements must be made in such cases beforehand.

Preparing to get underway **1605** The preceding articles have dealt with the preparations made in the planning stages by the navigator in advance of the day prescribed for getting underway. It is assumed that the navigator has conferred with the captain and that the latter has approved of the details of the plan proposed by the navigator, or that any changes directed by him have been incorporated into the final plan. There remain, however, certain other preparatory steps to be taken which have properly been postponed until the overall plan has been decided upon; the systematic accomplishment of these is no less important to the execution of a safe passage than was careful voyage planning.

Gyrocompass A typical ship's organization book prescribes that the gyrocompass be started at least four hours before getting underway in order that the gyro may settle on the meridian. Many experienced navigators prefer to start the gyrocompass well in advance of this minimum. This provides sufficient time to detect and correct any minor mechanical or electrical malfunctioning before getting underway.

Degaussing equipment Prior to getting underway, the proper settings for a naval ship's degaussing equipment should be determined by referring to the special charts prepared for that purpose, and the engineering department informed of the coil readings to be preset before departure. This equipment is always used in wartime and at any other time when it is known that influence mines may be encountered in a specified area. At the direction of the navigator, the degaussing equipment is energized before leaving protected waters and periodic adjustments are made thereafter to the coil settings to maintain protection at a maximum.

Piloting team Prior to entering or leaving port, the navigator should assemble his piloting team for a briefing. (See Article 1510.) While the bearing takers and the bearing recorder will be most vitally concerned with the briefing, all other members of the piloting team and all members of the navigation department should also attend. During the briefing the navigator should point out all aids to navigation expected to be used, their name, appearance, and about where and when they will be sighted. All natural and man-made ranges are located in order that a check on the gyrocompass may be made whenever one is crossed. Any special information concerning soundings should be given to the echo-sounder operator at this time. This is also an excellent opportunity to brief the CIC officer on the plans for entering or leaving port.

It is advantageous that key members of the team be given the material covered in the briefing in written form in order that the detailed plan, the characteristics, and appearances of lights and other important features to be encountered not be trusted entirely to memory.

Equipment checking The organization book of a ship, as well as the navigator's sea detail bill, prescribe certain readiness tests of various items of ship's equipment in accordance with a pre-underway time schedule. Again, forehanded testing will permit time to repair any casualties uncovered during this phase. The master gyro is first checked for error, after which the gyro repeaters on the bridge are checked against the master gyro. The steering engine and related electric and hydraulic transmission systems are tested as are the engine order telegraph, the depth finder, the bridge radio, the navigation and signal searchlights, and the navigational lighting circuits, and appropriate check-off notations made in the list maintained to record such test results. After the special sea detail has been set and all stations are manned, this equipment should be re-checked and all remaining items on the check-off list attended to, such as external and internal communication circuits, the bridge PPI, and the whistle and siren. In addition, the navigator should personally ascertain that all necessary charts, publications, and plotting instruments are available at his chart desk and ready for use.

Gyro error With the piloting team on station, a round of bearings is taken and plotted on the chart, or a gyro observation of a range is obtained and the amount and direction of gyro error, if any is present, is determined. When known, CIC should be notified of the results and an appropriate entry made in the bearing book. When the gyro error steadies down and remains constant, the navigator may offset the parallel motion dial of his drafting machine used for plotting by the amount of this error. This procedure permits plotting the reported bearings as they are received from the bearing takers without the necessity of applying gyro error before plotting each line of position.

Final preparation The navigator should personally check to see that his piloting team is on station and in all respects ready to function. A well-organized and efficient team requires a minimum of supervision, but the navigator should ensure that the more experienced bearing taker is on that side of the ship which will pass the larger number of aids to navigation, or who will have to take two bearings for each fix. Any final instructions pertaining to frequency of fixes, depth readings, draft, minor changes in plan, or bearing order should be announced at this time. The draft report should be made to the conning officer and the officer of the deck, and entered in the ship's log. To conclude all of the multitudinous preparations made by the navigator since the receipt of the original movement order, the navigator reports his department "ready for sea" to the executive officer, signifying that every phase of navigational planning and final checking under his cognizance has been accomplished to the best of his knowledge and ability.

So far the navigator has been primarily concerned with the science of navigation in extracting information from a number of publications which will be of great value to him once the ship is underway. The manner in which the navigator employs the art of navigation—the practical use of the information made available to him from whatever source—will be the subject of the remainder of the chapter.

A typical passage

1606 The USS *Severn*, moored starboard side to Pier 4, U.S. Naval Shipyard, Philadelphia, Pennsylvania, had completed its overhaul and was awaiting orders to proceed to Norfolk, Virginia. On the afternoon of 7 August, the following message was received:

R 071900Z BT
FROM: COMDESRON
TO: USS SEVERN 1X99 BT
UNCLAS 11N03100//
WHEN RFS DEPART PHILANSY FOR NOB NORVA
DIRECT X SOA15 X MOOR PIER 4 PRIOR 090800A BT

Preliminary planning

The navigator noted that both the time of arrival and speed of advance had been specified. Estimating that the trip will take about 16 hours, the ship should depart Philadelphia during the afternoon of 8 August in order to arrive on schedule. This is the navigator's initial estimate of the time of departure, which will be corrected after the exact length of the trip and current data have been determined.

Since both Philadelphia and Norfolk are deep-water ports, there are no restrictions placed on the times of departure or arrival by the state of the tide. As the time of arrival at Norfolk is specified, only the time of departure can be varied to allow for conditions en route. On consulting the captain, the navigator learned that he desired to take departure from Delaware Lighted Horn Buoy "D" (at the outer end of the Delaware to Cape Henlopen Traffic Lane) for Lighted Whistle Buoy "2JS" and hence direct to North Chesapeake Entrance Lighted Whistle Buoy "NCA" (at the start of an inbound traffic lane). The passage is planned accordingly.

SOA

By reference to the table in *Coast Pilot 3* entitled "Atlantic Ocean Distances for Deep-Draft Vessels—Montreal, Canada to Panama Canal Zone," the distance from Philadelphia to Norfolk was found to be 269 miles. As the speed of advance was specified as 15 knots, the navigator decided to allow about 19 hours for the trip. This is more than the time computed using distance and SOA, but makes allowance for time expected to be lost in the transit of the Delaware River due to speed regulations and heavy traffic.

ETD The time of departure from Philadelphia is now determined by subtracting 19 hours from the ETA, 0800, on 9 August.

Time of arrival Norfolk	9 August	0800 (Plus 4)
Length of trip		19 hours
Time of departure Phila.	8 August	1300 (Plus 4)

Both Philadelphia and Norfolk are keeping Daylight Saving Time (+4 or Q). If Norfolk were keeping Standard Time (+5), departure from Philadelphia could have been delayed by one hour. In such planning the navigator must always allow for any difference in the time kept at the port of departure and at the port of arrival.

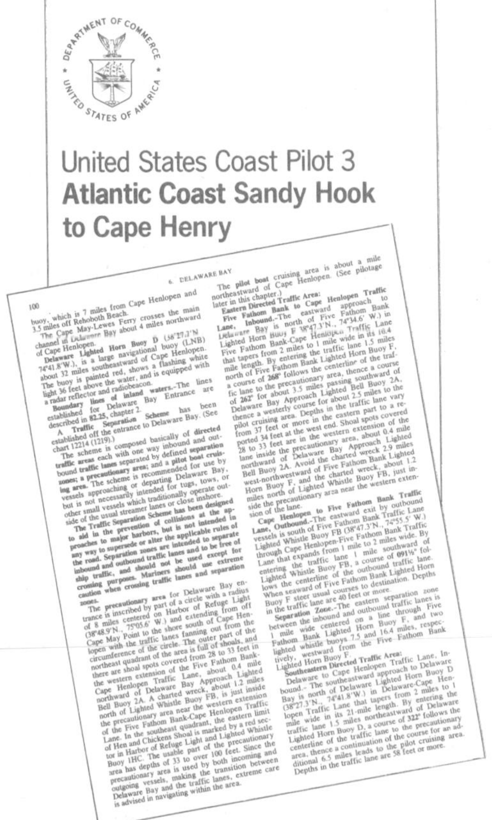

DEPARTMENT OF COMMERCE • UNITED STATES OF AMERICA •

United States Coast Pilot 3
Atlantic Coast Sandy Hook to Cape Henry

100 — 6. DELAWARE BAY

buoy, which is 7 miles from Cape Henlopen and 3.5 miles off Rehoboth Beach.

The Cape May-Lewes Ferry crosses the main channel in Delaware Bay about 4 miles northward of Cape Henlopen.

Delaware Lighted Horn Buoy D (38°27.3'N 74°41.8'W.), is a large navigational buoy (LNB) about 32 miles southeastward of Cape Henlopen. The buoy is painted red, shows a flashing white light 36 feet above the water, and is equipped with a radar reflector and radiobeacon.

Boundary lines of inland waters.-The lines established for Delaware Bay Entrance are described in **82.25**, chapter 2.

A **Traffic Separation Scheme** has been established off the entrance to Delaware Bay. (See chart 12214 (1219).)

The scheme is composed basically of **directed traffic areas** each with one way inbound and outbound **traffic lanes** separated by defined **separation zones; a precautionary area**; and a **pilot boat cruising area.** The scheme is recommended for use by vessels approaching or departing Delaware Bay, but is not necessarily intended for tugs, tows, or other small vessels which traditionally operate outside of the usual streamer lanes or close inshore.

The Traffic Separation Scheme has been designed to aid in the prevention of collisions at the approaches to major harbors, but is not intended in any way to supersede or alter the applicable rules of the road. Separation zones are intended to separate inbound and outbound traffic lanes and to be free of ship traffic, and should not be used except for crossing purposes. Mariners should use extreme caution when crossing traffic lanes and separation zones.

The **precautionary area** for Delaware Bay entrance is inscribed by part of a circle with a radius of 8 miles centered on Harbor of Refuge Light (38°48.9'N., 75°05.6' W.) and extending from off Cape May Point to the shore south of Cape Henlopen with the traffic lanes fanning out from the circumference of the circle. The outer part of the northeast quadrant of the area is full of shoals, and there are shoal spots covered from 28 to 33 feet in the western extension of the Five Fathom Bank-Cape Henlopen Traffic Lane, about 0.4 mile northward of Delaware Bay Approach Lighted Bell Buoy 2A. A charted wreck, about 1.2 miles north of Lighted Whistle Buoy FB, is just inside the precautionary area near the western extension of the Five Fathom Bank-Cape Henlopen Traffic Lane. In the southeast quadrant, the eastern limit of Hen and Chickens Shoal is marked by a red sector in Harbor of Refuge Light and Lighted Whistle Buoy 1HC. The usable part of the precautionary area has depths of 33 to over 100 feet. Since the precautionary area is used by both incoming and outgoing vessels, making the transition between Delaware Bay and the traffic lanes, extreme care is advised in navigating within the area.

The **pilot boat** cruising area is about a mile northeastward of Cape Henlopen. (See pilotage later in this chapter.)

Eastern Directed Traffic Area:

Five Fathom Bank to Cape Henlopen Traffic Lane, Inbound.-The eastward approach to Delaware Bay is north of Five Fathom Bank Lighted Horn Buoy F 38°47.3'N., 74°34.6' W.) in Five Fathom Bank-Cape Henlopen Traffic Lane that tapers from 2 miles to 1 mile wide in its 10.4 mile length. By entering the traffic lane 1.5 miles north of Five Fathom Bank Lighted Horn Buoy F, a course of **268°** follows the centerline of the traffic lane to the precautionary area, thence a course of **262°** for about 3.5 miles passing southward of Delaware Bay Approach Lighted Bell Buoy 2A, thence a westerly course for about 2.5 miles to the pilot cruising area. Depths in the traffic lane vary from 37 feet or more in the eastern part to a reported 34 feet at the west end. Shoal spots covered 28 to 33 feet are in the western extension of the lane inside the precautionary area, about 0.4 mile northward of Delaware Bay Approach Lighted Bell Buoy 2A. Avoid the charted wreck 2.9 miles west-northwestward of Five Fathom Bank Lighted Horn Buoy F, and the charted wreck, about 1.2 miles north of Lighted Whistle Buoy FB, just inside the precautionary area near the western extension of the lane.

Cape Henlopen to Five Fathom Bank Traffic Lane, Outbound.-The eastward exit by outbound vessels is south of Five Fathom Bank Traffic Lane Lighted Whistle Buoy FB (38°47.3'N., 74°55.5' W.) through Cape Henlopen-Five Fathom Bank Traffic Lane that expands from 1 mile to 2 miles wide. By entering the traffic lane 1 mile southward of Lighted Whistle Buoy FB, a course of **091½°** follows the centerline of the outbound traffic lane. When seaward of Five Fathom Bank Lighted Horn Buoy F steer usual courses to destination. Depths in the traffic lane are 40 feet or more.

Separation Zone.-The eastern separation zone between the inbound and outbound traffic lanes is 1 mile wide centered on a line through Five Fathom Bank Lighted Horn Buoy F, and two lighted whistle buoys 7.5 and 16.4 miles, respectively, westward from the Five Fathom Bank Lighted Horn Buoy F.

Southeastern Directed Traffic Area:

Delaware to Cape Henlopen Traffic Lane, Inbound.- The southeastward approach to Delaware Bay is north of Delaware Lighted Horn Buoy D (38°27.3'N., 74°41.8'W.) in Delaware-Cape Henlopen Traffic Lane that tapers from 2 miles to 1 mile wide in its 21-mile length. By entering the traffic lane 1.5 miles northeastward of Delaware Lighted Horn Buoy D, a course of **322°** follows the centerline of the traffic lane to the precautionary area, thence a continuation of the course for an additional 6.5 miles leads to the pilot cruising area. Depths in the traffic lane are 58 feet or more.

Figure 1606. U.S. *Coast Pilot 3* (cover and typical page).

Coast Pilot The section of *Coast Pilot 3* covering Delaware Bay and River below the starting point was carefully studied to obtain all pertinent information relating to the waters to be used. The navigator made particular note of the following:

Channels: Federal project depth is 40 feet from the sea through the main channel in Delaware Bay and River to the Philadelphia Naval Shipyard.

Speed: The Corps of Engineers has requested that vessels' speeds be limited when passing wharves and piers so as to avoid damage by suction or wave wash to property or persons; no specific maximum speed was prescribed.

Obstructions: At Mile 71, the Commodore John Barry Bridge has a clearance of 181 feet for a width of 1600 feet over the main channel and 190 feet at the center. At Mile 60, the Delaware Memorial Bridge has twin spans with a clearance of 188 feet for the middle 800 feet.

Fogs: Most frequent along this part of the Atlantic coast during months of December, January, and February, but may be encountered at any time of the year.

Rules of the Road: Inland Pilot Rules shall be followed inside of a line from Cape May Light to Harbor of Refuge Light; thence to the northernmost extremity of Cape Henlopen.

Traffic Separation Scheme: A TSS has been established off the entrance to Delaware Bay. The ship will be using the Southeastern Directed Traffic Area, Delaware to Cape Henlopen Traffic Lane, outbound. This lane is described in detail, together with the Separation Zone between it and the corresponding inbound lane. There is a Precautionary Area inscribed in part by a circle with a radius of 8 miles centered on the Harbor of Refuge Light and extending from off Cape May Point to the shore south of Cape Henlopen; the traffic lanes start at the circumference of this circle.

Local magnetic disturbance: Differences of as much as 2° to 5° from normal variation have been observed along the main channel from Artificial Island, Mile 44, to Marcus Hook, Mile 69.

A wealth of other information is available in this section of the *Coast Pilot,* but only that of direct concern in plotting the track down the bay has been noted above. In a similar manner, applicable portions of *Coast Pilot 3* were studied regarding the coastal passage and the entrance into Hampton Roads.

Chart preparation **1607** As this voyage will be entirely in U.S. coastal waters, the navigator consulted NOS *Nautical Chart Catalog 1* to obtain the numbers of charts to be used. These are shown as outlines on the small-scale charts. Figure 1607 shows the applicable portion for the overall passage from Philadelphia to Norfolk. Chart 12200 covers the offshore run at a scale of 1:416,944. Larger scale, more detailed charts that will be used for the passage are:

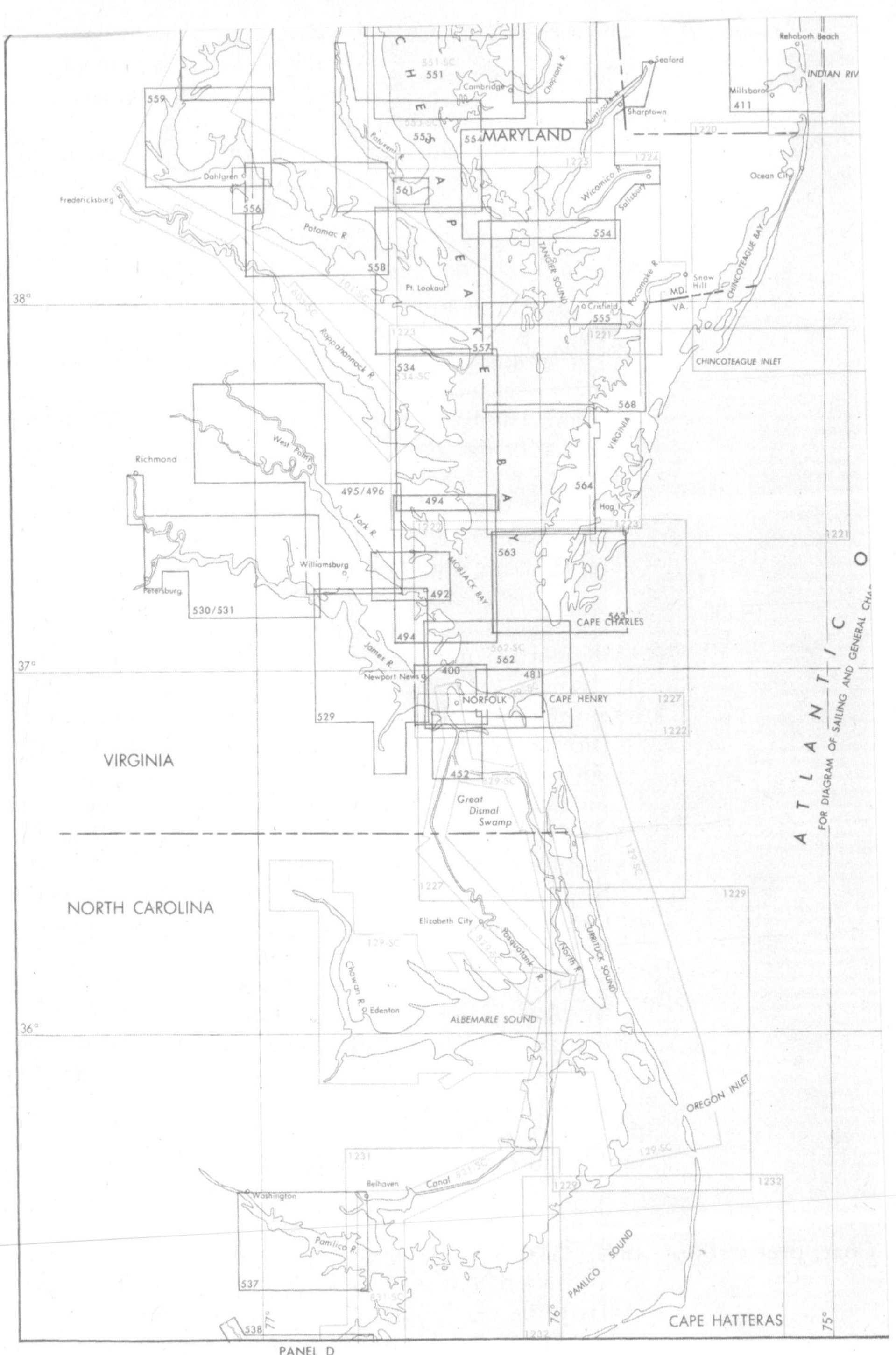

Figure 1607. Portion of NOS Chart Catalog No. 1.

12313	12214	12222
12312	12211	12254
12311	12210	12245
12304	12221	

Since all charts required were in Portfolio 12, it was a simple matter to obtain them from chart stowage. Comparing each chart with the edition data shown in Pub. No. 1-N-L, the navigator determined that all the charts he intended to use were in fact the latest edition.

Next, the Chart/Publication Correction Record card, DMAHC Pub. No. 8660/9, for each chart to be used was removed from the file and checked to determine which *Notices to Mariners* contained changes that must be applied to the charts. The latest issue of *Summary of Corrections,* Volume 1, together with any applicable individual *Notices to Mariners* since the date of the *Summary,* were consulted and the charts were brought up to date. Files of *Local Notices to Mariners* for the 3rd and 5th Coast Guard Districts were consulted as the information in these publications may be as much as several weeks fresher than in the weekly *Notices to Mariners*.

Plotting the track

1608 With all charts corrected up to date, the navigator was ready to plot his intended track, using as a guide information contained in *Coast Pilot 3*, the applicable *Fleet Guides*, and *Light List, Volume I.* These publications, before being used, were each checked to ensure that all changes had been entered.

Using a time of departure of 1300, and a speed of 10 knots until abeam of New Castle, the ETA at every turn point was calculated and labeled on the intended track. The navigator made a mental note that adjustments might have to be made to these ETAs as the passage was made down the river—a precise estimate cannot be made of the effect on speed made good by the necessity to slow to perhaps 6 knots from time to time when passing piers and wharves. After passing New Castle, a speed of 15 knots was assumed to determine the ETA at the remainder of the turning points. The effect of the river's current will be compensated for by appropriate adjustments in the ordered shaft revolutions. (It will be seen later in Article 1609 that the current was predicted to be as much as 1.8 knots, initially fair after the first 5 miles, but then turning foul.)

After plotting the track on all charts, the navigator computed the amount of advance and transfer for every turn, plotted the point at which the turn should commence, and located a landmark as near the beam as possible for use as a turning bearing. The turning point, turning bearing, and ETA were all noted on the chart. Two of these notations are illustrated in Figure 1608a.

Continuing this procedure, all notations concerning tracks, ranges, turning points, turning bearings, areas requiring a speed reduction, and the ETA at the various points were made on the remaining charts to be used.

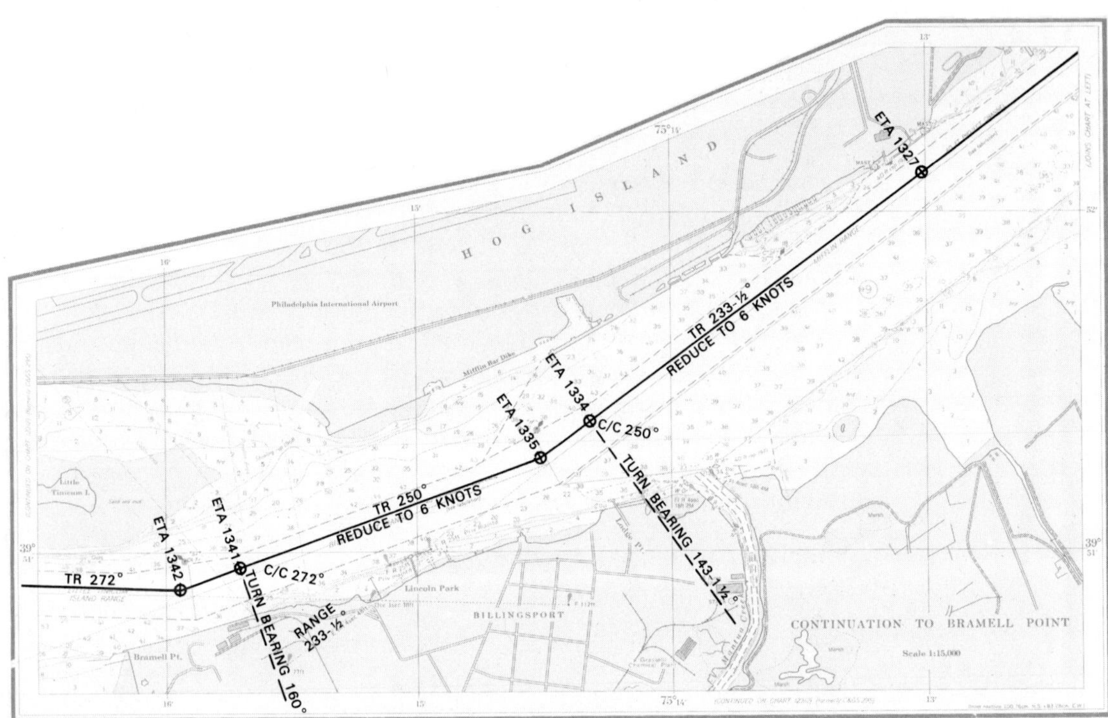

Figure 1608a. Intended track and notations shown on Chart 12313.

Ranges As the navigator plotted the recommended track on the chart, he observed that the Delaware River Main Channel was exceptionally well marked with buoys and that every leg of the channel was marked by both day and night ranges. A notation was made on the chart of the bearing of each of the fifteen ranges, observation of which would permit a continuous check of the gyro while in the confined waters of the river.

After passing the Cohansey River, Chart 12304 must then be used to plot the track until abeam of Cape Henlopen. The navigator was alert to the fact that with this chart the scale would change from 1:40,000 to 1:80,000. [A previous scale change would occur from 12313 to 12312, from 1:15,000 to 1:40,000.] Subsequently, the track was plotted on NOS charts 12214, 12211, 12210, and 12221; the track for these charts was derived from the overall offshore track on chart 12200. Departure was to be taken from Delaware Lighted Horn Buoy "D" at the end of the Traffic Separation Scheme for Jack Spot Lighted Whistle Buoy "2JS," then to the start of the North Chesapeake Bay Entrance Traffic Lanes.

NOS charts 12222, 12254, and 12245 were prepared for entry into Hampton Roads in the same manner as the initial charts for departure from Philadelphia.

While proceeding down the Delaware River for the first 40 miles, every channel axis is marked by ranges providing a ready means of observing the ship's position in relation to the center of the channel. After leaving the Liston Range, no more ranges are available and the navigator must employ other means to keep the ship in safe water.

Danger bearings Besides taking frequent fixes, the navigator had previously decided that danger bearings would be very useful. An examination of the chart showed that the red sectors of the principal lights coincided with danger bearings. The limits of these sectors were outlined in magenta and the exact bearing obtained from the *Light List.* The information concerning the sectors, danger bearings, and the description of each light structure, was placed in a box adjacent to the light symbol on the chart.

Lights A list of all lights that would be seen from sunset until sunrise was then prepared, giving information as to the name and number of the light, light characteristics, length of flash and eclipse, and its sound signal, if any. The computed visibility of all lights that would be sighted after sunset was determined for this ship, using a height of eye of 36 feet (11 m), and the arcs of visibility plotted on the chart as in Figure 1608b. From the intersection of the track with the arc of visibility, the predicted bearing and time of sighting was computed and added to the summary, an extract of which follows:

Expected Time of Sighting	Bearing	Name of Aid	Characteristic	Fog Signal
2021	139°	Delaware Lighted Horn Buoy "D"	Fl.W., 5 sec. vis. 14 mi.	Horn, 1 bl ev 15 sec. Rbn 298 kHz, (RK) Radar reflector
2025	132°	BW Buoy "DA"	Mo. (A) vis. 6 mi.	Whistle Radar reflector
2231	281°	Red Buoy "2JS"	Fl.W., 4 sec. vis. 6 mi.	Whistle
0453	305°	BW Buoy "NCA"	Mo. (A) vis. 6 mi.	Whistle Radar reflector

Arcs of visibility of the first two of these lights are shown in Figure 1608b. Since sunset occurs at 2003, both of these lights will become visible almost immediately after sunset if the visibility is clear. In this figure, note the safety lanes established for vessels entering and departing Delaware Bay; the appropriate lanes must be used by all ships.

Tides and currents **1609** The appropriate volumes of *Tide Tables* and *Tidal Current Tables,* as well as the *Tidal Current Charts* were next inspected.

Tide summaries were prepared for Philadelphia and Norfolk as follows, all times (+4) (Q).

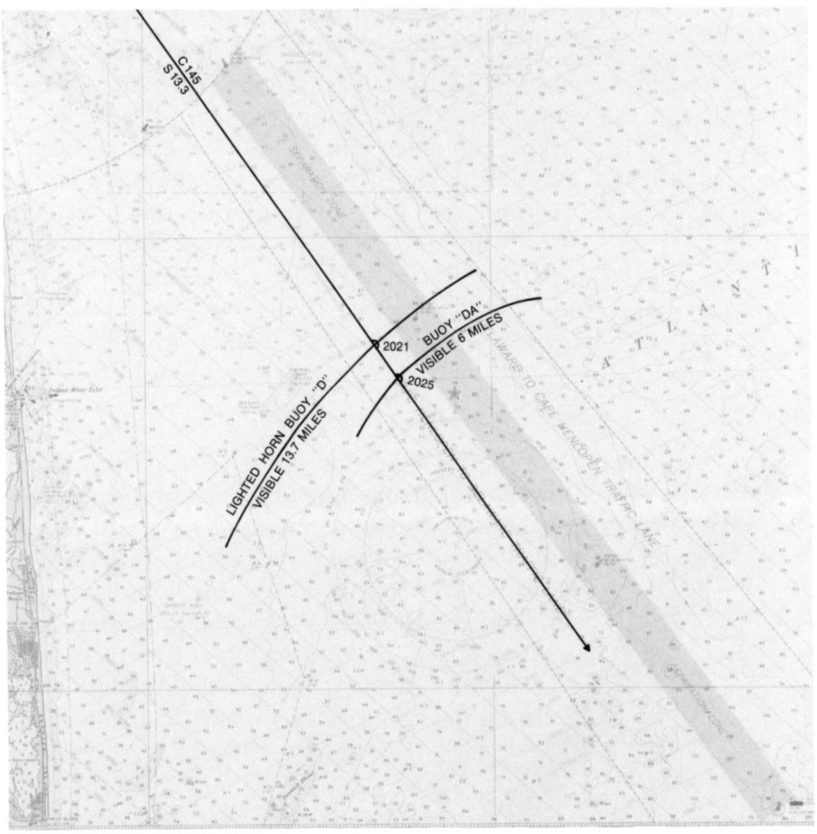

Figure 1608b. Arcs of visibility.

8 August **Philadelphia**			9 August **Norfolk (Sewell's Point)**		
Low water	0757	0.0 ft.	Low water	0329	−0.1 ft.
High water	1311	6.1	High water	0933	2.7
Low water	2007	0.2	Low water	1538	−0.1

Tidal current summaries were prepared for Delaware Bay Entrance and Chesapeake Bay Entrance as follows, all times (+4).

8 August **Delaware Bay Entrance**			9 August **Chesapeake Bay Entrance**		
Max. Flood	0617	1.6 kn.	Max. Ebb	0323	1.5 kn.
Slack, Ebb begins	0919		Slack, Flood begins	0641	
Max. Ebb	1221	1.7	Max. Flood	0910	0.9
Slack, Flood begins	1533				
Max. Flood	1830	1.8 kn.			
Slack, Ebb begins	2146				

From Table 2 of the *Tidal Current Tables,* the navigator found that the current at the Philadelphia Naval Shipyard would be negligible at the time of departure; a footnote to the table states that the "times of slack are indefinite," but it was noted that the time of departure was roughly midway between times of maximum currents, 1002 and 1606.

At Norfolk, the current was calculated to be at a maximum flood at 0735 at Sewell's Point; setting 195°, velocity 0.5 kn.

Using the publication *Tidal Current Charts–Delaware Bay and River,* the navigator determined the velocity and direction of the current at various points along the river for the estimated time of passage. Figure 1609a is a tidal current chart for a typical hour of the trip. These charts are related to the time of maximum or slack current at the entrance to the bay; the appropriate one must be used for each hour in the current cycle.

Using the Current Diagram

Reference was next made to the Current Diagram for Delaware Bay and River which is included in the *Tidal Current Tables.* The starting point was estimated (the Shipyard is at Mile 81), and the starting time, 1300, was found to be 2^h 33^m "before flood begins at Delaware Bay Entrance." Consideration was then given to the speed to be run during the initial legs of the trip down the Delaware River, with consideration being given to the fact that speed must be limited when passing wharves and piers. As an estimate, sufficiently accurate for use with the Current Diagram, speed would average 10 knots to New Castle and 15 knots thereafter. Appropriate speed lines were drawn on the Current Diagram (Figure 1609b); these showed a fair current could be anticipated to about Mile 28, then a foul current for the remainder of the distance to the Delaware Bay Entrance. These conditions would be about as favorable as could be expected, inasmuch as it is not possible to "ride" a favorable current all the way when a vessel is outbound (as might be possible when inbound up the bay and river).

Completing the planning

1610 The navigator then prepared his notebook, listing in chronological order every event of interest for the passage. Examples of typical entries are as follows:

Estimated Time	Event
1300	Underway.
1315	Set course 274°, speed 10.
1318	C/C to 233°.5 on the Miflin Range.
1328	Reduce speed to 6 knots off Hog Island Billingsport.
1334	C/C to 250° on the Billingsport Range.
1341	C/C to 272° on the Tinicum Range.
	(Intervening entries omitted)
1723	R "32" Qk Fl Bell abeam. C/C to 156° (Cross Ledge Range)
1736	Cross Ledge Lt abeam. C/C to 145° (Miah Maull Range)
	(Intervening entries omitted)
1919	"4" Fl Bell abeam. Special sea and anchor detail secured.
2003	Sunset.

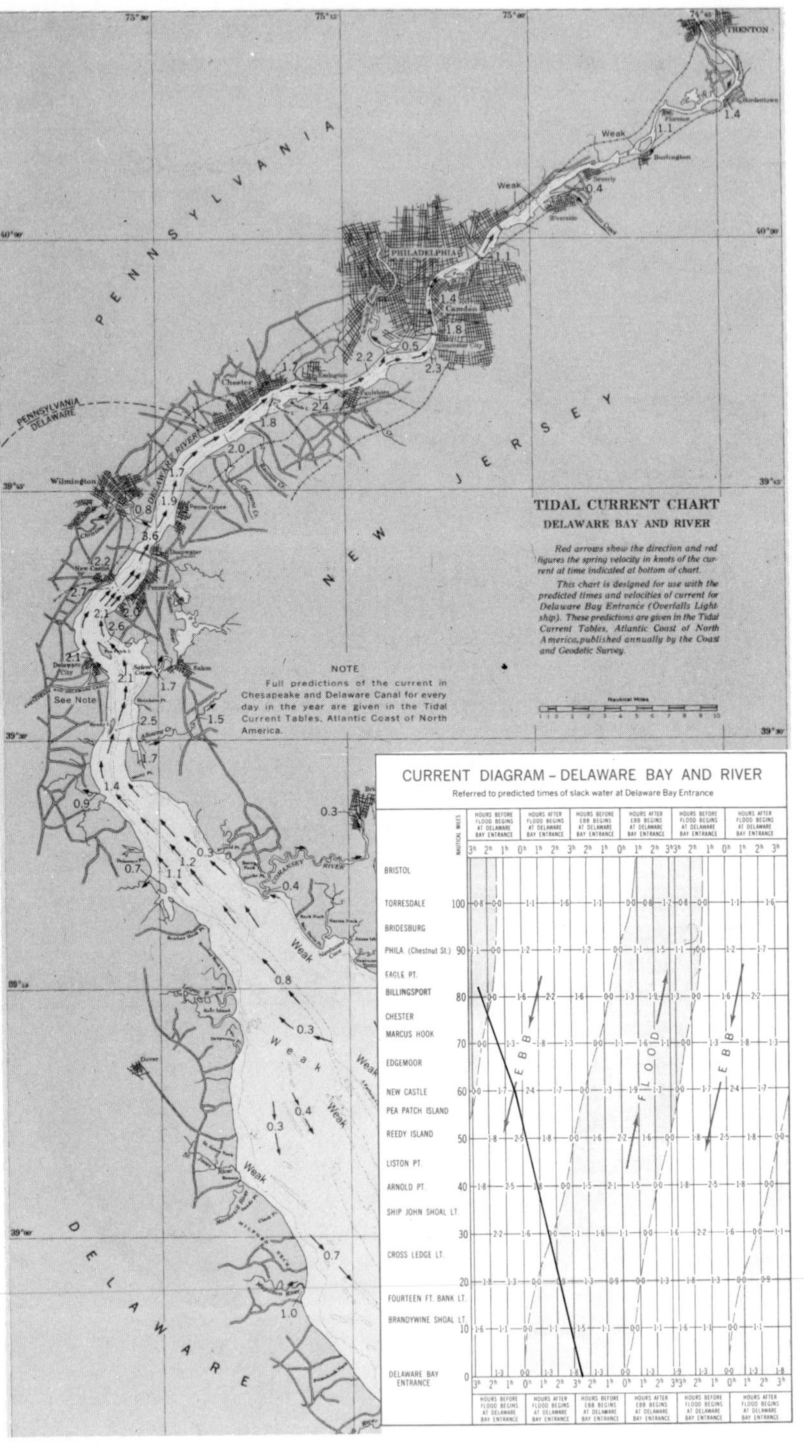

Figure 1609a. *Tidal Current Chart* for Delaware Bay and River for one particular hour of a tidal cycle. (Background). Figure 1609b. Current diagram for Delaware Bay and River. (Insert).

Based on the navigational planning as completed, a listing of all navigational events for the entire voyage is prepared, similar to that shown above. Such a listing is invaluable, especially when it is expected that the ship will be in pilot waters for an extended period of time, for it permits the assistant navigator or the officer of the deck to anticipate each item as the passage progresses, and permits the navigator greater freedom for supervision and observation.

Underway from Philadelphia to Norfolk

1611 Prior to getting underway, all equipment checks mentioned in Article 1605 were completed, and all personnel concerned in the piloting team and the CIC piloting team were briefed and given last minute instructions. Gyro error was determined to be zero.

The ship got underway on time, and as the trip down the bay progressed, the assistant navigator plotted fixes on the chart every three minutes, while the navigator exercised supervision over the entire team, evaluated the information, and made recommendations to the commanding officer regarding changes of course and speed to carry out the voyage safely. Heavy river traffic slowed the ship so that by the time New Castle was reached, a speed of 8 rather than 10 knots had been made good. Since sufficient margin had been allowed in the planning phase, this caused no difficulties except for an adjustment to the schedule for arrival at subsequent significant points along the track. At 2125 departure was taken from Delaware Lighted Horn Buoy "D," and the SOA was adjusted to arrive at North Chesapeake Entrance Lighted Whistle Buoy at 0520 (+4)(Q).

Once the adjusted SOA for the next phase of the trip was known, the expected time of sighting each light was inserted in the summary prepared earlier, and one copy provided for the commanding officer, one for the officer of the deck, and one retained for the navigator's use. Using this same information, the data for the Captain's Night Orders were prepared and sent to the commanding officer. See Figure 1611. This data included the expected times of arrival at each turning point, with the new course and the bearing of aids used as markers for the course change, and any other pertinent data of interest to the safe navigation of the ship.

ETA	C/C to	Name	Distance	Bearing
2138	182°	Lighted Horn Buoy "D"	1.6 miles	044°
2314	218°	Buoy "2 JS"	0.5 mile	270°
		(intervening entries omitted)		
0243	—	Chesapeake Light	17 miles	195°
0530	251°	Lighted Whistle Buoy "NCA"	0.2 miles	140°

Figure 1611. Extracts from navigation data for preparation of night orders.

Entering port at Norfolk

1612 At 0603 Cape Henry Light was passed abeam to port and the special sea detail was set. Since Norfolk was the home port of the ship, no detailed briefing of the piloting team was necessary. Again, the assistant navigator did the actual plotting on the chart, while the navigator kept a continuous check on all the various phases of navigating the ship into port.

The piloting team was functioning smoothly and the ship proceeded up the channel without incident. At 0705, speed was reduced after passing Fort Wool.

The tug and pilot met the ship as scheduled, and the first line was secured to the pier at 0749. The piloting team and all equipment except the gyro were secured after all lines were doubled-up. The navigator, knowing that the stay in Norfolk would be short, decided not to secure the gyro.

Summary

1613 The first part of this chapter was devoted to summarizing in general terms the preparation and planning necessary for the safe travel of a ship from one port to another. The latter part of the chapter demonstrated the application of these procedures to a typical voyage of a naval ship from Philadelphia to Norfolk, primarily emphasizing the navigational planning aspects of the passage. Although much of this chapter is typical, the procedures used are not exclusive, and no attempt has been made to describe all of the work done by the navigator and the piloting team. For a merchant ship or a yacht, the procedures would be somewhat abridged in recognition of the fewer persons available to carry out the functions described. It is emphasized, however, that the basic planning and en route activities remain wholly valid and must be carried out. Navigation, like any other professional skill, requires thorough preparation and careful execution to be successful. Careless or incomplete work can endanger not only ships, but the lives of many people and is a blemish on the pride and record of a professional mariner. If you understand all of the procedures and techniques necessary to complete a voyage such as is described here, you have mastered the mechanics of the navigational profession in pilot waters; the polish and precision of the professional navigator will come only with experience.

17 Radar Navigation

Introduction **1701** Radar (*RA*dio *D*etecting *A*nd *R*anging) as used for navigation is a system of determining distances by measuring the time between the transmission and return of an electromagnetic signal which has been reflected back to the receiver by a "target." The returned signal may be reflected as an "echo"; alternatively, it may be retransmitted by a *transponder* triggered by the original signal. A transponder generates a signal automatically, when interrogated by a signal of the appropriate frequency. Bearings may also be obtained by radar, but these are less precise than visual bearings and less accurate than distance measurements.

Equipment Radar equipment consists of five major components:

Transmitter. An oscillator which produces electromagnetic waves of energy. Super high frequencies (SHF) are used, generally 3,000 to 10,000 megahertz, but sometimes as high as 30,000 MHz; these are wavelengths of 10, 3, and 1 cm, respectively.

Modulator. Circuitry to turn the transmitter on and off so that the energy is sent out in *pulses* of about one microsecond (one millionth of a second) or less. Approximately 500 to 3000 very accurately timed pulses are transmitted each second by most radars of the type used for surface navigation, depending upon the range scale being used. The *timing base* circuitry in the modulator also controls and synchronizes several functions of the receiver and indicator units.

Antenna. A physical structure used to transmit the outgoing pulse and receive the returned signal. Antennas must be highly directional and capable of rotation; they can be relatively large and are often quite complex. A single antenna is used for both transmitting and receiving. Typical rotation rates are 15 to 25 rpm, clockwise, but some models may have faster or slower speeds. (Some radars can be set to "sector scan" within set limits.)

Receiver. Electronic circuitry to amplify the very weak incoming signal and demodulate it for display. A *duplexer,* or electronic switch, with a *transmit-receiver tube* (T/R tube) is provided between the receiver and antenna to electronically disconnect the receiver and thereby prevent damage during the interval of transmission of the energy pulse.

Indicator. Presents the information in a form for interpretation. It consists essentially of a cathode ray tube (CRT), the face or screen of which is commonly referred to as the *scope* (Figure 1701a), and various timing circuits and controls. In the scope a stream of electrons is directed toward a fluorescent screen, appearing there as a dot of light. Various types of presentation are used on CRTs, but for radar navigation only one type is generally employed; this presentation is called a *Plan Position Indicator* (PPI).

A typical system arrangement for the five parts of a radar system is shown in Figure 1701b.

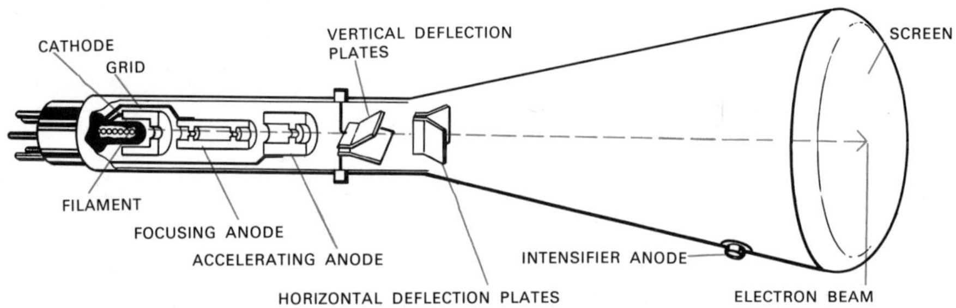

Figure 1701a. Diagramatic sketch of a cathode ray tube (CRT) using electrostatic deflection. Many radars use CRTs with magnetic deflection obtained from coils placed at the neck of the CRT.

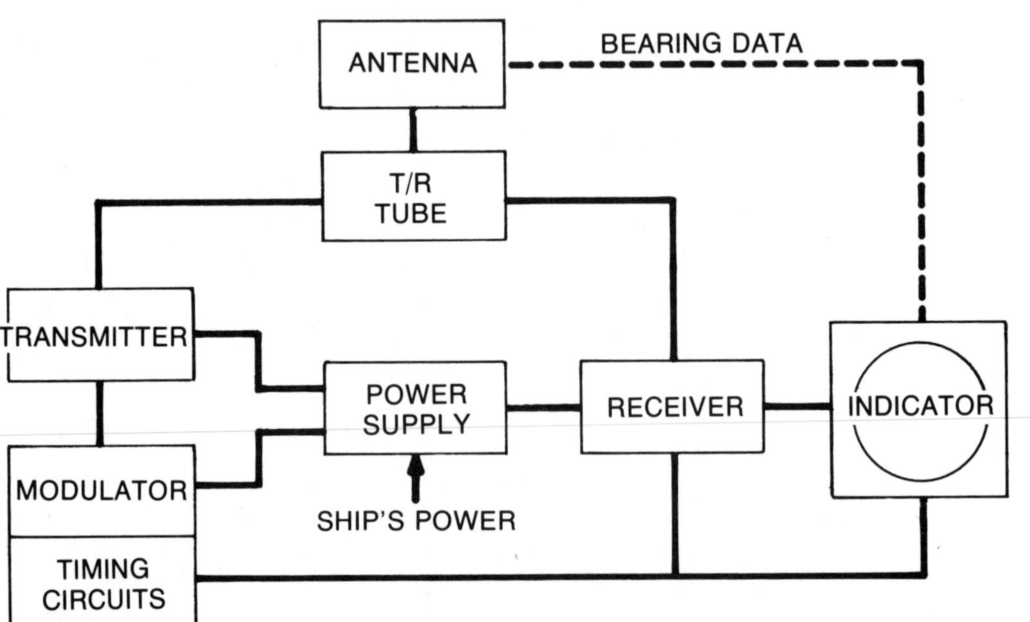

Figure 1701b. Major components of a typical radar set.

Display On the PPI scope, a faint radial line represents the outgoing beam of energy, a line which starts at the "own ship's" position at the center of the screen and extends to the outer edge, rotating in bearing in synchronization with the rotation of the antenna. Around the outer edge of the PPI scope are bearing indications, clockwise from 000° at the top.

When the radiated energy from the antenna strikes a target, a weak echo is returned, is amplified, and causes a spot or area of the PPI scope to glow; the distance out from the center of the scope to this spot or area is a measure of the distance from the ship to the target. This spot or area on the screen (called "blips" or "pips") will continue to glow, with slowly decaying brightness, after the radial line has continued to sweep around the face of the scope; on most sets, it will be "repainted" by the next sweep of the beam at about the time that it is fading from sight. Thus a continuous chart-like picture of the surrounding area will be presented without undue smearing of the old traces into the new; see Figure 1701c. The bright areas surrounding the transmitting ship's ("own ship") position at the center of the screen is *clutter* caused by *sea return* which is described in Article 1702.

On simpler radar sets, the display on the PPI screen is aligned so that 000° is dead ahead and thus all radar bearings are relative. On ships equipped with gyrocompasses, it is normal for gyro heading information to be fed into the radar system. The display can then present either relative bearings or true bearings (with north at the top of the screen) at the option of the operator.

The bearing of specific blips on the indicator scope can be estimated against the outer scale, usually as the spot is repainted by the sweeping beam. For more precise directions, a *bearing cursor* can be used; this is a faint radial line of light that can be manually rotated by the radar operator to alignment with the spot on the scope, the bearing then being read from a dial.

Some models of radar will permit a *true-motion* type of display. In such a mode of operation, one's own ship is no longer at the center of

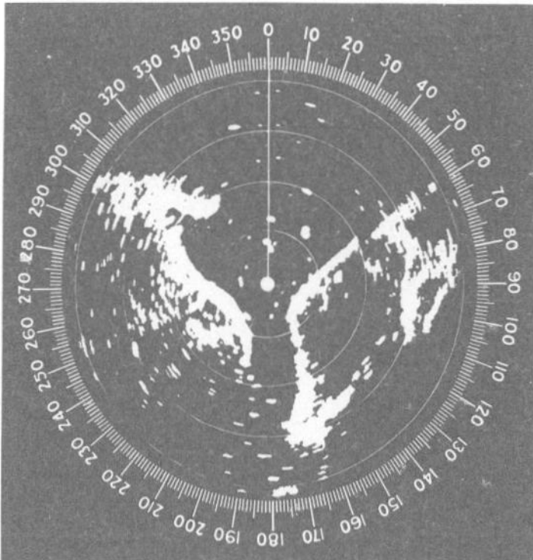

Figure 1701c. Radar PPI presentation.

the display. Here, the center of the screen remains a fixed point and a true-motion picture is painted of all targets, including the vessel on which the radar is located. (The fixed point of the screen's center must be advanced as the own-ship position approaches the outer limits of the screen.)

Radar sets have a number of *range scales,* the distance to the outer edge of the sweep on the PPI display, such as $\frac{1}{4}$, $\frac{1}{2}$, 1, 2, 4, 8, 16, and 32 miles. The number of different range scales and the maximum range scale available on any particular radar set are determined by its design; these characteristics are selected to match the size and employment of the vessel on which a radar is installed. The shorter ranges are used for close-in navigation, and the longer range scales to initially detect aids to navigation, landfalls, and other vessels. Most radars have several *range rings* that can be illuminated to give a rough measure of distance from own ship. For more precise measurements, a set may have a *range strobe* (a spot of light which can be moved in and out along the bearing cursor) or a *variable range ring;* these are manually controlled by the operator who places them over the desired spot and reads distance from a dial.

Some radar sets, particularly military models, may have a second type of display in addition to the PPI scope. Typically, this is a linear-base presentation with a portion of the range scale expanded. Such an *M-scope* display permits very accurate measurements of range with good discrimination between targets at nearly equal ranges; this capability is often of use in navigation.

Accuracy

1702 Many factors affect the operational characteristics of radar. The accuracy of positions obtained by radar varies considerably with different types of radar and with the skill of the operator. In general, the accuracy of radar fixes compares favorably with those obtained by other methods. The limitations of each radar set should be thoroughly understood by those who are depending on its information. Some of

Beam width

the factors affecting the accuracy are beam width, pulse length, mechanical adjustment, and interpretation of return. Radar signals, while directional, are transmitted as narrow, fan-shaped beams. While a beam may be less than 1° in width, it may be 20° or more in the vertical dimension; this greater vertical dimension permits illumination of targets from close to the ship out to the radar horizon and allows for the pitching and rolling motion of the ship. See Figures 1702a and b. Echoes are received continuously as the beam sweeps across a *target,* or reflecting surface. The center of the arc thus indicated is the desired bearing. On the PPI scope the effect is to cause a target to appear wider than it actually is. On each side its width is increased by about

Resolution in bearing

half the beam width, or slightly less. If two or more targets are relatively close together at about the same range, their widened pips may merge, appearing as a single pip of a larger target. The minimum difference in bearing between two objects at the same range that can be

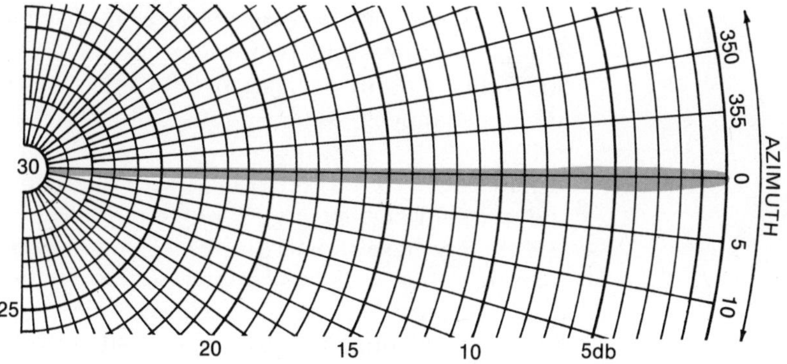

Figure 1702a. Horizontal radiation pattern (typical).

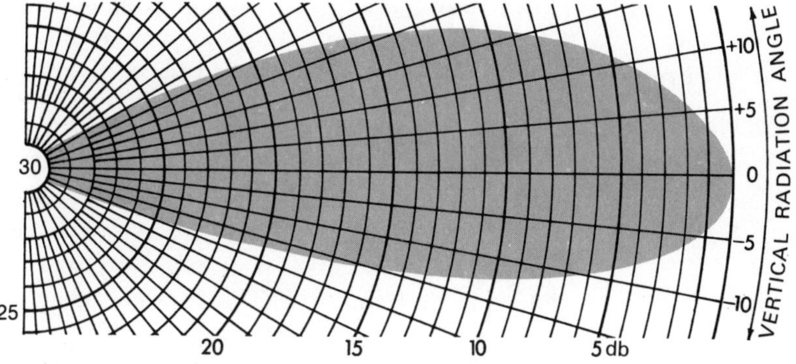

Figure 1702b. Vertical radiation pattern (typical).

separated by a radar is called its *resolution in bearing.* The ability to make this separation is directly dependent on beam width. A number of piles, rocks, or small boats near a shore may appear as a solid line, giving a false impression of the position of the actual shore line.

Pulse length The outgoing pulse of radio energy has a finite length and this affects the depth of the reflected signal in a manner generally similar to the widening by the beam width. Thus, a signal of one microsecond duration reflected from a flat, perpendicular surface continues to be received for one microsecond. The depth of such a pip is equal to half the distance traveled by the signal in one microsecond, or 492 feet (150 m). The shorter the pulse, the more accurate is the depth of the pip.

Resolution in range This is the minimum difference in range between two objects on the same bearing that can be separated by a radar. The ability to make this separation is dependent primarily on pulse length, but to some extent also on the pulse shape and the fidelity of the receiver. False interpretation may occur when two or more targets appear as a single long one, or when a ship, buoy, or rock is near shore and is not separated from it on the PPI.

Pulse length also determines the *minimum range* of the radar, a characteristic of considerable importance when navigating close to buoys and other aids to navigation (and other vessels) when proceeding along a channel.

Frequency

It may be stated as a generality that radars operating near the top of the normal radar frequency range of 9500 MHz may more easily be designed to have shorter pulse length and narrower beam width and therefore to give rather better resolution in both bearing and range than do those operating in a lower frequency band. On the other hand, for an equal output of power, sets operating at lower frequencies can acquire targets at somewhat longer ranges. The useful operational range of a given set depends not only on the frequency employed, but also on the height of the antenna above water, the power output, and its power of resolution. Low-frequency radar, as a rule, permits better target acquisition in areas of heavy rain, and also tends to have a smaller area masked by *sea return* or *clutter*. Sea return is caused by a portion of the transmitted signal being reflected by waves. It occurs principally in the area immediately surrounding the ship, and can mask targets within its area. On the other hand 3-cm radars operating at peak pulse powers far below the allowable maximum can detect targets at the horizon range of most radar antenna installations. A 3-cm radar at 25-kw peak pulse power can detect large ships at ranges above 60 miles (110 km) under certain atmospheric conditions.

Sea return

Sensitivity time control

On modern radar sets special circuits are included with appropriate manual settings to permit improved resolution in both range and bearing. A *sensitivity time control* (STC) circuit (for clutter control) changes the gain characteristics of the receiver at close-in ranges. This circuit is valuable in reducing sea-return saturation at close ranges so that nearby targets can be seen; it does not affect targets beyond the limit of its time base. A *fast time constant* (FTC) circuit provides differentiation of the received signals and also helps to reduce *rain clutter*, the pale echoes on the PPI scope caused by rainfall. Often a change from the normal *horizontal polarization* of the antenna to *circular polarization* will reduce clutter from rain or sea return at a cost of slightly weakened pulses.

Fast time constant circuit

On many radars, different values for pulse length and repetition rate are used on different ranges. For example, a pulse repetition rate of 1500 pulses per second and a pulse length of 0.1 microseconds is used on some sets for ranges under approximately 4 miles (7½ km); this is changed to 750 pulses per second and 0.5 microseconds for longer ranges.

Frequency and wavelength

1703 The great majority of marine surface-search radars, as well as the radar beacons designed for use in conjunction with them, operate in the frequency band of 3,000 to 10,000 MHz. Radars are frequently described by the approximate wavelength they employ. Thus, a *10-cm* radar is one operating in the frequency range of *3,000 to 3,246 MHz,* a *5-cm* radar uses the *5,450 to 5,825 MHz* band, and a *3-cm* radar is in the *9,320 to 9,500 MHz* band.

In the selection of a radar set for a vessel (or which set to use if more than one is on board), certain factors must be considered, such as:

Propagation conditions for the different wave lengths.

Size of antenna systems for the desired resolution and necessary gain (concentration of energy).

Comparative cost of components and complexity of design.

The first factor, propagation, is the one factor affecting radar performance over which man has no control. Reliability of coverage regardless of meteorological conditions is an important consideration for navigational radars. Fog has a negligible effect on the strength of either 3-, 5-, or 10-centimeter signals. Rainfall is more serious, as the signal strength weakens more or less linearly with the density of the precipitation. The amount the signal is weakened is called the *attenuation constant* and varies approximately as the square of the frequency. This means that the effective range of the higher frequency 3-centimeter sets may be considerably less than the 10-centimeter sets during periods of rainfall. When the precipitation is heavy and the distance to the target is great, the effect becomes more serious. During cloudbursts a complete radar blackout may temporarily occur on the 3-centimeter set.

Another early disadvantage of the 3-centimeter sets was the great sea return, or clutter, that is inherent at this shorter wavelength. The main beam, or *major lobe,* at 3 centimeters "grazes" the surface of the sea at a very low angle. Rough seas near the ship reflect more of the incident energy which tends to clutter up the scope, masking the weaker targets' images. However, the higher "grazing" angle of a 10-centimeter beam is more likely to miss buoys and other small targets. In favor of the 3-centimeter sets, it should be added that the effects of sea return and heavy rain which were so detrimental in early sets have largely been overcome by the development of the special operating circuits and controls described, and by the use of circular polarized antennas and high power. It is also generally held that the total percentage of time during which heavy rainfall occurs is so small that reduced performance during these limited periods is acceptable as a trade-off in return for better definition and resolution of targets for navigational purposes.

Most small craft, such as yachts and the smaller commercial fishermen, use 3-cm radar so as to obtain maximum resolution in bearing and range; in most instances, they have neither the antenna height nor the power available to work at long ranges. Liners, large tankers, and freighters frequently are equipped with both 10-cm radar for target acquisition at maximum ranges, and 3-cm radar for use in piloting during periods of poor visibility. U.S. Navy surface-search radars operate on wavelengths of 5 cm and 3 cm.

Mechanical adjustment

1704 Radar sets are sensitive instruments requiring accurate adjustment. Any error in the adjustment causes an error in echo interpretation. It is of the utmost importance that every user be completely familiar with the operator's manual for that set. Repairs should only be attempted by thoroughly experienced and licensed personnel.

Interpretation

1705 Even with considerable training an operator may not always find it easy to interpret an echo properly. Here are some of the factors which make the problem more difficult.

As stated earlier, beam width limits *resolution in bearing* and will cause a target to appear wider than it actually is. False interpretation may occur when two or more targets appear as a single long one, or when a ship, buoy, or rock is near shore and is not separated from it due to the resolution in range of the radar set.

False shore lines may appear on a PPI for any of several reasons. In Figure 1705a false shore lines appear at *B* because of a pier, at *C* because of several small boats, and at *D* because of heavy surf over a shoal. Figure 1705b is a chart of the area shown in Figure 1705a. The echoes of *A* and *G* make these appear as islands, where actually they are areas of high ground on the mainland. A shore line may be falsely indicated some distance inland if there are bluffs or cliffs back of a low and flat or gently sloping beach.

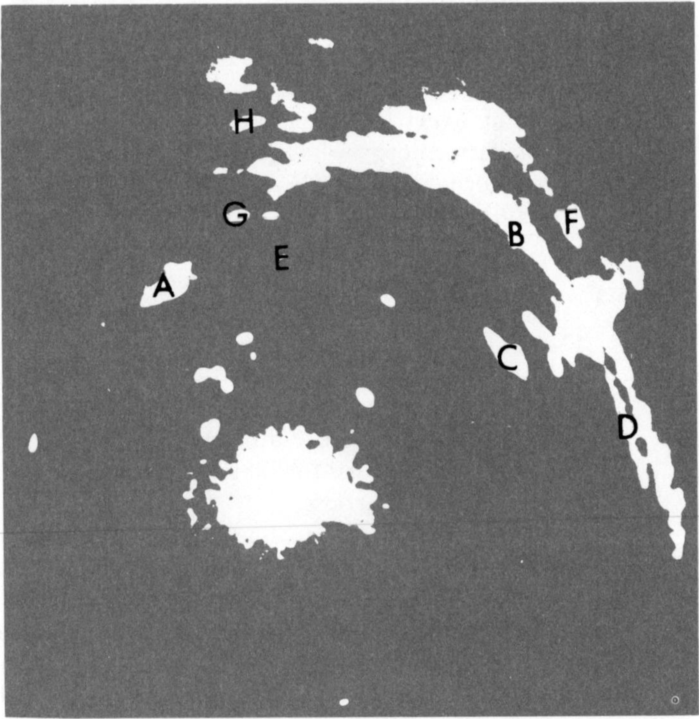

Figure 1705a. PPI pattern, ship off Pt. Loma, California.

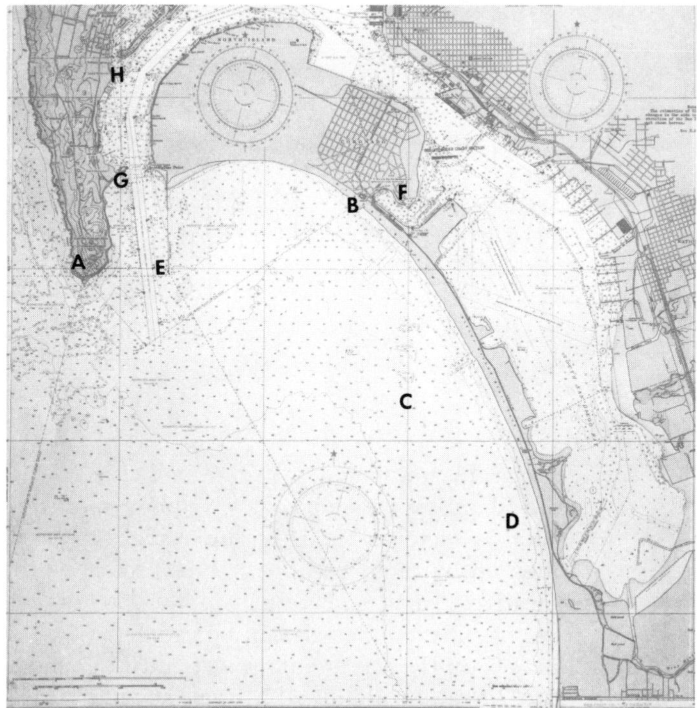

Figure 1705b. Chart of area shown in Figure 1705a.

Shadows (Figure 1705c) occur behind prominent objects. That is, no echo is returned from a surface that is completely shielded from radar pulses by higher targets nearer the antenna. Hence, mountains, towers, etc., inshore can be seen only if they extend above nearer objects by essentially direct line of sight. Thus, a valley parallel to a high shore line will not return an echo, although the higher land on either side may be seen. Similarly, a rock or small boat too far beyond the horizon to be seen will not return an echo, although a high mountain beyond it can be picked up. Until the operator is thoroughly familiar with the interpretation of all echoes on the radar screen, he should take every opportunity to compare the picture shown on the PPI with the actual land area it portrays. Particular attention should be given to noting the difference in the appearance of echoes caused by buoys and by ships.

By comparing the screen with a chart of the area it will be noted that shore lines and prominent points will appear as bright areas against a dark background. The reflected echo will be very much like the actual view of the area. Small objects such as buoys will appear as small illuminated areas when picked up at a distance. The image will increase in size as range decreases in much the same way that it would appear visually larger at close range. At close range a buoy might give a stronger return than a small vessel situated at a greater distance; this is particularly true if the buoy is fitted with a *radar reflector* as an ever-

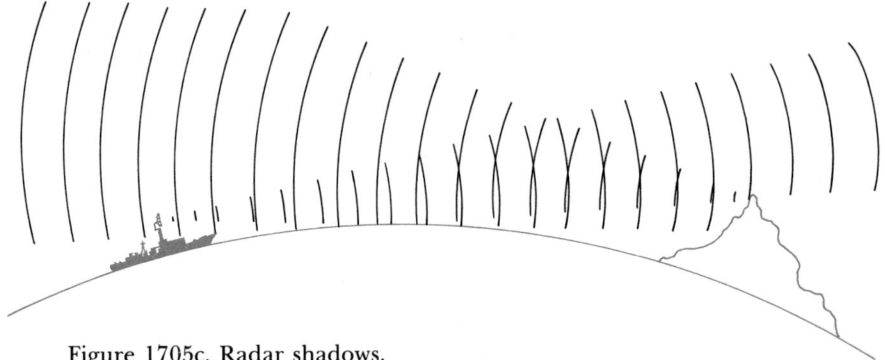

Figure 1705c. Radar shadows.

increasing number now are. (Small craft, particularly those of wood and fiberglass which have a very poor natural reflectivity, may hoist a radar reflector in their rigging at night or in fog when in waters frequented by radar-equipped ships.) Such a reflector despite its comparatively small size, returns a very strong echo. With practice, the size of different vessels can be estimated by the relative size of their images on the screen; allowance must be made for range. Low flying aircraft can be identified by their speed of travel. High coastlines and mountain areas near the sea can be picked up at the extreme range of the equipment. Storm areas and rain squalls are easily recognized by their mass and hazy definition.

Radar interference *Interference from another radar-equipped vessel* may occasionally appear on the screen as a patterned series of small dots. This effect is especially pronounced at the longer range scales. These dots appear to move to and from the center of the screen, often in long sweeping curves, sometimes in a straight line.

Ghost images of several types appear occasionally. They are easy to identify as they maintain a fixed relationship with respect to the true image, they have more of an arc-like appearance than the true image, and they have a tendency to "smear." They are not generally troublesome, as they are easily recognized. They should be noted, with their probable cause, to assist in future recognition.

Range limitations **1706** Both minimum and maximum range is limited. The minimum range is dependent on several factors. Excessive *sea return,* or echo from nearby water, and other obstructions nearby also affect the minimum effective range. Sea return can be reduced by judicious tuning, reducing the signal strength of close-in echoes which, however, reduces maximum range. Sea return becomes less with increased range because of the change in the angle of incidence, more of the signal being reflected away from the ship and less returned in the form of an

Minimum range echo. The minimum range is to a considerable extent a function of the frequency; a 3-cm radar may have a minimum range as short as 15 yards. Pulse length is also a determining factor as an echo from the leading edge of an outgoing pulse obviously cannot be received until the trailing edge of that pulse has cleared the antenna and the T/R switch has functioned to restore the signal path into the receiver.

Sea-return saturation at close range

The STC (sensitivity time control) provides the operator with a means of controlling the receiver sensitivity near minimum operating range. The best results in reducing sea return and other clutter such as that caused by rain, snow, or sleet can generally be achieved by careful adjustment of both the STC and the fast time constant control (FTC).

Maximum range

Maximum range is usually limited by the curvature of the earth to the line of sight or slightly more, because high-frequency radio waves travel in a straight line and do not follow the earth's curvature, except under abnormal atmospheric conditions. The approximate maximum range at which any given target will return an echo can be determined by means of Table 8, *Bowditch,* in the same manner used for determining the distance at which lights can be expected to be seen at sea (Article 511); this figure may be increased by about 15 percent to allow for the slight curvature of radar waves over the horizon. The navigator should be alert to unusual ranges which may be obtained when temperature inversion exists in the atmosphere.

Radar fixes

1707 Radar can be used in several ways to obtain position. Well-determined positions are labeled as *fixes* and less reliable ones as *EPs,* depending on the judgment of the navigator after experience with his equipment.

The accuracy of radar or radar-assisted position fixes follows in descending order:

Radar ranges and visual bearings of prominent isolated objects;

Radar ranges of several radar-conspicuous objects plotted as position circles;

Radar range and radar bearing of a single charted feature;

Radar bearings of two or more charted features.

Radar lines of position, no matter how they are determined, are plotted and labeled in the same manner as visual LOPs; see Chapter 11. The only difference occurs in plotting radar bearings of tangents when the radar beam width must be taken into consideration. For this specific case a correction of one-half the beam width may be applied in the direction of the land. An example of this would be a radar with a beam width of 4° giving a bearing of 045° on the left tangent of a point of land. The actual bearing to be plotted on the chart would be 047°.

If a series of radar fixes are being plotted simultaneously with visual fixes, a different symbol, a small triangle, may be used for the radar fixes so that they may be readily distinguished from the visual fixes plotted with the usual small circle.

Advantages of radar

1708 Radar has several advantages over other navigational aids for piloting:

It can be used at night and during periods of low visibility, when most other methods are limited or not available at all.

Navigation by radar is often more accurate than other methods of piloting during periods of reduced visibility.

Fixes may be available at greater distances from land than in most methods of piloting.

A fix can be obtained from a single object, since both range and bearing are provided. (This is less desirable than a fix by range to two or more objects.)

Fixes can be obtained rapidly. With the PPI, a continuous position is available.

It may be used with great effect to assist in the prevention of collision during periods of low visibility.

It can be used to locate and track heavy storms.

Limitations of radar

1709 As a navigational aid, radar is subject to certain limitations and disadvantages:

It is subject to mechanical and electrical failure.

There are both minimum and maximum range limitations.

Interpretation of the information presented on the scope is not always easy, even after considerable training.

Charts do not always give information necessary for identification of radar echoes.

It is often less accurate than visual piloting; i.e., a radar bearing is less precise than a visual bearing. (Distance measurements, however, can be quite precise.)

Buoys, small boats, etc., may not be detected, especially if a high sea is running, or if they are near shore or other objects.

It requires transmission of signals from the vessel.

Military and commercial radar developments

1710 Radar sets, while all consisting of the basic major components listed in Article 1701, vary widely in design according to the primary use for which each model is designed. In the U.S. Navy, the variations run from extremely high frequency, high power, strictly line-of-sight radar for control of the ship's armament, to a much lower frequency, long-range radar for tracking aircraft. Somewhere in between lies navigational radar. Radar aboard naval vessels usually employs a *north up* presentation, that is, true north appears at the center of the top of the scope. Many commercial radar sets give relative indications only (own ship's head up) or have a switch to change from north up to a *ship's-head-up* presentation. Most military radars show own ship at the center of the scope with both fixed and moving targets having relative motion on the scope when own ship is in motion. Several commercial models now present *true motion* with both own ship and other moving target images moving across the scope while land areas, fixed buoys, etc., remain motionless. Still another innovation permits an off-center relative motion display with own ship position remaining motionless but offset from the center of the scope to permit a maximum view of the area lying in a desired relative direction, usually ahead.

Use of short-wave, high-definition radar

1711 The 3-cm band radar (9500 MHz range) has come into general use both in the navies of the world, and with the merchant services as an adjunct to longer-wave radar. The high quality of the resolution it gives makes it particularly useful in pilotage. Naval vessels of nearly all sizes and classes are now fitted with 3-cm radar and can enter or leave port under conditions of zero visibility. Some merchant ships are now equipped with dual radar installations consisting of either a 10-cm and a 3-cm radar or two 3-cm sets. This practice is even gaining favor with many operators of seagoing tugs and larger fishing vessels in the United States.

Fishing fleets operating from U.S. ports are now widely equipped with the 3-cm band radar in order to allow greater mobility when fog, haze, or darkness might otherwise hinder operation. Smaller transistorized versions of the 3-cm band radar are available for use by yachtsmen in boats as small as 30 feet.

Navy surface radar

1712 The Navy's search radar, like that used by the Coast Guard, Army, and Air Force, differs from commercial radar, in that it is almost invariably equipped for Identification, Friend or Foe (IFF) operation, which is described in Article 1713. Naval vessels commonly use their *surface-search* radars for navigation; these are currently models of the SPS-10 and SPS-53 series. The newer SPS-55 series, a 3-cm radar, is being installed in major combatant ships, particularly aboard new construction. A brief discussion of these three radars follows.

SPS-10 series radar

1713 The SPS-10D operates in the 5450 to 5825 MHz band; the beacon receiver uses 5450 MHz. It is a 5-cm radar, and currently the most widely used surface-search set in the U.S. Navy. Range and bearing information is displayed on a 10-inch (25.4 cm) PPI scope, and provision is made for transponder beacon and IFF operation.

IFF

IFF returns a predetermined coded identification signal automatically. Similarly, if own ship's IFF is properly challenged, it will also return such a signal automatically. A pulse type of emission is used, the pulse length varying from 0.25 to 1.3 microseconds; the beacon pulse length is 2.5 microseconds. Depending upon the pulse length employed, pulse rate varies between 625 and 650 cycles per second, while the beacon uses 312 to 325 cycles per second. Bearing resolution is less than one degree with a range resolution on the short pulse of 50 yards (45.7 m) and on the long pulse of 275 yards (251 m). This radar is generally supplied without the transponder beacon interrogator, but when used for beacon operation is constitutes a complete electronic navigation system. In beacon operation the radar set generates and transmits electromagnetic microwave pulses which activate the strategically located navigational aid beacons. These beacons, when activated, transmit a microwave signal, coded for identification, which is received by the radar thus permitting the ship to be precisely located relative to an exactly known position. The SPS-10 presents either north or ship's heading at the top of the scope. Heading from the ship's gyrocompass can be used to show a ship's heading marker (SHM) on the PPI. This circuit provides a momentary marker flash on the PPI the instant the reflector faces the direction of the ship's heading. On relative bearing the ship's heading marker appears at 000° on the PPI; on true bearing it indicates own ship's course relative to true north. Either true or relative bearing can therefore be read from the screen. Normally, the set will acquire surface targets at ranges slightly greater than the visual line of sight from the antenna. Except under unusual conditions, it permits target identification within a rain area. The SPS-10 may be described as a medium range, high-definition, surface-search radar.

SPS-53 **1714** The SPS-53 is a surface-search radar in the 9345–9405 MHz band; its maximum range is 32 miles (59.3 km). Since it is typical of late model radars now being used in the U.S. Navy and U.S. Coast Guard, the function of the various components will be discussed in greater detail than for other models. The pedestal-mounted antenna contains a horizontally polarized, slotted waveguide radiating element. The "control-indicator" unit contains a 10-inch (25.4 cm) PPI tube. A signal data converter provides true and relative bearing inputs to the control indicator for display.

The RF energy output of the transmitter is conducted by a waveguide to the antenna where, after making a transition in the antenna pedestal, the energy is applied to the slotted array and then radiated in a fan beam pattern. The antenna rotates at 15 RPM and provides search capability for both surface and low-flying targets.

The transmitted energy which strikes a target is reflected back to the antenna. The antenna returns a portion of this reflected energy to the receiver via the waveguide. The detected echo pulse is amplified in the receiver and delivered to the control-indicator unit as a video signal whose amplitude is controlled at a desired level. The amplified video signal is coupled to the grid of the cathode ray tube, causing the echo signal to be converted into visual intelligence on the PPI screen where the signal appears as a bright spot.

Antenna The feedhorn, containing the slotted array radiating element, produces a vertical beam width of 20° and a horizontal beam width of 1.6° at the half-power points. The 20° height of the beam is sufficient to allow for the ship's pitch and roll which might otherwise cause the radar beam to miss a target. The above designation is based on a 5-ft. (1.5 m) antenna. Larger antennas which produce a smaller horizontal beam width are supplied on some models of the SPS-53A.

Receiver transmitter The RF pulse width of 0.1 microsecond with a pulse repetition rate of 1500 pulses per second used at short range, may be switched to 0.5 microseconds and 750 pulses per second for improved long-range performance.

Control indicator The main display unit, shown in Figure 1714, contains all the system controls. The set is turned on at this unit, the receiver is controlled, and true or relative bearing operation may be selected. The unit can

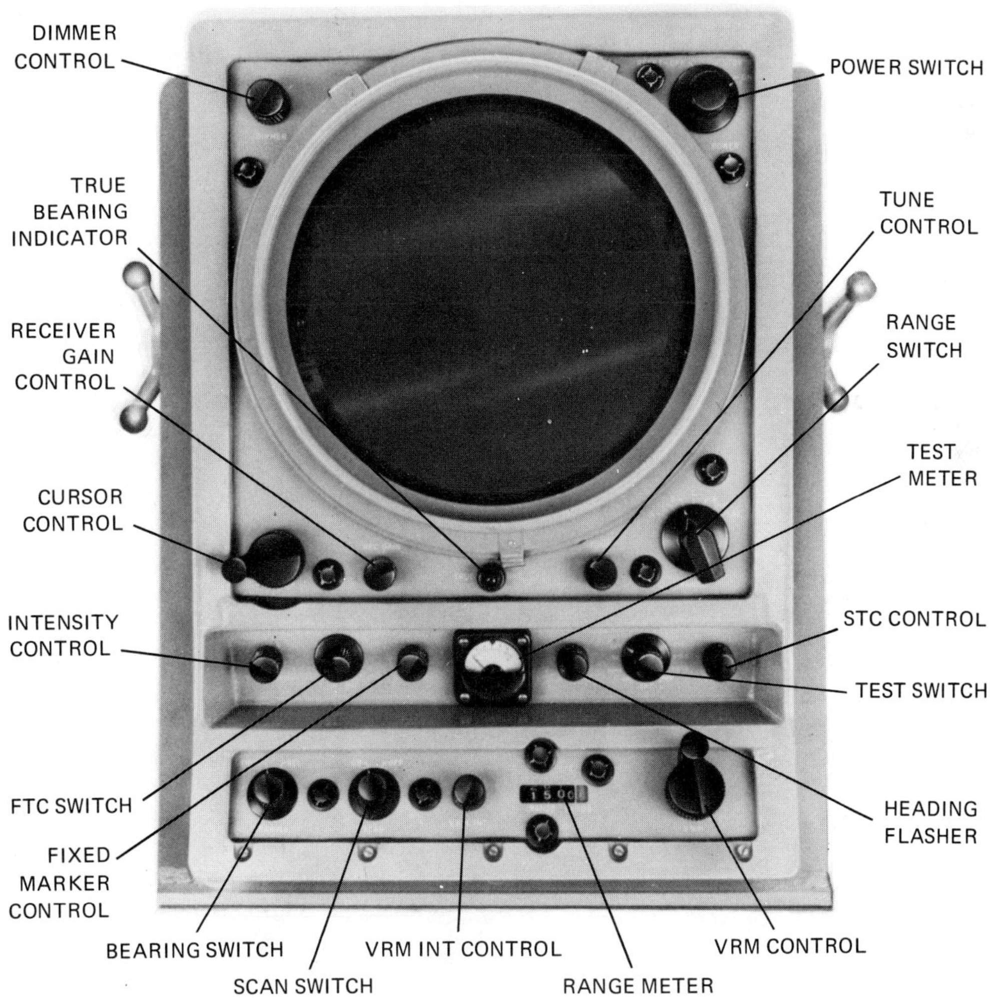

Figure 1714. AN/SPS-53 Radar showing front panel controls.

be pedestal mounted. Provision is also made for table-top, overhead, or bulkhead mounting.

A 10-inch magnetic-deflection, electrostatic-focus, cathode-ray tube provides a PPI presentation. A hood is provided for daytime viewing. Range scales available are: 0.5, 1, 2, 4, 8, 16, and 32 nautical miles, providing a wide choice of areas to be scanned. Scales are multiples of 2, so that perspective is not lost when switching scales. Calibrated range markers are provided; the distance represented by the range markers varies with the setting of the range switch. For example, the four markers will be at 1,000 yard intervals with a range setting of 2 miles, and at 16,000 yards with a range setting of 32 miles.

Surrounding the radar screen is an azimuthal or bearing ring calibrated in degrees. A bearing cursor which intersects the azimuth ring can be rotated in either direction and aligned with an object on the screen to determine the object's bearing relative to the ship's heading. A ship's heading flasher momentarily brightens the screen each time the PPI sweep goes through zero degrees relative, creating a definite line on the screen to indicate the ship's heading. Figure 1714 shows the location of controls on the SPS-53. The operator must be completely familiar with the use of these controls, if he is to obtain optimum information from the scope picture.

SPS-55

1715 The SPS-55 is the newest surface-search radar; it has excellent capabilities for assisting in navigation. This radar operates in the 9.05–10.0 GHz band with 120 kW peak power. A 6-foot (1.8 m) antenna, which rotates at 16 rpm, provides a beam-width of 1.5° horizontally and 20° vertically; the antenna is actually a dual unit, back-to-back with one end-fed slotted waveguide radiating horizontally polarized pulses, and the other side circularly polarized pulses.

Two pulse repetition rates, 750 and 2250 pps, are available, with corresponding pulse lengths of 1.0 and 0.12 microseconds. These are set at the control panel; they are not automatically switched with the range selected as in some radar equipment. The minimum range is 50 yards (46 m) or 200 yards (183 m) for short or long pulses respectively; the corresponding range resolution figures are 75 feet (23 m) and 550 feet (168 m).

The various range scales are selected at the associated indicator unit which is not a part of the SPS-55. The indicator has a 10-inch (25.4 cm) PPI scope and controls that are generally similar to other radar sets.

Commercial radar

1716 Typical of modern commercial radar sets is the SI-TEX/KODEN Model 23. This 3-cm radar operates at a frequency of 9410± 45 MHz with a peak power of 10kW. There are eight selectable range scales from $\frac{1}{4}$ to 48 miles (0.46 km to 89 km), with the added capability of viewing the area from 24 out to 72 miles (44 to 133 km) on the 48-

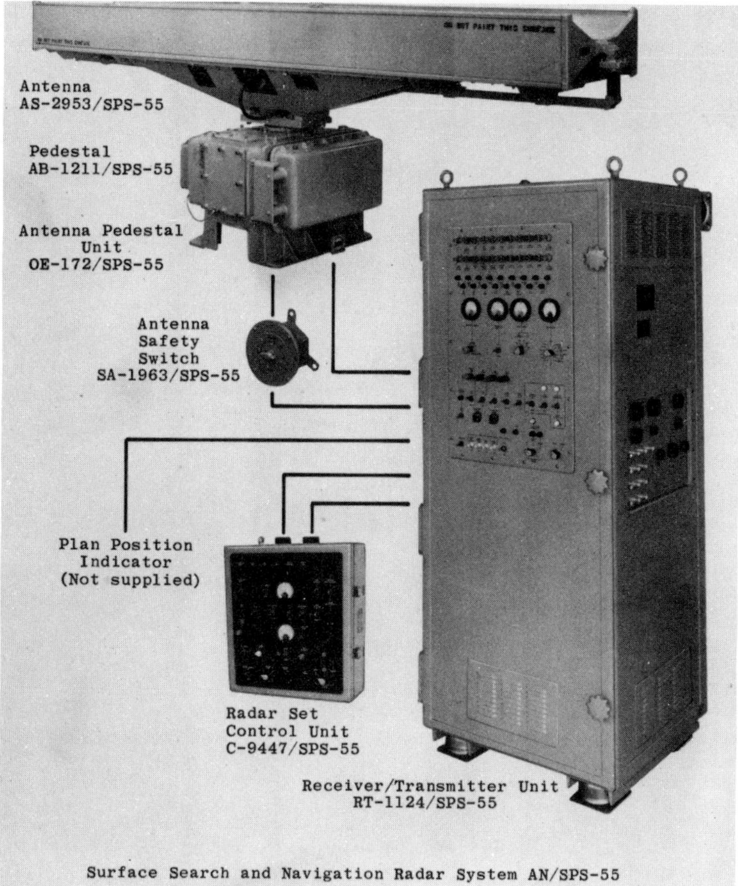

Figure 1715. AN/SPS-55 Radar.

mile range setting by operating a special "Extension" switch; the minimum range is 25 yards (22.9 m). The display has fixed range rings appropriate to the range scale being used, plus a variable range ring with digital readout from 0.2 to 80 miles (0.37 to 148 km). The sweep center can be offset up to approximately 17 percent of the range scale being used, extending the maximum range to as much as 84 miles (156 km). Two different pulse lengths (0.07 and 1.3 μs) and two pulse repetition rates (550 and 1650 pps) are switched automatically with selection of the range scale.

The display is a 10-inch (25.4 cm) PPI scope with a viewing hood for use in high ambient light conditions (the digital range readout is within this hood). There is a manually rotated cursor for bearing measurements. Bearing accuracy is better than 1°; bearing discrimination varies from 2.4° to 1.2° dependent upon the size of the antenna used. The presentation can be oriented either relative to the ship's head or true north up, with optional automatically positioned head and stern

Figure 1716. Commercial radar, SI-TEX/KODEN Model 23.

flashes. Front panel knobs are provided for receiver gain, variable sensitivity time control (STC), and switchable fast time control (FTC), as well as display and range ring brightness. The display may be tabletop mounted or installed on a free-standing pedestal.

Slotted waveguide antennas are available with widths of 3, 4, and 6 feet (0.9, 1.2, 1.8 m), having horizontal beamwidths of 2.4°, 1.8°, and 1.2°, respectively; polarization is horizontal. In all cases, the vertical beamwidth is 25° and the antenna rotates at 20 RPM.

The Model 23 makes extensive use of solid-state electronics, including an integrated circuit IF amplifier. Input primary electric power may be 14 to 40 volts DC (165 to 190 W). or 115 or 230 volts AC (320W).

1717 Radar adapts itself quite readily to uses other than for navigation. As was previously pointed out, the military uses vary from fire control to tracking aircraft at long distances. Other uses include tracking weather disturbances, surveying, etc. However, in all probability, the most important use of radar is to avoid the danger of collision.

Collision avoidance By means of radar-supplied data, proper plotting procedures, and common sense, information on the movements of other vessels can be properly evaluated. The conning officer can thus make decisions regarding course and speed changes in sufficient time to avoid the risk of collision.

The mariner must always bear in mind that even though other vessels may be detected by radar, there are no absolutely positive means of relating fog signals to objects detected by radar. The International Rules of the Road (1972) are specific and clear regarding the use of radar for collision avoidance in conditions of reduced visibility; if fitted on the vessel, radar must be used including systematic observations and plotting (Rule 7), but radar is not a substitute for a "proper lookout" (Rule 5). The use of radar does *not* legally justify greater speeds under conditions of restricted visibility.

Warning on use of radar One of the most essential factors in the use of radar for collision avoidance is the use of proper procedures for all available plotting information, as described in Chapter 14. As one knowledgeable mariner so aptly stated: "Many collisions have occurred because ships' officers were too busy to plot; but none, of which I have knowledge, has occurred because the officers were too busy plotting."

Radar reflectors and beacons **1718** The use of a *radar reflector*—three flat metallic plates at right angles to each other, called a corner reflector—greatly enhances the strength of a radar echo. This enables the detection of a small or nonmetallic object at greater range and/or enables it to be picked out of sea return. Radar reflectors are extensively used on buoys and other aids to navigation, and on small craft, especially those of wood or fiberglass construction.

Radar beacons As useful as radar reflectors are, these are only *passive* devices, limited in the extent that they can enhance a radar echo. For stronger returns, and for positive identification, an *active* device, a *radar beacon,* is required. Such equipment transmits a signal that is much stronger at the receiving antenna than a mere reflected pulse; this signal can be *coded* for identification.

Ramarks Radar beacons can be of two different designs, ramarks and racons. *Ramarks* are *continuously transmitting* beacons that display on the PPI scope a bright radial line or narrow sector on the bearing of the ramark; see Figure 1718a. There are two general types of ramarks; one operates within the marine radar frequency band, the other transmits in the adjacent radar "beacon" band on a frequency of 9310 MHz.

A ramark operating in the frequency band of radar equipment provides the advantage that no additional receiver is needed on the ship; the disadvantage is that the ramark design is more complex as it must *sweep* all frequencies in the band 9,320–9,500 MHz.

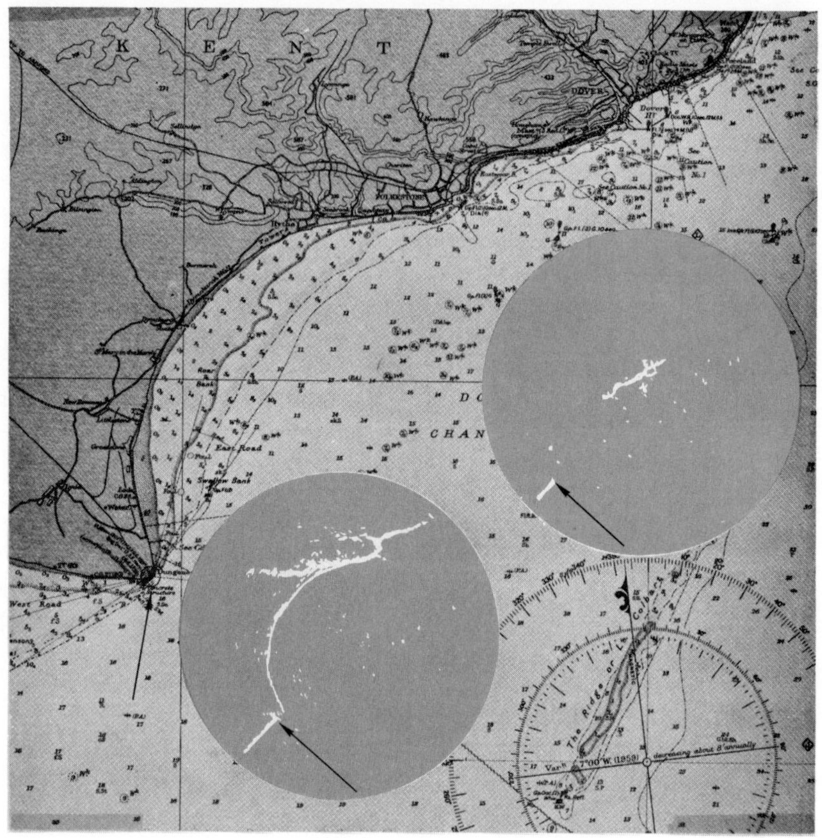

Figure 1718a. Radar beacon presentation off Dungeness, England.

There are two methods of providing identification—by having the radial line on the PPI broken up into dots and dashes, or by transmitting the signal only during some of the revolutions of its antenna and suppressing it during the next few revolutions (time coding). Specific identification by either method is achieved by assigning different codes to various ramarks. Time coding has a disadvantage for marine navigation in that a half-minute or so may be required to complete identification.

Ramarks operating in the beacon band are simpler, but require that the ship have either a separate receiver or a means of temporarily shifting the main radar set receiver from its normal working frequency to 9,310 MHz.

Racons *Racons* transmit a pulse or pulses, but only when *triggered* by receipt of a pulse from a ship's radar; they not only give a stronger return than a reflector, they can be coded for positive identification and range measurement to the beacon.

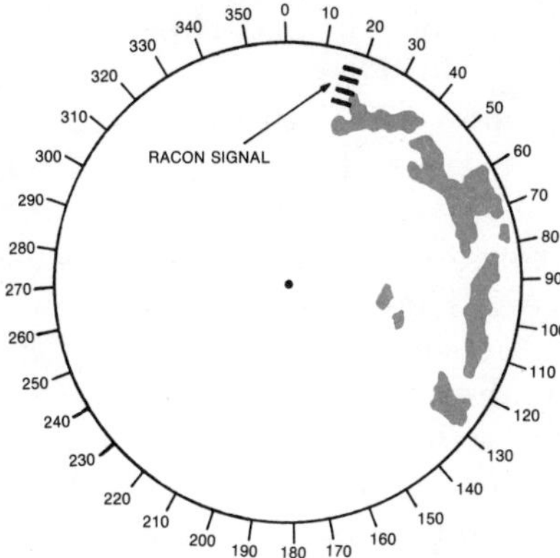

Figure 1718b. Racon signals as seen on a PPI scope.

In order to identify a racon, it is designed so that the reply to the received pulse consists of a number of pulses transmitted at selected intervals; these appear on the ship's PPI scope as segments of concentric arcs, Figure 1718b. The number of segments and their distance apart form the identification code. The usual procedure is that the racon can receive any frequency in the radar band and transmits on a frequency in the beacon band. Thus the ship's radar must have the same capabilities as those mentioned above for ramark reception.

Since the racon reply pulses are initiated by the ship's radar pulses, the racon signal is in synchronism with the PPI display and the range measurement is made to the inner edge of the pulse nearest the center of the scope. A correction, however, must be made as it takes an appreciable time for the racon to react to the incoming pulse, causing the range to appear greater than it actually is. The true range is found by subtracting this difference, which can be the same for all racons. The bearing of the racon is taken to the middle of the arcs.

A racon is a saturable device and cannot reply to all received pulses over a certain number. Moreover, when interrogated by several radar sets simultaneously, interference from the replies to other ships' pulses occurs on the PPI display.

Future outlook **1719** The future outlook for radar and for radar-associated navigation is extremely bright. Research and development in the field of high-resolution radar, combined with VHF-FM voice radio communications directly from one ship's bridge to the other ship's bridge (Channel 13, 156.65 MHz) is expected to materially reduce the possibility of collision during reduced visibility, as well as for in-port pilotage. Utilization of enlarged and brightened pictures on the PPI scope for examination of the presentation by several persons at the same time, day or night, without the restriction of the viewing hood and visor, is coming into increasingly wide use in commercial and military radar. Traffic separation schemes are being increasingly established at ports around the world. These combine buoyed traffic lanes and separation zones with shore-based surveillance radar and direct voice radio advice on ship movement for the greater safety of all vessels in the area.

Charts especially prepared for radar navigation in restricted waters are coming into use. These charts show buoys and other aids to navigation, as well as the shore line and radar-visible landmarks as they would appear on the radar screen of a vessel in the channel, with the range scale set to a stated distance. Such charts permit the navigator to locate himself both accurately and rapidly, and also permit ready differentiation between buoys and small craft.

Radar reflectors are now standard on most buoys and are being added to many minor lights; they are increasingly becoming part of the equipment of smaller vessels as their safety value is more widely recognized. More and more use is being made of radar beacons on prominent navigational landmarks.

With these developments, radar will come into ever increasing use both for navigation and collision avoidance aboard the great majority of vessels plying the rivers, bays, and oceans of the world. Transistors and microminiaturization will help to bring down both size and cost to the point where radar can be used aboard almost all powered vessels, regardless of size.

18 Navigational Astronomy

Introduction **1801** The subject of astronomy, the science of the stars and other celestial bodies—their size, composition, location, movements, etc.—is a fascinating subject full of facts that defy comprehension; it can be studied for a lifetime.

Astronomy is perhaps the oldest science to which man has devoted his attention. Probably primitive men gazed at the night sky in awe and wonderment, and folklore and legend reflect their interest in the heavenly bodies. The progress of the science of astronomy is closely associated with the history of the human race. Each of the great civilizations of the ancient world has recorded its findings in this field. The Egyptians, Babylonians, Chinese, Hindus, Mayas, and Aztecs all pursued the science of astronomy, which they associated with their religious beliefs. These studies were recorded and have been well researched, and the science of astronomy has been greatly advanced in recent years by scientists using the wonders of modern technology.

Here, however, consideration of this vast subject area must be limited to *navigational astronomy*—those aspects of astronomy of interest and value to a navigator in fixing his position and directing the course of his vessel.

The universe **1802** The universe is generally considered to be infinite in size. Modern technology has made possible telescopes which have greatly increased man's ability to see farther into the vast reaches of space. As a result, an immense number of galaxies have been discovered. Galaxies of stars are now observed at distances of approximately ten billion trillion (10^{22}) miles.

Units of distance Special units of measurement have been created for expressing such vast distances. In the measurement of distances within the solar system, the *astronomical unit* (AU) is used. To express distances to bodies outside the solar system, two terms are used, the *light-year,* and the *parsec.*

The value of the astronomical unit is approximately 93 million statute miles* (150 million km), the average distance between the earth and the sun.

* In this chapter only, distances will be stated in statute miles, as used in texts on astronomy, rather than in nautical miles.

Light-year The light-year is roughly 5.89 trillion miles (9.47 trillion or 9.47×10^{12} km); this is the distance that light travels in one year. The speed of light is approximately 186,282 miles (299,792.50 km) per second, and one year is equivalent to approximately 31.6 million seconds.

Parsec *Parsec* (from the words *parallax* and *second*) is the distance at which a body, viewed from the earth and from the sun, will differ in apparent position by one second of arc. This amounts to about 19.1 trillion (1.91×10^{13}) miles (3.07×10^{13} km), or 3.24 light-years. Since this value is less than the distance from earth to Rigil Kentaurus, the navigational star nearest to our solar system at a distance of about 4.3 light-years, any star viewed from the sun and from the earth will differ in direction by less than one second of arc. This small angle is known as the star's *heliocentric parallax* (not to be confused with *geocentric parallax*).

Each galaxy is an assemblage of perhaps 100 billion stars, dust clouds, and masses of thin gas in rotation, held together by gravitational force in a lens-shaped formation. A typical galaxy may be some 100,000 light-years in diameter, tapering in thickness from 15,000 light-years at the center to about 5,000 light-years near the rim. Most galaxies are spiral in shape (see Figure 1802).

Magnitude The brightness of a celestial body is expressed in terms of *magnitude.* The magnitude ratio is derived from Ptolemy's division of the visible stars into six groups according to brightness. The first group is considered to be 100 times brighter than the sixth group. Thus, the

Figure 1802. Photograph of a typical spiral galaxy.

magnitude ratio is computed as the fifth root of 100 or 2.512, and a zero magnitude body is 2.512 times brighter than a first magnitude body, which is 2.512 times brighter than a second magnitude body, etc. With this scale, the two brightest stars, Sirius and Canopus, have negative magnitudes of −1.6 and −0.9 respectively. Some are *variable stars* whose brightness varies slightly or considerably over regular or irregular intervals; for example, Betelgeuse varies in brightness by more than a factor of two over an irregular period.

The Milky Way

1803 Our own galaxy, the Milky Way, derives its name from the milky appearance of the night sky to the unaided eye as an observer looks along its major axis. This milky appearance is caused by the concentration of stars—uncounted and uncountable—in this area. The Milky Way is considered to be about average among galaxies in star population. The stars are not evenly distributed; they tend to be concentrated in two spiral arms extending outward from the center, with the whole galaxy in rotation. It is about 100,000 light-years in diameter, has a maximum thickness of some 10,000 light-years, and contains, perhaps, 100 billion stars.

The stars of the Milky Way revolve around the center of the galaxy at speeds which decrease with increased distance from the center. At a distance of roughly 27,000 light-years from the center, the speed of revolution is approximately 140 miles per second (225 km/s). At this distance, near the inner edge of one of the spiral arms of the Milky Way and about halfway between the "top" and the "bottom" of the galaxy, there is a quite ordinary star, as stars go, but one of supreme importance to man—it is the *sun.*

The stars which make up the Milky Way galaxy vary greatly in size. The largest known star is Antares (Alpha Scorpii) with a diameter about 428 times that of our sun; the smallest, 48 light-years distant was discovered only in recent years. Our sun, an average-sized star is approximately 864,400 miles (1.39×10^6 km) in diameter.

Apart from our own star, the sun, the navigator is concerned only with stars within our galaxy and, astronomically speaking, in our immediate neighborhood. The *Nautical Almanac* and the *Air Almanac* (Chapter 23) tabulate data on a total of 173 stars suitable for use in celestial navigation. Only 58 of this total are normally used; these are the 57 so-called "selected stars," plus Polaris, which is conveniently located for the determination of latitude in the northern hemisphere.

The stars are not the only celestial bodies employed in navigation. The planets of our solar system and the moon (see Article 1805) are also valuable to the navigator. Some of these bodies, with the sun, are suitable at times for daytime observations. However, the navigator's use of the bodies within the solar system differs from his use of the stars in two respects, both due to the vast difference in distance.

First, for navigation purposes, rays of light from any star may be considered to be parallel throughout the solar system. For example,

Rigil Kentaurus, the nearest navigational star, is more than four light-years distant; the second nearest navigational star and the brightest in the sky, Sirius, is twice that distance. Rigil Kentaurus, observed from opposite points on the earth's orbit around the sun (Figure 1803), would differ in angle by approximately 1.5 seconds of arc. The navigator is not equipped to measure angles to this precision. Thus, in the observation of a star, *horizontal parallax* (also called geocentric parallax), that difference in apparent direction or position of a celestial body when observed from a point on the surface of the earth from the theoretical direction from the center of the earth (see Figure 1805d), may be disregarded. For navigational purposes the stars can be considered as being at an infinite distance, while the sun, moon, and planets are at finite distances. The moon is only about 1¼ light seconds distant from the earth, and the sun is less than 8½ light minutes away; these relatively close distances necessitate a correction for parallax.

Horizontal parallax

Secondly, stars may be considered, for navigational purposes, as point sources of light with no measurable diameter when viewed through a sextant telescope. The sun, at an average distance from the earth of 93,000,000 miles (1.5×10^8 km), is considered to be equivalent in mass to an average star.

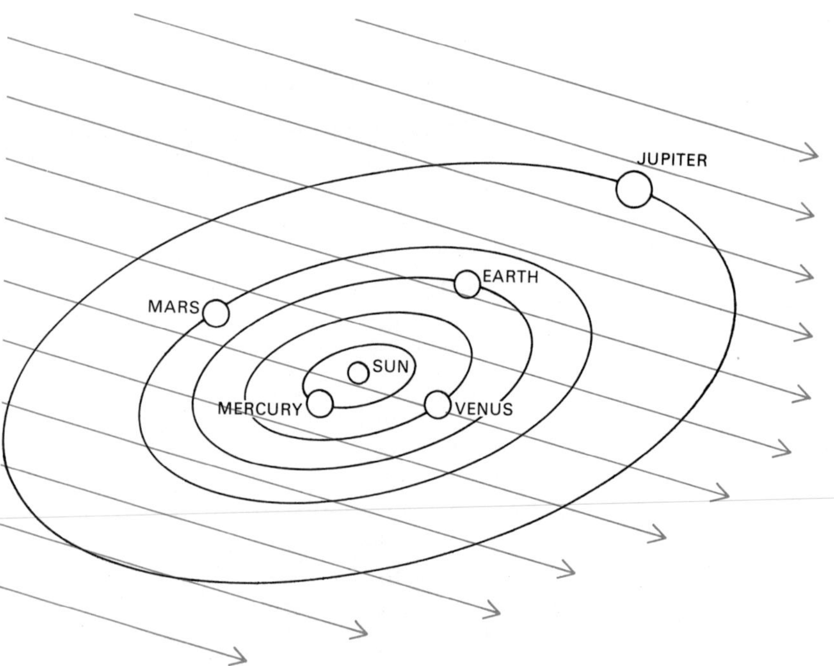

Figure 1803. Light rays from stars are essentially parallel all across the solar system.

Semidiameter As a result of the nearness of the sun and the moon, a correction is necessary for *semidiameter*—which adjusts for the difference between an observation on the upper or lower edge, called *limb*, of the body and a true measurement to the center of the body. The semidiameter of planets, limited to not more than about 32 *seconds* of arc, is seldom considered in marine navigation.

The sun **1804** The center of our solar system, a rotating mass of burning gases radiating energy at a fantastic rate, is called the sun. Every second it converts millions of tons of matter into energy, and it has been doing this for some five billion years. Its surface temperature is about 10,000 degrees Fahrenheit, and it is in a constant state of agitation, emitting eruptions of burning gas to distances sometimes as much as hundreds of thousands of miles, before they fall back to the surface.

A solar phenomenon of great interest is the *sun spot,* which appears dark on the surface of the sun. Sun spots are masses of comparatively cooler gas, sometimes 50,000 miles (80,000 km) in diameter.

Magnetic storms on the earth, which interfere with the propagation and reception of radio signals, are related to sun spots, which in recent times have occurred in eleven-year cycles.

The sun rotates about its axis, but due to its gaseous composition, the rotation is faster near the equator (25 days) than near the poles (34 days).

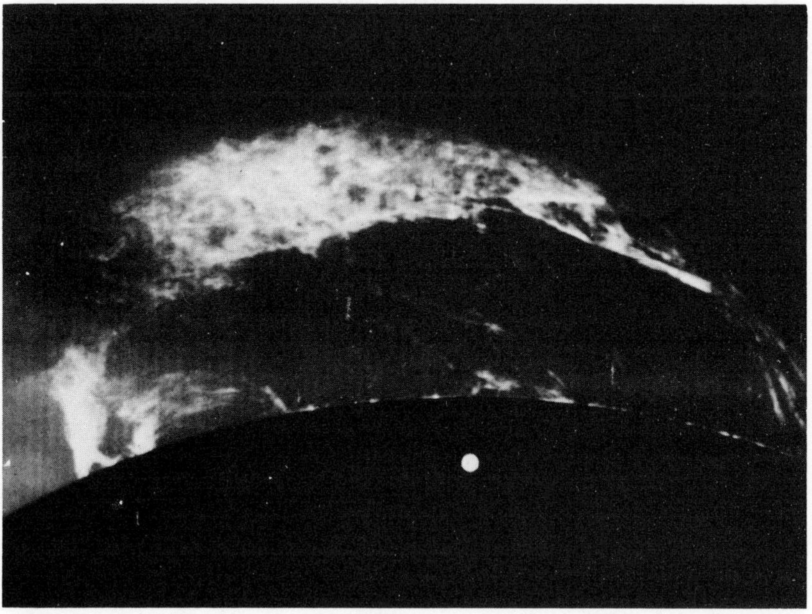

Figure 1804. The surface of the sun. (Dot indicates comparative size of the earth.)

The solar system **1805** The solar system consists of nine known major planets and thousands of planetoids or asteroids, traveling in elliptical orbits about the sun. Of these major planets, only Venus, Mars, Jupiter, and Saturn are normally used in navigation. Mean distances of the planets from the sun range from 67 million miles (1.08×10^8 km) for Venus, to 886 million miles (1.43×10^9 km) for Saturn; the periods required by each to complete a revolution around the sun vary from about 225 days for Venus, to $29\frac{1}{2}$ years for Saturn.

Pluto, the most remote of the planets, is about $5\frac{1}{2}$ light hours, or about 3,670 million miles (5.90×10^9 km), from the sun and requires more than 248 years to complete a revolution.

Motions in the solar system All celestial bodies *rotate* on their *axes* and *revolve* in their *orbits.* The solar system as a whole moves with the sun as it travels through space.

All the planets rotate from west to east, including the earth. They revolve in ellipses of quite slight eccentricities in which the common center of mass of the sun and the body concerned is at one of the two focuses. For a moon, the focus is the common center of mass of that satellite and its parent body.

The subject of the motions of celestial bodies in their orbits (paths of the smaller mass called the *body,* around the larger mass called the *primary*) is a complex one. The speed of a celestial body in its orbit varies in such a way that the line joining it with its primary sweeps over *equal areas* in equal times. Figure 1805a represents the orbit of a celestial body around its primary. It could represent the orbit of a planet about the sun, or a satellite around a planet. Whatever the body, its orbit is an ellipse. The law governing speed in orbit is illustrated by the shaded areas of Figure 1805a, each of which represents an equal area of the ellipse. Because of the eccentricity of the ellipse, exaggerated somewhat here for emphasis, the line joining the body and the primary sweeps over equal areas only if the body moves faster as it approaches closer to the primary. Thus the speed of a celestial body is greatest when it is nearest the primary, and least when it is farthest from it.

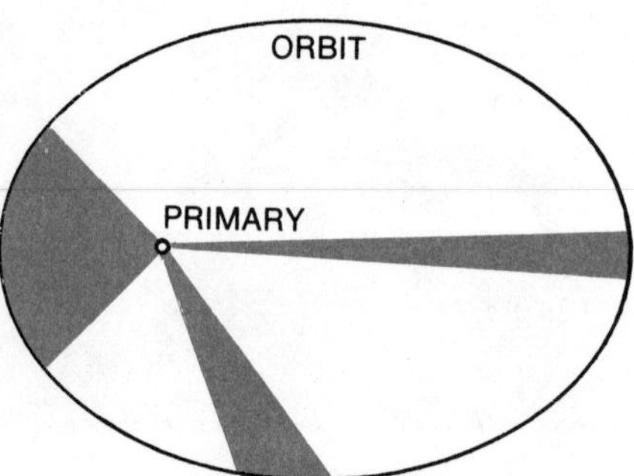

Figure 1805a. The elliptical orbit of a celestial body around its "primary."

Actually, the primary for any celestial body is affected by that body, causing the primary itself to revolve in a small ellipse which is a miniature counterpart of the orbit of the body, the two masses having a common focus. This is illustrated, in a general way, by Figure 1805b. In the earth-sun system, this focus is within the sun and very near its center. For the earth-moon pair, the focus is within the earth at about three-fourths radius from the center of the earth. The orbit of the earth in relation to that of the moon is of particular significance in relation to the basic causes of tides (Article 903).

The eccentricity of the earth's orbit about the sun is not great, but it is enough to result in a substantial change in the latter's apparent diameter. At *perihelion,* the point of nearest approach which follows the winter solstice (Article 1813) by 10 to 12 days, the apparent diameter of the sun is approximately 32.6 minutes of arc. At *aphelion,* the point of greatest separation, which follows the summer solstice by about the same time interval, the apparent diameter is about 31.5 minutes. *Perihelion* and *aphelion* are illustrated in Figure 1805b.

The moon The earth's only natural satellite, the moon, is at an average distance of about 239,000 miles (385,000 km) from the earth. Its orbit is, of course, elliptical; a moderate degree of eccentricity results in a distance of approximately 221,000 miles (356,000 km) at *perigee,* and 253,000 miles (407,000 km) at *apogee.* As with the sun, this change in distance causes a variation in apparent diameter of the moon, as viewed from the earth, between 29.4 and 33.4 minutes of arc. The diameter of the moon is roughly 2,160 miles (3,480 km). Its period of revolution about

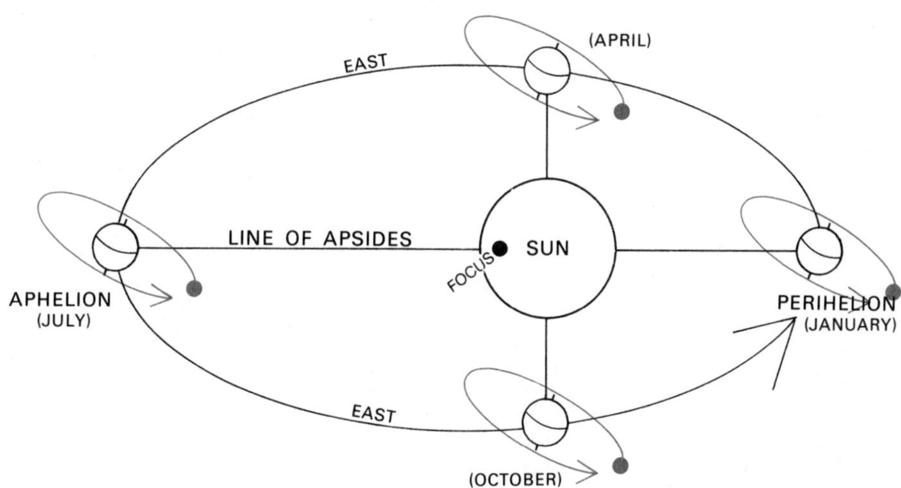

Figure 1805b. The body and its primary travel elliptical paths about a common focus.

the earth and its axial rotation are the same, $27\frac{1}{3}$ days, thus it always presents essentially the same face to the earth.

The moon illustrates why the navigator, in measuring altitudes, cannot use the nearest bodies in the solar system exactly as he does the stars. The altitude of the upper or lower limb of the body, as measured with the sextant, must be corrected to read as though made to the center of the body. The moon's visible diameter changes in value as it moves in orbit from perigee to apogee. The semidiameter, illustrated in Figure 1805c, must be applied as a correction to the sextant altitude.

The altitude observed by the navigator is measured up from the sea horizon, but it must be corrected to read as though it had been made at the center of the earth. This correction for horizontal parallax (Figure 1805d) has a maximum value for bodies near the horizon, decreasing to zero for a body directly overhead. The greatest correction for horizontal parallax is on observations of the moon as it is the nearest body used for navigational observations.

The nearer planets, Venus and Mars, are at times observed at distances less than that of the sun. The distance of Venus varies from 0.28 astronomical units to 1.72 astronomical units; Mars, from 0.38 to 2.66 astronomical units. Venus, almost equal in diameter to the earth, pro-

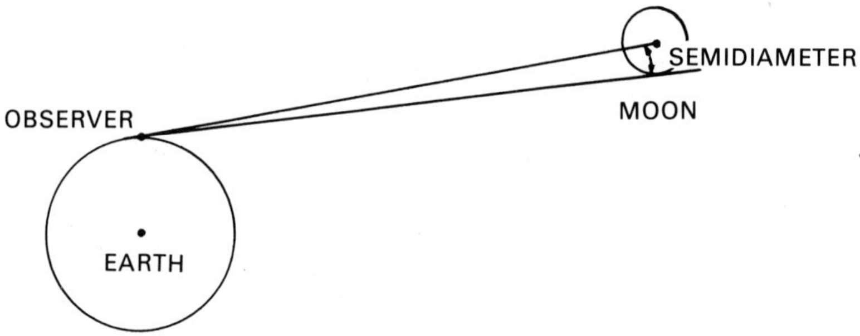

Figure 1805c. Semidiameter (scale greatly exaggerated).

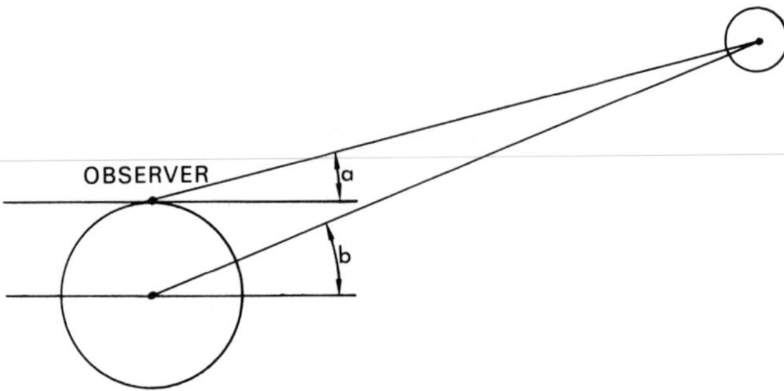

Figure 1805d. Parallax due to observer not being at center of the earth.

Planet	Mean Distance from Sun: Millions of Miles	Mean Distance from Sun: Astronomical Units	Mean Diameter (in miles)	Sidereal Period	Axial Rotation	Known Satellites
Mercury	36	0.4	3,008	88 days	60^d	none
Venus	67	0.7	7,700	224.7 days	$247^d \pm 5$	none
Earth	93	1.0	7,918	365.24 days	23^h56^m	1
Mars	142	1.5	4,215	687 days	24^h37^m	2
Jupiter	484	5.2	86,800	11.86 years	9^h50^m	12
Saturn	887	9.5	71,500	29.46 years	10^h14^m	10
Uranus	1783	19.2	31,700	84.02 years	10^h49^m	5
Neptune	2794	30.1	31,000	164.8 years	15^h40^m	2
Pluto	3666	39.4	3,500±	248.4 years	6.4^d?	none

Figure 1805e. Distance, diameter, and other data on planets.

vides an observable disc, rather than a true point of light, when nearest the earth. The sidereal period of revolution for Venus is only 224.7 days; for the earth it is 365.2 days. The maximum brilliance, as observed from the earth, occurs about 36 days prior to and after the inferior conjunction of the two planets, at which time it approaches a magnitude of −4.4. The minimum magnitude is about −3.3. For a considerable portion of the time, Venus is favorably situated for daytime celestial fixes in combination with lines of position acquired by sun or moon observations. Horizontal parallax is a small factor in planet observations.

Other planets may be observed during daylight hours, subject to the telescope used and atmospheric conditions. Jupiter varies in magnitude from −1.4 to −2.5, Mars from 1.6 to −2.8, Mercury from 1.1 to −1.2. These bodies compare very favorably in brilliance with the 57 selected stars which range from comparatively faint Zubenelgenubi, with a magnitude of 2.9, to the brightest star, Sirius, with a magnitude of −1.6. The light from a planet is usually somewhat steadier than that from a star. The full moon has a magnitude varying slightly around −12.6; the magnitude of the sun is about −26.7.

Like the moon, the sun varies in apparent size, depending on the earth's position in its elliptical orbit. Geocentric parallax, a value much smaller than that involved in moon observations, due to the much greater distance of the sun, amounts to approximately 0.1′ between altitudes 0° and 65°.

Data on the nine principal planets are given in Figure 1805e. It is interesting to note that the majority of the principal planets have satellites, or "moons," rotating about them. These satellites, like the planets themselves, are relatively cold bodies, and shine only due to the light reflected from them.

Minor planets and asteroids

1806 Minor planets and asteroids differ from the principal planets chiefly in size and number; they are not of navigational significance. While Mercury, the smallest principal planet, is only about 3,100 miles

(4,990 km) in diameter, the largest minor planet has a diameter of only 480 miles (770 km). Over 3,000 minor planets have been discovered, but many thousands more are believed to be circling the sun.

Most of the minor planets are in orbits lying between those of Mars and Jupiter. It is speculated that they may be the remains of a former principal planet, as there is mathematical support for the theory that such a planet once orbited there.

Meteors and meteorites

1807 The so-called "shooting stars" are small, solid bodies of the solar system, usually no larger than a grain of sand, which enter the earth's atmosphere and are heated to incandescence by friction. They are observed only when they enter the atmosphere. Most *meteors* are completely vaporized as they travel through the atmosphere. The small percentage which are not completely destroyed and strike the surface as solid particles are called *meteorites.* Most are composed largely of nickel and iron; the remainder are stone.

Some meteors are apparently small asteroids, which were drawn out of their elliptical orbits about the sun by the earth's gravity. Others, possibly remnants of comets, seem to travel in quasi-parabolic orbits; these latter are believed to cause the "showers of shooting stars" which occur periodically. Most meteors are believed to weigh only a small fraction of an ounce, but some can be of great size, and it seems probable that the large crater near Winslow, Arizona, was caused by a meteorite which weighed some 50,000 tons (4.5×10^7 kg).

Meteors enter the atmosphere at an estimated rate of 100 million a day. The dates of prominent annual meteor showers are listed in most astronomical texts. At such times, the observer may see ten or more, and on rare occasions sometimes hundreds, in an hour; the hours between midnight and dawn are the best for observation.

Comets

1808 Comets are composed chiefly of frozen methane, ammonia, and water, with clusters of meteoric material in the nucleus. They travel in orbits which are elliptical (if periodic), parabolic, or hyperbolic. When a comet first becomes visible, it shines only by light reflected from the sun but, as it approaches the sun, solar radiation excites the gases within the comet and it becomes partly self-luminous.

As a comet approaches within 100 million to 200 million miles (1.6 to 3.2×10^8 km) of the sun, a tail generally begins to form as the result of the impact of the nucleus of the comet with the charged particles of the "solar wind." The tail may grow in length to 100 million miles (1.6×10^8 km) at perihelion and then gradually recede as the comet moves away from the sun.

This tail is always directed away from the sun (Figure 1808) so that it precedes the comet as the latter gets farther away from the sun. Occasionally a comet is sufficiently brilliant to be seen in broad daylight, although this is a rare occurrence.

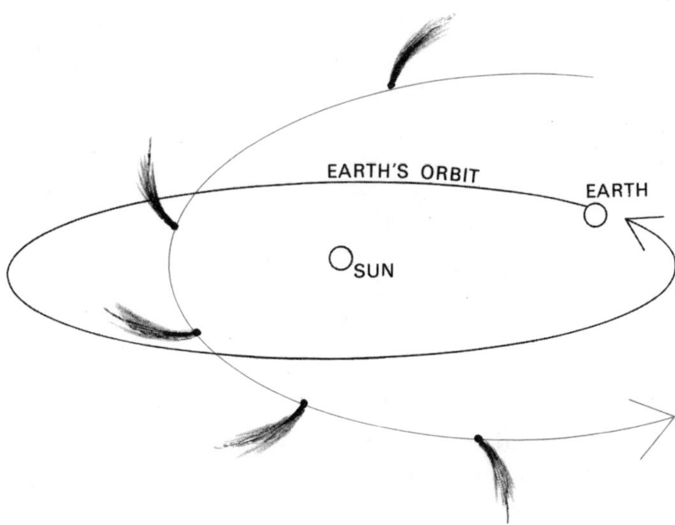

Figure 1808. Path of Cunningham's Comet. The tail of a comet always points away from the sun.

Comets are fairly plentiful in the solar system, and on most nights during the year at least one can be seen with a telescope. In general, they take many years to complete their orbits about the sun. Halley's comet, which is the best known, has a period of 76 years, and will next be visible in 1986.

Revolution and rotation of the earth

1809 The earth revolves about the sun in a slightly elliptical orbit; it is about 91,400,000 miles (1.47×10^8 km) from the sun in January, and 94,500,000 miles (1.52×10^8 km) in July. It rotates 360° about its axis once in 23 hours 56 minutes; this is termed the *sidereal day,* and differs from the solar day, which averages 24 full hours, because of the earth's motion in its orbit. This difference between the sidereal and solar days is illustrated in Figure 1809.

At position (1) the sun is over the meridian M; rotation is counterclockwise in this diagram. When the earth has arrived at position (2) in its orbit, it has rotated 360° on its axis, but the sun is still east of the meridian M, and will not be on the meridian until the earth has rotated for an additional period averaging four minutes. This period varies slightly during the year, and depends on the earth's position in its orbit.

Inclination of the earth

The earth's equator is inclined about 23.5° to its orbit (Figure 1813a), the north pole being inclined towards the sun from the latter part of March to the latter part of September. During the balance of the year, the south pole is inclined towards the sun. The resultant apparent annual path of the sun among the stars is called the *ecliptic.* This in-

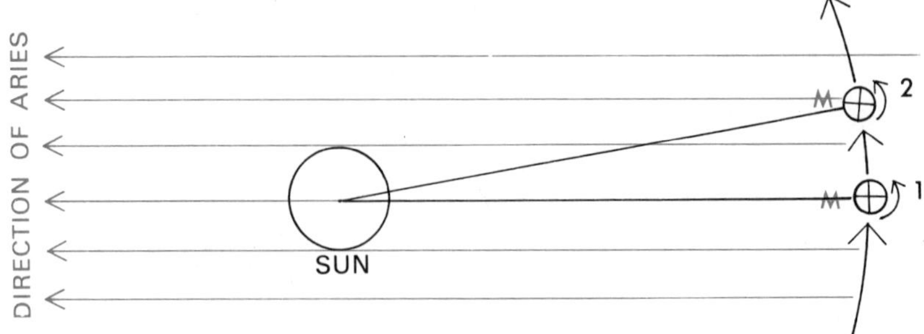

Figure 1809. Sidereal and solar days.

clination of the equator causes the change of seasons. The earth's axis remains rigidly inclined in space due to rotation of the mass, just as a spinning gyroscope's axis is rigid.

The earth's atmosphere

1810 The *atmosphere* of the earth is a great blanket of air, consisting principally of 78 percent nitrogen and 21 percent oxygen, with very small amounts and traces of other gases and contaminants. Half of the atmosphere is concentrated within about 3½ miles (5½ km) of the surface; the remainder thins out to an altitude of roughly 1000 miles (1600 km).

Atmospheric diffusion

Without the diffusing effect of the atmosphere, the stars and the sun would be visible at the same time. However, the molecules which make up the atmosphere, aided by suspended dust, scatter the sun's light in all directions, and make it difficult to see the stars. Astronauts report that at altitudes of over 100 miles (160 km) they are still unable to see most stars in daytime, but that from true "outer space" they can. The short wavelength blue light from the sun is particularly affected by this scattering, thus giving the sky its characteristic blue color.

When a celestial body is near the horizon, its light must pass through a greater volume of air than when it is overhead, as is shown in Figure 1810. This causes additional scattering, and permits very little blue light to reach the observer, leaving only the long wavelength red light. This causes the reddish-orange appearance of the sun and moon near the horizon.

Refraction of light

The atmosphere also causes light rays to be *refracted,* or bent, as they enter it from space; this refraction of the sun's rays prolongs the twilight. In addition, except when a celestial body is directly overhead, refraction affects its apparent altitude, causing it to appear higher than it actually is. Refraction increases as altitude decreases; under "standard" atmospheric conditions it amounts to 34.5′ at zero altitude. The entire disc of the sun can be visible after the upper limb has, in fact, passed below the horizon. The atmosphere also reduces the ap-

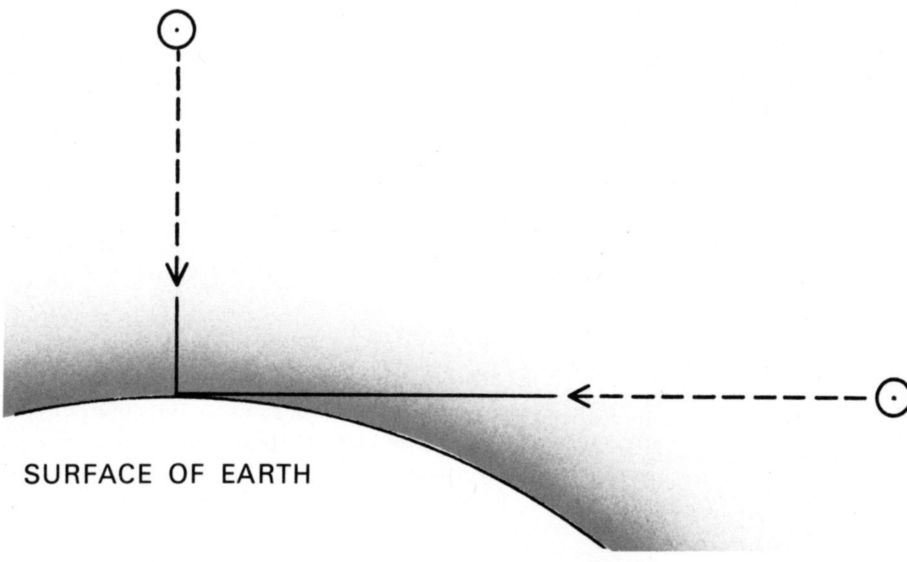

Figure 1810. At low altitudes, the sun's rays travel through greater distances in the earth's atmosphere and the characteristic red color is a result.

parent brightness of celestial bodies, again having its greatest effect when the body is on the horizon, and its light rays are passing through the maximum distance and density of air. As its altitude decreases from 90° to 5°, a star's brightness may be reduced by a full magnitude. Atmospheric turbulence often causes the light from a star to twinkle; the light from planets usually does not appear to do so, as they are comparatively near the earth, and have appreciable size, rather than being mere point sources of light.

Motions of the earth

1811 The earth in company with the entire solar system revolves around the axis of our galaxy. This motion has very little effect upon the apparent motion of the celestial bodies across the heavens. But there are three major and two minor types of earth motion or changes which affect the apparent paths of these bodies. The three major motions of the earth are *rotation* about its axis, *revolution* around the sun, and *precession*. The two minor motions are *wandering* of the terrestrial poles, and *variations* in the speed of rotation. These motions will be considered in the following articles.

Effects of the earth's rotation

1812 The daily rotation of the earth on its axis causes the principal apparent motion of the heavenly bodies across the sky from east to west. This motion is: parallel to the plane of the earth's equator; occurs in circles whose centers are on the earth's axis or its extension; and is at an almost constant rate. These circles are called diurnal or daily circles. To be visible to an observer a body must, of course, be above his *celestial horizon,* which may be considered as a plane passing through the center of the earth, and perpendicular to a line connecting the observer's position and the earth's center (see Figure 1812a). The plane of his horizon therefore changes as he changes latitude. If he is located at one of the poles his horizon is parallel to the equator. If the body's brightness and atmospheric conditions are ignored its visibility depends both upon the position of the body's diurnal circle, relative to the observer's latitude, and its location on that circle. The *declination* of a body on the celestial sphere (see Article 1902) is identical to the latitude of the point on earth directly under the celestial body. This is referred to as the *geographical position* (GP) of the body. Declination and GP will be discussed in greater detail in Chapter 19. The apparent motion of the celestial bodies caused by the rotation of the earth on its axis results in the GP of the body moving westward along

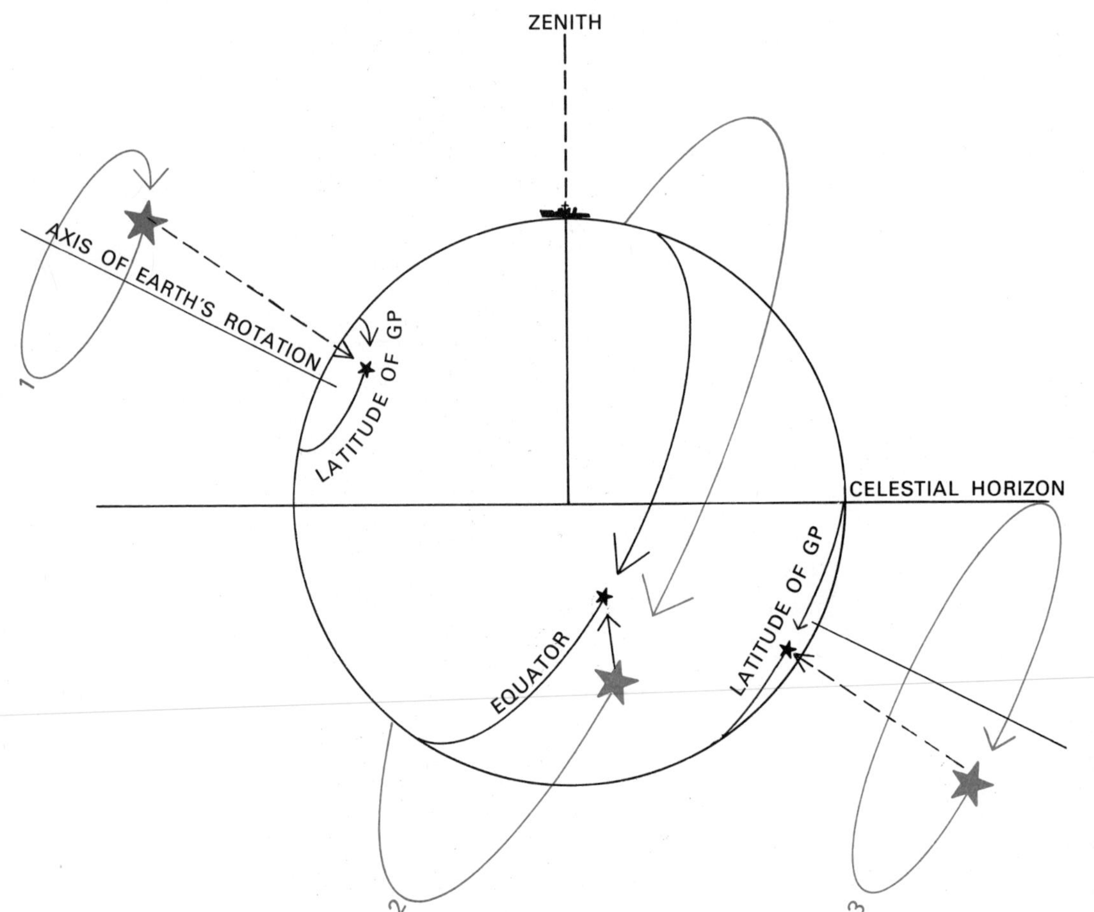

Figure 1812a. Diurnal circles.

a parallel of latitude equivalent in angular value to the declination of the body.

Figure 1812b illustrates three stars with declinations of 0°, 30° S, and 60° N. As the earth rotates, the GPs of the bodies will trace lines across the earth following the equator, the 30° south parallel of latitude, and the 60° north parallel of latitude respectively.

As illustrated in Figure 1812a, an observer is in 30° north latitude; the plane of his horizon is shown as passing through the earth's center; circle 1 represents the apparent daily path or diurnal circle of a body having a declination of approximately 80° north. In moving along its diurnal circle it is therefore constantly above some point on the 80th parallel of north latitude. Note that for the observer in latitude 30° north this body never sets below the horizon. This, of course, will be equally true for all bodies having a declination of 60° or more north (90° minus observer's latitude of 30°). All such bodies will bear due north of the observer at the highest and lowest points on their diurnal circles, and since they do not set below the horizon they are referred to as *circumpolar* stars. Figure 1812c depicts the trace of circumpolar stars, showing their path around the earth's axis extended.

A star with a declination of 30° north (not shown in Figure 1812a) will be above the horizon for about 14 hours and 40 minutes of the day. It rises over the horizon well north of east and will pass directly overhead and set north of west. Circle 2 represents the diurnal circle of a star having a declination of 0°; it circles the equator. It rises

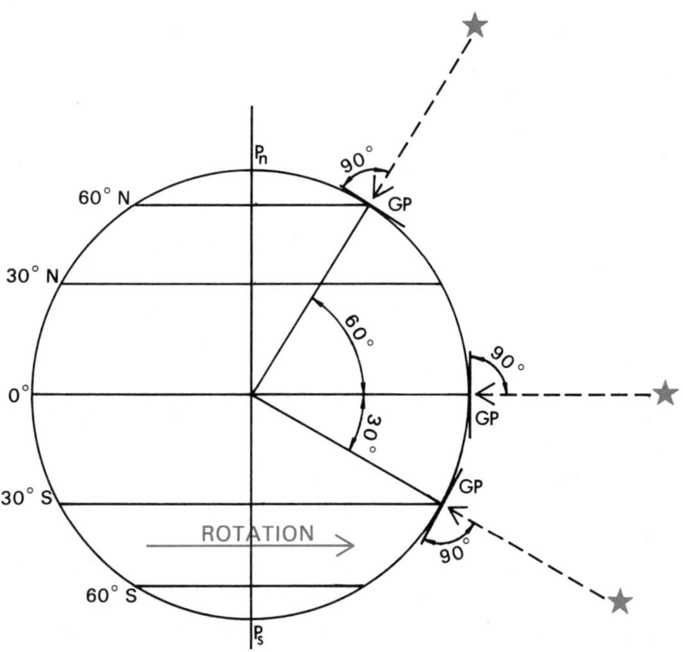

Figure 1812b. The declination of a star equals the latitude of its GP.

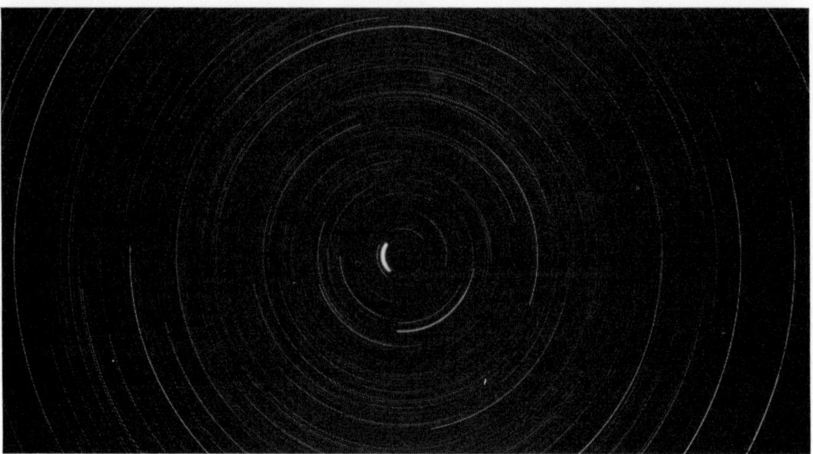

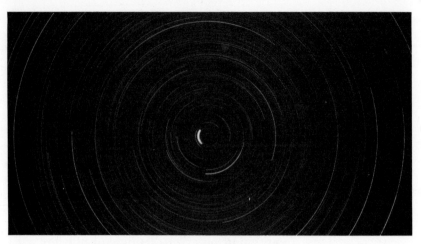

Figure 1812c. Observatory photograph of circumpolar stars.

due east of the observer, is due south of him when it reaches its maximum altitude of 60° and sets due west. It is above the horizon for 12 hours. Circle 3 represents the diurnal circle of a body with 60° south declination. Such a body or any with a declination greater than 60° south would never appear above the horizon for an observer in latitude 30° north.

The declination of each star changes so slowly that over a period of many years an observer in a given latitude will have essentially the same continuous view of the diurnal circle of that star. On the other hand, the declination of each body of the solar system changes with comparative rapidity, and thus the apparent motions of these bodies changes at a similar rate. The declination of the sun, moon, and navigational planets varies between approximately 25° north and 25° south, and at any time their diurnal circles will lie between these limits.

Day and night

One of the principal effects of the earth's rotation on its axis is the alternating phenomena known as day and night. Since the earth is approximately a sphere, half of it will be in sunlight and half in darkness at any given time. The length of the period of day or night varies with the observer's location on the surface of the earth as a result of the inclination of the earth's axis as discussed in Articles 1809 and 1813.

Effects of the earth's revolution

1813 The annual revolution of the earth about the sun is illustrated in Figure 1813a which also shows the 23.5° inclination of the equator to the earth's orbit. About 21 June each year the north pole is at its maximum inclination towards the sun, and the declination of the latter is 23.5° *north.* As the earth moves on in its orbit about the sun, the northerly declination of the sun decreases slowly, and reaches 0° about

23 September; it continues to decrease at a constant rate until about 22 December, when it reaches 23.5° *south,* its maximum southerly declination. Moving on from this point, the declination increases at a constant rate, reaching 0° again about 21 March, and 23.5° north on 21 June.

First point of Aries The points of maximum declination are called the *solstices;* the points of 0° declination are called the *equinoxes.* These words are derived from the Latin, solstice meaning "sun standing still," and equinox meaning "equal night." The point in space at which the March equinox occurs is also called the *first point of Aries* (♈), or simply *Aries;* it is an important reference point in the system of celestial coordinates. It derives its name from the fact that when the celestial coordinate system was first established, the sun entered the constellation Aries as it passed from south to north declination. It has kept the name although this point has moved due to the earth's precession (Article 1815).

The annual change in the sun's declination explains the changing seasons experienced on earth; they are caused by the angle at which the sun's rays strike the earth, and the comparative length of daylight and darkness. In this connection the times of 0° declination are generally termed the vernal (spring) and the autumnal equinoxes; the time of maximum north declination is the summer solstice, and the time of maximum south declination is the winter solstice for the northern hemisphere; summer and winter are reversed for the southern hemisphere.

The revolution of the earth about the sun also affects the apparent positions of the stars, which surround the solar system on all sides. The ones which can be seen from the earth on a given night are those in a direction generally opposite to that of the sun. Because of this the

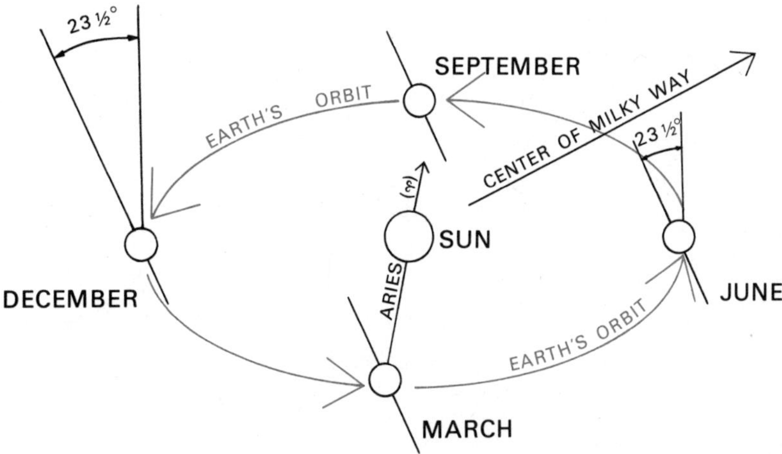

Figure 1813a. The annual revolution of the earth around the sun.

stars appear to make one complete revolution around the earth each year independently of their nightly revolution due to the earth's rotation on its axis; each succeeding night at the same time at a given place, each star will be almost one degree farther west; it requires an average of 365¼ days to complete the revolution of 360°. The early astronomers grouped the stars into arbitrary *constellations;* the twelve constellations along the plane of the ecliptic through which the sun passes during the year are called the *zodiac.* The zodiac as such has no navigational significance.

Superior planets

Motion of planets

The combination of the revolutions of the earth and of the planets about the sun results in the comparatively rapid change of position of the planets. Mars, Jupiter, and Saturn, whose orbits lie outside that of the earth, are termed *superior planets.* The superior planets appear to move steadily westward with respect to the sun, meaning that they rise earlier and cross the observer's meridian earlier on each succeeding day. They emerge from behind the sun as morning twilight bodies and continue to rise earlier each day until they again disappear behind the sun, last being seen as evening twilight bodies. With respect to the stars, the superior planets appear to move constantly eastward from night to night, except when they are nearest the earth. At this time their motion is *retrograde,* appearing to move westward among the stars. Figure 1813b illustrates the retrograde motion of a superior planet. When the earth is at E_1, E_2, E_3, etc., the superior planet is at P_1, P_2, P_3 etc., and appears at positions 1, 2, 3, etc., at the left.

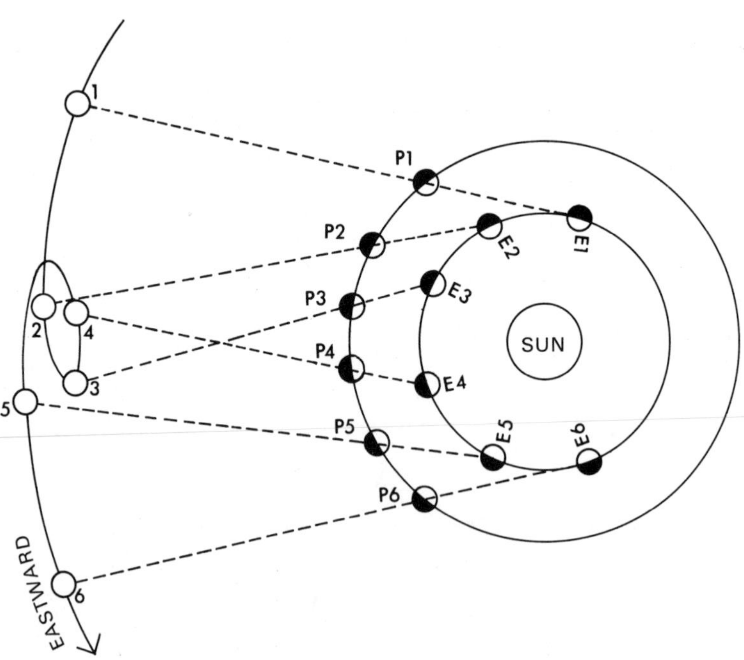

Figure 1813b. Retrograde motion of a superior planet.

Inferior planets Mercury and Venus are termed *inferior planets,* as their orbits lie inside that of the earth. They appear to oscillate with respect to the sun. Venus always appears comparatively near the sun, it alternates as a morning and evening planet, often popularly referred to as the "morning star" or "evening star," because it rises and sets within about three hours of sunrise and sunset.

Mercury is a bright celestial body, but because of its closeness to the sun it can be seen only rarely, and its coordinates are therefore not listed in the *Nautical Almanac.*

The planets shine by the reflected light of the sun; the inferior planets go through all the same phases as the moon (Article 1814), being "full" when on the opposite side of the sun from the earth, and "new" when on the same side. The superior planets never pass between the earth and sun, and are never seen in the "new" phase; they vary only between "full" and "gibbous" when viewed through a telescope.

Effects of the moon's revolution **1814** The most obvious effect of the moon's revolution about the earth is the cycle of *phases* through which it passes. Like the planets, the moon shines by the sun's reflected light. Excluding possible eclipses, the side facing the sun is lit, and the opposite side is dark; the moon's appearance from the earth depends on its orientation relative to the earth and sun.

Phases of the moon The moon passes through its cycle of phases during a 29.5 day *synodic period.* The synodic period of a celestial body is its average period of revolution with respect to the sun, as seen from the earth. It differs from the 360° sidereal period because of the motions of the earth and the body in their orbits. Figure 1814 illustrates the positions of the moon relative to the sun and earth during its synodic period, and the resulting phases. When the moon is between the sun and the earth, its sunlit half faces away from the earth, and the body cannot be seen; this is the *new moon.* As it revolves in its orbit, (counterclockwise in Figure 1814) an observer on earth first sees a part of the sunlit half as a thin crescent, which will then *wax* or grow slowly through first quarter, when it appears as a semicircle. After passing through the first quarter, it enters the *gibbous* phase until it becomes full, and the entire sunlit half can be seen. From full it is said to *wane,* becoming gibbous to the last quarter, and then crescent until the cycle is completed.

Age of the moon The *age of the moon* at a given time is the number of days which have passed since the preceding new moon, and is an indication of the phase, and therefore of the amount of light it sheds. The full moon rises in most latitudes about the same time the sun sets, and sets when the sun rises; the new moon rises and sets with the sun. On the average, the moon rises about 50 minutes later each day, although the

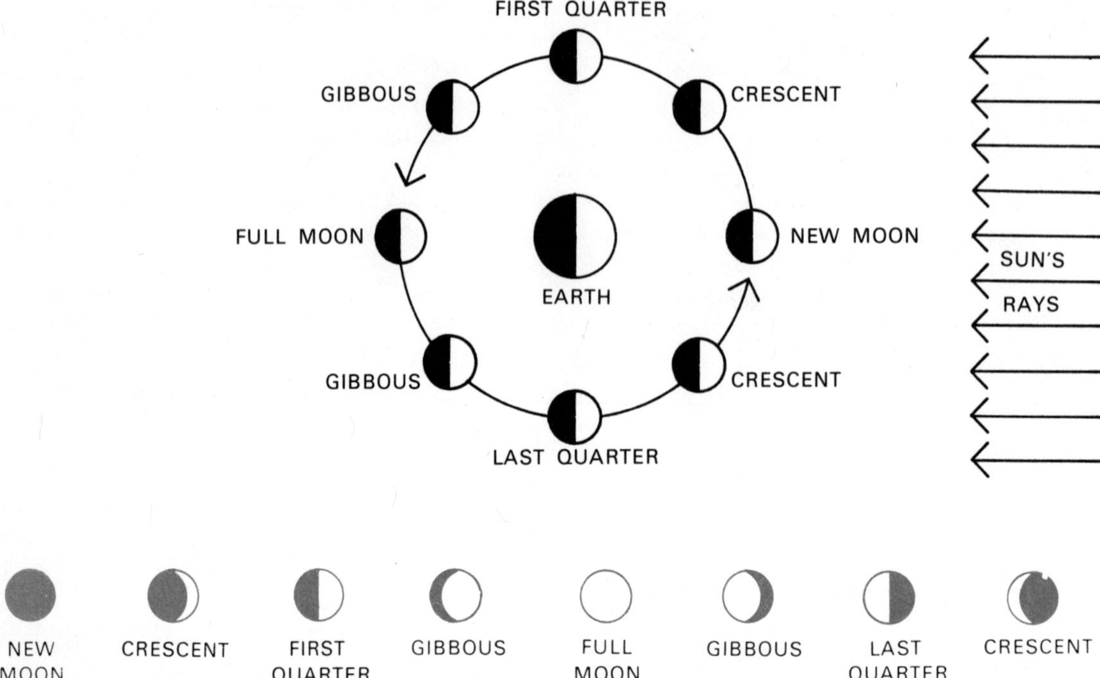

Figure 1814. Phases of the moon; symbols below.

interval varies considerably. The full moon which occurs near the time of the autumnal equinox actually has a small retardation, rising earlier each day. The illuminated limb of the moon is always towards the sun with the *cusps* or points directed away from the sun.

Solar and lunar eclipses Other effects of the moon's revolution about the earth are *solar* and *lunar eclipses,* which occur when the sun, the earth, and the moon are in line. The earth and the moon both cast shadows into space, in a direction away from the sun. A solar eclipse occurs whenever the shadow of the moon falls on a part of the surface of the earth, blocking light from the sun. As determined by the alignment of the three bodies, an observer on the earth may witness a total eclipse, or only a partial eclipse if part of the disc of the sun is visible. A solar eclipse is defined as *annular* when the moon's distance from the earth is sufficiently great to permit a narrow ring of sunlight to appear around the moon. A lunar eclipse occurs when the moon passes through the shadow of the earth; it, too, may be partial or total.

Effects of precession **1815** The earth is, in effect, a gigantic gyroscope, and is subject to the laws of gyroscopic motion. However, it is not a perfect sphere and has a bulge about its equator which is inclined at 23.5° to the plane of its orbit. The moon and sun exert gravitational forces on the earth, and these forces would tend to make the polar axis perpendicular to the plane of its orbit. Due to its rotation the earth resists these strong forces but reacts like a gyroscope when external force is applied. It precesses in a direction which is at right angles to the direction of the external force.

This precession causes a slow rotation of the earth's axis about an axis projected outward at right angles to the plane of its orbit, therefore slowly tracing a circle on the celestial sphere. The period of precession is about 25,800 years. Figure 1815 shows this path in space, and indicates various stars with the dates at which they will replace Polaris as the Pole Star.

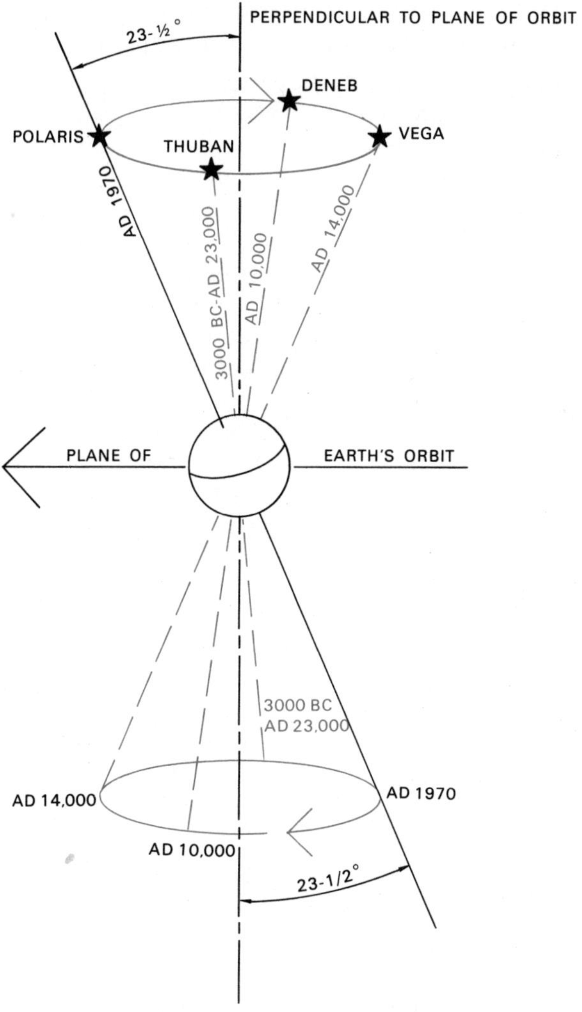

Figure 1815. Precession of the earth.

Precession of the equinoxes As noted before, the apparent location of the sun among the stars when its declination is 0° is termed an *equinox;* this occurs each spring and fall. The gyroscopic action of the earth causes a *precession of the equinoxes;* this is at a rate of about 50 seconds of arc per year and is in a westerly direction—that is, clockwise from the north. This is the *opposite* direction to both the earth's rotation and its revolution. The period of the earth's precession is not uniform due to the varying positions of the moon relative to the earth's equator and some small effects of other bodies; this slight variation is termed *nutation.*

Minor earth motions **1816** In addition to the major motions described above, there are several motions of the earth of minor importance. Two of the more significant in navigation are the *wandering of the terrestrial poles* and the *variations in speed of rotation* of the earth.

The north and south terrestrial poles, or the points where the earth's axis of rotation theoretically pierces the earth's surface, are not stationary. Instead, they wander slightly in somewhat circular paths. The movement is believed to be caused by meteorological effects. Each pole wanders in an area smaller than a baseball diamond, and neither has been known to move more than 40 feet (12 m) from its average position. The phenomenon is also called "variation in latitude."

The rotational speed of the earth on its axis is steadily decreasing by a small amount, causing the length of the day to increase at the rate of about 0.001 second a century. There are also small irregular changes in the rotational period, the causes of which are uncertain. With the introduction of atomic time standards which keep absolute time, variations in the speed of rotation of the earth—which affect its rotational position and hence astronomical observations—are of interest to the navigator; see Chapter 22 for further discussion of the differences between "perfect" time and "correct" time for navigational use.

Summary **1817** Navigational astronomy is that part of astronomy in general which is of interest and use to a navigator. It is concerned primarily with the *apparent motion* of celestial bodies. These apparent motions are *relative* motions as caused by the actual movements of the bodies as seen from the earth. Their apparent positions in space are tabulated in *almanacs* (Chapter 23), and are used by a navigator in solving the navigational triangle to determine his position (Chapters 24–27).

19 Introduction to Celestial Navigation

Definition

1901 Celestial navigation may be defined as the art of navigation with the aid of the sun, moon, planets, and the major stars. In order to practice this art, the navigator, until comparatively recent times, had to be well versed in spherical trigonometry. Now with the availability of modern inspection tables, which offer precomputed solutions of the spherical triangle, and programmable personal electronic calculators, he needs little mathematical skill beyond the ability to do simple addition and subtraction. He should, however, be familiar with the various concepts and assumptions upon which celestial navigation is based; these will be discussed in this and subsequent chapters.

Earth and the celestial sphere

1902 In celestial navigation, the earth is assumed to be a perfect sphere, located at the center of the universe. The universe is assumed to be a second sphere of infinite radius concentric with the earth. It is called the *celestial sphere,* and all heavenly bodies are considered to be located on it. The nearest of the "fixed stars" is at a distance of over six billion times the radius of the earth, resulting in this radius being negligible when using the "fixed stars" in celestial navigation.

Rotation of the earth

The earth's rotation from west to east causes the celestial sphere to appear to rotate slowly in the opposite direction, causing the bodies to rise in the east, cross the observer's meridian, and then set in the west.

These assumptions ignore the vast variation in the distances of these bodies, and the fact that the earth is an oblate spheroid rather than a true sphere. Because of the latter, a number of the relationships stated herein are close approximations, rather than exact statements of fact. However, no significant error is introduced in celestial navigation, as it is usually practiced, by considering the earth as a sphere.

Celestial poles, equator, and meridians

The earth's center is thus considered to be at the center of the celestial sphere, and the axis of its poles, extended outward, form the north and south *celestial poles.* Similarly, the plane of the equator is extended outward to form the *celestial equator* on the sphere, and any of the earth's meridians can also be projected out to form *celestial meridians.*

Celestial coordinates

1903 In Chapter 2, the earth's system of coordinates—latitude and longitude—was discussed; by means of these coordinates the location of any spot on earth can be precisely stated. A similar system of coordinates exists for the celestial sphere, by means of which a heavenly body can be located exactly on that sphere. The plane of reference is the *celestial equator* (the equinoctial) which is perpendicular to the axis formed by a line extending from the north celestial pole through the center of the earth and its poles to the south celestial pole. The celestial equivalent of latitude is *declination* (Dec.). It may be defined as angular distance north or south of the celestial equator (Figure 1903a). It is expressed in degrees and minutes of arc, generally to the nearest tenth of a minute, and is labeled N or S to indicate the direction of measurement. Declination is one of the coordinates for stating the location of any heavenly body.

Declination

Hour angle

The other celestial coordinate, equivalent to longitude on earth, is *hour angle. Greenwich hour angle* (GHA) is the angular distance of a celestial body west of the celestial meridian of Greenwich. GHA is measured in arc from 0° to 360° and is stated in degrees and minutes to the nearest tenth (in this it differs from longitude which is measured

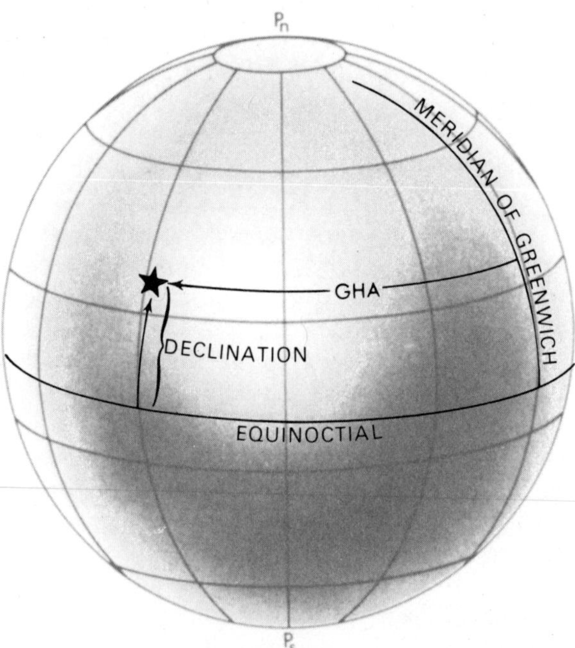

Figure 1903a. Equinoctial coordinates.

east or west to 180°). This celestial meridian of Greenwich is formed by projecting the plane of the Greenwich meridian outward to the celestial sphere. Like all meridians, it is a great circle, in that it is formed on the sphere by a plane passing through the center of the sphere, as discussed in Chapter 2.

The observer's meridian is also projected out to the celestial sphere (Fig. 1903b) and, like the meridian of Greenwich, it forms an important reference in celestial navigation. Just as the special name of celestial meridian is given to the arc of a great circle on the celestial sphere which passes through the poles and remains fixed with respect to the earth, so the special name of *hour circle* is given to the arc of a great circle on the celestial sphere which passes through the celestial poles and a celestial body, and *moves with the body.*

Hour circle

Meridian angle (t)

Local hour angle (LHA) is measured from 0° to 360° in arc *westward* from the observer's meridian to the hour circle of the celestial body. In some celestial computations *meridian angle* (t) is used. It is equivalent to LHA except that it is measured from 0° to 180° east or west from the observer's meridian to the hour circle of the body. Meridian angle, like longitude, is labeled with the suffix E or W, depending on whether the direction of measurement is east or west.

To determine LHA of a body apply longitude to the value of GHA by *adding* east longitude or *subtracting* west longitude.

The use of GHA relates the celestial sphere to the revolving earth by referring all values of hour angle to the earth's Greenwich merid-

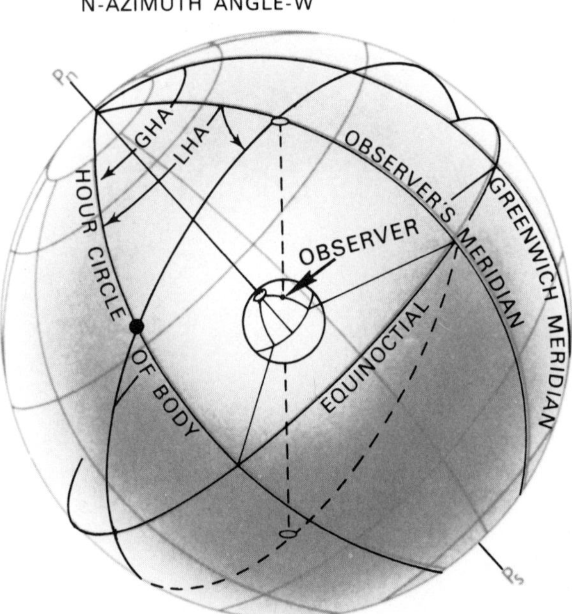

Figure 1903b. Celestial meridian, hour circles, and hour angle.

ian. The GHA of every celestial body is therefore constantly changing with time, as the earth containing the Greenwich meridian rotates around its axis. If the solar system, with the earth and navigational planets revolving around the sun, is ignored, there is a reference coordinate for locating the star positions in their east-west relationship to each other. Just as the meridian of Greenwich serves as the fixed reference on earth for terrestrial coordinates, so, on the celestial sphere, the hour circle through the *first point of Aries* (♈) is the fixed reference. In Chapter 18 on Navigational Astronomy, Aries was described as the point in space represented by the vernal equinox.

Sidereal hour angle (SHA) is measured westward from the hour circle of Aries from 0° through 360°. All of the fixed stars can be positioned in space by their SHA and declination (see Figure 1903c). (Astronomers use *right ascension* (RA) which is equivalent to SHA but measured eastward from the hour circle of Aries and expressed in units of time rather than arc; the navigator need not be concerned with the use of right ascension.) To tabulate the GHA of all the navigational stars in the *Almanac* would require publishing extremely large volumes. The GHA of the first point of Aries is therefore tabulated for various increments of time and the slowly changing SHA and declination of the navigational stars are listed separately. GHA of a star equals the GHA of Aries plus the SHA of the star. GHAs of the sun, moon, and navigational planets are tabulated separately as they move through the fixed pattern of the stars on the celestial sphere.

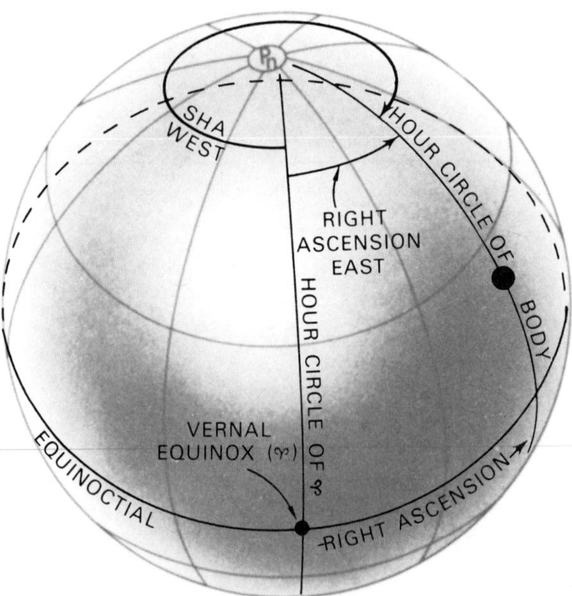

Figure 1903c. Sidereal hour angle (SHA) and right ascension.

Horizon system of coordinates

1904 A second system of coordinates is required in the practice of celestial navigation; this is termed the *horizon system of coordinates.* It differs from the celestial system in that it is based on the position of the observer, rather than on the celestial equator. The reference plane of the horizon system is the observer's *celestial horizon* (Figure 1904a); this plane passes through the center of the earth, and is perpendicular to a line drawn from the position of the observer to the earth's center. This line, when extended outward from the earth's center through the observer's position, defines his *zenith* on the celestial sphere (Figure 1904a). The zenith will be exactly 90° above the celestial horizon; it could also be defined as the point on the celestial sphere directly above the observer. Extended in the opposite direction through the earth's center, this line marks the observer's *nadir* on the celestial sphere. The imaginary line from zenith to nadir forms the axis of the observer's celestial horizon system. The celestial horizon is parallel to the plane of the observer's visible horizon at sea. The visible horizon, also called the sea horizon, and sometimes the natural horizon, is the line at which, to an observer, sea and sky appear to meet.

This concept is important, as the celestial horizon is the reference plane to which the navigator's observations are referred. It is illustrated in Figure 1904b.

Altitudes of *all* celestial bodies above the celestial horizon differ from those measured with the marine sextant aboard ship because of the height of the observer's eye above the visible horizon. The higher above the ocean surface the observer is situated, the more the visible horizon will be depressed below the true horizontal plane at his eye

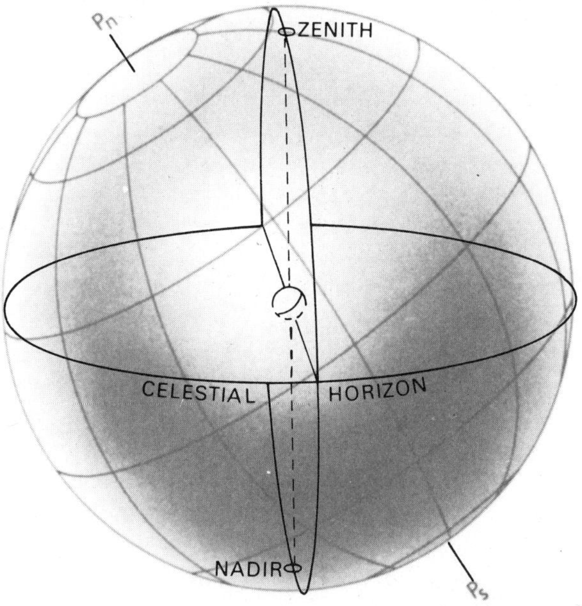

Figure 1904a. Zenith, nadir, and celestial horizon.

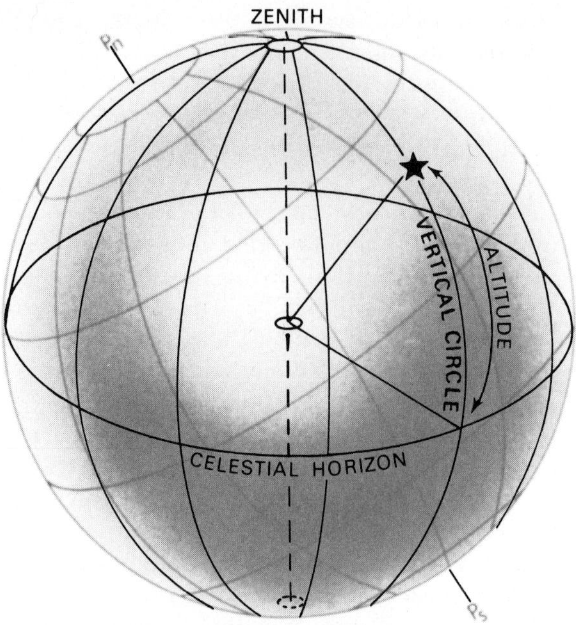

Figure 1904b. Altitude measured above celestial horizon.

level. This causes the measured altitude of the body observed to read higher than its true altitude. A correction for the *dip of the horizon,* as it is termed, must be made to the measured altitude, as will be described in Chapter 21.

A second correction is required for observations of the bodies within the solar system—the sun, moon, and planets. These bodies are much nearer the earth than are the fixed stars, which are considered to be at infinity; the light from such a body does not reach the earth in parallel rays, but diverges from the body's surface at a finite distance. The result is that a measurement of altitude taken at a point on the earth's surface will not be the same as an altitude measured from the center of the earth (center of the celestial sphere). The altitude of the body—sun, moon, or planet—above the celestial horizon will be greater than its altitude above the horizontal at the observer's eye, except when the body is on his zenith. This difference in altitude is called *parallax.* The required correction to the altitude as measured above the visible horizon is described in Chapter 21.

Altitudes of bodies, as measured with a sextant, and adjusted for dip (and parallax and other factors as appropriate), are angles above the plane of the celestial horizon, measured along a great circle, called the *vertical circle,* passing through the body as well as the observer's zenith and nadir; see Figure 1904b. In the celestial equator system of coordinates there can be an infinite number of hour circles, so, in the horizon system of coordinates, there can be an infinite number of vertical circles each passing through a given body on the celestial

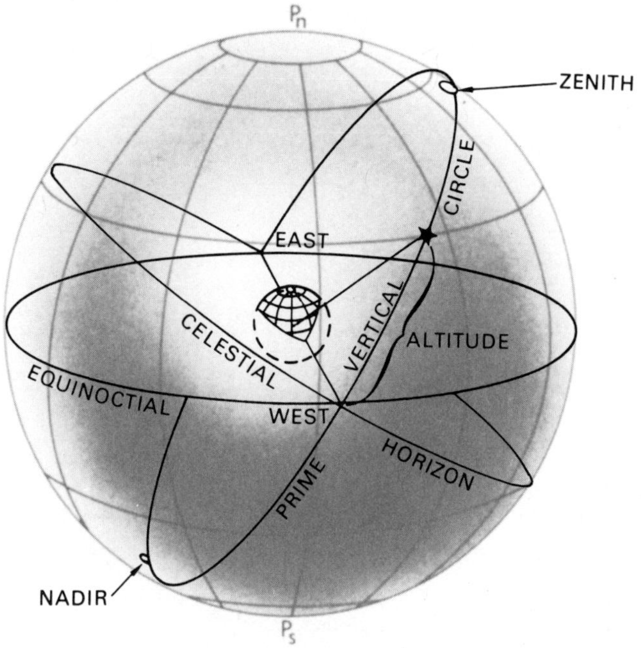

Figure 1904c. Horizon and equinoctial coordinates combined.

sphere. In addition to the vertical circle passing through the celestial body being observed, there is one other important vertical circle. This is termed the *prime vertical* and is that vertical circle which passes through the east and west points of the observer's celestial horizon. Figure 1904c shows the two systems of coordinates superimposed, with the altitude of a star shown on the prime vertical.

The astronomical triangle on the celestial sphere

1905 The *astronomical* or *celestial triangle* is an area on the celestial sphere defined by the observer's celestial meridian, the hour circle passing through the observed celestial body, and the vertical circle passing through that body. The celestial triangle is illustrated in Figure 1905. The vertices of the triangle are the celestial pole, the observer's zenith, and the position of the celestial body.

In Figure 1905 both the observer's zenith and the star being observed are shown in the northern hemisphere. The relationship of other possible positions will be discussed later in detail. It will be noted from this illustration that the angular distances representing two sides of the triangle are determined from the celestial equator system of coordinates, namely, the side defined as 90° minus Dec. and the one defined as 90° minus Lat. The third side, 90° minus altitude, has its angular distance determined by the altitude of the body above the celestial horizon and therefore it uses the horizon system of coordinates. The relationship of the two systems, as projected on the celestial

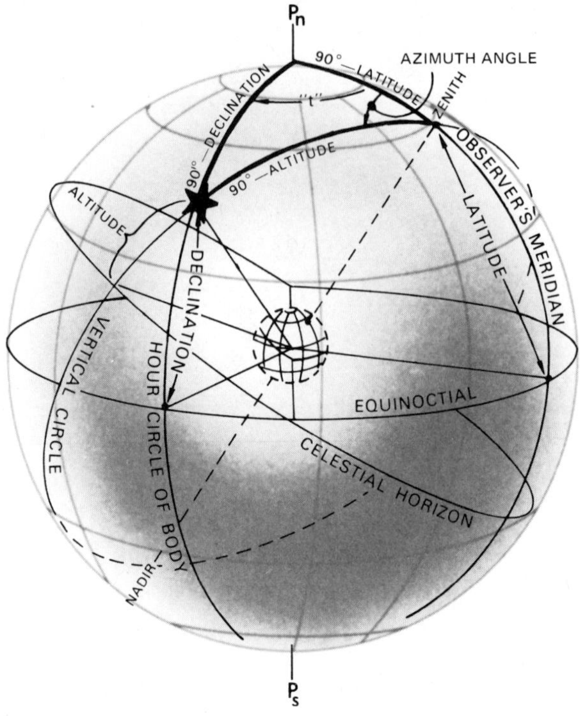

Figure 1905. Astronomical or celestial triangle.

sphere, should now be clear. Only two of the angles within the celestial triangle are used in celestial navigation. Meridian angle (t), previously defined, is shown in Figure 1905 as the angle at the pole between the observer's meridian and the hour circle of the body. *Azimuth angle* is the angle at the zenith between the celestial meridian of the observer and the vertical circle passing through the celestial body. Altitude and azimuth form the two horizon coordinates by means of which a celestial body is located with reference to the observer.

Geographical position (GP)

1906 This chapter has considered the heavenly bodies only in relation to their positions on the celestial sphere, in order to show the fundamentals of the celestial triangle concept, and to define the terms used in celestial navigation. The understanding of celestial navigation is greatly simplified if the apparent position of each heavenly body is considered to lie on the surface of the earth, rather than on another sphere. Imagine the earth to be a glass globe, with the observer located at its center. As the observer looks at a star or other celestial body its light rays pass through a single point on the earth's surface. This point is called the *geographical position* (GP) of the body (Figure 1906); it is moving constantly westward, but its precise position on the earth's surface can be determined for any instant of time from information

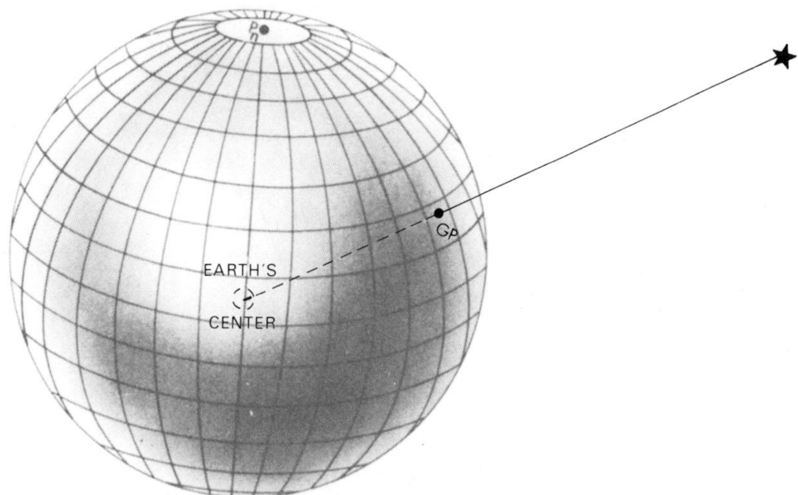

Figure 1906. Geographical position (GP) of a celestial body.

tabulated in an almanac (Chapter 23). Knowing the exact location of the GP of a body, the navigator can develop a line of position, by means of a sextant observation, very much as an LOP is obtained from observation of any landmark of known position on the earth's surface. To develop a celestial line of position, the navigator must obtain an accurate measurement of the altitude of a celestial body above the horizon. The following sections will explain the principles of developing such an LOP.

Circles of equal altitude

1907 To illustrate the basic concept involved in measuring an altitude, consider a pole of known height erected vertically on level ground, and stayed with a number of guy wires of equal length attached to the top of the pole and stretched taut to points on the ground equidistant from the base. The base of the pole establishes its GP. At the points where the guy wires meet the ground, angles are formed between the ground and the wires; these angles will be equal in value at each guy wire, and the points on the ground will describe a circle with the base of the pole at its center. It is evident then that anywhere on this circle the angle subtended by the height of the pole will be the same. This *circle of equal altitude* around the pole is illustrated in Figure 1907a.

In the case of the pole of known height, the distance from the base of the pole can be determined by plane trigonometry, if the angle it subtends is known. This is *partially analogous* to determining a ship's distance from the GP of a star by observing the star's altitude. However, the analogy is not completely valid, as the ship is on the curved surface of the earth, rather than on a flat plane, and instead of dealing

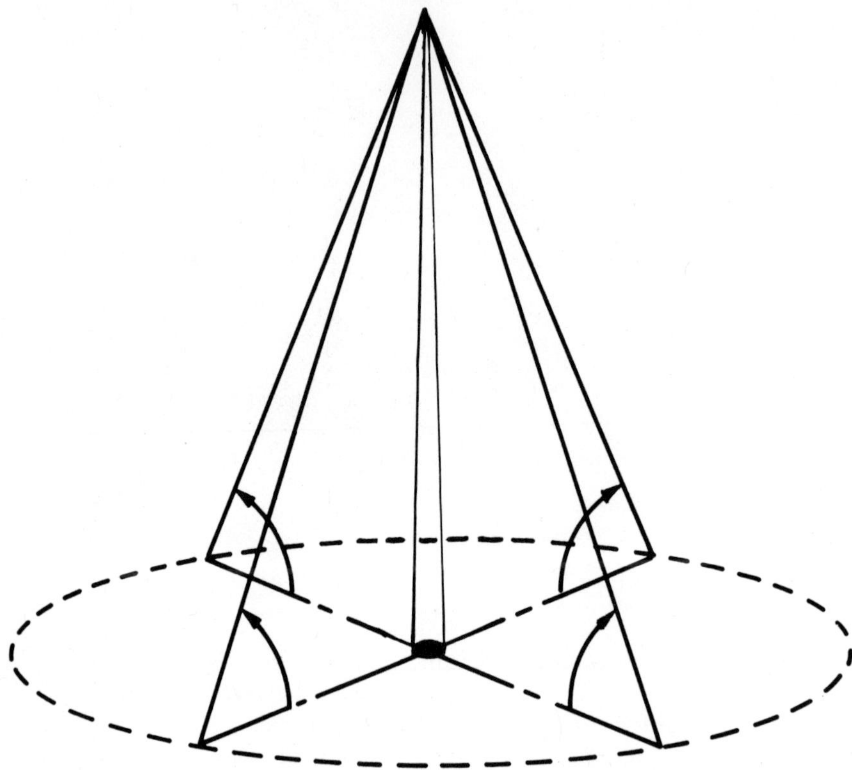

Figure 1907a. Circle of equal altitude around a pole.

with a pole of known height, the navigator is concerned with a celestial body considered (in the case of stars) to be situated at an infinite distance above its GP. It is, in fact, because of the curvature of the earth's surface that the navigator can determine his distance from the GP of a celestial body by measuring its altitude above the visible horizon.

The problem now involves angular measurement from a horizontal plane tangent to the earth's surface at the point of observation, followed by calculations in spherical trigonometry. As previously stated, most of the bodies used in navigation are at such great distances that their rays of light are parallel when they reach the earth. If the earth were flat, the angular altitude of each of these bodies would be the same at any point on the plane, regardless of distance from the GP, and the concept of circles of equal altitude would not be valid. However, the angular altitude the navigator actually uses is the angle between the lines of sight to the body and to the sea horizon. Because the earth's surface is curved, the observer's horizontal plane is tangent to the earth's surface at his position, and only at that one position on the surface of the earth. Hence, the angle between his horizon and the line of sight to a celestial body will vary if he moves his position toward or away from the GP of the body. This is illustrated in Figure 1907b, which shows the light rays from a celestial body intersecting two different horizon planes on the surface of the earth at the same instant of time. At point *A* the altitude of the body above the horizon plane is considerably less than at point *B* and the circle of equal altitude on which point *A* is located is farther away from the GP of the body than the circle of equal altitude passing through point *B*.

As the altitude varies in proportion to the observer's distance from the GP, he can convert coaltitude (an angular distance on a great circle) into linear distance from the GP, and this distance will in turn be the radius of the circle of equal altitude since 1′ of arc on a great circle equals 1 nautical mile. The entire circle is seldom drawn on the plotting chart as only a very short segment of its arc, in the area of the DR position, is needed. Due to the usually large radius of the circle, this short segment can, for practical purposes, be represented as a straight line, without causing material distortion. This small segment of a circle of equal altitude is a *celestial line of position.* Figure 1907c illustrates circles of equal altitude, or of position, derived from observations of two stars. One of the intersections of these two circles on the surface of the earth represents the navigator's position or "Fix." The other intersection of the two circles is located so far away from the DR position that in practical navigation there is no chance of error due to choosing the wrong intersection.

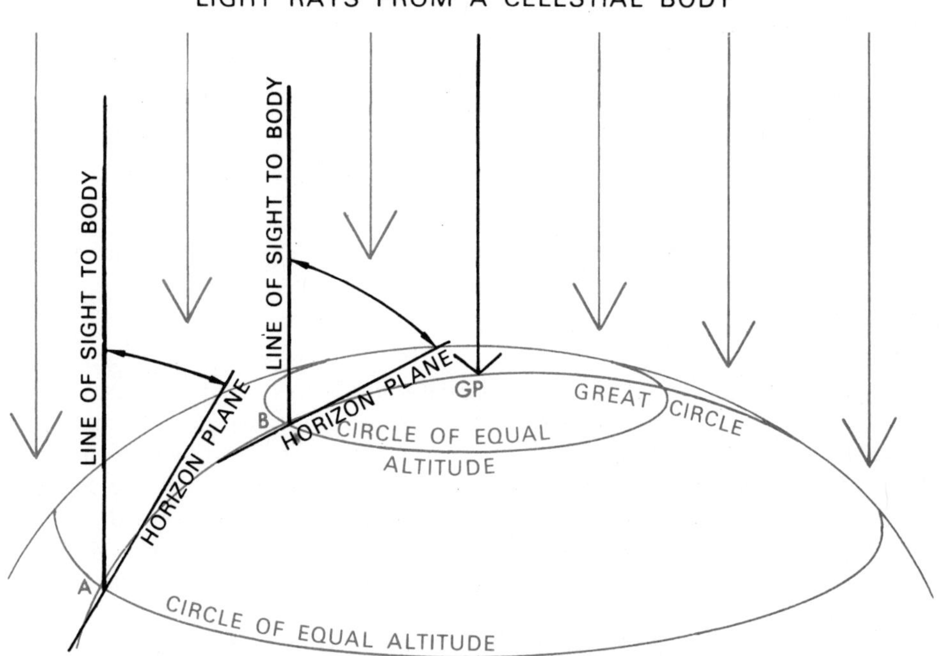

Figure 1907b. Parallel light rays, angle of elevation.

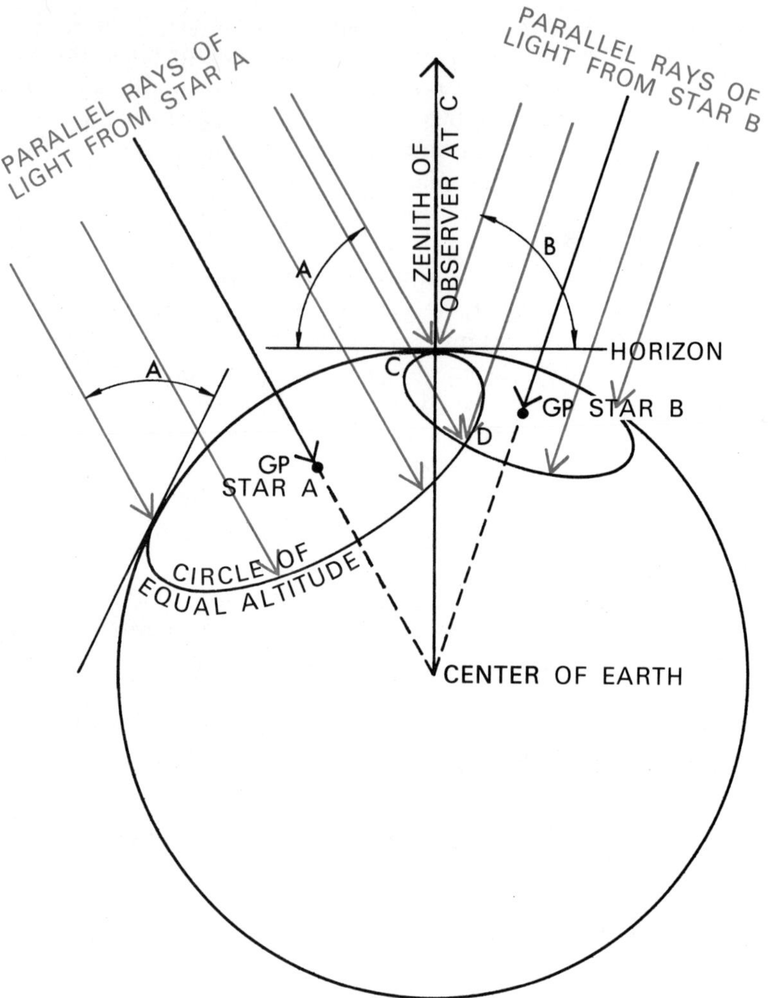

Figure 1907c. Circles of equal altitude for two stars. A—Altitude of star A from position of observer on circle of equal altitude. B—Altitude of star B from position of observer on circle of equal altitude. C and D—Two intersections of circles of equal altitude.

The navigational triangle represented on the earth's surface

1908 The *navigational triangle* on the earth's surface is the counterpart of the astronomical or celestial triangle on the celestial sphere, as described in Article 1905. It is the basis of celestial navigation, and as such it should be understood by every person who would call himself a "navigator." The navigational triangle is defined by three points on the earth's surface, and it is formed by the arcs of the great circles connecting these points (Figure 1909). These points are the position of the observer (*M*), the geographical position of the celestial body (GP), and the elevated pole. The elevated pole is the pole nearer the observer; it is the north pole for an observer in north latitude, and the south pole if he is in the southern hemisphere. It is called the elevated pole because it is the celestial pole above the observer's horizon. The GP may be in either the same or the opposite hemisphere to that of the observer.

Since the possible positions of *M* and GP are almost unlimited, the triangle may take a great variety of shapes. For any particular moment of time, a navigational triangle can be constructed connecting an observer at any location on the earth, the elevated pole, and the GP of any celestial body within the observer's field of view. Having a complete understanding of the triangle, the navigator is able to solve any problem of celestial navigation. He can fix his position at sea, check the accuracy of his compasses, predict the time of rising or setting of any body in the heavens, determine the times of the beginning and ending of twilight, and locate and identify celestial bodies. The solution of the navigational triangle *is* celestial navigation.

The sides of the navigational triangle

1909 The side of the triangle joining the observer and the elevated or nearer pole is called the *colatitude;* it is equal to 90° minus his latitude. The side joining the GP and the pole is called the *polar distance;* it is equal to 90° minus the body's declination, or 90° minus the latitude of the body's GP when referred to the surface of the earth. (When the latitude of the observer and the declination of the body are of *contrary names,* polar distance is 90° plus declination, or plus the latitude of the GPs of the bodies.) The side joining the GP and *M*, the position of the

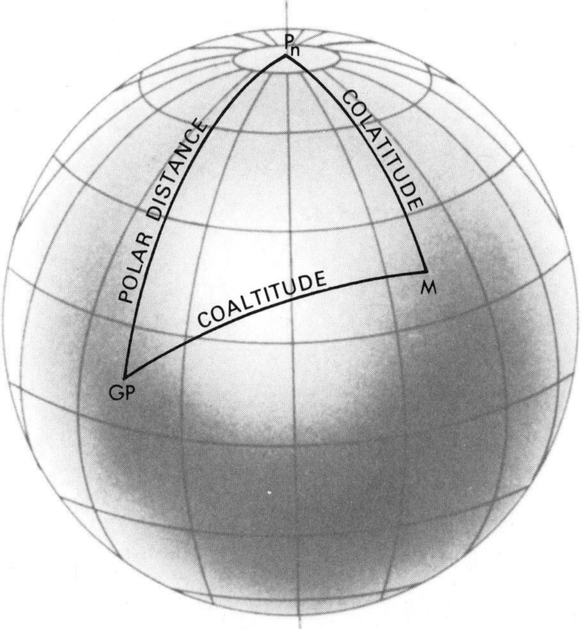

Figure 1909. Navigational triangle with sides labeled.

observer, is the *coaltitude,* sometimes called zenith distance, and it is equal to 90° minus the altitude of the body. Each of these sides is an arc of a great circle through the two points it connects, and its angular distance in minutes of arc is the distance in nautical miles between the two points on the surface of the earth. The triangle shown in Figure 1909 is for an observer in north latitude, with a celestial body setting to his west. Remember that two sides of the triangle, polar distance and colatitude, are defined by using the celestial equator system of coordinates, and the third side, coaltitude, is an arc of the vertical circle of the horizon system of coordinates. The three sides of the navigational triangle are illustrated and discussed in more detail in the following articles.

Colatitude **1910** Latitude, described in Chapter 2, is the angular distance north or south of the equator. It may also be defined as an angle at the center of the earth, measured along the observer's meridian from the equator to his position. Figure 1910 illustrates latitude and colatitude shown on the plane of the meridian of the observer. The line *QQ′* represents the equator and *O* the center of the earth. Since the maximum angle in the measurement of latitude is 90° (the latitude of the pole) it can be seen from the illustrations that colatitude will always be 90° minus the latitude.

Polar distance **1911** Since the geographical position, GP, of a body is a point on the earth's surface, it can be expressed in terms of latitude and longitude. Thus the side of the navigational triangle joining the GP and the pole

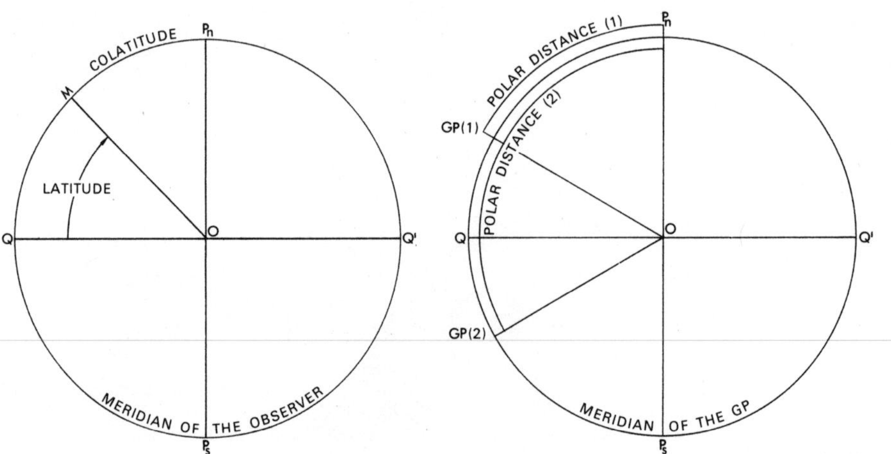

Figure 1910 (left). Coaltitude shown as angle at center of earth. Figure 1911 (right). Polar distance of $GP_1 = 90° - \text{Lat}$. For GP_2 polar distance = 90° + latitude of GP_2.

can be computed and used in the same manner as the side connecting the observer's position, *M*, and the pole. Although the observer is always on the same side of the equator as the elevated pole, at times he may observe a celestial body having a GP with a latitude of contrary name; that is, a navigator in north latitude may observe a celestial body whose GP is in south latitude or vice versa.

Polar distance, for a body having a GP in the same hemisphere as the observer's position, is shown in Figure 1911 to be 90° *minus* the latitude of the GP. For any body observed with a GP in the latitude of opposite name, the polar distance will be 90° *plus* the latitude of the GP, as illustrated in Figure 1911. In this illustration the line *QQ′* again represents the equator and point *O* on the center of the earth.

Coaltitude **1912** When a navigator observes a celestial body, he measures its angular altitude above the horizon. In Figure 1912a the observer, *M*, is shown at the top of a great circle representing the earth's circumference. This great circle joins the position of the observer and the GP of the celestial body; it is not a meridian (except in the rare case in which the GP falls on the observer's meridian) but a vertical circle on which the body's altitude is measured from the celestial horizon toward the zenith.

In Figure 1912a it can be seen that the light rays of a celestial body are assumed to be parallel, and that the angle (*h*) at the observer's visible horizon is the same as angle (*H*) at the center of the earth, measured from the celestial horizon. If altitude is illustrated as angle (*H*) in this figure, then it follows the coaltitude must be 90° minus the altitude. Although this presents no problem in the mathematical solu-

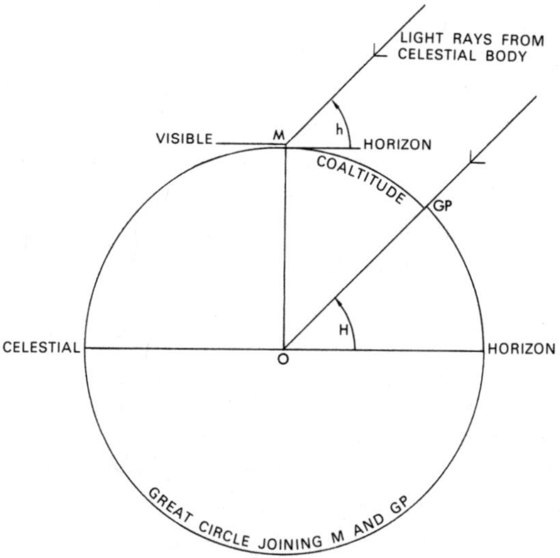

Figure 1912a. Coaltitude = 90° − altitude.

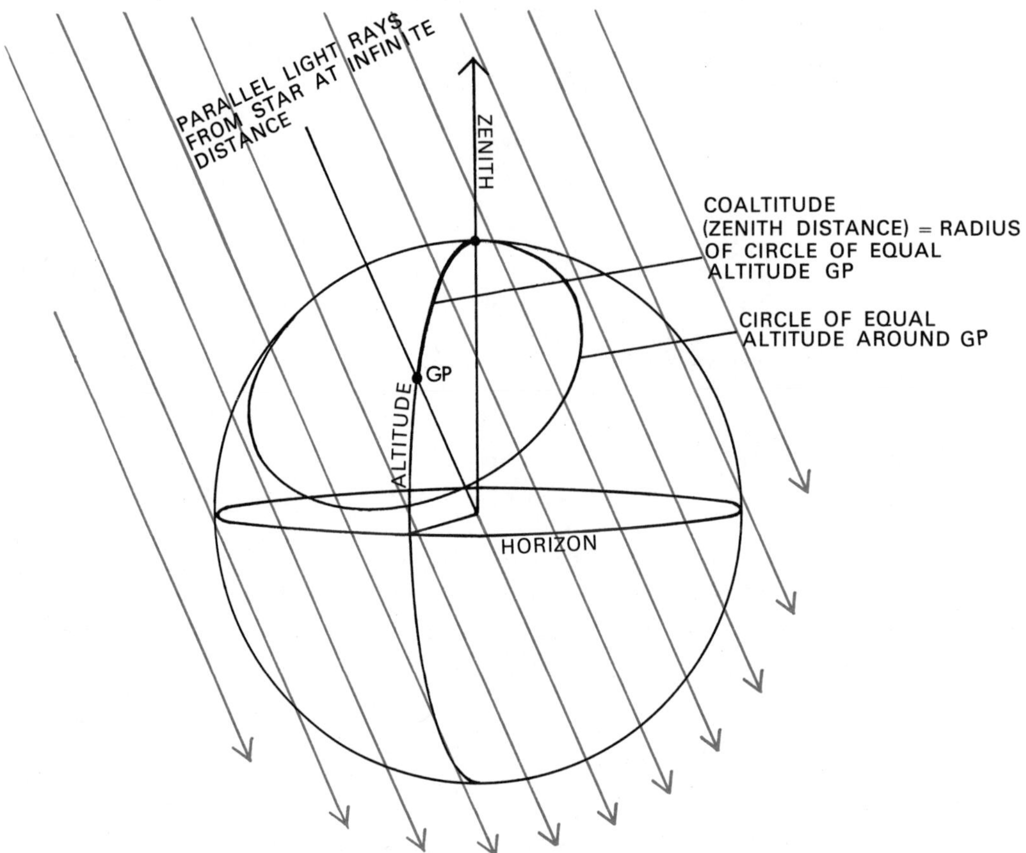

Figure 1912b. Coaltitude equals radius of circle of equal altitude.

tion of the triangle, the visualization of this third side of the navigational triangle sometimes proves difficult. Figure 1912b presents a graphic illustration in which the arc segment labeled coaltitude is shown as both 90° minus altitude and as the radius of the circle of the equal altitude. This is true in all cases when using the basic relationship of one minute of arc on a great circle on the surface of the earth equaling one nautical mile.

The angles in the navigational triangles

1913 In the navigational triangle, the angle at the pole between the meridian of the observer and the meridian of the GP is called the *meridian angle,* and labeled "t." Refer back to Figure 1903b, where this angle was labeled LHA. The local hour angle, LHA, is always measured in a westerly direction and from the meridian of the observer to the meridian of the GP, extending through an angle of 0° to 360°. In the computations involved in sight reduction it is more convenient to be able to measure this angle either east or west from the meridian of

Meridian angle

the observer, hence the designation meridian angle. Meridian angle is the "difference of longitude" between the position of the observer and the GP of the body.

The use of the *time diagram* is explained in Chapter 22. The meridian angle (t) is a vital part of the diagram. Figure 1913a illustrates the meridians of the observer and of the GP, with the resultant angle (t) as they will appear on a time diagram. The outer circle in this illustration represents the earth's equator as viewed from a point in space on an extension of the earth's axis beyond the south pole. (This pole is selected so as to place westerly directions to the left of north, and easterly to the right, a format familiar to a navigator from his use of charts.)

The center of this circle is labeled Ps to indicate the south pole. The lines in the illustration which connect both *M* and GP with the pole represent projections of meridians. *M* represents the intersection of the observer's meridian with the equator and GP represents the intersection of the meridian of the GP with the equator. In this diagram and in actual practice the meridian angle (t) is always measured from the observer's meridian toward the meridian of the GP and is labeled with the suffix "E" east or "W" west to indicate the direction of measurement. In a diagram of this type the use of the south pole does *not* imply that it is the elevated pole. The angle of intersection of the two meridians is identical at both poles.

Azimuth angle

The other important angle within the navigational triangle is the *azimuth angle* (Z), measured at the observer's position, between the observer's meridian and the vertical circle running through the position of the GP and that of the observer (Figures 1903b and 1905).

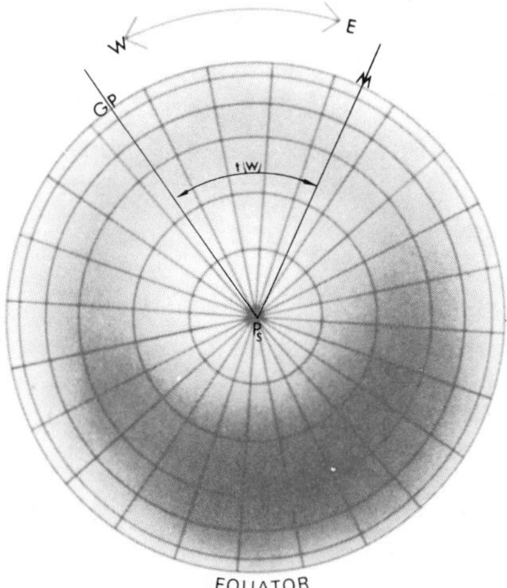

Figure 1913a. Meridian angle (t) measured westerly from the observer's meridian.

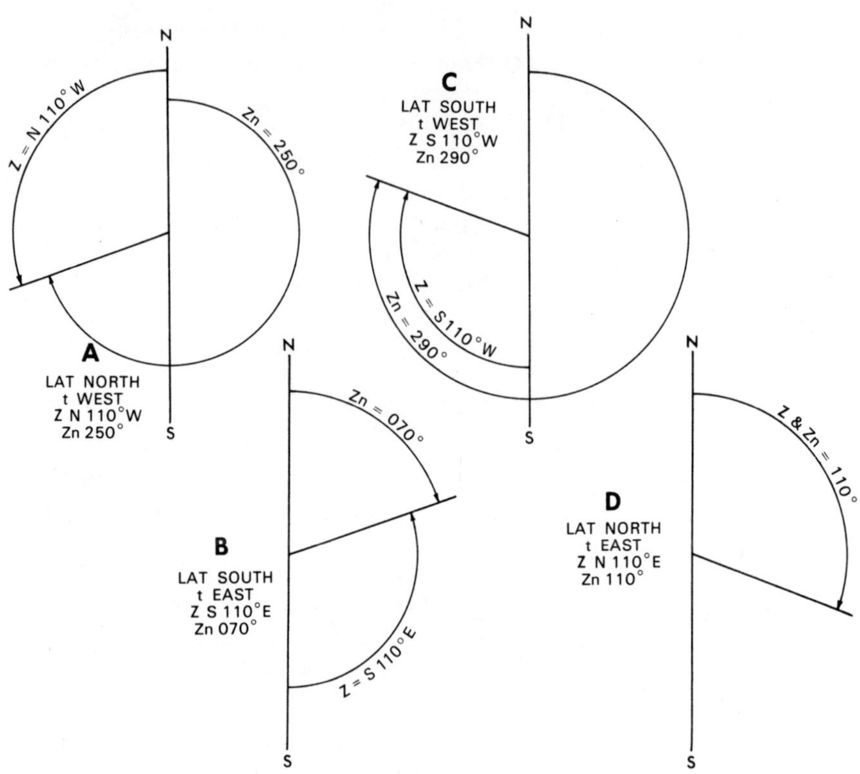

Figure 1913b. Azimuth angle (Z) and true azimuth (Zn).

Azimuth angle is always measured from the observer's meridian toward the vertical circle joining the observer and the GP. It is labeled with the prefix "N" north or "S" south, to agree with the name of the observer's elevated pole, and with the suffix "E" east or "W" west to indicate the direction of measurement. Labeling the azimuth angle in this manner is necessary as it may be measured from either the north or south poles, and either in an easterly or westerly direction. In the final plotting of position this angle is converted to *true azimuth* (Zn), which is measured clockwise from the north through 360°, as illustrated in Figure 1913b.

True azimuth

Parallactic angle

The third angle in the navigational triangle is called the *parallactic angle.* It is not used directly in the ordinary practice of celestial navigation, and need not be considered here.

Use of the navigational triangle

1914 To obtain a position at sea, a navigator observes the altitude of a celestial body and simultaneously notes the exact time to the nearest second. Knowledge of the time of observation enables him to determine the exact position of the GP of that body from data in the *Nautical* or *Air Almanac* (Chapter 23). Since the coaltitude has been previously described as equal to the radius of the circle of equal altitude, the position of the observer lies somewhere on the circumference of the circle of equal altitude. The observer's exact position cannot be determined by a single observation. If the bearing of the GP at the instant of observation could be obtained with the same accuracy as the altitude measurement, the position of the observer could be fixed mathematically. Unfortunately, at present it is not possible to measure azimuth with this degree of accuracy. A single observation only establishes that the observer is on the circle of equal altitude, a small segment of which can be assumed to be a straight line forming a line of position in the close vicinity of his most probable position at the time of the sight. To use the navigational triangle to determine position, the navigator begins by assuming that he is located at some selected point. This *assumed position* (AP) will be near the best *estimated position* (EP) that the navigator can determine (although on celestial navigation workforms this is commonly referred to as the DR latitude and longitude). For convenience in using precomputed tables and in plotting, both of which will be discussed in later chapters, the assumed position is usually not the same as either the estimated or DR position, but is chosen so that the latitude and the meridian angle are whole degrees.

Assumed position

Once an assumed position is selected and the GP of the celestial body at the exact time of observation is known, the coaltitude, polar distance, and meridian angle can easily be computed. With these two sides and included angle known, the process of *sight reduction* can be

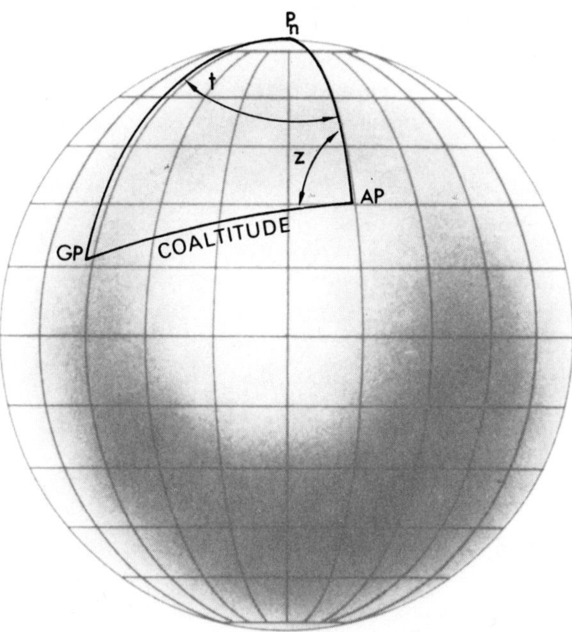

Figure 1914. Two sides and included angle known; solve for Z and coaltitude.

undertaken to determine coaltitude and azimuth angle; see Figure 1914. Modern "inspection" tables for sight reduction are conveniently arranged in a format that directly yields the desired value, altitude, rather than coaltitude.

Although a navigator using the precomputed tables will not use spherical trigonometry, the basic equations will be of use to those employing personal electronic calculators for sight reduction and are listed below.

Altitude $h = \sin^{-1} (\sin L \underline{\times} \sin d \underset{\sim}{+} \cos L \underline{\times} \cos d \underline{\times} \cos t)$

$$Azimuth\ Z = \sin^{-1}\left(\frac{\cos d \underline{\times} \sin t}{\cos h}\right)$$

where d is declination and + is interpreted as + when L and d are of opposite name (N and S) and as ~ (algebraic difference) when L and t are of the same name, with the smaller quantity being subtracted from the larger.

Computed altitude (Hc)

Observed altitude (Ho)

Altitude intercept (a)

1915 As discussed in the preceding article, if an assumed position for the observer and the actual position of the GP for the body are used, the spherical triangle can be solved by tables or equations to produce a *computed altitude;* this value (h in the equations) is now labeled *Hc*. The *observed altitude* obtained from the sextant observation with all corrections applied is labeled *Ho.* Hc and Ho are each proportional to the value of the radius of a circle of equal altitude, centered at the GP of the body, the first circle passing through the assumed position, the second through the observer's actual position. The difference between Hc and Ho is known as *altitude intercept* (*a*); this intercept represents the difference in length of the radii of the computed and observed circles of equal altitude. In Article 1907 it was shown that a small altitude angle places the circle of equal altitude, and therefore the LOP, farther away from the GP of the body than does a larger altitude. Accordingly, if Hc—the computed altitude—for the assumed position is greater than Ho—the observed altitude—the actual position from which the observation was made would be farther from the GP of the body than the assumed position. Similarly, if Ho is the greater, the actual position would be nearer the GP. The intercept, a linear distance, must always be labeled either with the suffix T (toward) or A (away from) the GP as plotted from the AP (Figure 1916).

Determining the vessel's position

1916 In addition to obtaining the value and direction of the intercept (a) in miles by solving the navigational triangle containing the AP, the navigator obtains the computed value of the azimuth angle (Z). By converting Z to direction measured from north (Zn), the navigator can conveniently plot on his chart the bearing of the GP from the AP. This azimuth line drawn through the assumed position would indicate the direction of the GP even though the latter is, in most cases, off the area of the chart being used. Since (a) is the difference in miles between the lines of position passing through the actual and assumed positions, the navigator can plot either toward or away for the value of (a) along this azimuth line. It is necessary to remember the direction of the intercept. From the description given in the preceding paragraph the phrase "Computed Greater Away" can be derived. A useful "memory aid" for CGA is "Coast Guard Academy"; another helpful acronym is "HoMoTo" for "Ho More Toward." The point on the azimuth line represented by marking off the intercept (a) is a point on the observer's circle of equal altitude. The celestial line of position is then drawn through this point and perpendicular to the azimuth line as shown in Figure 1916. Since a celestial LOP does not produce an absolute position or fix but merely a line on which the observer is located, at least two LOPs are required to obtain a fix. Three LOPs derived from different bodies will give a fix with a greater degree of confidence, and four or five LOPs are not too many. The position of the vessel is determined by the intersection of the LOPs, a point for

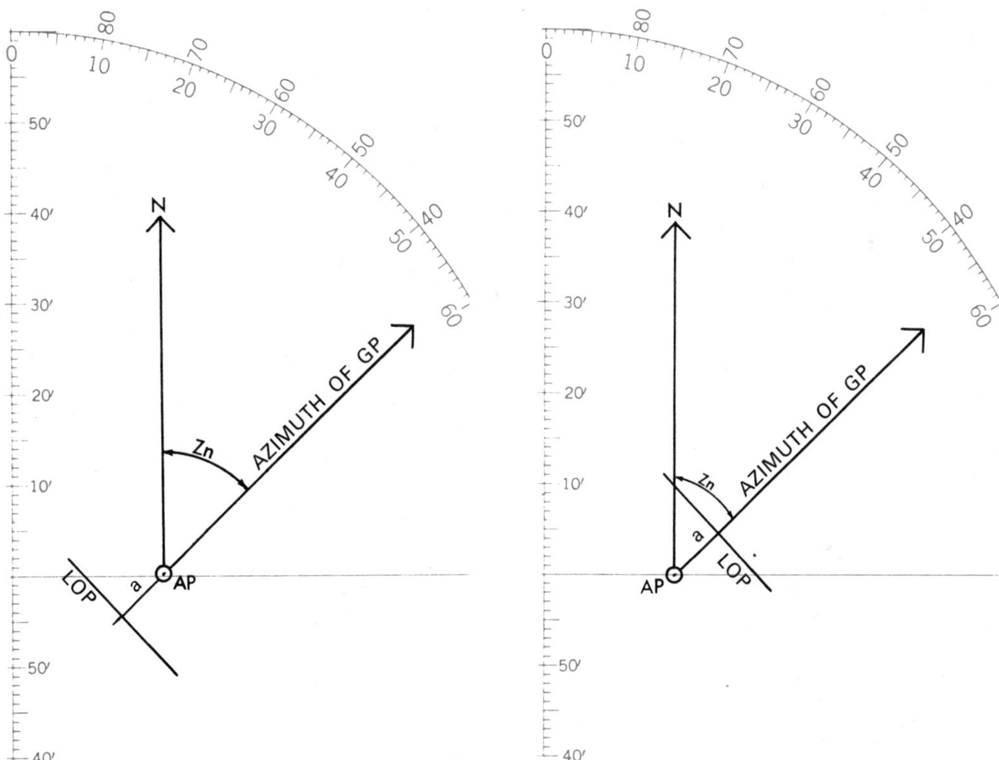

Figure 1916. The line of position plotted. Altitude intercept "a." Hc greater than Ho. "a" is *away* from the azimuth of the GP. Altitude intercept "a." Hc Less than Ho. "a" is *toward* the azimuth of the GP.

two lines and a single point for three or more lines if there is no error. In actual practice, however, three or more LOPs will seldom intersect at a point but will rather produce a small polygon often popularly referred to as a "cocked hat." It is normally assumed that the actual position of the ship is in the center of this figure, which can, for practical purposes, be estimated by eye; see also Article 2908. In some instances, there can be an "outside" or "exterior" fix in which the true position lies outside the polygon; see Article 2909 for details of this situation.

Coordinates on the plane of the observer's meridian

1917 The two systems of coordinates have been illustrated in this text to show their appearance both on the celestial sphere, and on earth. Both the horizon system and the celestial equator system of coordinates contain the celestial meridian of the observer, and celestial problems can be illustrated conveniently on the plane of the observer's meridian. Should a neophyte navigator become confused in the solution of a problem, he can often benefit by stopping to make sketches similar to these illustrations to clarify specific problems.

Horizon system of coordinates

In Figure 1917a the horizon system of coordinates is used. The circle represents the plane of the observer's meridian, the line NS is the celestial horizon with north at the left and south at the right. It is obvious that the center of the circle can be either the east or west point on the horizon, and the NS line contains a locus of points represent-

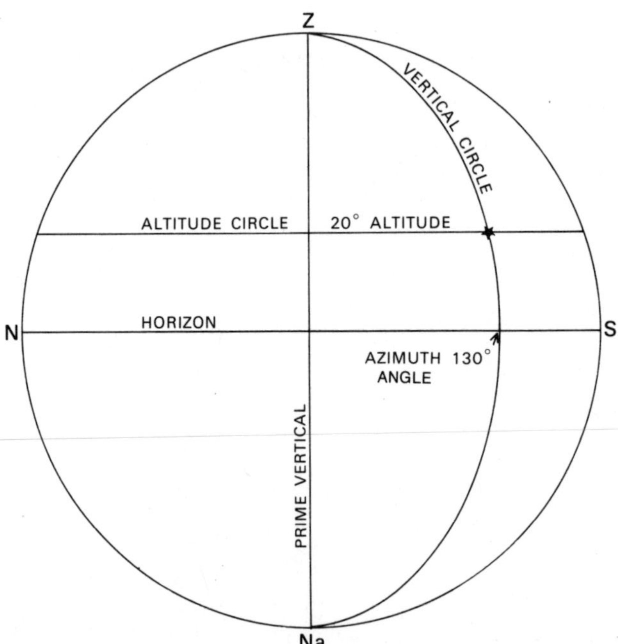

Figure 1917a. Horizon coordinates on the plane of the meridian.

ing all azimuths. Z represents the zenith of the observer, and Na the nadir. The line Z-Na passing through the zenith-nadir and the east-west point of the horizon is then, by definition, the prime vertical. Other vertical circles through celestial bodies will be shown on the diagram as ellipses passing through the observer's zenith, his nadir, and the celestial position of each body. The point where this line intersects the celestial horizon determines the azimuth angle of the body. Lines parallel to the horizon will represent lines of equal altitude. The position of any body can be plotted on the diagram in terms of altitude and azimuth.

Celestial equator system of coordinates Figure 1917b illustrates the celestial equator system of coordinates on the plane of the celestial meridian. In this case the line *QQ′* is the celestial equator containing a locus of points representing a position on all hour circles. Pn and Ps are the north and south poles respectively. The hour circle 90° from the meridian of the observer appears as the straight line Pn-Ps (its LHA is 90° or 270° and t is 90° E or W); all other hour circles appear as curved lines. Lines parallel to the celestial equator are lines of equal declination. The position of any body can then be located on this diagram in terms of declination and hour angle.

Combining the coordinate systems Combining the two systems of coordinates, if the observer were located at the north pole where his zenith and the north pole were identical, the diagrams could be superimposed on each other as drawn; this,

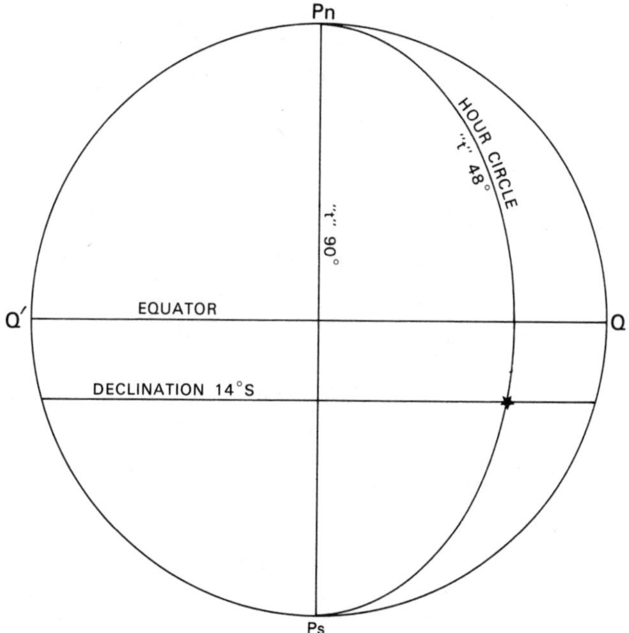

Figure 1917b. Celestial equator coordinates on the plane of the meridian.

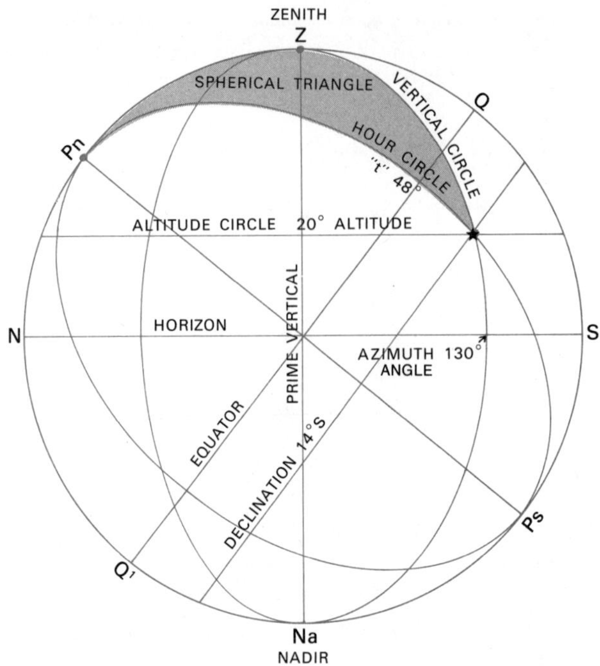

Figure 1917c. Combined coordinate systems.

obviously, is not a typical location for an observer on a ship. For all other positions of an observer, the elevated pole must be placed on the plane of the observer's celestial meridian at a point above the horizon equal to the latitude of the observer. Figure 1917c illustrates the diagrams of Figures 1917a and 1917b superimposed for a latitude of 40° N, with the area covered by the celestial triangle shaded.

Summary

1918 The basic theory of celestial navigation as it is usually practiced aboard ship has been presented in this chapter. The manner in which celestial navigation is actually practiced afloat is explained in subsequent chapters. Celestial navigation continues to be the only basic self-contained passive method for obtaining a position at sea. The art of celestial navigation is well documented and will be presented in a step-by-step operation involving the four basic tools: sextant, timepiece, almanac, and sight reduction tables. To master the art of navigation requires a thorough understanding of the basic concepts presented herein, as well as much practice in the use of the sextant. Sight reduction by means of a personal electronic calculator or a ship's computer requires an even greater understanding of and familiarity with the basic equations for altitude and azimuth.

20 Identification of Celestial Bodies

Introduction

2001 In order to solve the navigational triangle, the navigator must know the name of the celestial body he has observed, so that he can obtain its GHA, or SHA, and declination from the almanac. No difficulty is experienced in identifying the sun or moon, but the stars and planets can present a problem. Both appear to be point sources of light, and the only apparent differences between any two are in position and brightness, and in a few instances, much less obviously, in color.

The usual procedure in identifying stars and planets is to select, in advance of twilight, a number of these bodies, so located that lines of position obtained from them will result in a good fix. Only occasionally is an unknown body observed and identified afterward.

Most experienced navigators pride themselves on their ability to locate and identify the navigational stars; a portion of this chapter is intended to assist a neophyte navigator in learning the basic elements of star identification. He must, however, also learn to predetermine the approximate altitude and azimuth of the navigational bodies, so that they may be located without reference to other bodies. The modern sextant telescope enables the observer to sight a star in a comparatively bright sky when it is not visible to the unaided eye. Under such conditions he usually has the benefit of sharp horizon contrast, which permits accurate observations.

The "Star Finder and Identifier" 2102-D

2002 The Star Finder most used by navigators is generally referred to as "2102-D"; this was its "H.O." number when it was produced by the Navy Hydrographic Office. This Navy star finder is no longer available to nongovernment personnel, but identical units can be obtained from civilian sources which continue to use the same number for identification. The device is a development from the original "Rude Starfinder" created by Captain G. T. Rude, USC&GS; it is still referred to by some people by its original name.

The 2102-D Star Finder and Identifier is designed to permit a user to determine the approximate altitude and azimuth of those of the 57 "selected navigational stars" listed on the daily pages of the *Nautical* and *Air Almanacs* (Chapter 23) which are above his celestial horizon at any given place and time. With some minor additional effort, it can also be set up to indicate the positions of the navigational planets, other stars of interest, and even the sun and/or moon if desired. The Star Finder can also be used in the reverse operation—identification of an unknown body whose altitude and azimuth have been measured. The accuracy of this device is roughly ±3° to 5° in both altitude and azimuth.

The Star Finder consists of a *base* and ten circular *templates,* all contained in a case together with a sheet of instructions. The base, Figure 2002a, is a white opaque plastic disc, with a small pin at its center. On one side, the north celestial pole is shown at the center; on the opposite side the south celestial pole is at the center. On both sides the

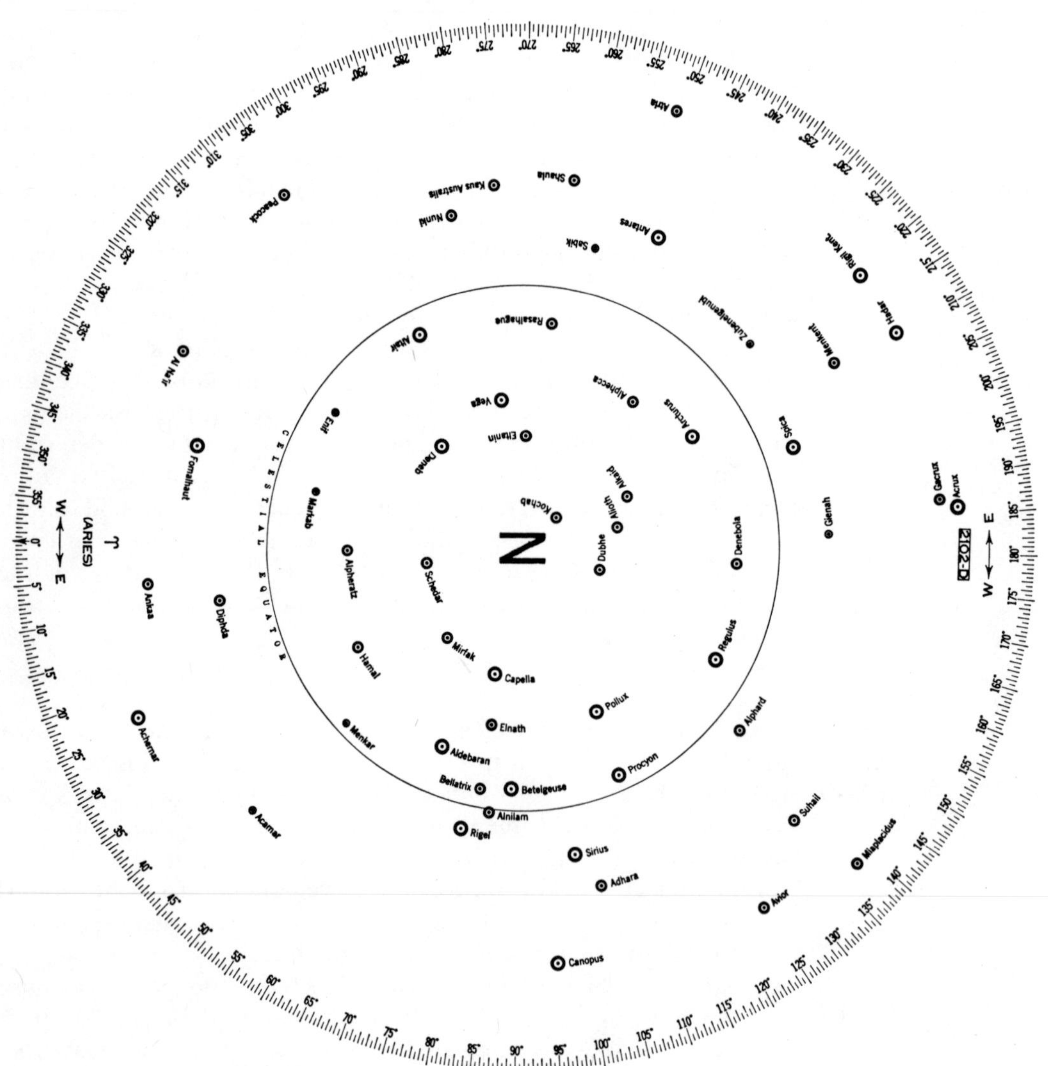

Figure 2002a. Star Finder; base only.

circumference is graduated in half degrees of LHA ♈, and labeled towards the east, at 5° intervals. All the stars are shown on each side of the base on a polar azimuthal equidistant projection extending towards the opposite pole. Each star is named, and the approximate magnitude is indicated by a symbol—a larger heavy ring for first magnitude, a smaller heavy ring for second magnitude, and a yet smaller and thinner ring for third magnitude. The celestial equator is shown as a circle about half the diameter of the base. Because of the distortion caused by the projection, the relative positions of the stars shown on the base do *not* correspond to their apparent positions in the sky, and the device cannot be compared directly with the heavens.

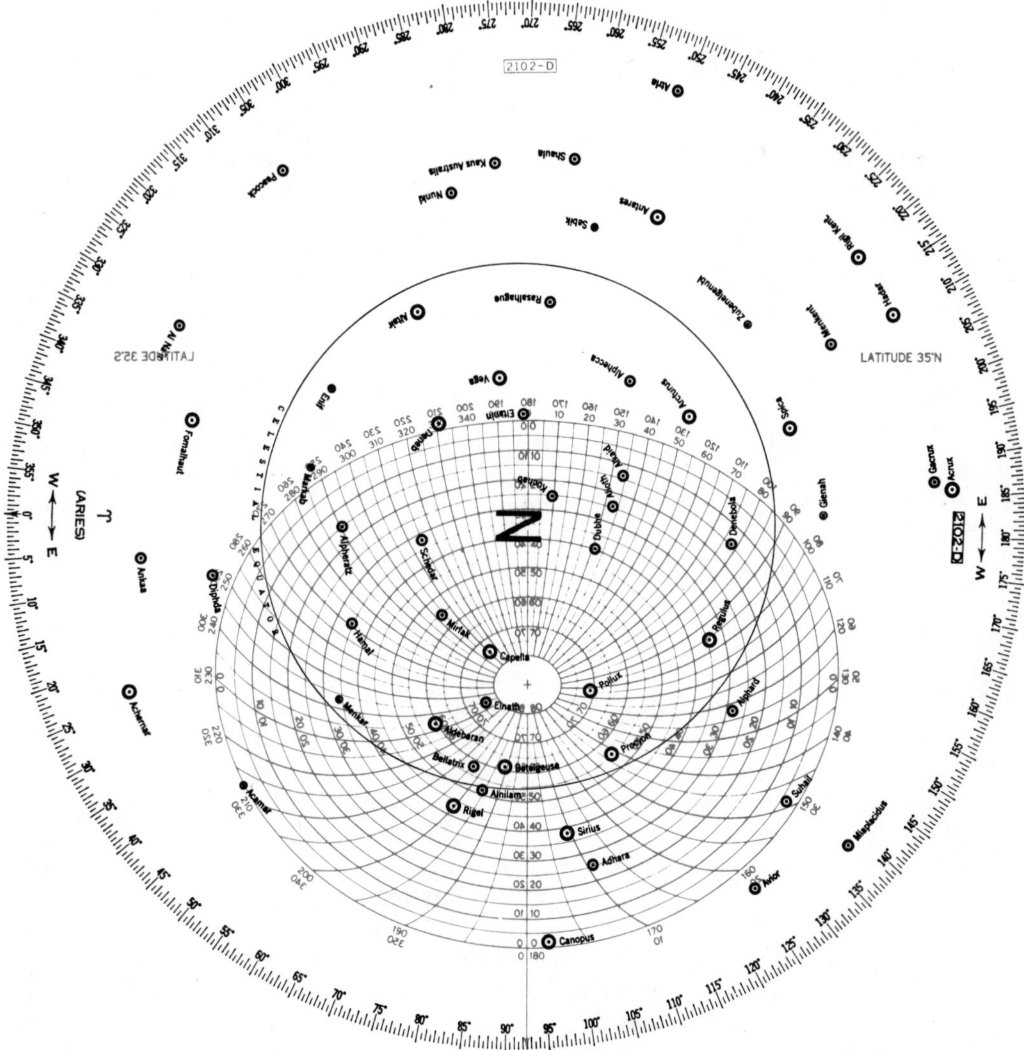

Figure 2002b. Star Finder; base with template for 35°N latitude in place.

There are ten templates of transparent plastic. Nine of these are printed with blue ink and are designed for apparent altitude and azimuth determinations, while the tenth, printed in red ink, is intended for the plotting of bodies other than the 57 selected stars on the base plate. There is one blue template for every 10° of latitude between 5° and 85°; one side of each template is for use in north latitudes, the other for south latitudes. Each of these "latitude" templates is printed with a set of oval blue *altitude* curves at 5° intervals, with the outermost curve representing the observer's celestial horizon, and a second set of radial *azimuth* curves, also at 5° intervals. The red template is printed with a set of concentric declination circles, one for each 10° of declination, and a set of radial meridian angle lines. In use, the appropriate template is placed on the star base much like a record on a phonograph turntable.

Figure 2002b shows the north side of the Star Finder with the template for 35° north latitude set for a LHA ♈ of 97.2°.

Use of the Star Finder for determining the altitude and azimuth

2003 The Star Finder is most convenient for determining which of the 57 selected stars will be favorably situated for observation at twilight and what their approximate altitudes and azimuths will be. First the LHA ♈ must be determined (Article 1903) for the mid-time of the period during which observations are to be made. (LHA ♈ equals GHA ♈ from an almanac minus west longitude, or plus east longitude; LHA ♈ can also be determined graphically with a small circular plastic device marked with multiple scales.) For morning sights, the beginning of civil twilight (Article 2711) or a time shortly thereafter is often used. For the evening, the time would be based on the ending of civil twilight. The most suitable time to select depends largely on the ability of the observer and the quality of his sextant, and can best be determined by experience.

The Star Finder is used as follows:

Example: A navigator, whose DR position at the time of the ending of civil twilight will be Lat. 37°14.8′ N, Long. 144°25.6′ E, determines the GHA of Aries to be 312°46.8′ at that time.

Required: The approximate altitudes and azimuths of all first magnitude stars which will be above the horizon at that time, using the Star Finder.

Solution: (Figure 2002b) First, determine LHA in the usual manner; in this case, 312°46.8′ + 144°25.6′ = 457°12.4′ − 360° = 97°12.4′. Next, select the blue-ink template for the latitude closest to the DR latitude. Place this on the star base so that the labels for both correspond to the name of the DR latitude. In this case the template for Latitude 35° N is selected and placed over the side of the star base which has the letter "N" at the center, as shown. Orient the template so that the arrow extending from the 0°–180° azimuth line points to the value on the base plate of LHA ♈ for the time desired; in this case, the arrow is aligned, as closely as possible by eye, with 97.2°.

Finally, note the approximate altitudes and azimuths of the desired celestial bodies. The approximate altitudes and azimuths of the first magnitude stars are tabulated below, in order of increasing azimuth.

Body	ha	Zn
Regulus	36°	101°
Pollux	73°	106°
Procyon	57°	148°
Sirius	39°	176°
Canopus	2°	181°
Betelgeuse	62°	200°
Rigel	43°	207°
Aldebaran	58°	243°
Capella	72°	315°

GHA ♈	312°46′.8
λ	144°25′.6 E
LHA ♈	97°12′.4

In this instance, there are a considerable number of first magnitude stars above the horizon, but they are not evenly distributed in azimuth. At sea, a navigator would include some tabulated stars of lesser magnitude to his north, such as Dubhe, Kochab, etc. He would probably not observe Canopus, except from necessity, due to its low altitude. Pollux and Capella might be difficult to observe, both being above 70° in altitude; Regulus and Mirfak would be easier to observe and give equivalent coverage in azimuth.

It is always wise to list more stars than the navigator actually expects to observe, as some may be obscured by clouds. The stars listed for observation should not be limited to those of the first magnitude; all the stars shown on the Star Finder are readily visible in clear weather. The stars should be selected so that good distribution in azimuth is obtained, and on the basis of altitude. The most convenient altitude band for observation lies roughly between 15° and 60°, but it is preferable to obtain observations considerably lower or higher than these approximate limits, rather than to have poor distribution in azimuth.

Using the Star Finder for determining the approximate altitudes and azimuths of planets

2004 The Star Finder may be used in the same manner to predetermine the position in the heavens of the planets—or of additional fixed stars, should this be required—if their positions are plotted on the star base. While the planets move in position relative to the stars, their positions so plotted will be satisfactory over a period of several days. Thus, for a vessel departing on a two-week passage, the positions of the planets could be plotted on the star base for a date approximately one week after departure.

To plot the position of a planet on the star base, the navigator first determines its declination for the desired time, as well as 360° minus its sidereal hour angle (SHA) as the relative positions of the stars are determined by their SHAs. This latter quantity is obtained by subtracting the GHA ♈ for the desired time from the GHA of the planet at that time, adding 360° to the GHA when necessary. This is equivalent to "right ascension" (Article 1903) expressed in units of arc (degrees) rather than units of time (hours). For example, suppose a navigator in south latitude wishes to plot Venus on the star base. From the *Nautical* or *Air Almanac* for a time near the middle of the observation period, he obtains the data shown below, and then determines 360° − SHA.

GHA Venus	222°40.2′	Dec. S 4°39.6′
GHA ♈	−213°29.3′	
SHA Venus	9°10.9′	
360° − SHA	350°49.1′	

This angle, and the declination, would be required to locate Venus on the star base: for plotting purposes, he would call them 350.8° and 4.5° south, respectively. (Alternatively, from the *Nautical Almanac* he could have directly read the SHA of Venus tabulated at the bottom of the left-hand page as an average for a three-day period and subtracted this value from 360°; this procedure is precise enough for Star Finder use.)

Next, the red plotting template is placed, south latitude side up, on the south (S) side of the star base. On the red template, a radial line is printed to represent every 10° of meridian angle, and a concentric circle is printed for every 10° of declination, with the median circle being the celestial equator. When in place on the base plate, this median circle should be concurrent with the celestial equator circle on the base plate. The solid circles within the celestial equator circle then represent declinations of the same name as the base plate, while the dashed circles outside the equator represent declinations of contrary name.

The index arrow is now aligned with 350.8°. The position of Venus is then plotted on the base by marking with a pencil through the cut-out slot at the proper point on the declination scale. In this case, south declination is on the side of the circle for the celestial equator toward the S pole at the center of the base; if the declination of the body had been of the *contrary* name to the name of the center of the base plate, it would have been plotted on the side of the equatorial circle away from the center. The proper symbol for Venus, ♀, is drawn in on the base after the template is removed. Figure 2004 shows the star base with the plotting template set at 350.8° and a mark for Venus at 4.5° south declination. The date for this plot should be marked in some clear area of the base as a reminder as to when the position will need to be recalculated and replotted.

Similar procedures will be followed to plot an unlisted star, the moon, or the sun. A star's plot will remain unchanged for an indefinite period, but any plot of the moon or sun must be corrected to a specific time of use.

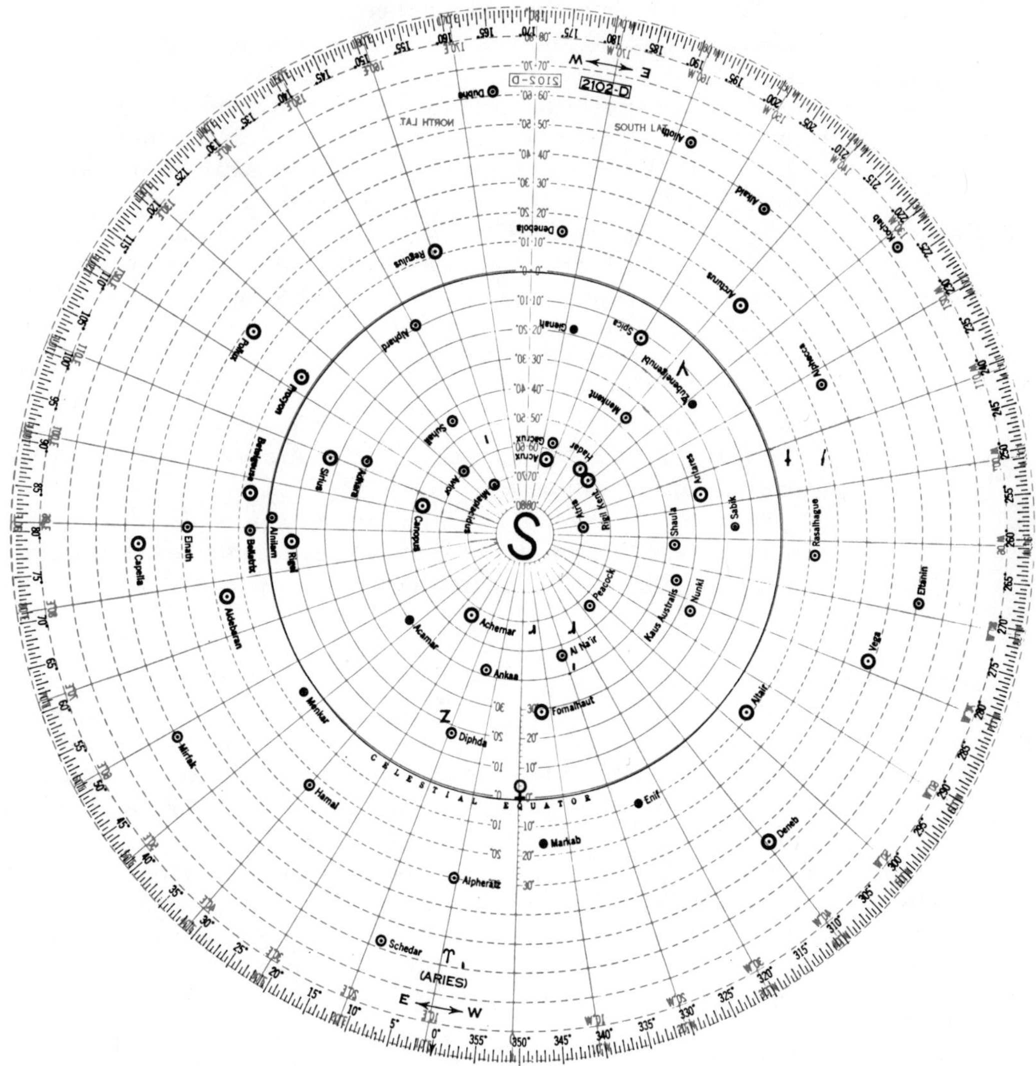

Figure 2004. Star Finder; base with red plotting template in place (shown here in blue).

Identifying unknown celestial bodies

2005 At times, the navigator will obtain an observation of an unknown body. In such a case, if *both its altitude and azimuth* are noted as well as the time of the observation, it may be identified by means of the Star Finder.

If the star is one of those shown on the base plate of the star finder the identification is quite simple. The index arrow of the blue template is aligned to the appropriate LHA ♈ for the time of the observation. The point of intersection of the altitude and azimuth curve of the body is then located on the blue template and the body listed on the star base at or quite near this position can usually be assumed to be the one observed.

The visible planets should have been plotted on the star base as outlined above, as the observed body may have been a planet rather than a star.

If no star or planet appears at or near that point, the red template can be used to determine the approximate Dec. and Sidereal Hour Angle (SHA) of the star. These two arguments can be located in the list of stars in the *Almanac* for proper identification.

To determine the SHA and Dec., the blue template is left in place properly aligned with LHA of Aries; the red template is then placed over the blue template and rotated until the slotted meridian is over the intersection of the altitude and azimuth curve obtained from the observation of the star. The Dec. is read off the scale along the slotted meridian, or its imaginary extension for large values of Dec. the quantity 360° minus SHA is read from the base plate underneath the arrow on the red template. This figure subtracted from 360° equals the SHA of the star.

With the declination and SHA known approximately, the list of stars in the *Nautical* or *Air Almanac* can be consulted for identification and exact values of these quantities.

Star identification by Pub. No. 229

2006 Although no formal star identification tables are included in DMAHC Pub. No. 229, *Sight Reduction Tables for Marine Navigation,* a simple approach to star identification is to scan the pages for the applicable latitude and for a combination of arguments which give altitude and azimuth angle for the unidentified body. Thus the approximate declination and LHA of the body are determined directly. The star's SHA is found from SHA star = LHA star − GHA ♈. With declination and SHA roughly known, the *Air* or *Nautical Almanac* is consulted for identification and exact values. The introductory pages of each volume of Pub. No. 229 describes this method, and an alternative, in greater detail.

Star charts and star diagrams

2007 In addition to the 2102-D Star Finder and Identifier, the identification of celestial bodies may be learned pictorially; remember that the Star Finder does *not* give a visualization of the heavens. *Sky charts* are photograph-like representations of the night sky at certain times of the year. *Sky diagrams* are drawings of the heavens as they would be seen from certain locations at various times. Although intended for the same purpose, there are differences in design and use.

Identification by star chart

Star charts are representations of the celestial sphere, or of parts of it, on a flat surface. On most charts, north is at the top and south at the bottom, but east is at the *left,* and west at the *right;* this is the reverse of the terrestrial chart presentation. If the chart is held overhead, and the N-S axis is properly oriented, this presentation approximates the appearance of the heavens. Some star charts are polar projections; these show the star groups around the pole and are especially helpful in visualizing the movement and relationship of circumpolar stars. Star charts are more often used for learning the identification of stars than in the normal practice of navigation at sea.

***Nautical Almanac* Star Charts** The *Nautical Almanac* star charts consist of four charts; one polar projection for each hemisphere, covering declinations 10° through 90°, of the same name, and two rectangular projections covering Dec. 30° N to 30° S, around the celestial sphere. See Figure 2007a.

A planetary diagram giving LMT of meridian passage of the planets is also given in the *Nautical Almanac.* By means of this diagram the approximate positions of the planets relative to the sun, and to each other, may be determined.

***Air Almanac* Star Charts** A fold-in, white-on-black star chart is located in the back of the *Air Almanac.* It presents the entire celestial sphere on a rectangular projection, the top and bottom edges representing the north and south celestial poles, respectively. This causes great distortion in the relative positions of stars near the poles, but provides a means of determining the order of appearance of the stars and constellations as they move across the heavens.

***Air Almanac* Sky Diagrams** The *Air Almanac* also contains a series of sky diagrams which show the appearance of the sky in various latitudes at different times of the day. They are helpful in selecting the most useful stars and planets for navigation, and for identifying prominent bodies when sighted. For each month, there is a series of diagrams for different latitudes (20° intervals from 70° N to 30° S) for two-hour intervals during the entire day.

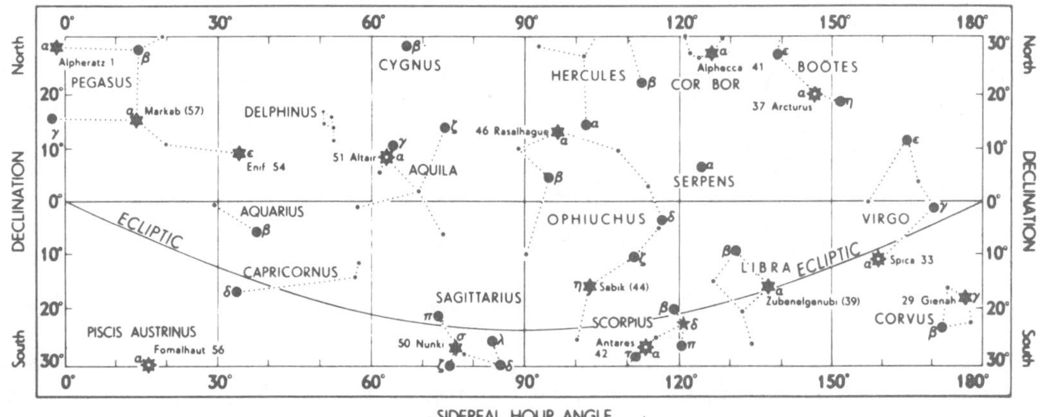

Figure 2007a. Star charts from the *Nautical Almanac.*

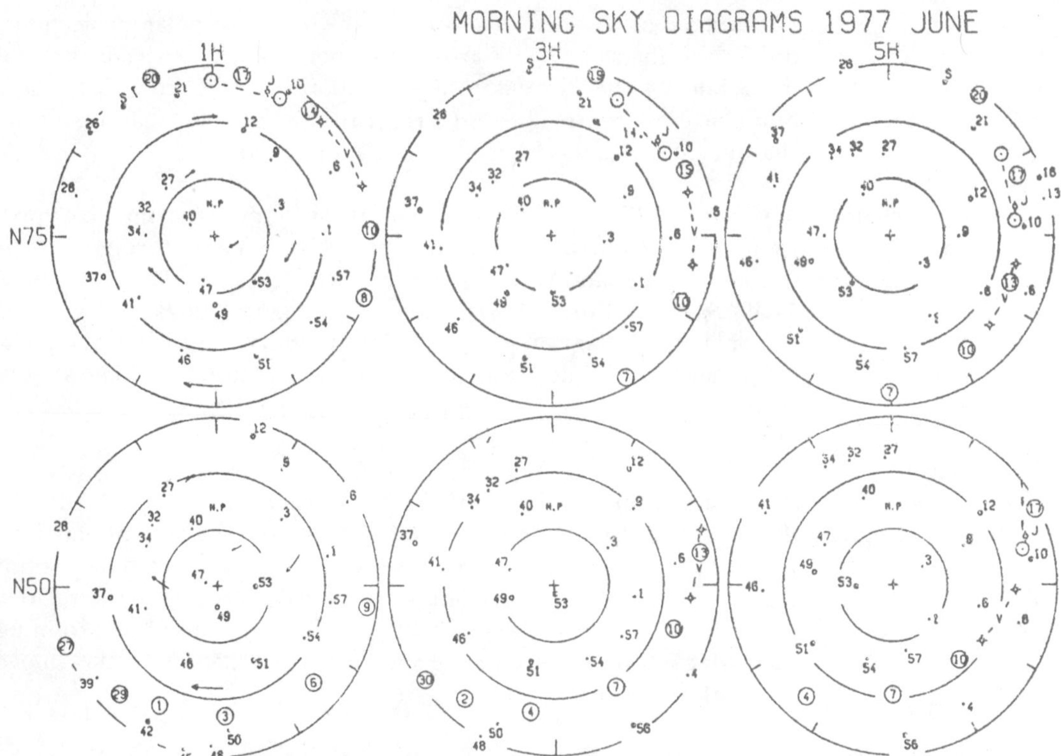

Figure 2007b. Sky diagrams from the *Air Almanac.*

The diagrams for a given latitude are in a horizontal row and show the changes as the day progresses. The appearance of the sky for different latitudes and different times is shown on a pair of facing pages; thus, the appearance of the sky for an intermediate latitude and/or time is easily visualized. A separate set of diagrams is included for the north polar region.

The sky diagrams of the *Air Almanac* have an advantage over sky charts as they are prepared for each month; they are immediately usable without reference to tables or calculations. The diagram for a specific month also allows the inclusion of the planets and the moon, in addition to the 57 selected navigational stars and Polaris; the north and south celestial poles are also shown as NP and SP where appropriate. Stars are shown by a symbol indicating their magnitude and a number for identification, planets are identified by a single-letter abbreviation, and the sun by its symbol. The position of the moon is shown separately for each day by a small circle around figures representing the day of the month. See Figure 2007b.

The positions of the stars and planets in each diagram are indicated for the 15th of the month and will usually serve for the entire month. If it is desired to allow for the motion of the stars during the month, it is necessary only to remember that a given configuration will occur at the beginning of each month one hour later than the time indicated, and at the end of the month one hour earlier. In those months during which Venus moves considerably with respect to the stars, the positions for the first and last of the month are shown; the position towards the west is for the first of the month.

As the sun moves with respect to the stars, its position is given for the first and last days of the month relative to the position of the stars and does not represent the true altitude and azimuth at those times; the position towards the west is for the first of the month. To obtain the altitude and azimuth of the sun at the beginning and end of the month, one must adjust the position of the sun by the amount the stars would have moved. The lengths of the arrows indicate the motion of the stars in 15 days. When the sun is above the horizon only the moon and Venus can be seen with the naked eye, but the positions of the stars are given for use with astro-trackers.

The moon moves so rapidly with respect to the stars that its position at a given time of the night varies appreciably from night to night, and it is necessary to show on each diagram a succession of positions for various days of the month. Three or four such positions are indicated and those for the intermediate dates may be estimated from those given. Since the moon moves completely around the sky in slightly less than a month, or a little over 13° in a day, it will appear on a given diagram for about half of each month. The position on the diagram for each successive night is always to the eastward; when it disappears off the eastern edge of the diagram it will reappear on the western edge about two weeks later, except occasionally on the polar diagrams.

The sky diagrams, used in conjunction with the star chart previously mentioned and a planet location diagram also included in each *Air Almanac,* are very effective in star identification; the latter two are used for detailed verification of the identification made with the sky diagrams.

It must be remembered that the sky diagrams of the *Air Almanac* are to be used flat on the chart table and that they show bearings as they appear on the navigator's chart, east to the right. The star chart and the planet location diagram, on the other hand, are designed to be held overhead for comparison with the sky, and on them east is to the left.

Star Charts **2008** Six numbered star charts are included in this chapter as Figures 2009 to 2014. They show all the brighter stars, necessarily with some repetition. The two charts of the polar regions are on the azimuthal equidistant polar projections; the others are on the transverse Mercator projection.

To use a polar chart, face the elevated pole and hold the correct chart with the name of the month on top. It will then be correctly oriented for LMT 2200 for that month. For each hour the LMT differs from 2200, rotate the chart one hour, as shown by the radial lines. These are labeled for LHA in *time units,* in which case it is called *local sidereal time* (LST), and for sidereal hour angle (SHA). The sidereal time indicates the direction of rotation, as earlier sidereal times occur at earlier solar times. The region about the *elevated* pole will be the only polar region visible.

To use a transverse Mercator star chart, hold it overhead with the top of the page toward north. The left edge will then be east, the right edge west, and the bottom south. The numbers along the central hour circle indicate declination and can be used to orient for latitude. The charts are made for LMT 2200 on the dates specified. For each half month later, subtract one hour to determine the time at which the heavens appear as depicted in the chart; for each half month earlier, add one hour to LMT 2200. The numbers below the celestial equator indicate local sidereal time; those above indicate sidereal hour angle. If the LMT of observation is not 2200, these can be used to determine which hour circle coincides with the celestial meridian. The lighter broken lines connect stars of some of the more easily distinguishable constellations. The heavier broken lines are shown to aid in the identification of stars of different constellations which have a spatial relationship to each other.

It should be kept in mind that the apparent positions of the stars are constantly changing because of the motions of the earth. If the observer changes his position on the earth, a further change in the apparent positions of the stars will result. Remember, too, that the limits of the transverse Mercator charts represent the approximate limits of observation only at the equator. Observers elsewhere will see below their elevated pole, and an equal amount of the opposite polar region will be hidden from view.

The approximate appearance of the heavens at any given time can be determined by obtaining LHA ♈ (from GHA ♈, tabulated in the almanacs, and the observer's longitude) and converting it to time units. The resulting LST is then found on the star charts. The celestial meridian on the transverse Mercator chart which is labeled with that time is the one which is approximately overhead. The same celestial meridian on the polar charts, labeled in the same way, is the one which is *up.* Thus if LHA ♈ is 225°, LST is 15^h. This appears on the transverse Mercator charts of both Figures 2010 and 2011. The stars to the east of the celestial meridian at this time appear in Figure 2011 (in the direction of increasing LST and decreasing SHA), and the stars to the west of the celestial meridian at this time appear in Figure 2010 (in the direction of decreasing LST and increasing SHA). By orienting each polar chart so that the celestial meridian labeled 15^h is up, the stars toward and beyond each celestial pole can be seen. An observer can view only half of the celestial sphere at a given time, of course, and the stars actually visible depend upon his latitude.

Ursa Major **2009** The *north polar region* (Star Chart 1, Figure 2009). Nearly everyone is familiar with the *Big Dipper,* the popular name for the constellation *Ursa Major* (the big bear). This is composed of seven stars in the shape of a dipper, with the open part toward the north celestial pole. For observers in the United States, most of the dipper is circumpolar and is therefore visible the year around. Dubhe, Alioth, and Alkaid are the stars of this constellation most used by navigators. Dubhe and Merak, forming part of the bowl of the dipper, are called the pointers, for if the line connecting them is extended northward, it passes very near Polaris, less than one degree from the north celestial pole. If the line is extended across the pole, it leads very near to Caph in *Cassiopeia.* These stars point straight *down* to Polaris in the evening

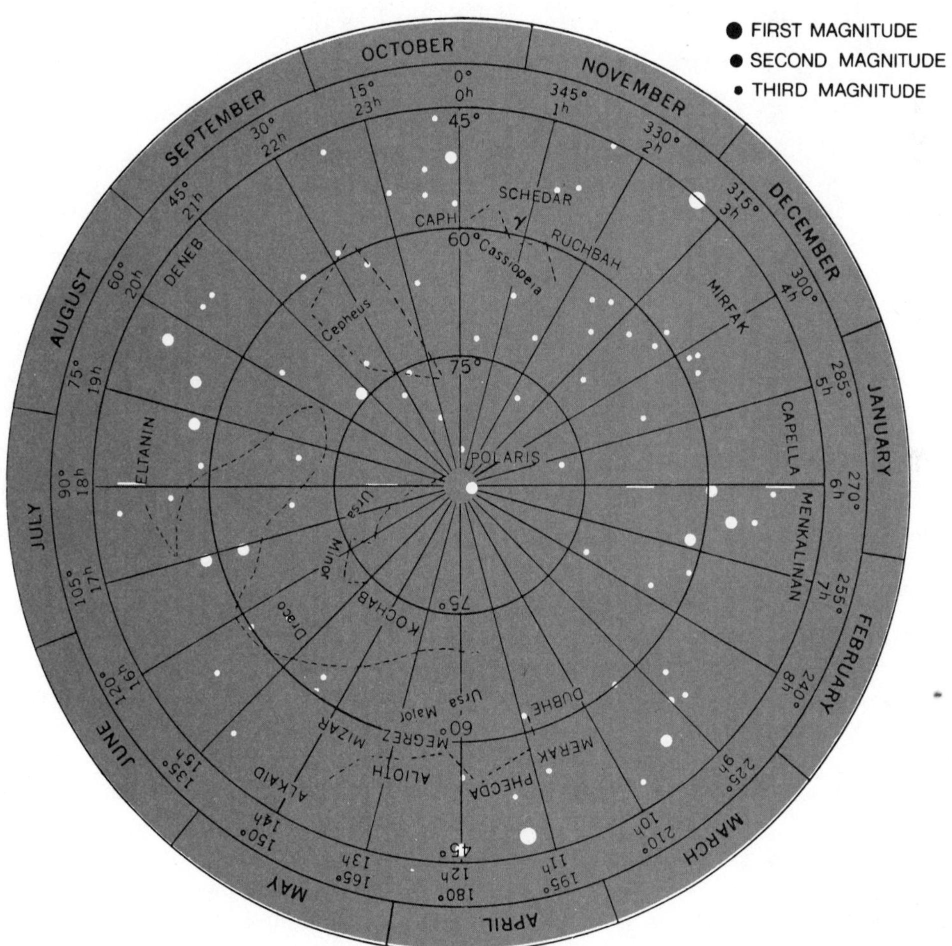

Figure 2009. Star Chart 1, the north polar region. Hold toward the north at 2200 LMT with the name of the month at the top.

sky of mid-April. By the middle of July they are to the left of Polaris. In mid-October they are directly below the pole, and three months later, in the middle of January, they are to the right. For other stars identified by means of the *Big Dipper,* see Article 2010.

Ursa Minor Polaris is part of the *Little Dipper*, as the constellation *Ursa Minor* (the little bear) is popularly known; this star is not conspicuous until the sky has become quite dark. Only Polaris at one end and Kochab at the other, both second-magnitude stars, are used by the navigator. The little dipper is roughly parallel to the big dipper, but upside down with respect to it. In the autumn the *Big Dipper* is under the *Little Dipper* and there is a folk saying that liquid spilling out of the little one will be caught by the big one. The handles of the two dippers curve in opposite directions, relative to their bowls.

Cassiopeia *Cassiopeia* (the queen). Across the pole from the handle of the *Big Dipper,* and approximately the same distance from Polaris, will be found *Cassiopeia's Chair.* The principal stars of this constellation form a well-defined *W* or *M,* depending on their position with respect to the pole. Schedar, the second star from the right when the figure appears as a *W,* is a second-magnitude star sometimes used by navigators. Second-magnitude Caph, the right-hand star when the figure appears as a *W,* is of interest because it lies close to the hour circle of the vernal equinox.

Draco *Draco* is about halfway from *Cassiopeia* to the *Big Dipper* in a westerly direction, but its navigational star Eltanin probably is more easy to identify by following the western arm of the *Northern Cross* as described in the *Scorpio* group (Article 2011).

Boötes, Virgo **2010** The *spring sky* (Chart 2, Fig. 2010). In the spring, the *Big Dipper* is above the pole, high in the sky, and serves to point out several excellent navigational stars. Starting at the bowl, follow the curvature of the handle. If this curved arc is continued, it leads first to Arcturus, the only navigational star in *Boötes* (the herdsman) and then to Spica in *Virgo* (the virgin), both first-magnitude stars much used by the navigator. A line northward through the pointers of the *Big Dipper* leads to Polaris. If this line is followed in the opposite direction, it leads in the general direction of Regulus, the end of the handle of the sickle
Leo in the constellation *Leo* (the lion). This much-used navigational star is of the first magnitude and the brightest star in its part of the sky. A line connecting Regulus and Arcturus passes close to second-magnitude Denebola (tail of the lion), sometimes used by navigators.

Corvus *Corvus* (the crow) resembles more nearly a quadrilateral sail. It is not difficult to find and contains the third-magnitude navigational star Gienah. Due south of *Corvus* is the *Southern Cross* (Article 2014).

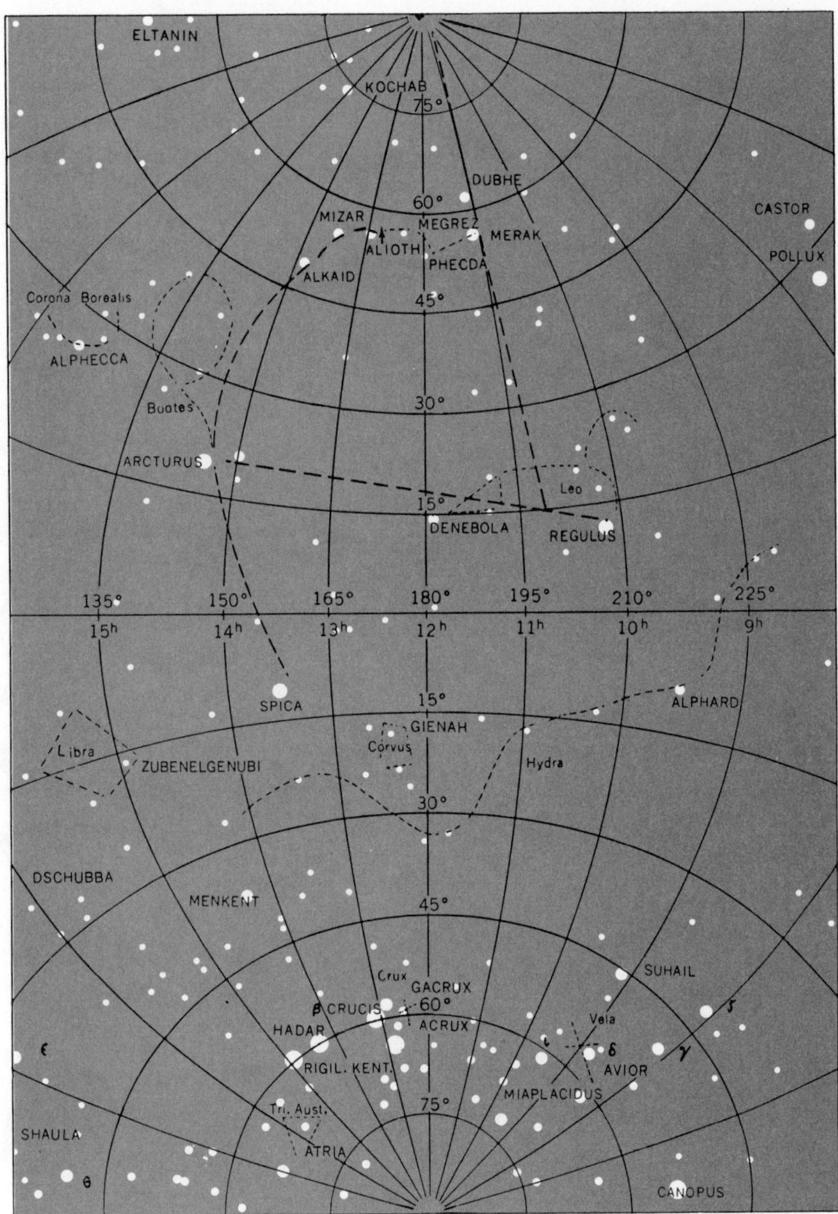

Figure 2010. Star Chart 2. The spring sky as seen at 2200 LMT on 22 April. Hold overhead with the top of the page toward the north.

Hydra The only navigational star in *Hydra* (the serpent), a long, inconspicuous constellation near *Corvus,* is the second-magnitude Alphard. This star is more easily identified by its being close to the extension of a line from the pointer of the *Big Dipper* through Regulus and extending southward.

Scorpio **2011** The *summer sky* (Star Chart 3, Figure 2011). *Scorpio* (the scorpion) is one constellation which resembles the animal for which it is named without too much imagination. The curve from Antares, the main navigational star, to Shaula is particularly suggestive of a scorpion's tail. Immediately to the east is a group forming the shape of a teapot with the star Nunki in the handle.

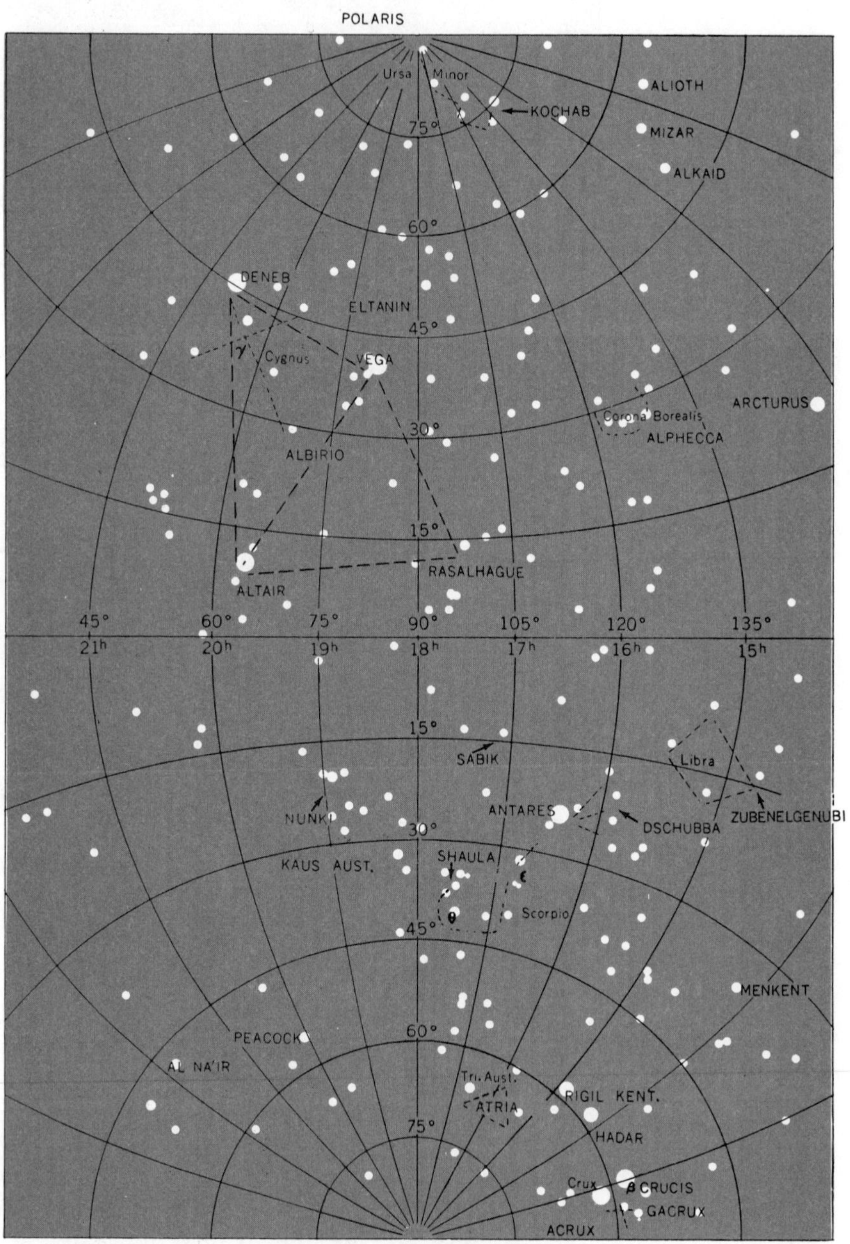

Figure 2011. Star Chart 3. The summer sky as seen at 2200 LMT on 22 July. Hold overhead with the top of the page toward the north.

To the north of these are the first-magnitude stars, Vega, Deneb, and Altair. They form a distinct right triangle (right angle at Vega) which many people use as an identification feature. However, each one is in a different constellation which should enable one to identify it without reference to any other stars. Deneb is in the northern cross

Cygnus (*Cygnus*); the eastern arm of the cross points to Enif, the western arm to Eltanin, and the bisectors of the lower right angles point to Altair and Vega. Altair is readily identified by the small stars on either side of it, sometimes called the guardians. It should be kept in mind, however, that the southern guardian is only a fourth-magnitude star and may not show too plainly on very hazy or bright moonlight nights. This configuration is unique and should identify Altair through a break in the overcast with no other stars showing. Vega may be identified under these conditions by an almost perfect parallelogram slightly to the south and east of it. Again, however, these are fourth magnitude stars and are not too distinct if the weather conditions are unfavorable.

Corona Borealis The northern crown (*Corona Borealis*) is a group of stars shaped like a bowl about two thirds of the distance from Vega toward Arcturus. This constellation forms a distinctive pattern and connects the dipper group to the northern cross to the east. Second-magnitude Alphecca in this group is sometimes used by navigators.

Rasalhague forms nearly an equilateral triangle with Vega and Altair. This second-magnitude star and third-magnitude Sabik, to the south, are occasionally used by navigators.

The Pegasus Group **2012** The *autumn sky* (Star Chart 4, Figure 2012) is marked by an absence of first-magnitude stars. The northern cross has moved to a position low in the western sky, and *Cassiopeia* is nearly on the meridian to the north. A little south of the zenith for most observers in the United States the great square of *Pegasus* (the winged horse) appears nearly on the meridian. The eastern side of this square, and Caph in *Cassiopeia,* nearly mark the hour circle of the vernal equinox. Alpheratz and Markab, second-magnitude stars at opposite corners of the square, are the principal navigational stars of this constellation. Second-magnitude Enif is occasionally used.

The square of *Pegasus* is useful in locating several navigational stars. The line joining the stars of the eastern side of the square, if continued southward, leads close to second-magnitude Diphda in *Cetus* (the sea monster). Similarly, a line joining the stars of the western side of the square, if continued southward, leads close to first-magnitude Fomalhaut. A line through the center of the square, if continued

Aries eastward, leads close to second-magnitude Hamal, in *Aries* (the ram). This was the location of the vernal equinox some 2000 years ago, when it was designated the "first point of Aries."

A curved line from Alpheratz through *Andromeda* leads to *Perseus.* The only navigational star frequently used in *Perseus* is the second-

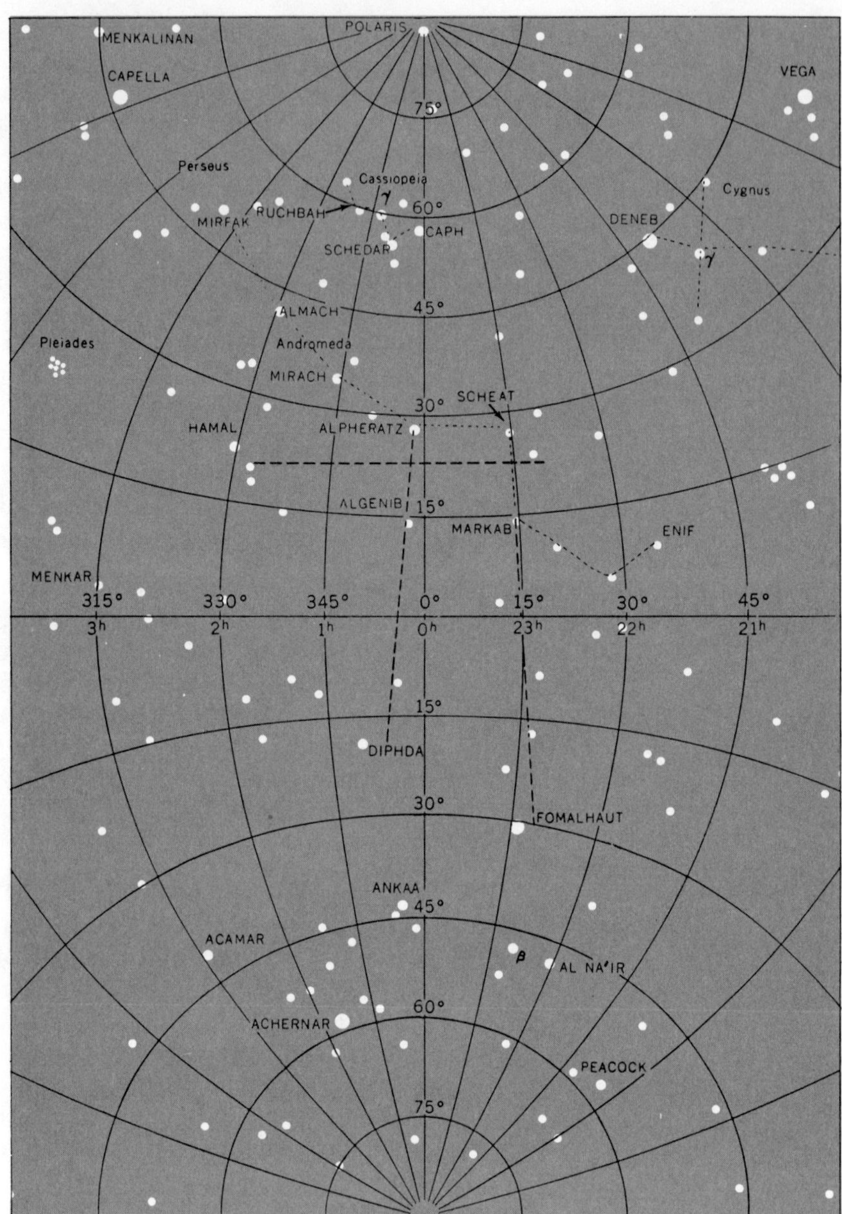

Figure 2012. Star Chart 4. The autumn sky as seen at 2200 LMT on 21 October. Hold overhead with the top of the page toward the north.

magnitude Mirfak. The curved line from Mirfak to Alpheratz forms a handle to a huge dipper of which the square of *Pegasus* is the bowl.

A line from Fomalhaut through Diphda extended about forty degrees leads to Menkar, an inconspicuous third-magnitude star in *Cetus;* and Ankaa, a second-magnitude star in *Phoenix,* is found about twenty degrees southeasterly from Fomalhaut. Both stars are listed among the navigational stars.

The navigational stars associated with *Pegasus* are Alpheratz, Markab, Diphda, Fomalhaut, and Hamal.

Capella, rising in the east as *Pegasus* is overhead, connects this group to the *Orion* group while Enif acts as a link to the west.

Orion **2013** The *winter sky* (Star Chart 5, Figure 2013). No other part of the sky contains so many bright stars. The principal constellation of this region is *Orion* (the hunter), probably the best-known constellation in the entire sky, with the exception of the big dipper. This figure is well known to observers in both northern and southern hemispheres, as the belt of *Orion* lies almost exactly on the celestial equator. Brilliant Rigel and first-magnitude Betelgeuse lie approximately equal distances below and above the belt, respectively.

Several good navigational stars may be found by the use of *Orion.* If the line of the belt is continued to the westward, it leads near first-magnitude, reddish Aldebaran (the "follower", so named because it follows the "seven sisters" of *Pleiades*), in the V-shaped head of *Taurus* (the bull). If the line of the belt is followed in the opposite direction, it leads almost to Sirius, the brightest of all the stars. This is the principal star in the constellation of *Canis Major,* the hunter's large dog. Starting with Sirius, a rough circle can be drawn through Procyon in *Canis Minor* (the little dog), Pollux and Castor in *Gemini* (the twins), Capella in *Auriga* (the charioteer), Aldebaran, Rigel, and back to Sirius. All of these except Castor are first-magnitude stars.

Pleiades
Taurus
Canis Major
Canis Minor

Several second-magnitude stars in the general area of *Orion* are bright enough for navigational purposes, but are seldom used because there are so many first-magnitude stars nearby. Four of these second-magnitude stars are listed among the principal navigational stars of the almanac. These are Bellatrix, just west of Betelgeuse; Alnilam, the middle star (actually, a spiral nebulae) in the belt; Elnath, in *Taurus;* and Adhara, part of a triangle in *Canis Major,* and just south of Sirius.

Nearly on the meridian far to the south the brilliant Canopus, second brightest star, is visible only to observers in the United States south of latitude 37½°. This star is part of the constellation *Carina* (the keel).

Crux **2014** The *south polar region* (Star Chart 6, Figure 2014). While the south polar region contains a number of bright stars, the person who travels to the southern hemisphere for the first time is likely to be disappointed by the absence of any striking configuration of stars similar to those with which he is familiar. The famed southern cross (*Crux*) is far from an impressive constellation and such a poor cross it might

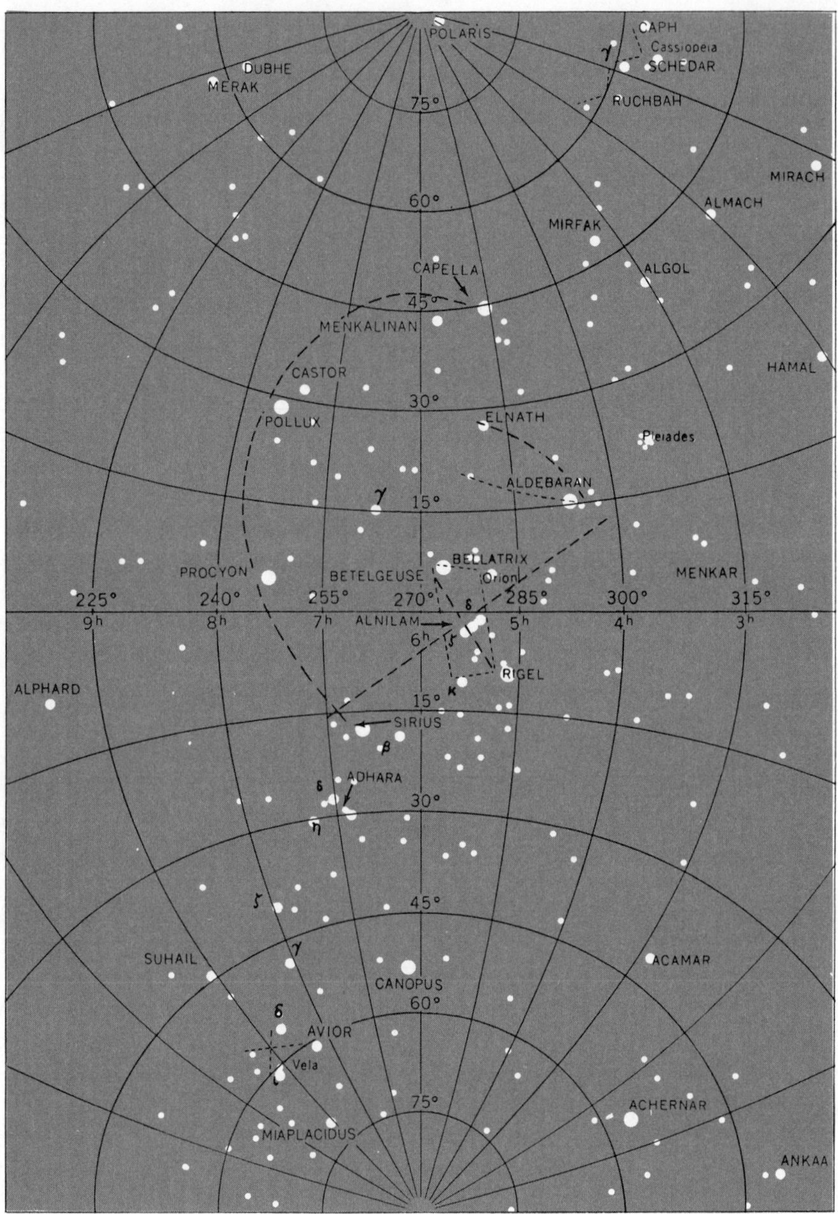

Figure 2013. Star Chart 5. The winter sky as seen at 2200 LMT on 21 January. Hold overhead with the top of the page toward the north.

easily be overlooked if two of its stars were not of the first magnitude. A somewhat similar "false cross" in the constellation *Vela* may be easily mistaken for the southern cross.

Canopus is almost due south of Sirius. The constellation *Carina,* of which Canopus is a part, was originally part of a larger constellation, *Argo* (the ship), which is now generally divided into *Carina* (the keel),

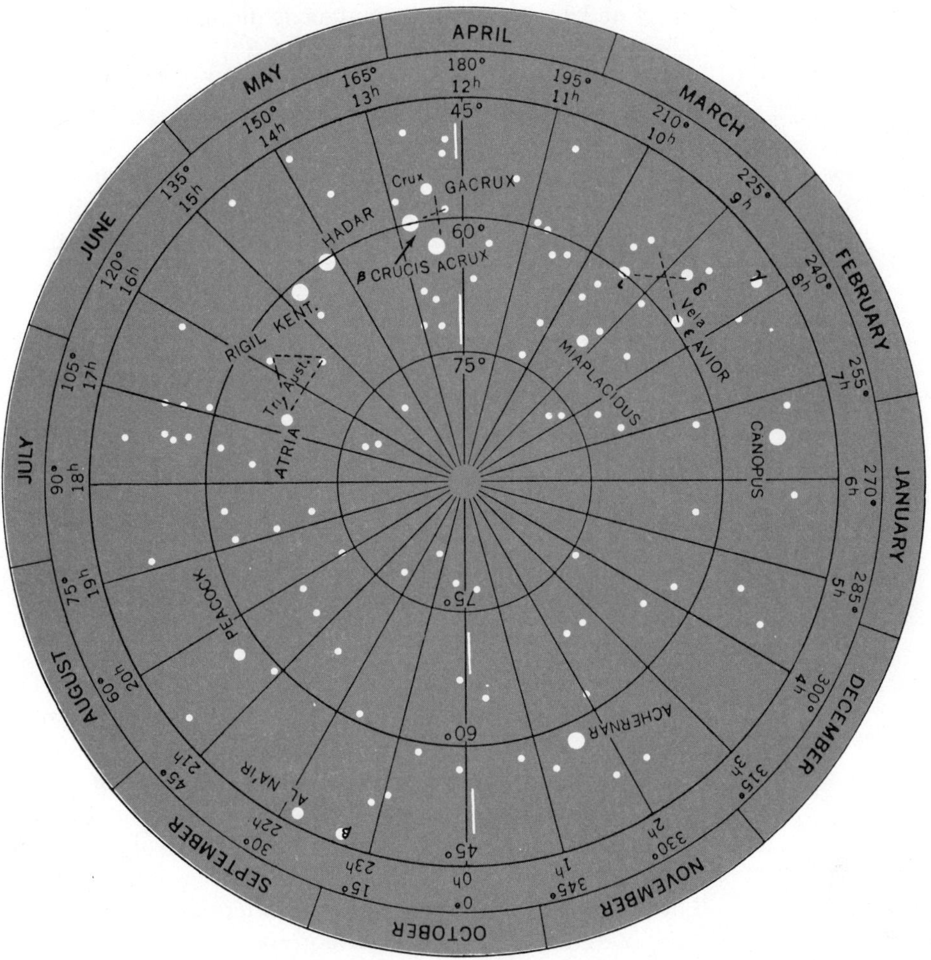

Figure 2014. Star Chart 6, the south polar region. Hold toward the south at 2200 LMT with the name of the month at the top.

Puppis (the stern), *Pyxis* (the mariner's compass), and *Vela* (the sails). Navigational stars included in *Argo* are, besides first-magnitude Canopus, Avior (part of the "false cross"), Suhail (Figures 2010 and 2013) and Miaplacidus, all second-magnitude stars.

Counterclockwise from *Argo* is *Crux,* the true southern cross. Acrux and Gacrux are listed among the principal navigational stars of the almanac. This constellation also contains the first-magnitude star β Crucis.

Centaurus Two more good first-magnitude stars lie in nearby *Centaurus* (the centaur). These are Rigil Kentaurus and Hadar. The second-magnitude Menkent at the other end of the constellation (Figures 2010 and

2011) is listed among the principal navigational stars and is used occasionally by navigators.

Near *Centaurus* and still in a counterclockwise direction around the pole is Atria, a commonly used navigational star in *Triangulum Australe*.

The half of the south polar region thus far described has a relatively large number of first- and second-magnitude stars. This area is actually a continuation of the bright area around *Orion,* as can be seen by referring to Figure 2013.

In the remaining section of the south polar region there are relatively few navigational stars. These are second-magnitude Peacock in *Pavo* (the peacock), second-magnitude Al Na'ir in *Grus* (the crane), and first-magnitude Achernar and third-magnitude Acamar (Figures 2012 and 2013) in *Eridanus* (the river). All of these constellations are faint and poorly defined. Of these stars Achernar and Peacock are good navigational stars. The other two are seldom used.

Summary **2015** The proper identification of a celestial body on which a sextant sight has been taken is an essential part of using that observation to obtain a line of position.

Many stars will become familiar "friends" to a navigator as he gains experience, but it is often desirable to prepare for morning or evening observations by recording a table of approximate altitudes and azimuths. Various methods can be used, but the 2102-D Star Finder and Identifier is probably the easiest and most direct. Planet locations can and should be added to the base plate to supplement the star information printed there.

There is also the problem of positive identification of an unknown celestial body used for an observation in order that the sight may be correctly reduced. Here the Star Finder method can be employed, or use can be made of precomputed sight reduction tables, sky charts, or sky diagrams.

Failure to obtain a reasonable line of position from a celestial observation can frequently be attributed to faulty identification, such as confusing a star for a planet or vice versa.

21 The Marine Sextant: Its Use, Adjustment, and Corrections

Introduction **2101** The first successful instrument developed for measuring the altitude of celestial bodies while at sea was the *cross-staff.* It was unique in that it measured altitude from the sea horizon; its disadvantage was that it required the user to look at the horizon and at the body at the same time. This must have been quite a feat, particularly when the body was well above the horizon; an experienced navigator, however, could for the first time determine the altitude of a body at sea with an accuracy of about one degree.

In 1590, the *backstaff*, or *Davis's quadrant*, shown in Figure 2101, was invented by John Davis—this was a great advancement over the cross-staff. To use this instrument the observer turned his back on the sun, and aligned a shadow cast by the sun with the horizon. Later designs of this instrument were fitted with a mirror so as to make possible observations of bodies other than the sun.

Today's *sextant* is an instrument designed to permit measurement of the angle between the lines of sight to two objects with great precision. It derives its name from the fact that its arc is approximately one-sixth of a circle; because of its optical principle, it can measure angles up to about 120°, or twice the value of the arc itself. Quintants and octants are similar instruments, named for the lengths of their arcs, but today it is the general practice to refer to all such instruments as sextants, regardless of the precise lengths of their arcs.

The optical principle of the sextant was first described by Sir Isaac Newton. However, its importance was not realized, and the information was long forgotten until it was applied to celestial navigation.

The double reflecting principle of the sextant, described hereafter, was independently rediscovered in 1730 by Hadley in England and Godfrey in Philadelphia; it made possible a high standard of accuracy in celestial navigation. The sextant and the compass remain the navigator's most important tools.

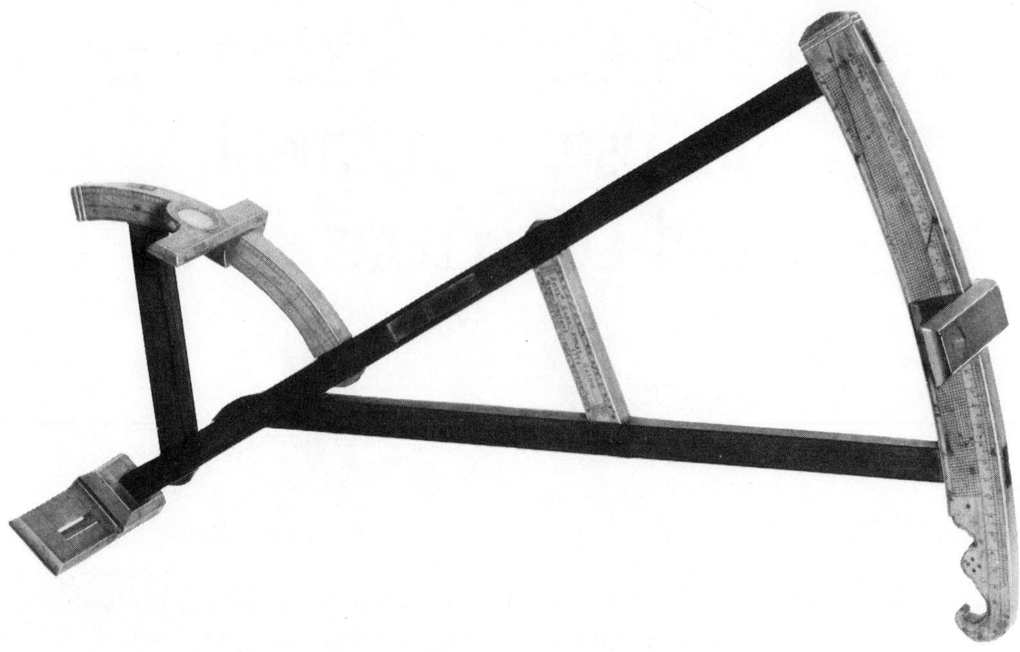

Figure 2101. Davis quadrant, 1775.

The marine sextant's components

2102 A marine sextant is illustrated in Figure 2102 with the principal parts labeled as follows:

A. The *frame,* on which the other parts are mounted. The frame is normally made of brass, but some "lightweight" models are of aluminum alloy.

B. The *limb* is the lower part of the frame and carries the *arc* (B′) graduated in degrees. The arc may be inscribed on the limb, or it may be inscribed on a separate plate permanently attached to the limb. The outer edge of the limb is cut into teeth which are engaged by the teeth of the *tangent screw* (not visible).

C. The *index arm,* of the same material as the frame, is pivoted at the center of curvature of the limb, and is free to move around it. Its lower end carries an *index* to indicate the reading in degrees on the arc.

D. The *micrometer drum* is used to make fine adjustments of the index arm. It is mounted on a shaft, having a pinion gear at the other end called the *tangent screw.* This tangent screw engages the worm teeth cut into the limb, and one full turn moves the index arm by one-half degree on the arc, thus changing the observed altitude by exactly one degree. The micrometer drum is generally graduated in minutes of arc. On some models there is only a single index mark for the micrometer drum, and fractions of a minute can only be estimated between graduations for whole minutes; see Figure 2102. On other models there is a vernier scale which permits readings to be taken to 0.1′ (or 0.2′); see Figure 2104. A few sextants may have vernier readings in

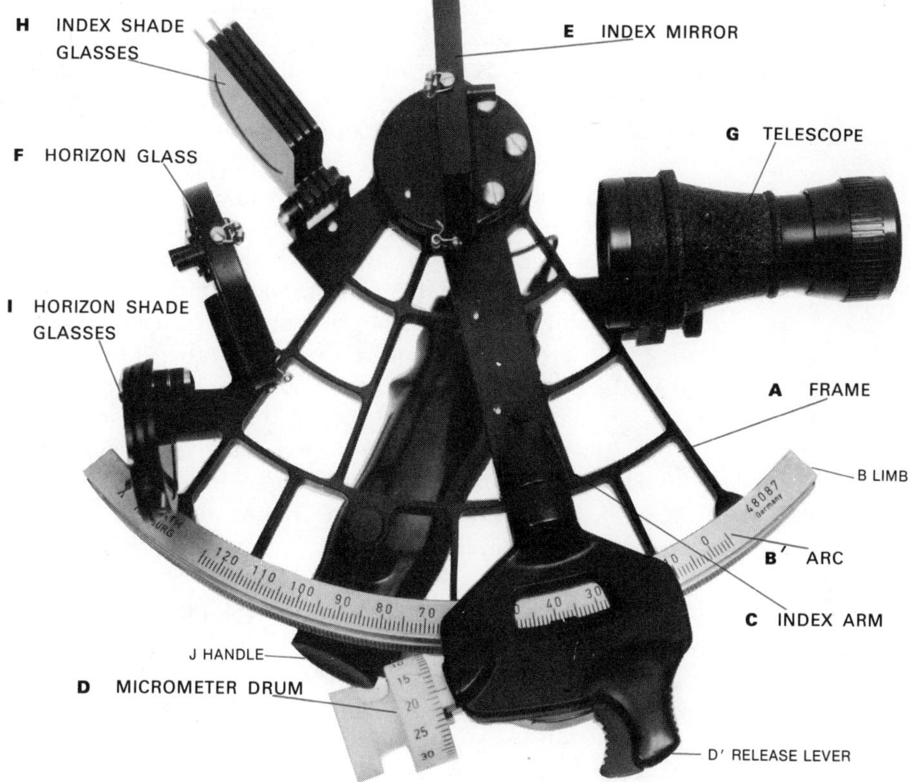

Figure 2102. Parts of a sextant.

tens of seconds of arc. The *release levers* (D′) are spring-loaded clamps that hold the tangent screw against the teeth of the limb. When squeezed together, they release the tangent screw and allow the index arm to be moved easily along the arc to roughly the desired setting (which is then refined by use of the micrometer drum when pressure on these levers is loosened).

E. The *index mirror* is mounted at the upper end of the index arm directly over the pivot point; it is perpendicular to the plane of the instrument.

F. The *horizon glass* is mounted on the frame. It, too, is precisely perpendicular to the plane of the instrument. When the index arm is set to exactly 0°, the horizon glass is parallel to the index mirror. The horizon glass is divided vertically into two halves. The part nearest the frame is silvered as a mirror, the other half is clear optical glass.

G. The *telescope* is mounted with its axis parallel to the plane of the arc. The magnification of the telescope permits the observer to judge contact between the celestial body and the sea horizon much more exactly than is possible with the unaided eye, and often makes it possible to pick up the image of a star when it cannot be seen by the unaided eye. Telescopes are adjustable for the characteristics of the individual observer's eye, and on some models, the telescope can be moved towards or away from the frame as conditions warrant.

H. The *index shade glasses* are of optically ground glass mounted perpendicular to the arc, and are pivoted, so that they can be swung out of the line of sight between the index and horizon mirrors. Two types of index shade glasses are employed on sextants. The first is a variable density polarizing filter; the second consists of four or more shade glasses of neutral tint and increasing density. The shade glasses are employed when making observations of the sun, and sometimes when observing a bright planet or star above a dimly lighted horizon.

I. The *horizon shades* are similar to the index shades, and serve to reduce the glare of reflected sunlight on the horizon.

J. The *handle,* usually of wood or plastic, is mounted on the frame at a location and angle for good balance and easy grip with the right hand. Some sextants provide for night lighting of the index marks of both the arc and micrometer drum; the batteries for such lights are within the handle.

Recent developments

A modernized sextant is under development that will provide a direct digital readout, eliminating the need for reading the arc plus the micrometer drum plus the vernier. It may be possible to electronically couple the data from such a sextant directly into a computer for sight reduction so that it is not even necessary to read the altitude! The computer would store the information from each of several sights as taken, figure the LOPs, and combine them to produce a complete celestial fix.

Such an ultra-modern sextant will have the capability of accepting a night-vision telescope for using the natural horizon after it is too dark to take sights in the usual manner; alternatively, a device providing an artificial horizon could be used.

Optical principle of the sextant

2103 The optics of the sextant are based on a system of double reflection, in that the image of the body observed is reflected from the upper, or index mirror, to the lower, or horizon mirror, and thence into the field of view of the sextant telescope, where it is brought into coincidence with the sea horizon, which is seen through the clear portion of the horizon mirror. The principle of optics involved is stated: *The angle between the first and last directions of a ray of light that has undergone two reflections in the same plane is twice the angle that the two reflecting surfaces make with each other.* This principle can be proven by geometry, and is illustrated in Figure 2103. The sextant arc, however, is engraved to show the actual altitude of the body, rather than the number of degrees the index arm has been moved from the 0° setting. In Figure 2103, angle *a*, the difference between first and last reflection, equals twice angle *b,* the angle between the reflecting surfaces. Angle *c* equals angle *d* and angle *e* equals angle *f,* the angles of incidence and reflection respectively, of the index and horizon mirrors.

Figure 2103. Optical principle of a sextant.

Artificial horizon sextants

2104 The "bubble sextant" has long been used by aviators for celestial observations. The vertical is established in these instruments by bringing the center of the observed body into coincidence with the center of a free-floating bubble. Most aviation artificial horizon sextants are fitted with an averaging device. This provides the determination of a mean of observations made over a considerable period of time, usually two minutes. On the latest models the observation may be discontinued at any time after the first thirty seconds and the average altitude determined. It is usually desirable, however, to use the full one- or two-minute observation as it is assumed that this will at least cover the complete period of natural oscillation of the aircraft in pitch and roll.

The aircraft bubble sextant is difficult to use aboard most surface vessels, particularly in a seaway, due to the constant and often violent accelerations that occur and the relatively short period of roll of a ship as compared to an aircraft. However, useful results have been obtained

Figure 2104. Sextant of modern design (C. Plath).

with them aboard large carriers, and partially surfaced submarines. The fleet ballistic missile submarines are now issued a marine sextant with special bubble attachment.

In the past thirty years considerable experimentation has been conducted with sextants fitted with gyroscopic artificial horizon systems. Such a system holds great promise but has not come into current usage.

The great advantage of an artificial horizon sextant is that it permits observations of celestial bodies when the sea horizon is obscured by darkness, fog, or haze. The accuracy obtainable with the bubble sextant lies in the range of minutes of arc, rather than the tenths of minutes obtained with a marine sextant using the natural horizon.

Other sextants

2105 The sextants described above are high-precision instruments and are quite expensive. Models of lesser precision and accuracy are available for navigators whose requirements are less demanding. Sextants are also made of very stable plastic materials with optics of good, but lesser, quality than those described in the preceding article. Such a sextant, sometimes carried as a back-up to a more refined instrument, can have a micrometer drum and read angles to a precision of 0.2′ with fully acceptable accuracy for ordinary navigation, yet cost one-tenth or less of the price of a first-line sextant.

There are also very simple plastic instruments often referred to as "practice" or "lifeboat" sextants. These operate on the same basic principles, but lack such features as a drum vernier, adjustable mirrors, and telescope; these can read angles no more precisely than 2′. Such sextants serve their intended purposes, however, and cost only a few dollars.

Reading a sextant scale

2106 In using a sextant to measure an angle, such as a celestial altitude, the spring release at the bottom of the index arm is disengaged, and the arm is moved until the body and the horizon are both seen in the field of view. The release is then freed so that the tangent screw re-engages the worm teeth on the arc, and the micrometer drum is turned until the body is brought into coincidence with the horizon.

To read the altitude, the position of the arm's index mark against the scale of degrees on the arc is first read. In Figure 2106, the index mark is located between 29° and 30°, indicating that the altitude will be 29° plus the reading of minutes and tenths obtained from the micrometer drum and its vernier respectively.

The index mark for the micrometer drum is the zero mark on the vernier. In Figure 2106, it is between the drum markings for 42′ and 43′, indicating that the altitude will be 42′ plus the number of tenths obtained from the vernier. To read the vernier, its graduation most nearly in line with a graduation on the drum is found. In Figure 2106,

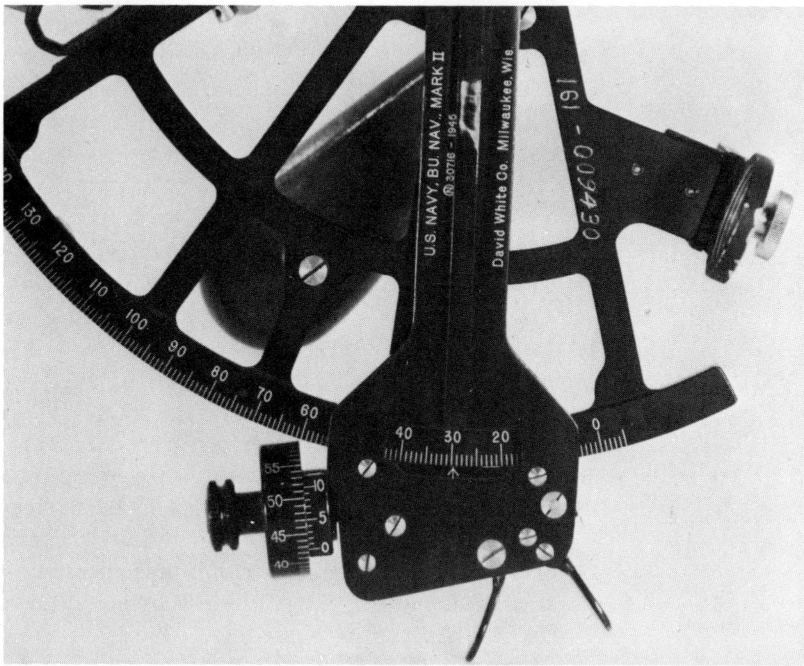

Figure 2106. Marine sextant, showing arc, micrometer, drum, and vernier.

this is 5 indicating a reading of 0.5′. Adding each of these components, the altitude is found to be 29°42.5′.

Considerable care must be exercised in reading the micrometer drum if the index mark for the index arm is very close to a graduation on the arc. If, for example, that index mark was apparently right opposite the 30° mark on the arc, and the micrometer drum read 57′ and some tenths, then the true reading for the sextant would be 29°57′, *not* 30°57′. Similar care must be used in reading the micrometer drum when the vernier scale is at its upper end near 8 or 9 tenths.

SEXTANT ERRORS AND ADJUSTMENTS

Instrument errors

2107 The sextant, being an optical-mechanical instrument, cannot be manufactured error-free. When a sextant is assembled by the manufacturer it is tested for *fixed instrument errors* and the combined values are recorded on a certificate attached to the inside of the sextant case. The error is usually listed for each 10° of the arc. Some manufacturers merely certify the instrument to be free of errors for practical use. This implies that the error nowhere exceeds approximately 10 seconds of arc. In modern precision sextants these nonadjustable errors are small, and may usually be ignored. Specifications for the Navy Mark II sextant require that no errors be greater than 35 seconds of arc. Since this exceeds a half minute of arc, or half mile on the earth's surface, correction should be applied to the sextant reading for any errors approaching this magnitude.

The mirrors are mounted in a manner permitting adjustment to maintain their perpendicularity to the sextant frame, and parallelism to each other. The line of sight of the telescope must be parallel to the plane of the sextant frame. Any necessary adjustment should, whenever possible, be accomplished in an optical repair shop.

Index error

2108 *Index error* should be determined each time the sextant is used. In the daytime, this is usually done by an observation of the horizon. The index arm is first set at 0° and with the sextant held in a vertical position, the horizon is observed. In nearly all instances, the horizon will not appear as a continuous line in the direct and reflected views; see Figure 2108a. The micrometer drum is adjusted until the reflected and direct images of the horizon are brought into coincidence, forming a straight unbroken line, as is shown in Figure 2108b. This operation should be repeated several times, the reflected image of the horizon being alternately brought down and up to the direct image. The value of the index error is read in minutes and tenths after each alignment, and the average of the readings is taken and used as the *index correction* (IC), with the appropriate sign. If the error is positive—the micrometer drum reads more than 0.0′—the sign of the correction is negative; conversely, if the micrometer drum reads less than 0.0′, the error is

Sign of IC

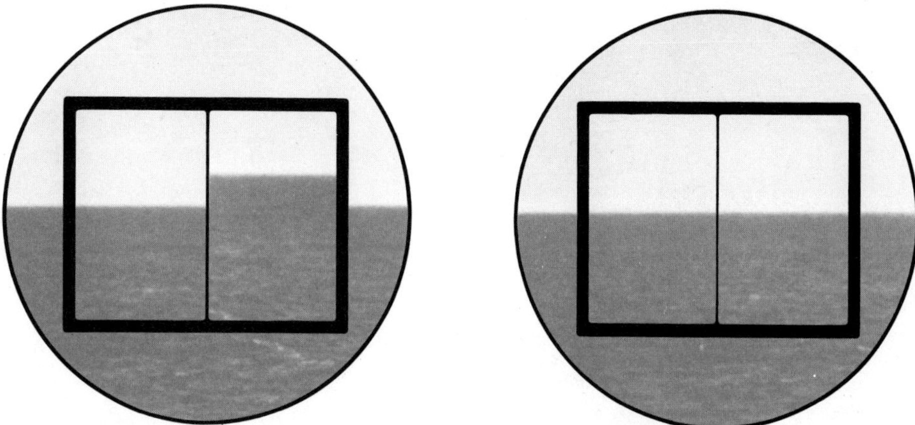

Figure 2108a. Sextant set at zero, with index error. Figure 2108b. Sextant set at zero, horizon in alignment as seen through sextant telescope.

negative and the sign of the correction is positive. If the average reading of the micrometer drum is 58.5′, the error is −1.5′ and the IC is +1.5′. If the index error is small, less than about 4.0′, it is best not to try to remove it. Where the error is negative, it is sometimes said to be "off the arc," conversely, when positive it is "on the arc."

At night the index error may be determined by observing a star. The direct and reflected images are brought into coincidence, or directly adjoining each other horizontally in the manner described above for the horizon. Quite frequently two observers will not obtain the same value for the index error; their findings will represent a combination of the actual index error and of each observer's *personal error* (see Article 2111).

The index error is caused by a lack of perfect parallelism between the index mirror and horizon glass, when the sextant is set at 0°. This lack of parallelism causes a greater error in observations than would a slight error in the perpendicularity of the mirrors.

Adjusting the mirrors To eliminate or reduce excessive index error, the *horizon* glass must be adjusted. On the Mark II Navy sextant the mirror is fixed within the mirror frame; adjustment is accomplished by moving the frame by means of two adjusting screws as shown in Figure 2108c. This adjustment is a trial and error process; one screw is first loosened by a small fraction of a revolution, and the other is tightened by an equal amount, and the process is repeated until the error is removed, or brought within an acceptable limit.

With the Plath and several other fine commercial sextants, the horizon glass is adjusted within the mirror frame. When holding the sextant vertical only the upper screw is used, as illustrated in Figure 2108d. The procedure just described is followed except that only the

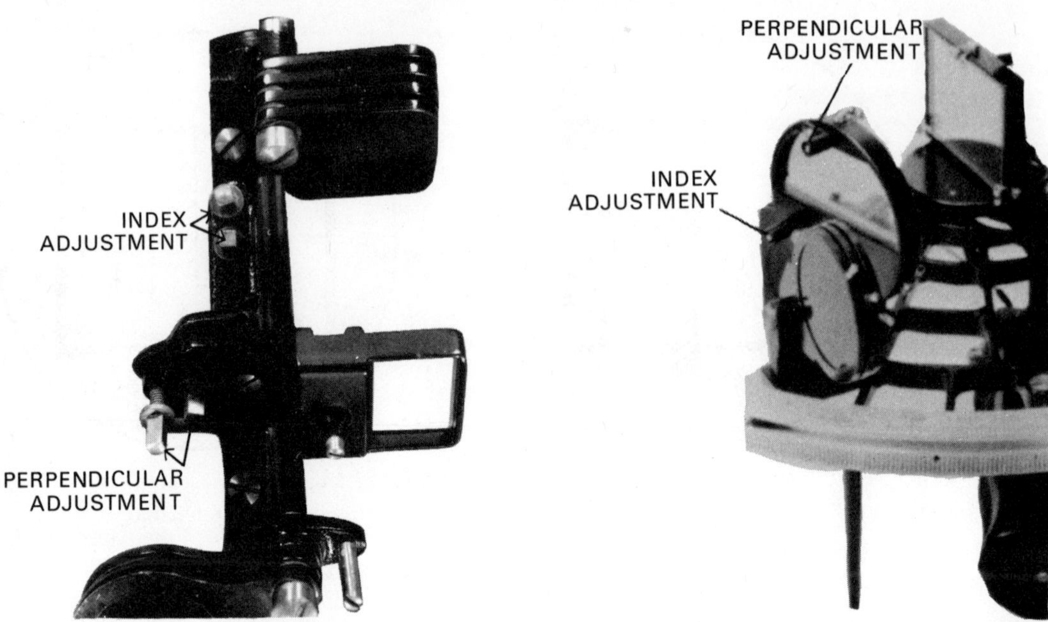

Figure 2108c. Adjustment screws, Navy Mark II sextant. Figure 2108d. Adjusting screws, Plath sextant.

one adjusting screw is turned slightly; this moves the mirror against the mounting springs. When the sextant is properly adjusted the horizon will appear as in Figure 2108b with the sextant reading zero.

Perpendicularity of mirrors

2109 The sextant should occasionally be checked to see that the mirrors are perpendicular to the sextant frame, and adjusted if a misalignment is found to exist. Index mirror alignment is checked by holding the sextant in the left hand with the index mirror towards the observer; he then looks into the index mirror and shifts the position of the sextant until the reflected image of the limb in the index mirror appears as a continuation of the limb as seen directly, looking past the index mirror. This is illustrated in Figure 2109a. If the reflected image is inclined to the limb as seen directly or is not in alignment with it, the index mirror is not perpendicular to the plane of the limb, and the alignment should be corrected by use of the adjusting screws on the back of the index mirror frame. Again, some sextants have two adjusting screws, one of which must first be loosened and the other tightened. On other sextants one adjusting screw is used which moves the mirror against retaining springs.

To check the perpendicularity of the horizon glass, the horizon should be sighted in the same manner as discussed in Article 2108, for determining the index error. The tangent screw is adjusted until the reflected and direct images of the horizon appear as a straight line

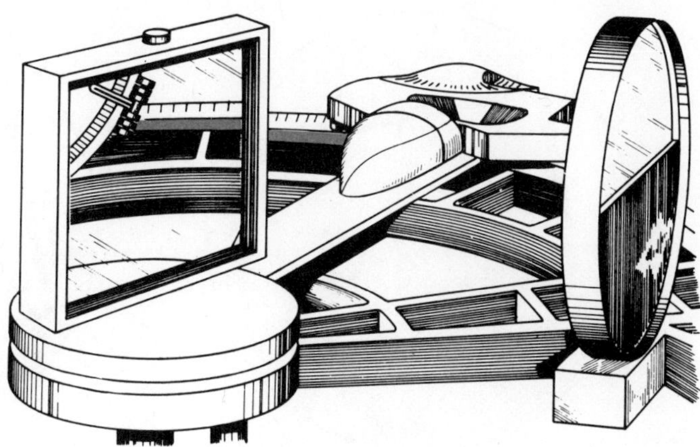

Figure 2109a. Checking perpendicularity of index mirror. Here the mirror is not perpendicular.

with the sextant in a vertical position. The sextant is then turned or rocked around the line of sight; the reflected horizon and the direct horizon should remain in exact alignment as in Figure 2109b. If they do not, as in Figure 2109c, the horizon glass needs adjustment to make it perpendicular to the plane of the limb. On the Navy Mark II sextant the two adjusting screws (Figure 2108c), are used to move the mirror frame assembly. Again, care must be used to loosen one before tightening the other. On sextants where the mirror is adjusted within the frame the adjusting screw farthest away from the sextant frame is used (Figure 2108d). When the mirror is properly adjusted the horizon will appear as a straight line while the sextant is rotated around the line of sight. To accomplish the adjustment at night the sextant is sighted directly at a star with the index set at 0°. When the tangent screw is turned, the reflected image of the star should move in a vertical line exactly through the direct image. If the line of movement is to one side or other of the direct image the horizon mirror is not perpendicular to the frame and should be adjusted (Figures 2109d and 2109e).

Proper sequence of adjustments

Since two different adjustments are made on the horizon glass, it is obvious that these adjustments are interrelated, and in making adjustment for the perpendicularity of the mirror, the index error will be affected. As a general rule it is best to remove the index error first, adjust for perpendicularity, and then check again for index error. Several consecutive adjustments may be necessary if the mirror is badly misaligned.

Telescope alignment

2110 If extreme difficulty is encountered in bringing a star down to the horizon as discussed in Article 2110, it is possible the line of sight of the telescope is not parallel to the plane of the sextant frame. This

Figure 2109b. Horizon glass perpendicular to sextant frame. Figure 2109c. Horizon glass not perpendicular to frame.

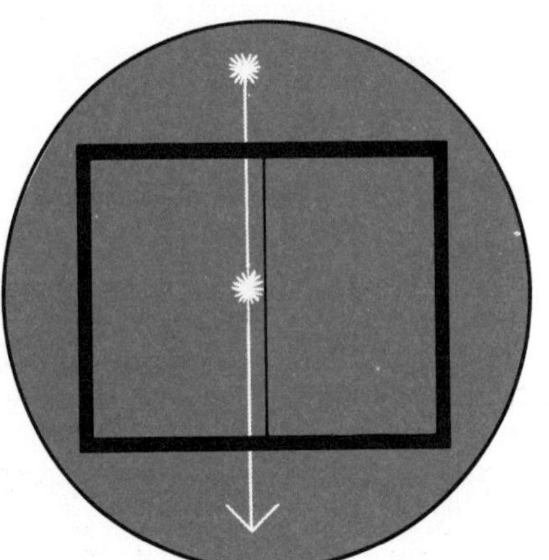
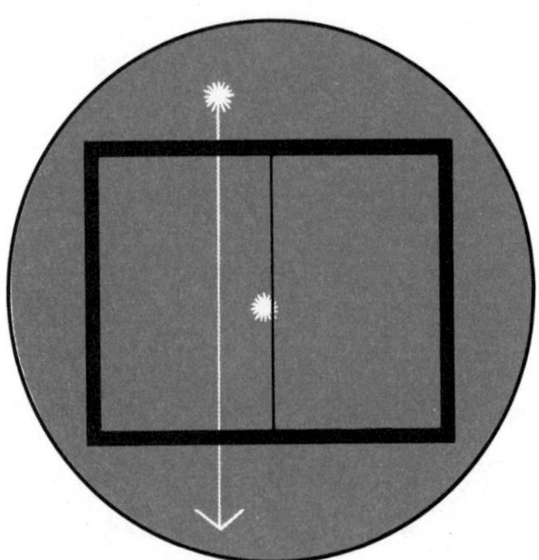

Figure 2109d. Reflected star image moves through direct image. Figure 2109e. Images not in line; horizon glass is not perpendicular.

is usually difficult to adjust aboard ship, but there is a quick practical check to determine if the telescope is out of alignment. The sextant is held in a horizontal position in the left hand with the horizon glass toward the observer, and the index arm set near 0°. The observer looks into the index mirror, holding the sextant in a position so that the reflected image of the center line of the horizon mirror is directly in line with the actual center line. In this position it should be possible to see straight through the telescope, the line of sight being the same as the path of light rays of a star when an observation is being made. If the telescope is out of alignment the observer will be unable to look straight

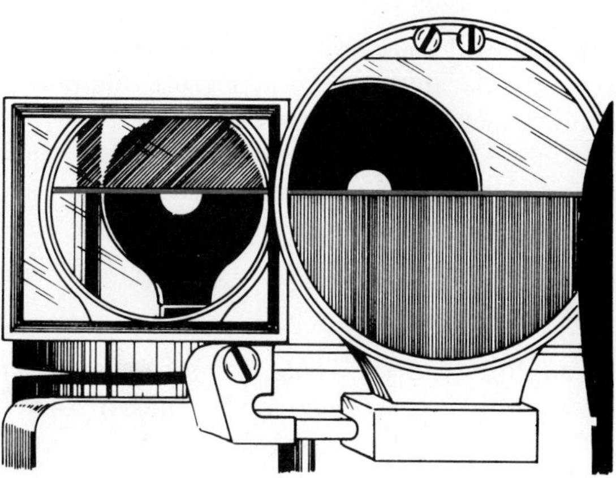

Figure 2110. Checking telescope alignment.

through it (Figure 2110). Some sextants have adjusting screws on the telescope for adjusting the line of sight; normally this should be accomplished in an optical shop.

Personal error

2111 After all adjustable errors have been reduced or eliminated insofar as possible, the sextant will probably still retain some residual, variable, adjustable error as well as a small fixed nonadjustable instrument error. Additionally, a small variable error called *personal error* may often be produced as a result of the eye of the observer acting in conjunction with the optical system of the sextant. This might be different for the sun and moon than for planets and stars, and might vary with the degree of fatigue of the observer, and other factors. For this reason, a personal error should be applied with caution. However, if a relatively constant personal error persists, and experience indicates that observations are improved by applying a correction to remove its effect, better results might be obtained by this procedure than by attempting to eliminate it from one's observations. The *personal correction* (PC) is the personal error with the sign reversed.

SEXTANT OBSERVATIONS

Horizon system coordinates

2112 As stated in Article 1904, celestial observations are made with reference to the horizon system of coordinates. The axis of this system is dependent on the position of the observer, and its reference plane is the celestial horizon. The celestial horizon passes through the center of the earth, and is perpendicular to the vertical circle passing from the observer's zenith on the celestial sphere, through his position and through the earth's center on to the observer's nadir.

Observing altitudes

2113 Altitude observations of celestial bodies are made in the plane perpendicular to the celestial horizon, along the vertical circle passing through the body. They are measured upward from the visible, or sea horizon, and a correction is applied which adjusts the sextant altitude to read as though the observed angle had been measured from the earth's center, above the celestial horizon. The plane of the visible horizon may, for all practical purposes, be considered to be parallel to the celestial horizon. Figure 2113a illustrates the principle of a celestial altitude measurement.

The altitude of a body above the visible horizon as read from the sextant is termed the *sextant altitude;* its symbol is hs.

To make an observation, the observer stands facing the body, holding the sextant vertically in his right hand, and centers the horizon in his field of view. He then frees the spring release, and moves the index arm until the body also appears in the field of view. The tangent screw is next allowed to engage the worm teeth on the arc, and the micrometer drum is turned until the horizon and the body are in coincidence.

Next, the sextant is tilted slightly from side to side slowly to determine that the sextant is being held vertically as is required for an accurate measurement. This rotation about the axis of the line of sight causes the body to swing like a pendulum across the horizon; this procedure is termed *swinging the arc;* see Figure 2113b. The lowest point indicated on this arc marks the correct position for the sextant; the micrometer drum is again turned until the body makes contact with the horizon at the bottom of its swing. At this instant, the time is noted and the sextant altitude is read off.

With practice, it is easy to determine when the body is on the vertical. The eye tends to extend the line of the sea horizon into the mirrored portions of the horizon glass, and the arc of the reflected image appears not only in the mirrored half of the horizon glass, but in the clear half as well.

Graphing sights

Skill in obtaining accurate altitudes comes only with practice. Some individuals are markedly more accurate observers than others, but experiments conducted for the Office of Naval Research clearly indicate that the accuracy of the best observers tends to increase with prac-

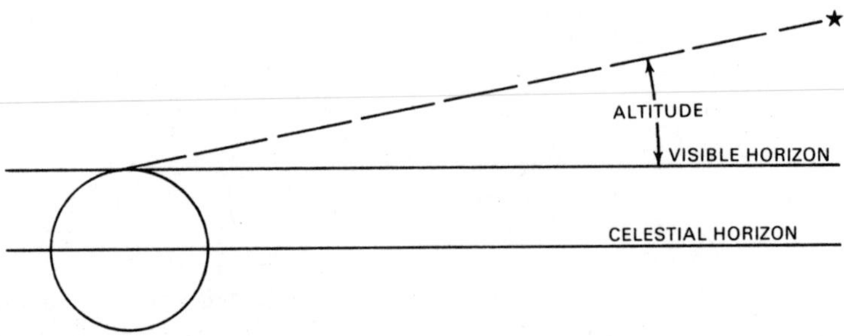

Figure 2113a. An altitude measurement.

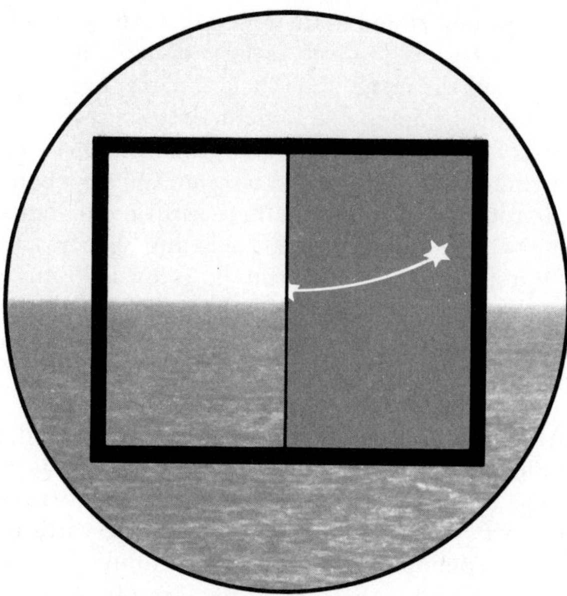

Figure 2113b. Swinging the arc.

tice. Each of five observers made over 3,000 sextant observations, and for each observer the mean of his second thousand observations was better than his first thousand, and the third thousand showed still further improvement. The novice observer may find that his sights do not yield satisfactory lines of position. Working with an experienced navigator may improve his technique, and it may be helpful for him to make a string of 10 or more observations of the same body in a period of less than three minutes. These sights should then be plotted on a large sheet of plotting paper, using a horizontal scale of one inch to ten seconds of time, and a vertical scale of one inch to one minute of arc, if possible. A "line of best fit" is then drawn through the string. The divergence of the individual sights from this line will tend to indicate the magnitude of the observer's random errors. The random error of a single sight is the greatest hazard to the accuracy of celestial navigation. Where accuracy is required, a single observation should not be relied on to obtain a line of position. It is far better practice to take at least three sights of each body, and for maximum accuracy an even greater number of observations should be made and graphed as described above. An altitude and time combination that lies on or near the mean line can then be selected as the sight to be reduced for the LOP.

Multiple observations

Suggestions that may be helpful in obtaining good sights are included in the following articles.

Sun observations

2114 As described in Article 2102, the sextant is fitted with index shade glasses, either of the variable density polarizing type, or neutrally tinted filters of varying degrees of density. To determine the degree of density best suited to the observer's eye under existing conditions, it is usually best first to look at the sun through the darkest index shade; if this dims the image too much, the next lightest shade should be tried. It should be noted that sometimes the best results are achieved by using two of the lighter filters, rather than a single dark one. When a polarizing filter is used, it should be set to full dark before looking at the sun; the rotatable portion can then be turned to lighten the image until the eye sees the image comfortably and clearly.

On a calm day, when the sun is low in altitude, the sea short of the horizon may reflect the sunlight so glaringly that it is desirable to employ a horizon shade. The most desirable shade must again be selected by trial and error.

The sun's limb After the proper shade or shades are selected, the observer sets the index arm to 0°, faces the sun, and proceeds as described in Article 2113 until the sun's *lower limb* is on the horizon; during this process the arc must be swung to establish the vertical. (The term "limb" is used to denote a portion of the circumference of the sun or moon.) At most altitudes, the best results are obtained by observing the sun's lower limb; however, at altitudes below about 5°, it is more desirable to observe the upper limb. In this case, the correction for *irradiation effect* should be applied to the sextant altitude, in addition to other corrections; see Article 2127. The procedure for observing the sun's upper limb is the same as for the lower limb. Figure 2114 shows the sun's lower limb on the horizon, as seen through a sextant telescope.

Figure 2114. Observing the sun, lower limb.

Observing LAN When practicing with the sextant, the neophyte navigator should observe the sun at local apparent noon (LAN). In most latitudes, the sun changes altitude but little for a period of several minutes before and after LAN. A string of 12 or more observations should be made, and the altitudes noted. After each sight, the micrometer drum should be moved so that the sun's image appears alternately above and below the horizon. It should then be brought to the horizon, and the arc should be swung until the sun's image is brought into coincidence with the horizon on the vertical. When the novice is able to obtain a consistent string of altitudes at LAN, he should take a series of sights in the afternoon, or morning, when the sun is changing rapidly in altitude. The procedure for making sun sights is outlined in Article 2114. These should, if possible, be graphed as outlined above; otherwise it should be determined that the change in altitude is consistent with the time interval between each pair of sights.

Moon observations **2115** Observations of the moon are made in the same manner as those of the sun, except that shades are not required during the daylight hours.

Because of the phases of the moon, upper limb observations are made about as frequently as those of the lower limb. Accurate observations of the moon can only be obtained if the upper or lower limb is brought to the horizon. This is not always possible, due to the moon's phase, and its position in the sky.

Carefully made moon observations, obtained during daylight hours, under good observational conditions, yield excellent LOPs. If the moon is observed at night, it may be desirable to shade its image somewhat, in order that the horizon not be obscured by the moon's brilliance.

Star and planet observations **2116** Observations of stars and planets are made at twilight. More experience in the use of the sextant is required to obtain good twilight sights than is needed in daylight. This is chiefly due to the fact that a star appears only as a point of light in the sextant telescope, rather than appearing as a body of considerable size, as does the sun or moon. In addition, the stars fade out in the morning, as the horizon brightens; in the evening this condition is reversed, and it is sometimes difficult to obtain a good star image and a well-defined horizon at the same time. However, the problem is considerably simplified when a well-designed sextant, fitted with a good telescope, is employed.

Three methods of bringing the star and the horizon together are possible. The first is to bring the star's image down to the horizon, the second is to bring the horizon up to the star, and the third is to predetermine the approximate altitude and azimuth of the selected star. Of the three methods, the third is usually the most satisfactory, as it often permits locating the star before it can be seen by the unaided eye.

Bringing a star down

To employ the first method, the sextant is set within about 2′ of 0°, and the line of sight is directed at the star, which will then appear as a double image. The index arm is then slowly pushed forward, while the sextant is moved downward, in order to keep the image of the body in the field of the telescope. When the index arm has reached the star's approximate altitude on the arc, the horizon will appear in the field. The micrometer drum is then allowed to engage the teeth on the arc, and the final contact is made by means of turning the drum, while rocking the arc to establish the vertical.

Some observers, when using a sextant with a small optical field of view, prefer to remove the telescope from the sextant while bringing the star down. The telescope should always be reinstalled before the altitude is read in order to obtain maximum accuracy.

The second method is sometimes employed when the horizon is bright, and the star is dim. To bring the horizon up to the star, the sextant is set at approximately 0°, and then held inverted in the left hand. The line of sight is then directed at the body, which will be seen through the clear portion of the horizon glass as shown in Figure 2116. The index arm is next adjusted until the horizon appears in the field of view and then allowed to lock to the arc, the sextant is righted, and the altitude is determined in the usual way.

Precomputed altitudes for sextant observations

The best practice for star observations, in most cases, is to determine in advance the approximate altitude and azimuth of the stars to be observed, by means of a star finder, such as the "Star Finder and Identifier" 2102-D, which is described in Article 2002. This predetermination of the approximate altitude permits full use to be made of the sextant telescope, which will usually make it possible to sight a star when it cannot be seen with the naked eye. Stars can thus be located at evening twilight, while the horizon is still clearly defined, and can be observed in the morning after they have faded from view of the unaided eye.

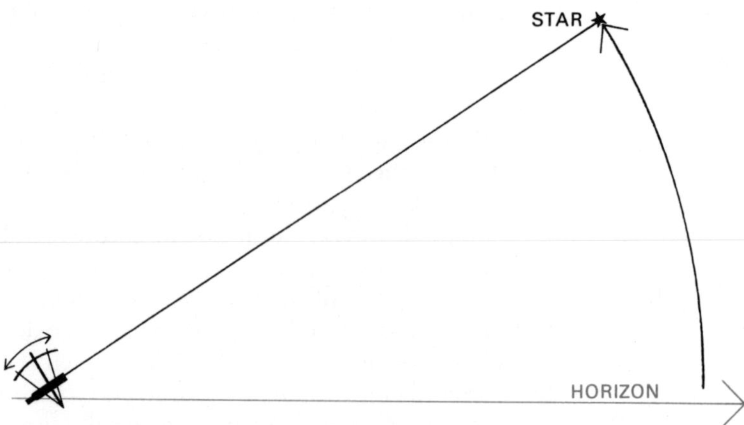

Figure 2116. Using the sextant inverted.

When using this method, the altitude of the body to be observed is taken from the star finder, and set on the sextant. The observer then faces in the direction of the body's azimuth, usually determined by sighting over a gyro repeater or magnetic compass, and directs his line of sight at the horizon. After locating the star, its altitude is determined in the regular manner.

Notes regarding celestial observations

2117 At times it is necessary to seize every opportunity to obtain one or more celestial observations, even under adverse conditions. Hints which may be helpful to the novice navigator in observing various bodies follow:

Sun. During extended periods of overcast, the sun may occasionally break through, appearing for only a minute or so. Under such conditions it is advisable to have a sextant set to the approximate altitude, with the telescope mounted, and located in a convenient spot where it can be picked up instantly if the sun appears. If necessary, the observer should be prepared to note his own time of observation rather than using another person for this. At times the sun shows through thin overcast, but its image is not sharply defined. It can nevertheless supply a helpful line of position.

When the sun is high in altitude, as it transits the observer's meridian at LAN, its change in azimuth during the hour or so preceding and following LAN is very rapid. This permits obtaining excellent running fixes over a comparatively short period of time. The first observation should be made when the sun bears about 45° east of the meridian. This should be followed by the conventional noon sight and another set of observations can be made when the sun is about 45° west of the meridian.

Low-altitude sun observations

Low-altitude sights of the sun (i.e., altitudes of 5° more or less) can be extremely helpful at times, and under most observational conditions will yield lines of position accurate to two miles or less, when carefully corrected. When making low-altitude sun sights, the upper limb will usually yield better observations than the lower. The correction for sun, lower limb (page A3 of the *Nautical Almanac*) may be used, or a more precise calculation may be made using the correction for refraction listed for stars in the *Nautical Almanac*, as well as a correction for semidiameter, as found in the daily pages of the *Nautical Almanac.* The correction for index error, dip of the horizon, and an additional refraction correction for nonstandard conditions, all given in the *Nautical Almanac*, should be used.

Moon. Observations of the moon can often be used for valuable daytime fixes when made in conjunction with observations of the sun. When moon sights are to be taken at night, it is advisable to make them from a point as low in the ship as possible. This will minimize errors caused by cloud shadows, which can shade the true horizon, and make the moon appear below its true position, causing the sextant altitude to read higher than it should.

Planets. Venus can frequently be observed with a sextant during daylight, particularly when its altitude is greater than that of the sun, and it is not too close to the latter in hour angle.

Daylight planet observations

To locate Venus during daylight, its position (declination and angle relative to Aries) should be carefully plotted on the "Star Finder and Identifier," 2102-D, as discussed in Article 2002. The latter is then set in the regular manner for the time of the desired observation and the corresponding DR position, and the approximate altitude and azimuth are read off.

Fixes based on sights of the sun, moon, and Venus made during daylight hours should be employed whenever possible.

The other planets, which are not as brilliant as Venus, are ordinarily observed only at twilight. Their positions may also be plotted on the Star Finder and Identifier, to aid in locating them in the sky. Twilight observation techniques, applicable to planets, are described in the following paragraph.

Stars. When the Star Finder and Identifier is employed, altitudes and azimuths of twelve or more stars, preferably with altitudes of 20° or more, should be listed in advance for the time of twilight. It is desirable to list considerably more stars than will actually be observed, as not all the stars may be visible at twilight, due to clouds.

The visibility of a star at twilight depends primarily on its magnitude, or brilliance, and on its altitude; to a considerably lesser extent it depends on its azimuth relative to that of the sun. Remember that the lower the tabulated magnitude of a star, the greater the brilliance. All other factors being equal, a low-magnitude star will be visible against a brighter sky than one of higher magnitude, and hence of less brilliance. If two stars are of equal magnitude, and have the same azimuth, the star with the higher altitude will appear to be the brighter. Due to the polarization of the sun's light rays, stars situated at 90° to the sun's azimuth will appear to be slightly brighter than stars of the same magnitude and altitude having nearly the same azimuth as the sun or lying about 180° from it. This is equally true, whether the sun be below or above the horizon.

The visibility of stars also depends on the sextant's mirrors, and on the quality and magnification of the telescope. The mirrors must be a size that permits using the full angular field of view of the telescope, as the larger the mirror, the larger is the bundle of light rays transmitted to the observer's eye; this is another way of saying the brighter will be the star's reflected image. In addition, the greater the magnification of the telescope, the more easily can the star be located against a bright sky; full daylight observations have been made of Sirius

(Mag. −1.6) and Arcturus (Mag. 0.2) with a sextant fitted with a 20-power telescope; typically, however, sextant telescopes are only of 2 to 8 power.

Often the position of the telescope relative to the sextant frame may be adjusted to fit varying conditions of illumination at twilight. Article 2102G stated that some sextant telescopes are not permanently fixed in relation to the frame, but that their axis may be moved in or out. This is generally true of sextants with small mirrors which have less light-gathering power. When the telescope is moved as close as possible to the frame, the maximum amount of light is reflected from the sky into the field of view. Conversely, when it is moved out from the frame, more light is transmitted from the horizon, and less from the sky. With a dim horizon, the telescope is moved out to the end of its travel. When the horizon is very dim, it may even be desirable to use a pale index screen, when observing a brilliant star or planet; this will facilitate obtaining an accurate contact between the body and the horizon. A navigator should experiment in positioning the telescope in order to obtain the optimum balance of lighting between the body and the horizon. It should be noted that a telescope with good light-gathering powers will permit the observer to see a sharply defined horizon, when it appears "fuzzy" to the naked eye.

It is, of course, desirable to observe stars against a sharply defined horizon, which implies a fairly bright sky. At evening twilight, the eastern horizon will fade first; as a general rule, therefore, it is best to observe stars situated to the eastward first. At morning twilight, the eastern horizon will brighten first and again it would be best to observe first those stars generally toward the east. With practice, a navigator should be able to determine the most desirable sequence of of star observation, balancing off the various factors involved, such as star magnitude and altitude, and horizon lighting.

Observations at night With a sextant telescope of good magnification and optical characteristics, it is possible to observe stars at any time on a clear night. However, the observer's vision must be completely dark adapted. Submariners during World War II regularly obtained very good star fixes in the middle of the night, using a sextant fitted with a 6-power prismatic telescope, having an objective lens 30 mm in diameter. Night vision telescopes are now available which use an electronic unit to amplify the small amount of ambient light available at night. These light amplification scopes can be adapted to sextants for night observations.

SEXTANT ALTITUDE CORRECTIONS

Sextant altitude **2118** The altitude of a celestial body, as measured with a marine sextant, is termed the *sextant altitude* (hs). It is the angle at the eye of the observer as measured in a vertical plane between the line of sight to

Observed altitude

the visible horizon, and the line of sight to the body. The *observed altitude* (Ho) of a celestial body is the hs corrected to read as though the altitude had been measured above the celestial horizon, at the earth's center, on a perpendicular plane passing through the observer's zenith and the body. The Ho is the altitude used in all celestial navigation. The significant corrections, and the order of their application to obtain Ho from hs, are described in the following articles. In order that these corrections may be applied in the correct order, an intermediate between hs and Ho is normally used. This intermediate is the *apparent altitude* (ha); its use is discussed in Article 2121.

In addition to those listed in the following articles, other corrections are theoretically necessary in order to obtain Ho; however, they are so small (and in some cases so difficult to determine), that no appreciable error arises from omitting their use. These additional corrections are described in *Bowditch,* DMAHC Pub. No. 9.

Nonadjustable instrument error
Instrument correction

2119 Nonadjustable instrument error is the sum of the nonadjustable errors—prismatic, graduation, and centering—of a sextant (Article 2107). The correction for these errors is called the *instrument correction* (I); it is determined by the manufacturer, and recorded on a certificate framed in the sextant box. It varies with the angle, may be either positive or negative, and is applied to all angles measured by that particular sextant.

Index error

2120 Index error is the residual error in a particular sextant, after the four adjustable errors have been corrected in so far as possible, as described in Article 2108. It is primarily caused by a slight lack of parallelism between the index mirror and horizon glass, when the instrument is set at zero. It is compensated for by applying the *index correction* (IC).

Index correction (IC)

The IC may be *positive* or *negative,* and is applied to *all* observations, whether celestial or terrestrial. When the IC is applied to the hs, the altitude is corrected to the value it would have if the instrument had no index error. The IC is not fixed, and its value should be determined each time the sextant is used.

Dip of the horizon (D)

2121 Dip of the horizon is customarily referred to merely as "the dip." The D correction is required because of the height of the observer's eye above the level of the sea.

Celestial altitudes obtained with the marine sextant are measured relative to the visible, or sea, horizon. As the earth is a spheroid, the higher the observer is situated above the surface, the more depressed the visible horizon will be below the celestial horizon or true horizontal at his eye. Figure 2121 shows two observers sharing a common zenith, but the observer at A'' is situated considerably higher than the ob-

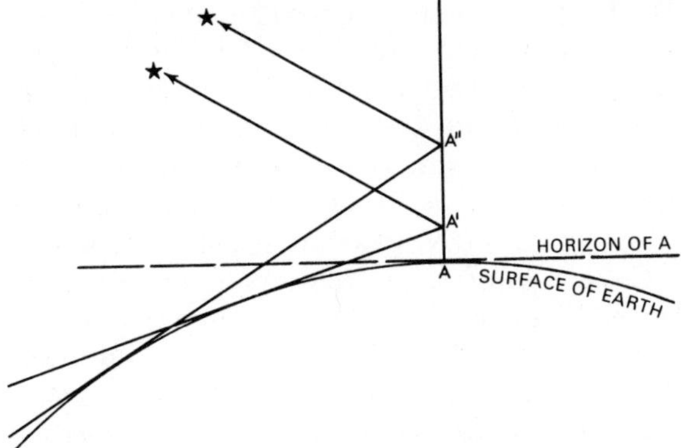

Figure 2121. Dip increases with height of eye above the water's surface.

server at A'; both are observing the same star. The observer's height of eye is greatly exaggerated in the figure for illustrative purposes. It is obvious that the star's hs will be considerably larger for the observer at A'', than for the one at A', and that the latter will have a larger hs than he would at the point A, on the water surface directly beneath him. The value of the dip may be defined as the excess over 90° of the angular distance from observer's zenith to his visible horizon, as the reference plane for determining altitudes of celestial bodies is the observer's celestial horizon, which is perpendicular to his zenith. The D correction must be made for this excess. As the magnitude of the correction depends upon the observer's height above the water, it is sometimes called the "height of eye correction."

The value of the dip correction is somewhat decreased by atmospheric refraction between the observer and the horizon. Refraction causes the visible horizon to appear slightly higher than it would if the earth had no atmosphere. This refractive effect is not constant, but depends on atmospheric and sea conditions, chiefly on the difference between the temperature of the air at the observer's eye level, and that directly adjacent to the surface of the water. If the air is colder at the observer's level, the horizon tends to be depressed slightly; conversely, if it is warmer it tends to be slightly elevated (Article 2129).

The D correction is always *negative,* and is applied to all celestial altitude observations. Its application to the hs corrects the latter to the value it would have if the visible horizon were a plane passing through the eye of the observer, and perpendicular to the line of his zenith.

Dip short of horizon In some situations, the full distance to the natural horizon is not available—another ship, land, or other obstruction blocks vision. In this instance a *dip short* observation must be made and the dip correction taken from a special table such as Table 22 in *Bowditch,* rather than from the *Nautical Almanac.* The distance to the foreshortened horizon must be accurately known and the height of eye becomes a more critical factor than with sights taken on a natural horizon.

Apparent altitude (ha) For purposes of routine navigation corrections to the sextant altitude can be applied in any order using the hs as entering argument in the various correction tables. Where greater accuracy is desired, however, or at low altitudes where small changes in altitude can result in significant changes in the correction, the order of applying the corrections is important. To obtain maximum accuracy, the three corrections so far discussed, for nonadjustable instrument error (I), index error (IC), and dip (D), are first applied to the hs. The hs so corrected is termed the *apparent altitude* (ha), and the value of ha is used in entering the tables to obtain corrections discussed in the following articles. In some books this value is termed *rectified altitude,* hr. For illustrative purposes in this chapter most of the corrections are shown as applied directly to hs. In Chapter 26, calculations for the complete celestial solution will use the apparent altitude, ha, as an intermediate value.

Refraction (R) **2122** Refraction is caused by the bending of a light ray as it passes from a medium of one density into one of a different density. The increasingly dense layers of the earth's atmosphere cause the rays to be bent more and more downward in the vertical plane, as they approach the surface. Refraction, therefore, causes a heavenly body to appear higher than its actual position, as shown in Figure 2122 (exaggerated for emphasis), except when the body is at the observer's zenith. In such a case, the light rays are traveling vertically, and there is no refraction.

The lower a body is located in altitude, the more atmosphere its light rays will penetrate in reaching the observer, and the greater, therefore, will be the refraction. This effect reaches its maximum at the horizon; in fact, when the sun's lower limb appears to touch the visible horizon at sunset, its upper limb is actually below the horizon.

The refractive effect is not absolutely constant but varies slightly with the density of the atmosphere. This is discussed further in Article 2123.

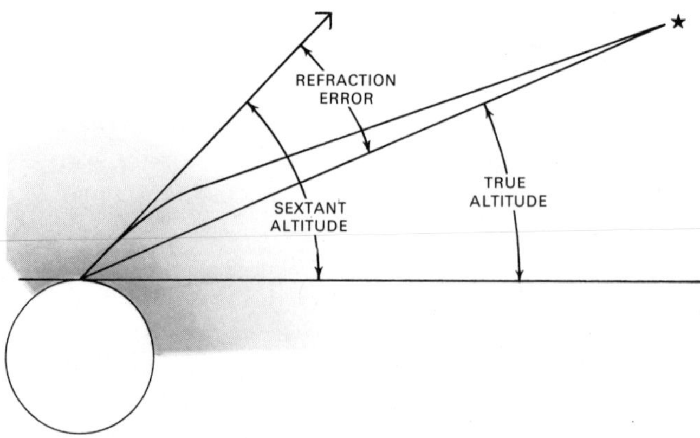

Figure 2122. Atmospheric refraction causes bending of light rays.

The R correction is always *negative*, and it is applied to all celestial altitude observations. Its application to the hs corrects the hs to the value it would have if the light rays from the body were not refracted by the earth's atmosphere.

Air temperature (T) and atmospheric pressure (B) corrections

2123 The R correction varies slightly with the density of the atmosphere; this, in turn, depends upon the air temperature and atmospheric pressure. The refraction correction table given in the *Nautical Almanac* is based on a standard or average atmospheric density, with a temperature of 50° Fahrenheit (10°C) and atmospheric pressure of 29.83 inches (1010 mb). An additional table of corrections is given in the *Almanac* to permit further correction for variations of temperature and pressure from the selected norms. The T and B corrections are ordinarily not required, except for low-altitude observations, unless temperature and pressure vary materially from the standard values. All observations at altitudes of 10° or less should be corrected for temperature and barometric pressure.

The *combined T and B* correction may be *positive* or *negative,* and is applied to all celestial altitudes when conditions require it, in addition to the R correction. When applied to the hs, the sextant altitude is corrected to the value it would have under conditions of a standard atmospheric density.

Semidiameter (SD)

2124 The values of Greenwich Hour Angle and Declination tabulated in all almanacs are for the centers of the various celestial bodies. Because an observer, using a marine sextant, cannot readily determine the center of the sun or moon, he measures the altitude of one of the limbs of these two bodies. The *semidiameter* (SD) is the angular distance between the limb of the sun or moon and the center as illustrated in Figure 2124. If a lower limb observation is made, the SD must be added to the hs to obtain the altitude of the center of the body; conversely, it is subtracted if the upper limb is observed.

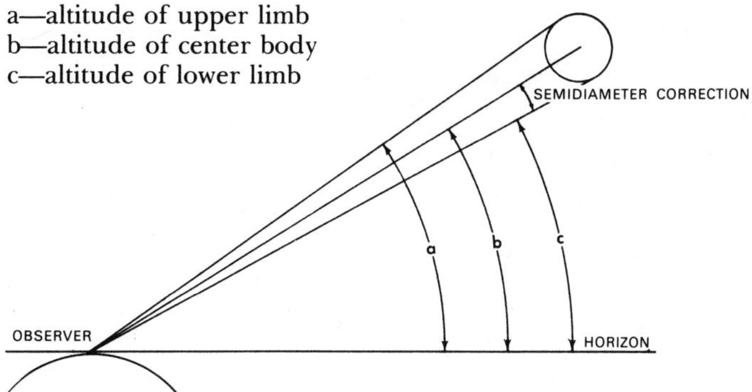

Figure 2124. Semidiameter correction for sun or moon. (Not to scale.)

The semidiameter varies with the distance of the body from the earth. The moon is comparatively near the earth and the changes in its distance as it revolves about the earth have a comparatively large effect on its SD. At certain times, the moon's SD may change significantly from day to day. The sun is much more distant and the eccentricity of the earth's orbit has a less pronounced effect on the sun's SD, which varies between about 15.8′ and 16.3′.

SD correction The SD correction is *positive* for a *lower limb* observation and *negative* for the *upper limb.* It is applied only to observations of the sun and moon when their altitudes are measured above the visible horizon. It is not applied to observations of stars or planets, as they have no significant apparent diameter when viewed through the telescopes normally used with sextants. When the SD is applied to the hs, the sextant altitude is corrected to the value it would have if the center of the body had been observed.

Augmentation (A) **2125** The semidiameter of a body varies with its distance from the observer. When a body is on the observer's horizon, its distance from him is greater than when it is at the zenith, the difference in distance being equal to the earth's radius. As the earth's radius is extremely small in comparison to the distance to the sun, augmentation has no significant effect on observations of that body. Augmentation for a

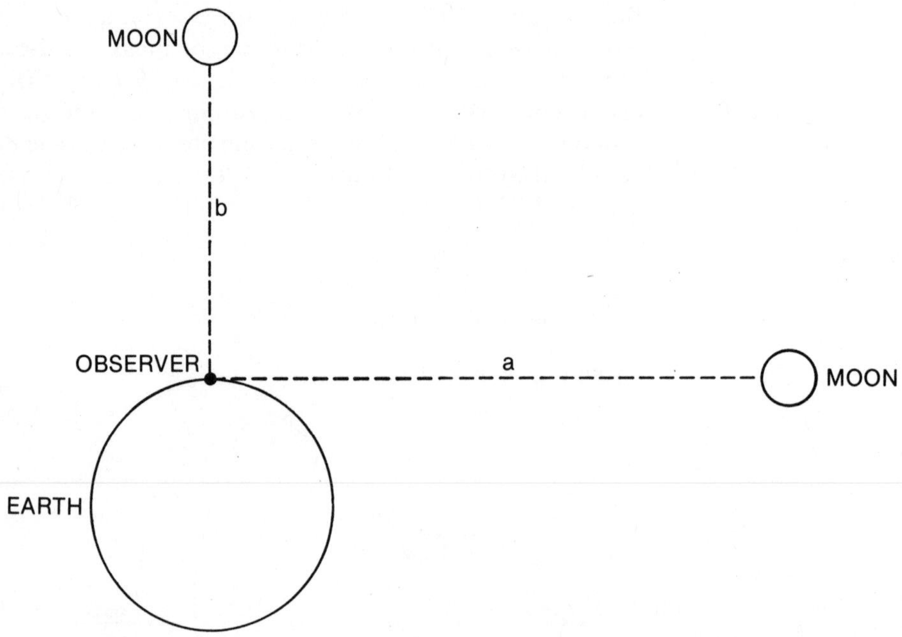

Figure 2125. Correction for augmentation; distance a is greater than b. (Not to scale.)

planet would vary with the relative position of that body and the earth in their orbits, but again is too small to be considered. Due to the comparative nearness of the moon, however, its augmentation from the observer's horizon to his zenith is about 0.3′ at mean lunar distance. Allowance for the moon's augmentation is made in the moon altitude correction tables given in the *Nautical Almanac.*

Phase (F) **2126** The planets go through phases which are quite similar to those of the moon. A planet's phase is not obvious to the naked eye, but a telescope does increase the phase effect, and affects the positioning of a planet on the horizon by the observer using a sextant. The phase correction is similar to the semidiameter correction for the sun and moon.

The phase correction (F) tabulated in the *Almanac* may be positive or negative. It is applied only to observations of Venus and Mars, as it is not significant for the other planets. When applied to hs, the sextant altitude is corrected to the value it would have if the center of the planet had been observed. A method of computing the phase and parallax correction for daylight observations of Venus is given in the *Nautical Almanac.*

Irradiation (J) **2127** *Irradiation* is the name applied to the optical illusion that causes the apparent size of a bright or light-colored object in juxtaposition with a darker one to appear larger than it actually is; conversely, the darker one appears smaller. Thus, when the sky is considerably brighter than the water, the horizon appears depressed. The apparent diameter of the sun is increased slightly by irradiation, and the brighter stars appear to have a measurable diameter. Altitudes of the sun's lower limb should not be affected as the irradiation effect on the sun and on the horizon are in the same direction and effectively cancel out. The effect on the upper limb of the sun, however, is opposite to that on the horizon, and a subtractive correction would be applicable. Quantitatively, it decreases with increasing telescope magnification, and with increasing altitudes. Irradiation corrections are not included in the tabulated values of Tables A2 and A3 of the *Nautical Almanac* and are seldom, if ever, calculated and applied in practical surface navigation.

Parallax (P) **2128** *Parallax* is the difference in the direction of an object at a finite distance when viewed simultaneously from two different positions. It enters into the sextant altitude corrections because hs is measured from the earth's surface, but Ho is calculated from the earth's center. Since the moon is the celestial body nearest the earth, parallax has its greatest effect on lunar observations.

The effect of parallax is illustrated in Figure 2128. If the moon is directly overhead, that is, with an altitude of 90°, there is no parallax,

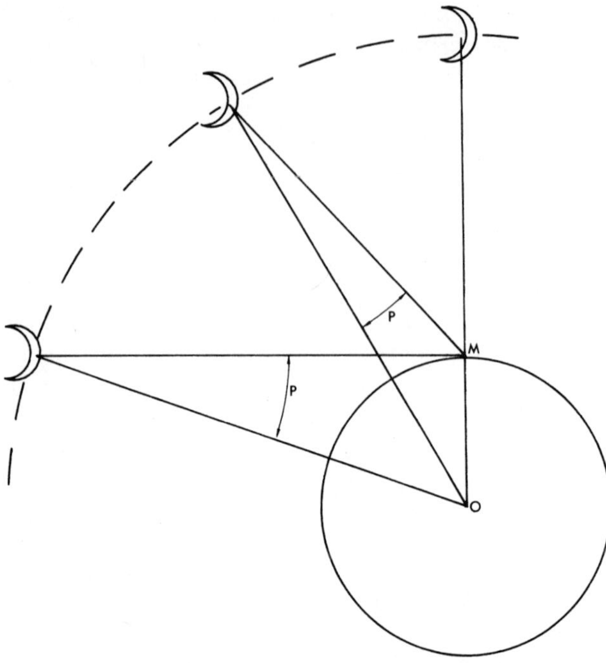

Figure 2128. Parallax correction varies with altitude of observed body. (Not to scale.)

as its direction is the same at the center of the earth as for the observer. As the moon decreases in altitude its direction from the observer begins to differ with its direction from the earth's center, and the difference in direction increases continuously until the moon sets. The same effect, of course, occurs in reverse when a body is rising. Parallax ranges from zero for a body with an altitude of 90° to a maximum when the body is on the horizon, with 0° altitude. At altitude 0°, it is called horizontal parallax (HP).

In addition to increasing as altitude decreases, parallax increases as distance to a celestial body decreases. Venus and Mars, when close to the earth, are also appreciably affected by parallax. The sun is slightly affected, the parallax correction for the sun being +0.1′ from zero altitude to 65°. All other celestial bodies are too far from the earth to require correction for parallax when observed with the sextant.

The correction for parallax is always positive, and is applied only to observations of the moon, sun, Venus, and Mars. When it is applied to hs, the sextant altitude is corrected to the value it would have if the observer were at the center of the earth.

Sea-air temperature difference correction (S)

2129 In discussing the dip of the horizon, it was pointed out that refraction affected the value of the dip. The various dip correction tables allow for this refraction, the allowance being based on a standard rate of decrease of pressure and temperature in the atmosphere with increased height above the surface. However, when there is a difference between the sea water and the air temperature *at the water surface,* the air in contact with the sea is warmed or cooled by the water, and the normal rate of decrease is upset.

This may alter the value of the dip. If the water is warmer than the air, the horizon is depressed and the dip is increased, resulting in sextant altitudes that are too great. As a correction to the hs, the sea-air temperature difference correction is negative when the water is warmer than the air. Conversely, when the air is warmer, the reverse is true, and the correction is positive. It is seldom used in routine navigation.

In practice, the air temperature is measured at the observer's height of eye, and the water temperature is determined preferably from a sample picked up by dip bucket, or from the intake water temperature. This is usually the most convenient method of approximating the temperatures. Various values have been placed on the effect resulting from this difference of temperatures. The Japanese Hydrographic Office, by considerable empiric testing, found the value to be 0.11′ per degree Fahrenheit; other values, ranging up to 0.21′ per degree Fahrenheit have been suggested.

To date the U. S. Navy has not taken an official stand on the use of sea-air temperature difference corrections. When the Japanese value of 0.11′ was applied to several hundred observations made along the Atlantic coast between the Virgin Islands and New England throughout a year, it proved to be generally satisfactory and improved some 98 percent of the observations.

Summary of corrections

2130 The foregoing sextant altitude corrections are summarized in Figure 2130. In the following section a description of the tables used to determine the corrections is given.

Applying corrections from the *Nautical Almanac*

2131 All observations made with a marine sextant must first be corrected for fixed or instrument error (I), index error (IC), and dip (D); a personal correction (PC) is applied if it is known to be applicable. The sextant altitude thus corrected is termed the apparent altitude, ha. This apparent altitude is used as the argument for entering the appropriate correction tables described in the following articles.

Determining apparent altitude

The I correction is obtained from the maker's certificate, furnished with the sextant. The IC should be determined each time the sextant is used, as described in Article 2109. The correction for dip is found in a table on the inside front cover of the *Nautical Almanac,* as well as on the book mark. This table, shown in Figure 2131, is entered with the observer's height of eye above the water in feet or meters; it is a *critical table* in that the tabulated value of dip is correct for any height of eye between those printed half a line above and half a line below. If the entering height of eye is an exact tabulated value, the correction half a line *above* it should be used.

Correction	Symbol	Sign	Increases with	Bodies*	Sextants*	Source
Instrument	I	±	changing altitude	S, M, P, ☆	M, A	sextant box
Index	IC	±	constant	S, M, P, ☆	M, A	measurement
Personal	PC	±	constant	S, M, P, ☆	M, A	measurement
Dip	D	−	higher height of eye	S, M, P, ☆	M	almanacs
Sea-air temp. diff.	S	±	greater temp. diff.	S, M, P, ☆	M	computation
Refraction	R	−	lower altitude	S, M, P, ☆	M, A	almanacs
Air temp.	T	±	greater diff. from 50° F	S, M, P, ☆	M, A	almanacs, table 23 H. O. 9
Atmospheric pressure	B	±	greater diff. from 29.83 in. mercury	S, M, P, ☆	M, A	Nautical Almanac table 24 H. O. 9
Irradiation	J	−	constant	S	M, A	Nautical Almanac
Semidiameter	SD	±	lesser dist. from earth	S, M	M, A	almanacs
Phase	F	±	phase	P	M, A	Nautical Almanac
Augmentation	A	±	higher altitude	M	M, A	Nautical Almanac
Parallax	P	±	lower altitude	S, M, P	M, A	almanacs

* Bodies: S refers to sun, M to moon, P to planets, ☆ to stars.
* Sextants: M refers to Marine, A to artificial horizon.

Figure 2130. Sextant corrections.

Correcting observations of the sun

2132 The *Nautical Almanac* gives critical value tables for the correction of observations of the sun, as illustrated in Figure 2131. The corrections are tabulated separately for the lower ($\underset{\smile}{\odot}$) and upper limb sun ($\bar{\odot}$) sights, and are in two columns, titled Oct.–Mar., and Apr.–Sept., to approximate the change in the sun's semidiameter throughout the year. These tables combine the corrections for *refraction, semidiameter,* and *parallax.* If a navigator wants maximum accuracy, he may apply these corrections individually, using the more precise value for semidiameter for the specific date as obtained from the daily pages of the *Almanac*. The steps to follow are:

Apply I, IC, and D corrections to obtain ha.

With the apparent altitude thus found, extract the R correction from the "Stars and Planets" correction table (Figure 2131).

Apply the SD correction obtained from the daily pages; this correction is positive for lower limb sights and negative for upper limb sights.

For altitudes below 65°, apply a positive correction of 0.1′ for parallax (P).

A2 ALTITUDE CORRECTION TABLES 10°-90°—SUN, STARS, PLANETS

SUN

OCT.—MAR. App. Alt.	Lower Limb	Upper Limb	APR.—SEPT. App. Alt.	Lower Limb	Upper Limb
° ′	′	′	° ′	′	′
9 34	+10·8	−21·5	9 39	+10·6	−21·2
9 45	+10·9	−21·4	9 51	+10·7	−21·1
9 56	+11·0	−21·3	10 03	+10·8	−21·0
10 08	+11·1	−21·2	10 15	+10·9	−20·9
10 21	+11·2	−21·1	10 27	+11·0	−20·8
10 34	+11·3	−21·0	10 40	+11·1	−20·7
10 47	+11·4	−20·9	10 54	+11·2	−20·6
11 01	+11·5	−20·8	11 08	+11·3	−20·5
11 15	+11·6	−20·7	11 23	+11·4	−20·4
11 30	+11·7	−20·6	11 38	+11·5	−20·3
11 46	+11·8	−20·5	11 54	+11·6	−20·2
12 02	+11·9	−20·4	12 10	+11·7	−20·1
12 19	+12·0	−20·3	12 28	+11·8	−20·0
12 37	+12·1	−20·2	12 46	+11·9	−19·9
12 55	+12·2	−20·1	13 05	+12·0	−19·8
13 14	+12·3	−20·0	13 24	+12·1	−19·7
13 35	+12·4	−19·9	13 45	+12·2	−19·6
13 56	+12·5	−19·8	14 07	+12·3	−19·5
14 18	+12·6	−19·7	14 30	+12·4	−19·4
14 42	+12·7	−19·6	14 54	+12·5	−19·3
15 06	+12·8	−19·5	15 19	+12·6	−19·2
15 32	+12·9	−19·4	15 46	+12·7	−19·1
15 59	+13·0	−19·3	16 14	+12·8	−19·0
16 28	+13·1	−19·2	16 44	+12·9	−18·9
16 59	+13·2	−19·1	17 15	+13·0	−18·8
17 32	+13·3	−19·0	17 48	+13·1	−18·7
18 06	+13·4	−18·9	18 24	+13·2	−18·6
18 42	+13·5	−18·8	19 01	+13·3	−18·5
19 21	+13·6	−18·7	19 42	+13·4	−18·4
20 03	+13·7	−18·6	20 25	+13·5	−18·3
20 48	+13·8	−18·5	21 11	+13·6	−18·2
21 35	+13·9	−18·4	22 00	+13·7	−18·1
22 26	+14·0	−18·3	22 54	+13·8	−18·0
23 22	+14·1	−18·2	23 51	+13·9	−17·9
24 21	+14·2	−18·1	24 53	+14·0	−17·8
25 26	+14·3	−18·0	26 00	+14·1	−17·7
26 36	+14·4	−17·9	27 13	+14·2	−17·6
27 52	+14·5	−17·8	28 33	+14·3	−17·5
29 15	+14·6	−17·7	30 00	+14·4	−17·4
30 46	+14·7	−17·6	31 35	+14·5	−17·3
32 26	+14·8	−17·5	33 20	+14·6	−17·2
34 17	+14·9	−17·4	35 17	+14·7	−17·1
36 20	+15·0	−17·3	37 26	+14·8	−17·0
38 36	+15·1	−17·2	39 50	+14·9	−16·9
41 08	+15·2	−17·1	42 31	+15·0	−16·8
43 59	+15·3	−17·0	45 31	+15·1	−16·7
47 10	+15·4	−16·9	48 55	+15·2	−16·6
50 46	+15·5	−16·8	52 44	+15·3	−16·5
54 49	+15·6	−16·7	57 02	+15·4	−16·4
59 23	+15·7	−16·6	61 51	+15·5	−16·3
64 30	+15·8	−16·5	67 17	+15·6	−16·2
70 12	+15·9	−16·4	73 16	+15·7	−16·1
76 26	+16·0	−16·3	79 43	+15·8	−16·0
83 05	+16·1	−16·2	86 32	+15·9	−15·9
90 00			90 00		

STARS AND PLANETS

App. Alt.	Corrⁿ
° ′	′
9 56	−5·3
10 08	−5·2
10 20	−5·1
10 33	−5·0
10 46	−4·9
11 00	−4·8
11 14	−4·7
11 29	−4·6
11 45	−4·5
12 01	−4·4
12 18	−4·3
12 35	−4·2
12 54	−4·1
13 13	−4·0
13 33	−3·9
13 54	−3·8
14 16	−3·7
14 40	−3·6
15 04	−3·5
15 30	−3·4
15 57	−3·3
16 26	−3·2
16 56	−3·1
17 28	−3·0
18 02	−2·9
18 38	−2·8
19 17	−2·7
19 58	−2·6
20 42	−2·5
21 28	−2·4
22 19	−2·3
23 13	−2·2
24 11	−2·1
25 14	−2·0
26 22	−1·9
27 36	−1·8
28 56	−1·7
30 24	−1·6
32 00	−1·5
33 45	−1·4
35 40	−1·3
37 48	−1·2
40 08	−1·1
42 44	−1·0
45 36	−0·9
48 47	−0·8
52 18	−0·7
56 11	−0·6
60 28	−0·5
65 08	−0·4
70 11	−0·3
75 34	−0·2
81 13	−0·1
87 03	0·0
90 00	

App. Alt.	Additional Corrⁿ
1977	
VENUS	
Jan. 1-Jan. 29	
°	′
47	+ 0·2
Jan. 30-Feb. 26	
46	+ 0·3
Feb. 27-Mar. 14	
11	+ 0·4
41	+ 0·5
Mar. 15-Mar. 23	
6	+ 0·5
20	+ 0·6
31	+ 0·7
Mar. 24-Apr. 19	
4	+ 0·6
12	+ 0·7
22	+ 0·8
Apr. 20-Apr. 28	
6	+ 0·5
20	+ 0·6
31	+ 0·7
Apr. 29-May 13	
11	+ 0·4
41	+ 0·5
May 14-June 8	
46	+ 0·3
June 9-July 23	
47	+ 0·2
July 24-Dec. 31	
42	+ 0·1
MARS	
Jan. 1-Nov. 12	
60	+ 0·1
Nov. 13-Dec. 31	
41	+ 0·2
75	+ 0·1

DIP

Ht. of Eye	Corrⁿ	Ht. of Eye
m	′	ft.
2·4	−2·8	8·0
2·6	−2·9	8·6
2·8	−3·0	9·2
3·0	−3·1	9·8
3·2	−3·2	10·5
3·4	−3·3	11·2
3·6	−3·4	11·9
3·8	−3·5	12·6
4·0	−3·6	13·3
4·3	−3·7	14·1
4·5	−3·8	14·9
4·7	−3·9	15·7
5·0	−4·0	16·5
5·2	−4·1	17·4
5·5	−4·2	18·3
5·8	−4·3	19·1
6·1	−4·4	20·1
6·3	−4·5	21·0
6·6	−4·6	22·0
6·9	−4·7	22·9
7·2	−4·8	23·9
7·5	−4·9	24·9
7·9	−5·0	26·0
8·2	−5·1	27·1
8·5	−5·2	28·1
8·8	−5·3	29·2
9·2	−5·4	30·4
9·5	−5·5	31·5
9·9	−5·6	32·7
10·3	−5·7	33·9
10·6	−5·8	35·1
11·0	−5·9	36·3
11·4	−6·0	37·6
11·8	−6·1	38·9
12·2	−6·2	40·1
12·6	−6·3	41·5
13·0	−6·4	42·8
13·4	−6·5	44·2
13·8	−6·6	45·5
14·2	−6·7	46·9
14·7	−6·8	48·4
15·1	−6·9	49·8
15·5	−7·0	51·3
16·0	−7·1	52·8
16·5	−7·2	54·3
16·9	−7·3	55·8
17·4	−7·4	57·4
17·9	−7·5	58·9
18·4	−7·6	60·5
18·8	−7·7	62·1
19·3	−7·8	63·8
19·8	−7·9	65·4
20·4	−8·0	67·1
20·9	−8·1	68·8
21·4		70·5

Ht. of Eye	Corrⁿ
m	′
1·0	− 1·8
1·5	− 2·2
2·0	− 2·5
2·5	− 2·8
3·0	− 3·0
See table ←	
m	′
20	− 7·9
22	− 8·3
24	− 8·6
26	− 9·0
28	− 9·3
30	− 9·6
32	− 10·0
34	− 10·3
36	− 10·6
38	− 10·8
40	− 11·1
42	− 11·4
44	− 11·7
46	− 11·9
48	− 12·2
ft.	′
2	− 1·4
4	− 1·9
6	− 2·4
8	− 2·7
10	− 3·1
See table ←	
ft.	
70	− 8·1
75	− 8·4
80	− 8·7
85	− 8·9
90	− 9·2
95	− 9·5
100	− 9·7
105	− 9·9
110	− 10·2
115	− 10·4
120	− 10·6
125	− 10·8
130	− 11·1
135	− 11·3
140	− 11·5
145	− 11·7
150	− 11·9
155	− 12·1

App. Alt. = Apparent altitude = Sextant altitude corrected for index error and dip.
For daylight observations of Venus, see page 260.

Figure 2131. *Nautical Almanac* correction tables for the sun, stars, and planets when at altitudes between approximately 10° and 90°.

The procedure for individual corrections is rarely used in practical navigation; the combined value will usually be applied as in the following example:

Example: A navigator observes the upper limb of the sun with a marine sextant on 5 June 1977 with a height of eye of 48 feet. The sextant reading is 51°58.4′. The instrument correction is −0.2′ and the sextant has an index error of 2.2′ "off the arc".

Required: Ho at the time of observation using the *Nautical Almanac.*

Solution: (1) Record I and IC; in this case, they are − 0.2′ and +2.2′. (2) Enter the *Nautical Almanac* "Dip" table with height of eye; extract and record the D correction; in this case, it is −6.7′. (3) Determine the net correction and apply it to hs to obtain ha. (4) Using ha, in this case, 51°53.7′, enter table A2 in the inside front cover of the *Nautical Almanac,* SUN, Apr–Sept, Upper Limb; extract the combined correction for refraction, parallax, and semidiameter; in this case, −16.6′. (5) Algebraically add this correction to ha to obtain Ho as 51°37.1′.

Answer: Ho 51°37.1′.

	+	$\bar{\odot}$	−
I			0.2′
IC	2.2′		
D			6.7′
Sum	2.2′		6.9′
Corr.		−4.7	
hs		51°58.4′	
ha		51°53.7′	
A2			16.6′
Corr.		−16.6′	
Ho		51°37.1′	

Correcting star observations

2133 In addition to the I, IC, and D corrections, star observations require only a correction for refraction, R. This is found in the appropriate table of the *Nautical Almanac,* headed "Stars and Planets."

Example: (Figure 2131) A navigator observes the star Zubenelgenubi with a marine sextant from a height of eye of 12 meters. The sextant altitude is 64°52.7′, and the instrument has an index error of 1.7′ "off the arc"; there is no applicable instrument correction.

Required: Ho at the time of observation.

Solution: (1) Record the IC. In this case it is +1.7′. (2) Enter the *Nautical Almanac* "Dip" table with height of eye, and extract and record the D correction. In this case it is −6.1′. (3) Determine the net correction and apply to hs to obtain ha. (4) Using ha, in this instance, 64°48.3′, enter the *Nautical Almanac,* Table A2, columns for "Stars and Planets"; extract the refraction correction, in this case −0.5′, and apply it algebraically to ha. Ho is found to be 64°47.8′.

Answer: Ho 64°47.8′.

	+	☆	−
IC	1.7′		
D			6.1′
Sum	1.7′		6.1′
Corr.		−4.4′	
hs		64°52.7′	
ha		64°48.3′	
A2-P			0.5′
Corr.		−0.5′	
Ho		64°47.8′	

Correcting observations of Jupiter and Saturn

2134 The planets Jupiter and Saturn, due to their comparatively great distance from the earth, may be treated as stars in the ordinary practice of navigation.

Example: A navigator observes the planet Jupiter with a marine sextant from a height of eye of 29 feet. The sextant altitude is 18°20.2′, and the instrument has an IC of +2.2′.

Required: Ho at the time of the observation.

Solution: (1) Record the IC. In this case, it is +2.2′. (2) Enter the "Dip" table with height of eye and extract and record the D correction. In this case, it is −5.2′. (3) Determine the net correction and apply it to hs to determine ha. (4) Using ha, in this case 18°17.2′, enter the *Nautical Almanac*—Table A2, Stars and Planets—extract the correction for refraction, in this instance −2.9′. (5) Algebraically add this correction to ha to obtain Ho which is 18°14.3′.

Answer: Ho 18°14.3′.

	+	JUPITER	−
IC	2.2′		
D			5.2′
Sum	2.2′		5.2′
Corr.		−3.0′	
hs		18°20.2′	
ha		18°17.2′	
A2			2.9′
Corr.		−2.9′	
Ho		18°14.3′	

Correcting observations of Venus and Mars

2135 Observations of Venus and Mars, in addition to being corrected for I, IC, D, and R, should be corrected for phase and parallax for observations inade during the period of twilight. These latter two corrections are combined, under the names of the planets, in the "Stars and Planets" correction table shown in Figure 2131.

Example: During morning twilight on 5 June 1977 a navigator with a marine sextant observes the planet Venus from a height of eye of 16.5 meters. The sextant altitude is 41°17.6′, and the instrument has an IC of − 0.5′.

Required: Ho at the time of the observation.

Solution: (1) Record the IC. In this case, it is −0.5′. (2) Enter the "Dip" table with height of eye and extract and record the D correction. In this case, it is −7.1′. (3) Determine the net correction and apply it to hs to obtain ha, in this case 41°10.0′. (4) Enter the *Nautical Almanac* Table A2—Stars and Planets—left-hand column and extract the refraction correction which is + 1.1′. (5); Enter the right-hand column of Stars and Planets and extract the additional correction. In this case +0.2′. (6) Determine the net correction to ha and apply it algebraically to determine Ho.

Answer: Ho 41°09.1′.

	+	VENUS	−
IC			0.5′
D			7.1′
Sum			7.6′
Corr.		−7.6′	
hs		41°17.6′	
ha		41°10′.0	
A2			1.1′
P add'l	0.2′		
Sum	0.2′		1.1′
Corr.		−0.9′	
Ho		41°09.1′	

Venus is occasionally observed in the daytime; for such observations the tabulated additional correction found in this table should *not* be used, as the magnitude and sign of the phase correction may differ from the tabulated value. If desired, for daylight observations of Venus, an additional correction may be derived from the equation given in the explanation section of the *Nautical Almanac.*

Correcting observations of the moon

2136 The tables for correcting observations of the moon are found on the inside back cover and the facing page of the *Nautical Almanac,* as shown in part in Figure 2136. These tables combine the corrections for refraction, semidiameter, augmentation, and parallax.

To correct observations of the moon, the I, IC, and D corrections are applied to the sextant altitude. The upper portion of the moon correction tables are then entered with the apparent altitude thus ob-

ALTITUDE CORRECTION TABLES 35°-90°—MOON

App. Alt.	35°-39° Corrⁿ	40°-44° Corrⁿ	45°-49° Corrⁿ	50°-54° Corrⁿ	55°-59° Corrⁿ	60°-64° Corrⁿ	65°-69° Corrⁿ	70°-74° Corrⁿ	75°-79° Corrⁿ	80°-84° Corrⁿ	85°-89° Corrⁿ	App. Alt.
′	° ′	° ′	° ′	° ′	° ′	° ′	° ′	° ′	° ′	° ′	° ′	′
00	35 56.5	40 53.7	45 50.5	50 46.9	55 43.1	60 38.9	65 34.6	70 30.1	75 25.3	80 20.5	85 15.6	00
10	56.4	53.6	50.4	46.8	42.9	38.8	34.4	29.9	25.2	20.4	15.5	10
20	56.3	53.5	50.2	46.7	42.8	38.7	34.3	29.7	25.0	20.2	15.3	20
30	56.2	53.4	50.1	46.5	42.7	38.5	34.1	29.6	24.9	20.0	15.1	30
40	56.2	53.3	50.0	46.4	42.5	38.4	34.0	29.4	24.7	19.9	15.0	40
50	56.1	53.2	49.9	46.3	42.4	38.2	33.8	29.3	24.5	19.7	14.8	50
00	36 56.0	41 53.1	46 49.8	51 46.2	56 42.3	61 38.1	66 33.7	71 29.1	76 24.4	81 19.6	86 14.6	00
10	55.9	53.0	49.7	46.0	42.1	37.9	33.5	29.0	24.2	19.4	14.5	10
20	55.8	52.8	49.5	45.9	42.0	37.8	33.4	28.8	24.1	19.2	14.3	20
30	55.7	52.7	49.4	45.8	41.8	37.7	33.2	28.7	23.9	19.1	14.1	30
40	55.6	52.6	49.3	45.7	41.7	37.5	33.1	28.5	23.8	18.9	14.0	40
50	55.5	52.5	49.2	45.5	41.6	37.4	32.9	28.3	23.6	18.7	13.8	50
H.P.	L U	L U	L U	L U	L U	L U	L U	L U	L U	L U	L U	H.P.
′	′ ′	′ ′	′ ′	′ ′	′ ′	′ ′	′ ′	′ ′	′ ′	′ ′	′ ′	′
57.0	4.3 3.2	4.3 3.3	4.3 3.3	4.4 3.4	4.4 3.4	4.5 3.5	4.5 3.5	4.6 3.6	4.7 3.6	4.7 3.7	4.8 3.8	57.0
57.3	4.6 3.4	4.6 3.4	4.6 3.4	4.6 3.5	4.7 3.5	4.7 3.5	4.7 3.6	4.8 3.6	4.8 3.6	4.8 3.7	4.9 3.7	57.3
57.6	4.9 3.6	4.9 3.6	4.9 3.6	4.9 3.6	4.9 3.6	4.9 3.6	4.9 3.6	4.9 3.6	5.0 3.6	5.0 3.6	5.0 3.6	57.6
57.9	5.2 3.7	5.2 3.7	5.2 3.7	5.2 3.7	5.2 3.7	5.1 3.6	5.1 3.6	5.1 3.6	5.1 3.6	5.1 3.6	5.1 3.6	57.9
58.2	5.5 3.9	5.5 3.8	5.5 3.8	5.4 3.8	5.4 3.7	5.4 3.7	5.3 3.7	5.3 3.6	5.2 3.6	5.2 3.5	5.2 3.5	58.2

Figure 2136. *Nautical Almanac* correction tables for moon observations.

tained, and the first correction is found under the appropriate altitude heading. The moon's HP (Horizontal Parallax) is next obtained from the daily pages of the *Almanac* for the time of the observation. HP is the entering argument to obtain the second correction from the lower portion of the tables. These tables are entered in the same vertical column as was used to obtain the first correction. Two values are listed in each column under the headings L and U for each tabulated value of HP; the L value is for observations of the moon's lower limb (☾̲), and the U for those of the upper limb (☾̄). The second correction is extracted under the appropriate heading. It should be noted that as HP is tabulated in increments of 0.3′, it is desirable to interpolate for nontabulated values of HP in obtaining the second correction.

Both the first and second corrections are *added* to the apparent altitude of all moon observations, but for *observations of the upper limb, 30.0′ is to be subtracted from the sum of the corrections.*

Example: A navigator observes the lower limb of the moon with a marine sextant from a height of eye of 7.6 meters. The sextant reading is 56°39.7′; there is no instrument or index error. The HP from the daily pages of the *Nautical Almanac* for the day concerned is found to be 57.6′.

Required: Ho for the time of observation.

Solution: (1) Record the IC. In this case there is no IC. (2) Enter the *Nautical Almanac* "Dip" table with height of eye, and extract and record the D correction. In this case it is −4.9′. (3) Apply the D correction to hs to obtain ha of 56°34.8′. (4) Enter the upper portion of the *Nautical Almanac* "moon" tables with ha and extract and record the first correction. In this case it is +41.8′. (5) Follow down the altitude column used in (4) above, and extract and record from the lower portion of the "moon" table the L correction for the HP found on the daily page. In this case HP is 57.6′ and L is +4.9′. (6) Sum the corrections and apply algebraically to ha to obtain Ho.

Answer: Ho 57°21.5′.

	+MOON−	
H.P. ☾	57.6′	
IC	0	
Dip (Ht 25′)		4.9′
Sum		−4.9′
hs	56°39.7′	
ha	56°34.8′	
First Corr.	41.8′	
L(HP = 57.6′) Moon	4.9′	
sum	+46.7′	0−
corr.	+ 46.7′	
ha	56°34.8′	
Ho	57°21.5′	

Correcting for nonstandard refraction

2137 The refraction corrections included in the various altitude correction tables in the *Nautical Almanac* are based on an air temperature of 50°F (10°C), and an atmospheric pressure of 29.83 inches (1010 millibars) of mercury. When atmospheric conditions vary from these standard values, the light from celestial bodies is refracted to a greater or lesser value than is stated in the tables.

Additional corrections for nonstandard conditions of refraction are given in the *Nautical Almanac*, Table A4, which is reproduced in Figure 2137. It is entered at the top with the temperature and a line is projected down vertically until it intersects with a horizontal line drawn in from the appropriate point on the pressure scale. The intersection of these two lines will fall within one of the diagonal lettered zones; the name of this letter establishes the vertical correction column to be used. Using the apparent altitude as the entering argument, the additional refraction correction is then found.

Ordinarily, except under extreme conditions, it is not necessary to use this table for altitudes above about 10°. However, due to the extremely rapid change in the value of the refraction at very low altitudes, it is desirable that this table be used for correcting such observations. Interpolation may be desirable at extremely low altitudes.

Example: A sextant observation of 7° is taken under conditions of air temperature +20°C and barometric pressure 1010 millibars.

Required: The additional correction for refraction.

Solution: Enter Table A4 of the *Nautical Almanac* for the stated conditions. These are found in area J of the upper portion. Following down column J to the line for an altitude of 7°, the correction is found to be +0.4′.

Answer: Additional refraction correction is + 0.4′.

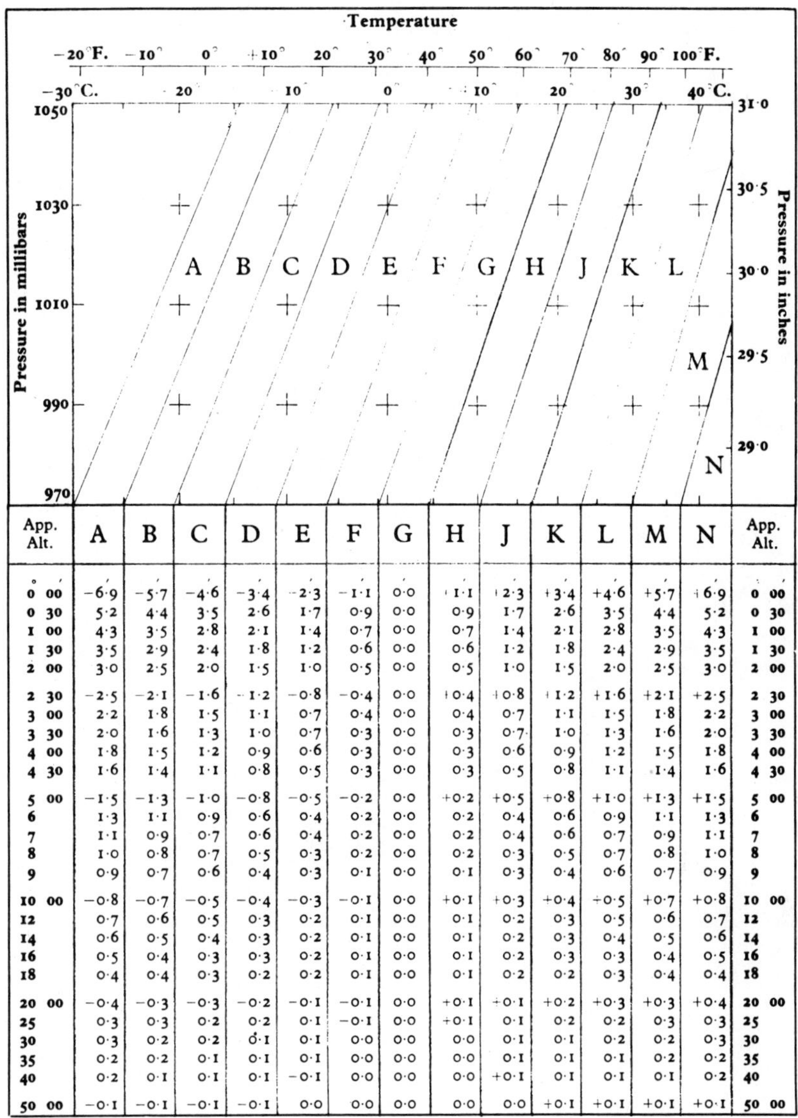

App. Alt.	A	B	C	D	E	F	G	H	J	K	L	M	N	App. Alt.
° ′	′	′	′	′	′	′	′	′	′	′	′	′	′	° ′
0 00	−6·9	−5·7	−4·6	−3·4	−2·3	−1·1	0·0	+1·1	+2·3	+3·4	+4·6	+5·7	+6·9	0 00
0 30	5·2	4·4	3·5	2·6	1·7	0·9	0·0	0·9	1·7	2·6	3·5	4·4	5·2	0 30
1 00	4·3	3·5	2·8	2·1	1·4	0·7	0·0	0·7	1·4	2·1	2·8	3·5	4·3	1 00
1 30	3·5	2·9	2·4	1·8	1·2	0·6	0·0	0·6	1·2	1·8	2·4	2·9	3·5	1 30
2 00	3·0	2·5	2·0	1·5	1·0	0·5	0·0	0·5	1·0	1·5	2·0	2·5	3·0	2 00
2 30	−2·5	−2·1	−1·6	−1·2	−0·8	−0·4	0·0	+0·4	+0·8	+1·2	+1·6	+2·1	+2·5	2 30
3 00	2·2	1·8	1·5	1·1	0·7	0·4	0·0	0·4	0·7	1·1	1·5	1·8	2·2	3 00
3 30	2·0	1·6	1·3	1·0	0·7	0·3	0·0	0·3	0·7	1·0	1·3	1·6	2·0	3 30
4 00	1·8	1·5	1·2	0·9	0·6	0·3	0·0	0·3	0·6	0·9	1·2	1·5	1·8	4 00
4 30	1·6	1·4	1·1	0·8	0·5	0·3	0·0	0·3	0·5	0·8	1·1	1·4	1·6	4 30
5 00	−1·5	−1·3	−1·0	−0·8	−0·5	−0·2	0·0	+0·2	+0·5	+0·8	+1·0	+1·3	+1·5	5 00
6	1·3	1·1	0·9	0·6	0·4	0·2	0·0	0·2	0·4	0·6	0·9	1·1	1·3	6
7	1·1	0·9	0·7	0·6	0·4	0·2	0·0	0·2	0·4	0·6	0·7	0·9	1·1	7
8	1·0	0·8	0·7	0·5	0·3	0·2	0·0	0·2	0·3	0·5	0·7	0·8	1·0	8
9	0·9	0·7	0·6	0·4	0·3	0·1	0·0	0·1	0·3	0·4	0·6	0·7	0·9	9
10 00	−0·8	−0·7	−0·5	−0·4	−0·3	−0·1	0·0	+0·1	+0·3	+0·4	+0·5	+0·7	+0·8	10 00
12	0·7	0·6	0·5	0·3	0·2	0·1	0·0	0·1	0·2	0·3	0·5	0·6	0·7	12
14	0·6	0·5	0·4	0·3	0·2	0·1	0·0	0·1	0·2	0·3	0·4	0·5	0·6	14
16	0·5	0·4	0·3	0·3	0·2	0·1	0·0	0·1	0·2	0·3	0·3	0·4	0·5	16
18	0·4	0·4	0·3	0·2	0·2	0·1	0·0	0·1	0·2	0·2	0·3	0·4	0·4	18
20 00	−0·4	−0·3	−0·3	−0·2	−0·1	−0·1	0·0	+0·1	+0·1	+0·2	+0·3	+0·3	+0·4	20 00
25	0·3	0·3	0·2	0·2	0·1	−0·1	0·0	+0·1	0·1	0·2	0·2	0·3	0·3	25
30	0·3	0·2	0·2	0·1	0·1	0·0	0·0	0·0	0·1	0·1	0·2	0·2	0·3	30
35	0·2	0·2	0·1	0·1	0·1	0·0	0·0	0·0	0·1	0·1	0·1	0·2	0·2	35
40	0·2	0·1	0·1	0·1	−0·1	0·0	0·0	0·0	+0·1	0·1	0·1	0·1	0·2	40
50 00	−0·1	−0·1	−0·1	−0·1	0·0	0·0	0·0	0·0	0·0	+0·1	+0·1	+0·1	+0·1	50 00

Figure 2137. *Nautical Almanac* additional refraction corrections for nonstandard conditions. The graph is entered with values of temperature and pressure to find a zone letter, A to L. Using the line for apparent altitude (sextant altitude corrected for dip) and column for the appropriate zone letter, a correction is taken from the table. This correction is to be applied to the apparent altitude *in addition* to the corrections for standard conditions.

Corrections from the *Air Almanac*

2138 The *Air Almanac* can be used to obtain corrections for each of the categories of possible error discussed in the preceding sections, but the *Nautical Almanac* is generally preferred in marine navigation because of the greater precision of the tabulated corrections. In the *Air Almanac*, the refraction correction for all bodies is extracted from

CORRECTIONS TO BE APPLIED TO SEXTANT ALTITUDE

REFRACTION

To be subtracted from sextant altitude (referred to as observed altitude in A.P. 3270)

$R_{\circ}$	Height above sea level in units of 1 000 ft. — Sextant Altitude: 0	5	10	15	20	25	30	35	40	45	50	55	$R_{\circ}$	$R = R_{\circ} \times f$ — f: 0·9	1·0	1·1	1·2
′	° ′	° ′	° ′	° ′	° ′	° ′	° ′	° ′	° ′	° ′	° ′	° ′	′	R ′	′	′	′
	90	90	90	90	90	90	90	90	90	90	90	90					
0													0	0	0	0	0
	63	59	55	51	46	41	36	31	26	20	17	13					
1													1	1	1	1	1
	33	29	26	22	19	16	14	11	9	7	6	4					
2													2	2	2	2	2
	21	19	16	14	12	10	8	7	5	4	2 40	1 40					
3													3	3	3	3	4
	16	14	12	10	8	7	6	5	3 10	2 20	1 30	0 40					
4													4	4	4	4	5
	12	11	9	8	7	5	4 00	3 10	2 10	1 30	0 39	+0 05					
5													5	5	5	5	6
	10	9	7	5 50	4 50	3 50	3 10	2 20	1 30	0 49	+0 11	−0 19					
6													6	5	6	7	7
	8 10	6 50	5 50	4 50	4 00	3 00	2 20	1 50	1 10	0 24	−0 11	−0 38					
7													7	6	7	8	8
	6 50	5 50	5 00	4 00	3 10	2 30	1 50	1 20	0 38	+0 04	−0 28	−0 54					
8													8	7	8	9	10
	6 00	5 10	4 10	3 20	2 40	2 00	1 30	1 00	0 19	−0 13	−0 42	−1 08					
9													9	8	9	10	11
	5 20	4 30	3 40	2 50	2 10	1 40	1 10	0 35	+0 03	−0 27	−0 53	−1 18					
10													10	9	10	11	12
	4 30	3 40	2 50	2 20	1 40	1 10	0 37	+0 11	−0 16	−0 43	−1 08	−1 31					
12													12	11	12	13	14
	3 30	2 50	2 10	1 40	1 10	0 34	+0 09	−0 14	−0 37	−1 00	−1 23	−1 44					
14													14	13	14	15	17
	2 50	2 10	1 40	1 10	0 37	+0 10	−0 13	−0 34	−0 53	−1 14	−1 35	−1 56					
16													16	14	16	18	19
	2 20	1 40	1 20	0 43	+0 15	−0 08	−0 31	−0 52	−1 08	−1 27	−1 46	−2 05					
18													18	16	18	20	22
	1 50	1 20	0 49	+0 23	−0 02	−0 26	−0 46	−1 06	−1 22	−1 39	−1 57	−2 14					
20													20	18	20	22	24
	1 12	0 44	+0 19	−0 06	−0 28	−0 48	−1 09	−1 27	−1 42	−1 58	−2 14	−2 30					
25													25	22	25	28	30
	0 34	+0 10	−0 13	−0 36	−0 55	−1 14	−1 32	−1 51	−2 06	−2 21	−2 34	−2 49					
30													30	27	30	33	36
	+0 06	−0 16	−0 37	−0 59	−1 17	−1 33	−1 51	−2 07	−2 23	−2 37	−2 51	−3 04					
35													35	31	35	38	42
	−0 18	−0 37	−0 58	−1 16	−1 34	−1 49	−2 06	−2 22	−2 35	−2 49	−3 03	−3 16					
40													40	36	40	44	48
		−0 53	−1 14	−1 31	−1 47	−2 03	−2 18	−2 33	−2 47	−2 59	−3 13	−3 25					
45													45	40	45	50	54
		−1 10	−1 28	−1 44	−1 59	−2 15	−2 28	−2 43	−2 56	−3 08	−3 22	−3 33					
50													50	45	50	55	60
			−1 40	−1 53	−2 09	−2 24	−2 38	−2 52	−3 04	−3 17	−3 29	−3 41					
55													55	49	55	60	66
				−2 03	−2 18	−2 33	−2 46	−3 01	−3 12	−3 25	−3 37	−3 48					
60													60	54	60	66	72
							−2 53	−3 07	−3 19	−3 31	−3 42	−3 53					

f	Temperature in °C.: 0	5	10	15	20	25	30	35	40	45	50	55	f	f: 0·9	1·0	1·1	1·2
	+47	+36	+27	+18	+10	+ 3	− 5	−13		For these heights no temperature correction is necessary, so use $R = R_{\circ}$				Where $R_{\circ}$ is less than 10′ or the height greater than 35 000 ft. use $R = R_{\circ}$			
0·9													0·9				
	+26	+16	+ 6	− 4	−13	−22	−31	−40									
1·0													1·0				
	+ 5	− 5	−15	−25	−36	−46	−57	−68									
1·1													1·1				
	−16	−25	−36	−46	−58	−71	−83	−95									
1·2													1·2				
	−37	−45	−56	−67	−81	−95											

Figure 2138. *Air Almanac* corrections for refraction, all bodies.

the same refraction table. When applicable, the effects of semidiameter, augmentation, phase, and parallax must be separately reckoned using data in the daily pages, and combined with the extracted refraction correction to form the total correction to ha for each body observed. An additional adjustment to the resulting line of position necessitated by the Coriolis effect on a fast-moving aircraft is also required in air navigation; tables for this correction are also contained in the *Air Almanac*.

Care of the sextant **2139** The modern marine sextant is a well-built, very precise optical instrument capable of rendering many years of service if it is properly maintained. Its usefulness can be greatly impaired, however, by careless handling or neglect. If the sextant is ever dropped, some error is almost certain to be introduced into all subsequent sightings.

When not in use, the sextant should always be kept secured in its case, and the case itself should be securely stowed in a location free from excessive heat, dampness, and vibration. In particular, the sextant should never be left unattended and unsecured on the chartroom table or any other high place. When outside its case, a sextant should only be picked up by its handle—never by the telescope, limb, or index arm.

Next to careless handling, moisture is the greatest enemy of a sextant. The mirrors and lens should always be wiped off before a series of observations because fogged optics make it very difficult to pick up dimmer stars; any moisture should also be wiped off before a sextant is placed back into its box after use. Lens paper should be used—cloth of any type tends to attract and retain dust particles that could scratch the mirror or lens surface; in particular, never use silk. Moisture in the sextant case can be controlled, at least partially, by keeping in the case a small bag of a desiccant, usually silica gel; the bag should occasionally be dehumidified by placing it in a moderately hot oven for a few hours.

Moisture has a particularly deleterious effect on the silvering of the mirrors and also on the graduations of the arc if they are on a bare, polished metal surface. Should resilvering of the mirrors become necessary, this task, like instrument alignment, is best left to an optical instrument repair facility. Materials can be obtained to perform resilvering aboard ship, however, and *Bowditch* contains a description of the resilvering procedure.

Lubrication is important, but must not be overdone. The teeth of the tangent screw and those on the limb should always be kept lightly coated with a thin film of oil. The graduations on an arc that is bare, polished metal should be protected with a thin film of petroleum jelly.

If the sextant is normally stowed in an air-conditioned space and the ship is operating in a humid climate, it is a good practice to bring the sextant in its case out into the open an hour or so before use to prevent condensation from forming on the mirror surfaces.

The sextant adjustments detailed in Articles 2108 and 2109 should be undertaken only by an experienced person and must be made with great care.

Summary **2140** The sextant is the basic tool for celestial navigation; it is an optical instrument of high precision and accuracy. The ability with which a navigator uses his sextant, and cares for it, is a good standard by which to judge his professional qualifications.

As great as the accuracy of a sextant may be, it is not without small errors. A navigator must understand these and how to make the necessary corrections; only with experience and the best of working conditions should he attempt any adjustments—these are best left to a qualified technician in a properly equipped shop.

While much can be written in a book on how to use a sextant in making celestial observations, only practical experience, and a lot of it, can really lead to a navigator's proficiency. Every opportunity should be taken to make observations, and these should be reduced to check their accuracy.

22 Time

Introduction **2201** This chapter will discuss the concept of time, and the manner in which the navigator uses time as a factor in his daily work, particularly in determining the coordinates of celestial bodies. It can be said that all navigation, whether piloting, dead reckoning, celestial, or radionavigation, is dependent upon the measurement and use of time.

Basis of time **2202** Most forms of time are based on the rotation of the earth, in relation to various celestial bodies. Due to the different rates of motion (Article 1809), these various forms of time may differ in the lengths of their standard unit, the *day,* which represents one rotation of the earth relative to the reference body.

Solar day The sun is the reference body most commonly used by man, and is the one chiefly used by the navigator; the period of the earth's rotation relative to the sun is called the *solar day.* The solar year is based on the period of the earth's revolution about the sun, which requires approximately 365¼ days. The *common year* is 365 days in length. In years exactly divisible by four, such as 1976 and 1980, known as *leap years,* an additional day—February 29—is usually inserted to adjust the calendar to the actual period of revolution. As the fraction in this period is not exactly ¼ of a day—it is some 11 minutes 14 seconds less—years ending in two zeros (1900, 2100) are not leap years, unless they are exactly divisible by 400 as are the years 2000 and 2400.

The other units of time, *month, week, hour, minute,* and *second* have origins deep in man's history. The ancient Egyptians used the rising of certain stars or star-groups to divide their calendar into ten-day periods. Such stars, or star-groups, rose successively at intervals of roughly 40 minutes, and so approximately 12 of them could be seen on any night. From this the night was divided into 12 hours and the entire day became 24 hours. The division of hours into 60 minutes of 60 seconds each was a development of the ancient Babylonian culture.

In the metric (SI) system of measurements, the *second* is the basic unit of time. Contrary to the usage for larger values of other metric units, prefixes such as "kilo" and "mega" are not used for longer periods of time; hours, days, and years are acceptable units in the metric system. For shorter periods of time, however, prefixes such as "milli" and "micro" are used, as in microsecond.

The month is now an arbitrary, irregular unit of time, but it was originally the moon's period of revolution around the earth. The week, as a quarter of a month, was derived from the moon's four phases.

Apparent solar time

2203 As stated in Article 2202, the sun has been the chief body by which man has controlled his life, since prehistoric times. He used *apparent solar time*, which he read from his sundial, as his criterion. Unfortunately, the apparent rotation of the sun around the earth, actually caused by the rotation of the earth on its axis, is not at a constant speed; as a result, the length of the *apparent day* varies throughout the year. This variation results, in part, from the fact that the revolution of the earth around the sun is in an elliptical orbit and thus is not at a constant speed; see Figure 1805a. A second cause of the variation in the length of a day is the tilt of the axis of the earth's rotation with respect to its plane of revolution around the sun (Figure 2203), causing the apparent path of the sun to be along the ecliptic.

This irregularity introduced numerous difficulties in an advancing civilization, and led to the introduction of "mean solar time."

Mean solar time

2204 To overcome the difficulties introduced by the nonuniform rate of apparent solar time, *mean solar time* was invented. This is based on an imaginary sun, termed the *mean sun*, which has an hour circle moving westward along the celestial equator at a constant rate. Mean solar time is nearly equal to the average apparent solar time; it is the time kept by ship's chronometers and the great majority of timepieces, and is also the argument used in almanacs in tabulating the coordinates of celestial bodies (Figure 2204).

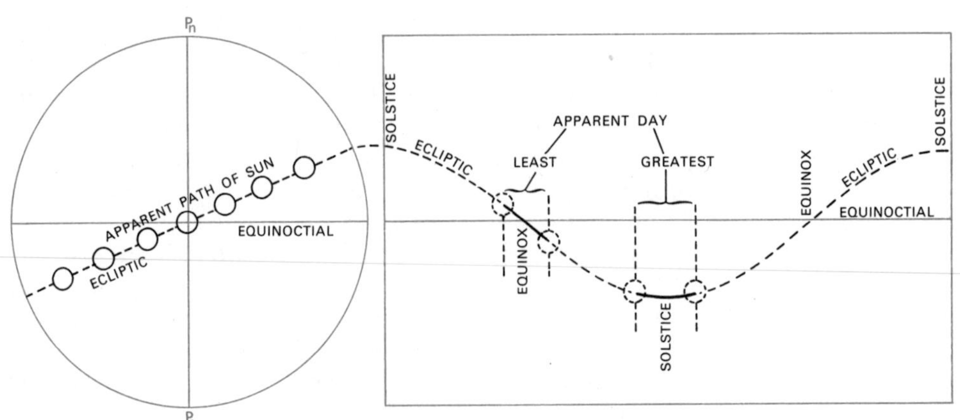

Figure 2203. Variation in length of apparent day due to obliquity of ecliptic.

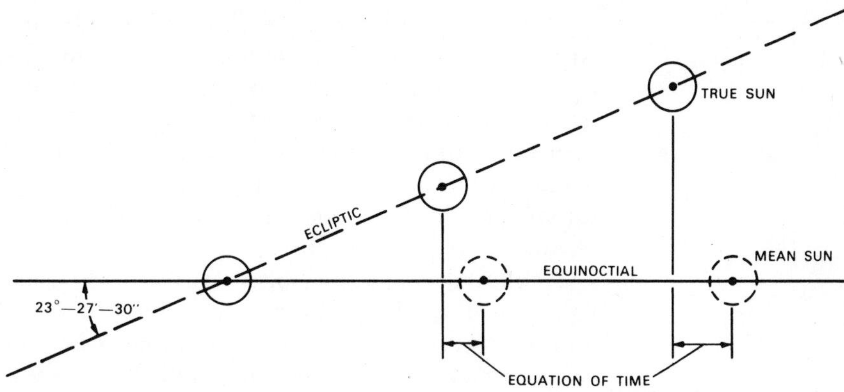

Figure 2204. Relationship of mean time to solar time.

The difference in length between the apparent and the mean day is never as great as a minute, but it is cumulative, and amounts to approximately a quarter-hour at certain times of the year.

Equation of time The difference between mean and apparent time at any instant is called the *equation of time.* Values are tabulated in the *Nautical Almanac* for noon and midnight each day; they are of little direct use in modern celestial navigation, except for the determination of the time of local apparent noon (Article 2702).

Notation of time in navigation

2205 The navigator states time on the basis of a 24-hour rather than on a 12-hour timepiece; this removes the danger of confusing "A.M." and "P.M." time. Also, he customarily works to the nearest second of time. To simplify handling and writing, hours, minutes, and seconds are expressed in that order, and are separated by dashes. Thus, a clock time of 10 hours, 57 minutes and 17 seconds P.M. is written 22-57-17. If the number of hours, minutes, or seconds is less than 10, a "0" is placed in front of each so that the hour, minutes, and seconds are each expressed by two digits; a time of 4 hours, 9 minutes, and 7 seconds A.M. is written as 04-09-07. Since the connotation of hours, minutes, and seconds is understood, no further labeling is required.

Upper and lower transit

2206 Transit signifies the instant a celestial body crosses or transits a given meridian. A meridian on the earth is a great circle, passing through the earth's geographical poles, at any given position.

The passage of a celestial body across the upper branch of the observer's meridian is called *upper transit;* in Figure 2206, the sun at *M* is shown at upper transit. Depending on the observer's latitude and the body's declination, at this instant the body is either due north, due south, or directly overhead of the observer. The passage of a celestial body across the lower branch of an observer's meridian is called *lower transit;* in Figure 2206, the sun is also shown at lower transit, at *m*. At this instant, the body will be either directly to his north, or south, or directly below him, again depending on his latitude and the body's declination. Bodies visible at the observer's position will be above the horizon at upper transit; the majority will be below the horizon at lower transit. Circumpolar stars may be above the horizon for both upper and lower transit for an observer who is not at the equator (Article 1812).

At all times, that hemisphere of the earth facing the sun is in sunlight, and the other is in darkness. The sun will be in upper transit on the central meridian of the half that is in sunlight, and it will be *midday* (noon) at that meridian; on the lower branch of the same meridian the sun will be in lower transit; at that instant it will be *midnight.* Lower transit of the mean sun simultaneously marks the end of one day (24-00-00), and the beginning of the next (00-00-00). For the observer at *M* in Figure 2206, this occurs when the mean sun is at *m*.

As the mean sun is considered to complete a revolution of 360° of arc about the earth in exactly 24 hours, it is evident that in one hour it will have traveled through 15°. In 6 hours it will have traveled through 90°, etc. Thus, there is a definite relationship between time and longitude; this will be discussed in Article 2208. The transits of celestial bodies and the resultant time-arc relationships are, for naviga-

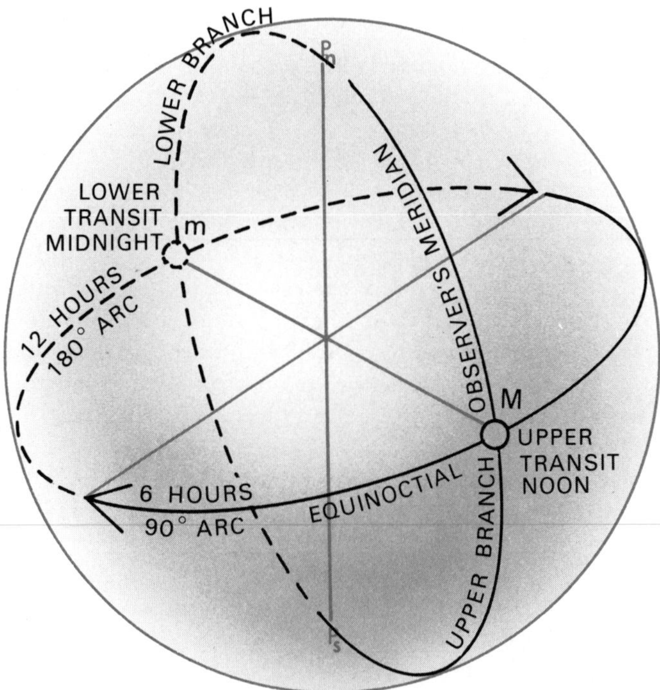

Figure 2206. Upper and lower transit.

tional purposes, generally sketched on a time diagram rather than pictorially as in Figure 2206. The use of a time diagram will be taken up in the following article.

Time diagrams **2207** The *time diagram* is a most useful aid in visualizing any time and date problem, and a navigator should be thoroughly familiar with the preparation of such a diagram.

Essentially, it is a simple sketch showing the relative positions of the meridians and hour circles involved in a particular problem. It consists of a circle representing the equator, straight lines from the center to the circumference, representing the meridians and hour circles of the problem, and appropriate labels. In drawing a time diagram, the earth is always considered to be viewed from a point in space beyond the south pole. *East* is in a *clockwise,* and *west* in a *counterclockwise* direction; all celestial bodies are therefore considered to revolve in a counterclockwise direction about the circle. All time problems in this text are illustrated with the use of a time diagram prepared in this manner. The basic elements of the time diagram are shown in Figure 2207a.

By convention, the observer's meridian is always drawn vertically, with the upper branch, *M,* shown as a solid line extending upward from the center. The lower branch, *m,* is shown as a broken line, extended downwards. In problems in which it is necessary to distinguish between local mean time and zone time (Article 2219), the *M-m* line represents the observer's meridian, and a *Z-z* line represents the central meridian of his time zone, and these meridians will be quite close together. However, local mean time is involved in only a comparatively small percentage of problems. In the majority of cases the central meridian of the zone is omitted. The approximate zone time (ZT) at *M* is shown by drawing in the hour circle of the sun (⊙) for the time in question. As shown in Figure 2207b, for an observer on the meridian

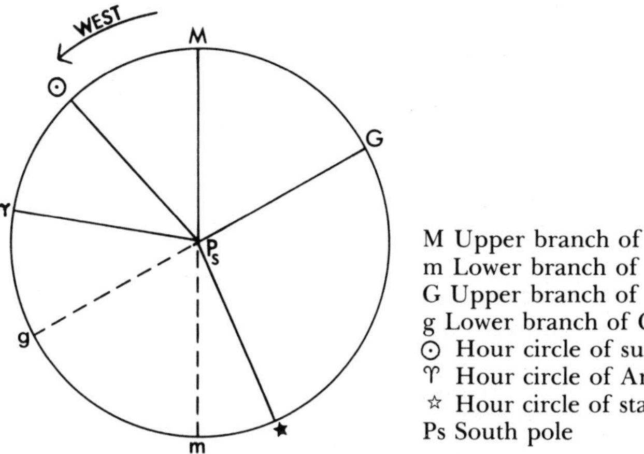

M Upper branch of observer's meridian.
m Lower branch of observer's meridian.
G Upper branch of Greenwich meridian.
g Lower branch of Greenwich meridian.
⊙ Hour circle of sun
♈ Hour circle of Aries
☆ Hour circle of star
Ps South pole

Figure 2207a. Elements of a time diagram.

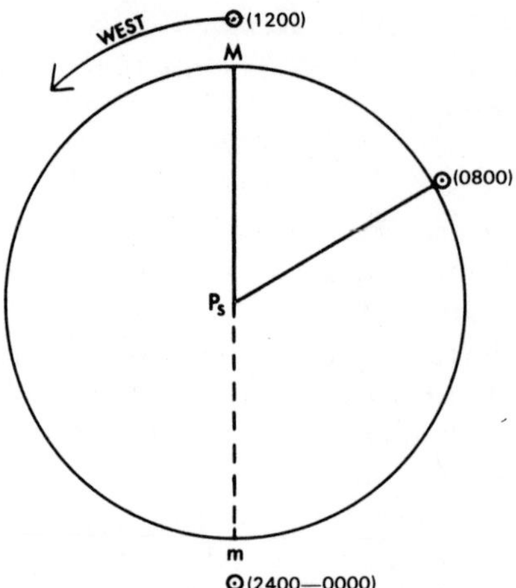

Figure 2207b. Time diagram illustrating the position of the sun at 2400-0000, 0800, and 1200.

M-m, the sun's 2400-0000 hour circle coincides with *m,* at 0800 it is 120° west or counterclockwise from *m*; at 1200 it coincides with *M* as it has moved through 180°. In Figure 2207a, the sun is shown at approximately 1500.

The time diagram may be thought of as the face of a 24-hour clock, with *m* representing ZT 2400-0000, while *M* represents 1200, and the hour circles of the sun and other celestial bodies moving in a counterclockwise direction.

Time and longitude

2208 The mean sun circles the earth's 360° of longitude in 24 hours, moving from east to west. In *one hour,* it passes over $\frac{1}{24}$ of the earth's meridians, or 15°. In *one minute* it covers $\frac{1}{60}$ of 15°, or 15 minutes of arc; in *four seconds* of time it covers one minute of arc, and in *one second,* it covers 0.25′ of arc.

The time-arc relationship may be summarized in tabular form.

Time	*Arc*
24 hours	360°
1 hour	15°
1 minute	15′
4 seconds	1′
1 second	0.25′

Due to the mean sun's motion from east to west, it is always *later* by local mean time at places to the observer's *east,* and *earlier* at those to his *west.*

The relationship between time and longitude can be used to determine the difference in local mean time (see Article 2211) between places in different longitudes. From the U.S. Naval Observatory in Washington, D.C. at longitude 77°04′ W, consider a ship in the

Mediterranean at longitude 19°58′ E, and the lighthouse at Point Loma, California, at longitude 117°15′ W. These meridians are shown in Figure 2208a, which again depicts the earth on a time diagram. West, the direction of the sun's motion, is in a counterclockwise direction. Ps-G represents the meridian of Greenwich, Ps-S that of the ship, Ps-N that of the Naval Observatory, and Ps-L that of the lighthouse. The difference in longitude between the ship and the observatory is 97°02′, since 19°58′ E + 77°04′ W = 97°02′, and the difference between the observatory and the lighthouse is 40°11′, since 117°15′ W − 77°04′ W = 40°11′. Converting these differences in longitude to time, we find that the difference in local time between the ship and the observatory is 6 hours, 28 minutes, and 08 seconds, and the difference between the observatory and the lighthouse is 2 hours, 40 minutes, and 44 seconds. Due to the sun's westerly motion, it is always later at the ship than at the other two positions. For example, when the local mean time at the observatory is 12-00-00, as shown by the sun over the meridian Ps-N in Figure 2208a, the local mean time at S is 18-28-08, and that at L is 09-19-16. If subtracting a time difference results in a change of date, it is convenient to add 24 hours to the numerically smaller time in making the computation. For example, if the local mean time at the Naval Observatory were 01-00-00 and it were desired to find the then local mean time at the Point Loma Lighthouse, 2-40-44 to the west, it is convenient to consider *0100 of today* as 0100 + 2400, or *2500* of the *preceding day*. Then it is 25-00-00 minus 2-40-44 = 22-19-16, the *preceding* day at the lighthouse.

In doing any arithmetical calculations with time, but especially when subtracting, a navigator must be mentally alert to the fact that there are 60, not 100, minutes in an hour, and 60 seconds in a minute. One gets so used to decimal calculations that it is very easy to slip up on this "60" situation when "borrowing" or "carrying."

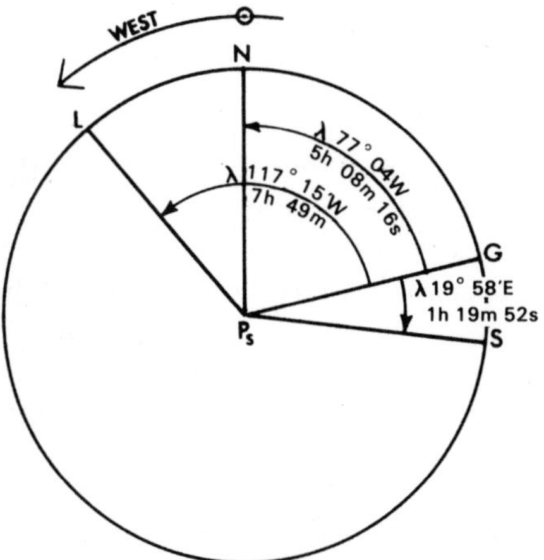

Figure 2208a. The difference in time between places is equal to the difference in their longitudes, converted to time units.

0°–59°		60°–119°		120°–179°		180°–239°		240°–299°		300°–359°			0′·00	0′·25	0′·50	0′·75
°	h m	°	h m	°	h m	°	h m	°	h m	°	h m	′	m s	m s	m s	m s
0	0 00	60	4 00	120	8 00	180	12 00	240	16 00	300	20 00	0	0 00	0 01	0 02	0 03
1	0 04	61	4 04	121	8 04	181	12 04	241	16 04	301	20 04	1	0 04	0 05	0 06	0 07
2	0 08	62	4 08	122	8 08	182	12 08	242	16 08	302	20 08	2	0 08	0 09	0 10	0 11
3	0 12	63	4 12	123	8 12	183	12 12	243	16 12	303	20 12	3	0 12	0 13	0 14	0 15
4	0 16	64	4 16	124	8 16	184	12 16	244	16 16	304	20 16	4	0 16	0 17	0 18	0 19
5	0 20	65	4 20	125	8 20	185	12 20	245	16 20	305	20 20	5	0 20	0 21	0 22	0 23
6	0 24	66	4 24	126	8 24	186	12 24	246	16 24	306	20 24	6	0 24	0 25	0 26	0 27
7	0 28	67	4 28	127	8 28	187	12 28	247	16 28	307	20 28	7	0 28	0 29	0 30	0 31
8	0 32	68	4 32	128	8 32	188	12 32	248	16 32	308	20 32	8	0 32	0 33	0 34	0 35
9	0 36	69	4 36	129	8 36	189	12 36	249	16 36	309	20 36	9	0 36	0 37	0 38	0 39
10	0 40	70	4 40	130	8 40	190	12 40	250	16 40	310	20 40	10	0 40	0 41	0 42	0 43
11	0 44	71	4 44	131	8 44	191	12 44	251	16 44	311	20 44	11	0 44	0 45	0 46	0 47
12	0 48	72	4 48	132	8 48	192	12 48	252	16 48	312	20 48	12	0 48	0 49	0 50	0 51
13	0 52	73	4 52	133	8 52	193	12 52	253	16 52	313	20 52	13	0 52	0 53	0 54	0 55
14	0 56	74	4 56	134	8 56	194	12 56	254	16 56	314	20 56	14	0 56	0 57	0 58	0 59

Figure 2208b. *Nautical Almanac* table "Conversion of Arc to Time" (extract).

In the interconversion of time and arc, the navigator is aided by a conversion table published in the *Nautical Almanac*, an extract of which is shown in Figure 2208b.

Greenwich Mean Time (GMT)

2209 *Greenwich Mean Time* (GMT) is mean solar time measured with reference to the meridian of Greenwich. The mean sun transits the lower branch of the meridian of Greenwich at GMT 00-00-00 and again at 24-00-00 (which is concurrently 00-00-00 of the following day); the mean sun transits the upper branch at 12-00-00. GMT is of great importance to the navigator, as it is the time used in almanacs as the argument for tabulating the coordinates of all celestial bodies. The choice of the meridian of Greenwich as the reference meridian for time is logical, as it is also the reference meridian used in reckoning longitude.

Universal time

2210 Although it was stated in Article 2204 that mean solar time was based on the *constant* motion of an imaginary sun, there are still slight variations. In contrast with this, man has developed a time standard that is almost perfectly constant. The *second,* the basic unit of time in the metric system, is defined in terms of atomic vibrations using cesium beam oscillators; the "clocks" of various observatories and standards agencies are coordinated throughout the world by the International Time Bureau.

The steady, internationally adjusted time is termed *Coordinated Universal Time* (UTC). This time scale meets the needs of most users; it is the time broadcast as radio time signals. Somewhat surprisingly, however, this near-perfect time is not the best for some purposes. In applications such as very precise navigation and satellite tracking, which must be referenced to the *actual* rotation of the earth, a time scale that speeds up and slows down with the earth's rotation rate must be used. This time scale is known as *UT1* and is inferred from astronomical observations.

To be responsive to the needs of such users, information is included in UTC broadcasts for adjustment to UT1. This increment, which may be either positive or negative, is termed DUT1 and is measured in tenths of a second. The relationships are as follows: UT1 = UTC + DUT1. The techniques used in transmitting it are explained in Article 2228.

For the navigator, and others who only need time to the nearest second, and to prevent DUT1 corrections from reaching too large a value, UTC is corrected by occasional corrections of exactly one second—a "leap second." These adjustments are inserted into UTC whenever needed to keep UTC time signals within ±0.9 seconds of UT1 at all times. Ordinarily, a positive leap second is required about once a year, usually at the end of December or June depending upon how the earth's rotation rate is behaving for that year.

For users who require the precision of time to the tenth of a second, UT1 can be calculated by adding the DUT1 correction. GMT is essentially UT1, but the fraction of a second difference from UTC is normally ignored by navigators (except that the insertion of a leap second must be taken into account in the determination of chronometer rate).

Local mean time (LMT)

2211 Just as Greenwich Mean Time is mean solar time measured with reference to the meridian of Greenwich, so *local mean time* (LMT) is mean solar time measured with reference to a given local meridian; this is the kind of time discussed in Article 2208.

Local mean time was the standard generally used after the introduction of time based on a mean sun, and every city kept time based on the mean sun's transit of its meridian. As a result, a number of different time standards were used in a comparatively small geographic area. Before the days of modern electronic communications, and when physical travel was at the speed of a man, a horse, or the flow of a river, such disparities in time over relatively small areas were of no real importance. However, when electrical and mechanical developments made communications essentially instantaneous and transportation quite rapid, the differences in local times could no longer be tolerated; this led to the introduction of zone time.

Zone time (ZT)

2212 The introduction of *zone time* served to straighten out the confusion caused by the multiplicity of different local mean times in a given area. In zone time, all the places in a given zone, or band of longitude, keep the same time, based on the local mean time of a single specified meridian, frequently the central meridian of the zone. Timepieces are reset only when moving into an adjoining time zone; they are advanced an hour if travel is to the east, and retarded an hour if to the west.

As a general rule, these zones are laid out so that they are not excessively wide; therefore, at no given place in the zone will the ZT vary greatly from the LMT, and the time will be in reasonably good agreement with the motions of the sun. At sea, the zones are usually bands of longitude 15° in width.

On land, the boundaries between adjacent time zones are generally irregular, reflecting political boundaries and commercial influences; see Article 2215.

Zone description (ZD)

2213 In general, at sea the central meridians selected for time zones are longitudes which are exact multiples of 15°. There are 24 of these central or "standard" meridians, each one hour apart, and the longitude boundaries of each zone are 7½° on each side of the zone's standard meridian, as shown in Figure 2213a.

The *zone description* (ZD) of a zone is the *correction* to be applied to the time of that zone to obtain GMT. For example, between longitudes 7½° east and 7½° west, the ZD is zero, and GMT will be used throughout the zone. In the zone bordered by longitudes 7° 30′ E and 22° 30′ E, the standard meridian is λ 15° E. ZT in this zone will differ from GMT by one hour, and the zone being *east* of the meridian of Greenwich, it will be one hour *later*. One hour is *subtracted* from ZT to obtain GMT, and the ZD is (−1). Similarly, in the zone bordered by longitudes 7°30′ W and 22°30′ W, the ZT

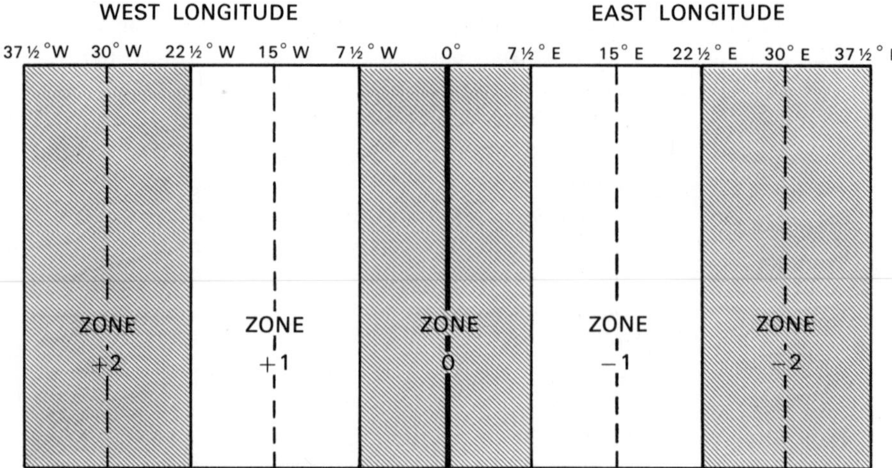

Figure 2213a. Time zone boundaries.

differs from GMT by one hour. But as this zone is *west* of Greenwich, it is one hour earlier, and the ZD is (+1), as one hour must be added to obtain GMT.

This procedure for determining the sign of time corrections for various zones is valid for any longitude; the sign of the ZD of any zone in *east* longitude is *minus,* and that of the ZD of any zone in *west* longitude is *plus.* The numerical value of the correction for a zone can be determined by dividing the longitude of its standard meridian by 15°. Thus, the zone having λ 135° W as its standard meridian will have a ZD of (+9), the zone having λ 75° E as its standard meridian will have a ZD description of (−5).

The ZD at a given position can be similarly determined. The longitude of the place is divided by 15°, and the whole number of the quotient is determined. If the remainder is less than 7°30′, the whole number quotient establishes the numerical value of the ZD; if it is greater than 7°30′, the numerical value of the ZD is one more than the whole number of the quotient. Thus in Lo 37°25.4′W, the ZD will be (+2), while in Lo 37°43.6′, the ZD will be (+3). These calculations refer to positions at sea where the zone boundaries are uniform; ashore, care must be taken with similar computations due to the frequently irregular boundaries of time zones.

Time zone plotter Figure 2213b illustrates one form of Time Zone Plotter. On this device, which would be more accurately described as a "computer," the time zones and their variations are shown for both hemispheres. There is also DMAHC Chart 76 which portrays this information on a Mercator chart of the world.

It will be noted that the 15°-wide zone centered on the 180th meridian is divided into two parts. The half in east longitude has a

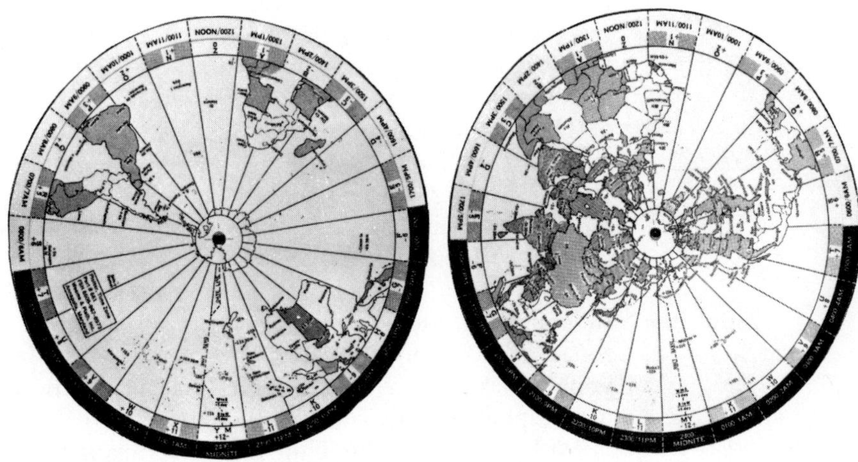

Figure 2213b. Time zone plotter.

ZD of (−12), and that in west longitude has a ZD of (+12). This division of the zone having the 180th meridian as its standard is necessitated by the convention of the *international date line*, discussed in Article 2217.

The letter designations shown in each time zone in Figure 2213b are those used by the U.S. Armed Forces in communications and operational planning for identification of the ZT in the various zones. These zone-descriptive letters have been widely adopted by other government and private activities. GMT (or Universal Time), which is zone time at Greenwich, is designated *Z* time. Zones to the east of Greenwich are designated alphabetically in order of increasing east longitude, commencing with *A*, and ending with *M*; the letter *J* is not used. Zones to the west of Greenwich are similarly designated, commencing with *N*, and ending with *Y* for the zone with ZD (+12). The use of these designations is discussed more fully in Article 2214.

Recording time and date in the Navy

2214 In Article 2205, the notation of time on a 24-hour basis in *navigation* was described, and it was stated that the navigator customarily worked and noted time to the nearest second; 23 hours, 14 minutes, and 21 seconds being written as 23-14-21.

For general use, the 24-hour clock is employed in the U.S. Armed Forces and by the civilian population in many foreign countries. Seconds are not needed and time is normally stated as a four-digit number without spaces; the first two representing the hours, from 00 to 24, and the latter two the minutes, from 00 to 59.

Hours and minutes less than ten are preceded by a zero, to maintain the four-digit system. Thus, 9:30 A.M. is written 0930, and 4:37 P.M. becomes 1637. When spoken, the former would be "oh-nine-thirty," and the latter "sixteen thirty-seven." Exact hours are said as "oh-five-hundred" or "seventeen hundred," for example. The times 1000 and 2000 are spoken "ten hundred" and "twenty hundred" respectively; not as "one thousand" or "two thousand." It is *incorrect* in nautical usage to add "hours" to the expression of time, as in "sixteen hundred hours."

The zone-description letters may be added to the four-digit statement of time. For example, a vessel off the east coast of the United States, keeping Eastern Standard Time (EST) could refer to the time of an event, for example, at "1715R"—*R* (Romeo) being the designator for zone (+5) which is EST.

Zulu time

In communications involving ships or activities in different time zones, it is common to use *Z*, or Greenwich Mean Time. This is popularly known as "Zulu Time," as Zulu is the international phonetic alphabet equivalent for the letter *Z*.

With the use of the Time Zone Plotter one can easily determine the time at any other location in the world. The time zone diagram is pivoted to rotate over the base of the instrument which contains a 24-hour time scale. Example: With the instrument set as in Figure 2213b, it is 0700 in Washington, D. C., Zone (+5). In Kodiak, Alaska, it is 0200, Zone (+10). In Tokyo it is 2100 the following day (Article 2216). If a message were received from a vessel near Kodiak with the time designation 0200W, it would be easy to convert this to time at any other location, by reading time on the base plate opposite the time zone description on the movable dial.

It is also frequently desirable in communications to indicate the date as well as time. This is accomplished by *prefixing* the time group, with its letter designator, with two digits which indicate the date of the current month. Thus, "121725 Z" would indicate a *date/time* of GMT 1725 on the 12th of the current month. If a month other than the current one is to be described, the date/time group with the appropriate designator is used, and the name of the desired month is added as a suffix. If a year other than the current one is to be indicated, it is indicated after the month. If the date/time example previously used were for May 1977, the full group would read 121725Z May 77.

Variations in zone description, standard and daylight saving time

2215 Zone time, based on uniform 15° bands of longitude, is a convenience at sea, but it can lead to complications on shore. For example, a city, or group of cities closely related by business ties, might lie astride the dividing line between zones. To avoid inconvenience to commerce and everyday life, such a territorial entity will often keep a single time that does not fully agree with the uniform zone system just described; boundaries between adjacent zones become quite irregular in many areas. This form of modified zone time is called *standard time.* In the 48 contiguous states of the U. S., it is designated as Eastern, Central, Mountain, and Pacific standard time. The "central" meridians of these zones are the 75°, 90°, 105°, and 125° of west longitude, respectively; the boundaries may be more or less than $7\frac{1}{2}$° from a central meridian. Similarly, a nation which overlaps into two or three time zones may choose to keep one single ZT throughout its territory, thus eliminating any time difference problem within the country (Figure 2213b).

Some places, for convenience, maintain a standard time which results in a ZD which is not a whole hour. The *Nautical Almanac,* under the heading "Standard Times," tabulates the zone descriptions used in many areas of the world; the list is kept corrected as new countries come into existence or changes in standard time are made. The use, however, of "daylight time" may in some situations affect the given ZT values.

Daylight time (DT), also called *daylight saving time* (DST) or *summer time*, is another variation of zone time. Due to the early rising of the sun in summer, a certain amount of daylight would be "lost" to most people if the ZD were not adjusted. To avoid this loss, in many areas it is customary to adopt the time of the next adjacent zone to the *east,* during the period DT is in effect. This results in sunrise and sunset occurring one hour later. Along the east coast of the United States, where the ZD is usually (+5), based on the 75th meridian, during daylight saving the ZD becomes (+4). Similarly, a place ordinarily using a ZD of (−9) might in summer advance its time so that the ZD is (−10).

Changing time and date aboard ship

2216 When a ship passes from one time zone into the next, it enters an area where it is desirable to keep a ZT differing by one hour from the previous one; if travel is towards the west, the ZT of the new zone will be one hour earlier than that of the old, and the ships clocks would be set back one hour. If the ship were traveling toward the east, the reverse would be true, and the clocks would be advanced one hour.

It is the navigator's duty to advise the captain when a new time zone is about to be entered; the latter will determine the time at which the ship's clocks will be reset. Zone time is used as a matter of convenience, and the time change is usually made with this in mind, to cause minimal dislocation of the ship's routine. The ZD does not change until the ZT is changed.

A ship steaming to the west sets its clocks back one hour in each new time zone; in a circumnavigation of the earth, it would therefore "lose" 24 hours. Conversely, if it were steaming around the world in an easterly direction it would "gain" 24 hours in circling the globe. A method adjusting for the day lost or gained is necessary, and this is described in the following article.

International Date Line

2217 The *International Date Line* follows the 180th meridian, with some offsets or variations so that it does not bisect an inhabited territory. The adjustment to the date is made at some convenient time before or after the vessel crosses the date line. If a vessel has been steaming *east,* its clocks have been steadily advanced, and this is compensated for by *reducing* the date one day. Conversely, a vessel steaming *west* has been setting back its clocks, so that the date is *advanced* one day. This date change is made by every vessel crossing the date line, regardless of the length of the voyage.

The change of date accounts for the two zone descriptions associated with the 15° band of longitude centered on the 180th meridian. That part of the zone in west longitude has a ZD of (+12), and that part in east longitude has a ZD of (−12). The ZT is the same throughout the zone, but the date is *one day later* in the half which is in east longitude than it is in the half which is in west longitude. For example, aboard a ship in λ 175° W at 0900 ZT on 3 February, GMT is determined to be 2100, 3 February, by applying the ZD of (+12). At the same instant, aboard a ship in λ 175° E,

ZT is 0900 on 4 February; by applying the ZD (−12), GMT is also found to be 2100, 3 February.

The date line is used as a convenience, just as zone time is used as a convenience, and the change of date is made in the area of the date line at a time when the ship's routine will be disturbed as little as possible. Frequently, it is convenient to change the date at the midnight falling closest to the time the ship crosses the date line. However, it would generally be considered undesirable either to repeat a Sunday or a holiday, or to drop one. Under such conditions, ships have found it convenient to operate for a period using a ZD of either (+13), or (−13). Regardless of when the line is crossed, the *sign* of the ZD remains unchanged until the date is changed.

To sum up: all changes in time and date are made solely for the purpose of convenience. The value of the zone time and the date used aboard ship are of comparatively little importance in themselves; what is important is that the navigator be able to determine the time and date at Greenwich, so that he can obtain the coordinates of celestial bodies from the almanac. Also, navigators should remember that the day which is added or subtracted when crossing the date line has *no effect on the Greenwich date.*

Using the time diagram

2218 In practical navigation, a navigator is concerned with using the preceding information on time to determine the GMT and date. The time diagram, introduced in Article 2207, is generally drawn roughly by the navigator for each celestial problem to assist in visualizing the problem. Since GMT is used, the Greenwich meridian is used on the diagram at an angular distance appropriate for the observer's longitude, east or clockwise from *M* if he is in west longitude, and west of *M*, if his longitude is east. The upper branch of the Greenwich meridian is drawn as a solid line and is labeled *G*, and the lower branch as a broken line and labeled *g*.

Figure 2218a shows on the left a time diagram for an observer in λ 60° W, with a ZT of about 1800. On the right, it shows a ZT of about 1800 for an observer in λ 15° E.

Since the sun is the basis of GMT as well as ZT, the approximate GMT can also be determined from a time diagram. In the time diagram in Figure 2218a, with the observer at λ 60° W, the sun (⊙) is approximately 90° west of the upper branch of the observer's meridian, *M,* and 150° or 10 hours west of the upper branch of the Greenwich meridian *G*; the GMT is therefore approximately 2200. Similarly, in the diagram at the right in this figure with the observer at λ 15° E, the sun is about 90° or six hours west of the local meridian *M,* but it is only about 75° or five hours west of the upper branch of the Greenwich meridian, *G*; the GMT is therefore about 1700. In this case, the sun will be at *g* in seven hours, which will signal the start of the next day for Greenwich.

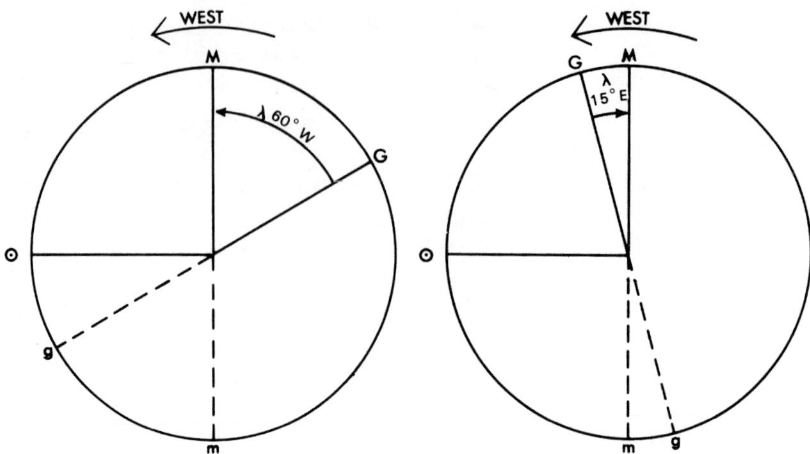

Figure 2218a. East and west longitude shown on a time diagram.

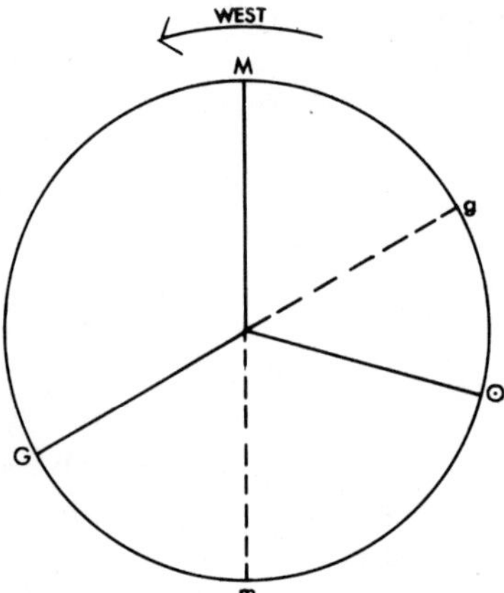

Figure 2218b. Time diagram illustrating a change in date.

The time diagram is particularly helpful when the date at the observer's meridian differs from that at another meridian, such as Greenwich. The time diagram in Figure 2218b shows an observer in λ 115° E, at approximately 0500 ZT. Here the sun has already passed the lower branch of the observer's meridian *m*, and a new day has begun for him. At this moment the sun must travel approximately 40°, or some 2 hours and 40 minutes, before it transits the lower branch of the meridian of Greenwich to start the new day there; the date at Greenwich is therefore *the day preceding* the date for the observer at *M*. Thus, if it is ZT 0500, 10 January, for the observer at *M*, the GMT is 2200, January 9.

A difference in dates is readily apparent when a time diagram is used, as *the dates at two meridians are always different if the sun's hour circle* falls between their lower branches, and the meridian whose lower branch is to the west of the sun's hour circle will always have the earlier date.

Zone Time (ZT) and Greenwich Mean Time (GMT)

2219 Zone time differs from Greenwich Mean Time by the zone description.

To correct ZT to GMT, apply the ZD to ZT with the *sign as shown.*

To convert GMT to ZT, apply the ZD to GMT with the *opposite sign.*

These conversions are illustrated in the following examples.

Example 1: A navigator aboard a ship at longitude 156°19.5′E observes the sun at 16-36-14 ZT on 26 April.

Required: GMT and date at the time of the observation.

Solution: First record the name of the body, the date based on ZT, and the ZT of the observation. Then sketch on a time diagram the relative positions of the observer, Greenwich, and the sun, to assist in visualizing the problem. Next, note the ZD of the time being kept aboard the ship (longitude divided by 15° as described in Article 2213). The ZD is (−)10 ("minus" because the observer is in east longitude; "10" because 156°19.5′ ÷ 15° = 10, remainder less than 7°30′). Then apply the ZD to ZT in accordance with its sign to determine GMT. Finally, record the date at Greenwich, which in this case is the same as the local date.

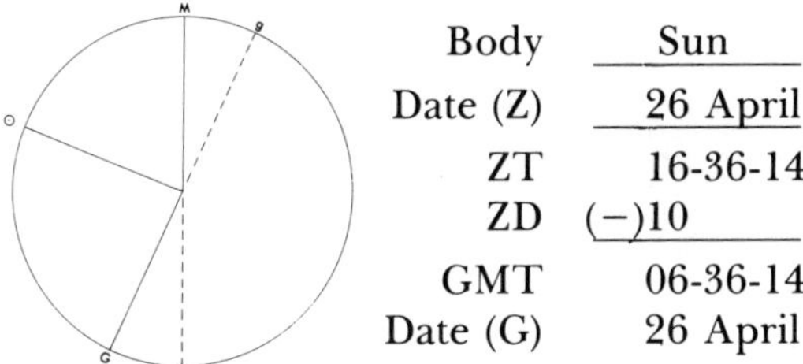

Body	Sun
Date (Z)	26 April
ZT	16-36-14
ZD	(−)10
GMT	06-36-14
Date (G)	26 April

Answer: GMT 06-36-14 on 26 April.

Example 2: A navigator aboard a ship at longitude 83°17.9′ W observes the star Arcturus at 19-15-29 ZT on 14 June.

Required: GMT and date at the time of the observation.

Solution: First record the name of the body, the date based upon ZT, and the ZT. Then sketch on a time diagram the relative positions of the observer, Greenwich, and the sun, to assist in visualizing the problem. Next, note the ZD, (if necessary, dividing the longitude by 15°, to the nearest whole number). The ZD is (+)6—("plus" because the observer is in west longitude; "6" because 83°17.9′ ÷ 15° = 5, remainder more than 7°30′). Then apply the ZD to ZT in accordance with its sign to determine GMT. Finally, record the date at Greenwich, which in this case is one day later than the local date—the sun has passed the Greenwich lower meridian (g) signaling the start of a new date there; it has not passed the lower branch of the local meridian which changes the local date.

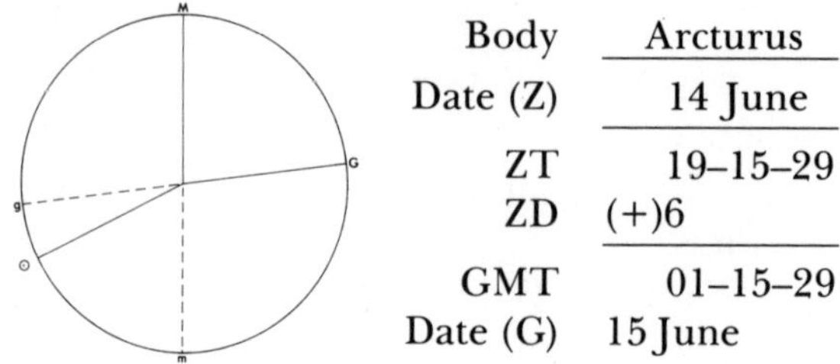

Body	Arcturus
Date (Z)	14 June
ZT	19–15–29
ZD	(+)6
GMT	01–15–29
Date (G)	15 June

Answer: GMT 01-15-29 on 15 June.

The relationship between Zone Time and Greenwich Mean Time can also be remembered by the following phrases:

Longitude west, Greenwich time best
Longitude east, Greenwich time least

in which "best" means greater and "least" means lesser.

Zone Time (ZT) and Local Mean Time (LMT)

2220 *Local mean time* (LMT) differs from zone time by the difference of longitude (dLo), expressed as time, between the meridian of the observer and the standard meridian of the zone. Local mean time is primarily of interest to the navigator in determining the zone time of phenomena such as sunrise and set, and moonrise and set.

If the observer is *east* of the central meridian of his zone, the phenomenon will occur for him before it will happen at the zone's central meridian. Conversely, if he is *west* of the standard meridian the phenomenon will occur *later,* and LMT at his position will be earlier than ZT.

The following examples will serve to clarify the use of LMT, and its relationship to ZT.

Example 1: The navigator of a ship at longitude 117°19.4′ W determines from the almanac that sunrise is at LMT 0658 on 26 October. (The times of phenomena such as sunrise are given in the almanacs only to the nearest minute.)

Required: ZT of sunrise and local date.

Solution: First, record the name of the phenomenon, the date based on LMT, and the LMT of the event. Then sketch on a time diagram the relative positions of the observer, the sun, and the central meridian of the time zone (Z-z), to assist in visualizing the problem. Next determine the difference in longitude (DLo) between the meridian of the observer and the central meridian of the zone, and convert to units of time, to the nearest minute. In this example the central meridian of the zone is 120° W (nearest whole multiple of 15°) and DLo equals 2°40.6′. Converting this value to time units by the rules of Article 2208, DLo equals 11 minutes (to the nearest minute). (A table for DLo time-units conversion is in each volume of the *Tide Tables.*) As the observer is east of the zone's central meridian, ZT is earlier than LMT, and the DLo, in time units, must be subtracted from LMT to obtain ZT.

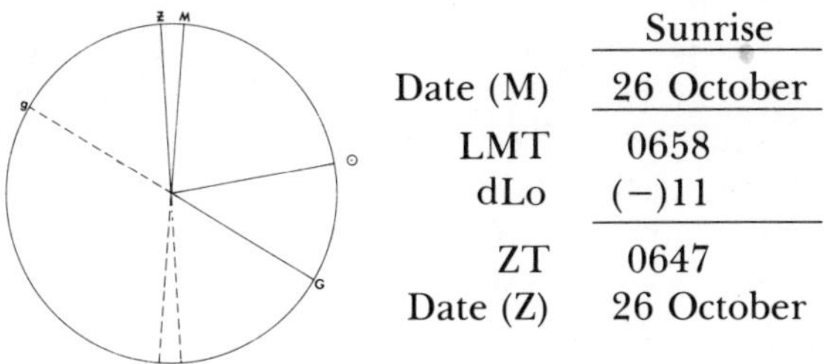

	Sunrise
Date (M)	26 October
LMT	0658
dLo	(−)11
ZT	0647
Date (Z)	26 October

Answer: ZT 0647 on 26 October.

Example 2: The navigator of a ship at longitude 38°58.5′ E determines from the almanac that moonset is at LMT 2347 on 26 January.

Required: ZT of moonset, including local date.

Solution: First record the phenomenon, the date based upon LMT, and the LMT of the phenomenon. Then sketch on a time diagram the relative positions of the observer, the central meridian of the zone, and the sun, to assist in visualizing the problem. Next, determine the difference of longitude between the meridian of the observer and that of the central meridian of the zone and convert to time units, to the nearest minute. In this case, the central meridian of the zone is 45° E and DLo equals 6°01.5′. Converting this to time units, DLo equals 24 minutes (to the nearest minute). Since the observer is west of the central meridian, ZT is later than LMT, and the DLo value must be added to LMT to obtain ZT.

Finally, record the date in the zone, which in this case is one day later than the date based upon LMT.

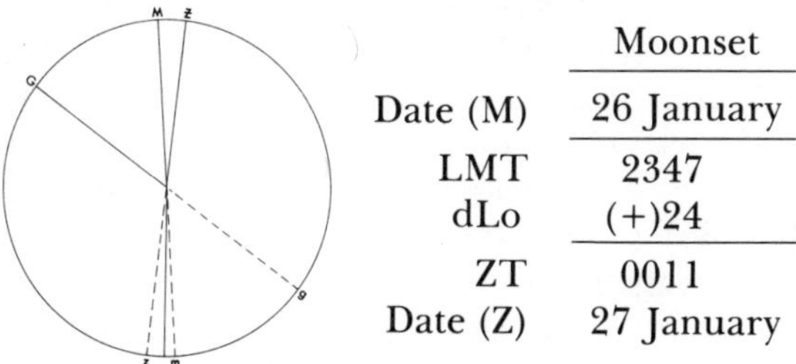

	Moonset
Date (M)	26 January
LMT	2347
dLo	(+)24
ZT	0011
Date (Z)	27 January

Answer: ZT 0011 on 27 January.

In the practice of modern navigation, the navigator ordinarily has little occasion to convert ZT to LMT.

Chronometers **2221** The keeping of accurate time aboard ship was impossible until the invention of the chronometer by John Harrison in the early eighteenth century. Hour or sand glasses were satisfactory for establishing the length of the watch aboard ship, but were useless for sustained time keeping. Probably the best shipboard timekeeper before the eighteenth century was the compass. Many compasses were designed especially for this purpose, with a vertical pin at the center of the card. The compass card was in effect a sundial, and the pin was the gnomon.

The chronometer was important because it was sufficiently accurate to permit determining longitude afloat. The sextant offered both convenience and accuracy in measuring altitudes, not only of the sun, but also of the moon, planets, and stars. Until about 1880, it was the general practice to compute position by the time sight method. A latitude was obtained from an observation of Polaris or of the sun's transit. This latitude was carried forward by dead reckoning and used in determining longitude by a subsequent observation; latitude and longitude were both calculated, rather than being determined from plotting lines of position (LOPs) on a chart, as is done today.

A traditional chronometer is a very accurate spring-driven timepiece, usually about 4 or 5 inches in diameter, mounted in a heavy brass case, which is supported in gimbals in a wooden case. The gimbals take up much of the ship's motion, so that the chronometer remains in a nearly horizontal position. The wooden case is usually mounted in a very heavily padded second case, designed to give maximum protection against shock, and sudden fluctuations of temperature. Chronometers are usually fitted with a detent escapement, and they beat, or tick, half-seconds, as compared to the five beats per second of most watches. This slow beat is of great convenience when comparing the instrument with radio time signals or other timepieces.

The great majority of chronometers have a 12-hour dial, see Figure 2221; a few instruments have been produced which have a 24-hour face. A "winding indicator," showing how many hours have elapsed since the instrument was wound, is universally employed. Most chronometers will run for 56 hours before running down, although 8-day models have been produced. However, *it is essential that the instrument be wound at the same time every day.*

Marine chronometers are almost invariably set to GMT; they may, however, be adjusted to keep sidereal time. They are never reset aboard ship; once the chronometer is started, the setting of the hands is not changed until it is scheduled for cleaning and overhaul. Due to the design of the escapement, a fully-wound mechanical chronometer will not start of its own accord. When a chronometer is to be started, the hands are set to the appropriate hour and minute of GMT. When the elapsed seconds of GMT agree with the second hand on the chronometer, the chronometer case is given a brisk horizontal turn through about 45°, and immediately turned back to its original position; this will start the movement.

The time indicated by the chronometer is chronometer time (C).

Quartz chronometers A development of modern science is the *quartz chronometer* in which a tiny quartz crystal is used to stabilize the frequency of an electronic

Figure 2221. Mechanical chronometer (Hamilton).

oscillator. The stability of these newer chronometers far surpasses that of older mechanical designs; kept at a reasonably constant temperature, they are capable of maintaining an excellent rate with the better models having a deviation of less than 0.01 seconds from their average daily rate which should not exceed 0.2 seconds per day. Many models have a sweep-second hand that can be advanced or retarded electronically in increments of one-tenth or one-hundredth of a second while the chronometer is running.

These quartz chronometers are powered by small "flashlight" batteries and thus do not require winding. They are highly resistant to shock and vibration and do not require gimbals; they may be mounted in a traditional box or on a bulkhead.

Quartz wristwatches A quartz-controlled movement is also used in most higher-quality wristwatches. Although the accuracy achieved will probably not be as great as that of a quartz chronometer, it is normally adequate for practical navigation, especially if certain precautions are taken. A uniform "environment" should be established for the watch, such as always wearing it, or always not wearing it and keeping it in the same protected place, or wearing it a consistent number of hours each day. Before such a timepiece is used for navigation, its time should be regularly compared to time of known accuracy (radio time signals or a chronometer) for a sufficient period to establish both the amount and stability of its *rate*; see Article 2224.

A useful feature found on many quartz wristwatches is an indication of the day of the month. If such a calender watch is set to Greenwich time *and date,* one calculation (and possible error) can be eliminated. Care must be taken with ordinary watch dials as to whether GMT is between 00 and 12 or between 13 and 24 hours, but this is easily worked out mentally by adding the ZD to the hours of local time. Most such watches will require a manual adjustment at the end of a month having less than 31 days in it.

Atomic time standards on board ship

With the ever-expanding use of highly sophisticated inertial and radionavigation systems and computers, there are more and more ships at sea equipped with their own atomic time standard. U.S. naval vessels, particularly nuclear-powered, missile-launching submarines, are often equipped with one or more cesium- or rubidium-beam devices for time information that are orders of magnitude more precise than mechanical or quartz chronometers. With on-board time data of such extreme accuracy, equipment and systems can be synchronized independently with signals received from land-based or satellite transmitters.

Errors in timepieces

2222 All timepieces are subject to certain errors, and at any given time every timepiece probably will indicate a time which is somewhat fast or slow with respect to the correct time.

If the *error* (E) of a timepiece is *fast* (F), meaning that the time indicated is later than the correct time, the amount of error must be *subtracted* to obtain the correct time. If the error is *slow* (S), meaning that the time indicated is earlier than the correct time, the amount of error must be *added* to obtain the correct time.

Watch error (WE) is the difference between the indication of a watch and the correct time at any instant. *Watch rate* is the amount by which a watch gains or loses in a specified time, usually 24 hours.

Chronometer error

2223 The difference between chronometer time and GMT at any instant is called *chronometer error* (CE), labeled (F) or (S) as the chronometer is fast or slow on the correct (Greenwich) time. Since chronometers are not reset aboard ship, the accumulated error may become quite large. This is not important if the error is accurately known.

Chronometer error is usually determined by means of a radio time signal; see Article 2228. The chronometer may be compared directly, or a watch may be used to avoid moving the chronometer.

Example 1: On 31 October, the navigator of a ship at λ 138° 36.6′ W desires to determine the chronometer error by means of a radio time signal, by direct comparison. A time signal at 2000 UTC is used; at the moment of the "tick," the chronometer read 7-46-27.

Required: The chronometer error on GMT.

Solution:

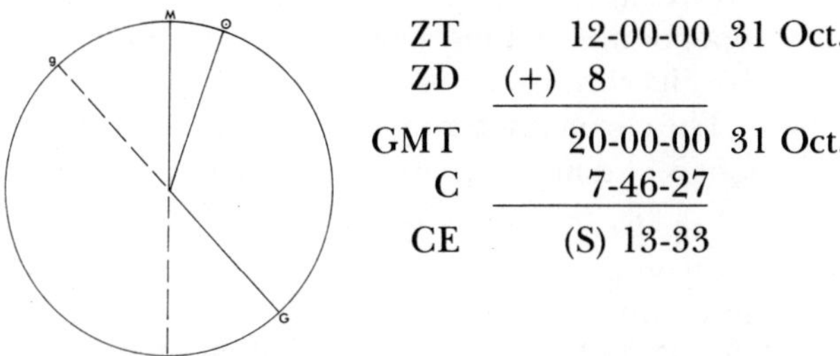

ZT	12-00-00	31 Oct.
ZD	(+) 8	
GMT	20-00-00	31 Oct.
C	7-46-27	
CE	(S) 13-33	

Answer: The chronometer is 13^m33^s slow on GMT.

Note that the GMT is 20^h, while the chronometer reads 7-46-27. The CE shown is correct, since the chronometer face is graduated to only 12^h. Hence, at GMT 20^h, the time in Greenwich is 8 P.M., as indicated approximately by the chronometer.

Example: On 10 July, the navigator of a ship at 46°30.4′ W longitude desires to obtain the chronometer error from a radio signal. A comparing watch, set approximately to ZT (+3), is used in the radio room to note the watch time of the signal. A time signal for 1700 UTC is used. At the moment of the tick, the comparing watch reads 2-01-30 P.M. A little later the comparing watch reads 2-04-20 P.M. at the instant the chronometer reads 4-38-00.

Required: The chronometer error on GMT.

Solution:

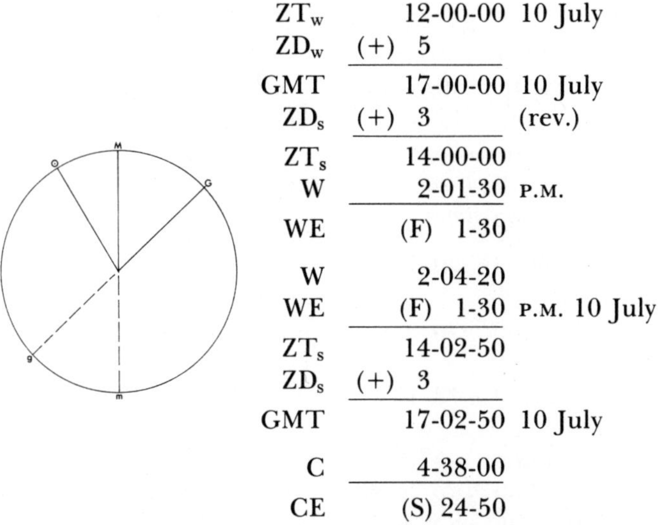

ZT_w	12-00-00	10 July
ZD_w	(+) 5	
GMT	17-00-00	10 July
ZD_s	(+) 3	(rev.)
ZT_s	14-00-00	
W	2-01-30	P.M.
WE	(F) 1-30	
W	2-04-20	
WE	(F) 1-30	P.M. 10 July
ZT_s	14-02-50	
ZD_s	(+) 3	
GMT	17-02-50	10 July
C	4-38-00	
CE	(S) 24-50	

Answer: The chronometer is 24^m50^s slow on GMT.

Chronometer rate **2224** The *rate* of a timepiece is the amount it gains or loses in a specified time. It is usually expressed as seconds and tenths of seconds per day, and is labeled "gaining" or "losing." Temperature is the main factor affecting fine timepieces; in general, their rates will increase with rising temperatures.

The nearly constant rate of a fine chronometer is its most important feature, as it makes safe navigation possible on a long voyage without dependence on time signals. While the rate should be as small as possible, its consistency is more important.

The chronometer rate is determined by comparison with radio time signals obtained several days apart.

Example 1: A navigator, desiring to determine the chronometer rate, compares the chronometer directly with a radio time signal at the same time on different days. On 6 April the chronometer reads 5-25-05 and on 16 April it reads 5-25-51.

Required: The chronometer error on each date and chronometer rate.

Solution:

ZT	12-00-00	6 April	GMT	17-00-00	16 April
ZD	(+) 5		C	5-25-51	
GMT	17-00-00	6 April	CE	(F) 25-51	16 April
C	5-25-05		CE	(F) 25-05	6 April
CE	(F) 25-05	6 April	diff.	46	
			rate	4.6	gaining

Answers: CE on 6 April is 25^m05^s fast on GMT. CE on 16 April is 25^m51^s fast on GMT. Chronometer rate over a ten-day period has been 4.6^s per day, gaining.

The chronometer rate provides a means of determining the chronometer error at any instant between time signals.

Example 2: At 1620 on 2 December the DR λ of a ship is 147°40.6′ W when the navigator prepares to observe the sun. He compares his watch with a chronometer which was 17^m27^s fast on GMT at ZT 1200 (when the ship was keeping (+5) zone time on 20 November. The chronometer rate is 0.7^s gaining.

Required: The chronometer error.

Solution:

ZT	12-00-00	20 Nov.		CE	(F) 17-27	20 Nov.
ZD	(+) 5			corr.	(+) 9	(12.4 × 0.7)
GMT	17-00-00	20 Nov.		CE	(F) 17-36	2 Dec.
ZT	16-20-00	2 Dec.		*Answer:* CE on 2 Dec. is 17^m36^s fast on GMT.		
ZD	(+)10					
GMT	2-20-00	3 Dec.				
GMT	17-00-00	20 Nov.				
Elapsed time	9-20-00 + 12	days				
	= 12.4 days					

Chronometer record

2225 The *Navigation Timepiece Rate Book* is issued to every U. S. naval vessel; it permits maintenance of complete records on three chronometers or other timepieces. These data include the daily error and the daily rate; each page has space for 31 daily entries. A portion of a sample page is reproduced in Figure 2225.

Complete instructions for the care, winding, and transportation of chronometers are given in the Navigation Timepiece Rate Book. An officer assuming navigational duty should familiarize himself with these instructions, as well as with pertinent information contained in an *OpNav Instruction*.

The standard chronometer in the Navy is returned to a chronometer pool every three years for cleaning, lubrication, and any other work that may be necessary.

It is the custom in the U. S. Navy for the senior quartermaster to wind the chronometers and check the rates every day at about 1130. This is reported to the officer of the deck, who in turn advises the captain that "the chronometers have been wound and compared" as part of the routine 1200 report.

Procedures on non-naval vessels will be less formal, but they should be carried out systematically in order that correct time will always be available for navigation and other purposes.

Comparing watch

2226 A *comparing watch* is a watch employed to time celestial observations, and to assist in checking a chronometer against a radio time signal. It is also sometimes called a *hack watch.* A good quality *split-second timer* makes the best comparing watch. It has two sweep second hands, one directly below the other, which can be started and stopped together, by means of a push button, usually mounted in the center of the winding stem. A second push button stops the lower of the two sweephands, permitting an accurate readout. When this button is

DATE	A					B					C					OBSERVATION	
YEAR 1977	MAKE HAMILTON; TYPE SC; SERIAL NO. 4327					MAKE HAMILTON; TYPE SC; SERIAL NO. 1278					MAKE HAMILTON; TYPE GCW; SERIAL NO. 843						
MONTH July	ERROR RELATIVE TO G.C.T. + = FAST − = SLOW			SUCCESSIVE DAILY RATES		ERROR RELATIVE TO G.C.T. + = FAST − = SLOW			SUCCESSIVE DAILY RATES		ERROR RELATIVE TO G.C.T. + = FAST − = SLOW			SUCCESSIVE DAILY RATES		LOCAL TIME TO NEAREST MINUTE	
DAY	±	MIN.	SECONDS	±	SECONDS	±	MIN.	SECONDS	±	SECONDS	±	MIN.	SECONDS	±	SECONDS	TIME	INITIALS
1	+	1	4.5		.	−	2	4.6		.	+	12	42.4		.	1155	[illegible]
2	+	1	6.0	+	1.5	−	2	3.8	+	0.8	+	12	40.0	−	2.4	1205	[illegible]
3	+	1	7.5	+	1.5	−	2	3.0	+	0.8	+	12	37.5	−	2.5	1140	[illegible]
4	+	1	9.0	+	1.5	−	2	2.2	+	0.8	+	12	35.1	−	2.4	1135	[illegible]
5	+	1	10.6	+	1.6	−	2	1.4	+	0.8	+	12	32.7	−	2.4	1120	[illegible]
6	+	1	12.1	+	1.5	−	2	0.5	+	0.9	+	12	30.2	−	2.5	1200	[illegible]

Figure 2225. Page extract, filled in, from *Navigation Timepiece Book* (NavSEC 9846/2).

pushed again, the stopped hand catches up with the running hand. These watches are also fitted with a small dial to indicate the elapsed time after the continuously running sweep hand was started.

Lacking a split-second timer, any fine watch with a sweep second hand makes a good comparing watch, as it facilitates reading time to the nearest second. A standard *stopwatch* may be used to advantage for this purpose.

Every watch used as a comparing watch should be checked regularly to determine that it will run free of appreciable error for the period of its normal maximum use; ordinarily this would be about 60 minutes.

A comparing watch can also be used in the determination of chronometer error and rate.

Second-setting watch

A *second-setting watch* also makes a satisfactory comparing watch. In these watches, the hour, minute, and second hand are all mounted concentrically; the hour hand usually reads out to 24 hours. On this type of watch, the second hand is stopped when the winding stem is pulled out, and the hour and minute hands can then be set to any desired time by turning the stem. When the stem is pushed back in, the watch is restarted. This type of watch may be set very accurately by means of a radio time tick. Other models combine the features of keeping GMT with a stopwatch mechanism and are referred to as navigational time and stopwatches. Due to the ready availability of the radio time tick for checking purposes, many smaller vessels and seagoing recreational craft do not carry a marine chronometer but depend on a high-quality watch or a mounted chronometer watch, plus radio time signals.

Timing celestial observations

2227 The coordinates of celestial bodies are tabulated with respect to GMT and date; it is therefore necessary that the navigator know the GMT and Greenwich date of each celestial observation. This is accomplished most simply by using a timepiece set precisely to GMT, and noting the time at the instant of each observation. This is far superior to using a watch set either to zone or chronometer time, as it both speeds the operation, and reduces the hazard of error.

A split-second timer, or lacking such, a stopwatch, should be used for celestial observations. The watch should, if possible, be started against a radio time signal (see Article 2228), using the tick which marks any exact minute; the GMT and Greenwich date at which the watch was started should be noted. If a radio time signal is unavailable, the watch should be started against the best chronometer. To do this, the local time zone description is applied to the ship's time to determine the Greenwich date, and whether the time there is A.M. or P.M. The updated chronometer error is then determined. The chronometer error must be applied to the chronometer time, *with the opposite sign*, in order to obtain GMT. With the error known, the watch

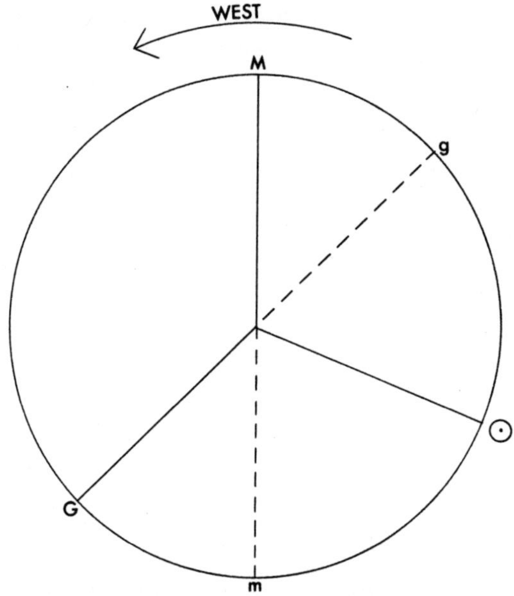

Figure 2227. Time diagram for a celestial observation with a stopwatch.
Ship's time and date 0543(-10) 7 April
GMT time and date 1943 6 April
Chronometer error + (fact) 2 min 41.5 sec
At GMT 19-45-00, a chronometer with a 12-hour dial will read
7 hours, 47 minutes, 41.5 seconds, and the comparing watch is started at this chronometer reading.

is started at the proper time. This procedure is illustrated in the following example.

Morning star observations are to be obtained, and the recorder's watch is to be started on a 5-minute increment of GMT. The ship's clocks are set to Zone (−10) time. (Calculations are shown in Figure 2227.)

TIME SIGNALS

Radio time signals

2228 *Radio time signals,* often called time ticks, are broadcast from many stations throughout the world. Complete information on the time signals of all countries is given in *Radio Navigational Aids,* DMAHC Publications No. 117A and 117B, and in various publications of the U. S. Naval Observatory and the National Bureau of Standards, an activity of the Department of Commerce.

The signals most commonly used by United States vessels are broadcast from the Bureau of Standards radio stations WWV at Fort Collins, Colorado, from WWVH on the island of Kauai, Hawaii, and from U. S. Navy stations in the United States, Canal Zone, and Australia. These signals have an accuracy far greater than is required for ordinary navigation.

Stations WWV and WWVH WWV and WWVH broadcast time signals continuously during each day. Frequencies and radiated power in kilowatts are as follows:

Frequency mHz	*Radiated power, kW.*	
	WWV	*WWVH*
2.5	2.5	5
5	10	10
10	10	10
15	10	10

The selection of frequency for best reception will depend on the time of day, and on atmospheric conditions. As a general rule, the 15 mHz band is satisfactory during the daylight hours, while the 5 mHz band is usually better at night.

Each second is marked by an audible "tick" (a 5-millisecond pulse of standard double-sideband amplitude modulation); however, the 29th and 59th seconds are not marked by a tick. Once each minute, time is announced by voice in the last 15 seconds of the minute. The two stations are distinguished by a female voice from WWVH between 15 and 7½ seconds before the minute, and a male voice from WWV between 7½ and 0 seconds before the minute. The time is stated as Coordinated Universal Time, which for ordinary navigational purposes can be used as GMT; see Article 2210. The format of the time announcement is the same from both stations; for example, just before 0310 UTC, the announcement, which is recorded, would be "At the tone, three hours, ten minutes, Coordinated Universal Time."

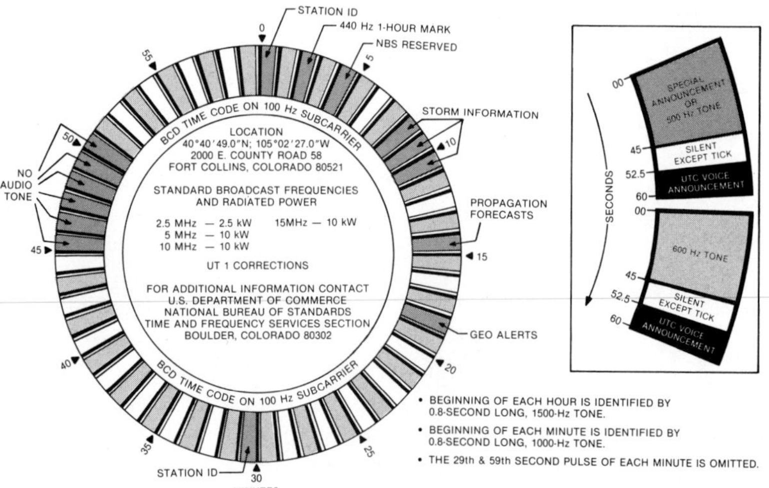

Figure 2228a. Signals from WWV.

The first pulse of each minute is longer, 800 milliseconds, for emphasis. The first pulse of each *hour* is further emphasized by being of a higher frequency (1500 Hz). The exact time is indicated by the *beginning* of each pulse. Pulses are transmitted in exact synchronization by WWV and WWVH, but propagation delays may result in their being received very slightly out of step if both stations are being heard at the same time.

Audio tones In alternate minutes during most of each hour, 500 or 600 Hz audio tones are broadcast. A 440 Hz tone, the musical note *A* above middle *C*, is broadcast once each hour. In addition to being a musical standard, the 400 Hz tone can be used to provide an hourly marker for chart recorders or other automated devices.

"Silent" periods There are "silent periods" with no tone modulation. However, the carrier frequency, seconds pulses, and time announcements continue. The main silent periods extend from 45 to 51 minutes after the hour on WWV and from 15 to 20 minutes after the hour on WWVH. An additional 3-minute period from 8 to 11 minutes after the hour is silent on WWVH.

Weather information on time broadcasts Weather information about major storms in the Atlantic and eastern North Pacific are broadcast in voice from WWV at 8, 9, and 10 minutes after each hour. Similar storm warnings covering the eastern and central North Pacific are given from WWVH at 48, 49, and 50 minutes after each hour. An additional segment (at 11 minutes after the hour on WWV and at 51 minutes on WWVH) may be used when there are unusually widespread storm conditions. These brief messages are designed to tell mariners of storm threats in their areas. If there are no

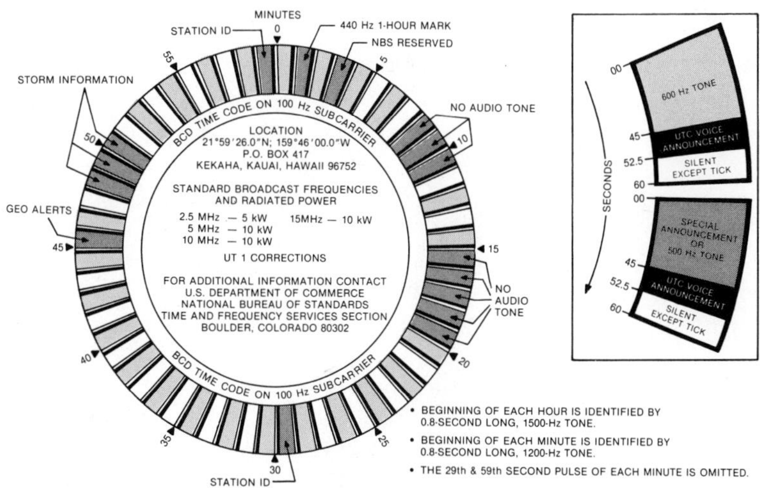

Figure 2228b. Signals from WWVH.

warnings in the designated areas, the broadcasts will so indicate. The ocean areas involved are those for which the U.S. has warning responsibility under international agreement. The regular times of issue by the National Weather Service are 0500, 1100, 1700, and 2300 UTC for WWV and 0000, 0600, 1200, and 1800 UTC for WWVH. These broadcasts are updated effective with the next scheduled announcement following the time of issue.

Using WWV and WWVH time signals

The signals broadcast from WWV and WWVH are in very useful form for the navigator. The tick transmitted every second is most useful for starting a stopwatch accurately. By beating every second with the incoming signal for about the final 15 seconds of the minute, with a little practice it is possible to start a stopwatch without a readable error; that is, with an error of less than one-fifth of a second.

If UT1 accuracy is required, the DUT1 correction may be noted and applied. This correction, in units of 0.1 second to a maximum of 0.8 second, are encoded into the broadcasts by using double ticks or pulses after the start of each minute. The 1st through the 8th ticks, when doubled, indicate a "plus" correction; doubled 9th through 16th ticks indicate a "minus" correction. For example, if the 1st, 2nd, and 3rd ticks are doubled, the correction is "plus" 0.3 seconds: UT1 = UTC + 0.3; if UTC is 08-45-17, then UT1 is 08-45-17.3. If the 9th, 10th, 11th, and 12th seconds had been doubled, the correction would have been "minus" 0.4 second and, in the above example, UT1 = 08-45-16.6.

Broadcasts by WWV and WWVH also contain information regarding radio propagation forecasts, geophysical alerts, and official announcements by federal agencies.

Navy time signals

U. S. Navy radio stations such as NAM (Norfolk, Virginia) and NPG (near San Francisco), broadcast time signals on varying frequencies from 22 to more than 21,000 kHz; occasionally other stations may also broadcast time signals. These transmissions are not continuous; frequencies and times are published in *Radio Navigation Aids*, DMAHC Pub. No. 117A and 117B. There are no voice announcements; time signals are transmitted each second of the minutes on-the-air except for the 29th second and those indicated in Figure 2228c. The beginning of each dash indicates the beginning of a second; the ends of the dashes are without significance. The seconds marked "60" in the figure are the zero seconds of the following minutes. DUT1 corrections are transmitted in Morse Code each minute during the interval between seconds 56 to 59.

Station CHU

Continuous time signals are broadcast by the Canadian station CHU, on 3,330, 7,335, and 14,670 kHz. Using single-sideband (A3H) modulation, voice announcements of the upcoming minute and hour of Eastern Standard Time (ZD+5) are made both in English and French. The 29th second tick is omitted, as are the 51st to 59th; during this

55	-		--	--	--	--					--
56	--	--		--	--	--					--
57	--	--	--		--	--					--
58	--	--	--	--		--					--
59	--										---

(1) The dashes indicate the seconds on which signals are transmitted.

(2) The seconds marked "60" are the zero seconds of the following minutes.

(3) The signals at the end of the transmissions, i.e., on the beginning of the hour or at the beginning of the half hour, are much longer than the others.

(4) In all cases the beginning of each dash indicates the beginning of a second.

(5) The ends of the dashes are without significance.

Figure 2228c. Coding of time signals from U.S. Navy radio stations.

latter period the voice announcement is made. These transmissions can be very useful to vessels off the Atlantic coast of North America.

Time signals of other nations Many foreign nations around the world broadcast time signals on a wide variety of frequencies and schedules; identifying information is given in some cases by Morse code and in other instances in voice. Details will be found in Pubs. No. 117A and 117B; changes are published in *Notices to Mariners.*

Time from Loran-C and Omega signals The pulsed signals of Loran-C and Omega electronic navigation systems are precisely timed to atomic standards. Highly accurate time information can be obtained from these transmissions, but this requires access to published technical data; in addition, coarse time information must be known as no identification of seconds or minutes is transmitted.

Time from NAVSAT signals A time check can also be obtained from the pulse, or "beep," at the end of each navigational satellite (Transit) transmission.

Summary **2229** The navigator makes direct use of three different kinds of time. These are Greenwich mean time, GMT; local mean time, LMT; and zone time, ZT. (Coordinated Universal Time, UTC, may be used for GMT in practical navigation applications.) All three are based upon the motions of the fictitious "mean sun." The mean sun is considered to revolve about the earth at the average rate of the apparent sun, making one complete revolution in 24 hours.

Solar time The reckoning of time is based upon the motion of the sun relative to a given meridian, the time being 2400–0000 at lower transit and 1200 at upper transit. In Greenwich mean time, the reference meridian is that of Greenwich; in local mean time, the reference meridian is that of a given place; in zone time, the reference meridian is the standard meridian of a given zone.

Sidereal time Article 1809 explained why the *sidereal day,* which is the time required for the earth to complete one rotation on its axis relative to the vernal equinox, is about 3 minutes and 56.6 seconds shorter than the mean solar day. As sidereal time indicates the position of the stars, their daily shift westward is therefore almost one degree every night. Because of *nutation* (see Article 1815), sidereal time is not perfectly constant in rate. Time based on the average rate is called *mean sidereal time.* There is no sidereal date.

Greenwich sidereal time (GST) uses the meridian of Greenwich as its terrestrial reference, while the observer's meridian is the reference for *local sidereal time* (LST).

Some timepieces, often reading in arc rather than in time, are adjusted to keep sidereal time. If set to GST they permit the navigator to read the GHA ♈, which is GST expressed in units of arc, directly from the timepiece at the instant of making a star observation, thus obviating the need to extract GHA ♈ and a correction thereto from the *Almanac.*

Time and longitude The difference between two times is equal to the difference of longitude of their reference meridians, expressed in units of time. GMT differs from LMT by the longitude of the place; GMT differs from ZT by the longitude of the standard meridian of the zone; LMT differs from ZT by the difference of longitude between the standard meridian of the zone and the meridian of the place. In applying a time difference, a place which is east of another place has a later time than that place, and a place which is west of another place has an earlier time than that place. In interconverting ZT and GMT, the navigator makes use of zone description in applying these rules. The ZD of a zone is the time difference between its standard meridian and GMT, and is given a sign to indicate the correction to ZT to obtain GMT. The sign is plus (+) for places in west longitude and minus (−) for places in east longitude.

23 Almanacs

Introduction

2301 The purpose of this chapter is to explain how the navigator, having observed a celestial body at a given time, obtains the Greenwich Hour Angle (GHA) and declination (Dec.) of the body at that time.

Although the *Air Almanac* is considered in this chapter, primary attention will be given to the *Nautical Almanac* which is normally the choice of the marine navigator.

Almanac history

2302 The early history of celestial observations and predictions has been briefly covered in Article 1801. Here we will consider how such predictions were developed for direct assistance to the navigator at sea. The Danish astronomer, Tycho Brahe, during the last half of the sixteenth century, spent over twenty years making accurate observations of the heavenly bodies. On the data thus amassed, Kepler based his laws of motion, which were the foundation both of modern astronomy and celestial navigation. The earliest compilations of astronomical calculations for nautical purposes dated from the fifteenth century and were private publications by individuals. The first official nautical *ephemeris* or *almanac* was published by the French in 1687; this was followed by the British *Nautical Almanac* in 1765 for the year 1767. In 1852, the United States Navy's Depot of Charts and Instruments published the first *American Ephemeris and Nautical Almanac* for the year 1855. This volume has appeared annually since then. In 1858, the *American Nautical Almanac* was published—the ephemeris section, of primary interest to astronomers, being omitted.

In 1933, the *Air Almanac* was first published in the United States. It was revolutionary, as Greenwich Hour Angle was substituted for Right Ascension; the hour angle, incidentally, was stated to 0.1′. This *Almanac* was discontinued in 1934, but produced again in 1937 by the Royal Greenwich Observatory in somewhat modified form, and published in the United States by the Weems System of Navigation. In 1941, the U. S. Naval Observatory resumed the publication of the *Air Almanac* in the United States.

The British and American editions of the *Nautical Almanac,* which are now identical in content, are produced jointly by Her Majesty's Nautical Almanac Office, Royal Greenwich Observatory, and by the Nautical Almanac Office, U. S. Naval Observatory, but are printed separately in the United States and Britain. The *Nautical Almanac* is prepared to the general requirements of the British Admiralty and the

United States Navy, but, of course, meets well the needs of other surface vessel navigators; its purpose is to provide, in convenient form, the astronomical data required for the practice of celestial navigation at sea.

The *Nautical Almanac* is also published, with minor modifications, by a number of foreign nations using their language for page headings, explanatory text, and notes.

Contents of the *Nautical Almanac*

2303 To find an observer's position on earth by observations of celestial bodies it is necessary to determine the position of the observer relative to the geographical positions of these bodies. The *Nautical Almanac* consists principally of data from which the Greenwich Hour Angle (GHA) and declination (Dec.) of all the celestial bodies used in navigation can be obtained for any instant of Greenwich Mean Time (GMT). In general these data are presented to the nearest one-tenth minute of arc, and one second of time. The Local Hour Angle (LHA) can then be obtained by means of the equations:

LHA

$$\text{LHA} = \text{GHA} - \text{west longitude}$$

and

$$\text{LHA} = \text{GHA} + \text{east longitude},$$

bearing in mind that 360° may be added or subtracted as required. LHA, like GHA, is always calculated in a westerly direction. For some methods of sight reduction *meridian angle* (t) is required; this is measured east or west from the observer's meridian to 180°, as discussed in Chapter 19. Meridian angle may be readily determined from LHA. Figure 2303 depicts the relationship between longitude (west), GHA, meridian angle (t), and SHA.

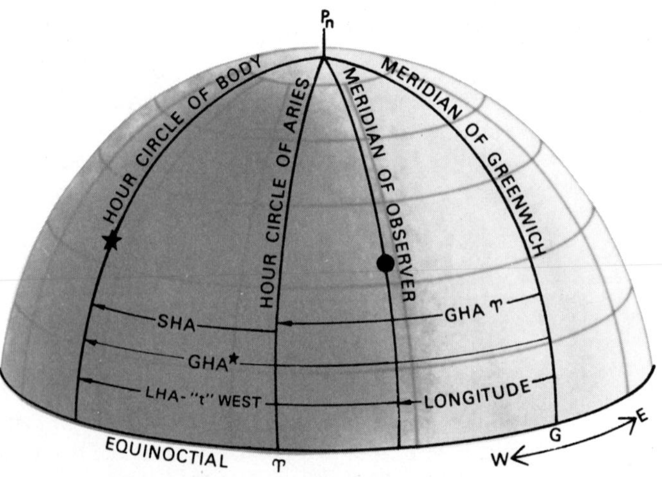

Figure 2303. Hour angles illustrated on a sphere.

***Nautical Almanac* format** **2304** The basic ephemeristic data for all navigational bodies of interest to the mariner covering a three-day period are presented on a pair of facing pages of the *Almanac.* The left-hand pages are used primarily for the tabulation of data for the stars and navigational planets. These bodies are of navigational interest primarily during morning and evening twilight. The right-hand pages present the ephemeristic data for the sun and moon, together with the times of twilight, sunrise, sunset, moonrise, and moonset. Sample almanac pages are shown as Figures 2304a and 2304b.

The extreme left-hand column of each page contains the dates, days of the week, and the hours of GMT for the three days. It should be noted carefully that the date *is that at Greenwich*; this may be one day earlier or later than the local date at the navigator's position as was explained in Article 2218.

***Nautical Almanac,* left page** Specifically, the left-hand page for each set of three days gives, for each hour, the GHA of Aries (♈) and the GHA and declination of the navigational planets—Venus, Mars, Jupiter, and Saturn. At the bottom of each column of data for a planet, there are the *v* and *d* values for that body; as these values change slowly, a single entry is given for the three-day period.

v* and *d The *d* values are the amount in arc by which Dec. changes during each hour; *v* values are the amount in arc by which GHA departs from the basic rate used in the almanac interpolation tables. The *v* and *d* values are for use with the interpolation tables, which are based on a constant rate of change. These latter tables, explained later in this article, are included to facilitate the interpolation of GHA and Dec. respectively for intermediate times.

Also on this page is a listing of the SHA of each planet and the time of its meridian passage, as well as the time of meridian passage of ♈.

A list of 57 selected stars, arranged in alphabetical order together with SHA and declination to the nearest one-tenth minute, is also given. These are the prime navigational stars selected for their magnitude and distribution in the heavens, and are the ones most frequently observed by a navigator.

All tabulations are in degrees, minutes, and tenths of minutes of arc.

***Nautical Almanac,* right page** Data for the sun and moon are presented on the right-hand page with GHA and Dec., tabulated to one-tenth minute of arc for each hour. For the moon, additional values for the horizontal parallax (HP) and of *v* and *d* are tabulated for each hour. The moon's rate of change of GHA and Dec. varies considerably. For the sun, *v* is omitted entirely and *d* is given only once at the bottom of the page for the three-day period.

Also shown on right-hand pages are data for each day covering the equation of time, meridian passage of the sun and moon, and the age

1977 JUNE 3, 4, 5 (FRI., SAT., SUN.)

G.M.T.	ARIES	VENUS −4.1		MARS +1.3		JUPITER −1.5		SATURN +0.6	
d h	G.H.A.	G.H.A.	Dec.	G.H.A.	Dec.	G.H.A.	Dec.	G.H.A.	Dec.
	° ′	° ′	° ′	° ′	° ′	° ′	° ′	° ′	° ′
3 00	251 20.1	225 19.6	N 8 27.0	225 15.5	N 9 38.9	179 21.4	N21 54.8	116 16.2	N18 02.6
01	266 22.6	240 20.0	27.6	240 16.2	39.6	194 23.2	54.9	131 18.4	02.5
02	281 25.1	255 20.4	28.3	255 16.9	40.3	209 25.0	55.0	146 20.7	02.5
03	296 27.5	270 20.8	·· 28.9	270 17.6	·· 41.0	224 26.9	·· 55.1	161 22.9	·· 02.4
04	311 30.0	285 21.2	29.5	285 18.3	41.6	239 28.7	55.1	176 25.2	02.3
05	326 32.4	300 21.6	30.1	300 19.0	42.3	254 30.6	55.2	191 27.4	02.3
06	341 34.9	315 22.0	N 8 30.7	315 19.7	N 9 43.0	269 32.4	N21 55.3	206 29.7	N18 02.2
07	356 37.4	330 22.4	31.3	330 20.4	43.7	284 34.2	55.4	221 31.9	02.2
08	11 39.8	345 22.8	31.9	345 21.1	44.4	299 36.1	55.4	236 34.2	02.1
F 09	26 42.3	0 23.2	·· 32.5	0 21.8	·· 45.1	314 37.9	·· 55.5	251 36.4	·· 02.0
R 10	41 44.8	15 23.6	33.1	15 22.5	45.7	329 39.8	55.6	266 38.7	02.0
I 11	56 47.2	30 24.0	33.7	30 23.2	46.4	344 41.6	55.7	281 40.9	01.9
D 12	71 49.7	45 24.3	N 8 34.3	45 23.9	N 9 47.1	359 43.5	N21 55.7	296 43.2	N18 01.9
A 13	86 52.2	60 24.7	34.9	60 24.6	47.8	14 45.3	55.8	311 45.4	01.8
Y 14	101 54.6	75 25.1	35.5	75 25.3	48.5	29 47.1	55.9	326 47.7	01.7
15	116 57.1	90 25.5	·· 36.1	90 26.0	·· 49.1	44 49.0	·· 56.0	341 49.9	·· 01.7
16	131 59.6	105 25.9	36.7	105 26.7	49.8	59 50.8	56.0	356 52.2	01.6
17	147 02.0	120 26.3	37.4	120 27.4	50.5	74 52.7	56.1	11 54.4	01.6
18	162 04.5	135 26.6	N 8 38.0	135 28.1	N 9 51.2	89 54.5	N21 56.2	26 56.7	N18 01.5
19	177 06.9	150 27.0	38.6	150 28.8	51.9	104 56.4	56.3	41 58.9	01.4
20	192 09.4	165 27.4	39.2	165 29.5	52.5	119 58.2	56.3	57 01.2	01.4
21	207 11.9	180 27.8	·· 39.8	180 30.2	·· 53.2	135 00.0	·· 56.4	72 03.4	·· 01.3
22	222 14.3	195 28.1	40.4	195 30.9	53.9	150 01.9	56.5	87 05.7	01.3
23	237 16.8	210 28.5	41.0	210 31.6	54.6	165 03.7	56.5	102 07.9	01.2
4 00	252 19.3	225 28.9	N 8 41.6	225 32.3	N 9 55.3	180 05.6	N21 56.6	117 10.2	N18 01.1
01	267 21.7	240 29.3	42.3	240 33.0	55.9	195 07.4	56.7	132 12.4	01.1
02	282 24.2	255 29.6	42.9	255 33.7	56.6	210 09.3	56.8	147 14.7	01.0
03	297 26.7	270 30.0	·· 43.5	270 34.4	·· 57.3	225 11.1	·· 56.8	162 16.9	·· 01.0
04	312 29.1	285 30.4	44.1	285 35.1	58.0	240 12.9	56.9	177 19.2	00.9
05	327 31.6	300 30.8	44.7	300 35.8	58.6	255 14.8	57.0	192 21.4	00.8
06	342 34.0	315 31.1	N 8 45.3	315 36.5	N 9 59.3	270 16.6	N21 57.1	207 23.7	N18 00.8
07	357 36.5	330 31.5	45.9	330 37.2	10 00.0	285 18.5	57.1	222 25.9	00.7
S 08	12 39.0	345 31.9	46.6	345 37.9	00.7	300 20.3	57.2	237 28.2	00.7
A 09	27 41.4	0 32.2	·· 47.2	0 38.6	·· 01.4	315 22.1	·· 57.3	252 30.4	·· 00.6
T 10	42 43.9	15 32.6	47.8	15 39.3	02.0	330 24.0	57.4	267 32.7	00.5
U 11	57 46.4	30 32.9	48.4	30 39.9	02.7	345 25.8	57.4	282 34.9	00.5
R 12	72 48.8	45 33.3	N 8 49.0	45 40.6	N10 03.4	0 27.7	N21 57.5	297 37.2	N18 00.4
D 13	87 51.3	60 33.7	49.7	60 41.3	04.1	15 29.5	57.6	312 39.4	00.4
A 14	102 53.8	75 34.0	50.3	75 42.0	04.7	30 31.4	57.7	327 41.7	00.3
Y 15	117 56.2	90 34.4	·· 50.9	90 42.7	·· 05.4	45 33.2	·· 57.7	342 43.9	·· 00.2
16	132 58.7	105 34.7	51.5	105 43.4	06.1	60 35.0	57.8	357 46.1	00.2
17	148 01.2	120 35.1	52.1	120 44.1	06.8	75 36.9	57.9	12 48.4	00.1
18	163 03.6	135 35.5	N 8 52.8	135 44.8	N10 07.4	90 38.7	N21 58.0	27 50.6	N18 00.0
19	178 06.1	150 35.8	53.4	150 45.5	08.1	105 40.6	58.0	42 52.9	18 00.0
20	193 08.5	165 36.2	54.0	165 46.2	08.8	120 42.4	58.1	57 55.1	17 59.9
21	208 11.0	180 36.5	·· 54.6	180 46.9	·· 09.5	135 44.3	·· 58.2	72 57.4	·· 59.9
22	223 13.5	195 36.9	55.3	195 47.6	10.1	150 46.1	58.2	87 59.6	59.8
23	238 15.9	210 37.2	55.9	210 48.3	10.8	165 47.9	58.3	103 01.9	59.7
5 00	253 18.4	225 37.6	N 8 56.5	225 49.0	N10 11.5	180 49.8	N21 58.4	118 04.1	N17 59.7
01	268 20.9	240 37.9	57.1	240 49.7	12.2	195 51.6	58.5	133 06.4	59.6
02	283 23.3	255 38.3	57.8	255 50.4	12.8	210 53.5	58.5	148 08.6	59.6
03	298 25.8	270 38.6	·· 58.4	270 51.1	·· 13.5	225 55.3	·· 58.6	163 10.9	·· 59.5
04	313 28.3	285 39.0	59.0	285 51.8	14.2	240 57.1	58.7	178 13.1	59.4
05	328 30.7	300 39.3	8 59.6	300 52.5	14.9	255 59.0	58.8	193 15.3	59.4
06	343 33.2	315 39.6	N 9 00.3	315 53.2	N10 15.5	271 00.8	N21 58.8	208 17.6	N17 59.3
07	358 35.7	330 40.0	00.9	330 53.9	16.2	286 02.7	58.9	223 19.8	59.2
08	13 38.1	345 40.3	01.5	345 54.6	16.9	301 04.5	59.0	238 22.1	59.2
S 09	28 40.6	0 40.7	·· 02.1	0 55.3	·· 17.5	316 06.4	·· 59.1	253 24.3	·· 59.1
U 10	43 43.0	15 41.0	02.8	15 56.0	18.2	331 08.2	59.1	268 26.6	59.1
N 11	58 45.5	30 41.4	03.4	30 56.7	18.9	346 10.0	59.2	283 28.8	59.0
D 12	73 48.0	45 41.7	N 9 04.0	45 57.4	N10 19.6	1 11.9	N21 59.3	298 31.1	N17 58.9
A 13	88 50.4	60 42.0	04.7	60 58.1	20.2	16 13.7	59.3	313 33.3	58.9
Y 14	103 52.9	75 42.4	05.3	75 58.8	20.9	31 15.6	59.4	328 35.6	58.8
15	118 55.4	90 42.7	·· 05.9	90 59.5	·· 21.6	46 17.4	·· 59.5	343 37.8	·· 58.8
16	133 57.8	105 43.0	06.6	106 00.2	22.2	61 19.2	59.6	358 40.0	58.7
17	149 00.3	120 43.4	07.2	121 00.9	22.9	76 21.1	59.6	13 42.3	58.6
18	164 02.8	135 43.7	N 9 07.8	136 01.6	N10 23.6	91 22.9	N21 59.7	28 44.5	N17 58.6
19	179 05.2	150 44.0	08.5	151 02.3	24.3	106 24.8	59.8	43 46.8	58.5
20	194 07.7	165 44.4	09.1	166 03.0	24.9	121 26.6	59.9	58 49.0	58.4
21	209 10.1	180 44.7	·· 09.7	181 03.7	·· 25.6	136 28.5	21 59.9	73 51.3	·· 58.4
22	224 12.6	195 45.0	10.4	196 04.4	26.3	151 30.3	22 00.0	88 53.5	58.3
23	239 15.1	210 45.3	11.0	211 05.1	26.9	166 32.1	00.1	103 55.7	58.3
Mer. Pass.	h m 7 09.5	*v* 0.4	*d* 0.6	*v* 0.7	*d* 0.7	*v* 1.8	*d* 0.1	*v* 2.2	*d* 0.1

STARS Name	S.H.A.	Dec.
	° ′	° ′
Acamar	315 39.3	S40 23.7
Achernar	335 47.4	S57 20.9
Acrux	173 39.3	S62 58.8
Adhara	255 34.2	S28 56.7
Aldebaran	291 20.9	N16 27.7
Alioth	166 44.3	N56 05.1
Alkaid	153 20.0	N49 25.7
Al Na'ir	28 17.7	S47 03.9
Alnilam	276 14.2	S 1 13.1
Alphard	218 22.9	S 8 33.8
Alphecca	126 33.7	N26 47.5
Alpheratz	358 11.7	N28 57.8
Altair	62 34.4	N 8 48.5
Ankaa	353 42.7	S42 25.5
Antares	112 59.2	S26 22.9
Arcturus	146 20.2	N19 18.1
Atria	108 24.8	S68 59.2
Avior	234 29.5	S59 26.6
Bellatrix	279 01.5	N 6 19.6
Betelgeuse	271 31.0	N 7 24.1
Canopus	264 08.7	S52 41.2
Capella	281 15.0	N45 58.4
Deneb	49 49.7	N45 11.9
Denebola	183 01.3	N14 41.9
Diphda	349 23.3	S18 06.6
Dubhe	194 25.0	N61 52.6
Elnath	278 47.3	N28 35.2
Eltanin	90 58.2	N51 29.5
Enif	34 13.6	N 9 46.3
Fomalhaut	15 53.9	S29 44.3
Gacrux	172 30.9	S56 59.5
Gienah	176 20.1	S17 25.2
Hadar	149 25.9	S60 16.1
Hamal	328 31.7	N23 21.2
Kaus Aust.	84 19.4	S34 23.6
Kochab	137 18.0	N74 15.1
Markab	14 05.4	N15 05.0
Menkar	314 43.7	N 4 00.0
Menkent	148 39.3	S36 15.7
Miaplacidus	221 45.7	S69 37.9
Mirfak	309 19.7	N49 46.7
Nunki	76 31.6	S26 19.4
Peacock	54 01.6	S56 48.2
Pollux	244 01.2	N28 04.8
Procyon	245 28.4	N 5 16.9
Rasalhague	96 31.3	N12 34.6
Regulus	208 12.5	N12 04.6
Rigel	281 38.5	S 8 13.8
Rigil Kent.	140 28.2	S60 44.6
Sabik	102 43.3	S15 41.8
Schedar	350 11.7	N56 24.6
Shaula	96 58.3	S37 05.2
Sirius	258 58.0	S16 41.3
Spica	158 59.7	S11 02.7
Suhail	223 12.6	S43 20.8
Vega	80 56.9	N38 45.8
Zuben'ubi	137 35.2	S15 56.9

	S.H.A.	Mer. Pass.
	° ′	h m
Venus	333 09.6	8 58
Mars	333 13.0	8 57
Jupiter	287 46.3	11 58
Saturn	224 50.9	16 09

Figure 2304a. *Nautical Almanac,* left hand daily page (typical).

1977 JUNE 3, 4, 5 (FRI., SAT., SUN.)

G.M.T.	SUN G.H.A.	SUN Dec.	MOON G.H.A.	v	MOON Dec.	d	H.P.
d h	° ′	° ′	° ′	′	° ′	′	′
3 00	180 30.4	N22 16.2	342 44.5	3.6	S18 46.2	1.2	61.1
01	195 30.3	16.5	357 07.1	3.6	18 45.0	1.2	61.1
02	210 30.2	16.8	11 29.7	3.7	18 43.8	1.4	61.1
03	225 30.1	·· 17.1	25 52.4	3.7	18 42.4	1.5	61.0
04	240 30.0	17.4	40 15.1	3.7	18 40.9	1.7	61.0
05	255 29.9	17.7	54 37.8	3.8	18 39.2	1.8	61.0
06	270 29.8	N22 18.1	69 00.6	3.8	S18 37.4	1.9	61.0
07	285 29.7	18.4	83 23.4	3.9	18 35.5	2.1	61.0
08	300 29.6	18.7	97 46.3	3.9	18 33.4	2.2	60.9
F 09	315 29.5	·· 19.0	112 09.2	3.9	18 31.2	2.3	60.9
R 10	330 29.4	19.3	126 32.1	4.1	18 28.9	2.5	60.9
I 11	345 29.3	19.6	140 55.2	4.0	18 26.4	2.6	60.9
D 12	0 29.2	N22 19.9	155 18.2	4.1	S18 23.8	2.7	60.8
A 13	15 29.1	20.2	169 41.3	4.2	18 21.1	2.9	60.8
Y 14	30 29.0	20.5	184 04.5	4.2	18 18.2	3.0	60.8
15	45 28.9	·· 20.8	198 27.7	4.3	18 15.2	3.1	60.8
16	60 28.8	21.1	212 51.0	4.4	18 12.1	3.3	60.7
17	75 28.7	21.4	227 14.4	4.4	18 08.8	3.4	60.7
18	90 28.6	N22 21.7	241 37.8	4.5	S18 05.4	3.5	60.7
19	105 28.5	22.0	256 01.3	4.5	18 01.9	3.7	60.7
20	120 28.4	22.3	270 24.8	4.6	17 58.2	3.7	60.6
21	135 28.3	·· 22.6	284 48.4	4.7	17 54.5	3.9	60.6
22	150 28.2	22.9	299 12.1	4.7	17 50.6	4.0	60.6
23	165 28.1	23.2	313 35.8	4.8	17 46.6	4.2	60.5
4 00	180 28.0	N22 23.5	327 59.6	4.9	S17 42.4	4.2	60.5
01	195 27.9	23.8	342 23.5	4.9	17 38.2	4.4	60.5
02	210 27.8	24.1	356 47.4	5.1	17 33.8	4.5	60.5
03	225 27.7	·· 24.4	11 11.5	5.1	17 29.3	4.6	60.4
04	240 27.6	24.7	25 35.6	5.1	17 24.7	4.8	60.4
05	255 27.5	25.0	39 59.7	5.3	17 19.9	4.8	60.4
06	270 27.4	N22 25.3	54 24.0	5.3	S17 15.1	5.0	60.3
07	285 27.3	25.6	68 48.3	5.4	17 10.1	5.0	60.3
S 08	300 27.1	25.9	83 12.7	5.4	17 05.1	5.2	60.3
A 09	315 27.0	·· 26.1	97 37.1	5.6	16 59.9	5.3	60.2
T 10	330 26.9	26.4	112 01.7	5.6	16 54.6	5.4	60.2
U 11	345 26.8	26.7	126 26.3	5.7	16 49.2	5.6	60.2
R 12	0 26.7	N22 27.0	140 51.0	5.8	S16 43.6	5.6	60.1
D 13	15 26.6	27.3	155 15.8	5.9	16 38.0	5.7	60.1
A 14	30 26.5	27.6	169 40.7	6.0	16 32.3	5.8	60.1
Y 15	45 26.4	·· 27.9	184 05.7	6.0	16 26.5	6.0	60.0
16	60 26.3	28.2	198 30.7	6.1	16 20.5	6.0	60.0
17	75 26.2	28.4	212 55.8	6.2	16 14.5	6.2	60.0
18	90 26.1	N22 28.7	227 21.0	6.3	S16 08.3	6.2	59.9
19	105 26.0	29.0	241 46.3	6.4	16 02.1	6.3	59.9
20	120 25.9	29.3	256 11.7	6.5	15 55.8	6.5	59.9
21	135 25.8	·· 29.6	270 37.2	6.5	15 49.3	6.5	59.8
22	150 25.7	29.9	285 02.7	6.7	15 42.8	6.6	59.8
23	165 25.5	30.1	299 28.4	6.7	15 36.2	6.8	59.7
5 00	180 25.4	N22 30.4	313 54.1	6.8	S15 29.4	6.8	59.7
01	195 25.3	30.7	328 19.9	6.9	15 22.6	6.9	59.7
02	210 25.2	31.0	342 45.8	7.0	15 15.7	7.0	59.6
03	225 25.1	·· 31.3	357 11.8	7.1	15 08.7	7.0	59.6
04	240 25.0	31.5	11 37.9	7.2	15 01.7	7.2	59.6
05	255 24.9	31.8	26 04.1	7.2	14 54.5	7.3	59.5
06	270 24.8	N22 32.1	40 30.3	7.4	S14 47.2	7.3	59.5
07	285 24.7	32.4	54 56.7	7.4	14 39.9	7.4	59.5
08	300 24.6	32.6	69 23.1	7.5	14 32.5	7.5	59.4
S 09	315 24.5	·· 32.9	83 49.6	7.6	14 25.0	7.6	59.4
U 10	330 24.4	33.2	98 16.2	7.7	14 17.4	7.6	59.3
N 11	345 24.2	33.5	112 42.9	7.8	14 09.8	7.8	59.3
D 12	0 24.1	N22 33.7	127 09.7	7.9	S14 02.0	7.8	59.3
A 13	15 24.0	34.0	141 36.6	8.0	13 54.2	7.9	59.2
Y 14	30 23.9	34.3	156 03.6	8.0	13 46.3	7.9	59.2
15	45 23.8	·· 34.5	170 30.6	8.2	13 38.4	8.0	59.1
16	60 23.7	34.8	184 57.8	8.2	13 30.4	8.2	59.1
17	75 23.6	35.1	199 25.0	8.3	13 22.2	8.1	59.1
18	90 23.5	N22 35.4	213 52.3	8.4	S13 14.1	8.3	59.0
19	105 23.4	35.6	228 19.7	8.5	13 05.8	8.3	59.0
20	120 23.3	35.9	242 47.2	8.6	12 57.5	8.3	58.9
21	135 23.1	·· 36.2	257 14.8	8.7	12 49.2	8.5	58.9
22	150 23.0	36.4	271 42.5	8.8	12 40.7	8.5	58.9
23	165 22.9	36.7	286 10.3	8.8	12 32.2	8.5	58.8
	S.D. 15.8	*d* 0.3	S.D. 16.6		16.4		16.1

Lat.	Twilight Naut.	Twilight Civil	Sunrise	Moonrise 3	Moonrise 4	Moonrise 5	Moonrise 6
°	h m	h m	h m	h m	h m	h m	h m
N 72	▭	▭	▭	■	01 33	01 02	00 50
N 70	▭	▭	▭	24 18	00 18	00 26	00 28
68	▭	▭	▭	23 40	24 00	00 00	00 11
66	////	////	01 00	23 13	23 40	23 57	24 09
64	////	////	01 51	22 52	23 24	23 46	24 02
62	////	////	02 22	22 35	23 11	23 36	23 55
60	////	01 18	02 45	22 21	22 59	23 28	23 50
N 58	////	01 55	03 04	22 09	22 49	23 20	23 45
56	////	02 20	03 19	21 59	22 41	23 14	23 40
54	01 11	02 40	03 32	21 49	22 33	23 08	23 36
52	01 45	02 57	03 44	21 41	22 26	23 03	23 33
50	02 09	03 11	03 54	21 34	22 20	22 58	23 30
45	02 50	03 39	04 15	21 18	22 06	22 47	23 22
N 40	03 19	04 00	04 32	21 05	21 55	22 39	23 16
35	03 41	04 17	04 46	20 54	21 46	22 31	23 11
30	03 59	04 32	04 59	20 44	21 37	22 24	23 07
20	04 26	04 55	05 20	20 27	21 23	22 13	22 59
N 10	04 48	05 15	05 38	20 13	21 10	22 03	22 52
0	05 06	05 32	05 55	19 59	20 58	21 54	22 45
S 10	05 22	05 49	06 11	19 45	20 46	21 44	22 39
20	05 38	06 05	06 29	19 31	20 33	21 34	22 32
30	05 53	06 23	06 49	19 14	20 19	21 22	22 24
35	06 01	06 33	07 01	19 04	20 10	21 16	22 19
40	06 10	06 44	07 14	18 53	20 01	21 08	22 14
45	06 20	06 57	07 30	18 40	19 49	20 59	22 08
S 50	06 31	07 12	07 50	18 24	19 36	20 48	22 00
52	06 36	07 19	07 59	18 17	19 29	20 43	21 57
54	06 41	07 26	08 09	18 08	19 22	20 38	21 53
56	06 47	07 35	08 21	17 59	19 14	20 32	21 49
58	06 53	07 44	08 35	17 48	19 05	20 25	21 44
S 60	07 00	07 55	08 51	17 36	18 55	20 17	21 39

Lat.	Sunset	Twilight Civil	Twilight Naut.	Moonset 3	Moonset 4	Moonset 5	Moonset 6
°	h m	h m	h m	h m	h m	h m	h m
N 72	▭	▭	▭	■	03 02	05 35	07 40
N 70	▭	▭	▭	02 35	04 17	06 10	08 00
68	▭	▭	▭	03 26	04 54	06 35	08 16
66	23 01	////	////	03 58	05 21	06 54	08 29
64	22 07	////	////	04 22	05 41	07 09	08 39
62	21 36	////	////	04 41	05 58	07 22	08 48
60	21 12	22 41	////	04 56	06 11	07 33	08 56
N 58	20 54	22 03	////	05 09	06 23	07 42	09 03
56	20 38	21 37	////	05 21	06 33	07 50	09 08
54	20 25	21 17	22 48	05 31	06 42	07 58	09 14
52	20 13	21 00	22 13	05 40	06 50	08 04	09 18
50	20 03	20 46	21 48	05 47	06 57	08 10	09 23
45	19 42	20 18	21 07	06 04	07 12	08 22	09 32
N 40	19 25	19 57	20 38	06 18	07 25	08 33	09 40
35	19 10	19 40	20 16	06 30	07 36	08 42	09 46
30	18 58	19 25	19 58	06 40	07 45	08 49	09 52
20	18 37	19 01	19 30	06 57	08 01	09 03	10 02
N 10	18 19	18 42	19 08	07 13	08 15	09 14	10 11
0	18 02	18 24	18 50	07 27	08 28	09 25	10 19
S 10	17 45	18 08	18 34	07 41	08 40	09 36	10 27
20	17 27	17 51	18 19	07 56	08 54	09 47	10 35
30	17 07	17 33	18 03	08 13	09 10	10 00	10 45
35	16 55	17 23	17 55	08 23	09 19	10 07	10 50
40	16 42	17 12	17 46	08 35	09 29	10 16	10 57
45	16 26	16 59	17 36	08 48	09 41	10 26	11 04
S 50	16 07	16 44	17 25	09 04	09 56	10 38	11 12
52	15 57	16 37	17 20	09 12	10 02	10 43	11 16
54	15 47	16 30	17 15	09 21	10 10	10 49	11 21
56	15 35	16 21	17 10	09 30	10 18	10 56	11 26
58	15 21	16 12	17 03	09 41	10 28	11 03	11 31
S 60	15 05	16 01	16 56	09 53	10 38	11 12	11 37

Day	SUN Eqn. of Time 00ʰ	SUN Eqn. of Time 12ʰ	SUN Mer. Pass.	MOON Mer. Pass. Upper	MOON Mer. Pass. Lower	Age	Phase
	m s	m s	h m	h m	h m	d	
3	02 02	01 57	11 58	01 12	13 43	16	◑
4	01 52	01 47	11 58	02 13	14 43	17	
5	01 42	01 37	11 58	03 12	15 39	18	

Figure 2304b. *Nautical Almanac,* right hand daily page (typical).

36^m INCREMENTS AND CORRECTIONS 37^m

36^m	SUN PLANETS	ARIES	MOON	v or d	Corr^n	v or d	Corr^n	v or d	Corr^n
s	° ′	° ′	° ′	′	′	′	′	′	′
00	9 00·0	9 01·5	8 35·4	0·0	0·0	6·0	3·7	12·0	7·3
01	9 00·3	9 01·7	8 35·6	0·1	0·1	6·1	3·7	12·1	7·4
02	9 00·5	9 02·0	8 35·9	0·2	0·1	6·2	3·8	12·2	7·4
03	9 00·8	9 02·2	8 36·1	0·3	0·2	6·3	3·8	12·3	7·5
04	9 01·0	9 02·5	8 36·4	0·4	0·2	6·4	3·9	12·4	7·5
05	9 01·3	9 02·7	8 36·6	0·5	0·3	6·5	4·0	12·5	7·6
06	9 01·5	9 03·0	8 36·8	0·6	0·4	6·6	4·0	12·6	7·7
07	9 01·8	9 03·2	8 37·1	0·7	0·4	6·7	4·1	12·7	7·7
08	9 02·0	9 03·5	8 37·3	0·8	0·5	6·8	4·1	12·8	7·8
09	9 02·3	9 03·7	8 37·5	0·9	0·5	6·9	4·2	12·9	7·8
10	9 02·5	9 04·0	8 37·8	1·0	0·6	7·0	4·3	13·0	7·9
11	9 02·8	9 04·2	8 38·0	1·1	0·7	7·1	4·3	13·1	8·0
12	9 03·0	9 04·5	8 38·3	1·2	0·7	7·2	4·4	13·2	8·0
13	9 03·3	9 04·7	8 38·5	1·3	0·8	7·3	4·4	13·3	8·1
14	9 03·5	9 05·0	8 38·7	1·4	0·9	7·4	4·5	13·4	8·2
15	9 03·8	9 05·2	8 39·0	1·5	0·9	7·5	4·6	13·5	8·2
16	9 04·0	9 05·5	8 39·2	1·6	1·0	7·6	4·6	13·6	8·3
17	9 04·3	9 05·7	8 39·5	1·7	1·0	7·7	4·7	13·7	8·3
18	9 04·5	9 06·0	8 39·7	1·8	1·1	7·8	4·7	13·8	8·4
19	9 04·8	9 06·2	8 39·9	1·9	1·2	7·9	4·8	13·9	8·5
20	9 05·0	9 06·5	8 40·2	2·0	1·2	8·0	4·9	14·0	8·5
21	9 05·3	9 06·7	8 40·4	2·1	1·3	8·1	4·9	14·1	8·6
22	9 05·5	9 07·0	8 40·6	2·2	1·3	8·2	5·0	14·2	8·6
23	9 05·8	9 07·2	8 40·9	2·3	1·4	8·3	5·0	14·3	8·7
24	9 06·0	9 07·5	8 41·1	2·4	1·5	8·4	5·1	14·4	8·8
25	9 06·3	9 07·7	8 41·4	2·5	1·5	8·5	5·2	14·5	8·8
26	9 06·5	9 08·0	8 41·6	2·6	1·6	8·6	5·2	14·6	8·9
27	9 06·8	9 08·2	8 41·8	2·7	1·6	8·7	5·3	14·7	8·9
28	9 07·0	9 08·5	8 42·1	2·8	1·7	8·8	5·4	14·8	9·0
29	9 07·3	9 08·7	8 42·3	2·9	1·8	8·9	5·4	14·9	9·1
30	9 07·5	9 09·0	8 42·6	3·0	1·8	9·0	5·5	15·0	9·1
31	9 07·8	9 09·2	8 42·8	3·1	1·9	9·1	5·5	15·1	9·2
32	9 08·0	9 09·5	8 43·0	3·2	1·9	9·2	5·6	15·2	9·2
33	9 08·3	9 09·8	8 43·3	3·3	2·0	9·3	5·7	15·3	9·3
34	9 08·5	9 10·0	8 43·5	3·4	2·1	9·4	5·7	15·4	9·4
35	9 08·8	9 10·3	8 43·8	3·5	2·1	9·5	5·8	15·5	9·4
36	9 09·0	9 10·5	8 44·0	3·6	2·2	9·6	5·8	15·6	9·5
37	9 09·3	9 10·8	8 44·2	3·7	2·3	9·7	5·9	15·7	9·6
38	9 09·5	9 11·0	8 44·5	3·8	2·3	9·8	6·0	15·8	9·6
39	9 09·8	9 11·3	8 44·7	3·9	2·4	9·9	6·0	15·9	9·7
40	9 10·0	9 11·5	8 44·9	4·0	2·4	10·0	6·1	16·0	9·7
41	9 10·3	9 11·8	8 45·2	4·1	2·5	10·1	6·1	16·1	9·8
42	9 10·5	9 12·0	8 45·4	4·2	2·6	10·2	6·2	16·2	9·9
43	9 10·8	9 12·3	8 45·7	4·3	2·6	10·3	6·3	16·3	9·9
44	9 11·0	9 12·5	8 45·9	4·4	2·7	10·4	6·3	16·4	10·0
45	9 11·3	9 12·8	8 46·1	4·5	2·7	10·5	6·4	16·5	10·0
46	9 11·5	9 13·0	8 46·4	4·6	2·8	10·6	6·4	16·6	10·1
47	9 11·8	9 13·3	8 46·6	4·7	2·9	10·7	6·5	16·7	10·2
48	9 12·0	9 13·5	8 46·9	4·8	2·9	10·8	6·6	16·8	10·2
49	9 12·3	9 13·8	8 47·1	4·9	3·0	10·9	6·6	16·9	10·3
50	9 12·5	9 14·0	8 47·3	5·0	3·0	11·0	6·7	17·0	10·3
51	9 12·8	9 14·3	8 47·6	5·1	3·1	11·1	6·8	17·1	10·4
52	9 13·0	9 14·5	8 47·8	5·2	3·2	11·2	6·8	17·2	10·5
53	9 13·3	9 14·8	8 48·0	5·3	3·2	11·3	6·9	17·3	10·5
54	9 13·5	9 15·0	8 48·3	5·4	3·3	11·4	6·9	17·4	10·6
55	9 13·8	9 15·3	8 48·5	5·5	3·3	11·5	7·0	17·5	10·6
56	9 14·0	9 15·5	8 48·8	5·6	3·4	11·6	7·1	17·6	10·7
57	9 14·3	9 15·8	8 49·0	5·7	3·5	11·7	7·1	17·7	10·8
58	9 14·5	9 16·0	8 49·2	5·8	3·5	11·8	7·2	17·8	10·8
59	9 14·8	9 16·3	8 49·5	5·9	3·6	11·9	7·2	17·9	10·9
60	9 15·0	9 16·5	8 49·7	6·0	3·7	12·0	7·3	18·0	11·0

37^m	SUN PLANETS	ARIES	MOON	v or d	Corr^n	v or d	Corr^n	v or d	Corr^n
s	° ′	° ′	° ′	′	′	′	′	′	′
00	9 15·0	9 16·5	8 49·7	0·0	0·0	6·0	3·8	12·0	7·5
01	9 15·3	9 16·8	8 50·0	0·1	0·1	6·1	3·8	12·1	7·6
02	9 15·5	9 17·0	8 50·2	0·2	0·1	6·2	3·9	12·2	7·6
03	9 15·8	9 17·3	8 50·4	0·3	0·2	6·3	3·9	12·3	7·7
04	9 16·0	9 17·5	8 50·7	0·4	0·3	6·4	4·0	12·4	7·8
05	9 16·3	9 17·8	8 50·9	0·5	0·3	6·5	4·1	12·5	7·8
06	9 16·5	9 18·0	8 51·1	0·6	0·4	6·6	4·1	12·6	7·9
07	9 16·8	9 18·3	8 51·4	0·7	0·4	6·7	4·2	12·7	7·9
08	9 17·0	9 18·5	8 51·6	0·8	0·5	6·8	4·3	12·8	8·0
09	9 17·3	9 18·8	8 51·9	0·9	0·6	6·9	4·3	12·9	8·1
10	9 17·5	9 19·0	8 52·1	1·0	0·6	7·0	4·4	13·0	8·1
11	9 17·8	9 19·3	8 52·3	1·1	0·7	7·1	4·4	13·1	8·2
12	9 18·0	9 19·5	8 52·6	1·2	0·8	7·2	4·5	13·2	8·3
13	9 18·3	9 19·8	8 52·8	1·3	0·8	7·3	4·6	13·3	8·3
14	9 18·5	9 20·0	8 53·1	1·4	0·9	7·4	4·6	13·4	8·4
15	9 18·8	9 20·3	8 53·3	1·5	0·9	7·5	4·7	13·5	8·4
16	9 19·0	9 20·5	8 53·5	1·6	1·0	7·6	4·8	13·6	8·5
17	9 19·3	9 20·8	8 53·8	1·7	1·1	7·7	4·8	13·7	8·6
18	9 19·5	9 21·0	8 54·0	1·8	1·1	7·8	4·9	13·8	8·6
19	9 19·8	9 21·3	8 54·3	1·9	1·2	7·9	4·9	13·9	8·7
20	9 20·0	9 21·5	8 54·5	2·0	1·3	8·0	5·0	14·0	8·8
21	9 20·3	9 21·8	8 54·7	2·1	1·3	8·1	5·1	14·1	8·8
22	9 20·5	9 22·0	8 55·0	2·2	1·4	8·2	5·1	14·2	8·9
23	9 20·8	9 22·3	8 55·2	2·3	1·4	8·3	5·2	14·3	8·9
24	9 21·0	9 22·5	8 55·4	2·4	1·5	8·4	5·3	14·4	9·0
25	9 21·3	9 22·8	8 55·7	2·5	1·6	8·5	5·3	14·5	9·1
26	9 21·5	9 23·0	8 55·9	2·6	1·6	8·6	5·4	14·6	9·1
27	9 21·8	9 23·3	8 56·2	2·7	1·7	8·7	5·4	14·7	9·2
28	9 22·0	9 23·5	8 56·4	2·8	1·8	8·8	5·5	14·8	9·3
29	9 22·3	9 23·8	8 56·6	2·9	1·8	8·9	5·6	14·9	9·3
30	9 22·5	9 24·0	8 56·9	3·0	1·9	9·0	5·6	15·0	9·4
31	9 22·8	9 24·3	8 57·1	3·1	1·9	9·1	5·7	15·1	9·4
32	9 23·0	9 24·5	8 57·4	3·2	2·0	9·2	5·8	15·2	9·5
33	9 23·3	9 24·8	8 57·6	3·3	2·1	9·3	5·8	15·3	9·6
34	9 23·5	9 25·0	8 57·8	3·4	2·1	9·4	5·9	15·4	9·6
35	9 23·8	9 25·3	8 58·1	3·5	2·2	9·5	5·9	15·5	9·7
36	9 24·0	9 25·5	8 58·3	3·6	2·3	9·6	6·0	15·6	9·8
37	9 24·3	9 25·8	8 58·5	3·7	2·3	9·7	6·1	15·7	9·8
38	9 24·5	9 26·0	8 58·8	3·8	2·4	9·8	6·1	15·8	9·9
39	9 24·8	9 26·3	8 59·0	3·9	2·4	9·9	6·2	15·9	9·9
40	9 25·0	9 26·5	8 59·3	4·0	2·5	10·0	6·3	16·0	10·0
41	9 25·3	9 26·8	8 59·5	4·1	2·6	10·1	6·3	16·1	10·1
42	9 25·5	9 27·0	8 59·7	4·2	2·6	10·2	6·4	16·2	10·1
43	9 25·8	9 27·3	9 00·0	4·3	2·7	10·3	6·4	16·3	10·2
44	9 26·0	9 27·5	9 00·2	4·4	2·8	10·4	6·5	16·4	10·3
45	9 26·3	9 27·8	9 00·5	4·5	2·8	10·5	6·6	16·5	10·3
46	9 26·5	9 28·1	9 00·7	4·6	2·9	10·6	6·6	16·6	10·4
47	9 26·8	9 28·3	9 00·9	4·7	2·9	10·7	6·7	16·7	10·4
48	9 27·0	9 28·6	9 01·2	4·8	3·0	10·8	6·8	16·8	10·5
49	9 27·3	9 28·8	9 01·4	4·9	3·1	10·9	6·8	16·9	10·6
50	9 27·5	9 29·1	9 01·6	5·0	3·1	11·0	6·9	17·0	10·6
51	9 27·8	9 29·3	9 01·9	5·1	3·2	11·1	6·9	17·1	10·7
52	9 28·0	9 29·6	9 02·1	5·2	3·3	11·2	7·0	17·2	10·8
53	9 28·3	9 29·8	9 02·4	5·3	3·3	11·3	7·1	17·3	10·8
54	9 28·5	9 30·1	9 02·6	5·4	3·4	11·4	7·1	17·4	10·9
55	9 28·8	9 30·3	9 02·8	5·5	3·4	11·5	7·2	17·5	10·9
56	9 29·0	9 30·6	9 03·1	5·6	3·5	11·6	7·3	17·6	11·0
57	9 29·3	9 30·8	9 03·3	5·7	3·6	11·7	7·3	17·7	11·1
58	9 29·5	9 31·1	9 03·6	5·8	3·6	11·8	7·4	17·8	11·1
59	9 29·8	9 31·3	9 03·8	5·9	3·7	11·9	7·4	17·9	11·2
60	9 30·0	9 31·6	9 04·0	6·0	3·8	12·0	7·5	18·0	11·3

Figure 2304c. *Nautical Almanac*, Increments and Correction page (typical).

and phase of the moon. Values are given for the semidiameter (SD) of the sun (for the three-day period) and of the moon (for each day).

Additionally, right-hand pages provide data on sunrise and sunset, moonrise and moonset, and the beginning and ending of twilight. The use of this data is discussed in Articles 2711–2716.

Interpolation To establish GHA and declination of the body for a time of observation other than the exact hour of GMT, it is necessary to interpolate—i.e., calculate intermediate values between those which appear in the hourly tabulation. For the intermediate time, stated in minutes and seconds past the whole hour printed in the tables, the change in GHA and Dec. are assumed to be at a uniform rate. This is not strictly true; however, the error involved is negligible when using the stars. The *v* and *d* corrections listed in the previous paragraph are applied for greater accuracy when using bodies within the solar system.

These increments and corrections are printed on tinted pages to facilitate locating them. A sample page is shown in Figure 2304c. The computations are based on standard apparent motions of the heavenly bodies around the earth, at the rate of 15° per hour for the sun and planets, 15°02.46′ for Aries, and 14°19.0′ for the moon. The values of the correction for *v* and *d* are then the excesses of the actual hourly motions over the above adopted values. They are generally positive, except for the *v* value for Venus which is sometimes negative. Increments and corrections are determined and applied as discussed in Article 2307.

Star positions The SHA and declination of 173 brighter stars, including the 57 navigational stars listed on the daily pages, are tabulated for each month near the end of the white section of the *Nautical Almanac.* No interpolation is needed and the data can be used in precisely the same way as those selected stars on the daily pages. The stars are arranged in ascending order of SHA.

Accuracy **2305** The tabulated values are in most cases correct to the nearest one-tenth minute, the exception being the sun's GHA, which is deliberately adjusted by up to 0.15′ to reduce the error caused by omitting the *v* correction. The largest imprecision that can occur in GHA or Dec. of any body other than the sun or moon is less than 0.2′; it may reach 0.25′ for the GHA of the sun, and 0.3′ for the moon. These are extremes; in actual use, it may be expected that less than 10 percent of the values of GHA and Dec. will have errors greater than 0.1′.

Errors in altitude corrections are generally of the same order as those for GHA and Dec., as they result from the addition of several quantities each rounded to 0.1′. The *actual* values, however, of dip and refraction at low altitudes may, in extreme atmospheric conditions, differ considerably from the mean values shown in the tables of the *Nautical Almanac.*

The time values shown are GMT, also referred to as UT1 (see Article 2210). This may differ from radio broadcast time signals, which are in UTC, by up to 0.8 seconds of time; step adjustments of exactly one second are made as required to prevent this difference from exceeding 0.8 seconds. Those who require the reduction of observations to a precision of better than one second of time must apply a correction, DUT1, which normally can be determined from the radio broadcast, to each time of observation. Alternatively, the DUT1 correction may be applied to the longitude reduced from the uncorrected time in accordance with the table below:

Correction to time signals	Correction to longitude
-0.8^s to -0.7^s	0.2′ to east
-0.6^s to -0.3^s	0.1′ to east
-0.2^s to $+0.2^s$	no correction
$+0.3^s$ to $+0.6^s$	0.1′ to west
$+0.7^s$ to $+0.8^s$	0.2′ to west

Additional tables in the *Nautical Almanac*

2306 A table is included within the *Nautical Almanac* for correcting sextant observations for atmospheric refraction. This table is based on standard conditions of barometric pressure and temperature; a second table gives additional corrections for nonstandard conditions. Tables for correcting for the dip of the horizon under standard conditions and a special table for moon correction are also included. These tables for correcting the sextant altitude are discussed in more detail in Chapter 21. These values do not change as a function of time as do the ephemeristic data in the *Nautical Almanac.*

Use of the tables

2307 The GMT of an observation is expressed as a day and an hour, followed by minutes and seconds. The tabular values of GHA and Dec., and, where necessary, the corresponding values of v and d, are taken directly from the daily pages for the day and hour of GMT; the hour used is always that *before* the time of observation. SHA and Dec. for selected stars are also taken from the daily pages.

The table of Increments and Corrections for the minutes component of the GMT of observation is then selected. The increment for GHA for minutes and seconds of GMT is taken from the line for the number of seconds and the column for the body concerned. The v correction is taken from the right-hand portion of the table for the same GMT minutes opposite the v value given on the daily pages. Both increment and v correction are to be added to the GHA value extracted from the daily page for the whole hour, except for Venus when the v value is prefixed with a minus sign; it is then subtracted.

For the Dec. there is no increment, but a d correction is applied in the same way as for v. Values of d on the daily pages are not marked

"+" or "−"; the sign must be determined by observing the trend of Dec. value.

Figure 2307 illustrates the determination and recording of data for the sun, moon, Mars, and the star Denebola. The data have been extracted from the daily pages of Figures 2304a and 2304b, and the Increments and Corrections page shown in Figure 2304c.

Example: (Figure 2307, sun column)

A navigator located at approximately 30° N, 60° W on 5 June ZT 09-36-35 (+4), having observed the sun needs to determine its GHA and Dec. from the *Nautical Almanac.*

Solution: (1) Determine GMT by adding the ZD to the ZT; GMT is 13-36-35. (2) On the right-hand page which includes the data on 5 June (Figure 2304b), find the column headed GMT and find the line for the whole hour "13" of the day indicated as "5 Sunday." (3) Follow across this line to the column for the sun; read and record the value for GHA (15°24.0′) and Dec. (N22°34.0′); note whether Dec. is increasing or decreasing at the next hour (it is increasing, and so the sign of the *d* correction will be +). (4) At the bottom of the Dec. column, read and record the *d* value (0.3′). (5) Turn to the yellow pages for Increments and Corrections and find the page which includes values for 36 minutes of GMT as indicated at the top of the page (Figure 2304c); find the line for 35 seconds and follow across to the Sun/Planets column; read and record the GHA increment (9°08.8′). [If time was measured more closely than to the nearest second, interpolate as required.] (6) In the column for *v* and *d* corrections, find the line for a *d* value of 0.3′; the *d* correction is read and recorded (0.2′); the sign was previously determined to be (+). (7) Add the GHA increment to the value of GHA for 13 hours GMT on 5 June: 15°24.0′

Body	SUN	MOON	DENEBOLA	MARS
Date (G)	5 JUN 77	5 JUN 77	5 JUN 77	5 JUN 77
GMT	13-36-35	09-37-08	23-36-56	23-37-22
GHA (h)	15° 24.0′	83° 49.6′	239° 15.1′	211° 05.1′
Incre (m/s)	9° 08.8′	8° 51.6′	9° 15.5′	9° 20.5′
V/V Corr	–	7.6/ +4.8′	–	0.7/ +0.4′
SHA			183° 01.3′	–
Total GHA	24° 32.8′	92° 46.0′	431° 31.9′	220° 26.0′
± 360°			71° 31.9′	
Tab Dec	N 22° 34.0′	S 14° 25.0′	N 14° 41.9′	N 10° 26.9′
d/d Corr	+0.3/ 0.2	7.6/ −4.8	–	+0.7/ +0.4′
True Dec	N 22° 34.2′	S 14° 20.2′	N 14° 41.9′	N 10° 27.3′

Figure 2307. Tabular solutions for GHA and declination using *Nautical Almanac.*

+9°08.8′ = 24°32.8′; this is the GHA of the sun for the time of observation. (8) Add the *d* correction to the value of Dec. for 13 hours GMT on 5 June; N22°34.0′ + 0.2 = N22°34.2′; this is the declination of the sun at the time of observation.

Solutions for other bodies Referring to Figure 2307 and the above procedure for determining GHA and Dec. for the sun, a similar procedure is followed for the other bodies. Following through the problem it will be noted that there is both a *v* and *d* correction for the moon in addition to the correction for minutes and seconds of time after the whole hour of GMT. The north declination of the moon was decreasing with time, resulting in the *d* correction being minus. In the Denebola problem the GHA ♈ plus SHA star produced a GHA Denebola of 431°31.9′ with the result that 360° was subtracted to produce a GHA of 71°31.9′. For the Mars observation, the north declination was increasing with time and the *d* correction was therefore (+). In both the Mars and moon observations, the declination was changing toward the north. In the first case, there was an increase in N Dec. and in the latter there was a decrease of S Dec.

***Nautical Almanac* summary** **2308** The coordinates of celestial bodies are tabulated in the *Nautical Almanac* with respect to Greenwich Mean Time. Using the GMT (or in practical terms, UTC) of an observation, the navigator extracts the GHA and Dec. of the body observed. The position of the body establishes one vertex of the navigational triangle: the navigator solves this triangle to obtain a line of position.

The GHAs of the sun, moon, planets, and Aries are tabulated in the *Nautical Almanac* for each hour of GMT, and tables of increments permit interpolation for the minutes and seconds of an observation. A small *v* correction factor applying to the GHA is also shown on the daily pages. The sum of the tabulated GHA, together with the increment for excess minutes and seconds, and the value of the *v* correction for these minutes and seconds, is the GHA of the body at the time of observation. The SHA of a star is added to the GHA of Aries to obtain the star's GHA. The SHA of the star is taken from the *Almanac* without interpolation.

The declinations of the sun, moon, and planets are also tabulated in the daily pages of the *Nautical Almanac* for GMT, as is a *d* factor. The correction to the declination for *d* is obtained from the table of increments for the excess minutes and seconds over the tabulated value. The declination of a star is taken from the *Nautical Almanac* without any correction.

In practice, the navigator always obtains *all* values of GHA and Dec., plus associated data, from the daily pages during one book opening. He then turns to the Increments and Corrections tables for the remaining data. This procedure materially shortens the time required to reduce observations.

Air Almanac contents **2309** The *Air Almanac* contains basically the same data as that of the *Nautical Almanac*. The arrangement is designed primarily for the use of aviators, being more convenient for a fast solution; however, small inaccuracies result for some bodies. It is becoming increasingly popular with surface navigators, but its use is not recommended when maximum accuracy is required in all observations.

The *Air Almanac* gives ephemeristic data for each ten minutes of GMT on the daily pages; and due to the great number of tabulations, it cannot conveniently be bound as a single volume covering an entire year. It is issued twice a year, each volume covering a six-month period of time. Two pages, the front and back of a single sheet, cover one calendar day (Figures 2309a and 2309b). Thus, at any one opening, the left-hand page contains the tabulation of data for every 10 minutes of time from 12 hours 0 minutes GMT to 23 hours 50 minutes of one day. Data from 0 hours 0 minutes to 11 hours 50 minutes of the following day are presented on the right-hand page. The daily data include GHA and Dec. of the sun, each to 0.1′, the GHA of Aries to 0.1′, and the GHA and Dec. of the moon and of the three planets most suitable for observation at that time, all to the nearest 1′. The volumes are bound with plastic rings to enable the aviator to tear out the daily pages for more convenient use. In addition, these daily pages give the time of moonrise and moonset, the moon's parallax in altitude, the semidiameters of the sun and moon, and the latter's age. At the bottom of each column of data (except GHA ♈), an hourly rate of change is given. For the declination of the moon, a "star" symbol following the rate tabulation indicates that a value derived at the end of a six-hour period, which is half of the time interval covered by the page, will be in error by at least two minutes of arc. These hourly rate tabulations are intended to facilitate computer input processing; they are not used in normal navigation calculations.

On the inside of the front cover there is a table to permit ready interpolation of GHA of the sun, Aries, and planets on the one hand, and of the moon on the other, for time increments between the 10-minute tabulated values of GHA. This table is repeated on a flap which can be folded out from the book. Both of these tables state arc to the nearest whole minute. For greater precision there is also included in the white section in the back of the *Almanac* a separate page for the interpolation of GHA sun and one for interpolation GHA Aries, each giving values of 0.1′ of arc. A star index of the 57 navigational stars in alphabetical order with their magnitudes, SHA, and Dec. to 1′ is given covering their average position for the six-month period of the *Almanac*. For those desiring greater precision, or for stars other than the 57 principal ones, separate tables are included in the white section giving SHA and Dec. of 173 stars to 0.1′ of arc for each month of the period covered by the *Almanac*. They are listed in ascending order of SHA and are intended for use with the astrotracker. The value of SHA is combined with GHA ♈ from the daily pages, to obtain GHA of the star.

Miscellaneous Tables in *Air Almanac*

2310 Various other tables, sky diagrams, and other data are included in the back of the book. As far as possible they are arranged in inverse order of use; that is, the most commonly used data are directly inside the back cover, therefore most easily located. A table is included in the back of the volume to assist in interpolating the time of moonrise and moonset for longitude.

Examples from the *Air Almanac*

2311 Sample daily pages from the *Air Almanac* are shown in Figures 2309a and 2309b; for comparison purposes, these are for dates included in the period covered by the sample pages from the *Nautical Almanac*. The table for interpolation of GHA is shown as Figure 2311a.

Figure 2311b illustrates the extraction of data from the *Air Almanac* for various bodies. Again, for comparison purposes, the same bodies and times are used as were illustrated in Figure 2307 for the *Nautical Almanac*.

Example: Obtain GHA and Dec. of the sun on 5 June ZT 09-36-35 (+ 4).

Solution: (1) Determine GMT by adding ZD to ZT; GMT is 13-36-35. (2) Locate the page which includes the second half of 5 June; locate the line for the hour and lesser 10-minute interval (13 30). (3) Follow across this line to the column headed "sun"; read and record the GHA (22°54.0′) and the Dec. (N 22°34.1′). (4) Turn to the table for "Interpolation of GHA" on the inside front cover of the *Almanac* (Figure 2311a) and pick out incremental correction in "Sun, etc." column for 6 minutes and 35 seconds (1°39′). Note: This is a quickly used table of critical values to the nearest 1′; if a value to 0.1′ is needed, there are also interpolation tables for GHA sun and GHA Aries in the white pages at the back of the *Air Almanac*. (5) Add the increment of GHA to the value from the daily page: 22°54.0′ + 1°39′ = 24°33′; this is the GHA of the sun for the time of observation.

It should be noted here that the *Air Almanac,* with entries for each 10 minutes of time, permits the GHA of the sun to be found more accurately than with the *Nautical Almanac* (unless special procedures are used with the latter). The reason for this is that the *Nautical Almanac,* with tabulated data only for each whole hour, lists GHA adjusted by as much as 0.15′ to minimize the error caused by ignoring any v correction, as stated in Article 2305.

In the *Air Almanac* tabulated declination is always used without interpolation; the tabular value for the GMT immediately *before* the time of observation is taken. In this example, this is N 22°34.1′.

U. S. Naval observatory publication, *Almanac for Computers*

2312 A recent product of the "computer age" is the U. S. Naval Observatory publication, *Almanac for Computers* (available for purchase directly from the U.S. Observatory, Washington, DC 20390). This small pamphlet contains mathematical expressions for various items of almanac data and tables of constants to be used in them, together with

(DAY 156) GREENWICH A. M. 1977 JUNE 5 (SUNDAY)

GMT	☉ SUN GHA	SUN Dec.	ARIES GHA ♈	VENUS −4.1 GHA	VENUS Dec.	MARS 1.3 GHA	MARS Dec.	SATURN 0.6 GHA	SATURN Dec.	☽ MOON GHA	MOON Dec.
h m	° ′	° ′	° ′	° ′	° ′	° ′	° ′	° ′	° ′	° ′	° ′
00 00	180 25.5	N22 30.4	253 18.4	225 38	N 8 57	225 49	N10 12	118 04	N18 00	313 54	S15 29
10	182 55.5	30.5	255 48.8	228 08		228 19		120 34		316 18	28
20	185 25.5	30.5	258 19.2	230 38		230 49		123 05		318 42	27
30	187 55.4	· 30.6	260 49.6	233 08	· ·	233 19	· ·	125 35	· ·	321 07	· 25
40	190 25.4	30.6	263 20.0	235 38		235 49		128 06		323 31	24
50	192 55.4	30.6	265 50.4	238 08		238 20		130 36		325 55	23
01 00	195 25.4	N22 30.7	268 20.9	240 38	N 8 57	240 50	N10 13	133 06	N18 00	328 20	S15 22
10	197 55.4	30.7	270 51.3	243 08		243 20		135 37		330 44	21
20	200 25.4	30.8	273 21.7	245 38		245 50		138 07		333 08	20
30	202 55.3	· 30.8	275 52.1	248 08	· ·	248 20	· ·	140 38	· ·	335 33	· 19
40	205 25.3	30.9	278 22.5	250 38		250 50		143 08		337 57	17
50	207 55.3	30.9	280 52.9	253 08		253 20		145 38		340 21	16
02 00	210 25.3	N22 31.0	283 23.3	255 38	N 8 58	255 50	N10 13	148 09	N18 00	342 46	S15 15
10	212 55.3	31.0	285 53.7	258 08		258 21		150 39		345 10	14
20	215 25.2	31.1	288 24.1	260 38		260 51		153 09		347 34	13
30	217 55.2	· 31.1	290 54.6	263 08	· ·	263 21	· ·	155 40	· ·	349 59	· 12
40	220 25.2	31.2	293 25.0	265 39		265 51		158 10		352 23	10
50	222 55.2	31.2	295 55.4	268 09		268 21		160 41		354 47	09
03 00	225 25.2	N22 31.3	298 25.8	270 39	N 8 59	270 51	N10 14	163 11	N17 59	357 12	S15 08
10	227 55.2	31.3	300 56.2	273 09		273 21		165 41		359 36	07
20	230 25.1	31.3	303 26.6	275 39		275 51		168 12		2 00	06
30	232 55.1	· 31.4	305 57.0	278 09	· ·	278 21	· ·	170 42	· ·	4 25	· 05
40	235 25.1	31.4	308 27.4	280 39		280 52		173 12		6 49	03
50	237 55.1	31.5	310 57.8	283 09		283 22		175 43		9 13	02
04 00	240 25.1	N22 31.5	313 28.3	285 39	N 8 59	285 52	N10 15	178 13	N17 59	11 38	S15 01
10	242 55.0	31.6	315 58.7	288 09		288 22		180 43		14 02	15 00
20	245 25.0	31.6	318 29.1	290 39		290 52		183 14		16 26	14 59
30	247 55.0	· 31.7	320 59.5	293 09	· ·	293 22	· ·	185 44	· ·	18 51	· 58
40	250 25.0	31.7	323 29.9	295 39		295 52		188 15		21 15	56
50	252 55.0	31.8	326 00.3	298 09		298 22		190 45		23 40	55
05 00	255 25.0	N22 31.8	328 30.7	300 39	N 9 00	300 53	N10 15	193 15	N17 59	26 04	S14 54
10	257 54.9	31.9	331 01.1	303 09		303 23		195 46		28 28	53
20	260 24.9	31.9	333 31.5	305 39		305 53		198 16		30 53	51
30	262 54.9	· 31.9	336 01.9	308 09	· ·	308 23	· ·	200 46	· ·	33 17	· 50
40	265 24.9	32.0	338 32.4	310 40		310 53		203 17		35 41	49
50	267 54.9	32.0	341 02.8	313 10		313 23		205 47		38 06	48
06 00	270 24.8	N22 32.1	343 33.2	315 40	N 9 01	315 53	N10 16	208 18	N17 59	40 30	S14 47
10	272 54.8	32.1	346 03.6	318 10		318 23		210 48		42 55	45
20	275 24.8	32.2	348 34.0	320 40		320 53		213 18		45 19	44
30	277 54.8	· 32.2	351 04.4	323 10	· ·	323 24	· ·	215 49	· ·	47 43	· 43
40	280 24.8	32.3	353 34.8	325 40		325 54		218 19		50 08	42
50	282 54.8	32.3	356 05.2	328 10		328 24		220 49		52 32	41
07 00	285 24.7	N22 32.4	358 35.6	330 40	N 9 01	330 54	N10 17	223 20	N17 59	54 57	S14 39
10	287 54.7	32.4	1 06.1	333 10		333 24		225 50		57 21	38
20	290 24.7	32.4	3 36.5	335 40		335 54		228 21		59 45	37
30	292 54.7	· 32.5	6 06.9	338 10	· ·	338 24	· ·	230 51	· ·	62 10	· 36
40	295 24.7	32.5	8 37.3	340 40		340 54		233 21		64 34	34
50	297 54.6	32.6	11 07.7	343 10		343 24		235 52		66 59	33
08 00	300 24.6	N22 32.6	13 38.1	345 40	N 9 02	345 55	N10 17	238 22	N17 59	69 23	S14 32
10	302 54.6	32.7	16 08.5	348 10		348 25		240 52		71 47	31
20	305 24.6	32.7	18 38.9	350 40		350 55		243 23		74 12	29
30	307 54.6	· 32.8	21 09.3	353 11	· ·	353 25	· ·	245 53	· ·	76 36	· 28
40	310 24.6	32.8	23 39.8	355 41		355 55		248 24		79 01	27
50	312 54.5	32.9	26 10.2	358 11		358 25		250 54		81 25	26
09 00	315 24.5	N22 32.9	28 40.6	0 41	N 9 02	0 55	N10 18	253 24	N17 59	83 49	S14 24
10	317 54.5	33.0	31 11.0	3 11		3 25		255 55		86 14	23
20	320 24.5	33.0	33 41.4	5 41		5 56		258 25		88 38	22
30	322 54.5	· 33.0	36 11.8	8 11	· ·	8 26	· ·	260 55	· ·	91 03	· 21
40	325 24.4	33.1	38 42.2	10 41		10 56		263 26		93 27	19
50	327 54.4	33.1	41 12.6	13 11		13 26		265 56		95 52	18
10 00	330 24.4	N22 33.2	43 43.0	15 41	N 9 03	15 56	N10 19	268 27	N17 59	98 16	S14 17
10	332 54.4	33.2	46 13.4	18 11		18 26		270 57		100 40	16
20	335 24.4	33.3	48 43.9	20 41		20 56		273 27		103 05	14
30	337 54.4	· 33.3	51 14.3	23 11	· ·	23 26	· ·	275 58	· ·	105 29	· 13
40	340 24.3	33.4	53 44.7	25 41		25 56		278 28		107 54	12
50	342 54.3	33.4	56 15.1	28 11		28 27		280 58		110 18	10
11 00	345 24.3	N22 33.5	58 45.5	30 41	N 9 04	30 57	N10 19	283 29	N17 59	112 43	S14 09
10	347 54.3	33.5	61 15.9	33 11		33 27		285 59		115 07	08
20	350 24.3	33.5	63 46.3	35 42		35 57		288 30		117 32	07
30	352 54.2	· 33.6	66 16.7	38 12	· ·	38 27	· ·	291 00	· ·	119 56	· 05
40	355 24.2	33.6	68 47.1	40 42		40 57		293 30		122 21	04
50	357 54.2	33.7	71 17.6	43 12		43 27		296 01		124 45	03
Rate	14 59.9	N0 00.3		15 00.3	N0 00.6	15 00.7	N0 00.7	15 02.3	S0 00.1	14 26.3	N0 07.3

Lat.	Moonrise	Diff.
N		
°	h m	m
72	01 02	−11
70	00 26	+03
68	00 00	08
66	23 57	07
64	23 46	10
62	23 36	11
60	23 28	13
58	23 20	14
56	23 14	15
54	23 08	16
52	23 03	17
50	22 58	18
45	22 47	19
40	22 39	20
35	22 31	21
30	22 24	23
20	22 13	24
10	22 03	26
0	21 54	27
10	21 44	28
20	21 34	30
30	21 22	31
35	21 16	32
40	21 08	33
45	20 59	35
50	20 48	36
52	20 43	37
54	20 38	38
56	20 32	39
58	20 25	40
60	20 17	41
S		

Moon's P. in A.

Alt. °	Corr. + ′	Alt. °	Corr. + ′
0		54	
	59		34
10		55	
	58		33
14		56	
	57		32
18		58	
	56		31
21		59	
	55		30
23		60	
	54		29
25		61	
	53		28
28		62	
	52		27
30		63	
	51		26
31		64	
	50		25
33		65	
	49		24
35		66	
	48		23
36		67	
	47		22
38		68	
	46		21
40		69	
	45		20
41		70	
	44		19
42		71	
	43		18
44		72	
	42		17
45		73	
	41		16
47		74	
	40		15
48		75	
	39		14
49		76	
	38		13
50		77	
	37		12
52		78	
	36		11
53		79	
	35		10
54		80	
	34		
55			

Sun SD 15′.8
Moon SD 16′
Age 18d

Figure 2309a. *Air Almanac,* right hand daily page (typical).

(DAY 156) GREENWICH P. M. 1977 JUNE 5 (SUNDAY)

GMT	☉ SUN GHA	SUN Dec.	ARIES GHA ♈	VENUS −4.1 GHA	VENUS Dec.	MARS 1.3 GHA	MARS Dec.	SATURN 0.6 GHA	SATURN Dec.	☽ MOON GHA	MOON Dec.
h m	° ′	° ′	° ′	° ′	° ′	° ′	° ′	° ′	° ′	° ′	° ′
12 00	0 24.2	N22 33.7	73 48.0	45 42	N 9 04	45 57	N10 20	298 31	N17 59	127 10	S14 01
10	2 54.2	33.8	76 18.4	48 12		48 28		301 01		129 34	14 00
20	5 24.2	33.8	78 48.8	50 42		50 58		303 32		131 59	13 59
30	7 54.1	· 33.9	81 19.2	53 12	· ·	53 28	· ·	306 02	· ·	134 23	· 57
40	10 24.1	33.9	83 49.6	55 42		55 58		308 33		136 47	56
50	12 54.1	34.0	86 20.0	58 12		58 28		311 03		139 12	55
13 00	15 24.1	N22 34.0	88 50.4	60 42	N 9 05	60 58	N10 21	313 33	N17 59	141 36	S13 54
10	17 54.1	34.0	91 20.8	63 12		63 28		316 04		144 01	52
20	20 24.0	34.1	93 51.3	65 42		65 58		318 34		146 25	51
30	22 54.0	· 34.1	96 21.7	68 12	· ·	68 28	· ·	321 04	· ·	148 50	· 50
40	25 24.0	34.2	98 52.1	70 42		70 59		323 35		151 14	48
50	27 54.0	34.2	101 22.5	73 12		73 29		326 05		153 39	47
14 00	30 24.0	N22 34.3	103 52.9	75 42	N 9 06	75 59	N10 21	328 36	N17 59	156 03	S13 46
10	32 54.0	34.3	106 23.3	78 12		78 29		331 06		158 28	44
20	35 23.9	34.4	108 53.7	80 43		80 59		333 36		160 52	43
30	37 53.9	· 34.4	111 24.1	83 13	· ·	83 29	· ·	336 07	· ·	163 17	· 42
40	40 23.9	34.4	113 54.5	85 43		85 59		338 37		165 41	40
50	42 53.9	34.5	116 24.9	88 13		88 29		341 07		168 06	39
15 00	45 23.9	N22 34.5	118 55.4	90 43	N 9 06	91 00	N10 22	343 38	N17 59	170 30	S13 38
10	47 53.8	34.6	121 25.8	93 13		93 30		346 08		172 55	36
20	50 23.8	34.6	123 56.2	95 43		96 00		348 39		175 20	35
30	52 53.8	· 34.7	126 26.6	98 13	· ·	98 30	· ·	351 09	· ·	177 44	· 34
40	55 23.8	34.7	128 57.0	100 43		101 00		353 39		180 09	32
50	57 53.8	34.8	131 27.4	103 13		103 30		356 10		182 33	31
16 00	60 23.7	N22 34.8	133 57.8	105 43	N 9 07	106 00	N10 23	358 40	N17 59	184 58	S13 30
10	62 53.7	34.9	136 28.2	108 13		108 30		1 10		187 22	28
20	65 23.7	34.9	138 58.6	110 43		111 00		3 41		189 47	27
30	67 53.7	· 34.9	141 29.1	113 13	· ·	113 31	· ·	6 11	· ·	192 11	· 26
40	70 23.7	35.0	143 59.5	115 43		116 01		8 42		194 36	24
50	72 53.7	35.0	146 29.9	118 13		118 31		11 12		197 00	23
17 00	75 23.6	N22 35.1	149 00.3	120 43	N 9 08	121 01	N10 23	13 42	N17 59	199 25	S13 22
10	77 53.6	35.1	151 30.7	123 13		123 31		16 13		201 49	20
20	80 23.6	35.2	154 01.1	125 44		126 01		18 43		204 14	19
30	82 53.6	· 35.2	156 31.5	128 14	· ·	128 31	· ·	21 13	· ·	206 39	· 17
40	85 23.6	35.3	159 01.9	130 44		131 01		23 44		209 03	16
50	87 53.5	35.3	161 32.3	133 14		133 31		26 14		211 28	15
18 00	90 23.5	N22 35.3	164 02.8	135 44	N 9 08	136 02	N10 24	28 45	N17 59	213 52	S13 13
10	92 53.5	35.4	166 33.2	138 14		138 32		31 15		216 17	12
20	95 23.5	35.4	169 03.6	140 44		141 02		33 45		218 41	11
30	97 53.5	· 35.5	171 34.0	143 14	· ·	143 32	· ·	36 16	· ·	221 06	· 09
40	100 23.5	35.5	174 04.4	145 44		146 02		38 46		223 30	08
50	102 53.4	35.6	176 34.8	148 14		148 32		41 16		225 55	06
19 00	105 23.4	N22 35.6	179 05.2	150 44	N 9 09	151 02	N10 25	43 47	N17 58	228 20	S13 05
10	107 53.4	35.7	181 35.6	153 14		153 32		46 17		230 44	04
20	110 23.4	35.7	184 06.0	155 44		156 03		48 48		233 09	02
30	112 53.4	· 35.7	186 36.4	158 14	· ·	158 33	· ·	51 18	· ·	235 33	· 01
40	115 23.3	35.8	189 06.9	160 44		161 03		53 48		237 58	13 00
50	117 53.3	35.8	191 37.3	163 14		163 33		56 19		240 23	12 58
20 00	120 23.3	N22 35.9	194 07.7	165 44	N 9 09	166 03	N10 25	58 49	N17 58	242 47	S12 57
10	122 53.3	35.9	196 38.1	168 14		168 33		61 19		245 12	55
20	125 23.3	36.0	199 08.5	170 45		171 03		63 50		247 36	54
30	127 53.3	· 36.0	201 38.9	173 15	· ·	173 33	· ·	66 20	· ·	250 01	· 53
40	130 23.2	36.1	204 09.3	175 45		176 03		68 51		252 26	51
50	132 53.2	36.1	206 39.7	178 15		178 34		71 21		254 50	50
21 00	135 23.2	N22 36.1	209 10.1	180 45	N 9 10	181 04	N10 26	73 51	N17 58	257 15	S12 48
10	137 53.2	36.2	211 40.6	183 15		183 34		76 22		259 39	47
20	140 23.2	36.2	214 11.0	185 45		186 04		78 52		262 04	46
30	142 53.1	· 36.3	216 41.4	188 15	· ·	188 34	· ·	81 22	· ·	264 29	· 44
40	145 23.1	36.3	219 11.8	190 45		191 04		83 53		266 53	43
50	147 53.1	36.4	221 42.2	193 15		193 34		86 23		269 18	41
22 00	150 23.1	N22 36.4	224 12.6	195 45	N 9 11	196 04	N10 27	88 54	N17 58	271 42	S12 40
10	152 53.1	36.5	226 43.0	198 15		198 35		91 24		274 07	39
20	155 23.0	36.5	229 13.4	200 45		201 05		93 54		276 32	37
30	157 53.0	· 36.5	231 43.8	203 15	· ·	203 35	· ·	96 25	· ·	278 56	· 36
40	160 23.0	36.6	234 14.2	205 45		206 05		98 55		281 21	34
50	162 53.0	36.6	236 44.7	208 15		208 35		101 25		283 46	33
23 00	165 23.0	N22 36.7	239 15.1	210 45	N 9 11	211 05	N10 27	103 56	N17 58	286 10	S12 31
10	167 53.0	36.7	241 45.5	213 15		213 35		106 26		288 35	30
20	170 22.9	36.8	244 15.9	215 45		216 05		108 56		290 59	29
30	172 52.9	· 36.8	246 46.3	218 16	· ·	218 35	· ·	111 27	· ·	293 24	· 27
40	175 22.9	36.9	249 16.7	220 46		221 06		113 57		295 49	26
50	177 52.9	36.9	251 47.1	223 16		223 36		116 28		298 13	24
Rate	14 59.9	N0 00.3		15 00.3	N0 00.6	15 00.7	N0 00.7	15 02.2	S0 00.1	14 27.4	N0 08.2

Lat.	Moon-set	Diff.
N		
°	h m	m
72	05 35	70
70	06 10	56
68	06 35	51
66	06 54	47
64	07 09	45
62	07 22	43
60	07 33	41
58	07 42	40
56	07 50	39
54	07 58	38
52	08 04	37
50	08 10	37
45	08 22	35
40	08 33	34
35	08 42	33
30	08 49	32
20	09 03	30
10	09 14	29
0	09 25	28
10	09 36	27
20	09 47	25
30	10 00	24
35	10 07	23
40	10 16	22
45	10 26	21
50	10 38	19
52	10 43	19
54	10 49	18
56	10 56	17
58	11 03	16
60	11 12	15
S		

Moon's P. in A.

Alt.	Corr.	Alt.	Corr.
°	+ ′	°	+ ′
0		54	
	59		34
7		55	
	58		33
12		56	
	57		32
16		57	
	56		31
19		58	
	55		30
22		60	
	54		29
24		61	
	53		28
27		62	
	52		27
29		63	
	51		26
31		64	
	50		25
32		65	
	49		24
34		66	
	48		23
36		67	
	47		22
38		68	
	46		21
39		69	
	45		20
41		70	
	44		19
42		71	
	43		18
43		72	
	42		17
45		73	
	41		16
46		74	
	40		15
47		75	
	39		14
49		76	
	38		13
50		77	
	37		12
51		78	
	36		11
53		79	
	35		10
54		80	
	34		
55			

Sun SD 15′.8

Moon SD 16′

Age 19d

Figure 2309b. *Air Almanac,* left hand daily page (typical).

STARS, JAN.—JUNE, 1977

No.	Name		Mag.	S.H.A.	Dec.
				° ′	° ′
7*	*Acamar*		3·1	315 39	S. 40 24
5*	*Achernar*		0·6	335 47	S. 57 21
30*	*Acrux*		1·1	173 39	S. 62 58
19	*Adhara*	†	1·6	255 34	S. 28 57
10*	*Aldebaran*	†	1·1	291 21	N. 16 28
32*	*Alioth*		1·7	166 44	N. 56 05
34*	*Alkaid*		1·9	153 20	N. 49 26
55	*Al Na'ir*		2·2	28 18	S. 47 04
15	*Alnilam*	†	1·8	276 14	S. 1 13
25*	*Alphard*	†	2·2	218 23	S. 8 34
41*	*Alphecca*	†	2·3	126 34	N. 26 47
1*	*Alpheratz*	†	2·2	358 12	N. 28 58
51*	*Altair*	†	0·9	62 35	N. 8 48
2	*Ankaa*		2·4	353 43	S. 42 26
42*	*Antares*	†	1·2	113 00	S. 26 23
37*	*Arcturus*	†	0·2	146 20	N. 19 18
43	*Atria*		1·9	108 26	S. 68 59
22	*Avior*		1·7	234 29	S. 59 26
13	*Bellatrix*	†	1·7	279 01	N. 6 20
16*	*Betelgeuse*	†	0·1–1·2	271 31	N. 7 24
17*	*Canopus*		−0·9	264 08	S. 52 41
12*	*Capella*		0·2	281 15	N. 45 59
53*	*Deneb*		1·3	49 50	N. 45 12
28*	*Denebola*	†	2·2	183 01	N. 14 42
4*	*Diphda*	†	2·2	349 23	S. 18 07
27*	*Dubhe*		2·0	194 25	N. 61 52
14	*Elnath*	†	1·8	278 47	N. 28 35
47	*Eltanin*		2·4	90 59	N. 51 29
54*	*Enif*	†	2·5	34 14	N. 9 46
56*	*Fomalhaut*	†	1·3	15 54	S. 29 45
31	*Gacrux*		1·6	172 31	S. 56 59
29*	*Gienah*	†	2·8	176 20	S. 17 25
35	*Hadar*		0·9	149 26	S. 60 16
6*	*Hamal*	†	2·2	328 32	N. 23 21
48	*Kaus Aust.*		2·0	84 20	S. 34 24
40*	*Kochab*		2·2	137 18	N. 74 15
57	*Markab*	†	2·6	14 06	N. 15 05
8*	*Menkar*	†	2·8	314 44	N. 4 00
36	*Menkent*		2·3	148 39	S. 36 16
24*	*Miaplacidus*		1·8	221 45	S. 69 38
9*	*Mirfak*		1·9	309 20	N. 49 47
50*	*Nunki*	†	2·1	76 32	S. 26 19
52*	*Peacock*		2·1	54 02	S. 56 48
21*	*Pollux*	†	1·2	244 01	N. 28 05
20*	*Procyon*	†	0·5	245 28	N. 5 17
46*	*Rasalhague*	†	2·1	96 32	N. 12 35
26*	*Regulus*	†	1·3	208 12	N. 12 05
11*	*Rigel*	†	0·3	281 38	S. 8 14
38*	*Rigil Kent.*		0·1	140 29	S. 60 44
44	*Sabik*	†	2·6	102 44	S. 15 42
3*	*Schedar*		2·5	350 12	N. 56 25
45*	*Shaula*		1·7	96 59	S. 37 05
18*	*Sirius*	†	−1·6	258 58	S. 16 41
33*	*Spica*	†	1·2	159 00	S. 11 03
23*	*Suhail*		2·2	223 12	S. 43 21
49*	*Vega*		0·1	80 57	N. 38 46
39	*Zuben'ubi*	†	2·9	137 35	S. 15 57

INTERPOLATION OF G.H.A.

Increment to be added for intervals of G.M.T. to G.H.A. of: Sun, Aries (♈) and planets; Moon

SUN, etc.		MOON	SUN, etc.		MOON	SUN, etc.		MOON
m s	° ′	m s	m s	° ′	m s	m s	° ′	m s
00 00	0 00	00 00	03 17	0 50	03 25	06 37	1 40	06 52
01	0 01	00 02	21	0 51	03 29	41	1 41	06 56
05	0 02	00 06	25	0 52	03 33	45	1 42	07 00
09	0 03	00 10	29	0 53	03 37	49	1 43	07 04
13	0 04	00 14	33	0 54	03 41	53	1 44	07 08
17	0 05	00 18	37	0 55	03 45	06 57	1 45	07 13
21	0 06	00 22	41	0 56	03 49	07 01	1 46	07 17
25	0 07	00 26	45	0 57	03 54	05	1 47	07 21
29	0 08	00 31	49	0 58	03 58	09	1 48	07 25
33	0 09	00 35	53	0 59	04 02	13	1 49	07 29
37	0 10	00 39	03 57	1 00	04 06	17	1 50	07 33
41	0 11	00 43	04 01	1 01	04 10	21	1 51	07 37
45	0 12	00 47	05	1 02	04 14	25	1 52	07 42
49	0 13	00 51	09	1 03	04 19	29	1 53	07 46
53	0 14	00 55	13	1 04	04 23	33	1 54	07 50
00 57	0 15	01 00	17	1 05	04 27	37	1 55	07 54
01 01	0 16	01 04	21	1 06	04 31	41	1 56	07 58
05	0 17	01 08	25	1 07	04 35	45	1 57	08 02
09	0 18	01 12	29	1 08	04 39	49	1 58	08 06
13	0 19	01 16	33	1 09	04 43	53	1 59	08 11
17	0 20	01 20	37	1 10	04 48	07 57	2 00	08 15
21	0 21	01 24	41	1 11	04 52	08 01	2 01	08 19
25	0 22	01 29	45	1 12	04 56	05	2 02	08 23
29	0 23	01 33	49	1 13	05 00	09	2 03	08 27
33	0 24	01 37	53	1 14	05 04	13	2 04	08 31
37	0 25	01 41	04 57	1 15	05 08	17	2 05	08 35
41	0 26	01 45	05 01	1 16	05 12	21	2 06	08 40
45	0 27	01 49	05	1 17	05 17	25	2 07	08 44
49	0 28	01 53	09	1 18	05 21	29	2 08	08 48
53	0 29	01 58	13	1 19	05 25	33	2 09	08 52
01 57	0 30	02 02	17	1 20	05 29	37	2 10	08 56
02 01	0 31	02 06	21	1 21	05 33	41	2 11	09 00
05	0 32	02 10	25	1 22	05 37	45	2 12	09 04
09	0 33	02 14	29	1 23	05 41	49	2 13	09 09
13	0 34	02 18	33	1 24	05 46	53	2 14	09 13
17	0 35	02 22	37	1 25	05 50	08 57	2 15	09 17
21	0 36	02 27	41	1 26	05 54	09 01	2 16	09 21
25	0 37	02 31	45	1 27	05 58	05	2 17	09 25
29	0 38	02 35	49	1 28	06 02	09	2 18	09 29
33	0 39	02 39	53	1 29	06 06	13	2 19	09 33
37	0 40	02 43	05 57	1 30	06 10	17	2 20	09 38
41	0 41	02 47	06 01	1 31	06 15	21	2 21	09 42
45	0 42	02 51	05	1 32	06 19	25	2 22	09 46
49	0 43	02 56	09	1 33	06 23	29	2 23	09 50
53	0 44	03 00	13	1 34	06 27	33	2 24	09 54
02 57	0 45	03 04	17	1 35	06 31	37	2 25	09 58
03 01	0 46	03 08	21	1 36	06 35	41	2 26	10 00
05	0 47	03 12	25	1 37	06 39	45	2 27	
09	0 48	03 16	29	1 38	06 44	49	2 28	
13	0 49	03 20	33	1 39	06 48	53	2 29	
17	0 50	03 25	37	1 40	06 52	09 57	2 30	
03 21		03 29	06 41		06 56	10 00		

*Stars used in H.O. 249 (A.P. 3270) Vol. 1.
†Stars that may be used with Vols. 2 and 3.

Figure 2311a. *Air Almanac,* tables on inside front cover.

Body	SUN	MOON	DENEBOLA	MARS
Date (G)	5 JUN 77	5 JUN 77	5 JUN 77	5 JUN 77
GMT	13-36-35	09-37-08	23-36-56	23-37-22
GHA (h + 10m)	22° 54′	91° 03′	246° 46′	218° 35′
Incre (m/s)	1° 39′	1° 43′	1° 44′	1° 51′
SHA	—	—	183° 01′	—
Total GHA	24° 33′	92° 46′	431° 31′	220° 26′
± 360°			71° 31′	
Tab Dec	N 22° 35′	S 14° 21′	N 14° 42′	N 10° 27′

Figure 2311b. Tabular solutions for GHA and declination, *Air Almanac.*

the necessary instructions. This publication can serve essentially as a complete alternative to the use of a *Nautical* or *Air Almanac.*

The *Almanac for Computers* is designed to facilitate the application of digital computation techniques to problems of astronomy and navigation that require the coordinates of celestial bodies. Although basically intended for use with computers—the tabular data are also available in machine-readable form on punched cards or magnetic tape—the procedures of this publication are within the capabilities of card-programmable personal calculators such as the Texas-Instruments models SR-52 and TI-59, and Hewlett-Packard models HP-65, -67, and -97.

For the navigator, direct calculations to essentially the full level of precision and accuracy of the *Nautical Almanac* are possible for all necessary data of the stars, Aries, planets, sun, and moon, including semidiameter and horizontal parallax where applicable. A given set of constants from the tables is usable for periods of 6 days for the moon, and 32 days for Aries, the sun, and the planets. It is a simple matter to update the constants for subsequent time periods. A set of constants for a star—data are tabulated for 176 stars, including the 57 "selected" stars—is valid for the full year of the publication.

The *Almanac for Computers* also provides for the direct calculation of such celestial phenomena of interest to navigators as sunrise, sunset, and twilight; moonrise and moonset; latitude by Polaris; longitude line of position; motion of body and observer; and others.

A separate section in *Almanac for Computers* is provided for the calculation of ephemeristic data of interest to astronomers, in units and to levels of precision and accuracy suited to their needs.

The use of *Almanac for Computers* is not advantageous to a navigator for the reduction of only a few observations. When, however, a considerable number of sights are to be reduced, it is quite convenient to obtain such necessary data as GHA Aries; sun GHA, declination, and semidiameter; or moon GHA, declination, semidiameter, and horizontal parallax by merely punching in the GMT on the keyboard of a personal calculator or general-purpose computer.

Other ephemeristic tabulations

2313 In addition to the *Nautical Almanac* and the *Air Almanac* many special tabulations of ephemeristic data have been made for specific purposes. A number of attempts have also been made to produce a long-term or perpetual almanac. Appendix H of Volume II of *Bowditch* (1975), DMAHC Publication No. 9, contains one version of a long-term almanac. In the explanation section of the *Nautical Almanac* a brief description is given of corrections which can be applied to use portions of the almanac in the succeeding year. These are generally considered to be emergency methods for use when a current edition of the *Almanac* is not available to the navigator.

Volume I of Pub. No. 249 contains information in Table 4 which will permit the computation of GHA ♈ for any time over a nine-year period; this table is updated for each edition of Volume I at five-year intervals. The value of GHA ♈ is determined by adding three tabulated quantities—for (a) month of year, (b) hour of day, and (c) minutes and seconds.

An excellent perpetual almanac is the one prepared in England by Her Majesty's Nautical Almanac Office. It is printed in the sight reduction tables, AP 3270, the British equivalent of Pub. No. 249. It is restricted to the sun and the entire ephemeris is presented in two pages. The presentation of data is both interesting and original.

Summary

2314 For a celestial sight reduction, the navigator must have data on the position of the heavenly body at the exact instant of his observation. On surface vessels, such data are normally taken from the *Nautical Almanac* published each year jointly by the U.S. Naval Observatory and the Royal Greenwich Observatory of England. (This same volume is also published by other countries for their naval and civilian navigators using identical tabulations with translated column headings and explanations.) In addition to positional data, the *Nautical Almanac* includes much useful information on the times of sunrise and sunset, moonrise and moonset, twilight, eclipse, civil time kept in foreign countries, etc.

The Naval Observatory also publishes the *Air Almanac* in semiannual editions. Essentially the same data is presented as in the *Nautical Almanac*, but in a manner better fitted for use aboard fast-moving vehicles. In most instances, a lesser degree of precision is provided, but one that is fully adequate for its applications. (Many surface-vessel navigators use the *Air Almanac*, as its degree of precision is adequate for high-seas navigation and is actually more comparable to the precision of routine sextant observations.) The *Air Almanac* also contains a sky chart and a number of sky diagrams.

In 1977, the Naval Observatory introduced its *Almanac for Computers* to provide equations and numerical constants from which celestial coordinates could be computed when needed, rather than taken from tables. These equations and data are suitable for use with a general-purpose computer aboard ship, or they may be used with advanced models of personal electronic calculators capable of receiving program and numerical information from magnetic cards. The initial issue of *Almanac for Computers* was well received and it has been republished in improved versions for succeeding years.

24 Sight Reduction Methods

Introduction **2401** Preceding chapters of this book have individually considered various aspects of determining a line of position from an observation of a celestial body. The purpose of this chapter is to continue the preparation for a complete solution by explaining the various methods currently in widest use. These include the use of the tables of DMAHC Pub. No. 229, the tables of Pub. No. 249, and the Ageton Method tables now in Pub. No. 9 (*Bowditch*, Volume II), as Table 35 (formerly published separately as H. O. 211). Examples of the use of these publications will be given in this chapter, with complete sight reductions in Chapters 26 and 27.

Early methods **2402** The most widely used sight reduction method in the last century was the time sight. A latitude line was obtained by means of an observation of Polaris, or the transit of the sun or of some other body. This latitude line was advanced to the time of an observation of a body located well to the east or west of the observer; the body most frequently used was the sun. With this assumed latitude, a longitude was calculated, originally in time, which gave the time sight its name. The accuracy of the time sight obviously depended on the accuracy of the assumed latitude.

This method remained popular with the merchant service up to World War II. The U. S. Navy was quick to see the advantages of the altitude intercept method of solution conceived by Marcq St.-Hilaire in 1875. For sight reduction by this method, the "cosine-haversine" equations were used for computed altitude and azimuth. These were derived from the classic equations:

Sine-Cosine equation

$$\sin H = \sin L \sin d + \cos L \cos d \cos t \qquad (1)$$

$$\sin Z = \frac{\cos d \sin t}{\cos H} \qquad (2)$$

where H is computed altitude
L is latitude
d is declination
t is meridian angle
z is azimuth angle

Note: In equation (1), the rules for naming the sign ($\pm$) may be stated as follows:

1. If t is less than 90°:
   a. and L and d have the same name, the sign is + and the quantities are added;
   b. and L and d have opposite names, the sign is ~ and the lesser quantity is subtracted from the greater.
2. If t is greater than 90°:
   a. and L and d have the same name, the sign is ~ and the lesser quantity is subtracted from the greater;
   b. and L and d have opposite names, the sign is + and the quantities are added.

These equations are used today when accuracy in reduction is paramount, and many of the "short methods" currently in use are based on them. They, or equations derived from them, are also used for the development of procedures and programs for sight reduction using electronic calculators (Appendix F).

Short methods

The cosine-haversine method remained in general use in the Navy until about 50 years ago, when Ogura in Japan developed a more convenient solution. This led to the production of other simplified methods, both in this country and abroad. These became known as the "short methods," and included among the American volumes, in the order of their development, the Weems *Line of Position Book,* H. O. 208 by Dreisenstok, and H. O. 211 by Ageton. These methods are still used by some navigators; the H. O. publications are no longer in print although both the Dreisenstok and Ageton tables are available commercially, and the Ageton tables have been incorporated into the 1975/77 edition of *Bowditch.* The only mathematical skill they demand of the user is the ability to add, subtract, and to interpolate between numbers in a column. They are convenient, in that in each case one small volume permits solution for any latitude, any declination, and any altitude. However, they have now been largely superseded by the "inspection tables," described in the following articles.

Inspection tables

2403 Modern sight reduction tables are of the inspection type. They are so called because altitude and azimuth are extracted for a given latitude, meridian angle, and declination by inspection, and no calculation is required. These tables are very much larger and heavier than the Dreisenstok and Ageton tables as they consist of vast numbers of precomputed solutions.

H.O. 214 was the basic inspection table for marine use for many years, but its publication has ceased and the tables are no longer generally available; it will not be considered in this book. H.O. 214 remains in some use by navigators who were schooled in its method and who have their own volumes; such use, however, grows less with each passing year.

Tables in current use *Sight Reduction Tables for Marine Navigation,* DMAHC Pub. No. 229, is now the primary inspection method used by surface navigators of the Navy, Coast Guard, Merchant Marine, and private yachts. *Sight Reduction Tables for Air Navigation*, DMAHC Pub. No. 249, is the primary method for air navigation and is also popular with some marine navigators. These tables, and the Ageton tables, will be discussed in the articles that follow.

Pub. No. 229 **2404** The set of tables, entitled *Sight Reduction Tables for Marine Navigation,* are generally referred to as "Pub. 229" (and sometimes by their former number, H.O. 229). They are inspection tables of precomputed altitudes and azimuths. The publication is a joint U.S.-British project involving the U.S. Naval Oceanographic Office (now, in part, the Defense Mapping Agency Hydrographic Center), the U. S. Naval Observatory, and the Royal Greenwich Observatory; volumes with identical tabular contents are published separately in England.

The Pub. No. 229 tables are published in six volumes, arranged by latitude. Each volume contains data for a 16° band of latitude, north or south, with an overlap of 1° between volumes; for example, latitude 30° appears in both Volumes 2 and 3. In each volume, the latitudes are separated into two "zones" as shown below.

Vol. No.	*First zone of latitude*	*Second zone of latitude*
1	0°–7°	8°–15°
2	15°–22°	23°–30°
3	30°–37°	38°–45°
4	45°–52°	53°–60°
5	60°–67°	68°–75°
6	75°–82°	83°–90°

Pub. No. 229 is designed to provide computed altitudes (Hc) correct to the nearest 0.1′ when all corrections are employed, and azimuth angle to 0.1° for all combinations of latitude, local hour angle (measured westward from the observer's celestial meridian through 360°), and declination at a uniform interval of 1° in each of these arguments. It may be used for reduction from a DR position to the same degree of precision, and directions for such reduction are given in each volume. However, it is primarily intended to be used with an *assumed position* (AP). The latitude of the latter is the integral degree nearest the vessel's DR or EP latitude; its longitude is selected to give a whole degree of *local hour angle* within 30′ of the vessel's DR or EP longitude. Among today's tables it is unique, in that if offers both the maximum degree of precision required by the navigator and also permits the reduction of an observation of *any* navigational body, at *any* altitude, including those of negative value; there are no limitations of latitude, hour, angle, or declination.

Entering arguments

The primary entering argument (page selection) within each zone of latitude is the local hour angle; it is prominently displayed at the top and bottom of each page. The horizontal argument heading each column is latitude, and the vertical argument is declination. For each value of the local hour angle, LHA, in the range 0° to 90° or 270° to 360° (corresponding to t less than 90°), there are two facing pages, which contain the tabulations for declination of 0° to 90° and for 8° of latitude.

Similar triangles

Note that the entering arguments (Lat., LHA, and Dec.) are *not* designated as north or south, east or west. The reason for this is illustrated in Figure 2404a, where four navigational triangles are shown on the surface of the earth. In each of the four triangles, the AP is at the same latitude north or south of the equator. If the numerical value of the latitude of the AP is assumed to be 33°, then the side between the AP and the pole in *each* triangle, the colatitude, is equal to an arc of 57°. Similarly, the GP in each triangle is at the same latitude, 14° (on the same side of the equator as the AP), making the polar distance in each triangle equal to 76°. Further, the four triangles illustrated are constructed so that the angular distance from the meridian of the AP to the meridian of the GP is equal in each case, making the numerical value of meridian angle, t, the same in all triangles. With the two sides and the included angle of all triangles being numerically equal, the values of computed altitude and azimuth angle obtained by solving each triangle will be numerically equal. Using Lat. = 33°, LHA = 34°, and Dec. = 14°, the numerical value of Hc (53°44.7′) and Z (113.4°) can be obtained from the tabular extract of Figure 2404b.

To determine the intercept, (a), for plotting the resulting lines of position, Hc is used in each case as obtained from the tables, but azimuth angle, Z, is usually converted to true azimuth, Zn, which differs

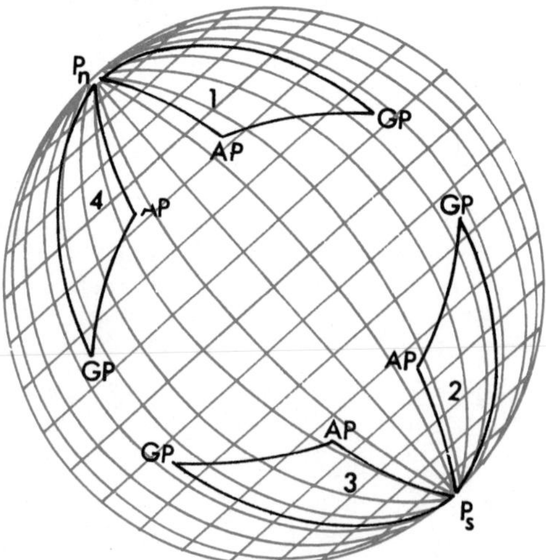

Figure 2404a. Four numerically equal celestial triangles.

34°, 326° L.H.A. **LATITUDE SAME NAME AS DECLINATION** N. Lat. {L.H.A. greater than 180°......Zn=Z; L.H.A. less than 180°............Zn=360°−Z}

Dec.	30° Hc	d	Z	31° Hc	d	Z	32° Hc	d	Z	33° Hc	d	Z	34° Hc	d	Z	35° Hc	d	Z	36° Hc	d	Z	37° Hc	d	Z	Dec.
°	° ′	′	°	° ′	′	°	° ′	′	°	° ′	′	°	° ′	′	°	° ′	′	°	° ′	′	°	° ′	′	°	°
0	45 53.2	+42.8	126.5	45 17.1	+43.7	127.4	44 40.4	+44.5	128.2	44 03.0	+45.3	128.9	43 25.0	+46.0	129.7	42 46.4	+46.7	130.4	42 07.3	+47.4	131.1	41 27.6	+48.0	131.7	0
1	46 36.0	42.3	125.5	46 00.8	43.2	126.4	45 24.9	44.0	127.2	44 48.3	44.8	128.0	44 11.0	45.6	128.8	43 33.1	46.3	129.5	42 54.7	47.0	130.2	42 15.6	47.7	130.9	1
2	47 18.3	41.7	124.5	46 44.0	42.6	125.4	46 08.9	43.4	126.2	45 33.1	44.3	127.1	44 56.6	45.1	127.9	44 19.4	45.9	128.6	43 41.7	46.6	129.4	43 03.3	47.3	130.1	2
3	48 00.0	41.1	123.4	47 26.6	42.0	124.3	46 52.3	43.0	125.2	46 17.4	43.8	126.1	45 41.7	44.6	126.9	45 05.3	45.4	127.7	44 28.3	46.2	128.5	43 50.6	46.9	129.3	3
4	48 41.1	40.5	122.3	48 08.6	41.5	123.3	47 35.3	42.4	124.2	47 01.2	43.3	125.1	46 26.3	44.2	126.0	45 50.7	45.0	126.8	45 14.5	45.7	127.6	44 37.5	46.5	128.4	4
5	49 21.6	+39.8	121.2	48 50.1	+40.8	122.2	48 17.7	+41.7	123.1	47 44.5	+42.7	124.1	47 10.5	+43.6	125.0	46 35.7	+44.5	125.8	46 00.2	+45.3	126.7	45 24.0	+46.1	127.5	5
6	50 01.4	39.0	120.0	49 30.9	40.1	121.1	48 59.4	41.2	122.1	48 27.2	42.1	123.0	47 54.1	43.0	123.9	47 20.2	43.9	124.9	46 45.5	44.8	125.7	46 10.1	45.6	126.6	6
7	50 40.4	38.4	118.9	50 11.0	39.4	119.9	49 40.6	40.5	120.9	49 09.3	41.5	121.9	48 37.1	42.5	122.9	48 04.1	43.4	123.8	47 30.3	44.3	124.8	46 55.7	45.2	125.6	7
8	51 18.8	37.5	117.6	50 50.4	38.7	118.7	50 21.1	39.8	119.8	49 50.8	40.8	120.8	49 19.6	41.9	121.8	48 47.5	42.9	122.8	48 14.6	43.8	123.7	47 40.9	44.6	124.7	8
9	51 56.3	36.7	116.4	51 29.1	37.9	117.5	51 00.9	39.0	118.6	50 31.6	40.2	119.7	50 01.5	41.2	120.7	49 30.4	42.2	121.7	48 58.4	43.2	122.7	48 25.5	44.1	123.7	9
10	52 33.0	+35.8	115.1	52 07.0	+37.1	116.3	51 39.9	+38.3	117.4	51 11.8	+39.4	118.5	50 42.7	+40.5	119.6	50 12.6	+41.6	120.6	49 41.6	+42.5	121.6	49 09.6	+43.6	122.6	10
11	53 08.8	35.0	113.8	52 44.1	36.2	115.0	52 18.2	37.5	116.1	51 51.2	38.7	117.3	51 23.2	39.8	118.4	50 54.2	40.8	119.5	50 24.1	42.0	120.5	49 53.2	42.9	121.6	11
12	53 43.8	34.0	112.4	53 20.3	35.3	113.6	52 55.7	36.6	114.9	52 29.9	37.8	116.0	52 03.0	39.0	117.2	51 35.0	40.2	118.3	51 06.1	41.2	119.4	50 36.1	42.3	120.5	12
13	54 17.8	32.9	111.0	53 55.6	34.4	112.3	53 32.3	35.7	113.5	53 07.7	37.0	114.8	52 42.0	38.3	116.0	52 15.2	39.4	117.1	51 47.3	40.6	118.3	51 18.4	41.7	119.4	13
14	54 50.7	31.9	109.6	54 30.0	33.4	110.9	54 08.0	34.7	112.2	53 44.7	36.1	113.4	53 20.3	37.3	114.7	52 54.6	38.7	115.9	52 27.9	39.8	117.1	52 00.1	40.9	118.2	14
15	55 22.6	+30.9	108.1	55 03.4	+32.3	109.4	54 42.7	+33.8	110.8	54 20.8	+35.2	112.1	53 57.6	+36.5	113.4	53 33.3	+37.7	114.6	53 07.7	+39.0	115.8	52 41.0	+40.2	117.0	15
16	55 53.5	29.6	106.6	55 35.7	31.2	108.0	55 16.5	32.7	109.3	54 56.0	34.1	110.7	54 34.1	35.6	112.0	54 11.0	36.9	113.3	53 46.7	38.2	114.5	53 21.2	39.4	115.8	16
17	56 23.1	28.5	105.0	56 06.9	30.0	106.4	55 49.2	31.6	107.8	55 30.1	33.1	109.2	55 09.7	34.5	110.6	54 47.9	36.0	111.9	54 24.9	37.3	113.2	54 00.6	38.6	114.5	17
18	56 51.6	27.2	103.4	56 36.9	28.9	104.9	56 20.8	30.5	106.3	56 03.2	32.0	107.8	55 44.2	33.5	109.2	55 23.9	34.9	110.5	55 02.2	36.3	111.9	54 39.2	37.7	113.2	18
19	57 18.8	25.9	101.8	57 05.8	27.6	103.3	56 51.3	29.2	104.8	56 35.2	30.9	106.2	56 17.7	32.5	107.7	55 58.8	34.0	109.1	55 38.5	35.4	110.5	55 16.9	36.7	111.8	19
85	34 06.1	−48.7	3.4	35 06.0	−48.7	3.4	36 05.9	−48.7	3.5	37 05.8	−48.7	3.5	38 05.7	−48.6	3.6	39 05.6	−48.6	3.6	40 05.5	−48.6	3.7	41 05.3	−48.4	3.7	85
86	33 17.4	49.1	2.7	34 17.3	49.0	2.7	35 17.2	48.9	2.7	36 17.1	48.9	2.8	37 17.1	48.9	2.8	38 17.0	48.9	2.8	39 16.9	48.8	2.9	40 16.9	48.8	2.9	86
87	32 28.3	49.2	2.0	33 28.3	49.2	2.0	34 28.3	49.2	2.0	35 28.2	49.2	2.1	36 28.2	49.2	2.1	37 28.1	49.1	2.1	38 28.1	49.1	2.1	39 28.1	49.1	2.2	87
88	31 39.1	49.5	1.3	32 39.1	49.5	1.3	33 39.1	49.5	1.3	34 39.0	49.4	1.4	35 39.0	49.4	1.4	36 39.0	49.4	1.4	37 39.0	49.4	1.4	38 39.0	49.4	1.4	88
89	30 49.6	49.6	0.7	31 49.6	49.6	0.7	32 49.6	49.6	0.7	33 49.6	49.6	0.7	34 49.6	49.6	0.7	35 49.6	49.6	0.7	36 49.6	49.6	0.7	37 49.6	49.6	0.7	89
90	30 00.0	−49.8	0.0	31 00.0	−49.8	0.0	32 00.0	−49.8	0.0	33 00.0	−49.8	0.0	34 00.0	−49.9	0.0	35 00.0	−49.9	0.0	36 00.0	−49.9	0.0	37 00.0	−49.9	0.0	90
	30°			31°			32°			33°			34°			35°			36°			37°			

34°, 326° L.H.A. **LATITUDE SAME NAME AS DECLINATION**

Figure 2404b. Pub. No. 229, typical "same name" page (extract).

for each triangle, since the true direction of the GP from the AP is different in each case. Referring to Figure 2404a, the Z in the first triangle is N and E, Zn therefore equals Z. In the second, the Z is S and E; Zn therefore equals 180° – Z. In the third, Z is S and W and Zn equals 180° + Z. In the fourth triangle Z is N and W; Zn therefore equals 360° – Z. When Zn and (a) are determined, the lines of position can be plotted using the methods described in Chapter 25.

The fact that four triangles can be solved by using one set of entering arguments makes it possible to save considerable space in an inspection table. Figure 2404a illustrates four such triangles, in each of which the AP and GP are on the same side of the equator; both north or both south. In these cases, the latitude and declination are said to have the *same name.* A *second set* of four triangles might be drawn so that in each triangle the AP is on one side of the equator, and the GP is on the other side. If the values of L, Dec., and t are numerically equal for each triangle, the resulting values of Hc and Z will also be numerically the same for all four triangles, and the solution of all four triangles can be achieved using one set of entering arguments, as before. For this second set of triangles, the latitude and declination are said to have *contrary names,* since they lie on opposite sides of the equator. (The organization and format of H. O. 214 were based on the principles outlined above.) Since each of the solutions obtained from the tables can apply to any of four triangles, the names north and south (for latitude and declination) or east and west (for meridian angle) are omitted in the tabulation, and must be applied by the navigator as appropriate for the particular triangle being solved. Solutions are provided for both sets of triangles by means of the tables being divided into two parts, *"Latitude Same Name as Declination"* and *"Latitude Contrary Name to Declination."*

For each opening of the tables of Pub. No. 229 the left-hand page is always limited to tabulations for declination and latitude of the same name. On the upper portion of the right-hand page are stated the tabulations for declination and latitude of contrary name; in the lower portions of these right-hand pages are stated tabulations for the supplementary values of LHA, those larger than 90° but less than 270° (t greater than 90°), for declinations of the same name as latitude. The upper and lower sections of each right-hand page are separated by horizontal lines in each column of data; these are known as the *Contrary-Same Lines*, or *C-S* Lines, and indicate the degree of declination in which the celestial horizon occurs (where the altitude reaches zero). Portions of a left- and right-hand page are shown as Figures 2404b and 2404c, respectively.

Assumed latitude and longitude For the assumed latitude (aL), the user selects the whole degree *nearest* his DR or estimated position. The user then selects an assumed longitude (aλ) which, when applied to the GHA of the body being observed, will yield a *whole degree* of LHA; *this assumed longitude (aλ) must lie within 30 minutes of arc of the best estimate of the ship's actual longitude at the time of the observation.*

Assumed longitude It is obvious that when a number of celestial bodies are observed at about the same time, as in a round of star sights, a different longitude will have to be assumed to obtain a meridian angle for each body. In most cases, all the assumed positions will lie along the same assumed parallel of latitude. (The exception occurs when a ship approaches nearer to an adjoining whole degree while observations are being made.) The longitudes assumed should all fall within about 60 minutes of one another, except in higher latitudes when the vessel's course and speed result in a rapid change of longitude, and the period required to obtain the observations is rather protracted.

To use the tables, the volume which includes the assumed latitude is selected, and the two pages listing the required LHA are found

LATITUDE CONTRARY NAME TO DECLINATION **L.H.A. 34°, 326°**

Dec.	30°			31°			32°			33°			34°			35°			36°			37°			Dec.
	Hc	d	Z	Hc	d	Z	Hc	d	Z	Hc	d	Z	Hc	d	Z	Hc	d	Z	Hc	d	Z	Hc	d	Z	
°	° ′	′	°	° ′	′	°	° ′	′	°	° ′	′	°	° ′	′	°	° ′	′	°	° ′	′	°	° ′	′	°	°
0	45 53.2	−43.3	126.5	45 17.1	−44.1	127.4	44 40.4	−44.9	128.2	44 03.0	−45.7	128.9	43 25.0	−46.4	129.7	42 46.4	−47.0	130.4	42 07.3	−47.7	131.1	41 27.6	−48.3	131.7	0
1	45 09.9	43.9	127.5	44 33.0	44.7	128.3	43 55.5	45.4	129.1	43 17.3	46.1	129.8	42 38.6	46.7	130.5	41 59.4	47.5	131.2	41 19.6	48.1	131.9	40 39.3	48.7	132.5	1
2	44 26.0	44.3	128.5	43 48.3	45.0	129.3	43 10.1	45.8	130.0	42 31.2	46.4	130.7	41 51.9	47.2	131.4	41 11.9	47.7	132.0	40 31.5	48.4	132.7	39 50.6	48.9	133.3	2
3	43 41.7	44.8	129.4	43 03.3	45.5	130.2	42 24.3	46.2	130.9	41 44.8	46.9	131.5	41 04.7	47.5	132.2	40 24.2	48.1	132.8	39 43.1	48.6	133.4	39 01.7	49.3	134.0	3
4	42 56.9	45.2	130.4	42 17.8	45.9	131.0	41 38.1	46.5	131.7	40 57.9	47.2	132.4	40 17.2	47.8	133.0	39 36.1	48.4	133.6	38 54.5	49.0	134.2	38 12.4	49.5	134.8	4
5	42 11.7	−45.6	131.2	41 31.9	−46.3	131.9	40 51.6	−47.0	132.6	40 10.7	−47.5	133.2	39 29.4	−48.1	133.8	38 47.7	−48.7	134.4	38 05.5	−49.2	134.9	37 22.9	−49.7	135.5	5
6	41 26.1	46.0	132.1	40 45.6	46.6	132.8	40 04.6	47.2	133.4	39 23.2	47.8	134.0	38 41.3	48.4	134.6	37 59.0	49.0	135.1	37 16.3	49.5	135.7	36 33.2	50.0	136.2	6
7	40 40.1	46.4	133.0	39 59.0	47.0	133.6	39 17.4	47.6	134.2	38 35.4	48.2	134.8	37 52.9	48.7	135.3	37 10.0	49.2	135.9	36 26.8	49.7	136.4	35 43.2	50.2	136.9	7
8	39 53.7	46.7	133.8	39 12.0	47.3	134.4	38 29.8	47.9	135.0	37 47.2	48.4	135.5	37 04.2	49.0	136.1	36 20.8	49.5	136.6	35 37.1	50.0	137.1	34 53.0	50.5	137.5	8
9	39 07.0	47.0	134.6	38 24.7	47.6	135.2	37 41.9	48.1	135.7	36 58.8	48.7	136.3	36 15.2	49.2	136.8	35 31.3	49.7	137.3	34 47.1	50.2	137.7	34 02.5	50.6	138.2	9
10	38 20.0	−47.4	135.4	37 37.1	−47.9	136.0	36 53.8	−48.5	136.5	36 10.1	−49.0	137.0	35 26.0	−49.4	137.5	34 41.6	−49.9	137.9	33 56.9	−50.4	138.4	33 11.9	−50.8	138.8	10
11	37 32.6	47.6	136.2	36 49.2	48.2	136.7	36 05.3	48.7	137.2	35 21.1	49.2	137.7	34 36.6	49.7	138.2	33 51.7	50.2	138.6	33 06.5	50.6	139.1	32 21.1	51.1	139.5	11
12	36 45.0	48.0	136.9	36 01.0	48.5	137.4	35 16.6	49.0	137.9	34 31.9	49.5	138.4	33 46.9	49.9	138.8	33 01.5	50.3	139.3	32 15.9	50.8	139.7	31 30.0	51.2	140.1	12
13	35 57.0	48.2	137.7	35 12.5	48.7	138.2	34 27.6	49.2	138.6	33 42.4	49.6	139.1	32 57.0	50.2	139.5	32 11.2	50.6	139.9	31 25.1	50.9	140.3	30 38.8	51.3	140.7	13
14	35 08.8	48.4	138.4	34 23.8	49.0	138.9	33 38.4	49.4	139.3	32 52.8	49.9	139.8	32 06.8	50.3	140.2	31 20.6	50.7	140.6	30 34.2	51.2	140.9	29 47.5	51.6	141.3	14
15	34 20.4	−48.8	139.1	33 34.8	−49.2	139.6	32 49.0	−49.6	140.0	32 02.9	−50.1	140.4	31 16.5	−50.5	140.8	30 29.9	−50.9	141.2	29 43.0	−51.3	141.5	28 55.9	−51.6	141.9	15
16	33 31.6	48.9	139.8	32 45.6	49.4	140.3	31 59.4	49.9	140.7	31 12.8	50.2	141.1	30 26.0	50.6	141.4	29 39.0	51.1	141.8	28 51.7	51.4	142.1	28 04.3	51.8	142.5	16
17	32 42.7	49.2	140.5	31 56.2	49.6	140.9	31 09.5	50.0	141.3	30 22.6	50.5	141.7	29 35.4	50.9	142.1	28 47.9	51.2	142.4	28 00.3	51.6	142.7	27 12.5	52.0	143.0	17
18	31 53.5	49.4	141.2	31 06.6	49.8	141.6	30 19.5	50.2	142.0	29 32.1	50.6	142.3	28 44.5	51.0	142.7	27 56.7	51.4	143.0	27 08.7	51.7	143.3	26 20.5	52.1	143.6	18
19	31 04.1	49.6	141.9	30 16.8	50.0	142.2	29 29.3	50.4	142.6	28 41.5	50.8	142.9	27 53.5	51.2	143.3	27 05.3	51.5	143.6	26 17.0	51.9	143.9	25 28.4	52.2	144.2	19
85	25 49.1	+50.5	3.1	26 49.0	+50.6	3.1	27 48.9	+50.6	3.2	28 48.8	+50.6	3.2	29 48.7	+50.7	3.2	30 48.7	+50.6	3.3	31 48.6	+50.7	3.3	32 48.5	+50.7	3.3	85
86	26 39.6	50.4	2.5	27 39.6	50.3	2.5	28 39.5	50.4	2.5	29 39.4	50.5	2.6	30 39.4	50.4	2.6	31 39.3	50.5	2.6	32 39.3	50.5	2.7	33 39.2	50.5	2.7	86
87	27 30.0	50.1	1.9	28 29.9	50.2	1.9	29 29.9	50.2	1.9	30 29.9	50.2	1.9	31 29.8	50.3	2.0	32 29.8	50.3	2.0	33 29.8	50.3	2.0	34 29.7	50.3	2.0	87
88	28 20.1	50.1	1.3	29 20.1	50.1	1.3	30 20.1	50.1	1.3	31 20.1	50.1	1.3	32 20.1	50.0	1.3	33 20.1	50.0	1.3	34 20.1	50.0	1.4	35 20.0	50.1	1.4	88
89	29 10.2	49.8	0.6	30 10.2	49.8	0.6	31 10.2	49.8	0.7	32 10.2	49.8	0.7	33 10.1	49.9	0.7	34 10.1	49.9	0.7	35 10.1	49.9	0.7	36 10.1	49.9	0.7	89
90	30 00.0	+49.6	0.0	31 00.0	+49.6	0.0	32 00.0	+49.6	0.0	33 00.0	+49.6	0.0	34 00.0	+49.6	0.0	35 00.0	+49.6	0.0	36 00.0	+49.6	0.0	37 00.0	+49.6	0.0	90
	30°			31°			32°			33°			34°			35°			36°			37°			

S. Lat. {L.H.A. greater than 180°......Zn=180°−Z; L.H.A. less than 180°............Zn=180°+Z} **LATITUDE SAME NAME AS DECLINATION** **L.H.A. 146°, 214°**

Figure 2404c. Pub. No. 229, typical "contrary name" page (extract).

within the appropriate latitude zone of this volume. The appropriate page is then selected for a declination having the same or the contrary name as the latitude. On this page, the vertical column headed by the integral degree of assumed latitude is next found. Declination is listed in vertical columns at the outer edge of each page; the integral whole degree of declination numerically *less* in value to the actual declination is located in this column. Horizontally across from this, in the latitude column, three sets of numerical values are tabulated. The first, under the sub-heading "Hc," is the calculated altitude stated to the nearest 0.1′; in the next column sub-headed "d," in smaller type, is the actual difference, with sign, to the tabulated altitude for the next higher degree of declination. The third column, subheaded "Z", tabulates the azimuth angle to the nearest 0.1°.

Column arrangement of Pub. No. 229

Rules are given on each page for the conversion of Z to Zn. Interpolation Tables, given on four pages inside the front and back covers of each volume, are provided to permit correcting the tabulated altitude for the first difference, d, between the actual declination, and the integral degree of declination, used as an entering argument. The interpolation tables are also designed to permit, where required, correction for the effect of a second difference; this allows full precision to be obtained in the calculated altitude. The linear interpolation tables are sufficiently accurate for altitudes below 60° and a second difference correction is not required. Above 60°, however, the accuracy of linear interpolation decreases, and a second difference correction will be necessary for some, but not all, reductions. The technique used is termed *double-second difference* and the corrections are listed in the form of tables of critical values at the right side of each block of figures on the pages of the Interpolation Table. In those cases in which second differences are significant, where omission of the correction for second difference might cause an error in excess of 0.25′ in the calculated altitude, the value of d is printed in italics, and is followed by a dot (see Figure 2404e).

Interpolation tables

Portions of these interpolation tables are shown in Figure 2404d. The main argument in entering these tables is the excess of the actual declination over the integral degree of declination used to enter the main body of the tables. This difference is tabulated in the vertical column at the left-hand edge of each table, under the heading "Dec. Inc." The other argument is the tabulated altitude difference d, which for convenience is divided into two parts, the first being a multiple of 10′ (10′, 20′, 30′, 40′, or 50′), and the second the remainder in the range 0.0′ to 9.9′ by tenths of minutes. This interpolation table is a great convenience to the navigator. Its use may occasionally lead to a small error in the Hc not exceeding 0.1′; such error is acceptable in the course of ordinary navigation.

First difference correction

The major portion of the correction to convert the tabulated altitude to the calculated altitude is called the *first difference correction.* It is obtained as the sum of two quantities:

The tabulated value corresponding to the Dec. Inc., and the tens of minutes of the altitude difference d, and

The tabulated value corresponding to the Dec. Inc., and the remainder of d in units and tenths. The units are to the right of the tens; note that the decimals here are a vertical argument.

The sum of these two quantities is applied to the tabulated altitude with the sign as shown in the d column of the main tables.

INTERPOLATION TABLE

Dec. Inc.	Altitude difference (d) Tens 10′	20′	30′	40′	50′	Decimals	Units 0′	1′	2′	3′	4′	5′	6′	7′	8′	9′	Double Second Diff.	and Corr.
28.0	4.6	9.3	14.0	18.6	23.3	.0	0.0	0.5	0.9	1.4	1.9	2.4	2.8	3.3	3.8	4.3	0.8	0.1
28.1	4.7	9.3	14.0	18.7	23.4	.1	0.0	0.5	1.0	1.5	1.9	2.4	2.9	3.4	3.8	4.3	2.4	0.2
28.2	4.7	9.4	14.1	18.8	23.5	.2	0.1	0.6	1.0	1.5	2.0	2.5	2.9	3.4	3.9	4.4	4.0	0.3
28.3	4.7	9.4	14.1	18.9	23.6	.3	0.1	0.6	1.1	1.6	2.0	2.5	3.0	3.5	3.9	4.4	5.6	0.4
28.4	4.7	9.5	14.2	18.9	23.7	.4	0.2	0.7	1.1	1.6	2.1	2.6	3.0	3.5	4.0	4.5	7.2	0.5
28.5	4.8	9.5	14.3	19.0	23.8	.5	0.2	0.7	1.2	1.7	2.1	2.6	3.1	3.6	4.0	4.5	8.8	0.6
28.6	4.8	9.5	14.3	19.1	23.8	.6	0.3	0.8	1.2	1.7	2.2	2.7	3.1	3.6	4.1	4.6	10.4	0.7
28.7	4.8	9.6	14.4	19.2	23.9	.7	0.3	0.8	1.3	1.8	2.2	2.7	3.2	3.7	4.1	4.6	12.0	0.8
28.8	4.8	9.6	14.4	19.2	24.0	.8	0.4	0.9	1.3	1.8	2.3	2.8	3.2	3.7	4.2	4.7	13.6	0.9
28.9	4.9	9.7	14.5	19.3	24.1	.9	0.4	0.9	1.4	1.9	2.3	2.8	3.3	3.8	4.2	4.7	15.2	1.0
																	16.8	
34.0	5.6	11.3	17.0	22.6	28.3	.0	0.0	0.6	1.1	1.7	2.3	2.9	3.4	4.0	4.6	5.2	0.8	0.1
34.1	5.7	11.3	17.0	22.7	28.4	.1	0.1	0.6	1.2	1.8	2.4	2.9	3.5	4.1	4.7	5.2	2.5	0.2
34.2	5.7	11.4	17.1	22.8	28.5	.2	0.1	0.7	1.3	1.8	2.4	3.0	3.6	4.1	4.7	5.3	4.1	0.3
34.3	5.7	11.4	17.1	22.9	28.6	.3	0.2	0.7	1.3	1.9	2.5	3.0	3.6	4.2	4.8	5.3	5.8	0.4
34.4	5.7	11.5	17.2	22.9	28.7	.4	0.2	0.8	1.4	2.0	2.5	3.1	3.7	4.3	4.8	5.4	7.4	0.5
34.5	5.8	11.5	17.3	23.0	28.8	.5	0.3	0.9	1.4	2.0	2.6	3.2	3.7	4.3	4.9	5.5	9.1	0.6
34.6	5.8	11.5	17.3	23.1	28.8	.6	0.3	0.9	1.5	2.1	2.6	3.2	3.8	4.4	4.9	5.5	10.7	0.7
34.7	5.8	11.6	17.4	23.2	28.9	.7	0.4	1.0	1.6	2.1	2.7	3.3	3.9	4.4	5.0	5.6	12.3	0.8
34.8	5.8	11.6	17.4	23.2	29.0	.8	0.5	1.0	1.6	2.2	2.8	3.3	3.9	4.5	5.1	5.6	14.0	0.9
34.9	5.9	11.7	17.5	23.3	29.1	.9	0.5	1.1	1.7	2.2	2.8	3.4	4.0	4.5	5.1	5.7	15.6	1.0
35.0	5.8	11.6	17.5	23.3	29.1	.0	0.0	0.6	1.2	1.8	2.4	3.0	3.5	4.1	4.7	5.3	17.3	1.1
35.1	5.8	11.7	17.5	23.4	29.2	.1	0.1	0.7	1.2	1.8	2.4	3.0	3.6	4.2	4.8	5.4	18.9	1.2
35.2	5.8	11.7	17.6	23.4	29.3	.2	0.1	0.7	1.3	1.9	2.5	3.1	3.7	4.3	4.9	5.4	20.6	1.3
35.3	5.9	11.8	17.6	23.5	29.4	.3	0.2	0.8	1.4	2.0	2.5	3.1	3.7	4.3	4.9	5.5	22.2	1.4
35.4	5.9	11.8	17.7	23.6	29.5	.4	0.2	0.8	1.4	2.0	2.6	3.2	3.8	4.4	5.0	5.6	23.9	1.5
35.5	5.9	11.8	17.8	23.7	29.6	.5	0.3	0.9	1.5	2.1	2.7	3.3	3.8	4.4	5.0	5.6	25.5	1.6
35.6	5.9	11.9	17.8	23.7	29.7	.6	0.4	0.9	1.5	2.1	2.7	3.3	3.9	4.5	5.1	5.7	27.2	1.7
35.7	6.0	11.9	17.9	23.8	29.8	.7	0.4	1.0	1.6	2.2	2.8	3.4	4.0	4.6	5.1	5.7	28.8	1.8
35.8	6.0	12.0	17.9	23.9	29.9	.8	0.5	1.1	1.7	2.2	2.8	3.4	4.0	4.6	5.2	5.8	30.4	1.9
35.9	6.0	12.0	18.0	24.0	30.0	.9	0.5	1.1	1.7	2.3	2.9	3.5	4.1	4.7	5.3	5.9	32.1	2.0
																	33.7	2.1
																	35.4	
	10′	20′	30′	40′	50′		0′	1′	2′	3′	4′	5′	6′	7′	8′	9′		

Dec. Inc.	Altitude difference (d) Tens 10′	20′	30′	40′	50′	Decimals	Units 0′	1′	2′	3′	4′	5′	6′	7′	8′	9′	Double Second Diff.	and Corr.
36.0	6.0	12.0	18.0	24.0	30.0	.0	0.0	0.6	1.2	1.8	2.4	3.0	3.6	4.3	4.9	5.5	0.8	0.1
36.1	6.0	12.0	18.0	24.0	30.1	.1	0.1	0.7	1.3	1.9	2.5	3.1	3.7	4.3	4.9	5.5	2.5	0.2
36.2	6.0	12.0	18.1	24.1	30.1	.2	0.1	0.7	1.3	1.9	2.6	3.2	3.8	4.4	5.0	5.6	4.2	0.3
36.3	6.0	12.1	18.1	24.2	30.2	.3	0.2	0.8	1.4	2.0	2.6	3.2	3.8	4.4	5.0	5.7	5.9	0.4
36.4	6.1	12.1	18.2	24.3	30.3	.4	0.2	0.9	1.5	2.1	2.7	3.3	3.9	4.5	5.1	5.7	7.6	0.5
36.5	6.1	12.2	18.3	24.3	30.4	.5	0.3	0.9	1.5	2.1	2.7	3.3	4.0	4.6	5.2	5.8	9.3	0.6
36.6	6.1	12.2	18.3	24.4	30.5	.6	0.4	1.0	1.6	2.2	2.8	3.4	4.0	4.6	5.2	5.8	11.0	0.7
36.7	6.1	12.3	18.4	24.5	30.6	.7	0.4	1.0	1.6	2.3	2.9	3.5	4.1	4.7	5.3	5.9	12.7	0.8
36.8	6.2	12.3	18.4	24.6	30.7	.8	0.5	1.1	1.7	2.3	2.9	3.5	4.1	4.7	5.4	6.0	14.4	0.9
36.9	6.2	12.3	18.5	24.6	30.8	.9	0.5	1.2	1.8	2.4	3.0	3.6	4.2	4.8	5.4	6.0	16.1	1.0
																	17.8	
42.0	7.0	14.0	21.0	28.0	35.0	.0	0.0	0.7	1.4	2.1	2.8	3.5	4.2	5.0	5.7	6.4		
42.1	7.0	14.0	21.0	28.0	35.1	.1	0.1	0.8	1.5	2.2	2.9	3.6	4.3	5.0	5.7	6.4		
42.2	7.0	14.0	21.1	28.1	35.1	.2	0.1	0.8	1.6	2.3	3.0	3.7	4.4	5.1	5.8	6.5	1.0	0.1
42.3	7.0	14.1	21.1	28.2	35.2	.3	0.2	0.9	1.6	2.3	3.0	3.8	4.5	5.2	5.9	6.6	3.0	0.2
42.4	7.1	14.1	21.2	28.3	35.3	.4	0.3	1.0	1.7	2.4	3.1	3.8	4.5	5.2	5.9	6.7	4.9	0.3
42.5	7.1	14.2	21.3	28.3	35.4	.5	0.4	1.1	1.8	2.5	3.2	3.9	4.6	5.3	6.0	6.7	6.9	0.4
42.6	7.1	14.2	21.3	28.4	35.5	.6	0.4	1.1	1.8	2.5	3.3	4.0	4.7	5.4	6.1	6.8	8.9	0.5
42.7	7.1	14.3	21.4	28.5	35.6	.7	0.5	1.2	1.9	2.6	3.3	4.0	4.7	5.5	6.2	6.9	10.8	0.6
42.8	7.2	14.3	21.4	28.6	35.7	.8	0.6	1.3	2.0	2.7	3.4	4.1	4.8	5.5	6.2	6.9	12.8	0.7
42.9	7.2	14.3	21.5	28.6	35.8	.9	0.6	1.3	2.1	2.8	3.5	4.2	4.9	5.6	6.3	7.0	14.8	0.8
43.0	7.1	14.3	21.5	28.6	35.8	.0	0.0	0.7	1.4	2.2	2.9	3.6	4.3	5.1	5.8	6.5	16.7	0.9
43.1	7.2	14.3	21.5	28.7	35.9	.1	0.1	0.8	1.5	2.2	3.0	3.7	4.4	5.1	5.9	6.6	18.7	1.0
43.2	7.2	14.4	21.6	28.8	36.0	.2	0.1	0.9	1.6	2.3	3.0	3.8	4.5	5.2	5.9	6.7	20.7	1.1
43.3	7.2	14.4	21.6	28.9	36.1	.3	0.2	0.9	1.7	2.4	3.1	3.8	4.6	5.3	6.0	6.7	22.7	1.2
43.4	7.2	14.5	21.7	28.9	36.2	.4	0.3	1.0	1.7	2.5	3.2	3.9	4.6	5.4	6.1	6.8	24.6	1.3
43.5	7.3	14.5	21.8	29.0	36.3	.5	0.4	1.1	1.8	2.5	3.3	4.0	4.7	5.4	6.2	6.9	26.6	1.4
43.6	7.3	14.5	21.8	29.1	36.3	.6	0.4	1.2	1.9	2.6	3.3	4.1	4.8	5.5	6.2	7.0	28.6	1.5
43.7	7.3	14.6	21.9	29.2	36.4	.7	0.5	1.2	2.0	2.7	3.4	4.1	4.9	5.6	6.3	7.0	30.5	1.6
43.8	7.3	14.6	21.9	29.2	36.5	.8	0.6	1.3	2.0	2.8	3.5	4.2	4.9	5.7	6.4	7.1	32.5	1.7
43.9	7.4	14.7	22.0	29.3	36.6	.9	0.7	1.4	2.1	2.8	3.6	4.3	5.0	5.7	6.5	7.2	34.5	1.8
																	36.4	
	10′	20′	30′	40′	50′		0′	1′	2′	3′	4′	5′	6′	7′	8′	9′		

The Double-Second-Difference correction (Corr.) is always to be added to the tabulated altitude.

Figure 2404d. Pub. No. 229, Interpolation Table (extract).

29°, 331° L.H.A. **LATITUDE SAME NAME AS DECLINATION**

N. Lat. {L.H.A. greater than 180°...Zn = Z; L.H.A. less than 180°........Zn = 360° − Z}

Dec.	75° Hc	d	Z	76° Hc	d	Z	77° Hc	d	Z	78° Hc	d	Z	79° Hc	d	Z	80° Hc	d	Z	81° Hc	d	Z	82° Hc	d	Z	Dec.
°	° ′	′	°	° ′	′	°	° ′	′	°	° ′	′	°	° ′	′	°	° ′	′	°	° ′	′	°	° ′	′	°	°
0	13 05.0	+59.5	150.2	12 12.9	+59.6	150.3	11 20.8	+59.6	150.4	10 28.6	+59.7	150.5	9 36.4	+59.7	150.5	8 44.1	+59.8	150.6	7 51.8	+59.9	150.7	6 59.5	+59.9	150.8	0
1	14 04.5	59.5	150.0	13 12.5	59.6	150.1	12 20.4	59.7	150.3	11 28.3	59.7	150.4	10 36.1	59.8	150.5	9 43.9	59.8	150.5	8 51.7	59.8	150.6	7 59.4	59.8	150.7	1
65	76 11.4	+50.4	120.9	75 39.1	+52.4	124.2	75 04.0	+54.0	127.3	74 26.4	+55.4	130.2	73 46.7	+56.4	132.8	73 04.9	+57.3	135.2	72 21.5	+58.0	137.5	71 36.6	+58.5	139.5	65
66	77 01.8	49.0	118.5	76 31.5	51.2	122.2	75 58.0	53.1	125.6	75 21.8	54.6	128.7	74 43.1	55.9	131.6	74 02.2	57.0	134.2	73 19.5	57.7	136.6	72 35.1	58.4	138.8	66
67	77 50.8	47.3	115.9	77 22.7	49.9	119.9	76 51.1	52.1	123.6	76 16.4	53.9	127.0	75 39.0	55.4	130.2	74 59.2	56.5	133.0	74 17.2	57.5	135.6	73 33.5	58.2	138.0	67
68	78 38.1	45.1	112.8	78 12.6	48.3	117.3	77 43.2	50.9	121.4	77 10.3	53.0	125.1	76 34.4	54.6	128.5	75 55.7	56.0	131.7	75 14.7	57.1	134.5	74 31.7	57.9	137.1	68
69	79 23.2	42.5	109.4	79 00.9	46.2	114.3	78 34.1	49.2	118.8	78 03.3	51.8	122.9	77 29.0	53.8	126.7	76 51.7	55.4	130.1	76 11.8	56.6	133.3	75 29.6	57.6	136.1	69
70	80 05.7	+39.4	105.4	79 47.1	+43.6	110.8	79 23.3	+47.3	115.8	78 55.1	+50.3	120.4	78 22.8	+52.7	124.6	77 47.1	+54.6	128.4	77 08.4	+56.2	131.8	76 27.2	+57.3	134.9	70
71	80 45.1	35.4	100.9	80 30.7	40.5	106.8	80 10.6	44.8	112.3	79 45.4	48.4	117.4	79 15.5	51.4	122.1	78 41.7	53.7	126.4	78 04.6	55.4	130.2	77 24.5	56.8	133.6	71
72	81 20.5	30.6	95.7	81 11.2	36.4	102.1	80 55.4	41.7	108.3	80 33.8	46.0	114.0	80 06.9	49.6	119.2	79 35.4	52.4	124.0	79 00.0	54.6	128.3	78 21.3	56.2	132.1	72
73	81 51.1	24.8	89.8	81 47.6	31.6	96.7	81 37.1	37.6	103.5	81 19.8	42.9	109.9	80 56.5	47.3	115.8	80 27.8	50.8	121.2	79 54.6	53.5	126.0	79 17.5	55.5	130.3	73
74	82 15.9	18.2	83.2	82 19.2	25.6	90.6	82 14.7	32.6	98.0	82 02.7	39.0	105.1	81 43.8	44.3	111.7	81 18.6	48.7	117.8	80 48.1	52.0	123.3	80 13.0	54.6	128.1	74
89	75 52.0	52.0	2.0	76 52.0	52.0	2.1	77 51.9	51.9	2.3	78 51.9	51.9	2.5	79 51.8	51.8	2.8	80 51.7	51.7	3.1	81 51.6	51.6	3.4	82 51.5	51.5	3.9	89
90	75 00.0	−52.9	0.0	76 00.0	−52.9	0.0	77 00.0	−53.0	0.0	78 00.0	−53.0	0.0	79 00.0	−53.1	0.0	80 00.0	−53.1	0.0	81 00.0	−53.2	0.0	82 00.0	−53.3	0.0	90
	75°			76°			77°			78°			79°			80°			81°			82°			

29°, 331° L.H.A. **LATITUDE SAME NAME AS DECLINATION**

Figure 2404e. Portion of a page from Pub. No. 229 with entries requiring double-second difference correction.

Double-second difference

The minor portion of the correction is for the *double-second difference.* This is the difference between the tabulated altitude differences (d) on the line directly above and the one directly below the value of d extracted from the table for the first difference. To illustrate: using Figure 2404e, enter the main tables with L 76° N, LHA 29°, and Dec. 69° N, Latitude Same as Declination. Note that the value of d is 46.2′, and that it is printed in italics, and followed by a dot; the double-second difference correction is therefore important. The value of d, for Dec. 68° (one line above the selected entry) is 48.3′, and for Dec. 70° (one line below) it is 43.6′; the difference of these values is 4.7′.

The interpolation tables also provide for obtaining the actual value of the double-second difference correction; it is obtained from the vertical column to the extreme right, headed "Double Second Diff. and Corr." This is a critical-type table. Enter it with the 4.7′ difference found above and obtain the actual value of the correction, 0.3′. *This correction is always additive.*

The value of the azimuth angle at times changes very materially with each degree of declination. It must, therefore, be corrected by interpolation for the actual value of the declination.

The following example illustrates the use of Pub. No. 229; it is based on the extracts of Figures 2404d and 2404e.

The calculated altitude and azimuth are required for an observation of a body having a declination of 69°34.8′ N, and a local hour angle of 29°; the assumed latitude is 76° N.

From the tables Latitude Same as Declination for Dec. = 69°, Hc = 79°00.9′, with d = 46.2′ (in italics and followed by a dot); Z = 114.3°. These must be corrected for the fractional part of declination using Figure 2404d.

Tabular Hc	79°00.9′	
First Diff Corr (Tens)	+23.2′	(for 40′)
First Diff Corr (Units and Decimals)	+ 3.6′	(for 6.2′)
Second Diff Corr	+ 0.3′	(previously calculated)
Exact. Hc	79°28.0′	

Z for 69° = 114.3°; Z for 70° = 110.8°; difference for 60′ = 3.5°.

Tabulated Z = N114.3W

− 2.0 $\left(-3.5° \times \frac{34.8}{60}\right)$

Z = N112.3W

Interpolation Zn = 247.7 (360° − Z)

Solution by Pub. No. 229 from a DR

2405 Pub. No. 229 can also be used for the reduction of an observation using the dead reckoning (DR) position rather than an assumed position (AP); this procedure, however, is more complex and difficult and it is rarely used. In principle, the method is the measurement of the difference in radii of two circles of equal altitude corresponding to the altitudes of the celestial body from two positions at the same time. One circle passes through the AP (selected, as usual, for whole degrees of latitude and LHA), and the second circle passes through the DR position (or other position from which the computed altitude is desired).

A graphic procedure is followed in which the Hc and intercept are first calculated in the usual way, followed by an offset correction to the plot. Full instructions on this procedure are given in the introductory pages of each volume. This method will give very satisfactory results except when plotting on a Mercator chart in high latitudes.

Possible errors arising from plotting from an assumed position

2406 Pub. No. 229, when used with an assumed position, offers sight reductions which are mathematically accurate. However, as with any sight reduction methods designed for use with an assumed position, and which tabulate latitude and meridian or hour angle by integral degrees, resulting lines of position may be somewhat in error under certain conditions. These errors tend to arise when the intercepts are long; they are caused by plotting the intercept and the line of position as rhumb lines on the chart, rather than as arcs of a great and small circle, respectively. These errors are not sufficiently large to require consideration in the ordinary practice of navigation at sea.

It has been found that for any given distance between the true and assumed position, the maximum perpendicular distance from the true position to the plotted line of position is roughly proportional to the tangent of the altitude. The error tends to increase with the altitude of the body, and it is roughly proportional to the square of the difference between the true and assumed positions. Other factors being equal, the error decreases as the latitude increases. In the vicinity of the equator, for an altitude of 75°, and a true position differing in both latitude and longitude by 30′ from the assumed position, the error will not exceed 1.0 miles; at latitude 60°, it will not exceed 0.7 miles, and the probable error would not be more than 0.3 miles. For an altitude of 60°, near the equator, the error will not exceed 0.5 miles. If the difference in both latitude and longitude between the true and assumed positions is reduced to 20′, the errors quoted above would be reduced by more than half.

The introductory pages of each volume include a "Table of Offsets" which gives the corrections to be applied to a straight line of position (LOP) as drawn on a chart or plotting sheet to provide a closer approximation of the arc of the circle of equal altitude. These corrections are offsets of points on the straight LOP plotted at right angles to it; these offset points are joined to obtain a better approximation of the arc of the *small* circle of equal altitude. Usually, the desired approximation of the arc can be obtained by drawing a straight line through two offset points. The magnitudes of these offsets are dependent upon altitude and the distance of the offset point from the intercept line.

Other uses of Pub. No. 229

2407 The tables of Pub. No. 229 can also be used in a number of secondary procedures. These include great-circle sailing problems, the solution of general spherical triangles, star identification, and the determination of compass error. Instructions for all these procedures are given in the introductory pages, together with several illustrative examples.

H. O. 229

The first printing of the *Sight Reduction Tables for Marine Navigation* occurred before the establishment of the Defense Mapping Agency and was designated as H. O. 229. Subsequent printings have borne the designation of DMAHC Pub. No. 229. The tabulated data are the same in all printings, but changes were made in the introductory pages when they became Pub. No. 229 (the "ABC" diagrams were omitted). Sight reductions are done in the same manner and produce the same results; other applications will give essentially the same results from either publication, but the procedures used may vary in details.

Pub. No. 249

2408 Another set of precomputed tables bear the name *Sight Reduction Tables for Air Navigation;* now designated as DMAHC Pub. No. 249, they are perhaps better known under their former name of "H. O. 249." As their name implies, they are designed for use by air navigators. However, they have also found favor with some surface navigators in cases where their greater speed and convenience offsets the less precise positional data so derived.

Volume I Selected Stars

These tables are published in three volumes. Similar to Pub. No. 229, they are inspection tables designed for use with an assumed position, but they differ from that publication in that altitude is stated only to the nearest whole minute of arc, and azimuth values are stated to the nearest whole degree. The first volume is designed for use with certain selected stars on a world-wide basis; all integral degrees of latitude, from 89° north to 89° south are included. The arguments for entering the tables in Volume I are the nearest whole degree of latitude, North or South, the LHA Aries, and the name of the star observed; with this entry, a calculated altitude, Hc, and a true azimuth, Zn, rather than azimuth angle, Z, are obtained. The LHA ♈ is obtained by applying to the GHA ♈ such an assumed longitude (within 30′ of DR or EP longitude) as will give a whole degree of LHA ♈.

For each degree of latitude and of LHA ♈, seven stars are tabulated; see Figure 2408a. The names of first-magnitude stars are printed in capital letters; those of second and third magnitude are in upper and lowercase letters. These stars are selected primarily for good distribution in azimuth, for their magnitude and altitude, and for continuity in latitude and hour angle; of these seven, three that are considered suitable for a three-star fix are identified by a diamond symbol (◆). The tabulated altitude and azimuth of the selected stars

LAT 42°N

LHA ♈	Hc	Zn	Hc	Zn	Hc	Zn	Hc	Zn	Hc	Zn	Hc	Zn	Hc	Zn
	♦Alpheratz		ALTAIR		Nunki		♦ANTARES		ARCTURUS		♦Alkaid		Kochab	
270	17 41	067	48 59	136	20 33	167	18 23	202	37 34	262	46 28	302	51 20	341
271	18 22	067	49 29	137	20 43	168	18 06	203	36 50	263	45 51	303	51 05	341
272	19 03	068	49 59	139	20 52	169	17 49	203	36 06	264	45 13	303	50 51	341
273	19 45	068	50 28	140	21 00	170	17 31	204	35 21	265	44 36	303	50 36	341
274	20 26	069	50 56	141	21 07	171	17 12	205	34 37	265	43 59	303	50 22	341
275	21 08	069	51 23	143	21 14	172	16 53	206	33 52	266	43 21	304	50 07	340
276	21 50	070	51 50	144	21 20	173	16 33	207	33 08	267	42 44	304	49 52	340
277	22 32	071	52 15	146	21 25	174	16 12	208	32 23	267	42 08	304	49 37	340
278	23 14	071	52 40	147	21 29	175	15 51	209	31 39	268	41 31	305	49 21	340
279	23 56	072	53 04	149	21 33	176	15 30	210	30 54	269	40 54	305	49 06	340
280	24 39	072	53 26	150	21 36	177	15 07	210	30 10	270	40 18	305	48 51	340
281	25 21	073	53 48	152	21 38	178	14 44	211	29 25	270	39 41	306	48 35	340
282	26 04	073	54 08	153	21 39	179	14 21	212	28 40	271	39 05	306	48 20	339
283	26 47	074	54 28	155	21 40	180	13 57	213	27 56	272	38 29	306	48 04	339
284	27 30	075	54 46	157	21 40	181	13 33	214	27 11	272	37 53	306	47 48	339
	♦Mirfak		Alpheratz		♦ALTAIR		Rasalhague		♦ARCTURUS		Alkaid		Kochab	
285	13 22	033	28 13	075	55 03	158	55 07	219	26 27	273	37 17	307	47 32	339
286	13 47	033	28 56	076	55 19	160	54 38	220	25 42	273	36 42	307	47 16	339
287	14 11	034	29 39	076	55 34	162	54 09	222	24 58	274	36 06	307	47 00	339
288	14 36	034	30 22	077	55 47	163	53 39	223	24 13	275	35 31	308	46 44	339
289	15 01	035	31 06	077	55 59	165	53 08	225	23 29	275	34 56	308	46 28	339
290	15 27	035	31 49	078	56 10	167	52 36	226	22 44	276	34 21	309	46 12	339
291	15 53	036	32 33	079	56 20	169	52 04	227	22 00	277	33 46	309	45 56	339
292	16 19	036	33 17	079	56 28	170	51 31	229	21 16	277	33 11	309	45 40	339

Figure 2408a. Pub. No. 249, Volume I (extract).

permits the use of this publication as a starfinder by presetting the sextant and observing in the tabulated direction.

The stars for which data are given in Volume I of Pub. No. 249 have continual slight changes in sidereal hour angle and declination due to the precession and nutation of the earth's axis of rotation. Editions of this publication contain tabulated data for a specific year, and an auxiliary table (Table 5) for corrections to be applied to an LOP or fix for years other than the base year. Editions are currently published every five years, but to provide for some overlap, the table of corrections covers a span of eight years. Each edition is designated with an *epoch year,* a multiple of five, but this is not necessarily the base year for which the tabulated data were calculated—the tables of the Epoch 1975.0 edition were calculated for 1974 with a corrections table making them usable for the years 1972 to 1979 inclusive.

Volume I has other auxiliary tables including altitude corrections for change in position of the observer (primarily for airborne observers) or change in position of the body between time of observation and fix. Polaris latitude and azimuth tables are provided, as well as a table of GHA ♈ to eliminate the need for an *Air Almanac.* Another auxiliary table facilitates conversion between arc and time units.

Pub. No. 249, Volumes II, and III Volumes II and III are generally similar in format to Pub. No. 229, except that Hc is tabulated only to the nearest whole minute and Z to the nearest whole degree. Both volumes list declination by integral degrees, but only for 0° to 29°; this covers all bodies of the solar system.

It is assumed Vol. I will usually be used for star sights, although stars with Dec. of 29° or less can be used with Vol. II and Vol. III; 29 of the 57 selected stars fall into this category. Volume II covers latitudes 0° to 39°, and Volume III covers latitude 40° to 89°. A portion of a page from Volume II is reproduced in Figure 2408b. The entering arguments are a whole degree of latitude, without name in these volumes, a whole degree of declination of same or contrary name to the latitude, and a whole degree of LHA. In the design of the tables it is intended that the *next smaller value* of declination be used. The tabulated values of LHA provide for negative altitudes, because of the large value of the dip at the high operating altitudes of modern planes, which permit the observation of bodies below the celestial horizon.

For each single set of entering arguments, the tables state an altitude expressed to the nearest whole minute of arc, under the heading "Hc." Adjoining this, under the heading *d*, is a value with sign, which is the difference in minutes between the tabulated altitude, and the altitude for a declination one degree higher, but at the same latitude, and for the same LHA. The third item, under the heading "Z", is the azimuth angle (not Zn as in Vol. I). The rule for converting Z to Zn is given on each page.

To correct the tabulated altitude for the difference between the true declination and that used as an entering argument, a multiplication table is included at the back of the book; a sample section is shown in Figure 2408c. By means of this table, the d value is multiplied by the difference between the true and tabulated declinations, and applied to the tabulated altitude according to the sign shown in the main table.

The "249" tables provide an excellent reduction method for the airborne navigator. Cloud cover rarely presents a problem at the altitudes presently used for long-distance flights, and the seven stars selected for any given time are usually all visible during the hours of

DECLINATION (19°-29°) CONTRARY NAME TO LATITUDE

	19°			20°			21°			22°			23°		
LHA	Hc	d	Z	Hc	d	Z	Hc	d	Z	Hc	d	Z	Hc	d	Z
	° ′	′	°	° ′	′	°	° ′	′	°	° ′	′	°	° ′	′	°
14	36 18	58	164	35 20	58	164	34 22	58	164	33 24	58	164	32 26	58	165
13	36 32	58	165	35 34	58	165	34 36	59	165	33 37	58	166	32 39	59	166
12	36 45	58	166	35 47	59	166	34 48	59	166	33 49	58	167	32 51	59	167
11	36 57	59	167	35 58	59	167	34 59	59	167	34 00	58	168	33 02	59	168
10	37 08	−59	168	36 09	−59	168	35 10	−59	169	34 11	−59	169	33 12	−59	169
9	37 18	60	169	36 18	59	170	35 19	59	170	34 20	59	170	33 21	59	170
8	37 27	60	171	36 27	59	171	35 28	60	171	34 28	59	171	33 29	59	171
7	37 34	59	172	36 35	60	172	35 35	59	172	34 36	60	172	33 36	59	172
6	37 41	59	173	36 42	60	173	35 42	60	173	34 42	59	173	33 43	60	173
5	37 47	−60	174	36 47	−60	174	35 47	−59	174	34 48	−60	174	33 48	−60	175
4	37 52	60	175	36 52	60	175	35 52	60	175	34 52	60	176	33 52	60	176
3	37 55	60	176	36 55	60	177	35 55	59	177	34 56	60	177	33 56	60	177
2	37 58	60	178	36 58	60	178	35 58	60	178	34 58	60	178	33 58	60	178
1	38 00	60	179	37 00	60	179	36 00	60	179	35 00	60	179	34 00	60	179
0	38 00	−60	180	37 00	−60	180	36 00	−60	180	35 00	−60	180	34 00	−60	180
	19°			20°			21°			22°			23°		

	24°			25°			26°			27°			28°			29°			
LHA	Hc	d	Z	Hc	d	Z	Hc	d	Z	Hc	d	Z	Hc	d	Z	Hc	d	Z	LHA
	° ′	′	°	° ′	′	°	° ′	′	°	° ′	′	°	° ′	′	°	° ′	′	°	
14	31 28	59	165	30 29	58	165	29 31	58	166	28 33	59	166	27 34	58	166	26 36	59	166	346
13	31 40	58	166	30 42	59	166	29 43	59	167	28 44	58	167	27 46	59	167	26 47	58	167	347
12	31 52	59	167	30 53	59	167	29 54	58	168	28 56	59	168	27 57	59	168	26 58	59	168	348
11	32 03	59	168	31 04	59	168	30 05	59	169	29 06	59	169	28 07	59	169	27 08	59	169	349
10	32 13	−60	169	31 13	−59	169	30 14	−59	170	29 15	−59	170	28 16	−59	170	27 17	−59	170	350
9	32 22	60	170	31 22	59	170	30 23	59	171	29 24	60	171	28 24	59	171	27 25	59	171	351
8	32 30	60	171	31 30	59	172	30 31	60	172	29 31	59	172	28 32	60	172	27 32	59	172	352
7	32 37	60	172	31 37	59	173	30 38	60	173	29 38	60	173	28 38	59	173	27 39	60	173	353
6	32 43	60	174	31 43	59	174	30 44	60	174	29 44	60	174	28 44	60	174	27 44	59	174	354
5	32 48	−60	175	31 48	−59	175	30 49	−60	175	29 49	−60	175	28 49	−60	175	27 49	−60	175	355
4	32 52	59	176	31 53	60	176	30 53	60	176	29 53	60	176	28 53	60	176	27 53	60	176	356
3	32 56	60	177	31 56	60	177	30 56	60	177	29 56	60	177	28 56	60	177	27 56	60	177	357
2	32 58	60	178	31 58	60	178	30 58	60	178	29 58	60	178	28 58	60	178	27 58	60	178	358
1	33 00	60	179	32 00	60	179	31 00	60	179	30 00	60	179	29 00	60	179	28 00	60	179	359
0	33 00	−60	180	32 00	−60	180	31 00	−60	180	30 00	−60	180	29 00	−60	180	28 00	−60	180	360
	24°			25°			26°			27°			28°			29°			

LAT 33°

DECLINATION (19°-29°) CONTRARY NAME TO LATITUDE LAT 33°

Figure 2408b. Pub. No. 249, Volume II (extract).

TABLE III.—Correction to Tabulated Altitude for Minutes of Declination

d / ′	1	2	3	4	5	6	7	8	9	10	11	12	13	14	15	16	17	18	19	20	21
0	0	0	0	0	0	0	0	0	0	0	0	0	0	0	0	0	0	0	0	0	0
1	0	0	0	0	0	0	0	0	0	0	0	0	0	0	0	0	0	0	0	0	0
2	0	0	0	0	0	0	0	0	0	0	0	0	0	0	0	1	1	1	1	1	1
3	0	0	0	0	0	0	0	0	0	0	1	1	1	1	1	1	1	1	1	1	1
4	0	0	0	0	0	0	0	1	1	1	1	1	1	1	1	1	1	1	1	1	1
35	1	1	2	2	3	4	4	5	5	6	6	7	8	8	9	9	10	10	11	12	12
36	1	1	2	2	3	4	4	5	5	6	7	7	8	8	9	10	10	11	11	12	13
37	1	1	2	2	3	4	4	5	6	6	7	7	8	9	9	10	10	11	12	12	13
38	1	1	2	3	3	4	4	5	6	6	7	8	8	9	10	10	11	11	12	13	13
39	1	1	2	3	3	4	5	5	6	6	7	8	8	9	10	10	11	12	12	13	14

37	38	39	40	41	42	43	44	45	46	47	48	49	50	51	52	53	54	55	56	57	58	59	60	d / ′
0	0	0	0	0	0	0	0	0	0	0	0	0	0	0	0	0	0	0	0	0	0	0	0	0
1	1	1	1	1	1	1	1	1	1	1	1	1	1	1	1	1	1	1	1	1	1	1	1	1
1	1	1	1	1	1	1	1	2	2	2	2	2	2	2	2	2	2	2	2	2	2	2	2	2
2	2	2	2	2	2	2	2	2	2	2	2	2	2	3	3	3	3	3	3	3	3	3	3	3
2	3	3	3	3	3	3	3	3	3	3	3	3	3	3	3	4	4	4	4	4	4	4	4	4
22	22	23	23	24	24	25	26	26	27	27	28	29	29	30	30	31	32	32	33	33	34	34	35	35
22	23	23	24	25	25	26	26	27	28	28	29	29	30	31	31	32	32	33	34	34	35	35	36	36
23	23	24	25	25	26	27	27	28	28	29	30	30	31	31	32	33	33	34	35	35	36	36	37	37
23	24	25	25	26	27	27	28	28	29	30	30	31	32	32	33	34	34	35	35	36	37	37	38	38
24	25	25	26	27	27	28	29	29	30	31	31	32	32	33	34	34	35	36	36	37	38	38	39	39

Figure 2408c. Pub. No. 249, Volume II or III (extract).

darkness. The procedures result in a degree of precision of fix that is in keeping with that of observed altitudes obtained with a sextant using a pendulous mirror, or some other artificial horizon, such as a bubble.

It is also a satisfactory method for small vessels making long ocean voyages. Stowage space in such craft is limited, and the three volumes give worldwide coverage. Of the 173 navigational stars tabulated in the *Nautical Almanac,* 75 are suitable for use with Volumes II and III; 29 of these 75 are among the selected stars. In its degree of precision, Pub. No. 249 is comparable with the accuracy of the sextant observations that can be obtained aboard a small craft in rough water. (On sailing craft, there may be problems as to the direction in which sights can be taken as a result of the blocking of vision by the sails. The availability of seven selected stars well distributed in azimuth should, however, permit the obtaining of enough celestial LOPs to get a fix.) The navigator of a large surface vessel, on the other hand, can and should obtain a higher order of precision in his celestial navigation than is possible with the use of these tables; Pub. No. 229 (or H. O. 214) should be the reduction method of his choice.

The Ageton Method

2409 A volume entitled *Dead Reckoning Altitude and Azimuth Table* was formerly published as H. O. 211 and is now included in DMAHC Pub. No. 9 (*Bowditch*), Volume II, as Table No. 35; these are referred to as the *Ageton* tables after their original designer. They are also available as separate tables from commercial publishers in a small volume of roughly 50 pages. There is a single table of log secants and log cosecants (× 100,000), stated for each 0.5′ of arc. It is suitable for worldwide use with any declination, and for any altitude. As its name implies, it is intended for use from a DR position. A partial page is shown in Figure 2409a.

In this method, two right triangles are formed by dropping a perpendicular from the celestial body to the celestial meridian of the observer. The right angle falls on the celestial meridian at a point which may lie either inside or outside of the navigational triangle. The right triangles are then solved for altitude and azimuth angle from equations derived from Napier's rules.

′	22° 30′		23° 00′		23° 30′		24° 00′		24° 30′		′
	A	B	A	B	A	B	A	B	A	B	
10	41412	**3491**	40516	**3651**	39641	**3815**	38786	**3983**	37951	**4155**	20
	41397	**3494**	40501	**3654**	39626	**3818**	38772	**3986**	37937	**4158**	
11	41382	**3496**	40486	**3657**	39612	**3821**	38758	**3989**	37924	**4161**	19
	41367	**3499**	40471	**3659**	39597	**3824**	38744	**3992**	37910	**4164**	
12	41352	**3502**	40457	**3662**	39583	**3826**	38730	**3995**	37896	**4167**	18
	41337	**3504**	40442	**3665**	39569	**3829**	38716	**3998**	37882	**4170**	
13	41322	**3507**	40427	**3667**	39554	**3832**	38702	**4000**	37869	**4173**	17
	41307	**3509**	40413	**3670**	39540	**3835**	38688	**4003**	37855	**4176**	
14	41291	**3512**	40398	**3673**	39525	**3838**	38674	**4006**	37841	**4179**	16
	41276	**3515**	40383	**3676**	39511	**3840**	38660	**4009**	37828	**4182**	
15	41261	**3517**	40368	**3678**	39497	**3843**	38645	**4012**	37814	**4185**	15
	41246	**3520**	40354	**3681**	39482	**3846**	38631	**4015**	37800	**4187**	
16	41231	**3523**	40339	**3684**	39468	**3849**	38617	**4017**	37786	**4190**	14
	41216	**3525**	40324	**3686**	39454	**3851**	38603	**4020**	37773	**4193**	
17	41201	**3528**	40310	**3689**	39439	**3854**	38589	**4023**	37759	**4196**	13
	41186	**3531**	40295	**3692**	39425	**3857**	38575	**4026**	37745	**4199**	
18	41171	**3533**	40280	**3695**	39411	**3860**	38561	**4029**	37732	**4202**	12
	41156	**3536**	40266	**3697**	39396	**3863**	38547	**4032**	37718	**4205**	
19	41141	**3539**	40251	**3700**	39382	**3865**	38533	**4035**	37704	**4208**	11
	41126	**3541**	40236	**3703**	39368	**3868**	38520	**4037**	37691	**4211**	
20	41111	**3544**	40222	**3705**	39353	**3871**	38506	**4040**	37677	**4214**	10
	41096	**3547**	40207	**3708**	39339	**3874**	38492	**4043**	37663	**4217**	
21	41081	**3549**	40192	**3711**	39325	**3876**	38478	**4046**	37650	**4220**	9
	41066	**3552**	40178	**3714**	39311	**3879**	38464	**4049**	37636	**4222**	
22	41051	**3555**	40163	**3716**	39296	**3882**	38450	**4052**	37623	**4225**	8
	41036	**3557**	40149	**3719**	39282	**3885**	38436	**4055**	37609	**4228**	
23	41021	**3560**	40134	**3722**	39268	**3888**	38422	**4057**	37595	**4231**	7
	41006	**3563**	40119	**3725**	39254	**3890**	38408	**4060**	37582	**4234**	
24	40991	**3565**	40105	**3727**	39239	**3893**	38394	**4063**	37568	**4237**	6
	40976	**3568**	40090	**3730**	39225	**3896**	38380	**4066**	37554	**4240**	
25	40961	**3571**	40076	**3733**	39211	**3899**	38366	**4069**	37541	**4243**	5
	40946	**3573**	40061	**3735**	39197	**3902**	38352	**4072**	37527	**4246**	
26	40931	**3576**	40046	**3738**	39182	**3904**	38338	**4075**	37514	**4249**	4
	40916	**3579**	40032	**3741**	39168	**3907**	38324	**4078**	37500	**4252**	
27	40902	**3581**	40017	**3744**	39154	**3910**	38311	**4080**	37486	**4255**	3
	40887	**3584**	40003	**3746**	39140	**3913**	38297	**4083**	37473	**4258**	

Figure 2409a. Pub. No. 9 (*Bowditch*), Volume II (1975), Table 35 (extract).

In Figure 2409b the navigational triangle is shown with the parts of the triangle lettered.

In right triangle *PMX,* t and d are known. *R* may be found from equation (1). Knowing *R* and d, *K* may be found by equation (2). *K* is then combined algebraically with *L* to obtain ($K \sim L$).

In triangle *ZMX,* sides *R* and ($K \sim L$) are now known. Hc may be found by equation (3). The azimuth, Z, is computed by equation (4).

All equations are in terms of secants and cosecants. The table is arranged in parallel *A* and *B* columns, the *A* columns containing log cosecants multiplied by 100,000 and the *B* columns log secants multiplied by 100,000. This device has greatly simplified the arithmetic of solution.

The tabulation of functions for every half-minute of arc throughout the table is employed so that, in ordinary use, interpolation will not be necessary.

The procedure necessary to obtain the calculated altitude and azimuth by the Ageton method is described in detail in *Bowditch,* Volume

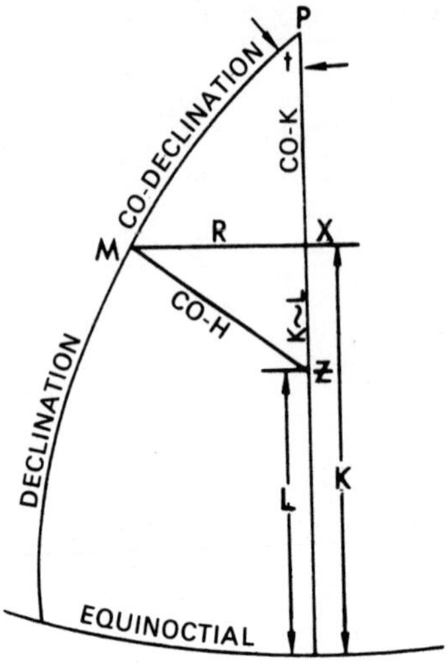

Figure 2409b. The celestial triangle as solved by the Ageton method.

P. Pole.
Z. Zenith of observer. The azimuth (angle PZM) is also called Z.
M. Heavenly body observed.
L. Latitude of observer.
d. Declination of body M.
t. (or LHA). Local hour angle of body M.
H. Altitude of body M.
R. Perpendicular let fall from M on PZ. This is an auxiliary part.
X. Intersection of R with PZ.
K. Arc from X to the equinoctial. This is an auxiliary part introduced to facilitate solution.

The following equations have been derived:

From triangle PMX—

1. $\csc R = \csc t \sec d$.
2. $\csc K = \dfrac{\csc d}{\sec R}$

From triangle ZMX—

3. $\csc Hc = \sec R \sec (K \sim L)$.
4. $\csc Z = \dfrac{\csc R}{\sec Hc}$

II, and in the separate publications of the table. The example shown in Figure 2409c illustrates the reduction of an observation by this method; the work form used will be found convenient, as it indicates where the *A* or *B* values taken from the tables are entered and how they are combined.

Example: A navigator whose DR position is L 33°21.3′ N, λ 65°26.2′ W observes the sun at a time when its t is 14°12.5′ W, and its Dec., is 22°37.4′ S. After appropriate corrections are applied to the hs, the Ho is 32°28.7′. (See Figure 2409c. The *A* and *B* values on the line for "dec." are taken from the extract of Figure 2409a; other values of *A* and *B* are from pages not shown.) In obtaining Hc he does not interpolate as the value for *K* was not near 90°. If, however, the value for *K*

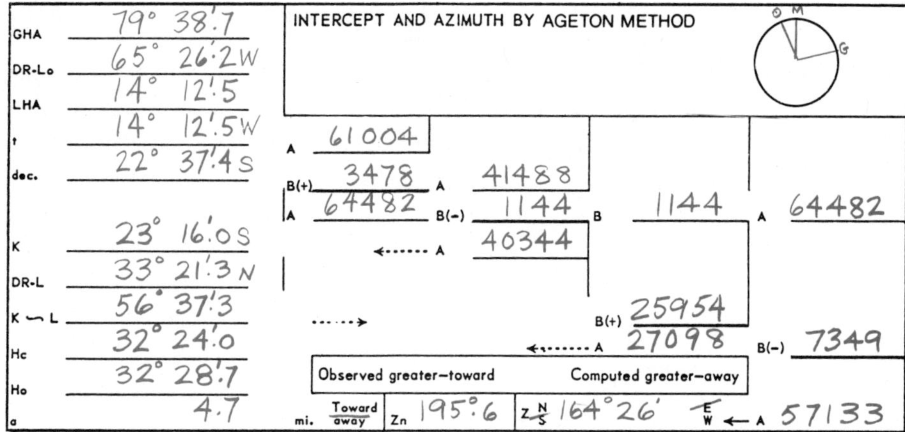

GHA	79° 38'.7
DR-Lo	65° 26'.2W
LHA	14° 12'.5
t	14° 12'.5W
dec.	22° 37'.4S
K	23° 16'.0S
DR-L	33° 21'.3N
K ~ L	56° 37'.3
Hc	32° 24'.0
Ho	32° 28'.7
a	4.7

INTERCEPT AND AZIMUTH BY AGETON METHOD

A 61004
B(+) 3478
A 64482

A 41488
B(-) 1144
A 40344

B 1144
B(+) 25954
A 27098

A 64482
B(-) 7349
A 57133

Observed greater–toward / Computed greater–away

mi. Toward/away — Zn 195°.6 — Z N/S 164°26' E/W

Figure 2409c. Form with sight reduction by Ageton method.

had been within a few degrees of 90°, the accuracy of the solution would have been inadequate without interpolation; it is good practice to either discard such sights or interpolate the *B* value in the second column of the form from the *A* value in the first column.

Summary **2410** The corrected sextant altitude must be *reduced* to obtain the information that will establish a celestial line of position. This reduction may be computed, or precomputed "inspection" tables may be used.

The computation method of sight reduction uses basic equations of spherical trigonometry. This method reached the peak of its popularity with the simplified procedures of the H. O. 208 and H. O. 211 publications. They have been largely superseded now by the inspection tables of H. O. 214, Pub. No. 229, and Pub. No. 249. These allow for a faster solution with less likelihood of computational errors. (The tables of H. O. 214 are no longer published, having been superseded by Pub. No. 229, but they are still used by some navigators). The choice between Pubs. No. 229 and 249 is largely a matter of personal preference, although the "229" tables will allow a more precise determination of position and, at least in theory, should be given preferential consideration in marine navigation.

With the recent widespread popularity of small, personal electronic calculators, there has been a rekindling of interest in sight reduction by computation using the classic equations (somewhat rearranged to fit the keyboards and procedures of the calculators). This is a fully feasible method with key-programmable calculators; with card-programmable models, it is quick, easy, and highly accurate. There are also available specialized models of hand-held electronic calculators that have internal sight reduction programs built into their circuitry.

A competent navigator should be "at ease" with several methods of sight reduction. Any use of calculators must be accompanied with a thorough understanding of the mathematical processes being employed.

25 Celestial Lines of Position

Introduction **2501** A prior chapter has shown how the navigator, having obtained an altitude of a celestial body, can determine the circle of equal altitude passing through his position. Only seldom is he able to plot this circular line of position directly on his chart; he must, therefore, be able to construct a portion of the circle on his chart in the vicinity of the ship's DR position. The purpose of this chapter is to explain the techniques whereby celestial altitudes are converted into celestial lines of position, and how fixes and running fixes are obtained from such lines. Celestial lines of position are usually plotted on special charts called *plotting sheets.* In the interest of simplification, however, the term *chart* will be used throughout this chapter.

Line of position An American, Captain Thomas H. Sumner, discovered the line of position in 1837. Due to thick weather, when approaching the English coast, he had been unable to obtain any observations. About 10 A.M. the sun broke through, and he procured an altitude which he reduced to obtain the longitude. However, the latitude he used for the reduction was in doubt; he solved for longitude twice more, each time using a different latitude. After plotting the three positions on a chart he was surprised to find that a straight line could be drawn through them. He correctly deduced that his position must lie somewhere along this line, which happened to pass through a light off the English coast. He turned the ship and sailed along that line until the light appeared, thus establishing his position exactly.

Sumner's discovery of the line of position was a great step forward in celestial navigation. Its greatest weakness lay in the fact that to obtain such a line of position, a sight had to be worked twice, using different latitudes. In 1875, Commander Marcq de St.-Hilaire of the French Navy, introduced the altitude difference, or intercept method, which has become the basis of virtually all celestial navigation. In this method, the altitude and azimuth, or direction of a body, are calculated for a given instant of time and for a location where the vessel is supposed to be. The difference between the altitude as observed by sextant, and the calculated altitude is then determined: this difference, which is called the intercept, will be in minutes of arc.

A line is then drawn through the position, corresponding in direction to the calculated azimuth. The intercept is next laid off along the azimuth line, one nautical mile being equal to one minute of arc. It is measured towards the body if the observed altitude is greater than the calculated, and away if it is less. All that remains is to draw the line of position at right angles to the azimuth line.

Terrestrial and celestial lines of position compared

2502 In piloting, the navigator may obtain a line of position in any of several ways; usually such lines represent bearings of a landmark or seamark. In celestial navigation a line of position is a small segment of a circle, which represents distance in nautical miles from the GP of the observed body; it is somewhat similar to the circular line of position obtained from a radar range in piloting. This distance is obtained by converting the altitude of the observed body into miles on the surface of the earth; this distance must then be transformed into a line of position which can be plotted on the appropriate chart. Both celestial and terrestrial lines of position are used in essentially the same manner, and may be advanced or retired as required; usually they are advanced so as to result in a common time for two or more LOPs taken in sequence rather than simultaneously.

Lines of position from high altitude observations

2503 As shown in Chapter 19 the radius of a circle of equal altitude is equal to the coaltitude, or 90° minus the altitude. If a body is observed at a very high altitude, the radius will be small, and the resulting circle of equal altitude can be plotted directly on a chart. The center of this circle will be the GP of the body, and the radius will equal the coaltitude. In practice, only that portion of the circle which lies in the vicinity of the ship's DR position is drawn.

There are two reasons why this direct method of plotting celestial lines of position is not suitable for most celestial observations. The first is that the radii of most circles of equal altitude are very long. For example, for an altitude of 50°, the coaltitude, and therefore the radius, is 40°, which equals 2,400 nautical miles (4,445 km), and for an altitude of 20°, the radius is 4,200 nautical miles (7,778 km). A chart that would permit plotting radii of such magnitudes would be of such small scale that it would not yield the accuracy in position required in practical navigation.

Secondly, distortion is apparent on the commonly used Mercator projection, and increases with the latitude of the GP. The distortion of such a circle is illustrated in Figure 2503a.

If, however, the body is very high in altitude, the coaltitude will be small enough to plot on a navigational chart, and the distortion will be negligible. There is no precise answer as to how great the altitude should be to permit direct plotting as a "high-altitude observation." Typically, all sights with an observed altitude of 87° or more are classed as high-altitude observations and the resulting LOP is plotted directly; the radius in this case would not exceed 180 miles (333 km).

Example: The 1137 DR position of an observer is L 5°30.5′ N, λ 139°57.7′ E, at which time he determines the Ho of the sun to be

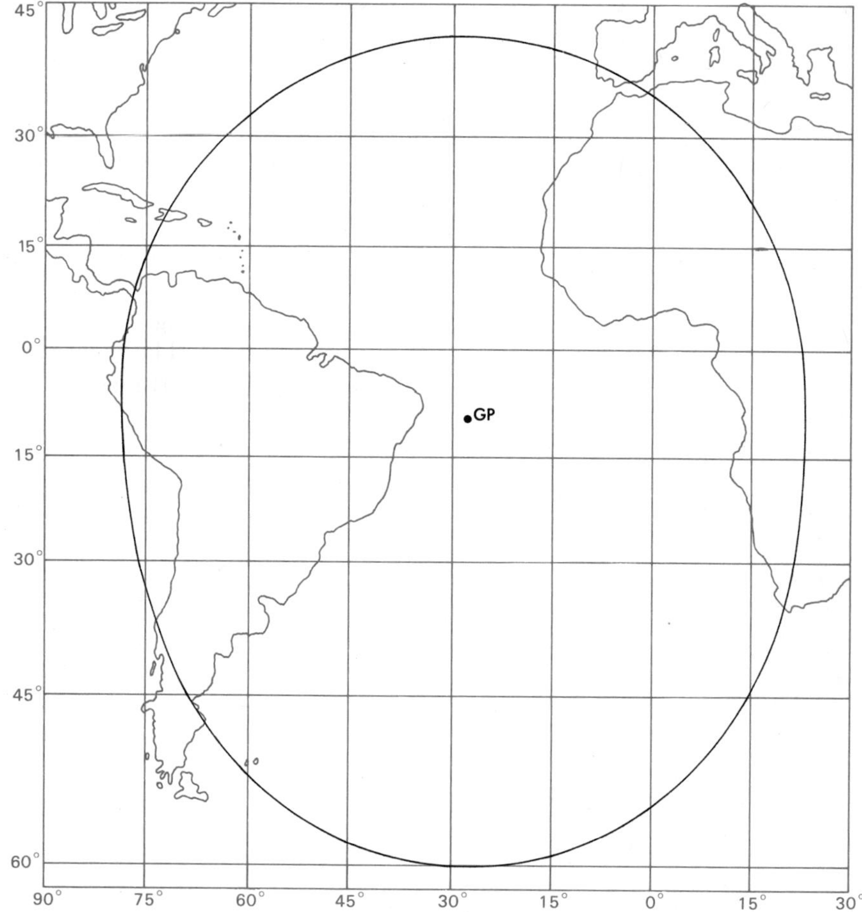

Figure 2503a. Circle of equal altitude plotted on a Mercator chart.

88°14.5′. The GP of the sun for this time is determined from an almanac to be L 7°14.9′ N, λ 140°26.2′ E.

Required: The plot of the 1137 LOP.

Solution: (Figure 2503b) Plot and label the 1137 DR position and the GP, using the latitudes and longitudes given. Since the radius of the circle of equal altitude equals the coaltitude, subtract the observed altitude from 90°, and convert the difference into minutes of arc, which equal nautical miles.

	90°00.0′
Ho	88°14.5′
Radius	1°45.5′ = 105.5 nautical miles (195.4 km)

Using a radius of 105.5 miles (shown by the broken line), construct an arc with the GP as the center, drawing only that segment which lies in the vicinity of the DR position. Label the resulting line of position as shown, except for the radius shown in this figure which is normally not drawn.

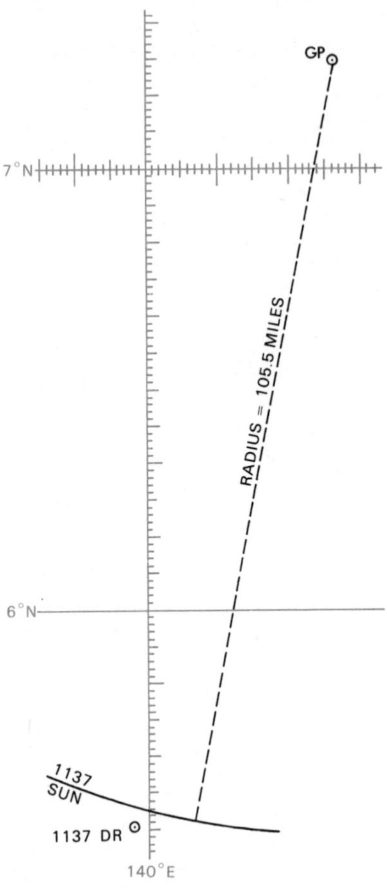

Figure 2503b. Plot of the LOP from a high-altitude observation.

In actual practice, it is difficult to obtain accurate observations at very high altitudes, since when the sextant is rocked, the observed body travels almost horizontally along the horizon, making it difficult to establish the vertical. However, at midday in the tropics, the navigator must make his LAN observation of the sun, regardless of its altitude, in order to obtain a latitude line of position.

Lines of position from other than high altitude observations

2504 The great majority of celestial observations are made at altitudes which do not permit direct plotting, as described above; for these, a different method must be employed. This method is usually based on the use of an assumed position (AP), and the solution of the navigational triangle associated with it.

It has been stated that the navigational triangle may be defined by the AP, the elevated pole, and the GP of the body. By solving the triangle, the altitude and azimuth of the body at the AP at the time of observation may be computed. In Figure 2504a the circle represents the circle of equal altitude for an observer at *M* and the point AP is the assumed position selected for the particular observation. By solving the triangle containing AP, the navigator determines the length of the side AP-GP, or coaltitude, which is the radius of the circle of equal altitude through the AP (not shown in Figure 2504a).

If the altitude (Ho) obtained by the observer at M *is greater than the altitude computed (Hc) by solving the triangle, the observer must be closer to the GP than is the AP; if it is less, he must be farther away.* Also, the difference in the radii of the two circles of equal altitude, as illustrated in Figure 2504b, is equal to the difference between the coaltitudes obtained from Ho and Hc, respectively. *The difference is the intercept* (*a*), and is expressed in nautical miles, which equals the difference expressed in minutes of arc.

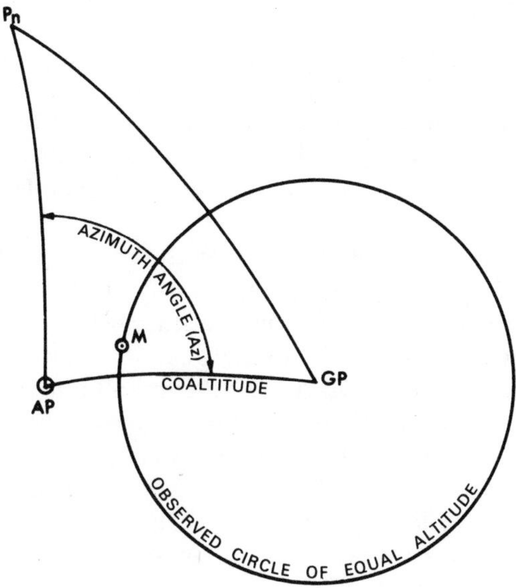

Figure 2504a. A circle of equal altitude and the navigational triangle associated with one AP.

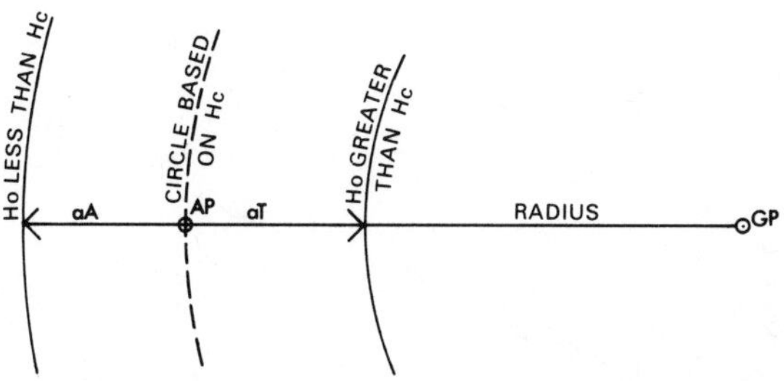

Figure 2504b. The relationship of the altitude difference, (a), to the AP and to the observed circle of equal altitude.

Azimuth for the LOP

In solving the triangle, the value of the *azimuth angle* (Z) is also obtained; this is used to determine the true direction or *azimuth* (Zn) of the body from the AP. If the Ho is greater than the Hc, a line representing Zn is plotted from the AP toward the GP; if Hc is the greater, the line will be plotted as the reciprocal of Zn, or away from the GP. This line is a part of the radius of a circle of equal altitude; by laying off a distance equal to (a) along this line, a point on the observed circle of equal altitude is determined. If Ho is greater than Hc, (a) is always labeled T (toward); if it is less, the label is A (away). A useful memory aid in labeling (a) is *Coast Guard Academy* for *Computed Greater Away;* also *HoMoTo,* for *Ho More Toward.*

To sum up, to plot a celestial LOP the following must be known:

The position of the AP;
Azimuth of the body, Zn;
The intercept, (a).

The intercept, (a), lies along a partial radius of a circle of equal altitude; it is plotted from the AP in the direction Zn, or towards the body, if labeled T (Ho greater than Hc). If labeled A (Hc greater than Ho), it is plotted in the direction of the reciprocal of Zn. The length of (a) in miles is equal to the difference between Ho and Hc in minutes of arc.

The line of position on which the observer is located is perpendicular to the intercept and passes through its terminus. Actually, this LOP is an arc of a circle of equal altitude; however, for most observations, the radius of the circle is so large that the curvature of the LOP is not significant. The LOP resulting from all but very high altitude observations may, therefore, be drawn as a straight line; the resulting error is insignificant in the ordinary practice of navigation. Figure 2504c illustrates the approximation made by using a straight line rather than an arc for plotting a celestial LOP. If a more precise solution is required, the circle can be closely approximated by plotting "offsets" from the straight LOP as covered by Article 2406 and the introductory pages to any volume of DMAHC Pub. No. 229.

The following example will illustrate that portion of the navigator's work which has just been discussed. The actual plot, as laid down on

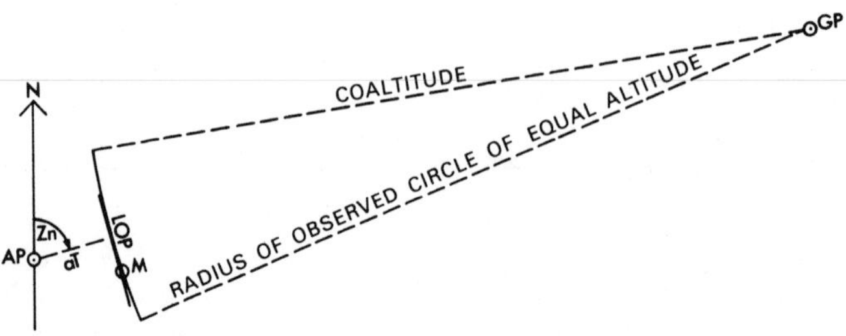

Figure 2504c. Plot of the same LOP from the AP and from the GP.

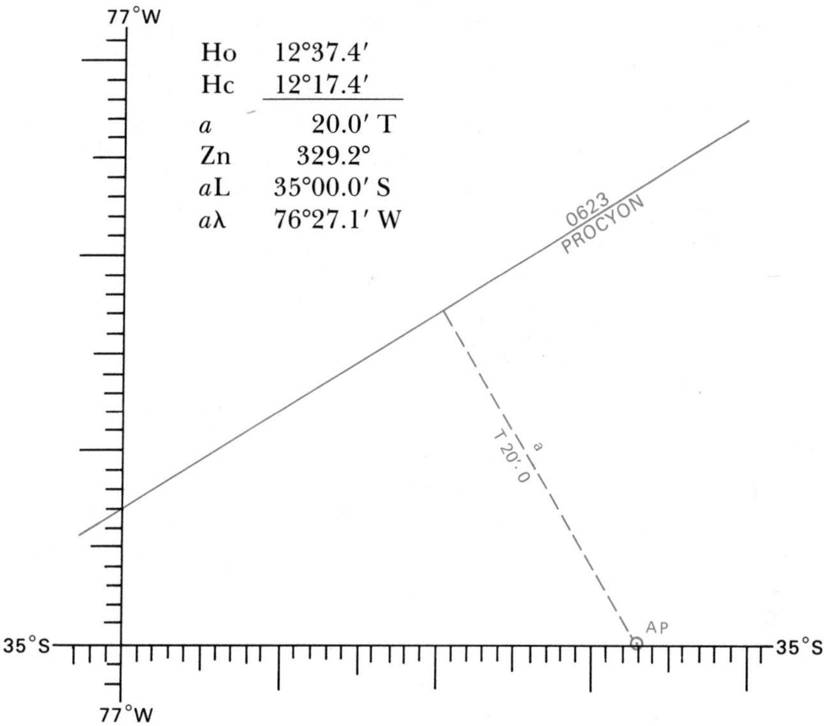

Figure 2504d. Plot of a celestial LOP.

the chart, is shown in Figure 2504d. Note that only two lines are drawn; the dashed line, from the AP, which is the intercept, and the heavy line, which is the LOP. The latter is labeled in accordance with standard practice, the ship's time of the observation being shown above, and the name of the body observed below. In normal practice, the intercept is not labeled; the time may be omitted from the LOP if it is used for a fix that is labeled with time.

Example: At 0623 a navigator determines the Ho of the star Procyon to be 12°37.4′. Selecting a point at L 35°00.0′ S and λ 76°27.1′ W as his assumed position, he computes Hc to be 12°17.4′ and Zn to be 329.2°.

Required: The plot of the 0623 celestial LOP.

Solution: (Figure 2504d).

First, determine (a) by comparison of Hc with Ho, and designate it "To" or "Away" in accordance with whether Ho or Hc, respectively, is the greater. Plot the AP, using aL and aλ given. From the AP draw a broken line either toward or away from the direction of the GP, as indicated by Zn and the label of (a). Measure the distance (a) along this line, and at the point so determined, construct a perpendicular. This perpendicular is the 0623 LOP; it is labeled with the time of the observation above the LOP and with the name of the body below the LOP, as shown in Figure 2504d.

The celestial fix **2505** In piloting, a navigator can fix his position by taking bearings of two or more landmarks or other aids to navigation in rapid succession. For practical purposes, it is assumed that these bearings are taken simultaneously, and no adjustment of the lines of position is required. In celestial navigation, observations cannot be taken as rapidly as in piloting, with the result that the lines of position obtained must usually be adjusted for the travel of the ship between sights. This means that what is termed a *fix* in celestial navigation is actually constructed using the principles of the running fix used in piloting, since lines of position are advanced or retired to a common time. It is customary to consider the position resulting from observations obtained during a single round of sights as a fix, with the term *running fix* being reserved for a position obtained from observations separated by a considerable period of time, typically more than 30 minutes.

Each celestial line of position requires an AP, a segment of the radius (determined by Zn) equal to (a) in length, and the actual LOP constructed perpendicular to the Zn line through the point found using (a) (unless the high-altitude technique is used). If three successive celestial observations were taken with small time intervals between them, the resulting APs with their associated lines of position could readily be plotted. To obtain a celestial fix, however, each would have to be advanced or retired to the time desired for the fix, making proper allowance for the travel of the ship during the intervening time. This could be done, as in piloting, by moving each LOP for the correct distance and direction. Because of the larger number of lines required to plot a celestial fix in this manner in a comparatively small area of the chart or plotting sheet, many navigators prefer to *advance the AP rather than the line of position,* thereby plotting the LOP only once. This is the method that will be used throughout this book; it is illustrated in the following examples.

Example 1: The 0515 DR position of a ship on course 176°, speed 14.5 knots, is L 35°09.2′ S, λ 119°13.7′ E. About this time the navigator observes the stars Antares, Acrux, and Regulus, with the following results:

Body	ANTARES	ACRUX	REGULUS
Time	0515	0519	0525
a	20.3 T	18.1 T	7.0 A
Zn	093.6°	189.5°	311.0°
aL	35.00.0′ S	35°00.0′ S	35°00.0′ S
aλ	118°56.0′ E	119°17.9′ E	119°27.9′ E

Required: The plot of the 0525 celestial fix.

Solution: (Figure 2505a) Plot the 0515 DR position and the DR track from 0515 to 0525. Plot the DR position for the time of each observation. Plot the AP of the earlier sight (Antares) and advance it in the direction and for the distance corresponding to the travel of the ship between the 0515 DR position and the 0525 DR position (2.4

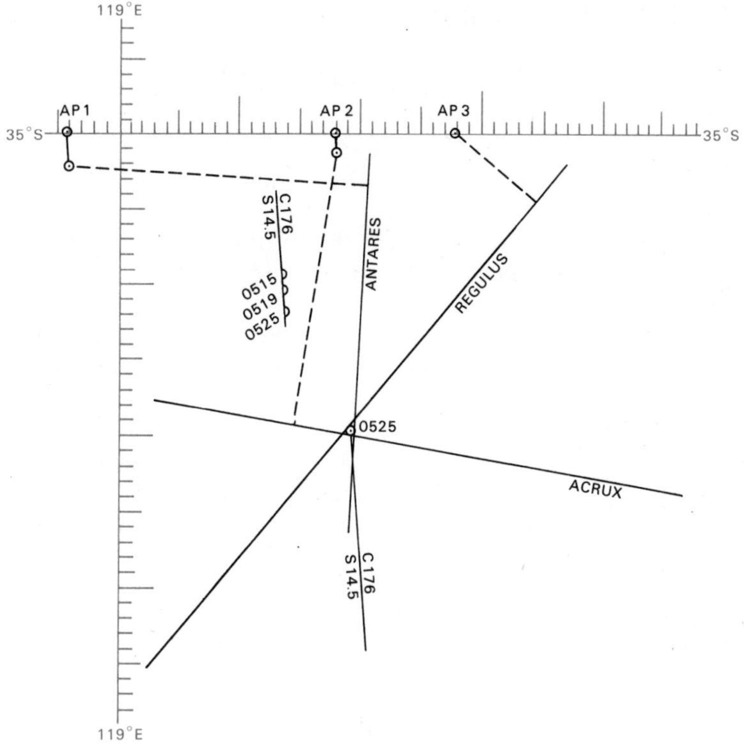

Figure 2505a. Three LOPs resulting in a celestial fix.

miles in direction 176°). From the advanced AP so obtained, plot the 0515–0525 LOP, labeling it as shown. Note that the line joining the original AP and the advanced AP is plotted as a solid line, and that the advanced AP is *not* labeled. Next, plot the AP of Acrux and advance it for the direction and distance the ship has traveled between 0519 and 0525 (1.4 miles in direction 176°). Plot and label the 0519–0525 Acrux LOP from the advanced AP. Finally, plot the AP for the Regulus sight, and from it plot the 0525 Regulus LOP. The intersection of the three lines of position (or the center of the small triangle so formed) is the 0525 fix. (Note that to reduce the "clutter" of the plot, times are omitted on the individual LOPs and are shown only for the DR positions and the final fix.)

When a change of course or speed occurs between the times of the observations used in plotting a fix, the procedure used for advancing or retiring a line of position is the same as that used in piloting (Article 1112). This is illustrated in the following example.

Example 2: The 0500 DR position of a ship on course 250°, speed 20 knots, is L 35°11.0′ N, λ 78°17.0′ W. At 0535 course is changed to 190°. During morning twilight the navigator observes two bodies with results as follows:

Body	DENEB	VENUS
Time	0525	0550
a	8.1 A	5.3 T
Zn	058.5°	123.9°
aL	35°00.0′ N	35°00.0′ N
aλ	78°09.0′ W	78°27.5′ W

Required: The plot of the 0550 celestial fix.

Solution: (Figure 2505b) Plot the 0500 DR position and the DR track until 0550, indicating the DR position for the time of each observation. Plot the AP of the earlier sight (Deneb) and advance it in the direction and for the distance corresponding to the travel of the ship between the 0525 DR position and the 0550 DR position (7.3 miles in direction 213.4°, as shown by the broken line marked "CMG" for "course made good"). From the advanced AP so obtained, plot the 0525–0550 LOP, labeling it as shown. Plot the AP of the Venus sight, and from it plot the 0550 LOP. The intersection of the two lines of position is the 0550 fix.

A fix obtained using the results of high-altitude observations is plotted in a manner similar to that described above, except that the GP of the body is adjusted if necessary. The method of advancing a high-

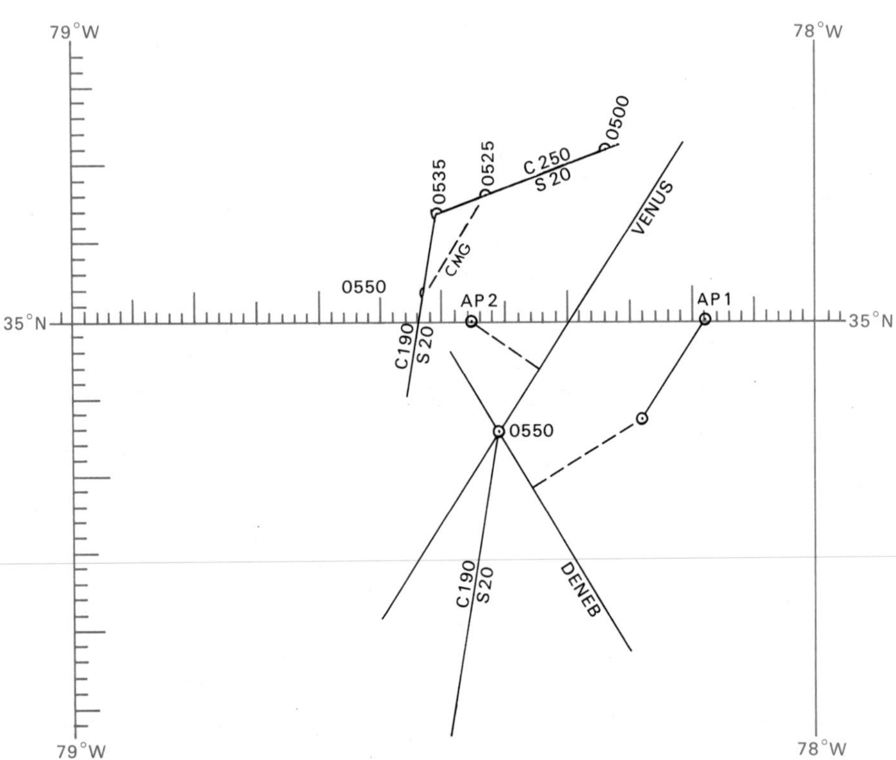

Figure 2505b. A celestial fix with a change of course between observations.

altitude celestial line of position by advancing its GP is explained in the following example.

Example 3: The 1200 DR position of a ship on course 270°, speed 20.0 knots, is L 23°20.0′ N λ 75°08.4′ W. About this time, the navigator observes the sun twice, with the following results:

Body	SUN	SUN
Time	1154	1206
Ho	88°33.6′	88°00.8′
L GP	22°07.7′ N	22°07.7′ N
λ GP	74°04.2′ W	77°04.2′ W

Required: The plot of the 1206 fix.

Solution: (Figure 2505c) Plot the DR track from 1154 to 1206, indicating the 1154 and 1206 DR positions. Plot the 1154 position of the sun's GP, and advance it for the direction and distance from the 1154 DR position to the 1206 DR position (4.0 miles in direction 270°). Determine the radius of the observed circle of equal altitude about the GP by subtracting the Ho from 90°00.0′. The radius is 86.4 miles (since 90°00.0′–88°33.6′ = 1°26.4′ = 86.4 mi.). With this radius, and using the advanced GP as the center, swing an arc through the area containing the DR position. This is the 1154–1206 line of position,

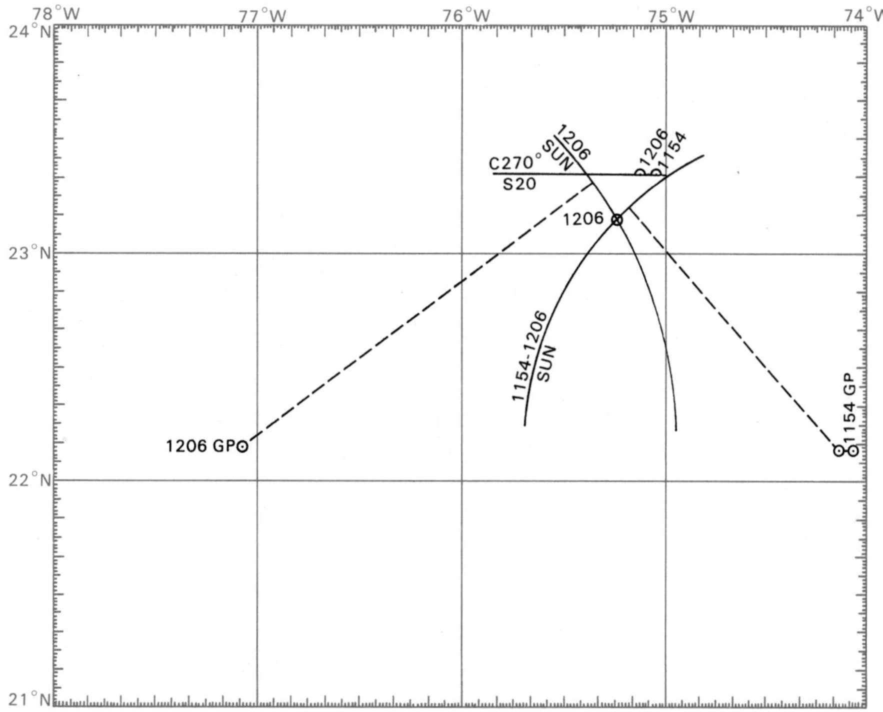

Figure 2505c. A celestial fix using high-altitude observations.

and is labeled as shown. Plot the 1206 GP of the sun, and determine the radius of the circle of equal altitude about it by subtracting the Ho from 90°00.0′. The radius is 119.2 miles (since 90°00.0′–88°00.8′ = 1°59.2′ = 119.2 mi.). With this radius, and using the 1206 GP as a center, swing an arc through the area containing the DR position. The intersection of the two lines of position is the 1206 fix.

Note that there are two possible intersections of two circles of equal altitude, only one of which is shown. In ordinary circumstances, that intersection nearer the DR position is the fix. In the case shown in Figure 2505c, there is no doubt as to the correct intersection, as the body passed to the south of the observer, and the intersection to the north of the GP used must be the fix. Where doubt exists and the navigator is unable to determine which intersection to use, commence a DR track from both positions, assuming the ship to be on the DR track from both positions, and assuming the ship to be on the DR track that is more dangerous until confirmation is obtained.

Running celestial fix

2506 When the times of the observations used are separated by a considerable interval (more than 30 minutes in a normal situation), the result is a *celestial running fix* (R Fix). The observations may be of different bodies, or successive sights of the same body. Since the time elapsed between observations used to obtain a running fix is usually at least an hour, and frequently considerably longer, the LOP obtained from the earlier observation is plotted for the information it provides. This LOP is then advanced (rather than the AP) to the time of the later observation to establish the R fix, using the same methods employed in establishing an R fix in piloting.

There is no absolute limit on the maximum time interval between observations used for a celestial running fix. This must be left to the discretion of the navigator who will give consideration to how accurately he knows his course and speed made good during that time interval. In most instances, however, three hours might be considered a practical limit.

It should be noted that in summer, when the sun transits at high altitudes, it changes azimuth very rapidly before and after transit; excellent running fixes may thus be obtained within reasonable periods of time.

Example 1: The 0930 DR position of a ship on course 064°, speed 18.0 knots, is L 33°06.4′ N, λ 146°24.5′ W. The navigator observes the sun twice during the morning, with results as follows:

Body	SUN	SUN
Time	0942	1200
a	6.2 A	27.9 A
Zn	134°.2	182°.5
aL	33°00′.0 N	33°00′.0 N
aλ	146°24′.9 W	145°38′.0 W

Required: The plot of the 1200 running fix.

Solution: (Figure 2506a) Plot the 0930 DR position, and the DR track to 1200, indicating the 0942 and the 1200 DR positions. Plot the AP with its associated LOP for 0942. Advance the LOP for the distance and direction from the 0942 DR position to the 1200 DR position (41.4 miles in direction 064°), and label it as shown. Plot the AP and from it the LOP for the 1200 sun observation, labeling it as shown. The intersection of the 0942–1200 LOP and the 1200 LOP is the 1200 running fix. (In this plot, the time is labeled on the 0942 LOP and on the 0942–1200 advanced LOP to ensure proper identification.)

When a change of course or speed occurs between the times of the observations used for obtaining a running celestial fix, the procedures used are the same as those employed in advancing the first LOP to obtain a running fix in piloting.

Using the same observations as in example 1 of this article, the following example illustrates how a running fix is obtained when both course and speed are changed between observations.

Example 2: The 0930 DR position of a ship on course 064°, speed 18.0 knots, is L 33°06.4′ N, λ 146°24.5′ W. At 1100 course is changed to 030°, and speed is reduced to 13.5 knots. During the morning, the navigator observes the sun twice, with results as follows:

Body	SUN	SUN
Time	0942	1200
a	6.2 A	27.9 A
Zn	134.2°	182.5°
aL	33°00.0′ N	33.00.0′ N
aλ	146°24.9′ W	145°38.0′ W

Required: The plot of the 1200 running fix.

Solution: (Figure 2506b) Plot the 0930 DR position and the DR track to 1200, indicating the 0942 and the 1200 DR positions. Plot the 0942 LOP, and advance it for the distance and direction from the 0942 DR position to the 1200 DR position (35.4 miles in the direction 052°). Label it as shown. Plot and label the 1200 LOP. The intersection of the 0942–1200 LOP and the 1200 LOP is the 1200 running fix.

Where a current of known set and drift exists, the position of the running fix may be adjusted to allow for the effect of the current during the time elapsed between the first and second observation.

The errors inherent in the running celestial fix are the same as those for the terrestrial running fix. However, the magnitude of the errors tends to be greater in the celestial fix. There are three reasons for this:

The celestial LOP is rarely as accurate as the terrestrial LOP;

Information on set and drift is not available at sea to the same degree of accuracy as is usual along a coast or in pilot waters; and

In celestial navigation, the time required to obtain the running fix is usually longer than that required in piloting, thus errors in

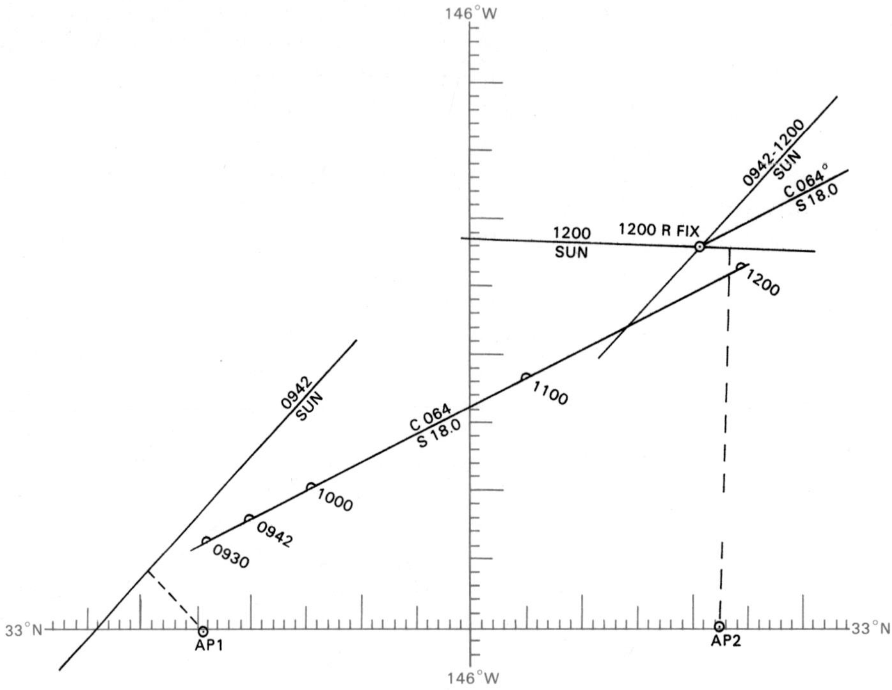

Figure 2506a. A celestial running fix.

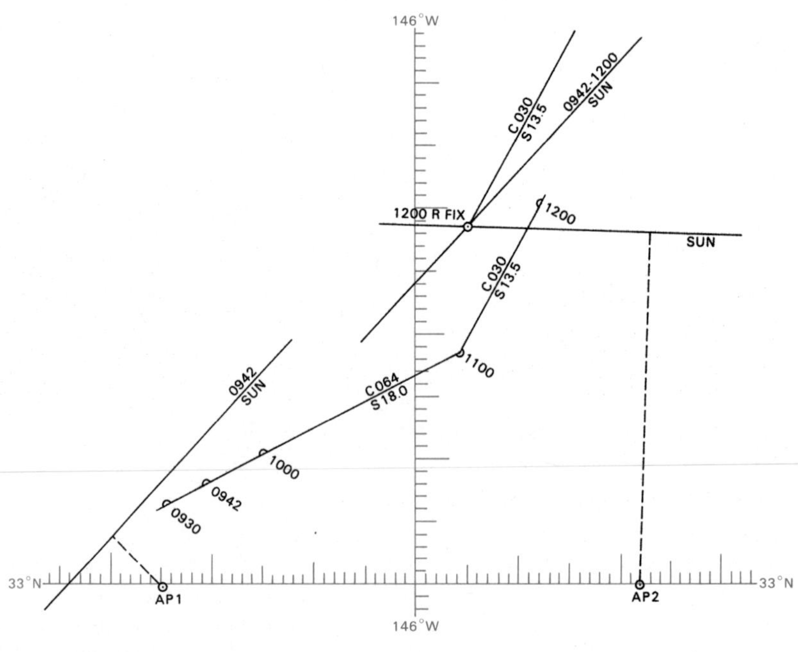

Figure 2506b. A celestial running fix with change of course and speed between observations.

courses and distances made good affect the accuracy to a greater extent. However, a running celestial fix is frequently the best obtainable indication of position at sea, and is helpful to the navigator.

Labeling celestial lines of position and fixes

2507 A neat, carefully labeled plot of navigational information is characteristic of a good navigator. All lines of position and fixes should be drawn and labeled in such a way that no doubt ever exists as to their meaning. The illustrations in this chapter are all drawn and labeled in conformance with the standards that have been generally agreed upon by the various U. S. instructional activities. These standards are:

Assumed position or geographical position. The AP or GP used with an LOP is always marked by an encircled dot and may be labeled "AP" or "GP," as appropriate and numbered consecutively.

Advanced AP or GP. The direction and distance an AP or GP is advanced is always shown by a solid line or lines, the end point of which is encircled but not labeled. This is the advanced AP or GP from which an advanced LOP is plotted.

Azimuth line. The direction of the LOP from the AP used to plot the line is always shown by a broken line extending from the AP to the LOP, as indicated by the magnitude and direction of (a); no labels.

Line of position. A line of position, whether a straight line or an arc, is always shown by a solid line and labeled with the name of the body "below" the line. The ship's time of the observation may be labeled "above" the LOP, or may be omitted to reduce chart clutter if time is close to that shown at the fix (see below). If the LOP has been advanced or retired for a running fix, the time of observation and the time to which it has been adjusted are both shown; for example, "1210–1420" for a 1210 line of position advanced to 1420.

Fix. The position found by a fix is encircled and labeled with the time, such as "0726" placed horizontally; the word "fix" is understood and need not be labeled. If a small polygon is formed by an inexact intersection of more than two lines, an encircled dot may be added to indicate the position.

Running fix. The position found by a running fix is marked in the same manner as a fix, but is labeled as to its special nature, as "1628 R Fix" placed horizontally.

Fixes involving celestial and other lines of position

2508 A line of position, however obtained, is merely an indication of the position of a ship, and must be crossed with one or more other lines to fix the position. A major objective of all forms of navigation is the determination of position—so that the vessel can safely and efficiently be directed from where it is to the desired destination. A navigator should, therefore, use any and all lines of position that he can obtain.

Thus, the navigator might cross a Loran or Omega LOP with an LOP obtained from a celestial body. The LOP from Consol bearings may be similarly employed. In like manner, a navigator making a landfall might cross a celestial or some other LOP with a depth curve shown on his chart, determining by echo sounder the time when the curve is crossed. When only one LOP is obtainable at sea, a sounding or series of soundings may be helpful in determining the general area of the ship's position. Article 1119 describes how soundings may be used in this connection.

All LOPs will not be of the same order of accuracy, but with experience the navigator learns to evaluate the resulting fix. *It is vital that no opportunity be lost to acquire information which may be helpful in determining the ship's position.*

Summary **2509** The first step in obtaining a celestial LOP is to measure the altitude of the body above the horizon. Ordinarily, the navigator then solves the navigational triangle containing his AP. The difference between the altitude thus computed and the observed altitude is the intercept, (a).

The intercept is then measured from the AP in the direction determined by Zn; Zn is the direction of the body's GP from the AP. The intercept will be measured toward (T) the body's GP from the AP if Ho is greater than Hc; it will be measured along the reciprocal away from (A) the GP if Hc is the greater. A line drawn perpendicular to (a) at its terminus is the LOP.

A fix is obtained when two or more lines of position are crossed, after being adjusted to a common time. If the observations are obtained over a relatively brief time, roughly 30 minutes or less, this is usually done by advancing the APs of the earlier observations for the ship's run to the time of the final observation; the LOPs are then plotted from the advanced APs. The resulting position is termed a *fix.* If the observations are obtained over a longer period of time, the first LOP is plotted when it is obtained, and is then advanced to the time of the later observation, as in piloting. The intersection of the first with the second LOP yields a *running fix.*

The careful navigator will seize every opportunity to acquire information which will be of help in fixing the ship's position. In addition to celestial lines of position, he may use lines obtained by electronics, and from soundings. At twilight, in clear weather, he should observe a minimum of five stars, well distributed in azimuth. He will make three observations of each body; normally, only one will be reduced to obtain a line of position. Should the resulting LOP seem to be in error, he may then reduce one of the other observations as a check. The rate of change of altitude in a series of observations of the same body should be directly proportional to the period of time between them. This gives a good check on the consistency of observations and, therefore, of their probable reliability.

26 The Complete Celestial Solution

Introduction

2601 Preceding chapters have dealt individually with all aspects of determining a line of position from an observation of a celestial body. The purpose of this chapter is to present the complete solution for a line of position, using the *Nautical Almanac* and the tables of DMAHC Pub. No. 229, and other methods. The steps involved will be reviewed briefly in the order in which they are taken. Following this, the same sights will be reduced by other methods for comparison purposes.

Almanac data for these solutions can be found in Chapter 23. Data from Pubs. No. 229 and 249, as well as Table 35 of Pub. No. 9, Volume II, should be taken from the publication concerned.

It should be noted that the observations taken are reduced in a columnar format. A navigator may use any form or format with which he is "comfortable"; it is the result, not the process, that is important. The columnar format, however, is highly recommended as it permits a logically progressive flow of data and calculations in the reduction. Further, it facilitates multiple reductions on a single page, each of which may use some of the same data, such as IC and Dip.

The combined coordinate systems

2602 In chapter 19 the theory of the navigational triangle was explained with reference to positions on the earth's surface; in this case, the vertices of the triangle were the elevated pole, the position of the observer, and the GP of the body. However, in some respects, it is more convenient to consider the triangle with reference to positions on the celestial sphere. In this sense, it is formed by a combination of the celestial equator system of coordinates and the horizon system of coordinates. The vertices of the triangle are now the celestial pole, the observer's zenith, and the body itself, which is located by its coordinates. Note that the navigational triangle as envisioned on the celestial sphere is simply a projection of the navigational triangle as envisioned on the earth. Angles and angular distances are identical in each case.

On the celestial sphere shown in Figure 2602, the blue lines and labels refer to the triangle portrayed on the sphere, and the black lines and labels refer to the triangle depicted on the earth. In solving the navigational triangle, the navigator first obtains the position of the celestial body at a given time with reference to the celestial equator

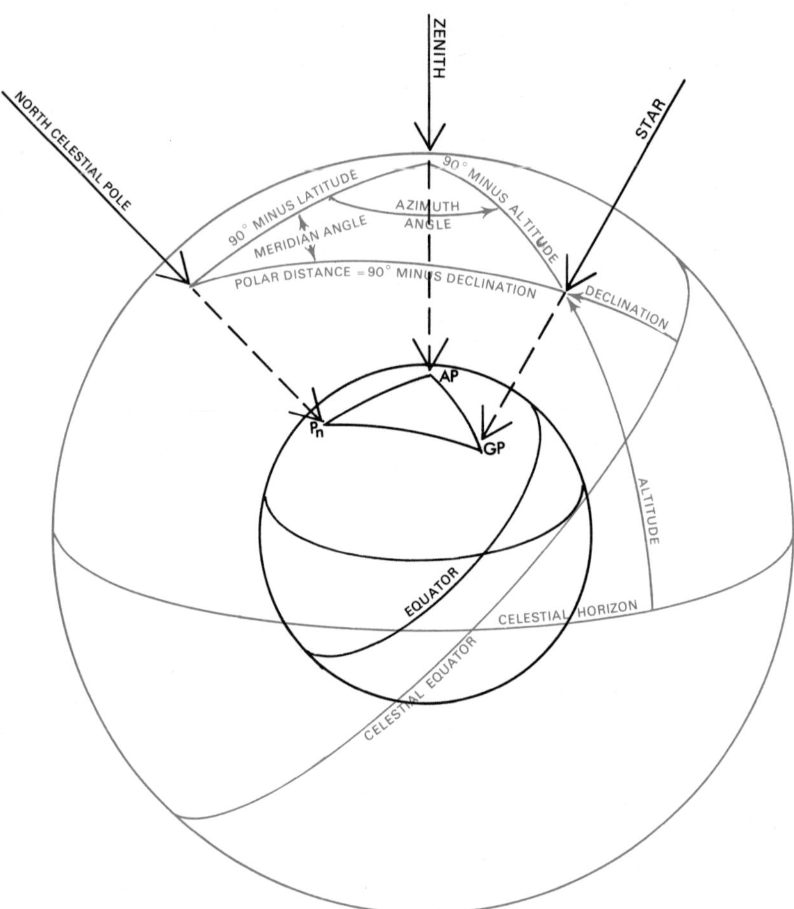

Figure 2602. The combined coordinate systems.

system of coordinates, by obtaining GHA and Dec. from the *Nautical Almanac.* This establishes the position of the body (and the GP), and defines the relationship of that position to both of the celestial poles. The navigator then selects the proper assumed position (AP), which is in the near vicinity of his DR position. This selection establishes two points on the celestial sphere, both of which may be located in either the celestial equator or the horizon system of coordinates. One point is that occupied by the AP (and its zenith), and the other is the celestial pole nearer the AP. The celestial pole selected is identical with one of the poles used in conjunction with declination in the celestial equator system, and is used in determining both the colatitude and the polar distance sides of the navigational triangle. The pole used is usually called the *elevated pole,* as it is the one elevated above the horizon of the observer. The meridian angle, defined when the AP is selected, determines the angle at the pole between the great circle joining the pole and the zenith, and the great circle joining the pole and the celestial body. Knowing the colatitude, the polar distance, and the meridian angle, the triangle can be solved in terms of the horizon system of coordinates to determine the angle at the zenith, which is azimuth angle, and the arc from the zenith to the body, which is the computed coaltitude. By converting the computed coaltitude to computed altitude (Hc) and comparing it with the observed altitude (Ho) to obtain the altitude difference (a), and by converting the azimuth angle (Z) to true azimuth (Zn), the navigator is able to plot the resulting celestial line of position.

Complete solutions for celestial observations

2603 A navigator will save time, and perhaps reduce the possibility of an error, if he extracts the pertinent data for all bodies from the daily pages of the *Nautical Almanac* at one page opening, when working multiple sights for a fix. Similarly, the *v* and *d* corrections, as well as the increments of GHA for minutes and seconds for each body, should be obtained at a single use of the increments and corrections table.

While no additional corrections for nonstandard atmospheric conditions are used in the following examples, a navigator must always bear in mind that these should be included when weather conditions so warrant.

A typical day's work

2604 The examples of this chapter will represent typical portions of a single day's work in celestial navigation for a navigator; for consideration of what comprises a full day's work, see Article 3004. The computations are shown on a typical work form; see Figures 2604a and c. Modifications may be made, and an individual navigator should develop a format that is best suited to his procedures. The lines of position and resultant fix from the morning observations will be shown as a single plot in Figure 2604b.

The situation is that of a salvage tug accompanying a partially disabled tanker; the course is 288°, speed 6.8 knots. At 0400 (time zone +1) on 5 June 1977, the ship's DR position is Lat. 41°02.8′ N, Long. 14°38.0′ W.

Complete solution for a planet observation

When observing a planet, the navigator measures the sextant altitude of the center of the body and records the time and date of the observation. He also checks the index error of the instrument.

The navigator enters the Index Correction (IC), as determined from the sextant, on the form; any corrections for instrument or personal errors would be entered at this time. Using the *Nautical Almanac* (Table A2 or the bookmark) and his height of eye, he determines the Dip correction and enters it on the form. He next applies these corrections to the sextant altitude (hs) to obtain apparent altitude (ha) which will be used in determining all further corrections. He now determines and records the altitude corrections(s) for refraction from the "Stars and Planets" column of Table A2 or the bookmark, including the "add'l" value for Venus or Mars; these are added to ha to yield observed altitude (Ho).

He then converts the time to GMT and Greenwich date, and enters the appropriate daily pages of the *Nautical Almanac* to obtain the GHA and declination at the whole hours of GMT, and the *v* and *d* values for the period, noting the sign of the *d* value by inspection. The *v* is always plus except for Venus when it can be either plus or minus. (The values of *v* and *d* are normally taken from the bottom of each column; they can also be determined specifically by subtraction between adjacent values of GHA or declination, respectively. Occasionally a difference of 0.1′ will be found between these two procedures; this will not make a significant difference in the results.) Turning to the appropriate "Increments and Corrections Table," he obtains the increments of GHA for minutes and seconds, and the corrections to GHA and declination for the *v* and *d* values, respectively. Applying these values to those obtained from the daily pages, he obtains the GHA and Dec. of the planet at the time of observation.

The navigator then selects the AP, based on the best estimate of his position, and uses the aλ to determine LHA in whole degrees.

Entering Pub. No. 229 with the integral degrees of LHA, aL, and Dec., the navigator obtains the tabular value for computed altitude (Hc), *d* (noting the sign of the *d* value by inspection), and azimuth angle (Z) for the entering arguments. Z is corrected by mental interpolation for the actual value of declination. The correction to the tabulated Hc for Dec. Inc. and *d* is then taken from inside the front or back cover of Pub. No. 229 and applied to the tabulated value; a double-second difference correction is applied if *d* is printed in italics and followed by a dot. These corrections give the computed altitude, Hc, for the exact declination of the body.

This corrected Hc is then compared with Hc to determine (a). The azimuth angle, Z, is converted to azimuth, Zn. The navigator now completes the reduction by using Zn and (a) to plot the LOP from the AP.

Example 1: On 5 June 1977, the 0417 position of the ship is Lat. 41°03.4′ N, Long. 14°40.4′ W. At 04–17–21 by a watch that is 8 seconds fast, the planet Venus is observed from a height of eye of 21 feet, with a sextant having an IC of +0.2′. The observed sextant altitude is 21°13.4′.

Required: The AP, (a), and Zn using the *Nautical Almanac* and Pub. No. 229.

Answer: (Solution is shown in column 1 of Figure 2604a.)

aL 41°00.0′ N
aλ 14°57.7′ W
a 10.1′ Toward
Zn 096.4°

Note: This example includes, for the sake of completeness of illus-

Sight Reduction using Pub. 229	W M E m	W M E m	W M E m
Body	VENUS	MOON LL	SUN LL
IC	+ 0.2 -	+ 0.2 -	+ 0.2 -
Dip (Ht 21 ')	4.4	4.4	4.4
Sum	-4.2	-4.2	-4.2
hs	21 13.4	18 56.0	19 17.5
ha	21 09.2	18 51.8	19 13.3
Alt. Corr	2.5	62.4	
Add'l.	0.3		
H.P. ( )		7.2	
Corr. to ha	-2.2	+ 1 09.6	+ 13.3
Ho (Obs Alt)	21 07.0	20 01.4	19 26.6
Date	5 JUN 77	5 JUN 77	5 JUN 77
DR Lat	41 03.4 N	41 07.9 N	41 07.9 N
DR Long	14 40.4 W	14 58.7 W	14 58.7 W
Obs. Time	04-17-21	06-24-43	06-25-23
WE (S+, F-)	-8F	-8F	-8F
ZT	04-17-13	06-24-35	06-25-15
ZD (W+, E-)	+1	+1	+1
GMT	05-17-13	07-24-35	07-25-15
Date (GMT)	5 JUN 77	5 JUN 77	5 JUN 77
Tab GHA / v	300 39.3 / +0.4	54 56.7 / +7.4	285 24.7 /
GHA incr'mt.	4 18.3	5 52.0	6 18.8
SHA or v Corr.	0.1	3.0	
GHA	304 57.7	60 51.7	291 43.5
±360 if needed			
aλ (-W, +E)	14 57.7 W	14 51.7 W	14 43.5 W
LHA	290	46	277
Tab Dec / d	N8 59.6 / +0.6	S14 39.9 / -7.4	N22 32.4 / +0.3
d Corr (+ or -)	+0.2	-3.0	+0.1
True Dec	N8 59.8	S14 36.9	N22 32.5
a Lat (N or S)	41 N Same ~~Cont.~~	41 N Same ~~Cont.~~	41 N Same ~~Cont.~~
Dec Inc / (±)d	59.8 / +39.2	36.9 / -49.0	32.5 / +36.4
Hc (Tab. Alt.)	20 17.9	20 29.2	19 19.9
tens / DS Diff.	29.9	-24.6	16.3
units / DS Corr.	9.1 / +	-5.5 / +	3.5 / +
Tot. Corr. (+ or -)	+39.0	-30.1	+19.8
Hc (Comp. Alt.)	20 56.9	19 59.1	19 39.7
Ho (Obs. Alt.)	21 07.0	20 01.4	19 26.6
a (Intercept)	10.1 ~~A~~ T	2.3 ~~A~~ T	13.1 A ~~T~~
Z	N 96.4 E	N 132.2 N	N 76.8 E
Zn (°T)	096.4°	227.8°	076.8°

Figure 2604a. Sight reductions using Pub. No. 229; planet, moon, and sun.

tration, a watch error in the calculations. Often in ordinary navigation the use of radio time signals and a comparing watch (or stopwatch) makes this step unnecessary.

Complete solution for a moon observation

When observing the moon, the navigator measures the sextant altitude of either the upper or lower limb of the body, and records the time and date of the observation. He also checks the index error of the instrument.

He then converts the time to GMT and Greenwich date, and enters the appropriate daily pages of the *Nautical Almanac* to obtain the GHA, *v* value, which for the moon is always (+), declination, *d* value (noting the sign of the *d* value by inspection), and HP for the nearest whole hour of GMT. Turning to the appropriate "Increments and Corrections Table," he obtains the increments of GHA for minutes and seconds, and the corrections to GHA and declination for the *v* and *d* values, respectively. Applying these values to those obtained from the daily pages, he obtains the GHA and Dec. of the moon at the time of the observation.

The navigator records the IC on his form. Using the *Nautical Almanac*, he determines the Dip correction for his height of eye; he records this value and the corrections for altitude and HP from the "Altitude Correction Tables—Moon." The latter two corrections are always additive, but if the upper limb is observed, an additional correction of −30′ is made. These corrections are combined with hs to obtain ha and then Ho.

The navigator then selects the AP, based on the best estimate of his position, and uses the aλ to determine LHA in whole degrees.

Entering Pub. No. 229 with integral degrees of LHA, aL and Dec., he obtains the tabulated altitude for the value of entering arguments, *d* and its sign, and Z. Z is corrected by visual interpolation for the actual value of the declination. The correction to the tabulated altitude for Dec. Inc. and *d* is then taken from a multiplication table inside the cover of Pub. No. 229 and applied to ht (the tabulated value of h), as is the double-second difference correction if *d* is printed in *italic* type, to obtain Hc.

Hc is then compared with Ho to find (a). By converting Z to Zn, the navigator can then use Zn and (a) to plot the LOP from the AP.

Example 2: On 5 June 1977, the 0625 DR position of the ship is Lat. 41°07.9′ N, Long. 14°58.7′ W. At 06–24–43 (the watch remains 8 seconds fast), the lower limb of the moon is observed to be 18°56.0′. (The height of eye and IC are as before, 21 feet and +0.2′ respectively).

Required: The AP, (a), and Zn using the *Nautical Almanac* and Pub. No. 229.

Answer: (Solution is shown in column 2 of Figure 2604a.)

aL 41°00.0′ N
aλ 14°51.7′ W
a 2.3′ Toward
Zn 227.8°

Complete solution for a sun observation

When observing the sun, the navigator measures the sextant altitude of either the upper or lower limb of the body, and records the time and date of the observation. He also records the index error of the sextant.

The values of I and IC, with their appropriate signs, would be entered in the form, as would the correction for Dip, obtained from the *Nautical Almanac*. These would be combined with hs to obtain ha.

He then converts the time to GMT and Greenwich date, and enters the appropriate daily pages of the *Nautical Almanac* to obtain the GHA and declination at the whole hours of GMT, and the *d* value for the period (noting the sign of the *d* value by inspection). If maximum accuracy were desired, he would also note the SD of the sun from the daily pages.

Ordinarily, the ha is corrected by means of the sun altitude correction tables on the inside front cover of the *Nautical Almanac,* which include corrections for a nominal value of semidiameter, refraction, and parallax. Alternatively, the value of the semidiameter found at the bottom of the sun column in the daily pages of the *Nautical Almanac* may be used together with the value of the refraction correction found under the heading "Stars and Planets," and an additional correction of +0.1′ for parallax to be used for altitude of 65° and less. These corrections are applied to ha to obtain Ho.

Having entered the GHA and declination for the whole hours of GMT, the navigator now turns to the appropriate page of the Increments and Corrections table, and obtains the increments of GHA for minutes and seconds and the correction to the declination for the *d* value. Applying these values to those obtained from the daily pages, he obtains the GHA and Dec. of the sun at the time of the observation.

With the *Nautical Almanac* still open, the navigator notes the value of IC (as determined from the sextant) and extracts the appropriate value of D. These are combined with hs to obtain ha. The appropriate correction for $\underline{\odot}$, or $\overline{\odot}$, taken from the Sun Table, is then applied to ha to obtain Ho.

The navigator then selects the AP, based on the best estimate of his position, and uses the aλ to determine LHA in whole degrees.

Entering Pub. No. 229 with integral degrees of LHA, aL, and Dec., he obtains the tabulated altitude for the value of the entering arguments, *d* and its sign, and Z. Z is corrected by visual interpolation for the actual value of the declination. The correction to the tabulated altitude for Dec. Inc. and *d* is then taken from a multiplication table inside the covers of Pub. No. 229 and is applied to the tabulated computed altitude, as is the double-second difference correction if *d* is printed in italic type; this is now computed altitude, Hc, for the exact value of declination.

Hc is then compared with Ho to determine (a). Z is converted to Zn. At this time the navigator can plot the LOP from the AP by using Zn and (a).

Example 3: From the same DR position as in the preceding example, the lower limb of the sun is observed at 06–25–23; sextant reads 19°17.5′.

Required: The AP, (a), and Zn using the *Nautical Almanac* and Pub. No. 229.

Answer: (Solution is shown in column 3 of Figure 2604a.)

aL	41°00.0′ N
aλ	14°43.5′ W
a	13.1′ Away
Zn	076.8°

The above reduction was made for refraction under standard conditions. This is not always so; for example, if the temperature were 90° F (32.2° C) and the barometric pressure were 29.23″ (990 mb), the refraction correction would have to be calculated in more detail. Using Table A4, a correction of +0.3′ is found; this is combined with a value of +15.8′ for semidiameter, −2.8′ from the "Stars and Planets" column of Table A2, and a parallax correction of +0.1′ for the sun's altitude being less than 65°. The correction by this procedure is +13.4′. In this case, the difference is of minor significance, but it would be greater in more extreme conditions of temperature and/or barometric pressure, and at lower apparent altitudes.

The 0625 fix from the moon and sun observations is shown in Figure 2604b. The AP for the moon LOP was not advanced because of the short interval between observations and the slow speed of the vessel.

Complete solution for a star observation

Two star observations are reduced in the following examples. Note that the Alkaid reduction (Example 4) requires a double-second difference correction.

When observing a star, the navigator measures the sextant altitude of the body and records the time and date of the observation. He also checks the index error of the instrument.

The navigator enters the IC on the form and then the Dip correction as determined from the *Nautical Almanac* for his height of eye. He applies these (and any corrections for instrument or personal errors) to hs to obtain ha. The altitude correction is found in the "Stars and Planets" column of Table A2 or the bookmark; this is added to ha to give Ho.

He then converts the time to GMT and Greenwich date, and enters the appropriate daily pages of the *Nautical Almanac* to obtain the GHA of Aries at the whole hours of GMT, and the SHA and declination of the star for that period. Turning to the appropriate Increments and Corrections table, he obtains the increments of GHA of Aries for minutes and seconds. Adding this value to the GHA of Aries and SHA of the star obtained from the daily pages, he obtains the star's GHA at the time of the observation. The Dec. is the value tabulated on the daily page.

The navigator then selects the AP, based on the best estimate of his position, and uses the aλ to determine LHA in whole degrees.

Entering Pub. No. 229 with integral degrees of LHA, aL, and Dec., he obtains the tabulated altitude for the value of the entering argument, *d* and its sign, and Z. The correction to tabulated altitude for *d* and Dec. Inc. is then taken from the multiplication table in Pub. No. 229, and applied to ht, as is the double-second difference correction if *d* is printed in *italic* type, to obtain the exact Hc. The navigator corrects Z by visual interpolation for the actual value of the declination.

Hc is then compared with Ho to determine (a). By converting Z to Zn, the navigator can then use Zn and (a) to plot the LOP from the AP.

Example 4: On 5 June 1977, the 2003 DR position of the ship is Lat. 41°34.8′ N, Long. 17°00.5′ W. At 20–03–06 (watch error 10 seconds fast), the star Alkaid is observed from a height of eye of 21 feet with a sextant having an IC of +0.2′. The sextant altitude is 77°39.3′.

Required: The AP, (a), and Zn, using the *Nautical Almanac* and Pub. No. 229.

Answer: (Solution is shown in column 1, Figure 2604c.)

aL	42°00.0′ N
aλ	17°14.2′ W
a	10.4′ Away
Zn	047.9°

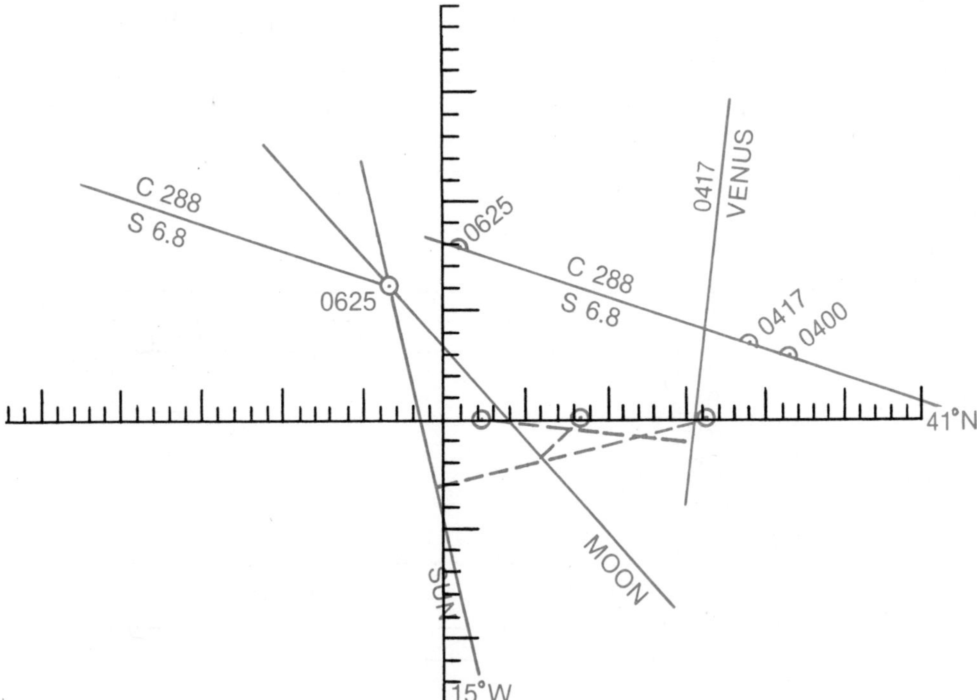

Figure 2604b. Plot of LOPs from sight reductions of Figure 2604a.

Sight Reduction using Pub. 229		(M / W E / m)			(M / W E / m)		
Body		ALKAID			CAPELLA		
IC		+ 0.2		-	+ 0.2		-
Dip (Ht 21 ')			4.4			4.4	
Sum			- 4.2			-4.2	
hs		77	39.3		15	27.0	
ha		77	35.1		15	22.8	
Alt. Corr			0.2			3.5	
Add'l.							
H.P. ( )							
Corr. to ha			-0.2			-3.5	
Ho (Obs Alt)		77	34.9		15	19.3	
Date		5 JUN 77			5 JUN 77		
DR Lat		41	34.8 N		41	34.8 N	
DR Long		17	00.5 W		17	00.5 W	
Obs. Time		20-03-06			20-04-08		
WE (S+, F-)			-10 F			-10 F	
ZT		20-02-56			20-03-58		
ZD (W+, E-)		+1			+1		
GMT		21-02-56			21-03-58		
Date (GMT)		5 JUN 77			5 JUN 77		
Tab GHA	v	209	10.1		209	10.1	
GHA incr'mt.		0	44.1		0	59.7	
SHA or v Corr.		153	20.0		281	15.0	
GHA		263	14.2		491	24.8	
±360 if needed					131	24.8	
aλ (-W, +E)		17	14.2	W	17	24.8	W
LHA		346			114		
Tab Dec	d	N 49	25.7		N45	58.4	
d Corr (+ or -)							
True Dec		N49	25.7		N45	58.4	
a Lat (N or S)		42 N	Same ~~Cont.~~		42 N	Same ~~Cont.~~	
Dec Inc	(±)d	25.7		-32.0	58.4		+42.6
Hc (Tab. Alt.)		77	58.6		15	02.1	
tens	DS Diff.	-12.6		6.9	+38.9		
units	DS Corr.	- 0.8		+0.4	+ 2.5		+
Tot. Corr. (+ or -)		-13.3			+41.4		
Hc (Comp. Alt.)		77	45.3		15	43.5	
Ho (Obs. Alt.)		77	34.9		15	19.3	
a (Intercept)			10.4	A ~~T~~		24.2	A ~~T~~
Z		N	47.9 E		N	41.2 W	
Zn (°T)		047.9°			318.8°		

Figure 2604c. Sight reductions using Pub. No. 229; stars.

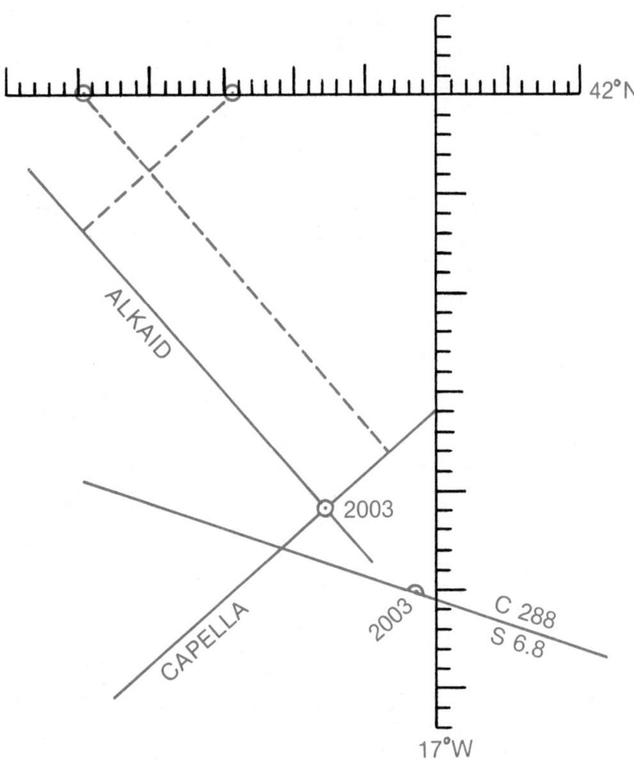

Figure 2604d. Plot of LOPs from sight reductions of Figure 2604c.

Example 5: Shortly after the above observation, a sight is taken on a second star, Capella. The height of eye, IC, and watch error are the same as before; the time is 20–04–08; the sextant reading is 15°27.0′.

Required: The AP, (a), and Zn using the *Nautical Almanac* and Pub. No. 229.

Answer: (Solution is shown in column 2 of Figure 2604c.)

aL	42°00.0′ N
aλ	17°24.8′ W
a	24.2′ Away
Zn	318.8°

The lines of position from the above observations and the 2003 fix are shown in Figure 2604d.

Reduction by Pub. No. 249

2605 As has been noted before, some navigators prefer the greater ease and speed gained through the use of the *Air Almanac* and Pub. No. 249, accepting the lesser degree of precision of the results. (Actually, either almanac could be used with either set of sight reduction tables, but in normal practice, the *Nautical Almanac* is paired with Pub. No. 229 and the *Air Almanac* with Pub. No. 249.

To illustrate the use of the *Air Almanac* and Pub. No. 249 tables, several of the same observations as in the preceding article will be reduced by that method.

The *Air Almanac* has been described in Chapter 23, and the Pub. No. 249 tables in Chapter 24. Here attention will be focused on their use with particular reference to the differences between the procedures of the preceding article and those of the *A.A.*/249 method. Comparisons will be made between the results obtained by use of the two different methods.

Solution of a planet observation by *A.A.*/249

In using the *Air Almanac* for the reduction of a planet observation, the navigator first enters on his form the IC, the Dip correction (found on the inside back cover) and the refraction correction (from the page facing inside back cover; for marine navigation, use the left-hand column "0" for 0 feet elevation above the earth's surface). (Note that sextant altitude and corrections are summed to the nearest minute rather than tenth of a minute.) He next locates the applicable daily page and then the line for the GMT just before the time of observation, remembering that tabular entries in the *A.A.* are for each 10 minutes of GMT. The values for GHA and declination are taken from this line and entered on the form. An increment of GHA for the balance of the time is taken from the inside front cover; the same column is used for the sun, Aries, and planets, with a different column for the moon. The GHA of the body is the sum of the angle from the daily page and the increment.

The navigator now selects an assumed position (AP) which has a whole degree of latitude and will yield a whole degree of LHA when its longitude is combined with the GHA of the body.

Volume II or III of Pub. No. 249 is selected as determined by the ship's latitude. The appropriate volume is entered with integral degrees of latitude, declination, and LHA; values are obtained for Hc, and *d* to the nearest minute and Z to the nearest degree; the declination correction is obtained from Table 5 at the back of the volume and is applied to Hc with the proper sign.

The comparison of corrected Hc and Ho to obtain the intercept (a) and the conversion of Z to Zn is the same as in Article 2604.

Example 1: On 5 June 1977, the 0417 position of the ship is Lat. 41°03.4′ N, Long. 14°40.4′ W. At 04–17–21 by a watch that is 8 seconds fast, the planet Venus is observed from a height of eye of 21 feet with a sextant having an IC of +0.2′. The observed sextant altitude is 21°13′.

Required: The (a) and Zn using the *Air Almanac* and Pub. No. 249.

Answer: (Solution is shown in column 1 of Figure 2605a.)

a 10′ Toward
Zn 096°

Note that this is a solution of the same observation that was reduced by use of the *Nautical Almanac* and Pub. No. 229 in Example 1 of Article 2604. The results can be roughly compared without plotting, as the assumed positions are the same except for a fraction of a minute of longitude. The differences in intercept and azimuth, 0.1′ and 0.4° are negligible.

Reduction of a moon observation by *A. A.*/229 In using the *Air Almanac* for reduction of a moon observation, the navigator proceeds as above for the IC, dip, and refraction corrections. From the daily pages, he obtains GHA and declination, plus two other values. Semidiameter is read from the box at the lower right corner and entered on the form; this is combined with the first three corrections to get a value which is used to enter the critical-value table "Moon's P in A" to get the correction for parallax. This final correction is added to obtain Ho.

The tabular value of GHA for the moon is incremented for the balance of time beyond the tabular entry (using a value from the column headed "Moon"); no correction is required to the tabulated declination. An AP is determined as before, so as to give an integral value of LHA when the longitude is subtracted (W) or added (E). Volume II or III of Pub. No. 249 is now used to determine tabular Hc which is corrected for *d* and Z. Intercept and Zn are found in the usual manner.

Example 2: On 5 June 1977, the 0625 DR position of the ship is Lat. 41°07.9′ N, Long. 14°58.7′ W. At 06–24–43 (the watch remains 8 seconds fast), the lower limb of the moon is observed to be 18°56′. The height of eye and IC are as before, 21 feet and +0.2, respectively. (These data are the same as Example 2 of Article 2604.)

Required: The (a) and Zn using the *Air Almanac* and Pub. No. 249.

Answer: (Solution is shown in column 2 of Figure 2605a.)

a 2′ Toward
Zn 228°

Here again, compare the results of this reduction with those obtained from the *N.A.*/229 solution in the preceding article. The differences are slight and without significance in high-seas navigation.

Reduction of a sun observation by *A.A.*/249 The procedures for determining the Ho of the sun are basically the same as those just described for the moon, except that there is no parallax correction to the sextant altitude. The procedures for GHA, declination, and LHA are the same for the sun as for the moon.

No example will be shown for the reduction of a sun observation by A.A./249; the reader may wish to solve this for himself and compare the slight differences with the N.A./229 method.

Reduction of a star observation by *A.A.*/249 In the reduction of a star observation, the navigator uses the *Air Almanac* as before to find the dip and refraction corrections and combines them with IC and the sextant reading to obtain Ho to the nearest minute.

Body	VENUS	MOON LL
IC	+0.2	+0.2
Dip (Ht.21′)	-4	-4
Ro	-2	-3
S.D.		+16
Sum	-6	+9
hs	21 13	18 56
P in A (Moon)		+56
Ho	21 07	20 01
Date	5 JUN 77	5 JUN 77
DR Lat	41 03.4 N	41 07.9 N
DR Long	14 40.4 W	14 58.7 W
Obs Time	04-17-21	06-24-43
WE	-8F	-8F
ZT	04-17-13	06-24-35
ZD	+1	+1
GMT	05-17-13	07-24-35
Date (GMT)	5 JUN 77	5 JUN 77
Tab GHA	303 09	59 45
GHA incrmt	1 48	1 06
SHA		
GHA	304 57	60 51
± 360		
a λ (−W, +E)	14 57	14 51
LHA	290	46
Tab Dec	N 9 00	S 14 37
a Lat	41N S~~C~~	41N ~~S~~C
Dec Inc	00	37 -49
Tab Hc	20 57	20 29
Dec corr	00	-30
Hc	20 57	19 59
Ho	21 07	20 01
a	10 A̶ T	2 A̶ T
Z	N 96 E	N 132 W
Zn	096°	228°

Figure 2605a. Sight reductions using Pub. No. 249, Volume III.

If the star observed is not one of the 57 "selected stars," the procedure is the same as previously discussed for Volumes II and III of Pub. No. 249.

If, however, the star is one of the 57 selected stars, the unique procedure of Volume I of Pub. No. 249 can be employed. These tables are entered with whole degrees of latitude and LHA of Aries, and the name of the star, if it is one of the seven tabulated for the latitude and LHA ♈ concerned. Values of Hc and Z can be read directly and the intercept and Zn obtained with great ease and speed.

Note that when Volume I can be used, no incremental corrections of any kind are required. After the LHA and assumed latitude have been determined, a simple table "look-up" is all that is necessary to find Hc and Z. The LHA ♈ can be found from either the *Air Almanac* or the *Nautical Almanac;* note that here in the *Air Almanac* the tabular value is carried to the tenth of a minute, and this degree of precision is correspondingly used in the value of assumed longitude. The assumed latitude is simply the whole degree of latitude nearest the DR position of the vessel at the time of the sight. The GHA ♈ can also be found from Pub. No. 249 without the use of either almanac. Values are taken from Table 4 for the month and year, the hour of the day, and the minutes of the hour; these three values are added together to get the GHA ♈ to the nearest whole minute of arc.

Example 3: On 5 June 1977, the 2004 DR position of the ship is 41°34.8′ N, Long. 17°00.5′ W. At 20–04–08 watch time, a sight was taken on the star, Capella. The height of eye was 21 feet, the IC was +0.2′, and the watch error was 10 seconds fast. The sextant reading was 15°26′.

Required: The AP, (a), and Zn using the *Air Almanac* and Pub. No. 249, Volume I.

Answer: (Solution is shown in Figure 2605b.)

aL 42°
aλ 17°10′ W
a 16′
Zn 319°

The line of position just calculated is subject to a correction for the effects upon the tabulated altitude of progressive changes in the declination and SHA of the star due to the precession of the equinoxes, including nutation. Such a correction should be included if the year of the observation is other than the base year of the tables used. Corrections are given in Table 5 of Pub. No. 249, Volume I, for two years before the base year and for five years afterwards. The tables used in the above example are designated as "Epoch 1975.0" and have a base year of 1974. As the year of the sight reduced above is not the base year, a "P&N" correction should be applied for the slight progressive changes in the declination and SHA of the body as a result of the precession of the equinoxes, including nutation. For the appropriate year, 1977, Table 5 is entered for the nearest values of LHA and lati-

Body	CAPELLA		
IC	+0.2		
Dip	4		
Sum	−4		
Hs	15 27		
Ha	15 23		
Alt Corr.	−4		
Ho (obs alt.)	15 19		
Date	5 JUN 77		
DR Lat	41 34.8N		
DR Long	17 00.5W		
Obs Time	20-04-08		
WE (S+, F-)	−10 F		
ZT	20-03-58		
ZD (W+, E-)	+1		
GMT	21-03-58		
Date (GMT)	5 JUN 77		
Tab GHA γ	209 10		
GHA incr'mt.	1 00		
GHA γ	210 10		
Aλ (-W, +E)	17 10		
LHA γ	193		
A Lat	42 N		
Hc	15 35		
Ho	15 19		
a T A	16 ~~T~~ A	T A	T A
Zn	319°		
P&N Corr.	2 mi 120°		

Figure 2605b. Sight reductions using Pub. No. 249, Volume I.

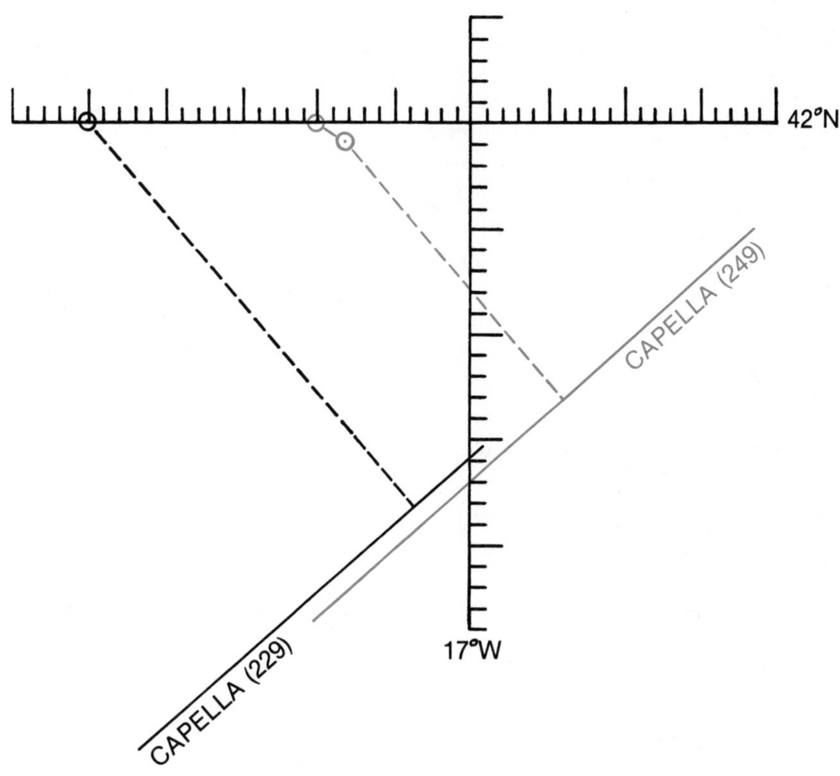

Figure 2605c. Plot of LOPs from reductions of same sight by Pub. No. 229 and by Pub. No. 249, Volume I.

tude (180° and N40° in this case); interpolation is not used. In the example above, the line of position should be adjusted 2 miles, 120° when plotted. (If several LOPs were determined, a single P&N correction could be applied to the fix, rather than to each LOP individually.) The P&N correction is applicable *only* to sight reductions made with Volume I of Pub. No. 249.

Note that although the Zn can be compared directly with the solution by Pub. No. 229, the intercept value cannot be directly compared as it is drawn from a quite different assumed position. Figure 2605c shows the LOP as produced by the two methods; the difference is apparent, but slight.

Reduction by Ageton method

2606 Because of the greater time and effort required, the Ageton method—using Table 35 of *Bowditch*, Volume II, or the old H. O. 211 tables—is seldom a primary method of sight reduction. The fully qualified navigator should, however, be competent in its use. This method uses the DR position rather than an assumed position and the intercept distance is thus a relatively direct measure of the accuracy of the DR position. The Ageton method has a considerable advantage for small craft or lifeboat use as multiple large volumes such as those of Pub. No. 229 are not required. (The Ageton tables can be copied from *Bowditch,* Volume II; they are also published commercially as a slim booklet).

Sextant corrections and almanac data are determined as before, and time calculations are made in the same manner. *Bowditch* Table 35, or other Ageton table, is entered for the various angular values, recording the entry for *A* or *B,* or both, as appropriate; note carefully the instruction "When LHA (E or W) is *greater* than 90°, take *K* from *bottom* of table."

The GHA of the body is entered on the form and from this is subtracted the DR longitude to obtain the LHA and t angle. The *A* value for t is found in the tables and entered on the form. The value of declination is entered followed by both the *B* and *A* values. Addition, as shown on the form, yields an *A* value (which is copied again in the fourth column); the corresponding *B* value is located in the tables and entered in columns 2 and 3. Further additions and subtractions are carried out as shown in Figure 2606a, ending in a value for Hc and Z from which (a) and Zn can be derived.

A single reduction will be shown here to illustrate the complete solution by the Ageton method; the observation of the star Capella, previously used, is selected as a typical example.

Example: On 5 June 1977, the 2004 DR position of the ship is Lat. 41°34.7′ N, Long. 17°01.0′ W. At 20–04–08, (watch is 10 seconds fast), the star Capella is observed from a height of eye of 21 feet with a sextant having an IC of +0.2. The sextant reading is 15°27.0′.

Required: The (a) and Zn using the *Nautical Almanac* and the Ageton method of reduction (Table 35 of *Bowditch,* Volume II).

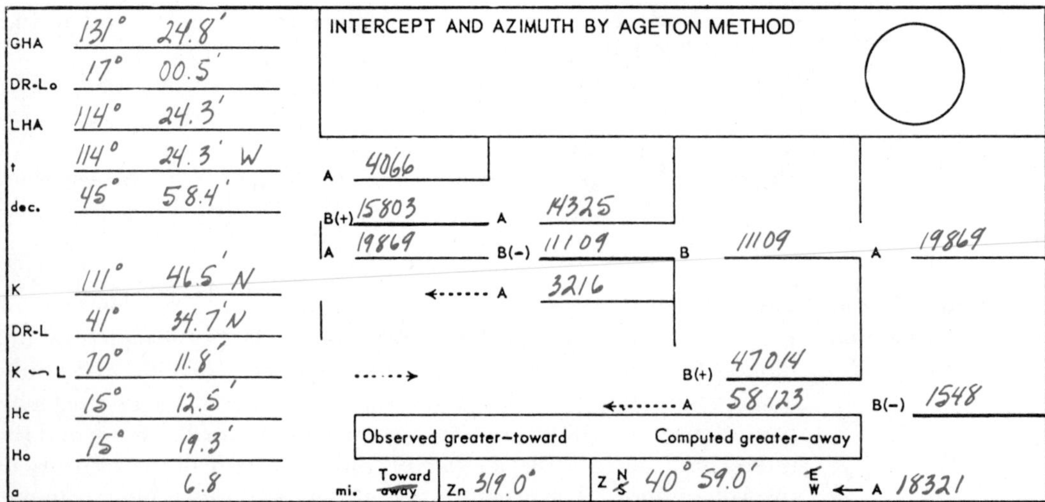

INTERCEPT AND AZIMUTH BY AGETON METHOD

GHA	131° 24.8′
DR-Lo	17° 00.5′
LHA	114° 24.3′
t	114° 24.3′ W
dec.	45° 58.4′
K	111° 46.5′ N
DR-L	41° 34.7′ N
K ∼ L	70° 11.8′
Hc	15° 12.5′
Ho	15° 19.3′
a	6.8

A 4066
B(+) 15803 A 14325
A 19869 B(−) 11109 B 11109 A 19869
←······ A 3216
······→ B(+) 47014
←······ A 58123 B(−) 1548
Observed greater–toward Computed greater–away
mi. Toward ~~away~~ Zn 319.0° Z N 40° 59.0′ W ← A 18321

Figure 2606a. Sight reduction by Ageton method.

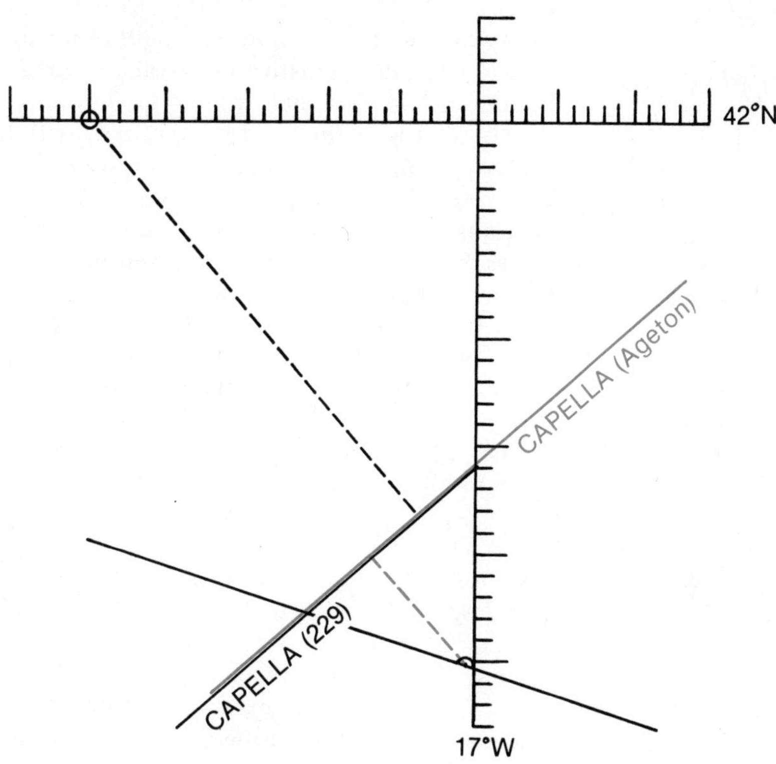

Figure 2606b. Plot of LOPs from reductions of same sight by Pub. No. 229 and by Ageton method.

Solution: The following data are extracted from the *Nautical Almanac* and are the same as those in Example 5 of Article 2604; Ho 15°19.3′; GHA 131°24.8′; Dec. N 45°58.4′. The solution by Ageton method is shown in Figure 2606a.

Answer: a 6.8′ Toward
Zn 319.0°

Note that the intercept value obtained from the Ageton method is quite different than that resulting from reduction by Pub. No. 229 or 249. This results, of course, from the use of the DR position rather than an assumed position. Sight reduction by the Ageton method can be compared to the results of the other methods only by means of a plot of the corresponding LOPs; see Figure 2606b.

Solutions by electronic calculator

2607 As mentioned in Chapter 24, celestial observations can be reduced by computation using a small hand-held electronic calculator. This is more easily done for multiple sights if the calculator can be programmed to repeat the same mathematical processes successively for different input data; it is most easily accomplished if the calculator is "card-programmable," with the process steps recorded for quick insertion into the machine (or if a specialized calculator that has built-in programs is used).

No examples are given here of sight reduction by calculator, as the programs and manipulative steps will be dependent upon the specific unit used. No set of sight reduction tables will be needed; a *Nautical* or *Air Almanac* may or may not be required. With the more widely used card-programmable models, the procedures consist of a sequence of program cards, with data being keyed in manually for each program; the calculator internally stores the results of one program that will be used as partial input for the next program. The final output is a value of intercept and azimuth for a single reduction, or the coordinates of the fix if two or three reductions have been made with internal storage of the separate intercepts and azimuths.

It is again emphasized that a navigator must *not* depend solely on an electronic hand calculator to the exclusion of a capability to reduce sights by other means (and he must have available the necessary tables for such other means).

Summary **2608** In this chapter, complete solutions have been shown for various celestial observations that are *part* of a navigator's daily work at sea; some observations were reduced by two or more methods to permit comparison of the results. The basic method of sight reduction used the *Nautical Almanac* and Pub. No. 229. Parallel reductions for some sights were made using the *Air Almanac* and Pub. No. 249; one example was shown to illustrate the Ageton method (formerly H. O. 211). The applicability of personal electronic calculations was discussed in general terms.

While typical, the examples of this chapter are far from being all-inclusive and are only samples of the work in celestial navigation done each day, weather permitting, by a navigator at sea. (For more on a normal "day's work," see Article 3004.) Special cases of observations and reductions are covered in Chapters 27 and 28.

27 Latitude and Longitude Observations; Celestial Phenomena

Introduction

2701 A latitude observation is obtained when the celestial body is either due north or south of the observer. When reduced, such an observation yields an LOP extending in an east-west direction; this is termed a *latitude line.* A longitude observation is obtained when the observed body is either east or west of the observer. The resulting LOP is termed a *longitude line,* as it extends in a north-south direction. The former will be discussed first in this section; it has much to recommend it, as a celestial body changes altitude very slowly at transit, except at very high altitudes. Ordinarily, a skilled observer can obtain a considerable number of observations of a transiting body which will be almost identical in altitude. When one of these observations is reduced, great reliance can be placed on its accuracy.

Any celestial body will yield a latitude line when observed at transit. However, the two bodies most commonly used are the sun and Polaris. The sun transits the observer's meridian at *local apparent noon* (LAN); the *LAN* observation is extremely important in navigation, chiefly because it can usually be relied on to yield the most dependable celestial LOP of the day. The sun should be observed at LAN as a matter of routine aboard every vessel.

A latitude line can also be determined from an observation not at LAN but within 28 minutes of that time; see Article 2704.

Determining the time of LAN

2702 To determine the time of LAN accurately, the navigator, while the sun is still well to his east, enters the *Nautical Almanac* for the appropriate day, and finds the tabulated GHA of the sun which is nearest to, but east of, the DR longitude, and he notes the GMT hour of this entry. He then turns to his chart, and for this GMT, he determines difference of longitude in minutes between the sun's GHA and the ship's longitude at the hour of GMT found in the *Nautical Almanac.* This difference is meridian angle east (tE). The next step is to determine the instant when the sun's hour circle will coincide with the ship's longitude; this establishes the time of LAN, and is accomplished by combining the rate of the sun's change of longitude with that of the ship. The sun changes longitude at an almost uniform rate of 15°, or 900′ per hour. The rate of the ship's change of longitude per hour is usually determined by measurement on the chart.

If the ship is steaming towards the east, its hourly rate of change of longitude is added to that of the sun; if it is steaming west, the rate of change is subtracted from that of the sun.

All that remains is to divide the meridian angle east expressed in minutes, found above, by the combined rate of change of longitude. The answer, which will be in decimals of an hour, should be determined to three significant places. Multiplied by 60, minutes and decimals of minutes are obtained; the latter may be converted to seconds by again multiplying by 60. The answer will be mathematically correct to about four seconds; when added to the hour of GMT obtained from the *Nautical Almanac,* it will give the GMT of the sun's transit (LAN) at the ship. Any error in DRλ will, of course, affect the accuracy. The zone description may be employed to convert the GMT of LAN to ship's time. The above procedure can conveniently be written as the following equation:

$$\text{Interval to LAN} = \frac{\text{tE in minutes of arc}}{900' \text{ arc} \pm \text{ship's movement in longitude per hour}}$$

This procedure is illustrated in the following example.

Example: On 5 June 1977, the navigator of a ship proceeding on course 281°, speed 11.5 knots, plans to observe the sun at LAN. At 1145 (+1), he notes that the 1200 DR position will be Lat. 41°17.7′ N, Long. 20°51.6′ W.

Required: The ZT of transit of the sun.

Solution: (Figure 2702). The ship's 1200 DR longitude will be 20°51.6′ W. Entering the *Nautical Almanac* with this value and for this date, 5 June 1977, the nearest, but lesser, GHA of the sun is found; this is 15°24.0′ for 1300 GMT, which is 1200 ship's time. (If the longi-

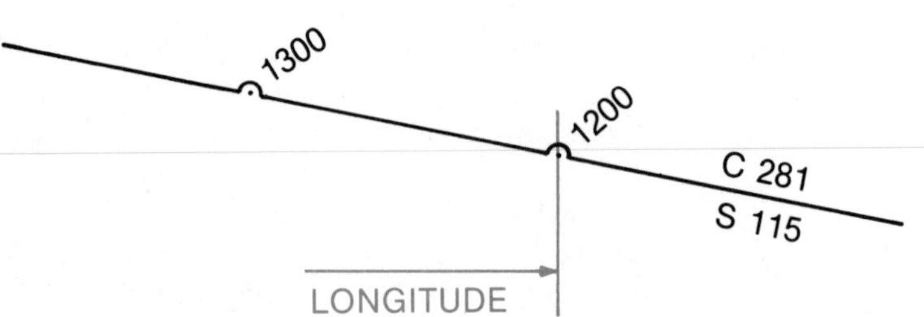

Figure 2702. Plot for calculating time of LAN.

tude had been east, it would have been subtracted from 360° to get the angular distance west of Greenwich for entry into the *Nautical Almanac.*)

The difference in longitude between the ship and the sun at 1200 (+1) equals 20°51.6′ minus 15°24.0′ or 5°27.6′ or 327.6′. This value is used for tE.

By inspection of the plot of the ship's DR longitude for 1200 and 1300 (Figure 2702) the hourly change of longitude, in minutes of arc, is found to be 15.0′. This change is in a *westerly* direction; it will therefore be subtracted from the sun's change which is 900′ per hour. The combined hourly rate of change is 900′ minus 15.0′, or 885.0′ per hour. The value of tE is next divided by this combined rate, 327.6 ÷ 885.0′, to find the time, in decimal fractions of an hour, after 1200 ship's time at which transit will occur. The answer, rounded off, is 0.37; in minutes 0.37 × 60 = 22.2 minutes or 22 minutes 12 seconds. This is added to 1200 (+1) to get the time of transit, or LAN.

Answer: 12–22–12 ZT.

Alternate method of determining LAN

The time of local apparent noon (LAN) can also be determined from calculations using the time of meridian passage of the sun as tabulated for each day on the right-hand pages of the *Nautical Almanac;* see Figure 2304b. This time is given for the meridian of Greenwich, but the rate of change is so slight that it can be used at any longitude without significant error.

The navigator obtains the tabulated value of meridian passage from the *Nautical Almanac;* this is local meridian time (LMT). He then plots the DR position for the vessel for that time in zone time (ZT). He next determines the longitude difference between the DR position and the central meridian of the time zone being used, and converts this to time units. This time difference is applied to the LMT of meridian passage, adding if the DR position is west of the central meridian, subtracting if it is east. The time thus obtained is the first estimate of ZT of transit of the sun.

If the ship is moving, further computation is required. The navigator plots a new DR position for the first estimate of the ZT of LAN as determined above. Using this new DR longitude, he computes a new ZT correction to the tabulated LMT of meridian passage; this is the second estimate of the ZT of LAN and is used for observations.

This procedure is illustrated using the same situation as in the prior method.

Example: On 5 June 1977, the navigator of a ship proceeding on course 281°, speed 11.5 knots, plans to observe the sun at local apparent noon.

Required: The ZT of transit of the sun.

Solution: The navigator determines from the *Nautical Almanac* that meridian passage is at 1158. He also determines that the ship's longitude at that zone time will be 20°51.1′ W. This is 5°51.1′ west of the central meridian of the (+1) time zone; converted to time units, this is 23^m24^s; rounded to 23 minutes and adding to 1158, the first estimate is 1221.

The DR longitude for 1221 ZT is 20°56.9′ W. The time difference for 5°56.9′ is 23^m48^s. This is rounded to 24 minutes and added to 1158, giving 1202.

Answer: 1222 ZT.

Note that this procedure computes values to the nearest minute only, consistent with the *Nautical Almanac* tabulations of the time of meridian passage. This is sufficiently precise, as the time of LAN will be used only as the approximate center time for a series of observations.

A determination of the time of LAN is especially necessary when a ship is steaming on a generally northerly or southerly course at speed. For a ship proceeding towards the south, the sun will continue to increase its altitude for a considerable period *after* it actually has crossed the ship's meridian, and an observation made at the moment when it reaches its maximum altitude will yield a latitude which may be considerably in error.

Under most conditions, however, the sun will appear to "hang" for an appreciable period of time at LAN; that is, it will not change perceptibly in altitude. To obtain a latitude line at LAN, the navigator usually starts observing about two minutes before the time of transit, and continues to obtain sights until the altitude begins to decrease. The average of the three or four highest altitudes can be used for the reduction (or a graph can be plotted of altitude vs. time). On a northerly or southerly course several altitudes may be taken before and after that calculated time of transit to ensure that an unpredictable random error did not occur in the sight taken at time of transit.

Solution for meridian altitudes

2703 While meridian altitudes may be solved routinely by means of the inspection tables such as Pub. No. 229, using an assumed latitude, LHA 0°, and a tabulated declination as entering arguments, such tables are not necessary to obtain a solution.

The method of solution is the same for all celestial bodies observed on the upper branch of the meridian; at this instant each azimuth is precisely 000.0°, or 180.0°. In terms of the navigational triangle, it is a special case, in that the elevated pole, the observer's zenith, and the celestial body are all on the same great circle. The LOP obtained from a meridian observation is an exact latitude line.

The semicircle in Figure 2703a represents that half of the observer's meridian extending from the north point to the south point of his celestial horizon; it is also occupied by a celestial body (in this case the sun) at the instant of transit. This article will discuss the transit of the sun, as it is most frequently observed. However, any celestial body observed when precisely on the navigator's meridian may be used, and the method of reduction would be the same as that outlined here for the sun.

In this diagram, *Z* represents the observer's zenith, *Q* is the equator, P_n is the north pole, here the elevated pole, *N* and *S* represent the north and south points of the observer's horizon, respectively, and ⊙ the sun on the meridian. The angle *z* is the zenith distance of the sun, that is, 90° minus the observed altitude; *L, Dec.*, and *Ho* are the observer's latitude, the declination, and the observed altitude, respectively. The same labeling is used in all diagrams on the plane of the observer's meridian.

Zenith distance (z) In reductions to the meridian, *z is named for the direction of the observer from the body;* that is, if the observer is south of the body, the z is named *south.* The latitude may then be obtained by applying the angular value of the z to the declination, *adding if they are of the same name, and subtracting the smaller from the larger if the names are contrary.* The latitude will have the same name as the remainder; for example, if the z is 42° N and the declination is 18° S, the latitude equals 42° N minus 18° S, or 24° N.

Figure 2703a is drawn for an observer in north latitude, who is north of the sun; the observed altitude of the sun at transit is 71°. The z, therefore, is 90° minus 71°, or 19°N. The sun's declination at the time of transit is 21° N. As the declination is north, and as the observer is north of the sun, z and Dec. are added (19° N + 21° N) to give the observer's latitude, 40° N. Figure 2703b illustrates a case where the

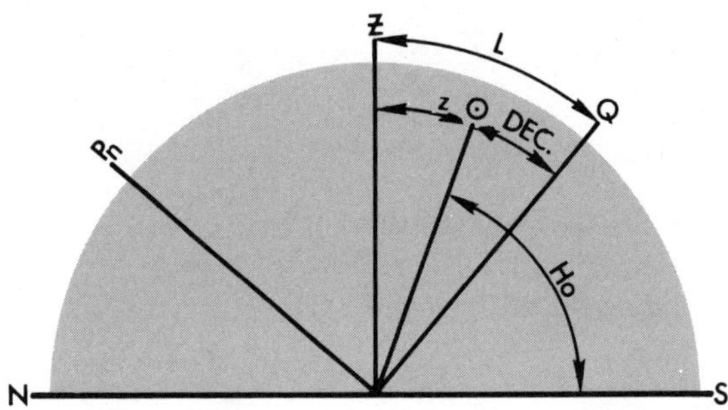

Figure 2703a. Lat. = z + Dec.

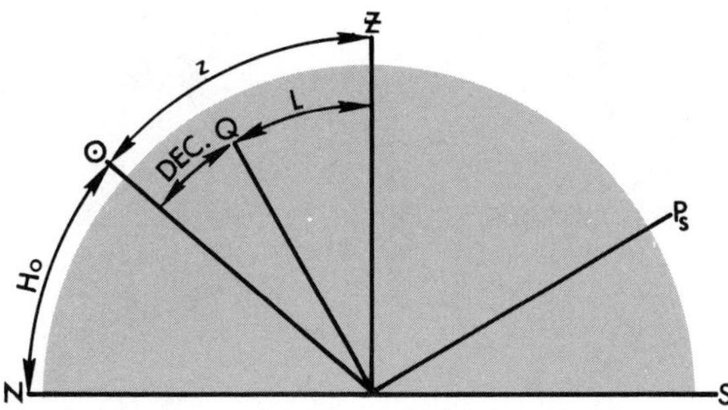

Figure 2703b. Lat. = z − Dec.

observer's latitude and the declination are of opposite name. The Ho is 40°, and the sun is north of the observer, giving a z of 50° S, and the declination is 20° N. In this case Dec. is subtracted from the z (50° S − 20° N) to yield a latitude of 30° S.

Figure 2703c shows an L and Dec. of the same name, but Dec. greater than L. The Dec. is 21° N; Ho is 78°, giving a z of 12° S. Therefore, z is subtracted from Dec. (21° N − 12° S) to yield a latitude of 9° N.

The procedure for the determination of latitude from an observation of the sun at LAN can be summarized in the following two rules:

> If the zenith distance and declination are of the *same* name, they are *added;* the *sum* is the latitude of the observer.
>
> If the zenith distance and declination are of *contrary* name, the smaller value is *subtracted* from the larger; the *difference* is the latitude, with the sign of the larger value.

Solution for lower branch meridian altitudes

When a body is observed at *lower transit*, or on the lower branch of the meridian, the solution differs from that for the upper branch, in that polar distance (p) is used, rather than z; p is the angular dis-

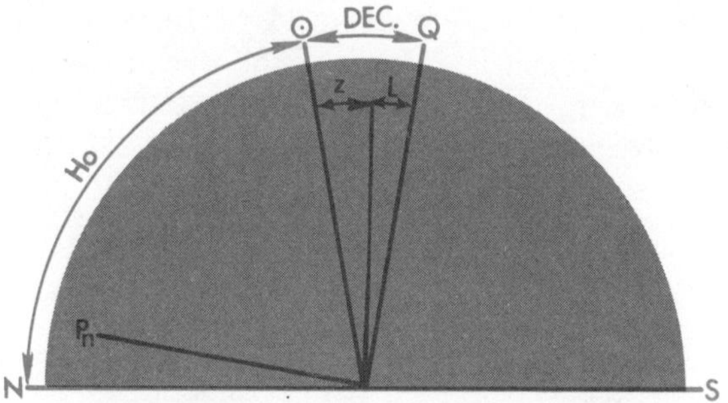

Figure 2703c. Lat. = Dec. − z.

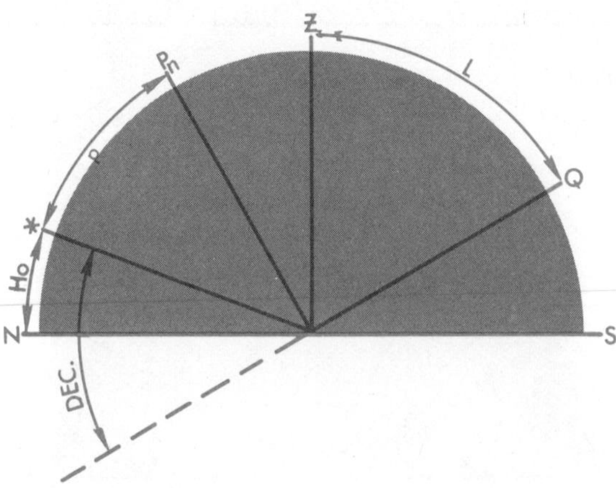

Figure 2703d. Lat. = Ho + p

tance of the body from the pole or 90° minus Dec. At lower transit, the observer's latitude is equal to the observed altitude plus the polar distance, or L = Ho + p. In Figure 2703d a star with a declination of 50° N is observed at lower transit at an Ho of 20°. L therefore equals 20° + 40°, or 60° N.

Reduction to the meridian using *Bowditch* Tables 29 and 30

2704 A latitude line of position can be obtained from any observation made within 28 minutes of the time of either upper or lower transit, provided the altitude of the body is between 6° and 86°, the latitude is not more than 60°, and the declination is not greater than 63°. This is termed a *reduction to the meridian*, or *ex-meridian* reduction. The calculations use Tables 29 and 30 in *Bowditch,* Volume II.

An initial *altitude factor* (a) is taken from Table 29 using the ship's latitude and the body's declination. For an upper transit, a left-hand page is used if the latitude and declination are of the same name; a right-hand page is used if they are of contrary names. For a lower transit the factor is taken from below the heavy lines on the last three right-hand pages of Table 29.

The factor (a) derived from Table 29 is used to entered Table 30, together with the time difference from LAN (or meridian angle t in units of arc). Table 30 is entered twice, for the whole units of (a) and for the tenths of that factor; these values are summed. The total is a correction to be applied to the observed altitude, adding for an upper transit or subtracting for a lower transit, to yield meridian altitude at the time of transit.

Latitude by Polaris

2705 The latitude of a place is equal to the altitude of the elevated pole, as is illustrated in Figure 2705. Both the latitude of the observer, *QOZ* and the altitude of the pole *NOPn* equals 90° minus *PnOZ.* Thus if a star were located exactly at each celestial pole, the corrected altitude of the star would equal the observer's latitude.

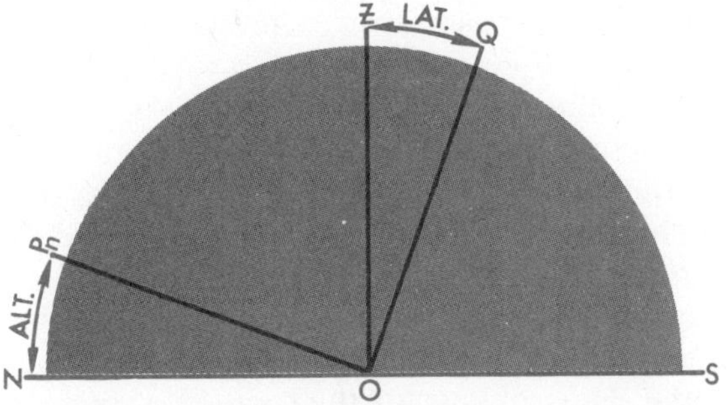

Figure 2705. Latitude equals altitude of elevated pole.

No star is located exactly at either pole, but Polaris is less than a degree from the north celestial pole. Like all stars, it alternately transits the upper and lower branches of each celestial meridian in completing its diurnal circle. Twice during every 24 hours, as it moves in its diurnal circle, Polaris is at the same altitude as the pole, and at that moment no correction would be required to its observed altitude to obtain latitude. At all other times a correction, constantly changing in value, must be applied. The value for any instant may be obtained from the Polaris tables in the *Nautical Almanac,* the entering argument being LHA ♈. The correction is tabulated in three parts; the first is the basic correction applicable under all conditions. This correction, designated a_0 in the *Nautical Almanac,* compensates for the component of the distance between the position of Polaris in its diurnal circle and the north celestial pole, measured along the observer's celestial meridian. The second correction, a_1, is for the DR latitude of the observer, and corrects for the angle at which he views the star's diurnal circle. The third correction, a_2, is for the date and corrects for the small variations in the position of the star in its diurnal circle in the course of a year.

Solution of a Polaris observation by *Nautical Almanac*

2706 A latitude line of position can be obtained from an observation of Polaris using only the *Nautical Almanac* (or *Air Almanac*) to reduce the observation. An azimuth can also be obtained; see Article 2806.

The three Polaris correction tables comprise the last three white pages at the back of the *Nautical Almanac.* A portion of these tables, showing the arrangement of the three corrections a_0, a_1, and a_2, is reproduced in Figure 2706a. It must be borne in mind that *these three corrections are in addition to the usual corrections applied to all sextant observations to obtain Ho.*

As with any body, the sextant altitude is obtained, and the time and date are recorded. The index error is checked.

Using the GMT and Greenwich date, the appropriate daily pages of the almanac are entered, and the GHA of Aries for the minutes and seconds are obtained. These are added to the tabulated value to obtain the GHA of Aries at the time of the observation. The DR longitude at the time of observation is applied (subtract west, add east) to get LHA Aries. Note that an assumed position is not used.

To solve a Polaris observation for latitude, find the value of LHA Aries in the column headings across the top of the tables; these are divided into groups of 10°. Then follow down this column until opposite the single degree of value of LHA ♈ as tabulated in the left-hand column; the exact value for a_0 is then found for the minutes of LHA ♈ by interpolation. Staying in the same vertical column, the value of a_1 is then found in the middle part of the table for the nearest tabulated latitude, without interpolation. Next, the a_2 correction is found in the same column for the current month, again no interpolation.

POLARIS (POLE STAR) TABLES, 1977
FOR DETERMINING LATITUDE FROM SEXTANT ALTITUDE AND FOR AZIMUTH

L.H.A. ARIES	120°–129°	130°–139°	140°–149°	150°–159°	160°–169°	170°–179°	180°–189°	190°–199°	200°–209°	210°–219°	220°–229°	230°–239°
	a_0	a_0	a_0	a_0	a_0	a_0	a_0	a_0	a_0	a_0	a_0	a_0
°	° ′	° ′	° ′	° ′	° ′	° ′	° ′	° ′	° ′	° ′	° ′	° ′
0	0 57·0	1 05·7	1 14·3	1 22·3	1 29·7	1 36·0	1 41·3	1 45·3	1 47·9	1 49·1	1 48·7	1 46·8
1	57·9	06·6	15·1	23·1	30·3	36·6	41·8	45·6	48·1	49·1	48·6	46·6
2	58·7	07·5	15·9	23·9	31·0	37·2	42·2	45·9	48·3	49·1	48·4	46·3
9	04·9	13·4	21·5	29·0	35·5	40·8	45·0	47·7	49·0	48·8	47·1	43·9
10	1 05·7	1 14·3	1 22·3	1 29·7	1 36·0	1 41·3	1 45·3	1 47·9	1 49·1	1 48·7	1 46·8	1 43·5
Lat.	a_1	a_1	a_1	a_1	a_1	a_1	a_1	a_1	a_1	a_1	a_1	a_1
°	′	′	′	′	′	′	′	′	′	′	′	′
0	0·2	0·2	0·2	0·3	0·4	0·4	0·5	0·6	0·6	0·6	0·6	0·5
10	·2	·2	·3	·3	·4	·5	·5	·6	·6	·6	·6	·5
20	·3	·3	·3	·4	·4	·5	·5	·6	·6	·6	·6	·6
30	·4	·4	·4	·4	·5	·5	·6	·6	·6	·6	·6	·6
66	1·0	1·0	0·9	·9	·8	·7	·7	·6	·6	·6	·6	·7
68	1·1	1·1	1·0	0·9	0·9	0·8	0·7	0·6	0·6	0·6	0·6	0·7
Month	a_2	a_2	a_2	a_2	a_2	a_2	a_2	a_2	a_2	a_2	a_2	a_2
	′	′	′	′	′	′	′	′	′	′	′	′
Jan.	0·6	0·6	0·6	0·5	0·5	0·5	0·5	0·4	0·4	0·4	0·4	0·4
Feb.	·8	·7	·7	·7	·6	·6	·5	·5	·5	·4	·4	·4
Mar.	0·9	0·9	0·9	·8	·8	·7	·7	·6	·6	·5	·5	·4
Apr.	1·0	1·0	1·0	0·9	0·9	0·9	0·8	0·8	0·7	0·7	0·6	0·5
May	0·9	1·0	1·0	1·0	1·0	1·0	0·9	0·9	·9	·8	·7	·7
June	·8	0·9	0·9	0·9	1·0	1·0	1·0	1·0	·9	·9	·9	·8
Oct.	0·3	0·3	0·3	0·3	0·4	0·4	0·5	0·5	0·6	0·6	0·7	0·7
Nov.	·2	·2	·2	·2	·2	·2	·3	·3	·4	·4	·5	·6
Dec.	0·3	0·2	0·2	0·2	0·2	0·2	0·2	0·2	0·2	0·3	0·3	0·4

Latitude = Apparent altitude (corrected for refraction) $-1° + a_0 + a_1 + a_2$

The table is entered with L.H.A. Aries to determine the column to be used; each column refers to a range of 10°. a_0 is taken, with mental interpolation, from the upper table with the units of L.H.A. Aries in degrees as argument; a_1, a_2 are taken, without interpolation, from the second and third tables with arguments latitude and month respectively. a_0, a_1, a_2 are always positive. The final table gives the azimuth of *Polaris.*

Figure 2706a. *Nautical Almanac,* Polaris Tables (extract).

The arrangement of the tables is such that these three corrections are always *positive* (additive), *but an additional constant negative of 1° is finally applied* to determine the total correction at the time and latitude of the observation. The total correction, therefore, can be negative in some instances.

Customarily, the navigator uses the latitude thus obtained to draw a latitude LOP. If his DR longitude is reasonably accurate, this latitude line will yield acceptable accuracy. If there is considerable uncertainty as to the ship's longitude, the azimuth of Polaris should be determined. This will be found at the bottom of the Polaris tables, the entering arguments being the nearest 10° of LHA ♈, and the nearest tabulated latitude; no interpolation is required. The LOP is then drawn through the computed latitude and the DR longitude, perpendicular to this azimuth.

Example: During morning twilight on 5 June 1977, at approximately 0352 (+1), a navigator observes Polaris. The ship's DR position is Lat. 41°02.5′ N, Long. 14°36.9′ W. The sextant has an IC of +0.2′;

	+	−
IC	0.2	
Dip (Ht 21')		4.4
Sum		-4.2
hs	41	14.2
ha	41	-10.0
Alt. Corr		-1.1
TB (hs<10°)		
Ho	41	08.9
Date	5 JUN	77
DR Lat.	41°	02.5'N
DR Long	14°	36.9'W
Obs time	03-52-16	
WE (S+, F−)		8F
ZT	03-52-08	
ZD (W+, E−)	+1	
GMT	04-52-08	
Date (GMT)	5 JUN 77	
Tab GHA ♈	313	28.3
GHA Incrmt	13	04.1
GHA ♈	326	32.4
DR Long	14	36.9 W
LHA ♈	311	55.5
a_0	51.9	
a_1	0.5	
a_2	0.3	
Add'n'l		60.0
Sub total	51.9	60.0
Corr to Ho		-8.1
Ho	41	08.9
Lat	41°	00.8'N
True Az		
Gyro Brg		
Gyro Error		

Figure 2706b. Calculation of latitude from a Polaris observation using *Nautical Almanac.*

the watch is 8 seconds fast; the height of eye is 21 feet. The sextant altitude at 03–52–16 watch time is 41°14.2′.

Required: The latitude at the time of observation, using the *Nautical Almanac.*

Answer: (Solution is shown in Figure 2706b.)

Lat. 41°00.8′

Solution of a Polaris observation by *Air Almanac*

2707 An observation of Polaris can also be reduced for a latitude line of position by use of the *Air Almanac.*

Various Q corrections are tabulated for critical values of LHA ♈ (which is found from GHA ♈ and DR longitude in the normal manner). The Q value is applied to the corrected sextant altitude to directly yield latitude.

Example: During morning twilight on 5 June 1977, at approximately 0352 (+1), a navigator observes Polaris. The ship's DR position

IC	+ 0.2 –	
Dip (Ht.21')	4	
Sum	– 3.8	
hs	41 - 14	
ha	41 - 10	
Alt Corr	– 1	
TB (hs <10°)		
Ho	41° 09'	
Date	5 JUN 77	
DR Lat	41° 02.5' N	
DR Long	14° 36.9' W	
Obs time	03-52-16	
WE	8F	
ZT	03-52-08	
ZD	+1	
GMT	04-52-08	
Date GMT	5 JUN 77	
Tab GHA ♈	326 00	
Incrmt	0 32	
GHA ♈	326 32	
DR Long	14 37	
LHA ♈	311 55	
Q	–8	
Ho	41 09	
Lat.	41° 01' N	

Figure 2707. Calculation of latitude from a Polaris observation using *Air Almanac.*

is Lat. 41°02.5′ N, Long. 14°36.9′ W. The sextant has an IC of +0.2′; the watch is 8 seconds fast; the height of eye is 21 feet. The sextant altitude at 03–52–16 watch time is 41°14′.

Required: The latitude at the time of observation, using the *Air Almanac.*

Answer: (Solution is shown in Figure 2707).

Lat. 41°01′ N.

Note that this value, to the nearest whole minute of latitude, is essentially the same as that obtained, to the nearest tenth of a minute, by use of the *Nautical Almanac;* several fewer steps were required by use of the *Air Almanac.*

Observations for longitude

2708 Longitude observations were in general use until the altitude difference or intercept method, devised in 1875 by Marcq de St.-Hilaire, was accepted. The longitude obtained was predicated on a latitude; the latter was usually obtained from a LAN sun observation, and carried forward or back by DR to obtain the longitude. The calculated longitude was therefore accurate only if the DR latitude was accurate. Subsequently, as the accuracy of chronometers was improved, celestial bodies were observed on the *prime vertical,* that is, when their azimuth was exactly 090.0° or 270.0°; this method yielded considerably increased accuracy.

Presently, observations intended solely to yield longitude are seldom required or made. If one is to be made, the most convenient method involves the use of an inspection table, usually Pub. No. 229, to determine the time at which the observation should be made. In the case of Pub. No. 229, it is entered with values of latitude and declination, and the LHA is determined for the time at which the azimuth equals 90.0° (or 270.0°). The GMT at which this LHA, converted to GHA by applying DR longitude, occurs can then be obtained from the *Nautical Almanac.* For the best results, interpolation should be made for t, Dec., and L. The process is feasible but laborious and consequently is not often done.

Observations on the beam, bow, and stern

2709 Observations made directly on the beam are helpful in determining whether the ship is on the desired track line, while observations obtained dead ahead or astern show how far she has advanced. The sun is the body most commonly used in making such observations. Here, again, Pub. No. 229 may be used to advantage. It is entered with the appropriate latitude and declination, as outlined in Article 2708, and the desired azimuth angle, relative to the ship's head, stern, or beam is found. The time for the observation is then determined as for a longitude observation.

Summary, latitude, longitude, and special case observations

2710 Observations yielding latitude lines are conventional aids used to assist in determining position at sea. The bodies most frequently observed for this purpose are the sun and Polaris. The sun, observed at upper transit, yields a latitude line, which ordinarily can be relied on as the most accurate LOP of the day, as the horizon at noon is usually very well defined, and the sun's rate of change of altitude is then usually very slow. Any celestial body may be observed at upper or lower transit, and a latitude line obtained.

Polaris observations, when fully corrected, yield an LOP which ordinarily may be plotted as a latitude line.

Observations, usually of the sun, when made dead ahead or astern, or on the beam, yield information which can be very helpful to the navigator.

PHENOMENA

Introduction

2711 Sunrise is the first appearance of the sun's *upper* limb above the visible horizon; similarly, sunset is the disappearance of the upper limb below the horizon. Due chiefly to the effect of refraction, as the upper limb appears to touch the horizon, it is actually more than

30.0′ below the celestial horizon. The times of moonrise and moonset are similarly determined, by the contact of the upper limb with the horizon.

Twilight is the period before sunrise when darkness is giving way to daylight, and after sunset, when the opposite is true. Three kinds of twilight are defined below; the darker limit of each twilight occurs when the *center* of the sun is the stated number of degrees below the celestial horizon. A navigator is concerned only with civil and nautical twilight.

Twilight designations

Twilight	*Lighter Limit*	*Darker Limit*	*At Darker Limit*
Civil	$\bar{\odot}$ 0°	−6°	Horizon clear and bright stars visible
Nautical	$\bar{\odot}$ 0°	−12°	Horizon vague
Astronomical	$\bar{\odot}$ 0°	−18°	Full night

The conditions at the darker limits are relative and vary considerably under different atmospheric conditions. The duration of twilight is chiefly a function of the observer's latitude; it increases with an increase in latitude.

In the *Nautical Almanac,* the GMT of sunrise and sunset, and the beginnings of morning and endings of evening civil and nautical twilight are tabulated for every three-day period, at various latitudes along the meridian of Greenwich (0° λ), the second of the three being the reference day. The GMT of moonrise and moonset for 0° λ are similarly tabulated in a separate column for each day.

The Local Mean Time (LMT) of sunrise, sunset, and twilight for a given date and latitude are essentially the same in any longitude. This is due to the fact that for a period of one day the change in declination, and more important, the rate of change in hour angle, of the sun is comparatively small. For moonrise and moonset an additional interpolation for longitude is needed.

In the back of each volume of the *Air Almanac,* tables will be found giving the times of sunrise and sunset, and the darker limits of civil twilight; times of moonrise and moonset are given on the daily pages. In addition, the *Tide Tables* (published by the National Ocean Survey) include tables for the LMT of sunrise and sunset, with a convenient table for the reduction of LMT to ZT. Moonrise and moonset are tabulated daily for specific cities rather than by latitude.

Sunrise and sunset

2712 The GMT of sunrise and sunset for the middle day of the three on each page opening in the *Nautical Almanac,* is tabulated to the nearest minute for selected intervals of latitude from 72° N to 60° S. An extract from this table is shown in Figure 2712a. The tabulated times are generally used to obtain the ZT of the phenomena by one of two

Lat.	Sunset	Twilight		Moonset			
		Civil	Naut.	3	4	5	6
°	h m	h m	h m	h m	h m	h m	h m
N 72	□	□	□	■	03 02	05 35	07 40
N 70	□	□	□	02 35	04 17	06 10	08 00
68	□	□	□	03 26	04 54	06 35	08 16
66	23 01	////	////	03 58	05 21	06 54	08 29
64	22 07	////	////	04 22	05 41	07 09	08 39
62	21 36	////	////	04 41	05 58	07 22	08 48
60	21 12	22 41	////	04 56	06 11	07 33	08 56
N 58	20 54	22 03	////	05 09	06 23	07 42	09 03
56	20 38	21 37	////	05 21	06 33	07 50	09 08
54	20 25	21 17	22 48	05 31	06 42	07 58	09 14
52	20 13	21 00	22 13	05 40	06 50	08 04	09 18
50	20 03	20 46	21 48	05 47	06 57	08 10	09 23
45	19 42	20 18	21 07	06 04	07 12	08 22	09 32
N 40	19 25	19 57	20 38	06 18	07 25	08 33	09 40
35	19 10	19 40	20 16	06 30	07 36	08 42	09 46
30	18 58	19 25	19 58	06 40	07 45	08 49	09 52
20	18 37	19 01	19 30	06 57	08 01	09 03	10 02
N 10	18 19	18 42	19 08	07 13	08 15	09 14	10 11
0	18 02	18 24	18 50	07 27	08 28	09 25	10 19
S 10	17 45	18 08	18 34	07 41	08 40	09 36	10 27
20	17 27	17 51	18 19	07 56	08 54	09 47	10 35
30	17 07	17 33	18 03	08 13	09 10	10 00	10 45
35	16 55	17 23	17 55	08 23	09 19	10 07	10 50
40	16 42	17 12	17 46	08 35	09 29	10 16	10 57
45	16 26	16 59	17 36	08 48	09 41	10 26	11 04
S 50	16 07	16 44	17 25	09 04	09 56	10 38	11 12
52	15 57	16 37	17 20	09 12	10 02	10 43	11 16
54	15 47	16 30	17 15	09 21	10 10	10 49	11 21
56	15 35	16 21	17 10	09 30	10 18	10 56	11 26
58	15 21	16 12	17 03	09 41	10 28	11 03	11 31
S 60	15 05	16 01	16 56	09 53	10 38	11 12	11 37

Day	SUN			MOON			
	Eqn. of Time 00ʰ	Eqn. of Time 12ʰ	Mer. Pass.	Mer. Pass. Upper	Mer. Pass. Lower	Age	Phase
	m s	m s	h m	h m	h m	d	
3	02 02	01 57	11 58	01 12	13 43	16	
4	01 52	01 47	11 58	02 13	14 43	17	◐
5	01 42	01 37	11 58	03 12	15 39	18	

Figure 2712a. *Nautical Almanac* portion of a daily page showing evening phenomena; morning phenomena are shown in a similar manner on facing page.

possible methods. The GMT of sunrise or sunset may be considered to be its LMT, and therefore its ZT on the standard meridian of any zone. To obtain the ZT of the phenomena at the ship, it is only necessary to convert the difference of longitude between the standard meridian and the ship into time, adding this difference if the ship is west of the standard meridian and subtracting if it is east. Each degree of longitude will be 4 minutes of time, and each 15′ of longitude 1 minute of time. The same result can be obtained by taking from the table the GMT at the required latitude, and applying to this the longitude converted to time, to give GMT of the phenomena at the local meridian, and finally applying the zone description with the sign reversed. Interpolation for latitude is made by means of a table near the back of the *Nautical Almanac;* a portion of this is reproduced in Figure 2712b. When more precise times of sunrise and sunset are desired, they may be obtained by interpolating for the correct day, in addition to the regular interpolation for latitude.

At times, in high latitudes, the sun remains continuously either below or above the horizon. In the former case, the symbol ■ appears in place of a time; in the latter, the symbol ▭ is substituted for the time. These symbols are seen in Figure 2712a where the sun does not set in high latitudes, and the moon, at extreme latitudes, did not come above the horizon on 3 June.

TABLES FOR INTERPOLATING SUNRISE, MOONRISE, ETC.

TABLE I—FOR LATITUDE

Tabular Interval			Difference between the times for consecutive latitudes															
10°	5°	2°	5m	10m	15m	20m	25m	30m	35m	40m	45m	50m	55m	60m	1h 05m	1h 10m	1h 15m	1h 20m
° ′	° ′	° ′	m	m	m	m	m	m	m	m	m	m	m	m	h m	h m	h m	h m
0 30	0 15	0 06	0	0	1	1	1	1	1	2	2	2	2	2	0 02	0 02	0 02	0 02
1 00	0 30	0 12	0	1	1	2	2	3	3	3	4	4	4	5	05	05	05	05
1 30	0 45	0 18	1	1	2	3	3	4	4	5	5	6	7	7	07	07	07	07
2 00	1 00	0 24	1	2	3	4	5	5	6	7	7	8	9	10	10	10	10	10
2 30	1 15	0 30	1	2	4	5	6	7	8	9	9	10	11	12	12	13	13	13
3 00	1 30	0 36	1	3	4	6	7	8	9	10	11	12	13	14	0 15	0 15	0 16	0 16
3 30	1 45	0 42	2	3	5	7	8	10	11	12	13	14	16	17	18	18	19	19
4 00	2 00	0 48	2	4	6	8	9	11	13	14	15	16	18	19	20	21	22	22
9 00	4 30	1 48	4	9	13	18	22	27	31	35	39	43	47	52	0 55	0 58	1 01	1 04
9 30	4 45	1 54	5	9	14	19	24	28	33	38	42	47	51	56	1 00	1 04	1 08	1 12
10 00	5 00	2 00	5	10	15	20	25	30	35	40	45	50	55	60	1 05	1 10	1 15	1 20

Table I is for interpolating the L.M.T. of sunrise, twilight, moonrise, etc., for latitude. It is to be entered, in the appropriate column on the left, with the difference between true latitude and the nearest tabular latitude which is *less* than the true latitude; and with the argument at the top which is the nearest value of the difference between the times for the tabular latitude and the next higher one; the correction so obtained is applied to the time for the tabular latitude; the sign of the correction can be seen by inspection. It is to be noted that the interpolation is not linear, so that when using this table it is essential to take out the tabular phenomenon for the latitude *less* than the true latitude.

TABLE II—FOR LONGITUDE

Long. East or West	Difference between the times for given date and preceding date (for east longitude) or for given date and following date (for west longitude)																	
	10m	20m	30m	40m	50m	60m	1h + 10m	1h + 20m	1h + 30m	1h + 40m	1h + 50m	1h + 60m	2h 10m	2h 20m	2h 30m	2h 40m	2h 50m	3h 00m
°	m	m	m	m	m	m	m	m	m	m	m	m	h m	h m	h m	h m	h m	h m
0	0	0	0	0	0	0	0	0	0	0	0	0	0 00	0 00	0 00	0 00	0 00	0 00
10	0	1	1	1	1	2	2	2	2	3	3	3	04	04	04	04	05	05
20	1	1	2	2	3	3	4	4	5	6	6	7	07	08	08	09	09	10
30	1	2	2	3	4	5	6	7	7	8	9	10	11	12	12	13	14	15
40	1	2	3	4	6	7	8	9	10	11	12	13	14	16	17	18	19	20
50	1	3	4	6	7	8	10	11	12	14	15	17	0 18	0 19	0 21	0 22	0 24	0 25
60	2	3	5	7	8	10	12	13	15	17	18	20	22	23	25	27	28	30
70	2	4	6	8	10	12	14	16	17	19	21	23	25	27	29	31	33	35
80	2	4	7	9	11	13	16	18	20	22	24	27	29	31	33	36	38	40
90	2	5	7	10	12	15	17	20	22	25	27	30	32	35	37	40	42	45
100	3	6	8	11	14	17	19	22	25	28	31	33	0 36	0 39	0 42	0 44	0 47	0 50
110	3	6	9	12	15	18	21	24	27	31	34	37	40	43	46	49	0 52	0 55
120	3	7	10	13	17	20	23	27	30	33	37	40	43	47	50	53	0 57	1 00
130	4	7	11	14	18	22	25	29	32	36	40	43	47	51	54	0 58	1 01	1 05
140	4	8	12	16	19	23	27	31	35	39	43	47	51	54	0 58	1 02	1 06	1 10
150	4	8	13	17	21	25	29	33	38	42	46	50	0 54	0 58	1 03	1 07	1 11	1 15
160	4	9	13	18	22	27	31	36	40	44	49	53	0 58	1 02	1 07	1 11	1 16	1 20
170	5	9	14	19	24	28	33	38	42	47	52	57	1 01	1 06	1 11	1 16	1 20	1 25
180	5	10	15	20	25	30	35	40	45	50	55	60	1 05	1 10	1 15	1 20	1 25	1 30

Table II is for interpolating the L.M.T. of moonrise, moonset and the Moon's meridian passage for longitude. It is entered with longitude and with the difference between the times for the given date and for the preceding date (in east longitudes) or following date (in west longitudes). The correction is normally *added* for west longitudes and *subtracted* for east longitudes, but if, as occasionally happens, the times become earlier each day instead of later, the signs of the corrections must be reversed.

Figure 2712b. *Nautical Almanac,* tables for interpolating the times of rising and setting of the sun and moon, and of twilight.

Latitude correction

To determine the time at a latitude which is not tabulated, Table I is entered, following the instructions listed below the table. It should be pointed out that the correction table is not linear and that information from the daily pages is always taken for the tabulated latitude smaller than the actual latitude. The entering arguments are:

Latitude difference between the tabulated latitude and the actual one.

Time difference between the times of the occurrence at the tabulated latitudes on either side of the one for which the information is desired.

The latitude interval between tabular entries for sunrise and sunset varies with the latitude concerned, being 10° near the equator, 5° in mid-latitudes, and 2° in higher latitudes. Table I has columns at the left for each of these intervals. The *latitude difference* between the actual latitude and the smaller tabulated latitude is determined and used to select the appropriate line of Table I. For example, if the interval between tabulated latitudes is 2°, and the latitude for which the information is desired is 0°24′ greater than the smaller tabulated latitude, the "Tabular Interval" column headed 2° is entered; 0°24′ is found on the fourth line down. If the tabular interval were 5°, a latitude difference of 0°24′ would be located approximately on the second line down; if it were 10°, this same latitude difference would be located approximately on the first line. The *time difference* is used to determine the column of Table I that is to be used; the time correction is taken directly from the table, with interpolation if necessary to obtain the time of the phenomenon to the nearest minute. The correction thus obtained is applied to the GMT of the phenomenon for the *smaller* tabulated latitude, originally extracted from the daily pages; the sign of the correction is determined by inspection.

To this sum, the longitude converted from arc to time is applied as described, to obtain the ZT of the phenomenon for the latitude and longitude.

Sample problem, sunset

Example: Find the ZT of sunset on 5 June 1977 at Lat. 41°34.1′ N Long. 16°46.1′ W using the *Nautical Almanac* (Figures 2712a and b).

Solution: Enter the appropriate daily page of the *Nautical Almanac* (Figure 2712a) and extract and record the LMT of sunset for the next lesser tabulated latitude. In this case, the next lesser latitude is 40° N and the LMT of sunset at that latitude is 1925. Then note the difference of latitude between the tabulated values above and below the latitude for which information is desired, and the difference in the times of the phenomenon between these latitudes including its sign. In this instance, the tabular interval is 5° and the time difference is $+17^m$ (1925 at Lat. 40° N and 1942 at Lat. 45° N). Next, enter Table I of "Tables for Interpolating Sunrise, Moonrise, etc." (Figure 2712b) and obtain the correction to the tabulated LMT. In this example, the latitude difference, 41°34.1′ minus 40°00.0′ or 1°34.1′, is applied to the column for Tabular Interval of 5°. The time difference is found between the columns for 15^m and 20^m. Interpolating by eye to the nearest minute, the correction is $+5^m$. Finally, apply this correction to the LMT for the lesser tabulated latitude (40°) to obtain the LMT of sunset at the given latitude, and convert this time to ZT. For this example, the LMT of sunset at Lat. 41°34.1′ N is 1925 + 5 = 1930; the ZT is 1930 + 7^m (for 1°46.1′ longitude west of zone central meridian; using the table "Conversion of Arc to Time" to nearest whole minute of time) = 1937.

Sunset

N 45°	1942	
N 40°	1925	
Diff for 5°	17	min.
Table I Lat. Corr.	+ 5	min.
1925 + 5 =	1930	
dLo Corr.	+ 7	
ZT	1937	

Answer: The ZT of sunset is 1937.

The above example was done directly from the tabulated data of the *Nautical Almanac* without correction for the fact that 5 June is not the center date of the *Almanac* pages for "1977 June 3, 4, 5" nor for the difference in longitude between the ship and Greenwich. Such procedure will yield a time of sunrise or sunset sufficiently accurate for the usual uses to which such information is put. If, however, a more precise determination of the time of these phenomena is needed, corrections can be calculated in accordance with procedures explained in the *Nautical Almanac*. In the above example, because of the time of year and latitude, such a correction is negligible; in months near the equinoxes and at high latitudes, corrections can be as much as 6 to 8 minutes.

The procedure for obtaining the time of sunrise from the *Nautical Almanac* is the same as that explained above for sunset.

The procedures of the *Air Almanac* are illustrated in the following example.

Example: Find the ZT of sunset on 5 June 1977 at Lat. 41°34′ N, Long. 16°46′ W using the *Air Almanac* (Figure 2712c).

Solution: The tabular data for sunrise, sunset, and civil twilight are given in the "white pages" of the *Air Almanac* at three-day intervals for the longitude of Greenwich and latitude intervals of 10°, 5°, or 2° similar to the *Nautical Almanac*. These figures may be used for other longitudes without correction. The nearest date is used but interpolation is done for the actual latitude. The *Air Almanac* data for this example are as follows:

	June
Lat.	4
N45	1942
N40	1925

SUNSET

May 23	May 26	May 29	June 1	June 4	June 7	June 10	June 13	June 16	June 19	June 22
h m	h m	h m	h m	h m	h m	h m	h m	h m	h m	h m
□	□	□	□	□	□	□	□	□	□	□
□	□	□	□	□	□	□	□	□	□	□
23 06	□	□	□	□	□	□	□	□	□	□
22 06	22 19	22 32	22 46	23 01	23 16	23 36	□	□	□	□
21 33	21 42	21 51	21 59	22 07	22 14	22 21	22 26	22 29	22 32	22 33
21 08	21 16	23	29	21 35	21 41	21 45	21 49	21 52	21 54	21 54
20 49	20 56	21 02	21 07	21 12	21 16	21 20	21 23	21 26	21 27	21 28
34	39	20 44	20 49	20 53	20 57	21 01	21 03	21 05	21 07	21 07
20	25	30	34	38	41	20 44	20 47	20 48	20 50	20 50
20 09	13	17	21	25	28	30	33	34	35	36
19 59	20 03	20 06	10	13	16	18	20	22	23	24
19 50	19 53	19 57	20 00	20 03	20 06	20 08	20 10	20 11	20 12	20 13
31	34	37	19 39	19 42	19 44	19 46	19 47	19 49	19 50	19 50
15	18	20	23	25	26	28	29	31	32	32
19 02	19 05	19 07	19 08	19 10	19 12	13	15	16	17	17
18 51	18 53	18 55	18 56	18 58	18 59	19 00	19 02	19 03	19 04	19 04
18 32	18 33	18 35	18 36	18 37	18 38	18 39	18 40	18 41	18 41	18 42
16	16	17	18	19	19	20	21	22	22	23
18 00	18 01	18 01	18 01	18 02	18 02	18 03	18 04	18 04	18 05	18 05
17 45	17 45	17 45	17 45	17 45	17 46	17 46	17 46	17 47	17 47	17 48
29	28	28	28	28	28	28	28	28	29	30
17 11	17 10	17 09	17 08	17 07	17 07	17 07	17 07	17 07	17 08	17 08
17 00	16 59	16 57	16 56	16 56	16 55	16 55	16 55	16 55	16 55	16 56
16 48	46	45	43	42	41	41	41	41	41	42
34	32	30	28	26	25	25	24	24	24	25
16	13	11	16 09	16 07	16 05	16 04	16 04	16 03	16 03	16 04
16 08	16 05	16 02	15 59	15 57	15 56	15 54	15 54	15 53	15 54	15 54
15 59	15 55	15 52	49	47	45	44	43	42	42	43
49	45	41	38	35	33	31	30	30	30	30
37	32	28	25	21	19	17	15 16	15 15	15 15	15 16
15 23	15 18	15 13	15 09	15 05	15 02	15 00	14 59	14 58	14 57	14 58

Figure 2712c. *Air Almanac,* Sunset Tables (extract).

The LMT of sunset at Lat. 41°34′ N is found by interpolation to be 1930. Adjusting for longitude, the ZT is 1930 + 7^{m} (for 1°46′ longitude east of zone central meridian) = 1937.

Answer: ZT of sunset is 1937.

Note that in this example the ZT of sunset is the same whether the *Air Almanac* or the *Nautical Almanac* is used. In some instances, slight differences will occur between the two procedures, but these are of minor practical significance.

Sunrise-Sunset Computer In addition to the tabular methods discussed here, the data can be determined to an accuracy better than 2 minutes by the use of a special Sunrise-Sunset Computer (Figure 2712d). Ephemeristic data for the

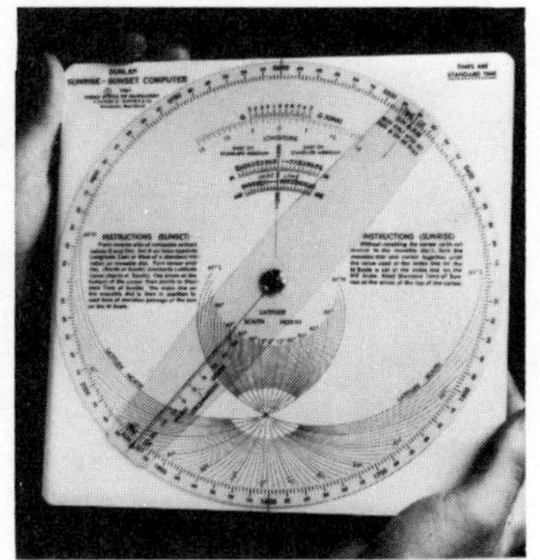

Figure 2712d. A sunrise-sunset computer.

Sunset

S 10°	1752
S 20°	1741
Diff. for 10°	− 11 min.
Table 1 Lat. Corr.	− 8 min.
1752—8 min.	= 1744
Long. Corr.	− 4 min.
	1740

sun are printed on the back of the computer and for purposes of this problem can be considered to be repetitive each year. Declination and *G* are tabulated, *G* being the GHA of the sun for 1200 GMT with the first two figures omitted for brevity. For example, GHA of 359.1° would be 9.1° and 001.7° would be 1.7°. With this ephemeristic data and the DR latitude and longitude, the four entering arguments are set on the face of the computer in accordance with the printed instructions. The time of meridian passage of the sun is also indicated on the computer.

Twilight calculations **2713** In celestial navigation, morning and evening twilight are the most important times of the day, as ordinarily these are the only periods during which a fix may be obtained by nearly simultaneous lines of position from observations of a number of celestial bodies. At the darker limit of nautical twilight, when the sun's center is 12° below the celestial horizon, the horizon is usually only dimly visible, except to an observer with dark-adapted vision, or who is using a telescope of superior light-gathering power. At the darker limit of civil twilight, when the sun's center is 6° below the celestial horizon, during good weather the bright stars are readily discernible to the practiced eye, and the horizon is clearly defined. This is approximately the mid-time of the period during which star observations should ordinarily be made.

The time of the darker limit of civil or nautical twilight is obtained from the *Nautical Almanac* in the same manner that sunrise and sunset data are obtained. The GMT of the phenomenon at the closest tabulated latitude is taken from the daily pages, interpolation for latitude is made in Table I, and the ZT of the phenomenon at the desired latitude is then obtained by applying the longitude in time, as discussed in Article 2712.

When twilight lasts all night, as happens at times in high latitudes, the symbol //// is shown in place of a time; see higher latitudes of Figure 2712a.

Example: Find the ZT of the ending of civil twilight on 5 June 1977 at latitude 41°36.0′ N, Long. 16°54.0′ W using the *Nautical Almanac*.

Solution: Enter the appropriate daily page of the *Nautical Almanac* (Figure 2712a) and extract and record the LMT for the end of civil twilight for the next lesser tabulated latitude. In this case, the next lesser latitude is 40° and the LMT at that latitude is 1957. Then note the difference between the tabulated values of latitude on either side of the latitude for which the information is desired, and the difference in time of the phenomenon between these tabulated latitudes, and its sign. In this case the tabular interval is 5° and time difference is $+21^m$ (1957 at 40° N and 2018 at 45° N). Next, enter Table I (Figure 2712b) and obtain the correction to LMT. This is found on a line for 1°36′ in the 5° Tabular Interval Column (between 1°30′ and 1°45′) and a column for 21^m time difference (between 20^m and 25^m); it is $+7^m$. Finally, apply this correction to the LMT of the lesser latitude (40°) to obtain the LMT at the desired latitude, and convert this time to ZT. In this example, the LMT of the end of civil twilight at Lat. 41°36.0′ N is 1957 + 7 = 2004; the ZT 2004 + 8^m (for 1°54.0′ of longitude west of zone central meridian) = 2012.

Civil Twilight

N 45°	2018	
N 40°	1957	
Diff for 5°	21	min
Table I Lat. Corr.	+ 7	min
1957 + 7 =	2004	
dLo Corr.	+ 8	min
	2012	

Answer: ZT of the ending of civil twilight is 2012.

The procedures for finding the ending of nautical twilight, or the beginning of civil or nautical twilight are similar to the example shown above.

The beginning or ending of civil twilight can be found from the *Air Almanac* following the instructions contained in that publication; the procedures are generally the same as illustrated for sunrise or sunset as described in Article 2912.

Moonrise and moonset

2714 The times of moonrise and moonset are found by first interpolating for the latitude at which they are required, as was done with the sun. However, there must be a second interpolation for longitude, as the times of moonrise and moonset differ considerably from day to day, and at any longitude other then 0° these phenomena will fall somewhere between the times tabulated for consecutive days on the 0° meridian. This is due to the fact that the change in hourly rate of increase of GHA for the moon is not precisely 15° per hour which would be assumed if longitude were merely converted to time as in the case of the sun.

Always remember that the tabulated times of moonrise and moonset are their GMTs at the longitude of Greenwich (0° λ); an observer in east longitude will experience each phenomenon before it occurs at 0° longitude. The GMT of moonrise and moonset in *east* longitude is found by interpolating between the tabulated time for the given day, and the tabulated time for the *preceding* day. For *west* longitude the reverse holds true, and the GMT at a given meridian in west longitude is found by interpolating between the tabulated time for the given day, and the tabulated time for the *following* day. (It is for this reason that the *Nautical Almanac* shows moonrise and moonset times for *four* days, the three days of the daily page plus the next day.)

However, before interpolating for longitude, the times of the required phenomenon on the two days involved must first be interpolated for the required latitude using Table I, Figure 2712b. The interpolating for longitude is then made using Table II of the "Tables for Interpolating Sunrise, Moonrise, Etc." An extract from this table is shown in the lower part of Figure 2712b. GMT is converted to ZT in the usual manner.

Sample problem, moonset

Example: Find the ZT of moonset on 5 June 1977 at Lat. 41°12.4′ N, Long. 15°17.1′ W using the *Nautical Almanac* (Figures 2712a and b).

Solution: Enter the appropriate daily page of the *Nautical Almanac* and extract and record, for the next smaller tabulated latitude, the LMT of the phenomenon at the Greenwich meridian on the given date. In this case the LMT at Greenwich, tabulated for Lat. 40° N is 0833 on 5 June. Then extract the equivalent time on the *preceding day if in east longitude,* or on the *following day if in west longitude.* In this example, the LMT at Greenwich, again using 40° N, is 0940 on 6 June, the later day being taken since the position for which information is desired is in west longitude. Then determine the interval between tabulated values of latitude on either side of the one for which information is desired, and the time difference and its sign between the tabulated LMT at each of these latitudes for each of the two days involved. In this case the tabular interval for both days is 5° and the difference in time is -11^m on 5 June and -8^m on 6 June. Next enter Table I and obtain the correction for latitude to the tabulated LMT at the longitude of Greenwich. The correction is -2^m on 5 June, and -2^m on 6 June. Then apply these corrections to the lesser tabulated latitude (40°), thus completing interpolation to the nearest minute of time for the exact latitude on each day. In this case, the LMT at the longitude of Greenwich at Lat. 41°12.4′ N is 0831 on 5 June and 0938 on 6 June.

To interpolate for longitude, enter Table II with the longitude (east or west) in the left-hand column, and the difference between the LMT at each date in the line at the top of the table. In this case the longitude is approximately 15° and the time difference is 1^h07^m (0938 − 0831). Then obtain the correction from the table, using eye interpolation as necessary. In this case the correction to the nearest minute is 3^m. Apply the correction to the LMT of the phenomenon on the date for which the information is desired, in such a way that the time arrived at falls between the LMT at Greenwich on the two dates in question. In most cases this will mean that the correction is added if the longitude is west, and subtracted if it is east. In this case, the correction is added, making the LMT of moonset at the observer's meridian 0834 (since 0831 + 3 = 0834) on 5 June. Finally, convert this LMT to ZT; 0834 + 1^m (correction for 0°17.1′ of longitude west of zone central meridian) = 0835.

Moonset

N 40°	0833	5 June
N 45°	0822	
Diff for 5°	− 11	
Table I Lat. Corr.	− 2	
LMT(G) 0833 − 2 =	0831	5 June
N 40°	0940	6 June
N 45°	0932	
Diff for 5°	− 8	
Table I Lat. Corr.	− 2	
LMT(G) 0940 − 2 =	0938	6 June
LMT(G)	0831	5 June
Diff between days	1 07	
LMT(G)	0831	5 June
Table II Corr.	+ 3	
LMT(L)	0834	5 June
dLo Corr.	+ 1	
ZT	0835	5 June

Answer: The ZT of moonset is 0835.

The procedure for obtaining the time of moonrise from the *Nautical Almanac* is the same as explained above for moonset.

Calculations for the local times of moonrise and moonset can also be done using the *Air Almanac.* On each daily page there are data for the 0° longitude occurrence at various latitudes, plus a column headed "Diff." which gives the half-way difference in order to correct for a longitude other than Greenwich. The correction to be applied to the tabulated GMT of moonrise or moonset is given in the table F4 on the flap headed "Interpolation of Moonrise, Moonset for Longitude" (Figure 2714). This table is entered with Diff. and longitude, and the correction, selected without interpolation, is applied with the sign indicated. This correction cannot be made in extreme conditions, when a symbol (*) is shown in the Diff. column.

Example: Find the ZT of moonset at Lat. 41°12′ N, Long. 15°17′ W using the *Air Almanac* (Figures 2712c and 2714).

F4 INTERPOLATION OF MOONRISE, MOONSET

FOR LONGITUDE

Add if longitude *west*
Subtract if longitude *east*

Longi-tude	Diff.*					
	05	10	15	20	25	30
°	m	m	m	m	m	m
0	00	00	00	00	00	00
20	01	01	02	02	03	03
40	01	02	03	04	06	07
60	02	03	05	07	08	10
80	02	04	07	09	11	13
100	03	06	08	11	14	17
120	03	07	10	13	17	20
140	04	08	12	16	19	23
160	04	09	13	18	22	27
180	05	10	15	20	25	30

Figure 2714. *Air Almanac,* Table F4 for interpolating time of moonrise and moonset (extract).

Solution: Using the exact date and interpolating for latitude, the time is found to be 0830 and the difference 34 minutes. Using the nearest Table F4 arguments, Long. 20°, difference 30^m, a correction of 3^m is found. As the difference is positive and the longitude is west, the correction is additive; the LMT is 0830 + 3 = 0833. The ZT is 0833 + 1 (for longitude 17′ west of central meridian) = 0834.

Answer: ZT of moonset is 0834.

Note that this differs from the time found from the *Nautical Almanac* by one minute; the difference is of no practical significance.

The moon appears to make a revolution about the earth in a period averaging 24h 50m; that is to say that moonrise and moonset occur, *on the average,* about fifty minutes later on successive days. However, any given period may vary considerably from the average, and under certain conditions moonrise may occur twice during a single day, or may not occur at all. If moonrise occurs twice on the same day, both times are tabulated in the *Nautical Almanac* and *Air Almanac;* for example, 0002/2355. If moonrise does not occur before midnight of a day, it may be tabulated for that day, but, for example, as 2413. This means that moonrise at the tabulated latitude will not occur at all on the stated day, but at 0013 on the next day. As discussed in Article 1814, the phenomenon can occur earlier on successive days. Considerable care must be exercised in interpolation.

Determining the times of phenomena aboard a moving ship

2715 In the preceding articles, the methods of obtaining the times of these phenomena at a fixed position have been discussed. Usually, the navigator must determine these times aboard a moving ship.

To obtain the required time, he first examines his DR track in conjunction with the latitudes and GMT tabulated for the desired phenomenon in the *Nautical Almanac.* He selects the tabulated latitude nearest his DR position for the approximate time of the phenomenon and notes the tabulated GMT. This GMT he treats as his ZT (i.e. GMT 1144 he writes as ZT 1144), and determines the DR position for this ZT. Since LMT and ZT seldom differ by more than 30 minutes this method is sufficiently accurate for the initial DR. Using the latitude and longitude thus found, he determines the ZT of the phenomenon for this position, as described in the preceding articles. This is his *first estimate.*

The navigator next determines a new DR position for the ZT of the first estimate, and calculates the time of the phenomenon for this new position, interpolating for date, latitude, and longitude as may be necessary; this is the *second estimate.*

Ordinarily, this second estimate will give an acceptably accurate time for the phenomenon. However, if the two DR positions should prove to differ considerably in longitude, a new determination of the first estimate should be made.

Usually at sea, the maximum obtainable precision is required only for the time of sunrise and sunset; ordinarily, 2 or 3 minutes leeway are permissible in predicting the times of the other phenomena. The "Tables for Interpolating Sunrise, Moonrise, Etc." in the back of the *Nautical Almanac* are used, and longitude to the nearest 15′ may be used in converting to time, i.e., to the nearest minute.

Example: On 5 June 1977, the 1600 DR position of a ship is Lat. 33°23.3′ N, Long. 65°19.4′ W. The vessel is on course 255°, speed 20 knots.

Required: The ZT of sunset to the nearest whole number, using the *Nautical Almanac* (Figure 2712a and b).

Solution: (Figure 2715). By examination of the DR plot and the almanac, the navigator notes that in the band of latitude between 30° N and 35° N, sunset will occur at some time after 1858. At that time, the tabulated latitude nearest to his DR is 35° N. He notes that for this latitude sunset occurs at 1910; he also notes that for latitude 30° N, sunset occurs at 1858, or 12 minutes earlier.

He next plots his expected DR position for 1910; this turns out to be Lat. 33°06.9′ N, Long. 66°32.6′ W.

Using this DR position, he computes the time of sunset by entering the table on the daily page for latitude 30° and extracting the time of 1858. The latitude correction from Table I is + 8^m and the correction for difference in longitude between the DR and the central meridian of the time zone is +26 minutes (dLo of 6°32.6′). Adding 1858 + 8 + 26 results in a ZT of 1932 as the *first estimate.*

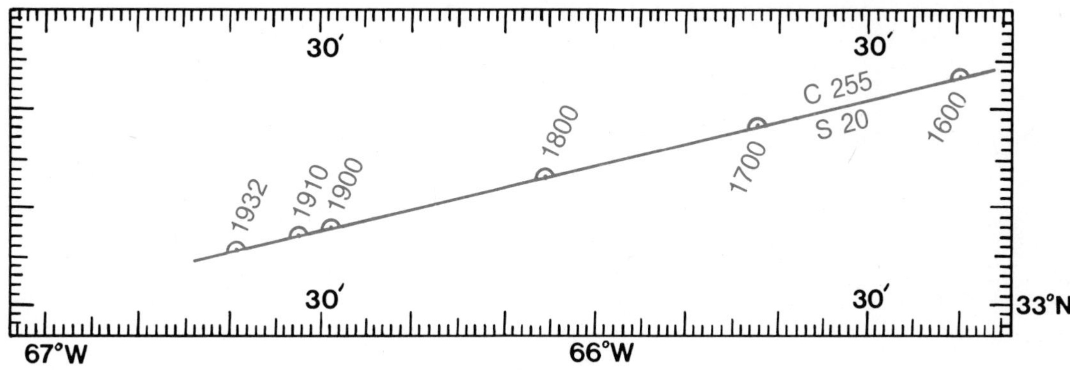

Figure 2715. Plot for determination of ZT of sunset for a moving vessel.

He plots the 1931 DR position, finding it to be Lat. 33°05.0′ N., Long. 66°41.0′ W; now the difference in longitude from the central meridian (computed to the nearest 15′ of arc) is 6°45′, resulting in a recomputed value for dLo correction of +27 minutes. The ZT is adjusted for this additional minute and 1933 is the *second estimate*.

Answer: ZT of sunset is 1933.

1910 DR Lat. 33°06.9′ N
Long. 66°32.6′ W

Sunset

N30°	1858	
N 35°	1910	
Diff for 5°	+ 12	
Table I Lat. Corr.	+ 7	
LMT = 1858 + 8 =	1906	
dLo Corr.	+ 26	
ZT	1931	1st Est.
LMT	1906	
dLo Corr.	+ 27	
ZT	1933	2nd Est.

Problems involving the times of sunrise, moonrise, moonset, and twilight for a moving ship are solved in a similar manner.

Finding the time of moonset on a moving ship

2716 Moonrise or moonset would be determined aboard ship by combining the method set forth in Article 2714 with the above. The following example illustrates the solution.

Example: (Figure 2716). On the evening of 5 June 1977, a ship's 2000 DR position is Lat. 16°52.6′ N, Long. 62°19.4′ W. The course is 063°, speed 20 knots.

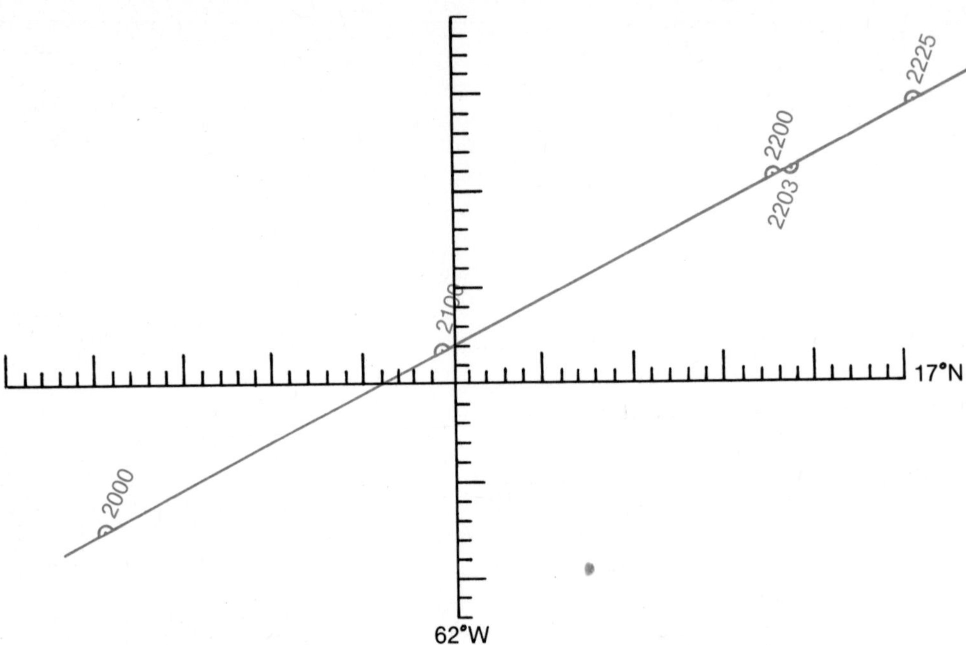

Figure 2716. Plot for determination of ZT of moonrise for a moving vessel.

Required: The ZT of moonrise on the night of 5–6 June, using the *Nautical Almanac* (Figures 2712a and b).

Solution: (Figure 2716). An inspection of the moonrise tables for 5 and 6 June, latitudes 10° N and 20° N, shows that the time of moonrise will be approximately 2230, 5 June. For latitude 10° N and longitude 0°, the time of moonrise will be 2203. The DR position for this time is plotted and found to be Lat. 17°11.2′ N, Long. 61°41.2′ W. Next the time of moonrise for this position is calculated as the first estimate; this is 2225. The ship's DR position for the time of the first estimate is plotted and found to be Lat. 17°14.5′ N, Long. 61°34.4′ W. The time of moonrise is recalculated for this revised DR position using the same procedures as in obtaining the first estimate; this gives the second estimate of moonrise, 2224.

Answer: The ZT of moonrise is 2224.

Moonrise

Calculations of first estimate: Lat. 17°11.2′ N., Long. 61°41.2′ W.

20° N.	2213	5 June
10° N.	2203	
Diff for 10°	+ 10	
Table I Lat. Corr.	+ 7	
2203 + 7 =	2210	LMT, Long. 0°

20° N.	2259	6 June
10° N.	2252	
Diff for 10°	+ 7	
Table I Lat. Corr.	+ 5	
2252 + 5 =	2257	LMT, Long. 0°
	2210	
	+ 47	

LMT (Long. 0°)	2210	5 June
Table II Long. Corr.	+ 8	
LMT (Ship)	2218	
dLo (1°41.2′ W)	+ 7	
ZT	2225	1st Estimate

Calculation for second estimate: Lat. 17°14.5′ N., Long. 61°34.4′ W.

10° N.	2203	5 June
Table I Lat. Corr.	+ 7	
	2210	LMT, Long. 0°

10° N.	2252	6 June
Table I Lat. Corr.	+ 5	
	2257	LMT, Long. 0°
	2210	
	+ 47	

LMT (Long. 0°)	2210	5 June
Table II Long. Corr.	+ 8	
LMT (Ship)	2218	
dLo (1°34.4′ W)	+ 6	
ZT	2224	2nd Estimate

Summary **2717** The GMTs of various phenomena at specified latitudes along the Greenwich meridian are tabulated on the daily pages of the *Nautical Almanac* (and in the *Air Almanac* in a somewhat different format). For the sun phenomena, these values of GMT are almost exactly equal to the ZT along the standard meridian of each time zone, as the rotation of the earth causes the sun to appear to move westward at the rate of 15° per hour and the standard meridians of the time zones are established at 15° intervals. The navigator first determines the GMT of the desired phenomenon for the required latitude along the meridian of Greenwich and applies the difference in longitude—converted to time—between his position and the standard meridian to obtain the Zone Time.

For moonrise and moonset, the tabulated LMT must be interpolated for both latitude and longitude to obtain the LMT at the required position; it is then converted to ZT.

To find the time of these phenomena for a moving ship, the DR latitude is first determined for the approximate expected time of the required phenomenon. The tabulated latitude nearest to the DR latitude is located in the *Nautical Almanac* and the tabulated time is used to establish a DR position for that time. A *first estimate* of the time of the phenomenon is then computed from the tables. Using the ZT thus obtained, a new DR position is plotted, and the time is corrected for the difference between the first and second DR positions; this is the *second estimate,* the time used by the navigator for the phenomenon concerned.

A useful procedure is to determine for morning and evening twilight those stars that will transit the observer's meridian in the time period during which sights can be taken.

28 Compass Error at Sea

Introduction **2801** A prudent navigator, when underway and weather conditions permit, checks the error of his compass once each day; for U.S. naval vessels, regulations require that this be done. Good practice, however, calls for a compass check at least twice a day, whenever possible. A check should be made immediately if there is any reason to suppose that a compass has been damaged, or is malfunctioning. Thus far, the celestial navigation portion of this book has been concerned with the solution of navigational triangles to obtain LOPs and fix the position of the vessel. It is frequently necessary, however, for a navigator to solve navigational triangles for other purposes. This chapter will consider the solution of a navigational triangle to determine true azimuth, and from this, the compass error at sea.

Compass error at sea is determined by azimuth observations of celestial bodies; the sun is the body most frequently observed. Such observations should be made when the sun is low in altitude, preferably under 20°. All navigators and their assistants should be trained to obtain accurate azimuth observations, and make the necessary calculations.

Azimuth observations **2802** Azimuth observations of celestial bodies are made using an *azimuth circle,* bearing circle, or similar device. An azimuth circle (Figure 704) is an instrument whose principal components are a small, hinged, concave mirror and a shielded prism which is located on the ring opposite the mirror. When the instrument is used to observe the sun's azimuth, the azimuth circle is fitted over a gyrocompass repeater, or the bowl of a magnetic compass, and aligned so that the prism is directly between the mirror and the sun. When the hinged mirror is properly adjusted in the plane of the vertical circle of the sun, a thin, vertical beam of sunlight is cast upon a slit in the prism shield and refracted downward onto the compass card. The line of sunlight on the card indicates the compass azimuth of the sun at that time. Two leveling bubbles are provided with the azimuth circle, as the instrument must be horizontal to indicate an accurate compass azimuth.

An azimuth observation of a star or planet is made using the sight vanes of an azimuth circle or bearing circle, in a manner similar to that used for observing terrestrial bearings (Article 704). The moon may be observed for azimuth using either the mirror-prism method or the sight vane method. Because of the difficulty in seeing the leveling bubbles during darkness, azimuth observations are usually restricted to the sun. A pelorus can also be used to determine the azimuth measurements.

In practice, the navigator observes the azimuth of a celestial body and notes the time of the observation. He then solves the navigational triangle for his position, and determines the true azimuth of the body at the time of the observation. The difference between the true and observed azimuths, properly labeled E or W, is the compass error.

In general, the lower the celestial body, the more accurate the azimuth observations. For most practical purposes an accuracy to the nearest one-half degree is normally sufficient.

Exact azimuth by inspection tables

2803 The inspection tables for sight reduction, Pub. No. 229, make excellent azimuth tables. (Pub. No. 249 tables cannot be used for obtaining exact azimuths as tabulations are only to the nearest whole degree.)

When Pub. No. 229 is used to determine true azimuth for the purpose of checking the compass, triple linear interpolation usually must be made in order to obtain the required accuracy. The *d* values in Pub. No. 229 apply only to *altitude,* and should not be used when interpolating for azimuth.

Example: The azimuth of the sun is observed at 06–25–42 on 5 June 1977. The 0625 position has been fixed at Lat. 41°06.1′ N, Long. 15°03.1′ W. The azimuth obtained by using a gyro repeater is 076.0°.

Required: Gyro error, using Pub. No. 229 to obtain exact true azimuth.

Solution: (Figure 2803). It is first necessary to determine the exact values of LHA, Dec., and L for the instant of observation of the azimuth. These values are determined as for working a sight, except that the *actual* position of the ship is used rather than an assumed position. Thus the DR longitude, 15°03.1′ W, is used to determine the exact value of LHA at the time of observation. The exact value of Dec. is found to be N22°32.5′ by use of the *Nautical Almanac* in the usual manner. The DR latitude is taken as the exact value of L at the time of observation. (If a fix obtained from observations and complete reductions at about this time shows the DR position to be significantly in error, the more accurate values of Lat. and Long. of the fix can be used.)

With the exact values of LHA, Dec., and L determined, the appropriate page of Pub. No. 229 is entered for the "tab" values, those tabulated entering arguments *nearest* to the exact values. In this case, they are LHA 277, Dec. N 23°, and L 41° N. With these "tab" values as entering arguments, the proper page (the "same name" section in this case) is entered and the tabulated azimuth angle, Z, 76.4° is recorded. This value of Z is the *tabulated* ("tab") value, to which the corrections resulting from the necessary interpolation are applied to obtain the

EXACT AZIMUTH USING Pub. 229

Body	☉	
DR L	41°	06.1′ N
DR λ	15°	03.1′ W
Date (L)	5 JUN 77	
ZT	06 - 25 - 42	
ZD (+ or -)	+1	
GMT	07 - 25 - 42	
Date (G)	5 JUN 77	
Tab GHA	285°	24.7′
Inc'mt	6°	25.5′
GHA	291°	50.2′
DR λ	- 15°	03.1′ W
LHA	276°	47.1
		d(+/-)
Tab Dec	N22° 32.4′	+ 0.2′
d corr	+ 0.1′	
Dec	N22° 32.5′	

	EXACT Deg	EXACT Min	Z DIFF. (+ or -)	CORR. (+ or -)
LAT	41	06.1	+ 0.3	0.0
LHA	276	47.1	-0.6	-0.1
DEC	22	32.5	+0.8	+ 0.4
			Total (±)	+0.3
			Tab Z	76.4
			Exact Z	76.7
			Exact Zn	076.7
			Gyro/Compass Brg	076.0
			Gyro/Compass Error	0.7 E

NORTH LAT

LHA greater than 180° .... Zn = Z
LHA less than 180° .... Zn = 360° - Z

SOUTH LAT

LHA greater than 180° .... Zn = 180° - Z
LHA less than 180° .... Zn = 180° + Z

Figure 2803. Determination of exact azimuth and gyro error using Pub. No. 229.

azimuth angle for the exact values of LHA, Dec., and L at the moment of observation. Interpolation is made separately for the difference between each of the exact values and the corresponding "tab" values of LHA, Dec., and L; and the algebraic sum of the resulting corrections is applied to the value of tab Z to obtain the exact azimuth angle at the moment of observation. It is normally considered sufficiently accurate to reduce these corrections to the nearest tenth of a degree.

An interpolation is made between LHA 277° (Z 76.4°) and LHA 276° (Z 75.8°). The change in Z is −0.6° for a change in LHA of 1° (60′); this is known as the "Z diff." Since the exact value of LHA is 276°47.1′, or 12.9′ less than the "tab" value of LHA, the difference in the value of Z corresponding to this difference in LHA is $\frac{12.9'}{60'}$ of the difference for a 1° change in LHA. Thus the "corr," which is the correction to apply to the value of tab Z because of the difference between the exact value of LHA and the tab value, is equal to $-0.6° \times \frac{12.9'}{60}$ or −0.1°.

An interpolation for declination is made between 23° (Z 76.4°) and 22° (Z 77.2°) in the same manner as above: 77.2° − 76.4° = +0.8° (Z diff); the exact declination is 60′ − 32.5′ = 27.5′ less than the tab declination of 23°; the correction is $+0.8° \times \frac{27.5}{60} = +0.4°$.

A similar interpolation is made for latitude between 41° (Z 76.4°) and 42° (Z 76.7°): 76.7° − 76.4° = +0.3°; the exact latitude is 6.0′ greater than the tab latitude of 41°; the correction is $+0.3° \times \frac{6.0}{60} =$ 0.0°.

By applying the algebraic sum of the LHA, Dec., and L corrections, as determined above, to the tab Z, the exact azimuth angle at the moment of observation is found to be N 76.7° E, which converts to a Zn of 076.7°. The gyro error is found by comparing this exact azimuth with that obtained by observation, 076.0°. Thus 076.7 minus 076.0 equals 0.7°; as the compass is "least" (lesser in value than the true value), the error is "east."

Answer: Gyro error is 0.7° E.

Note that although exact azimuth is calculated to the nearest tenth of a degree, the gyro repeater used for taking the bearing is calculated only to whole degrees; and readings are not possible to a greater precision than a half-degree, or perhaps a quarter-degree. Thus, gyro error in the above example should more properly be stated as 0.5° E.

In solving problems for exact azimuth using Pub. No. 229, the multiplication of the fractional amount by the amount of the "diff" to obtain the appropriate correction can be accomplished readily by establishing a proportion with dividers on a log scale of speed or distance, such as is found on some charts and on Maneuvering Board paper, and is discussed briefly in Article 1404. In establishing the fractions involved, it is well to remember that the denominator of the fractional part of LHA, Dec., and L is always 60′, since the tabulated entering arguments of LHA, Dec., and L are always 1° apart.

Azimuth by other tabular methods

2804 Exact azimuths may also be calculated using the now-obsolete publications H.O. 214, H.O. 211, H.O. 208, or by the use of various other tables, such as the Weems *Line of Position Book.* As with the inspection tables, these methods permit simultaneous solution for both azimuth and altitude.

Other tables that may be used to obtain a true value of azimuth are DMAHC Pub. No. 260, *Azimuths of the Sun and Other Celestial Bodies of Declination 0° to 23°,* and Pub. No. 261, *Azimuth of Celestial Bodies, Declination 24° to 70°.* Pub. No. 260, popularly known as the "Red Azimuth Tables" because of the color of the binding used for most printings, and Pub. No. 261, called the "Blue Azimuth Tables" for the same reason, contain tabulations of azimuth to the nearest *minute* of arc for every ten minutes of time. Present shipboard equipment does not provide azimuth readings of such a high degree of precision, nor is such precision needed for practical navigation. Instructions for the use of the azimuth tables are contained in each of these publications.

Azimuth by amplitude

2805 When using an azimuth to check a compass, a low altitude is most desirable, as it is both easy to observe and gives the most accurate results. An *amplitude* observation is one made when the center of the observed body is either on the *celestial* or *visible horizon,* i.e., it is in the act of rising or setting. In the latter case a correction is applied to the observation in order to obtain the corresponding amplitude when the center of the body is on the celestial horizon. The sun is the body most frequently observed in obtaining an amplitude. However, the moon, a planet, or a bright star having a declination not exceeding 24° may also be used. Amplitudes should be avoided in high latitudes.

Amplitude may be defined as angular distance measured N or S from the prime vertical to the body on the celestial horizon. It is given the prefix E (east) if the body is rising, and W (west) if it is setting; the suffix is N if the body rises or sets north of the prime vertical, as it does with a northerly declination, and S if it rises or sets south of the prime vertical, having a southerly declination.

If a body is observed when its center is on the celestial horizon, the amplitude may be taken directly from Table 27 in *Bowditch* (Figure 2805a).

When observing amplitudes with a height of eye typical of ships' bridges, two assumptions can be made that will yield results sufficiently accurate for practical purposes. The first is that when the *sun's lower limb* is about two-thirds of a diameter above the *visible* horizon, its center is on the *celestial* horizon. The second is that when the *moon's upper limb* is on the visible horizon, its center is on the *celestial* horizon. This apparent anomaly is due to the sun's parallax being very small (0.1′) as compared to the refraction, which at this altitude amounts to about 34.5′, whereas the moon parallax is large (between 54.0′ and 61.5′, depending on the date), while the refraction is about 34.5′

When planets or stars are on the celestial horizon, they are about one *sun* diameter, or some 32.0′ above the visible horizon.

TABLE 27
Amplitudes

Latitude	Declination													Latitude
	18°0	18°5	19°0	19°5	20°0	20°5	21°0	21°5	22°0	22°5	23°0	23°5	24°0	
°	°	°	°	°	°	°	°	°	°	°	°	°	°	°
0	18. 0	18. 5	19. 0	19. 5	20. 0	20. 5	21. 0	21. 5	22. 0	22. 5	23. 0	23. 5	24. 0	0
10	18. 3	18. 8	19. 3	19. 8	20. 3	20. 8	21. 3	21. 8	22. 4	22. 9	23. 4	23. 9	24. 4	10
15	18. 7	19. 2	19. 7	20. 2	20. 7	21. 3	21. 8	22. 3	22. 8	23. 3	23. 9	24. 4	24. 9	15
20	19. 2	19. 7	20. 3	20. 8	21. 3	21. 9	22. 4	23. 0	23. 5	24. 0	24. 6	25. 1	25. 6	20
25	19. 9	20. 5	21. 1	21. 6	22. 2	22. 7	23. 3	23. 9	24. 4	25. 0	25. 5	26. 1	26. 7	25
30	20. 9	21. 5	22. 1	22. 7	23. 3	23. 9	24. 4	25. 0	25. 6	26. 2	26. 8	27. 4	28. 0	30
32	21. 4	22. 0	22. 6	23. 2	23. 8	24. 4	25. 0	25. 6	26. 2	26. 8	27. 4	28. 0	28. 7	32
34	21. 9	22. 5	23. 1	23. 7	24. 4	25. 0	25. 6	26. 2	26. 9	27. 5	28. 1	28. 7	29. 4	34
36	22. 5	23. 1	23. 7	24. 4	25. 0	25. 7	26. 3	26. 9	27. 6	28. 2	28. 9	29. 5	30. 2	36
38	23. 1	23. 7	24. 4	25. 1	25. 7	26. 4	27. 1	27. 7	28. 4	29. 1	29. 7	30. 4	31. 1	38
40	23. 8	24. 5	25. 2	25. 8	26. 5	27. 2	27. 9	28. 6	29. 3	30. 0	30. 7	31. 4	32. 1	40
41	24. 2	24. 9	25. 6	26. 3	26. 9	27. 6	28. 3	29. 1	29. 8	30. 5	31. 2	31. 9	32. 6	41
42	24. 6	25. 3	26. 0	26. 7	27. 4	28. 1	28. 8	29. 5	30. 3	31. 0	31. 7	32. 5	33. 2	42
43	25. 0	25. 7	26. 4	27. 2	27. 9	28. 6	29. 3	30. 1	30. 8	31. 6	32. 3	33. 0	33. 8	43
44	25. 4	26. 2	26. 9	27. 6	28. 4	29. 1	29. 9	30. 6	31. 4	32. 1	32. 9	33. 7	34. 4	44

Figure 2805a. Table 27, Amplitudes, from *Bowditch,* Volume II.

If a body is observed on the *visible* horizon, the *observed* value is corrected by a value taken from *Bowditch* Table 28 (Figure 2805b), according to the rule: For the *sun,* a *planet*, or a *star* apply the correction to the observed amplitude in the direction away from the elevated pole thus increasing the azimuth angle; for the *moon*, apply *half* the correction *toward* the elevated pole. The entering arguments for both tables are latitude and declination (Table 28 was computed for a height of eye of 41 feet (12.5 m) but may be used for other values without significant error.)

If desired, the correction can be applied with reversed sign to the value taken from Table 27, for comparison with the uncorrected observed value. This is the procedure used if amplitude or azimuth is desired when the celestial body is on the visible horizon.

Example: The DR latitude of a ship is 41°03.8′ N when the declination of the sun is N 22°31.9′. The sun, when centered on the visible horizon, bears 059.5 by gyro, giving a compass amplitude of E 30.5° N.

Required: The gyro error.

Solution: By interpolation in Tables 27 and 28 (Figures 2805a and 2805b).

True amplitude	E 30.5° N	(Table 27)
Correction	– 0.7°	(Table 28, sign
	E 29.8° N	reversed)
Zn	60.2°	
Compass	59.5°	
Error	0.7° E	

Answer: Gyro error is 0.7° E; or in more realistic terms 0.5° E since, as noted above, observations will be possible only to nearest half-degree.

TABLE 28

Correction of Amplitude as Observed on the Visible Horizon

Latitude	Declination 0°	2°	4°	6°	8°	10°	12°	14°	16°	18°	20°	22°	24°	Latitude
°	°	°	°	°	°	°	°	°	°	°	°	°	°	°
0	0. 0	0. 0	0. 0	0. 0	0. 0	0. 0	0. 0	0. 0	0. 0	0. 0	0. 0	0. 0	0. 0	0
10	0. 1	0. 1	0. 1	0. 1	0. 1	0. 1	0. 1	0. 1	0. 1	0. 1	0. 1	0. 1	0. 1	10
15	0. 2	0. 2	0. 2	0. 2	0. 2	0. 2	0. 2	0. 2	0. 2	0. 2	0. 2	0. 2	0. 2	15
20	0. 3	0. 3	0. 3	0. 3	0. 3	0. 3	0. 3	0. 3	0. 3	0. 3	0. 3	0. 3	0. 3	20
25	0. 3	0. 3	0. 3	0. 3	0. 3	0. 4	0. 3	0. 3	0. 3	0. 3	0. 3	0. 3	0. 3	25
30	0. 4	0. 4	0. 4	0. 4	0. 5	0. 4	0. 4	0. 4	0. 4	0. 4	0. 4	0. 5	0. 5	30
32	0. 4	0. 4	0. 4	0. 4	0. 5	0. 4	0. 4	0. 4	0. 4	0. 4	0. 5	0. 5	0. 5	32
34	0. 5	0. 5	0. 5	0. 5	0. 5	0. 5	0. 5	0. 5	0. 5	0. 5	0. 5	0. 5	0. 5	34
36	0. 5	0. 5	0. 5	0. 5	0. 5	0. 5	0. 5	0. 5	0. 6	0. 5	0. 6	0. 6	0. 6	36
38	0. 6	0. 6	0. 6	0. 6	0. 6	0. 6	0. 6	0. 6	0. 6	0. 6	0. 6	0. 6	0. 6	38
40	0. 6	0. 6	0. 6	0. 6	0. 6	0. 6	0. 6	0. 6	0. 6	0. 6	0. 7	0. 7	0. 7	40
42	0. 6	0. 6	0. 6	0. 6	0. 7	0. 7	0. 7	0. 7	0. 7	0. 7	0. 7	0. 7	0. 7	42
44	0. 7	0. 7	0. 7	0. 6	0. 6	0. 7	0. 7	0. 7	0. 8	0. 8	0. 8	0. 8	0. 9	44
46	0. 7	0. 7	0. 7	0. 7	0. 7	0. 8	0. 8	0. 8	0. 8	0. 8	0. 8	0. 9	0. 9	46
48	0. 8	0. 8	0. 8	0. 8	0. 8	0. 8	0. 8	0. 8	0. 9	0. 9	1. 0	1. 0	1. 0	48

Figure 2805b. Table 28, Correction of Amplitudes as Observed on the Visible Horizon from *Bowditch,* Volume II.

A personal electronic calculator can be used instead of the *Bowditch* tables. If the observation is made when the center of the body is on the celestial horizon using the procedures given above for the sun and moon (no Table 28 correction required), true amplitude (A) can be found from the equation

$$A = \sin^{-1}\left(\frac{\sin d}{\cos L}\right)$$

If the body is observed when its center is on the visible horizon, the equation is

$$A = \sin^{-1}\left(\frac{\sin d - \sin L \sin 0.7^\circ}{\cos L \cos 0.7^\circ}\right)$$

where -0.7° is the value for the altitude of the body used in the preparation of Table 28.

Azimuth by Polaris

2806 The true azimuth of Polaris is tabulated in the *Nautical Almanac* for northern latitudes up to 65°. Polaris, the "north star," is always within about 2° of true north in these latitudes, and observations of it provide a convenient means of checking the compass, with little interpolation needed. An extract from the *Nautical Almanac* Polaris azimuth table, which appears in the almanac at the foot of the Polaris latitude tables, is shown in Fig. 2806.

The entering arguments in the *Nautical Almanac* azimuth table for Polaris are: (1) LHA of Aries and (2) latitude (at intervals of 5°, 10°, or 20°). Eye interpolation is made if necessary.

Example: The navigator of a ship at Lat. 41°39.2′ N, Long. 17°07.6′ W observes Polaris when the GHA is 210°25.3′. The observed azimuth by gyro repeater (GB) is 359.0°.

Required: Gyro error by Polaris, using *Nautical Almanac* Polaris Table.

POLARIS (POLE STAR) TABLES, 1977
FOR DETERMINING LATITUDE FROM SEXTANT ALTITUDE AND FOR AZIMUTH

L.H.A. ARIES	120°–129°	130°–139°	140°–149°	150°–159°	160°–169°	170°–179°	180°–189°	190°–199°	200°–209°	210°–219°	220°–229°	230°–239°
Lat.	AZIMUTH											
°	°	°	°	°	°	°	°	°	°	°	°	°
0	359·2	359·2	359·2	359·3	359·4	359·5	359·6	359·7	359·9	0·0	0·2	0·3
20	359·1	359·1	359·2	359·2	359·3	359·5	359·6	359·7	359·9	0·0	0·2	0·3
40	358·9	358·9	359·0	359·1	359·2	359·3	359·5	359·7	359·9	0·0	0·2	0·4
50	358·7	358·7	358·8	358·9	359·0	359·2	359·4	359·6	359·8	0·1	0·3	0·5
55	358·5	358·6	358·7	358·8	358·9	359·1	359·3	359·6	359·8	0·1	0·3	0·5
60	358·3	358·4	358·5	358·6	358·8	359·0	359·2	359·5	359·8	0·1	0·4	0·6
65	358·0	358·1	358·2	358·4	358·6	358·8	359·1	359·4	359·7	0·1	0·4	0·7

Figure 2806: Polaris azimuth table from *Nautical Almanac* (extract).

Solution: Using the exact DR longitude (note that an assumed position is *not* used), determine the LHA ♈ for the time of observation. Turn to the three pages of Polaris Tables located just forward of the yellow pages, toward the back of the *Nautical Almanac,* and locate the column heading encompassing the computed value of LHA ♈. In this case it occurs on the second page of Polaris tables, an extract of which is given in Figure 2806. (In this figure the azimuth tables appear directly below the columnar headings, whereas the azimuth portion of the tables is actually at the extreme bottom of the table.) Using the column with a heading of LHA ♈ 190°–199° follow down the column to the appropriate latitude. Using interpolation by eye for latitude, the value of 359.7° is found; this is the true azimuth of Polaris. The gyro error is determined by comparing this with the azimuth observed using the gyro repeater.

DR Lat	41°39.2′ N	
DR Long.	17°07.6′ W	
GHA ♈	210°25.3′	
DR Long.	17°07.6′ W	
LHA ♈	193°17.7′ W	
Zn	359.7°	(from Table)
GB	359.0°	
GE	0.7° E	

Answer: Gyro error 0.7° E. Due to the limitations in the precision with which the compass or a repeater can be read, this would be rounded off to the nearest half-degree, or 0.5° E.

In practice, it is difficult to observe Polaris accurately for azimuth unless the ship is in a lower latitude, due to the difficulty of observing accurate azimuths at higher altitudes; this difficulty is increased if the ship is rolling. However, Polaris serves as a useful check on the compass at any time it can be observed, as an azimuth observation of approximately 000° indicates that the compass is reasonably free of error.

Curve of magnetic azimuths

2807 The deviation of a magnetic compass on various headings is determined by *swinging ship.* During the process of swinging ship at sea, it is desirable to be able to obtain the magnetic azimuth of the sun at any moment, without the delay that would result if it were necessary to select each azimuth by triple interpolation from the tables. For this reason, it is common practice to determine in advance the magnetic azimuths at intervals during the period of swing, and to plot these against time on cross-section paper, fairing a curve through the points. The curve can be constructed by means of azimuths from Pub. No. 229 or from other appropriate tables.

To construct the curve, the navigator first determines the true azimuth for the approximate mid-time of the period during which the ship is to be swung, using the method of Article 2803. During the time devoted to swinging the ship, the latitude and declination remain essentially constant, and the only one of the three entering arguments to change appreciably is meridian angle. Since meridian angle changes at the nearly constant rate of 1° for each four minutes of time, the azimuth at a time four minutes before or after the mid-time of the swing can be obtained by entering Pub. No. 229 with the same values of Dec. and L used previously but with a t value 1° greater or less, and applying the same correction to the tabulated value as that used for the mid-time. In practice, the change in azimuth in four minutes (1° of t) is usually quite small, and sufficient accuracy is obtained by determining the azimuth at intervals of eight minutes (2° of t). Thus, having determined the correction to the tabulated azimuth for the mid-time of the swing, the navigator has only to enter Pub. No. 229 with the same values of declination and latitude, and a meridian angle two degrees greater or less, and apply the previously found correction to the tabulated Z to determine the true Z eight minutes earlier or later. A series of such computations provides values of true azimuth at intervals throughout the swing. By converting these values to magnetic azimuth, the navigator can plot this information on cross-section paper and fair a curve through the points, from which the magnetic azimuth can be taken at any time during the period. The above method will provide acceptable accuracy if the total time period is not overly long or close to the time of LAN. For more accurate results, the determination of a separate correction for each solution is recommended.

Example: A ship is to be swung between 1630 and 1730 ZT to determine magnetic compass deviation. The 1700 DR is Lat. 41°28.3′ N, Long. 16°34.2′ W. At that time the declination of the sun will be N 22°35.4′ and its meridian angle will be 73°49.3′. The variation in the area is 14°32′ W.

ZT	t	Tab	Tab Z	Corr	Z	Zn	Var	Mag Zn
	°	°	°		°	°		°
1628	65.8	66	86.6	↑	N87.3W	272.7	↑	287.7
1636	67.8	68	85.4		86.1	273.9		288.4
1644	69.8	70	84.2		84.9	275.1		289.6
1652	71.8	72	82.9		83.6	276.4		290.9
1700	73.8	74	81.7	+0.7°	82.4	277.6	14.5°W	292.1
1708	75.8	76	80.5		81.2	278.8		293.3
1716	77.8	78	79.3		80.0	280.0		294.5
1724	79.8	80	78.2		78.9	281.1		295.6
1732	81.8	82	77.0	↓	77.7	282.3	↓	296.8

Figure 2807a. Table of magnetic azimuth.

Required: A curve of magnetic azimuths for use during the swing.

Solution: Determine the correction to tabulated azimuth angle and the true azimuth for the mid-time of the swing. The correction to tabulated azimuth angle is +0.7° and the true azimuth is 277.6°. Record this information on the middle line of a form such as Figure 2807a, and then record ZT at eight-minute intervals before and after the mid-time to provide for the full period of the swing. In this case the time range is from 1628 to 1732. Next to each ZT, record t at that time. Since the sun is setting during the period of the swing, t

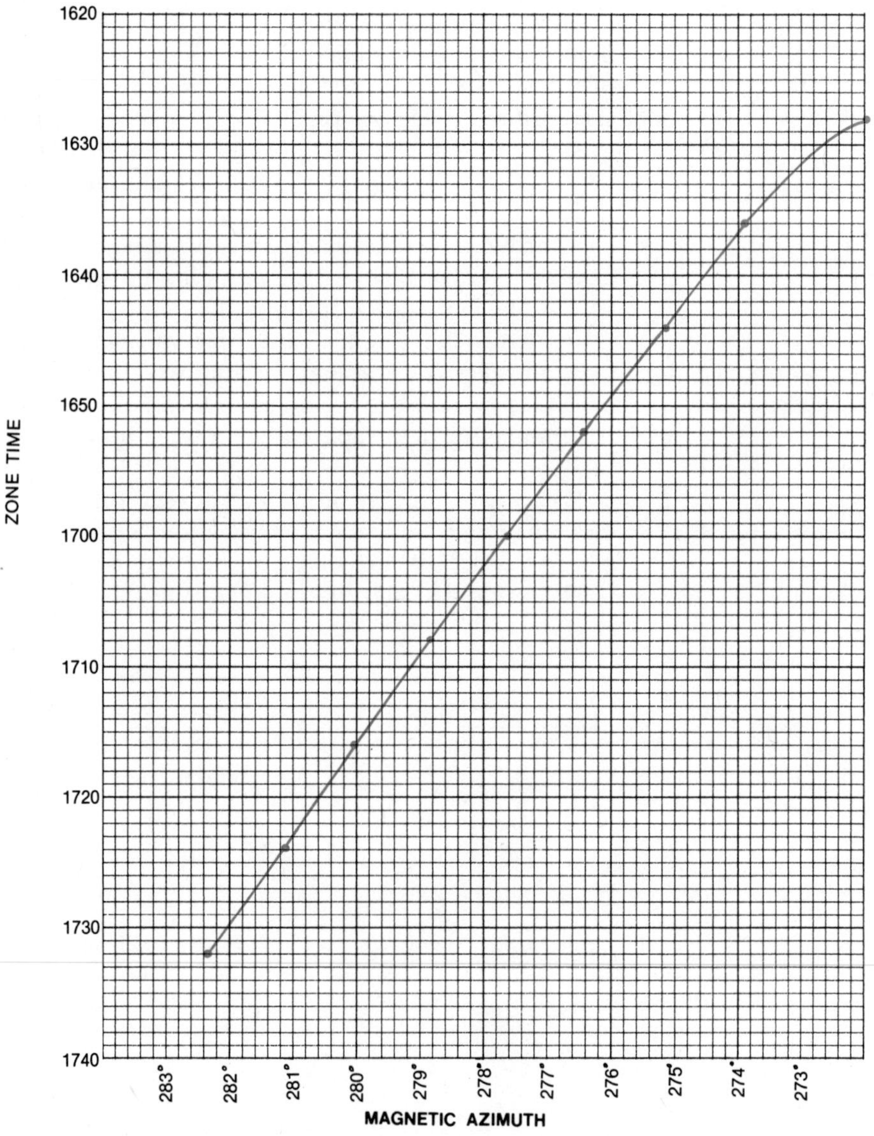

Figure 2807b. A curve of magnetic azimuths.

increases with time in this situation, from 65.8° to 81.8°. Take the nearest whole degree of value, which is the tab LHA value in each case. Then obtain the tabulated Z from Pub. No. 229 for each tab LHA and the constant values of Lat. and Dec. (which are 41° N and N 23°, respectively, in this case), and apply the correction for the mid-time (+ 0.7° in this example) to each tabulated Z to obtain the exact Az for each ZT. Next, convert each Z to Zn and apply the variation for the locality to determine the magnetic azimuth of the sun at each ZT. Finally, plot the magnetic azimuths against zone time on graph paper, as shown in Figure 2807b.

Answer: See Figure 2807b.

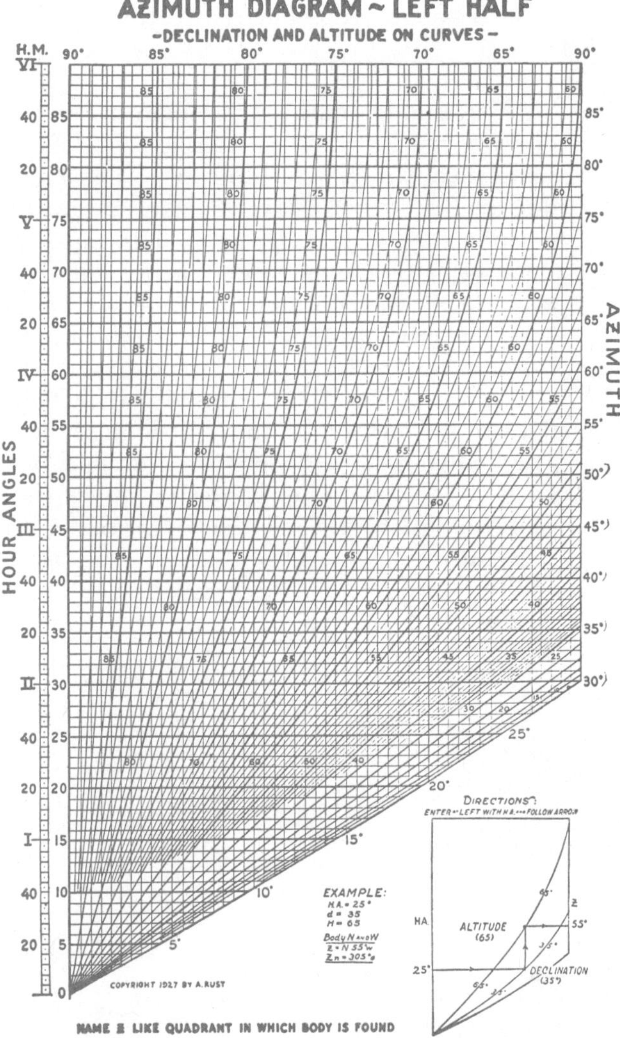

Figure 2808. Armistead Rust azimuth diagram, left half; declination and altitude on curves.

It might be noted here that the above procedure is probably more "academic" than practical as it will seldom be that a ship at sea will have the time to devote to the maneuvers of swinging ship.

For an explanation of the use of magnetic azimuths in obtaining deviations of the magnetic compasses aboard ship, see Article 421.

Azimuths by diagram

2808 Various azimuth diagrams have been produced over the years, to permit a graphic determination of azimuth; the Weir diagram was long used by the Navy.

Currently the most commonly used azimuth diagram is that designed by Armistead Rust, a portion of which is reproduced in Figure 2808. This diagram is included in the Weems *Line of Position Book,* as an alternate to computation for determining azimuth.

Summary

2809 Compass error is determined at sea by observing the azimuth of a celestial body and comparing the observed value with the exact value, as obtained by computation. The azimuth obtained for plotting an LOP is not sufficiently accurate for this purpose, and interpolation must be made for t, Dec., and Lat. to obtain the exact azimuth when using inspection tables such as Pub. No. 229. This is done by triple linear interpolation, with entering arguments to the nearest 0.1°. The exact azimuth of Polaris, which is always close to 000° (for latitudes up to 65° N), can be obtained from tables in the *Nautical Almanac.* In solutions for exact azimuth by Pub. No. 229 or by Polaris, the best estimate of the ship's position is always used rather than an assumed position. A reasonably accurate curve of magnetic azimuths, for use in swinging ship, is conveniently obtained by determining the exact azimuth for the mid-time of the period, and applying a constant correction to the tabulated values for the Dec. and L of the mid-time, and for t values which differ from that of the mid-time by whole numbers of degrees.

29 The Sailings

Introduction **2901** The term *the sailings* refers collectively to various mathematical methods of solving problems involving course, distance, difference of latitude, difference of longitude, and departure. These mathematical solutions were in general use until comparatively recent years due to a lack of adequate chart coverage of much of the world. The modern navigator usually solves these problems by measurement on a chart, as this graphic method provides a rapid solution of practical accuracy. Occasionally, however, it becomes necessary to obtain the solution by computation or by table.

Great-circle, mid-latitude, and Mercator are the only sailings to be discussed in this chapter. A more complete discussion of the various sailings will be found in *Bowditch,* DMAHC Publication No. 9; Volume II (1975) of that publication contains tables relating to the sailings with examples of their use.

Preliminary considerations **2902** It must be kept constantly in mind that all solutions of sailing problems are made with true directions. Throughout this book, *all directions given are true unless specifically stated otherwise.*

Before proceeding with a discussion of the sailings, it is advisable to be thoroughly familiar with the terms to be employed. In Chapter 2, the following terms were introduced: latitude (L), difference of latitude (l), longitude (Lo or λ), difference of longitude (DLo), departure (p), distance (D or Dist), course (Cn from mathematical solutions; C as used for plotting), great circles, and rhumb lines. The latitude and longitude of the point of departure will be designated L_1 and λ_1, respectively, and the coordinates of the destination, L_2 and λ_2. The latitude and longitude of the vertex of a great circle (point on circle farthest from the equator) is L_v and λ_v.

Departure (symbol p) is the linear measure, in nautical miles, of an arc of a parallel included between two meridians. The term distinguishes it from difference of longitude (DLo) which is the *angular* measure of the same arc. Regardless of the latitude, the difference of longitude between two meridians remains the same, but the departure between those meridians varies with the parallel on which it is measured. Thus, in Figure 2902 the difference of longitude between the meridians is constant, whereas the departure becomes less as the poles are approached. Departure may be marked east (E) or west (W) according to how it is made.

Figure 2902 illustrates the relationship of DLo and departure at various latitudes. At the equator DLo and departure are identical and equal to the difference in longitude in minutes. The distance between the meridians becomes less with increased latitude and varies as the *cosine* of the latitude—at 60°, the departure is one half of that at the equator (cos 60° = 0.5), and the distance around the earth at the sixtieth parallel is one half the distance around the earth at the equator. The relationship of DLo and p is expressed by the equation, p = DLo cos L, or DLo = p sec L.

Course angle (symbol C) is the inclination of the course line to the meridian, measured from 0° at the reference direction (*north* or *south*) *clockwise* or *counterclockwise* through 90° or 180°. It is labeled with the reference direction (N or S) as a prefix, and the direction of measurement from the reference direction (E or W) as a suffix. The rules for determining the labels and the numerical limits vary with the method of solution. Course angle (C) is converted to *course* (Cn) by following the instructions of the labels. For example:

N 40° E = 000° + 40° = 040°
S 50° E = 180° − 50° = 130°
S 30° W = 180° + 30° = 210°
N 15° W = 360° − 15° = 345°

Middle or *mid-latitude* (Lm) is the latitude of a point which normally is found by taking the *mean* value of L_1 and L_2, both being on the same side of the equator. (A more exact definition exists for "mid-latitude" but it is difficult mathematically and the difference is of no practical significance.)

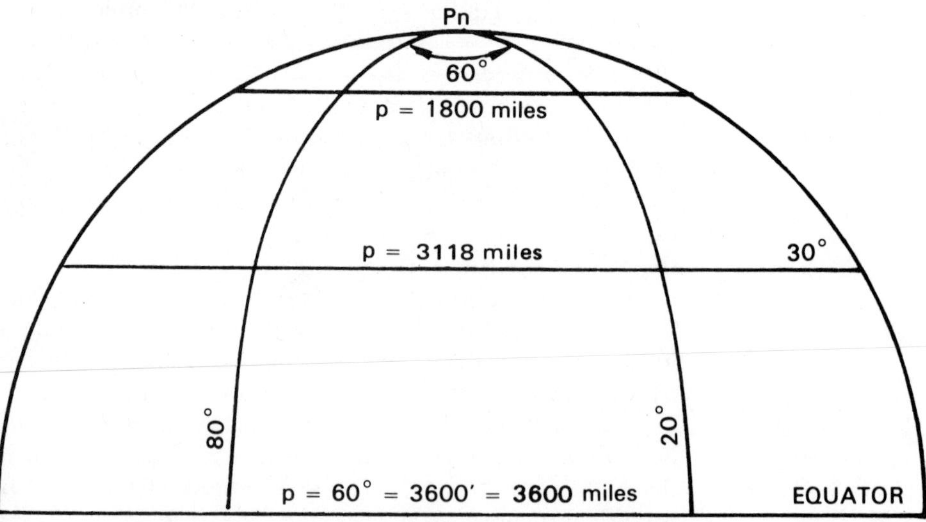

Figure 2902. Departure and difference in longitude.

Meridional parts (M). The length of a meridian on a Mercator chart, as expanded between the equator and any given latitude, expressed in units of 1′ of arc of the equator, constitutes the number of meridional parts of that latitude. The meridional parts used in the construction of Mercator charts and in Mercator sailing are tabulated in Table 5 of *Bowditch,* Volume II. In Mercator sailing, M_1 represents the meridional parts of the latitude of the point of departure, and M_2 the parts of the latitude of the destination.

Meridional difference (m). This represents the absolute difference $M_1 \sim M_2$ ($M_1 - M_2$ or $M_2 - M_1$ as determined by which is the larger).

The various sailings

2903 Several of the more often used "sailings" will be considered in this chapter. The method that gives the most accurate results, and is unlimited in its applications, is *great-circle sailing;* the "cost" of these advantages is a longer mathematical solution of greater complexity. Several other methods involve shorter solutions and give less precise results, although still within acceptable limits for practical navigation; these procedures, which yield rhumb lines, include *mid-latitude sailing* and *Mercator sailing.*

Other "sailings" of less general usefulness, are covered in Volumes I and II of *Bowditch.* Among these are *plane* and *traverse sailings* in which a small area of the earth's waters is considered to be a flat, or plane, surface with the obvious simplifications in the mathematics of the solution; plane sailing is for a single "leg" and traverse sailing is for two or more legs of a complex set of rhumb lines. *Parallel sailing* is a method involving the interconversion of departure and difference of longitude for a vessel proceeding due east or west; it is now generally obsolete. *Composite sailing* is a modification of great-circle sailing to limit the maximum latitude that otherwise would be reached.

Comparison of rhumb lines and great circles

2904 A course line plotted on a Mercator chart is a rhumb line; it makes the same angle with all the meridians it crosses. The chief advantage the rhumb line offers is that a ship following it does not have to change course between departure and destination. It is adequate for most purposes of navigation, except in high latitudes, and except for long bearing lines, such as those obtained by a radio direction finder.

A *great circle* is formed by the intersection of the surface of a sphere and a plane passing through the center of the sphere. The shortest distance between two places is measured along the great-circle arc passing through them. However, this arc will cross each meridian at a slightly different angle; it cannot be drawn on a Mercator chart as a straight line, but would be represented by a curve. The *vertex* is the point of greatest latitude through which the great-circle arc passes.

The equator and meridians are great circles, but they may also be considered as special cases of the rhumb line. Arcs both of meridians and of the equator appear as straight lines on a Mercator chart.

The difference between the great-circle distance and the rhumb-line distance between two places may amount to several hundred miles. For example, the great-circle distance from Sydney, Australia, to Valparaiso, Chile, is 748 miles (1385 km) shorter than the rhumb-line distance. It is obvious that while the rhumb line is most convenient, it should not be used for all long passages.

Under certain circumstances the great-circle track is *not* materially shorter than the rhumb line between two places. These may be summarized as follows:

1. For a short distance, the rhumb line and great circle are nearly coincident. The difference is about one mile for two places 350 miles apart on the 40th parallel of latitude.
2. The rhumb line between places that are near the same meridian is very nearly a great circle.
3. The equator is both a rhumb line and great circle. Parallels near the equator are very nearly great circles. Therefore, *in low latitudes,* a rhumb line is very nearly as short as a great circle.

The decision to use or not to use great-circle sailing depends on whether the distance to be saved is sufficient to justify the trouble involved, as well as on other considerations, such as the latitude of the vertex, and anticipated weather, currents, etc., along the different routes.

Mid-latitude sailing

2905 The procedures for *mid-latitude* sailing are based on approximations which simplify the mathematics of the problem, and which yield somewhat less accurate answers than are obtainable by more rigorous and time-consuming reductions. For ordinary purposes, however, they yield results more accurate than are obtainable in ordinary navigation.

Typical mid-latitude sailing problems are: (1) knowing latitude and longitude of points of departure and destination, solving for course and distance; or (2) knowing latitude and longitude of point of departure, and course and distance made good, solving for the latitude and longitude of the point reached.

Note carefully that when the course line crosses the equator, the problem *must* be broken down into two separate triangles of north and south latitude and solved separately.

The basic equations for mid-latitude sailing are:

$$\text{p} = \text{DLo (in minutes of arc)} \times \cos \text{Lm} \quad (1)$$

$$\text{C} = \tan^{-1} (\text{p} \div l) \text{ where } l = \text{difference of latitude in minutes of arc} \quad (2)$$

$$\text{Dist} = l \times \sec \text{C} \quad (3)$$

The use of these equations for the solution of a problem of the first type referred to above is shown in the following example:

Solution:	L_1	8°48.9′ S	λ_1	89°53.3′ W
	L_2	17°06.9′ S	λ_2	104′51.6′ W
	l	8°18.0′ S	DLo	14°58.3′ W
	l	498.0′ S	DLo	898.3′ W
	$\frac{1}{2}l$	4°09.0′ S		
	Lm	12°57.9′ S		

DLo	898.3′W	log	2.95342			
Lm	12°57.9′S	log cos	9.98878 − 10			
p	875.4 mi W		2.94220			
l	498.0′S	− log	2.69723		log	2.69723
C	S60°21.9′W	log tan	0.24497		log sec	0.30586
(2) Dist	1007.1					3.00309
(1) Cn	240.4°					

The solution above is shown through use of logarithms. It can be easily and quickly solved with a small electronic calculator having trigonometric functions. Equations (1) and (2) above would be used as shown, but equation (3) might be changed to

$$\text{Dist} = l \div \cos C \qquad (3a)$$

to better match normal keyboard functions, angles may have to be converted to degrees and decimal fractions.

If the calculator does not have keys for trigonometric functions, values for them can be found in Table 31 of *Bowditch,* Volume II.

When the latitude and longitude of the point of departure and the course and distance steamed are given, the latitude and longitude of the point of arrival may be found by using the following equations:

$$l = \text{Dist} \times \cos C \qquad (4)$$

$$p = \text{Dist} \times \sin C \qquad (5)$$

$$\text{DLo} = p \times \sec \text{Lm} \qquad (6)$$

$$\text{or DLo} = p \div \cos \text{Lm} \qquad (6a)$$

With l having been found, $\frac{1}{2}l$ is applied to the latitude of the point of departure to find Lm. The latitude and longitude of the point of arrival are found by applying l and DLo, in accordance with their names, to the latitude and longitude respectively of the point of departure.

Example: A vessel at Lat. 37°01.2′ N, Long. 75°53.7′ W proceeds on a rhumb-line course 072.5° for a distance of 850 miles.

Required: (1) Latitude and (2) longitude of point reached at end of run.

Solution (by calculator):

$$l = \text{Dist} \times \cos C$$
$$= 850 \times \cos 72.5° = 255.6' \text{ N}$$
$$= 4°15.6' \text{ N}$$
$$p = \text{Dist} \times \sin C$$

	$= 850 \times \sin 72.5° = 810.7'$ E		
l	4°15.6′ N	$\frac{1}{2}l$	2°07.8′ N
L_1	37°01.2′ N		37°01.2′ N
(1)L_2	41°16.8′ N		
L_m			39°09.0′ N

DLo = p ÷ cos L_m
= 810.7′ ÷ cos 39°09.0′ = 1045.4′
= 17°25.4′ E
75 53.7 W

(2) 58°28.4′ W

Answer: Lat. 41°16.8′ N; Long. 58°28.4′ W.

Mercator sailing **2906** The determination of course and distance on a Mercator chart constitutes a graphic solution of a *Mercator sailing* problem. This sailing may also be solved by computation.

The equations for Mercator sailing are:

$$C = \tan^{-1} (DLo \div m) \quad (1)$$

$$Dist = l \times \sec C \quad (2)$$

$$\text{or } Dist = l \div \cos C \quad (2a)$$

where m is the absolute difference between M_1 and M_2 as taken from Table 5 of *Bowditch.*

These equations can be conveniently arranged for solution as shown in the following example:

Example: Find the course and distance by Mercator sailing from Cape Flattery Light, Washington, to Diamond Head, Oahu, Hawaiian Islands.

Cape Flattery Light	L_1	48°23.5′ N
	λ_1	124°44.1′ W
Diamond Head	L_2	21°15.1′ N
	λ_2	157°48.7′ N

Solution:					
L_1	48°23.5′ N	M_1	3309.2	λ_2	157°48.7′ W
L_2	21°15.1′ N	M_2	1296.9	λ_1	124°44.1′ W
l	27°08.4′ S	M	2012.3	DLo	33°04.6′ W
l	1628.4′ S			DLo	1984.6′ W

By calculator:

C = tan⁻¹ (DLo ÷ m)
= $\tan^{-1}$ (1984.6 ÷ 2012.3) = $\tan^{-1}$ 0.98623
= 44.6029° = S 44°36.2′ W

C_n = 180° + 44°36.2′
= 224.6°

Dist = l ÷ cos C = 1628.4 ÷ cos 44.6001°
= 2287.0 mi

In mercator sailing, the limits of C are 0° to 90°, labeled N or S to agree with l and E or W to agree with DLo. To convert C to Cn, follow the instructions of the labels. In the above example, start at S (180°). The course is 44°36.2′ to the west, or 180° + 44°36.2′ = 224°36.2′; this is recorded as 224.6°. It is customary to solve for Distance and C to a precision of 0.1′ but to record Cn only to a precision of 0.1°.

These equations can also be used for determining the latitude and longitude of the destination if the course and distance are known, but if the course is near 090° or 270°, an appreciable error in DLo may result.

Mercator sailing problems can also be solved by means of Volume II of *Bowditch* by using values from Table 3 in accordance with instructions in Article 1007 of that publication.

Characteristics of great circles

2907 Every great circle of a sphere bisects every other great circle. Therefore every great circle, if extended around the earth, will lie half in the northern hemisphere and half in the southern hemisphere, and the midpoint of either half will be farthest from the equator. This point, where a great circle reaches its highest latitude, is called the *vertex*.

A great circle between two places on the same side of the equator is everywhere nearer the pole than the rhumb line. If the two places are on different sides of the equator, the great circle between them changes its direction of curvature, relative to the rhumb line, at the equator. If the two places are equal distances on opposite sides of the

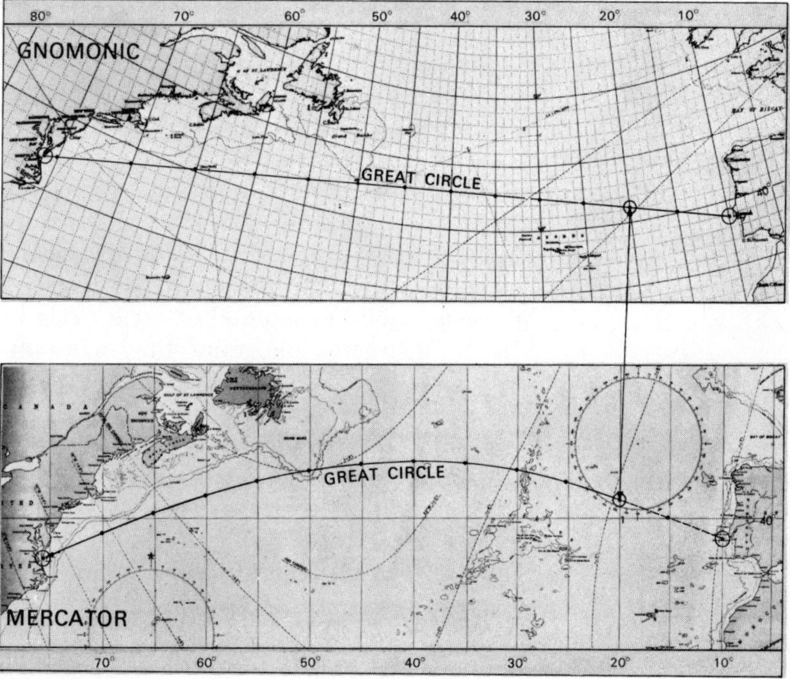

Figure 2907. Transferring a great circle from a gnomonic chart to a Mercator chart.

equator, the great circle will bisect the rhumb line between them at the equator.

Since the direction of a great circle is constantly changing, the course of a ship attempting to follow such a curved path would have to be continually changed. As this is obviously impractical, the course is changed at intervals, so that a ship follows a series of rhumb lines. Since for a short distance a rhumb line and a great circle are nearly coincident, the result is a close approximation of the great circle. This is generally accomplished by determining points at regular intervals along the great circle, plotting them on a Mercator chart or plotting sheet, and steaming the rhumb lines between the points (see Figure 2907).

It should be apparent that the equator and the meridians are special cases, and that many of the statements regarding great circles do not apply to them. If the course lies along one of these great circles, the solution may be made mentally, since the course is constant (these special great circles being also rhumb lines), and the distance is the number of minutes of DLo in the case of the equator and *l* in the case of a meridian.

Great-circle sailing by chart: gnomonic projection

2908 The Defense Mapping Agency Hydrographic Center publishes a number of charts at various scales which use the gnomonic projection, covering the usually navigated portions of the earth. The point of tangency is chosen for each chart to give the least distortion for the area to be covered. Any great circle appears on this type chart as a straight line. Because of this property, the chart is useful in great-circle sailing.

However, since the meridians are not shown as parallel lines, no ordinary compass rose can be provided for use in measuring direction over the entire chart, and since angles are distorted, they cannot be measured by protractor. Latitude and longitude at a particular point on the chart must be determined by reference to the meridians and parallels in the immediate vicinity of the point. Hence, a gnomonic chart is not convenient for ordinary navigational purposes. Its practical use is limited to solution of great-circle sailing problems.

In use, a straight line connecting the point of departure and the destination is drawn on the chart (upper half of Figure 2907). The great circle is then inspected to see that it passes clear of all dangers to navigation. If this requirement is met, the courses are then transferred to a Mercator chart by selecting a number of points along the great circle, determining their latitude and longitude, and plotting these points on the Mercator chart. These points are then connected by straight lines to represent the rhumb-line courses to be steered. The two arrows of Figure 2907 indicate a corresponding position on the two charts. It can be seen in Figure 2907 that points have been chosen at intervals of 5° of longitude to facilitate the picking off of points and plotting them on the Mercator chart. At this interval the error in using rhumb lines to approximate the great circle is small.

It will be noted that the rhumb-line segments determined in the manner just described are chords of the great circle, as plotted on the Mercator chart. The course and distance for steaming each segment can be determined by measurement on the Mercator chart. Courses and distances of tangents to the great circle can be determined directly from the great-circle charts, but the method is somewhat involved and can best be understood by studying the explanation given on each gnomonic chart. The chord method is easier and is commonly used in practice.

The great-circle distance of a voyage is sometimes determined from a gnomonic chart for comparison with the rhumb-line distance in determining which method will be used.

The great-circle track should be checked on a pilot chart for any potential hazards. If it extends into high latitudes, consideration should be given to modifying it to *composite sailing* in which a great circle track is followed from the point of departure to a *limiting latitude,* thence along that parallel to a point from which another great circle track will take the ship to her destination.

Great-circle sailing by chart: Lambert conformal projection

2909 Although most marine navigators use the combination of gnomonic and Mercator charts for great-circle sailing, the use of the Lambert conformal projection is beginning to receive attention. The advantage of the Lambert conformal chart for this purpose is that both great-circle distance and courses for segments of the great circle may be obtained by direct measurement, saving a transfer of points from the gnomonic to the Mercator projection. As stated earlier, any straight line on a Lambert conformal chart is a close approximation to a great circle, and angles are truly represented on this projection. Although direction can therefore be measured directly on the chart, protractors or plotters must be used, as the meridians are not shown as parallel lines. The course, a rhumb line, of each segment of a great circle is measured at its midpoint.

Since the distance scale of a Lambert conformal chart is so nearly constant that a fixed scale can be used without appreciable error, distance may be measured either by means of the latitude scale (as on a Mercator chart), by distance scales if printed on the chart, or by use of a special protractor plotter made to the scale of the chart. This latter method permits rapid measurement of both course and distance.

The illustration in Figure 2909 is on the base plate of National Ocean Survey Chart 3071. This chart was prepared for air navigation and its number does not fit into the standard nautical chart numbering system; it is, however, very useful for marine navigation as it has Loran lines and other helpful information. NOS publishes a series of these charts covering areas of the world with high-density air traffic. Note that the distance from A to B (430 miles or 796 km) is measured with dividers directly on the latitude scale, while the course at any point is determined by use of a protractor to measure the angle with the meridian at that point.

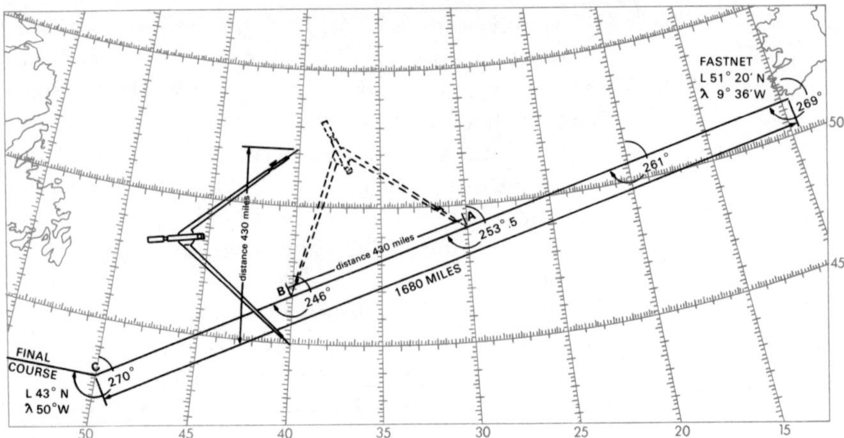

Figure 2909. Great-circle sailing on a Lambert projection chart.

Because of the advantages noted, and since this projection is suitable for general navigational purposes, charts based on this projection are replacing both gnomonic and Mercator charts to some extent, especially for air navigation. Plotting charts are commercially available on the Lambert conformal projection, made for specific latitudes, which may be used for any longitude.

Great-circle sailing by conversion angle

2910 If the difference in the direction of the great circle and rhumb line is known, this difference, called the *conversion angle,* can be applied to either one to obtain the other. In any great-circle sailing the angle which the great circle makes with the meridian at the starting point is referred to as the initial great-circle direction. In many texts it is referred to as the initial great-circle course even though the course by definition must be a rhumb line.

Conversion angles are tabulated in Table 1 of *Bowditch,* Volume II. If the distance does not exceed approximately 2000 miles (3700 km) *and* both points (departure and destination) lie on the same side of the equator, the conversion angle can be found to practical accuracy by the equation:

$$\text{Conversion angle} = \tan^{-1} (\sin \text{Lm} \times \tan \tfrac{1}{2} \text{DLo})$$

This equation can be solved graphically by a simple construction as shown in Figure 2910. Draw any line *AB*. Draw a second line, *AC,* making an angle with *AB* equal to the mid-latitude between the point of departure and the destination. From the intersection measure, to any convenient scale, a number of linear units equal to one-half the number of degrees of DLo, thus locating *D*. From *D* drop a perpendicular to the line *AB*. The number of linear units in this perpendicular, to the same scale used for $\frac{1}{2}$DLo, is the number of degrees of the conversion angle.

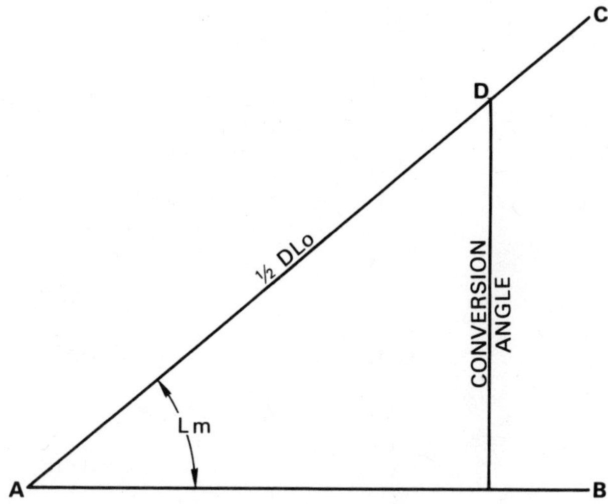

Figure 2910. Conversion angle determined graphically.

The sign of the conversion angle in any given case will be apparent if it is remembered that the great circle is nearer the pole than the rhumb line. For instance, in north latitude if the destination is east of the point of departure, the conversion angle is minus (−); if to the west, it is plus (+).

In practice the conversion angle is usually modified to provide chord courses. This is done by dividing the conversion angle by the number of legs to be used and *subtracting* this from the conversion angle before it is applied to the Mercator (rhumb line) course. At the end of the first leg a new solution must be made for the next leg. This is somewhat more trouble than using a great-circle chart, but eliminates the necessity of a lengthy computation if no great-circle chart is available.

Distance is determined by measuring the length of each rhumb-line leg and adding the figures so obtained.

Great-circle sailing by computation: the problem

2911 In Figure 2911, *C* represents the point of departure (L_1, λ_1), *B* the destination (L_2, λ_2); *P* is the pole nearest *C*, and *EQ* the equator. The great circles through *PC* and *PB* are meridians. Since latitude is the angular distance of a place north or south of the equator, measured along a meridian, *PC*, the angular distance from the pole to *C*, the point of departure, is $90° - L_1$, or the colatitude. Similarly, *PB* is the colatitude of the destination. However, the term *colatitude,* as used with respect to the destination, is $90° \pm L_2$, since *P* is chosen as the pole nearest the point of departure. That is, if *B* and *C* are on the same side of the equator, or of the same *name,* the latitude of *B* may be considered (+) and the colatitude = $90° - L_2$. However, if *B* is of opposite name,

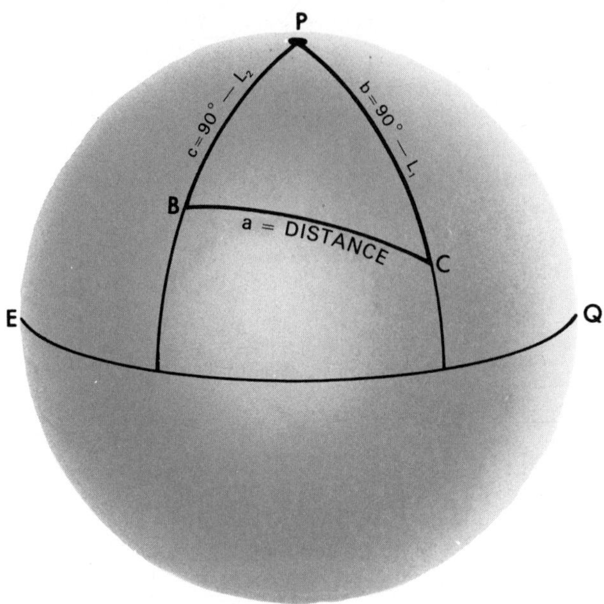

Figure 2911. The navigational triangle as used in great-circle sailing.

or on the opposite side of the equator from C, it may be considered (−) in which case the colatitude is $90° - (-L_2)$, or $90° + L_2$.

If C and B are connected by a great circle, a spherical triangle is formed. The length of the arc of the great circle between C and B is the great-circle distance between these two points. The initial direction from C to B is the angle PCB. The angle BPC is the DLo, designated t when used in the special case as part of the navigational triangle illustrated in Figure 2911. This is the same triangle used in the solution of celestial observations, C then being the assumed position of the observer and B the point on the earth directly under the celestial body observed. Hence, any method of solution devised for one of these problems can be used for the other. However, some methods devised for solution of celestial observations are better adapted to the solution of great-circle sailing problems than others.

The solution of a great-circle sailing problem involves computation for the distance and initial direction, the position of the vertex, and the coordinates of points along the track. Computation is somewhat tedious, but the results are accurate and this method sometimes constitutes the only method available.

Great-circle sailing by computation; distance and initial direction

2912 Refer to Figure 2912. A perpendicular dropped from the destination, B, to the meridian, PC, through the point of departure, C, will divide the oblique navigational triangle PBC into two right spherical triangles. The length of the perpendicular is designated R, and the foot of the perpendicular y. The latitude of point y is designated K, which is always on the same side of the equator as B. The arc Cy represents the *difference* of latitude of points C and y, regardless of which is greater or whether or not both are on the same side of the equator.

This is designated as $K \sim L_1$. (Here the symbol $\sim$ is used to mean the *algebraic* difference.) Thus, if both K and L_1 have the same name, the smaller is subtracted from the larger, but if they are of opposite name, their numerical values are added. The value $K \sim L_1$ has no sign or name, being merely a difference. The side Py is co $- K$.

If the point of departure and the destination are known, L_1, L_2, and t $(\lambda_2 - \lambda_1)$, are the values available for use in the solution. The problem is to find the distance (the side D in Figure 2912) and the angle at C.

These can be found by the following equations:

$$\csc \mathrm{R} = \csc t \sec \mathrm{L}_2 \tag{1}$$

$$\csc \mathrm{K} = \frac{\csc \mathrm{L}_2}{\sec \mathrm{R}} \tag{2}$$

$$\sec d = \sec R \sec (K \sim \mathrm{L}_1) \tag{3}$$

$$\csc \mathrm{C} = \frac{\csc R}{\csc d} \tag{4}$$

The derivation of these equations is explained in *Bowditch.* Any table of log secants and log cosecants can be used for the solution by these equations, but they are most conveniently arranged in Table 35

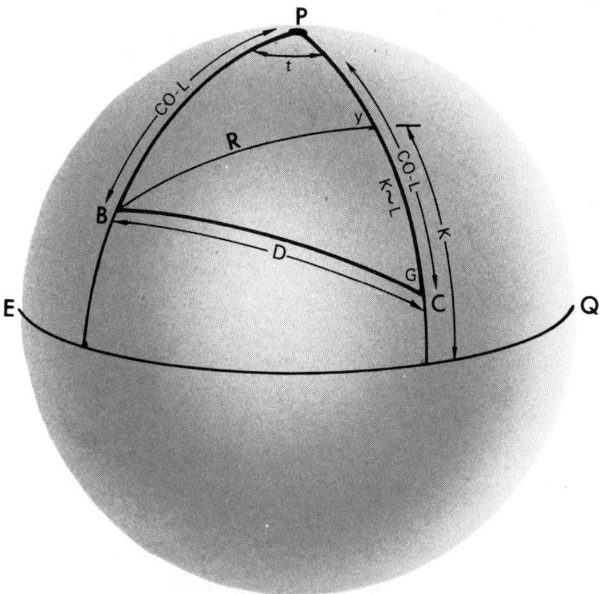

Figure 2912. The navigational triangle divided into two right spherical triangles by a perpendicular from the point of destination to the meridian of the point of departure.

of *Bowditch,* Volume II. (These tables of the "Ageton method" were published for many years as a separate volume, H.O. 211.) In Table 35, column "A" contains log cosecants multiplied by 10^5 and column "B" contains log secants similarly multiplied by 10^5. These values are intended for use without interpolation in most instances, the accuracy being sufficient for practical navigation. In situations, however, where t is near 90°, the results may not be accurate enough; it is advisable to interpolate if t is between 85 and 95°.

Numerous rules for naming the triangle parts north or south, and for entering the tables at the top or bottom of the page must be carefully followed. These rules and the equations and method of solution for determining the great-circle distance, the initial direction, the vertex, and additional points along the track are given in Article 1012 of *Bowditch,* Volume II and will not be repeated here. A single complete solution is presented for illustrative purposes in the following article.

Great-circle sailing by computation: complete solution

2913 A complete solution for all aspects of the mathematical solution of a great-circle sailing problem using *Bowditch* Table 35 is given in the example below. The equations and the terminology used are as given in the instructions of Article 1012, *Bowditch,* Volume II.

Example: (1) Find the initial great-circle direction and distance from Land's End, England (50°04.0′ N, 5°45.0′ W) to St. John's, Newfoundland (47°34.0′ N, 52°40.0′ W) by computation using Table 35 of *Bowditch.* (2) Find the latitude and longitude of the vertex. (3) Find the latitude and longitude of points along the great circle at distance intervals of 5° (300 miles) along the great circle, measured in both directions from the vertex.

Solution:

(1)			Add	Subtract	Add	Subtract
	λ_2	52°40.0′ W				
	λ_1	5°45.0′ W				
	t	46°55.0′ W	A 13646			
	L_2	47°34.0′ N	B 17087	A 13191		
			A 30733	B 6041	B 6041	A 30733
	K	58°01.0′ N		A 7150		
	L_1	50°04.0′N				
	$K \sim L_1$	7°57.0′			B 419	
	D	30°29.0′			B 6460	A 29475
	Cn	283.7°		C N76°16.5′ W		A 1258
	Dist	1829.0 mi				

(2)			Add	Subtract
	L_1	50°04.0′ W	B 19253	
	C	N 76°16.5′ W	A 1258	B 62477
	L_v	51°25.5′ N	B 20511	A 10691
	t_v	17°40.0′ W		A 51786
	λ_1	5°45.0′ W		
	λ_v	23°25.0′ W		

(3) d_{v-x}	5°	10°	15°	20°
L_v	A 10691	10691	10691	10691
d_{v-x}	(+)B 165.6	665	1506	2701
L_x	A 10856.6	11356	12197	13392
L_x	51°09.0′ N	50°21.0′ N	49′02.5′ N	47′16.5′ N
d_{v-x}	A 105970	76033	58700	46595
L_x	(−)B 20254	19511	18342	16846
t_{v-x}	A 85716	56522	40358	29749
t_{v-x}	7°59.0′	15°47.5′	23°15.5′	30°16.5′
λ_v	23°25.0′	23°25.0′	23°25.0′	23°25.0′
λ_x	15°26.0′ W	7°37.5′ W	—	— $(\lambda_v - t_{v-x})$
λ_x	31°24.0′ W	39°12.5′ W	46°40.5′ W	53°41.5′ W $(\lambda_v + t_{v-x})$

Note: For some L_x there are two λ_x, one east and one west of the vertex.

In calculations such as the above, it is well to write down the entire form for all parts before doing any of the computation. The mind is thus freed of thinking of what to do next and can focus on the mechanics of the computation. Also, it will be noted that the same quantity sometimes appears in several places. In part (1), for instance, C is found from its A function. In part (2) both A and B functions are needed. If the B function is picked out at the same time C is being found, it will save going again to the same place in the table in the solution of part (2). The same A value found in part (1) is used in part (2). The same A value found in part (1) is used in part (2) regardless of whether it is a tabulated number.

It will be noted that but one point is found at distances of 15° and 20° from the vertex, since the points to the east are beyond the point of departure. The number of points needed can be determined by dividing the distance interval (in this example 5° or 300 miles) into the total distance. In determining the number of computations, the position of the vertex must be considered. In some problems the vertex will be located beyond the destination, but its position must be determined in order to calculate the points along the great circle.

Checking great-circle computations

2914 Mathematical errors frequently occur when a great-circle problem is computed in the foregoing manner. It is advisable to check the answers for gross errors with a small calculator using the following equations. Distances over 1,800 miles (3300 km) and course angles between 0° and 70°, and between 110° and 180°, can be solved with considerable accuracy.

$$D = 60 \cos^{-1} [(\sin L_1 \times \sin L_2) + (\cos L_1 \times \cos L_2 \times \cos t)] \quad (1)$$

$$C = \sin^{-1} [(\cos L_2 \times \sin t) \div \sin D] \quad (2)$$

$$L_v = \cos^{-1} (\cos L_1 \times \sin C) \quad (3)$$

$$t_v = \sin^{-1} (\cos C \div \sin L_v) \quad (4)$$

$$D_v = \sin^{-1} (\cos L_1 \times \sin t_v) \tag{5}$$

$$L_x = \sin^{-1} (\sin L_v \times \cos D_{v-x}) \tag{6}$$

$$t_{v-x} = \sin^{-1}(\sin D_{v-x} \div \text{Cos } L_x) \tag{7}$$

Note: Equation (1) above assumes that L_1 and L_2 are both of the same name (both north or both south). If they are contrary (the course crossing the equator) insert L_2 as a negative quantity. In equation (2), d is in angular units, D ÷ 60. These are not the only formats used for such equations; other forms may be found in other sources.

A partial solution by calculator of the previous example yields results as follows:

$$\begin{aligned} D &= 60 \cos^{-1} [(\sin 50°04.0' \times \sin 47°34.0') \\ &\quad + (\cos 50°04.0' \times \cos 47°34.0' \times \cos 46°55.0')] \\ &= 1828.98 \text{ miles} \end{aligned}$$

$$\begin{aligned} C &= \sin^{-1} (\cos 47°34.0' \times \sin 46°55.0') \\ &\quad \div \sin (1828.98 \div 60) \\ &= \text{N } 76.275° \text{ W} = \text{N } 76°16.5' \text{ W} \end{aligned}$$

$$\begin{aligned} L_v &= \cos^{-1} (\cos 50°04.0' \times \sin 76°16.5') \\ &= 51.423° = 51°25.4' \text{ N} \end{aligned}$$

$$\begin{aligned} t_v &= \sin^{-1} (\cos 76°16.5' \div 51°25.4') \\ &= 17.667° = 17°40.0' \text{ W} \end{aligned}$$

$$\lambda_1 = \underline{5°45.0' \text{ W}}$$

$$\lambda_v = 23°25.0' \text{ W}$$

Equations (5) through (7) could be similarly solved by calculator for the latitude of intermediate points specified by longitude or longitude intervals to either side of the vertex. (Calculator programs are also available for the computation of the latitude of any point on the great-circle track specified in terms of its longitude (without reference to the vertex).)

Great-circle sailing computation by Pub. No. 229

2915 The tables of DMAHC Pub. No. 229 are readily adaptable to solutions of great-circle sailing problems, as the point of departure and the destination can always be found on the same page.

Pub. No. 229, and the use of its interpolation tables, is described at some length in Article 2404; it will be dealt with only briefly here, to describe its use for finding the great-circle distance and initial direction. By entering the tables with latitude of departure as "latitude," latitude of destination as "declination," and difference of longitude as "LHA," the tabular altitude and azimuth angle may be extracted and converted to distance and course.

The tabular azimuth angle (or its supplement) becomes the initial great-circle course angle, prefixed N or S for the latitude of departure, and suffixed E or W depending upon the destination being east or west of point of departure.

If all entering arguments are integral degrees, the altitude and azimuth angle are obtained directly from the tables without interpolation. If the latitude of destination is nonintegral, interpolation for the additional minutes of latitude is done as in correcting altitude for any declination increment; if either the latitude of departure or difference of longitude, or both, are nonintegral, the additional interpolation is done graphically.

Since the latitude of destination becomes the declination entry, and all declinations appear on every page, the great-circle solution can always be extracted from the volume which covers the latitude of departure.

Great-circle solutions belong in one of the four following cases:

Case I—Latitudes of departure and destination of same name and initial great-circle distance less than 90°.

Case II—Latitudes of departure and destination of contrary name and great-circle distance less than 90°.

Case III—Latitudes of departure and destination of same name and great-circle distance greater than 90°.

Case IV—Latitudes of departure and destination of contrary name and great-circle distance greater than 90°.

The introductory pages of Pub. No. 229 provide instructions for the solution of each of these cases. The solution of a Case I problem will be shown below; for comparison purposes, this is the same problem as was worked previously by Table 35 of *Bowditch* and by calculator.

Example: Find the initial great-circle course and distance from Land's End, England (50°04.0′ N, 5°45.0′ W) to St. John's, Newfoundland (47°34.0′ N, 52°40.0′ W) by computation using Pub. No. 229.

Solution: (1) Since the latitude of the point of departure, the latitude of the destination, and the difference of longitude (DLo) between the

47°, 313° L.H.A. LATITUDE SAME NAME AS DECLINATION N. Lat. {L.H.A. greater than 180°......Zn=Z; L.H.A. less than 180°..........Zn=360°−Z}

Dec.	45°			46°			47°			48°		
	Hc	d	Z	Hc	d	Z	Hc	d	Z	Hc	d	Z
0	28 49.9	+48.4	123.4	28 16.7	+48.9	123.9	27 43.1	+49.5	124.3	27 09.1	+50.0	124.7
1	29 38.3	48.1	122.7	29 05.6	48.7	123.2	28 32.6	49.3	123.7	27 59.1	49.9	124.1
2	30 26.4	47.9	122.0	29 54.3	48.5	122.5	29 21.9	49.1	123.0	28 49.0	49.7	123.5
3	31 14.3	47.6	121.3	30 42.8	48.3	121.8	30 11.0	48.9	122.3	29 38.7	49.4	122.8
4	32 01.9	47.5	120.6	31 31.1	48.1	121.1	30 59.9	48.7	121.7	30 28.1	49.3	122.2
5	32 49.4	+47.1	119.9	32 19.2	+47.8	120.4	31 48.6	+48.4	121.0	31 17.4	+49.1	121.5
6	33 36.5	46.9	119.2	33 07.0	47.6	119.7	32 37.0	48.3	120.3	32 06.5	48.9	120.8
7	34 23.4	46.6	118.4	33 54.6	47.3	119.0	33 25.3	47.9	119.6	32 55.4	48.6	120.1
8	35 10.0	46.3	117.6	34 41.9	47.0	118.2	34 13.2	47.8	118.9	33 44.0	48.4	119.4
9	35 56.3	46.1	116.9	35 28.9	46.8	117.5	35 01.0	47.4	118.1	34 32.4	48.1	118.7
45	57 14.7	+16.9	72.9	57 31.6	+18.7	74.4	57 47.0	+20.4	75.9	58 00.8	+22.2	77.5
46	57 31.6	15.4	71.1	57 50.3	17.1	72.6	58 07.4	19.0	74.2	58 23.0	20.8	75.7
47	57 47.0	13.8	69.3	58 07.4	15.6	70.8	58 26.4	17.4	72.4	58 43.8	19.2	73.9
48	58 00.8	12.2	67.5	58 23.0	14.0	69.0	58 43.8	15.8	70.5	59 03.0	17.7	72.1
49	58 13.0	10.5	65.6	58 37.0	12.4	67.1	58 59.6	14.2	68.7	59 20.7	16.0	70.2
80	51 16.2	−34.2	11.7	52 14.9	−33.9	12.0	53 13.6	−33.7	12.2	54 12.2	−33.4	12.5
81	50 42.0	35.1	10.4	51 41.0	34.8	10.6	52 39.9	34.5	10.9	53 38.8	34.3	11.1
82	50 06.9	35.8	9.1	51 06.2	35.7	9.3	52 05.4	35.5	9.5	53 04.5	35.3	9.8
83	49 31.1	36.7	7.9	50 30.5	36.5	8.1	51 29.9	36.3	8.2	52 29.2	36.1	8.4
84	48 54.4	37.4	6.7	49 54.0	37.3	6.8	50 53.6	37.2	7.0	51 53.1	37.0	7.1
85	48 17.0	−38.1	5.5	49 16.7	−38.0	5.6	50 16.4	−37.9	5.7	51 16.1	−37.7	5.8
86	47 38.9	38.8	4.3	48 38.7	38.7	4.4	49 38.5	38.6	4.5	50 38.4	38.6	4.6
87	47 00.1	39.4	3.2	48 00.0	39.4	3.3	48 59.9	39.3	3.3	49 59.8	39.2	3.4
88	46 20.7	40.1	2.1	47 20.6	40.0	2.2	48 20.6	40.0	2.2	49 20.6	40.0	2.2
89	45 40.6	40.6	1.0	46 40.6	40.6	1.1	47 40.6	40.6	1.1	48 40.6	40.6	1.1
90	45 00.0	−41.2	0.0	46 00.0	−41.2	0.0	47 00.0	−41.2	0.0	48 00.0	−41.2	0.0
	45°			46°			47°			48°		

49°			50°			51°			52°			Dec.
Hc	d	Z	Hc	d	Z	Hc	d	Z	Hc	d	Z	
26 34.7	+50.6	125.1	26 00.0	+51.1	125.5	25 25.0	+51.6	125.9	24 49.6	+52.1	126.3	0
27 25.3	50.4	124.5	26 51.1	50.9	125.0	26 16.6	51.4	125.4	25 41.7	51.9	125.8	1
28 15.7	50.2	123.9	27 42.0	50.8	124.4	27 08.0	51.3	124.8	26 33.6	51.7	125.2	2
29 05.9	50.1	123.3	28 32.8	50.6	123.8	27 59.3	51.1	124.2	27 25.3	51.7	124.6	3
29 56.0	49.9	122.7	29 23.4	50.4	123.1	28 50.4	51.0	123.6	28 17.0	51.5	124.1	4
30 45.9	+49.6	122.0	30 13.8	+50.3	122.5	29 41.4	+50.8	123.0	29 08.5	+51.3	123.5	5
31 35.5	49.5	121.4	31 04.1	50.0	121.9	30 32.2	50.6	122.4	29 59.8	51.2	122.9	6
32 25.0	49.3	120.7	31 54.1	49.9	121.2	31 22.8	50.4	121.8	30 51.0	51.0	122.3	7
33 14.3	49.0	120.0	32 44.0	49.6	120.6	32 13.2	50.3	121.1	31 42.0	50.8	121.7	8
34 03.3	48.8	119.3	33 33.6	49.5	119.9	33 03.5	50.0	120.5	32 32.8	50.6	121.0	9
58 13.0	+24.0	79.1	58 23.5	+25.9	80.7	58 32.4	+27.7	82.3	58 39.7	+29.4	83.9	45
58 37.0	22.6	77.3	58 49.4	24.4	78.9	59 00.1	26.2	80.6	59 09.1	28.0	82.2	46
58 59.6	21.1	75.5	59 13.8	22.9	77.1	59 26.3	24.7	78.8	59 37.1	26.6	80.5	47
59 20.7	19.5	73.7	59 36.7	21.4	75.3	59 51.0	23.3	77.0	60 03.7	25.1	78.7	48
59 40.2	17.9	71.8	59 58.1	19.7	73.5	60 14.3	21.7	75.1	60 28.8	23.6	76.9	49
55 10.7	−33.0	12.9	56 09.2	−32.7	13.2	57 07.6	−32.4	13.5	58 05.9	−32.0	13.9	80
54 37.7	34.1	11.4	55 36.5	33.8	11.7	56 35.2	33.5	12.0	57 33.9	33.2	12.3	81
54 03.6	35.0	10.0	55 02.7	34.8	10.2	56 01.7	34.5	10.5	57 00.7	34.3	10.8	82
53 28.6	36.0	8.6	54 27.9	35.8	8.8	55 27.2	35.6	9.0	56 26.4	35.3	9.3	83
52 52.6	36.8	7.3	53 52.1	36.6	7.4	54 51.6	36.5	7.6	55 51.1	36.3	7.8	84
52 15.8	−37.6	6.0	53 15.5	−37.6	6.1	54 15.1	−37.4	6.3	55 14.8	−37.3	6.4	85
51 38.2	38.5	4.7	52 37.9	38.3	4.8	53 37.7	38.2	4.9	54 37.5	38.2	5.1	86
50 59.7	39.2	3.5	51 59.6	39.1	3.6	52 59.5	39.1	3.6	53 59.3	38.9	3.7	87
50 20.5	39.9	2.3	51 20.5	39.9	2.3	52 20.4	39.8	2.4	53 20.4	39.8	2.5	88
49 40.6	40.6	1.1	50 40.6	40.6	1.2	51 40.6	40.6	1.2	52 40.6	40.6	1.2	89
49 00.0	−41.2	0.0	50 00.0	−41.2	0.0	51 00.0	−41.3	0.0	52 00.0	−41.3	0.0	90
49°			50°			51°			52°			

47°, 313° L.H.A. LATITUDE SAME NAME AS DECLINATION

Figure 2915a. Pub. No. 229, "same name" page (extract).

point of departure and destination are not integral degrees, the solution is effected from an adjusted point of departure or assumed position of departure chosen as follows: the latitude of the assumed position (AP) is the integral degree of latitude nearest to the point of departure; the longitude of the AP is chosen to provide integral degrees of DLo. This AP, which should be within 30′ of the longitude of the point of departure, is at latitude 50° N, longitude 5°40.0′ W; the DLo is thus 47°. (2) Enter the tables with 50° as the latitude argument (Same Name), 47° as the LHA argument, and 47° as the declination argument. (3) From page 96 of Pub. No. 229, Volume 4 (Figure 2915a), extract the tabular altitude, altitude difference, and azimuth angle; interpolate altitude and azimuth angle for the declination increment using Figure 2915b. The Dec. Inc. is the number of minutes that the actual latitude of the destination exceeds the integral degrees used as the declination argument.

		ht (Tab. Hc)	d	Z
LHA 47°, Lat. 50° (Same), Dec. 47°		59°13.8′	+22.9′	77.1°
Dec. Inc. 34.0′, d + 22.9′	Tens	11.3′		
	Units	1.7′		
Interpolated for Dec. Inc.		59°26.8′		C N76.1° W
Initial great-circle course from AP				Cn 283.9°

Great-circle distance from AP (90° − 59°26.8′ = 30°33.2′) 1833.2 n.mi.

Dec. Inc.	Altitude Difference (d)																Double Second Diff. and Corr.
	Tens					Decimals	Units										
	10′	20′	30′	40′	50′	↓	0′	1′	2′	3′	4′	5′	6′	7′	8′	9′	
34.0	5.6	11.3	17.0	22.6	28.3	**.0**	0.0	0.6	1.1	1.7	2.3	2.9	3.4	4.0	4.6	5.2	0.8 0.1
34.1	5.7	11.3	17.0	22.7	28.4	**.1**	0.1	0.6	1.2	1.8	2.4	2.9	3.5	4.1	4.7	5.2	2.5 0.2
34.2	5.7	11.4	17.1	22.8	28.5	**.2**	0.1	0.7	1.3	1.8	2.4	3.0	3.6	4.1	4.7	5.3	4.1 0.3
34.3	5.7	11.4	17.1	22.9	28.6	**.3**	0.2	0.7	1.3	1.9	2.5	3.0	3.6	4.2	4.8	5.3	5.8 0.4
34.4	5.7	11.5	17.2	22.9	28.7	**.4**	0.2	0.8	1.4	2.0	2.5	3.1	3.7	4.3	4.8	5.4	7.4 0.5
																	9.1 0.6
34.5	5.8	11.5	17.3	23.0	28.8	**.5**	0.3	0.9	1.4	2.0	2.6	3.2	3.7	4.3	4.9	5.5	10.7 0.7
34.6	5.8	11.5	17.3	23.1	28.8	**.6**	0.3	0.9	1.5	2.1	2.6	3.2	3.8	4.4	4.9	5.5	12.3 0.8
34.7	5.8	11.6	17.4	23.2	28.9	**.7**	0.4	1.0	1.6	2.1	2.7	3.3	3.9	4.4	5.0	5.6	14.0 0.9
34.8	5.8	11.6	17.4	23.2	29.0	**.8**	0.5	1.0	1.6	2.2	2.8	3.3	3.9	4.5	5.1	5.6	15.6 1.0
34.9	5.9	11.7	17.5	23.3	29.1	**.9**	0.5	1.1	1.7	2.2	2.8	3.4	4.0	4.5	5.1	5.7	17.3 1.1
																	18.9 1.2
35.0	5.8	11.6	17.5	23.3	29.1	**.0**	0.0	0.6	1.2	1.8	2.4	3.0	3.5	4.1	4.7	5.3	20.6 1.3
35.1	5.8	11.7	17.5	23.4	29.2	**.1**	0.1	0.7	1.2	1.8	2.4	3.0	3.6	4.2	4.8	5.4	22.2 1.4
35.2	5.8	11.7	17.6	23.4	29.3	**.2**	0.1	0.7	1.3	1.9	2.5	3.1	3.7	4.3	4.9	5.4	23.9 1.5
35.3	5.9	11.8	17.6	23.5	29.4	**.3**	0.2	0.8	1.4	2.0	2.5	3.1	3.7	4.3	4.9	5.5	25.5 1.6
35.4	5.9	11.8	17.7	23.6	29.5	**.4**	0.2	0.8	1.4	2.0	2.6	3.2	3.8	4.4	5.0	5.6	27.2 1.7
35.5	5.9	11.8	17.8	23.7	29.6	**.5**	0.3	0.9	1.5	2.1	2.7	3.3	3.8	4.4	5.0	5.6	28.8 1.8
35.6	5.9	11.9	17.8	23.7	29.7	**.6**	0.4	0.9	1.5	2.1	2.7	3.3	3.9	4.5	5.1	5.7	30.4 1.9
35.7	6.0	11.9	17.9	23.8	29.8	**.7**	0.4	1.0	1.6	2.2	2.8	3.4	4.0	4.6	5.1	5.7	32.1 2.0
35.8	6.0	12.0	17.9	23.9	29.9	**.8**	0.5	1.1	1.7	2.2	2.8	3.4	4.0	4.6	5.2	5.8	33.7 2.1
35.9	6.0	12.0	18.0	24.0	30.0	**.9**	0.5	1.1	1.7	2.3	2.9	3.5	4.1	4.7	5.3	5.9	35.4
	10′	20′	30′	40′	50′		0′	1′	2′	3′	4′	5′	6′	7′	8′	9′	

Figure 2915b. Pub. No. 229, interpolation table (extract).

(4) Using the Pub. 229 graphical method for interpolating altitude for latitude and LHA increments, the course line is drawn from the AP in the direction of the initial great-circle course from the AP (283.9°). As shown in Figure 2915c, a line is drawn from the point of departure perpendicular to the initial great-circle course line or its extension. (5) The required correction, in units of minutes of latitude, for the latitude and DLo increments is the length along the course line between the foot of the perpendicular and the AP. The correction as applied to the distance from the AP is −4.3; the great-circle distance is 1828.9 nautical miles. (6) The azimuth angle interpolated for declination, LHA, and latitude increments is N76.3°W; the initial great-circle course from the point of departure is 283.7°.

The accuracy of Pub. No. 229 in calculating great-circle distance and initial direction is indicated by the fact that the actual distance, rigorously computed, is 1828.98 miles and the initial direction is 283°43.5′, giving an error of less than 0.1 miles and less than 0.1 degrees.

Points along a great-circle route by Pub. No. 229

If the latitude of the point of departure and the initial great-circle course angle are integral degrees, points along the great circle are found by entering the tables with the latitude of departure as the latitude argument (Same Name), the initial great-circle course angle as

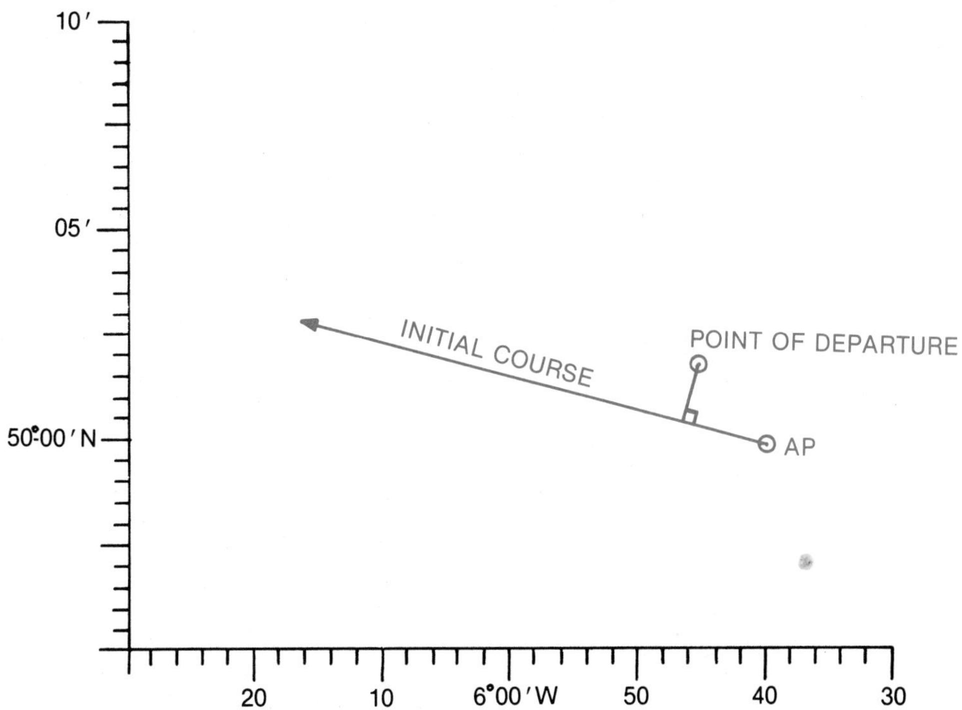

Figure 2915c. Correction of great-circle distance when using Pub. No. 229.

76°, 284° L.H.A. **LATITUDE SAME NAME AS DECLINATION** N. Lat. {L.H.A. greater than 180°......Zn=Z; L.H.A. less than 180°............Zn=360°−Z}

Dec.	45°			46°			47°			48°			49°			50°			51°			52°			Dec.
	Hc	d	Z	Hc	d	Z	Hc	d	Z	Hc	d	Z	Hc	d	Z	Hc	d	Z	Hc	d	Z	Hc	d	Z	
°	° ′	′	°	° ′	′	°	° ′	′	°	° ′	′	°	° ′	′	°	° ′	′	°	° ′	′	°	° ′	′	°	°
0	9 51.0	+43.0	100.0	9 40.5	+43.7	100.2	9 29.8	+44.5	100.3	9 19.0	+45.1	100.5	9 07.9	+45.9	100.7	8 56.8	+46.5	100.8	8 45.4	+47.2	101.0	8 33.9	+47.8	101.1	0
1	10 34.0	42.9	99.3	10 24.2	43.7	99.5	10 14.3	44.3	99.7	10 04.1	45.1	99.8	9 53.8	45.7	100.0	9 43.3	46.4	100.2	9 32.6	47.1	100.3	9 21.7	47.7	100.5	1
2	11 16.9	42.8	98.6	11 07.9	43.5	98.8	10 58.6	44.3	99.0	10 49.2	44.9	99.2	10 39.5	45.7	99.3	10 29.7	46.3	99.5	10 19.7	47.0	99.7	10 09.4	47.7	99.9	2
3	11 59.7	42.7	97.9	11 51.4	43.5	98.1	11 42.9	44.2	98.3	11 34.1	44.9	98.5	11 25.2	45.6	98.7	11 16.0	46.3	98.9	11 06.7	46.9	99.1	10 57.1	47.6	99.3	3
4	12 42.4	42.6	97.1	12 34.9	43.3	97.4	12 27.1	44.0	97.6	12 19.0	44.8	97.8	12 10.8	45.5	98.0	12 02.3	46.2	98.2	11 53.6	46.8	98.4	11 44.7	47.5	98.6	4
70	46 18.0	+6.5	28.7	47 10.5	+7.2	29.2	48 02.7	+8.0	29.8	48 54.7	+8.7	30.3	49 46.3	+9.5	30.9	50 37.6	+10.4	31.5	51 28.6	+11.2	32.2	52 19.2	+12.0	32.9	70
71	46 24.5	5.4	27.3	47 17.7	6.1	27.8	48 10.7	6.8	28.3	49 03.4	7.6	28.8	49 55.8	8.3	29.4	50 48.0	9.0	30.0	51 39.8	9.9	30.6	52 31.2	10.8	31.3	71
72	46 29.9	4.3	25.8	47 23.8	5.0	26.3	48 17.5	5.7	26.8	49 11.0	6.3	27.3	50 04.1	7.1	27.8	50 57.0	7.9	28.4	51 49.7	8.6	29.0	52 42.0	9.4	29.7	72
73	46 34.2	3.3	24.4	47 28.8	3.8	24.8	48 23.2	4.4	25.3	49 17.3	5.1	25.8	50 11.2	5.8	26.3	51 04.9	6.5	26.8	51 58.3	7.3	27.4	52 51.4	8.0	28.0	73
74	46 37.5	2.1	22.9	47 32.6	2.7	23.3	48 27.6	3.3	23.8	49 22.4	4.0	24.3	50 17.0	4.6	24.7	51 11.4	5.3	25.3	52 05.6	5.9	25.8	52 59.4	6.7	26.4	74
75	46 39.6	+1.0	21.5	47 35.3	+1.6	21.9	48 30.9	+2.2	22.3	49 26.4	+2.7	22.7	50 21.6	+3.3	23.2	51 16.7	+3.9	23.7	52 11.5	+4.6	24.2	53 06.1	+5.4	24.7	75
76	46 40.6	−0.1	20.0	47 36.9	+0.4	20.4	48 33.1	+0.9	20.8	49 29.1	1.5	21.2	50 24.9	2.1	21.6	51 20.6	2.7	22.1	52 16.1	3.3	22.6	53 11.5	3.9	23.1	76
77	46 40.5	1.3	18.5	47 37.3	−0.8	18.9	48 34.0	−0.3	19.3	49 30.6	+0.2	19.6	50 27.0	+0.8	20.0	51 23.3	1.3	20.5	52 19.4	1.9	20.9	53 15.4	2.5	21.4	77
78	46 39.2	2.3	17.1	47 36.5	1.9	17.4	48 33.7	1.4	17.7	49 30.8	−0.9	18.1	50 27.8	−0.5	18.5	51 24.6	+0.1	18.9	52 21.3	+0.6	19.3	53 17.9	+1.1	19.7	78
79	46 36.9	3.4	15.6	47 34.6	3.0	15.9	48 32.3	2.6	16.2	49 29.9	2.2	16.6	50 27.3	1.7	16.9	51 24.7	−1.3	17.3	52 21.9	−0.8	17.6	53 19.0	−0.3	18.1	79
80	46 33.5	−4.6	14.2	47 31.6	−4.2	14.4	48 29.7	−3.8	14.7	49 27.7	−3.4	15.0	50 25.6	−3.0	15.3	51 23.4	−2.6	15.7	52 21.1	−2.1	16.0	53 18.7	−1.7	16.4	80
81	46 28.9	5.6	12.7	47 27.4	5.3	13.0	48 25.9	5.0	13.2	49 24.3	4.7	13.5	50 22.6	4.3	13.8	51 20.8	3.9	14.1	52 19.0	3.5	14.4	53 17.0	3.1	14.7	81
82	46 23.3	6.7	11.3	47 22.1	6.4	11.5	48 20.9	6.1	11.7	49 19.6	5.8	12.0	50 18.3	5.5	12.2	51 16.9	5.2	12.5	52 15.5	4.9	12.7	53 13.9	4.4	13.0	82
83	46 16.6	7.8	9.9	47 15.7	7.6	10.0	48 14.8	7.3	10.2	49 13.8	7.1	10.4	50 12.8	6.8	10.6	51 11.7	6.5	10.9	52 10.6	6.2	11.1	53 09.5	5.9	11.4	83
84	46 08.8	8.9	8.4	47 08.1	8.6	8.6	48 07.5	8.5	8.7	49 06.7	8.2	8.9	50 06.0	8.0	9.1	51 05.2	7.7	9.3	52 04.4	7.5	9.5	53 03.6	7.3	9.7	84
85	45 59.9	−9.9	7.0	46 59.5	−9.8	7.1	47 59.0	−9.6	7.3	48 58.5	−9.4	7.4	49 58.0	−9.2	7.6	50 57.5	−9.1	7.7	51 56.9	−8.8	7.9	52 56.3	−8.6	8.1	85
86	45 50.0	11.0	5.6	46 49.7	10.8	5.7	47 49.4	10.7	5.8	48 49.1	10.6	5.9	49 48.8	10.4	6.0	50 48.4	10.2	6.1	51 48.1	10.1	6.3	52 47.7	9.9	6.4	86
87	45 39.0	12.0	4.2	46 38.9	11.9	4.2	47 38.7	11.8	4.3	48 38.5	11.7	4.4	49 38.4	11.7	4.5	50 38.2	11.5	4.6	51 38.0	11.4	4.7	52 37.8	11.3	4.8	87
88	45 27.0	13.0	2.8	46 27.0	13.0	2.8	47 26.9	12.9	2.9	48 26.8	12.8	2.9	49 26.7	12.8	3.0	50 26.7	12.8	3.0	51 26.6	12.7	3.1	52 26.5	12.6	3.2	88
89	45 14.0	14.0	1.4	46 14.0	14.0	1.4	47 14.0	14.0	1.4	48 14.0	14.0	1.5	49 13.9	13.9	1.5	50 13.9	13.9	1.5	51 13.9	13.9	1.5	52 13.9	13.9	1.6	89
90	45 00.0	−15.0	0.0	46 00.0	−15.0	0.0	47 00.0	−15.0	0.0	48 00.0	−15.1	0.0	49 00.0	−15.1	0.0	50 00.0	−15.1	0.0	51 00.0	−15.1	0.0	52 00.0	−15.1	0.0	90
	45°			46°			47°			48°			49°			50°			51°			52°			

76°, 284° L.H.A. **LATITUDE SAME NAME AS DECLINATION**

Figure 2915d. Pub. No. 229, "same name" page (extract).

the LHA argument, and 90° minus distance to a point on the great circle as the declination argument. The latitude of the point on the great circle and the difference of longitude between that point and the point of departure are the tabular altitude and azimuth angle respondents, respectively.

Required. A number of points at 300-mile intervals along the great circle from latitude 50° N, longitude 5° W when the initial great-circle course angle is N 76° W.

Entering the tables (Figure 2915d) with latitude 50° (Same Name), LHA 76°, and with successive declinations of 85°, 80°, 75°, . . . the latitudes and differences in longitude from 5° W are found as tabular altitudes and azimuth angles respectively.

Distance n. mi. (arc)	300(5°)	600(10°)	900(15°)	1200(20°)
Latitude	51.0° N	51.4° N	51.3° N	50.6° N
DLo	7.7°	15.7°	23.7°	31.5°
Longitude	12.7° W	20.7° W	28.7° W	36.5° W

Note. If the respondents are abstracted from across the C-S line, the DLo is the supplement of the tabular azimuth angle; the tabular altitudes correspond to latitudes on the side of the equator opposite from the latitude of departure.

Summary **2916** The "sailings" are mathematical procedures involving computations between latitude and longitude of the departure point, course and speed, and latitude and longitude of the destination. In general, two of these three pairs will be known and solution will be for the third pair.

30 The Practice of Celestial Navigation at Sea

Introduction **3001** Chapter 16, "The Practice of Piloting," explained the navigation of a ship from her berth or anchorage to the point where she took her departure, a coastal passage to the entrance to her next port, and then on to her berth or anchorage there. This chapter is concerned with the practice of navigation on the high seas, when out of sight of land and seamarks. At sea, the proper practice of celestial navigation is of the utmost importance. Even in areas where electronic navigation systems provide good coverage, celestial navigation must not be neglected; electronic systems or individual pieces of equipment may suddenly become unavailable. The prudent navigator uses *every* available means of fixing his position.

Navigation at sea **3002** At sea, it is usually impossible to fix position with the same accuracy as can be obtained in piloting; however, the navigator must make every effort to obtain the most accurate fixes possible, and to maintain an accurate DR and EP between fixes. Every opportunity to obtain celestial observations should be seized.

Every available means of obtaining positioning data should be employed. Loran, Omega, satellite navigation systems, radio direction finders, Consol, Decca, the echo sounder, and other electronic equipment should be used whenever conditions permit.

The navigation team **3003** In the following article a typical minimum day's work in celestial navigation at sea is outlined. The ship's "navigation team" will be discussed here in terms of the personnel available on a U.S. naval vessel; the same general functions will be performed on merchant ships and yachts, but with many less people being involved.

Aboard many naval vessels, a considerable share of this work will be performed by the quartermasters. For example, the senior quartermaster usually winds and compares the chronometers, and azimuth observations are usually made and reduced by quartermasters, who usually also prepare the lists of stars to be observed. The organization of the navigation team, and the duties of the individual quartermasters who are a part of it, will depend on their training and natural abilities.

The senior quartermasters are frequently good sextant observers, and their sights can be most helpful in augmenting those of the navigator. The navigator should encourage and train his quartermasters to become proficient in all aspects of navigation, and particularly as celestial observers. The greatest limiting factor on the accuracy of celestial navigation is the quality of the sextant observation, and consistently reliable observations can only be obtained after much practice. A quartermaster who can obtain good celestial observations is of great value to his ship and to the Navy.

Practice sights. Training in this field should start with LAN sights when the sun is moving slowly in altitude. Next, observations should be made when its altitude is changing more rapidly; with practice, sights should be obtained every 10 to 15 seconds. These may be plotted on graph paper, using $\frac{1}{2}$ inch or 1 inch to a minute of arc and to 10 seconds of time; a "line of best fit" is then drawn in, which serves to indicate the random errors of the individual observations. Such graphing will soon enable the navigator to identify his best-qualified observers.

The navigator should also see to it that the quartermasters are trained as recorders. An observation is worthless if the altitude or time is misrecorded.

The training of quartermasters is one of the highly important duties of a navigator.

The day's work in celestial navigation

3004 Details of the navigating team's work during a day at sea vary with the navigator and the ship, as well as with other factors, but a typical *minimum* day's work during good weather might include the following:

Plot of dead reckoning throughout the day.

Computation of the time of the beginning of morning civil twilight, and preparation of a list of stars and planets in favorable positions for observation at that time, with the approximate altitude and azimuth of each body.

Observation of selected celestial bodies and solution of the observations for a fix during morning twilight.

Preparation of a position report based upon the morning twilight fix.

Azimuth of the sun to determine compass error.

Observation of the sun for a morning sun line (and of Venus and the moon, if available).

Winding of chronometers, and determination of chronometer error, by radio time ticks.

Observation of the sun at LAN (and of the moon if it is available) to obtain a ZT 1200 position (running fix or fix), or as near LAN as possible in the event of overcast.

Computation of the day's run, from the preceding noon to the present noon.

Preparation of a position report based upon the ZT 1200 position.

Observation of the sun for an afternoon sun line (and of Venus and the moon, if available).

Azimuth of the sun to determine compass error.

Computation of the time of ending of evening civil twilight, and preparation of a list of stars and planets in favorable positions for observation at that time, with the approximate altitude and azimuth of each body.

Observations of the celestial bodies selected and solution of the observations for a fix during evening twilight. If only one or two bodies can be obtained, the afternoon sun line can be advanced and combined with the evening stars for a running fix.

Preparation of a 2000 position report based upon the evening twilight fix and any other positioning data.

Preparation of the check-off list for the Captain's Night Order Book.

Notes on the day's work

Venus can frequently be observed in the morning, when it is well west and higher than the sun. Similarly, it can be observed in the afternoon, if it is well east, and therefore considerably higher than the sun.

When the sun is high at transit, it is changing rapidly in azimuth. This permits excellent running fixes to be obtained by combining late morning and early afternoon sun lines with LAN.

During prolonged periods of overcast, the sun does at times break through for a short time. Under such conditions, an observer should be ready to obtain an observation without delay. Under such conditions, the sun should be observed even if it is veiled by thin cirrus; rarely does such blurring of the sun's limb cause an error of as much as one minute of arc.

Morning twilight observations

3005 The LMTs of the beginning of morning nautical and civil twilights, and of sunrise, are tabulated in the *Nautical Almanac,* and they are used by the navigator principally to assist him in planning for morning twilight observations. He does this by determining the time at which civil twilight begins (Article 2712), and obtaining LHA ♈ for that time. By setting his Star Finder for that LHA ♈, he can determine the approximate altitudes and azimuths of celestial bodies which will be visible at that time.

A table like that shown in Figure 3005a is useful in preparing to observe celestial bodies during twilight, as it is of great assistance in locating them in both azimuth and altitude. In addition, it permits the selection of bodies with azimuths which will be particularly helpful. A

Star	Magnitude	H	Zn
		° ′	°
Capella	0.2	10 45	036.4
*Mirfak	1.9	27 25	046.2
Schedar	2.5	52 22	047.9
Hamal	2.2	25 50	081.1
*Alpheratz	2.2	50 55	093.0
Diphda	2.2	12 00	127.2
Formalhaut	1.3	14 22	155.2
*Enif	2.5	57 43	161.3
Nunki	2.1	16 18	210.6
*Altair	0.9	53 49	212.9
*Ralsahague	2.1	36 11	254.5
Vega	0.1	61 49	278.1
*Alphecca	2.3	22 21	287.0
Deneb	1.3	84 07	314.2
Alkaid	1.9	19 33	318.8
Alioth	1.7	18 21	330.4
*Kochab	2.2	38 21	339.5
Dubhe	2.0	15 51	345.9

Figure 3005a. Morning stars, 5 June 1977. DR Lat. 41° 02.6′N, Long. 14° 37.1′W. Civil twilight 0354.

body ahead or astern will yield an LOP which makes a *speed line,* thus giving a check on the ship's advance. Similarly, a body observed on the beam will produce an approximate *course line.*

Programs are available for some models of personal electronic calculators that, for an input of latitude, longitude, and date, will compute the time of morning (or evening) civil twilight and the stars that will then be visible, listing altitude to the nearest 1′ and azimuth to nearest 0.1°. Figure 3005a was prepared by such a procedure. Alternatively, a given time can be entered into the calculator and the same star positional information calculated.

In general, the bodies selected should be well distributed in azimuth. Good practice calls for observing a minimum of five bodies; six or seven are more desirable. Of these, four should be reduced, and the resulting LOPs should be advanced for the run between observations. If the resulting quadrangle is of reasonable size, its center is taken as the position of the fix; if not, the other observations are reduced to obtain data for a better position. However, when all the bodies observed lie within 180° of azimuth, the *bisector method,* described in Article 3009, should be used in establishing the fix, which may be *external* rather than *internal.*

The table should include many more bodies than the navigator expects to observe, as some may be obscured by cloud cover. Bodies in the altitude range between 15° and 65° are in general the most satisfactory to observe. Azimuth should also be taken into consideration, so that the bodies observed differ by roughly equal amounts in azimuth. The most desirable bodies for observation should be marked by asterisks on the star table, to signify that they are the first choice for observation, as is shown in Figure 3005a. The marked stars are selected to get good distribution in azimuth, and as being at good altitudes for observation. Polaris, which should be observed, both for a line of position and for a check on the compass, is not on the list, as its azimuth will be within about a degree of north, and its altitude will be about the same as the DR latitude.

Rate of change of altitude When there is broken cloud cover, considerable time is often consumed in obtaining observations of a round of stars. As daylight increases, the stars become increasingly difficult to locate, particularly with the naked eye, and allowance must be made for the change in their altitudes. Bodies to the east or west will change altitude much more rapidly than those to the north or south; for example, in the list, Alpheratz with an azimuth near 090° at twilight will be increasing in altitude at a rate of about 11.3′ per minute of time, while Dubhe will be decreasing in altitude at a rate of only about 3.1′. Alpheratz, therefore, could well have moved out of the field of view of the sextant telescope, if no allowance is made for its motion. The rate of change of altitude in a minute of time may be obtained by the equation:

ΔH per minute = 15 × cos Lat × sin Z, where Z is the angle between the meridian and the body.

This equation was used in preparing the nomogram shown in Figure 3005b, which has been found to be helpful.

During morning twilight, the eastern horizon is the first to become sharply defined, and as a general rule, bodies in that direction are observed first. This procedure may be modified by the brightness of a particular body, which may make it visible in the east for some time after all other bodies are hidden from view by the approaching daylight. Conversely, it may be desirable to observe a relatively dim star to the westward as soon as the horizon is clear under it, as it may otherwise be lost to view. In general, the later a star or planet is observed during morning twilight, the more accurate will be its LOP, as the observation will then be made with the most sharply defined horizon. The inexperienced navigator must, however, guard against waiting too long, as the body may then be too faint to observe. For this reason, it is often desirable to make an observation of a body as soon as conditions permit, and then a second one of the same body as late as possible.

No difficulty should be experienced in identifying the bodies observed during morning twilight, as the navigator usually has ample opportunity to study them before taking his sights. If any doubt does exist, its azimuth should be noted and recorded for possible use in identifying the body later.

In checking the index error of the sextant, one should use a moderately bright star before making the observations, or the clearest part of the horizon after making the observations.

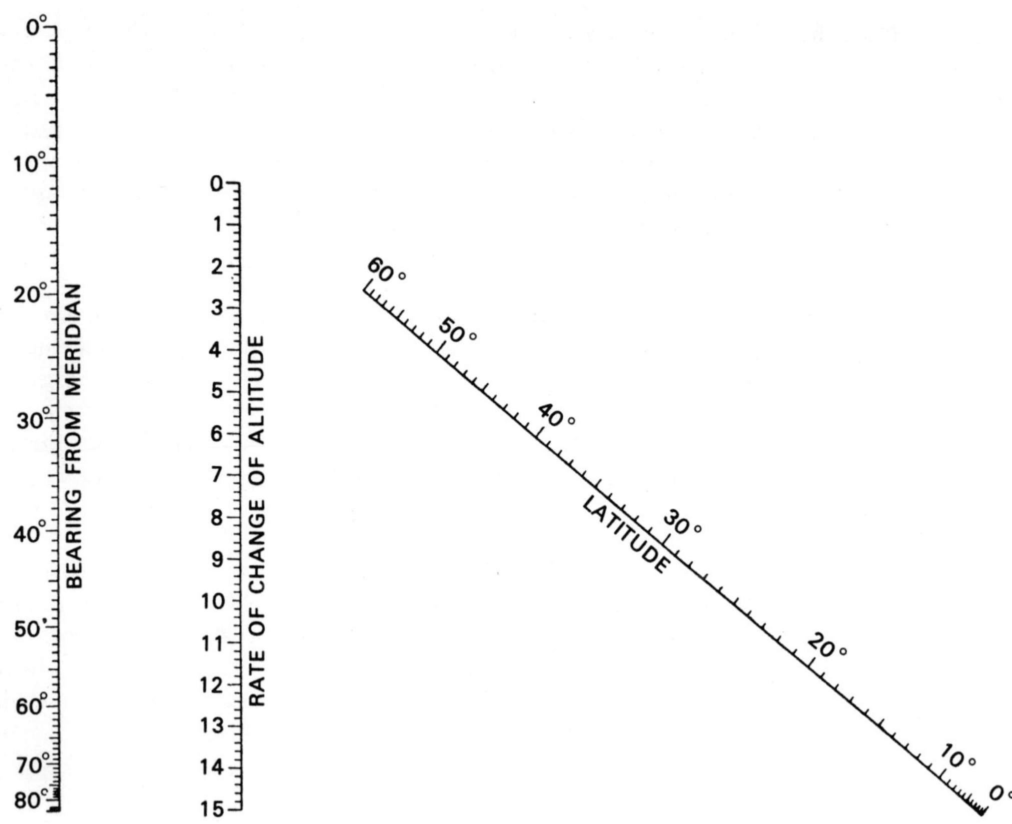

Figure 3005b. Nomogram for determining the change in altitude of a body per minute of time.

Daylight observations **3006** The usual observations made at sea include two azimuths made for compass checks.

Azimuth observations The sun is the body most frequently used for this purpose; the most accurate observations may be made when it is rising or setting as it is then moving comparatively slowly in azimuth, and minimal error is introduced by any tilt in the azimuth circle. Under conditions where it is very difficult to obtain accurate azimuths with an azimuth circle, it is wise to make an amplitude observation.

Altitude sights When quartermasters who are capable observers are available, it is good practice to observe the sun at frequent and regular intervals; some ships make hourly observations. Even if all these sights are not reduced immediately, it does make valuable data available in the event of sudden overcast.

As stated in Article 3004, Venus and the moon should be observed whenever possible in conjunction with the sun to obtain a forenoon fix.

Noon fix If only one morning sun sight is to be observed it should be taken with two thoughts in mind. One is that the resulting LOP is to be advanced to noon to obtain a running fix, and the other is that the LAN observation will yield a latitude line, or an approximate latitude line in the event that the sun cannot be observed exactly at LAN. It is desirable that the two LOPs intersect at an angle of 45° or more; on the other hand, the morning sun observation should not be obtained so early that there can be much error due to uncertainty as to the ship's speed and course in advancing it to noon. The two factors depend on the latitude of the observer and the sun's declination. Pub. No. 229 can be used to determine the rate of change of the sun's azimuth, and therefore how long before noon the observation should be made.

LAN should be observed as a matter of routine aboard all ships. It offers the most accurate celestial line of position, as the sun is not changing altitude perceptibly at LAN, and the horizon is usually sharply defined. In addition to the LAN sight, it may be desirable to obtain a sun line exactly at ZT 1200, so that it will not have to be adjusted to determine the ZT 1200 position, or it may be obtained at another convenient time. Many navigators prefer to make an observation at about ZT 1145, so that it and the morning sun line can be advanced to 1200 and the running fix at that time determined and submitted by 1200. A meridian altitude observation can, of course, be obtained only at the time of transit unless the appropriate correction is applied from *Bowditch* Table 28.

The conditions governing the afternoon sun-line observations are similar to those which apply to the morning sun line. A longitude line in the afternoon is useful for determining the time at which to make evening twilight observations, and, since in mid-latitudes it generally will be taken rather late in the afternoon, it affords a good speed check for a vessel on an easterly or westerly course.

The above discussion is based upon the assumption that good weather prevails, and that the navigator can observe the sun at any time. If the sky is overcast, he should not ignore the possibility of obtaining an LOP at any time when the sun might be visible. With skillful use of the sextant shade glasses, the sun often can be observed when behind thin clouds.

If the moon can be observed during daylight, its LOP should be crossed with a sun line obtained at the same time, unless the two bodies are at nearly the same or reciprocal azimuths. Care must sometimes be taken when observing the moon that the correct limb is observed. Venus can often be seen during daylight, when it is higher in altitude than the sun, if the navigator knows its approximate altitude and azimuth, and less frequently Mars and Jupiter can be seen.

A small error, due to phase and parallax, will occur in daytime observations of Venus if the equation given in the "Explanation" section of the *Nautical Almanac* is not employed. For observations of Venus and Mars obtained between sunset and sunrise, the "additional correction," found inside the front cover of the *Almanac,* should be used to compensate for phase and parallax.

Sun correction tables

The *Sun Correction Tables,* on the inside front cover of the *Nautical Almanac,* should be used for correcting sextant altitudes except when maximum accuracy is desired. The semidiameter of the sun is averaged in the tables for two six-month periods. Greater accuracy can be obtained by using the refraction correction, listed under "Stars and Planets," and the sun's semidiameter obtained from the bottom of the appropriate page in the *Almanac.* To these, a parallax correction +0.1′ should be added for altitudes up to 65°.

Low-altitude sights

Low-altitude sun sights, that is, observations of the sun in the altitude range of from 0° to 5°, have acquired a reputation for unreliability that they do not deserve. Refraction is somewhat uncertain at low altitudes; however, except under very unusual atmospheric conditions, such sights usually yield acceptable results. To illustrate: 266 observations of the sun were made at altitudes between 0° and 5°; 183 of these yielded LOPs that were within 0.5 miles of the true position, 53 lay between 0.5 and 1.0 miles, 30 were in error by more than 1.0 miles, and only two were in error by more than 2.0 miles, the greatest error being 2.2 miles. These observations were, of course, fully and carefully corrected.

Low-altitude sun sights must be corrected carefully. The fixed sextant error, the IC, and the dip are applied to the sextant altitude (hs) before the refraction correction is taken from the Stars and Planets column of Table A3; the semidiameter is taken from the daily pages of an almanac, and + 0.1′ is used as the parallax correction. The "Additional Corrections" to the Altitude Correction Tables in the *Nautical Almanac* should also be used for all low-altitude observations.

It should be noted here that, for some observers, the upper limb of the sun is both easier to observe and yields somewhat more accurate results at low altitudes than does the lower limb.

High-altitude sights

High altitude sun sights, that is, observations of the sun at altitudes greater than 80°, are generally difficult to obtain accurately due to the difficulty of establishing the vertical. A compensatory advantage, however, is the near absence of observational error from refraction.

When the sun's declination is near the vessel's latitude, morning sun observations make possible the determination of longitude with considerable accuracy. This, in turn, makes possible a highly accurate prediction of the time of local apparent noon, and a high altitude LAN observation can frequently be made with great accuracy.

An azimuth circle is placed on a gyro repeater on the side of the bridge on which the sun will transit, and is aligned with the north-south points of the gyro repeater card. The sextant index arm is set to the expected altitude at LAN, and the observer then steps back from the pelorus, and places himself so that the azimuth circle vanes are in line when seen through the horizon glass of the sextant. The sun's altitude is obtained for LAN when its image is in contact with the horizon at a point directly above the vanes.

Such a high-altitude LAN observation can be of considerable value, as under such conditions all other sun lines obtained during the day will lie generally in a north-south direction.

Care should be taken in plotting very high altitude observations, those with sextant altitudes of roughly 87° or more. The curvature of the circular line of position becomes so great that a straight line is not a satisfactory approximation. In such cases, it is preferable to plot the entire circle using the geographical position (GP) of the body as the center and the zenith distance (90° – hs) as the radius. This graphic solution eliminates any need for the use of sight reduction tables. Two circular LOPs can be drawn for observations separated by a short period of time; the DR position will guide the navigator as to which of the two intersections should be used for the fix.

Sea-air temperature

Sea-air temperature difference correction. (Article 2129). A difference between the sea surface temperature and that of the air in contact with it tends to affect the value of the dip correction. The latter is calculated for "standard conditions," and these are distorted when the air in contact with the sea is warmed or cooled by the water. The result is not serious when a number of bodies well distributed in azimuth are observed, as it may generally be assumed that the anomaly is constant, and will apply equally to each of the bodies observed.

However, when only the sun is available for observation, as is usually the case in the daytime, this anomaly can affect the accuracy of the LOP. This is equally true for several bodies located in a limited sector of azimuth; however, in such a case, the use of bisectors (Article 3009) is helpful.

For best results sea water should be picked up in a canvas dip bucket at some point well forward in the ship; in actual practice, the intake water temperature, as obtained from the engine room, is used. This is compared with the dry bulb temperature measured at the level where the observations are made. The correction is subtractive when the air is colder than the water (i.e., the sextant altitude will be too great), and additive when the water is colder than the air (Article 2129). This correction should be used only when experienced judgment indicates that it will result in improved observations.

Evening twilight observations

3007 Evening twilight observations are similar to morning twilight observations, with the important difference to the inexperienced navigator that there is little opportunity to identify the bodies in advance of observation. Under these conditions, the approximate altitude and azimuth are particularly helpful in locating the bodies, and the azimuth of a body which has been observed for altitude, but not positively identified, should always be noted.

In the evening the stars and planets in the east are usually observed first, subject to their brightness, as that area of the sky darkens first.

Dark-adapted vision

Night observations. Star observations can be made successfully on clear nights, provided the observer's vision is *dark adapted* and if the sextant telescope and mirrors have reasonably good optical qualities. During World War II it was found that if the human eye was exposed to no light other than dull red for a considerable period of time, its night perception was considerably increased. This proved to be of great value to many navigators in the fleet submarines, which, when in enemy waters, could surface only during the hours of complete darkness. With dark-adapted vision, and using a sextant fitted with a prismatic telescope having a 30-mm objective lens, and a magnification of 6×, they obtained satisfactory star fixes. The 6 × 30 telescope is acceptable for night use, but the 7 × 50 is superior, as it has about twice the light-gathering power of the 6 × 30.

In making night observations, it is vital that the readout light on the sextant and the recorder's flashlight be fitted with red bulbs. Red lamp dye is available commercially, and flashlight bulbs dipped in it have proven satisfactory for night use.

Light amplification telescopes

Light amplification or night-vision telescopes developed as sniper scopes for the Army will, when mounted on a sextant, provide a view of the horizon on a dark night.

Astigmatizing shade

When observing bright stars or planets with a dim horizon, it is often desirable to use a pale sun shade to reduce the body's brilliance. An *astigmatizing shade* is also frequently helpful under such conditions. This is a prism which elongates the image of a star into a thin horizontal line. Astigmatizers are fitted on many sextants.

There is considerable risk of obtaining a false altitude when observing a brilliant moon, or a star or planet near the moon in azimuth, as the moonlight may give a false horizon. This risk is reduced if such observations are made from a point as low as possible in the ship, and it is also wise to have the recorder check the horizon under the moon through 7 × 50 binoculars to see if the illuminated water is actually at the horizon.

Accuracy of celestial lines of position and fixes

3008 The accuracy of an LOP obtained by celestial navigation is only rarely equal to that of the average LOP obtained in piloting. The reasons for this are numerous, and the major ones have been commented upon at appropriate places in this text. Ordinarily, therefore, a navigator should consider a single celestial LOP to be accurate only within about two miles in either direction. This is considering error in altitude measurement only, and might be increased by a mistake in timing, computation, or plotting. With experience and the cultivation of sound judgment in such matters, the navigator will be able to evaluate some sights as being more accurate than this, and some as probably being less accurate. Also, the accuracy of celestial observations increases with practice; a research program disclosed some years ago that the accuracy of observers in making celestial observations continued to improve even after more than 2,000 observations had been made. Expert observers, under good conditions, expect a multiple star fix to yield a position accurate within a quarter of a mile.

The following discussion of the theory of error may be helpful in evaluating positioning data.

A fix or running fix in celestial navigation is determined by two or more lines of position, each of which may be in error. If two lines are crossed at an angle of 90° and each has a possible error of two miles, the situation illustrated in Figure 3008a results.

The navigator selects the point where LOP *A-B* intersects LOP *X-Y* as his fix, but if each line is in error by two miles, he will be at one of the corners of the square shown by the broken lines, 2.8 miles from his fix. If one of the lines is in error by two miles and the other is without error, his actual position will be at the intersection of one of the solid lines and one of the broken lines, 2.0 miles from his fix.

If two lines are crossed at an angle of 30° and each has a possible error of two miles, the situation illustrated in Figure 3008b results.

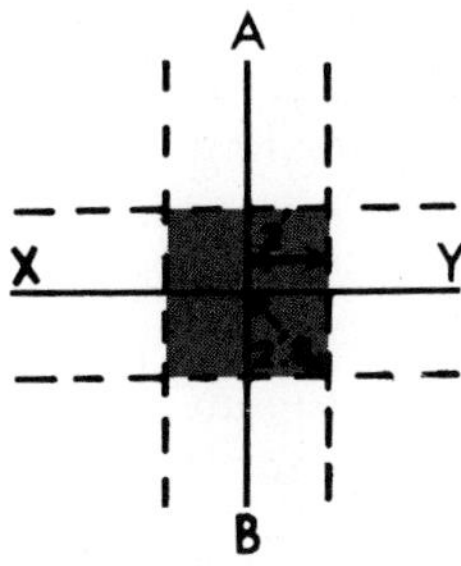

Figure 3008a. Possible error in a fix from two lines of position differing in azimuth by 90° if each LOP has a possible error of two miles.

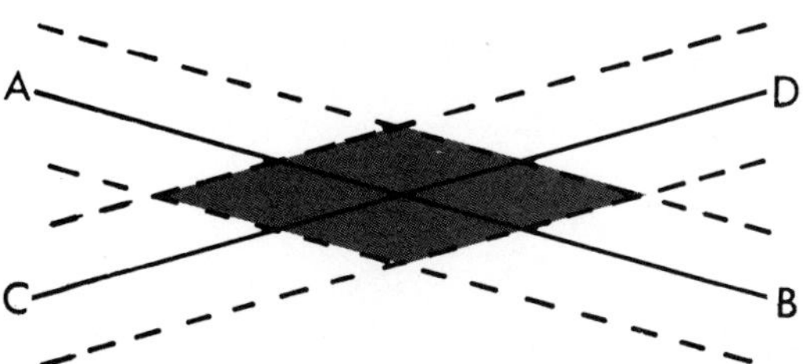

Figure 3008b. Possible error in a fix from two lines of position differing in azimuth by 30° if each LOP has a possible error of two miles.

The navigator selects the point where LOP *A-B* intersects LOP *C-D* as his fix, but if each line is in error by two miles, he will be at one of the corners of the parallelogram shown by the broken lines, either 2.1 or 7.7 miles from his fix. If one of the lines is in error by two miles and the other is without error, his actual position will be at the intersection of one of the solid lines and one of the broken lines, or 4.0 miles from his fix.

From the above discussion it can be seen that, when two lines of position are obtained, the navigator may place the most confidence in the resulting fix when the lines intersect at angles of 90°, or nearly 90°, all other factors being equal. A 90° intersection in a *running fix,* however, may not give as reliable a position as can be obtained from two lines of a *fix* which cut at a smaller angle, because of the possible error in advancing the earlier LOP for a running fix.

Whenever possible, the navigator uses at least three lines of position to obtain a fix. If these lines intersect at angles of 60° and each has a possible error of two miles, the situation illustrated in Figure 3008c results. The navigator selects the point where the three lines intersect as his fix, but if each line is subject to error of up to two miles, his actual position may be anywhere within the shaded hexagon of the figure, at a maximum distance of 2.3 miles from the plotted fix.

The accuracy of a fix is not materially increased by plotting more than four lines of position, if the lines can be relied on to be equally accurate, and are approximately evenly distributed in azimuth. In practice, the usable stars are never perfectly located in azimuth, and five or more lines will usually yield a better idea of the most probable position, than will three. When the bodies observed all lie within 180° of azimuth of one another, *bisectors,* which are discussed in the next article, should be drawn and used.

In Figure 3008c the three solid lines are shown intersecting at a point. In practice, this rarely happens, and the navigator takes the center of the small figure usually formed as being his fix. The point

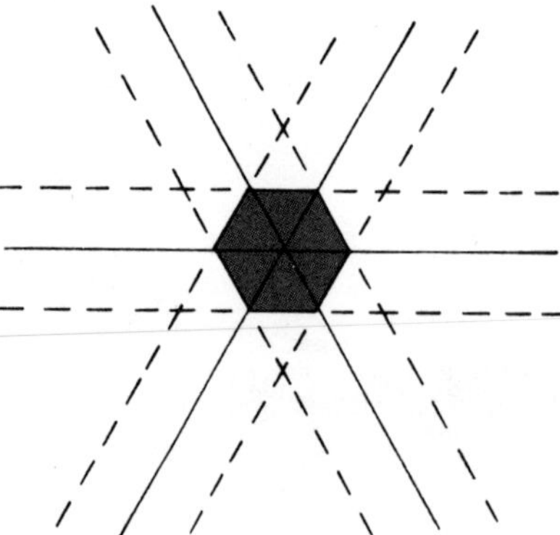

Figure 3008c. Possible error in a fix from three lines of position differing in azimuth by 120° if each has a possible error of two miles.

selected is equidistant from all sides of the figure. It can be determined geometrically or by computation, but in practice the navigator estimates it by eye. The size of the figure obtained is not necessarily an indication of the accuracy of the fix.

When the navigator can select three or more bodies to be observed for a fix (as when observing stars), he can guard against a *constant* error in altitude by observing bodies at equal intervals of *azimuth.* A constant error in altitude causes all lines of position to be in error by the same amount and in the same direction, relative to the bodies being observed. When bodies are observed at equal intervals of azimuth, a constant error will either increase or decrease the size of the figure formed when the lines are plotted, but will have no effect on the center of the figure. Thus, three stars differing in azimuth by 120° (not 60°), or four stars differing by 90° should be observed, or five stars differing by 72°, etc. Theoretically, a four-star fix from bodies differing in azimuth by 90° (as N, S, E, and W) should produce only two lines of position, but in all probability a small rectangle will be the result; the center of the rectangle, determined by eye, can be taken as the fix.

The factor that has the greatest effect on a single observation is usually *random error.* The reliability of an individual line of position can be considerably improved by making several observations of the same body, and averaging the times and altitudes before solving for an LOP; this tends to average out the random errors. Alternatively, if five or more observations of the same body are taken in quick succession, and its azimuth is noted by gyro, the accuracy of the individual observations may be determined by comparing the change of altitude between observation; the rate of change in altitude per second of time being equal to 0.25 × cos Latitude × sine of the angle between the body and the meridian. If the rate of change is steady for several sights one of these should be selected for reduction. This equation may be solved extremely rapidly with an electronic calculator.

An alternate method is to make three observations in quick succession and to solve and plot each one. If two LOPs are then in close agreement and a third differs considerably, it is usually safe to assume that the correct LOP lies mid-way between the two lines which are in agreement. The method is not as tedious as it may at first seem, particularly if solutions are made in parallel columns, as usually the only difference in the solutions are in minutes and seconds of time and the resulting differences in GHA and aλ. Ordinarily, multiple observations are limited to sun lines, as the several bodies observed for a twilight fix serve as a check on each other.

In fixing or estimating the position of a ship, the navigator should not ignore the DR or EP, as these positions are based on other navigational information which may be more or less accurate than a given LOP. A DR or EP should be considered a *circle* with radius equal to the navigator's estimate of its accuracy, if knowledge of course and speed are considered to be equally good. If the navigator believes that one of these is known more accurately than the other, the DR or EP should be considered a small *ellipse*, with its minor axis extending in the direction indicated by the more accurately known quantity and its major axis extending in the direction indicated by the less accurately known quantity.

From the above, it can be seen that the interpretation of celestial lines of position can be a complex subject—one which calls for sound judgment on the part of an experienced navigator.

LOP bisectors

3009 When a number of bodies with azimuths *all lying within a horizontal 180° sector of arc* are observed, a constant error (both magnitude and sign) may yield misleading results if the fix is assumed to lie within the polygon formed by the LOPs; this is often called an "internal" fix. Such constant errors could result from an uncorrected personal error or from unusual terrestrial refraction, which causes the value of the dip, as obtained from the *Nautical Almanac,* to be considerably in error. This may lead to the fix lying *outside* the polygon, resulting in an "external" fix rather than the usual internal one. Where multiple LOPs well distributed in azimuth are obtained, this problem does not arise, as in this case the error may be assumed to affect all LOPs about equally.

Where three or more observations are made of bodies with azimuths within 180° of each other, it is wise to use *LOP bisectors* to determine the fix. Each angle formed by a pair of position lines is bisected, the bisector being drawn in the direction of *the mean of the azimuths* of the two bodies.

For example, assume that due to cloud cover, it was possible to observe only three stars, the respective azimuths being as follows: star No. 1, 224°; No. 2, 002°; and No. 3, 254°. The resulting LOPs are plotted in Figure 3009. Note that arrows have been added to each LOP showing the direction of the celestial body; this is desirable for any plot.

LOPs 1 and 2 will be bisected in the direction 292°—112°:

$$\frac{(224° + 000°)}{2} = 112°$$

LOPs 1 and 3 will be bisected in the direction 240°—060°:

$$\frac{(224° + 256°)}{2} = 240°$$

and LOPs 2 and 3 will be bisected in the direction 308°—128°. In Figure 3009 these bisectors are drawn in as blue lines.

The most probable position for the fix lies at the center of the small triangle formed by the three bisectors, rather than in the triangle formed by the three LOPs. Note that this external fix shows an apparent greater "error" than is shown by assuming the center of the original triangle, but this is not actually so.

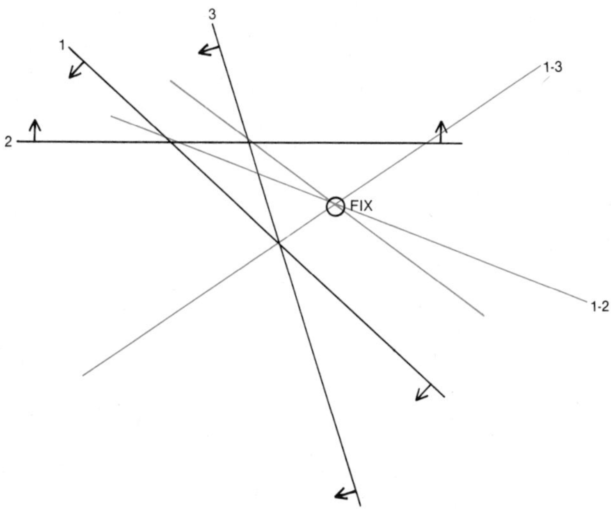

Figure 3009. The use of bisectors showing the external fix (LOPs in black, bisectors in blue).

It can be seen in Figure 3009 that the external fix is a point equidistant from each LOP in the same direction, "away" in this example. Such a point can be estimated by eye, taking care to always be on the same side of each LOP as indicated by the arrows. This technique is more practical at sea than calculating the bisector directions and cluttering up the plot with several additional lines; it should be sufficiently accurate for practical navigation.

The "external" fix should be found and used *only* when there is good reason to believe that there is an error in each observation of constant magnitude and direction. Barring this, the navigator is safer to use the internal fix.

A much more rigorous and detailed mathematical consideration of navigational errors can be found in Appendix Q of *Bowditch*, Volume II (1975).

Errors resulting from selection of the AP

A careful investigation made some years ago in Great Britain showed that for an observer located at the equator when the difference between the true and assumed positions is 30′ in both latitude and longitude, and the altitude of the body observed was 75°, the maximum error will not exceed 1.0 mile; this maximum error will not be more than 0.7 miles at latitude 60°, and the probable error would be about half this amount. For an altitude of 60° at the equator the error will not exceed 0.5 miles. Being roughly proportional to the square of the difference between the true and assumed positions, if the true position is within 20′ of latitude and longitude of the AP, the errors would be less than half those cited.

It is obvious that these errors are of no great concern in the ordinary course of navigation. They are cited only to show that under special conditions, when the utmost accuracy is required, a reduction should be made from the EP. The use of an electronic hand calculator, which provides trigonometric functions and other calculations to many decimal places, can yield an accuracy of better than 0.1′; this is better than the limit of precision of sextant observations.

Position reports

3011 A ship's navigator customarily submits position reports to the captain at least three times each day. In the U.S. Navy this is done at ZT 0800, ZT 1200, and ZT 2000. The information required is the zone time and date of the report; the latitude and longitude, and the time the position was last determined; the method used (where a combination of methods are used it is customary to indicate the method having the predominant effect upon the accuracy of the position); the set and drift since the last well-determined position; distance made good since the last report (indicate time of last report, and distance in miles); the destination, its distance in miles, and the ETA; the true heading; the error of the master gyro; the variation; the magnetic compass heading, with an indication of which compass is in use; the deviation as most recently determined; the deviation according to the current Nav Ships 3120/4 table; whether or not degaussing is energized; and any appropriate remarks, such as the clocks having been advanced or retarded since the last report.

The latitude and longitude given are always for the time of the report, while the time at which the last well-determined position was obtained is given in the "determined at" block. Some commanding officers prefer that the time given in connection with the distance made good be the preceding 1200 rather than the time of the last report, since this gives a ready indication of the miles steamed during the elapsed portion of the "navigational day."

The distance made good and distance to go are ordinarily obtained by measurement on the chart, with dividers, if the distance is not too great, or they can be computed, as explained in Chapter 29.

Gyro and magnetic compass errors are based upon the most recent accurate azimuth observation. Variation is obtained from the pilot chart or sailing chart.

Summary

3012 In this chapter the routine celestial navigation work of the navigator at sea has been listed. While typical, it is not all inclusive, and all of the work done by the navigator and his assistants has not been described.

Only the mechanics of the practice of navigation can be given in a book, and the would-be "navigator" who has mastered this book has mastered *only* the mechanics. The efficiency, accuracy, and judgment of a good professional navigator comes only with experience, and never really ceases to increase with more and more experience. The mark of a good navigator is not as much his ability to obtain accurate information as it is his ability to evaluate, interpret, and correctly use the information that is available to him.

31 Principles of Radionavigation

Introduction

3101 *Electronics* may be defined as the science and technology relating to the emission, flow, and effects of electrons in a vacuum, through a semiconductor, and through appropriate circuitry. *Radionavigation*, as discussed in this chapter, is considered to mean navigation by means of electronic equipment and radio-wave emissions received from an outside source.

The *radio time signal* was the first such aid to come into use. It made precise time available to the navigator for use in connection with celestial navigation. Subsequently, he was able, on request, to obtain radio bearings from a limited number of shore stations. On some coasts, the direction-finding stations were linked by landline telegraph so that a fix could be determined from several radio bearings and transmitted by radio to the ship; often, though, only one radio line of position was available. This system of shore direction-finding stations is now nearly extinct, having been replaced by ship-borne *radio direction finders* (RDF), which permit the navigator to obtain a bearing on any radio station which is transmitting signals. In many coastal areas, he is able to obtain several such bearings, which enable him to determine his position with considerable accuracy. The wide employment of radio direction finders led to the introduction of the term *radionavigation.* Although the term *electronic navigation* is sometimes used in lieu of radionavigation, it is less precise, as it technically would include the use of any electronic device—depth sounder, log, gyrocompass, etc.—for navigation.

Extensive research has been carried out in this field over the past several decades. The development of long-range airplanes established a need for suitable radionavigation systems. Subsequently, the need arose for systems suitable for Fleet Ballistic Missile submarines, and recently systems have been required for the navigation and guidance of space vehicles.

Dead reckoning and positioning systems

These needs were, in each instance, twofold: systems for position fixing (radionavigation systems), and systems for carrying forward a dead-reckoning position from the last fix (inertial systems, Chapter 35). For the latter systems, extremely sensitive and accurate, but expensive, gyros and accelerometers were designed. For position fixing, highly accurate instruments for determining the time of travel of radio signals have been produced, as well as for the measurement of altitude angles of celestial bodies by automatic electro-optical and radiometric tracking. In addition, equipment for measuring the *Doppler shift* of very precisely timed radio signals transmitted by artificial satellites has yielded excellent results. The Doppler shift (named for the Austrian scientist who reported the effect in 1842) is the apparent change in frequency of radiated energy when the distance between the source and the receiver is changing.

In piloting, excellent position fixing is being achieved by both radar and sonar, as currently instrumented. Bathymetric navigation, or navigation by means of continuous soundings of the ocean bottom analyzed by a computer, holds great promise. However, it requires data in the form of very precise bathymetric charting of the operating area.

The ideal navigation system has yet to be developed. Such a system should be worldwide, self-contained, passive, completely reliable, and highly accurate. Currently, the most promising systems, although they do not meet all the above requirements, are Omega, discussed in Chapter 33, and Satellite Navigation, discussed in Chapter 34. Omega uses radio signals from land-based transmitting systems, while the Satellite Navigation system depends on signals from a satellite traveling in a precisely determined orbit.

Basic phenomena

3102 The following brief discussion of electronic fundamentals assumes that the reader has some knowledge of basic physics, or has access to appropriate reference books; it is not possible to cover the subject of electronics in detail in a volume such as this.

Hertz (Hz) and cycles per second

For many decades, alternating current frequency was expressed in "cycles per second." This seemed the natural term to indicate the complete reversal of the polarity of the voltage and the direction of flow of the current in alternating current circuits. In recent years, however, this term has been replaced with *hertz* which is synonymous with "cycles per second"; the older term is still used by some persons, but less and less each year. The new term honors the German scientist, Heinrich Hertz. Larger units are formed in the same manner as for others of the metric system; see Appendix D.

1 kilohertz (kHz) = 1,000 hertz (Hz)
1 Megahertz (mHz) = 1,000,000 Hz
or 1,000 kHz
1 Gigahertz (gHz) = 1,000,000,000 Hz
or 1,000,000 kHz
or 1,000 MHz

Basic alternating current theory states that a varying magnetic field, resulting from the flow of alternating current in a circuit, induces a voltage in a conductor placed within the field. In fact, voltage is induced even when there is no conductor in the field. Such a voltage, induced into space is, in effect, an electric field. Thus, a varying electric field is created in space by a varying magnetic field. The varying electric field in turn sets up a displacement current, which gives rise to a magnetic field. The varying magnetic field creates an electric field and so on. The process whereby they mutually induce one another is called *electromagnetic induction.* The combination is called the *electromagnetic field;* this effect occurs at all alternating frequencies.

Electromagnetic induction

Once the initial field is created, it becomes independent of further electrical input. When the current stops, the field can continue to survive and to propagate itself on out into space, because of the self-sustaining exchange process.

In an electomagnetic radiation field, the electric field lines close on themselves. They are not attached to charges, and the magnetic field lines are not related to current in conductors. The fields are truly independent, as if cut adrift in space.

There is also a connotation of motion in the process. The complete theory was developed about a hundred years ago by James Clerk Maxwell. He correlated a set of four simultaneous partial differential equations, which describe the interrelation of the electric and magnetic components of electromagnetic fields, and their relation to electric currents and voltages. These equations stand today as the theoretical basis of electromagnetism, and by their use all problems of electromagnetic fields and radiation can be solved. They are: Ampere's circuital law; Gauss's theorem for the electric field; Gauss's theorem for the magnetic field; and Faraday's law on electromotive force.

These laws, formulated by others, but combined by Maxwell within the concept of the displacement current, facilitate the computation of electromagnetic propagation. To compute the velocity of waves of electromagnetic energy traveling outward into space from the point at which they are created, the characteristics of the medium through which they travel must be considered. The Maxwell equations predict that electromagnetic field velocity should be equal to the reciprocal of the square root of the product of the permeability and the permittivity of the medium in rationalized meter-kilogram-second (RMKS) units.

Permeability

Permeability may be defined as the ratio of magnetic induction to magnetizing force. It is a measure of the magnetic induction produced by a unit value of magnetizing force. Permeability is expressed in *henrys* per meter (a term named after Joseph Henry, an American physicist), and may be considered an inductance value.

Permittivity

Permittivity is the ratio of electric flux density to electric field intensity. Relative permittivity of a medium is the ratio of its value of permittivity to that of empty space. It is sometimes referred to as dielectric constant, and may be considered a capacitance value. The permittivity of a substance is expressed in *farads* per meter.

Permeability of empty space is considered to be equal to 1.26×10^{-6} *henrys* per meter; permittivity of empty space is equal to 8.85×10^{-12} *farads* per meter. Then, in accordance with Maxwell's laws, in empty space:

$$\text{electromagnetic wave velocity} = \frac{1}{\sqrt{1.26 \times 8.85 \times 10^{-18}}}$$

or 3×10^8 meters per second.

Maxwell noted that this velocity very closely approximated the measured velocity of light, suggesting that light is a form of electromagnetic radiation. To illustrate the relationship of velocity, wave length, and frequency, consider the measurement of time in the transit of one complete cycle of an electromagnetic field at a specific point on the earth's surface. In the period of time of this measurement, a minute fraction of a second, a complete wavelength of the electromagnetic field would have moved across the point at which the measurement was made. The measured time is the elapsed time required for the electromagnetic field to be moved a distance equal to the wavelength of the field.

Wavelength vs. frequency

The time of completion of one full cycle is therefore equal to the velocity divided by the wavelength. The frequency, the number of times *per second* the signal completes one full cycle, is given in hertz units. The relationship can be visualized as the greater the wavelength the lower the frequency. The transmission characteristic of a given electronic system is stated either as wavelength or frequency. The relationship as discussed briefly above can be stated as a simple equation:

$$\lambda = \frac{300}{F}$$

in which λ is the wavelength in meters, F is the frequency in megahertz, and the constant 300 is the velocity of light in meters per microsecond.

Absorption

Absorption accounts for the loss of some of the energy of electromagnetic waves propagated through space which contains material that is not a perfect insulator. In both radio and light waves, the losses caused by absorption are the result of the conversion of some of the field energy into heat, through the collisions of electrons, excited by the electric field, with other particles in the material. The computation of this loss is similar to the computation of power loss in an electrical circuit due to resistance. If the electromagnetic field were radiated into a pure vacuum, no work would be performed by the energy of the field, and its intensity would be maintained. The alternating electric and magnetic fields would continue to be propagated by each other with the same magnitude of energy as that of the initial radiation.

For example, if an electromagnetic field is radiated from an antenna near the surface of the earth, the electrons in the gas atoms of the atmosphere begin to move under the force of the electric field. The greater the length of time that the force continues in one direction, i.e., the lower the frequency of the radiated field, the greater will be the velocity attained by the electrons during each half cycle of the radiated energy. If the movement of the freed electrons were unobstructed, the power expended in their acceleration would be returned to the electromagnetic wave by the magnetic field which their own motion would produce. However, the electrons, moving at high velocity, collide with atoms of gas and other particles in the atmosphere, thus dissipating significant power in the heat generated by the collisions.

Permittivity and permeability values vary slightly with atmospheric density. Therefore, in accordance with Maxwell's rules, electromagnetic radiation velocity is slightly reduced by increased atmospheric density, or by other material in the propagation medium.

Ground waves and sky waves

3103 The preceding article has discussed briefly the radiation of an electromagnetic field from an antenna into the atmosphere. It next becomes necessary to consider how this field travels outward.

Electromagnetic energy, as transmitted from the antenna, radiates outward in all directions. A portion of this energy proceeds out parallel to the earth's surface, while the remainder travels upwards as well as outwards, until it strikes one or more layers of ionized gases in the *ionosphere* (see Article 3107) and is reflected back to earth; this normally occurs only once but may be repeated as shown by "sky wave 2" in figure 3103a. (These are at times referred to as "one-hop" and "two-hop" sky waves.) That portion of the radiated energy which follows along the surface of the earth is called the *ground wave;* the

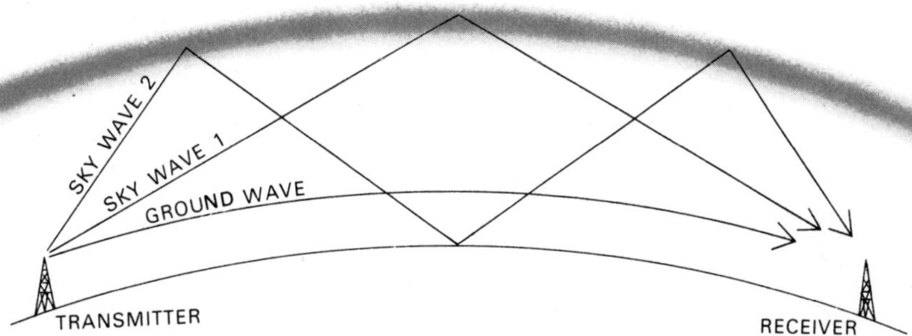

Figure 3103a. Radio ground-wave and sky-wave propagation paths. (The vertical distances in this figure have been exaggerated for clarity, as the distance between the transmitter and receiver is normally hundreds of miles while the ionosphere is only 85 to 100 miles above the earth.)

energy transmitted at higher angles is termed *sky waves.* The ionosphere and its effect on radio waves is considered in more detail later in this chapter.

In the employment of low frequencies, ground waves become very important, and the conductivity of the earth's crust becomes a major factor in signal attenuation (the decrease in amplitude of a wave or current with increasing distance from the source of transmission) by absorption, and its effects on propagation velocity. Because of this conductivity, the electromagnetic field to some extent penetrates the earth's surface. The lower limit of the wave is slightly impeded by its penetration into this medium of increased conductivity, while the upper portion of the wave is not so affected. This results in the lines of force leaning away from the signal source, causing the movement of the electromagnetic wave to curve with the curvature of the earth's surface. It must be remembered that the lines of force of the electric field are perpendicular to the lines of force of the magnetic field, and the direction of motion of the electromagnetic wave is perpendicular to both. (Figure 3103b.)

It is this tendency to follow the earth's curvature that makes possible the transmission of ground waves over great distances. Combined with this curvature of the motion of the electromagnetic wave is the energy loss through absorption in the penetration of the earth's surface. This latter effect necessitates the use of high power to achieve long-distance transmission of the ground wave.

The variation in the characteristics of the surface of land areas complicates the prediction of its effects on ground-wave transmission. The conductivity of the ocean surface is quite constant and propagation velocity over ocean areas can be predicted quite accurately.

Only low-frequency radio transmissions curve sufficiently to follow the earth's surface over great distances. Electromagnetic fields at higher frequencies do not penetrate as deeply into the surface, and so encounter less impedance of velocity from the ground. They are slightly curved, but not enough to provide ground-wave signals at great distances from the transmitting antenna.

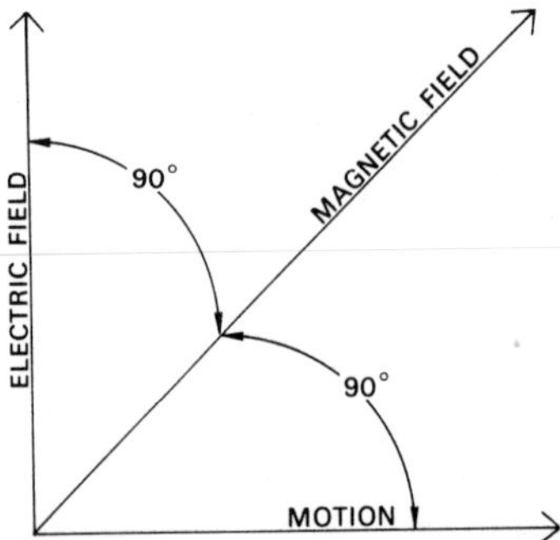

Figure 3103b. Vector relationship of the electric and magnetic fields and of the motion of the electromagnetic wave.

The *polarization* of the radio wave is described in terms of the orientation of the electric field with respect to the earth, either *horizontal* or *vertical;* for special applications, polarization can also be *circular* or *elliptical* with the plane of polarization rotating about the axis of propagation. In any radio system, the transmitting and receiving antennas will normally have the same polarization if they are to be most effective.

Reflection and refraction

3104 Long-distance transmission of high-frequency radio waves can be achieved by reflection and refraction of the electromagnetic waves from ionized layers in the upper atmosphere.

Radio waves and light waves are both forms of electromagnetic waves, differing only in frequency. Some of the laws learned in the science of optics are also applicable to radio waves.

Any surface can reflect light waves. If the surface is smooth and polished, the light is reflected in a *specular* fashion, as by a mirror. Reflection from a rough surface is *diffuse.* Dull, dark-colored surfaces reflect poorly. When a surface reflects only a portion of the light, the rest is absorbed, and the energy of the absorbed light wave is converted into heat in the material.

Radio waves are also reflected, specularly from smooth surfaces and diffusely from rough surfaces. Surfaces of good conductors reflect, and poor conductors absorb. The waves pass through some materials which are electrical insulators, such as glass. Most materials do not completely reflect or completely absorb radio waves, but are imperfect reflectors, or, as poor conductors, still reflect a small portion of the wave.

In both light and radio waves, the reflection capability depends upon the magnitude of the surface irregularities, as compared to the wavelength of the electromagnetic wave. A sea of ten-foot waves would reflect specularly a radio wave of several hundred meters in length, but a radio signal of a few centimeters wavelength would be reflected diffusely.

When a radio wave is reflected specularly, the character of the wave front is unchanged. As in the behavior of light rays reflected from a sextant mirror, the angle of reflection is equal to the angle of incidence. When reflected from a rough surface, the incident wave front breaks up and is randomly reflected in different directions.

In free space, an electromagnetic wave travels in a straight line; however, when traveling through an area containing matter or material particles, the wave may be bent or *refracted.* The light from a celestial body, entering the atmosphere at an oblique angle, bends increasingly downward as it continues into an atmosphere of increasing density. Similarly, bending in the direction of travel of a radio wave occurs when the wave passes from one medium to another of different permittivity or permeability. Thus, when a wave front enters a medium of different characteristic at an oblique angle, the change in velocity affects the first portion of the wave front entering the new medium before the remainder of the wave is affected, and the alignment of the wave front is changed. The direction of travel, as previously stated, is perpendicular to the wave front, therefore the direction of travel changes toward the direction of reduced velocity.

Diffraction

3105 When an electromagnetic wave, either radio or light, is partially obstructed by an object of opaque material, the area behind the object is shadowed as the unobstructed portion of the wave front continues in its original direction. In the case of light waves, a shadow is cast by the object; waves which would otherwise reach this area are blocked.

According to Maxwell's equations, the wave-front portion at the edge of the obstructing object does not completely hold to its original direction. A small portion of the energy is propagated into the shadow area. This phenomenon is called *diffraction* (Figure 3105). Maxwell's equations predict the intensity of the field to be found in the shadow area.

Interference

3106 If two or more radio waves arrive simultaneously at the same point in space, *interference* results. The combination of such waves is in accordance with the principle of superposition of fields. Each field may be represented by a vector, indicating spatial direction and intensity.

The resultant field direction and intensity of either the electric fields or of the magnetic fields may then be determined by following the rules for vector addition.

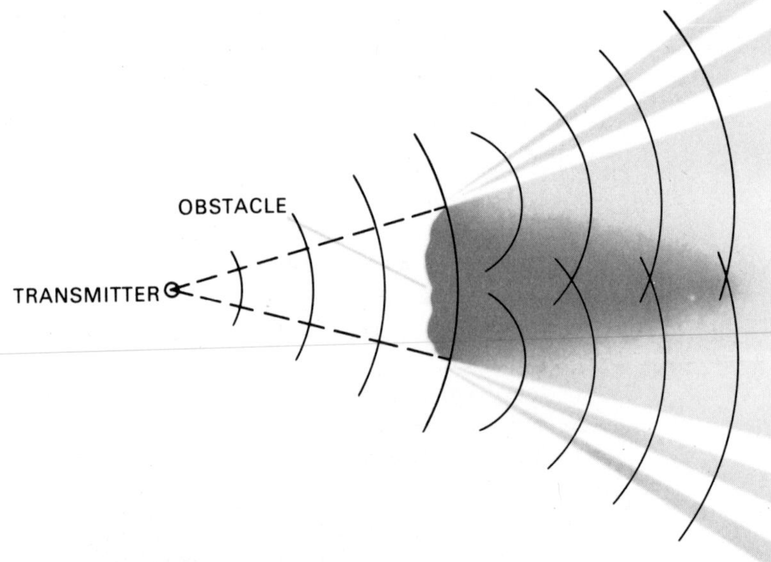

Figure 3105. Diffraction of a wave front.

Ionization **3107** The daylight portion of the earth's atmosphere is subjected to bombardment by intense ultra-violet rays of the sun. At extremely high altitudes in the atmosphere, the gas atoms are comparatively sparse. Electrons are excited by the powerful ultra-violet electromagnetic forces which reverse polarity approximately 10^{17} times per second. This violent oscillation causes the electrons to separate from the positive ions with which they were combined. These freed electrons would eventually find their way to other electron-deficient atoms, but this is prevented by the continuing forces of the ultra-violet rays while in direct sunlight. The region of the upper atmosphere, generally above 30 miles (55 km), where the free ions and electrons exist in sufficient density to have an appreciable effect on radio-wave travel, is called the *ionosphere*; the ionization effect reaches its maximum when the sun is at its highest.

Layers of ionization The electrons and ions are not uniformly distributed in the ionosphere, but rather tend to form layers. These change, disappear, combine, and separate as they are affected by the local time of day, season of the year, and the level of sun-spot activity; the layers are also at times affected by apparent random changes from moment to moment. Four such ionized layers (Figure 3107) are involved in the phenomenon of radio-wave propagation. Each layer has thickness with the most intense ionization at the center, tapering off above and below. The greater the intensity of ionization in any layer, the greater is the bending back towards earth of the radio waves; lower frequencies are more easily reflected than are higher frequencies which have a greater tendency to penetrate the ionosphere and "escape" into space.

D-layer The ionized layer nearest the earth's surface is termed the *D-layer;* its density is considerably less than any of the other three and it has more of an absorbing than reflecting effect. This layer, which occurs at heights of 30 to 50 miles (55 to 90 km) above the earth apparently exists only during daylight hours and disappears completely at night.

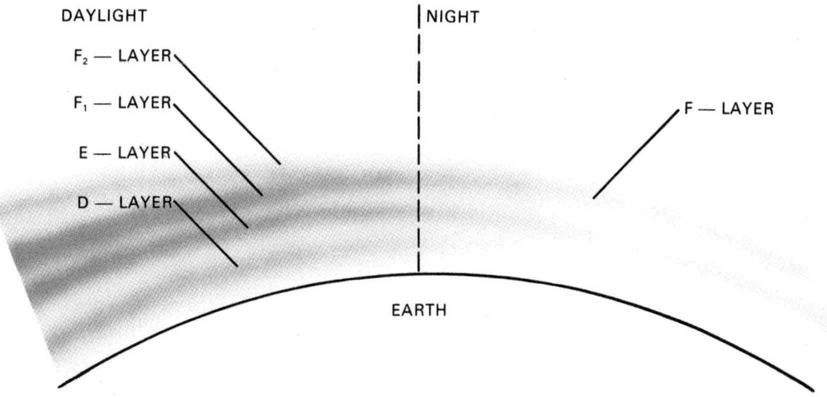

Figure 3107. Layers of ionization; during daytime (left) and at night (right).

E-layer Located at a height of about 65 miles (120 km), the *E-layer* remains during the night, but with somewhat decreased intensity. Its density is greatest in the region beneath the sun. Irregular areas of very high ionization occur during a large percentage of the time. These areas are referred to as *Sporadic E;* they occur at night as well as in daylight.

F_1-layer The F^1-*layer* occurs only in daylight, the freed electrons and ions apparently rejoining to form the normal atoms and molecules of the rarefied air as the stress of the sun's ultra-violet rays diminishes. This layer is usually between 95 and 135 miles (175 to 250 km) above the earth's surface.

F_2-layer The F_2-*layer* varies in both height and density; the variation is diurnal, seasonal, and related to the level of sun-spot activity. It is found at altitudes of 160 to 215 miles (300 to 400 km), where the atmospheric density is extremely low and results in a more complicated diurnal pattern. Due to the molecular collision rates in the very low density of the air at these altitudes, solar energy may be stored for many hours. The gas atoms are relatively few and far between. The release of electrons during the periods of high ultra-violet intensity leaves them moving freely for hours after the sun has disappeared below the horizon. In this condition collisions between free electrons and gas atoms cause other electrons to be dislodged, even during the hours of darkness. Solar energy may be stored in this manner for many hours at these levels.

Some diurnal pattern is discernible at the high levels of the atmosphere. There is a tendency for the F_1 and the F_2 layers to merge during darkness, at a height of about 160 miles (300 km). After sunrise, the upper portion of the layer is again intensified by the sun's rays, and the F_1 layer increases in density as it lowers.

Radio-wave propagation is affected by the various ionized layers in accordance with the wave length or frequency of the radio transmission, and the height and density of the layers of ionization. The ionized layers may either be conducive to the sky-wave transmission of the electromagnetic energy to the area of desired reception, or may hinder or even prevent such transmission, as will be discussed in the following paragraphs.

Electromagnetic frequency spectrum

3108 Radiation in electronics is in the form of electromagnetic waves called *radio waves.* Electromagnetic fields occur at all alternating frequencies. The electromagnetic frequency spectrum extends from a single reversal of polarity per second, through the radio frequency spectrum, infrared frequencies, visible light frequencies, ultraviolet ray, X-ray, and Gamma-ray spectrums to approximately 10^{15} MHz. A diagram of the *electromagnetic* frequency spectrum is shown in Figure 3108a.

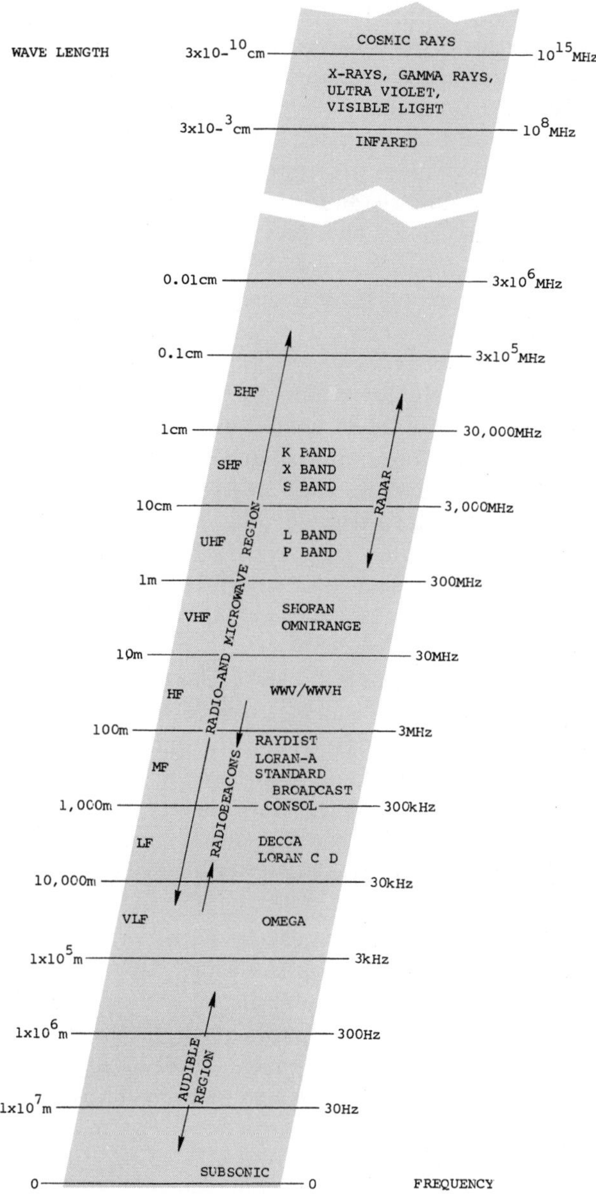

Figure 3108a. Frequency spectrum.

Radio frequency spectrum

The *radio* frequency spectrum extends from 3 kilohertz (kHz) to 300 gigahertz (GHz). This spectrum is divided into eight frequency bands to be described here. (There are two other, lower frequency bands that are not of present interest to this book: VF, or voice frequencies, 300 to 3000 hertz, and ELF, extremely low frequencies, 30 to 300 hertz.)

Very Low Frequency (VLF)

The *VLF band* includes those frequencies below 30 kHz down to approximately 10 kHz. The primary advantage in employing frequencies in this band is the reliability of propagation over great distances by the use of high power. VLF ground waves may be propagated for distances as great as 8,000 miles (15,000 km) facilitating determination of distance by measuring the time of travel of the wave.

VLF sky waves are reflected from the ionosphere with comparatively little loss of energy due to the short distance traveled within the ionized layer. However, the ensuing reflection from the earth's surface undergoes significant loss by absorption, especially over land areas. Diffraction is also greater in the VLF band than in the higher frequencies. VLF waves will, however, penetrate the surface of the earth (land or water) and hence are used for transmissions to submarines. In the lower part of the VLF band, signals may be received with good readability at depths of 40 to 50 feet (12 to 15 m).

It is much more difficult and expensive to obtain antenna efficiency at these frequencies than at higher ones. Radiation of high power, which is required if good reliability over long distances is to be realized, becomes very costly.

The primary navigational use of the VLF band is for the Omega system discussed in Chapter 33.

Low Frequency (LF)

The *LF band* (30 to 300 kHz) is not reflected as efficiently by the ionosphere. Ground losses increase as the frequency is increased and diffraction decreases. However, the antennas for use in the LF band are usually more efficient than those in the VLF band. Good ground-wave propagation is still possible over moderate distances. LF signals are usable, to a limited degree, for transmissions to submerged submarines; at 100 kHz, usable signals are available for a short distance beneath the surface.

Navigational time-measurement systems employing the LF band are able to use first-hop sky waves, by applying a correction to compensate for the additional distance of travel of the sky wave. The accuracy obtainable by use of first-hop sky waves is not as good as that obtained with ground waves, although satisfactory for most navigational purposes. For positioning accuracy of less than a mile, ground-wave reception is necessary.

The primary navigational uses of the LF band are: radiobeacons, Loran C and D, Consol, and Decca (all described in Chapter 32).

Medium Frequency (MF)

The *MF band* extends from 300 kHz to 3 megahertz (MHz). Frequencies in this band provide reliable ground-wave propagation over distances of up to approximately 700 miles (1300 km). Daytime ionosphere absorption is high, and limits sky-wave propagation. Long distance sky-wave transmission is possible at night. Antenna requirements are not as stringent as they are in the VLF and LF bands.

The primary navigational systems operating in the MF band are Consol and Raydist; the older Loran-A system also operates in this band. Some radiobeacons operate on frequencies near the lower limit of this band.

High Frequency (HF)

The *HF band* (3 MHz to 30 MHz) is employed in long-distance communication, made possible by the ionized layers in the ionosphere. At these frequencies, antenna efficiency is much more easily obtained than at the lower frequencies. Communications over long distances are possible with moderate transmitter power. However, frequencies must be selected with respect to the conditions prevailing at the moment. Under some conditions, the higher frequencies travel great distances in the ionosphere before being refracted sufficiently to reflect the wave back to earth. Signals entering the ionosphere at an angle of incidence which prevents their being refracted back towards the earth penetrate the ionized layers and are lost in space. In daylight, energy propagated at the lower frequencies of this band has high absorption losses and fades out a short distance from the source. Higher frequencies, during hours of darkness, if reflected at all, return to earth at great distances from the transmitting antenna, so that they skip over distances of several hundred or more miles. Little or no signals will be received in this "skip zone"; see Figure 3108b.

An example of the need to select proper frequencies will be found when receiving a National Bureau of Standards time signal from station WWV (see Article 2228). This signal can be readily received by day on a standard radio set at 15 MHz at a location 1300 miles (2400 km) from Colorado, but the 5 MHz signal must be tuned in at night.

Frequencies in the HF band do not propagate with suitable characteristics for obtaining distance or bearings, for they are used chiefly for communications.

Very High Frequency (VHF) and Ultra High Frequency (UHF)

Frequencies in the *VHF band* (30 to 300 MHz) and the *UHF band* (300 to 3,000 MHz) are widely used for communications. They are basically *line-of-sight* frequencies as their range is ordinarily limited by the curvature of the earth to distances approximately equal to those at which the top of one antenna could be seen from the top of the other

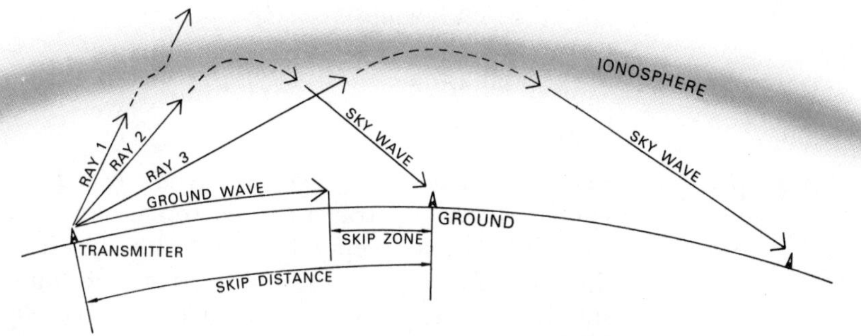

Figure 3108b. The effect of the ionosphere on radio-wave propagation.

under ideal weather conditions. VHF and UHF frequencies are also used to some extent for communications over several hundred miles in what is termed a *scatter mode* of operation. A small portion of very high power electromagnetic waves in the 30 to 60 MHz frequency range are scattered by particles in the ionosphere and returned to earth, permitting signal reception at ranges of 600 to 1,200 miles (1100–2200 km).

A similar scatter effect can be obtained in the *troposphere* by emissions in the 400 to 4,000 MHz range. The troposphere is much nearer the earth than the ionosphere, being situated below the stratosphere. By means of tropospheric scatter, ranges of about 600 miles (1100 km) have been obtained.

For navigational purposes, VHF and UHF frequencies provide good line-of-sight propagation at moderate transmitter power. Systems using VHF include the air navigation techniques of Omni/DME and Shoran. In the lower part of the VHF band will be found the TACAN military air navigation system; some radars use frequencies in the upper regions of the UHF band.

Super High Frequency (SHF) and Extremely High Frequency (EHF)

The *SHF band* (3,000 to 30,000 MHz) and the *EHF band* (30,000 to 300,000 MHz) are used for precise distance measurements and for radar, within line-of-sight range. The employment of SHF frequencies for radar has resulted in significantly improved definition over the UHF systems. Power requirements are moderate, and very efficient antennas can be employed.

Ducting and irregularities

3109 Many irregularities occur, especially at the higher frequencies, in the propagation of electromagnetic waves. A phenomenon called *radio refractive ducting* occurs over much of the radio frequency spectrum, but particularly on frequencies of the VHF and UHF bands. This phenomenon seems to occur more over oceans than over land, and is generally associated with a temperature inversion at a very low altitude, perhaps 200 or 300 feet (60–90 m), and a sharp decrease in moisture content of the warm air. Very long ranges have been reported when low-power UHF transmitters were employed in experiments with these phenomena. Ducting can be responsible for limiting as well as extending the range of radio transmissions.

Hyperbolic navigation systems

3110 *Hyperbolic navigation systems* are based on the theory that the known velocity of travel of electromagnetic waves through space is constant, within acceptable limits. Although it is possible to measure the time of travel of a radio wave from the transmitting antenna to a ship, it is the capability of measuring the *time difference* in the arrival of signals from two separate stations that makes feasible the determination of position.

A major advantage of the hyperbolic navigation systems is that position line data may be computed in advance of its use, and plotted or printed on charts, at convenient units of time-difference value, eliminating the necessity for the navigator to make such computations. A disadvantage lies in the deterioration of accuracy inherent in spherical hyperbolic system geometry.

The hyperbola is the locus of the points at which synchronized signals from the two transmitters comprising a system will arrive at a constant time difference. This time difference is expressed in *microseconds,* or millionths of a second. The receivers employed in these systems therefore provide a readout in microseconds of time difference.

In Figure 3110 signals from stations *S* and *M* transmitted simultaneously would have no time difference but would arrive simultaneously at any point along the center line, as all points along this line are equidistant from points *S* and *M*. All other lines, represented by hyperbolas, would represent points of equal time difference. (In actual hyperbolic navigation systems the transmission for the slave station *S* is delayed rather than being simultaneous with the master

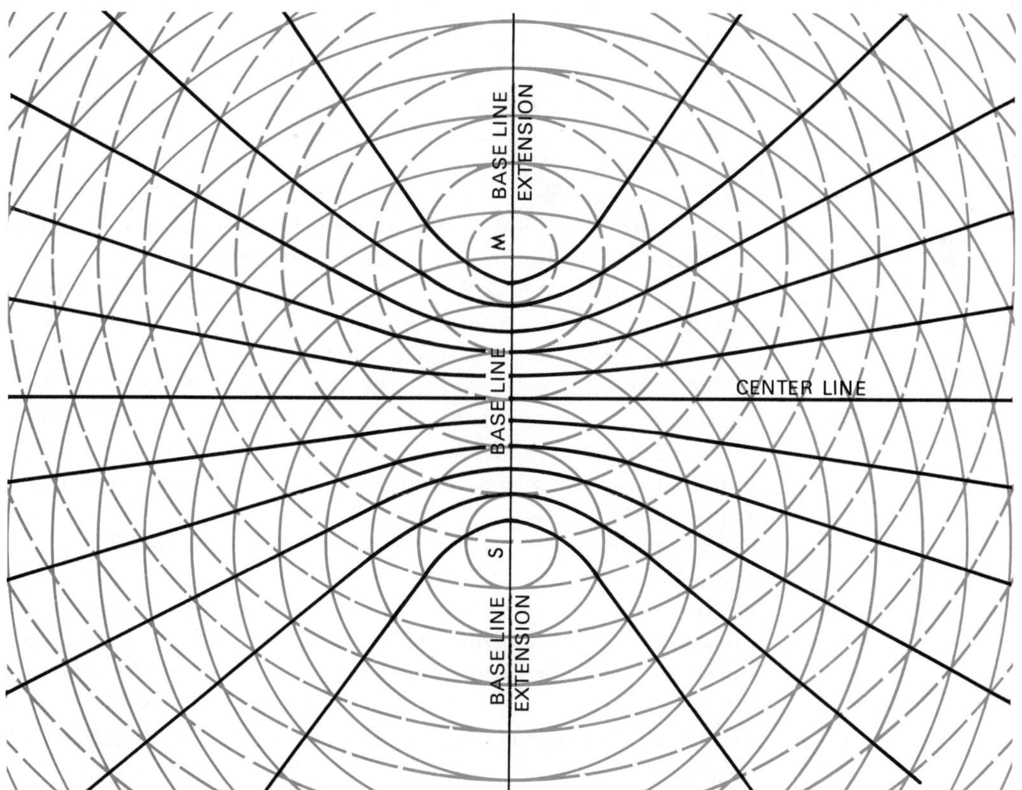

Figure 3110. A family of hyperbolic lines of position.

M.) The figure represents hyperbolic lines on a plane surface. The appearance of the lines on a navigation chart, which represents a portion of the spherical surface of the earth, will vary somewhat with the chart projection used.

The computation of hyperbolas for a given pair of stations is tabulated for the navigator, giving the coordinates at which each hyperbola intersects a whole meridian or parallel, whichever is applicable. Charts, on which the hyperbolas are printed, are commonly employed. Tables may be used if suitable charts are not at hand, but these are much more cumbersome and slower. Receivers are available that include a computer, or that can be coupled into a computer and coordinate converter, to provide a direct readout in terms of latitude and longitude.

Two types of time-difference measurement are employed in hyperbolic systems. In one, the matching of electromagnetic wave envelopes of pulses transmitted from the two stations is measured in time difference, resulting in a coarse measurement which locates the receiver on a hyperbolic line with known geographical coordinates. In the other system, matching the electromagnetic wave *phase* provides a fine measurement within an area or lane defined by two time-difference hyperbolas, in addition to the coarse measurement obtained by time difference. In phase-matching systems, extreme accuracy is possible under favorable conditions. A precision of about 0.05 microseconds can be obtained, which is equivalent to about 50 feet (15 m). This precision is, of course, degraded by system geometry as distance from the base line between the station increases.

To establish position, a ship or aircraft employs two or more pairs of stations to acquire two or more intersecting position lines. As with other methods of determining position by means of intersecting lines of position, precision in positioning varies with the angle of intersection of the lines. Where lines cross at right angles, the area of most probable position is circular, with its center at the intersection of the lines. Where the lines intersect at an acute angle, the area of most probable position is elliptical; the minor axis of this ellipse will be equal to the diameter of the circle formed when the intersection is at 90°. The major axis will be greater; the ratio of its length to the diameter of the circle varies with the cosine of the angle of the intersection.

The development of the first electronic, hyperbolic navigational systems began about 1940. Due to the urgent requirements brought about by World War II, Loran-A came into general military use only a few years later. Following that war, Loran-A was also widely used by merchant shipping, fishing vessels, and some recreational craft. In U.S. waters, a phase-out of Loran-A in favor of Loran-C and Omega began in the mid-1970s. Loran-D and Decca are other hyperbolic systems.

Short-range hyperbolic systems designed for survey and oceanographic use are Decca Survey and Raydist, among others.

Rho-Theta navigation

3111 *Rho-Theta navigation,* or, more specifically, range-direction navigation, utilizes a combination of circular or ranging systems for distance measurements, together with azimuthal or directional measuring systems (Figure 3111). The *Omnirange* (VOR) system in general use for aviation throughout the U.S. provides bearing information. A large number of the stations are equipped with distance-measuring equipment (DME) to provide a complete rho-theta system. The military version is known as TACAN. These systems are sufficiently accurate for general navigation purposes, but are limited to a line-of-sight range. (As these systems are used by aircraft, often at tens of thousands of feet altitude, line-of-sight ranges may be 100 to 200 miles (185 to 370 km).

The principle of Omnirange navigation is based on the phase comparison between two radiated radio-frequency signals, with the phase varying with a change in azimuth. One of these two signals is nondirectional, with a constant phase throughout 360° of azimuth. This signal is utilized as the reference phase. The other signal rotates and varies in phase with change in azimuth; it is the variable phase signal.

Special receiver and display equipment on the aircraft translates the received signal into usable information for the pilot, including an indication as to whether the measured direction is "TO" or "FROM" the ground station.

Repeatability and predictability

3112 In the design of all electronic position systems two major factors are carefully taken into consideration for precision work: *repeatability* and *predictability.* The first problem, repeatability, is the ability of a system to repeat a position. In other words, if the position of a point on the surface of the earth is given in coordinates of the system at one time, "how closely may we return to that exact position at some later time?"

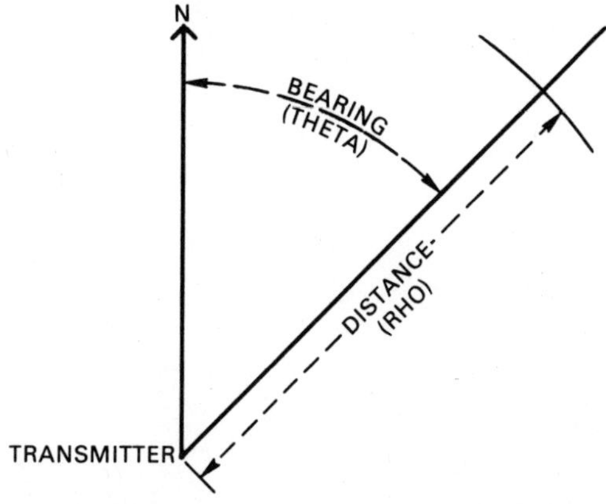

Figure 3111. Rho-Theta system of position determination.

The second problem, that of predictability, is one of knowing, given the atmospheric conditions, the propagation characteristics of the signal. Predictability is influenced primarily by refraction in the atmospheric medium, and by the conductivity of the surface. One of the basic limitations on predictability versus repeatability is the integrity of the geodetic positioning of the transmitter stations. A minor displacement of an antenna position can cause a major error in prediction of a service area point. Of interest is the geodetic datum, the method of measuring geodetics, the spheroid used, etc. Also a problem in predictability is the translation of coordinates, i.e., hyperbolic to orthogonal and the rigor of the mathematics used.

32 Basic Radionavigation Systems

Introduction **3201** The principles of radio waves and their propagation were discussed in Chapter 31. Here we will consider their application to certain basic radionavigation systems; more complex systems incorporating advanced technology will be covered in later chapters.

The primary advantages of radionavigation systems are their long-range and all-weather availability. Such systems provide information on a vessel's position at sea far beyond such physical aids to navigation as coastal landmarks and lightships. Many radionavigation systems will provide position fixing to a higher degree of accuracy than celestial observations, but their real advantage is their lack of any need for clear skies and a visible horizon.

On the negative side of radionavigation systems are their complex equipment, need for electrical power, and the fact that signals must be radiated (primarily a disadvantage in time of war). The degrees of complexity will vary considerably in the "basic" systems classification —from simple radio direction finders to automatic signal-acquiring-and-tracking Loran receivers, for example. Well-maintained equipment will have a high degree of reliability, but failures can, and do, occur, frequently at just the "wrong" time. Also to be considered is the fact that even more complex equipment is based on shore as part of the system and thus is outside the mariner's control as regards operation and maintenance. Alternate sources of power will often be available for shipboard navigational equipment, but the possibility of a total loss of power must not be overlooked in emergency plans.

Even the most enthusiastic supporters of radionavigation recognize it has limitations and that it will probably never completely replace other methods any more than the gyrocompass, valuable as it is, has replaced the magnetic compass. Keep constantly in mind that the methods discussed in this chapter are navigational *aids* and that it is still important to know how to use other methods.

Radio communications **3202** Although message traffic is the primary function of radio communications, the navigator can also be served in other ways. Probably the most important application is that of time signals (Article

2228). Weather information is disseminated both as a part of time-signal broadcasts and in special transmissions for that purpose alone. Information on the establishment or disestablishment of, or changes to, aids to navigation are transmitted regularly, including announcements of scheduled interruptions in service for various stations or radionavigation systems.

Much information of interest and value to a navigator will be found in DMAHC Publications No. 117A and 117B, *Radio Navigational Aids.* Information on weather broadcasts will be found in the publication *Worldwide Weather Broadcasts* of the National Oceanic and Atmospheric Administration. Systems in U.S. waters will be covered by the various volumes of the USCG *Light Lists;* see Article 603.

Radio direction finding

3203 The simplest and most widespread of radionavigation systems is that of *radio direction finding* (RDF). Equipment for RDF will be found on most medium-size or larger recreational craft, on fishing vessels of all sizes, and on all ocean-going ships. The extent of regular use of RDFs may vary with the availability of more sophisticated equipment, but it remains a basic radionavigation system.

In the early days of RDF, the actual direction finder was located on shore, taking bearings on transmissions from a ship and then radioing such information to the navigator. Often coastal networks were established and several simultaneous measurements could yield a fix. Such a network existed along the U.S. coasts during the 1920s and 1930s; shore-based direction finder service is still available in a few foreign locations.

Modern RDF systems for marine navigation use shore-based non-directional transmitters and direction-sensitive antennas with ship-based receivers. Thus the *radio bearing* is taken aboard the vessel and plotted directly. Bearings are best taken from *marine radiobeacons* which are designed and constructed solely for this purpose, but they can also be taken on commercial broadcasting stations (standard AM band), aeronautical radiobeacons, and some other stations. (The ability to DF on other ship stations using medium and high frequencies was essentially lost with the conversion to single-sideband modulation; direction finding on VHF-FM channels is limited to expensive specialized equipment.) A bearing obtained from any of these sources can be used in the same manner as any other line of position. The exact location of the transmitting antenna must be known; nautical charts will show all marine radiobeacons and will often show the position of aeronautical radiobeacons and some commercial broadcast stations (whose antennas are frequently *not* in the town or city whose name is used in station identification).

Typically, a radio direction finder makes use of the directional properties of a loop antenna. If such an antenna is parallel to the direction of travel of the radio waves, the signal received is of maximum strength. If the loop is perpendicular to the direction of travel, the signal is of minimum strength or entirely missing. When a dial is attached to such a loop antenna, the direction of the antenna and hence the direction of the transmitter can be determined. The pointer indicates the direction of the transmitter from the receiver when the loop is perpendicular to this direction, when the minimum signal is heard. The minimum, generally called the "null," rather than the maximum, is used because a sharper reading is thus obtained. Since radio waves travel a great circle, a correction must be applied for plotting on a Mercator chart. A Lambert chart permits direct plotting of all radio bearings.

The correction to be applied to convert a great-circle direction to the rhumb-line direction for plotting on a Mercator chart can be obtained from a correction Table in Pub. No. 117A or B, or in *Bowditch,* Table 1.

Arbitrary rules are sometimes given to determine whether or not a radio bearing should be corrected before plotting; these are based on the relative positions of the transmitter and receiver. The amount of the correction depends on the latitude and the difference of longitude. A bearing from a transmitter 200 miles (370 km) away near the equator or in a nearly north-south direction from the receiver may require a smaller correction than if the distance is 25 miles (46 km) in an east-west direction in high latitudes. The only way to be sure is to enter a correction table and determine the magnitude of the correction.

Having found the correction, it is necessary to determine its sign before applying it to the observed bearing. This is easy to determine if it is remembered that the *great-circle direction is always nearer the pole than the Mercator direction.* Do not try to remember any other rule. Draw a small diagram, mentally or otherwise, for each problem and determine the sign from it. Figure 3203 illustrates the four possible situations. The important thing to remember is that the sign depends on the relative position of the *receiver* and the *transmitter,* regardless of which is the ship.

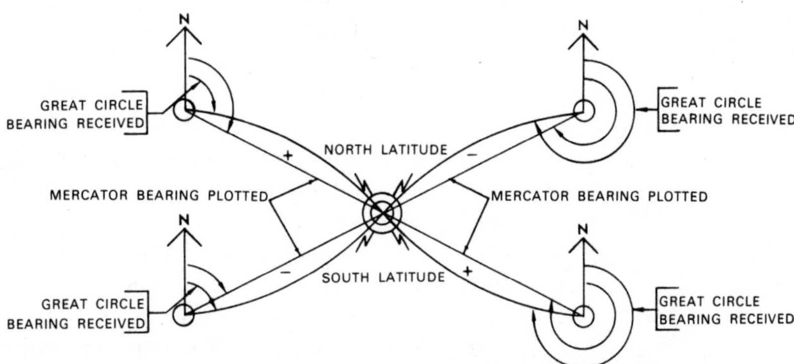

Figure 3203. Diagram for determination of the sign of a conversion angle.

Marine radiobeacons

3204 Many nations operate radiobeacons along their coasts to aid maritime navigation. These transmitting stations are employed both to extend navigational assistance beyond visual range and to replace visual observations at closer distances when fog or other "thick weather" exists. They operate in the upper part of the medium frequency (MF) band and the lower part of the high frequency (HF) band. For purposes of identification, simple characteristics of dots and dashes are used—these are usually, but not always, intended to be read as letters and/or numbers in standard Morse code.

Types of radiobeacons

Radiobeacons have been divided into three specific classifications.

Directional radiobeacons which transmit radio waves in beams along fixed bearings.

Rotating radiobeacons by which a beam of radio waves is revolved in azimuth in a manner similar to the beam of light sent out by certain lighthouses.

Circular radiobeacons which send out waves of approximately uniform strength in all directions so that ships may take radio bearings of them by means of the ship's radio direction-finder sets. This is the most common type of radiobeacon.

Full information on the location of marine radiobeacons, frequencies, characteristic identifying signals, hours of operation, type of service, and range is given in DMAHC Pub. No. 117A for Atlantic and Mediterranean waters and in Pub. No. 117B for the Pacific and Indian Ocean areas; information on radiobeacons in U.S. waters is contained in USCG *Light Lists.* (The existence of radiobeacons is indicated in *Coast Pilots* and DMAHC *Lists of Lights,* but no operational details are given.) The location of marine radiobeacons is shown on nautical charts by the letters "R Bn" near a chart symbol, the circle of which is *not* indicative of the expected range of radio reception. As influenced by the space available on the chart, some other information may be given, such as frequency and characteristic signal. Reference should be made to the appropriate publication(s) for full information before any radiobeacon is used. Although any transmitting station can be used, the signal must first be properly identified and the station antenna accurately located.

The U.S. Coast Guard operates about 200 marine radiobeacons in the frequency band 285–325 kHz. Most of these are located at, or very close to, a primary seacoast light, a lightship, offshore light tower, or large navigational buoy; some are located at secondary lights. Where the antenna is separated from the visual aid, the publication listing gives the direction and distance. Another category is that of the low-powered "marker" beacons usually located at the entrance to a harbor or on an offshore large navigational buoy.

To extend the usefulness of marine radiobeacons to ships and aircraft employing automatic radio direction finders, U.S. marine radiobeacons on the Great Lakes, Atlantic, and Pacific coasts have been

Freq. kHz	Group Sequence	Station	Characteristic	Range (mile)	Lat. (N) ° ′ ″	Long. (W) ° ′ ″
286	I	HIGHLAND	HI (•••• ••)	100	42 02 24	70 03 40
	II	NANTUCKET L. S.	NS (▬• •••)	100	40 30 00	69 28 00
	III	FIRE ISLAND	RT (•▬• ▬)	100	40 37 48	73 13 09
	IV	AMBROSE	T (▬)	100	40 27 32	73 49 52
	V	GREAT DUCK ISLAND	GD (▬▬• ▬••)	50	44 08 32	68 14 47
	VI	EXECUTION ROCKS	K (▬•▬)	20	40 52 41	73 44 18
	VI	MANANA ISLAND	MI (▬▬ ••)	100	43 45 48	69 19 38

Figure 3204. Sequenced operation of radiobeacons.

modified to transmit a continuous carrier signal during the entire radiobeacon operating period with keyed modulation providing the characteristic signal. Unless a beat frequency oscillator is installed, the continuous carrier signals are not audible to the operator of an aural null direction finder. A 10-second dash has been included in the characteristic of these radiobeacons, to enable the navigator using a conventional aural null direction finder to refine his bearing.

Marine radiobeacons are assigned to specific radio frequencies; stations on the same frequency are spaced geographically far enough from each other to avoid interference, or they are operated on a time-sharing basis. Major beacons of the U.S. Coast Guard operate either continuously or as part of a sequenced group. Those in any group transmit on the same frequency and are assigned a specific minute of a six-minute cycle; for example, a radiobeacon assigned sequence II, would transmit during the 2nd, 8th, 14th, 20th, etc., minute of each hour. There may be less than six beacons in a group; one station may transmit in two segments, or there may be no signals on some segments. Sequenced groups are being eliminated in favor of continuous operation on different frequencies.

The operation of a typical group of sequenced radiobeacons is shown in Figure 3204. These are off the New England coast, all operating on 286 kHz. (Another beacon operates on this frequency, but is far away at the Dry Tortugas in the Gulf of Mexico.)

RDF equipment **3205** Radio direction-finding equipment can be either manual (RDF) or automatic (ADF). In the former case, the antenna is rotated by hand until a direction is obtained. The point of minimum signal (null), rather than the maximum, is used as it is sharper and can be judged more precisely. The loop, or other style, antenna can be mounted on top of the receiver or separately. There will be two positions of the antenna, 180° apart, which will give a null; a separate "sense" antenna is used to resolve the ambiguity (unless the correct direction is readily apparent from other information such as the DR position).

Automatic direction finders rotate a loop either mechanically or electronically. A direct-reading visual display continuously indicates the bearing of the transmitter being received, corrected for ambiguity; the operator of an ADF set needs only to tune it to the correct frequency and confirm the identification of the station.

RDFs and ADFs for low and medium frequencies are normally tunable across one or more bands; some models may contain one or more crystals to ensure rapid and accurate tuning. Direction finders for VHF use will be automatic in operation and crystal controlled on specific channels.

Radio direction finder stations

3206 In some foreign countries radio direction-finder equipment is installed at points ashore and these radio direction-finder stations will take radio bearings on ships when requested, passing that information by radio. Such stations are also called radio compass stations, and can be located by reference to Pub. No. 117A or B, or by the letters "RDF" placed near a radio station symbol on a chart.

Bearings taken by radio direction-finder stations, and reported to the ships, are corrected for all determinable errors except the difference between a great circle and a rhumb, and are normally accurate within 2° for distances under 50 nautical miles (93 km).

Accuracy of RDF bearings

3207 The accuracy of RDF bearings depends on the following factors.

Strength of signals. The best bearings can be taken on vessels whose signals are steady, clear, and strong. Weak signals give inaccurate bearings at best.

Personal error. The skill of the operator is perhaps the most important factor in obtaining accurate readings. Frequent practice is essential if this source of error is to be reduced to a minimum.

RADIO NAVIGATIONAL AIDS — RADIO DIRECTION-FINDER AND RADAR STATIONS

200F. Radio Bearing Conversion Table

Correction to be applied to radio bearing to convert to Mercator bearing

Difference of longitude

Mid. lat.	0.5°	1°	1.5°	2°	2.5°	3°	3.5°	4°	4.5°	5°	5.5°	6°	6.5°	7°	7.5°	Mid. lat.
°	°	°	°	°	°	°	°	°	°	°	°	°	°	°	°	°
4	- - -	- - -	- - -	- - -	0.1	0.1	0.1	0.1	0.2	0.2	0.2	0.2	0.2	0.2	0.3	4
5	- - -	0.1	0.1	.1	.1	.1	.2	.2	.2	.2	.2	.3	.3	.3	.3	5
6	- - -	.1	.1	.1	.1	.2	.2	.2	.2	.3	.3	.3	.3	.4	.4	6
7	- - -	.1	.1	.1	.2	.2	.2	.3	.3	.3	.3	.4	.4	.4	.5	7
8	- - -	.1	.1	.1	.2	.2	.2	.3	.3	.4	.4	.4	.5	.5	.5	8
9	- - -	.1	.1	.1	.2	.2	.2	.3	.3	.4	.4	.5	.5	.6	.6	9
10	- - -	.1	.1	.1	.2	.2	.3	.4	.4	.4	.5	.5	.6	.6	.6	10
11	- - -	.1	.1	.2	.2	.3	.3	.4	.4	.5	.5	.6	.6	.7	.7	11
12	.1	.1	.1	.2	.3	.3	.4	.4	.5	.5	.6	.6	.7	.7	.8	12

Figure 3207. Radio Bearing Conversion Table.

Radio deviation. Direction finders are subject to *radio* (or *RDF*) *deviation* which affects the accuracy of their readings in much the same manner as magnetic compass deviation, although for different reasons. Incoming waves are picked up by metallic objects, particularly items of rigging, and re-radiated in such a way as to cause incorrect nulls on the vessel's RDF. Calibration for these errors can be accomplished by observing simultaneous radio and visual bearings on various headings and preparing an RDF deviation table. Any known source of signals can be used, but special radiobeacon calibration stations are operated by the Coast Guard at several points on all U.S. coasts. Deviation errors should be checked at intervals, particularly after the ship's structure has been altered or major changes have been made in electrical wiring. Bearings should be taken when other antennas and movable equipment such as davits, cranes, etc. are in the same condition as during calibration.

Reciprocal bearings. With some equipment it is not apparent from which of two directions differing by 180° the bearing is coming. The best-known grounding case in U.S. history, the Point Honda disaster, took place in 1923 when seven destroyers were wrecked because they used a reciprocal bearing taken by the radio compass station then located at Point Conception, California. It is usually possible to tell which bearing to use by the dead-reckoning position of the ship, but if there is any doubt, take several bearings and note the direction of change. The station should draw aft. *If a reciprocal bearing is obtained, do not attempt to obtain the correct bearing by adding or subtracting 180°.* The radio deviation correction will probably not be the same.

Night effect. Within half an hour of sunrise and sunet, and to a lesser extent throughout the night, radio bearings may be less accurate than at other times, due largely to polarization effect. This is manifested by a broadening and shifting of the minimum signal.

Land effect. When a radio signal crosses a shore line at an oblique angle, or if it passes over an island or peninsula of high land, the direction of travel may be bent a slight amount in a manner similar to the refraction of light. When a bearing is taken under these conditions, it should be considered of doubtful accuracy.

Plotting errors. In addition to the usual errors of plotting, two additional sources of error must be guarded against. First, be careful to plot from the correct position. If the bearing is observed aboard ship, it must be plotted from the position of the transmitting antenna; if observed at a radio compass station, it must be plotted from the position of the *receiving* antenna. *These locations are not always the same,* nor do they always coincide with a light having the same name. Second, radio waves travel great circles and if they are to be plotted on a Mercator chart, a correction may have to be applied to convert the great circle to the corresponding rhumb line between the broadcasting and receiving antennas. A correction is usually not necessary providing the range is under 50 miles (93 km). If necessary, the correction will be found in Table 1 of *Bowditch* or in DMAHC Pub. No. 117A or B.

Plotting RDF bearings

3208 Radio bearings are plotted and labeled in the same manner as visual bearings. RDF bearings are, however, usually much less precise and accurate; a position found with one or more radio bearings must be identified as an RDF fix or as an estimated position (EP). A new DR track is not customarily plotted from an EP, but a course line should be drawn to determine whether or not there is any possibility of the ship standing into danger. A series of estimated positions obtained from RDF bearings and supplemented by a line of soundings can often locate a vessel's position with acceptable accuracy.

LORAN

Loran systems

3209 Several related, but distinctly separate, radionavigation systems are categorized under the overall heading of Loran, an acronym for *Lo*ng *Ra*nge *N*avigation.

Theory of operation

The technical principle that distinguishes the various versions of Loran from most other hyperbolic navigation systems is the use of pulse emissions. This permits the nonambiguous measurement of time differences of signals from different stations and further provides the means for discrimination at the receiving location between ground waves and sky waves. The ability to select and use a particular transmission provides maximum accuracy consistent with the system's inherent geometric configuration.

Loran employs transmitting stations at fixed points, which send carefully synchronized signals. These travel at the speed of light (161,875 nautical miles per second, 299,793 km/s) and cover one nautical mile in 6.18 microseconds (μs).

The time interval between transmission of signals from a pair of Loran stations is very closely controlled; all Loran-C stations, for example, operate with an atomic time standard of extremely high accuracy and stability. To understand the principle of operation, assume this difference is zero and that two stations, M and S (Figure 3209) broadcast signals simultaneously. A ship at A, equidistant from the two stations, receives both signals at the same time. A ship at A' also receives the signals simultaneously, since it is also equidistant from the stations. The locus of all points equidistant from the two stations is called the *center line*. It is the perpendicular bisector of the *base line*, the great circle joining the two stations.

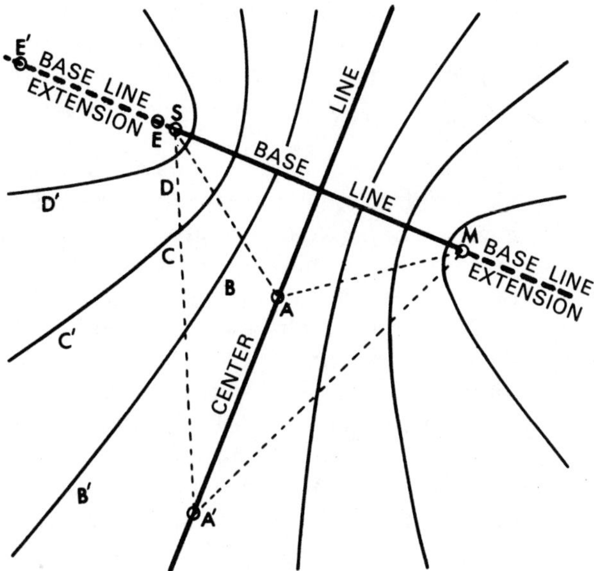

Figure 3209. The basic principle of hyperbolic radionavigation.

Consider, now, a ship at *B,* closer to *S* than *M.* The signal from *S* is received first. At some other point *B'*, where the difference in distance from *M* and *S* is the same as at *B,* the time difference is the same. The locus of all points with this time difference is a hyperbola, since this curve defines all points with a constant difference in distance from two fixed points. These lines do not appear as true hyperbolas on most charts because of chart distortion and the earth's spheroidal shape.

If the time difference is greater, the ship is on another hyperbola, at *C* or *C'*, still closer to *S.* A still greater difference puts the ship at *D* or *D'*. If the difference is equal to exactly the time needed for a signal to travel from *M* to *S,* the ship is somewhere on the *base line extension* at *E* or *E'*.

Any number of hyperbolas could thus be drawn indicating various time differences.

If the signal from *M* is received first, the ship is nearer *M.* For every curve to the left of the center line there is a similar but reversed curve to the right. Since the time differences thus define definite fixed curves, they can be either plotted on a chart or their coordinates tabulated. In practice, both methods are used. In actual practice there is a precise time delay between the transmission of the signal from the slave following that from the master station.

At any given point, then, one line of position can be obtained from one pair of stations. To obtain a fix, at least one additional line is needed from another pair of stations or from other means, such as celestial observations.

Loran-A **3210** The initial system was termed simply *Loran* until the development of later versions; it then became *Loran-A,* or "standard Loran." This system operates on medium frequency (MF) channels between 1850 and 1950 kHz. Both ground-wave and sky-wave reception are used, giving different ranges, day and night, and different accuracies of fixes. Daytime use of ground waves extends out to about 500 miles (925 km) with fixes accurate to 1.5 miles (2.8 km) over 80 percent of the coverage area (accuracy is greatest along the *base line* between the two transmitting stations). The use of sky waves extends the daytime range out to as much as 1200 miles (2,225 km) and as much as 1400 miles (2600 km) at night; the accuracy of sky-wave fixes is roughly 5 to 7 miles (9–13 km).

Loran-A stations are located at separations of 250 to 600 miles (460–1100 km). At one time, there were 83 Loran-A stations in operation giving coverage of both the North Atlantic and North Pacific Oceans, the Gulf of Mexico, and the North Sea, with some extensions into adjacent waters and land areas; this number is now gradually being reduced (see Article 3211).

Loran-A receiving equipment was produced in many models including both manual and automatic tracking sets. These were, and, to some extent, still are, widely used on small craft, fishing vessels, merchant ships, and naval vessels, as well as in aircraft. Charts were overprinted with Loran-A lines of position for direct plotting, or positions could be determined from the use of Loran-A tables. Often three or more Loran-A pairs could be received, or Loran lines could be combined with lines of position obtained from other navigational procedures.

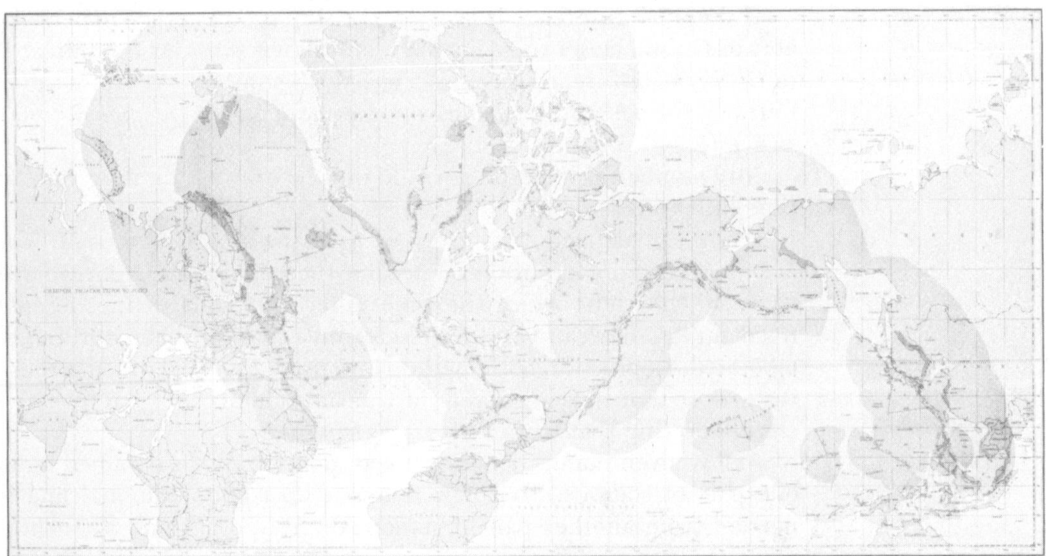

Figure 3210. Loran-A coverage diagram in the mid-1970s.

National Plan for Navigation **3211** In the mid-1970s, a study was made of the navigational needs of various types of vessels when operating in harbors, coastal waters, and on the high seas. This was carried further into a study of the various navigation systems best suited to meet these needs. One of the major conclusions of the *National Plan for Navigation* was a decision to adopt Loran-C for the "Coastal Confluence Zone (CCZ)," waters having an inner boundary at harbor entrances and an outer boundary at 50 miles (92.6 km) offshore, or the outer edge of the continental shelf (100 fathom curve), whichever is greater. Loran-A service would be phased out after the new system was well established. This decision made unnecessary the replacement of aging Loran-A transmitters and allowed a considerable reduction in the number of stations, with consequent savings in manpower and operating costs. It also introduced a new system having greater accuracy and with an over-land capability.

Loran-C **3212** Loran-C is a pulsed, hyperbolic, long-range electronic navigation system. It operates on a single frequency centered on 100 kHz.

The need for an accurate long-range navigation system was recognized during World War II, after the development of Loran-A. Between 1952 and 1956 extensive tests were conducted on this system, and the first operational chain was established along the East Coast of the United States in 1957. Since then Loran-C coverage has been greatly expanded, with the area of coverage in mid-1977 as shown in Figure 3212. (Greater detail is shown on Chart 5130.) Ultimately, some 45 stations in 12 chains are planned, giving complete coverage of U.S. coastal waters and a large portion of the northern hemisphere. (A separate, but compatible, Loran-C system is operated by the U.S.S.R.) The change-over from Loran-A to Loran-C has brought the extension of the latter system into many areas, such as the U.S. Pacific coast, which previously did not have such service. An overlap period of roughly two years, during which both systems were operated, was provided to facilitate the change-over by users of Loran-A; charts were made available that were printed on both sides, with Loran-A lines on one side and Loran-C lines on the other.

Characteristics **3213** Loran-C is similar to Loran-A, in that it is a pulsed, hyperbolic system of radionavigation available to ships and aircraft by day or night, in all weather conditions, over land and sea. In Loran-A a single RF pulse is transmitted in each repetition interval. In Loran-C a multipulse transmission is used. Each station radiates a group of eight pulses spaced 1,000 microseconds apart. Additionally, the master station transmits a ninth pulse principally for identification. Multiple pulses are used so that more signal energy is available at the receiver, improving significantly the signal-to-noise ratio without having to increase the peak power capability of the transmitters. Loran-C can

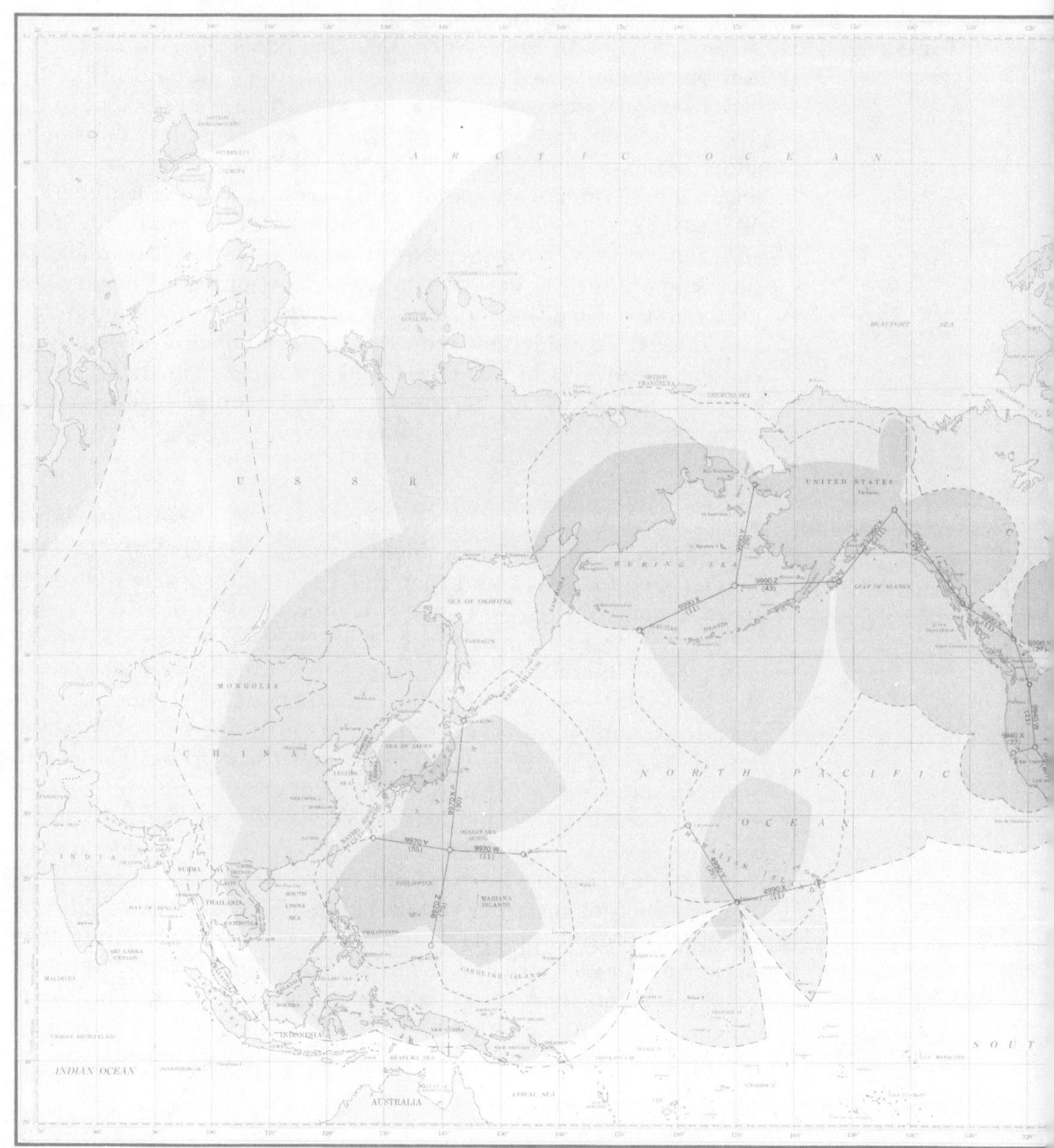

Figure 3212. Loran-C coverage diagram, late 1970s.

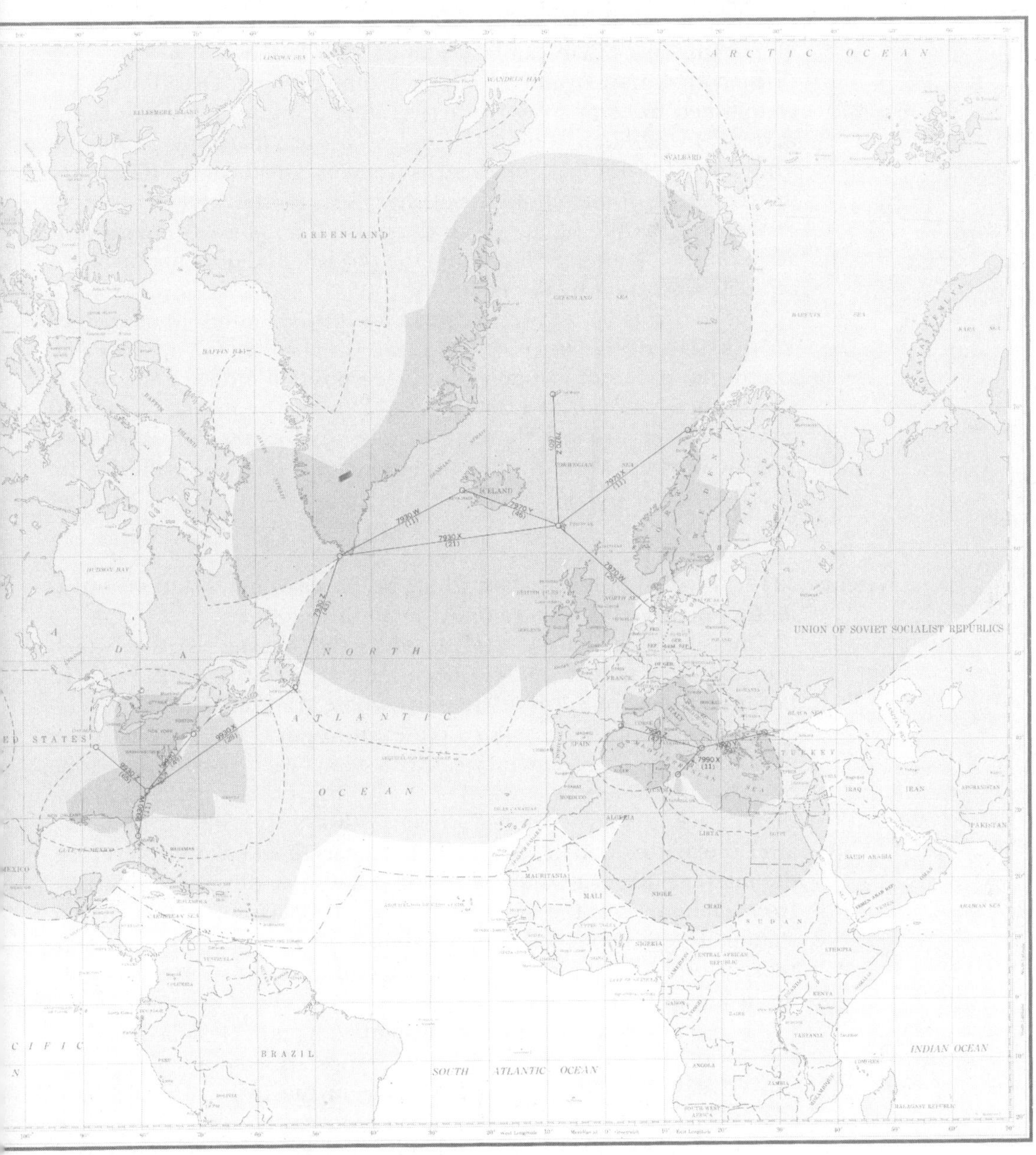
ARCTIC OCEAN
GREENLAND
SVALBARD
ICELAND
NORWEGIAN SEA
7970 Z (65)
7970 X (11)
7970 Y (46)
7970 W (20)
7930 W (11)
7930 X (21)
7930 Z (43)
NORTH
ATLANTIC
OCEAN
UNION OF SOVIET SOCIALIST REPUBLICS
FRANCE
SPAIN
TURKEY
7990 X (11)
IRAQ
IRAN
PAKISTAN
LIBYA
ALGERIA
MAURITANIA
MALI
NIGER
CHAD
SUDAN
NIGERIA
ETHIOPIA
KENYA
9930 X
9930 Z
MEXICO
BRAZIL
SOUTH ATLANTIC OCEAN
INDIAN OCEAN

supply position information to a higher degree of accuracy and at greater distances than can be obtained with Loran-A.

In both Loran-A and Loran-C, a time-difference reading is accomplished by comparing the arrival time of pulses from two transmitters. In addition, Loran-C employs a cycle-matching technique for greater precision. A rough measurement is made of the difference in arrival time of the pulsed signals and this is refined by a comparison of the phase of the signal within the pulse. The phase comparison is accomplished automatically within the receiver and does not involve a separate operation by the navigator.

Due to the use of a lower frequency—100 kHz rather than 1850 or 1950 kHz—and an increased baseline distance, 1,000 miles (1,850 km) or more, Loran-C is able to provide position information of reasonable accuracy out to 1,200 miles (2,225 km) by means of ground waves, and out to more than 3,000 miles (5,550 km) with sky waves. The power of a Loran-C transmitter varies with the specific station and is between 250 kW and 3 MW.

Basic system **3214** In any Loran-C "chain" there are three or more stations transmitting pulses which are radiated in all directions.

One of the stations is designated as the "master" station which transmits the master pulse; the others are *secondary* stations. (In Loran-A these were "slave" stations whose transmissions were triggered by receipt of the master pulse; in Loran-C the high accuracy of atomic time and frequency controls allows each station to operate on schedule independently—hence the use of "secondary" rather than "slave.") The secondary stations always transmit in sequence after the master station with fixed, predetermined delays. Therefore, the master pulse is always received first and time differences increase from a minimum at the secondary station to a maximum at the master station. The locations of a constant time difference between the reception of the master pulse group and that of a secondary station establish a Loran LOP.

The time difference remains constant along a hyperbolic line, and a series of lines of constant time difference are computed for each pair of stations; data is made available in the form of charts and tables. When the navigational position of a vessel is desired, the time difference of a pair of stations is determined from the Loran receiver, and, by consulting the charts and/or tables, interpolating where necessary, the LOPS can be plotted corresponding to the measured values.

Pulse characteristics When a pulse is transmitted, the amplitude of the signal starts at zero, rises to a maximum, and then recedes back to zero; all this, of course, occurs in an extremely brief time. This pulse shape can be varied. In Loran-C there is a fast build-up of amplitude to the peak, and the leading edge of the pulse is used for timing signals. Figure 3214 illustrates an idealized pulse shape and the sampling point as

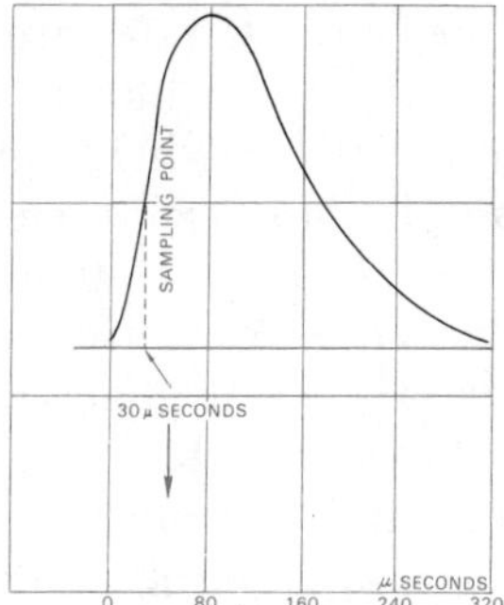

Figure 3214. Loran-C pulse shape showing sampling point.

determined by the circuitry of the receiver. The shape of the pulse also allows the receiver to identify one particular cycle of the pulse. This is essential to prevent whole-cycle ambiguities in time-difference measurement and allows the high accuracy of the phase measurement technique to be achieved.

The purpose of the sampling point being on the leading edge of the pulse is to differentiate between ground and sky waves. The ground-wave signals of the same pulse will always be received first when signals are being picked up from both paths. The sky-wave lag can be as short as 35 microseconds (μs), making it necessary to use the leading edge of the pulse to ensure that the ground wave is measured before being contaminated by the effects of the sky wave signal. The ability to use ground waves without contamination from the sky wave permits use of visual techniques in time-difference measurements, and permits the use of long base lines with high accuracy synchronization between master and slave stations.

The sky-wave lag can also be as great as 1000 μs, and in such cases it would contaminate the ground-wave signal of the next succeeding pulse if the technical characteristics of the Loran-C system did not provide protection.

Within each of the multipulse groups from the master and slave stations, the phase of the RF carrier is changed with respect to the pulse envelope in a systematic manner from pulse to pulse. The phase of each pulse in an eight- or nine-pulse group is changed in accordance with a prescribed code so that it is either in phase (+) or 180° out of phase (−) with a stable 100 kHz reference signal. The phase code used at a master station is different from the phase code used at a secondary, but all secondaries use the same code. Contamination by preceding sky waves without phase coding would nullify the effect of sampling only the ground wave, thereby degrading the inherent accuracy of the system. The use of phase coding also provides the receiver with the necessary information for an automatic search for the master and secondary signals. Automatic search can be used for convenience or when the signal-to-noise ratio of the received signals precludes visual identification. Phase coding also provides some protection from interference from non-Loran signals.

A large percentage of the Loran-C rates are compatible with the Loran-A system rates and, with proper modification of the Loran-A receiver to permit reception of the 100-kHz signal, envelope matching of these signals is possible. Since RF cycle matching is not incorporated in Loran-A receivers, a "fine" time-difference measurement is not possible with the Loran-A receiver and, consequently, the accuracy is less than when the 100-kHz signal is received on a Loran-C receiver fully capable of cycle matching.

The use of pulse groups and extremely precise timing at each Loran-C station makes possible the sharing of the same frequency by all stations in the system. Identification of particular groups of stations must be provided by some means other than channel selection. Accordingly, provision has been made in the Loran-C system for as many as 78 different pulse *group repetition intervals,* abbreviated as GRI. (In theory there could be some 10,000 GRI, but practical considerations lead to the use of not more than 78; actually, even fewer are needed.) Each station transmits one pulse group—nine pulses for the master station and eight for each secondary station in each group repetition interval.

Station location

3215 A Loran-C chain is composed of a master transmitting station, two or more secondary stations, and, if necessary, system area monitoring (SAM) stations. The transmitters are located so that signals from the master and at least two secondary stations may be received through the desired coverage area. (In some instances, a common site is used for a secondary station of two different chains, or for the master of one chain and a secondary of another chain.) For convenience, the master station is designated by the letter *M,* and the secondary stations are designated *W, X, Y,* or *Z.*

For any Loran-C chain, a GRI is selected that will not cause mutual (crossrate) interference with adjacent chains. The designation of a

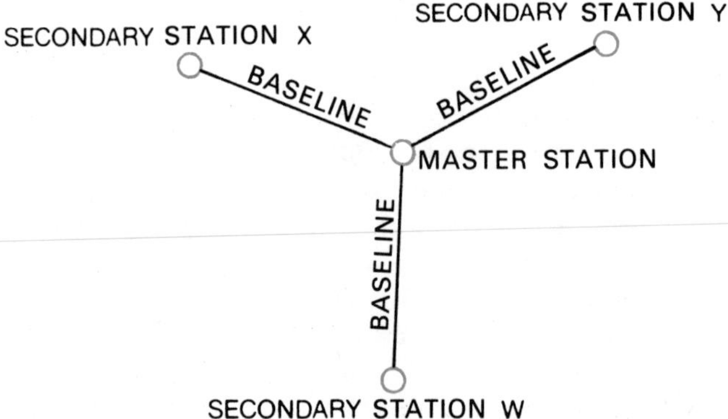

Figure 3215a. Loran-C star configuration of one master and three secondary stations.

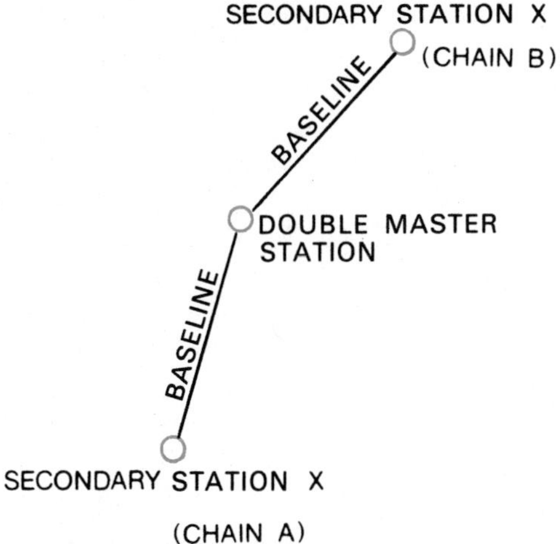

Figure 3215b. Loran-C triad configuration with a "double master" station functioning in two chains.

Loran-C rate is by the first four digits of the specific GRI; for example, a GRI of 99300 microseconds is rate 9930 (this was formerly designated as rate SS7). A specific pair, which produce a set of lines of position, are identified by the rate and the letter of the secondary station used with the master; for example 9930-X.

Chain operation

3216 The master transmitter's ninth pulse in each group is used for visual identification of the master and for "blink." Blinking is used to warn users that there is an error in the transmission of a particular station or stations; it is accomplished by turning the ninth pulse off and on in a specified code as shown in Figure 3216. The secondary station of the unusable pair also blinks by turning off and on the first two pulses of its pulse group. Most modern receivers automatically detect secondary station blink only, as this is enough to trigger alarm indicators.

Synchronization control

3217 All transmitting stations are equipped with cesium frequency standards. The extremely high accuracy and stability of these standards permit each station to establish its own time of transmission without reference to another station.

The objective for control of a Loran-C chain is to keep the observed time difference (TD) of each master-secondary pair constant at any location throughout the coverage area. Frequency offsets in the cesium standards and changes in propagation conditions can cause the observed TD to vary. Therefore, one or more SAM stations are established in the area with precision receiving equipment to monitor continuously the TDs of the master-secondary pairs. In some in-

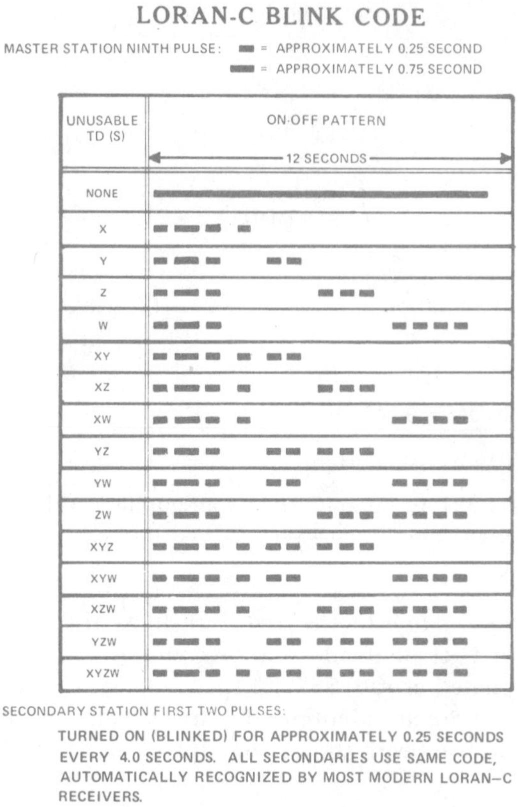

LORAN-C BLINK CODE

MASTER STATION NINTH PULSE: ▬ = APPROXIMATELY 0.25 SECOND
▬▬ = APPROXIMATELY 0.75 SECOND

UNUSABLE TD (S)	ON-OFF PATTERN (12 SECONDS)
NONE	
X	
Y	
Z	
W	
XY	
XZ	
XW	
YZ	
YW	
ZW	
XYZ	
XYW	
XZW	
YZW	
XYZW	

SECONDARY STATION FIRST TWO PULSES:

TURNED ON (BLINKED) FOR APPROXIMATELY 0.25 SECONDS EVERY 4.0 SECONDS. ALL SECONDARIES USE SAME CODE, AUTOMATICALLY RECOGNIZED BY MOST MODERN LORAN–C RECEIVERS.

Figure 3216. Loran-C blink code.

stances, a transmitting station is suitably located and can perform the monitoring function. A control TD is established during system calibration. When the observed TD varies from the control TD by more than one-half the prescribed tolerance, the SAM directs a change in the timing of the secondary station to remove the error. If the observed TD becomes different from the control TD by more than the established tolerance, then a "blink" is ordered to alert all users that the time difference is not usable.

Loran-C position accuracies

3218 Position accuracy degrades with increasing distance from the transmitting stations as a result of variation in propagation conditions, losses over the signal path, and internal receiver conditions. Accuracies cannot be stated absolutely, but using range as the distance to the master station of the pair, ground-wave accuracies may be generally stated as:

at 200 miles (370 km), 50–300 feet (15–90m)
500 miles (925 km), 200–700 ft (60–210m)
750 miles (1390 km), 300–1,100 ft (90–340m)
1,000 miles (1850 km), 500–1,700 ft (150–520m)

Accuracies are stated as a range of distances, rather than fixed amounts, as the value will vary with the position of the receiver with respect to the master and secondary stations, variations from standard propagation conditions, and other factors.

The transmitters of some Loran-C chains are located inland from the coasts—in a few instances, several hundred miles or more. The overland path of the signals results in phase shifts that are difficult to predict accurately. Initial editions of charts with Loran-C lines of position are based on theoretical predictions rather than actual measurements. These lines bear a correct relationship to each other, but the grid as a whole may be offset from true locations by $\frac{1}{4}$ to 2 miles; the problem is, of course, greater on large-scale charts. As soon as adequate field measurements can be taken from known positions, the charts are corrected in later editions.

Sky-wave reception gives greater range, of course, but lesser accuracy. At 1,500 miles (2,780 km), position accuracy may be as poor as 10 miles (18 km), at 2,000 miles (3,700 km), it may degrade to as much as 17 miles (31 km); these are "worse condition" values and sky-wave accuracies are often better.

The relatively high order of positional accuracy of Loran-C permits its use in the early stages of collision avoidance. System errors such as those due to propagation conditions equally affect vessels in the same area and a comparison of Loran-C fixes will yield separation distances to a relatively high degree of precision.

A worldwide Loran-C coverage diagram is published as DMAHC Chart No. 5130. Geographic limits are shown for 95 percent fix accuracy (two standard deviations) of 1500 feet (457 m) from ground wave signals with signal-to-noise ratios of 1:3 and 1:10. Limits are also shown for sky-wave coverage that will yield a fix of specified lesser accuracy.

Loran-C reception

3219 A "full service" Loran-C receiver will provide both automatic signal acquisition and cycle matching for maximum positional accuracy. As a master station is common to two or more pairs, the receiver can be designed to automatically give two time differences for two lines of position, and to automatically track these signals once they have been acquired. The receiver will give a direct readout of the time differences; if two pairs are being tracked, a single digital display will alternately show each time difference, or there may be a dual display to give both readings simultaneously. Some Loran-C receivers provide a direct readout in latitude and longitude; some models may be coupled to an X-Y coordinate converter which will plot the ship's track.

Like all radionavigational systems, Loran-C can be bothered by interference. The effect of interference is to make it difficult to acquire the Loran-C signals and/or to make the readings fluctuate more than usual. Most manufacturers provide tunable filters which can be used to minimize such interferences. If a user is always going to remain in the same general area (an approximate 100-mile radius from a center point), it will probably never be necessary to readjust these filters once they are properly set by the manufacturer or his local representative.

If the user is going to travel great distances, it will be necessary for the operator to learn how to readjust the filters. This is not a difficult task once the operator has received some initial training.

To start the acquisition process of the receiver, the GRI of the Loran-C chain to be used is entered into the set. With the long baselines of this system, a single GRI is used over a wide area, such as the U.S. Atlantic and Gulf coasts, or the U.S. Pacific coast. The speed at which the receiver will find the Loran-C signals depends upon the signal strength and how much noise is present. In some receivers, the operator can speed up the process by preselecting the approximate Loran-C readings he expects to read. Most modern receivers will be automatically tracking within five minutes of initial turn-on, and will continue to track until the receiver is turned off. If the vessel is at a known location (at a pier and ready for departure, for example) it will be obvious when the receiver is providing the correct information. In any event, most receivers show some type of an alarm which remains lighted until the receiver is tracking properly.

Initially, acquiring Loran-C signals when arriving from far out at sea (several hundred miles or more) is a more difficult problem than the one of a vessel made fast to a pier where the Loran-C readings are known. Thus, the receiver may take a little longer to acquire the signals. When first entering a Loran-C coverage area, the receiver should be checked frequently to ensure that all the alarm lights are extinguished. Sometimes, due to weak signals and high noise, the receiver alarms will go out even though the receiver is not tracking precisely. However, as the vessel continues to enter the stronger signal area, the receiver will automatically recognize that it has made an error and will give the operator an alarm light. This should occur well before entering coastal waters.

Loran-C plotting

3220 Determining a vessel's position from Loran-C data is quite simple. A Loran-C chart of the area is examined for the time delays labeled on the various lines of position. Read one Loran-C time difference from the receiver and find the pair of lines which lie on either side of this value; interpolate by eye for the exact LOP. The same procedure is followed for the second time difference as indicated by the receivers; the position is at the intersection of these lines to the accuracy determined by the range and other factors.

In some instances, one or both of the following conditions may cause difficulties for the navigator:

a. The lines of position are almost parallel, thus making it difficult to determine accurately the vessel's position.

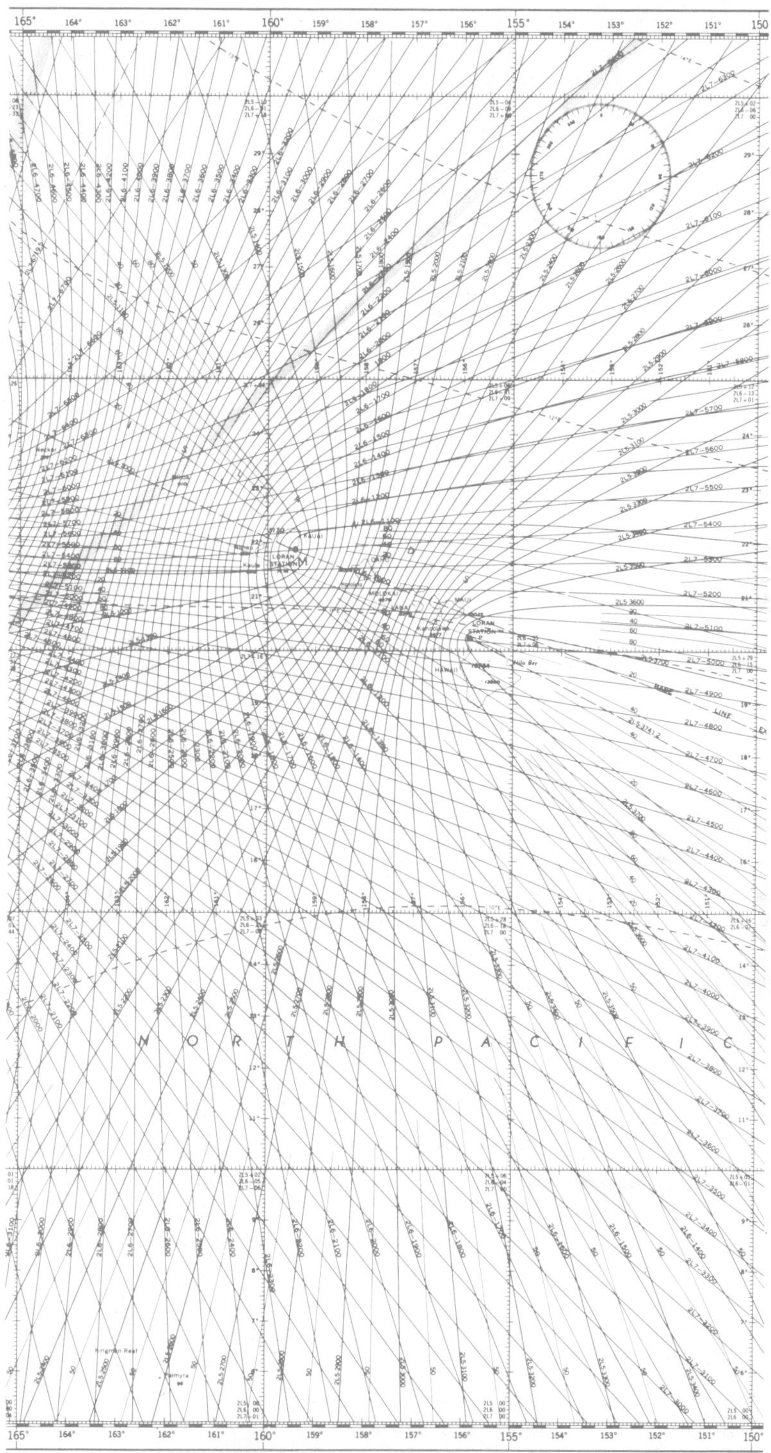

Figure 3220. Chart with Loran-C lines of position (extract).

b. A small change in the Loran-C reading will cause a large change in the position of the corresponding LOP (i.e., the lines are spaced farther apart than are other sets on the same chart).

If either or both of these things happen, the proper procedure is to relock one channel of the receiver to a different secondary station signal, using the manufacturer's operating instructions. To determine which signal to use, examine the chart and find a set of LOPs which results in a good crossing angle (greater than 30°) with the other Loran-C LOP and/or which shows a small change in position for small changes in time-difference readings.

Loran-C charts are published by both the Defense Mapping Agency Hydrographic Center and the National Ocean Survey. If a chart with Loran-C lines overprinted is not available, time differences can be translated into geographic coordinates for plotting on conventional charts by the use of tables (DMAHC Pub. No. 221 series).

Loran-C plotting charts for North Polar regions are published by DMAHC as Charts No. 820 through 825; these are, however, not for sale to the public.

There are several advanced models of Loran-C receivers available with specialized features. One will provide digital data output to a position plotter that will automatically and continuously plot the vessel's position in N-S and E-W coordinates to any selected chart scale within wide limits; this will permit precise return over a previous track for buoy placement, offshore drilling or research tasks, or other applications.

Another highly sophisticated receiver contains an internal microcomputer that will process the Loran-C signals and provide output directly in terms of latitude and longitude to a resolution of 0.01′. It is capable of storing in its memory the location of up to ten Loran-C chains and the direct output of position data eliminates the necessity for having Loran-C charts, or plotting from Loran-C lines if such charts are available. The internal microprocessor can also supply outputs such as course and speed being made good (computed from changes in the Loran-derived positions), direction and distance to a previously entered destination, distance off course to right or left of direct track to destination, time to go to reach destination at present speed, and a warning signal just before the preset destination is reached (such as for a change-of-course point). Once started with accurate time, this receiver can function as a chronometer with an error no greater than about two seconds per month. The equipment contains highly sophisticated self-testing circuitry to give a navigator confidence in its output information. It is capable of operating on pairs of secondary stations without a master, adding to its flexibility.

Repeatability **3221** The Loran-C system provides excellent *repeatability;* a Loran-C fix taken many times at a known location will give positions normally varying less than 300 feet (91 m), and often less than 50 feet (15 m).

Thus the knowledge of previously obtained readings at a specific location can be extremely useful if the navigator wants to return to that spot at a later date; the readings can be used for his return rather than values of latitude and longitude.

The repeatability capability of Loran-C makes it useful in inshore and harbor navigation where data has previously been taken and recorded. Used in this manner, Loran-C may be employed where its accuracy when used with over-printed charts is not adequate for safe navigation. This local knowledge can be very helpful to the navigator, but he should also make full use of other navigational aids available to him. As every prudent navigator realizes, complete faith should *never* be placed solely on *one* system.

Other uses of Loran-C

3222 The inherent stability of the transmitted signals makes the Loran-C system extremely useful for various additional purposes besides precise electronic navigation.

It can serve as a long-range distribution system for time information (UTC) with an accuracy in the order of one microsecond.

It makes possible relative time standardization and synchronization between widely separated receiving locations to accuracies of a few microseconds.

It is useful for electromagnetic wave propagation studies.

These services can be utilized in conjunction with, but without adversely affecting, navigational accuracy. Utilization of this time standard, with knowledge of the exact location of the transmitting stations, allows updating of SINS navigational equipment (Chapter 35).

Loran-C can be used to track vehicles, whether they be on land, sea, or in the air. The most common use to date has been to track weather balloons, with results which have exceeded the performance of balloon-tracking radar systems and have done so at significantly reduced cost.

The basis for vehicle location systems is retransmission of the Loran-C signals from the vehicle to a master receiver located at a base station. With the sophisticated and expensive equipment located at the base station, only inexpensive retransmission modules need be installed in the vehicles. By processing the retransmitted Loran-C signals, the time difference readings which exist at the vehicle can be determined, thus providing vehicle position on an absolute basis or with respect to the base station.

This retransmission technique is being studied as a possible means of locating vessels in distress, and directing search and rescue ships and aircraft to their assistance. It is also being considered as a method of locating ships in the outer areas of a Vessel Traffic System when they are beyond the range of shore-based radars.

As previously noted, a Loran-C receiver can be designed to yield its output data in the form of signals that may be fed into a computer.

The computer converts Loran-C time difference to geographic coordinates. By entering the desired destination or en route points in the computer, steering information can be generated (e.g., range and bearing to destination, off-track indication, etc.) This information can also be used to drive a vessel's autopilot.

Loran-C for harbors and harbor entrance areas

3223 The current Coast Guard Loran-C program will meet some of the requirements for navigation in "Harbors and Harbor Entrance Areas (HHE)"—another geographic subdivision in the National Plan for Navigation. However, the wide-area Loran-C system for the CCZ (Coastal Confluence Zone) was not designed primarily to have the more precise capability required for the HHE. Studies and experiments are being conducted on possible refinements, including differential Loran-C, signal enhancement by low-powered local transmitters, and complete low-powered local "mini-chains."

Differential Loran-C consists of monitoring the minute variations in signals that occur at a specific location, and then transmitting corrections to local users. Experiments have shown this technique to be effective for increasing the accuracy and effectiveness of Loran-C. Differential techniques show great promise of improving, even further, the usefulness of the already highly stable Loran-C signals.

A local low-power transmitting station can be used in areas where the CCZ stations do not provide sufficient signal strength to permit rapid and accurate signal processing. This method may also be used for improvement in the intersection angles of lines of position (LOPs). The navigator of a vessel might use signals from a high-powered CCZ station some distance away in combination with signals from a local low-powered transmitter to obtain the desired quantity and quality of LOPs.

An experimental mini-chain of four 100-watt stations has already been established and studied. Results obtained were sufficient to warrant further trials and evaluation.

Loran-D

3224 Some years ago, the need developed for a low-frequency, hyperbolic navigation system which would be semimobile. Loran-D, a pulsed-type system, was developed to fill this need. It is designed to be readily transportable, so that new lines of position can be furnished in a new area as the need develops, and to minimize downtime required to correct equipment failures.

Like Loran-C, Loran-D operates in the low-frequency band, in the range 90–110 kHz, and its signal characteristics are very similar to those of Loran-C. Three or four transmitting stations operate together on a time-shared basis to provide ground-wave signals of high accuracy over a range of about 500 miles. Under good conditions it will establish position to one-tenth of a mile at a range of 250 miles from the transmitters. Its signals are equally dependable, whether over land or water.

Primarily, Loran-D differs from Loran-C in its signal, which uses repeated groups of 16 pulses, spaced 500 microseconds apart.

The system is highly resistant to electronic jamming. This characteristic, and its extreme mobility—stations can be set up anywhere within 24 hours—make it extremely useful when areas of operation are changing rapidly. The system is equally satisfactory for use aboard naval vessels and high speed aircraft.

OTHER SYSTEMS

Decca **3225** The *Decca* hyperbolic radionavigation system is unique in that in many areas it is privately owned and operated, supported by funds derived from the sale and lease of receiving equipment used on board ships and aircraft. Decca uses phase comparison for the determination of distance from the transmitters, with one master and three (or four) slaves in each chain; see Figure 3225a. Ideally, the slaves would be equally spaced around the circumference of a circle having a radius of 70 to 80 miles (130–150 km), and centered on the master station.

For purposes of identification, the slaves are designated *purple, red,* and *green* (and *orange,* if a fourth is used). Each of the stations transmits a continuous wave at a different frequency within the band 70–

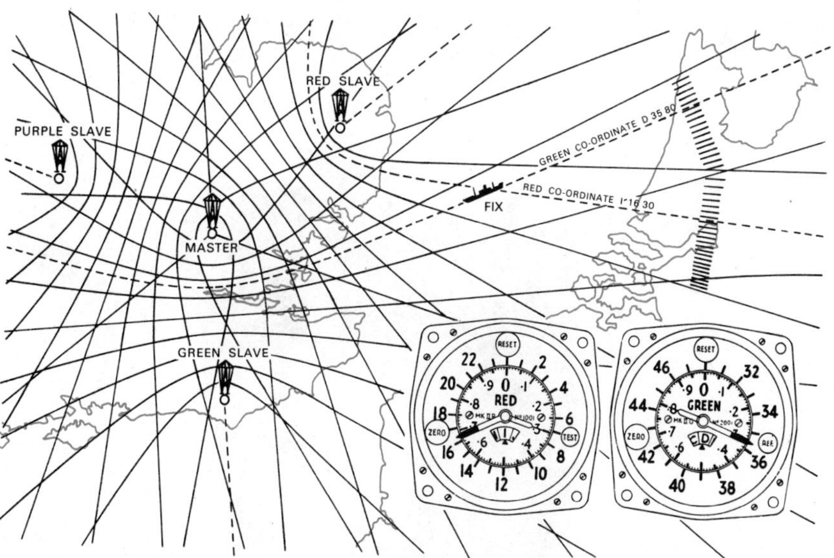

Figure 3225a. Decca lattice for the English Channel.

130 kHz; the frequencies are related in the ratio of 5, 6, 8, and 9 (and 8.2 if an orange station is used).

With the continuous harmonically related carrier frequencies, the phase relationship of the signals conveys the information necessary to determine hyperbolic position.

A typical receiver includes three essentially identical units, one for each frequency. Internal circuitry provides for comparison of the phase of the signal from each slave with that of the master.

Decca charts are published, showing hyperbolas printed in colors to agree with the colors of the slaves. Two slaves provide a fix; the third provides a check on the others, and permits positioning in areas unfavorable to one of the other slaves. To determine a position, it is only necessary to read three dials called *Decometers,* and locate the intersection of the two or three lines indicated. No matching of signals or manipulation of dials is required. As with any phase relationship system the phases of the signals transmitted by master and slave are compared, rather than the travel times. The phase comparison gives a precise measure of the fractional part of a wave-length, or lane, but no indication of the total number of whole lanes existing. An auxiliary means of keeping track of the number of whole lanes is essential. The Mk 21 shipboard receiver, Figure 3225b, has a digital Lane Identification Display for this purpose. Lane identification can also be accomplished from an accurate DR plot on the chart.

The average reliable operational day and night range of Decca is about 250 miles (460 km). At this distance the average error in a line of position is approximately 150 yards (137 m) in daytime, and about 800 yards (730 m) at night.

Decca coverage extends over much of Western Europe, the Persian Gulf, the Indian subcontinent, the Far East, Australian waters, and the Canadian maritime provinces.

Figure 3225b. Decca Mk 21 marine receiver and Model 350 T Track Plotter.

For air navigation a Decca Flight Log Display, Figure 3225c, is available when an automatic system is installed in the aircraft. This roller map display is an X-Y plotter using true coordinates and a strip map showing the exact location of the aircraft at all times.

Consol

3226 *Consol* is a long-range radionavigation system which requires no special receiving equipment. There are stations in several European countries, but none in North America.

Signals are between 190 and 370 kHz and may be received on any LF/MF radio receiver, including most direction finders. If a loop antenna is used, the best results will be obtained by adjusting the antenna to the approximate position of maximum signal; if a communications receiver is used, the automatic gain control must be turned off. A receiver with narrow-band selectivity characteristics will give the most satisfactory results under the normally prevailing conditions of atmospheric noise and other interference; the use of a beat frequency oscillator (BFO) is desirable.

Basic principles

Hyperbolic lines, when extended, approach more and more a definite straight line, the asymptote. In general, at distances more than 12 times the length of the base line, the lines can be considered as straight. Consol has a very short base line, roughly 2½ miles (4 to 5 km), and is sometimes referred to as a "collapsed hyperbolic" system. The system must *not* be used at distances *less than* 25 miles (46 km) from the transmitting station; beyond this, the lines are, for all practical purposes, straight and are used to obtain a bearing with respect to the mid-point of the base line.

Consol stations

A Consol station consists basically of a medium-frequency radio transmitter with a special directional antenna system having three antennas

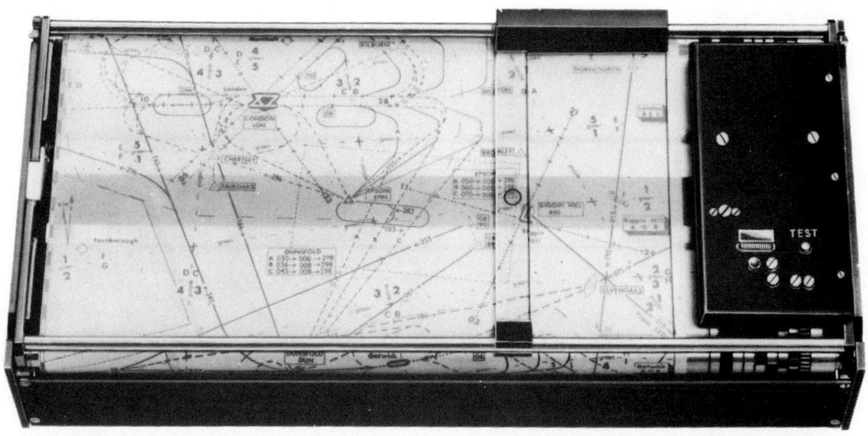

Figure 3225c. Decca Type 966 Flight Log Display Head.

in line, evenly spaced at distances on the order of three times the wave length of the signals. Consol bearings have a maximum accuracy along the perpendicular bisector of the base line of the three antennas; accuracy decreases as the base line extension is approached. Useful coverage is thus limited to two arcs, each of about 120° extent; see Figure 3226a.

The radiation pattern in each coverage area consists of alternate sectors of dot and dash signals, each sector being about 15° wide. This pattern rotates so that a so-called *equisignal* between the dot and dash sectors moves through one sector's width during the keying cycle. The rotation ceases at the end of the cycle and the pattern reverts to its original position for the next cycle. Consequently, an observer will hear the equisignal once in each keying cycle and his angular position in the pattern sector is determined by the number of dot or dash characters heard before the equisignal. The call sign of the station and a long dash are transmitted between keying cycles. The total cycle is

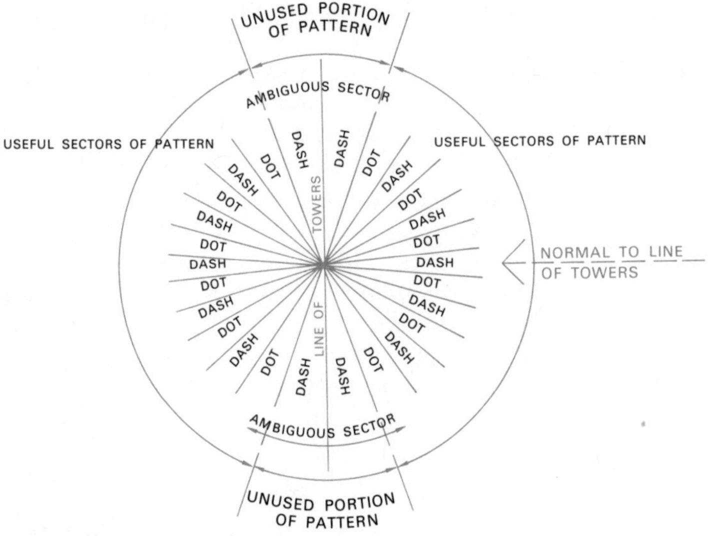

Figure 3226a. Polar diagram of Consol pattern.

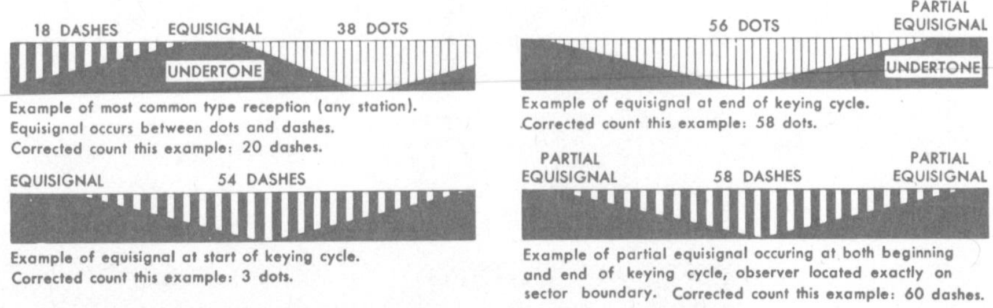

Figure 3226b. Examples of Consol dot-dash sequences as received on different bearings.

usually 60 seconds with a keying cycle of 30 seconds, but some variations will exist from station to station. Full characteristics of each station are given in Chapter 7 of DMAHC Publication No. 117A.

Obtaining a Consol bearing It is not difficult to obtain a bearing from a Consol station. The following procedure is adapted from DMAHC Pub. No. 117A.

Tune to the desired beacon on any radio receiver capable of receiving medium-frequency carrier-wave transmissions on the appropriate frequency. Automatic gain control must be off, and the beat frequency oscillator turned on. If a radio direction finder is used, the loop antenna should be rotated to the position of maximum reception of the Consol signal during the period of counting. To suppress interference or for other reasons, it may be necessary to rotate the loop away from this position. If this is done it should not be rotated more than 45° from the position of maximum reception. When rotated to, or near to, the position of minimum reception an error in the count may be introduced, particularly at ranges of less than 300 miles (555 km) at night.

Listen for the continuous signal and identify the station by the call sign. Then count the number of dots and dashes which follow. A total of 60 dot and dash characters should be heard in each keying cycle. In practice this is rarely the case, since the exact change from dots to dashes (or from dashes to dots) is masked by the width of the equisignal. This period of masking is generally known as the "twilight zone." Consequently the actual count must be corrected to allow for the characters lost in the equisignal. The total observed count should therefore be subtracted from 60 and half the difference added to each of the dot and dash counts.

Example:

Observed count: 12 dots, 44 dashes.
$12 + 44 = 56$
$60 - 56 = 4$ add 2 dots, 2 dashes
True count: 14 dots, 46 dashes.

When the number of characters lost in the twilight zone is large, some operators find that dots are easier to distinguish than dashes and also that the signal fading into the noise can be followed to a lower level than that to which the signal has to rise before being detected again. Considerable practice often makes it possible to eliminate errors arising from the above.

There will be an ambiguity unless the bearing of the beacon is known to within ±10°. The approximate bearing can be obtained by taking a direction-finder bearing of the long dash if the reliability of the DR position is doubtful. In using this method the possibility of "night-effect" (Article 3207) on the direction finder must be allowed for. Since, however, a comparatively rough bearing is satisfactory this will seldom be serious, but the usual precautions (such as observing any tendency of the bearing to wander, etc.) must be taken to avoid gross errors.

Using a Consol count Charts are available with Consol lines overprinted for various dot and dash counts. DMAHC Pub. No. 117A contains tables giving the true bearings for various dot and dash counts.

If these bearings are plotted on a Mercator chart, an additional correction must be made since a radio wave follows the great circle, a curved line on the Mercator projection. A portion of this conversion table is shown in Figure 3226d. On a Lambert chart the bearings are plotted directly.

Range and accuracy During periods of low interference levels, ranges over the sea of 1,000 miles (1,850 km) by day and 1,200 miles (2,200 km) by night may normally be expected about 90 percent of the time. In general, when ground waves are received, the error over water does not exceed about one-third degree along the perpendicular to the base line, nor about two-thirds of a degree at an angle to the perpendicular. Stated in linear units, this is an error of about 1 mile (1.85 km) for each 180 miles (333 km) from the station along the perpendicular, and for each 90 miles (167 km) along the bearing line 60° from the perpendicular. This error can usually be reduced considerably by taking a number of readings and getting an average bearing. (A wide variation in successive counts is an indication of sky wave-ground wave interference. These bearings should be used with great caution, or disregarded altogether.)

While Consol cannot be considered a precision system, it is suitable for ocean navigation off the European continent and can be quite useful in some special situations, such as for ships approaching the Straits of Gibraltar from the west, and for ships operating in the western Mediterranean. Bearings should be used with increasing caution as the proximity of possible danger becomes greater. Errors may be expected to be greater at night.

7510.3 Stavanger Consol Station—Dash Sectors

Count of dashes	True bearings from station										
0	035.6	057.0	077.0	098.4	127.4	186.6	215.6	237.0	257.0	278.4	307.4	006.6
1	035.4	056.8	076.8	098.2	127.1	186.9	215.8	237.2	257.2	278.6	307.7	006.3
2	035.2	056.7	076.7	098.0	126.7	187.3	216.0	237.3	257.3	278.8	308.1	005.9
3	035.0	056.5	076.5	097.9	126.4	187.6	216.1	237.6	257.5	279.0	308.4	005.6
4	034.8	056.3	076.3	097.7	126.1	187.9	216.3	237.7	257.7	279.2	308.8	005.2
5	034.6	056.2	076.2	097.5	125.8	188.2	216.5	237.8	257.8	279.4	309.1	004.9
6	034.4	056.0	076.0	097.3	125.4	188.6	216.7	238.0	258.0	279.6	309.5	004.5
7	034.2	055.8	075.8	097.1	125.1	188.9	216.9	238.2	258.2	279.8	309.8	004.2
8	034.0	055.6	075.7	096.9	124.8	189.2	217.1	238.3	385.4	280.0	310.2	003.8
54	024.3	047.7	068.0	088.4	112.5	201.5	225.6	256.0	266.3	289.7		
55	024.1	047.5	067.8	088.2	112.3	201.7	225.8	246.2	266.5	289.9		
56	023.9	047.4	067.7	088.1	112.0	202.0	225.9	246.3	266.6	290.1		
57	023.7	047.2	067.5	087.9	111.8	202.2	226.1	246.5	266.8	290.3		
58	023.4	047.0	067.3	087.7	111.5	202.5	226.3	246.7	267.0	290.6		
59	023.2	046.8	067.2	087.5	111.3	202.7	226.5	246.8	267.2	290.8		
60	023.0	046.7	067.0	087.3	111.0	203.0	226.7	247.0	267.3	291.0		

Figure 3226c. Consol dash count to bearing conversion table (extract).

7510. **Stavanger (LEC).** 58°37'32"N., 5°37'49"E.
FREQ.: 319 kHz, A1. POWER: 650 W.
CHARACTERISTIC SIGNAL: Call sign 4.5 sec., long dash 19.2 sec., silent 2.5 sec., keying cycle 30 sec., silent 3.0 sec. Total time 40 sec.
HOURS OF TRANSMISSION: Continuous.
REMARKS: Coverage areas – 350° to 140° and 170° to 320°. Bearing of line of aerials: 336°59'20". Distance between aerials: 8,885 f

7510.1 Stavanger Consol Station—Conversion Table

Difference of longitude	Latitude of Observer																		
	0°	5°	10°	15°	20°	25°	30°	35°	40°	45°	50°	55°	60°	65°	70°	75°	80°	85°	90°
0	0.0	0.0	0.0	0.0	0.0	0.0	0.0	0.0	0.0	0.0	0.0	0.0	0.0	0.0	0.0	0.0	0.0	0.0	0.0
5	1.9	1.9	2.0	2.0	2.0	2.1	2.1	2.1	2.1	2.1	2.1	2.1	2.1	2.1	2.1	2.0	1.9	1.7	0.0
10	3.8	3.9	4.0	4.0	4.1	4.1	4.2	4.2	4.2	4.2	4.2	4.2	4.3	4.3	4.2	4.0	3.8	3.4	0.0
15	5.7	5.8	5.9	6.0	6.1	6.2	6.3	6.3	6.3	6.4	6.4	6.4	6.4	6.4	6.2	6.0	5.7	5.1	0.0
75	31.1	31.7	32.2	32.6	32.9	33.2	33.5	33.6	33.7	33.7	33.6	33.5	33.1	32.6	31.8	30.7	28.8	25.6	0.0
80	33.6	34.2	34.7	35.1	35.5	35.8	36.0	36.2	36.2	36.2	36.1	35.9	35.5	34.9	34.1	32.8	30.8	27.3	0.0
85	36.2	36.8	37.3	37.7	38.1	38.4	38.6	38.8	38.8	38.8	38.6	38.3	37.9	37.2	36.3	34.9	32.8	28.9	0.0
90	38.8	39.5	40.0	40.5	40.8	41.1	41.3	41.4	41.4	41.4	41.2	40.8	40.3	39.6	38.6	37.0	34.7	30.6	0.0

Corrections to be *added* to the Great Circle bearing to obtain the Mercator bearing when the observer is to the East of the station and *subtracted* when the observer is to the West of the station.

Figure 3226d. Radio bearing conversion table for a specific Consol station (typical).

Omnirange navigation

3227 An aircraft navigation system, VHF Omnidirectional Range, or "Omni" for short, has some application to marine navigation. As the name indicates, it operates in the very high frequency band between 108 and 118 MHz. Omni signals are, as the name indicates, radiated in an all-around pattern and enable the user to get a highly precise bearing on the transmitting station.

A special Omni receiver (quite small and lightweight, but not inexpensive) is required; its operation is quite simple. A direct reading is shown on the face of the indicator, together with an indication of whether it is "To" or "From" the station. The course may be set into the receiver and it will then show any deviation to the right or left.

Ranges are quite limited for surface vessels due to the use of VHF frequencies (line of sight plus a small percentage for bending over the horizon). Although Omni stations are located for their usefulness to aircraft, many of them will be found close enough to the coastline that they can be received at sea. Omni is thus most useful for "landfall navigation" or obtaining a line of position during coastal passages. (There are, however, many stretches of coastal waters without Omni coverage.)

Summary

3228 Radionavigation systems provide valuable assistance to a navigator on the high seas or in coastal waters as he can then fix his position even under weather conditions that preclude celestial observations or visual piloting. The offsetting disadvantage is that complex electronic equipment is required both on the ship and ashore, gear that must be operated and maintained properly.

Direction finding on marine radiobeacons has been somewhat replaced by more sophisticated systems, but remains a basic technique and is still widely used by smaller and less elaborately equipped vessels. Loran-A is scheduled to be phased out of the U.S. system of electronic navigation aids by the early 1980s, but stations will remain in operation in some foreign areas. Loran-C is the system adopted for the U.S. "coastal confluence zone"—defined as 50 miles (92.6 km) offshore or out to the edge of the continental shelf (100-fathom line), whichever is greater. (Omega is its high seas counterpart; see Chapter 33.)

Other radionavigation systems available in some waters include Decca, Consol, and Omni.

A navigator must be knowledgeable as to which radionavigation systems are available in the waters traveled by his vessel—their capabilities and limitations. He must be able to efficiently use all equipment fitted on his ship for the reception of the signals of such systems, but he must not develop a dependence on the availability and accuracy of any system. Radionavigation systems may become unavailable or ineffective due to loss of ship's power, propagation irregularities, equipment malfunction, or other causes. It is essential that a navigator be skilled in dead reckoning, piloting, and celestial navigation. He must not place his reliance solely on radionavigation systems; he must be able to navigate successfully with the basic tools of the trade—compass and sextant. In the words of the Bible, he must know "the way of a ship in the midst of the sea."

33 Omega Navigation System

Introduction **3301** The fundamental principles of the Omega Navigation System date back to the late 1940s, but many years of development and refinement were required before practical implementation was begun. Omega was developed by the U.S. Navy to provide a world-wide, all-weather positioning system for ships, aircraft, and submarines, both surfaced and submerged, with a nominal accuracy of one mile in daytime and two miles at night. (Expansion of the Loran-C system was not feasible due to the very large number of stations that would have to be built and operated.) The Omega electronic navigation system is also used by many non-naval vessels from small yachts to the largest of tankers.

The Omega system **3302** The Omega Navigation System involves the use of land-based transmitting stations, special Omega receivers, propagation correction tables, and special charts or plotting sheets, or tables that allow plotting on conventional charts.

Omega is a global system of eight transmitting stations; two of them are located on U.S. soil, while the other six are operated in cooperation with partner countries. The transmitters, each radiating 10 kilowatts of power, are so situated that a user will be able to receive signals from at least three stations; normally from four to as many as six stations will be received. This multiple reception will result in an even greater number of signal-pairs, each of which provides a line of position. Thus LOPs can be selected for optimum crossing angles. (Any two signals may be used as a pair; there are no "master" and "secondary" stations as with Loran-C.) The availability of signals from a number of transmitters will also do much to ensure at least a minimum number of pairs even at times of unfavorable propagation conditions. Theoretically, the system will provide full global coverage, but economic and political considerations have resulted in transmitter locations that are somewhat less than ideal. Near, but not quite, world-wide coverage will be obtained when all eight transmitters are in the air; the final permanent station, in Australia, is scheduled for operation in late 1980.

Omega receivers are characterized by simplicity of operation, ease of use of the information obtained, simple and compact installation, and acceptable cost. They are so designed that almost any marine navigator with a minimum of training can obtain a fix in a few minutes.

When a ship is within range of three or more stations, the Omega receiver, once set, will continually display a series of lane values, or numbers, on its panel indicator. These numbers roughly correspond to the lines of position (LOPs) on the Omega plotting chart.

The marine navigator records the lane values displayed by his receiver and applies the proper correction data as obtained from the appropriate Propagation Correction Tables (if the corrections have not already been entered into the receiver); see Article 3307. He then plots the information on an Omega chart or plotting sheet to establish his ship's position.

In most airborne Omega systems the above procedure is completely automatic and is pilot-operable. Automatic systems, with output data directly in terms of latitude and longitude, are coming into greater shipboard use as a result of advancements in microprocessor design.

Omega signals can be received out to maximum usable ranges of 4,000 to 10,000 miles (7,400 to 18,500 km) from the transmitters, depending upon the bearing of the receiver from the transmitter and favorable sky-wave conditions. Shorter ranges can be expected at reception points west of stations located near the magnetic equator. Signals are also severely attenuated when a propagation path crosses land which is overlaid with a thick sheet of ice, such as Greenland or Antarctica.

System description

3303 Omega is a very low frequency (VLF) hyperbolic radionavigation system using phase-difference measurements of continuous wave (CW) radio signals. These VLF signals can be transmitted over great distances; only six transmitting stations will make the system available in nearly all parts of the globe, with two other stations for redundancy and coverage during repair of an inoperative station.

Omega differs from most other hyperbolic systems, such as Loran A, in that it uses a phase-difference technique, rather than a time-difference principle. (Loran-C uses cycle matching, but this is merely for a more precise measurement of time differences. Decca uses phase-comparison techniques, but is on higher frequencies and is a relatively short-range system.)

The basic Omega measurement is the phase difference of 10.2 kHz signals transmitted from two or more stations. (As will be seen later, the various Omega stations transmit in sequence rather than continuously. As it is received, each signal is compared with an internal reference oscillator with these measurements being stored internally for subsequent comparison in various pairs.) The phase difference of a station pair yields a hyperbolic line of position (Article 3110). A fix can be obtained by using additional LOPs obtained from further phase-difference measurements made on the signals of other pairs of transmitters. At VLF frequencies, sky-wave propagation is reliable and the velocity of propagation is predictable with errors of only a few microseconds.

The wavelength of the 10.2 kHz signal is approximately 16 miles; phase readings repeat twice for each wavelength or once for every eight miles (Figure 3303a). The intervals between zero phase-difference readings are called *lanes*. Along a base line between two stations the lane is eight miles in width; this gradually increases away from the base line to approximately 12 nautical miles. A specific phase difference establishes a line of position within one (any one) of these lanes; the counters on the phase indicators on the ship's receiver are set at the beginning of a voyage, and subsequently count the numbers of lanes traversed. In the more sophisticated receivers provisions are made for resolving lane ambiguities and deriving a fix without prior knowledge of position (Article 3304).

As the hyperbolic lines represent the locus of points at which the differences in the distances from the transmitting stations are equal, and as these distances are measured in units of time, representing distances traveled by the radio waves, the relative times of the transmission of signals from all Omega stations must be determined with the utmost precision and accuracy. Each Omega station transmits in a fixed sequence with the length of the transmission in each ten-second period varying between 0.9, 1.0, 1.1, and 1.2 seconds from station to station; these differences aid in the identification of the specific Omega transmitting station. In addition to broadcasting a continuous-wave (no modulation) signal on the basic 10.2 kHz frequency, each Omega station also transmits on three other navigational frequencies, 11.05, 11.33, and 13.6 kHz. The radio frequencies and the timing of the transmissions are governed by extremely accurate cesium frequency standards (four at each station) that are checked and synchro-

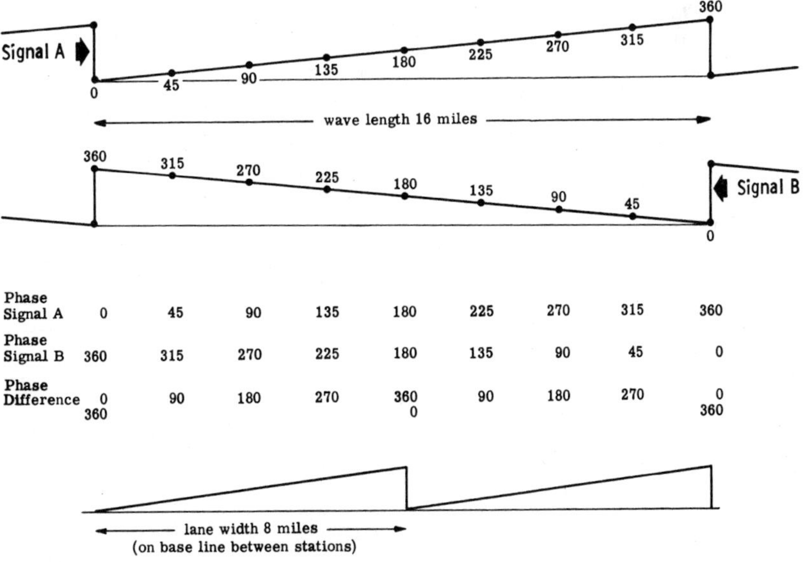

Figure 3303a. Omega 10.2 kHz phase difference measurement.

nized by reference to the U.S. Naval Observatory Master Clock. (The UTC leap-second adjustments, discussed in Article 2210, are *not* made to the Omega time epoch, and "Omega time" may be as much as five to ten seconds different from UTC.)

The older navigation systems use pulses emitted in the required time relationship, as in Loran, or continuous harmonically related carrier frequencies, in which the phase relationship conveys the time information, as in Decca. With a pulse system, all Loran stations in a network can transmit on the same radio frequency at different times. However, when continuous carriers are employed, the frequencies used by the various stations must differ, so that they can be identified, while retaining a common basis in time. This leads to the requirement for the harmonic relationship.

Omega to some extent combines both methods. Measurements are made of the relative phase of bursts of a steady carrier transmitted on the same radio frequency at different times. The use of a single frequency is advantageous, since phase shifts within the receiver are of no concern, as they remain the same for all signals. Aside from the very low frequency employed, the chief distinction between Omega and the older systems is the time-sharing of continuous carrier bursts of relative phase. Each Omega station transmits in a fixed sequence pattern, so only one station is transmitting on each navigational frequency at any time. Eight stations can share a ten-second period, and the receiver can identify each station by its place in the sequence as well as by the exact time duration of its signal; see the portion of Figure 3303b relating to 10.2 kHz transmissions. Note also that when one

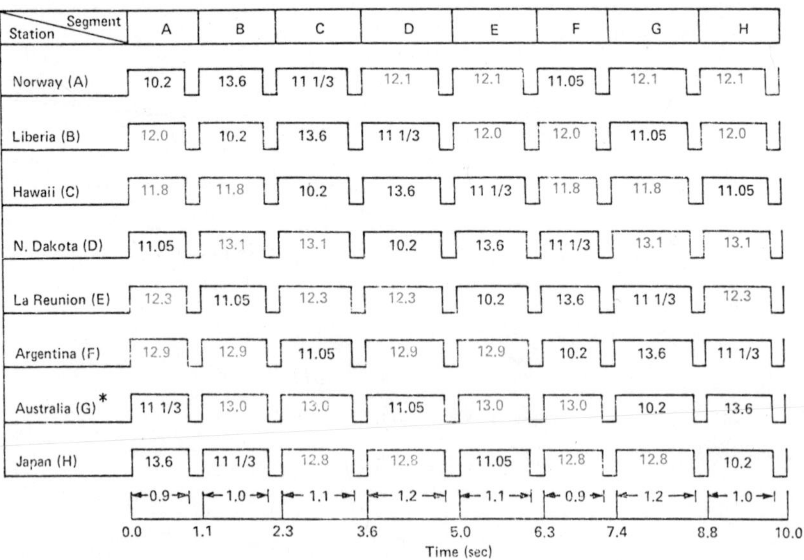

Figure 3303b. Omega signal format.
*Segment G. has been used for the interim station in Trinidad until Australia becomes operational.

station is transmitting on 10.2 kHz in its assigned time slot, a second station is transmitting on 13.6 kHz, a third station on 11.33 kHz, and a fourth station on 11.05 kHz.

Each Omega station *may* also transmit on additional frequencies for purposes not related to conventional marine navigation. These "unique" frequencies are shown as f_1 to f_8 in Figure 3303b; they can be ignored by the navigator at sea.

In addition, Omega differs from other hyperbolic navigation systems in that any two stations from which signals can be received may be paired to furnish a line of position. The navigator may therefore select stations whose signals will yield lines of position crossing nearly at right angles. This geometrical excellence, coupled with the range of choices available to the navigator, results in an accuracy in positioning that varies little with geographical location.

In the Omega system, the transmitting stations are located approximately 6,000 miles from one another. With a network of eight stations, at least four stations should be available to the navigator at any point on earth, thus yielding a minimum of six possible LOPs. If six stations could be received, he would have a theoretical choice of 15 LOPs.

The U.S.S.R. operates a radionavigation system much like Omega; this consists of three stations using two sets of three frequencies each in the VLF band between 11.9 and 15.6 kHz.

Lane identification

3304 As discussed above, the measurement of the difference in phase of two received signals, which were synchronized in time at the transmitting station, can produce a line of position which can be posi-

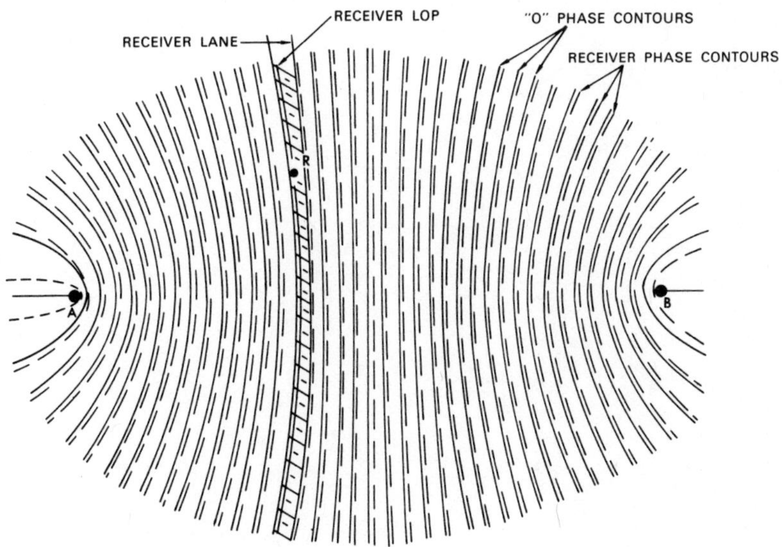

Figure 3304a. Omega lane pattern.

tively identified with a band or lane one-half the wavelength in width (Figure 3304a). It is therefore mandatory to know in which lane the vessel is located. The Omega receiver provides a counter, or printout on a graph, to furnish the navigator with data on the number of lanes which have been crossed since the start of the counter. Lane identification therefore presents no serious problems for vessels, provided there is no interruption in the continuous receipt of Omega signals.

Any ambiguity in lane identification can be resolved by using the transmission from two stations on a second Omega frequency, 13.6 kHz. This frequency has a wavelength which is exactly one-third shorter than that of the basic frequency, 10.2 kHz. The phase synchronization is adjusted so that one contour of the higher frequency coincides with one contour of the lower frequency. Every *fourth* 13.6 kHz contour will now coincide with every *third* 10.2 kHz contour, thus establishing a pattern of broad lanes, each extending over three lanes

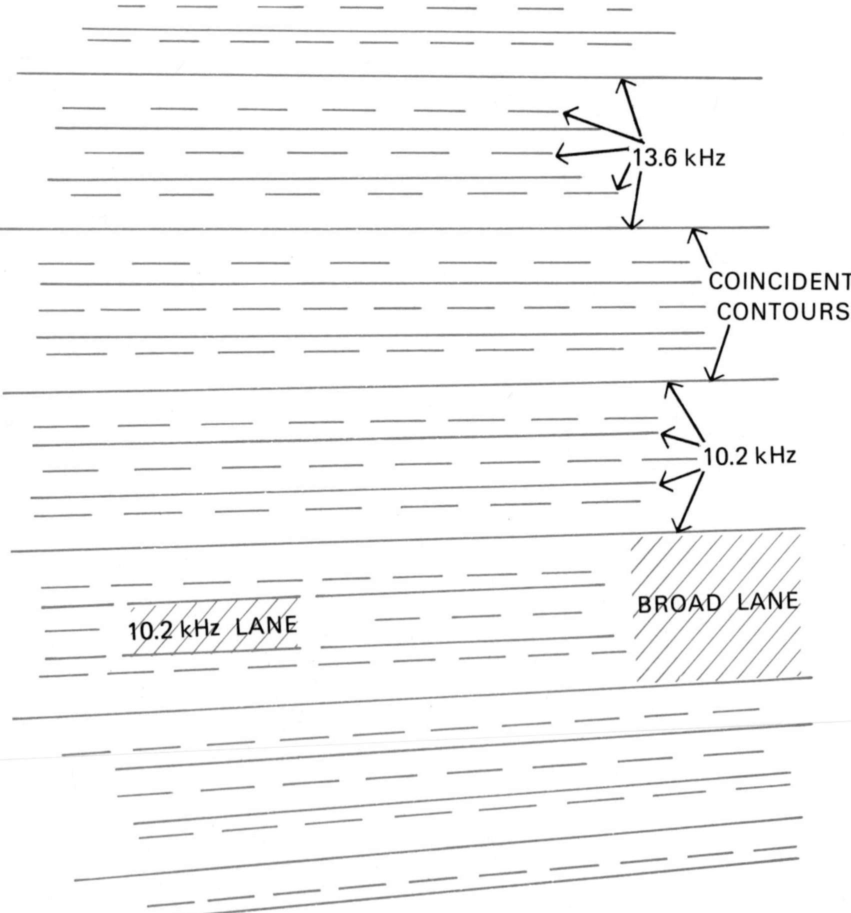

Figure 3304b. Principles of lane resolution.

of the basic 10.2 kHz pattern, or over a width of twenty-four miles. This is illustrated in Figure 3304b.

It can thus be determined from the difference of the two phase indications in which of the three 10.2 kHz lanes forming the broad lane the observer is located. If the difference is less than one-third hertz, he is in the first lane; if between one and two-thirds, he is in the middle lane; and if between two-thirds and one hertz, he is in the third lane.

A third frequency of 11.33 kHz is also transmitted by all Omega stations; see Figure 3303b. The difference between the frequency of this signal and that of the basic 10.2 kHz signal—1.13 kHz—provides for lane ambiguity resolution to 72 miles; see Figure 3304c. The fourth navigational frequency of 11.05 kHz extends lane resolution out to 288 miles.

Many Omega navigation receivers can receive only the 10.2 kHz basic signals. With these an accurate DR track must be maintained and it may be necessary to employ celestial or other electronic navigation systems to restart an Omega lane count if an interruption to continuous tracking occurs. (Positional accuracy is the same whether one, two, or three frequencies are being received, provided proper lane identification is known; the additional frequencies serve only to resolve questions of lane identification.)

Omega stations may also transmit on other frequencies during the periods of each ten-second cycle when they are silent on 10.2, 11.05, 11.33, and 13.6 kHz. These "unique frequency" transmissions are not now of direct interest to marine navigators.

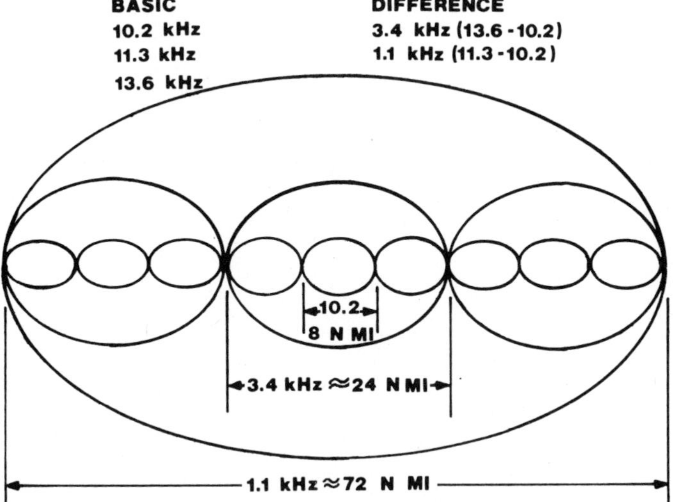

Figure 3304c. Lane resolution relationship using three frequencies.

Omega charts

3305 Omega navigational charts published by DMAHC are small-scale nautical charts on which are overprinted the hyperbolic lines of constant phase difference between various transmitter pairs. (Any two stations that can be received can constitute a pair, with a consequent set of hyperbolic lines.) Each Omega chart has two or more sets of lines to permit the navigator to select those that will give him suitable intersection angles—90° for two lines, 120° for three lines, etc. Lines are printed in different colors for greater ease of identification; they are designated by the letters of the station pair and the lane numbers (three or four digits). Lines of position are normally printed for every third lane of any pair. In the margin of the chart, there will be a listing of the Omega pairs for which lines of position are shown on the chart; these are color coded similarly to the printed lines. The station pairs are listed in order of probable best reception.

Omega navigation charts are in the DMAHC 7500 and 7600 series (the "7600 series" extends to 7714). Use of the 7600 series is preferable, except where the interim station in Trinidad is used, as this appears only on charts of the 7500 series. These Omega charts have no overlap and there are often differences in the station pairs shown on adjacent charts as each carries only those LOPs considered best for that chart's general area. Omega lines of position have been added to a number of DMAHC conventional nautical charts; such lines will be added to all DMAHC charts at a scale of 1:300,000 or smaller as they are routinely reprinted in new editions. Omega lines also appear on some foreign charts.

Since the base line between Omega stations is on the order of 6,000 miles (11,000 km), charted LOPs show relatively little curvature. In some areas, as near a base line bisector, these LOPs may become essentially straight. This characteristic simplifies the navigator's job, particularly in interpolating for percentage of lane between two Omega lines.

Omega position tables

3306 Omega charting coordinate tables (called Omega "lattice" tables in some publications) are simply Omega lines of position in tabular form. If a navigator so desires, or if he lacks an Omega chart, he may simply plot his Omega information directly onto a convenient chart or plotting sheet. A separate table is used for each station pair for each specific geographic area. These tables are published by DMAHC as part of the Pub. No. 224 series; a lattice table for a specific pair might be numbered 224(107) A-C, where the "1" indicates the 10.2 kHz frequency, the "07" denotes Omega area 07, and "A-C" names the stations of the pair. (The "Omega areas" are unique to this navigational system and should not be confused with other "areas" or "regions" used with marine navigational charts and publications.)

Each page of an Omega charting table has a number of columns of geographic coordinates for the specific Omega lane value shown at the heading of that column; see Figure 3306. In most instances, the readings are tabulated at intervals of one degree of latitude (or longitude). Each column lists all the points, in latitude and longitude, required to plot an Omega line of position; latitude always appears to the left of longitude. Omega hyperbolic lines of position are so nearly straight lines, except when near to a transmitter, that the tabulated points can be joined by straight lines. The Omega lattice tables also include a table of bearings to each of the stations concerned from various points, defined in terms of latitude and longitude.

Since Omega lines of position from each pair of stations fan out in all directions, it is sometimes necessary to tabulate the latitude at which the lines intersect meridians; at other times it is necessary to tabulate the longitudes at which the lines intersect parallels of latitude.

For the entire area of coverage, points are listed at intervals of one degree of latitude or longitude from the equator to 60° of latitude, north and south. From 60° latitude to 80° latitude the interval is one degree of latitude or two degrees of longitude; from 80° to 90° latitude the interval of listing is one degree of latitude or five degrees of longitude.

Close to the transmitting stations, where the lines curve sharply, additional points are inserted at intervals of 15 minutes of arc. The spacing of the points has been chosen so that the navigator may safely use a straight line between any two adjacent tabulated points. Within approximately 20 miles (37 km) of a transmitting station, the curvature of the lines is excessive, and the navigator is cautioned that straight line segments will introduce appreciable errors. A plot of three consecutive points will always show the amount of curvature present and indicate the true line.

T	A-C 985		A-C 986		A-C 987		A-C 988		A-C 989		T
Lat ° ′	° ′	Δ	° ′	Δ	° ′	Δ	° ′	Δ	° ′	Δ	Long ° ′
20 N	96 44.2W	124	96 56.6W	124	97 09.0W	124	97 21.5W	124	97 34.0W	124	
21 N	97 17.2W	125	97 29.7W	124	97 42.1W	125	97 54.7W	125	98 07.2W	125	
22 N	97 50.9W	125	98 03.5W	125	98 16.1W	126	98 28.7W	125	98 41.2W	125	
23 N	98 25.6W	125	98 38.2W	126	98 50.9W	126	99 03.5W	126	99 16.2W	126	
24 N	99 01.1W	127	99 13.8W	127	99 26.6W	127	99 39.3W	126	99 52.0W	127	
25 N	99 37.6W	127	99 50.4W	128	100 03.3W	128	100 16.0W	127	100 28.8W	128	
26 N	100 15.1W	128	100 28.1W	129	100 41.0W	128	100 53.8W	128	101 06.7W	129	
27 N	100 53.8W	130	101 06.9W	129	101 19.8W	129	101 32.7W	129	101 45.8W	130	
28 N	101 33.7W	131	101 46.8W	130	101 59.8W	130	102 12.9W	131	102 26.0W	131	
29 N	102 14.8W	132	102 28.0W	132	102 41.2W	131	102 54.3W	132	103 07.6W	132	
30 N	102 57.3W	133	103 10.5W	132	103 23.8W	133	103 37.2W	133	103 50.6W	133	
31 N	103 41.2W	134	103 54.6W	134	104 08.0W	134	104 21.5W	135	104 35.1W	134	
32 N	104 26.6W	135	104 40.2W	136	104 53.9W	136	105 07.5W	136	105 21.1W	135	
33 N	105 13.8W	137	105 27.6W	137	105 41.4W	138	105 55.2W	137	106 09.0W	137	
34 N	106 02.9W	138	106 16.8W	139	106 30.8W	139	106 44.8W	139	106 58.7W	139	
35 N	106 53.8W	141	107 08.0W	141	107 22.2W	141	107 36.3W	141	107 50.5W	141	
36 N	107 47.0W	143	108 01.4W	144	108 15.8W	143	108 30.2W	143	108 44.6W	143	
37 N	108 42.6W	145	108 57.2W	145	109 11.8W	145	109 26.4W	146	109 41.0W	146	
38 N	109 40.7W	148	109 55.6W	148	110 10.4W	148	110 25.3W	148	110 40.2W	149	
39 N	110 41.6W	151	110 56.8W	151	111 11.9W	151	111 27.0W	151	111 42.3W	152	
40 N	111 45.7W	154	112 01.1W	154	112 16.5W	154	112 32.1W	155	112 47.6W	155	
41 N	112 53.1W	157	113 08.9W	158	113 24.7W	158	113 40.6W	158	113 56.5W	159	
42 N	114 04.3W	161	114 20.5W	162	114 36.8W	162	114 53.1W	162	115 09.4W	163	
43 N	115 19.8W	166	115 36.5W	166	115 53.2W	167	116 09.9W	167	116 26.7W	168	
	43 30.5N	-126	43 17.8N	-126	43 05.2N	-127	42 52.4N	-127	42 39.7N	-127	116 W
	44 14.3N	-123	44 01.9N	-123	43 49.6N	-123	43 37.2N	-124	43 24.7N	-124	117 W
	44 56.1N	-120	44 44.0N	-120	44 31.9N	-121	44 19.8N	-121	44 07.6N	-121	118 W
	45 36.0N	-117	45 24.2N	-118	45 12.3N	-118	45 00.5N	-118	44 48.6N	-119	119 W

Figure 3306. Omega lattice table (extract).

Omega is primarily a long-range radionavigation system and has limitations at relatively close-in ranges. These result from propagation complications as well as the excess curvature of lines considered above. On Omega charts, lines of position are shown dashed within 450 miles (830 km) of a transmitter. Difficulties can be avoided by using distant pairs of transmitters; for example, a ship near Honolulu should use signals from the Norway and North Dakota stations, but not those from the transmitter in Hawaii.

Additional information on the construction of the tables, and their use in navigation without a special Omega chart, will be found in the front page of each publication.

Propagation corrections

3307 Basic to the operation of the Omega navigation system is the stability of the propagation characteristics of VLF radio waves over great distances, plus the fact that the slight changes that do occur can generally be predicted quite accurately. The VLF Omega frequencies radiate from the transmitting stations to the receiver along the normal channel between the earth's surface and the ionosphere. As the ionosphere changes its height from day to night, the path of wave travel varies, and the apparent signal speed also varies from day to night; periods of about two hours at morning and evening twilight show rapid and considerable changes in propagation characteristics. The Omega charts are constructed using standard daytime phase velocity of propagation. Propagation corrections (PPCs) must be applied to each Omega receiver reading to compensate for such deviations from standard conditions. PPCs are calculated in advance and are published in tables for transmitting stations; these tables are part of the DMAHC Pub. No. 224 series. A specific correction table might be designated Pub. No. 224 (112-C)B where the first "1" indicates its applicability to the 10.2 kHz frequency (a "2" would indicate corrections for 3.4 kHz, the difference of frequency between 10.2 and 13.6 kHz), the "12" denotes the Omega area (as with lattice tables), the "C" designates it as a correction table (rather than a lattice table), and the "B" names the station concerned. A brief introduction, which also describes the arrangement and application of the corrections, together with illustrative examples, precedes the tabular data within each PPC table. An extract is shown in Figure 3307; a graph from this table is also shown. Such graphing is of convenience to a navigator when remaining in the same general vicinity for some time.

It should be noted that propagation correction tables are published for the 3.4 kHz difference frequency as this is what is used for lane ambiguity resolution. PPC tables are now published for the 13.6 kHz navigational frequency and similar tables may at a later date be calculated and published for the other basic and difference frequencies.

These are the only corrections that need to be applied to the receiver display in order to obtain valid readings. Some models of "automatic" Omega receivers have the capability of internally generat-

10.2 KHZ OMEGA PROPAGATION CORRECTIONS IN UNITS OF CECS — LOCATION 16.0 N 60.0 W — STATION A NORWAY

DATE	GMT 00	01	02	03	04	05	06	07	08	09	10	11	12	13	14	15	16	17	18	19	20	21	22	23	24
1-15 JAN	-77	-79	-78	-79	-79	-79	-80	-81	-81	-75	-20	9	-12	-11	-7	-8	-10	-18	-23	-35	-47	-63	-74	-78	-77
16-31 JAN	-75	-76	-76	-77	-77	-77	-77	-78	-76	-71	-19	5	-12	-9	-4	-4	-7	-13	-21	-29	-40	-55	-68	-73	-75
1-14 FEB	-77	-78	-78	-79	-79	-79	-79	-76	-69	-59	-8	-1	-11	0	2	0	-2	-8	-16	-24	-36	-54	-70	-75	-77
15-29 FEB	-74	-76	-76	-77	-76	-76	-74	-68	-57	-46	0	-1	-2	5	8	5	4	-1	-8	-19	-30	-48	-66	-73	-74
1-15 MAR	-87	-89	-87	-88	-89	-87	-80	-72	-62	-56	-6	-13	-5	2	4	4	1	-7	-16	-27	-38	-59	-78	-86	-87
16-31 MAR	-84	-86	-84	-83	-85	-79	-71	-60	-51	-40	-2	-9	2	6	10	10	9	4	-6	-18	-30	-49	-70	-80	-84
1-15 APR	-83	-85	-84	-84	-79	-69	-64	-57	-44	-32	-6	-9	1	3	9	9	5	5	-1	-11	-21	-41	-67	-77	-83
16-30 APR	-78	-77	-78	-75	-69	-62	-55	-46	-32	-21	-4	-6	3	5	9	14	14	12	6	-1	-13	-26	-56	-70	-78
1-15 MAY	-78	-81	-81	-75	-74	-65	-55	-47	-34	-20	-11	-7	1	4	7	9	9	8	5	-3	-12	-28	-53	-71	-78
16-31 MAY	-75	-79	-80	-79	-75	-63	-55	-45	-31	-16	-9	-3	5	8	9	9	9	9	7	4	-5	-21	-47	-66	-75
1-15 JUN	-72	-75	-76	-77	-72	-58	-49	-36	-24	-6	-2	2	8	10	13	12	12	11	12	11	5	-12	-41	-63	-72
16-30 JUN	-67	-73	-75	-75	-70	-59	-48	-37	-25	-7	-2	2	7	9	11	10	11	9	9	8	5	-4	-35	-60	-67
1-15 JUL	-58	-63	-61	-61	-60	-50	-38	-29	-18	7	9	10	13	15	17	17	16	13	14	12	11	11	-12	-48	-58
16-31 JUL	-60	-66	-65	-63	-63	-53	-47	-36	-24	-1	6	6	9	12	13	14	14	12	11	8	7	6	-13	-48	-60
1-15 AUG	-76	-80	-80	-78	-69	-65	-59	-50	-39	-12	-4	-4	-1	2	5	4	4	1	-1	-6	-10	-13	-25	-62	-76
16-31 AUG	-74	-79	-79	-74	-70	-64	-61	-52	-37	-12	-2	-2	1	3	6	4	4	3	0	-6	-12	-19	-32	-61	-74
1-15 SEP	-71	-75	-74	-72	-68	-63	-59	-49	-36	-7	7	3	7	8	10	11	10	8	2	-6	-14	-24	-34	-61	-71
16-30 SEP	-73	-76	-75	-73	-73	-70	-63	-54	-40	-9	9	4	6	9	10	10	9	4	-1	-9	-18	-28	-41	-67	-73
1-15 OCT	-81	-82	-77	-80	-80	-77	-70	-60	-45	-16	9	2	6	8	9	8	6	1	-5	-13	-21	-30	-54	-76	-81
16-31 OCT	-81	-81	-80	-80	-81	-81	-75	-66	-54	-23	10	2	5	8	8	7	5	-2	-7	-14	-23	-34	-68	-79	-81
1-15 NOV	-78	-79	-79	-80	-80	-80	-77	-71	-61	-31	17	4	1	6	7	6	3	-3	-7	-14	-27	-47	-72	-80	-78
16-30 NOV	-73	-75	-75	-76	-78	-76	-75	-74	-69	-42	22	10	-1	5	6	5	3	-1	-7	-15	-29	-51	-69	-74	-73
1-15 DEC	-72	-75	-75	-75	-78	-77	-76	-75	-74	-55	16	20	0	3	5	5	5	-2	-8	-22	-39	-57	-71	-70	-72
16-31 DEC	-72	-73	-73	-73	-72	-71	-72	-72	-76	-65	-2	23	2	2	2	4	4	-3	-11	-21	-38	-57	-68	-73	-72

Figure 3307. Omega propagation correction table (extract).

ing and applying propagation corrections from data entered on magnetic tape cassettes.

Continuing efforts are being made to refine the predicted propagation corrections through research and constant monitoring so as to develop more accurate figures. Correction tables are published in new editions when significantly improved data are determined; only the latest edition of correction (and chart position) tables should be used. Interim changes or corrections to the tables may be disseminated by messages on the radio broadcasts of navigational warnings.

Receivers

3308 In using Omega, a receiver on board the vessel must be capable of determining the phase of the Omega signals in the presence of the usual ambient noise and interference. The format of the signal permits many different modes of receiver operation ranging from an oscilloscope display of the signal timing, with manual alignment of the multiplexing function, to computer-type receivers capable of performing all functions and presenting position in the form of geographical coordinates without external aid.

To determine position the operator and receiver must be able to:

Recognize the total transmitted pattern to identify the transmission of a given set of stations.

Isolate the signal components,

Determine the relative phases of the isolated signal components with accuracy,

Use the phase reading to determine a line of position or a fix.

To obtain a line of position when the approximate DR position is known, it is only necessary to read the receiver display, note the Greenwich Mean Time, and note these data on the work sheet. The appropriate correction table for the general area is then entered, and the diurnal correction for the GMT and date are extracted and noted on the work sheet. This correction is added to the reading taken from the receiver display; the sum provides the required datum for plotting the line of position on the Omega chart. A fix can be obtained in two or three minutes.

Figure 3308a shows a typical Navy receiver for Omega signals. Graphic recorders provide a continuous record of lane readings and there is a built-in oscilloscope to aid in synchronization and troubleshooting. Another Navy receiver, the AN/BRN-7 for submarines, has additional internal circuitry and can directly display position in latitude and longitude; it can receive all three Omega frequencies. Figure 3308b shows a commercial receiver which displays LOP information

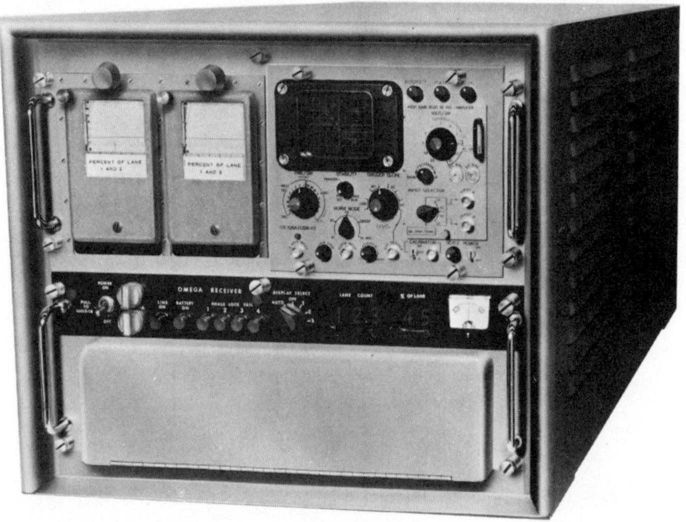

Figure 3308a. AN/SRN-12 Omega shipboard navigation receiver.

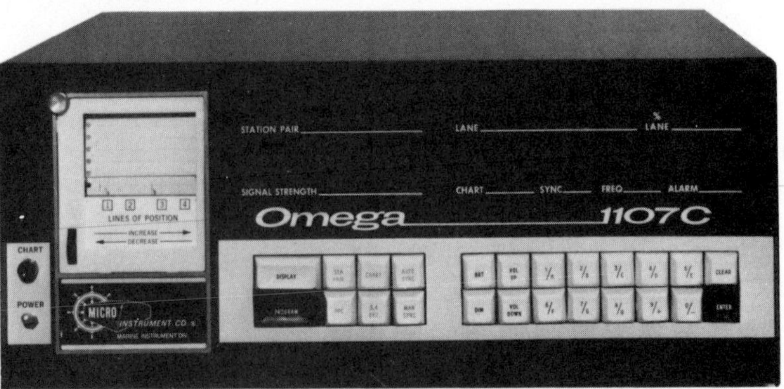

Figure 3308b. Commercial model of Omega receiver.

by a digital readout to .01 lane (1 centilane); PPCs can be pre-inserted by means of the keyboard in order that the lane readings can be used directly without further arithmetic. At the option of the navigator, a single LOP may be displayed, or up to five LOPs cycled at the rate of one every five seconds; the receiver can also feed into a strip-chart recorder for a permanent record. The receiver continuously monitors all transmitting stations, identifies each, and indicates those whose signal-to-noise ratio is adequate for use. (This receiver uses only the 10.2 kHz signals; lane ambiguity must be resolved within 4 miles.) Trackable stations are indicated by lamps on the front panel display. Warning and alarm signals operate whenever there is a malfunction or other problem. Dual power sources, AC and battery, can be used to guard against any loss of lane count during temporary primary power outages.

Antennas for Omega receivers can be very simple in design. Vertical whip antennas, 8 to 10 feet in height, are generally used for shipboard installations. Several special types of antennas are used with aircraft receivers.

Obtaining an Omega fix

3309 The procedures for obtaining an Omega position will vary somewhat with the specific equipment being used. General procedures can be given here, but reference must be made to the receiver's instruction manual, plus the material in the propagation correction tables.

In all instances wherever possible, the Omega receiver should be turned on and synchronized while the vessel is at a known position, such as at a pier or in an anchorage. The pairs of transmitters which give acceptable signal strengths are then determined. The propagation corrections for each *station* are determined individually from the appropriate tables for the applicable GMT date and time. Next the corrections for each *pair* of stations are computed from the individual values by subtracting the PPC for the second station from that for the first station; because this is *algebraic* subtraction, due regard must be given to a minus sign on either or both of the correction values. These pair correction values are either entered into the receiver or retained for manual application. The correct lane count is entered into the receiver for the known position; the receiver will then automatically track future lane crossings and show percent of lane for each station pair as the voyage progresses.

For each fix, the receiver is read for each pair to be used and the corrected values are plotted on an Omega chart (or are used with Omega position tables to derive geographic coordinates for plotting on a conventional chart). This process is somewhat simpler than positioning by Loran and is much faster than obtaining a fix from celestial observations.

If track is lost during the voyage for any reason, the navigator must then redetermine his position as he did in port and enter the new cor-

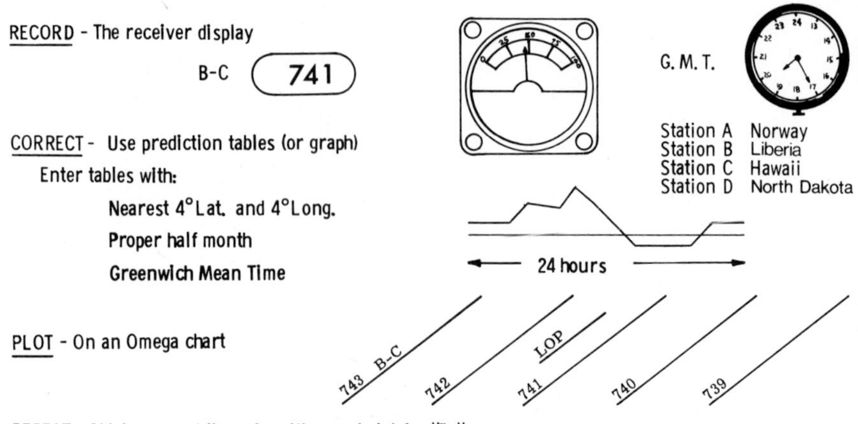

RECORD - The receiver display
B-C
741
G. M. T.
Station A Norway
Station B Liberia
Station C Hawaii
Station D North Dakota
CORRECT - Use prediction tables (or graph)
Enter tables with:
Nearest 4°Lat. and 4°Long.
Proper half month
Greenwich Mean Time
24 hours
PLOT - On an Omega chart
743 B-C
742
741
LOP
740
739

REPEAT - Obtain second line of position and plot for 'fix'.

OMEGA WORK SHEET

Greenwich Mean Time			Date: 12 Apr	Time: 1925
Receiver	B-D	A-D	A-C	B-C 741.49
Correction				-.08
Line of Position				741.41

Figure 3309. Omega operation (AN/SRN-12).

rected whole lane counts for his selected station pairs. If the Omega receiver is a single frequency unit, this redetermined position must be correct to within four miles. In other words, with a lane width of nominally eight miles, the navigator must know his position within half of this lane width in order to determine the proper whole lane count. If his Omega receiver is a dual frequency unit, that is, receives Omega signals on 10.2 and 13.6 kHz, an additional lane width of 24 nautical miles is provided. In this case the navigator need only know his correct position within ±12 miles, or half of the 24-mile land width, in order to receive lane ambiguity. If it has a capability to receive 11.33 kHz signals also, then the "known" position need only be within ±36 miles of the correct location; or within ±144 miles if all four frequencies, including 11.05 kHz, can be received.

Omega need not be used separately from other navigational procedures; it works well in combination with selected daily celestial observations. As Omega involves complex electronic equipment, a prudent navigator maintains his skill with the sextant and sight reduction tables.

As with Loran-C, highly sophisticated models of Omega receivers are available. One such set has an internal microprocessor which is loaded with data from an ordinary audio tape cassette; this includes propagation corrections, making unnecessary the use of lengthy tables for such data. An initial position must be entered by means of the keyboard, but then the receiver will continuously display position in latitude and longitude, and will also print out on paper tape the date, time, latitude, and longitude at selected time intervals from one to nine times each hour. If a destination is entered using the keyboard, the unit will compute course and distance for either a rhumb-line or great-circle path; if speed is entered manually, transit time will also be calculated. After starting with the correct time, the receiver will function as a chronometer with an accuracy to within one or two seconds per year. As Omega navigation is dependent upon continuous reception of signals to avoid a loss of lane count, automatic switchover to an internal rechargeable battery occurs on any interruption of primary power, and an alarm signal is sounded.

Omega accuracy

3310 The accuracy of an Omega position is directly related to the accuracy of the propagation correction constants. The published tables are dependent upon the accuracy of predictions, accuracies which increase with continued operation of the system. Monitoring stations build up millions of hours of data which are analyzed by complex computational procedures to establish refinements to the predictions which are initially made on theoretical and empirical principles. Only after years of data collection and analysis, the process is termed "validation," will it be possible to realize the true worldwide Omega system accuracy of one to two miles (1.8–3.7 km) based on one standard deviation, or 68 percent of positions within the stated limits.

Differential Omega

3311 The one to two miles nominal accuracy of the Omega system is adequate for the high seas, but it is not precise enough for coastal areas. Omega accuracy can be improved to approximately one-half nautical mile (0.9 km), or better, by the technique known as *differential Omega.* This technique is based on the principle that propagation corrections will be the same for all receivers within a local area of perhaps 100–200 miles (185–370 km) radius. A monitor station whose location is known precisely develops highly refined values of propagation corrections on a continuous basis; these are then transmitted to ships with Omega receivers via any radio communications link. When these more accurate PPCs are applied to the shipboard Omega receiver, positions can be fixed to within 0.25 miles (0.5 km) at distances of 50 miles (93 km) from the monitoring station, degrading to about 0.5 miles (0.9 km) at 200 miles (370 km) distance.

Although differential Omega is valuable for its 2:1 or better improvement in accuracy under normal operating conditions, its true worth is achieved at times of sudden ionospheric disturbances (SIDs) and polar cap disturbances (PCDs) when its accuracy is retained while that of the basic system is seriously degraded; at such times the improvement by the differential technique may be as great as 10:1.

Differential Omega also provides an excellent quality of *repeatability,* the capability to return to a position previously occupied; the

PPC may change from day to day, but fresh data from the monitoring station will ensure the same degree of accuracy on successive applications.

Micro-Omega The *Micro-Omega* system is a form of differential Omega in which the adjusted sky-wave corrections for actual propagation conditions are transmitted continuously and are automatically applied to the "standard" Omega receiver. The data link uses single sideband modulation on a carrier frequency near 1.8 MHz with a nominal range of 350 miles (648 km) by day and 200 miles (370 km) at night. The Micro-Omega system is directly compatible with Omega charts, and existing Omega receivers can be updated to Micro-Omega with a simple add-on converter.

Other differential techniques The actual, real-time propagation corrections can be transmitted on any radio frequency, LF to VHF, that will cover the desired area. One system broadcasts the data by modulating a subcarrier applied to the signals of an LF radiobeacon. Such a technique has the advantage of not requiring continuous use of a dedicated channel in the already overcrowded radio spectrum, but this can be offset by the lack of continuous data if the radiobeacon transmits only intermittently as part of a sequenced group (see Article 3204).

Summary **3312** In general, the advantages and disadvantages of Omega are those of any radionavigation system. The navigator has a relatively simple, fast, and accurate method of determining his position regardless of time of day or weather conditions. On the other hand, he is entirely dependent upon complex electronic equipment, much of which is far distant and not under his control.

Omega has a specific advantage in that it is essentially a worldwide system without gaps in its coverage; thus one relatively small, lightweight, and acceptably priced piece of equipment can be used wherever a vessel travels. Another Omega advantage is that there are only eight stations in the system and these provide considerable redundancy; a fix can normally be obtained even if one or two, or even more, of the transmitters are off the air.

Information on the current status of each transmitting station of the Omega Navigation System is broadcast once each hour by the standard time and frequency stations, WWV (at 16^m after the hour) and WWVH (at 47^m after the hour). A recorded telephone message with the same information is available by dialing (202) 245-0298; a similar message can also be received via telex if prior arrangements are made for payment of message charges.

34 Satellite Navigation

Introduction **3401** The *Navy Navigation Satellite System* developed for the U.S. Navy is generally referred to as NAVSAT. It originated within the Navy as Project Transit and was developed to fulfill a requirement established by the Chief of Naval Operations with an objective stated as follows: "Develop a satellite system to provide accurate all-weather, world-wide navigation for naval surface ships, aircraft, and submarines." The system was then developed by the Applied Physics Laboratory of the Johns Hopkins University under a Navy contract. It is a highly accurate, passive, all-weather, worldwide navigational system, suitable for subsurface and surface navigation as well as for use in aircraft. NAVSAT became operational for Polaris submarines in 1964 and was released for civilian use in 1967. It is widely used on major combatant vessels of the U.S. Navy and on commercial ships of the United States and many foreign nations. It is suitable for use on vessels of any size, including yachts, when it is economically justifiable; shipboard receivers and related equipment are several times more expensive than other systems such as Omega and Loran. Equipment for receiving NAVSAT signals is now manufactured in at least six countries and marketed in many more.

Doppler shift **3402** The measurement of radio signals transmitted by NAVSAT is based on the *Doppler shift* phenomenon—the apparent change in frequency of the radio waves received when the distance between the source of radiation (in this case the satellite) and the receiving station is increasing or decreasing because of the motion of either or both. The amount of shift in either case is proportional to the velocity of approach or recession. The frequency is shifted upward as the satellite approaches the receiving station and shifted downward as the satellite passes and recedes. The amount of this shift depends on the exact location of the receiving station with respect to the path of the satellite. Accordingly, if the satellite positions (orbits) are known, it is possible by a very exact measure of the Doppler shift in frequency to calculate the location of the receiver on earth. The Doppler shift is also affected by the earth's rotation, but this effect is allowed for and corrected by a computer in providing the fix.

The accuracy obtained by using this Doppler shift technique is possible because the quantities measured, frequency and time, can readily be determined to an accuracy of one part in a billion.

Components of the system

3403 The NAVSAT system (Figure 3403a) consists of one or more satellites, ground tracking stations, a computing center, an injection station, Naval Observatory time signals, and the shipboard receiver and computer.

Satellite data

Each satellite is placed in a nominally circular polar orbit at an altitude of about 600 miles (1100 km), orbiting the earth in approximately 105 minutes. Only one satellite is used at any given time to determine position. The satellite stores data which is updated from a ground injection station approximately every twelve hours; it broadcasts the following data every two minutes:

Fixed and variable parameters describing its own orbit.
A time reference.

Two frequencies, 150 and 400 MHz, are employed because the ionosphere, which is a dispersion medium, bends and also stretches radio waves, causing the satellite to seem closer than it actually is. Each frequency is somewhat differently affected, and by comparing the Doppler signals received on the two frequencies, precise allowance can be made for the ionosphere's effect on the waves. (A single-frequency receiver, 400 MHz only, can be used with a savings in cost and complexity; its accuracy in position fixing is less, but still much more than required for high-seas navigation.)

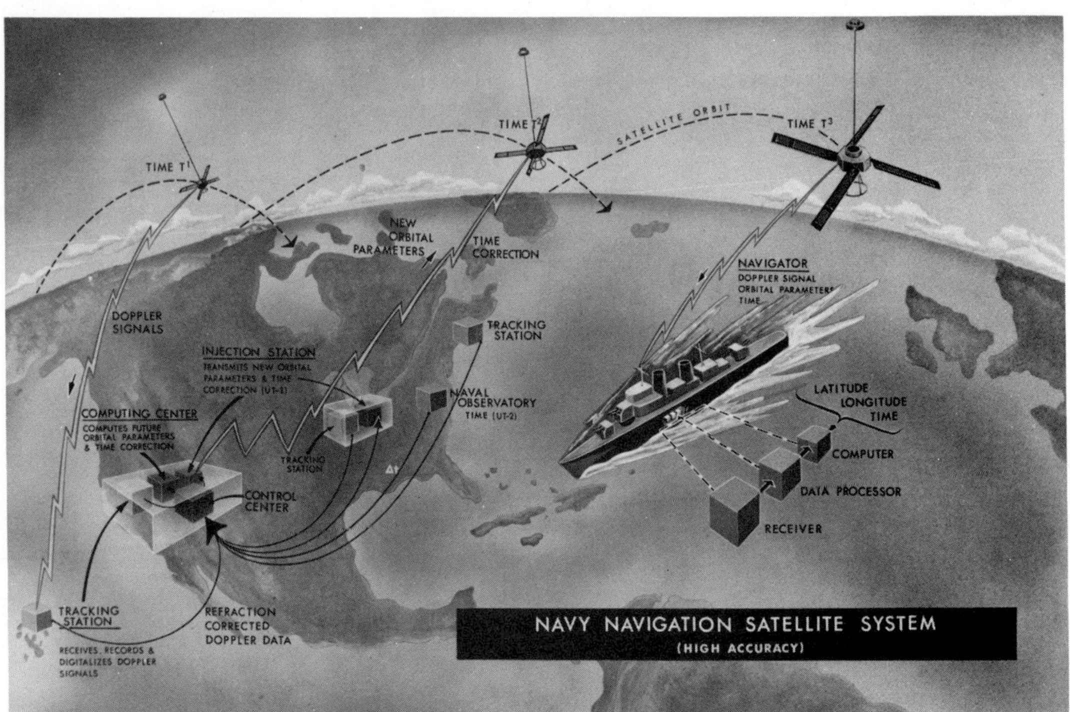

Figure 3403a. Components of the NAVSAT (Transit) system.

The parameters broadcast by the satellite describe its orbit as a function of time; the variable parameters are correct for the two-minute time interval for which they are transmitted and for those intervals immediately preceding and following that time period. Signals will normally be received for ten to fifteen minutes during each "pass" of a satellite within range of a ship; this results in five to seven repetitions of the transmitted message for increased accuracy. Data is also included in each broadcast period that will allow an approximation of the orbit if there has been an interruption in the receipt of data. The time reference is synchronized with corrected universal time (UT_1) from the Naval Observatory. A simplified block diagram of satellite functions is shown in Figure 3403b.

The satellites (Figure 3403c), sometimes referred to as "birds," are completely transistorized; they are octagonal in shape, and have four windmill-like vanes which carry solar cells. They are gravity-gradient

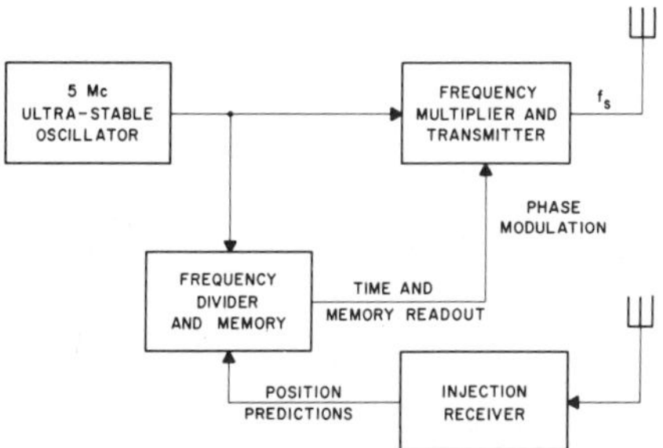

Figure 3403b. Block diagram of Transit satellite.

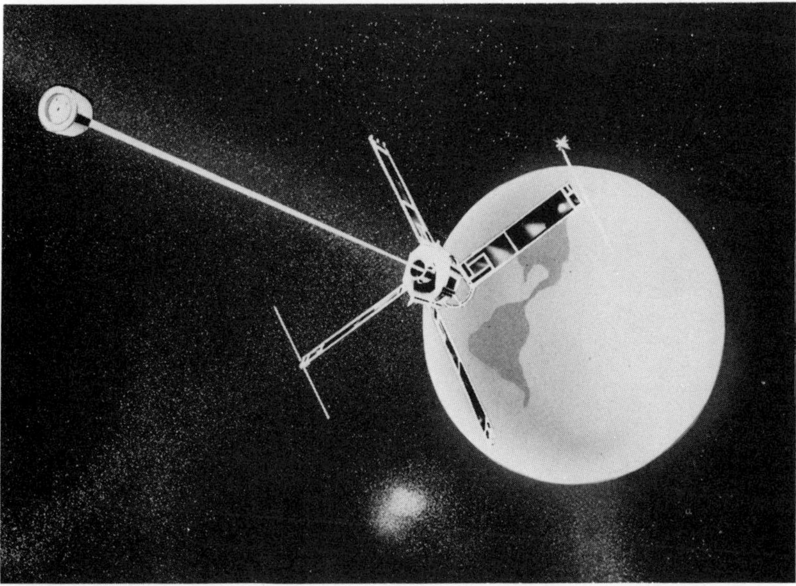

Figure 3403c. Transit satellite.

stabilized, so that the directional antennas are always pointed downwards, towards the earth.

Figure 3403d shows an idealized view of four satellites in orbit around the earth. This constellation of orbits forms a "birdcage" fixed in space within which the earth rotates; a NAVSAT receiver thus passes in turn under each orbit. It is obvious that an increase in the number of satellites will increase the frequency with which a fix may be obtained. In actuality, however, the distribution of orbits is not as ideal as shown in Figure 3403d. Orbits are not precisely polar, and they will precess with time. Satellites have a working life of many years —ten or more in some instances—but precession is not equal among them. Orbits may get closed together or farther apart, upsetting the ideal uniform distribution; more than four satellites may be required to ensure adequate coverage.

Position fixing A satellite fix may be obtained when the satellite's maximum altitude, relative to the observer, is above 15°, and less than 75°. As a general rule, each satellite will yield four fixes a day—two on successive orbits, and two more on successive orbits some twelve hours later. Ideally, a NAVSAT fix could be obtained about every 90 minutes. However, this sequence may be disturbed, as the satellite, while above the horizon, may pass at too great or too small an altitude relative to the observer to permit obtaining a position.

NAVSAT users are kept informed as to the operational status of the satellites, of the insertion of new satellites into service, and the withdrawal of satellites by SPATRAK messages originated by the U.S. Naval Astronautics Group, Pt. Mugu, California.

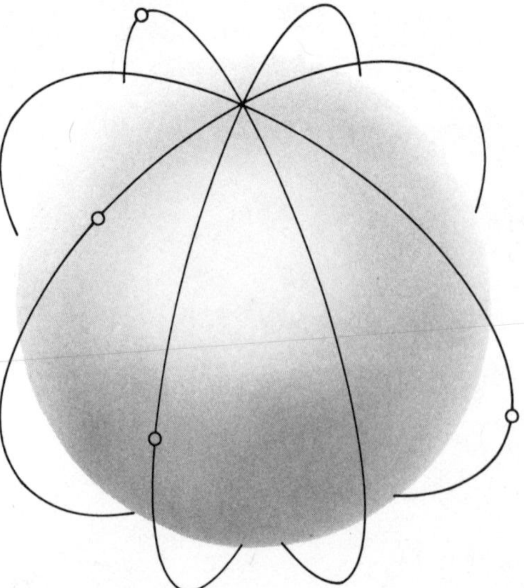

Figure 3403d. Coverage (idealized) with four satellites.

The need for daily satellite updating

3404 A planet in deep space follows a fixed path around its parent body in accordance with Newton's Laws of Motion. Its orbit is Keplerian, or perfectly elliptical, and its position can be predicted exactly for any given future instant of time. A NAVSAT satellite moves under the earth's gravitational attraction in accordance with the same laws, but as it operates at an altitude of about 600 miles, it is subjected to external forces which produce orbital irregularities, or *perturbations.* To make the system acceptable, these perturbations must be accurately predicted, so that the satellite's position can be determined for any instant of time.

The most important of these forces is caused by the earth's shape; the earth is not a sphere, but an oblate spheroid, and, in addition, its gravitational field is irregular. Figure 3404 shows the earth's gravity model, as sensed by a NAVSAT satellite. The satellite is also subject to slight atmospheric drag, as it is not operating in a complete vacuum. Other external forces which affect it are the gravitational attraction of

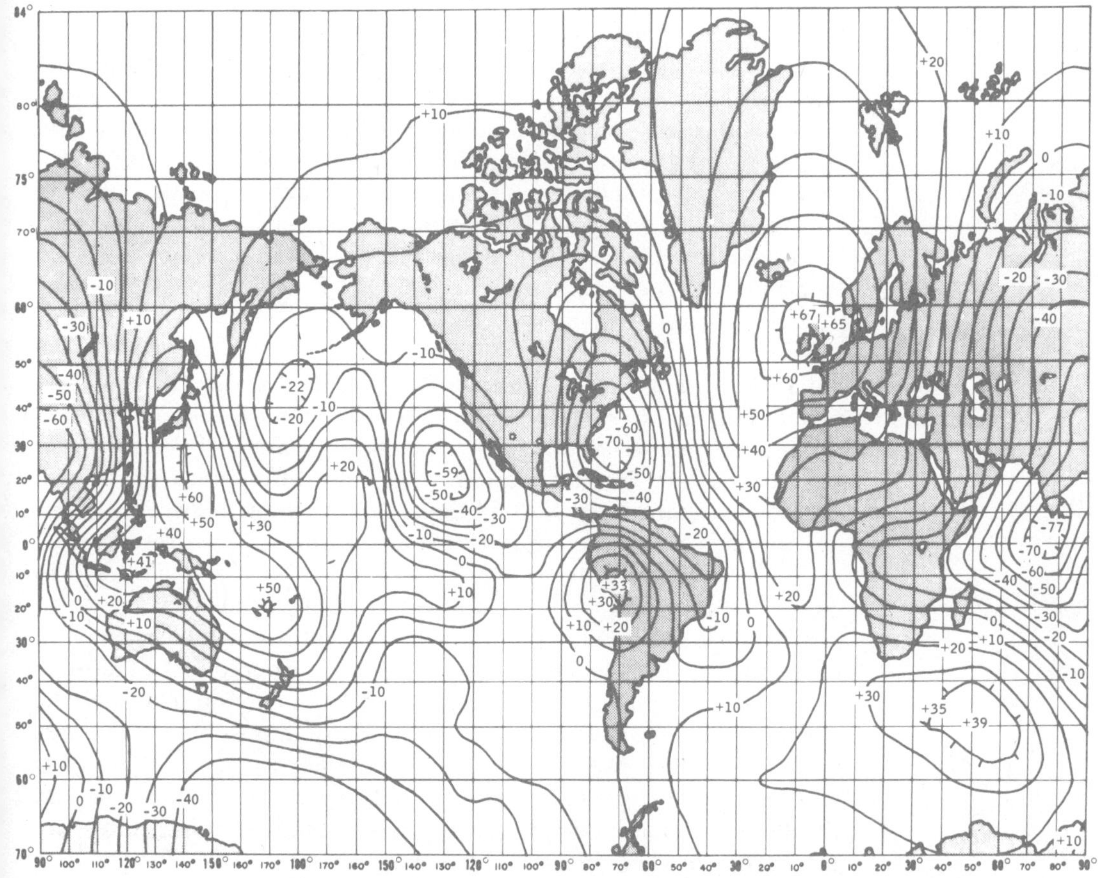

Figure 3404. Contoured plot of mean deviation of sea level.

the sun and the moon, solar photon pressure and solar wind, and electrostatic and electromagnetic forces caused by the satellite's interaction with charged particles in space and in the earth's magnetic field.

Fortunately, all the forces causing perturbations are either sufficiently constant or so localized that they can be reduced to equations which can be programmed into orbital computations.

Satellite tracking stations To determine the precise orbit of each satellite in the system, ground tracking stations are established at exactly determined positions in Hawaii, California, Minnesota, and Maine. These stations regularly monitor the Doppler signal as a function of time. Concurrently, the U.S. Naval Observatory monitors the satellite's time signal for comparison with corrected Universal Time (UT_1). The resulting information is transmitted to the computing center for processing.

As the satellite is essentially moving as a planet, and as the perturbations in its orbit are determined by the computer, of all the possible paths permitted by Newton's Laws, only one can result in a particular curve of Doppler shift. Thus, at any instant of time, the position of the satellite relative to the known location of the tracking station can be determined very precisely.

The computing center, having received these data, computes an orbit for the satellite that best fits the Doppler curve obtained from the tracking stations. This orbital information is extrapolated to give satellite positions for each two minutes of UT_1 for the following sixteen hours, and these data are supplied to the injection station for transmission to the satellite about every twelve hours, for storage and retransmission on schedule. The satellite is in effect a relay station which stores and transmits the data computed at ground stations, which are inserted in its memory system.

Ship velocity information **3405** In systems such as Loran or Omega a fix is derived from at least two station "pairs," each with its own base line. In the case of the Navy Navigation Satellite System a receiver obtains signals from only one satellite at a time. Instead of measuring range differences from several stations simultaneously, NAVSAT measurements are between sequential positions of the satellite as it passes. This process requires from ten to fifteen minutes, during which the satellite travels some 2,400 to 3,600 miles (4,400 to 6,700 km), providing an excellent base line.

Because NAVSAT measurements are not instantaneous, motion of the ship during the satellite pass must be considered in the fix calculation. Also, because the satellites are in constant motion relative to the earth, simple charts with lines of position are impossible to generate. Instead, each satellite transmits a set of orbital parameters, permitting its position to be calculated quite accurately as a function of time. By combining the calculated satellite positions, the range difference measurements between these positions, and information regarding motion of the ship, an accurate position fix can be obtained. Because the calculations are both complex and extensive, a small digital computer is always a part of the receiving equipment. As satellite navigation does not yield continuous positional information (such as Omega), the computer can also be used to keep a dead-reckoning track between each satellite fix. Speed and heading can be entered manually if not available from other sources. It is preferable, however, to use automatic speed and heading signals to describe the ship's motion.

Ship motion computer inputs

3406 To obtain a fix, the ship's *estimated position* and *velocity of movement* must be entered in the computer. The accuracy of the estimated position is not of great importance; however, the accuracy with which the velocity can be established is important, as will be seen in the following discussion.

On ships equipped with the Ships Inertial Navigation System (SINS) described in Chapter 35, the two-minute synchronization signal received from the satellite can be transmitted on SINS. In some installations this signal causes the SINS to print out ship's position data coinciding with the two-minute Doppler count. In other installations the SINS general purpose computer is used to solve the NAVSAT problem rather than employing a separate computer.

If inertial equipment is not available to supply automatic information on the ship's movement to the computer, the course and speed from the gyrocompass and EM log are inserted in the computer. This, of course, is a potential source of error, as the system, for high accuracy, requires an input of the ship's true velocity—that is, her speed and direction of travel relative to the surface of the earth.

Unfortunately, accurate information on the existence of a current and its set and drift are rarely available to the navigator. In round numbers, the error in a NAVSAT fix will be about 0.25 miles (0.46 km) for every knot of unknown velocity. A velocity north (or south) error causes a considerably larger error in the fix than a velocity east (or west) error.

Required shipboard computer input

The computer insertions can be made in various forms. They may be in the form of an estimated position at a given time plus course and speed, estimated positions at two minute intervals, distance moved in X-Y coordinates, etc. The geographic accuracy of an estimated position is not of vital importance, but accurate velocity *is* required. Thus, when two estimated positions are used, the location of the second position must be accurately described relative to the first. The computer must also be fed such initial data as antenna height above the *geoid* as corrected for local variations, time and date, and the proper computer program; the first items are entered by use of the keyboard, the program by magnetic tape.

Shipboard NAVSAT equipment

3407 Typical NAVSAT shipboard equipment used by a navigator consists of a receiver, a computer, and an input/output unit, normally a keyboard with printer and/or video screen. Equipment used aboard a U.S. Navy ship is shown in Figure 3407a. The AN/BRN-3 equipment (Figure 3407b) used in fleet ballistic missile submarines is larger

Figure 3407a. AN/SRN-9 shipboard receiver for satellite navigation.

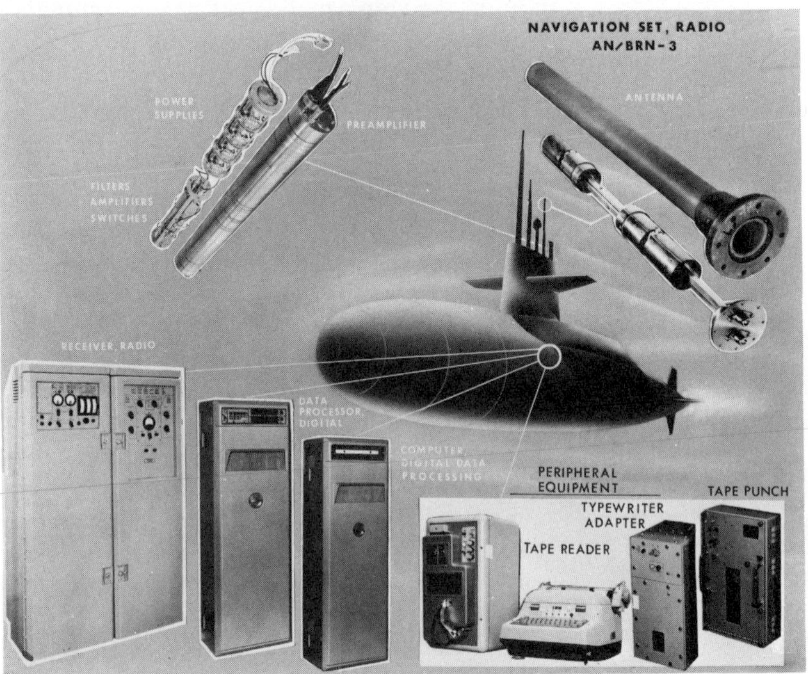

Figure 3407b. AN/BRN-3 equipment for submarine use of satellite navigation signals.

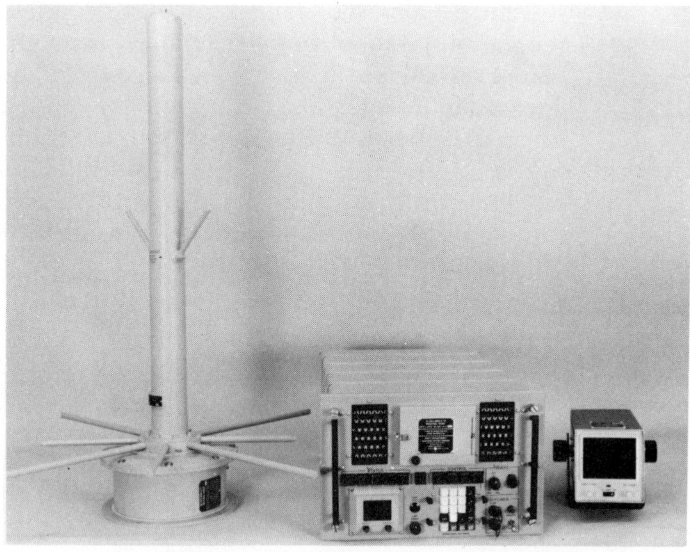

Figure 3407c. Commercial model of satellite navigation receiver.

and somewhat more complex, as both the operation and self-test capability are more fully automated. The BRN-3 is not an integrating Doppler system, as it obtains approximately one-second samples of the signal rather than integrating over a longer period. However, from the navigator's viewpoint they perform similar functions. A typical commercial receiver is shown in Figure 3407c.

How a fix is obtained

3408 The fix determined by the ship's computing system is based on the Doppler frequency shift which occurs whenever the relative distance between a transmitter and a receiver is changing. Such a change occurs whenever a transmitting satellite passes within range of a radio receiver on earth, and consists of a combination of the motion of the satellite in its orbit, the motion of the vessel over the surface of the earth, and the rotation of the earth about its axis. Each of these motions contributes to the overall Doppler frequency shift in a characteristic way. An increase in frequency occurs as the satellite approaches the ship, in effect compressing the radio waves en route. The received frequency exactly equals the transmitted frequency at the point of closest satellite approach, where for an instant of time there is no relative motion directly along the vector from the satellite to the receiver. The received frequency then decreases as the satellite recedes from the ship's position, thereby expanding the radio waves between them. The shape of the curve of frequency differences and its time of reception depend both on the receiver's position on earth and the satellite's location in space. The reception of these Doppler signals and the resulting computer computations form the basis of the satellite navigation system.

Figure 3408a shows in a simplified form the relationship of time, range, and position. In the diagram, t_1 through t_5 represent the position of the satellite in orbit at the successive transmissions which occur at two-minute intervals. S_1 through S_5 represent the slant range between the satellite and the ship. p_1 through p_5 represent the position of the ship referenced to the time at which the receiver recognizes the satellite synchronization signal $t_1 + \Delta t_1$ through $t_5 + \Delta t_5$, where Δt represents the time interval for the signal to travel from the satellite to the receiver aboard ship.

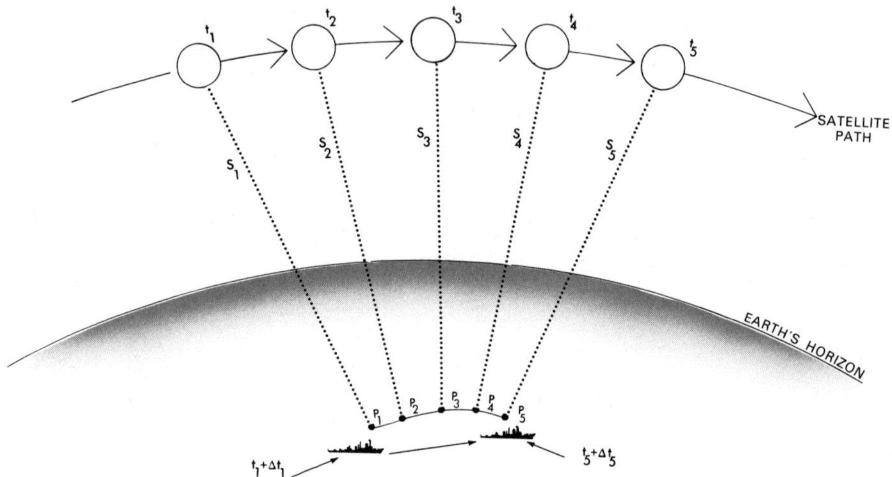

Figure 3408a. Integrated Doppler measurements of satellite signals.

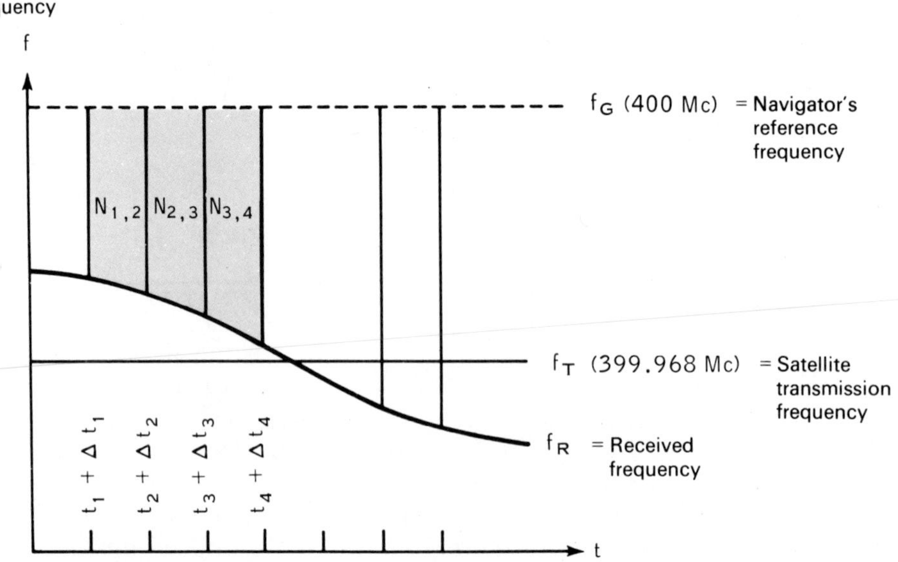

Figure 3408b. Frequency variation with time as measurement of slant range changes.

The integral Doppler measurements (Figure 3408b) are simply the count N 1–2 of the number of cycles received between $t_1 + \Delta t_1$, and $t_2 + \Delta t_2$, the count N 2–3 of the number of Doppler cycles between $t_2 + \Delta t_2$ and $t_3 + \Delta t_3$, and so on for all two-minute intervals during the satellite pass.

Four or five two-minute Doppler counts are obtained during a typical satellite pass. Each Doppler count consists of a constant plus a measured slant range difference between the receiver and the satellite at positions defined by the navigation message. The measured range differences are truly known only if the constant but unknown frequency difference, ΔF, between the satellite's oscillator and the receiver's reference oscillator can be determined.

To calculate a position fix, the Doppler counts and the satellite message are fed to a digital computer. The computer is also provided with an initial estimate of the ship's latitude and longitude and an estimate of the frequency difference ΔF. The computer then compares calculated range differences from the known satellite positions to the estimated ship's position with those measured by the Doppler counts, and the navigation fix is obtained by searching for and finding those values of latitude, longitude, and ΔF which make the calculated range differences agree best with the measured range differences. Because the geometry is complicated, only simple, linearized equations are used, and the computations are performed repeatedly until the solution converges. Many repetitions are normally required, and a fix is obtained within a few minutes on typical small digital computers.

Output data **3409** An AN/SRN-9 NAVSAT receiver output is on printed tape. Figure 3409a depicts an output of satellite orbit data and Figure 3409b illustrates a typical printout of positional information. (The explana-

	Units	*Title and Symbol*
++1281.0815	Minutes	Time of Perigee (t_p)
+ .4275817	Deg/Min	Mean Satellite Motion − 3 ($\dot{M} - 3$)
+ 320.2034	Degrees	Argument of Perigee (ϕ_p)
+ .0021431	Deg/Min	Argument of Perigee Change Rate ($1\dot{\phi}1$)
+ 0.011115	None	Eccentricity
+ 07374.01	Kilom.	Orbit Semi Major Axis (A_0)
+ 211.8482	Degrees	Right Ascension of the Ascending Node (ω_N)
− .0000636	Deg/Min	Right Ascension Change Rate ($\dot{\omega}_N$)
+ 0.015707	None	Cosine of the Inclination Angle
+ 134.2802	Degrees	Right Ascension of Greenwich at Time of Perigee (ω_G)
+ 0.999877	None	Sine of the Inclination Angle
3977492.	Cycles	(Doppler Count)

Figure 3409a. Tape printout from a receiver showing satellite orbit.

Tape		Result
+ 0390977		Latitude: 39°09.7782′ North
82		
− 0765383	Fix Result	Longitude: 76°53.8350′ West
50		
+ 3196219		Offset Frequency: 31,962.19 Cycles

Figure 3409b. Tape printout of vessel's position.

Figure 3409c. Video display of satellite navigation information.

tions shown at the right in each of these illustrations are, of course, not printed on the tape.) Figure 3409c shows how computer output can be displayed on a video screen.

Time signals **3410** The time signal transmitted by the satellite, which occurs at the two-minute mark, is accurate to better than 0.02 seconds. It may be used conveniently as an accurate chronometer check. With the NAVSAT receiver locked to the satellite signal, the two-minute signal will be heard as a "beep."

NAVSAT accuracy **3411** NAVSAT fixes have a high order of accuracy and repeatability. For a fixed location, a dual-frequency receiver can be expected to give a fix within 50 yards (46 m) and a single-frequency receiver to within 100 yards (91 m). As previously noted, accuracy of fix for a vessel underway is dependent upon precise and accurate knowledge of own ship's motion. Typically, a Transit fix of a moving vessel can be as accurate as 0.1 mile (185 m).

NAVSTAR Global Positioning System (GPS)

3412 A second-generation satellite navigation system under development is known as the NAVSTAR Global Positioning System (GPS). When operational, the NAVSTAR system will ensure the accessibility of updated navigation signals worldwide. NAVSTAR satellites, orbiting 10,898 miles (20,183 km) above the earth will broadcast continuous time and position messages. This highly sophisticated tri-service project is designed to provide extremely accurate instantaneous position (three-dimensional), velocity, and time information with lower-cost user equipment of reduced size and weight and with considerably improved performance and reliability.

Signals are received from any four NAVSTAR satellites (one-way ranging). These are demodulated, time-correlated, and processed to derive precise time, position, and velocity information. These data can be presented in a variety of ways to meet the different requirements of various users. GPS, when fully operational, is to provide position within 8 meters (8.7 yd) horizontally and 10 meters (10.9 yd) vertically; velocity to 0.1 knot; and time to a fraction of a microsecond. These highly precise data are achieved only from signals which have been "coded" for military security; "clear" or uncoded signals will provide less precise positioning information, about 200 meters (219 yards), but this is still more than adequate for ordinary offshore navigation. (During periods of war or international crisis, the uncoded signals can be turned off to prevent their use by hostile forces, while the secure, high-precision coded signals remain usable by friendly units.)

The Global Positioning System is composed of:

Satellites—twenty-four in all, that complete two revolutions of the earth per day, transmitting continuously.

Control Stations—consisting of a master station and a few monitor sets located in the U.S. that control and fine tune the satellites when they pass over each day.

User Equipment—light-weight, small, and relatively inexpensive receivers that may be installed on ships, aircraft, and ground vehicles, or carried as a man-pack.

The NAVSTAR program is divided into three phases, depending upon the number of satellites orbited. In Phase I six "birds" will provide periodic three-dimensional coverage for the United States. During Phase II additional satellites will be launched providing a worldwide, two-dimensional navigation capability with position within 300 meters (328 yards) and velocity within 2 knots. The Phase III configuration, consisting of 24 satellites in three orbital planes, will supply real-time, three-dimensional navigation information to users around the world. The system is scheduled for the mid-1980s.

Summary **3413** Satellite navigation is practical and advantageous for vessels of all types when militarily or economically justifiable. It is available worldwide and is not affected by weather conditions, including local thunderstorms. It requires shipboard equipment which is relatively expensive and complex, but which is not difficult to operate. It provides positional information to a high degree of accuracy and precision if supplied with correct information of own vessel's motion with respect to the bottom.

35 Inertial Navigation

Definition

3501 *Inertial navigation* is defined by J. M. Slater in *Newtonian Navigation* as the process of directing the movements of a rocket, ship, aircraft, or other vehicle from one point to another, based on sensing acceleration of the vehicle in a known spatial direction with the aid of instruments that mechanize the Newtonian Laws of Motion, and integrating acceleration to determine velocity and distance (position).

Ship's Inertial Navigation System (SINS)

3502 The *Ship's Inertial Navigation System* (SINS) has been developed by the U.S. Navy as an accurate, all-weather, dead-reckoning system. It employs gyroscopes, accelerometers, and associated electronics to sense turning rates and accelerations associated with the rotation of the earth, and with ship's movement relative to the surface of the earth.

Since Newton's Laws of Motion remain valid throughout the entire range of speeds of any naval vessel, inertial navigation, which is based on these laws, can be of tremendous assistance to a navigator. The inertial systems can furnish a wide range of information in addition to position coordinates. They provide a continuous readout of latitude, longitude, and ship's heading, as well as information on roll, pitch, and velocity, which is useful for the stabilization of other instruments. They are capable of extreme accuracy; their accuracy depends directly on how faithfully the component gyroscopes and accelerometers mechanize the laws of motion. Constant advances are being made both in the design and manufacturing processes of this precision instrumentation. In addition, every effort is made to locate and eliminate every possible source of error, no matter how minute. The SINS system is of necessity extremely complex compared to other navigational methods—consequently, it has a high initial cost and requires expert maintenance and operating personnel.

Generally similar, but often somewhat less elaborate, inertial systems are available for civilian applications requiring very high accuracies, such as offshore geophysical surveys. These are used with externally referenced systems, primarily the Transit navigational satellite system described in Chapter 34.

Background

3503 Inertial navigation systems were originally developed for aircraft; subsequently they came into use in spacecraft. The Ship's Inertial Navigation System was developed for the Polaris submarines; its use has now been extended to include surface ships and attack-class submarines.

This chapter is intended to cover only the basic principles of SINS, so that its advantages and disadvantages may be better understood, as well as its relationship to more conventional surface navigation. No mechanical or electronic system should ever be relied upon to give absolute continuous solution of the navigational problem, but rather to present intelligent information to assist the navigator in the performance of his duties. The general principles of inertial navigation are, of course, equally applicable to any equipment developed for use on a naval or commercial vessel—air, surface, or subsurface.

Among the earliest applications of inertial navigation was the installation by Sperry Gyroscope Division of Sperry Rand Corporation of an MIT-designed Ship's Inertial Navigation System aboard the USS *Compass Island* in the fall of 1956. This was part of an evaluation program which led to the design and fabrication of SINS systems for submarines. Practical inertial navigation for shipboard use was inaugurated with the installation of the N6A Inertial Navigators, built by Autonetics, a Division of North American Aviation, Inc., in the submarines *Nautilus* and *Skate,* for their transpolar voyages in 1958. These units had originally been designed for missile use but were found acceptable for use in submarines.

Concept **3504** Inertial systems derive their basic name from the fact that gyroscopes and accelerometers (described in Article 3505) have a sense of inertia in that they have a tendency to maintain their orientation in accordance with Newton's Laws. Any deviation from their original orientation can be sensed and measured with proper instrumentation. Accelerometers measure the individual components of horizontal and vertical accelerations, while the gyroscopes stabilize the accelerometers in a desired orientation. A computer, which is also included in the system, determines position and velocity by integrating the acceleration components sensed in the vehicle and also calculates orientation corrections caused by motion over the earth, rotation of the earth, and other factors.

Chapter 4 discussed the basic concept of the gyroscope in introducing the principles of the north-seeking gyrocompass. In inertial systems three gyro axes (Article 3506) are used to establish a stable platform for the accelerometers. The platform must remain horizontal with reference to the surface of the earth, while the gyroscopes, in their gimbaled mounts, are generally torqued so as to have two horizontal axes and one vertical axis. They are generally not fixed in space, although they could be in certain configurations. Certain errors in SINS increase with time, so that after an extended period the readout data become unacceptable; the system must then be corrected or updated. This is achieved by the *systems approach,* in which the inertial system with its own internal monitoring is supplemented by external sources of data on position, attitude, and velocity. These data sources have limited errors which are not a function of elapsed time; they include celestial trackers, radiometric sextants, Loran and other radionavigation systems, navigation satellites, speed logs, etc.

Accelerometers **3505** Inertial navigation is based on the sensing of movement of the vehicle and integrating this movement or acceleration with respect to time to determine velocity and distance (position). The stable platform established by means of gyroscopes is used to establish the horizontal for the accelerometers. In actual practice, the accelerometers need not be physically mounted on the gyro platform; they can be installed on an accelerometer platform controlled by the gyros.

Acceleration sensing instruments may be of three basic types:

An *accelerometer* in which the output is a measure of acceleration;

A *velocity meter*—a single-integrating device with an output signal proportional to velocity; and

A *distance meter*—a double-integrating device with an output signal proportional to distance traveled.

The term *accelerometer* is often used to denote any one of these instruments. The principle of the accelerometer may be illustrated by the use of a pendulum or a leveling bubble. Although a simple bubble would not measure acceleration to an accuracy needed in an inertial navigation system, it can be used to illustrate the basic concept of the effects of acceleration. For this illustration consider the bubble in an ordinary carpenter's level. Like the accelerometer, it cannot disginguish between the force of gravity and that of acceleration caused by movement. In Figure 3505a at *A*, the level is shown both at rest and with one end raised. In the latter case the bubble moves to a new position due to the force of gravity on the liquid. At *B*, the same unit is shown at rest and in motion in the direction of the arrow. The bubble moves off-center only during a change in velocity—that is, during a period of acceleration or deceleration; at rest or at a constant velocity it remains centered.

The gyro-stabilized platform, or the gimbaled gyros, with no torque applied, will remain fixed relative to space rather than relative to the surface of the earth. If this were the case, then in Figure 3505a at *C*, the arrows would indicate the direction in space to which a platform is aligned. On the left, the accelerometer, represented by the carpenter's bubble-level, is shown level with the earth at the equator. The direction of the gravity vector is 90° from the plane of the gyro platform. As the vehicle changes latitude, as shown on the right, the direction of the gravity vector will still be toward the center of the earth, but it will no longer be 90° from a space-oriented platform, thus creating a movement of the bubble by the force of gravity in a similar manner as shown at *A*. To avoid sensing this gravity component, the platform is generally maintained level as it is moved over the surface of the earth.

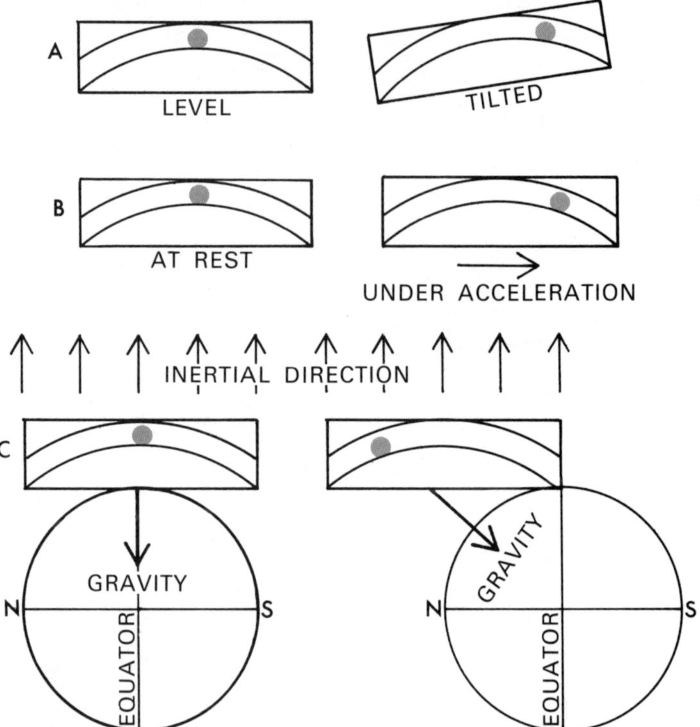

Fiture 3505a. Gravity and acceleration effects on a bubble.

This is accomplished by appropriate torquing of the gyroscopes. An actual accelerometer is much more complex than the carpenter's level, but it is similar in that it usually has only one sensitive axis, like the bubble which can only move along the glass tube.

Figure 3505b illustrates the principle of the accelerometer *integrated* for velocity and distance. Velocity in the technical sense is a measure both of speed and direction. Acceleration similarly is a measure both of magnitude and direction. In this case, the mass (m) in the accelerometer is illustrated as free to move along a rod which determines the sensitive axis, but with the mass operating against a spring restraint. Such an instrument could be calibrated in terms of gravity by orienting the rod vertically with respect to the earth's surface, rather than horizontally. If the accelerometer is neither vertical nor horizontal with respect to the earth, the mass will be deflected to indicate a component of acceleration proportional to the sine of the tilt angle.

In the horizontal position, and while undergoing acceleration, the mass moves against the spring restraint until a point of equilibrium is reached whereby force (f) is equal to mass (m) multiplied by acceleration (a), or $f = ma$. This equation is universally valid in inertial space, except where velocity approaches the speed of light, when mass no longer remains constant. In Figure 3505b the accelerometer indica-

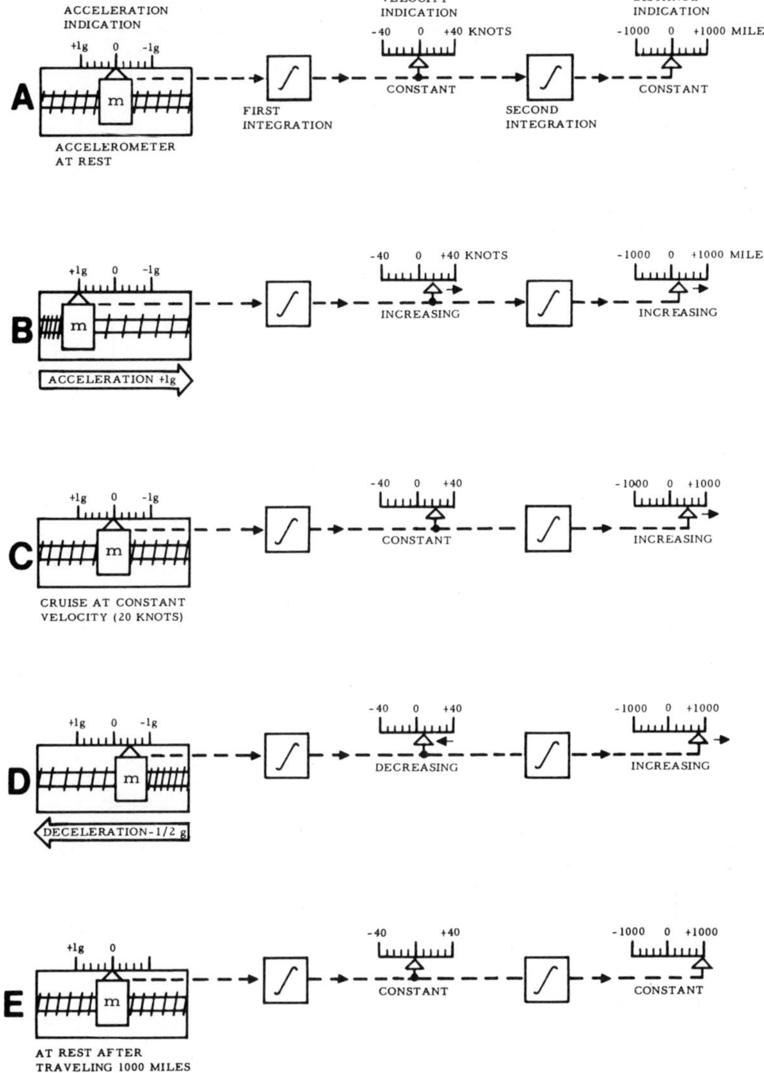

Figure 3505b. Illustrations of accelerometer action and integration for velocity and distance.

tion will be zero when the vehicle is stationary, or when it moves at a constant velocity. An accelerometer with *double integration* will give a readout for distance as well as for velocity. By following through the illustrations in Figure 3505b, the sequence of events can be seen in five steps. At *A,* the vehicle is at rest; the accelerometer read *0,* and the velocity and distance indicators have been zeroed. At *B,* the vehicle is accelerating at the rate of 1 *g* as indicated by the accelerometer; acceleration is being integrated to yield velocity, which is increasing; velocity is being integrated to yield distance, which is beginning to be indicated. At *C,* acceleration has ceased; the accelerometer indicates *0;*

velocity is constant at 20 knots and continues to be integrated for increasing distance. At *D,* deceleration is occurring at the rate of 0.5 *g* as sensed by the accelerometer; this "negative acceleration" is integrated to decrease the velocity, but as the velocity is still in a forward direction, its integration continues to yield increasing distance. Finally, at *E,* the deceleration has been applied for a sufficient time to reduce the velocity to *0* and then has ceased; as there is no longer a velocity to be integrated, no further change in direction takes place—the vehicle is now at rest 1,000 miles from its starting point. Velocity and distance are thus seen as the first and second integrations of the output of the accelerometer with respect to time.

In an inertial system, the accelerometer will normally contain at least the first stage of integration to produce an output signal indicating velocity. The instrument can then be referred to as a velocity meter; velocity is of greater interest to the navigation system than is acceleration, per se. The second integration is readily performed in the computer of the SINS system to give distance. The sensing element in the accelerometer is subject to various vibrations and accelerations, so that if an elementary accelerometer were used, the signal strength would change rapidly and would indicate frequent shifts from acceleration to deceleration. This can be seen if a bubble level is moved across a table by hand; the bubble will fluctuate rapidly back and forth. The integrating accelerometer smooths out these rapid changes and produces a steady velocity signal which is more readily accommodated by the system's digital computer.

A "perfect" accelerometer would be unaffected by rotation about its sensitive axis; it would measure only the force, or resultant vector of two or more forces, that is along the direction of its sensitive axis.

The centering of the floating element is generally accomplished by torque feedback.

Gyroscopes

3506 A gyroscope is, in effect, a miniaturized version of the earth, used to hold the inertial platform in alignment. When affected by disturbing torques it cannot maintain direction in space as well as the earth does, due to its much smaller mass, which is only partially offset by its much higher speed of rotation. For this reason it is necessary to use several motors and gear drives or direct-drive torquers to drive the gimbals in response to the gyroscopes signals to maintain platform stabilization. A "package" consisting of three gyroscopes, two for the horizontal axes, and one for azimuth can control the alignment of a platform from which accelerometer measurements are made. The velocity meters (accelerometers) can be mounted on the gyro-stabilized platform. Velocity signals from these accelerometers are used to precess or torque the gyroscopes in their respective axes. This feedback from one instrument to the other produces an oscillation, which can best be visualized by considering a simple pendulum which has motion across the vertical when any force is applied to it, rather than simply moving to a new position and stopping. The inertial system is so designed that the oscillatory period T equals $2\pi(R/g)^{\frac{1}{2}}$, where R is earth's radius and g is the surface acceleration of gravity; this is the so-called *Schuler period,* or *84-minute pendulum.* With the system tuned to this 84-minute period, as the platform is moved at any angular velocity in any direction about the earth, the leveling gyroscopes are torqued to cause precession at exactly the same velocity, and thereby maintain the accelerometer platform in a level plane.

Schuler period

Rate integrating gyroscope

Three rate gyros are normally used on the platform, the z axis of the platform being vertical. Axes x and y may be aligned north and east or in other azimuthal directions, depending upon the coordinates used in designing the system.

The basic sensing element of a modern SINS system, such as the Mark 3 Mod 5, is the *rate integrating gyroscope* (Figure 3506a). The accuracy of the SINS data output depends largely upon the ability of the gyro to maintain its orientation; this ability, while based to a great extent on the internal construction of the gyro, also depends upon the accuracy of calibration and alignment of the system, which are the responsibility of the shipboard operator. Basic information on gyroscopic precession was given in Chapter 4. It is summarized here, and is illustrated in Figure 3506b when applied to a gyroscope having a single degree of freedom. For a given torque around the input axis (IA), a given angular rate of precession about the output axis (OA) is generated, assuming the angular momentum of the wheel stays constant. The rule for precession is: a spin axis (SA) precesses about the output axis (OA) towards the input axis (IA) about which the torque is applied. In other words, with the force exerted by a torque acting

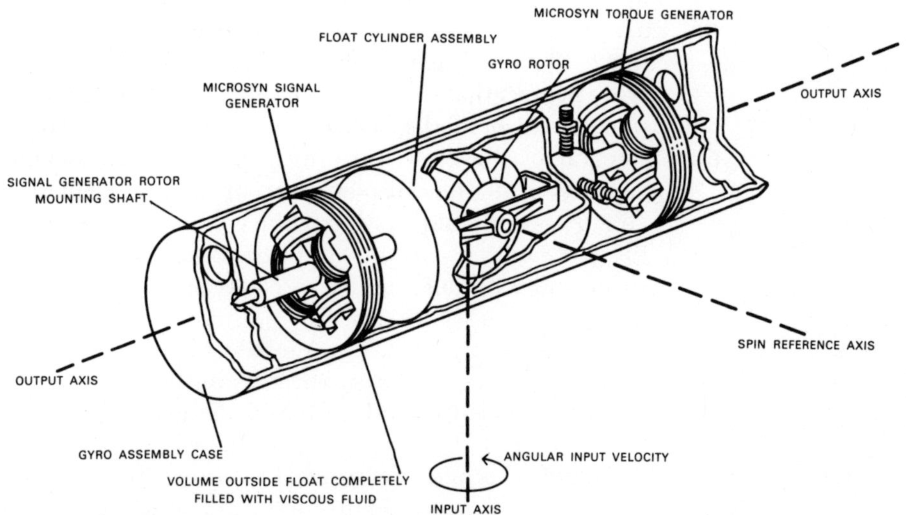

Figure 3506a. Rate integrating gyro.

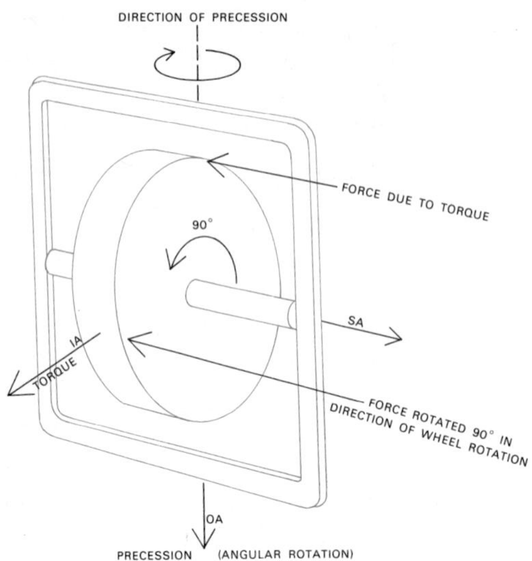

Figure 3506b. The rule for precession.

directly on the wheel, the precession of the wheel is in the direction of the force rotated around 90° in the direction of wheel rotation, as shown in Figure 3506b.

The gyroscope is damped to cause the rate of precession to match linearly the rate of input axis rotation. For example, for a *10 arc minute per hour* input rate the gyro precesses at 10 arc minutes every hour. The high-precision gyroscopes used in SINS are capable of precessing linearly in response to input torques covering a range of seconds of arc per hour to several degrees of arc per second of time. The first value defines the minimum sensitivity of the unit, and the latter the maximum rate of roll, pitch, or azimuthal rate change, to which the gyro is designed to respond. The total displacement about the output axis is the same as the total angle through which the input axis is rotated. The rate integrating gyroscope (Figure 3506a) derives its name from the fact that the output of the pickoff signal is the summation, or integration, of all the rates causing precession; the output angle is the integral of the input rate integral. The gyro pickoff output signal represents the total displacement of the *float* element, containing the spinning wheel and its supporting gimbal, with respect to its case. This displacement is caused by applied-control precessional torques, gyro drift, and external angular rates acting on the case about the input axis.

The gyro output drives a gimbal which applies a rotation about the input axis, always restoring the gyro output to a null. Thus the sum of the rates applied to and acting on the gyro must be zero.

Rate gyroscope A simplified schematic of a *rate gyroscope,* having a single degree of freedom, is shown in Figure 3506c. The precessional rotation about the output axis is restrained by a spring. The amount of precession around the output axis is in this case a function of the *rate* of rotational motion around the input axis rather than the *amount* of rotation, as in the integrating rate gyroscope. The rate of rotation around the input axis results in an output torque which is opposed by a restraining force illustrated by the spring device. The gyro will precess through angle θ until the precessional torque is balanced by the force exerted by the spring. It follows, then, that as long as the *rate* of input remains constant the gyro will maintain its position. When the rate of input decreases the gyro will feel the force of the spring applied as an input torque, and this torque will cause the rotor to return to its normal position. The angle θ is always proportional to the angular input rate.

The assembled system

3507 Two basic principles can be stated which summarize the use of gyroscopes and accelerometers in an inertial system.

Linear momentum of a mass remains constant unless an external force is applied.

Angular momentum of a rotating mass remains constant unless an external torque is applied.

By practical application of the first principle, if acceleration is precisely measured, and is integrated twice with respect to time, then the distance traveled is determined. Applying the second principle a gyroscope can be used to determine the direction of travel. Having determined both distance and direction, a dead-reckoning navigation system is created.

Figure 3507a shows the schematic of a gimbaled inertial design using separate gyroscopes and accelerometers for the three axes *x, y,* and *z*.

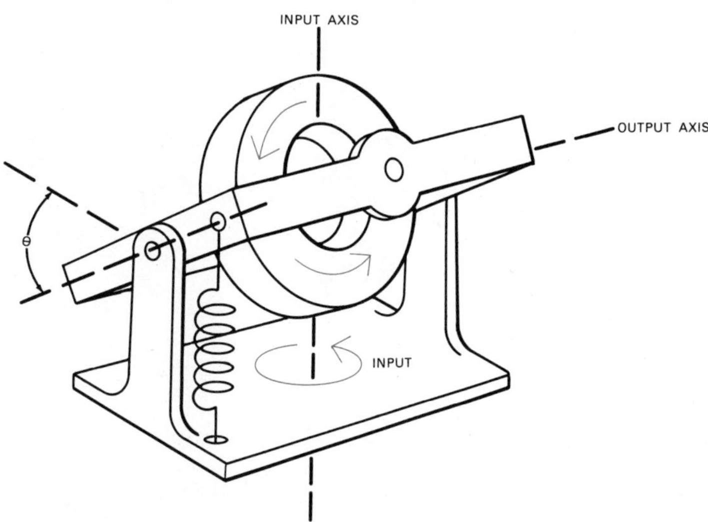

Figure 3506c. Schematic of a rate gyro.

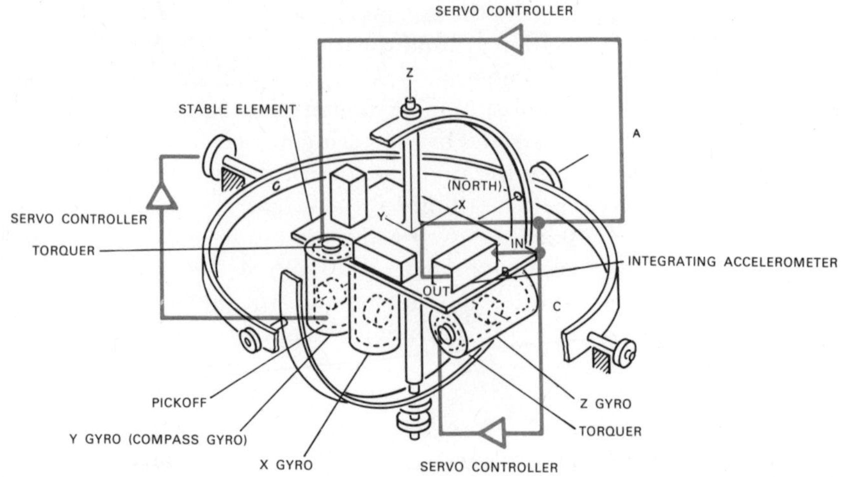

Figure 3507a. Components of an inertial guidance platform.

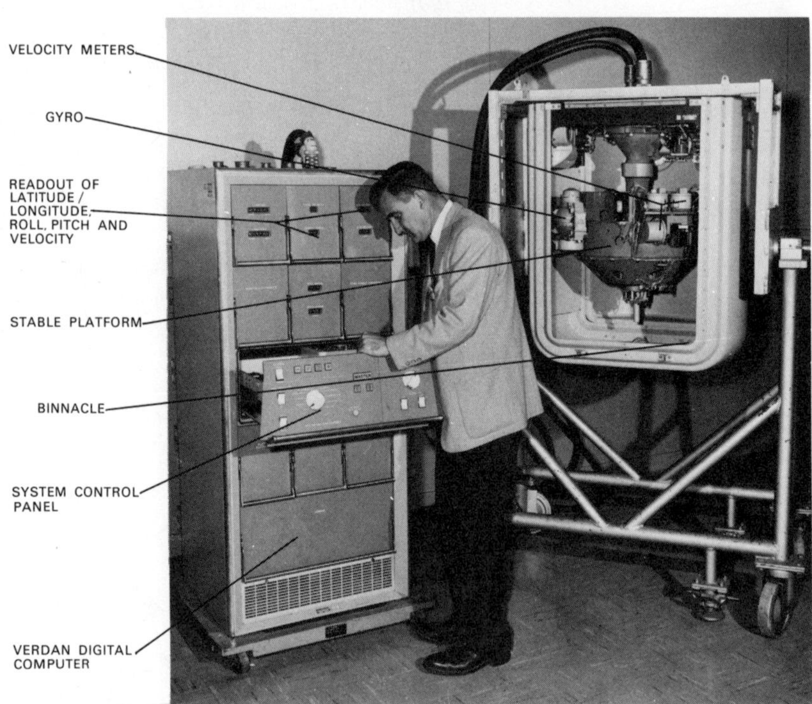

Figure 3707b. Mark 2, Mod. 1 Inertial Autonavigator.

Figure 3507b shows a complete inertial navigation system, the Autonetics Mark 2, Mod 1 *Inertial Autonavigator.* The arrangement of the internal component parts is visible, with the cover removed from the binnacle. In the cabinet at the left of the photograph the top section contains windows for the readout of latitude, longitude, roll,

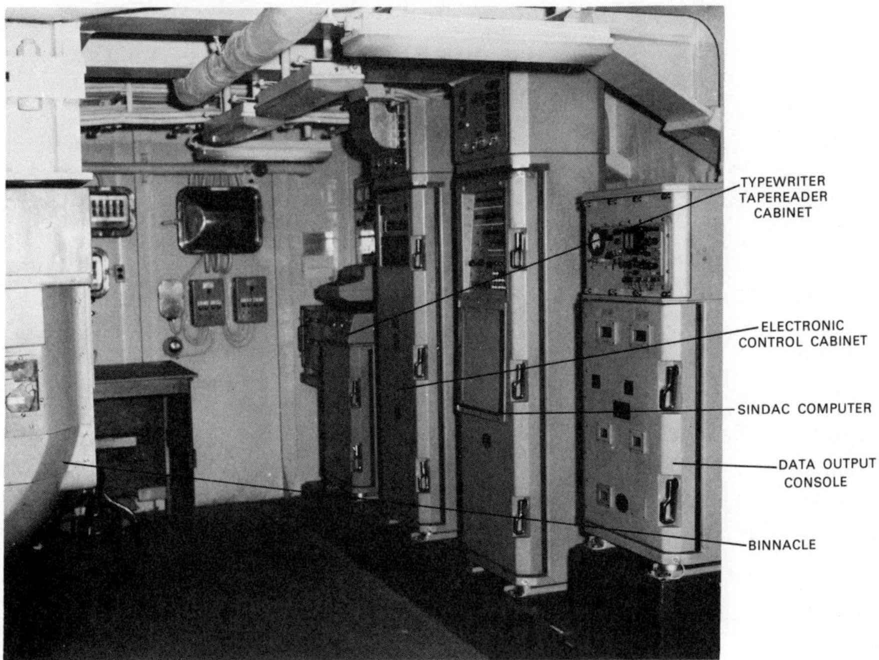

Figure 3507c. Mark 3, Mod. 5 SINS.

pitch, and velocity. The central section contains the system control panel, and the lower section holds a digital computer designated VERDAN (Versatile Digital Differential Analyzer).

Figure 3507c shows the SINS Mark 3 Mod 4 installed aboard ship; other Mods are essentially similar. The binnacle is at the left, and the various consoles with their functions marked are at the right. Another piece of equipment, not illustrated, is the AN/WSN-1(V)2 Dual MINISINS.

Errors in inertial navigation

3508 Inertial systems are not subject to the various errors of dead-reckoning navigation outlined in Article 1201, grouped together under the heading "current." In theory the inertial system is limited in ultimate accuracy only by the degree of perfection of the instrumentation used. Imperfections can, of course, arise in many of the various parts of the assembled system.

When the inertial system is used aboard ship over a considerable period of time, the dominant error sources are the gyro-loop uncompensated drift rates. These drift rates are composed of many variables, depending on the mechanization and configuration of the system. They may be due to imperfections in manufacturing, to instabilities arising subsequent to the installation of the system, or they can be caused by vehicle movement or position. The ultimate result, however, is that they appear as gyro platform drift, causing erroneous presentation of the output data. The principal known causes of this apparent gyro drift are outlined below.

Article 3505 stated that an accelerometer is sensitive only to acceleration along one axis. If two accelerometers are mounted with their sensitive axes at right angles to one another, they can be used to measure any arbitrary acceleration in the plane in which they are mounted. Assuming for the sake of simplicity that the system is so designed that one accelerometer is mounted with a north-south axis while the other is in the east-west axis, then in measuring accelerations along any course each will measure one component of the acceleration. These components can be integrated separately and interpreted as distances traveled north-south or east-west from the assumed starting point.

Errors in alignment

Obviously, an exact initial alignment of the platform is necessary. If there is a misalignment in azimuth of the system, and the ship is steaming on a precise course of 000°, the east-west accelerometer will detect a very slight signal which will produce an erroneous indication that the ship has moved slightly either to the east or west, and the north distance readout will be slightly too low.

Earth rate

As the earth completes one rotation about its axis in 24 hours, the accelerometer platform must be continuously adjusted to remain level with respect to the earth during this entire period. If the platform is permitted to tilt, the accelerometer will sense a component of gravity. This adjustment for the computed earth rate is automatically applied to the platform by the computer system. While the computed earth rate may equal in *magnitude* the true earth rate, if its *direction* is incorrect due to a misalignment of the platform in heading, there will be an error in the rate supplied to the platform. The resultant error in the accelerometer platform position is generally known as the 24-hour error since it is based upon erroneous sensing of the daily rotation of the earth.

Aligning the platform using earth rate

The fact that the computed earth rate must match the true is used in aligning the inertial platform. With the system at rest the platform is leveled and aligned as closely as possible in azimuth. The accelerometer outputs are then monitored, and any indicated acceleration is considered to be due to platform tilt caused by residual error in the azimuth alignment. Azimuth alignment is then corrected until no measurable platform tilt occurs. When this procedure is followed, the platform has been aligned by using the earth's rate of rotation as a reference.

The inertial package when carried over the surface of the earth is affected by both the curvature of the earth and by gravity. When the computer arrives at an incorrect value of the angular distance traveled by the vehicle, due to incorrect alignment or because of other errors in the system, it will supply an incorrect signal to the drive motor used for leveling the accelerometer platform. This causes the accelerometer, which cannot distinguish between gravity and vehicle acceleration, to sense a gravity component, and an erroneous acceleration signal is fed back through the closed loop. This attempt of the system to correct itself produces an undamped oscillation which, in a properly designed system, would have a period approaching 24 hours (Figure 3508).

Gyro drift Since a gyroscope cannot be constructed to be mechanically perfect, some drift rate will always be present. This drift of the platform tends to produce an acceleration error which increases linearly with time. Due to the closed feedback loop, the earth curvature is actually an asset rather than a liability. The accelerometer platform oscillates about a zero mean error as described in the preceding paragraph rather than building up a linear error. Nevertheless, as indicated in Figure 3508, there will be a consistent and often random build-up of error with respect to time, due to gyro drift, producing a position error.

Miscellaneous errors The precise requirements of an inertial system make it necessary to take secondary effects into account; these are caused by Coriolis effect, and the earth's shape, which is not perfectly spherical. These error sources are automatically compensated for by the computer. For long periods of inertial navigation, dynamic coupling between various parts of the system produces a small rate error which must also be considered.

It must be realized that error sources can better be described statistically than as constants. Using this concept, the long-term build-up of errors can be determined and reduced more readily than by attempting to evaluate and use only constant error sources.

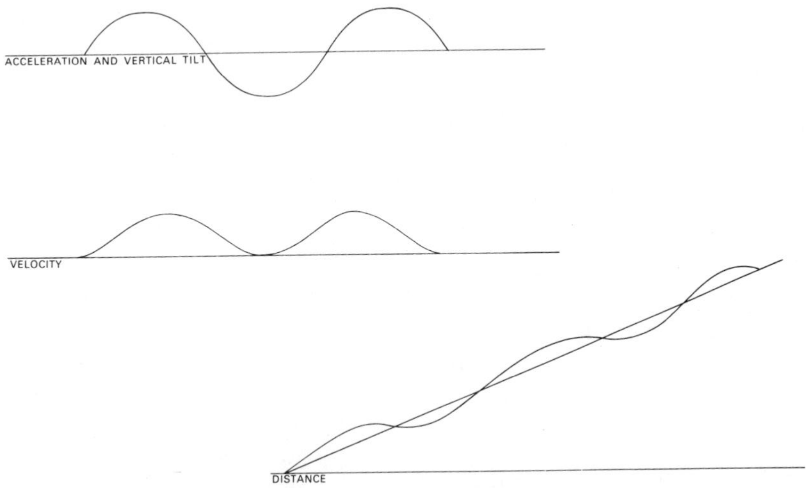

Figure 3508. System errors plotted against time.

Reset procedures

3509 The early methods of resetting the system were based on the assumption that the drift rate remained constant during the sampling period. This did not prove entirely satisfactory because accurate drift rate measurements can be made only at intervals, and it was not always true that the drift rate was essentially constant, or that any random errors were accurately known. Accurate position information, external to the inertial system, is needed and is used to recalibrate or reset the SINS, regardless of the reset technique. These data are fed through the computer which computes and applies proper torquing to the stabilized platforms. All of the data fed to the computers needs to be smoothed out, as frequent resetting, or the use of data which may itself be inaccurate, can create errors in determining and correcting the drift rate of the system.

Kalman filter theory

A theory developed by R. E. Kalman and generally referred to as the "Kalman filter" makes it feasible to include the randomness of the system as well as of the reference source in the reset formula. A detailed explanation of the theory is beyond the scope of this text. It involves complex differential equations; in practice these are solved by the computer.

Monitoring gyro

3510 New methods of monitoring the SINS gyros are constantly being developed. One method of determining the drift rate is by employing a *monitoring gyro.*

Including a monitor (a rate gyro) in the system improves performance because it senses and supplies data to the computer on any uncompensated fixed or slowly varying components of drift in the x and y gyros; a significant reduction in the random error component is also obtained. The monitoring technique utilizes a redundant gyro mounted on a rotating platform. An integrating rate gyro, with high-gain feedback from pickoff to torquer, is used to effectively yield an accurate rate gyro. This platform, an integral part of the *heading* gimbal, rotates about an axis parallel to the heading gimbal axis, and does not compensate the z axis, or *heading* gyro. Reversal of the direction of the input axis of the monitor inertial component, with respect to the navigational component, represents the basic technique used. Case reversal is instrumented by successively positioning the monitor table to each of the four quadrant positions, under control of the computer program. The monitoring gyro provides an output at each quadrant which is equal to the difference between the gyro-applied torque and the sensed torque. The torque applied from the computer to the monitor gyro is the same as the torque computed for the gyro being monitored. Since the SINS system computes the ship's position from accelerations resulting from the ship's movement, it is important that gyro drift be known as accurately as possible. The monitoring gyro improves overall performance of the system by detecting gyro drift that has not been compensated.

System updating 3511 Due to the errors just discussed, inertial navigation systems must have the capability of being updated or reset through the computer. Continuous compensation can be made for a known gyro drift. Discrete position information obtained, for example, from a NAVSAT, Omega, Loran-C, bathymetric, or celestial fix, can also be used to damp the system by manual or automatic insertion of the position into the computer.

The process of navigation involves various coordinate systems. Regardless of the system of coordinates chosen for the internal operation of the system, the computer must deal with three reference systems, as well as with the vector angles defining the angular relationship of the reference systems. These vector angles can be described in an overly simplified manner as follows:

1. The vector angle relating the platform coordinate system, defined by the sensitive axes of the inertial instruments on the platform, to a true coordinate system such as latitude and longitude.
2. The vector angle relating the computer coordinate system, defined by information available to the computer, to a true coordinate system.
3. The vector angle relating the platform coordinate system to the computer coordinate system.

This latter vector angle can in part be attributed to the misalignment of the platform, resulting in a slightly different set of coordinates from those programmed in the computer. The interrelationship of vector angles in the coordinate systems outlined above can always be stated as:

$$\text{vector no. } 1 = \text{no. } 2 + \text{no. } 3$$

Stellar inertial navigation A star tracker mounted on an inertial system can be used for determining a celestial fix, but even more importantly, it can be used to determine the platform drift rate representing a major portion of the vector angle described in no. 3. The star tracker could be physically mounted on the stable element of the inertial system; in actual use it is often remotely located. A computer in the system can automatically compute elevation angle or altitude, and azimuth angle, from the ephemeristic data stored in its memory section, and from its knowledge of ship's position. Disregarding errors in driving the telescope, it would be possible to point the telescope directly at the star, provided the coordinate system stored in the computer and the platform coordinates were coincident. The platform-mounted telescope will, however, have a pointing error equivalent to vector angle no. 3.

The telescope on the star tracker generally scans around or across the line of sight to the star. In this process it does have the ability to track the star, thereby permitting a determination of the deviation in altitude and azimuth angles from those computed. These error data, extrapolated over a period of time, can be used in determining drift rate of the gyro platform. In this monitoring system it is necessary to use either two trackers tracking different stars, or one tracker alternately tracking two stars. This is because the star tracker, when used as a monitor, must be capable of measuring the angular deviation between the actual line of sight to the star and the computed line. The tracker can measure only components normal to the line of sight; it cannot detect angular errors about the line of sight. However, the error components obtained from two stars can be resolved in the computer to determine the total error.

Since the stellar-monitored system has the capability of determining a gyro drift rate, it can be used for *alignment* of the platform attitude, as well as to correct the *computed* azimuth orientation without physically rotating the platform. It must be remembered that the stellar monitor system will introduce its own slight error caused by refraction compensation errors, ephemeristic errors, timing errors, and mechanical pointing errors. They may be considered as essentially constant while tracking a star for a short period of time. While alternately tracking two stars, the stellar-monitoring error will generally be random in nature.

Coordinate systems

3512 Previous articles have mentioned various coordinate systems relating to inertial navigation. The gyros in the inertial system are the inertial instruments which define the frame of reference in which acceleration is measured. This frame of reference is mathematically described by the particular coordinate system chosen, and mechanically defined by causing the gyro to precess at angular rates as dictated by the coordinate system. The design and arrangement of components and the coordinate system employed within the instrumentation is not strictly a navigational function and will not be discussed in detail. The readout on a SINS system is normally given in the familiar terms of latitude and longitude even though the computer may go through various conversions and computations to arrive at this readout. The operating manual for the SINS Mark 3 Mod 5 explains the operation of that particular instrumentation on the basis of the following three coordinate systems, which are familiar to the navigator, and will be reviewed briefly.

The *ship's coordinate system* is defined by the longitudinal axis, the athwartship axis, and the vertical or deck-to-keel axis, which, in the case of a submarine, can be defined as the optical axis of the main periscope. The angular quantities measured in the ship's coordinate system are relative bearing or relative azimuth, and elevation—the angle measured in a vertical plane from the deck plane to the line of sight. The ship's coordinate system is related to the horizontal plane in the local geographic coordinate system by the angles of roll, pitch, and heading.

The *local geographic coordinate system* is located at the ship's position

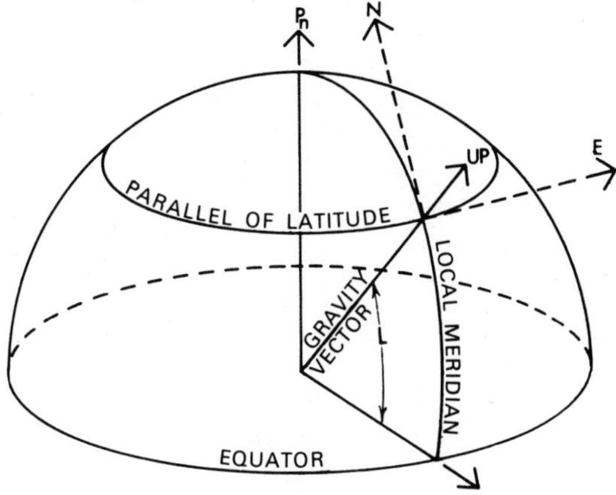

Figure 3512a. Geographic coordinate system.

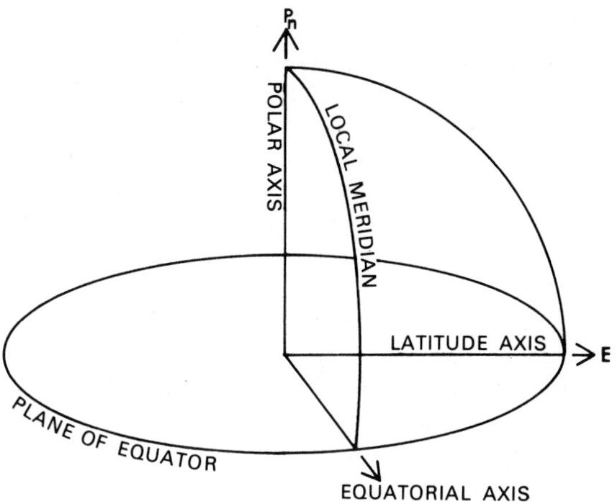

Figure 3512b. Equatorial coordinate system.

and is based on the direction of the vertical and the direction of north (Figure 3512a). The quantities measured in the local geographic system are velocity north, velocity east, and *depth* when used in a submarine. Heading is measured about the vertical from north clockwise to the projection in the horizontal plane of the ship's fore and aft axis. It can be considered as a local coordinate system, and the angle relating this system to the equatorial coordinate system is latitude.

The *equatorial coordinate system* consists of the earth's polar axis, the intersection of the plane of the ship's local meridian with the plane of the equator, and an axis directed east perpendicular to both these axes (Figure 3512b). The intersection of the equatorial coordinate system axes is therefore at the center of the earth. The latitude axis and the east axis of the local geographic system are parallel. Ship's motion in longitude is measured about the polar axis of this system, while motion in latitude is measured about the latitude axis.

Computers **3513** Due to the technical and mathematical complexity of inertial navigation systems, a computer must be included as an integral part of the overall system. Within this chapter, various references have been made to the functions of the computer. The computers used in modern SINS systems are usually general-purpose digital computers, but they are used in a very special purpose application. The words "general purpose" merely imply that the computer could be programmed without a hardware change to solve any general problem instead of the specific computations related to inertial navigation.

The computer for a SINS system could be analog rather than digital although the digital type is at present the more widely used, and its functions will vary somewhat depending upon the acceleration instruments employed, the system accuracy required, and the choice of coordinate system. In general, the computer will send torquing signals to the gyros and accelerometers, in addition to computing present position and velocity.

Summary **3514** Inertial navigation is a field in which technology advances rapidly. A variety of systems are already in operation, ranging from those designed for ballistic missiles, in which guidance is needed for only a very short period of time (which can be measured in seconds), to those designed for nuclear submarines, which may cruise for many weeks. It is difficult to predict the optimum configurations that will be used in any future system.

In addition to providing a self-contained navigation system, data from any inertial system can be used for other navigational applications. The Navy Navigation Satellite System requires an input of ship's motion into the solution, and this can be obtained accurately from the inertial system. On aircraft carriers, SINS is used to transfer precise ship's velocity and position to the inertially equipped aircraft before launching. This transfer of information is required for gyrocompass alignment of the aircraft inertial systems.

It is vitally important to always remember that for all the precision and accuracy of inertial systems, the output is merely an estimated position and not a fix. Only external means (visual bearings, NAVSAT, celestial, etc.) will provide the exact location of a vessel at a given time. The best inertial equipment still must be updated at intervals, as frequently as circumstances permit. The navigator who puts blind faith in the output of his inertial systems invites disaster.

36 Bathymetric Navigation

Introduction

3601 *Bathymetric Navigation* may be defined as the branch of navigation that uses the topography of the ocean floor to obtain positioning data by sonic or ultrasonic echoes returned from the ocean floor even at the greatest depths. A vessel's position is determined with respect to known locations of geological features of the ocean bottom.

Since the days of man's first ventures onto the waters, the mariner's major concern has been grounding; the sounding pole—followed by the sounding line, or *lead*—was perhaps the earliest navigational tool. From these developed the deep-sea lead which could be used at greater depths. The base of this lead was concave, so that the hollow could be "armed" with tallow, thus yielding both a sounding and a sample of the bottom sediment to assist in determining position. Such soundings could be obtained in the vicinity of the continental shelf but only at comparatively long intervals, due to the time consumed in recovering a fifty- or seventy-pound lead and a hundred or more fathoms of line by hand. Later, even greater depths could be measured with a *sounding machine* that used fine steel wire and mechanical methods for retrieving the weight and sounding bottles at its end. (Due to currents and the forward motion of the ship, the sounding wire was normally not vertical and so its length did not give a true indication of depth. The sounding bottles measured pressure at the bottom which could be translated to a measurement of depth.) The sounding machine allowed accurate measurements of considerable depths, but only a very few measurements could be taken in an hour of continuous effort. Today, a navigator can quickly and easily obtain an accurate measurement of depth, and a recorded profile of the bottom if he so wishes.

Principles of echo sounding

3602 The modern *electronic depth sounder,* also called an *echo sounder,* ("Fathometer" is a trademarked name applicable only to equipment from one manufacturer) generates an underwater sound-wave signal, and measures the duration of the time elapsing between the generation of the signal and the reception of the echo return from the bottom. This time lapse is converted to a readout of units of depth, usually stated in fathoms, although feet are used in many echo sounders designed for small craft. Many foreign charts, and newer charts from the Defense Mapping Agency Hydrographic Center, use meters and fractions of a meter to indicate depths; a depth-finder scale in metric units is desirable. Most echo sounders for large ships operate in the audible range of about 20 to 20,000 Hertz; such models are termed *sonic* depth finders. Now, however, the trend is towards using higher frequencies, in order to reduce interference from ship noise, and such instruments are termed *ultrasonic.*

The speed of sound through sea water varies with the salinity of the water, its temperature, and the pressure (depth). This variation is not very great, and most echo-sounding equipment of American manufacture is calibrated for a speed of sound of 4,800 feet per second (1,463 m per second). At sea, the actual speed of travel of sound is nearly always greater than this calibrated speed, and the error introduced lies on the side of safety, except where the water is fresh or extremely cold.

Transducer

The *transducer,* located on a horizontal portion of a ship's bottom plating, near the keel, transmits the acoustic signal when activated electrically. The sound energy used to determine depth is projected in the shape of a cone. Aboard most large ships, including U.S. naval vessels, the echo-sounding equipment generates a cone of 30° to 60° apex angle. The area of the bottom covered by such a cone of sound waves is a function of the depth; in deep water, this area can be quite large. The returning echo is picked up by a transducer (usually the same one that sent out the pulse, but not necessarily so), converted into electrical energy, amplified, and presented visually. Elapsed time between the transmission of the pulse and reception of its echo is displayed as depth. Typically, a depth sounder gives depth under the transducer; this is essentially at keel depth on ships, but usually is less on small craft; the actual depth is, of course, the indicated depth plus the depth of the transducer below the water's surface. Alternatively, a depth sounder can be calibrated to indicate directly the depth of the water as measured from the surface; this technique aids in navigation application, but gives less-obvious warnings of potential grounding.

The trend in the development of newer echo-sounding equipment is toward narrower beams, obtained by using higher frequencies or larger transducers, or both. Higher frequencies, however, have a disadvantage of greater attenuation and lesser depth range; practical installation considerations place a restraint on transducer size. For survey work, complex arrays of multiple transducers may be used; transducers may be stabilized to counter ship's rolling and pitching motions that could result in erroneous data.

Readout

The readout of depth is presented in somewhat different form by various sounders. In a typical instrument, a circular electric light tube is mounted vertically; this tube flashes briefly at the instant the sonic signal is transmitted, and again when the echo is received. In front of the light tube, and mounted concentrically with it, is an opaque shield that rotates at a predetermined speed. This shield has a narrow radial slot, which allows the light to be seen at only one point each time it flashes. Adjacent to the shield is a circular scale calibrated in units of depth. The depth finder shows the first flash of light at the zero point on the scale, and the second flash indicates the depth of water. Different scales may be available for use at various depths; the speed of rotation of the opaque shield is adjusted to match the scale being used. The U.S. Navy's AN/UQN-1 depth finder is shown in Figure 715a; its display is on a cathode-ray tube as well as a strip recorder. The newer, redesigned, and improved AN/UQN-4 is shown in Figure 3602a; it is described in Article 3603. Depth sounders for small craft frequently use a rotating arm at the outer end of which is a small neon bulb or light-emitting diode. This flashes for the "zero" pulse and again when the echo is received, in the same manner as described above for larger models. Other sounders show depth by an electrical meter or a direct-reading digital display.

Some echo sounders are also equipped with a *recorder* which produces a graphic trace of the depths encountered; this trace is called a *bottom profile.* The recorder consists of a wide paper tape, graduated in depth and time units, and a moving arm equipped with a stylus, which

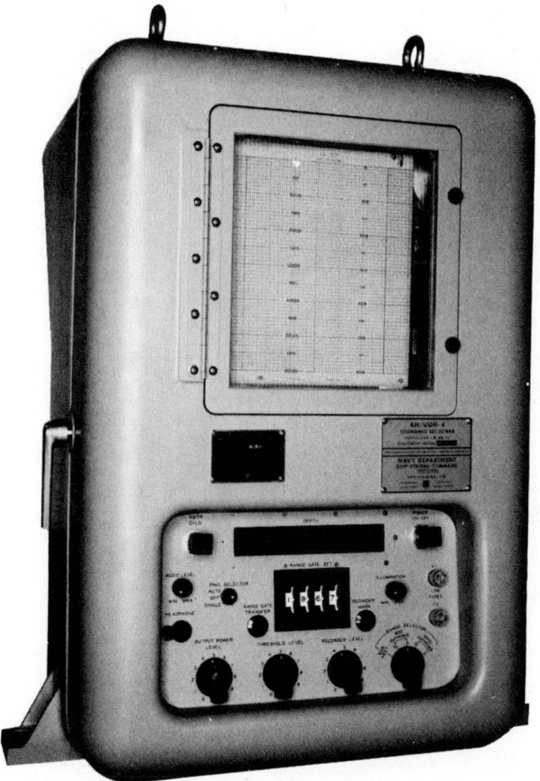

Figure 3602a. AN/UQN-4 Depth Finder.

makes one sweep over the tape for each sounding. When an echo is received, the stylus makes a dot or short line on the tape. For greater clarity of bottom features, the vertical scale is exaggerated by a predetermined ratio. A typical bottom profile is shown in Figure 3602b.

In theory, echoes are returned from the bottom from all points within the sound cone; in actual use, the first echoes tend to mask the later ones, and there may be an appreciable delay between the return of the first and the later echoes. It must be borne in mind that the first return will come from that portion of the bottom which is *nearest* the ship, and that *this portion is not necessarily directly below the ship*. This phenomenon is known as a *side echo.* Subsequent returns will be from other portions of the bottom. In comparatively shallow water, *multiple returns* may occur when the bottom is a good sound reflector. The echo returns from the bottom and is recorded as the depth, but it is also reflected for a second trip downward by the water's surface, and then back up for a second reading. Two or more returns can occur in shallower water, particularly when the bottom is of hard material such as sand or rock. Reducing the echo-sounder gain will usually remove indications of multiple return.

Side Echo

Multiple returns

Another phenomenon which may be puzzling is the appearance at times of a false bottom, suspended in the water. This is caused by echoes returned from the *deep scattering layer,* also called the *phantom bottom.* In daytime it is encountered at depths of about 200 fathoms (366 m); it usually moves nearer the surface at night. It is caused by echoes reflected from light-shunning plankton and other minute marine life. At times, this layer is sufficiently dense to mask echoes from the actual bottom. Schools of fish, or a single large fish, also return an echo, making the echo sounder particularly useful to fishermen. Any sharp discontinuity within the water causes sound to be reflected, and an echo sounder often can detect the boundary of a layer of fresh water overlying heavier salt water.

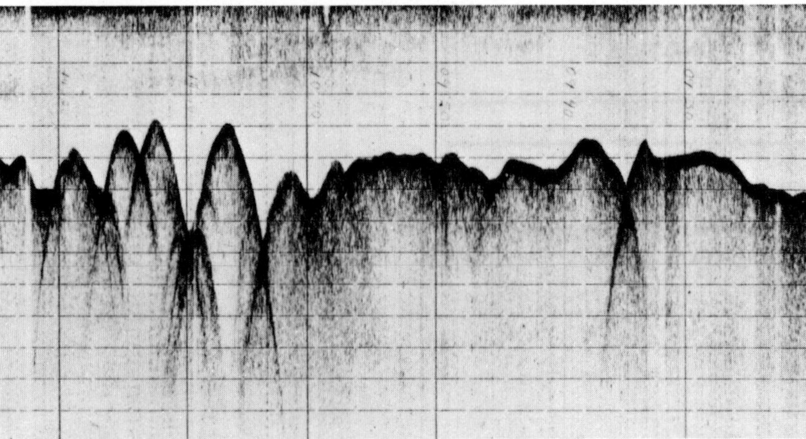

Figure 3602b. A typical bottom profile.

A rocky bottom reflects almost all the sound striking its surface, while soft mud tends to absorb it, thus returning a weaker signal. A layer of mud or silt overlying rock frequently yields two echoes.

The navigator must always bear in mind that depths shown on charts may be inaccurate due to changing bottom conditions, such as silting or the formation of sandbars since the survey was made. It is also possible that protruding underwater obstacles may have been missed during the survey. It is important to use the depth sounder continuously in a deep-draft vessel approaching shallow water or operating on soundings. Modern surveys are, however, much more accurate and reliable than those conducted before the introduction of electronic positioning systems. Electronic systems permit not only an accurate establishment of the survey vessel's position but extend the range of operations farther from shore. More important, they are able to maintain an automatic plot of positions related to time. By use of a depth sounder in place of the old hand lead a continuous recording of depths is made and is correlated with the position of the survey vessel.

The AN/UQN-4 echo sounder

3603 The AN/UQN-4 precision echo sounder is a standard model in use by the U.S. Navy; it has features typical of commercial sounders used on merchant ships.

The UQN-4 is essentially an improved version of the basic UQN-1, described in Article 715. Like the latter instrument, it transmits on a frequency of 12 kHz; it differs from them primarily in that both the transmitting and receiving circuitry are entirely solid state, and in that the cathode ray tube readout has been replaced by a numerical readout, which shows the depth stated either in feet or fathoms.

The transducer beam width is 30°. The signal frequency is crystal controlled; emission consists of a pulsed CW signal, with a maximum peak output of 1,000 watts. The pulse duration and repetition rate are given in the following table. Two pulse lengths are available for each of the deeper range settings.

Range	*Short Pulse*	*Long Pulse*	*Pulse Repetition Rate*
600 feet	0.33 ms		120 per minute
600 fathoms	2.46 ms	26.67 ms	20 per minute
6,000 fathoms	20.00 ms	160.00 ms	2 per minute

In lieu of automatic transmission (auto pinging), the operator can key a single pulse manually. In addition to the numerical depth readout, the UQN-4 has a strip chart recorder, which is greatly improved over previous models.

The UQN-4 has two additional features which are not available on its predecessors. It is fitted with a draft adjustment, which permits the depth readout to be adjusted so that it states depth below the lowest portion of the ship, such as a sonar dome, and provision is made for automatic tracking. A selected depth is set manually into the numerical depth readout circuit. A *Lost Tracking Indicator* is illuminated whenever a depth of 200 feet (61 m) greater or less than the preset depth is encountered.

The echo sounder as a navigational tool

3604 Soundings shown on DMAHC charts are obtained by echo sounders using an assumed standard velocity of sound in sea water and are uncorrected for any variation in salinity, density, or temperature. This lack of correction is desirable because conditions in any given area remain reasonably constant, and thus the subsequent echo-sounder readings of a ship may be directly compared with the charted values.

In bathymetric navigation, the wide-beam characteristics of a typical depth sounder may actually be advantageous. Often a sea-bottom feature would go undetected by a ship not directly over it were it not for the wide cone of sounding pulses. Because of the cone configuration, the deeper such a feature lies, the greater the horizontal distance at which the ship can locate it. From the bathymetric navigation standpoint, the fact that such an off-track feature is recorded at a depth greater than its true depth is a meaningful clue to its position. The minimum depth recorded by a ship over a seamount will be identical to that shown on the chart only if the ship passes directly over the top, assuming that the charted depth is in fact correct. If the top of the seamount still lies within range of the sound cone, it will be recorded even though the ship is to one side. However, the minimum depth will be recorded deeper than shown on the chart because of the greater oblique distance from the transducer. Within a range of values, the difference in minimum depths (between charted and recorded values) will yield distance horizontally from the ship to the projected point of the seamount top at the surface.

Line of soundings

In ordinary navigation when using the echo sounder, the *line-of-soundings* method may be used to advantage as an aid in determining position. The manner of employing this method depends largely on the chart covering the area.

Either of the two methods requires a piece of transparent paper or plastic, on which is drawn a straight line representing the ship's course. If bottom contour lines are printed on the chart, the depth values of the contour lines should be noted; assume that these are given for every 20 fathoms. The echo sounder is now turned on, and when a sounding of a multiple of 20 fathoms true depth is obtained, a mark is made at one end of the heading line on the tracing paper, the depth is noted opposite the mark at one side of the line, and the time at the other. When the depth changes by 20 fathoms, the time is again noted, and using the latitude scale of the chart, the ship's run for the time interval is calculated, and another mark is made at the appropriate distance from the first, and depth and time are again noted. After this process has been repeated several times, the paper is placed on the chart in the vicinity of the ship's DR position, with the ship's heading line oriented in the proper direction. It is now moved across the chart, with the heading line always oriented in the proper direction, until the depth marks on the paper agree with the contour lines on the chart. The ship's position may now usually be determined with considerable accuracy; see Article 1119.

Note that if the echo sounder reads depth under the keel, the soundings must be adjusted to represent depth below the surface. In this case, if the vessel draws 24 feet (4 fathoms), use echo-sounder readings of 16 fathoms, 36 fathoms, 56 fathoms, etc.

When contour lines are not shown on the chart, it is best to mark off the line on the paper in equal distances, each distance representing the ship's advance for a convenient period of time. On small-scale charts these distances should be greater than when a large-scale chart is used. When a number of soundings have been recorded, the paper is oriented and moved across the chart in the same manner as described above, to determine the most probable position.

The National Ocean Survey is producing a series of *bathymetric maps* of the waters adjacent to portions of the coast of the United States. These maps extend seaward somewhat beyond the 100-fathom curve, and show the contour of the bottom in considerable detail. Such maps can be of great assistance in fixing position by means of the depth finder.

Even where a line of soundings cannot be matched to a chart or bathymetric map, echo-sounder data can be of value to a navigator. While an isolated measurement of depth cannot, of itself, yield a position due to the repetition of the same depth at many spots, it can provide "negative" information which questions the validity of a fix obtained by other means and starts the navigator on a search for better data.

Use of bottom "land marks" in navigation

3605 Charted "landmarks" on the ocean floor can often assist the navigator in determining position. Such marks include *submarine canyons, trenches, troughs, escarpments, ridges, seamounts,* and *guyots.* These terms in general describe submarine topographical features which are similar to their counterparts found on dry land. An escarpment is a long steep face of rock, or long submarine cliff. A seamount is an elevation of relatively small horizontal extent rising steeply towards, but not reaching, the surface. A guyot is a flat-topped seamount, rather similar to the mesas found in the southwestern United States. Canyons are found off most continental slopes; they are relatively steepsided, and their axes descend steadily. A canyon, when crossed approximately at right angles, is easily recognized on a depth sounder or recorder. It will serve to establish a line of position, and the maximum depth noted, when crossing the axis, may further aid in determining position. Trenches, troughs, ridges, and escarpments are often found on the ocean bottom, which may be otherwise featureless; they can also be useful in yielding a line of position. Many guyots occur in the Pacific, and are useful in positioning. A line of position may also be obtained when crossing the line of demarcation between an ocean basin, which is usually very flat, and the surrounding bottom mass.

Precise positioning by means of seamounts

3606 If the apex of an isolated seamount is located by means of the echo sounder, a precise position can be determined. If several seamounts are located in the same area, identification must be made by individual shape as well as minimum depth.

Article 3602 stated that the echo sounders on many vessels typically generate a 60° cone of sounding pulses. The geometry of such a cone will now be considered in terms of isolated features on the sea bed such as a seamount; this is known as the *side-echo technique* (the name is something of a misnomer in this case as the technique actually concerns position to one side of a feature rather than the phenomenon previously discussed under this name.) Basically, the technique involves two passes near a seamount at right angles with each other. The point of minimum depth on each track is noted and lines at right angles to the track are drawn at these points; the intersection of these lines locates the seamount with respect to the ship.

Although the procedures are not difficult, several important concepts must be kept in mind. Seamounts (or seaknolls) are large features. The notion that they are steepsided, as seen on echograms with large vertical exaggerations, must be dispelled. The tops are never so sharp or well defined as they appear on the echogram. Charted values indicating a unique minimum depth can be incorrect; the depth can be wrong; or (more probably) it may have been charted in the wrong position. Knowledge of whether the feature was compiled from a survey or from random tracks is essential for confidence in use of the reference chart. One records the minimum sounding of a seamount identical to the depth on the chart when the ship passes directly over the top or very close to it. A recorded value shallower than seen on the chart indicates that the chart is in error (or the sounding gear is in error, or it is the wrong seamount). It is desirable to know the nature of the equipment used by the ship(s) that produced the data upon which the chart is based, and of course one must know the limitations of his own equipment. All of these must be kept in mind. There is also the possibility of using incompatible features, and an isolated seamount is best chosen despite the greater difficulty in initial detection.

The 60° sound cone

The first echo return comes from the portion of the sea bed which is nearest the ship, and this portion is not necessarily directly below the ship; in such a case, the depth finder is indicating a side echo. This can be very helpful because, if the seamount apex lies within the sound cone the depth recorded by the depth finder cannot exceed the depth of the apex multiplied by 1.154. In addition, the horizontal distance from the apex to the ship cannot exceed half the depth indicated by the depth finder (Figure 3606a). (These factors must be modified if the depth sounder being used has a cone of sound pulses other than 60°.)

Ordinarily, to obtain a fix by means of locating the summit of a seamount, a position some distance away is determined as accurately as possible, and then a course is set for the apex. The distance of the departure position from the apex will depend in part on the existing current, sea, and wind conditions.

Figure 3606b shows the contour lines surrounding the apex of a seamount. Assume that a ship obtained a good running fix due south of the apex, and is approaching on a course of 000°. It is possible that this course will take the ship directly over the summit, in which case

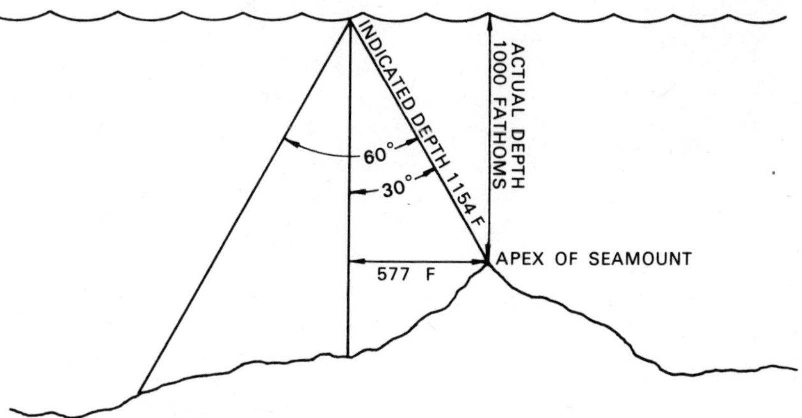

Figure 3606a. The geometry of a 60° sound cone.

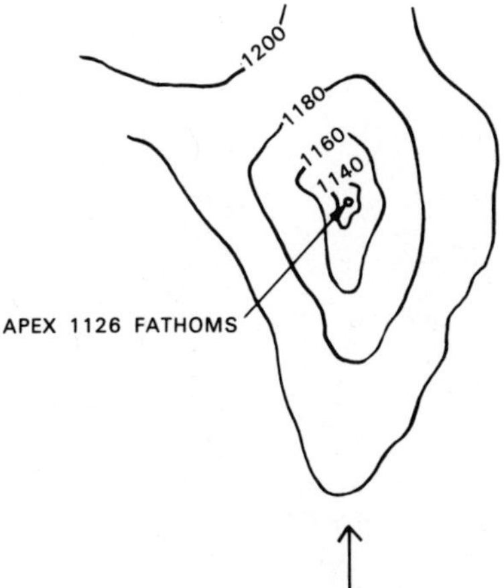

Figure 3606b. Bottom contour chart.

the depth finder will give a minimum reading of 1126 fathoms (the depth at the summit), and provide a fix. Unfortunately, this seldom occurs.

Figure 3606c shows the DR plot as the ship approaches the location of the summit. Soundings are recorded every minute on the plot and also the minimum sounding obtained; times are omitted in this figure for clarity. The shallowest sounding obtained is 1169 fathoms, and a line is drawn at right angles to the heading line for this sounding. As the soundings begin to increase, it is obvious the ship has passed the area of the summit; a right turn is made to come to a course of 270°, crossing the original track at an angle of 90°. The turn to starboard is adjusted so that the new course will pass as close as possible to the summit's assumed position. Soundings are again noted every minute, as is the minimum sounding, which is 1149 fathoms. A perpendicular to the ship's course line is again drawn for this minimum sounding.

The intersection of the two perpendicular lines passing through the minimum recorded depths locates the summit of the seamount relative to the ship; the direction and distance separating the intersection of these two lines from the charted position of the seamount is the offset of the ship's track from the seamount. Adjustment of the track may be accomplished by shifting all recorded times and soundings by the direction and distance of the offset.

It is possible that the selected track will pass so far to the side of the seamount that the top lies *outside* the cone of sounding pulses. This is apparent if the navigator observes a minimum depth greater than 1,300 fathoms; this means that the ship was more than 1,300 yards to the side of the top. For a 60° sound cone, the geometry of the situa-

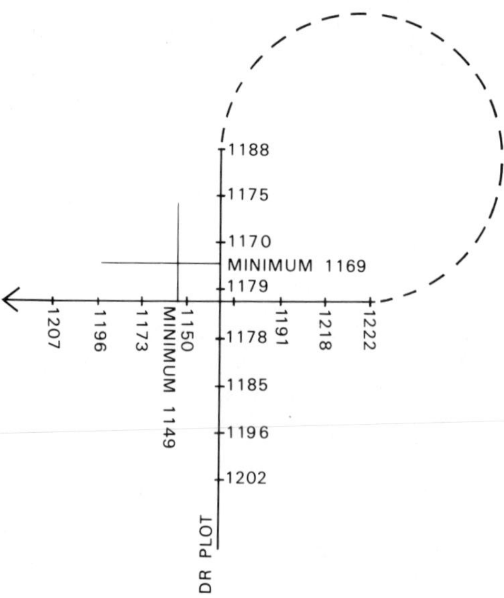

Figure 3606c. Determining position by means of a seamount.

tion leads to this rule of thumb: the deepest value recorded with the seamount top still retained within the cone is twice the distance from ship to seamount top horizontally. Obviously, it is to the advantage of the navigator to choose, if a choice is possible, a seamount with deep minimum depth, other considerations being equal. In the event that the top does not lie within the sound cone, the ship's position can be determined only approximately. It would be desirable to make another pass on a reciprocal course, displaced to one side as indicated by the approximate position, to attempt a more precise location of the seamount top.

It should also be noted that this method, while entirely feasible, requires that the vessel be diverted from her track towards her destination in order to make the second pass by the seamount at right angles to the first passing. Such a diversion is not normally welcomed by captains, and for ships on normal ocean passages this method is rather more theoretical than practical.

Contour advancement

3607 Somewhat similar to the line-of-soundings method is the *contour advancement technique.* If the area has been precisely surveyed and compiled, this technique will yield highly accurate and repeatable results. No bathymetric anomalies such as seamounts, canyons, or ridges are required; but some variation in depths is necessary. In this case it is the slopes that are of interest. Ideally, a slope of more than one degree, but no more than four or five degrees, is required. The slope should not be constant because this method will not work if the linear distance between contours is equal.

In noting that some slope is required, the presence or absence of contours and the scale of chart used must be kept in mind. Areas that appear devoid of contours and flat on one chart may, upon use of a larger-scale chart, show some relief or slope. After finding that a given area is not absolutely level, the contour advancement method is facilitated by use of the largest-scale chart available.

Refer to Figure 3607a as the base chart. The DR track is shown as a dashed line, with observed depths marked off at increments equal to the charted contour interval. These data were obtained while the ship was steaming across the area, using the 700-fathom curve as reference contour. This is a time-distance plot and is based on ship speed and recorded depths. For example, if the ship had been steaming in the same direction for several miles (over this slope), it would be recording incremental depths differing in time from the recording of the charted depths. The recorded contour crossings are merely extended to the area on this chart and plotted in relative position on the DR track.

By starting with the 700-fathom curve as the first one crossed, the curve is traced onto an overlay and becomes the *reference contour.* The assumed track is also indicated on the overlay. The next step is to shift the overlay in the direction of travel until the reference contour (700

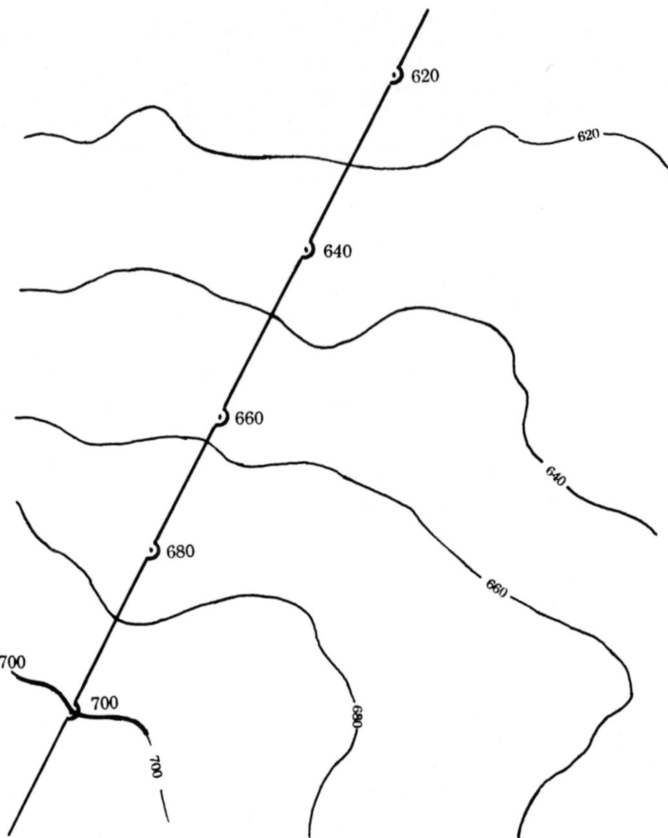

Figure 3607a. Chart extract showing DR track and successive depth contours.

fathoms) matches the plotted (not contoured) position of the next depth for which a contour exists (680 fathoms). Now the 680-fathom curve is traced. It should intersect the reference contour at one or more positions. The overlay is again advanced along the direction of travel to the point where the reference contour intersects the plotted 660-fathom curve. This contour (660 fathoms) is now traced. The three contours that are now traced should intersect at a point off the assumed track. Or, some triangle of error will be indicated which can be further defined by continuation of the "advancement." The intersection of lines becomes the position which is used to adjust the ship's track. This adjustment is a linear shift of the DR track and is a fix modified by the time (and therefore positional) lag after determination.

This description may appear complex in the absence of an overlay. Actually, the technique is a simple one and easy to master. Figure 3607b depicts the overlay after the contours have been traced by advancement of the 700-fathom curve.

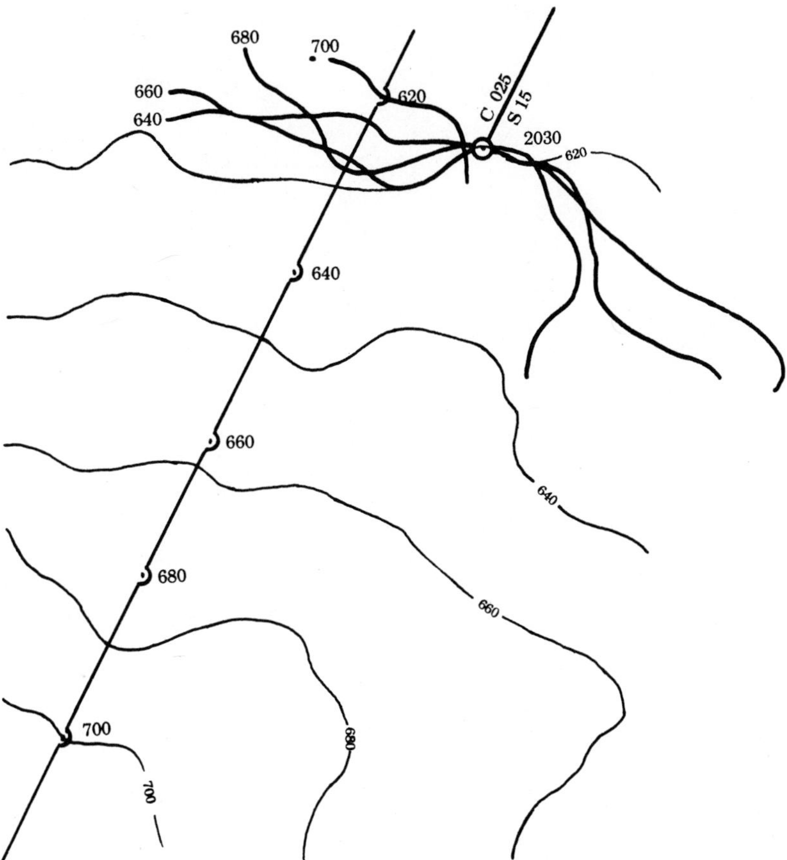

Figure 3607b. Transparent overlay showing contours successively advanced and position of ship at common intersection.

Sonar in piloting **3608** *Sonar* (SOund NAvigation Ranging) operates in the same manner as the echo sounder, except that it radiates its signal in a generally horizontal, rather than a vertical, direction. Excellent ranges on underwater objects may be obtained with sonar, and as the sonar transducer can be rotated horizontally, accurate bearings may also be obtained.

Sonar can be of great assistance in piloting in thick weather, particularly in rocky areas.

For example, when the harbor of Newport, Rhode Island, is closed due to very heavy fog, a ship returning to port can come to anchor out of the channel south of Brenton Reef and west of Seal Ledge in a very precisely determined position. Subsequent changes in sonar ranges and bearings would give immediate notice, should she drag her anchor (Figure 3609).

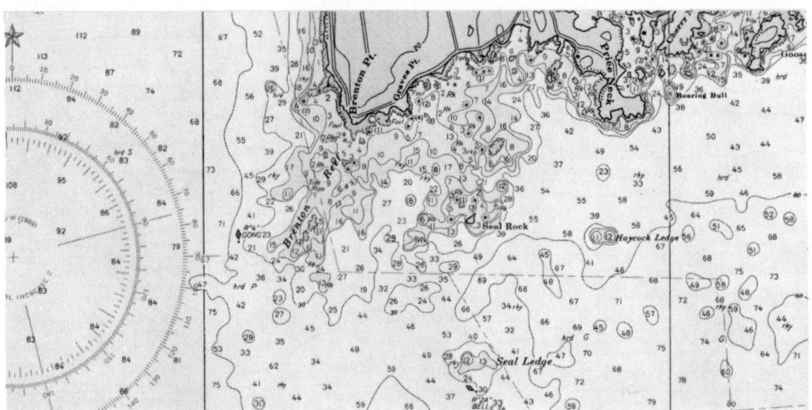

Figure 3609. Use of sonar in piloting.

In arctic regions, sonar is sometimes helpful in locating ice when steaming at slow speed, as approximately nine-tenths of the ice mass is located below the water surface. Large bergs may sometimes be detected at a range of 6,000 yards or more, but the service range is usually less. Growlers may be picked up at ranges of between 1,000 and 2,000 yards; even smaller pieces may be detected in time to avoid them.

During the latter part of World War II sonar made it possible for U.S. submarines to penetrate defensive mine fields laid by the Japanese. Moving submerged at slow speeds, the submarines were able to detect the anchored mines, and thus thread their way through the fields.

Summary **3609** Bathymetric navigation is an advanced technique of the general art and science of positioning ships at sea, but one whose potential should not be overlooked by any navigator, especially for specialized situations. The instrumentation developed for NASA's range instrumentation ships is only a first step in the use of modern technology in this field; the possibilities of computer applications are almost limitless. An interesting device developed by the Navy for its Deep Submersible Rescue Vehicle program is the altitude/depth sonar, which shows the vehicle's altitude above the ocean bottom and the depth below the surface for cruising and search purposes. Nuclear submarines cruising beneath polar ice packs use sounding equipment both upward and downward, as well as ahead.

Bathymetric navigation is a developing technique and continued refinements and improvements can be expected in the future, both in equipment and procedures.

37 Doppler Navigation

Introduction **3701** If the direction and distance traveled by a ship *relative to the earth* could be continuously and accurately determined, position information would be available at all times following departure from a known location. Several methods of making such measurements have been developed for marine navigation; these are subject to continued refinement, and new techniques are being researched. One procedure for determining direction and distance uses inertial navigation, discussed in Chapter 35. Another method is *Doppler Navigation* using acoustic waves. Doppler navigation using electromagnetic (radio) waves has proven highly satisfactory in air navigation.

The Doppler method, based on a change of frequency caused by motion, is named for Christian Doppler, who described the frequency change, or shift, in 1842. The classic example used to illustrate the Doppler shift is the sound of a fast-moving locomotive's whistle. As the locomotive approaches, the pitch of the sound seems to rise; as the locomotive moves away, the pitch seems to sink. For a long time, the Doppler shift was of real interest only to astronomers and science teachers. When, however, technology had progressed to the point where acoustic and electromagnetic radiation could be produced and controlled, it was realized that the Doppler effect could be used to measure velocity (and when velocity is known, it can be integrated to obtain distance from a starting point).

Acoustic Doppler navigation systems are capable of giving a constant readout of speed and distance traveled to a high degree of accuracy. Some models can additionally show speed on the athwartship axis for a measurement of offsetting influences such as current. In shallower waters—depths less than 250 feet (76 m)—some Raytheon units can be switched to a "mooring mode" in which speeds on both the fore-and-aft and athwartship axes can be resolved down to 0.01 knot to facilitate docking, anchoring, or mooring to a buoy.

A limitation of Doppler navigation systems is the depth of water under the vessel. Typically, units can operate from bottom echoes in waters no deeper than 1,500 feet (460 m). In greater depths "water-mass tracking" must be employed, using reflections from particulate matter in the water with somewhat reduced accuracy of speed and distance measurements.

Doppler systems can simultaneously be used for depth measurement, often with a preset alarm capability. All information derived from the system—speed, distance traveled, and depth—can be transmitted in digital form to a navigational computer. Here, distance can be combined with heading information from a gyrocompass for an accurate continuing computation of latitude and longitude.

Mechanics of the Doppler shift

3702 In order to comprehend the principles of Doppler navigation, the mechanics of the Doppler shift must be understood. The same principles hold good regarding the Doppler shift for all waves of the frequency spectrum, whether they be the waves of visible light, with which the astronomer is concerned, the electromagnetic waves used by the jet aircraft navigator, or the acoustic (sound) waves used in marine navigation.

For purposes of illustration, this article will first consider the sound energy as being transmitted horizontally through the water, rather than diagonally downwards, as is the case in marine Doppler navigation. If the sonic projector shown in Figure 3702a is considered as being stationary in the water while transmitting sound on a frequency f, the transmitted radiation in the form of sound waves moves away from the transmitter at the speed of sound, C. This speed is affected primarily by the temperature, salinity, and density of the sea water. The transmitted radiation travels outward in the form of waves, alternating between pressure crests and troughs. The distance between consecutive crests or troughs is the *wavelength*, λ, of the acoustic wave.

The wavelength is equal to the speed of sound divided by the frequency, or $\lambda = C/f$. Therefore, in a period of time t each pressure crest travels a distance d equal to C multiplied by t. In the illustration it can be seen that the wavelength in feet (λ) and the distance (d) that a given pressure crest has traveled are one and the same.

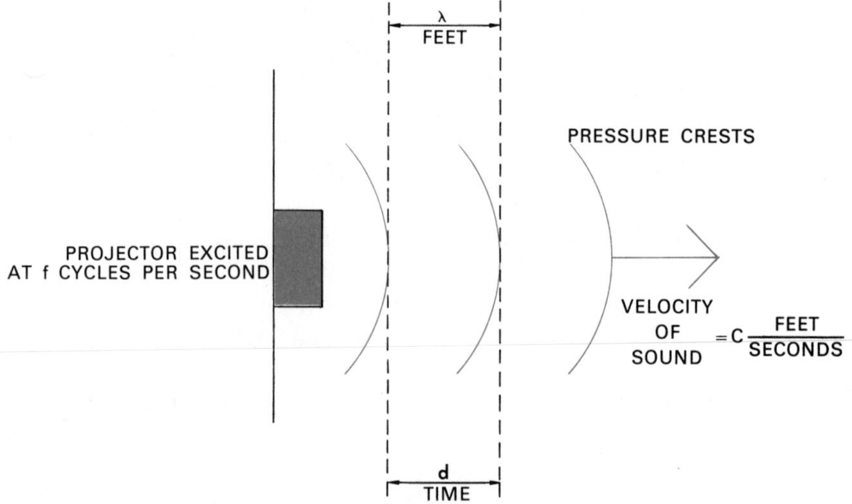

Figure 3702a. Pattern of acoustic waves transmitted from a stationary underwater projector.

Figure 3702b depicts a ship carrying the projector moving through the water at a velocity *V*, and the resulting wave being monitored at a fixed point some distance away from the projector. When transmitted at the same fixed frequency (*f*, as above), the waves, with their pressure crests, are generated at the same time intervals or frequency. The pressure crests are closer together in the water due to the forward velocity of the vessel. The new compressed wavelengths, λ', are equal to the prior undisturbed wavelengths minus the distance traveled at velocity v between pressure crests. Since wavelength and frequency vary inversely in any medium having a fixed speed of sound, the shortened wavelength caused by the ship's velocity results in an increase in frequency received at the monitoring point. Stated somewhat differently, the motion of the source of sound waves toward the stationary observer results in a greater number of pressure crests reaching the observer; this means a higher frequency of the acoustic waves. The change in frequency is known as the *Doppler shift.*

If the stationary observer in Figure 3702b is replaced by a reflector, as shown in Figure 3702c, the transmitted energy will be reflected back to the ship. By adding a hydrophone, or receiver, the distance to the object can be determined by measuring the elapsed time between transmission of an outgoing signal and the return of the echo, a sonar distance. In addition, by measuring the Doppler shift of the echo, the ship's speed relative to the reflector can be determined.

In Doppler navigation the ocean floor is normally used as a reflector, as no reflective surfaces are available in the horizontal plane. A highly directional sound projector and hydrophone are therefore depressed to a predetermined angle below the horizontal. If a second projector and hydrophone, facing in the opposite direction to the first

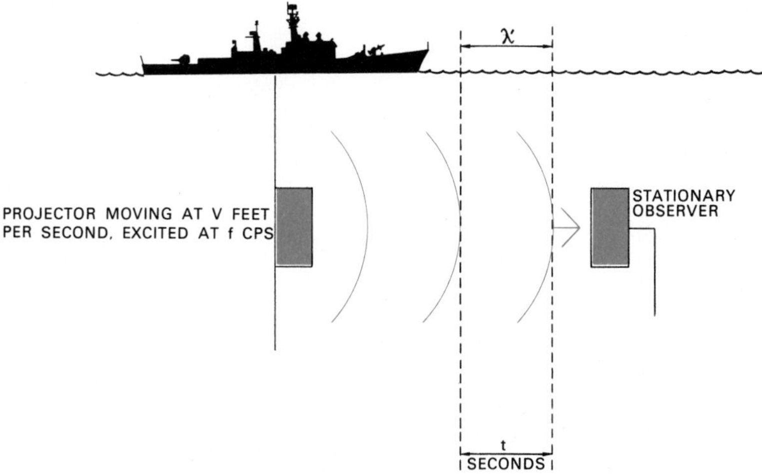

Figure 3702b. Pattern of acoustic waves transmitted from a moving underwater projector.

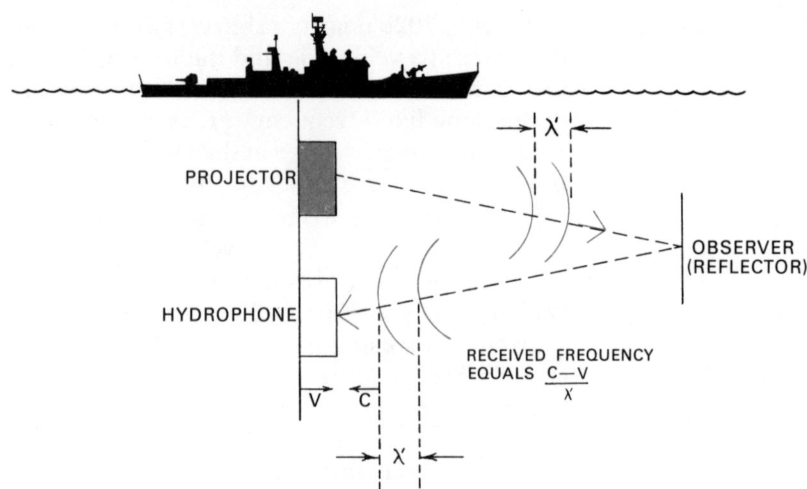

Figure 3702c. Pattern of acoustic waves reflected back to a moving transmitter/receiver.

pair and depressed to the same angle, are added, the Doppler shift, as received by the two hydrophones, can be compared. If the Doppler shift, as obtained from the after hydrophone is subtracted from the shift as obtained from the forward hydrophone, the value of the shift due to horizontal motion will be doubled; in addition, any shift due to vertical motion will be canceled. It follows that if four projectors and hydrophones equally distributed in bearing are employed, relative direction and distance measurements can be very precisely determined. In some systems, only three projector/receiver units are used, with one being used on both axes.

Sonic signals transmitted through sea water

3703 So far, only the Doppler shift has been considered, with no thought to the medium—sea water—through which it is transmitted. The existing characteristics of the water can have a significant effect on Doppler navigation, the major considerations being their effect on the *speed of sound,* on *signal attenuation,* and on *volume reverberation.*

Speed of sound

As was stated in Article 3702, the wavelength, λ, of a transmitted sound wave is equal to the speed of sound, C, divided by the frequency, f, or $\lambda = C/f$. The *speed of sound* in water is affected by such factors as salinity, temperature, and pressure, which increases with depth. It can vary by approximately 3 percent on either side of the standard value, which is generally taken as 4,935 feet per second (1504 m/s) in sea water near the surface with a temperature of 60° F (15.6° C) and salinity of 34 parts per thousand. Note that this speed differs from the more-rounded figure of 4800 feet per second (1463 m/s) commonly used in echo-sounding and bathymetric navigation.

An uncompensated variation in the speed of sound as great as 3 percent could cause an unacceptable error in a Doppler navigation system. Errors resulting from such a cause can be largely eliminated by transmitting a signal on a constant wavelength rather than on a constant frequency, or by constantly adjusting the depression angle of the transmitter and hydrophone array to compensate for a change in the velocity of sound. Both methods offer certain advantages, but neither is generally considered to be the ultimate answer to the problem. The two methods have been combined with considerable success in some Doppler instrumentation.

Signal attenuation The acoustic energy of the sonic signal is dissipated as it passes through the water; this phenomenon is called *signal attenuation.* As path losses increase with increased frequency, due to signal attenuation, tradeoffs between power and frequency must always be taken into consideration in the design of Doppler navigational equipment.

Volume reverberation *Volume reverberation* is the term used to describe the acoustic energy that is returned from debris, bubbles, minute marine life, or thermal gradients in the water, rather than from the bottom. The noise caused by volume reverberation can at times drown out the echo reflected from the bottom. This effect is used to advantage with some types of Doppler equipment, as discussed in Article 3705.

The Doppler navigator **3704** The Doppler navigational system as originally developed by the Raytheon Company employed four beams of sonic energy, spaced 90° apart. These beams were directed outward and downward at equal angles of inclination from the horizontal. The sonic energy was transmitted from *transducers*, which were activated by an electrical signal from the transmitter. In addition to radiating the outgoing sonic signal, the transducers served as hydrophones, in that they also picked up the echo of the signal, reflected from the ocean floor, and converted the acoustic echo into electrical energy. This energy passed into the receiver, where it was amplified, and the input from the four transducers was compared to produce the Doppler frequency. It also determined the relative strength of the frequencies, thus providing a sense of motion and its direction.

If the transducer array remained fixed in bearing relative to the ship's center line, motion would be stated relative to the ship's coordinate system; that is, the readout would show motion relative to the vessel's heading and would indicate speed over the bottom and cross track errors (lateral displacement relative to the track). To make it a true navigational system, a transducer array can be constantly oriented to true north by the ship's gyrocompass, which also serves to stabilize the array, and maintain it in a horizontal plane, regardless of any roll or pitch. Motion is thus indicated in the north-south and east-west directions, and readout is both the true direction and distance traveled from a point of departure expressed as distance north or south and east or west as shown in Figure 3704. Therefore the system can present a constant indication of position, expressed as latitude and longitude, and can also continuously plot position on a chart, using an X-Y coordinate plotter.

Accuracy Geometric arrangement and sonic factors, both of which affect the performance of the system, have been discussed briefly. Another limitation on the accuracy of the system is the heading accuracy supplied by the gyrocompass employed. A high-quality gyrocompass under good operational conditions will have a bearing uncertainty of 0.1°, or about six minutes of arc. The Doppler navigational system using a heading reference in which this error remained constant would indicate a position to about 0.17 percent of the distance traveled from the departure, and the ship might be to the right or left of the intended track by this amount. As the errors introduced by the gyro usually tend to be random rather than constant, they average out to a considerable extent. Many runs have been made with this equipment to a considerably higher degree of accuracy than the 0.17 percent error would seem to indicate.

The chief limitation in Doppler navigation using the ocean floor as a reflector is not system accuracy, but rather that it is effective only in depths not exceeding approximately 1,500 feet (460 m) due to signal attenuation; accuracy degrades somewhat with increasing depth.

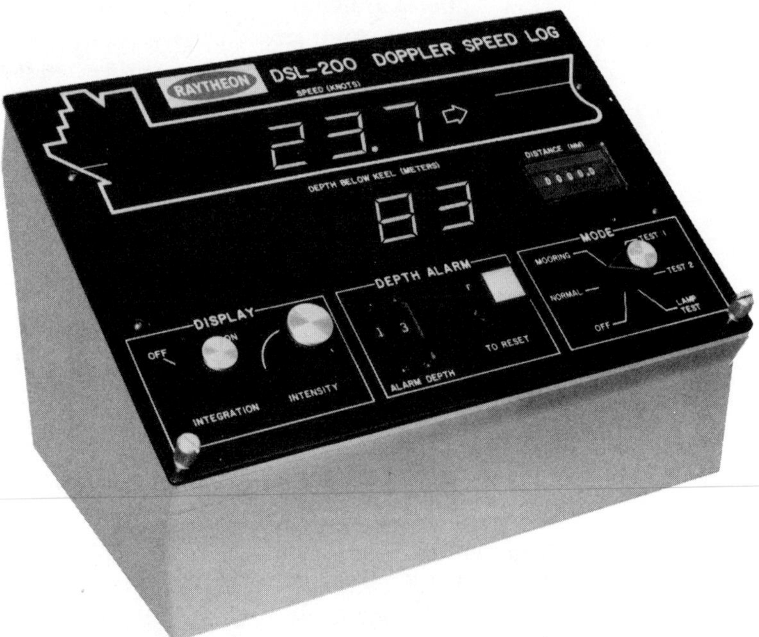

Figure 3704. Doppler system readout showing speed, distance traveled, and depth, with depth alarm available.

Doppler navigational system for maintaining an accurate DR plot at sea

3705 Volume reverberation was mentioned in Article 3703 as sometimes having an adverse effect on the Doppler navigational system, as the echo returning from the ocean floor was masked by an echo from thermal gradients, stratified layers of minute marine life, etc. Because of this volume reverberation in sonar transmissions, with a CW transmitter, part of the acoustic energy is reflected back and produces a signal level, at the receiver, that is higher than the noise level. Consequently Doppler navigation is possible *relative to the water mass,* regardless of water depth.

Volume reverberation is not an unmixed liability, as it makes possible use of the Doppler navigational system as a highly accurate DR system at any sea depths. Motion is sensed relative to the water mass, and is accurately read out as a change in position. This equipment can be extremely helpful at sea in indicating deviations from the intended heading, such as steering errors.

Second generation Doppler navigational equipment

3706 A new generation of Doppler navigational instrumentation has been developed with two very different types of vessels primarily in mind; these are the "super-jumbo" tankers, displacing 300,000 tons or more, and research submarines, often termed deep-submergence vehicles.

These two highly diverse types have one characteristic in common —they are little affected by wave action. At its operating depths, the deep submergence vehicle will be quite unaffected by surface conditions, while the giant tanker, due to its enormous size, is much less affected than are most other surface ships.

Due to this greatly improved stability, the Doppler system developed for these ships does not employ the gyro-stabilized pendulous array of transducers described in the preceding articles. Instead, the four transducers are rigidly affixed to the ship's bottom plating, in such a position that under normal conditions of loading, their axes are directed downwards at a specific angle; usually they are located well forward of the midships point. Stabilization is achieved internally by electronic means.

This system of mechanically fixed transducers will perform the same functions and permit the same degree of accuracy as discussed above, and the system should greatly benefit both types of vessels. The deep submergence vehicle, operating in a medium which cuts off almost all conventional types of navigation, is no longer at the mercy of bottom currents of unknown set and drift. It can complete an accurate and detailed survey of the ocean floor, and return to the point from which the survey was started.

For the giant tanker, this equipment furnishes a continuous and accurate DR plot at sea; it is of even greater benefit when entering or operating in port. Due to the great draft of these ships, often well in excess of 80 feet (24 m), they cannot rely on the usual markers to keep in safe waters. Instead, they must often restrict their movements to a limited portion of the normally used channel. The Doppler system will be of the greatest assistance in such operations, and can often warn of potential trouble before it can be detected by plotting visual bearings.

Doppler in docking tankers

3707 Pilots and conning officers have frequently experienced difficulty in sensing slight lateral motion in these big ships during the final stages of coming alongside a berth. Due to the tremendous inertia involved, serious damage can result from even a comparatively slight contact with a pier or camel.

To detect such slight motion, a more sensitive "mooring mode" can be used, or a pair of auxiliary transducers may be installed well aft. These are placed on the athwartships axis, and are intended solely to detect lateral or turning motion when coming alongside a pier and when the engines are stopped. Propeller noise would seriously affect their efficiency when underway.

Summary

3708 Doppler navigation using acoustic waves is a highly specialized form of marine navigation. Practical equipment has been developed and is in regular use, but further development is likely. It seems highly probable that performance and efficiency can be further improved. Doppler navigation will probably continue to be limited to specialized ships, but for them it should prove to be a most useful adjunct to their normal navigation equipment and techniques.

38 Navigational Computers

Introduction **3801** The basic methods used for obtaining navigational positioning information have not changed appreciably over the years, although some of the tools or instruments have. Acronyms and terms such as NAVDAC, MINDAC, VERDAN, MARDAN, SINS, INS, analog, and digital, are necessary to the navigator's vocabulary. These terms relate to computers; how computers affect the navigator, and some of the computers used in navigation, are described in this chapter.

Computers in navigation **3802** A computer is an electronic calculator especially designed for the solution of complex mathematical problems. When separate subsystems are combined to make a single complex navigational system, such as SINS (Chapter 35), the solution becomes much too involved and lengthy for the navigator to undertake using the old conventional methods. Therefore computers, with their essential mathematical programming and information storage capability, are employed to do the navigator's work. Computers are now installed in aircraft, submarines, and, in limited numbers, in surface vessels. They may be programmed for one specific task, as for Loran-C or Omega supplying a continuous latitude-longitude readout on an *x-y* plotter or on dials, or for a series of tasks, as when used in the *Integrated Navigation System* or INS (Article 3807). In order to provide answers to the various navigational problems, either an *analog* or a *digital* computer, or a combination of both, may be required.

Analog computers **3803** The *analog computer* solves a particular physical problem instantaneously through the use of an equivalent electrical circuit which is mathematically identical to the physical problem; that is, the electrical circuit selected is *analogous* to the problem.

It should be noted that the solution of the physical problem by the analog computer is instantaneous; in other words, the electrical analog produces a continuous solution at every instant of time. Generalizing, analog computers may be said to yield instantaneous solutions to time-varying physical problems. The analog computer is not versatile; if the physical problem itself, rather than merely its parameters, is changed, a new analog must be designed. Analog computers are therefore usually designed to furnish repeated solutions for a very specific type of problem. It is obvious that the accuracy of the solution of a physical problem by an electrical analog is limited by the circuit component tolerances. The limited versatility and precision of analog computers has led to the concentration of developmental work on digital computers.

Digital computers **3804** The *digital computer* may be defined as a machine which calculates the solution of a mathematical problem to any desired degree of numerical accuracy through a prearranged sequence or algorithm of simple arithmetic operations such as addition, subtraction, multiplication, and division. Most digital computers employ the *binary* code which uses only two digits, 0 and 1; electronically this can be off and on, pulse and no pulse, or high and low levels of voltage.

Several important advantages and disadvantages inherent in digital computers should be noted. The digital computer forms the solution through a sequence of arithmetic operations known as *instructions.* A *program* is defined as an ordered sequence of instructions. The digital computer performs only one of these operations or instructions at a time.

Clearly, the digital computer solution is *not* instantaneous, as it obviously requires a finite time to form and sum the first terms of the series expansion. However, it is important to note that the solution can be made more accurate by merely summing more terms. Finally the input variable need not be continuous; that is, the independent variable is treated as a discrete value, and the solution is the numerical result of the summation for that value.

The finite time required for the digital computer solution must be less than the time between significant changes of the input variable; otherwise, the solution would be seriously in error. Fortunately, the computation frequency of an electronic digital computer can be made much greater than the frequency of changes for most variables in the real world. The functions can be accomplished at the rate of 10 million or more operations per second.

A major advantage of the digital computer over the analog computer is its versatility. Analog computers usually require a hardware change to solve a new problem of a different form, but the digital computer may be reprogrammed to solve a new problem merely by rearranging the existing instructions already fed into the computer, or by preparing new instructions. In other words, a new problem of a different form merely requires a "software" change to the program of a digital computer.

NAVDAC **3805** The *NAV*igation *D*ata *A*ssimilation *C*omputer (NAVDAC) is a real-time (precise time or clock time), general-purpose, digital computer originally designed for the Polaris submarine program. This computer has four primary functions:

Functions *Coordination*—the control of all equipment in the entire system.
Data gathering for fixes from external fix sources.
Processing of fix data for reduction to SINS reset parameters.
Resetting SINS and *monitoring* results.

From these four functions it can be seen that NAVDAC is an integrator for the various navigational instruments, including the inertial system, velocity measuring devices, gyrocompasses, electronic navigation systems such as NAVSAT, Loran-C, Omega, and celestial altitude measuring instruments, etc. It is, in fact, the central system for combining the individual components into a single operating system. Data from the individual input sources are processed by NAVDAC, drawing, when necessary, on its data storage or "memory" component, and the resultant information is used to determine the corrections to be applied to SINS, to indicate ship's position, etc. The data storage component has a tremendous capacity; for example, it stores the sidereal hour angle and declination for each of about 200 stars. All data are regularly updated, as required.

Since NAVDAC uses more than one fix-determining input, it is able to filter the data received, correlate and weigh it, make logical and statistical decisions, perform coordinate conversions, and generate control functions. Consequently, a standard of accuracy and reliability previously unattainable is possible by means of the redundancy from multiple data sources. In addition to all this, the computer is able to carry out self-checking procedures for verifying the large number of computations that it has undertaken. NAVDAC has provided the accuracies commensurate with the requirements of marine navigation.

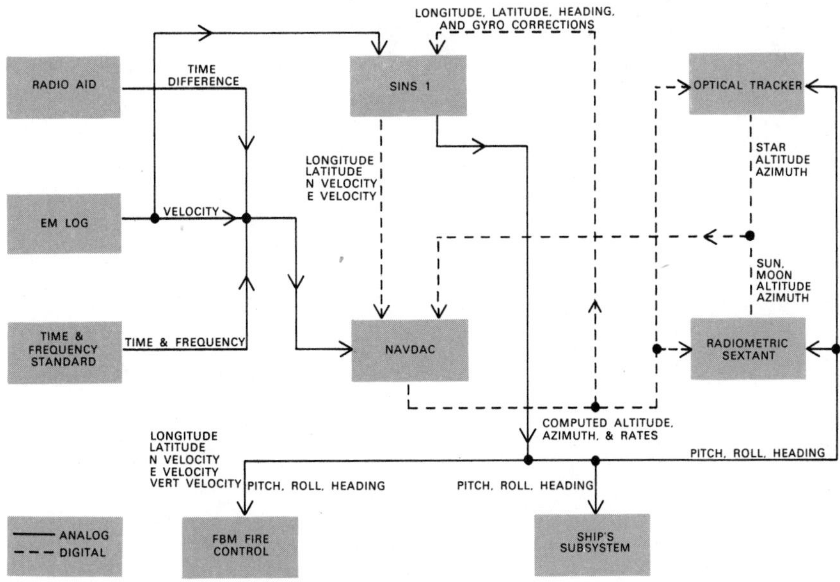

Figure 3805a. Block diagram of navigation system with NAVDAC.

Figure 3805a shows the role of NAVDAC in the operational system, together with its inputs and outputs, as well as its employment of both analog and digital computer information. Figure 3805b shows the NAVDAC data flow with input from an external electronic navigation system. Operation with any other system would differ only in the source and type of input. The function of the NAVDAC computer has been described as it is representative of the computer solution required for navigation of modern nuclear submarines. Other computers provide similar solutions. A later version, the MARDAN computer, used with the Autonetics N7F SINS, has a self-contained buffer allowing intercommunication with the other computers. It has a capacity of 4,096 words and a speed of up to 400 iterations per second. The Sperry SINDAC computer was shown in Figure 3507c, in a shipboard installation.

MINDAC **3806** The *M*iniature *I*nertial *N*avigation *D*igital *A*utomatic *C*omputer (MINDAC) is a general-purpose digital computer in a SINS system designed primarily to calculate present ship's position from heading and velocity input data, and to provide appropriate bias and torquing signals to the gyros in order to keep the SINS inertial platform aligned to the vertical. In addition, it provides periodic readout of the ship's velocity and position to the central data processor, and resets the platforms to the correct position when necessary at the operator's command.

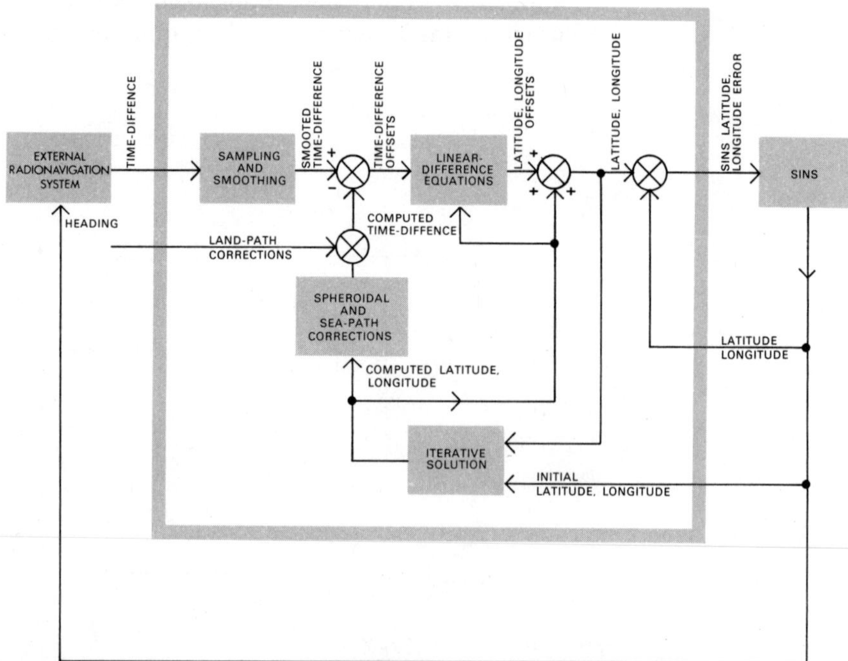

Figure 3805b. NAVDAC operation with input from an external radionavigation system.

While there are other computers that perform these same functions, MINDAC is the primary inertial platform alignment computer designed for use in the Integrated Navigation System described hereafter. It is also used aboard submarines and aircraft carriers with the Sperry Mk 3 Mod 6 SINS.

INS-Integrated Navigation System

3807 The *I*ntegrated *N*avigation *S*ystem (INS) consists of a Ship's Inertial Navigation System (SINS), to which are added an automatic star tracker, a multi-speed repeater, and instrumentation to provide accurate data on attitude (roll, pitch, and heading) for radar stabilization. The system also supplies velocity (north, east, or vertical), and latitude and longitude coordinates for ship control and navigation. The system is used aboard the NASA range instrumentation ships, which supplement the range-tracking stations established ashore in various parts of the world. For effective space-vehicle tracking and control, the positions of the tracking stations must be established to the closest possible tolerance; the navigational accuracy requirements for the range instrumentation ships are therefore unusually stringent.

As may be seen in Figure 3807, the INS receives inputs from a number of sources, processes the data, positions the star tracker (for day and night observations) and gives an output of navigation data and heading. This enables the proper positioning of the tracking equipment (radar) for immediate acquisition of the spacecraft. INS is a subsystem of the complete *S*hip's *P*osition and *A*ttitude *M*easurement *S*ystem, the components of which are also shown in Figure 3807.

Future computer use

3808 Other navigational computers are being developed; many of these are of a less-sophisticated type than those described. Such computers fall under two headings—those designed solely for navigation and those intended for general shipboard use on a shared-time basis. The latter type is of very considerable interest to operators of large commercial vessels, as it fits in well with the present trend towards automation in such ships.

It seems probable that all naval vessels of the destroyer type as well as many of the larger military planes, will, within the next decade, be equipped with digital computers designed for navigation. Such a computer might give a continuous DR readout in latitude and longitude, based on data received from the gyrocompass and ship's log, as does the *D*ead *R*eckoning *A*nalyzer *I*ndicator (DRAI) currently in use. However, with the computer, the DR position could be updated on command from the navigator, based on any navigational data obtained, even a single line of position. In such a case, the computer would select the most probable position, and give, in effect, an EP. The computer would have its own time source, in the form of a quartz crystal clock or even a cesium atomic time standard, and a memory section capable of storing the SHA and Declination of a limited num-

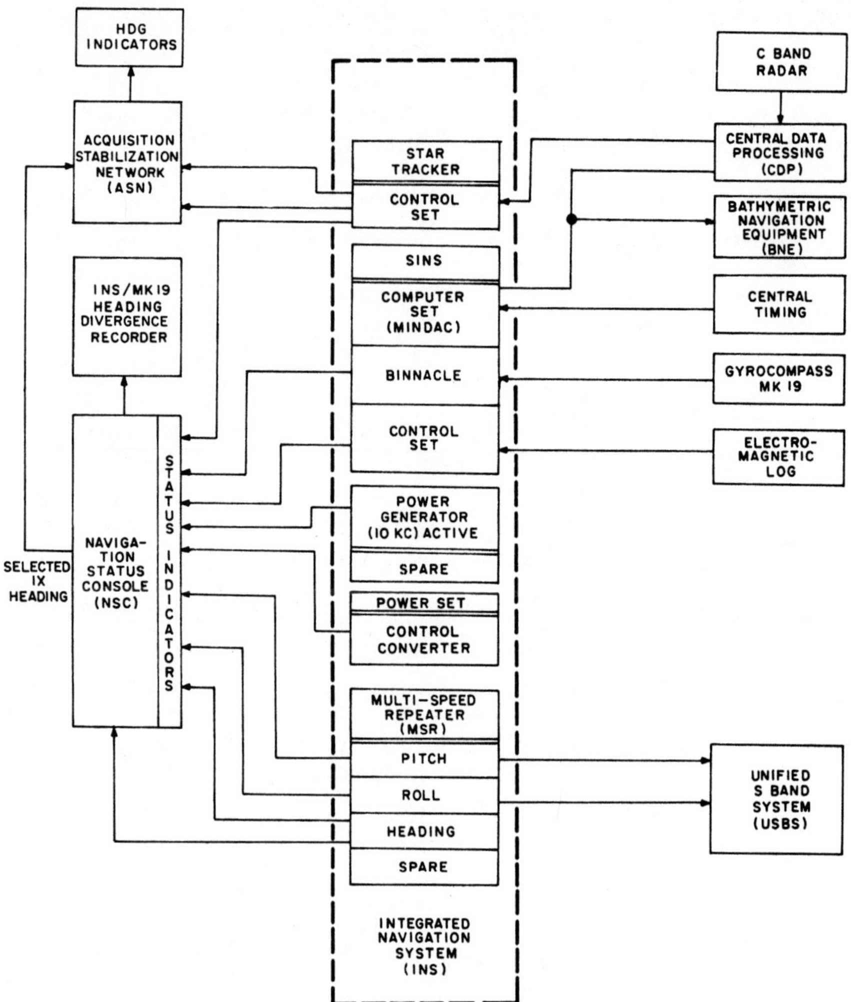

Figure 3807. INS data and signal inputs and outputs from and to external equipment.

ber of stars—those currently in use for morning and evening observations. GHA and Dec. of the sun, moon, and planets would be entered in the computer by means of a typewriter keyboard as required.

The computer would have a remote electronic readout of the altitude shown on the sextant; the latter would be fitted with a button to signal when the body was on the horizon, and the computer would note both time and altitude, and almost instantaneously reduce the sight for computed altitude and azimuth, and determine the intercept. Several observations would yield a satisfactory fix automatically, the computer being able to differentiate between an internal and external fix (Article 3009).

The navigator could thus take a considerable number of observations of each body, without ever losing it from view, and these observations would be averaged by the computer in order to determine an excellent fix.

When used with an electronic navigational system, such as Omega or Loran-C, it is possible for the computer to update position automatically and continuously, based on signals received from two or more stations. Such computers, programmed for use with Loran-C, are currently in use in aircraft.

Such a computer would have the capability of solving both plane and spherical triangles. Given ranges and bearings, obtained by radar, of a moving ship, it could determine the range, bearing, and time of the closest point of approach, and enable the conning officer to determine any required change in course or speed well before any danger of collision arose. Maneuvering board problems could be solved with equal speed. Great-circle distance and the initial heading for any destination from the ship's position could be determined almost instantaneously.

Computers in the merchant service

3809 *Data loggers* have been used with success to monitor the performance of both the main and auxiliary power plants aboard merchant ships for many years. Their function is to scan perhaps 300 or more test points at a rate of 2 to 25 or so points per second, depending on the required control. The scanning sensors are transducers which have high-speed response, and which convert measurements into electrical signals. These signals are converted by the data logger for display, and an alarm may be actuated if any signal exceeds a safe value.

Data loggers

The data logger has greatly increased power-plant efficiency; however, unlike the computer, it cannot exert any control function. The growing trend towards automation in the merchant service and the decreasing cost of computers, combined with increased reliability, versatility, and flexibility, all lead towards the increased use of computers in merchant ships. These computers are generally of the multipurpose type, and are programmed to serve several or all the ship's departments. In the engine room, such a computer can carry out all the functions of a data logger, and, in addition, it can be programmed to take immediate corrective action when required. The fresh water supply can be monitored, and the evaporaters started as needed. All in all, it can make possible a reduction of a number of men in the engineering spaces of a ship.

The computer can also be extremely valuable for navigation. In merchantmen, the mate on watch traditionally has performed all the navigator's duties during his tour on the bridge. Sight reduction and plotting can be time consuming, and sometimes have to be slighted when other immediate problems demand attention. The computer can be programmed to do all this; in fact, if desired, it could be designed to perform all the navigational functions described in Article 3808.

Of particular interest to commercial operators is the use of the computer for ship weather routing (Chapter 41). The computer's memory section can store data on the ship's resistance moment, performance under various conditions of load, draft, sea state, and the resulting motion. Based on these data, and an input of weather and sea state reports, the computer can supply an immediate recommendation on the optimum course and speed to be employed.

It is expected that this ability of the computer to recommend optimum course and speed under conditions of adverse weather, as well as the improved accuracy in navigation it permits, will lead to greatly increased economy of operation.

Trend to automation The trend towards automation in the merchant marine is worldwide, and is resulting in increasing economy of operation. A Japanese supertanker of 205,000 deadweight tons operates with a crew of only 32 men, as compared to the 42-man crew required for a slightly older 130,000-ton tanker. The *SS Mormacargo* in 1964 was the first U.S. flag merchant ship to have engine controls operated directly from the bridge, thus permitting complete ship control by one man. It seems probable that in the future merchantmen will have all monitoring and computer readouts presented in consoles in the wheelhouse.

Summary **3810** The computers discussed in this chapter have yielded standards of accuracy and speed of solution that would have seemed incredible to the navigator only a few years ago; they are representative of the finest navigational computers presently available. However, the state of the art in the field of computers is advancing extremely rapidly, particularly in microminiaturization; and new computers, combining greater accuracy, versatility, reliability, and speed with lesser space and power requirements are becoming available.

Personal electronic calculators of hand-held size have been developed to such an advanced capability that they can almost be considered small computers. These devices can be programmed from their keyboards or from instructions stored on magnetic cards or plug-in modules; they have considerable storage capacity in memory registers and can read data in and out from magnetic cards. Some models can provide printed outputs of programs, results, etc. Several specialized calculators are available with all necessary programs permanently wired into their circuitry. (See Appendix F.)

The steady advance of technology, particularly in solid-state electronics, can be expected to exert a continuing influence on instrumentation and data processing in all branches of navigation.

39 Lifeboat Navigation

Introduction **3901** The preceding chapters have dealt with navigation as practiced aboard a well-equipped vessel. Lifeboat navigation is very different; only minimal facilities are available for the navigator, and even the basic instruments, such as a sextant, may be lacking. In addition, lifeboat navigation differs in that it is impossible to travel any considerable distance to windward even in a powered lifeboat, and in that any destination must be carefully selected. It is also impossible to bring a lifeboat in to a beach through heavy surf without risking the loss of all hands; this has a direct bearing on the selection of a landfall and navigation toward it.

As long as ships ply the seas, ships will be lost, and the prudent navigator must plan ahead for the possibility that his ship may be one of them. He cannot expect that there will be sufficient time to organize his equipment after the word is passed to abandon ship. In addition to being thoroughly familiar with the use of available equipment, he must be able to improvise and must know what is possible if either sextant, watch, reduction tables, or almanac is lost.

Procedure after abandoning ship *The first consideration after abandoning ship is to determine whether to remain as close as possible to the scene, or try to reach land or a heavily traveled shipping lane.* This decision will generally depend on whether or not a distress signal was sent, and acknowledged, before the ship was abandoned, and when help might be expected.

If no assistance can be expected, the navigator must always bear in mind that long voyages in poorly equipped lifeboats can be made, as proved by Captain Bligh, of HMS *Bounty,* who sailed 3,000 miles when cast adrift in an open boat. He must also remember that morale is a factor of the highest importance if a long journey is to be completed successfully.

Preparation for an emergency **3902** The best way to lessen the degree of an emergency is to always be prepared for it. When the emergency occurs, it may be too late to "plan"; only "execution" is possible. There are several ways to prepare for the emergency of abandoning ship. The surest way is to make up an emergency navigational kit for each lifeboat and life raft, place it in a waterproof container, and lash it securely in place. The following items are desirable even if they cannot all be included in a kit for each lifeboat.

Charts. The best charts for lifeboat use are pilot charts for the area to be traveled. Both winter and summer charts should be included. The aircraft position charts, published by the National Ocean Survey, are also excellent. They are prepared on the Lambert conformal conic projection; in addition to variation, they give data permitting the plotting of lines of position from Consol stations, if within an area of coverage, and if a radio receiver is available. Other plotting materials that may prove useful include a pad of Maneuvering Board sheets (the 10-inch DMAHC Chart 5091 will be more convenient in a lifeboat than the 20-inch Chart 5092) and sheets of graph paper, preferably graduated in five or ten lines per inch.

Sextant. If possible, the ship's sextant should be taken into a lifeboat. If this is not possible, there are inexpensive plastic ones that should be in each boat; these are sufficiently precise and accurate for lifeboat navigation.

Almanac and star chart. If at all possible a *Nautical Almanac* and a *Star Finder* should be available. Failing the latter, charts in the *Nautical Almanac* may be used, although many navigators prefer the star chart included in the *Air Almanac;* the star chart from an old almanac may be saved for emergency use. A *Long-term Almanac* is included in *Bowditch,* Volume II (1975), Appendix H. With the instructions for its use and auxiliary tables, it comprises six pages and supplies ephemeristic data on the sun and 30 of the selected stars. It does not become outdated and is surprisingly accurate; the maximum error in altitude computed by it should not exceed 2.0′ for the sun, and 1.3′ for the stars. It is wise to have these pages photocopied and included with each set of sight reduction tables to be used in boats. It is necessary to include copies of the refraction and dip tables from the *Nautical Almanac,* as these tables are not a part of the *Bowditch Long-term Almanac.* Copies of almanacs for recent years can be put in lifeboat navigation kits with instructions on the simple corrections to be applied for use in the current year. These are usable for the sun, Aries, and stars, with data being sufficiently accurate for emergency situations.

Tables. Although the two volumes of *Bowditch* constitute a considerable bulk to take into a lifeboat, consideration should be given to such action because of the vast amount of information contained therein. As an alternative, only Volume II with its tables, plus Chapter XXVI of Volume I, could be taken into the boats.

Volume II of *Bowditch* now includes the Ageton tables for sight reduction, formerly published separately as H.O. 211. These are the most compact set of tables for sight reduction; they are used from a DR position, which is sometimes advantageous in lifeboat navigation.

For vessels operating only in a relatively limited ocean area, or along repeated routes, photocopy extracts could be made of just those pages of Pub. No. 229 or 249 that might be needed.

A 10-inch slide rule with sine/cosine scales permits a rapid reduction of observations for altitudes and azimuths. Equations for use with slide rules are given in Article 3912. Altitudes to 30° may be solved to an accuracy of about 2′ if care is used; an accuracy of roughly 5′ may be obtained up to 50°. Electronic hand calculators, which have almost completely replaced slide rules in recent years, are of no value in lifeboats because of their dependence upon batteries that will quickly become discharged with no power source for recharging.

Battery-powered radio. A small transistorized radio receiver can be of great value in obtaining time signals, especially if it has a short-wave band. It should be used sparingly to conserve battery power; spare batteries should be brought into the lifeboat if available and time permits.

EPIRB. Although not directly related to the navigation effort being made in the lifeboat, each such craft should be equipped with an *Electronic Position Indicating Radiobeacon* (EPIRB). This small unit transmits a distinctive signal on the emergency frequencies (121.5 and 243.0 MHz) guarded by long-range civil and military aircraft; it can be received by high-flying planes out as far as 200 miles (370 km). An EPIRB can serve not only to alert authorities of a ship sinking, but also subsequently as a navigation aid for aircraft and ships searching for survivors.

Radar reflector. Folding radar reflectors are available, made of metal mesh or aluminum sheets. Such a reflector returns a strong echo, and will make it much easier for search craft to locate a lifeboat by radar, particularly if the reflector is elevated. Aluminum kitchen foil may serve as a substitute but with much less effectiveness.

Plastic bags. Fairly heavy plastic bags, such as are used for packaging ice cubes, are invaluable for storing books, instruments, radio, etc., and keeping them dry in a lifeboat.

Notebook. Various items of general information from this chapter and any other desired information should be copied in advance. *Do not depend on memory.* Enough blank pages should be left to permit computations and a log to be kept.

Plotting equipment. Be sure to include pencils, erasers, a protractor (very important), and some kind of straightedge, preferably one graduated in inches. Dividers and compasses may prove useful, but are not essential. A knife or some means of sharpening pencils should be provided.

American flag merchant ships are required by law to keep much equipment in their lifeboats; however, this is all survival gear, and includes no navigational equipment beyond a simple magnetic compass.

In addition to water, rations, and equipment such as a jacknife, bailers, boathooks, buckets, etc., the required equipment includes a first aid kit, two signaling mirrors, storm oil, a sea anchor or drogue, a fishing kit, lifesaving signals or flares, a signaling whistle, and a desalting kit.

In addition to physical items of equipment, knowledge of certain facts is most useful and may be of great value under some conditions. Typical of such items are:

Positions. The approximate latitude and longitude of several ports, islands, etc., in the area in which the ship operates. This will prove useful if no chart is available. In addition, the approximate position of the ship should be known at all times. A general knowledge of the charts of the region in which the ship operates is often useful.

Currents. A general knowledge of the principal ocean currents in the operating area is valuable if no current chart is available.

Weather. A general knowledge of weather is useful. The particular information of value in emergencies is a knowledge of prevailing winds at different seasons in the operating area, and the ability to detect early signs of approaching storms and predict their paths relative to the course of the lifeboat.

Stars. The ability to identify stars may prove valuable, particularly if no star chart is available.

Whatever plan is adopted for preparation in case of an emergency, be sure there is a definite plan. Do not wait until the order to "abandon ship" to decide what to do. It may then be too late.

Abandoning ship

3903 When the abandon ship order is given, the amount of preparation that can be made for navigation will depend on the time available. There is usually some warning. There are some things that must of necessity be left to the last moment, but it is not wise to add unnecessarily to the list. All actions in support of lifeboat navigation that will be required in an actual emergency should be a part of every abandon-ship drill.

A check-off list should be available without a search. The number of items on it will depend on the degree of preparation that has been made. The following minimum list assumes that a full navigational kit is available in the lifeboat. Anything short of this should be taken into consideration in making the check-off list. Before leaving the ship, check the following:

Watch error. Determine the error and write it down. Be sure you know what kind of time your watch is keeping. Do not attempt to set it, but see that it is wound. It may be possible to take along a chronometer. Wristwatches of the "quartz" type, especially if their rate is known, may provide time of fully sufficient accuracy for lifeboat navigation; they do not require winding and generally are quite water-resistant, making them suitable for the wet environment of a boat.

Date. Check the date and write it down in the notebook, note the zone time being maintained.

Position. Write down the position of the ship. If possible, record also the set and drift of the current and the latitude and longitude of the nearest land in several directions. It may be easier to take along the chart or plotting sheet giving this information.

Navigational equipment. Check the navigational equipment in the boat. Look particularly to see that there is a compass, chart, and watch. If anything is missing, is it possible to get it from the ship? Do not abandon the ship's sextant. If a portable radio is available, take it along.

See that all equipment is properly secured before lowering the boat.

Getting organized

3904 The first few hours in a lifeboat may prove the most important. If medicine for seasickness is available, take it at once, even before leaving the ship, if possible.

There must be a definite understanding of who is to be in charge, not to exercise autocratic rule, but to regulate the cramped life in the lifeboat and avoid confusion. Extreme fairness and equality are important if good teamwork and high morale are to be maintained.

If there are several boats in the water, considerable advantage is to be gained by their staying close together, if possible.

Before setting out on any course, it is important to make an *estimate of the situation.* Do not start out until you know where you are going, and determine this carefully and deliberately. This may be the most important decision of the entire journey. Make it carefully.

First, determine the number of watches available and determine as accurately as possible the error of each watch. Learn from each owner all that is available regarding the rate and reliability of his timepiece. Record this information and establish a regular routine for winding the watches and checking them.

Record the best-known latitude and longitude of the point of departure and the time of day. Let this be the beginning of a carefully kept log.

In choosing the first course, carefully study all factors. *Do not set the course until you are sure the best possible one has been determined.*

A number of factors will influence the decision. If a pilot chart is available, study it minutely and be sure you are thoroughly familiar with the average current and prevailing winds to be expected. Consider the motive power available and the probable speed. It may be better to head for land some distance away, if wind and current will help, than for nearby land which will be difficult to reach.

Note the location of the usually traveled shipping routes. These are shown on the pilot chart. If more than one suitable course is available, choose the one that will take you nearest to well-traveled shipping routes. Remember, in selecting a course, that the upwind range of even a powered lifeboat is very limited. Captain Bligh knew that there were islands within about 200 miles upwind, but he knew he could not reach them; his decision to take the long 3000-mile downwind journey made survival possible.

Consider the size and height of any nearby land, and the navigation equipment available. Remember that the horizon is quite close when the observer is standing in a lifeboat: the distance to the horizon in miles is about 1.15 times the square root of the height of eye in feet. Consider the probable accuracy with which positions can be determined. A small low island some distance away may be extremely hard to find with crude navigational methods; it may be advantageous to head for a more distant, but higher and more easily seen, landfall.

If the destination is on a continental land mass at a known latitude, it is often wise to direct one's course toward a point somewhat north or south of that place, and then when land is reached, run south or north along the coastline to the objective. This will eliminate the uncertainty as to which way to turn that will exist if land is reached at what is believed to be the correct latitude, but the destination is not sighted.

Will accurate time be available? Remember that the latitude can be determined accurately without time, but the longitude will be no more accurate than the time. If there is any question of the ability to maintain reasonably accurate time (each four seconds error in time results in 1′ error in the longitude), do not head straight for the destination, but for a point that is certain to take the boat to the east or west of the destination, and when the latitude of the destination has been reached, head due east or west and maintain the latitude. This method was successfully used for centuries before the invention of the chronometer.

If adequate distress signals were sent before abandoning ship, and it is to be expected that rescue ships or planes will conduct a search, it will probably be best to remain near to the last reported position of the ship.

Having decided upon the course to follow and the probable average speed, including help from current and wind, estimate the time of reaching the destination and set the ration of water and food accordingly.

Determine the knowledge, ability, and aptitude of all aboard and assign each definite responsibilities. *Establish a definite routine.*

Morale **3905** An important part of the trip back to safety is the maintaining of a high morale. With great determination and cool judgment almost any difficulty can be overcome. This is proved by many great tales of the sea. The story of Captain Bligh, previously mentioned, is perhaps one of the greatest illustrations of the value of patience and determination.

A regular routine and a definite assignment of duties is valuable from the standpoint of morale. Include in the routine regular periods for reading aloud from the Bible if one is available. This will not only provide a means of occupying time, but will constitute a source of encouragement and add to the faith and determination of the crew. Remember, also, the high value placed on prayer by those who have been through the experience of abandoning a ship at sea.

Morale and navigation are closely interrelated. Good health and morale will materially aid in the practice of good navigation. The capability to navigate adequately will definitely contribute toward hope of survival, an essential ingredient of good morale.

Dead reckoning

3906 *Dead reckoning* is always important, but never more so than when in a lifeboat. Determine as accurately as possible the point of departure and keep a record of courses, speeds, estimated currents, and leeway. Do not be too quick to abandon a carefully determined EP for an uncertain fix by crude methods. Unless really accurate methods of navigation are available, consider all positions as EP's and carefully evaluate all information available. The real test of a navigator is how accurately he can evaluate the information at hand and from it determine the true position of his vessel. Upon this ability may depend the question of whether the lifeboat arrives at its destination.

Take full advantage of all conditions. When the wind is favorable, make all the distance possible in the desired direction. It may sometimes be advantageous to change course slightly to make greater speed in a direction differing somewhat from the desired course. If the wind is definitely unfavorable, put out a sea anchor and reduce the leeway.

Attempt to keep a plot of the track of the boat. Plotting in an open boat may be difficult; it may be easier to keep account of movements mathematically by means of the traverse table in Article 3909.

Direction

3907 At the very start of the voyage it is well to check the accuracy of the compass on the course to be steered. The variation can be determined from the pilot chart, but to find the deviation, if this is not accurately known, locate a bit of wreckage in the water or throw overboard a life preserver or other object that will not drift too much with the wind and take the reciprocal magnetic course to the one desired. After this has been followed for some distance (a half mile to a mile), turn and steer for the object. If there is no deviation, the compass course will be the reciprocal of that first steered. If it is not, the desired compass course is half way between the reciprocal of the first course and the compass course back to the object.

Underway the compass error should be checked at regular intervals. In the northern hemisphere Polaris can be considered to be due north except in very high latitudes (above L 60° N the maximum error is greater than 2°). When Polaris is directly above or below the pole the azimuth is 000° in any latitude. When the sun, or any body, reaches its highest altitude, it can be considered to be on the celestial meridian, bearing 180° or 000°. These are true directions, and yield compass error directly, not deviation.

If an almanac and a method of computation are available, the true direction of any body can be determined at any time, by the usual methods of computing azimuth.

If a compass is not available, an approximation of a straight course can be steered by towing a line secured at the gunwale amidships. If the boat deviates from a straight track, the line will move away from its neutral position approximately parallel to the side of the boat. With a cross sea this method is least accurate but may be better than nothing at all. Do *not* steer by a cloud on or near the horizon; these move with the wind and a curved, rather than straight, track will result.

At night the boat can be kept on a reasonably straight course north, east, or west by steering for Polaris or a body near the prime vertical.

Speed **3908** Throughout the trip, speed should be determined as accurately as possible. Ability to estimate speed will be developed by practice. One crude method of measuring the speed is to throw a floating object overboard at the bow and note the time required for the boat to pass it. For this purpose a definite distance should be marked off along the gunwale. Make this as long as convenient, but an easily used length—25 feet, 16.7 feet, 20 feet, 10 feet, etc.—a length that will facilitate calculations. A boat traveling 100 feet (30.5 m) in 1 minute is moving at a speed of 1 knot. If possible, mark off a length that is divisible into 100 (or 30.5) a whole number of times. If, for example, the length marked off is 25 feet (7.6 m) and an object is thrown over at the forward mark, it should be opposite the second mark in 15 seconds if the boat is making 1 knot, 7.5 seconds if 2 knots, 5 seconds if 3 knots, etc. If the distance is 16.7 feet, the time should be 10 seconds for 1 knot, 5 seconds for 2 knots, etc. A table or curve of speed vs. time can easily be made. Speed determined in this way is relative to the *water* and not speed made good over the bottom.

Since the objects available for throwing overboard may be scarce, attach a light line to the object and secure the other end to the boat, so that it can be recovered and used again. A small drogue can be improvised from light cloth and light cord, such as a fishing line, which makes a good log line. Knot the line at intervals similar to those listed above or multiples of these. As the drogue is streamed aft, with the line permitted to run out freely, the time between the passage of two knots through the hand is noted. The drogue should be some distance astern before starting to take time; the knot at which time is started should therefore be 25 feet (7.6 m) or so forward of the drogue. *Be sure the line can run out freely.*

Even without a watch, the method can still be used. A member of the crew who has practiced with a chronometer, such as a quartermaster who has been responsible for checking a comparing watch with a chronometer, may have become quite proficient at counting seconds and half seconds. A half-second counter can be improvised by making a simple pendulum. Attach any small heavy weight to a light line. If the pendulum is 9.8 inches long (24.9 cm) to the center of the weight, the period (over and back) is 1 second. If the length is 39.1 inches (99.3 cm) long, the period is 2 seconds.

Traverse table **3909** A simple traverse table may have many uses. In the table below, the course is given in the first four columns, the difference of latitude in minutes per mile distance along the course in the fifth, and the departure or miles east or west per mile distance in the sixth. To find *l* and p multiply the tabulated value by the distance.

Course				*l*	p
°	°	°	°		
000	180	180	360	1.00	0.00
005	175	185	355	1.00	0.09
010	170	190	350	0.98	0.17
015	165	195	345	0.97	0.26
020	160	200	340	0.94	0.34
025	155	205	335	0.91	0.42
030	150	210	330	0.87	0.50
035	145	215	325	0.82	0.57
040	140	220	320	0.77	0.64
045	135	225	315	0.71	0.71
050	130	230	310	0.64	0.77
055	125	235	305	0.57	0.82
060	120	240	300	0.50	0.87
065	115	245	295	0.42	0.91
070	110	250	290	0.34	0.94
075	105	255	285	0.26	0.97
080	100	260	280	0.17	0.98
085	095	265	275	0.09	1.00
090	090	270	270	0.00	1.00

This table can be used for the solution of any right triangle. For the distance covered by a lifeboat during one day, the earth can be considered a plane without appreciable error. Apply the difference in latitude to the latitude at the beginning of the run. To convert p to DLo, multiply p by the factor taken from the table below. The midlatitude is the entering argument. Both difference of latitude and difference of longitude are in minutes. The course indicates the direction in which to apply them.

Lm	p to DLo	Lm	p to DLo	Lm	p to DLo
°		°		°	
0	1.00	30	1.15	60	2.00
5	1.00	35	1.22	65	2.37
10	1.02	40	1.30	70	2.92
15	1.04	45	1.41	75	3.86
20	1.06	50	1.56	80	5.76
25	1.10	55	1.74	85	11.47

A photocopy of these above two tables should be made and fastened into the notebook which is a part of the lifeboat navigation kit.

Example: A lifeboat leaves Lat. 28°37′ S, Long. 160°12′ E and follows course 240° for 80 miles.

Required: The latitude and longitude at the end of this run.

Solution: Enter the first table with C 240° and find $l = 0.50$, p = 0.87. Since the distance is 80 miles, the difference in latitude is 80 × 0.50 = 40′. Since the course is 240°, this is a southerly change; hence the latitude after the run is 28°37′ S + 40′ S = 29°17′ S.

Enter the second table with the mid-latitude 29° S and take out "p to DLo" as 1.14 by interpolation. The DLo is then 80 × 0.87 × 1.14 = 79′; this is westerly. Thus, the longitude after the run is 160°12′ E − 79′ W = 158°53′ E.

Answer: Lat. 29°17′ S, Long. 158°53′ E.

If desired, the values of l and p can be found graphically by constructing the triangle of Figure 3909a. A Maneuvering Board (Chapter 14) is useful for this purpose, but not essential. The conversion from p to DLo can also be made graphically, as shown in Figure 3909b. However, it is usually as easy to plot directly on a chart or plotting sheet as to make graphical solutions in the way just described.

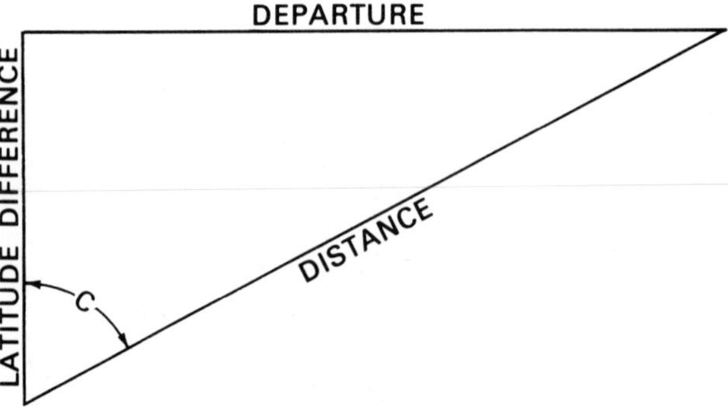

Figure 3909a. Traverse sailing.

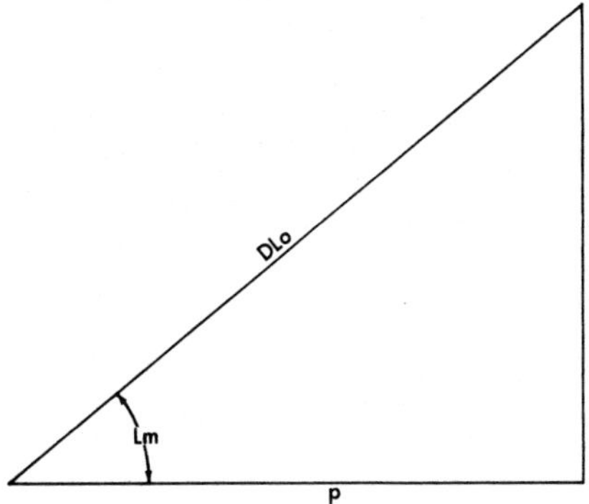

Figure 3909b. Converting p to dLo graphically.

Measuring altitudes **3910** If a sextant is available, altitudes of celestial bodies are measured as described in Chapter 21. Be sure to determine the index correction. To assure optimum observations, when using a sextant in a lifeboat or in any other small craft, the observer should obtain his altitude at the instant the crest of a wave is directly under his position in the boat. If no sextant is available altitudes can be measured in several ways, including the following:

Protractor. A protractor, a Maneuvering Board fastened securely to a board, or any graduated circle or semicircle can be used in any of several ways. The astrolabe used before the sextant was invented employed the same principle as the methods described hereafter.

In Figure 3910a a weight is attached to the center of curvature by a string that crosses the outer scale. If an AN plotter (Article 312) is used, a hole for attaching the string is already provided. The observer sights along the straightedge of the protractor, *AB,* towards the body. Another person reads the point on the scale where it is crossed by the string. This is the zenith distance if the protractor is graduated as shown in Figure 3910a; the altitude is 90° minus this reading. In Figure 3910a, the reading is 62° and hence the observed altitude is 28°. Several readings should be taken, some with the protractor reversed; all of these are averaged for a more accurate value. This method should not be used for the sun unless the eyes are adequately protected.

In Figure 3910b the weight is attached to a pin at the center of curvature and the protractor held horizontally, as indicated by the string crossing at 90°. The assistant holds the protractor and keeps the string on 90°. The observer moves a pin, pencil point, or other thin object along the scale until this pin and the center one are in line with the body. The body is then in direction *AB*. When the protractor is used in this way, the altitude is indicated directly. In Figure 3910b an altitude of about 48° is being measured. This method should not be used for the sun unless the eyes are protected.

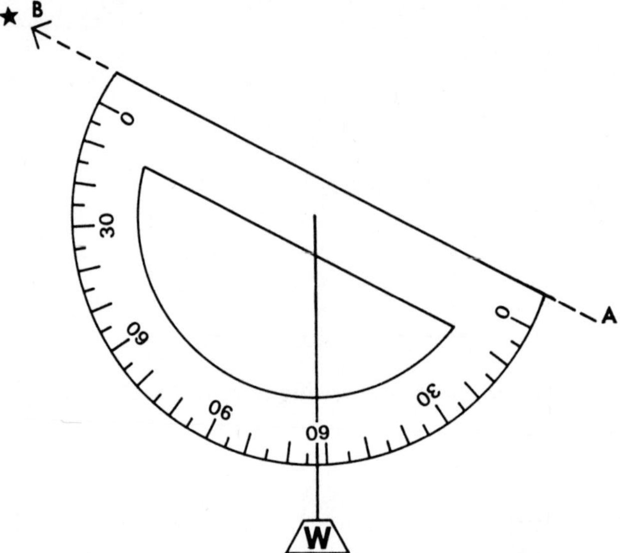

Figure 3910a. Measuring zenith distance with a protractor.

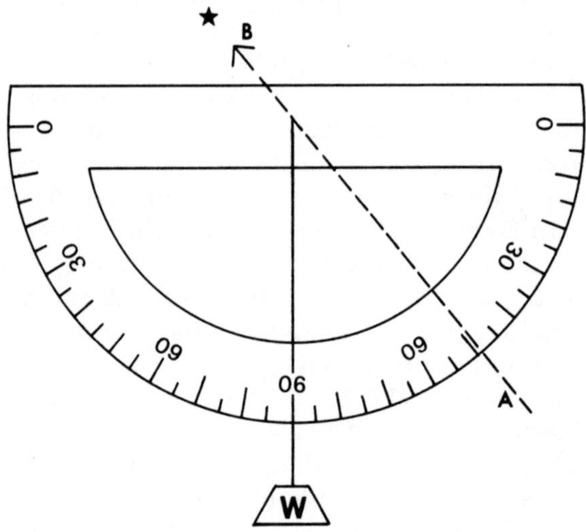

Figure 3910b. Measuring altitude with a protractor.

For the sun either of the above methods can be used if a pin is mounted at the plane of the protractor. In the first method the reading is made when the shadow of the pin falls on 0°. In the second method the reading is made at the shadow.

There are several other variations of the use of the protractor. In the second method the weight can be omitted and the assistant can sight along the straightedge at the horizon. An observation can be made without the assistant if the weight is attached at the scale at 90°

and a loop of string placed over the pin at the center of curvature for holding the device. If preferred, the handle can be attached at 90° on the scale and the weight at the center of curvature, the protractor being inverted. The first method can be used without an assistant if the string is secured in place by the thumb and forefinger when the observation is made.

If no protractor is available, but there is handy a Maneuvering Board pad, one of these sheets may be fastened to any flat surface that can be raised to eye level. The same procedures are used as with a more conventional protractor; pins stuck into the board make sighting easier and more accurate.

If no scale graduated in degrees is available, place two pins or nails in a board and attach a weight to *B* by means of a string (Figure 3910c). Sight along *AB* and line up the two pins with the body. If the sun is being observed, hold the board so that the shadow of *B* falls on *A*. When *A* and *B* are lined up with the body, secure the string in place with the thumb and forefinger. From *A* draw *AC* perpendicular to the string. The traverse table can then be used to find the angle, entering the difference of latitude column with length *BC* or the departure column with *AC*. In either case the length is given in units of *AB*. That is, if *AB* is 10 inches, the length *BC* or *AC* in inches is divided by 10 before entering the table. A simple way is to divide *AC* by *BC* and use the table below, entering the L/H column with *AC*/*BC*.

Length of shadow. If a bucket or other container is available, altitudes of the sun can be determined by measuring the length of a shadow. Drive a nail or other pointer in a board and float the board on water. The top of the pointer should be pointed for accurate results. If a nail is used, drive it through the board and turn the board over. Measure carefully the length of the shadow. Turn the board approximately

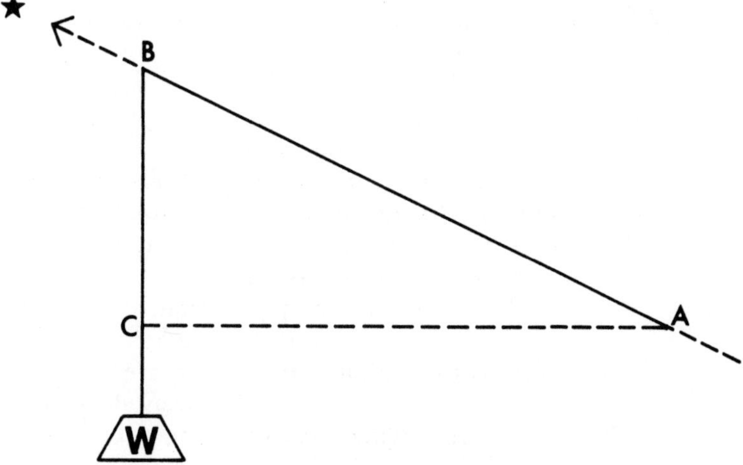

Figure 3910c. Measuring altitude without a protractor.

180° in azimuth and measure again. Divide the average of the two readings by the height of the pin and enter the following table (or any table of natural cotangents) to find the altitude.

Alt.	L/H	Alt.	L/H	Alt.	L/H
°		°		°	
5	11.430	35	1.428	65	0.466
10	5.671	40	1.192	70	0.364
15	3.732	45	1.000	75	0.268
20	2.747	50	0.839	80	0.176
25	2.145	55	0.700	85	0.087
30	1.732	60	0.577	90	0.000

In this table L is the length of the shadow and H is the pin height.

Example: The length of the shadow of a pin 4 inches long is 6.3 inches, or similar dimensions in metric units.

Required: The altitude of the sun.

Solution: $L/H = 6.3 \div 4 = 1.575$. Interpolating in the table, the altitude is found to be 32.6°.

Answer: h = 33°.

Note: In all calculations of lifeboat navigation, care must be taken *not* to carry the calculations to a finer degree of precision than is warranted by the input data. In the above example, the length of the pin was stated to be 4 inches—this is one significant figure. It would be unwarranted, with such an imprecise statement of one element of the equation, to state altitude to the tenth of a degree, three significant figures in this example; even the exactness of "33 degrees" is less than justified by this method and with this data. In lifeboat navigation it is self-delusion (perhaps dangerously so) to carry calculations to the same degree of refinement as done on a large ship. Even if a marine sextant and exact time by radio is available, the movement of a small boat, the uncertainty of the height of the observer's eye, and similar factors, do not justify position measurements more precise than a whole minute and azimuths to a whole degree, and even this precision is subject to question.

When using any of the methods described, several observations should be made and the average used, with the average time. If possible, reverse the device for half the readings.

Whatever method is used, *measure* the altitude, however crude the method. Do not attempt to estimate it, for estimates are seldom as accurate as the crudest measurement. If a damaged sextant is available, try to repair it. If the mirrors are broken, plain glass held in place by chewing gum or anything else available will usually be satisfactory.

Before leaving the measurement of altitudes, it might be well to point out that at sunrise or sunset the observed altitude (Ho) is − 50′. To this must be added (numerically) the dip correction.

Correction of measured altitudes

3911 If altitudes are measured from the visible horizon, they are corrected in the usual way, as explained in Chapter 21. Altitudes of the sun should be corrected for refraction, mean semidiameter, and dip. Altitudes of stars should be corrected for refraction and dip. If a weight is used to establish the vertical, or if the length of a shadow is measured, there is no correction for dip. If the sun's altitude is measured by means of a shadow, whether the length of the shadow is measured or the shadow falls across a scale or another pin, the center of the sun is measured, and hence no correction for semidiameter is needed. Approximate altitude corrections can be found as follows:

Alt.	°	5		6		7		8		10		12		15		21		33		63		90
Corr.	′		9		8		7		6		5		4		3		2		1		0	

Refraction. The critical type table shown above provides refraction corrections from 5° to 90°. If crude methods of observing the altitudes are employed, it may be sufficiently accurate to apply the correction only to the nearest 0.1°. For this procedure, altitudes above 20° can be considered to have no correction and those between 5° and 20° to have a correction of 0.1°. Observations below 5° should not be made if they can be avoided. The correction for refraction is always subtractive, and must be applied to observations of all bodies, regardless of the method used.

If a slide rule is available, the refraction correction for altitudes above 10° may be found accurately by multiplying the cotangent of the altitude by 0.96.

Mean semidiameter. The mean semidiameter of the sun is 16′ and the actual value does not differ from this by more than 0.3′. If the lower limb is observed, the correction is (+) and if the upper limb is observed, the correction is (−).

Dip. The correction for dip, in minutes of arc, is equal to the square root of the height of eye in feet, to sufficient accuracy for lifeboat use. (The *Nautical Almanac* tables do not give a dip correction for height of eye less than 8 feet or 2.4 m). This correction is used for all bodies whenever the visible horizon is used as a reference; it is always (−). Dip may be determined more exactly with a slide rule; multiply the square root of the height of eye in feet by 0.97, or the square root of the height of eye in meters by 1.76.

Parallax. No correction is made for parallax, unless the moon is used, for it is too small to be a consideration for lifeboat navigation when other bodies are observed.

Horizon sights

3912 A line of position may be obtained without a sextant or other altitude-measuring instrument by noting the time a celestial body makes contact with the visible horizon. The body most suitable for such observations is the sun, and either the upper or lower limb may be used; the best practice would be to time both when they contact the horizon, and use the mean of the two resulting intercepts. A pair of binoculars, if available, will assist in determining the instant of contact.

Such observations will usually yield surprisingly accurate results; they will certainly be more satisfactory than lines of position obtained from measurements made by improvised altitude measuring devices.

The uncorrected altitude is noted as 0°0′, and carefully corrected for dip, refraction, and semidiameter. The correction for dip is made by adding its value numerically to the value of the refraction correction. Thus if the semidiameter is 16.0′, and the height of eye is 6 feet 6 inches, the corrections to an upper limb sun horizon sight would be as follows:

Height of eye 6′6″	Dip	− 2.5′
0° H, Refraction		−34.5′
$\bar{\odot}$	SD	−16.0′
Correction		53.0′

The corrected altitude would be 0° minus 53.0′ or −53.0′. Under nonstandard atmospheric conditions, the additional corrections for temperature and barometric pressure should be applied, if a thermometer and barometer are available; in actual lifeboat circumstances, however, this is unlikely.

The sight may be reduced by the tables of Pub. No. 229 or the Ageton (H.O. 211) tables in *Bowditch,* Volume II. It must be remembered that when *both* Ho and Hc are negative, the intercept will be *"towards" if Ho is numerically less than Hc,* and vice versa.

Very low altitude sights may also be reduced very rapidly by means of a slide rule having sine/cosine scales using the equation

$$\sin Hc = \sin L \sin D \underset{\sim}{+} \cos L \cos d \cos t.$$

Hc is negative, if its sine is negative. Accurate solutions may be obtained at very low latitudes; as at altitudes below 2°, a sine may be read to about 0.2′ on a 10-inch slide rule. Azimuth angle may be obtained by means of the equation:

$$\sin Z = \frac{\cos d \sin t}{\cos Hc}$$

At very low altitudes, the division by cosine Hc may be ignored, as in such cases the cosine approaches unity. (See Article 2402 for naming the sign.)

Any low-altitude observations may yield results that are in error by a few miles under conditions of abnormal terrestrial refraction. However, Captain P. V. H. Weems, USN (Retired) made ten horizon sights at sea on six different occasions, which gave an average error of 1.95 miles (3.6 km) and a maximum error of 4.0 miles (7.4 km).

An azimuth of the sun should be obtained at the same time the horizon sight is made, as a check on the accuracy of the compass.

The green flash The *green flash* is a common phenomenon in the tropics, and occurs at the moment the sun's upper limb touches the horizon. It is caused by refraction of the light waves from the sun, as they pass through the earth's atmosphere. These light waves are not refracted, or bent, equally, the longer waves of red light being least refracted, the shorter blue and violet waves being more refracted. The red, orange, and yellow light is cut off by the horizon when the blue and violet light is still momentarily visible. These blue and violet rays cause the green flash.

It is estimated that at sea in the tropics, the green flash may be seen as often as 50 percent of the time; it is, of course, easier to observe at sunset. The green flash usually lasts for a period of between one-half and one second.

Using the time of the green flash to obtain a line of position is merely a variation of the horizon sight described in the previous article. It is somewhat easier to use the time of the flash than to determine the instant the sun's upper limb disappears below the horizon when there is no green flash.

The green flash sight is corrected and reduced similarly to the horizon sight, described above.

Lines of position **3913** If tables are available for computation of Hc, lines of position are used in the usual way, as explained in Chapter 25. However, if no such tables are available, latitude and longitude should be determined separately, as was done before the discovery of the line of position by Captain Sumner in 1837.

If accurate time is not available, it will not be possible to determine the longitude. In this case no attempt should be made to steer directly for the destination, unless a whole continent is involved. Instead, the course should be set for a point well to the eastward or westward of the destination and when the latitude has been reached, a course of 090° or 270°, as appropriate, should be followed, as mentioned earlier in the chapter. If a single wrist watch is used for time and the journey is likely to be a long one, the time may be of questionable accuracy before the end of the voyage. If the watch is in error by 1 minute, the longitude will be inaccurate by 15′. If the destination is a small island, the course should be set for a point 50 to 100 miles (93–185 km), or more, according to the maximum reasonable error in time, to the eastward or westward. In making this estimate allow for large watch rates, since the rate in a lifeboat will probably not be the same as aboard ship. Watches controlled by quartz crystals will give consistently better results than others.

Finding latitude **3914** The latitude of a position can be determined in the northern hemisphere by means of an altitude observation of Polaris, and in any latitude by means of meridian altitudes, as explained in Chapter 27.

Latitude by Polaris. If no Polaris correction table is available, the correction can be estimated in the following way: A line through Polaris and the north celestial pole, if extended, passes between ϵ Cassiopeia and Ruchbah (the two left-hand stars of *Cassiopeia* when it appears as a W) on one side and Alkaid and Mizar (the last two stars in the handle of the big dipper) on the other. In both constellations these are the trailing stars in the counterclockwise motion about the pole. Polaris is on the side of the pole toward *Cassiopeia.* The correction depends only on the angle this line makes with the vertical. The accompanying critical type table gives the correction. If *Cassiopeia* is above Polaris, the correction is (−); if the *Big Dipper* is above, the correction is (+). If no correction table is available, it may be possible to estimate the correction from the relative positions of the two constellations. In Figure 3914a the angle is 40° and from the table the correction is found to be 0.8°. Since *Cassiopeia* is above the pole, the correction is −0.8°.

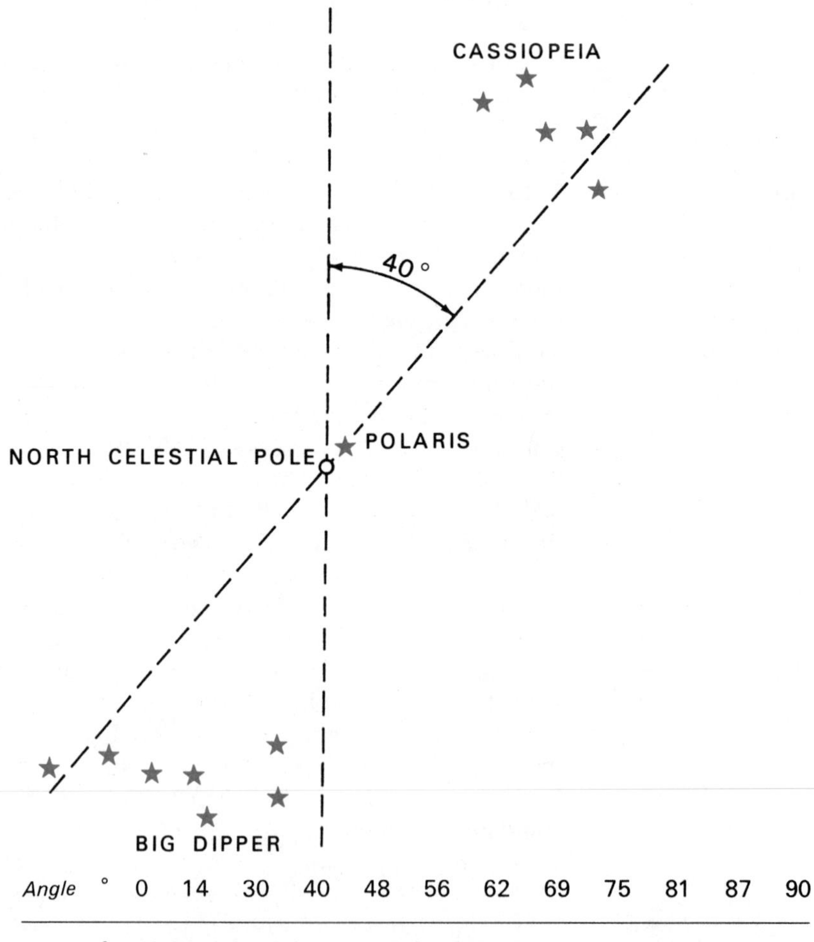

Angle °	0		14		30		40		48		56		62		69		75		81		87		90
Corr. °		1.0		0.9		0.8		0.7		0.6		0.5		0.4		0.3		0.2		0.1		0.0	

Figure 3914a. Estimating the Polaris correction.

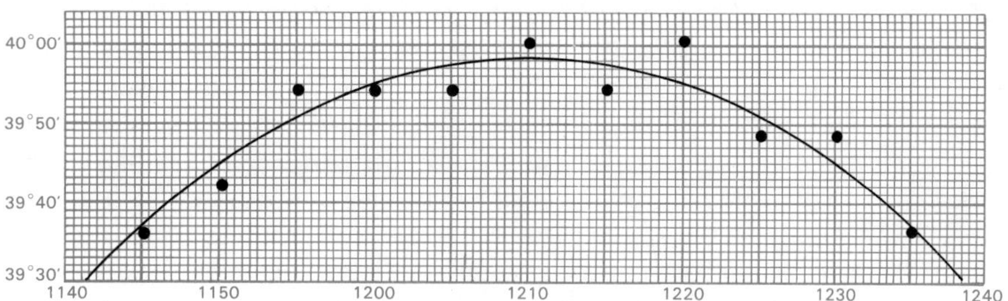

Figure 3914b. Curve of altitudes near meridian transit (typical).

Meridian altitude. At lifeboat speed most accurate results by the meridian altitude method are usually obtained by observing the highest altitude. For this purpose a number of observations should be made before and after meridian transit. If cross-section paper is available, plot the altitude vs. time and fair a curve through the points. A typical curve is shown in Figure 3914b. Although the highest altitude measured is 40.0°, the meridian altitude is found to be 39°58′. For this plot altitudes were observed to the nearest 0.1° at five-minute intervals. If preferred, altitudes can be observed at less frequent intervals, perhaps each half hour, during the entire day. At a stationary point the curve should be symmetrical before and after meridian transit. At lifeboat speeds it should approach symmetry. The highest altitude is independent of time, which is used only to space the observations. If time is not available, make the observations at any desired interval. Approximately equal intervals can be estimated by using a pendulum, as explained in Article 3908, or by counting at an even speed to any desired amount.

When the meridian altitude has been determined, combine it with the body's declination to find the latitude, as explained in Chapter 27.

The latitude can also be found by the duration of daylight, as described in Article 3916.

Finding declination of the sun

3915 If the declination of the sun is not available, the approximate value can be found as follows:

Draw a circle, the larger the better, and draw horizontal and vertical diameters. Label the left intersection of the diameter and the circle March 21 and the right intersection September 23. Label the top of the circle June 22 and the bottom December 22. Divide each quadrant into a number of spaces equal to the number of days between the limiting dates. Divide the vertical *radius* into 23.45 linear units with 0 at the center, positive above the center and negative below the center. To find the declination, draw a horizontal line from the date to the vertical diameter and read off the declination in degrees. See Figure 3915. A compass rose or a Maneuvering Board form is convenient for this purpose. If the latter is used, consider the radius 1 and multiply the

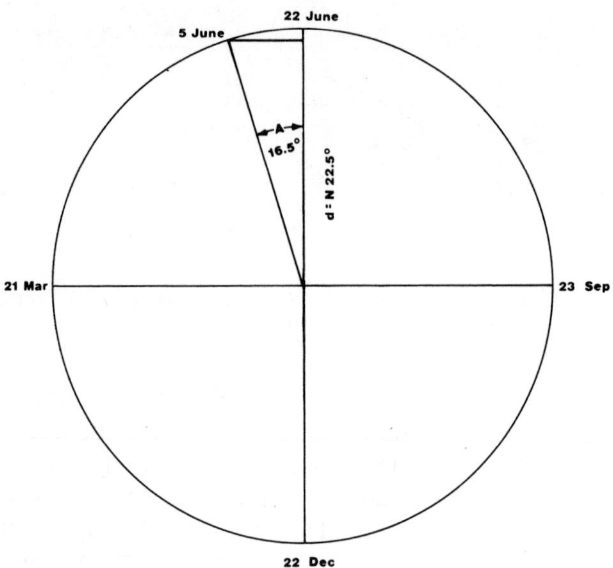

Figure 3915. Determination of approximate declination of the sun graphically.

reading by 23.45 to find the declination. The maximum error of this method is about half a degree; not good, but better than nothing at all.

The declination can also be found by means of the traverse table, as follows: Refer to Figure 3915. Find the angle A between the radius to the nearest solstice (June 22 or Dec. 22) and the given date. Enter the traverse table with this as a course and take out l, the difference of latitude. Multiply this value by 23.45 and the answer is declination in degrees. To find the angle A, find the number of days in the quadrant involved and the number of days between the given date and the nearest solstice. Divide the latter by the former and multiply by 90°. For example, in Figure 3915 there are 93 days between March 21 and June 22 and 36 days between May 17 and June 22.

$$A = \frac{36}{93} \times 90° = 34.8°.$$

From the traverse table the value of l is 0.82. The declination is

$$\text{Dec.} = 0.82 \times 23.45° = 19.2°.$$

Obtaining the longitude

3916 In Figure 3914b the highest point on the curve represents meridian transit, or LAN; it can be seen that the time of transit is 1210. At this moment, the sun is the same distance west of Greenwich as the observer, and if a table of GHA of the sun is available, or if the equation of time is known, the approximate longitude can be determined.

Without a fairly accurate timepiece there is, of course, no method for determining longitude.

The time of meridian transit can be found by picking off two points on this curve at which the altitude is the same, and noting the respective times; meridian transit occurs midway between them.

Greater accuracy may be obtained if the observations for equal altitude are made when the sun's rate of change of altitude is greater than that shown in Figure 3914b; say an hour before and after transition in this case. The curve as illustrated is not necessary. The best practice would be to obtain a series of altitudes before transit, plotting them against time then drawing in a line of best fit, which over a period of a few minutes would be represented by a straight line. Then, after transit, the sextant would be reset to the last and highest altitude obtained before LAN, and when the sun reached this altitude, a new series of sights would be begun. These also should be plotted. Note that actual observations do not have to be used; equal altitudes, with their times, may be taken from the lines of best fit.

This method can be used with any body. If no means of measuring an altitude is available, the instant at which the body bears 180° or 000° true should be noted.

If a star is used, it is necessary to have its GHA. If its SHA is known, its GHA can be found approximately, by knowing that GHA ♈ in time units equals GMT on 23 September. GHA ♈ in time units is 90° more than GMT on 22 December, 180° more on 21 March, and 270° more on 22 June. GHA ♈ in time units gains approximately 4 minutes per day on GMT. The GHA of a star is equal to GHA ♈ + SHA.

The equation of time can be found approximately from the table below.

Linear interpolation in this table does not produce very accurate results because of the uneven variation of the equation of time. The value varies from year to year, also, as does declination, but almost repeats every four years. If an almanac is available, it should be used.

Date	Eq. T	Date	Eq. T	Date	Eq. T
	m s		m s		m s
Jan. 10	−7 29	May 10	+3 41	Sept. 10	+2 53
20	11 02	20	3 39	20	6 25
30	13 21	30	2 42	30	9 51
Feb. 10	14 21	June 10	+0 50	Oct. 10	12 51
20	13 53	20	−1 16	20	15 05
28	12 43	30	3 23	30	16 15
Mar. 10	10 30	July 10	5 08	Nov. 10	16 04
20	7 41	20	6 10	20	14 25
30	4 39	30	6 19	30	11 25
Apr. 10	−1 27	Aug. 10	5 19	Dec. 10	7 20
20	+1 01	20	3 24	20	+2 33
30	2 47	30	−0 43	30	−2 25

Example: The altitude of the sun is 30° at $11^h21^m14^s$ and again at $12^h06^m32^s$ on 15 July. The watch is keeping + 9 ZT.

Required: Find the longitude, using the equation of time table above.

Solution: The time of transit is midway between the two times given, or at $11^h43^m53^s$. The GMT is 9 hours later, or $20^h43^m53^s$. The equation of time on 15 July is -5^m39^s. Hence, the Greenwich apparent time (GAT) is $20^h43^m53^s - 5^m39^s = 20^h38^m14^s$. The GHA is equal to GAT $\pm 12^h$, or $8^h38^m14^s = 129°33.5'$. This is the longitude.

Answer: Long. 129°34′ W. (Although times are shown to have been measured to the precision of the nearest second, note that the altitude of the sun is only stated to the nearest *degree,* implying a relatively crude and inexact technique. In this instance, longitude should be given only to the nearest minute, and that degree of precision is of doubtful validity.)

If the only watch should run down, it can be started again approximately by working this problem in reverse. That is, start with the best estimated longitude and find the GAT, then the GMT, and finally the ZT. Set the watch according to this time. Do this at the first opportunity after the watch runs down, while the EP is still reasonably good.

Longitude can also be determined by the time of sunrise or sunset, if a sunrise-sunset table is available. The process is somewhat similar to that just described for meridian transit. Find the LMT of sunrise or sunset from the table. Note the exact watch time of the phenomenon and from this find the GMT. The difference between GMT and LMT is the longitude. This depends on a knowledge of the latitude. It has the advantage that no equipment but a watch and sunrise-sunset table is needed. However, it is not very accurate, and the longitude obtained will not be as reliable as that taken from a horizon sight line of position, using the same latitude.

The latitude can be determined in this way, too, but even less accurately. Near the equinox, it is practically worthless and of little value at any time near the equator. To use the method the times of sunrise *and* sunset are noted and the total period of daylight determined. This is a function of the latitude on any given date. The latitude having this length of daylight is determined from the almanac. This is perhaps the least accurate way of finding the latitude and should be used only when there is no means of measuring the altitude. The time need not be accurate, for only the *duration* of daylight is needed.

Estimating distance

3917 If land or a ship is seen, it may be of value to know its approximate distance. To determine this, it is necessary to know approximately its height or some other dimension. If an object of known height (such as a mountain peak) appears over the horizon, the distance in nautical miles from the top of the object to the horizon is equal to $1.15\sqrt{H}$, where H is the height of the object above sea level in feet. This is approximately equal to 8/7 of the square root of the height in feet of the object. (The expression is $2.08\sqrt{H}$ when H is in meters.) To this must be added the distance from the observer to his horizon found in the same way for his height of eye.

Example: A mountain peak 2000 feet high appears over the horizon of an observer whose eye is 8 feet above sea level.

Required: The distance of the mountain peak from the observer.

Solution: The distance from the top of the mountain to the horizon is $1.15\sqrt{2000} = 51.4$ miles. The distance from the observer to the horizon is $1.15\sqrt{8} = 3.3$ miles. Hence, the distance of the mountain is $51.4 + 3.3 = 54.7$ miles.

Answer: D = 55 miles, approximately. (The degree of precision with which the height of the mountain and the height of eye in a moving small boat are known does not permit a more exact statement of distance, regardless of the refinement of the calculations.)

If an object is fully visible and its height is known, or if the length between two visible points is known, the distance can be found by simple proportion. Hold a scale at arm's length and measure the length subtended by the known height or length. Distance is then found by the proportion

$$\frac{D}{d} = \frac{H}{h} \qquad \text{or} \qquad D = \frac{dH}{h}$$

where D is the distance in feet, d is the distance in inches of the rule from the eye, H is the height (or length) of the object in feet and h is the length of the rule subtended by the object in inches. See Figure 3917. If H is in miles, the distance D is also in miles. If H is in feet and D is desired in nautical miles, the formula becomes

$$D = \frac{dH}{6000h}$$

Example: An island 1.2 miles long subtends a length of 3.5 inches for an observer holding a rule 21 inches from his eye.

Required: The distance of the island from the observer.

Solution: Solving the formula.

$$D = \frac{dH}{h} = \frac{21 \times 1.2}{3.5} = 7.2 \text{ miles.}$$

Answer: $D = 7$ miles, approximately.

In using this method with a length, be careful to use the length *at the visible height* (the shore line and a low beach may be below the horizon) and be sure that the length is perpendicular to the line of sight (which may not be the same as the greatest length). If a height is employed, be sure the *visible* height is used.

A variation is to measure the angle subtended and determine the length graphically. That is, in Figure 3917, if the angle at E is known, the distance D at height H can be determined by drawing a figure to scale.

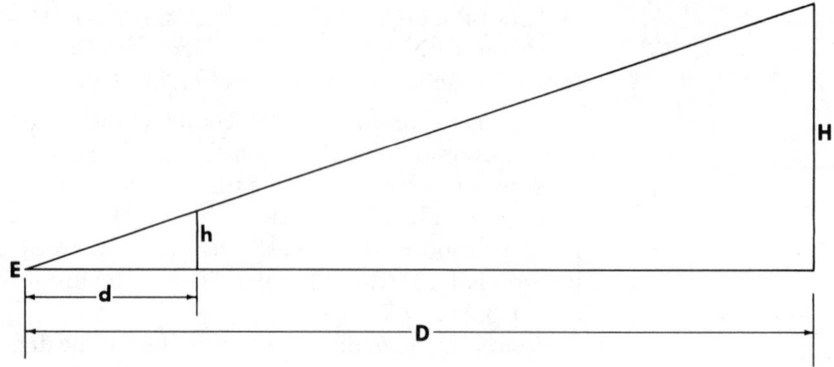

Figure 3917. Finding distance by simple proportion.

Miscellaneous

3918 The position of the celestial equator is indicated in the sky by any body of 0° declination. The sun's declination is 0° about 21 March and 23 September. The star δ Orionis (the northernmost star of *Orion's* belt) is nearly on the celestial equator. Such a body indicates the approximate east point of the horizon at rising and the west point at setting, at any latitude.

A great circle through Polaris, Caph (the leading star in *Cassiopeia*), and the eastern side of the square of *Pegasus* (Alpheratz and Algenib) represents approximately the hour circle of the vernal equinox. The local hour angle of this circle is the LHA ♈ . The LHA ♈ in time units can also be determined approximately by knowing that the autumnal equinox (about 23 September) LHA ♈ and LMT are identical. Every half a month thereafter the LHA ♈ in time units *gains* one hour on LMT. Hence, on 15 January it is approximately 7^h30^m fast on LMT.

Protect the watch and wind it regularly. If a watertight container is available, that is a good place for the watch, especially while launching the lifeboat, but make sure that this container is inside a compartment or is secured to the lifeboat by a lanyard.

In the interest of being picked up at the earliest possible time, remember that metal is a better radar reflector than wood, and the higher the reflector the greater the range at which it might be picked up. If there is a possibility that radar-equipped planes or ships are searching for your lifeboat, try to rig up some kind of metal corner reflector that will produce a stronger pip on the rescuer's radar screen. Also, do not forget to weigh the possibility of rescue in determining to leave the vicinity of the stricken ship and in setting the course.

Keep out of the direct rays of the sun as much as possible to avoid sunburn, dehydration of the body, eye infection, and eye strain. Good physical condition is a prerequisite to good navigation under difficult conditions.

Rig a sail, even if one must be improvised.

Navigation without instruments **3919** The ancient Polynesians were able to navigate successfully, without mechanical instruments or timepieces, by using their knowledge of the heavens and the lore of the sea. Few persons today have acquired this knowledge, hence this chapter has been principally devoted to using, or improvising, instruments and methods familiar to most naval and merchant marine officers and quartermasters.

The declination of any star is equal to the latitude of the point on earth directly beneath the star, the GP, and for lifeboat accuracy the declination of the stars can be assumed to remain fixed. This is the key to no-instrument celestial navigation. In the South Atlantic, for example, Alphard will pass overhead at Ascension Island. Farther north Alkaid passes over Land's End, England; Newfoundland; Vancouver Island; south of the Aleutians, and over the Kuril Islands, north of Japan.

A rough determination of latitude can therefore be made by observing the passing of a star of known declination directly overhead. (The determination of "directly overhead" is not easily done; use the opinions of several persons for an average result.) By comparing the star's declination with the known latitude of land areas, a position east or west of the land areas can be determined. Ancient navigators were able to sail to the proper latitude, then sail east or west to a known island by this process.

Directions to land can be determined by observing the flight of birds or by typical cloud formations over islands. A steady course can be steered by maintaining a constant angle with the direction of swells or wave motion. Nearby land can sometimes be detected by sounds or even by a particular smell. A complete dissertation on using the lore of the sea and sky for navigation is beyond the space limitation of this text but is mentioned to illustrate the necessity of using any available data or knowledge when routine navigation methods are not available.

Summary **3920** Anyone spending a part of his life at sea or over the water should consider it good insurance to be adequately prepared for an emergency. A man does not refuse to buy fire insurance for his house just because he hopes it will never burn down, or even because relatively few houses do burn. The cost of insurance is too inexpensive and the consequences of a fire too great to ignore this important item. As long as there is a possibility, however remote, of having to abandon ship, a suitable preparation for this emergency is good insurance. His very life and those of others may depend on his preparation. It may be too late when the order to abandon ship is given.

One of the essential items of preparation is a thorough knowledge of *fundamentals.* Practically all of the information given in this chapter consists of applications of fundamentals.

A major decision is whether to remain in the area of the abandoned ship, or make way for the nearest land or shipping lanes. If a distress message has been sent and acknowledged, efforts should be made to stay in the vicinity reported. If the distress is unknown to the authorities, plans should be made to proceed toward land or areas of greater concentration of shipping where there would be a greater probability of being sighted and rescued.

Once you have boarded a lifeboat or life raft, make a careful estimate of the situation. The methods to be used and the procedure to be followed depend on the particular situation, what tools and information are available. Use the most accurate methods available. Do not, however, be misled by the level of detail to which your calculations can be taken; remember the relative crudity of your instruments and the difficult conditions under which they are used. Carry calculations only to a justifiable degree of precision, and label them "approximate" when appropriate; plan further actions with a full awareness of the inexactness of your information. Use imagination and ingenuity in making use of the materials at hand. If more than one method of doing anything is available, check one method against another.

Establish a regular routine and keep busy. *Navigate* with whatever means are available; do not guess if there is any way of making a measurement or estimate.

Maintain good morale at all cost. Be *determined* to reach safety and do not permit conversation to become pessimistic. Good leadership qualities are never more important than at such a time.

40 Polar Navigation

The polar regions **4001** No single definition is completely satisfactory in defining the limits of the *polar regions.* Astronomically, the parallels of latitude at which the sun becomes circumpolar, at about latitudes 67.5° north and south, are considered the lower limits. Meteorologically, the limits are irregular lines which, in the Arctic, coincide approximately with the tree line. For purposes of this book, the polar regions will be considered to extend from the geographical poles to latitude 70°. The *subpolar regions* are a transitional area extending for an additional 10° to latitude 60°.

Arctic geography **4002** The *Arctic Ocean* is a body of water, a little smaller in area than the United States, which is almost completely surrounded by land. Some of this land is high and rugged, and covered with permanent ice caps; part of it is low and marshy when thawed. Permanently frozen ground underneath, called *permafrost,* prevents adequate drainage, resulting in large numbers of lakes and ponds and extensive areas of *muskeg,* soft spongy ground with characteristic growths of certain mosses, and tufts of grass or sedge. There are also large areas of *tundra,* low treeless plains with vegetation consisting of mosses, lichens, shrubs, willows, etc., and usually having an underlying layer of permafrost.

Greenland Greenland is mountainous, and notable for its many *fjords*—long, narrow, and often deep arms of the sea lying between mountains. Its northern portion is covered with a heavy ice cap. The northernmost point of land is Kap Morris Jesup, which is about 380 miles (700 km) from the geographic pole.

The central part of the Arctic Ocean is a basin with an average depth of about 12,000 feet (3,660 m); the bottom is not level, and there are a number of seamounts and deeps. The greatest depth is probably something over 16,000 feet (4880 m); at the pole the depth is 14,150 feet (4310 m). Surrounding the polar basin is an extensive continental shelf, broken only in the area between Greenland and Spitsbergen. The many islands of the Canadian archipelago lie on this shelf. The Greenland Sea, east of Greenland, Baffin Bay, west of Greenland, and the Bering Sea, north of the Aleutians, all have their independent basins. Due to ice conditions, surface ships cannot penetrate to the pole but have successfully reached quite high latitudes.

Antarctic geography

4003 The *Antarctic,* or south polar region, is in marked contrast to the Arctic in physiographical features. It is a high mountainous land mass, about twice the area of the United States, surrounded by the Atlantic, Pacific, and Indian Oceans. An extensive polar plateau, covered with snow and ice, is about 10,000 feet (3,050 m) high. The average height of Antarctica is about 6,000 feet (1,830 m) which is higher than any other continent, and there are several mountain ranges with peaks rising to more than 13,000 feet (3,960 m). The height at the South Pole is about 9,500 feet (2,900 m).

The barrier presented by land and tremendous *ice shelves* in the Ross Sea prevents ships from reaching very high latitudes. Much of the coast of Antarctica is high and rugged, with few good harbors or anchorages.

Polar coordinates

4004 Many of the concepts of measurement which are used in normal navigation take on new meanings, or lose their meaning entirely, in the polar regions. In temperate latitudes man speaks of north, south, east, and west when he refers to direction; of latitude and longitude; of time; of sunrise and sunset; and of day and night. Each of these terms is normally associated with specific concepts and relationships. In the polar regions, however, each of these terms has a somewhat different significance, requiring a reappraisal of the concepts and relationships involved.

In temperate latitudes, the lengths of a degree of latitude and a degree of longitude are roughly comparable, and meridians are thought of as parallel lines, as they appear on a Mercator chart, or as nearly parallel lines. Not so in polar regions, where meridians radiate outward from the pole like great spokes of a gigantic wheel, and longitude becomes a coordinate of direction. A plane circling the pole might cover 360° of longitude in a couple of minutes. Each of two observers might be north (or south) of the other if the north (or south) pole were between them. At the north pole all directions are south, and at the south pole all directions are north. A visual bearing of a mountain peak can no longer be considered a rhumb line. It is a great circle, and because of the rapid convergence of meridians, must be plotted as such.

Time as used in temperate zones has little meaning in polar regions. As the meridians converge, so do the time zones. A mile from the pole the time zones are but a quarter of a mile apart. At the pole the sun rises and sets once each year, the moon once a month. The visible stars circle the sky endlessly, essentially at the same altitudes; only half the celestial sphere is visible from either pole. The planets rise and set once each sidereal period (from 225 days for Venus to

29½ years for Saturn). A day of 24 hours at the pole is not marked by the usual periods of daylight and darkness, and "morning" and "afternoon" have no significance. In fact, the day is not marked by any observable phenomenon except that the sun makes one complete circle around the sky, maintaining essentially the same altitude and always bearing south (or north).

Our system of coordinates, direction, and many of the concepts so common to our daily lives are man-made. They have been used because they have proved useful. If they are discarded near the poles, it is because their usefulness does not extend to these regions. A new concept must be devised for use in the polar regions. It should differ as little as possible from familiar methods, while taking full cognizance of changed conditions.

Navigation in the polar regions

4005 Probably the only real trick to navigating in higher latitudes is to use every known method, and evaluate the results by weighing the value of each shred of positional evidence gathered. No method used is really new or unique, rather the application of method to unique problems.

Navigational problems in polar and subpolar regions are most easily considered in these categories: chart projections, environmental factors, determining direction, determining distance, and fixing position.

Charts

4006 The familiar Mercator chart projection will normally not be used in higher latitudes since distortion becomes so great as the poles are approached. Variations of the Mercator projection can be used, thus retaining some advantages without the unacceptable distortion imposed by having tangency of the cylinder occur at the Equator. This is done *by rotating the tangent cylinder through 90°*. If this is done, the cylinder is tangent to a meridian, which becomes the "fictitious equator." Parallels of latitude become oval curves, with the sinusoidal meridians extending outward from the pole. The meridians change their direction of curvature at the pole. Within the polar regions the parallels are very nearly circles and the meridians diverge but slightly from straight lines. The distortion at L 70° is comparable to that at L 20° on an ordinary Mercator chart. Within this region a straight line can be considered a great circle with but small error. If the cylinder is tangent to a meridian, the projection is called *transverse Mercator*. If it is placed tangent to an oblique great circle, the projection is termed *oblique Mercator*.

Other projections used in polar regions are the stereographic, gnomonic or great circle, azimuthal equidistant, and the modified Lambert conformal. Near the pole, all of these and the transverse Mercator projection are so nearly alike as to be difficult to distinguish by eye. All are suitable, and all can be used with a grid. On the gnomonic chart a great circle is a straight line, and on the others it is very nearly so. Distance and grid direction are measured in the accustomed manner.

In practice these polar charts are used in a manner similar to the Lambert for measuring course and distance and plotting position (Chapter 3).

The real problem of polar charts does not involve the projection to be used. The latitude and longitude lines can be drawn to the same accuracy as on any other chart, but the other information shown on polar charts is sometimes far from accurate. These regions are being traveled more and more, and publications and charts are improving, but many areas have not been accurately surveyed. The result is that in less-traveled areas coastlines are inaccurate or missing, topography is unreliable, and soundings are sparse. Lines of magnetic variation are located principally by extrapolation. Even the positions of the magnetic poles are only generally known, and may vary irregularly. One of the major problems of navigation is the production of accurate charts for polar regions. The navigator must, therefore, be acutely aware of the accuracy (or lack of accuracy) of his charts, and take greater than usual precautions to ensure that a safe course is steered. Any advance warning device is most useful, and should be fully used. Coastal topography or irregular soundings may presage pinnacles some distance offshore, and if ice conditions permit use of sonar or a forward-looking echo sounder, these should be employed.

A straight line across a polar chart can be considered a great circle within the limits of practical navigation. On the transverse Mercator chart this is a fictitious rhumb line making the same angle with fictitious meridians.

The most easily used projection for polar ship operations is usually considered to be the Lambert conformal. Plotting is a bit of a problem, but land masses are most accurately portrayed, and courses steamed in ice being somewhat tortuous, the advantages of a rhumb line course being a straight line are not missed. For this or any other of the usual high-latitude chart projections, an AN or aircraft plotter is most convenient (Article 720).

Grid direction

4007 Some navigators consider that in polar regions it is convenient to discard the conventional directions of true north, east, etc., except for celestial navigation, and substitute grid north, grid east, etc. That is, directions can be given in relation to the common direction of all fictitious grid meridians across the chart. The relationship between grid direction and true direction depends on the orientation of the grid. The system generally accepted places grid north in the direction of the north pole from Greenwich, or 000° on the Greenwich meridian is 000° grid (at both poles). With this orientation the interconversion of true and grid directions is very simple. If G is grid direction and T is true direction, in the northern hemisphere,

$$G = T + \lambda W$$
$$G = T - \lambda E$$
$$T = G - \lambda W$$
$$T = G + \lambda E.$$

In the southern hemisphere the signs are reversed. It is not necessary to remember all of these equations, for the last three follow naturally from the first. Grid direction of a straight line remains constant for its entire length, while true direction changes continually.

In Figure 4007 the grid direction from *A* to *B* is 057° and from *B* to *A* is 237°, the reciprocal. However, at *A*, longitude 20° W, the true direction is 037° ($T = G - \lambda W = 57° - 20° = 37°$). At *B*, longitude 100° E, the direction is not 237°, but 237° + 100° = 337°.

It is most convenient to give all directions in relation to grid north. Even azimuths of celestial bodies can be converted to grid directions, if desired, both for plotting lines of position and for checking the directional gyro. If wind directions are given in terms of the grid, confusion is minimized, for a wind blowing in a constant grid direction is following widely different true directions over a relatively short distance near the pole. Since drift correction angle relative to a grid course is desired, wind direction should be given on the same basis. A grid direction is indicated by the letter *G* following the direction, as Zn

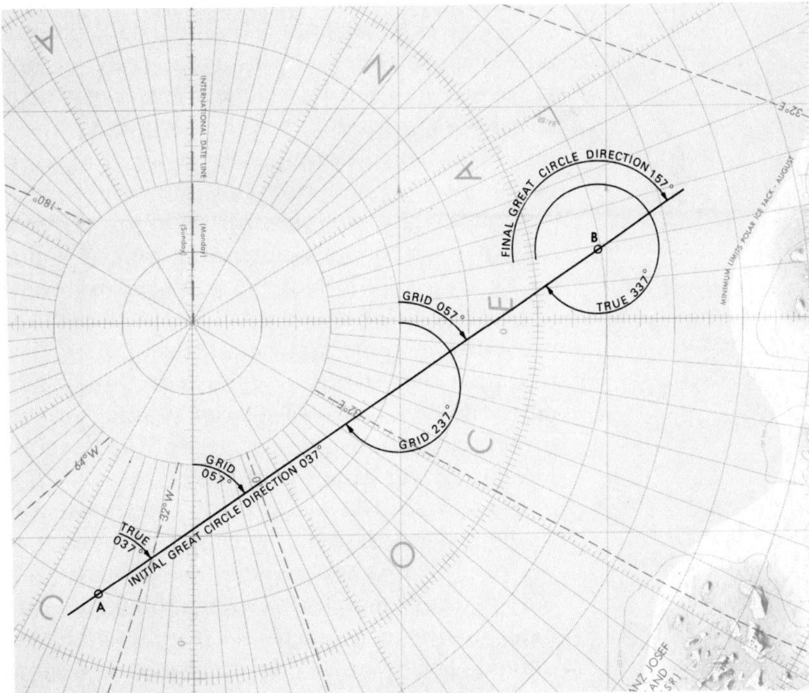

Figure 4007. Grid navigation.

068° G, or by placing the letter *G* before the nature of the direction, as GH 144°, for grid heading 144°.

The lines of equal magnetic variation all pass through the magnetic pole and the geographic pole, the former because it is the origin of such lines, and the latter because of the convergence of the meridians at that point. Convergency, however, can be combined with variation to obtain the difference between grid direction and magnetic direction at any point. This difference is called *grid variation* or *grivation.* Lines of equal grid variation can be shown on a polar chart in lieu of lines of ordinary variation. These lines pass through the magnetic pole but disregard the geographic pole. Hence, even when a magnetic compass is used, grid navigation is easier than attempting to maintain true directions.

Grid sailing as described may be useful for air navigation but is not likely to be needed for surface ship operations, because 82° N is the probable limit of navigation and speeds are usually so low that other more normal plotting methods can be effectively used.

Environmental factors

4008 The effects of polar operations in navigation are many and varied. A thorough study of *Sailing Directions* or *Coast Pilots* is necessary, including those available from other countries. For example, the Danish *Pilot* for Greenland contains some excellent land profiles; *Aircraft charts* can also be very useful, since the topography shown is an essential factor in marine navigation. The *Ice Atlas,* DMAHC Pub. No. 700S3, gives good average seasonal data although up-to-date information from satellite, long-range aircraft, or helicopter ice reconnaissance is more useful. In some areas, it may be necessary to work from aerial photographs or preliminary charts, and soundings will be lacking. Whatever the circumstance, the navigator must plan ahead and obtain all information from whatever source.

Occasionally, a review of old *Cruise Reports,* or even accounts by early explorers, will yield useful data. A volume of *Sailing Directions for Antarctica,* Pub. No. 27, has been published. It contains a large amount of information that recent expeditions into the area have proved to be quite accurate, if incomplete.

Rather than paraphrase the many authoritative references available on the higher latitudes, a brief summary of the more prevalent features is presented as a reminder of the general environment in which navigation will be accomplished.

Seasonal conditions. Normally cruises will be scheduled during the daylight periods, that is, during the summer months for the area involved. During these periods the sun may not set at all, and consequently there may be no navigational twilight. Ice conditions will be more favorable, as will the weather generally except at the turn of the seasons. Fog at the ice edge is frequently encountered, and good radar navigation is imperative. Warm-water currents also cause fog, not just at the ice edge but near cooler land masses as well. There may be days with below-freezing temperatures, or raw and damp days, but for the most part the weather will be cool and pleasant. Gales are few. Cold-weather precautions should be taken, but mosquitos may be encountered in Northern Ellesmere Island in August. Aside from the *Sailing Directions* and other sources already suggested, there are several Army Engineer manuals on cold-weather operations, and the *Naval Arctic Operations Handbook* (in two parts). There is a special series of *Ice Plotting Charts and Sheets* for the arctic area. There is additional information in the ATP, NWP, and NWIP series for those to whom such publications are available.

Cruising in the off season, though unlikely, is possible and is apt to increase as ship capabilities and the needs of commerce expand. Severe low temperatures, ice conditions, and gales may be expected, especially at the turn of the season. During the dark period, there may be enough light to take good celestial sights although there may be no actual navigational twilight. The mid-winter period will probably be clear and very cold. Bare flesh will stick to metal instruments. Elaborate cold-weather precautions are essential for engineering equipment as well as personnel.

Magnetic anomalies and *storms* are prevalent, the *Aurora* (Borealis and Australis) will be visually attractive but troublesome to communications and magnetic compasses.

Mirage effect. This phenomenon, due to abnormal refractions, occurs whenever there is a severe discontinuity between surface and air temperatures. In summer in the north, for example, when the water and ice are much colder than the air above, multiple images may be seen. Landfalls may appear many miles before they are expected.

Piloting and DR. Unknown tides and currents, or ice conditions, will make a good DR very hard to keep. Close observations for any clues of set and drift are most useful; for example, grounded icebergs may show tidal erosion as well as a wake. If observed for long periods, they serve as a rough tide gauge. Depth can also be estimated from grounded bergs, using 1 foot (or meter) above the waterline as equal to 6 feet (or meters) below. Pit logs may not be practical, but timing objects passing alongside can give a rough indication of speed through the water or ice.

Upon entering a harbor or unfamiliar waters it is good practice to send a small boat ahead with a portable echo sounder and a radiotelephone for communications.

One of the principal hazards to marine navigation in polar regions is ice. In some regions icebergs are very numerous. In the upper part of Baffin Bay, for instance, south of Cape York, literally hundreds of icebergs may be visible at one time. During periods of darkness or low visibility, radar is essential in avoiding collision. This method is usually quite adequate, icebergs often being picked up before they are capable of being seen. *Growlers* are the chief hazard to marine navigation. These are small icebergs, about the size of a small house, usually broken from larger ones. When the sea is smooth, it is usually possible to detect growlers in time to avoid them without difficulty, but if the sea is rough, they may not be picked up because of excessive sea return near the ship. It must be remembered that about 90 percent of an iceberg is *below* the surface of the water, so that in a rough sea, a growler is practically awash. Sonar has proved useful in detecting the presence of such ice. Broken ice presents no particular difficulty, but when heavy pack ice is encountered, further progress is usually impossible. Sometimes a *lead* or strip of open water where the ice has cracked and drifted apart permits a ship to continue for some distance into pack ice.

Fog is somewhat frequent in some polar regions during the summer, but is seldom of long duration. Most of the precipitation in the summer is in the form of rain, which is quite plentiful in some areas and is usually light but steady. Overcast conditions can persist for days.

To summarize, piloting in polar regions is fraught with difficulties and at best yields only a general indication of position. However, it is a most important method of marine navigation in these regions.

Direction **4009** The determination of *direction* is perhaps the single most difficult problem. Magnetic compasses become largely useless due to the large and somewhat unpredictable variations and magnetic storms encountered. Gyrocompasses with proper speed and latitude corrections entered are reasonably accurate, but directive force weakens as the poles are approached. Flux gate gyros have been recommended, but are usually available only in aircraft.

Any gyroscopic device will degrade in accuracy in higher latitude, and will lose all directive effect at the geographic poles. It is therefore necessary to take almost continuous error observations on a celestial body, normally the sun. One practical method is to mount an *astrocompass* on the ship's centerline (if offset, mount lubber's line parallel to the center line). An astrocompass is illustrated in Figure 4009. A sun compass can be useful, but needs a shadow from the sun to give useful data. The astrocompass can be used with the sun or *any other body.*

The *sky compass,* operating on polarized sunlight, has been successfully used. It is valuable in that the sun need not be seen, therefore an overcast does not mean a total loss of direction; a clear zenith, however, is needed for full accuracy. The usual azimuths can also be used, of course, and precomputed tables or curves make the process practical and timely. Since acceleration errors in gyrocompasses (from turns or abrupt speed changes) are greater in high latitudes, timely error determination is essential.

Bearings Bearings may be difficult to plot over long distances, due to the problems encountered with chart projections, but considering the bearings as great circles and plotting them as such according to the chart projection employed will solve the problem (use radio-bearing correction

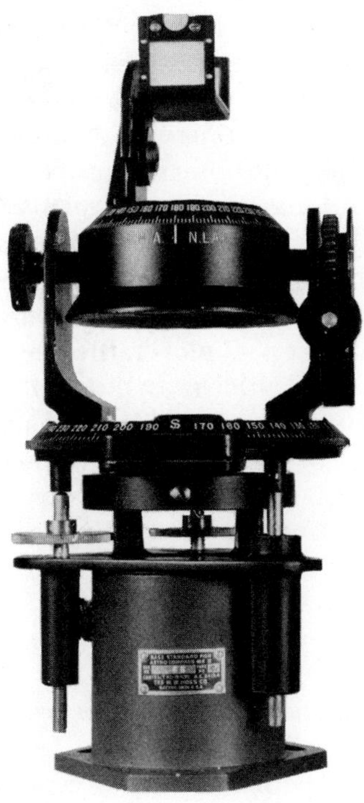

Figure 4009. Astrocompass.

procedure). Bearings generally may be a problem due to poor charting. In this case, redundancy of observations is important, and an attempt to fix the position of objects with the ship stopped, to give good visual or radar navigational references for a stretch of steaming, is recommended. Piloting practices should be thoroughly reviewed.

Distance **4010** Determining distance may also require some ingenuity. *Distance off* may be measured by radar, or by stadimeter or sextant if heights are known. *Distance to go* will depend on good fixes and good charts. *Distance run* will require the use of some of the older piloting techniques (such as doubling the angle on the bow if running on a steady course and speed), or a chip log, or timing the passage of objects alongside the ship for a known distance. Fixed, or almost stationary objects such as bergs, can also be used and plotted on a Maneuvering Board as known fixed targets to solve for own course and speed; radar can be useful for this purpose. Recall, however, that drifting bergs are offset by Coriolis force, the rule of thumb being that the offset is 30° to 40° to the right of the wind in the northern hemisphere. In open water, pit logs or engine turns can be used as usual with only normal problems as to accuracy. To prevent damage, pit logs and retractable sonar gear must be retracted when entering ice.

Dead Reckoning

4011 A DR plot must be carefully and attentively kept, particularly in ice. Every movement of the vessel must be recorded with the best possible accuracy. Some ships operating in ice detail one or two men full time to this task alone. At times the ship's movements may be too erratic to permit plotting, and the average course and speed must be carefully estimated. An *automatic course recorder* is very useful if the gyro corrections are known. Speed must be estimated or obtained as described above. With practice, a useful estimate of speed can be made by an experienced man. Since many polar cruises require close navigation, it is better to keep up all plots rather than to prepare historical records after the fact. The latter records are also desirable, but timely fixes and good DR projections are operationally necessary for safe navigation at the present moment. It is frequently good practice to proceed very deliberately, or even stop, in order not to lose track. If a DRT has a dummy log input, speed estimates can be entered and a track without set can be developed easily.

Fixing position

4012 *Fixing position* can be quite an adventure, and occasionally there will be considerable doubt. Skillful piloting is essential, in addition to a good DR plot. The navigator must never miss an opportunity for an LOP; he can not know when there will be another available. He must obtain all information possible even though some of it may be incomplete or of questionable accuracy. An alert conning officer may notice uncharted dangers or those on the track if the ship is off course. Occasionally land, water, or ice reflections can be useful in navigating as well as conning and the watch officer may be the one to observe them first.

Visual methods of position fixing are always good, particularly as charts of polar areas improve, but there will be an almost total absence of such aids to navigation as buoys, beacons, lights, and sound signals.

Radar can serve as a warning device as well as for navigation. A good rule is to use only radar ranges. One helpful technique, particularly in first establishing a position in an unfamiliar area, is to prepare a tracing of the PPI picture, which can then be matched with the chart. Many targets should be plotted on the tracing; target separation should, when possible, be about 5°. This will simplify matching the tracing to the chart, as any error in bearings will not affect the accuracy of determining the ship's position; position is determined by matching the contours on the tracing to those on the chart, rather than by the use of bearings.

One useful wrinkle when using radar in ice is to reduce radiated power. This reduces range but increases ice definition (resolution), so that leads are more easily perceived. Some radars have an automatic setting for this, others would require reducing magnetron current. Shorter wavelength radars now available also give better resolution, and vessels may have sets of this type available.

Celestial navigation **4013** Celestial navigation is of prime importance in polar regions, although its practice may be very different from that to which the navigator is accustomed. He must acquire new techniques, familiarize himself with new tools, accustom himself to functioning in a very different environment, and never miss the opportunity to obtain a line of position.

Navigation during the summer months involves the problem of positioning the vessel by altitude measurements of the sun only (except for occasional use of the moon), as continuous daylight prevents any observations of stars or planets. A navigator, therefore, must depend almost solely on single lines of position of the sun. In very high latitudes, a particular difficulty may arise twice a year. After the sun has set below the horizon, (or shortly before it rises for the summer) there may be a period of days or even several weeks when the sun is not available yet the sky is too bright for observation of other bodies; at this time, it will not be possible to make any use of celestial navigation.

Tools and techniques which have been found useful will be discussed in the following paragraphs. But first consider *time,* on which all celestial navigation is based, as the importance of time itself is somewhat affected in the polar regions.

Time In previous chapters the importance of time was stressed, since each four seconds of error of the navigational watch may introduce an error of as much as one minute of longitude. At the equator this is 1 mile (1.85 km); at latitude 60°, it is 0.5 mile (0.93 km); at latitude 88°, it is only 0.035 miles (65 m). Thus at this latitude, a watch error of 2 minutes would introduce a maximum error of about 1 mile (1.85 km). That is, the maximum change of altitude of a body, at a fixed point of observation, is one minute of arc in two minutes of time, and the average error is not more than half this amount. Thus, for celestial navigational purposes precise time is of little consequence in polar regions. At the pole all bodies circle the sky at a constant altitude, except for a very slow change due to the changing declination. Because time zones lose their significance near the poles, it is customary to keep all timepieces set to GMT while in polar regions.

Navigators in temperate climates usually avoid observations of bodies below 15° and most of them never observe bodies lower than 10°. In polar regions the only available body may not exceed an altitude of 10° for several weeks. At the pole the maximum altitude of the sun is 23°27′; the moon and planets may exceed this value by a few degrees. Hence, in polar regions there is no lower limit to observations.

The reason for avoiding low altitudes in temperate latitudes is the variable amount of refraction to be expected. In polar regions refraction varies over much wider limits than in lower latitudes. Because of the low temperatures in polar regions, the refraction correction for sextant altitudes should be adjusted for temperature, or a special refraction table for this area should be used. Refraction is known to vary with temperature and barometric pressure, but there are other factors which are imperfectly known. Refractions of several *degrees* have occasionally been observed, resulting in the sun appearing several days before it was expected in the spring, or continuing to appear for days after it should have disappeared below the horizon. Since abnormal refraction affects both the refraction and dip corrections, bubble sextant altitudes, if the average of a number of observations is used, are sometimes more reliable in polar regions than marine sextant altitudes.

Tools and techniques

The marine sextant is the basic tool for polar navigation, although it is difficult at times to obtain a good horizon. Sun and moon observations will usually be made at lower altitudes than the navigator is accustomed to using; they must be carefully corrected for refraction. As for all observations made in the polar regions, the "Additional Corrections" for nonstandard temperature and barometric pressure, contained in the *Nautical Almanac,* should be applied. An artificial horizon can be improvised when required. The conventional mercury horizon can rarely be used even aboard a stationary ship; it can, however, be used to advantage on the ice. For ship use, a pan of lubricating oil makes an acceptable horizon. It may be placed on a leveled gyro repeater, and should be shielded from the wind, if necessary.

When the horizon is poorly defined and a star at high altitude is visible, it may be desirable to take both direct and *back* (or *over-the-shoulder*) sights. In this latter technique, the observer faces *away* from the body and measures the *supplement* of the altitude (180° − sextant reading = observed altitude). The arc that appears when "rocking" the sextant is inverted, with the highest point on the arc the position of perpendicularity; practice is required for accuracy in taking back sights. The results of the direct and back sights are compared, and usually averaged.

Bubble sextant

An aircraft bubble sextant, or a marine sextant with bubble attachment (Article 2104) can be used advantageously in the polar regions. It takes some practice to become accustomed to its use, and a considerable number of sights of each body should always be taken and averaged. Results obtained with the bubble sextant will be improved if there is no ship's motion; it may be desirable to take all way off the ship while sights are being made. Some navigators suspend the bubble sextant from a spring, to help damp out undesired motion.

The best celestial fixes are obtained by erecting a theodolite on shore, or on firm ice. If it is equipped with a 30-power telescope, high-magnitude fixed stars, situated at reasonably high altitudes, should be visible on clear days, even with the sun above the horizon. This is particularly true if they lie approximately 90° from the sun in azimuth. For nighttime star observations, the theodolite serves best if it is fitted with a prismatic astrolabe.

During the long polar day, which at Thule, Greenland, in latitude 76°32′ N, lasts for four months, the only body regularly available is the sun, which circles the sky, changing azimuth about 15° each hour. The moon will at times give a second line of position; when it is near the new or full phase, such a line will be nearly parallel to the sun line, and hence of little value in fixing a position. An average of several observations of the sun, obtained every two hours, provides a series of running fixes. Even better practice is to make observations every hour, and establish the most probable position for each hour.

The best celestial fixes are usually obtained from star observations made during twilight. With increased latitude, the period of twilight lengthens, permitting additional time for observation. With this increase the period when the sun is just below the horizon also lengthens, and it may be difficult to pick up stars or planets unless a sextant with a high-magnification telescope and large mirrors is available.

In the Arctic, with such an instrument, Capella, Deneb, and Vega should be among the first stars visible, particularly when situated approximately at right angles in azimuth to the position of the sun below the horizon. In the Antarctic, the first stars to look for are Rigel Kentaurus, Acrux, Canopus, Hadar, and Achernar. The brighter planets will be the next bodies to become visible, if they are high in declination. A bright aurora may delay the observation of stars and planets after sunset; at times, however, it may assist in defining the horizon. With dark-adapted vision, and good sextants, navigators can frequently obtain excellent observations throughout the polar night. The moon should, of course, be observed whenever it is available. Polaris, because of its high altitude and difficult azimuth determination, has very limited use.

Other conditions besides long periods of darkness complicate the problem of locating the horizon in high latitude. Low fog, frost smoke, or blowing snow may veil the horizon when the sun is clearly visible. Nearby land, hummocked sea ice, or an extensive ice foot may be troublesome, particularly at low heights of eye. As previously stated an artificial horizon sextant can be most helpful under such conditions, and can supply good lines of position, if the observer is practiced in its use and averages a number of observations.

When using the marine sextant aboard ship, the value of the dip correction should be determined by the height of eye *above the ice at the horizon*. This can usually be established with reasonable accuracy by observing nearby ice. Due to the frequently considerable anomalies in refraction, the tabulated refraction should always be corrected for temperature and barometric pressure. When stars are available, several, well distributed in azimuth, should be observed to minimize errors due to abnormal refraction. The center of the geometric figures formed by the LOPs should be taken as the fix. Any error in dip or refraction will alter the size of the polygon, but will not appreciably change the location of its center. Other difficulties experienced aboard ship include the fact that false horizons sometimes appear, and during summer, when ships are most likely to be in polar regions, the sky in some areas is usually overcast. Also, a geographical position is not as important to a ship as a position relative to adjacent land, which may not be accurately charted. When stars are available, it is good practice to observe those of relatively high altitudes, since they are least affected by abnormal refraction.

The plotting of lines of position in polar regions is no more difficult than elsewhere. However, it must be remembered that an azimuth line is in reality a great circle. In moderate latitudes it is approximated on a Mercator chart by a rhumb line. Over the short distance involved no appreciable error is introduced by this practice. Similarly, the line of position, actually part of a small circle on the earth, is also drawn as a straight line without loss of accuracy unless the altitude is very high, when it is actually drawn as a circle. These are discussed in more detail in Chapter 25.

In polar regions rhumb lines are not suitable because they no longer approximate great circles. This is shown in Figure 4013a in which a fix is plotted on a Mercator plotting sheet in the usual way. The solid lines show the actual lines that should be used. In Figure 4013b this same fix is shown plotted on a transverse Mercator chart. Note that both the azimuth line and the line of position are plotted as straight lines, as on a Mercator chart near the equator. The AP is

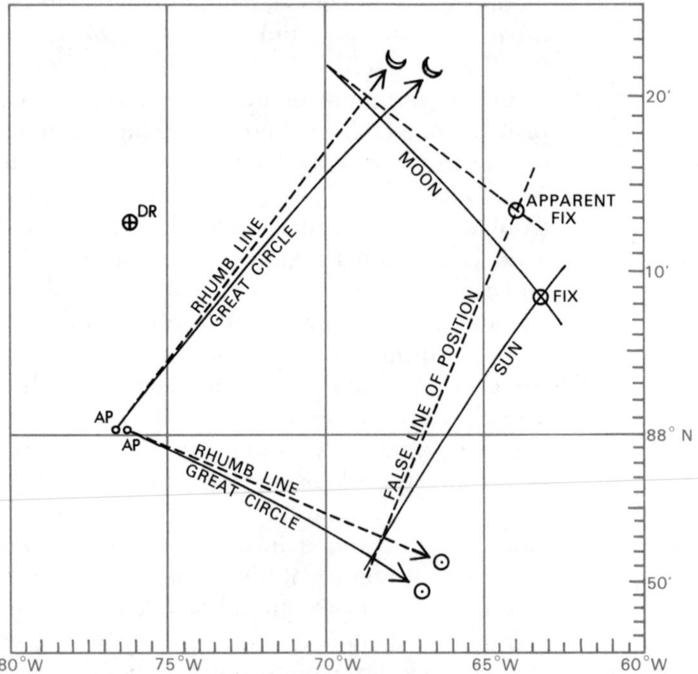

Figure 4013a. High-latitude celestial fix plotted on a Mercator plotting sheet.

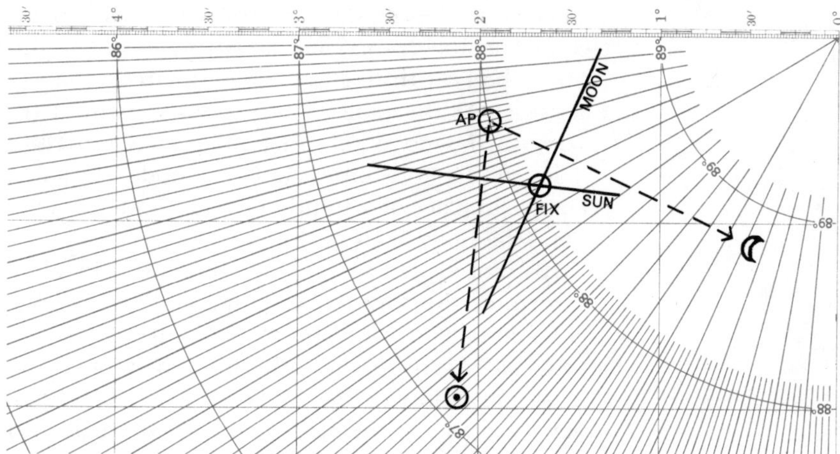

Figure 4013b. The celestial fix of Figure 4013a plotted on a transverse Mercator chart.

selected as in any latitude and located by means of the graticule of actual latitude and longitude. The fix is also given in terms of geographical coordinates. In plotting the azimuth line, the direction can be converted to grid azimuth, or plotted directly by means of true azimuth. If the latter method is used, be careful to measure the direction from the meridian of the AP. An aircraft plotter or protractor is usually used for this purpose.

Sextant altitudes are corrected the same in polar regions as elsewhere, except that refraction should be corrected for temperature, or a special refraction table used, as indicated above. Coriolis corrections, needed for bubble sextant observations made from a moving craft, reach extreme values near the poles and should not be neglected.

Computed altitude can be calculated in polar regions by any of several methods, including the Ageton tables now in Volume II of *Bowditch* as Table 35. It can be determined more easily, however, by Pub. No. 229. If its standard of accuracy is acceptable, Pub. No. 249 offers a rapid reduction, but Volume I is restricted to a limited number of stars. The Weems *Star Altitude Curves* are available for the north polar regions. These are printed on the Mercator projection from latitude 50° S to latitude 80° N, and on the stereographic projection between latitude 80° N and the north pole. These, also, are restricted to certain stars.

If a body near the zenith is observed, the line of position is plotted as a circle, with the GP as the center, as in any latitude.

Pole as assumed position

One special method of plotting lines of position is available above 80° latitude. By this method the pole is used as the AP. The Hc can then be determined by means of the almanac. The altitude of a body is its angular distance from the horizon; the declination is its angular distance from the celestial equator. At the pole the horizon and celestial equator coincide, making the altitude equal to the declination. This is why a body with fixed declination circles the sky without change in altitude. At the pole all directions are south (or north) and hence azimuth has no significance. The lines radiating outward from the pole, similar to azimuth lines in moderate latitudes, are meridians. Hence, in place of azimuth, GHA is used, for it indicates which "direction" the body is from the pole.

To plot a sight by this method, enter the almanac with GMT and determine the body's declination and GHA. Using the declination as Hc, compare it with Ho. If Ho is greater, it is a "Toward" case, as usual. Measure the altitude difference, (a) from the pole along the meridian indicated by the GHA, and at the point so found erect a perpendicular to the meridian. If Hc is greater, an "Away" case, measure (a) along the meridian 180° from that indicated by the GHA, or *away* from the body (Figure 4013c).

This method was first suggested at least as early as 1892, but there is no evidence of its having been used until some thirty years later. In the early days of air exploration in polar regions the method was quite popular, but with the development of modern tabular methods, it has fallen into disuse, except within 2° of the pole, or above latitude 88°, where it is sometimes used. This, of course, is a very small area. If a ship is near the meridian of the GP of the body (or its reciprocal), the method is entirely accurate at any latitude, even though the altitude

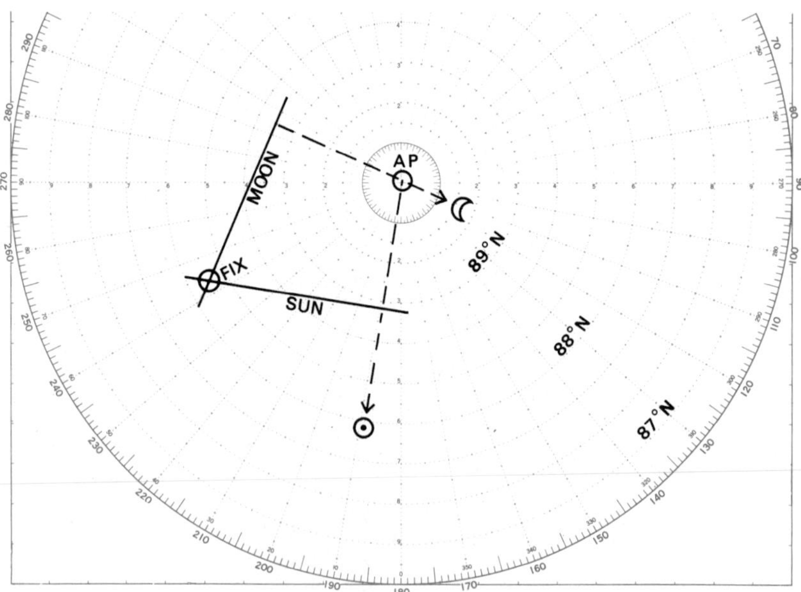

Figure 4013c. The celestial fix of Figure 4013a plotted on a maneuvering board sheet used as an azimuthal equidistant chart. The pole is used as the assumed position.

difference might be quite large, for this is simply a different way to plot meridian altitudes. However, the straight line used as the line of position is actually the arc of a small circle on the earth. The radius of the circle depends on the altitude of the body. For bodies near the horizon, the straight line of position, a close approximation of a great circle, can be used for some distance from the meridian of the GP without appreciable error. However, as the altitude increases, the discrepancy becomes larger. Tables have been prepared to show the distance from the straight line to the circle of equal altitude at different altitudes and for several hundred miles from the meridian of the GP, on a polar stereographic projection. With modern methods available, the pole is not generally used as the AP in an area where such a correction is needed.

Lines of position are advanced in the same manner as in lower latitudes. If a grid course is being followed, the AP or line of position is advanced along the grid course. The use of the pole as the AP does not complicate this practice.

Various other methods of using celestial navigation in polar regions have been suggested. Among these are the use of sets of altitude curves for different bodies printed on transparent paper or plastic, to be used as a template over the chart; these methods also include the use of various types of computers.

From overall considerations, tables such as Pub. No. 229 or Pub. No. 249 are the best for celestial navigation in polar regions.

Electronic navigation

4014 Other means of fixing position are electronic systems, radiating from sources external to the ship:

Radiobeacons, when available, can be used. Watch for plotting errors due to chart projection, and for attenuation over ice or snow. Radio direction finders may be used to effect a rendezvous between ships or aircraft. On the surface, this is particularly useful in fog when there are many radar returns such as from icebergs. Radio reception in high latitudes suffers from ionospheric disturbances, but the short distances involved here should make RDF use possible. It is important that the radio deviation tables be kept up to date.

Consol, available in a small portion of the polar regions, is useful but not precise, as is true of any bearing device at extreme range.

Loran-A (1850–1950 kHz) is usable in the Arctic, but the coverage is greatly restricted. Ground-wave coverage extends into the edge of the sub-Arctic in several places, but into the Arctic in the Baffin Bay, Denmark Straits, and Norwegian Sea only as shown on Chart No. 5131. The sky-wave coverage extends some distance beyond that of the ground-wave coverage.

Loran-C (100 kHz) is available in some portions of the polar regions, and is quite precise when properly used. See Chart No. 5130 for coverage.

Omega (10–14 kHz) is a global hyperbolic system that will give position information accurate to 1 to 2 miles (1.8 to 3.7 km) in all areas, including the polar regions. See Chart No. 5132 for coverage.

Navigational satellites give excellent fixes, but not continuously, with good precision and reliability. They are essential for polar vessels, and receiver-computers are available to civilian navigators.

Inertial navigation systems will prove very useful in polar cruising, but must be updated periodically from external sources of information. Inertial systems have been used as the primary means of navigation by submarines transiting the pole under the ice.

Sunrise, sunset, moonrise, moonset

4015 Sunrise, sunset, moonrise, and moonset, as stated in Article 4004, do not have the same significance in polar regions as in lower latitudes. At the pole the change in altitude of a body is occasioned only by a change in declination. Since the maximum rate of change of declination of the sun is about 1′ per hour, and the sun is about 32′ in diameter, the entire sun would not be visible for about 32 hours after "sunrise," or the moment of first appearance of the upper limb, if refraction remained constant. In a plane high above the pole the sun might be visible more than a week before it appears on the ground. Because of large variations in refraction, even the *day* of sunrise is difficult to predict in polar regions.

Ordinary sunrise, sunset, moonrise, and moonset tables are not available above 72° N or 60° S latitudes, nor would they be of much value if they were published. The method usually used is that provided by graphs in the *Air Almanac* as shown in Figures 4015a, b, and c; comparable diagrams are not found in the *Nautical Almanac.*

The semiduration of sunlight is found by means of the graph in Figure 4015a. The manner of its use is illustrated by the dashed lines.

Example: Find the LMT of sunrise and sunset at L 78° on March 8. Find the GMT if the observer is in λ 93° W.

Solution: From 8 March on the scale at the bottom of the graph draw a line vertically upward to the top of the diagram. To the nearest minute the time indicated by the dots is 1211. This is the LMT of meridian transit, or the center of the period of sunlight. Next, draw a horizontal line from L 78° N at the left (or right) margin to intersect the vertical line. At the point of intersection interpolate by eye between the curves. The semiduration of sunlight so found is 4^h40^m. Hence, the sun will rise 4^h40^m before meridian transit, or at 0731, and set 4^h40^m after meridian transit, or at 1651. The GMT is 6^h12^m *later,* so that sunrise occurs at 1343 and sunset 2303. These values, of course, are approximations.

Answers: Sunrise, LMT 0731, GMT 1343; sunset, LMT 1651, GMT 2303.

The duration of civil twilight is found in a similar manner by the use of Figure 4015b.

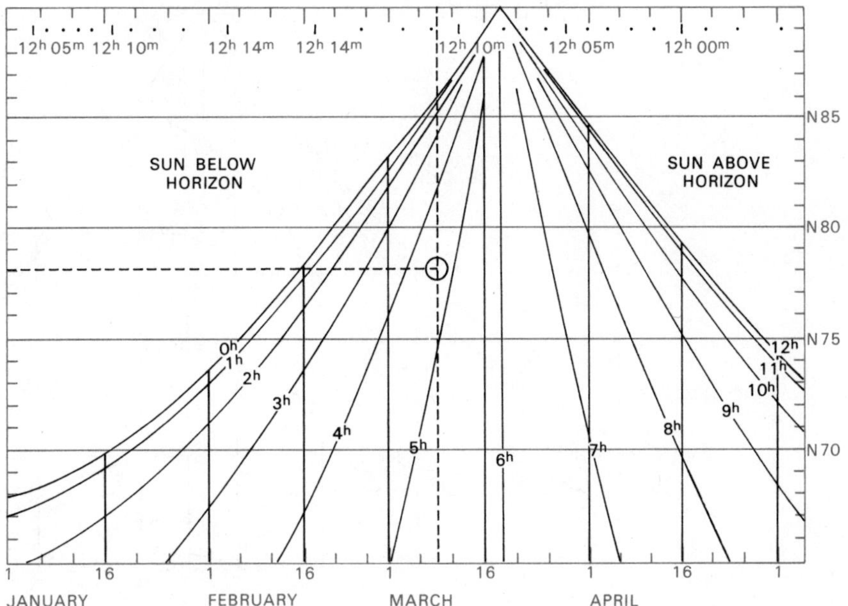

Figure 4015a. Semiduration of sunlight graph from the *Air Almanac.*

Example: Find the LMT and GMT of beginning of morning twilight and ending of evening twilight for the example above.

Solution: Draw a vertical line through 8 March and a horizontal line through L 78° N. At the intersection interpolate between the two curves. The value found is about 1^h45^m. Hence, morning twilight begins 1^h45^m before sunrise and evening twilight ends 1^h45^m after sunset.

Answers: Morning twilight, LMT 0546, GMT 1158; evening twilight, LMT 1836, GMT 2448 or 0048 the following day.

The time of moonrise and moonset is found from Figure 4015c in a manner similar to finding sunrise and sunset. The time of transit of the moon, of course, is not always near 1200 but may be any time during the day. The phase of the moon is shown by its symbol, the open symbol being full moon and the black symbol new moon.

Example: Find the LMT, ZT, and GMT of both moonrise and moonset at L 76° N, λ 70° W on 12 January, and the phase this day.

Solution: The vertical line through 12 January indicates that the moon will be on the celestial meridian at LMT 0425. The semiduration of moonlight is 8^h00^m. Hence, moonrise occurs 8 hours before the LMT of 0425, or at 2025 the day before, and moonset at 1225. Similarly, for the following day moonrise occurs at 2230 the day before and moonset occurs at 1130. The next moonrise will occur at 0100 on 14 January.

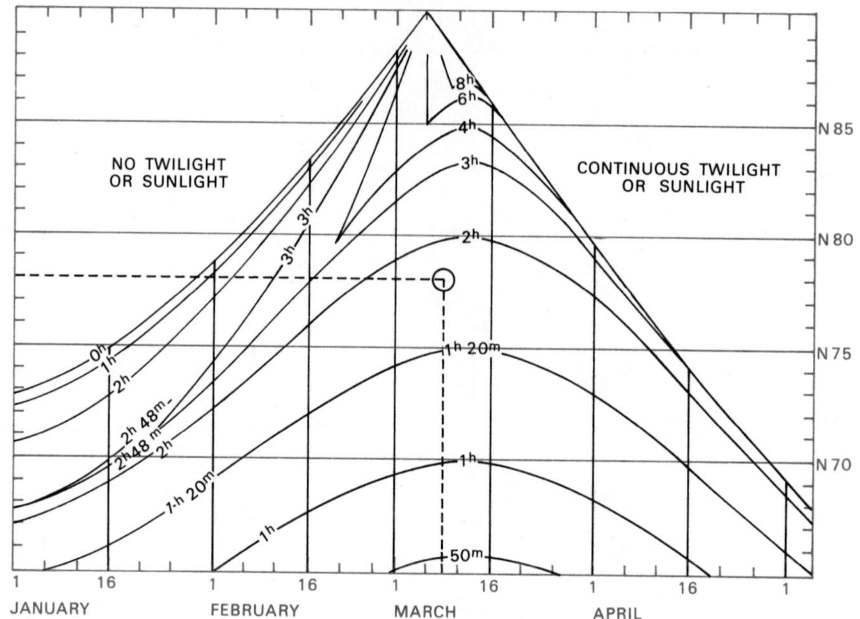

Figure 4015b. Duration of twilight graph from the *Air Almanac.*

	Moonrise			Moonset	
Tab	2230	12 Jan.	Tab	1225	12 Jan.
Tab	0100	14 Jan.	Tab	1130	13 Jan.
Diff	150		Diff	55	
150 × 70.0/360	(+) 29		55 × 70.0/360	(−) 11	
LMT	2259		LMT	1214	
$d\lambda$	(−) 20		$d\lambda$	(−) 20	
ZT	2239	12 Jan.	ZT	1154	12 Jan.
ZD	(+) 5		ZD	(+) 5	
GMT	0339	13 Jan.	GMT	1654	12 Jan.

The phase is gibbous, about two days before last quarter.

Answers: Moonrise, LMT 2259, ZT 2239, GMT 0339 (13 Jan.); moonset, LMT 1214, ZT 1154, GMT 1645; phase, gibbous, about two days before last quarter.

There are comparable graphs for sunlight, twilight, and moonlight for the south polar region. These are not printed in the almanacs but are avilable free from the U.S. Naval Observatory in Washington, D.C., in U.S. Naval Observatory Circular No. 147 (or subsequent circulars in the same series for later years).

Land navigation

4016 Land navigation of vehicles which cross the surface of the ice is not essentially different from that of aircraft or marine vessels, with one important exception. The navigator of the ice vehicle can stop and

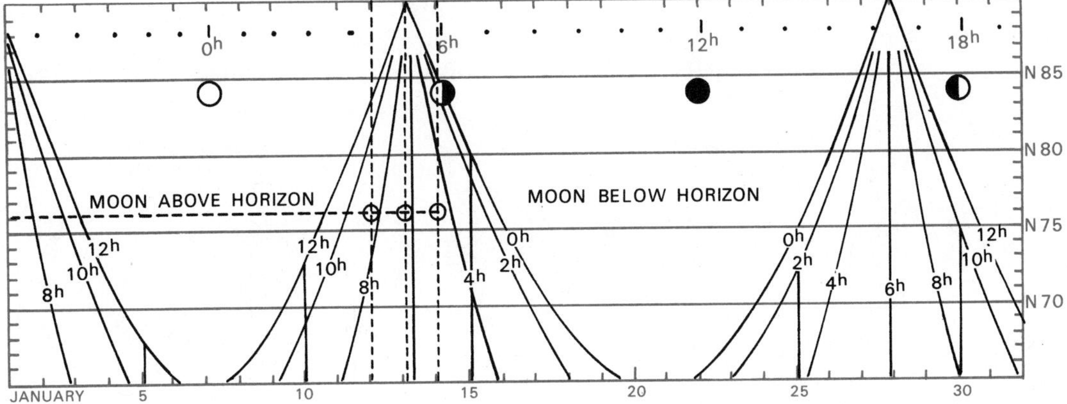

Figure 4015c. Semiduration of moonlight graph from the *Air Almanac.*

obtain a stable platform for measuring altitudes, directions, etc., without being bothered by bubble acceleration or vibration.

Navigation of such vehicles usually consists of proceeding by dead reckoning for a convenient period (often several days) and checking the position by accurate celestial observation at favorable times. At such times the accuracy of the compass is also checked. An aircraft type flux gate compass is generally most suitable for maintaining direction, except in the immediate vicinity of the magnetic poles, where it is usually necessary to steer for prominent landmarks and check the direction at frequent intervals. Dead reckoning in land vehicles is complicated by the necessity of frequently changing course to avoid obstructions.

Summary **4017** Throughout this chapter emphasis has been placed on the problems and difficulties to be encountered in polar regions, not to frighten people away, but to emphasize the need for an understanding of the conditions to be met and for adequate planning and preparation before entering the regions. This having been done the polar regions can be navigated with confidence.

Planning is important in any operation; it is vital to the success of polar navigation. The first step to adequate planning is the acquisition of maximum data on the operational area. *Sailing Directions* should be procured. The Defense Mapping Agency Hydrographic Center and the Cold Weather Programs Office in the Environmental Services Division, Office of the Chief of Naval Operations, should be consulted to obtain any pertinent data. Planning should not be confined solely to navigational matters; the navigator should seek information on ice, climate, and weather, as well as information gathered from previous operations in the area. A bubble sextant should be obtained, and the navigator should familiarize himself with its operation. Forecasts on anticipated ice and weather conditions should be obtained before departure, and updated by radio whenever possible. The entire cruise may well be unusual and interesting, as well as professionally challenging. The navigator's role is vital to the safety of the vessel, and his skillful and ingenious use of a variety of navigation methods will contribute significantly to the success of the operation.

41 Ship Weather Routing

Introduction **4101** *Ship weather routing* can be defined as the process of selecting an optimum track for a transoceanic passage by making long-range predictions of the effects of wind, waves, and currents. It has been defined more generally as the art of taking advantage of all available meteorological and hydrographic information in order to obtain the safest and most economical passage for a ship.

Optimum Track Ship Routing **4102** In the U.S. Navy, weather routing is called *Optimum Track Ship Routing* (*OTSR*) and is done by Fleet Weather Centrals based on analytical studies made at the Fleet Numerical Weather Center, Monterey, California. Several commercial meteorological activities provide similar services for merchant ships and yachts.

Purpose of weather routing As shown in earlier chapters, the shortest distance between any two points on the surface of the earth is the arc of the great circle connecting them. Although this represents the shortest linear distance, it may not represent the most desirable track for the vessel; another route may produce a least time track. In the case of passenger vessels, the optimum route is quite often one which will maintain the maximum conditions of passenger safety and comfort. In other operations, minimum fuel consumption may be the determining factor; or, in the case of some cargo vessels, particularly those carrying deck loads, the optimum track may be one which will present the least hazard to the cargo. In general, routes are prepared which combine these considerations. It has always been recognized by seamen that waves, whether breaking seas or swells, have the greatest adverse effect on the movement of a ship through the water. Optimum track routing is therefore normally used to route ships along a track to avoid areas where the waves are expected to be the highest.

The desirability of optimum track routing cannot be overemphasized. During the month of February, 1965, a group of insurance underwriters reported that due to bad weather, 105 merchant ships sustained hull or cargo damage of sufficient seriousness to result in insurance claims. During the same month, bad weather was a contributing factor in the total loss of 7 ships and damage to 253 others.

Fundamentals of routing

4103 The basic inputs to any ship routing process are present weather conditions and forecasts; forecasts may be short-range (roughly a week), extended-range (a week to a month), and long-term (more than a month). From such forecasts, predictions are made of probable sea states. Other inputs are vessel type, speed, extent of loading, and nature of cargo.

The output from the weather routing advisory service is normally in the form of an *initial route recommendation,* prepared and made available to the ship two or three days in advance of the planned sailing date. Subsequently, the advisory service may recommend advancing or delaying the day or hour of departure. Also available from advisory services are generalized *planning routes* that are developed more from seasonal data than from present and forecast weather patterns.

After a ship sails, its progress along the recommended route is monitored with respect to developing weather patterns. *Diversions* are recommended in terms of change of course or speed to avoid or minimize the effects of adverse weather and sea conditions—conditions that might require a speed reduction by one-third or an increase in transit time of six hours or more. A recommendation of storm *evasion* may be made if conditions become dangerous enough that the planned route should be disregarded and the ship should take independent action to avoid hazardous conditions.

An essential element of any ship weather-routing system is an efficient two-way communications system. By having the ship report present conditions, the advisory agency can confirm or modify its forecasts; by receiving changes in routing, the ship can take advantage of knowledge more recent than that which went into the initial route recommendation.

Predictions of sea conditions

4104 Standard wave-forecasting techniques are used to derive predictions of wave heights from the isobaric pattern of winds on the weather chart. Empirical tests have been made to determine ship speed versus wave conditions for various types of vessels; this information is further divided into the effect of head seas, following seas, and beam seas. Figure 4104a shows a typical graph presenting this information.

Synoptic wave charts are prepared showing the size and type of waves over large areas of the ocean. Data for the preparation of these charts is gathered from commercial and military vessels, and from the meteorological services of various governments. *Prognostic* wave charts are more widely used than the synoptic charts for route selection, because wind and wave conditions often change rapidly at a given point—as in the vicinity of a rapidly moving cold front. They are prepared from sea-level atmosphere charts, as well as from data in the synoptic charts. Figure 4104b is a section of a typical prognostic wave chart of the North Atlantic.

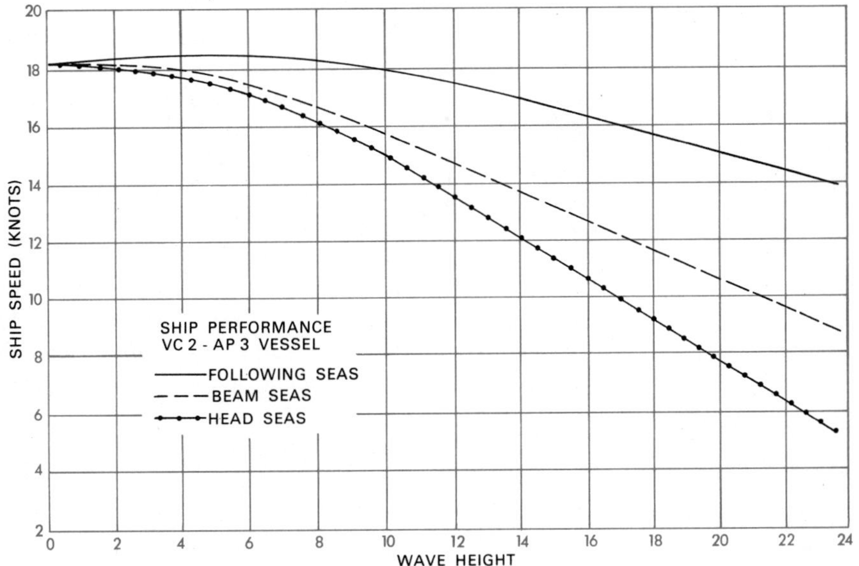

Figure 4104a. Relationship between wave heights and ship's speed made good.

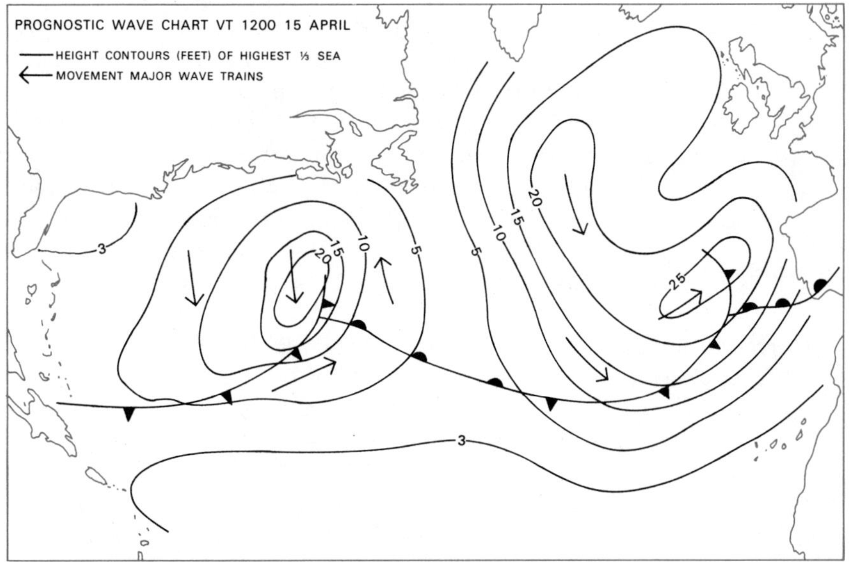

Figure 4104b. Prognostic wave chart.

Figure 4104c shows a surface pressure system lying along a ship's proposed track, *A-B,* and the distribution and direction of waves connected with this pressure system. The barometric pressures are in millibars; the wave lengths are in feet (1 foot = 0.3 m). The *isopleth* lines give the mean wave heights for waves within each area. The

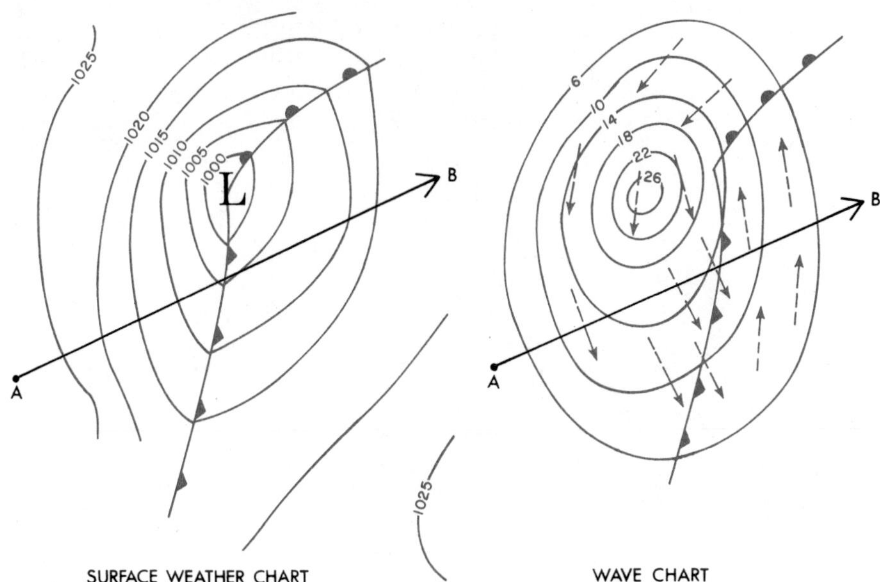

Figure 4104c. Surface pressure system and associated wave heights.

pressure system and wave pattern are assumed to remain static for each 24-hour period.

The various techniques of forecasting sea conditions are constantly being improved. The use of upper air charts and jet stream analysis has proven valuable for longer term predictions covering the duration of a voyage. Significant upper air meteorological features often appear on the upper level charts before they are reflected in surface conditions, thus permitting the analysis and the forecasting of marine weather. Ocean areas that will become hazardous may thus be determined before the condition actually develops.

Currents, wind, and waves

4105 The effects of ocean currents on the movement of a ship in relation to the earth would be easy to determine if the exact current set and drift were known; as the ship moves through the water the entire water mass is also being moved by the current effect. By adding the vectors representing the ship's course and speed and the set and drift of the current, the ship's movement relative to the earth could be precisely determined. This is quite similar to the wind drift problem of an aircraft in which the track of the aircraft over the earth is the result of the two vectors representing heading and air speed, and wind direction and velocity. However, there is one important difference

Current

affecting a ship in the ocean current problem. The ship is not completely immersed in the moving medium; approximately one-third of the hull is immersed and affected by the current, while the remainder of the hull is being affected by air resistance. This latter effect is negligible at low speeds and in no-wind conditions, but it becomes more serious as the relative wind speed increases. Ship movement can be aided by a favorable current, but the prediction of the location and velocity of such a current at a given time is not in most cases accurate enough to be the determining factor in optimum track ship routing. Currents help in the final determination of a route where the wind and wave conditions also suggest the same choice.

Wind effect Wind effect on the movement of a vessel is difficult to compute. It varies with the ship's type, load, and on the direction and strength of the wind relative to the exposed hull and superstructure; container ships with their massive deckloads are particularly affected by surface winds. It is known that for a given wind velocity, a head wind will slow the movement of a vessel more than a following wind will increase her speed; in fact, if a following wind produces moderate to large waves, forward movement will be slower rather than faster. See Figure 4104a.

Wave effect The wave effect on a vessel is also difficult to determine and the computations of mathematical models seldom agree with empirically derived values. This is due in part to the fact that uniform wave heights are used in computation while a great range of heights is actually present in a storm, and also because a captain often decreases his ship's speed in order to avoid the adverse effects of violent motion. The prediction of wave effects on different types of vessels represents the result of large numbers of empirical tests analyzed to produce average values. A combination of reported wave heights and wind values from prognostic charts is used to draw isopleths, or lines of equal wave heights, on the chart. Details of theory and the construction of wave charts to apply these values to actual operations is beyond the scope of this book; additional information will be found in DMAHC Pubs. No. 148, 192, 602, and 604.

Guidance for ship weather routing in various ocean areas can be found in *Bowditch* (1977), Volume I, Articles 2405 and 2406. These generalized statements are based on the overall probability of storm generation at various seasons of the year; they provide a base of information to which can be applied specific extended and long-range forecasts for more exact ship routing. The goal of careful route planning is to minimize the later need for diversion.

Construction of a least time track **4106** Either as an adjunct of weather routing advice, or in lieu thereof, a ship that has the capability of receiving and printing facsimile radio weather charts can benefit from the construction of "least time" tracks like those prepared ashore by a routing service prior to departure.

The basic concept involves the determination of a day's run that would be obtained on various courses. A great circle is normally drawn on the chart between point of departure, or present position if at sea, and the destination. Diverging lines radiating from the point of origin represent the possible tracks, as shown in Figure 4106a. Using a chart of average wave height and the ship's performance curve to determine speed on the various tracks, a 24-hour passage can be computed for each possible track. The points on each line representing a 24-hour passage are then connected with a smooth curve which represents the loci of possible positions of the vessel after one day's travel. Additional diverging tracks are then drawn, the origin of each being perpendicular to curve S_1 at its starting point. Using the wave chart for the second day, the second day's run is constructed and a curve S_2 is drawn through these points. A point of tangency of an arc, centered at the destination *B*, to curve S_2 would indicate the point nearest the destination that can be reached after two days steaming.

When good meteorological forecasts are available, least time tracks can be prepared for several days in advance; such advanced plans, however, should be rechecked each day as additional weather forecasts are received. Figure 4106b shows a plot carried forward for five

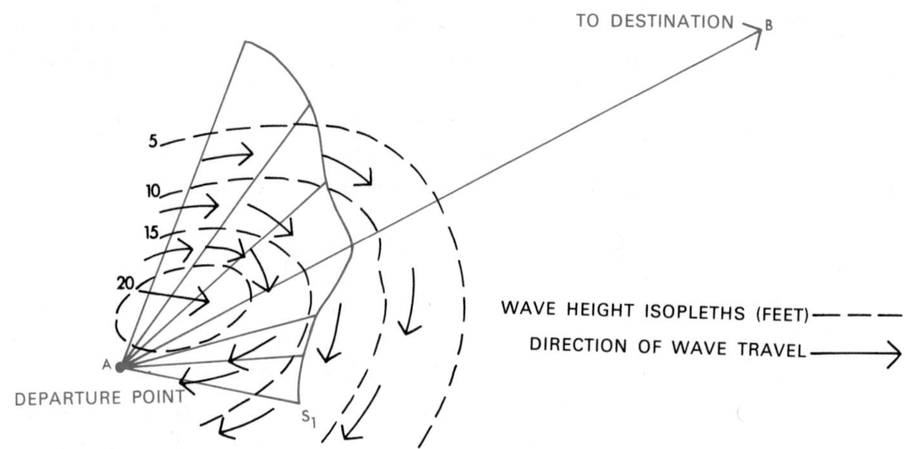

Figure 4106a. Possible routes for first day's travel (black lines outward from *A*).

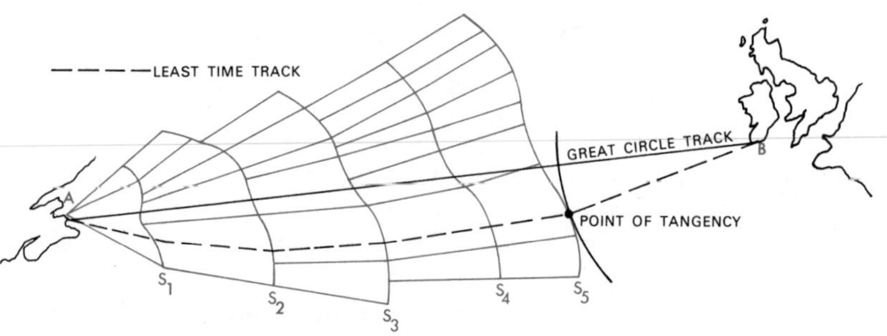

Figure 4106b. Least time track prepared for five days' travel.

days. The least time track is plotted in reverse from the farthest point of advance (found in the preceding paragraph as the point of tangency) back to the point of origin. Each section of the intended track will be perpendicular to the respective curves.

Computers now being introduced aboard merchant vessels digest weather and sea data inputs, and present an almost instantaneous accommodation as to the optimum course and speed to permit maximum safety and economy. The use of computers aboard ship is discussed in more detail in Chapter 38.

Routing to avoid storms

4107 For an extended trip it may be impossible to avoid all storms; sometimes the vessel will be able to avoid the actual storm center, but not all the storm seas and swells associated with the system. The use of long-range forecasts and all available weather data to avoid storms is an art which is mastered by a thorough understanding of navigation and meteorology. The following examples illustrate the use of weather routing on a long voyage using the forecasts of the movements of storm centers expected to be encountered.

Figure 4107a shows a developed semistationary storm and a series of deepening lows in the northern hemisphere. A ship is bound to the westward from *A* to *B*.

Prolonged heavy head seas are to be expected to the south and southwest of the storm center, and moderate head seas to the south and southwest of the center of the second low-pressure area.

To avoid these head seas, a marked diversion to the north of the storm center is indicated; this new path, shown as a dotted line, should also take the ship to the north of the second low.

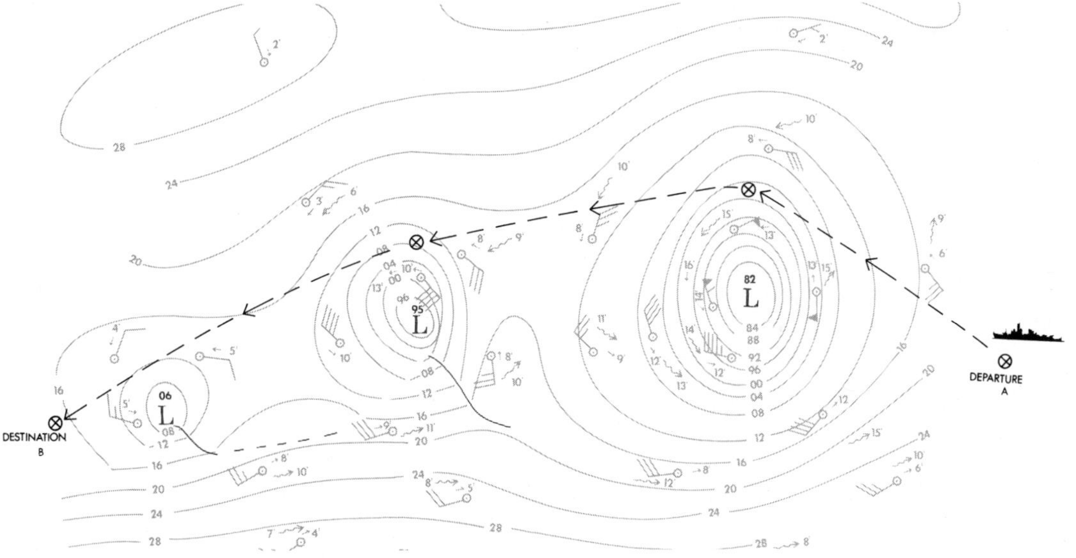

Figure 4107a. Storm avoidance.

Another situation is the existence of a very intense northern hemisphere storm pattern with a series of lows that will be moving northeastward along a cold front. In this case, it is not possible to pass safely to the north of the storm. The ship therefore should divert well to the south. This will cause continuous head winds, but will avoid possible damage due to heavy seas.

A reduced speed *after* adverse weather and sea conditions are encountered will probably mean a longer time of exposure for the ship and her crew and cargo. The objective of weather routing and storm avoidance planning is to make any necessary diversion early enough and of great enough magnitude to entirely avoid the threatening conditions; a greater distance may have to be traveled, but if speed can be maintained (or nearly so), then little delay may result.

Transmissions of weather data

4108 Various U.S. Navy radio stations, and foreign stations also, transmit facsimile weather charts and other data on regular schedules. Weather broadcasts by radiotelephone and radiotelegraph are made by many stations throughout the world. NOAA publication *Worldwide Marine Weather Broadcasts* furnishes a complete listing of such transmissions.

Results of optimum ship routing

4109 Experience indicates that considerable savings in time and fuel are usually obtained by using Optimum Track Ship Routing, and that damage can frequently be avoided. The many variables involved, and the uncertainty of the time which would have been used in following a great circle make exact comparisons impossible. From the experience gained in thousands of crossings, it is apparent that the savings in time, fuel, and passenger and cargo safety, as well as reduced cargo and ship damage, have made this system very worthwhile, and the navigator should familiarize himself with the techniques required for optimum ship routing. In order to gain this familiarization, the Defense Mapping Agency Hydrographic Center Special Publication, SP-1, *Application of Wave Forecasts to Marine Navigation,* should be consulted.

The use of a weather routing service is purely advisory to the navigator and captain of a ship. The captain fully retains his responsibility for the safe and efficient movement of his vessel.

Appendix A Abbreviations

Included in this appendix are the abbreviations and symbols that are commonly used in the practice of navigation. The abbreviations and symbols used on charts are described in Chart No. 1, which is included as Appendix G.

A ampere; amplitude; augmentation; away (altitude difference).
a altitude intercept (altitude difference, Hc Ho); assumed.
a_0, a_1, a_2, First, second, and third Polaris sight-reduction correction (from *Nautical Almanac*).
AA *Air Almanac.*
AC alternating current.
ADF automatic direction finder.
AF audio frequency.
aL assumed latitude.
aLo assumed longitude.
A.M. amplitude modulation.
Amp amplitude.
AP assumed position.
App apparent.
atm atmosphere.
AU astronomical unit.
Aug augmentation.
Az azimuth angle. (Z also used.)
aλ assumed longitude.
B bearing; bearing angle; barometric correction (altitude).
BFO beat frequency oscillator.
Bn beacon.
C Celsius (centigrade); chronometer time; compass (direction); correction; course (vessel); course angle.
C & GS Coast and Geodetic Survey.
CB compass bearing.
CC chronometer correction; compass course.
CCZ Coastal Confluence Zone.
CE chronometer error; compass error.
CH compass heading.

Note: Some variations in capitalization may occur.

CIC Combat Information Center.
cm centimeter.
CMG course made good.
Cn course (as distinguished from course angle).
CNO Chief of Naval Operations.
co- the compliment of (90° minus).
COA course of advance.
COG course over ground.
co-L colatitude.
comp compass.
corr correction.
cos cosine.
cot cotangent
CPA closest point of approach.
Cpgc course per gyro compass.
cps cycles per second.
Cpsc course per standard compass.
CP stg c course per steering compass.
CRT cathode ray rube.
csc cosecant.
Cus course (aircraft). (The following are preferable: CC, GC, MC, TC).
CW continuous wave.
C-W chronometer time minus watch time.
Dev. inc. declination increment.
D deviation; dip (of horizon); distance; drift (current).
d declination; difference; distance.
DB danger bearing.
DC direct current.
Dec. declination.
Dec. inc. declination increment.
deg degree.
Dep departure.
Dest destination.
Dev deviation.
DG degaussing.
diff difference.
dist distance.
D. Lat. Difference of latitude.
DLo Difference of longitude (arc units).
DMAHC Defense Mapping Agency Hydrographic Center.
DME distance measuring equipment.
DR dead reckoning, dead reckoning position.
Dr drift.
DRA dead reckoning analyzer.
DRAI dead reckoning analyzer indicator.
DRM direction of relative movement.
DRT dead reckoning tracer.
DSD Double-second difference.
DST daylight saving time.
dur duration.
DUT_1 time signal correction.
dλ difference of longitude.

E East; error.
e Earth (wind triangle and relative movement problems), base of Naperian logarithms.
EHF extremely high frequency.
EM log electromagnetic log.
EP estimated position.
EPI electronic position indicator.
Eq. T equation of time.
est estimated.
ETA estimated time of arrival.
ETD estimated time of departure.
F Fahrenheit; fast; phase correction (altitude).
f frequency; latitude factor.
fath fathom, fathoms.
FBM Fleet Ballistic Missile (submarine).
FM frequency modulation.
fm fathom, fathoms.
ft foot, feet.
FTC fast time constant (radar).
G Greenwich, Greenwich meridian (upper branch); grid.
g Greenwich meridian (lower branch); acceleration due to gravity.
GAT Greenwich apparent time.
GB grid bearing.
GC grid course.
GE gyro error.
GH grid heading.
GHA Greenwich hour angle.
GHz gigahertz.
GMT Greenwich mean time.
Govt government.
GP geographical position.
GPS Global Positioning System.
Gr Greenwich.
GRI group repetition interval.
GST Greenwich sidereal time.
GV grid variation.
GZn grid azimuth.
h altitude (astronomical); height above sea level.
ha apparent altitude.
HA hour angle.
Hc computed altitude.
Hd head.
Hdg heading.
HE height of eye.
HF high frequency.
HHW higher high water.
HLW higher low water.
H.O. Hydrographic Office, U.S. Navy (now a part of the Defense Mapping Agency Hydrographic Center).
Ho observed altitude.
Hor horizontal.
HP horizontal parallax.

H_{pgc} heading per gyro compass.
H_{psc} heading per standard compass.
H_{pstgc} heading per steering compass.
hr hour.
hrs hours.
hs sextant altitude.
Ht height.
ht tabulated altitude.
Ht. eye height of eye.
HW high water.
Hz hertz (cycle per second).
I instrument correction.
IC index correction.
IFF identification friend or foe.
IFR instrument flight rules.
IMU inertial measurement unit.
in inch, inches.
INS integrated navigation system.
J irradiation correction.
K knot; knots; Kelvin (temperature).
kc kilocycles (kilohertz).
kHz kilohertz.
km kilometer, kilometers.
kn knot, knots.
kt knot; knots
kW kilowatt.
L latitude; lower limb correction for moon (from *Nautical Almanac*).
L_1 latitude of departure.
L_2 latitude of destination.
l difference of latitude.
LAN local apparent noon.
LAT local apparent time.
lat latitude.
LEM lunar excursion module.
LF low frequency.
LHA local hour angle.
LHW lower high water.
LL lower limb.
LLW lower low water.
Lm mid-latitude; mean latitude.
LMT local mean time.
log logarithm; logarithmic.
$\log_e$ natural logarithm (to base e).
$\log_{10}$ common logarithm (to base 10).
Lo(λ) longitude.
long longitude.
LOP line of position.
LST local sidereal time.
Lv latitude of vertex.
LW low water.
λ_1 longitude of departure.
λ_2 longitude of destination.

λv longitude of vertex.
M magnetic; maneuvering ship (in relative plot of relative movement problems; meridian (upper branch); meridional parts.
m maneuvering ship (in speed triangle of relative movement problems); meridian (lower branch); meridional difference; meters.
mag magnetic; magnitude.
max maximum.
MB magnetic bearing.
mb millibars.
MC magnetic course.
Mc megacycles.
Mer. Pass. meridian passage.
MF medium frequency.
MH magnetic heading.
MHHW mean higher high water.
MHW mean high water.
MHWN mean high water neaps.
MHWS mean high water springs.
MHz megahertz.
mi mile, miles.
mid middle.
min minute, minutes.
MINDAC Miniature Inertial Navigational Digital Automatic Computer.
MLLW mean lower low water.
MLW mean low water.
MLWN mean low water neaps.
MLWS mean low water springs.
mm millimeter.
mph miles (statute) per hour.
MPP most probable position.
ms millisecond.
MZn magnetic azimuth.
N North.
NA *Nautical Almanac.*
Na nadir.
NASA National Aeronautics and Space Administration.
naut nautical.
NAVDAC Navigational Data Assimilation Computer.
NAVSAT Navy navigation satellite system.
NAVSTAR Global Positioning System.
nm nautical mile, nautical miles.
n mi nautical mile, nautical miles.
NOAA National Oceanic and Atmospheric Administration.
NOS National Ocean Survey.
NRL Naval Research Laboratory.
Nt M nautical mile.
ONC Operational Navigational Charts.
P atmospheric pressure; parallax; planet; pole.
p departure; polar distance.
PC personal correction.
PD polar distance; position doubtful.
pgc per gyro compass.

P in A parallax in altitude.
Pit log Pitot-static log.
PM pulse modulation.
Pn North pole; North celestial pole.
Pos position.
posit position.
PPC propagation correction.
PPI plan position indicator.
PRF pulse repetition frequency.
PRR pulse repetition rate.
Ps South pole; South celestial pole.
psc per standard compass.
p stg c per steering compass.
Pt point.
pub publication.
PV prime vertical.
Q Polaris correction.
QQ′ celestial equator; equator.
R reference craft (relative movement problems); refraction.
r reference ship (in speed triangle of relative movement problems).
RA right ascension.
RB relative bearing.
R Bn radiobeacon.
RDF radio direction finder.
rel relative.
rev reversed.
RF radio frequency.
R Fix running fix.
RIS range instrumentation ship.
RMS root mean square.
RPM revolution per minute.
S sea-air temperature difference correction; slow; South; speed.
s second, seconds.
SD semidiameter.
sec secant; second, seconds.
SH ship's head (heading).
SHA sidereal hour angle.
SHF super high frequency.
SI international system of units (metric).
sin sine.
SINS Ship's Inertial Navigation System.
SMG speed made good.
SOA speed of advance.
SOG speed over the ground.
SRM speed of relative movement.
SSCNS Ship's Self-Contained Navigation System.
STC sensitivity time control.
St.M statute mile.
T air temperature correction; temperature; time; toward (altitude difference); true (direction).
t meridian angle; elapsed time.
Tab tabulated value.

tan tangent.
TB true bearing; combined temperature-barometric correction.
TC true course.
TD time difference (Loran).
$\mathbf{T_G}$ ground-wave reading (Loran).
$\mathbf{T_{GS}}$ ground-wave-sky-wave reading (Loran).
TH true heading.
TR track.
Tr transit.
$\mathbf{T_S}$ sky-wave reading (Loran).
$\mathbf{T_{SG}}$ sky-wave-ground-wave reading (Loran).
TZn true azimuth.
U upper limb correction for moon (from *Nautical Almanac*).
UHF ultra high frequency.
UL upper limb.
UT Universal Time (UT_1, UT_2).
UTC Coordinated Universal Time.
V variation; vertex.
v excess of GHA change from tabulated value for one hour.
Var variation.
vel velocity.
VHF very high frequency.
vis visibility.
VLF very low frequency.
VOR very high frequency omnirange.
W watch time; West.
w wind (wind triangle problems).
WAC World Aeronautical Chart.
WE watch error.
X parallactic angle.
yd yard.
yr year.
Z azimuth angle; zenith.
z zenith distance; zone meridian (lower branch).
ZD zone description.
Zn azimuth (as distinguished from azimuth angle).
ZT zone time.
Δ a small increment, or the change in one quantity corresponding to a unit change in another variable.
λ longitude; wave length (radiant energy).
μ**s** microsecond.
π ratio of circumference of circle to diameter = 3.14159+.

Appendix B
Symbols

Positions	⌓	dead reckoning position.
	⊙	fix.
	⊡	estimated position.
	△	symbol used for one set of fixes when simultaneously fixing by two means, e.g., visual and radar; sometimes used for radionavigation fixes.
Mathematical symbols	$+$	plus (addition).
	$-$	minus (subtraction).
	$\pm$	plus or minus.
	$\sim$	absolute difference (smaller subtracted from larger).
	$\times$	times (multiplication).
	$\div$	divided by (division).
	x^2	square of number x.
	x^3	cube of number x.
	x^n	nth power of number x.
	$\sqrt{\ }$	square root.
	$\sqrt[n]{\ }$	nth root.
	$=$	equals.
	$\neq$	not equal to.
	$\approx$	nearly equal to.
	$>$	is greater than.
	$<$	is less than.
	$\geqslant$	is equal to or greater than.
	$\leqslant$	is equal to or less than.
	∞	infinity.
	.....	repeating decimal.

Appendix C
Standards of Precision and Accuracy; Mathematical Rules

Standards of precision and accuracy

C-01 The adoption of a set of standards for the precision and accuracy of navigational measurements must be tempered somewhat by their application to a specific vessel in a specific set of circumstances. A large ship will be navigated more precisely than a small boat; a vessel of any size more accurately in good weather than in a storm.

Precision

C-02 In navigation, "precision" is used to mean the fineness of the degree of measurement; thus a value of 12.0 is a more *precise* value than one of 12; the former has three significant digits, the latter has two.

In some scientific fields, "precision" is related to the degree to which a given set of measurements of the same sample agree with their mean; this definition is not applicable in navigation.

Accuracy

Accuracy relates to the closeness of a measured value to the true (correct, exact) value.

Precision and accuracy are not the same, and only the correct terms should be used in each instance. A measured value should not be stated to a degree of precision that is greater than the accuracy of its measurement.

Any quantity derived by interpolation from a table should be expressed to the same degree of precision as are the tabulated values.

Any quantity derived from a mathematical calculation should not be expressed to any higher degree of precision than that of the *least* precise term used in the calculation.

Levels of precision

C-03 The levels of precision of measurement and calculation used in this book are:

Altitude	0.1′
Azimuth	0.1°
Bearing	0.1°

Compass Error	0.5°
Current: Set	1°
Drift	0.1 knot
Course	0.1°
Deviation	0.5°
Distance	0.1 mile
Height of tide	0.1 foot
Latitude	0.1′
Longitude	0.1′
Speed	0.1 knot
Time DR	1 minute
Celestial	1 second
Variation	0.5°

In expressing any quantity to *tenths*—when there are no tenths—the ".0" should be shown to indicate the degree of precision; for example,

15 miles—means to the nearest mile;
15.0 miles—means to the nearest 0.1 mile.

Rounding off **C-04** In this book, the following rules have been used to round off the results of mathematical computations which contain digits without significance.

1. If the digit to be rounded off is a "4" or less, it is dropped or changed to a zero. (633 is rounded to 630; 1.24 is rounded to 1.2.)

2. If the digit to be rounded off is a "6" or larger, the preceding digit is raised to the next higher value and the rounded digit is dropped or changed to zero.

1.27 is rounded to 1.3
787 is rounded to 790

3. If the final digit is a "5," the preceding digit is *increased* or *decreased* so that it will be an *even* number and the rounded digit is dropped or changed to zero.

1.25 is rounded to 1.2
1.35 is rounded to 1.4
425 is rounded to 420
775 is rounded to 780

4. If more than one digit is to be rounded off, these digits are *not* rounded off separately in sequence. For example, 1.348 is rounded to 1.3 in one operation, and *not* in steps, first to 1.35 and then to 1.4.

Appendix D
The Metric System

Introduction **D-01** The "Metric Conversion Act of 1975" declared the policy of the United States to be an increased use of the metric system of measurement on a voluntary basis, with the goal of "a nation predominantly, although not exclusively, metric." This edition, therefore, introduces metric units as parenthetical equivalents to the customary (English) units. Some charts are now using metric units for depths and heights, although it is expected that nautical miles and knots will continue in use for many years.

The modern metric system **D-02** The correct name for the "metric" system is the *International System of Units,* abbreviated as *SI* (from the name in French). This is a thoroughly modernized metric system based on very precise standards and relationships between units. SI provides a logical and consistently interrelated system of measurement for science, industry, commerce, and other areas of human effort, including, of course, navigation.

The modern metric system is built upon a foundation of seven base units, plus two supplementary units.

The base units **D-03** The *base units* and their symbols are:

Quantity	SI unit name	Symbol
Length	meter†	m
Mass (weight)	kilogram	kg
Temperature	kelvin	K‡
Time	seconds	s
Electric current	ampere	A
Amount of substance	mole	mol
Luminous intensity	candela	cd

†The spelling in SI is "metre" but "meter" has been adopted for U.S. use.

‡The commonly used unit of temperature is the "degree Celcius," °C (formerly called "centigrade"); the size of the unit is the same, the zero point is different. If kelvins are used, note that the unit is "kelvin (K)" and not "degree kelvin (°K)."

The supplementary units

D-04 The *supplementary units* and their symbols are:

Quantity	SI unit name	Symbol
Plane angle	radian	rad
Solid angle	steradian	sr

Unit symbols should be used rather than abbreviations; e.g., "A" rather than "amp" for ampere. Unit symbols are not changed for the plural form. Most symbols are written in lower-case letters; exceptions are those named after persons in which cases the symbol is capitalized. Periods are not used after symbols (except at the end of a sentence). In the expression of a quantity, a space is left between the numerical value and the symbol; e.g., 35 mm rather than 35mm, but a hyphen is normally inserted in the adjectival form; e.g., 35-mm film. No space is left, however, between a numerical value and the symbols for degrees, minutes, or seconds.

In the field of navigation, the SI units most often encountered will be those of length, time, and angular measurement; note that the unit of time is the same in both metric and customary (English) systems.

Derived units

D-05 SI units for all other quantities are *derived* from the above nine base and supplementary units. All are defined as products or ratios without numerical factors. Some are expressed in terms of the base units concerned; others have been given special names of their own.

Typical of the derived units that are combinations of the base units are:

Quantity	SI unit name	Symbol
Area	square meter	m^2
Volume	cubic meter	m^3
Density	kilogram per cubic meter	kg/m^3
Speed, velocity	meter per second	m/s
Acceleration	meter per second squared	m/s^2

Typical of derived units with special names are:

Quantity	SI unit name	Symbol	Expression in terms of other units
Frequency	hertz	Hz	s^{-1}
Force	newton	N	kg · m/s
Pressure, stress	pascal	Pa	N/m^2
Energy, work	joule	J	N · m
Power	watt	W	J/s
Electrical potential	volt	V	W/A
Electrical resistance	ohm	Ω	V/A

Some derived units combine base and special names; typical of these are:

Quantity	SI unit name	Symbol
Electrical field strength	volt per meter	V/m
Specific energy	joule per kilogram	J/kg

Derived units resulting from multiplication are normally written out with a space between units; e.g., newton meter (acceptable, but less desirable is the hyphenated form, "newton-meter"). With symbols, a raised dot (·) is used to indicate the product of the two units; e.g., N · m; an exception is watt hour which is written "Wh" without the raised dot.

Powers may be expressed as words, such as "squared" or "cubed," which follow the names of units. An exception is that powers expressed as words may precede the names of units of area and volume.

In division, the word "per" is used rather than a solidus (/) when units are spelled out; e.g., meter per second, not meter/second. When symbols are used, any of the following forms may be used; m/s or $\frac{m}{s}$ or $m \cdot s^{-1}$.

Multiples and submultiples **D-06** Units larger and smaller than the base and derived units are formed by adding prefixes decimally to make multiples and submultiples. The symbol for the prefix is added to the symbols for the base or derived unit.

1,000,000,000	10^9	giga	G
1,000,000	10^6	mega	M
1,000	10^3	kilo	k
100	10^2	hecto	h
10	10^1	deka	da
0.1	10^{-1}	deci	d
0.01	10^{-2}	centi	c
0.001	10^{-3}	milli	m
0.000,001	10^{-6}	micro	μ

There are others—larger multiples and smaller submultiples—than those shown above (for a total of 16 prefixes), but these are of little or no interest in navigation.

It is important to note that the kilogram is the only SI unit that integrally includes a prefix. Because double prefixes are not to be used, the standard prefixes, in the case of mass, are to be used with gram (g) and not with kilogram (kg).

Retained customary units **D-07** Certain "customary" (English) units that are not a part of the SI (metric) system are in such wide use that it is not practical to abandon them. Among those accepted for continued use with SI units in the United States are:

degree, angle (°)	= (π/180) rad
minute, angle (′)	= (1/60)° = (π/10,800) rad
second, angle (″)	= (1/60)′ = (π/848,000) rad
liter (L*)	= 1 dm = 10^{-3} m
metric ton (t)	= 10^3 kg

In those cases where their usage is well established, certain other customary units will continue to be acceptable "for a limited time, subject to future review." Of interest to navigators in this category are:

Nautical mile
Knot
bar, millibar (atmospheric pressure)

Unacceptable units **D-08** The Metric Conversion Act of 1975 authorizes the Secretary of Commerce to make "interpretations and modifications" of the International System of Units for U.S. usage. Several such official decisions have been made; these form the basis for the preceding articles. Metric units, symbols, and terms not in accordance with the published decisions are no longer acceptable for continued use in the United States. The officially acceptable list includes many units not discussed above, but, as previously stated, these are generally not used in navigation.

Conversion **D-09** As long as both "customary" and "metric" units are in wide use, a navigator will be faced with the task of converting from one to the other. The conversion factors shown here have been rounded off for practical use and do not, in most instances, yield exact values. (The metric equivalents shown in this book have been rounded to roughly the same degree of precision of value as the customary unit.)

Customary units to metric

Known value	Multiplied by	To find
inches (in)	25.4	millimeters (mm)
feet (ft)	0.3048	meters (m)
yards (yd)	0.9144	meters (m)
statute miles (s mi)	1.609	kilometers (km)
nautical miles (n mi)	1.852	kilometers (km)

*The international symbol for liter is the lowercase letter "l" which can easily be confused with the numeral "1"; accordingly, the symbol "L" is recommended for U.S. use.

Known value	Multiplied by	To find
ounces, weight (oz)	28.35	grams (g)
pounds (lb)	0.4536	kilograms (kg)
ounces, liquid (oz)	30.28	milliliters (mi)
quarts (qt)	0.9464	liters (L)
gallons (gal)	3.785	liters (L)
Fahrenheit temperature (°F)	5/9 after subtracting 32	Celsius temperature (°C)
Metric units to Customary		
centimeters (cm)	0.3937	inches (in)
meters (m)	3.281	feet (ft)
meters (m)	1.094	yards (yd)
kilometers (km)	0.6214	statute miles (s mi)
kilometers (km)	0.5400	nautical mi (n mi)
grams (g)	0.03527	ounce (weight) (oz)
kilograms (kg)	2.205	pounds (lb)
milliliters (ml)	0.03302	ounces (liq.) (oz)
liters (L)	1.057	quarts (qt)
liters (L)	0.2642	gallon (gal)
Celsius temperature (°C)	9/5 then add 32	Fahrenheit temperature (°F)

Procedures for conversion

When converting from customary units to metric, or from metric to customary, care must be taken not to have a converted value implying a higher degree of precision than the original value. The number of digits retained in the converted value should be such that precision is not exaggerated. For example, a length of 250 feet converts exactly to 76.2 m. If, however, the 250-foot length has been obtained by rounding to the nearest 10 feet, the converted value should be stated as 76 m; if it has been obtained by rounding to the nearest 50 feet, the metric length should be given as 80 m.

The proper conversion procedure is to multiply the given quantity, customary or metric, by the conversion factor in full exactly as given above, and then to round the product to the appropriate number of significant digits (for rounding, see Article C-04). For example, to convert 15.2 feet to meters, multiply 15.2 by 0.3048 and obtain 4.63296; this is rounded to 4.63 m. Do not round either the conversion factor or the quantity before multiplying them.

Conversion by calculator

Conversion in either direction between customary and metric units is easily accomplished using a personal electronic calculator such as those described in Appendix F. Ordinary multiplication can be performed using the conversion factors listed above, or other appropriate values. Many more advanced models, however, are internally programmed for direct keyboard conversions without reference to the factor involved.

Appendix E
Conversion Table for Feet, Fathoms, and Meters

Meters	Feet	Fathoms	Meters	Feet	Fathoms	Feet	Meters	Feet	Meters	Fathoms	Meters	Fathoms	Meters
1	3.28	0.55	61	200.13	33.36	1	0.30	61	18.59	1	1.83	61	111.56
2	6.56	1.09	62	203.41	33.90	2	0.61	62	18.90	2	3.66	62	113.39
3	9.84	1.64	63	206.69	34.45	3	0.91	63	19.20	3	5.49	63	115.21
4	13.12	2.19	64	209.97	35.00	4	1.22	64	19.51	4	7.32	64	117.04
5	16.40	2.73	65	213.25	35.54	5	1.52	65	19.81	5	9.14	65	118.87
6	19.69	3.28	66	216.54	36.09	6	1.83	66	20.12	6	10.97	66	120.70
7	22.97	3.83	67	219.82	36.64	7	2.13	67	20.42	7	12.80	67	122.53
8	26.25	4.37	68	223.10	37.18	8	2.44	68	20.73	8	14.63	68	124.36
9	29.53	4.92	69	226.38	37.73	9	2.74	69	21.03	9	16.46	69	126.19
10	32.81	5.47	70	229.66	38.28	10	3.05	70	21.34	10	18.29	70	128.02
11	36.09	6.01	71	232.94	38.82	11	3.35	71	21.64	11	20.12	71	129.84
12	39.37	6.56	72	236.22	39.37	12	3.66	72	21.95	12	21.95	72	131.67
13	42.65	7.11	73	239.50	39.92	13	3.96	73	22.25	13	23.77	73	133.50
14	45.93	7.66	74	242.78	40.46	14	4.27	74	22.56	14	25.60	74	135.33
15	49.21	8.20	75	246.06	41.01	15	4.57	75	22.86	15	27.43	75	137.16
16	52.49	8.75	76	249.34	41.56	16	4.88	76	23.16	16	29.26	76	138.99
17	55.77	9.30	77	252.62	42.10	17	5.18	77	23.47	17	31.09	77	140.82
18	59.06	9.84	78	255.91	42.65	18	5.49	78	23.77	18	32.92	78	142.65
19	62.34	10.39	79	259.19	43.20	19	5.79	79	24.08	19	34.75	79	144.48
20	65.62	10.94	80	262.47	43.74	20	6.10	80	24.38	20	36.58	80	146.30
21	68.90	11.48	81	265.75	44.29	21	6.40	81	24.69	21	38.40	81	148.13
22	72.18	12.03	82	269.03	44.84	22	6.71	82	24.99	22	40.23	82	149.96
23	75.46	12.58	83	272.31	45.38	23	7.01	83	25.30	23	42.06	83	151.79
24	78.74	13.12	84	275.59	45.93	24	7.32	84	25.60	24	43.89	84	153.62
25	82.02	13.67	85	278.87	46.48	25	7.62	85	25.91	25	45.72	85	155.45
26	85.30	14.22	86	282.15	47.03	26	7.92	86	26.21	26	47.55	86	157.28
27	88.58	14.76	87	285.43	47.57	27	8.23	87	26.52	27	49.38	87	159.11
28	91.86	15.31	88	288.71	48.12	28	8.53	88	26.82	28	51.21	88	160.93
29	95.14	15.86	89	291.99	48.67	29	8.84	89	27.13	29	53.04	89	162.76
30	98.43	16.40	90	295.28	49.21	30	9.14	90	27.43	30	54.86	90	164.59
31	101.71	16.95	91	298.56	49.76	31	9.45	91	27.74	31	56.69	91	166.42
32	104.99	17.50	92	301.84	50.31	32	9.75	92	28.04	32	58.52	92	168.25
33	108.27	18.04	93	305.12	50.85	33	10.06	93	28.35	33	60.35	93	170.08
34	111.55	18.59	94	308.40	51.40	34	10.36	94	28.65	34	62.18	94	171.91
35	114.83	19.14	95	311.68	51.95	35	10.67	95	28.96	35	64.01	95	173.74
36	118.11	19.69	96	314.96	52.49	36	10.97	96	29.26	36	65.84	96	175.56
37	121.39	20.23	97	318.24	53.04	37	11.28	97	29.57	37	67.67	97	177.39
38	124.67	20.78	98	321.52	53.59	38	11.58	98	29.87	38	69.49	98	179.22
39	127.95	21.33	99	324.80	54.13	39	11.89	99	30.18	39	71.32	99	181.05
40	131.23	21.87	100	328.08	54.68	40	12.19	100	30.48	40	73.15	100	182.88
41	134.51	22.42	101	331.36	55.23	41	12.50	101	30.78	41	74.98	101	184.71
42	137.80	22.97	102	334.65	55.77	42	12.80	102	31.09	42	76.81	102	186.54
43	141.08	23.51	103	337.93	56.32	43	13.11	103	31.39	43	78.64	103	188.37
44	144.36	24.06	104	341.21	56.87	44	13.41	104	31.70	44	80.47	104	190.20
45	147.64	24.61	105	344.49	57.41	45	13.72	105	32.00	45	82.30	105	192.02
46	150.92	25.15	106	347.77	57.96	46	14.02	106	32.31	46	84.12	106	193.85
47	154.20	25.70	107	351.05	58.51	47	14.33	107	32.61	47	85.95	107	195.68
48	157.48	26.25	108	354.33	59.06	48	14.63	108	32.92	48	87.78	108	197.51
49	160.76	26.79	109	357.61	59.60	49	14.94	109	33.22	49	89.61	109	199.34
50	164.04	27.34	110	360.89	60.15	50	15.24	110	33.53	50	91.44	110	201.17
51	167.32	27.89	111	364.17	60.70	51	15.54	111	33.83	51	93.27	111	203.00
52	170.60	28.43	112	367.45	61.24	52	15.85	112	34.14	52	95.10	112	204.83
53	173.88	28.98	113	370.73	61.79	53	16.15	113	34.44	53	96.93	113	206.65
54	177.17	29.53	114	374.02	62.34	54	16.46	114	34.75	54	98.76	114	208.48
55	180.45	30.07	115	377.30	62.88	55	16.76	115	35.05	55	100.58	115	210.31
56	183.73	30.62	116	380.58	63.43	56	17.07	116	35.36	56	102.41	116	212.14
57	187.01	31.17	117	383.86	63.98	57	17.37	117	35.66	57	104.24	117	213.97
58	190.29	31.71	118	387.14	64.52	58	17.68	118	35.97	58	106.07	118	215.80
59	193.57	32.26	119	390.42	65.07	59	17.98	119	36.27	59	107.90	119	217.63
60	196.85	32.81	120	393.70	65.62	60	18.29	120	36.58	60	109.73	120	219.46

From DMAHC Pub. No. 9, Volume II, Table 21.

Appendix F
The Use of Electronic Calculators in Navigation

Introduction **F-01** In the early 1970s, advancements in solid-state electronics made possible small "hand-held" or "pocket" *electronic calculators.* These could add, subtract, multiply and divide. Numbers were displayed by small *light-emitting diodes* for direct reading. The very small amount of power required was supplied by internal batteries. Initially, such units were quite limited in their capabilities and were rather expensive, thus restricting the extent of their use.

Subsequently, the development of small "personal" calculators has been literally astounding. Models soon appeared that had internal magnetic memories for the "scratch pad" recording of intermediate results. Then came *scientific* (or *slide rule*) models that could directly compute squares and square roots, had stored constants such as π, and which had the capability for direct calculations involving trigonometric functions. The next step was the introduction of *programmable* calculators with memories capable of storing a limited number of operational sequences; these greatly facilitate the repetition of complex problems using different input data; see Article F-04. Programmable models also include multiple data memories for the storage of various input data or intermediate results. Further along in the hierarchy of existing types, are the *card programmable* models. With these, the steps of a program can be quickly and flawlessly entered by the insertion of a small magnetic card that is read and passed out the other side of the calculator. The use of such cards can also be extended to the input of data and the extraction of results for storage and later use. Several models of programmable calculators can provide an optional paper tape printout of the stored program, a trace of the calculations as they progress through a problem, or a print of the results only. In various designs, this capability is either built into the unit or achieved by coupling the hand calculator to a separate printer. Related to "programmable" calculators are the *stored program* models that have several programs permanently built into their memories; such units are very easy to use, but are limited to the specialized applications for which they were manufactured, plus simple, nonprogrammed arithmetic and trigonometric calculations.

Caution An individual's ability to use an electronic calculator for the solution of navigation problems must *not* be substituted for the ability to solve such problems by other means *without* the assistance of a calculator.

A calculator is a marvelous device, but it is quite complex and relatively fragile. A navigator may be able to use a calculator, and gain from such use, but *he should not be entirely dependent upon it.*

Characteristics of calculators

F-02 Slide rules normally calculate with from two to four significant digits, depending on the nearer end of the scale—a higher level of precision between 1 and 2 than between 9 and 10. In contrast, electronic calculators commonly calculate to a level of precision as great as from six to twelve digits (depending on the model) regardless of the place of the number on a scale of 1 to 10; many models provide for rounding down to a preselected number of decimal places, if desired. In all applications, especially in navigation, caution must be exercised that this very high degree of precision in calculation does not lead the user to place a higher degree of confidence in his results than is warranted by the level of precision and accuracy of input data; for example a calculator might be quite capable of producing a dead-reckoning position to degrees, minutes, and hundredths of minutes—yet this level of precision would not be justified if speed were only known to the nearest knot or course to the nearest degree. Calculator-derived solutions to celestial observations might yield a fix to a hundredth of a minute, yet if the sextant observation had been made under difficult conditions, the position might be valid only to the nearest minute, if even to that level of precision. While calculator results can be accepted as fully accurate (provided that the proper inputs and functions have been keyed in), judgment must be used in their interpretation and application.

Electronic calculators using light-emitting diode (LED) displays may be difficult to read in bright sunlight; this can be a limitation to their use in a marine environment. A few models are made with liquid crystal displays (LCD), which are easily read in bright light conditions but are not seen in darkness; this design has some disadvantages and has not been applied to the more advanced models. A recent development is vacuum fluorescent displays, an attempt to combine the advantageous features of both LED and LCD designs.

Types of calculators

F-03 Small electronic calculators suitable for use in the solution of various navigational problems can be roughly divided into several types.* These will be listed in order of increasing capabilities; those in each group include the capabilities of those in lower categories.

Type A—Calculators with the basic four functions (+, −, ×, ÷), possibly with the capability for squares and square roots, and perhaps including one memory register.

*These type groupings are arbitrary and are used here solely for convenience in this appendix.

Type B—Calculators with the capability for direct calculations with trigonometric (and inverse trig) functions, and various powers and roots; angles may be in degrees or radians (and possibly also in grads). These calculators may have more than one memory, and if so, each may be separately addressed.

Models at the upper end of this category may have special keys for polar-to-rectangular conversion, and the inverse. Some Type B calculators are internally programmed for a limited number of conversions between customary and metric units, and/or several basic statistical functions. Numbers may be entered and displayed either in conventional format or in *scientific notation*—expressed as a number (mantissa) that has a single digit to the left of its decimal point followed by a variable number of digits to the right of the decimal point as selected by the user, plus a power-of-ten (exponent). This makes possible calculations involving very large and very small quantities.

The number of functions has now reached the point where it is no longer possible to have a separate key for each and remain a "pocket" or "hand-held" calculator. Two functions are assigned each key, selected by a *second function* or *shift* key much the same as is done on a typewriter for uppercase letters and special characters.

Type C—Calculators that can be programmed, capable of receiving and storing a series of up to several hundred instructions. Normally, but not in all cases, the "program" is lost when the calculator is turned off, and the unit must be reprogrammed when it is next used. In a few models, however, the calculator can retain, for several days or weeks, the program and any internal data. This is a considerable advantage, but only one such program can be retained if more than one is being used; other programs would have to be manually reentered as in other Type C units.

Calculators in the Type C category may have either one or two shift keys to provide added keyboard capacity.

Some Type C calculators (and a few Type B models) have a key for *engineering notation* in which the power-of-ten exponent is used only in multiplies of three, corresponding to the prefixes of the metric system (see Article D-06). This limitation requires that there may be one, two, or three digits to the left of the decimal point in the mantissa. Calculators not having a key for direct display in engineering notation can accomplish conversion from scientific notation by use of a simple subroutine.

Type D—Calculators that are capable of receiving programs from small magnetic cards; these programs will have been previously recorded on the cards, either on the calculator with which they are being used or on a similar unit. Additionally, problem data can be entered into or recorded from storage registers by use of similar magnetic cards. Calculators of this type are capable of being programmed for relatively sophisticated techniques, such as subroutines, conditional branching, flags, indirect addressing, etc. Multiple memories are included, and models are available with a print-out capability either integrally or with an accessory unit. There may be as many as three shift keys.

Originally all personal calculators with storage capabilities had "volatile" memories, the contents of which were lost when the unit was switched off—and most models are still subject to this limitation. A later development, however, is a memory register that is nonvolatile to a degree and will retain its stored program and/or data for a period of days, or even several weeks, after the calculator is turned off following a period of use.

A major advancement in personal calculator design occurred in 1977 with the introduction of solid-state, semiconductor memory units in the form of small plug-in modules or cartridges. A single module less than 0.8 inch (2 cm) square can hold as many as 5,000 program steps and replace an entire "library" of as many as 25 programs on magnetic cards. In addition, the basic internal memory registers were increased in number and provision was added for varying the proportion of registers between the use for program steps and for data storage. One model retains and expands the capability of also using magnetic cards. This combination of cards programmed by the user and plug-in modules programmed by the manufacturer makes a very powerful hand-held personal calculator.

Type-E—Calculators with built-in programs for navigation including celestial sight reduction; almanac data may be stored internally or may be acquired from external sources. (This internal programming is often referred to as "firmware" in contrast to the external programs, "software," of key and card programmable models.) Type E calculators, sometimes referred to as "hardwired" models, usually also have some general calculating capability, but they are really specialized models for limited applications.

Specific models

In this appendix reference to specific models will be avoided as much as possible due to the rapid advancement in calculator design and the frequent introduction of new models with subsequent discontinuance of older designs.

Data entry techniques

F-04 In the development of small calculators, two quite different techniques have come into being for the entry of data into the devices. One is generally termed *algebraic entry* and the other is named *Reverse Polish Notation* (for reasons that need not be considered here). The various calculator manufacturers have adopted one procedure or the other; strong proponents speak for each technique, and usually against the other, although both are quite suitable for use in all calculations.

It is beyond the scope of this appendix to discuss either algebraic or Reverse Polish Notation (RPN) in detail; such information can best be obtained from the instruction manual for the calculator being used. In very broad terms, it might be said that RPN provides a somewhat more "powerful" programming technique, but at a cost of greater complexity in use. RPN, with its more difficult procedures, is more easily used by individuals with mathematical experience. Algebraic entry, with its "plain English" approach, is more easily understood by the average person.

Calculator programs **F-05** Any mathematical problem can be solved using an electronic calculator by merely pressing the proper keys in sequence to enter the data and perform the mathematical operations; this is true whether the problem is short or long, simple or complex. The sequence of steps taken, the keys pressed, is a *program,* although this term is not normally used unless the sequence is thought out and reduced to writing in advance of execution. If the problem is lengthy or complex, or the same problem is to be solved repeatedly with different data, *programming* in advance is desirable both from the time saved and the reduction of possibility of error. A program simply consists of a statement of the sequence of operations that will be repeated in each solution of the problem, with appropriate entry points for the insertion of data. Programming is merely logical thinking, the organization of the flow of the various steps of the solution. For most complex solutions, there is no one single "best program"; the efforts of different individuals will result in somewhat different programs, all of which should yield the same answer to the problem.

The effort required to prepare an efficient program for the solution of a problem is quickly repaid by the ease with which the problem is solved a second or third or more times. With the card-programmable Type D models, this advantage reaches its maximum; the program need be manually prepared and keyed into the calculator only once, no matter how many times it is needed.

The many navigational problems that can be solved more easily, quickly, and accurately with an electronic calculator—and the many different models that can be used—make it impractical to cover programming in detail in this appendix. That topic could fill a book, and indeed several have been written. In broad terms, a navigator wishing to solve a program with his calculator should first search for the appropriate equation. This can be as simple as D = ST or it can be as complex as $\sin h = \sin L \sin d \underset{\sim}{+} \cos L \cos d \cos t$ and

$$\sin Z = \frac{\cos d \sin t}{\cos h},$$

or even more complex. The equation is then broken down into a series of mathematical functions and machine operations depending upon the basic nature of the calculator being used (the use of algebraic entry or RPN, the number of memories available, etc.). When the program has been written down on paper, it should be keyed into the calculator and then run, preferably with simple data, or with data that will yield a known solution. If, or when, the program checks out, it is recorded on paper or on a magnetic card. From then on, the program can be run as many times as needed, inserting new data as appropriate. With Type D calculators, the program recorded on a magnetic card can be reinserted into program memory at a later date in only a few second's time. Quite often the solution of a complex problem will require the use of a series of program cards. These are inserted at appropriate times in the solution of the problem, with the intermediate results being carried forward in the calculator's data memory registers. With the most recent models, the related programs will all be in a single plug-in module. Individual programs are accessed when needed by pressing two or three keys on the keyboard, or these operations can be a part of a "master program."

Programs for various models of calculators have been prepared by the manufacturers to cover a wide variety of applications; some are furnished with the unit when it is purchased and others can be bought separately as the need arises. Such programs may have been either developed by the manufacturer or contributed by users. Other programs are often available from formal or informal groups of owners of similar model calculators. Users frequently can improve on or extend purchased programs, or write their own for problems for which nothing has been published. No prior education or experience in computer programming is required for the level involved with the small calculators being considered here. It is, however, valuable to observe certain basic procedures. The first step is to identify the equations that will be needed in the preparation of the program for the solution of the navigational problem(s) at hand. These usually can be found in a standard text or reference work such as this book, *Bowditch,* etc. They may not be in the best format for calculator solution and may have to be rearranged algebraically. In other cases, a new equation may have to be developed by extension or a combination of basic relationships.

When the required mathematical expressions are known, the next step is to develop the procedures for their use; this is sometimes termed the *algorithm.* Although not strictly necessary, it is often helpful to prepare a *flow chart* (or *flow diagram*), especially if branching or subroutines are involved, or if multiple related programs are to be used. A flow chart outlines what is happening, and in what sequence, when a program is running; it is a graphic representation of the reasoning behind the structure of the program. A complete flow diagram will include not only the instructions placed in the calculator's memory, but also what must be done manually on the keyboard, such as starting the program and inserting data. More on flow charts and diagrams will be found in the instruction books of applicable calculators.

Calculators in navigation

F-06 For a number of decades, a slide rule was of considerable assistance to a navigator trained in its use; time and effort was saved, and accuracy was enhanced. Now, however, the slide rule is all but replaced by the personal electronic calculators which can supply the solution to navigational problems from simple distance-speed-time calculations to the determination of a fix from multiple celestial observations.

Type A calculators are generally limited to the solution of the most simple problems. A slight gain in speed may be achieved, but the principal advantage is in accuracy, *if* care is taken in keying-in the data and functions to be executed. The time required to look up trigonometric values in tables makes the use of these simple calculators impractical for more complex problem solving.

The trigonometric capability of the Type B calculators makes possible their use with such problems as current sailing or positioning using two bearings on the same object; and their use makes the solution easier, quicker, and more accurate. At the upper end of calculators in this class are models with features especially useful in navigational applications, such as multiple memories, rectangular-polar coordinate conversion, and conversion between degrees-minutes-seconds and decimal degrees. Type B calculators have the capability of reducing celestial observations, but the length of the process and the necessity to perform each step individually for each reduction generally make such application rather tedious.

Celestial sight reductions can be done on Type B calculators, but are more readily accomplished on the programmable Type C and Type D models; the D units are the easiest to use since the necessary programs can be entered by passing a magnetic card through the calculator, or accessed in a plug-in module by merely pressing several keys on the keyboard. These calculators are also useful in the solution of problems involving dead reckoning, currents, and the "sailings"—great circle, rhumb line, composite, etc. Calculations can be made for the most probable position based on one or two or more lines of position. Relative motion problems, too, are very suitable for calculator solution.

Celestial sight reductions can be even more quickly and easily done on the Type E calculators, units that are already internally programmed and require only the entry of the input data. These models can also be used to solve problems involving some types of the sailings.

Need for use of the *Nautical Almanac* (or *Air Almanac*) in celestial navigation solutions may or may not be eliminated by the calculator programs; this is determined by the particular model and its available programs. Type D calculators are ideally suitable for the direct computation of almanac data from the U.S. Naval Observatory publication, *Almanac for Computers,* using pre-recorded magnetic cards for the entry of both programs and mathematical constants.

It should be noted that there are two different approaches possible in the reduction of celestial observations, procedures that are nearly the opposite of each other. With a Type E (or Type D with suitable program cards) the answer can be obtained by merely pressing a few keys to enter the raw input data. No knowledge of celestial triangles nor of the use of precomputed tables (Pub. No. 229 and 249) is necessary; it has become "push-button" navigation. On the other hand, a navigator knowing the geometry involved and the basic equations can use his Type B, C, or D calculator to solve the equations and obtain the answers needed. The "push-button navigator" runs the risk of being completely incapable of sight reduction if his calculator breaks down or his batteries fail. His more knowledgeable counterpart, however, can continue to function in such circumstances, albeit more slowly and with more mental effort, using the precomputed sight reduction tables or even simple tables of sine and cosine values. It is for this reason that preprogrammed calculations (internally or externally) are not allowed in most scholastic and licensing examinations. The "push-button-only" navigator is not a safe navigator; the "fully-qualified" navigator, who is knowledgeable in both techniques, can use the "easy-quick" method when available, but he is fully competent to meet situations in which the only "calculator" available is his own brain.

Summary

F-07 This appendix has dealt with small personal electronic calculators more in generalities than specifics, as this is a very rapidly advancing field of technology. The capabilities of today's calculators make models of just a few years ago appear quite crude and obsolete, while the capabilities of the calculator of a few years in the future cannot even be guessed.

Caution

It is emphasized that the only safe way to use an electronic calculator for the solution of navigational problems is with a full knowledge and understanding of the basic equations. Blind reliance on programs prepared by other people, or on purchased prerecorded magnetic cards or plug-in modules, can only lead to disaster in emergency situations. Calculators can be a great help, but the only "brain" available to solve the problem is that gray matter in the navigator's skull.

Index

Chart No. 1

United States of America

Nautical Chart Symbols and Abbreviations

SIXTH EDITION
JULY 1975

Prepared jointly by

DEPARTMENT OF COMMERCE
National Oceanic and Atmospheric Administration
National Ocean Survey *(Formerly Coast and Geodetic Survey, and U.S. Lake Survey)*

DEPARTMENT OF DEFENSE
Defense Mapping Agency
Hydrographic Center

GENERAL REMARKS

This publication (CHART NO. 1) contains symbols and abbreviations that have been approved for use on nautical charts published by the United States of America. The buoyage systems used by other countries often vary from that used by the United States. Charts produced by the Defense Mapping Agency Hydrographic Center (DMAHC) will show the colors, lights, and other characteristics in use for the area of the individual chart. Certain modified reproduction charts distributed by DMAHC will also show the shapes and other distinctive features that may vary from those illustrated in this chart. Terms, symbols, and abbreviations are numbered in accordance with a standard form approved by a 1952 resolution of the International Hydrographic Organization (IHO). Although the use of IHO-approved symbols and abbreviations is not mandatory, the United States has cooperated to adopt many IHO-approved symbols for standard use on U.S. nautical charts. Alphanumeric style differences in the first column of the following pages indicate symbol and abbreviation status as follows:

VERTICAL FIGURES indicate those items for which the symbol and abbreviation are in accordance with resolutions of the IHO.

SLANTING FIGURES indicate those symbols for which no IHO resolution has been adopted.

SLANTING FIGURES UNDERSCORED indicate IHO and U.S. symbols do not agree.

SLANTING FIGURES ASTERISKED indicate that no symbol has been adopted by the United States.

SLANTING FIGURES IN PARENTHESES indicate that the items are in addition to those appearing in the "Glossary of Cartographic Terms", SP No. 22, 3rd Edition, 1951, IHO, and subsequent revisions.

† All changes since the July 1972 edition of this publication are indicated by the dagger symbol in the margin immediately adjacent to the item identification of the symbol or abbreviation affected.

BUILDINGS. A conspicuous feature on a building may be shown by a landmark symbol with a descriptive label. (See I 8b, 36, 44, 72.) Prominent buildings that are of assistance to the mariner may be shown by actual shape as viewed from above (see I 3a, *19*, *47*, 66), and may be marked "CONSPICUOUS".

BUOYS and BEACONS. On entering a channel from seaward, buoys on starboard side are red with even numbers, on port side black with odd numbers. Lights on buoys on starboard side of channel are red or white, on port side white or green. Mid-channel buoys have black-and-white vertical stripes. Junction or obstruction buoys, which may be passed on either side, have red-and-black horizontal bands. This system does not always apply to foreign waters.

The position of a fixed beacon is represented by the center of the beacon symbol or the circle at the base of the symbol. The approximate position of a buoy is represented by the dot or circle associated with the buoy symbol. The approximate position is used because of practical limitations in positioning and maintaining buoys and their sinkers in precise geographical locations. These limitations include, but are not limited to, inherent imprecisions in position fixing methods, prevailing atmospheric and sea conditions, the slope of and the material making up the seabed, the fact that buoys are moored to sinkers by varying lengths of chain, and the fact that buoy body and/or sinker positions are not under continuous surveillance, but are normally checked only during periodic maintenance visits which often occur more than a year apart. The position of the buoy body can be expected to shift inside and outside the charting symbol due to the forces of nature. The mariner is also cautioned that buoys are liable to be carried away, shifted, capsized, sunk, etc. Lighted buoys may be extinguished or sound signals may not function as a result of ice, running ice or other natural causes, collisions, or other accidents. For the foregoing reasons, a prudent mariner must not rely completely upon the charted position or operation of floating aids to navigation, but will also utilize bearings from fixed objects and aids to navigation on shore. Further, a vessel attempting to pass close aboard always risks collision with a yawing buoy or with the obstruction the buoy marks.

COLORS are optional for characterizing various features and areas in the charts.

DEPTH contours and soundings are shown in meters on an increasing number of new charts and new editions; the depth unit is stated on all charts.

HEIGHTS of land and conspicuous objects are given in feet above Mean High Water, unless otherwise stated in the title of the chart.

IMPROVED CHANNELS are shown by limiting dashed lines with the depth and date of the latest examination placed adjacent to the channel except when the channel data is tabulated.

LETTERING styles and capitalization as indicated in Chart No. 1 are not always rigidly adhered to on the charts.

LONGITUDES are referred to the Meridian of Greenwich.

OBSOLESCENT SYMBOLIZATION on charts will be revised to agree with the current preferred usage as soon as opportunity affords.

SHORELINE shown on charts represents the line of contact between the land and a selected water elevation. In areas affected by tidal fluctuation, this line of contact is usually the mean high-water line. In confined coastal waters of diminished tidal influence, a mean water level line may be used. The shoreline of interior waters (rivers, lakes) is usually a line representing a specified elevation above a selected datum. Shoreline is symbolized by a heavy line (A 9).

APPARENT SHORELINE is used on charts to show the outer edge of marine vegetation where that limit would reasonably appear as the shoreline to the mariner or where it prevents the shoreline from being clearly defined. Apparent shoreline is symbolized by a light line (A 7, C 17).

U.S. COAST PILOTS, SAILING DIRECTIONS, LIGHT LISTS, RADIO AIDS, and related publications furnish information required by the navigator that cannot be shown conveniently on the nautical chart.

U.S. NAUTICAL CHART CATALOGS and INDEXES list nautical charts, auxiliary maps and related publications, and include general information relative to the charts.

Some differences may be observed between Chart No. 1 and symbols shown on certain reproductions of foreign charts and special charts. Foreign symbols may be interpreted by reference to the Symbol Sheet or Chart No. 1 of the originating country. A glossary of foreign terms and abbreviations is generally given on charts on which they are used, as well as in the Sailing Directions.

TABLE OF CONTENTS

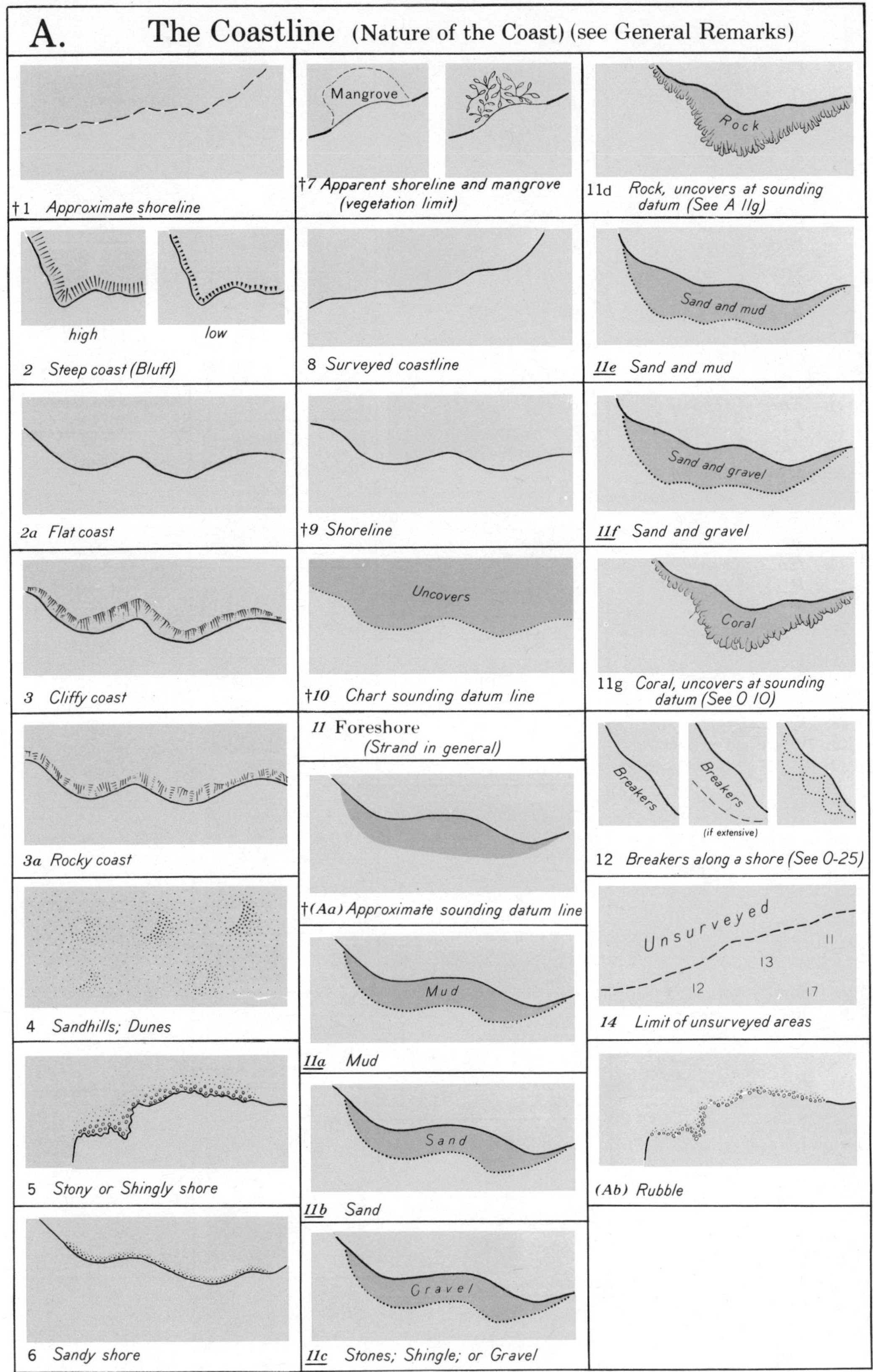

NOTE: Areas shown in gray tint are shown in yellow tint on charts published by the National Ocean Survey.

B. Coast Features

1	*G*	*Gulf*
2	*B*	*Bay*
(Ba)	*B*	*Bayou*
3	*Fd*	*Fjord*
4	*L*	*Loch; Lough; Lake*
5	*Cr*	*Creek*
5a	*C*	*Cove*
6	*In*	*Inlet*
7	*Str*	*Strait*
8	*Sd*	*Sound*
9	*Pass*	*Passage; Pass*
	Thoro	*Thorofare*
10	*Chan*	*Channel*
10a		*Narrows*
11	*Entr*	*Entrance*
12	*Est*	*Estuary*
12a		*Delta*
13	*Mth*	*Mouth*
14	*Rd*	*Road; Roadstead*
15	*Anch*	*Anchorage*
16	*Hbr*	*Harbor*
16a	*Hn*	*Haven*
17	*P*	*Port*
(Bb)	*P*	*Pond*
18	**I**	*Island*
19	**It**	*Islet*
20	**Arch**	*Archipelago*
21	**Pen**	*Peninsula*
22	**C**	*Cape*
23	**Prom**	*Promontory*
24	**Hd**	*Head; Headland*
25	**Pt**	*Point*
26	**Mt**	*Mountain; Mount*
27	**Rǵe**	*Range*
27a		*Valley*
28		*Summit*
29	**Pk**	*Peak*
30	**Vol**	*Volcano*
31		*Hill*
32	**Bld**	*Boulder*
33	**Ldǵ**	*Landing*
34		*Tableland (Plateau)*
35	*Rk*	*Rock*
36		*Isolated rock*
(Bc)	*Str*	*Stream*
(Bd)	*R*	*River*
(Be)	*Slu*	*Slough*
(Bf)	*Lag*	*Lagoon*
(Bg)	*Apprs*	*Approaches*
(Bh)	*Rky*	*Rocky*
†(Bi)	Is	*Islands*
†(Bj)	Ma	*Marsh*
†(Bk)	Mg	*Mangrove*
†(Bl)	Sw	*Swamp*

C. The Land (Natural Features)

1 *Contour lines (Contours)*

1a *Contour lines, approximate (Contours)*

2 *Hachures*

2a *Form lines, no definite interval*

2b *Shading*

3 *Glacier*

4 *Saltpans*

5 *Isolated trees*

5a *Deciduous or of unknown or unspecified type*

5b *Coniferous*

5c *Palm tree*

5d *Nipa palm*

5e *Filao*

5f *Casuarina*

5g *Evergreen tree (other than coniferous)*

6 *Cultivated fields*

6a *Grass fields*

7 *Paddy (rice) fields*

7a *Park; Garden*

8 *Bushes*

8a *Tree plantation in general*

9 *Deciduous woodland*

10 *Coniferous woodland*

10a *Woods in general*

11 *Tree top height (above shoreline datum)*

12 *Lava flow*

13 *River; Stream*

14 *Intermittent stream*

15 *Lake; Pond*

16 *Lagoon (Lag)*

17 *Marsh; Swamp*

18 *Slough (Slu.)*

19 *Rapids*

20 *Waterfalls*

21 *Spring*

D. Control Points

No.	Symbol	Abbreviation	Description
1	△		*Triangulation point (station)*
1a			*Astronomic station*
2	⊙	*(See In)*	*Fixed point (landmark, position accurate)*
(Da)	○	*(See Io)*	*Fixed point (landmark, position approx.)*
3	· 256		*Summit of height (Peak) (when not a landmark)*
(Db)	256		*Peak, accentuated by contours*
(Dc)	256		*Peak, accentuated by hachures*
(Dd)			*Peak, elevation not determined*
(De)	⊙ 256		*Peak, when a landmark*
4	⊕	Obs Spot	*Observation spot*
***5**		BM	*Bench mark*
6	View X		*View point*
7			*Datum point for grid of a plan*
8			*Graphical triangulation point*
9		Astro	*Astronomical*
10		Tri	*Triangulation*
(Df)		C of E	*Corps of Engineers*
12			*Great trigonometrical survey station*
13			*Traverse station*
14		Bdy Mon	*Boundary monument*
(Dg)	◇		*International boundary monument*

E. Units

No.	Abbreviation	Meaning
†*1*	hr, h	*Hour*
†2	m, min	*Minute (of time)*
†3	sec, s	*Second (of time)*
4	m	*Meter*
4a	dm	*Decimeter*
4b	cm	*Centimeter*
4c	mm	*Millimeter*
4d	m^2	*Square meter*
4e	m^3	*Cubic meter*
5	km	*Kilometer*
6	in	*Inch*
7	ft	*Foot*
8	yd	*Yard*
9	fm	*Fathom*
10	cbl	*Cable length*
†11	M, Mi, N Mi	*Nautical mile*
12	kn	*Knot*
†12a	t	*Tonne (metric ton = 2,204.6 lbs.)*
12b	cd	*Candela (new candle)*
13	lat	*Latitude*
14	long	*Longitude*
14a		*Greenwich*
15	pub	*Publication*
16	Ed	*Edition*
17	corr	*Correction*
18	alt	*Altitude*

No.	Abbreviation	Meaning
19	ht; elev	*Height; Elevation*
20	°	*Degree*
21	′	*Minute (of arc)*
22	″	*Second (of arc)*
23	No	*Number*
†**(Ea)**	St M, St Mi	*Statute mile*
†**(Eb)**	μsec, μs	*Microsecond*
(Ec)	Hz	*Hertz (cps)*
(Ed)	kHz	*Kilohertz (kc)*
(Ee)	MHz	*Megahertz (Mc)*
†**(Ef)**	cps, c/s	*Cycles/second (Hz)*
(Eg)	kc	*Kilocycle (kHz)*
(Eh)	Mc	*Megacycle (MHz)*
†**(Ei)**	T	*Ton (U.S. short ton = 2,000 lbs.)*

F. Adjectives, Adverbs, Nouns, and Other Words

No.	Abbreviation	Meaning
1	gt	*Great*
2	lit	*Little*
3	Lrg	*Large*
4	sml	*Small*
5		*Outer*
6		*Inner*
7	mid	*Middle*
8		*Old*
9	anc	*Ancient*
10		*New*
11	St	*Saint*
12	conspic	*Conspicuous*
13		*Remarkable*
14	D, Destr	*Destroyed*
15		*Projected*
16	dist	*Distant*
17	abt	*About*
18		*See chart*
18a		*See plan*
19		*Lighted; Luminous*
20	sub	*Submarine*
21		*Eventual*
22	AERO	*Aeronautical*
23		*Higher*
23a		*Lower*
24	exper	*Experimental*
25	discontd	*Discontinued*
26	prohib	*Prohibited*
27	explos	*Explosive*
28	estab	*Established*
29	elec	*Electric*
30	priv	*Private, Privately*
31	prom	*Prominent*
32	std	*Standard*
33	subm	*Submerged*
34	approx	*Approximate*
35		*Maritime*
36	maintd	*Maintained*
37	aband	*Abandoned*
38	temp	*Temporary*
39	occas	*Occasional*
40	extr	*Extreme*
41		*Navigable*
42	N M	*Notice to Mariners*
(Fa)	L N M	*Local Notice to Mariners*
43		*Sailing Directions*
44		*List of Lights*
(Fb)	unverd	*Unverified*
(Fc)	AUTH	*Authorized*
(Fd)	CL	*Clearance*
(Fe)	cor	*Corner*
(Ff)	concr	*Concrete*
(Fg)	fl	*Flood*
(Fh)	mod	*Moderate*
(Fi)	bet	*Between*
(Fj)	1st	*First*
†*(Fk)*	2nd, 2d	*Second*
†*(Fl)*	3rd, 3d	*Third*
(Fm)	4th	*Fourth*
(Fn)	DD	*Deep Draft*
(Fo)	min	*Minimum*
(Fp)	max	*Maximum*
†*(Fq)*	N'ly	*Northerly*
†*(Fr)*	S'ly	*Southerly*
†*(Fs)*	E'ly	*Easterly*
†*(Ft)*	W'ly	*Westerly*
†*(Fu)*	Sk	*Stroke*
†*(Fv)*	Restr	*Restricted*

G. Ports and Harbors

1	Anch	*Anchorage (large vessels)*
2	Anch	*Anchorage (small vessels)*
3	Hbr	*Harbor*
4	Hn	*Haven*
5	P	*Port*
6	Bkw	*Breakwater*
6a		*Dike*
7		*Mole*
8		*Jetty (partly below MHW)*
8a		*Submerged jetty*
(Ga)		*Jetty (small scale)*
9	Pier	*Pier*
10		*Spit*
11		*Groin (partly below MHW)*
12	ANCH PROHIBITED; ANCH PROHIB	*Anchorage prohibited (screen optional)(See P 25)*
12a		*Anchorage reserved*
12b	QUARANTINE ANCHORAGE; QUAR ANCH	*Quarantine anchorage*
13	Spoil Area	*Spoil ground*
(Gb)	Dumping Ground	*Dumping ground*
(Gc)	80 83 Disposal Area 85 depths from survey of JUNE 1972 90 98	*Disposal area*
(Gd)	Ⓟ	*Pump-out facilities*
14	Fsh stks	*Fisheries; Fishing stakes*
14a		*Fish trap; Fish weirs (actual shape charted)*
14b		*Duck blind*
15		*Tuna nets (See G 14a)*
15a	Oys	*Oyster bed*
16	Ldg	*Landing place*
17		*Watering place*
18	Whf	*Wharf*
19		*Quay*
20		*Berth*
20a	14	*Anchoring berth*
20b	3	*Berth number*
21	Dol	*Dolphin*
22		*Bollard*
23		*Mooring ring*
24		*Crane*
25		*Landing stage*
25a		*Landing stairs*
26	Quar	*Quarantine*
27		*Lazaret*
*28	Harbor Master	*Harbormaster's office*
29	Cus Ho	*Customhouse*
30		*Fishing harbor*
31		*Winter harbor*
32		*Refuge harbor*
33	B Hbr	*Boat harbor*
34		*Stranding harbor (uncovers at LW)*
35		*Dock*
36		*Drydock (actual shape on large-scale charts)*
37		*Floating dock (actual shape on large-scale charts)*
38		*Gridiron; Careening grid*
39		*Patent slip; Slipway; Marine railway*
39a	Ramp	*Ramp*
40	Lock	*Lock (point upstream) (See H 13)*
41		*Wetdock*
42		*Shipyard*
43		*Lumber yard*
44	Health Office	*Health officer's office*
45	Hk	*Hulk (actual shape on large-scale charts) (See O 11)*
46	PROHIBITED AREA; PROHIB AREA	*Prohibited area (screen optional)*
46a	10	*Calling-in point for vessel traffic control*
47		*Anchorage for seaplanes*
48		*Seaplane landing area*
49	Under construction	*Work in progress*
50		*Under construction*
51		*Work projected*
(Ge)	Subm ruins	*Submerged ruins*

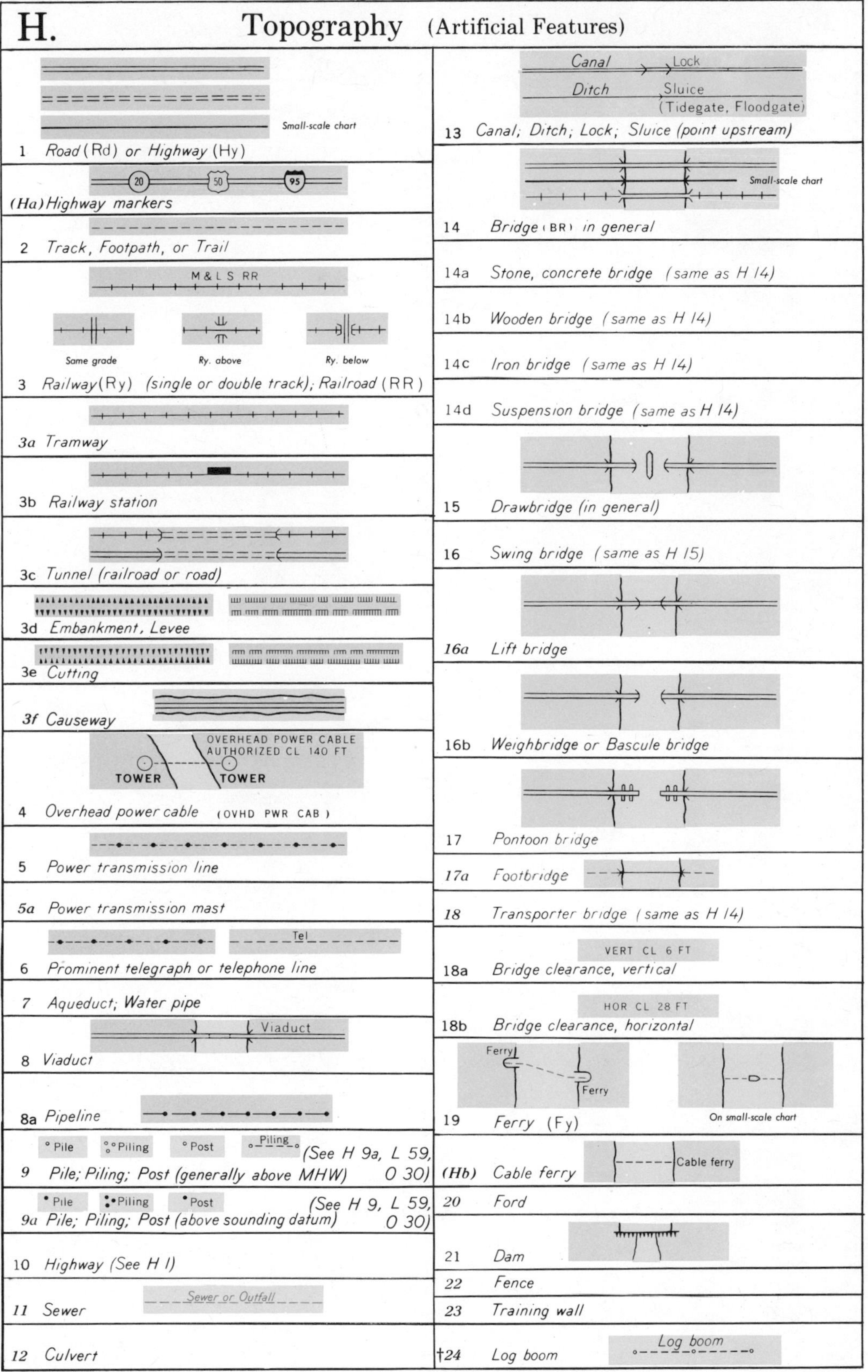
H. Topography (Artificial Features)
Small-scale chart
1 Road (Rd) or Highway (Hy)
20
50
95
(Ha) Highway markers
2 Track, Footpath, or Trail
M & L S RR
Same grade
Ry. above
Ry. below
3 Railway (Ry) (single or double track); Railroad (RR)
3a Tramway
3b Railway station
3c Tunnel (railroad or road)
3d Embankment, Levee
3e Cutting
3f Causeway
OVERHEAD POWER CABLE
AUTHORIZED CL 140 FT
TOWER
TOWER
4 Overhead power cable (OVHD PWR CAB)
5 Power transmission line
5a Power transmission mast
Tel
6 Prominent telegraph or telephone line
7 Aqueduct; Water pipe
Viaduct
8 Viaduct
8a Pipeline
Pile
Piling
Post
Piling
(See H 9a, L 59, O 30)
9 Pile; Piling; Post (generally above MHW)
Pile
Piling
Post
(See H 9, L 59, O 30)
9a Pile; Piling; Post (above sounding datum)
10 Highway (See H 1)
Sewer or Outfall
11 Sewer
12 Culvert
Canal
Lock
Ditch
Sluice
(Tidegate, Floodgate)
13 Canal; Ditch; Lock; Sluice (point upstream)
Small-scale chart
14 Bridge (BR) in general
14a Stone, concrete bridge (same as H 14)
14b Wooden bridge (same as H 14)
14c Iron bridge (same as H 14)
14d Suspension bridge (same as H 14)
15 Drawbridge (in general)
16 Swing bridge (same as H 15)
16a Lift bridge
16b Weighbridge or Bascule bridge
17 Pontoon bridge
17a Footbridge
18 Transporter bridge (same as H 14)
VERT CL 6 FT
18a Bridge clearance, vertical
HOR CL 28 FT
18b Bridge clearance, horizontal
Ferry
Ferry
On small-scale chart
19 Ferry (Fy)
Cable ferry
(Hb) Cable ferry
20 Ford
21 Dam
22 Fence
23 Training wall
Log boom
†24 Log boom

I. Buildings and Structures (see General Remarks)

No.	Symbol	Abbreviation	Meaning
1			*City or Town (large scale)*
(Ia)			*City or Town (small scale)*
2			*Suburb*
3		Vil	*Village*
3a			*Buildings in general*
4		Cas	*Castle*
5			*House*
6			*Villa*
7			*Farm*
8			*Church*
8a		Cath	*Cathedral*
8b	⊙ SPIRE	Spire	*Spire; Steeple*
9			*Roman Catholic Church*
10			*Temple*
11			*Chapel*
12			*Mosque*
12a			*Minaret*
(Ib)			*Moslem Shrine*
13			*Marabout*
14		Pag	*Pagoda*
15			*Buddhist Temple; Joss-House*
15a			*Shinto Shrine*
16			*Monastery; Convent*
17			*Calvary; Cross*
17a	Cem		*Cemetery, Non-Christian*
18			*Cemetery, Christian*
18a			*Tomb*
19			*Fort (actual shape charted)*
20			*Battery*
21			*Barracks*
22			*Powder magazine*
23	Airport		*Airplane landing field*
24			*Airport, large scale (See P-13)*
(Ic)			*Airport, military (small scale)*
(Id)			*Airport, civil (small scale)*
25			*Mooring mast*
26	King St	St	*Street*

No.	Symbol	Abbreviation	Meaning
26a	Locust Ave	Ave	*Avenue*
26b	Grand Blvd	Blvd	*Boulevard*
27		Tel	*Telegraph*
28		Tel Off	*Telegraph office*
29		PO	*Post office*
30		Govt Ho	*Government house*
31			*Town hall*
32		Hosp	*Hospital*
33			*Slaughterhouse*
34		Magz	*Magazine*
34a			*Warehouse; Storehouse*
35	⊙MON °Mon		*Monument*
36	⊙CUP °Cup		*Cupola*
37	⊙ELEV °Elev		*Elevator; Lift*
(Ie)		Elev	*Elevation; Elevated*
38			*Shed*
39			*Zinc roof*
40	Ruins °Ru		*Ruins*
41	⊙ TR °Tr		*Tower*
(If)	⊙ ABAND LT HO		*Abandoned lighthouse*
42	⊙ WINDMILL		*Windmill*
43			*Watermill*
43a	⊙ WINDMOTOR		*Windmotor*
44	⊙CHY °Chy		*Chimney; Stack*
45	⊙S'PIPE °S'pipe		*Water tower; Standpipe*
46			*Oil tank*
47		Facty	*Factory*
48			*Saw mill*
49			*Brick kiln*
50			*Mine; Quarry*
51	°Well		*Well*
52			*Cistern*
53	⊙ TANK °Tk		*Tank*
54			*Noria*
55			*Fountain*

I. Buildings and Structures (continued)

No.	Symbol	Abbreviation	Meaning
61		Inst	*Institute*
62			*Establishment*
63			*Bathing establishment*
64		Ct Ho	*Courthouse*
65	[symbol]	Sch	*School*
(Ig)	[symbol]	HS	*High school*
(Ih)	[symbol]	Univ	*University*
66	[symbols]	Bldg	*Building*
67		Pav	*Pavilion*
68			*Hut*
69			*Stadium*
70		T	*Telephone*
71	[symbols]		*Gas tank; Gasometer*
72	⊙GAB °Gab		*Gable*
73			*Wall*
74			*Pyramid*
75			*Pillar*
76			*Oil derrick*
(Ii)		Ltd	*Limited*
(Ij)		Apt	*Apartment*
(Ik)		Cap	*Capitol*
(Il)		Co	*Company*
(Im)		Corp	*Corporation*
(In)	⊙		*Landmark (position accurate)(See D 2)*
(Io)	○		*Landmark (position approximate)(See Da)*

J. Miscellaneous Stations

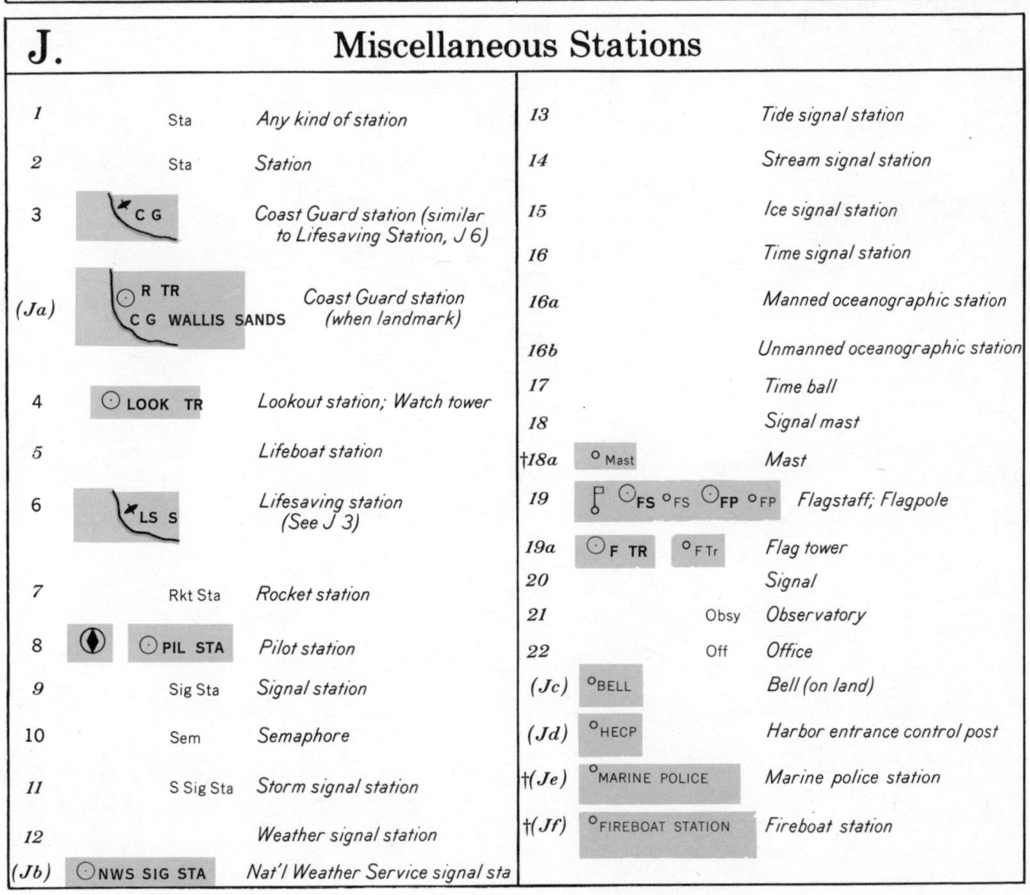

No.	Symbol	Abbreviation	Meaning
1		Sta	*Any kind of station*
2		Sta	*Station*
3	C G		*Coast Guard station (similar to Lifesaving Station, J 6)*
(Ja)	⊙ R TR C G WALLIS SANDS		*Coast Guard station (when landmark)*
4	⊙ LOOK TR		*Lookout station; Watch tower*
5			*Lifeboat station*
6	LS S		*Lifesaving station (See J 3)*
7		Rkt Sta	*Rocket station*
8	[symbol] ⊙ PIL STA		*Pilot station*
9		Sig Sta	*Signal station*
10		Sem	*Semaphore*
11		S Sig Sta	*Storm signal station*
12			*Weather signal station*
(Jb)	⊙NWS SIG STA		*Nat'l Weather Service signal sta*
13			*Tide signal station*
14			*Stream signal station*
15			*Ice signal station*
16			*Time signal station*
16a			*Manned oceanographic station*
16b			*Unmanned oceanographic station*
17			*Time ball*
18			*Signal mast*
†18a	○ Mast		*Mast*
19	[symbol] ⊙FS ○FS ⊙FP ○FP		*Flagstaff; Flagpole*
19a	⊙F TR ○F Tr		*Flag tower*
20			*Signal*
21		Obsy	*Observatory*
22		Off	*Office*
(Jc)	○BELL		*Bell (on land)*
(Jd)	○HECP		*Harbor entrance control post*
†(Je)	○MARINE POLICE		*Marine police station*
†(Jf)	○FIREBOAT STATION		*Fireboat station*

K. Lights

No.	Symbol/Abbreviation	Description	No.	Abbreviation	Description
1		*Position of light*	29	F Fl	*Fixed and flashing light*
2	Lt	*Light*	30	F Gp Fl	*Fixed and group flashing light*
(Ka)		*Riprap surrounding light*	30a	Mo	*Morse code light*
3	Lt Ho	*Lighthouse*	31	Rot	*Revolving or Rotating light*
4	 AERO / AERO	*Aeronautical light (See F-22)*	41		*Period*
4a		*Marine and air navigation light*	42		*Every*
5	Bn / Bn	*Light beacon*	43		*With*
6		*Light vessel; Lightship*	44		*Visible (range)*
8		*Lantern*	†(Kb)	M; Mi; N Mi	*Nautical mile (See E-11)*
9		*Street lamp*	(Kc)	m min	*Minutes (See E-2)*
10	REF	*Reflector*	†(Kd)	s; sec	*Seconds (See E-3)*
11	 Ldg Lt / Ldg Lt	*Leading light*	45	Fl	*Flash*
12	 RED / RED	*Sector light*	46	Occ	*Occultation*
13	RED / GREEN / RED / GREEN	*Directional light*	46a		*Eclipse*
			47	Gp	*Group*
14		*Harbor light*	48	Occ	*Intermittent light*
15		*Fishing light*			
16		*Tidal light*	49	*SEC*	*Sector*
17	 Priv maintd	*Private light (maintained by private interests; to be used with caution)*	50		*Color of sector*
21	F	*Fixed light*	51	Aux	*Auxiliary light*
22	Occ	*Occulting light*	52		*Varied*
23	Fl	*Flashing light*	61	Vi	*Violet*
23a	Iso E Int	*Isophase light (equal interval)*	62		*Purple*
24	Qk Fl	*Quick flashing (scintillating) light*	63	B	*Blue*
25	Int Qk Fl I Qk Fl	*Interrupted quick flashing light*	64	G	*Green*
			65	Or	*Orange*
25a	S Fl	*Short flashing light*	66	R	*Red*
26	Alt	*Alternating light*	67	W	*White*
27	Gp Occ	*Group occulting light*	67a	Am	*Amber*
28	Gp Fl	*Group flashing light*	67b	Y	*Yellow*
28a	S-L Fl	*Short-long flashing light*	68	*OBSC*	*Obscured light*
28b		*Group short flashing light*	68a	*Fog Det Lt*	*Fog detector light (See Nb)*

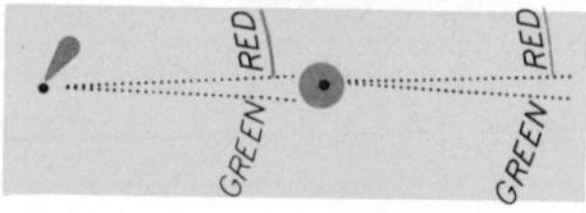

K. Lights (continued)

69		*Unwatched light*
70	Occas	*Occasional light*
71	Irreg	*Irregular light*
72	Prov	*Provisional light*
73	Temp	*Temporary light*
(Ke)	D; Destr	*Destroyed*
74	Exting	*Extinguished light*
75		*Faint light*
76		*Upper light*
77		*Lower light*
78		*Rear light*
79		*Front light*
80	Vert	*Vertical lights*
81	Hor	*Horizontal lights*
(Kf)	VB	*Vertical beam*
(Kg)	*RGE*	*Range*
(Kh)	Exper	*Experimental light*
(Ki)	TRLB	*Temporarily replaced by lighted buoy showing the same characteristics*
(Kj)	TRUB	*Temporarily replaced by unlighted buoy*
(Kk)	TLB	*Temporary lighted buoy*
(Kl)	TUB	*Temporary unlighted buoy*

L. Buoys and Beacons
(see General Remarks)

† (new standard symbols)

	Symbols	
1		*Approximate position of buoy*
†2		***Light buoy***
†3	BELL BELL BELL	***Bell buoy***
†3a	GONG GONG GONG	***Gong buoy***
†4	WHIS WHIS	*Whistle buoy*
†5	C C	*Can or Cylindrical buoy*
†6	N N	*Nun or Conical buoy*
†7	SP SP	*Spherical buoy*
†8	S S	*Spar buoy*
†8a	P P	*Pillar or Spindle buoy*
†9		*Buoy with topmark (ball) (see L-70)*
†10		*Barrel or Ton buoy*
†(La)		*Color unknown*
†(Lb)	FLOAT FLOAT	*Float*
†12	FLOAT FLOAT FLOAT	*Lightfloat*
13		*Outer or Landfall buoy*
†14	BW BW	*Fairway buoy (BWVS)*
†14a	BW BW	*Midchannel buoy (BWVS)*
†15	R "2" R "2" R "2"	*Starboard-hand buoy (entering from seaward)*
†16	"1" "1"	*Port-hand buoy (entering from seaward)*
†17	RB RB RB	*Bifurcation buoy (RBHB)*
†18	RB RB RB	*Junction buoy (RBHB)*
†19	RB RB RB	*Isolated danger buoy (RBHB)*
†20	RB RB G G G G G	*Wreck buoy (RBHB or G)*
†20a	RB RB G G	*Obstruction buoy (RBHB or G)*
†21	Tel Tel	*Telegraph-cable buoy*
22		*Mooring buoy (colors of mooring buoys never carried)*
22a		*Mooring*
22b	Tel Tel	*Mooring buoy with telegraphic communications*
22c	T T	*Mooring buoy with telephonic communications*
†23		*Warping buoy*
†24	Y Y	*Quarantine buoy*
24a		*Practice area buoy*
†25	Explos Anch Explos Anch	*Explosive anchorage buoy*
†25a	AERO AERO	*Aeronautical anchorage buoy*
†26	Deviation Deviation	*Compass adjustment buoy*
†27	BW BW	*Fish trap (area) buoy (BWHB)*
†27a		*Spoil ground buoy*
†28	W W	*Anchorage buoy (marks limits)*
†29	Priv maintd Priv maintd	*Private aid to navigation (buoy) (maintained by private interests, use with caution)*

L. Buoys and Beacons (continued)

No.	Symbol	Abbr.	Description
29 (cont.)		R	Starboard-hand buoy (entering from seaward)
		B	Port-hand buoy
30			Temporary buoy (See Ki, j, k, l)
30a			Winter buoy
†31			Horozontal stripes or bands HB
†32			Vertical stripes VS
†33			Checkered Chec
†33a		Diag	Diagonal bands
41		W	White
42		B	Black
43		R	Red
44		Y	Yellow
45		G	Green
46		Br	Brown
47		Gy	Gray
48		Bu	Blue
48a		Am	Amber
48b		Or	Orange
†51			Floating beacon
52	△RW Bn △W Bn △R Bn		Fixed beacon (unlighted or daybeacon)
	▲Bn		Black beacon
	△Bn		Color unknown
(Lc)	MARKER Marker		Private aid to navigation
53		Bn	Beacon, in general (See L 52)
54			Tower beacon
55			Cardinal marking system
56	△ Deviation Bn		Compass adjustment beacon
57			Topmarks (See L 9, 70)
58			Telegraph-cable (landing) beacon
59	Piles Piles		Piles (See O 30; H 9, 9a)
			Stakes
	Stumps		Stumps (See O 30)
			Perches
61	CAIRN Cairn		Cairn
62			Painted patches
63	TR		Landmark (position accurate) (See D 2)
(Ld)	Tr		Landmark (position approximate)
64		REF	Reflector
65	MARKER		Range targets, markers
†(Le)	W Or W Or W Or W Or		Special-purpose buoys
66			Oil installation buoy
67			Drilling platform (See Of, Og)
70			Note: TOPMARKS on buoys and beacons may be shown on charts of foreign waters. The abbreviation for black is not shown adjacent to buoys or beacons.
(Lf)	Ra Ref		Radar reflector (See M 13)

Symbols and abbreviations for buoyage to be introduced into European waters from April 1977.

Buoys and Beacons
IALA Buoyage System 'A'

The combined Cardinal and Lateral System (Red to Port)

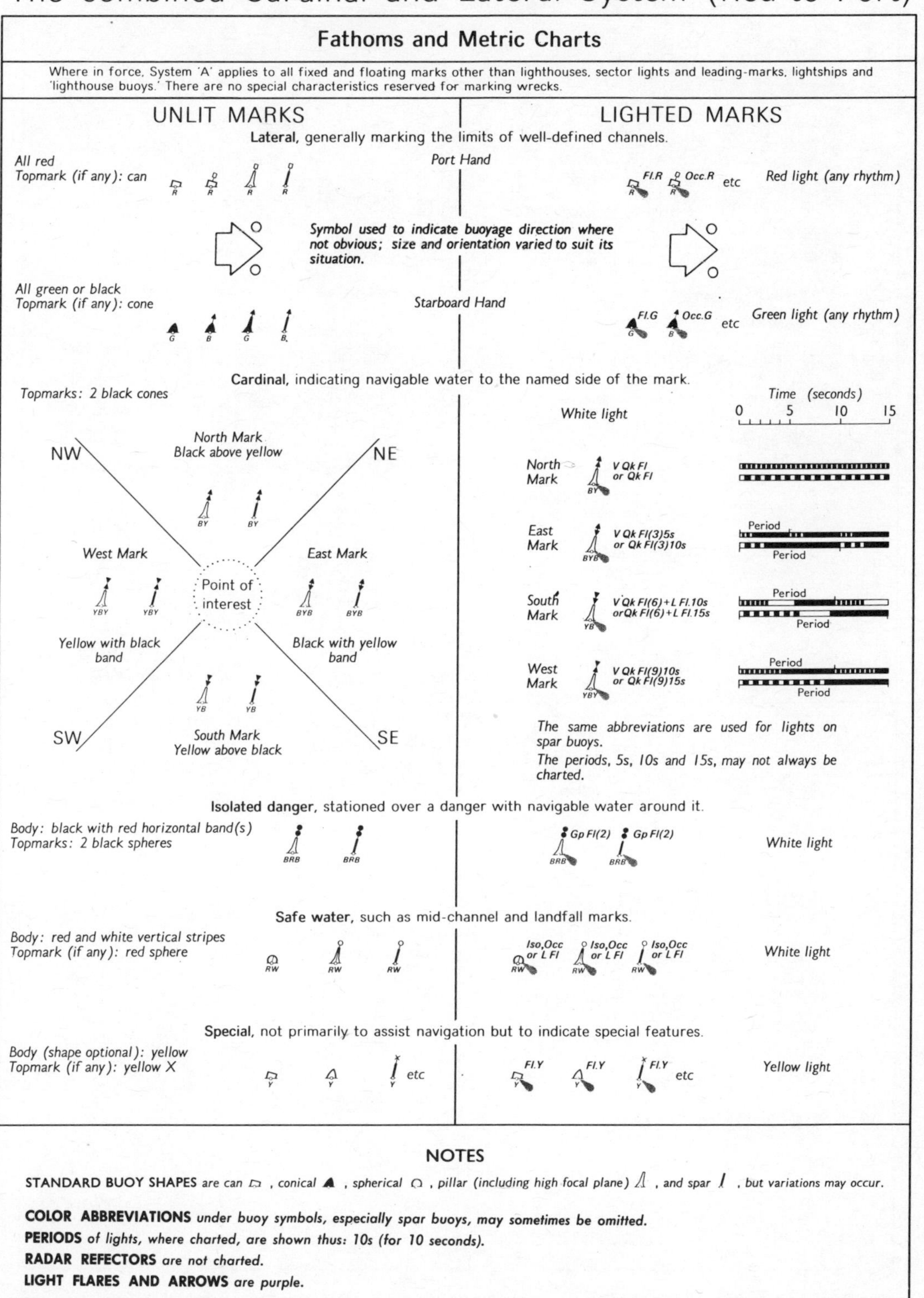

M. Radio and Radar Stations

No.	Symbol	Description
1	R Sta	*Radio telegraph station*
2	RT	*Radio telephone station*
3	R Bn	*Radiobeacon*
4	R Bn	*Circular radiobeacon*
5	RD	*Directional radiobeacon; Radio range*
6		*Rotating loop radiobeacon*
7	RDF	*Radio direction finding station*
†(Ma)	ANTENNA (TELEM) TELEM ANT	*Telemetry antenna*
(Mb)	R RELAY MAST	*Radio relay mast*
(Mc)	MICRO TR	*Microwave tower*
9	R MAST R TR	*Radio mast* *Radio tower*
9a	TV TR	*Television mast; Television tower*
10	R TR (WBAL) 1090 KHZ	*Radio broadcasting station (commercial)*
10a	R Sta	*QTG radio station*
11	Ra	*Radar station*
12	Racon	*Radar responder beacon*
13	Ra Ref	*Radar reflector (See L-Lf)*
14	Ra (conspic)	*Radar conspicuous object*
14a		*Ramark*
15	D F S	*Distance finding station (synchronized signals)*
16	AERO R Bn 302	*Aeronautical radiobeacon*
17	Decca Sta	*Decca station*
18	Loran Sta Venice	*Loran station (name)*
19	CONSOL Bn 190 kHz MMF	*Consol (Consolan) station*
(Md)	AERO R Rge 342	*Aeronautical radio range*
(Me)	Ra Ref Calibration Bn	*Radar calibration beacon*
(Mf)	LORAN TR SPRING ISLAND	*Loran tower (name)*
(Mg)	R TR F R Lt	*Obstruction light*
†(Mh)	RA DOME DOME (RADAR) Ra Dome Dome (Radar)	*Radar dome*
†(Mi)	uhf	*Ultrahigh frequency*
†(Mj)	vhf	*Very high frequency*

N. Fog Signals

No.	Symbol	Description
1	Fog Sig	*Fog-signal station*
2		*Radio fog-signal station*
3	*GUN*	*Explosive fog signal*
4		*Submarine fog signal*
5	*SUB-BELL*	*Submarine fog bell (action of waves)*
6	*SUB-BELL*	*Submarine fog bell (mechanical)*
7	*SUB-OSC*	*Submarine oscillator*
8	*NAUTO*	*Nautophone*
9	*DIA*	*Diaphone*
10	*GUN*	*Fog gun*
11	*SIREN*	*Fog siren*
12	*HORN*	*Fog trumpet*
13	*HORN*	*Foghorn*
13a	*HORN*	*Electric foghorn*
14	*BELL*	*Fog bell*
15	*WHIS*	*Fog whistle*
16	*HORN*	*Reed horn*
17	*GONG*	*Fog gong*
18		*Submarine sound signal not connected to the shore (See N 5,6,7)*
18a		*Submarine sound signal connected to the shore (See N 5,6,7)*
(Na)	*HORN*	*Typhon*
(Nb)	*Fog Det Lt*	*Fog detector light (See K 68a)*

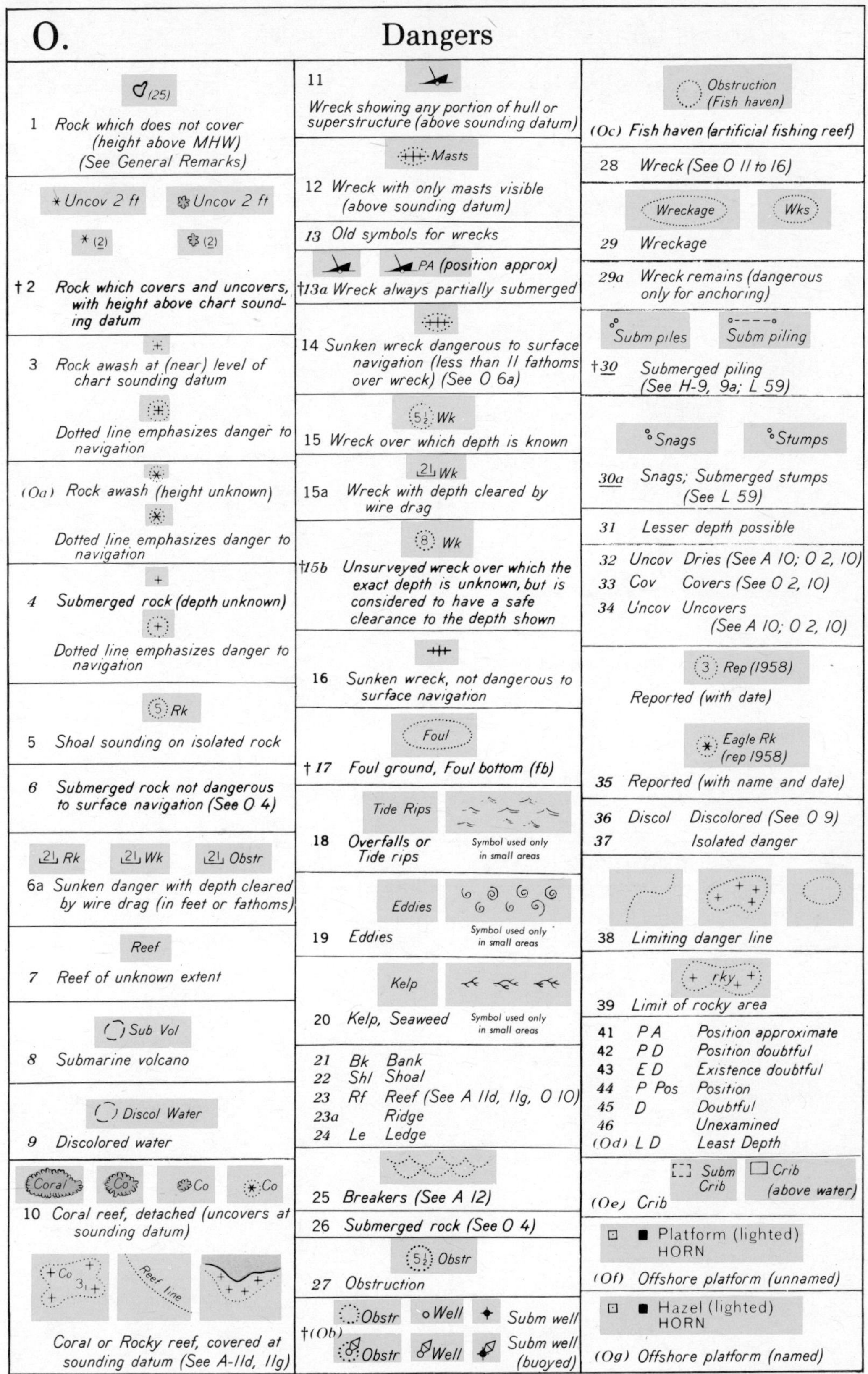

O. Dangers

No.	Symbol	Description
1	(25)	Rock which does not cover (height above MHW) (See General Remarks)
†2	Uncov 2 ft; Uncov 2 ft; (2); (2)	Rock which covers and uncovers, with height above chart sounding datum
3		Rock awash at (near) level of chart sounding datum
		Dotted line emphasizes danger to navigation
(Oa)		Rock awash (height unknown)
		Dotted line emphasizes danger to navigation
4	+	Submerged rock (depth unknown)
	(+)	Dotted line emphasizes danger to navigation
5	(5) Rk	Shoal sounding on isolated rock
6		Submerged rock not dangerous to surface navigation (See O 4)
6a	21 Rk; 21 Wk; 21 Obstr	Sunken danger with depth cleared by wire drag (in feet or fathoms)
7	Reef	Reef of unknown extent
8	Sub Vol	Submarine volcano
9	Discol Water	Discolored water
10	Coral; Co; Co; Co	Coral reef, detached (uncovers at sounding datum)
	Co 3₁; Reef line	Coral or Rocky reef, covered at sounding datum (See A-11d, 11g)
11		Wreck showing any portion of hull or superstructure (above sounding datum)
12	Masts	Wreck with only masts visible (above sounding datum)
13		Old symbols for wrecks
†13a	PA (position approx)	Wreck always partially submerged
14		Sunken wreck dangerous to surface navigation (less than 11 fathoms over wreck) (See O 6a)
15	(5½) Wk	Wreck over which depth is known
15a	21 Wk	Wreck with depth cleared by wire drag
†15b	(8) Wk	Unsurveyed wreck over which the exact depth is unknown, but is considered to have a safe clearance to the depth shown
16		Sunken wreck, not dangerous to surface navigation
†17	Foul	Foul ground, Foul bottom (fb)
18	Tide Rips (Symbol used only in small areas)	Overfalls or Tide rips
19	Eddies (Symbol used only in small areas)	Eddies
20	Kelp (Symbol used only in small areas)	Kelp, Seaweed
21	Bk	Bank
22	Shl	Shoal
23	Rf	Reef (See A 11d, 11g, O 10)
23a		Ridge
24	Le	Ledge
25		Breakers (See A 12)
26		Submerged rock (See O 4)
27	(5½) Obstr	Obstruction
†(Ob)	Obstr; Well	Subm well
	Obstr; Well	Subm well (buoyed)
(Oc)	Obstruction (Fish haven)	Fish haven (artificial fishing reef)
28		Wreck (See O 11 to 16)
29	Wreckage; Wks	Wreckage
29a		Wreck remains (dangerous only for anchoring)
†30	Subm piles; Subm piling	Submerged piling (See H-9, 9a; L 59)
30a	Snags; Stumps	Snags; Submerged stumps (See L 59)
31		Lesser depth possible
32	Uncov	Dries (See A 10; O 2, 10)
33	Cov	Covers (See O 2, 10)
34	Uncov	Uncovers (See A 10; O 2, 10)
	(3) Rep (1958)	Reported (with date)
35	Eagle Rk (rep 1958)	Reported (with name and date)
36	Discol	Discolored (See O 9)
37		Isolated danger
38		Limiting danger line
39	rky	Limit of rocky area
41	PA	Position approximate
42	PD	Position doubtful
43	ED	Existence doubtful
44	P Pos	Position
45	D	Doubtful
46		Unexamined
(Od)	LD	Least Depth
(Oe)	Subm Crib; Crib (above water)	Crib
(Of)	Platform (lighted) HORN	Offshore platform (unnamed)
(Og)	Hazel (lighted) HORN	Offshore platform (named)

NOTE: The symbol for 15b above has been changed to the following: (8) Wk

P. Various Limits, etc.

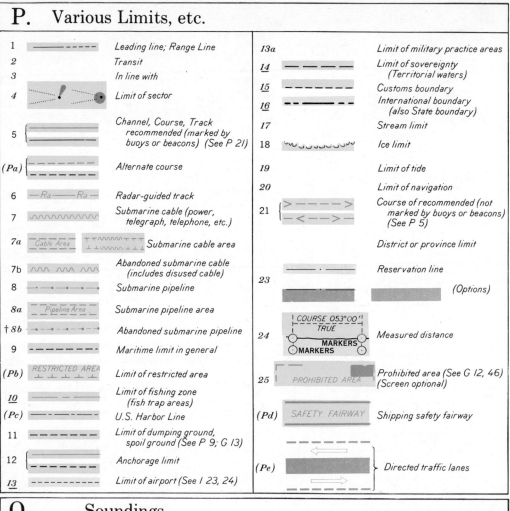

No.	Symbol	Description
1		Leading line; Range Line
2		Transit
3		In line with
4		Limit of sector
5		Channel, Course, Track recommended (marked by buoys or beacons) (See P 21)
(Pa)		Alternate course
6	Ra Ra	Radar-guided track
7		Submarine cable (power, telegraph, telephone, etc.)
7a	Cable Area	Submarine cable area
7b		Abandoned submarine cable (includes disused cable)
8		Submarine pipeline
8a	Pipeline Area	Submarine pipeline area
† 8b		Abandoned submarine pipeline
9		Maritime limit in general
(Pb)	RESTRICTED AREA	Limit of restricted area
10		Limit of fishing zone (fish trap areas)
(Pc)		U.S. Harbor Line
11		Limit of dumping ground, spoil ground (See P 9; G 13)
12		Anchorage limit
13		Limit of airport (See I 23, 24)
13a		Limit of military practice areas
14		Limit of sovereignty (Territorial waters)
15		Customs boundary
16		International boundary (also State boundary)
17		Stream limit
18		Ice limit
19		Limit of tide
20		Limit of navigation
21		Course of recommended (not marked by buoys or beacons) (See P 5)
		District or province limit
23		Reservation line
		(Options)
24	COURSE 053°00' TRUE MARKERS MARKERS	Measured distance
25	PROHIBITED AREA	Prohibited area (See G 12, 46) (Screen optional)
(Pd)	SAFETY FAIRWAY	Shipping safety fairway
(Pe)		Directed traffic lanes

Q. Soundings

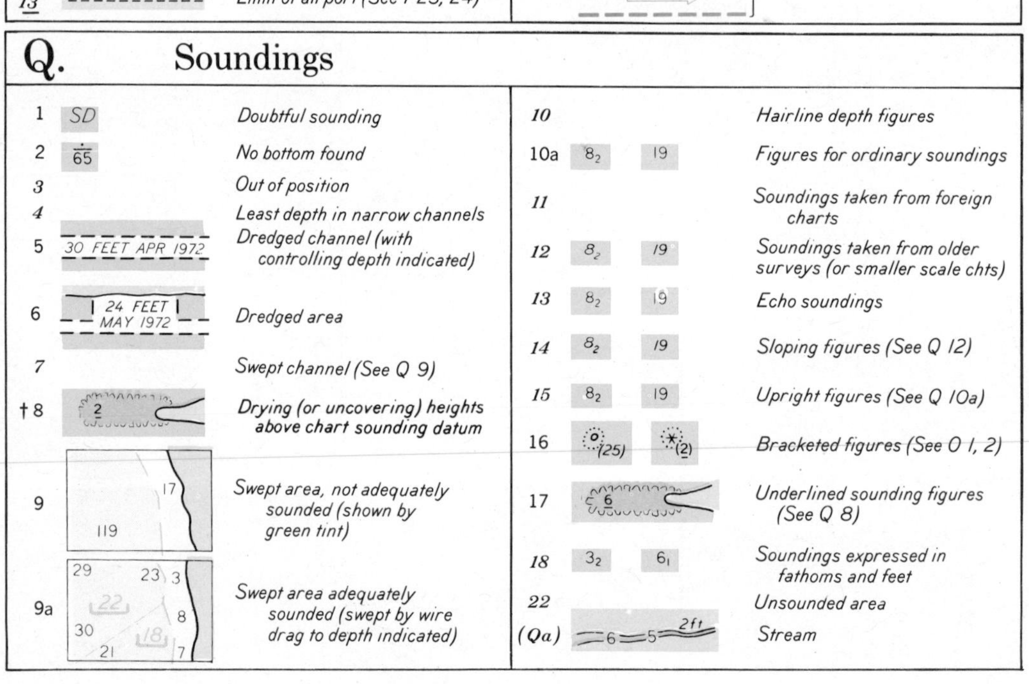

No.	Symbol	Description
1	SD	Doubtful sounding
2	65	No bottom found
3		Out of position
4		Least depth in narrow channels
5	30 FEET APR 1972	Dredged channel (with controlling depth indicated)
6	24 FEET MAY 1972	Dredged area
7		Swept channel (See Q 9)
† 8	2	Drying (or uncovering) heights above chart sounding datum
9	17 119	Swept area, not adequately sounded (shown by green tint)
9a	29 23 3 22 8 30 18 21 7	Swept area adequately sounded (swept by wire drag to depth indicated)
10		Hairline depth figures
10a	8_2 19	Figures for ordinary soundings
11		Soundings taken from foreign charts
12	8_2 19	Soundings taken from older surveys (or smaller scale chts)
13	8_2 19	Echo soundings
14	8_2 19	Sloping figures (See Q 12)
15	8_2 19	Upright figures (See Q 10a)
16	(25) (2)	Bracketed figures (See O 1, 2)
17	6	Underlined sounding figures (See Q 8)
18	3_2 6_1	Soundings expressed in fathoms and feet
22		Unsounded area
(Qa)	6 5 2ft	Stream

R. Depth Contours and Tints (see General Remarks)

Feet	Fm / Meters	Feet	Fm / Meters
0	0	300	50
6	1	600	100
12	2	1,200	200
18	3	1,800	300
24	4	2,400	400
30	5	3,000	500
36	6	6,000	1,000
60	10	12,000	2,000
120	20	18,000	3,000
180	30	Or continuous lines, with values	5 (blue or black) 100
240	40		

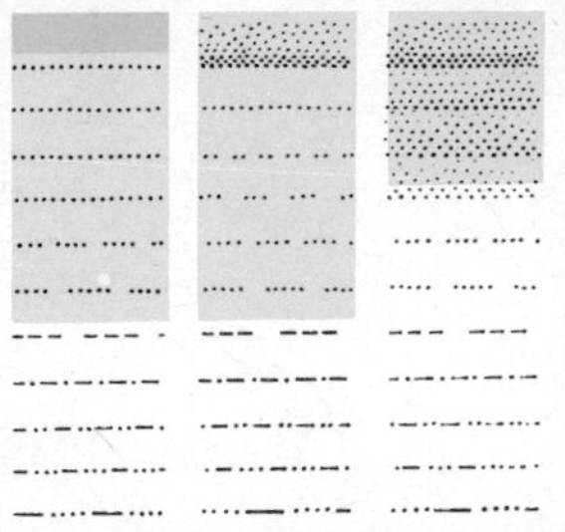

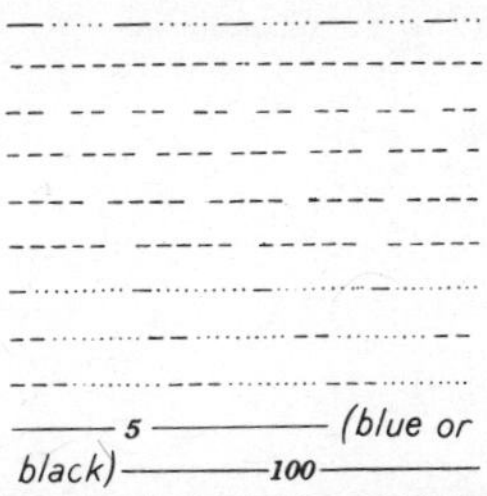

S. Quality of the Bottom

1	*Grd*	*Ground*
2	*S*	*Sand*
3	*M*	*Mud; Muddy*
4	*Oz*	*Ooze*
5	*Ml*	*Marl*
6	*Cl*	*Clay*
7	*G*	*Gravel*
8	*Sn*	*Shingle*
9	*P*	*Pebbles*
10	*St*	*Stones*
11	*Rk; rky*	*Rock; Rocky*
11a	*Blds*	*Boulders*
12	*Ck*	*Chalk*
12a	*Ca*	*Calcareous*
13	*Qz*	*Quartz*
13a	*Sch*	*Schist*
14	*Co*	*Coral*
(Sa)	*Co Hd*	*Coral head*
15	*Mds*	*Madrepores*
16	*Vol*	*Volcanic*
(Sb)	*Vol Ash*	*Volcanic ash*
17	*La*	*Lava*
18	*Pm*	*Pumice*
19	*T*	*Tufa*
20	*Sc*	*Scoriae*
21	*Cn*	*Cinders*
21a		*Ash*
22	*Mn*	*Manganese*
23	*Sh*	*Shells*
24	*Oys*	*Oysters*
25	*Ms*	*Mussels*
26	*Spg*	*Sponge*
27	*K*	*Kelp*
28	*Wd*	*Seaweed*
	Grs	*Grass*
29	*Stg*	*Sea-tangle*
31	*Spi*	*Spicules*
32	*Fr*	*Foraminifera*
33	*Gl*	*Globigerina*
34	*Di*	*Diatoms*
35	*Rd*	*Radiolaria*
36	*Pt*	*Pteropods*
37	*Po*	*Polyzoa*
38	*Cir*	*Cirripedia*
38a	*Fu*	*Fucus*
38b	*Ma*	*Mattes*
39	*fne*	*Fine*
40	*crs*	*Coarse*
41	*sft*	*Soft*
42	*hrd*	*Hard*
43	*stf*	*Stiff*
44	*sml*	*Small*
45	*lrg*	*Large*
46	*stk*	*Sticky*
47	*brk*	*Broken*
47a	*grd*	*Ground (Shells)*
48	*rt*	*Rotten*
49	*str*	*Streaky*
50	*spk*	*Speckled*
51	*gty*	*Gritty*
52	*dec*	*Decayed*
53	*fly*	*Flinty*
54	*glac*	*Glacial*
55	*ten*	*Tenacious*
56	*wh*	*White*
57	*bk*	*Black*
58	*vi*	*Violet*
59	*bu*	*Blue*
60	*gn*	*Green*
61	*yl*	*Yellow*
62	*or*	*Orange*
63	*rd*	*Red*
64	*br*	*Brown*
65	*ch*	*Chocolate*
66	*gy*	*Gray*
67	*lt*	*Light*
68	*dk*	*Dark*
70	*vard*	*Varied*
71	*unev*	*Uneven*
(Sc)	*S/M*	*Surface layer and Under layer*
76	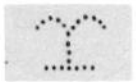	*Freshwater springs in seabed*

T. Tides and Currents

1	HW	High water
1a	HHW	Higher high water
2	LW	Low water
(Ta)	LWD	Low-water datum
2a	LLW	Lower low water
3	MTL	Mean tide level
4	MSL	Mean sea level
4a		Elevation of mean sea level above chart (sounding) datum
5		Chart datum (datum for sounding reduction)
6	Sp	Spring tide
7	Np	Neap tide
7a	MHW	Mean high water
8	MHWS	Mean high-water springs
8a	MHWN	Mean high-water neaps
8b	MHHW	Mean higher high water
8c	MLW	Mean low water
9	MLWS	Mean low-water springs
9a	MLWN	Mean low-water neaps
9b	MLLW	Mean lower low water
10	ISLW	Indian spring low water
11		High-water full and change (vulgar establishment of the port)
12		Low-water full and change
13		Mean establishment of the port
13a		Establishment of the port
14		Unit of height
15		Equinoctial
16		Quarter; Quadrature
17	Str	Stream
18	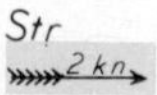 2 kn	Current, general, with rate
19	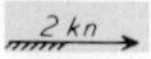 2 kn	Flood stream (current) with rate
20	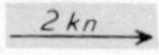 2 kn	Ebb stream (current) with rate
21	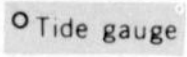 Tide gauge	Tide gauge; Tidepole; Automatic tide gauge
23	vel	Velocity; Rate
24	kn	Knots
25	ht	Height
26		Tide
27		New moon
28		Full moon
29		Ordinary
30		Syzygy
31	fl	Flood
32		Ebb
33		Tidal stream diagram
34	 Ⓐ Ⓑ	Place for which tabulated tidal stream data are given
35		Range (of tide)
36		Phase lag
(Tb)	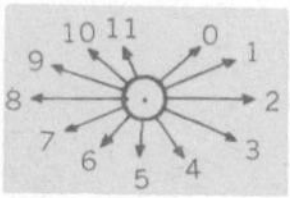	Current diagram, with explanatory note

U. Compass

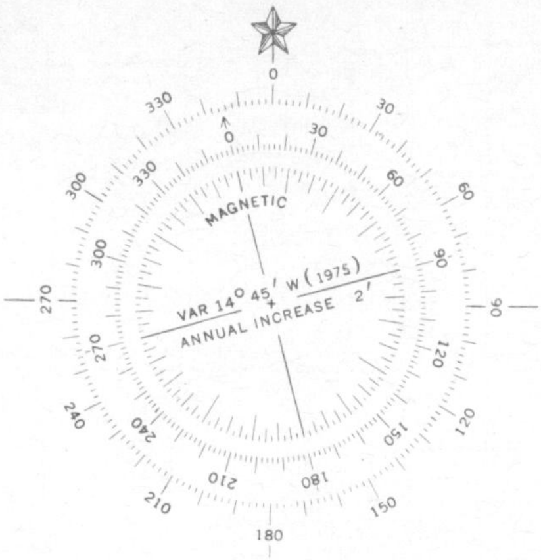

Compass Rose

The outer circle is in degrees with zero at true north. The inner circles are in points and degrees with the arrow indicating magnetic north.

1	N	North
2	E	East
3	S	South
4	W	West
5	NE	Northeast
6	SE	Southeast
7	SW	Southwest
8	NW	Northwest
9	N	Northern
10	E	Eastern
11	S	Southern
12	W	Western
21	brg	Bearing
22	T	True
23	mag	Magnetic
24	var	Variation
25		Annual change
25a		Annual change nil
26		Abnormal variation; Magnetic attraction
27	deg	Degrees (See E-20)
28	dev	Deviation

Index of Abbreviations

A

aband	Abandoned	F 37
ABAND LT HO	Abandoned lighthouse	If
abt	About	F 17
AERO	Aeronautical	F 22; K 4
AERO R Bn	Aeronautical radiobeacon	M 16
AERO R Rge	Aeronautical radio range	Md
alt	Altitude	E 18
Alt	Alternating (light)	K 26
Am	Amber	K 67a; L 48a
anc	Ancient	F 9
Anch	Anchorage	B 15; G 1, 2
Anch prohib	Anchorage prohibited	G 12
Ant	Antenna	Ma
approx	Approximate	F 34
Apprs	Approaches	Bg
Apt	Apartment	Ij
Arch	Archipelago	B 20
Astro	Astronomical	D 9
AUTH	Authorized	Fc
Aux	Auxiliary (light)	K 51
Ave	Avenue	I 26a

B

B	Bay	B 2
B	Bayou	Ba
B, b, bk	Black	L 42; S 57
Bdy Mon	Boundary monument	D 14
BELL	Fog Bell	N 14
bet	Between	Fi
B Hbr	Boat harbor	G 33
Bk	Bank	O 21
Bkw	Breakwater	G 6
Bl	Blast	
Bld, Blds	Boulder, Boulders	B 32; S 11a
Bldg	Building	I 66
Blvd	Boulevard	I 26b
BM	Bench mark	D 5
Bn	Beacon (in general)	L 52, 53
BR	Bridge	H 14
Br, br	Brown	L 46; S 64
brg	Bearing	U 21
brk	Broken	S 47
Bu, bu	Blue	K 63; L 48; S 69
BWHB	Black and white horizontal bands	L 27
BWVS	Black and white vertical stripes	L 14, 14a

C

C	Can, Cylindrical (buoy)	L 5
C	Cape	B 22
C	Cove	B 5a
Ca	Calcareous	S 12a
Cap	Capitol	Ik
Cas	Castle	I 4
Cath	Cathedral	I 8a
cbl	Cable length	E 10
cd	Candela	E 12b
C G	Coast Guard	J 3, Ja
ch	Chocolate	S 65
Ch	Church	I 8
Chan	Channel	B 10
Chec	Checkered (buoy)	L 33
CHY	Chimney	I 44
Cir	Cirripedia	S 38
Ck	Chalk	S 12
Cl	Clay	S 6
CL	Clearance	Fd
cm	Centimeter	E 4b
Cn	Cinders	S 21
Co	Company	Il
Co	Coral	S 14
Co Hd	Coral head	Sa
concr	Concrete	Ff
conspic	Conspicuous	F 12
C of E	Corps of Engineers	Df
cor	Corner	Fe
Corp	Corporation	Im
Cov	Covers	O 33
corr	Correction	E 17
cps, c/s	Cycles per second	Ef
Cr	Creek	B 5
crs	Coarse	S 40
Cswy	Causeway	H 3f
Ct Ho	Courthouse	I 64
CUP	Cupola	I 36
Cus Ho	Customhouse	G 29

D

D	Doubtful	O 45
DD	Deep Draft	Fn
D, Destr	Destroyed	F 14; Ke
dec	Decayed	S 52
deg	Degrees	U 27
dev	Deviation	U 28
Diag	Diagonal bands	L 33a
D F S	Distance finding station	M 15
Di	Diatoms	S 34
DIA	Diaphone	N 9
Discol	Discolored	O 36
discontd	Discontinued	F 25
dist	Distant	F 16
dk	Dark	S 68
dm	Decimeter	E 4a
Dol	Dolphin	G 21
DRDG RGE	Dredging Range	

E

E	East, Eastern	U 2, 10
Ed	Edition	E 16
ED	Existence doubtful	O 43
elec	Electric	F 29
elev	Elevation	E 19
ELEV	Elevator, Lift	I 37
Elev	Elevation, Elevated	Ie
E'ly	Easterly	Fq
Entr	Entrance	B 11
E Int	Isophase light (equal interval)	K 23a
Est	Estuary	B 12
estab	Established	F 28
Exper	Experimental (light)	Kh
exper	Experimental	F 24
explos	Explosive	F 27

Abbreviations

Explos Anch	Explosive Anchorage (buoy)	L 25
Exting	Extinguished (light)	K 74
extr	Extreme	F 40

F

F	Fixed (light)	K 21
Facty	Factory	I 47
Fd	Fjord	B 3
F Fl	Fixed and flashing (light)	K 29
F Gp Fl	Fixed and group flashing (light)	K 30
Fl	Flash, Flashing (light)	K 23, 45
fl	Flood	Fg; T 31
fly	Flinty	S 53
fm	Fathom	E 9
fne	Fine	S 39
Fog Det Lt	Fog detector light	K 68a; Nb
Fog Sig	Fog signal station	N 1
FP	Flagpole	J 19
Fr	Foraminifera	S 32
FS	Flagstaff	J 19
Fsh stks	Fishing stakes	G 14
ft	Foot	E 7
Ft	Fort	I 19
F TR	Flag tower	J 19a
Fu	Fucus	S 38a
Fy	Ferry	H 19

G

G	Gulf	B 1
G	Gravel	S 7
G, Gn, gn	Green K 64; L 20, 20a, 45; S 60	
GAB	Gable	I 72
Gl	Globigerina	S 33
glac	Glacial	S 54
GONG	Fog gong	N 17
Govt Ho	Government House	I 30
Gp	Group	K 47
Gp Fl	Group flashing	K 28
Gp Occ	Group occulting	K 27
Grd, grd	Ground	S 1, 47a
Grs	Grass	S 28
gt	Great	F 1
gty	Gritty	S 51
GUN	Explosive fog signal	N 3
GUN	Fog gun	N 10
Gy, gy	Gray	L 47; S 66

H

HB	Horizontal bands or stripes	L 31
Hbr	Harbor	B 16; G 3
Hd	Head, Headland	B 24
HECP	Harbor entrance control post	Jd
Hk	Hulk	G 45
HHW	Higher high water	T 1a
Hn	Haven	B 16a; G 4
Hor	Horizontal lights	K 81
HOR CL	Horizontal clearance	H 18b
HORN	Fog trumpet, Foghorn, Reed horn, Typhon	N 12, 13, 13a, 16, Na
Hosp	Hospital	I 32
hr, h	Hour	E 1
hrd	Hard	S 42
H S	High School	Ig
ht	Height	E 19; T 25
HW	High water	T 1
Hy	Highway	H 1
Hz	Hertz	Ec

I

I	Island	B 18
I Qk, Int Qk	Interrupted quick	K 25
in	Inch	E 6
In	Inlet	B 6
Inst	Institute	I 61
Irreg	Irregular	K 71
ISLW	Indian spring low water	T 10
Is	Islands	Bi
Iso	Isophase	K 23a
It	Islet	B 19

K

K	Kelp	S 27
kc	Kilocycle	Eg
kHz	Kilohertz	Ed
km	Kilometer	E 5
kn	Knots	E 12; T 24

L

L	Loch, Lough, Lake	B 4
La	Lava	S 17
Lag	Lagoon	Bf; C 16
lat	Latitude	E 13
LD	Least Depth	Od
Ldg	Landing, Landing place	B 33; G 16
Ldg Lt	Leading light	K 11
Le	Ledge	O 24
Lit	Little	F 2
LLW	Lower low water	T 2a
LNM	Local Notice to Mariners	Fa
long	Longitude	E 14
LOOK TR	Lookout station, Watch tower	J 4
lrg	Large	F 3; S 45
LS S	Lifesaving station	J 6
Lt	Light	K 2
lt	Light	S 67
Ltd	Limited	Ii
Lt Ho	Lighthouse	K 3
LW	Low water	T 2
LWD	Low water datum	Ta

M

M, Mi	Nautical mile	E11; Kb
M	Mud, Muddy	S 3
m	Meter	E 4, d, e
m^2	Square meter	E4d
m^3	Cubic meter	E4c
m, min	Minute (of time)	E2; Kc
Ma	Marsh	Bj
Ma	Mattes	S 38b
mag	Magnetic	U 23
Magz	Magazine	I 34
maintd	Maintained	F 36
max	Maximum	Fp
Mc	Megacycle	Eh
Mds	Madrepores	S 15

Mg	Mangrove	Bk
MHHW	Mean higher high water	T 8b
MHW	Mean high water	T 7a
MHWN	Mean high-water neaps	T 8a
MHWS	Mean high-water springs	T 8
MHz	Megahertz	Ee
MICRO TR	Microwave tower	Mc
mid	Middle	F 7
min	Minimum	Fo
Mkr	Marker	Lc
Ml	Marl	S 5
MLLW	Mean lower low water	T 9b
MLW	Mean low water	T 8c
MLWN	Mean low-water neaps	T 9a
MLWS	Mean low-water springs	T 9
mm	Millimeter	E 4c
Mn	Manganese	S 22
Mo	Morse code light	K 30a
mod	Moderate	Fh
MON	Monument	I 35
Ms	Mussels	S 25
μsec, μs	Microsecond (one millionth)	Eb
MSL	Mean sea level	T 4
Mt	Mountain, Mount	B 26
Mth	Mouth	B 13
MTL	Mean tide level	T 3

N

N	North; Northern	U 1, 9
N	Nun; Conical (buoy)	L 6
N M, N Mi	Nautical mile	E 11
NAUTO	Nautophone	N 8
NE	Northeast	U 5
N'Ly	Northerly	Fq
NM	Notice to Mariners	F 42
No	Number	E 23
Np	Neap tide	T 7
NW	Northwest	U 8
NWS	National Weather Service Signal Station	Jb

O

OBSC	Obscured (light)	K 68
Obs Spot	Observation spot	D 4
Obstr	Obstruction	O 27
Obsy	Observatory	J 21
Occ	Occulting (light), Occultation	K 22, 46
Occ	Intermittent (light)	K 48
Occas	Occasional (light)	F 39; K 70
Off	Office	J 22
Or, or	Orange	K 65; L48b; S 62
OVHD PWR CAB	Overhead power cable	H 4
Oys	Oysters, Oyster bed	S 24; G 15a
Oz	Ooze	S 4

P

P	Pebbles	S 9
P	Pillar (buoy)	L 8a
P	Pond	Bb
P	Port	B 17; G 5
PA	Position approximate	O 41
Pag	Pagoda	I 14
Pass	Passage, Pass	B 9
Pav	Pavilion	I 67
PD	Position doubtful	O 42
Pen	Peninsula	B 21
PIL STA	Pilot station	J 8
Pk	Peak	B 29
Pm	Pumice	S 18
Po	Polyzoa	S 37
P O	Post Office	I 29
P, Pos	Position	O 44
priv	Private, Privately	F 30
Priv maintd	Privately maintained	K 17; L 29
Prohib	Prohibited	F 26
prom	Prominent	F 31
Prom	Promontory	B 23
Prov	Provisional (light)	K 72
Pt	Point	B 25
Pt	Pteropods	S 36
pub	Publication	E 15
P F	Pump-out facilities	Gd
PWI	Potable water intake	

Q

Quar	Quarantine	G 26
Qk Fl	Quick flashing (light)	K 24
Qz	Quartz	S 13

R

R	Red	K 66; L 15, 43
R	River	Bd
Ra	Radar station	M 11
Racon	Radar responder beacon	M 12
Ra (conspic)	Radar conspicuous object	M 14
RA DOME	Radar dome	Mh
Ra Ref	Radar reflector	Lf; M 13
RBHB	Red and black horizontal bands	L 17, 18, 19, 20, 20a
R Bn	Red beacon	L 52
R Bn	Radiobeacon	M 3, 4, 16
Rd	Radiolaria	S 35
rd	Red	S 63
Rd	Road, Roadstead	B 14; H 1
RD	Directional Radiobeacon, Radio range	M 5
RDF	Radio direction finding station	M 7
REF	Reflector	K 10; L 64
Rep	Reported	O 35
Restr	Restricted	Fv
Rf	Reef	O 23
Rge	Range	B 27
RGE	Range	Kg
Rk	Rock	B 35
Rk, rky	Rock, Rocky	S 11
Rky	Rocky	Bh
R MAST	Radio mast	M 9
Rot	Rotating (light), Revolving	K 31
RR	Railroad	H 3
R RELAY MAST	Radio relay mast	Mb
R Sta	Radio telegraph station, QTG Radio station	M1, 10a
RT	Radio telephone station	M 2

rt	Rotten	S 48
R TR	Radio tower	M 9
Ru	Ruins	I 40
RW Bn	Red and white beacon	L 52
Rv	Railway	H 3

S

S	Sand	S 2
S	South; Southern	U 3, 11
S	Spar (buoy)	L 8
Sc	Scoriae	S 20
Sch	Schist	S 13a
Sch	School	I 65
Sd	Sound	B 8
SD	Sounding doubtful	Q 1
SE	Southeast	U 6
sec, s	Second (time; geo. pos.)	E 3; Kd
SEC	Sector	K 49
Sem	Semaphore	J 10
S Fl	Short flashing (light)	K 25a
sft	Soft	S 41
Sh	Shells	S 23
Shl	Shoal	O 22
Sig Sta	Signal station	J 9
SIREN	Fog siren	N 11
Sk	Stroke	Fu
S-L Fl	Short-long flashing (light)	K 28a
Slu	Slough	Be; C 18
S'ly	Southerly	Fr
sml	Small	F4; S 44
Sn	Shingle	S 8
Sp	Spring tide	T 6
SP	Spherical (bouy)	L 7
Spg	Sponge	S 26
Spi	Spicules	S 31
S'PIPE	Standpipe	I 45
spk	Speckled	S 50
S Sig Sta	Storm signal station	J 11
St	Saint	F 11
St	Street	I 26
St	Stones	S 10
Sta	Station	J 1, 2
std	Standard	F 32
stf	Stiff	S 43
Stg	Sea-tangle	S 29
stk	Sticky	S 46
St M, St Mi	Statute mile	Ea
Str	Strait	B 7
Str	Stream	Bc; T 17
str	Streaky	S 49
sub	Submarine	F 20
SUB-BELL	Submarine fog bell	N 5, 6
Subm, subm	Submerged	F 33; Oa, 30
Subm Ruins	Submerged ruins	Gd
SUB-OSC	Submarine oscillator	N 7
Sub Vol	Submarine volcano	O 8
Subm W	Submerged Well	Ob
SW	Southwest	U 7
sw	Swamp	B 1

T

t	Tonne	E12a
T	Ton	Ei
T	Telephone	I 70; L 22c
T	True	U 22
T	Tufa	S 19
TB	Temporary buoy	L 30
Tel	Telegraph	I 27; L 22b
Telem Ant	Telemetry antenna	Ma
Tel Off	Telegraph office	I 28
Temp	Temporary (light)	F 38; K 73
ten	Tenacious	S 55
Thoro	Thorofare	B 9
Tk	Tank	I 53
TR	Tower	I 41
TRLB, TRUB,	TLB, TUB	Ki, j, k, l
Tri	Triangulation	D 10
TV TR	Television tower (mast)	M 9a

U

uhf	Ultra high frequency	Mi
Uncov	Uncovers; Dries	O 2, 32, 34
Univ	University	Ih
unverd	Unverified	Fb
unev	Uneven	S 71
μsec, μs	Microsecond (one millionth)	Eb

V

var	Variation	U 24
vard	Varied	S 70
VB	Vertical beam	Kf
vel	Velocity	T 23
Vert	Vertical (lights)	K 80
VERT CL	Vertical clearance	H 18a
vhf	Very high frequency	Mi
Vi, vi	Violet	K 61; S 68
View X	View point	D 6
Vil	Village	I 3
Vol	Volcanic	S 16
Vol Ash	Volcanic ash	Sb
VS	Vertical stripes	L 32

W

W	West, Western	U 4, 12
W, wh	White	K 67; L 41; S 56
W Bn	White beacon	L 52
Wd	Seaweed	S 28
Whf	Wharf	G 18
WHIS	Fog whistle	N 15
Wk	Wreck	O 15, 28
Wks	Wrecks, Wreckage	O 29
W Or	White and orange	Le
W'ly	Westerly	Ft

Y

Y, yl	Yellow	L 24, 44; S 61
yd	Yard	E 8
1st	First	Fj
2nd, 2d	Second	Fk
3rd, 3d	Third	Fl
4th	Fourth	Fm
°	Degree	E 20
′	Minute (of arc)	E 21
″	Second (of arc)	E 22

NAVIGATIONAL AIDS

IN

UNITED STATES WATERS

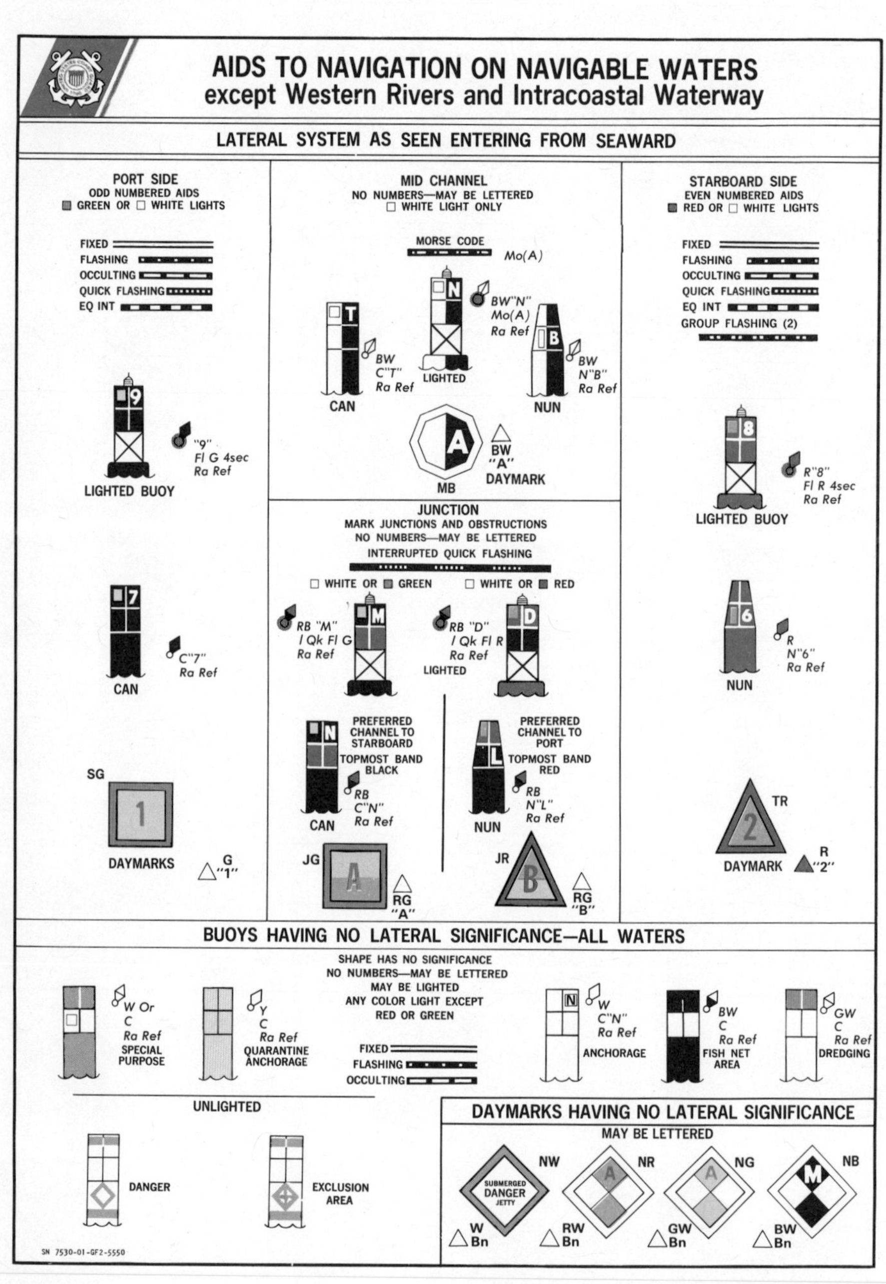

NOTE: Under column headed "Mid Channel" above, the bottom half of the black and red nun numbered "L" should be red; in other words, the top half red and black, and the bottom half red.

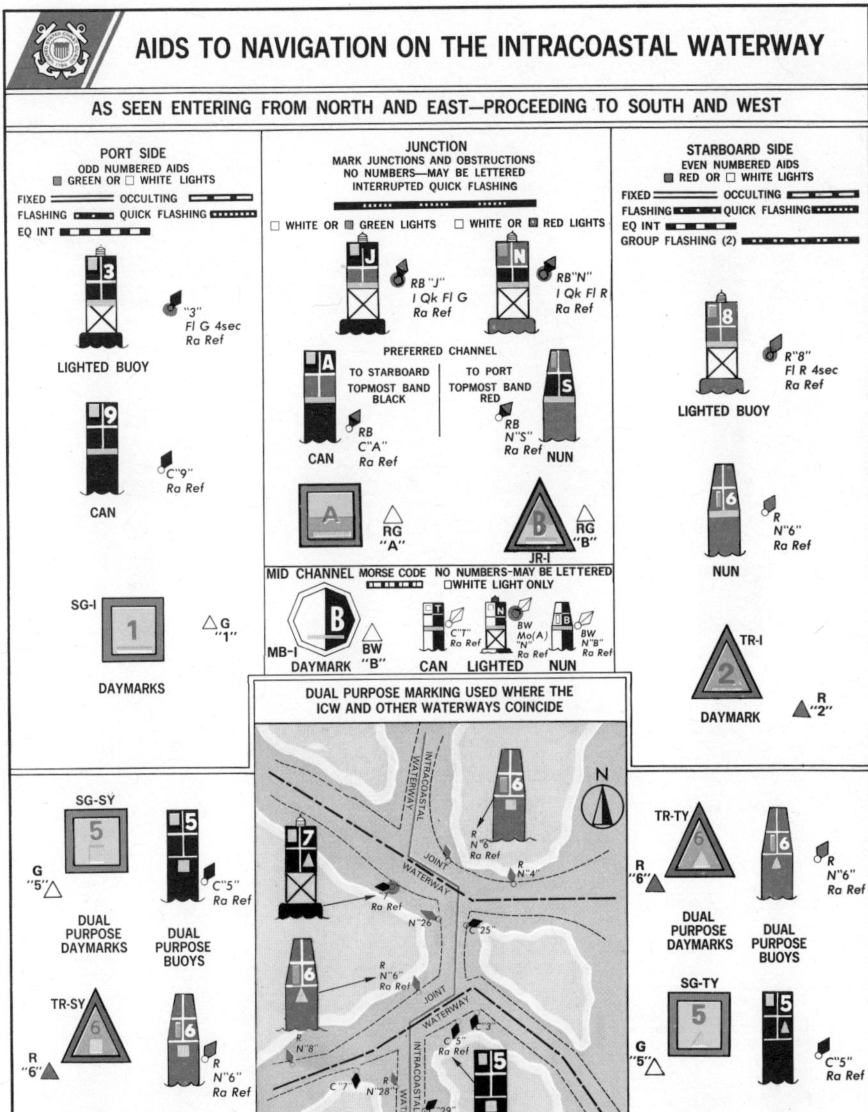
AIDS TO NAVIGATION ON THE INTRACOASTAL WATERWAY
AS SEEN ENTERING FROM NORTH AND EAST—PROCEEDING TO SOUTH AND WEST
PORT SIDE
ODD NUMBERED AIDS
GREEN OR WHITE LIGHTS
FIXED
OCCULTING
FLASHING
QUICK FLASHING
EQ INT
"3"
Fl G 4sec
Ra Ref
LIGHTED BUOY
C"9"
Ra Ref
CAN
SG-I
G
"1"
DAYMARKS
JUNCTION
MARK JUNCTIONS AND OBSTRUCTIONS
NO NUMBERS—MAY BE LETTERED
INTERRUPTED QUICK FLASHING
WHITE OR GREEN LIGHTS
WHITE OR RED LIGHTS
RB "J"
I Qk Fl G
Ra Ref
RB "N"
I Qk Fl R
Ra Ref
PREFERRED CHANNEL
TO STARBOARD
TOPMOST BAND
BLACK
TO PORT
TOPMOST BAND
RED
RB
C"A"
Ra Ref
CAN
RB
N"S"
Ra Ref
NUN
RG
"A"
JR-I
RG
"B"
MID CHANNEL
MORSE CODE
NO NUMBERS-MAY BE LETTERED
WHITE LIGHT ONLY
MB-I
DAYMARK
BW
"B"
C"T"
Ra Ref
CAN
BW
Mo(A)
"N"
Ra Ref
LIGHTED
BW
N"B"
Ra Ref
NUN
STARBOARD SIDE
EVEN NUMBERED AIDS
RED OR WHITE LIGHTS
FIXED
OCCULTING
FLASHING
QUICK FLASHING
EQ INT
GROUP FLASHING (2)
R"8"
Fl R 4sec
Ra Ref
LIGHTED BUOY
R
N"6"
Ra Ref
NUN
TR-I
DAYMARK
R
"2"
DUAL PURPOSE MARKING USED WHERE THE
ICW AND OTHER WATERWAYS COINCIDE
INTRACOASTAL WATERWAY
JOINT WATERWAY
N
R
N"6"
Ra Ref
R
N"4"
"7"
Ra Ref
N"26"
C"25"
R
N"6"
Ra Ref
R
N"8"
C"5"
Ra Ref
C"3"
C"7"
R
N"28"
C"29"
When following the ICW from New Jersey through Texas, a △ should be kept to your starboard hand and a ▢ should be kept to your port hand, regardless of the color of the aid on which they appear.
SG-SY
G
"5"
C"5"
Ra Ref
DUAL PURPOSE DAYMARKS
DUAL PURPOSE BUOYS
TR-SY
R
"6"
R
N"6"
Ra Ref
JG-SY
JR-SY
RG
"A"
SN 7530-01-GF2-5560
RG
"B"
TR-TY
R
"6"
R
N"6"
Ra Ref
DUAL PURPOSE DAYMARKS
DUAL PURPOSE BUOYS
SG-TY
G
"5"
C"5"
Ra Ref
JG-TY
JR-TY
RG
"C"
RG
"B"

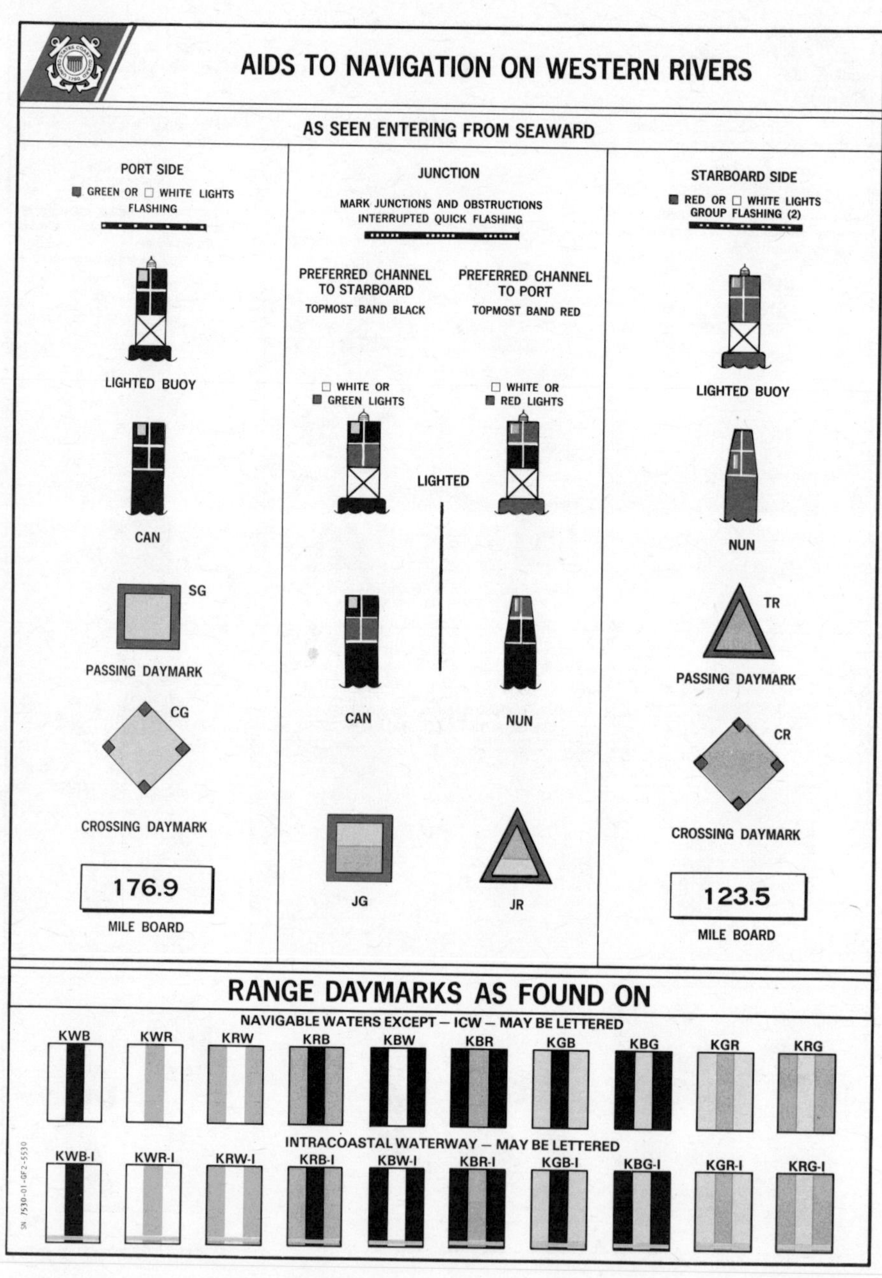

NOTE: Under the column headed "Junction" above, the bottom half of the "NUN" should be red; in other words, the top half red and black, the bottom half red.

UNIFORM STATE WATERWAY MARKING SYSTEM

STATE WATERS AND DESIGNATED STATE WATERS FOR PRIVATE AIDS TO NAVIGATION

REGULATORY MARKERS

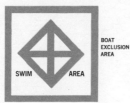

SWIM AREA

BOAT EXCLUSION AREA

EXPLANATION MAY BE PLACED OUTSIDE THE CROSSED DIAMOND SHAPE, SUCH AS DAM, RAPIDS, SWIM AREA, ETC.

DANGER

THE NATURE OF DANGER MAY BE INDICATED INSIDE THE DIAMOND SHAPE, SUCH AS ROCK, WRECK, SHOAL, DAM, ETC.

SLOW

NO WAKE

CONTROLLED AREA

TYPE OF CONTROL IS INDICATED IN THE CIRCLE, SUCH AS SLOW, NO WAKE, ANCHORING, ETC.

INFORMATION

FOR DISPLAYING INFORMATION SUCH AS DIRECTIONS, DISTANCES, LOCATIONS, ETC.

BUOY USED TO DISPLAY REGULATORY MARKERS

MAY SHOW WHITE LIGHT
MAY BE LETTERED

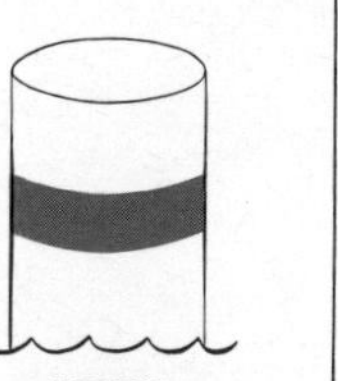

MOORING BUOY

WHITE WITH BLUE BAND

MAY SHOW WHITE REFLECTOR OR LIGHT

AIDS TO NAVIGATION

MAY SHOW WHITE REFLECTOR OR LIGHT

RED-STRIPED WHITE BUOY

MAY BE LETTERED
DO NOT PASS BETWEEN BUOY AND NEAREST SHORE

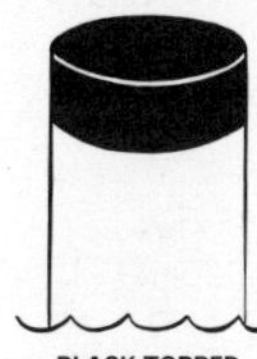

BLACK-TOPPED WHITE BUOY

RED-TOPPED WHITE BUOY

MAY BE NUMBERED

PASS TO NORTH OR EAST OF BUOY

PASS TO SOUTH OR WEST OF BUOY

CARDINAL SYSTEM

MAY SHOW GREEN REFLECTOR OR LIGHT

MAY SHOW RED REFLECTOR OR LIGHT

SOLID RED AND SOLID BLACK BUOYS

USUALLY FOUND IN PAIRS
PASS BETWEEN THESE BUOYS

PORT SIDE — LOOKING UPSTREAM — STARBOARD SIDE

LATERAL SYSTEM

SN 7530-01-GF2-5540

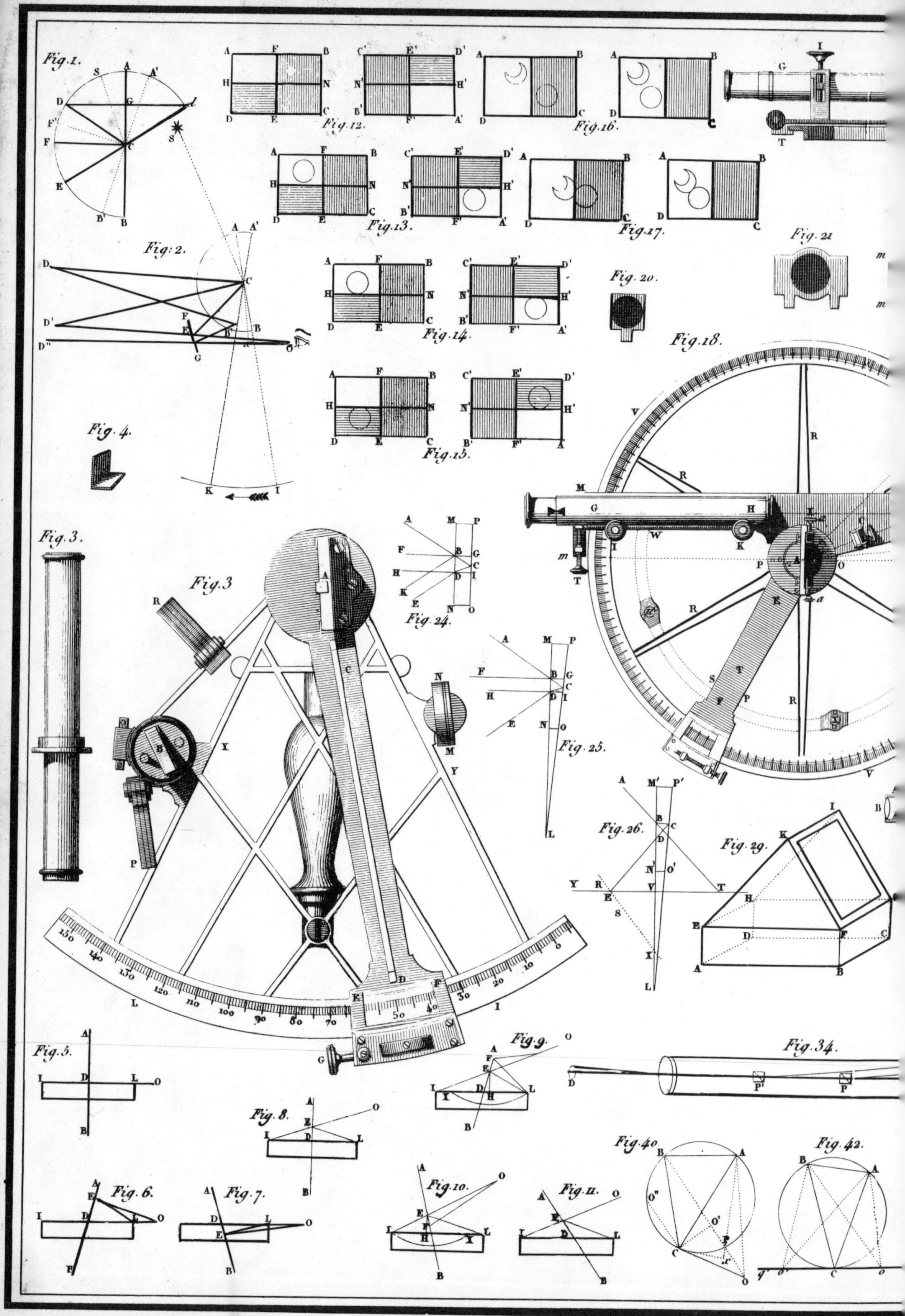
Fig. 1.
Fig. 12.
Fig. 16.
Fig. 13.
Fig. 17.
Fig. 2.
Fig. 14.
Fig. 20.
Fig. 21
Fig. 18.
Fig. 15.
Fig. 4.
Fig. 3.
Fig. 3
Fig. 24.
Fig. 25.
Fig. 26.
Fig. 29.
Fig. 5.
Fig. 9.
Fig. 34.
Fig. 8.
Fig. 40
Fig. 42.
Fig. 6.
Fig. 7.
Fig. 10.
Fig. 11.